$8.95

Politics and Government in the United States

Politics and Government in the United States

National, State, and Local Edition

EMMETTE S. REDFORD
UNIVERSITY OF TEXAS

DAVID B. TRUMAN
COLUMBIA UNIVERSITY

ANDREW HACKER
CORNELL UNIVERSITY

ALAN F. WESTIN
COLUMBIA UNIVERSITY

ROBERT C. WOOD
MASSACHUSETTS INSTITUTE OF TECHNOLOGY

Alan F. Westin COORDINATING EDITOR

Harcourt, Brace & World, Inc.

NEW YORK / CHICAGO / BURLINGAME

Preface

When five political scientists with approaches as diverse as those of the undersigned collaborate on a textbook, a few prefatory words are in order to explain what drew them together in the enterprise. We shared, first of all, a belief that there was a growing need for a text in American government to cover the ground between the lively but elementary volumes and the "single-theme" or behavioral texts, which are presented for introductory courses but appeal primarily to more advanced students. As more and more students come to college with better high school preparation in history and government, and as television deposits greater awareness of public events in student minds, we believe that deeper analytical insights can be gained in the basic course, as long as a foundation of information and description is also established.

Second, we believe that it is possible to improve the balance of "process," "institutional," and "substantive" analysis that now exists in the basic course. In the years of planning, drafting, and editing that went into this volume, we focused continuously on an integrated treatment of ideas, interests, processes, institutions, and programs throughout each major section of the text. We hope that this has resulted in the kind of multifaceted discussions that do, in fact, occur when public officials gather, formally or informally, to weigh alternatives, or when political scientists analyze these factors among themselves as professional students of government and politics. The aim, then, has been to approach in text form the reality of daily political analysis.

Beyond these brief observations, a few additional comments may be useful. We have used three "paired-themes" for the analysis of American government—the constant tensions between conflict and resolution, continuity and change, and power and consent. These are presented and discussed in Chapter 1. We have illustrated the book with political cartoons, as others have done, but we have included both liberal and conservative cartoons on the various problems illustrated.

As for the division of responsibility among the authors of the text, the planning and editing have been collegial. We have read one another's several drafts and have been painfully free with suggested substantive changes, improvements in language, and calls for revised or additional material. However, while Part I represents such an amalgam of writing that it must be called a joint effort, Part II has been primarily the work of Andrew Hacker, Part III of David Truman, Part IV of Alan Westin, Part V of Emmette Redford (with the exception of Chapter 21, which was written by Robert Wood), and Part VI of Robert Wood.

Finally, we are delighted to acknowledge the special aid that Richard Morgan of Columbia University has given to this book in a host of ways, from substantive writing to editorial assistance. For penetrating comments on the book as a whole, we are in the debt of Wallace Sayre, Austin Ranney, Richard Neustadt, and Hugh Douglas Price. For reading particular sections, we are debtors to Samuel Huntington, Michael Reagan, Eugene Skolnikoff, and Nancy Arnone Bord. For errors of commission or omission the authors themselves assume full responsibility.

E. S. R.

D. B. T.

A. H.

A. F. W.

R. C. W.

Contents

PART I

DEMOCRACY AND
THE AMERICAN WAY

1 / American Government at Work

When a painter begins work on a portrait or landscape, he usually starts with a rough sketch in charcoal, pencil, or chalk that attempts to capture the essential action and mood of the subject and fix them across the whole canvas as a guiding outline. Only then will the artist begin his detailed work on face, figure, clothing, ground, sky, or other components of the total study.

This procedure has much to recommend it for a textbook in American government. Before plunging into the description and analysis of the federal Constitution, party politics, Congress, or the Presidency, it is revealing to attempt a sketch of the American political system as a whole, with all its parts suggested in their most characteristic pattern. To do this, we have blocked in a portrait of one week in American government and politics—March 8–15, 1964—and have drawn up (from the newspaper and magazine stories of that period) a narrative account of what took place in eight leading "arenas" of American governmental life: the Presidency, Congress, the federal executive agencies, the national judiciary, party and election activity, interest groups, constitutional rights problems, and state-local government. We deliberately chose a typical rather than an exceptional week in American political life. No wars were declared, no heads of state were assassinated, no far-reaching federal laws were enacted, and there were no announcements of major scientific or medical discoveries. Problems and crises were those of the recurring, "constant" variety, and both the men and the machinery of American government could be caught in their "normal" patterns of action.

As we began work on such a sketch of the American political system, we soon realized that if a contemporary sketch would be useful, it would be even more helpful to have a similar sketch of the American political system at some earlier point in its history; thus contemporary American government could be contrasted with its image before nuclear weapons, instant radio communication, modern industrial systems, and a host of other twentieth-century developments had placed their imprint on our governmental processes.

One point of contrast could have been 1789, when the Constitution of the United States was ratified and the new federal government officially came into being; another could have been 1812, when we fought a minor naval war with Great Britain. Still other years for comparison might have been 1860 or 1865, taking the American nation either on the eve of the Civil War or just after that tragic ordeal had ended. Any of these dates—1789, 1812, 1860, 1865—would have provided us with the pre-industrial and pre-urban setting of late eighteenth- or mid-nineteenth-century America, and with the dominant attitudes toward society, government, and political life held by the Framers of our Republic or the political generation that followed them.

We decided finally that 1889 offered the best year for our comparison. The Constitution had been in effect one hundred years by then, and throughout the nation centenary celebrations of its promulgation marked a strong sense of national maturity and self-confidence. From a "frontier society" and an "upstart Republic" the United States had developed in its first hundred years into a rich and influential nation, and had done so while providing its white population, both native-born and immigrant, with more political and civil liberty than in any other country of the day. Thus the choice of 1889 allows us to depict American government on the eve of national modernization.

After we present these two sketches, we will try to suggest the basic constants and the major changes in the American governmental system in the seventy-five event-filled years between 1889 and 1964. We will also discuss the kinds of social, economic, political, and cultural forces that have been at the heart of these changes. Finally, we will suggest how political scientists take the journalistic raw materials typified by our survey of a week's press reports and organize them for disciplined analysis and judgment. In this regard, we will offer three sets of paired themes with which the reader of this text can analyze and understand both the day-to-day processes and the long-range developments of the American political system.

Panorama of Washington, looking northwest from the Capitol.

Politics and Government in the United States: March 8–15, 1889

1889 in the United States was a year of rising range wars in the West between cattle barons and sheepherders. Electric street lights, asphalt paving, telephones, and indoor bathtubs were just coming into use. It was 1889 when John L. Sullivan fought the last of the public bare-knuckle contests, defeating Jake Kilrain in a bloody seventy-five-rounder in New Orleans.

THE PRESIDENCY

The newly inaugurated President, Benjamin Harrison, a Republican who had served as a United States Senator from Indiana, spent most of the week greeting visitors to the White House. Many of these came to seek appointments to federal office, but thousands merely wished to shake hands with the new President, under the prevailing custom that the President shook hands with anyone who wished to meet him. The numbers grew so large, however (about 30,000 in a week), that Harrison decided to wave to the crowds from the White House portico rather than shake hands individually, a break with tradition that some observers thought might cause adverse public opinion.

When he had free time during the week, President Harrison worked on his message to Congress, which would set out the Republican Administration's position on such upcoming legislative issues as the new tariff bill, a silver purchase act, federal antitrust action, and civil service reform. The message was also expected to refer to tensions with Great Britain over American seal-

5

President Benjamin Harrison and his grandson, Benjamin Harrison McKee.

Methodist Episcopal Church (the largest American Negro church group), several hundred teachers attending meetings in Washington of the National Teachers' Association, and the "colored editors of America" (also meeting in Washington). Mrs. Harrison began her duties as first lady by receiving callers and attending the opening of an art exhibit at the Garfield Hospital. On Sunday the Harrisons went to church. (the President had decided to make surprise visits to various churches rather than attend any one regularly). Fulfilling a campaign promise, the President did no work on Sunday.

CONGRESS

In Congress, the 76 Senators and 325 Congressmen spent most of the week seeking patronage for their states and districts. More than half of the Senators and about a third of the Representatives called on the President in a single day, said the New York *Times*, as well as visiting Cabinet heads and other executive officers with positions to fill. The only Congressional committees which met were those on organization of the House and Senate, to nominate the various committee chairmen and members for the next (Fifty-first) Congress.

fishing rights in the Bering Sea and to conflicts with Germany as to paramount influence in the naval coaling station of Samoa.

During the week President Harrison greeted the bishops of the African

The Senate Chamber.

Senator Blair of New Hampshire in a speech to school superintendents called for "federal aid to education in the South." There was some speculation that the Republican Speaker of the House of Representatives, Thomas Reed of New York, might try to end the practice by which House Democrats sat silently when their names were read at a "quorum call" and thus forced an end to the day's session unless there were enough Republicans present to make up a quorum. Representative Townshend of Illinois died on March 10, and Washington went into official mourning. The Military Affairs Committee, of which he had been chairman, prepared the funeral ceremonies.

THE EXECUTIVE BRANCH

Among the new Cabinet members, Postmaster General Wanamaker and Secretary of State Blaine were busy with appointment matters, having more

RIGHT: *The first passenger elevator was installed in the Capitol by W. E. Hale. Hydraulic elevators like this one had been in use since the early part of the century; electric elevators began to appear in 1889.*

BELOW: *A New York City telephone exchange. In 1889 there were 211,500 telephones in the United States. The dial system was patented in that year.*

John L. Sullivan, left, and Jake Kilrain. The seventy-five-round fight lasted two hours and fifteen minutes.

positions to fill than the other departments. Secretary of State Blaine issued a statement denying sensational reports from San Francisco that an American ship had been sunk by a German torpedo near Samoa. Secretary of the Treasury Windom came into office faced with the problem of how to spend a federal surplus of some $48 million. Attorney General Miller received a dozen of the most prominent citizens of

the Territory of Idaho and pledged "to stand by them in their efforts to abolish polygamy in the Territory." Agents sent by the Department of the Interior reported their failure to discover any evidence of fraud in the disposal of timber on federal reservations in Wisconsin. The Interstate Commerce Commission was asked by a convention of state railroad commissioners to consider what could be done to prevent accidents caused by pin-and-link type railroad couplers. More than 6,000 men were being killed or maimed annually by these devices.

THE FEDERAL JUDICIARY

In the only significant federal court decision reported in the press during this week, a United States circuit judge in San Francisco held in the case of *Southern Pacific Railroad* v. *United States* that the United States Government was subject to suit by citizens in property claim cases even without the government's "sovereign consent" to be sued. The ruling was hailed as another proof that government was "under law" in the American Republic.

PARTY ACTIVITY

In the area of party activity, the defeated former President and Demo-

A contemporary print showing the pin-and-link coupling.

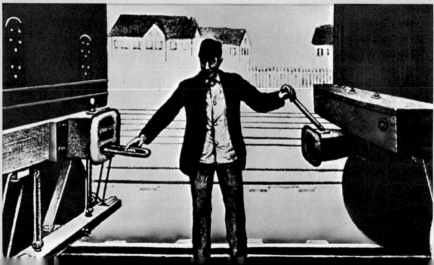

A family of settlers in front of their sod house in Custer County, Nebraska. Such houses were typical in Midwestern states and territories. The cow is not on the roof.

cratic party leader, Grover Cleveland, settled into law practice in New York City, moving from his home town of Buffalo. Despite his professions to the contrary, political experts doubted that he had any intention of forsaking his political career permanently.

In preparing for celebration of Jefferson's birthday on April 2, the National Association of Democratic Clubs announced that the Democrats were founded "upon Jeffersonian principles and in view of the fact that the Government . . . has passed into the hands of a party avowedly Federalist and acknowledging none of the restrictions of the Constitution, it is now especially important that the teachings of the great apostle of Democracy should again be solemnly invoked." Meanwhile, a bloody riot occurred between two rival factions in the Democratic caucus of the fourth ward in Troy, New York.

INTEREST GROUPS

Interest groups at work in March of 1889 included a delegation from Idaho which presented that Territory's claims to statehood to President Harrison, and the Philadelphia Wool Merchants, who demanded that Secretary of the Treasury Windom rectify a "flaw" in the tariff act of 1883 which was allowing "large and increasing importations of goods and wool." Two days later the Massachusetts Tariff Reform League called upon Congress, asking why it had "sacrificed the interests of New England to the greed of Pennsylvania." The meat packers of Minnesota sponsored a bill which would have made impossible the sale in Minnesota of any beef slaughtered outside the state. It was expected that Philip Armour of Chicago would fight the bill vigorously. The Texas state legislature discovered that schoolteachers and superintend-

The blizzard of 1888 had knocked down many of the telephone poles shown in this earlier view of Broadway in New York looking north. By 1889 underground cables were being laid, although overloaded poles remained.

ents were being paid by book publishers to lobby against a bill which would have reduced publishers' profits on textbooks. The Bakers' Union of New York called for a sixty-hour work week, while the African Methodist Episcopal convention closed with a prayer for better government in Washington.

CIVIL RIGHTS
AND CIVIL LIBERTIES

Civil rights issues already played a role in Washington in 1889, especially with a Republican returning to the White House. The president of the colored editors of America called upon "Ben Harrison, our President, and the Republican Party" to "Rip up with unabating fury the base pretensions of men who come to Congress over the bones of our people." The famous Negro writer, Frederick Douglass, told the editors that American Negroes should "assimilate" themselves with the white race rather than attempt to separate from it, and that the Negro should practice temperance and advance in "mechanical enterprise." In the South, the North Carolina legislature passed a literacy test for voting during this

The first commercially marketed typewriter came into common use in the 1880s.

10

President Harrison riding in a parade celebrating the one-hundredth anniversary of the promulgation of the Constitution.

week, over the vigorous opposition of Negroes and Republicans. It was generally agreed that the effect of the bill would be to assure the supremacy of the Democratic party and further weaken the political position of Southern Negroes. In a similar vein, in South Carolina several accused lynchers were convicted for the first time in that state's history; the persons convicted were Negroes.

STATE AND LOCAL GOVERNMENT

There was widespread action by state and local governments during this week. The New Jersey legislature defeated a bill to forbid the sale of ciga-

President Harrison being welcomed at New York's City Hall.

rettes as harmful to good health and morals. The Illinois legislature debated a proposed constitutional amendment to limit state taxes to those on land. New Hampshire sent to its voters a set of constitutional amendments, one of which would fix the salary of state legislators at $200 per session instead of on the per diem basis then in effect, in order to encourage shorter and more efficient sessions.

The most lively issue among the states concerned prohibition of liquor sales. New Hampshire voters resoundingly defeated a state prohibition amendment. To thwart prohibition efforts, the Rhode Island legislature voted for and the Minnesota legislature voted against submission of prohibition laws to popular referendums. In Maine, a dry state, a law was passed allowing doctors to prescribe up to a quart of liquor per patient for "medicinal purposes."

Another important issue during the week was voting reform. Indiana became the fourth state to adopt the Australian ballot system, the Montana Territory, scheduled to become a state that year, also adopted it, and the Rhode Island legislature brought this system up for consideration. New York passed a law making it illegal for a person to sell his vote. In Galveston, Texas, the city council battled over the question of private versus public electric lighting. The city finally decided to buy electric power from a private company.

"A Cold Reception Everywhere": an anti-Prohibition cartoon of 1889, showing the states that had defeated the measure.

J. Keppler in *Puck*

Sources for the events during March 8–15, 1889, were the New York *Times*, the *Nation*, *Harper's Weekly*, the Galveston *Daily News*, the Chicago *Daily Tribune*, and the Washington *Post* for that week.

Panorama of Washington, looking northwest from the Capitol.

Politics and Government in the United States: March 8–15, 1964

1964 began under the cloud of the assassination of John F. Kennedy in November, 1963. By March 8, Lyndon Johnson had been President of the United States for only fifteen weeks; thus the week of March 8–15 was still a time of adjustment to a new Administration—a situation that influenced, to some degree, most governmental and political activity.

THE PRESIDENCY

For Lyndon Johnson, the week was a time of consolidating his Presidency—settling into the White House seat of decisions, establishing his personality with foreign leaders, setting legislative priorities, and reassuring the public that there was both continuity and power in the new Administration. In his role of chief spokesman for American foreign policy and national defense, President Johnson dispatched Secretary of Defense Robert McNamara to South Vietnam on March 8, partly to gather information on the troublesome Vietnamese military situation and partly to reassure Premier Nguyen Khanh that his newly installed government had the "wholehearted support" of the Johnson Administration. The Cold War wound of divided Germany was reopened when a United States reconnaissance jet bomber that "strayed accidentally" across the East German frontier was shot down by Soviet fighters on March 10. President Johnson held a conference on the incident with Secretary of State Dean Rusk and McGeorge Bundy, the President's Special Assistant for National Security

13

Affairs. Latin-American affairs were a topic of major Presidential attention this week, with secret negotiations with Panama held in Washington over a crisis precipitated by anti-American riots directed against continued American control of the Panama Canal Zone. On still another foreign policy front, President Johnson announced that the United States would join Britain in paying half the costs of the United Nations' special peace force in Cyprus, which was desperately engaged in trying to avert full-scale war between Greek and Turkish Cypriots. While these actions were being taken, the President continued the Chief Executive's usual round of daily meetings with American officials and foreign representatives, conferring with General Maxwell Taylor (chairman of the Joint Chiefs of Staff), Charles E. Bohlen (United States Ambassador to France) Miguel Rubiero (Ghana's Ambassador to the United States), and many others.

President Johnson, in his plane, inspecting flood damage in the Ohio River Valley.

Wide World

In his role as chief legislative initiator in the federal system, President Johnson sent Congress several proposals designed to stem unemployment, including a bill to create a National Commission on Automation and Technological Progress. At 8:45 A.M. on March 10, the President had his weekly breakfast with Congressional leaders, during which the agenda of pending legislation, from foreign aid to the civil rights bill, was discussed. President Johnson signed into law the Presidential Transition Act, providing public funds for the President-elect to prepare for his administration in the period between election in November and his inauguration in January. The President also signed legislation extending the Federal Airport Act, and he received for his signature the Military Procurement Act for the fiscal year 1965, authorizing expenditures for aircraft, missiles, naval vessels, and military research and development projects.

In his capacity as head of the executive branch and chief administrator of the federal service, President Johnson sent a steady flow of nominations to the Senate, ranging from new members of the powerful Federal Reserve Board and Securities and Exchange Commis-

The President meeting with his top advisers in the Cabinet Room of the White House.

sion to military officers, postmasters, and District of Columbia commissioners. In keeping with his pledge to appoint fifty women to "top executive posts" during his first months in office, the President named Virginia M. Brown to the Interstate Commerce Commission and Mrs. Frankie M. Freeman to the Civil Rights Commission. Another aspect of the President's role as executive was demonstrated when Johnson took a three-and-a-half-hour helicopter ride to inspect the damage caused by a heavy flood through the Ohio River Valley on March 12. After inspecting the six-state area, Johnson held a conference with the governors of the states affected and authorized direct federal disaster aid through loans and special services.

Presidents are leaders of their parties, and as "Chief Democrat," President Johnson sent cordial letters to several "regular" Democratic party incumbents

The President signing the bill extending federal aid to airports for three years.

running for reelection to Congress from the Bronx area of New York City. The fact that these men were opposed for reelection by "reform" Democrats led by Mayor Robert Wagner underscored the President's problems with factional disunity in New York's Democratic politics. Party concerns came to the fore also on the question of whom the President should appoint to a vacancy in the United States Court of Appeals for the highly important Connecticut, Vermont, and New York Circuit. Some Connecticut Democrats were supporting Eugene Rostow, dean of the Yale Law School and a leading Democratic adviser. Other Democratic forces in Connecticut urged the promotion of Judge Robert Anderson of the Federal District Court in Connecticut; Judge Anderson was a Republican, but his promotion to the Circuit Court would leave a vacancy on the District Court in Connecticut, which the Democratic state organization then wanted filled by President Johnson with an Italian-American, reflecting strong pressure among the state's Italian-American population for "representation" on the federal bench.

In addition to these major activities, the President also fulfilled a host of ceremonial, social, and political roles as the official Chief of State. President Johnson visited the ailing General Douglas MacArthur at Walter Reed Hospital, presided over a White House reception for members of the House of Representatives and their wives, addressed the National Editorial Association, and attended a Requiem Mass in Washington for the late King Paul of Greece. Asked in an interview to characterize his political philosophy as "liberal" or "conservative," Johnson responded in the classic manner of the American political leader seeking to avoid the limiting aspects of ideological dog tags: "I suppose all of us want a better deal, don't we? . . . I have often said that I was proud that I was a free man first of all and an American second, and a public servant third and a Democrat fourth, in that order . . . . [Otherwise] I don't believe much in labels."

CONGRESS

In the first two and a half months of 1964, Congress had already enacted several major pieces of legislation, including a fairly generous foreign aid authorization, two important bills giving federal aid to education, and a huge "stimulator" tax cut of $11.5 billion. And the House of Representatives had overwhelmingly passed the strongest civil rights bill in a century. Whether the Senate would muster the two-thirds

The President attending the Requiem Mass for the late King Paul of Greece in the Greek Orthodox Cathedral of Saint Sophia.

16

majority needed to close off Southern debate and act on civil rights proposals was the central question in this second session of the nation's Eighty-eighth Congress.

The week of March 8–15 in Congress predictably mixed major legislative drama with grinding committee routine. The Senate Democratic leader, Mike Mansfield of Montana, formally called up the Administration's civil rights bill, guaranteeing equality in voting, employment, public accommodations, and education, and setting forth other rights for Negroes. Eighteen Southern Democratic Senators organized into three six-man teams that would alternate in a full-dress filibuster against the measure; they called it "a complete reversal of Federal policy and law [which] would override and strike down laws, customs, habits, practices, and the social order of millions of people in the United States." In other action by the full chambers, the House of Representatives gave final approval to a $17 billion military construction bill, the largest in peacetime history, and sent it to President Johnson for signature. However, the House defeated a bill to raise the wages of 1.7 million government employees, including a $10,000-a-year salary increase for the Congressmen themselves.

In Senate committee work, the Senate Space Committee gave final approval on March 10 for placement of a $60 million National Aeronautics and Space Administration electronics research center in the Boston area. Before the Senate Foreign Relations Committee, Secretary of State Dean Rusk defended the Administration's policy to create more flexible powers for the government in handling East-West trade; the Communist bloc is no longer a monolithic whole, he said, and different Communist countries show varying degrees of susceptibility to attempts at

Secretary of State Dean Rusk before the Senate Foreign Relations Committee.

either trade blockades or liberal trade agreements. The Senate Indian Affairs Subcommittee cut in half a $20 million assistance bill approved unanimously by the House as federal compensation for the flooding of the Seneca Indian Reservation in western New York.

In House committee work, the House Space Committee approved a $3.5 billion budget for manned space flights for the coming year, and the Armed Services Committee recommended $20.5 million for the expansion of the Military Academy at West Point. A Judiciary subcommittee, considering a bill to tighten protection of official visitors, heard testimony from a deputy legal adviser to the State Department that several threats were received against the life of French President Charles de Gaulle when he was in the United States for the funeral of President Kennedy.

As usual, the week's Appendix to the *Congressional Record* was filled with those editorials, daily columns, speeches, book reviews, letters, conven-

Daily Digest

HIGHLIGHTS

Senate debated motion to take up civil rights bill.

House cleared military procurement authorization for President.

Senate

Chamber Action

Routine Proceedings, pages 4599–4608

Bills Introduced: Six bills and one resolution were introduced, as follows: S. 2613-2618; and S. Con. Res. 72.

Page 4600

Bill Referred: H.R. 8000, proposed Interest Equalization Tax Act of 1963, was referred to Committee on Finance.

Page 4573

President's Communication—Automation: Communication from the President transmitting draft of proposed legislation to establish a National Commission on Automation and Technical Progress, with accompanying papers, was received and referred to Committee on Labor and Public Welfare.

Page 4599

King of Greece: Senate adopted unanimously S. Con. Res. 72, expressing condolences on the death of King Paul of Greece, and extending felicitations to his successor, King Constantine.

Page 4573

Civil Rights: Senate debated motion by Senator Mans-

Director of Defense Research and Engineering, and Gen. Bernard A. Schriever, Commander, Air Force Systems Command, Andrews AFB.

Committee will meet again tomorrow in executive session.

INDIANA DUNES LAKESHORE

Committee on Interior and Insular Affairs: On Saturday, March 7, Subcommittee on Public Lands concluded its hearings on S. 2249, providing for the establishment of the Indiana Dunes National Lakeshore, after receiving testimony from numerous witnesses.

ALLEGHENY RIVER PROJECT

Committee on Interior and Insular Affairs: Subcommittee on Indian Affairs, in executive session, approved for full committee consideration with amendment H.R. 1794 authorizing U.S. to take rights-of-way over lands within the Allegany Indian Reservation, N.Y., for the Allegheny River project (Kinzua Dam).

INVESTIGATION—SENATE EMPLOYEES

House of Representatives

Chamber Action

Bills Introduced: 12 public bills, H.R. 10295-10306; 2 private bills, H.R. 10307-10308; 3 resolutions, H.J. Res. 945 and 946, and H. Con. Res. 279, were introduced.

Page 4570

Bills Reported: Reports were filed as follows:

S. 1964, to increase the fee charged for learners' permits, filed on March 6 (H. Rept. 1219);

H.R. 10215, to extend sick leave benefits for D.C. police and firemen, U.S. Park Police, and White House Police, filed on March 6 (H. Rept. 1220);

H.J. Res. 888, authorizing promulgation of special regulations and granting of certain permits during Shrine Convention in District of Columbia in July 1965 (amended), filed on March 6 (H. Rept. 1221);

H.R. 5990, to amend the District of Columbia Charitable Solicitation Act, filed on March 6 (H. Rept. 1222);

H.R. 9962, to amend the act regulating the practice of podiatry relative to written theoretical examinations, filed on March 6 (H. Rept. 1223);

H. Con. Res. 189, naming the Southwest regional water laboratory of the Department of Health, Education, and Welfare at Ada, Okla., as the "Robert S. Kerr Water Research Center" (H. Rept. 1224);

S. 87, a private bill (H. Rept. 225);

Sick leave: H.R. 10215, to extend sick leave benefits for D.C. police and firemen, U.S. Park Police, and White House Police;

Podiatry: H.R. 9962, to amend the act regulating the practice of podiatry relative to written theoretical examinations;

Drivers' learners' permits: S. 1964, to increase the fee charged for learners' permits from $2 to $5.

Pages 4519–4524

Pacific Power: The conference report on S. 1007, guaranteeing electric consumers in the Pacific Northwest first call on electric energy generated at Federal hydroelectric plants in that area, was called up but objection was made to a request to insist on the House amendments and to agree to a further conference with the Senate.

Page 4535

Bills Referred: Two Senate-passed bills were referred to appropriate committees.

Page 4567

Quorum Call: During the proceedings of the House today one quorum call developed and it appears on page 4512.

Program for Tuesday: Adjourned at 2:44 p.m. until Tuesday, March 10, 1964, at 12 o'clock noon, when the House will consider H.R. 8070, to establish a Public Lands Law Review Commission (2 hours of debate).

Excerpts from the summary of Congressional action on March 9, 1964, as reported in the Congressional Record.

Demonstrators at the United States Embassy in Phnom Penh, Cambodia, on March 11.

tion resolutions, obituary notices, prayers, and court rulings that each Representative and Senator thought it important to bring to the attention of the nation (and his constituents) at public expense. Along with insertions dealing with national and local policies went a poem written to Richard Cardinal Cushing on his twenty-fifth anniversary as a bishop, the winning speech of a Florida high school senior in the Veterans of Foreign Wars' annual "Voice of Democracy" contest, a table showing the important tobacco-growing districts in the nineteen tobacco-growing states of the nation, and a press review of an art show by "a former cowboy from the town of Meeteetse in northern Wyoming."

THE EXECUTIVE BRANCH

Hundreds of actions affecting millions of Americans, and the nation as a whole, are taken each week by federal executive departments and independent reg-

ulatory agencies. During the week of March 8–15 the Department of Justice asked a federal court in Portland, Oregon, to forbid the four major swimsuit manufacturers in the United States from engaging in price-fixing agreements; another Justice Department motion to a federal court in Montgomery, Alabama, asked the judges to require that the Alabama State Board of Education eliminate the state's "dual school system, based on race."

The State Department sent a note to Prince Sihanouk of Cambodia, protesting the riots against the United States Embassy in the Cambodian capital, carried out by government-tolerated street mobs. A State Department representative at the United Nations submitted two draft treaties designed to protect astronauts in space-flight emergencies and to fix liability for damages caused by space accidents. At a penthouse suite in the State Department, the Assistant Secretary of State for African Affairs,

19

A diplomatic diversion: square dance in the State Department.

G. Mennen Williams, presided over a square dance for leading diplomats from the African states, calling out the steps in both English and French.

In reply to allegations that secret flights over Communist countries were standard American practice in the Far East, the Defense Department denied that the United States was carrying out RB-57 high-altitude reconnaissance flights over Communist China. On March 13, the Atomic Energy Commission conducted a "low-yield" underground nuclear explosion at its Nevada test site. A "small amount" of "very low-level" radioactive fall-out accidentally fell on Las Vegas, seventy miles away.

Secretary of Commerce Luther Hodges held a press conference to disclose details about the shipment of United States wheat sold to Russia in 1963 after its serious crop failures. Sec-

retary Hodges praised the "extremely cooperative attitude" of Soviet officials in the last-minute arrangements for ocean carriage of the wheat, and he echoed a rising view in many American business circles that it was time for "normalizing trade relations" with the Soviet Union.

Throughout the week, a special executive commission investigating the assassination of President John F. Kennedy heard witnesses to the Dallas shooting on November 22. Four persons who claimed to have seen a rifle protruding from the window of the Texas School Book Depository Building were questioned by the chairman, Chief Justice Earl Warren, and other commission members. The proceedings remained closed to the press and public.

The federal regulatory agencies were equally active in this period. The chairman of the Federal Trade Commission reassured cigarette industry officials on March 14 that the agency would consider "the economic aspects" before making a decision whether to require health warnings on cigarette packs and in advertisements. In other action, the

"Relighting the Flame."

Miller in the Des Moines *Register*

FTC dismissed charges of retail price fixing against the General Electric Company; however, the FTC said it would keep the company's merchandising plan under close scrutiny.

The Federal Power Commission, which had been studying a plan for a $130 million hydroelectric project in upper New York state, reported during the week that construction of the plant would have little adverse effect on the scenic beauty of the Hudson River Valley; the report rejected an opposite conclusion by the Scenic Hudson Preservation Conference.

An attempt to establish the airline industry's first minimum air cargo charter rates across the Atlantic met with tentative disapproval from the Civil Aeronautics Board on March 10. However, the CAB gave the airlines fifteen days in which to file data to support the proposed minimums adopted in December, 1963, by members of the International Air Transport Association.

Wide World

James R. Hoffa and his lawyer leaving the Federal Courthouse in Chattanooga, Tennessee, after being sentenced.

THE FEDERAL JUDICIARY

Federal courts throughout the nation issued several important decisions affecting American government and society during the week of March 8. The Supreme Court, citing the freedom-of-speech-and-press guarantees of the First Amendment, unanimously reversed a $500,000 libel judgment awarded in the Alabama courts against the New York *Times* and four Negro clergymen. The case concerned a full-page ad published in the March 29, 1960, edition of the *Times* by friends of integration leader Dr. Martin Luther King, Jr. This ad stated that police had ringed a local Negro college campus to subdue a student civil rights protest, and it charged "Southern violators" with bombing Dr. King's home and arresting him seven times. State officials, including then Governor John M. Patterson, had sued for libel. In its de-

cision, the Supreme Court held that public officials could not recover libel damages for criticism of their official performances unless they could prove that statements had been made with deliberate malice.

The role of courts in the American system of government was forcefully stated in a United States district court proceeding on March 12 when Teamsters' Union President James R. Hoffa was sentenced to eight years in prison and fined $10,000 for attempting to bribe a federal jury. In setting the sentence, presiding Judge Frank W. Wilson told the defendant, "You stand here convicted of seeking to corrupt the administration of justice. You stand here convicted of having tampered, really, with the very soul of this nation. You stand here convicted of having struck at the very foundation upon which everything in this nation depends, the very basis of civilization itself, and that is the administration of justice, because without a fair and proper and lawful administration of justice nothing else would be possible in this country."

A special three-judge federal court in Alabama declared on March 13 that Alabama's system of electing Congressional candidates was unconstitutional, and the state legislature was warned to redraw Congressional districts "within a reasonable time" after the start of the next legislative session.

In Los Angeles, a federal grand jury indicted the United States Steel Corporation, five other steel concerns, and eight company officers on charges of rigging bids and allocating sales of steel and concrete water pipe in ten Western states.

PARTY AND ELECTION ACTIVITY

The week of March 8 was especially significant for the 1964 Presidential election. New Hampshire on March 10 held its state Presidential primary—the first of seventeen states to do so—to elect delegates to the nominating conventions of the two major parties, scheduled for late summer. The New Hampshire primary was widely viewed as a test of voter reaction to the two "leading" candidates for the Republican nomination, Arizona's Senator Barry Goldwater and New York's Governor Nelson A. Rockefeller, both of whom were formally entered on the ballot and had campaigned vigorously in the Granite State for months. When all the ballots were counted, it was Henry Cabot Lodge, the United States Ambassador to South Vietnam, who scored an upset victory by winning a write-in vote of 35 percent of the total ballots cast. Goldwater, who before his campaign in the state had been given a 4-1 lead, received only 23 percent. We "must have goofed somewhere," the Senator told newsmen later. Rockefeller, whose divorce and remarriage had been considered by many as a major political handicap, won 22 percent of the vote. Richard Nixon, also a write-in candidate, received 17 percent. The consensus of political experts in Washington and of James Reston in

Senator Barry Goldwater campaigning in Milford, New Hampshire.

Governor George Wallace of Alabama surrounded by students of Wisconsin State College, Oshkosh, during his primary campaign.

the New York *Times* was that the primary results had destroyed any real chance for Goldwater to get the GOP nomination.

The New Hampshire primary also caused some furor within the Democratic party, since supporters of Attorney General Robert Kennedy had waged a campaign to get the state's Democrats to write in the name of the Attorney General for the Vice-Presidential nomination. There were rumors in Washington that the President was not pleased by the campaigning on behalf of his Attorney General, viewing the write-in drive as an effort to force the Kennedy candidacy on the President before the nominating convention. In another Democratic party development that week, Alabama's Governor George Wallace began his campaign in Wisconsin's Democratic Presidential preference primary against favorite son Governor

John Reynolds. While he did not expect to win, Wallace said he would gain enough votes to show that a strong segregationist would win a substantial vote among Northerners who were "fed up" with federal "favoritism" and "muscle" on behalf of Negroes.

In party and election matters below the national level, a New York *Times* report on March 15 described the growth of Republican strength in North Carolina and the possible effects of genuine two-party competition in this leading Southern state. From a party that was once dismissed by Carolina Democrats as "able to hold their conventions in a telephone booth," the state Republicans had registered 46.5 percent of the gubernatorial vote in 1960, and had won two Congressional seats and twenty-three places in the state general assembly. But with this prosperity had come factional disputes between liberal and conservative ele-

Robert G. (Bobby) Baker, left foreground, before the Senate Rules Committee.

ments and between pro-Negro and anti-Negro elements in the party.

One final set of political developments during the week of March 8 illustrated both the partisan and bipartisan aspects of politics within Congress. The Senate Rules Committee, after extensive hearings on the financial dealings of Robert Baker, former secretary to the Senate Democratic party, voted along strict party lines to end the hearings on Baker's possible misuse of his official position for personal profit. Democrats felt that the hearings had already explored all the useful avenues of evidence, while Republicans—deeply interested in suggestions of forged income-tax returns and Baker's close friendship with former Senate Majority Leader Lyndon Johnson—charged that the Democrats were attempting to "whitewash" the case. When the Senate opened debate on the civil rights bill, however, Senator Hubert Humphrey, the Democrat serving as floor manager for the Administration's proposal, called for a firm bipartisan effort and warmly praised the leading Senate Republicans. "This is not a partisan issue," said Humphrey, "and if we succeed, as I know we will, it will be because men like Senator Everett McKinley Dirksen, Senator Thomas H. Kuchel and other Republicans have put the interest of their country above any partisan advantage."

INTEREST GROUPS

During the week of March 8, the activities of civic interest groups were readily apparent. Some of the economic groups appearing before legislative bodies included witnesses who championed federal bills to restrict the import of foreign beef, veal, and lamb into the United States. On March 12, the Senate Finance Committee heard representatives of the American National Cattlemen's Association, the National Wool Growers Association, and the National Livestock Feeders Association support the proposed meat import restrictions. In other Congressional committee hearings during the week, the American Hospital Association asked for increased money to renew aging city hospitals rather than increased appropriations for rural hospital aid; the American Federation of Labor supported legislation to require all foreign steamship companies operating in American ports to list their country of registry in promotional advertising; the United Hebrew Immigrants Aid Society (HIAS) called on Congress to eliminate the present racial and religious bias in the national immigration laws; and the Motion Picture Theater Association joined other film and book groups in opposing bills to give District of Columbia police greater powers to censor "indecent" publications or performances.

Congressional leaders did not always remain passive under the pressures of various interest groups. On the civil rights front, for example, Senator J. Strom Thurmond of South Carolina challenged the right of the National Council of Churches of Christ, as an organization exempted from federal taxation and therefore barred from legislative activities, to continue its letter-writing campaign to Senators in behalf of a strong civil rights measure. In turn, Senator Hubert Humphrey of Minnesota attacked the Coordinating Committee for Fundamental American Freedoms, a group financed by Mississippi state funds, which had placed full-page advertisements entitled "$100 Billion Blackjack" in newspapers throughout the country. The ads called the pending civil rights measure a "blackjack" that would destroy the right of white Americans "to determine for themselves how they will live."

Other groups were busy with "educational" and "public opinion" campaigns during this week. The Elgin, Hamilton, and Bulova Watch Companies opened a nationwide campaign to prevent further reductions by the Tariff Commission in the tariff on Swiss watches. The Sierra Club, a leading conservationist group, announced it would fight federal proposals to build dams on the lower Colorado River; it claimed the dams would destroy priceless scenic landmarks and "violate our national park system." Americans for Constitutional Action, a right-of-center group, issued its annual index of the "conservatism rating" of Congressmen: its ratings turned out to be almost the exact reverse of the ratings of "liberalism" that Americans for Democratic Action, a left-of-center organization, had issued in January, 1964. A coalition of groups for elderly persons called on the World's Fair to set up a "Senior Citizen's Week" during which entrance fees would be reduced to $.25; there was no comment from Fair director Robert Moses. Heavy lobbying was reported at the Coliseum in New York during the International Flower Show over the selection of an official national flower for the United States. David Burpee, a registered agent for the marigold interests, engaged in sharp debates with spokesmen for the rose, gardenia, corn tassel, and sunflower.

CIVIL RIGHTS
AND CIVIL LIBERTIES

While civil rights for America's Negro population were being debated in Congress during the week, and while the courts were ruling on important legal issues of equality, events throughout the nation reminded citizens of the continuing political and civic ferment over the civil rights issue. Following an incident in November, 1963, when two Negro students were arrested for attempting to enter a concert hall in Jackson, Mississippi, to hear the London Royal Philharmonic Orchestra, a number of the nation's leading artists had spoken out against appearance before segregated audiences. Conductors George Szell and Leonard Bernstein and opera star Risë Stevens announced this week that they would not appear

Wide World

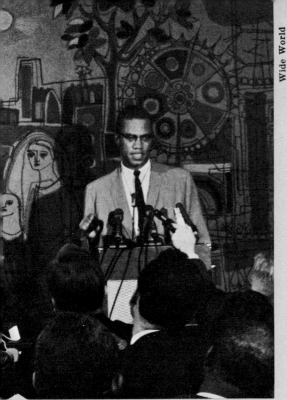

Malcolm X addressing newsmen at the Park-Sheraton Hotel, New York, March 12.

public referendum in Seattle, Washington. In California, Governor Edmund Brown denounced civil rights sit-ins as endangering efforts to defend a new state law forbidding housing discrimination against a real-estate-sponsored repeal campaign.

A rift within the Negro protest movement came to a climax during the week as Malcolm X, formerly a leading Black Muslim spokesman, broke with that organization to found his own movement, the Black Nationalists. In a press interview, Malcolm predicted that there would be more racial violence in 1964 than ever before. Meanwhile, what was coming to be called the "white backlash" against civil rights movements was also signaled in New York by a march across Brooklyn Bridge to New York City Hall by 15,000 persons (mostly housewives) from the Parents and Taxpayers Association protesting the city's plan for transporting children to equalize racial balances in the public schools.

In the area of civil liberties, involving conflicts over freedom of expression, due process, and religious liberty,

before such audiences in the future. Pianist Artur Rubenstein had urged that artists should "actively participate in fostering civil rights." As the artist boycott movement grew, the Student Nonviolent Committee approached the Pittsburgh Orchestra and sopranos Birgit Nilsson and Eleanor Steber during the week of March 8 with a request to cancel their appearances before segregated audiences this season.

On March 14, Maryland became the first Southern state to pass a statewide public accommodations law, as a result of strong pressure by Governor Tawes on a reluctant legislature; discussion on a similar bill was held before the Kentucky house of representatives. A fair housing bill, however, lost in a

Members of the Parents and Taxpayers Association crossing Brooklyn Bridge on their way to the New York City Hall.

UPI

Senators Allen Ellender of Louisiana, left, and John Stennis of Mississippi planning strategy to defeat Senate passage of the Civil Rights bill.

news developments ran their customarily wide gamut. A schoolgirl in Long Island, New York, was suspended from classes because she refused to participate in a civil defense drill; her parents said they would take the school's action to court. At the University of Illinois, the trustees were considering the case of Revilo P. Oliver, a fifty-five-year-old classics professor and member of the John Birch Society's National Council, whose article, "Marxmanship in Dallas," in the Birch Society magazine had accused President Kennedy of "collaborating" with Premier Khrushchev in a sham embargo of Cuba and concluded that the President's "memory will be cherished with distaste" by all true Americans. Whether Professor Oliver's extracurricular writings were grounds for disciplinary action by the University was the key issue at stake. In Pennsylvania, a court suit was filed by several parents against a school board which provided for a fifteen-minute compulsory study of the Bible as a "literary and historical exercise" each day. Such a system, the complaint said, violated the United States Supreme Court's 1963 ruling that religious exercises in the public schools were forbidden by the First Amendment's guarantee of separation between church and state.

In other civil liberties developments, the American Civil Liberties Union wrote to Attorney General Robert Kennedy, criticizing public statements by FBI Director J. Edgar Hoover that gave the prior criminal records of the men arrested for the kidnaping of Frank Sinatra, Jr. Such announcements, said the ACLU, endanger the right to impartial trial of persons suspected of crime.

STATE AND LOCAL GOVERNMENT

News at the state and local governmental level covered the full range of executive, legislative, administrative, judicial, party, interest group, and constitutional rights areas already discussed, sometimes in matters with only local appeal but at other times with sharp import for the nation as well. Dallas, Texas, made international headlines when a jury in the Third Criminal District Court for Dallas County found Jack Ruby guilty of killing Lee Harvey

New York police "frisking" an unidentified suspect on Lexington Avenue.

Oswald, the alleged assassin of President Kennedy, and sentenced him to die in the electric chair. His attorney, Melvin M. Belli, denounced the verdict as a "victory for bigotry" and pledged to appeal "to a court where there is justice and impartiality."

In the state legislatures, New Jersey held an inconclusive debate over the passage of a state sales tax. Bar Association and civil liberties groups in New York protested the signing by Governor Rockefeller of two laws allowing police to "stop and frisk" persons suspected of criminal activity and to enter a suspect's home without knocking when "quickly destroyable" evidence was being sought. The Mississippi house of representatives passed a bill to permit commitment of parents of illegitimate children to prison unless they submitted to voluntary sterilization. Several states debated plans to reapportion election dis-

tricts within their legislatures to conform to Supreme Court rulings that had struck down existing systems as unconstitutional. Some idea of the range of issues facing state legislators was the week's agenda of issues under debate in New York, which included state aid to local schools, liquor price controls, an ethics code for state legislators, regulation of abuses by companies giving trading stamps, and permission for family stores to remain open on Sundays in cases where the owners celebrated the Sabbath on another day.

At the local level, a bond issue for school expansion was defeated for the ninth time in Rockland County, New York, despite double sessions for almost half the children in public schools. The reason for the defeat was that one school district composed primarily of older residents with few children had been consolidated with a district having a housing boom and large school population. In Arkansas, the federal government was rebuffed in an attempt to close down gambling activities in Hot Springs; local residents making up a federal grand jury refused to indict persons charged with a federal gambling offense for using out-of-state checks to buy illegal gambling chips. Governor Orval Faubus had called control of gambling a "local issue" and had attacked federal intervention.

Gubernatorial and administrative agency problems were illustrated by efforts by Governor Hughes of New Jersey and state mediation officials to prevent a threatened strike of workers on New Jersey and interstate bus lines. Also during this week, Governor Hughes warned in a speech before the Port of New York Authority that the air traffic problem over the metropolitan New York area would reach "crisis proportions" by 1968 unless creative measures were taken now by the states involved.

Constants and Changes in the American Political System, 1889–1964

Looking over our sample weeks in 1889 and 1964 we can see many parallel aspects—Presidential concern over appointments to federal posts, party conflicts within Congress, factional rivalry within the parties, economic groups seeking special legislation to promote their interests, racial struggles in the South, federal-state rivalries, debates over the boundary between private and public services at the local level, and disputes with foreign powers. Obviously, the basic forms and institutions, and even most of the procedures, of contemporary American government in 1964 were those also in use during 1889.

Despite these striking elements of continuity, American government today is radically different from its 1889 ancestor. The key changes are in the relationships between the parts of the American governmental system and between government and the private sphere. Stated most simply, major shifts took place between 1889 and 1964 in four "great balances" of the system:

1. Foreign and defense policy matters increased greatly in importance over domestic affairs.
2. The President took on broad powers at the expense of traditional Congressional authority.
3. The federal government assumed responsibility for vast areas of regulation that once lay under the jurisdiction of state and local governments.
4. National, state, and local governments as a whole assumed responsibility for social, economic, and civic concerns that once were conducted by individuals or private groups.

The effect of these changed balances on the conduct of our political system will be discussed at length in many of the more specific chapters that follow. The basic point to be made here is that the 1889 example illustrated the American political system at the height of its classic era, while the week from 1964 showed the same system fundamentally altered by a changed social, technological, and international environment.

A good way to appreciate how marked this change in environment has been is to compare some of the bare statistics of American life in 1889 and 1964 and then sample some of the deeper forces at work in the seventy-five intervening years.

In 1889, the United States was a nation of sixty-two million persons, in forty-two states, with two out of three Americans living in rural communities. Twenty-five percent of the population was illiterate; most of this group was foreign-born or nonwhite. The annual federal budget was $230 million (excluding certain previously authorized expenditures), the public debt was $1.2 billion, and 30,000 civilians worked for the federal government, or one out of every 2,000 Americans. The nation's gross national product was $13.5 billion and the average work week in manufacturing was sixty hours. The military forces of the United States on active duty numbered about 40,000, with rifle, fieldpiece, and cavalry the dominant weapons of land war.

American troops were stationed solely in the Western Hemisphere, and the nation had no treaties pledging it to the defense of any other country. There was no foreign aid. Fifteen thousand persons graduated from college that year. Four cities had populations of over a half million. The average life expectancy of males was forty-five years, of females, forty-two and one half years. The federal government collected about $267 million yearly from all taxes levied. The fastest trip possible between New York and Chicago took 34 hours, and between Washington and Los Angeles 139 hours. Newspaper readers learned that a new "horseless carriage," the Benz auto, had been displayed that year at the Paris World's Fair, but horse and railroad were what made people and things go in 1889 and what set patterns of transportation, residence, and work.

In 1964, the United States had a population of over 190 million, in fifty states, with almost three out of every four Americans living in urban and suburban areas. Only 4.5 percent of the population was illiterate (by now, almost wholly nonwhites). The annual federal budget in 1964 was $99 billion, the public debt $312 billion, and more than two and a half million persons worked for the federal government, or one out of seventy-six Americans. The nation's gross national product was $554 billion, and the average work week in manufacturing was 40.4 hours. The military forces on active duty were almost 2.7 million men and women, in an era of intercontinental ballistic missiles and nuclear-firing atomic submarines. A significant number of American troops were stationed in nineteen foreign countries, and the nation had military alliances with forty-two countries. In 1963, $4.4 billion had been spent in foreign aid. Some 520,000 persons received college degrees in 1964. Twenty-one cities had populations of over a half million. The average life expectancy for men was 66.6 years, and for women 73.1 years. The federal government collected $99.4 billion in taxes. There were 66 million automobiles in the United States, and 74 percent of American families had at least one car. Jet flights between New York and Chicago took two hours, and between Washington and Los Angeles five and a half.

Between 1889 and 1964, then, immense changes took place in the American environment, in the technological ways of dealing with that environment, in the size and mixture of the American population, and in the relation of the United States to the international community. It would take far more space than we have here to explain, even briefly, all of the major changes, and many discussions later in the book will deal with these matters as they relate to particular institutions, processes, or policies. What we can do here is to select a few of the most revealing social changes since 1889 and indicate three things about them: the *nature* of the development, the way in which it gave rise to *political* issues, and the effects this had on the activities of American *government*.

THE EXPANSION OF KNOWLEDGE

Since the 1890s, man's knowledge of himself and his environment has undergone dramatic, surging increases. The most conspicuous has been in the physical realm, not only the discovery and harnessing of atomic energy and the revolutions in weaponry but also achievements in electronics, metallurgy, and related fields that have transferred the exploration of outer space from fiction to fact. Potentially as important are developments in biology, such as the biochemistry of the living cell, which promise to unlock the secrets of heredity. In the past two decades, information theory and computer technology have begun the revolution of automation, reducing the labor requirements in many manufacturing and office processes to a fraction of their previous level. Similarly our present sophistication as to the nature of illness is a post-1890s development—especially the relation of micro-organisms to disease—which underlies most of contemporary public health practice and many of the accomplishments of modern surgery. The list of recent break-throughs could be expanded to include developments in psychology that have made mental illness something to be cured rather than merely an affliction to be borne, as well as increased knowledge of man's social arrangements, extending to the conditions controlling economic growth and levels of productivity.

The national government stands at the center in this great expansion of knowledge. A nationally instituted program of government research in agricultural colleges and experiment stations, for example, was the leading factor in the growth of agricultural knowledge. Today, however, the national government activates and supports research and development on a scale unheard of even twenty-five years ago. In 1963 the federal government spent $12 billion, one third more than its total prewar annual budget, for research and development. Much of this is spent through the Department of Defense, the Atomic Energy Commission, and the National Aeronautics and Space Administration. But the National Science Foundation had a budget of $206 million in 1963, and the National Institutes of Health and a multitude of other government agencies are supporting research—some with very large sums of money. Contracts are made by the government with private companies, specially created research corporations (such as the RAND Corporation), universities, research bureaus, and individual scholars. Research and development, essential for national defense, economic growth, and cultural advance, thrive under government sponsorship and support.

Government, moreover, uses this expanded knowledge. The military and space programs are the most obvious examples. Illustrative, however, of other applications is the program of air traffic control of the Federal Aviation Agency, which cost $813 million in 1964. Illustrative, also, are the uses of automated devices in administrative operations—essential to the effective conduct of such large programs as social security, tax collection and record-keeping, and national defense.

The political effect of this expansion of knowledge has been to change the expectations of the American people (along with peoples in other advanced or developing nations). To know that large-scale preventive medicine is technically possible generates public expectations that money for research and medical services will be made available, if not by private effort, then by governmental action. The same is true of developing supersonic airplanes, miniaturizing circuitry for communication, or collecting statistics on seasonal unemployment. How quickly *government* should enter these fields to promote private activity by grants or subsidies, to regulate the activity of private operators, or even to take over the enterprise as a government monopoly has become a political issue, with contending groups of producers and users struggling to advance their own ideas and interests in relation to the expanding fields of knowledge.

Important also is the sudden change in the political role of the country's scientists. Barely three decades ago physicists and their colleagues were primarily university specimens, academic types pursuing work of probable but uncertain importance. They were certainly not significant actors on the governmental scene. Today the scientific aspects of weapons development, of rivalry in outer space, and hence of governmental budget and expenditure decisions are so large and so complex that the country's most competent scientists must play an important part in the making of governmental policy. How the scientist's governmental role is to be played and how it is to be related to the positions and powers of responsible elected officials thus have become questions of critical importance.

PRODUCTION TECHNOLOGY

When technological change occurs very rapidly, as it has in the past seventy-five years of our history, however much it increases the material well-being of society, in the long run it can also revolutionize whole industries and create vast manpower dislocations. This is best illustrated in agriculture. A depressed industry between the two world wars, it was again, as in the First World War, highly prosperous in the Second World War. Surpluses of agricultural commodities gave way to shortages and even to rationing of meats, fats, and canned foods. But an upward surge in production began about 1940. In 1860 one farm worker could supply fewer than 5 people. It took eighty years for this to double—rising by 1940 to 10.69 people. But by 1962 one farm worker could supply 27 people. This nearly threefold increase in productive power in twenty-two years is the result of growth in knowledge about soils, products, and agricultural methods, and the application of this knowledge and machinery to farm production. Farms are becoming factories; today 40 percent of them produce 87 percent of the output.

A prime economic effect of this achievement in farm technology has been that the country needs fewer farmers. The "excess" farm population should therefore move off the land into other occupations. Though this has been occurring (the farm population declined by nearly fifteen million people in the past two decades) the shift has not been swift enough to match increased productivity, since many persons have not wished to leave "farm life" for city work and an urban environment.

The political result has been a chronic national "farm problem" since at least 1920, involving not only farmers but consumers, manufacturers, transportation groups, and even foreign policy specialists. Clearly, no state alone could begin to deal with the farm problem, and the federal government has as yet found no acceptable solutions. If the natural processes of the market are allowed to operate, farm prices decline drastically, the incomes of all farmers deteriorate, and large numbers of people are literally driven out of agriculture. If farm prices are supported, movement off the farms is slowed, and surplus production piles up. If limits on production and marketing are attempted, migration can be stimulated and prices controlled to some degree, but the government is charged with bureaucratic meddling, with destroying the "family farm," and with attempting to "socialize" American agriculture.

The revolutionary effects of technology are apparent in other industries. The automobile has produced employment for millions in iron, steel, automotive, and other industries, in oil production, in gas stations, motels, and other local businesses. Similarly, as other products or new processes of production are developed, new opportunities for employment and investment are created. On the other hand, adverse effects are felt in other industries. This is illustrated by the bituminous coal industry, which produced in 1955 the same output as in 1940, but with half as many miners. New mechanical methods put 200,000 men out of work, and coal consumption itself declined with increased use of new fuels. Most of this change occurred within one decade. In a state like West Virginia, the chief producer of bituminous coal, the effects of such change have been intense. Some of the displaced workers moved out, with the result that West Virginia was one of the three states in the country that declined in population between 1950 and 1960. But many of them did not want to leave and had skills useful nowhere but in the coal industry. What to do about this stranded, poor, and increasingly embittered population became a serious government problem for the states, and, given limited state resources, for Washington as well.

Technological changes constantly affect employment opportunities in almost every kind of occupation. Automation, though a cost-reducing device and thus a contribution to higher standards of living, is a fearful word for workers. Technological developments in medicine bring specialization and group practice, and television may transform teaching practices and reduce manpower needs in education. Very few Americans are still self-employed; five out of every six dollars of income in this country are from wages and salaries. Job dependence is now the most familiar aspect of the American economic system. Because of this, and because the remaining self-employed (shopkeepers, dentists, etc.) are also quickly affected by declines in the economy, men expect government to follow policies which support maximum employment and economic growth. Large differences of opinion exist over the kinds of policies which will yield these results—for example, balanced or unbalanced budgets—and out of these differences arise issues of politics. But from the "full dinner pail" campaign of the Republicans in 1896, through the promise of two cars in every garage in the Hoover campaign of 1928 and the anti-Depression measures of the New Deal, to the present, government has been increasingly involved in the problems created by individual dependence on the state of the economy. And since no state can hope to deal alone with the problems presented, the search for solutions occurs within the national government.

Still another by-product of technological change has been the growth of large-scale corporate enterprises. A Federal Trade Commission study in 1950 showed that the 200 largest manufacturing corporations accounted for 40.5 percent of the national production. Another study showed that in 1958 four manufacturing companies in each of the following fields produced from 50 percent to 80 percent of the total production: motor vehicles and parts, steel works and rolling mills, aircraft engines, organic chemicals, cigarettes, tin cans and other tinware, synthetic fibers, and tractors. Large corporate enterprises are also characteristic of insurance, banking, transportation, utilities, and, more recently, retailing. They operate nationally, without respect to state boundaries. Giant national labor unions have arisen to deal with giant national corporate enterprises. At present about one third of all nonagricultural employees belong to unions. In 1960 three unions had over 1,000,000 members, four had 500,000 to 1,000,000, and fourteen had 200,000 to 500,000.

The figures on size do not reveal fully the power of corporate and union leaders. The corporate community's interests are reflected in the United States Chamber of Commerce, the National Association of Manufacturers, national trade associations, and other organizations, and most large unions are federated in the AFL-CIO. Such organizations are potent in the economy and in politics. Moreover, vast power is exerted through decisions in corporate boards of industries and in union-management negotiations. A strategic decision on wages or on price increases at one point in the economy —for example, within the steel or automobile industry—may set a pattern for wage or price increases throughout the nation and have more impact on the condition of the economy than decisions by Congress, the President, the Federal Reserve Board, or other government agencies.

The effect of these changes was just beginning to be felt in 1889. Congress enacted a weak regulatory statute for railroads in 1887, an antitrust statute of 1890 was enforced hesitantly, and the President intervened in a labor dispute for the first time in 1894. These dates, however, mark a transition in the functions of the national government. While it had previously left economic regulation to the states, except for the institution of banking regulation in 1863, in the next seventy-five years it would have an expanding agenda of problems generated by large-scale private organizations. It now has a large volume of statutes dealing with antitrust, collective bargaining, transportation and communications industries, banking, power and gas utilities, foods and drugs, and miscellaneous other industries. The states also have regulations in most of these fields as well as for insurance corporations. Still, how much governments should intervene in questions of economic policies such as pricing decisions or wage controversies, and what methods should be used, remain issues that divide both the American public and the experts who must work on the problems.

POPULATION CHANGES

Many basic changes have taken place in the composition and distribution of the "American people" since 1889, and these have had tremendous effects upon the functions of government, the responsibilities exercised at local, state, and national levels, and the politics of the nation.

Many of the changes are so recent that their phenomenal character and impact are rarely more than faintly appreciated. Historians date the disappearance of the "frontier" at 1890, and not until 1920 was a majority of the American population "urban," that is living in places with 2,500 or more inhabitants. Even as late as 1940 one out of every five persons was employed in agriculture. But in 1960 only one out of twelve was so employed, and 70 percent lived in urban centers. The most striking fact, however, is that urbanization has become metropolitanization. In 1960 nearly two thirds (63 percent) of the population lived in 202 large metropolitan areas, that is, in areas with more than 100,000 population, in comparison with 15 percent in 28 centers in 1890, and with 29 percent in 106 centers as late as 1950. Moreover, between 1950 and 1960 nearly all (97 percent) of the country's increase was in such areas. Another spectacular recent population movement has occurred in the metropolitan areas. While the growth of suburbs was relatively modest until 1940, in the forties about one half, and in the fifties two thirds, of the country's increase in population was in suburban portions of metropolitan areas.

The consequences of these changes are so important and so diverse that they receive attention in many chapters of this book. A few only may be mentioned here. Metropolitan government has become big government. Transportation, utility service, recreation, housing, crime, and other problems have far more extensive and complex dimensions in metropolitan than in rural or small urban areas. Moreover, as cities have found it difficult to finance their many functions they have turned first to the states and then to the national government for financial help. Other problems are created by the existence within the same metropolitan area of several governments that need to cooperate but are often in conflict with each other, and by the inability of central cities to enlist the interest and collect the taxes of those who live in the suburbs and work in the central city.

Urbanization has, moreover, brought new trends in politics. Many people carry with them general attitudes formed in a rural environment even after they have moved to cities. But new generations will adapt to their environment, and will come to think as urbanites. The effect of urbanization on politics has been delayed because of the carryover of rural attitudes and the underrepresentation of urban populations in legislatures. Congress has been more responsive to urban populations than have many state legislatures, and this has led metropolitan government leaders to turn to Washington for aid. Recent reapportionment decisions of the Supreme Court, if not reversed by constitutional amendment, will give the urban population a greater influence in Congress and state legislatures, particularly the latter. Urbanism also tends to increase the nationalization of politics. The classic cleavages in American politics were sectional—the Atlantic seaboard versus the Trans-Allegheny West, the North against the South, and the Trans-Mississippi West against the East. Although these differences have not disappeared, the politically significant cleavages are increasingly those within urban areas—retired taxpayers versus the parents of school children, employers versus employees, commuters versus full-time residents, and many others. Although the massive impact of urbanization and industrialization has not yet been fully felt, the tendency away from the sectionalism that characterized rural politics has been noticeable in Presidential elections. Moreover, mayors of large cities, whatever section of the country they live in, are likely to make common cause in their plea to Washington for attention to housing, the regulation of the price of natural gas, and other matters of interest to urban populations.

Another change in the population is in the proportions of the aged and children in the total population. Here again the changes have been spectacular in the last generation. The percentage of the aged increased from 3 percent in 1890, and less than 7 percent in 1940, to over 9 percent in 1960. A population explosion after the Second World War led to an increase in the percentage of persons under nineteen—from 30 percent in 1940 to 39 percent in 1960.

These changes are reflected in increased costs of government for support of the aged and for education of children and adolescents. Technological change, which has increased the life span and decreased the opportunities for employment of older persons, has meant that most persons reaching sixty-five (or frequently some earlier age) must have some kind of support other than earnings for five, ten, twenty, or more years after they retire. An increased number of children and technological changes have led to low employment opportunities for youth and to a need for longer periods of education. These trends have brought an amazingly large increase in the costs of education—not merely for children but for young adults who want college and professional education. In sum, changes in the composition of the population and accompanying technological changes mean that those of employment age must support more persons at other age levels, and one way is through taxes for support of public services.

Changes bring new issues in politics. Social security payments became an issue in the thirties, and the level and details of the system are still issues in the sixties. The new medicare issue has led to new tensions in politics, and if some form of medicare is adopted for older persons there will still be controversy about the amount and duration of payments, and perhaps also about extending the system to younger persons. Creating only slightly less tension are the issues about federal aid for education. Traditionally, education has been a local function. Yet the increasingly uneven distribution of financial resources among localities, the burden of local real estate taxes, and the desire to provide good educational opportunities for all has led to state support for education; and now the same unevenness of state resources, the difficulties of raising ample state taxes, and increased consciousness of the need for education have led to pressures for national support. The national government now supports education in many ways, but the issue of general aid presses upon the Congress in every session.

One of the most noticeable features of our population is its mobility. Increasingly, Americans are leaving their home towns and even their home states. The effect is to destroy local attachments, loyalty to states, and interest in local and state governments, bringing a decline of sectional cleavages and increasing the sense of national unity and the interest in national solutions for American problems. A man who is born in Massachusetts, serves in his nation's armed forces at several locations, gets a college degree in Michigan, and takes a job first in Colorado, then in Texas, and then in California is likely to be more interested in national than in local or state politics, and he is not likely to be much concerned over the preservation of local self-government or states' rights.

Mobility of population brings changes in the political balances of the country. The disproportionate growth of population in the West and Southwest compared to the remainder of the country has increased the importance of these areas in national politics. California, with a population growth of nearly 50 percent from 1950 to 1960 in comparison with 18.5 percent for the nation as a whole, now has forty electoral votes—only three less than New York. Florida, with a growth of 78.7 percent, and Texas with 24.2 percent become more important as pivotal states. The diminution of sectional issues in politics may, however, reduce the significance of these sectional changes.

One important example of the internal redistribution of population in recent years has been the emigration of Negroes from the South. As recently as 1920, more than 85 percent of the Negro population of the country lived in the region that the Bureau of the Census defines as the South (the eleven states of the Confederacy plus the District of Columbia and the five border states of Delaware, Maryland, West Virginia, Kentucky, and Oklahoma). In 1960 this proportion was only 59 percent.

Numerous political problems have stemmed from this migration. A sudden increase in the ethnic minority of an area is likely to result in tensions, especially if the newcomers begin to take over jobs from portions of the existing population. When this is aggravated by racial prejudice, which is no stranger in the North, the likelihood of discrimination and violence is sharply increased. Then too, the Negro migration is primarily a movement from rural areas in the South to cities in the North. Except for the absence of a language problem, these newcomers encounter all the difficulties of adjustment experienced by previous waves of immigrants from European farms to American cities, including those associated with inadequate education in the places from which they have come. These difficulties have been compounded by city segregation patterns: large numbers of whites have moved out of the cities to the suburbs and Negroes have filled up the "old core" of the metropolis. The net effect is that Negroes constitute an increasingly large fraction of the population in our largest cities. (In 1960 the proportions were 29 percent in Detroit, 26 percent in Philadelphia, 23 percent in Chicago, 14 percent in New York, and 13 percent in Los Angeles.) Thus almost all the most difficult problems facing the city governments—housing, urban renewal, education, the retention of a skilled labor supply, relations with state governments, etc.—are inevitably involved with the matter of racial discrimination. Since the Negro has free access to the ballot in the North, the Negro population can make its demands felt in local, state, and national elections. Mayors and mayoralty aspirants in cities with large Negro populations cannot ignore the spokesmen of these groups. Furthermore, the Negro vote in pivotal states such as Michigan, Pennsylvania, Illinois, New York, and California is also important in national elections. It is not an accident that the advocacy of civil rights by Northern members of Congress has increased as Negroes have settled in Northern cities or that recent Presidents and Presidential candidates of both parties have given at least verbal support to the claims of Negroes. Nor is it accidental that attitudes toward Negroes hitherto characteristic of the South should be revealed in the North. Governor Wallace of Alabama won a majority of the vote in certain sections of Indiana near Chicago in his 1960 primary campaign for President. The existence of this "white backlash" further demonstrates how mobility, along with urbanization and industrialization, is reducing the sectional differences in the country and producing a national politics in which voters divide along the same lines, though not in the same proportions, in all parts of the country.

THE INTERNATIONAL ENVIRONMENT

Few comparisons are more striking than the changes in the international environment between 1889 and 1964. Changes in weapons, transportation, communications, the relative power of different nations, and the expectations of peoples around the globe, as well as the emergence of new states and new conflicts in big-power politics, have all affected American government in our age.

The United States was relatively isolated through the nineteenth century—protected by the oceans and the British Navy from aggression from abroad. Then in 1898 it suddenly acquired an empire—Cuba, Puerto Rico, the Philippines, Hawaii. But neither the Spanish-American War nor the First World War materially changed the American conception that the destiny of the United States was to be shaped by its domestic conditions and institutions. But other forces had nevertheless destroyed the independence of the nation from the outer world, and its victory in the Second World War and its technological resources suddenly gave it a dominant position over half of the globe. The dominance is one of influence and responsibility rather than one of political subjugation; it is greater and at the same time more fragile than that of any empire that has been created by military conquest. This dominant position was not sought as a deliberate national policy. Had it occurred as a consequence of conscious choice and planning, the resulting problems would be somewhat easier to manage. The government's foreign policies might then rest upon a firm domestic consensus, reflecting a widely accepted understanding of the facts and circumstances affecting the country's international role. Instead, the domestic support for this empire that was not sought but cannot be abandoned had to be created after the responsibilities of world leadership were acquired. In the space of less than half a normal American lifetime the country has had to move from a position of security behind two ocean barriers—where it was free to concentrate upon domestic matters and had only a rudimentary foreign policy, almost no military establishment, and no strategic policy—to the role of being the military and diplomatic anchor of Western civilization.

A useful way to think of one critical feature of this impact is to visualize the national government as having suddenly acquired several hundred million new "semicitizens" outside the country's boundaries. They are clearly not full and legal citizens, and they cannot vote in American elections. But they or their leaders make choices that affect the fortunes of the United States as deeply as those made by American voters, corporations, labor unions, and other groups of citizens. First, the United States may be called upon to resolve conflicts among countries where American national interests are at stake. The threat of hostilities between India and Pakistan, among the Middle Eastern countries, or within Saigon, Cyprus, or the Congo would concern the security and well-being of the United States as clearly, if not as directly, as the state of our own economy. The means of resolution available to the United States when conducting negotiations with other sovereign nations are different from those used to handle domestic issues, but the need to reconcile conflicting interests is basically the same.

In the second place, conflicts of at least equal importance occur between sets of these new semicitizens and groups in the American citizenry. Sometimes these conflicts are quite overt. For example, suppose the Japanese, pressing to increase the exports upon which their island economy depends, began to ship quantities of textiles and finished wearing apparel into the United States at prices that undercut those in the American market. The textile and clothing industries in the United States would demand increased tariff protection or a system of import quotas. Organized clothing workers might refuse to work on textiles imported from Japan. They in turn would be supported by members of Congress from textile states—legislators whose votes might be essential for a continued foreign aid program from constituencies where voters were needed to maintain the administration in power. If they became alarmed at these threats, the Japanese, who currently buy more American goods than any other country in the world except Canada and the United Kingdom, might prepare to restrict American imports and might threaten to shift a sizable portion of their trade to the Chinese Communists. Should this shift occur, it would undermine American efforts to restrain Communist China by cutting off her trade with the free world.

Whether such conflicts are indirect or overt, they are as much a part of American politics as a dispute over public or private ownership of an electric power plant on the Columbia River. In this sense politics—the politics of imperial leadership—does not stop at the water's edge. It cannot, for the American government in its new role is compelled to contest for the loyalties of its new semi-citizens while maintaining those of its own citizens and attempting to bring the latter's attitudes into closer conformity with our country's international requirements.

As the preceding discussion implies, the recent changes in the American world position are accentuating certain purely domestic problems that have been touched upon in earlier sections of the chapter. Thus governmental concern with the decisions of large business and labor organizations—with all the controversy that such concern invites—is reinforced by awareness that the growth and stability of the American economy have become an essential element in the continued maintenance of American power and prestige in the contemporary world. Other centralizing tendencies are also reinforced. The decision of federal officials to attempt with increased vigor to eliminate racial segregation in the North and South and to enforce constitutionally guaranteed political rights can be explained as much by international as by domestic concerns. Each time an African diplomat is denied service in a restaurant because of his color, each time a dispute occurs such as the one in Little Rock in 1957, the handicaps of American leadership are increased. Correspondingly, each time vigorous action protects acknowledged civil rights—for example, when the national government enforced James Meredith's right to attend the University of Mississippi—the prestige and influence of America are reinforced throughout the world. Such matters can no longer be regarded as purely local affairs.

Some political consequences that stem from these changes in the American international position are of at least equal importance though they may be less dramatic. The requirements of national security in an age of nuclear weapons have, for example, altered the status of whole sectors of American society. The change in the position of the nation's scientists has already been mentioned. Similar changes have occurred in the position of military leaders and civilians associated with them in public or private capacities. Budget expenditures for national security in 1939–40 were only about 16 percent of a total federal budget of less than $10 billion. Just over twenty years later, 1960–61, they constituted more than half a budget nearly nine times as large. Such figures are indicators of a shift of power among groups in the population. They are not necessarily threatening, but they raise problems that are without precedent except during a major war. The military establishment's decisions on expenditures for basic scientific research affect the financial resources of all our major universities; their choices among alternative weapons systems and among competing bidders for development and production contracts involve tens of billions of dollars each year; and those choices not only affect the fortunes of major corporate enterprises but also control the prosperity of whole regions of the country and significantly affect the distribution of population.

Themes for an Analysis of American Government

Now that we have compared a week of American government in 1889 with one in 1964 and have examined some of the causes and effects of drastic social change on American government in the past seventy-five years, we are ready to turn to specific chapters on the facts, institutional theories, and political science techniques for analyzing contemporary American government.

Some books of political analysis have a "master theme" or set of key analytical judgments that constitute the organizing principle of the work. Such was Charles Beard's theory about the economic basis of American politics, or Frederick J. Turner's idea about the impact of the frontier on the American system. The great value of such a theme is that it brings order out of what may seem to be a chaos of facts and conflicting interpretations. The great danger of a single theme in a work of basic description is that it does not reflect properly the variety, divergencies, conflicts, and "inconsistencies" of a complex society—and especially a heterogeneous, pluralistic, and democratic nation such as the United States.

Given the twin dangers of chaos and oversimplification, there are still several themes that will illuminate and help students to organize the discussion of American government; analysis of these themes represents the dominant approach of the authors. We can identify three *tensions,* or competing sets of forces at work in American political life. These three pairs of opposing tendencies are as follows:

CONFLICT AND RESOLUTION

Politics deals with conflict. In a free society, individuals differ over the ends of governmental action and, in the United States in particular, over the means to achieve those ends that are agreed upon. Organized groups will line up on different sides of public issues according to their notions of what best serves their constituents' basic interests. Factions within a political party will not agree on who should be its candidate for the Presidency. Agencies within the federal executive branch will part company on the best way to deal with farm surpluses. Even Supreme Court Justices divide over interpretation of the nation's basic constitutional law.

Given the inevitability of disagreement, of opposing interests and opinions, one vital test of the American political system is its ability to resolve such conflicts with no more than an acceptable minimum of civic bitterness and disorder. Clearly, conflict is too creative a force in the economic, social, and political life of a free society to be suppressed; it results from the clash of ideas and interests coursing through the channels of a free society that can carry a people to new levels of progress. Yet, if government is to represent the whole people and conduct national affairs in an era of international peril, ways must be found to compromise differences, conciliate opposing groups, and develop machinery for containing political conflicts. How well American institutions are equipped today to resolve conflict is a vital concern in surveying the American political system.

CONTINUITY AND CHANGE

The original seven articles of the Constitution remain today as they were when written in 1787, and they have been modified only slightly by amendments in the past seventeen decades. The terms of Senators and Representatives have not changed since that time, and the mechanism of the Presidential veto is still used as was directed at the birth of the Republic. The Supreme Court continues to open its sessions with the same ceremonial flourishes that were employed when it convened for the first time under Chief Justice John Jay.

While Americans often point with pride to the dynamic quality of life in the United States, our present political system exhibits great continuity with the past. Precedents are not easily overturned, and institutions often demonstrate great inertia when called upon to adjust to changing conditions. Yet, as we have already underscored, there has been change since 1787, and a great deal of it has occurred in the past seventy-five years. As American society has grown larger, industrialized, more differentiated, and with a different "population mix," American government has had to assume new responsibilities and create new agencies to meet them. Thus part of the study of American institutions is to master the classic and continuing patterns while identifying what is new about our system and its processes, to analyze how the changes were made and what their individual effects have been on the classic balances of the system as a whole. Still another aspect of this tension between continuity and change is whether our government processes are changing fast enough to cope with sweeping socioeconomic changes at home and the rush of events in the international community. Every institution in our political system—from the local tax assessor's office to the National Security Council—and each pattern of behavior—from the way we nominate candidates for President to our techniques for resolving racial conflict—must be analyzed to see whether these ideas and instruments are adequate for our present condition. If change is not swift enough, allies in Southeast Asia may be lost to Communist expansion, California may not have enough water for its needs, in large cities across the country metropolitan areas may become decaying slums while suburbs collapse under inadequate planning. These tensions between continuity and change represent key perspectives for analyzing and evaluating our political system.

POWER AND CONSENT

One day a citizen receives a notice telling him to pay his taxes. Attached to this notice is a warning that if he does not pay them properly and promptly he will be subject to penalties at the hands of the government. Another day the same individual goes to the polls and casts a ballot for the men who will, among other things, levy taxes the next year. In the first instance the citizen is the target of governmental power; in the second he is able to exercise power of his own in electing his governors, thus expressing his consent to being governed. Government, then, is an agency of coercion—real, implied, or potential. But a democratic government rules with the consent of its citizens. This is not to suggest that all Americans are in full agreement with all the laws and regulations they must obey. But they have many opportunities—voting is only one—to convey their ideas and opinions to the men and institutions that exercise power. Some uses of power are more susceptible to public check than are others.

Today, with the complexity of such issues as automation, juvenile delinquency, or nuclear-war strategy, and with the "lead-time" for informing and "consulting" the citizenry about alternatives often curtailed by domestic or international crises, the very meaning of "consent of the governed" must be reexamined. Are dialogues between the party in power and the party in opposition, or between the government and the spokesmen for organized groups, a necessary and acceptable substitute for the kind of citizen democracy our ideology presupposes? How well is our checks and balances system working within government and in the sphere of industrial life? These are only some of the questions involved in the general inquiry as to how much American government is or in fact can be based on consent today and whether the avenues of consultation are open to all those who wish to use them.

Having described these three sets of conflicting forces as useful themes for analyzing American government, we are now ready to turn to that assignment in depth. We move from a section on the background of American government (the American political style, the Constitutional ground rules, and the changes in our system in its first seventeen decades) to a consideration of the American political process, the Presidency, the legislative process, the judicial process, civil rights and liberties, governmental functions, and the state and local political systems. How it works, why it works, and whether it is working well enough now become our entry points to the specific compartments of the American political system.

2 / The Social Basis
   of American Government

The starting point for understanding—and evaluating—the American political system is an appreciation of the environment in which it works. The ways and means by which Americans resolve conflict, achieve orderly change, and agree to submit to government authority are powerfully shaped by other patterns of our national behavior.

The methods we use to produce and consume material resources (the economic structure); to establish households and raise children (the family); to deal with other individuals and groups in the immediate geographical area (the community); to maintain contact and share experiences with other Americans across the continent and beyond (the society); all these patterns help determine how we conduct our public affairs. Political institutions and processes do not spring full-blown from the minds of philosophers, and constitutions are not the innovations of pure reason. Instead, they stem from a complex fabric of human relations, basic social attitudes and institutions, and respond to conditions and opinions arising from the environment. Until we know something of this broader fabric, we cannot account for how and why our politics works as it does.

National Character and the Process
of Political Socialization

"Character," "culture," "style" are shorthand terms for summarizing distinctive ways of life of particular groups of people in particular places. They can apply to an isolated South Sea Island tribe or to a large, complex nation like the United States. However used (and the precision and clarity of definition vary enormously), these notions refer to the nonbiological conditions of human life—the distinctive beliefs, customs, values, and skills that individuals *learn* early in life from *shared* experiences with others.

So courtship, marriage, the education of the young, the burial of the dead, the use of leisure time, the acceptance of new ideas—and the choice of leaders and the definition of their proper duties—may vary greatly from continent to continent, nation to nation, and even region to region. They represent different responses developed and transmitted across generations to the common requirements for sustaining human life: eating, sleeping, loving, working, playing.

When we identify the distinctive ways a group handles these activities, we are describing its culture or style (the principal behavior patterns for the total population) or its character (the likelihood that a person in the society will share a distinct combination of traits with other society members that a person in another culture would lack). When we inquire as to how individuals acquire these traits we are dealing with the process of socialization: the conditioning of the infant or the child to adjust his personality structure to the patterns of the larger group. Political culture and political socialization are *slices* of the larger human systems, the particular beliefs and practices that determine the activities carried out in common and the ways public power is obtained and applied.

Concepts of culture and socialization are especially important in studying the American political system. Elusive as these notions are at times, most observers since colonial times have been convinced that there is a unique American character. Our early physical isolation from other cultures, our rich endowment of natural resources, our pattern of immigration, the conditions of establishing organized communities, the role of the frontier have all been singled out as special variables contributing to a special culture. Although interpretations of the "real" American vary widely (each generation of scholars and commentators paints a somewhat different picture of our way of life), few dispute that the United States *is* different. And all agree that our special character, continued through socialization, has encouraged and reinforced our special political system.

Among the characteristics of the American societies most frequently singled out over the years as distinctive, five have special relevance to our politics: (1) our *de novo establishment* in the sense that people possessing the advanced techniques of organization and wealth production ventured into a continental wilderness and consequently became committed to equality; (2) our *affluence:* the rich bounty that nature provided this continent, and our skill in utilizing that bounty; (3) our *mobility:* the eagerness of Americans to advance in status and their readiness to pull up stakes and move on to greener pastures; (4) our *pragmatism:* the national disposition to try to find specific solutions to immediate problems of the day, rather than to seek general philosophical answers for all time; (5) our *pluralism:* the accommodation of diverse nationalities and ethnic and religious groups, influenced by the steady immigration of Europeans and others for more than three hundred years.

Other characteristics obviously set us apart from other nations, but down through the years foreign and native students have returned again and again to these dominant characteristics. Each of these characteristics has contributed to building a remarkably stable society and political system.

AMERICA AS THE FIRST "DEVELOPING NATION"

The initial impetus to a distinctive American character was the fact that the early settlers "began again." In the words of Louis Hartz, a contemporary observer, the nation was "born free," unfettered by an *ancien régime* and not bound by feudal notions of class and status. So its early institutions had marks of genuine originality. The town meeting, for example, was dictated more by its natural "fit" than by example of the English parish, and the American innovation of federalism was a then unique response to unique circumstances.

Perhaps the most striking quality derived from this abrupt break with the past is the American emphasis on equality. Alexis de Tocqueville, the famous young French aristocrat who set down his impressions of this country in the 1830s, singled out this atmosphere of egalitarianism as of prime importance. "Amongst the novel objects that attracted my attention during my stay in the United States," he wrote, "nothing struck me more forcibly than the general equality of condition among the people."

In most countries of Europe and in many other parts of the world, the man-in-the-street has been deferential to those of his fellow countrymen who are superior in birth and breeding. In such societies most people accept their allotted station in life and do not question the rights or privileges of those standing above them on the social scale. Americans, in contrast, are suspicious of those who claim to possess superior capacities or competence. A glance at the Letters-to-the-Editor column of any American newspaper will show that the judgment and even the credentials of educators, economists, scientists, foreign affairs specialists, and other supposed experts are constantly being questioned by laymen. A television repairman in Omaha sees nothing untoward in matching his own theories about the proper role of the Supreme Court against those of an Ivy League law school professor. A druggist in Pasadena will come to his own conclusions about our relations with various Latin-American countries, unimpressed by the views of the State Department. So the old colonial injunction "You're as good as any man and better than none" still rings true for many citizens. In modern language, it is most frequently translated as "equality of opportunity" for the able, energetic individual to get ahead.

Equality carries other connotations as well: conformity, commonness in tastes, and suspicion of the unusual opinion. De Tocqueville noted this when he wrote that the "manly and lawful passion for equality tends to elevate the humble to the rank of the great. But there exists also in the human heart a depraved taste for equality, which impels the weak to attempt to lower the powerful to their own level and reduces men to prefer equality in slavery to inequality with freedom." Contemporary analysts such as David Riesman see this aspect of our colonial endowment increasing in significance today. Never "tradition-directed," but formerly "inner-directed" in his striving for personal success, the modern American now seems to Riesman "other-directed," an organization man with built-in radar constantly seeking out and adjusting to the opinion of others.

But whether the ultimate effect of the "passion for equality" liberates or suffocates the individual, this predisposition seems to be a pervasive national trait, applicable to our family life and our business dealings, as well as our politics.

THE AFFLUENT SOCIETY

When the economist John Kenneth Galbraith called America "the affluent society" in the 1950s, he drew attention both to our present situation as compared to that of the rest of the world and to the rich resources with which we have always been endowed. Certainly the great majority of Americans not only are comfortable but also possess luxuries that are the envy of the world. The 1960 Census revealed that 74 percent of American families had washing machines, that 75 percent had a telephone and at least one car, and that 87 percent had television sets. The median family income for 1963 was over $6,200. The majority of our citizens have secure and well-paying jobs, and they have little to complain of so far as the economic system is concerned.

This affluence should not be counted simply in monetary terms. The proportion of white-collar jobs has been steadily rising: since 1955 more people have been employed in office, sales, and service work than in the actual processes of production. If American social classes are arranged in a pyramid, it is misshapen indeed: for the middle class now far outnumbers the working class, and, in economic terms, the moderately prosperous are far more numerous than the poor.

From this pattern have flowed a series of behavior patterns so powerful that they lead distinguished scholars such as David Potter to conclude that our material abundance decisively influences our life from cradle to grave. To him, the manner in which we feed and train our babies, build and heat our houses, and make our clothes is dependent on our wealth. So are the time we marry, the frequency of divorce, our choice of neighbors and jobs. These habits all reinforce the historic condition of equality and voluntarism in our personality structures. They rest upon a sufficiency of resources that makes the strict authoritarian control characterizing poorer societies unnecessary.

Not all observers make such a close and intimate association of national character and affluence as Potter does. But most attribute to it the American emphasis on material well-being as a mark of personal success and the American respect for private property. These dovetail neatly with that aspect of our egalitarian instinct that emphasizes individualism. Again De Tocqueville is instructive in discovering how early these traits appeared.

> When the distinctions of rank are confounded together and privileges are destroyed; when hereditary property is subdivided, and education and freedom widely diffused; the desire of acquiring the comforts of the world haunts the imagination.[1]

So materialism helps provide the American with a sense of identity that in traditional societies is supplied by family, birthplace, and occupation. The very ownership of goods—an automobile, a boat, a workshop, a swimming pool—gives stature to the individual personality. For material possessions not only provide new freedoms and enhanced comforts but they also lend to their owner a status and a definition of his own self.

Linked with emphasis on goods per se is our loyalty to our ways and means of producing and distributing our bounty.

> In no other country in the world is the love of property more active and more anxious than in the United States.[2]

---

[1] Alexis de Tocqueville, *Democracy in America* (New York, 1946), Vol. II, p. 137.
[2] *Ibid.*, p. 270.

The ideas of eighteenth-century economists and the worldly philosophy of Adam Smith found fertile ground in the young United States. Firmly embedded in our ideology is a commitment to capitalism, the free enterprise system for organizing and managing the economy. Among all principal groups in society there is acceptance of and even enthusiasm for the principle that property ought to be owned and directed by private individuals. There has never been a major socialist movement in the United States, and even in the depths of the Depression of the 1930s there was little support for radical changes in the country's economic system.

Several factors help explain why Americans identify themselves with the institutions of capitalism. The first is/affluence itself: the fact that this system of production and distribution has provided them with the highest standard of living in the world. Second, private ownership holds out the promise of rewards for those who are able to succeed in the system. Money, security, and comforts are available to those individuals who climb high in the business world, and opportunities for advancement are not confined to an exclusive class or stratum in the society. Third, capitalism is, in a meaningful sense, "democratic." Profits accrue to a company only if it gives the public what the public wants. Some commentators may argue that what the public wants (or thinks it wants) is a product of seductive advertising and subtle salesmanship. But the fact remains that Americans do feel that life is more comfortable and interesting with air-conditioning units, color television, electric can openers, and frozen dinners. Finally, and quite naturally, the system helps perpetuate itself by educating the citizens to the advantages of capitalism and the disadvantages of alternative methods of economic organization.

So far as political values are concerned, Americans have come to interpret the ownership of property as an area of freedom: a realm in which they can act as they please subject to minimum public restrictions. So the home owner takes pleasure in practices never allowed the tenant, hammering picture hooks in the plaster, changing walks, removing shrubs at will. And owning one's business appeals strongly as an escape from the role of employee. The path to independence is property ownership—a retail store, a manufacturing concern, a service establishment. Not only is one's own name over the door but everything inside the door is one's own property.

Affluence and the economic system that converts resources to consumer goods thus appear as positive political values. These factors also serve to make many Americans question critically any proposed change in government responsibilities. Public service and regulatory programs are established only after a clear demonstration of need, and usually with reluctance, for the private sector of the economy appears as the seedbed from which self-reliant, energetic citizens are grown.

This view of society persists even though the explanation for affluence and the economic system has now become vastly more complex. In an industrialized, job-dependent society, man's realization of affluence is more contingent on what the wage payment will buy than it is upon independent ownership of shops or farms. His financial protection depends upon social security and public benefit payments as well as on his savings. New developments in science and industry depend upon the billions of dollars in research money that is contributed annually from public funds and corporate treasuries more than from private research. Vast public projects conserve and expand the nation's natural resources. Ownership itself is now largely separated from management in big corporations, and the continued growth of the economy depends upon men holding key positions in industry, labor, and government. Even property values depend upon the condition of the economy as a whole. Yet despite these changes which are refashioning the economy, the American still accepts the basic freedoms of the capitalist system—to choose his employment, invest his money, and organize his own business—and the basic assumptions that affluence rests upon a vigorous private economy and that liberty depends on a balance between public and private power which strongly supports individual initiative.

THE UPWARD AND OUTWARD AMERICAN

Reinforcing the qualities of newness and equality, of affluence, its attendant goal of physical well-being, and its chosen instrument of capitalism is the fact that Americans seem forever in motion. They are on the move both physically and socially—for generations toward the frontier and for generations toward success.

The willingness of Americans to move physically has been manifested at every stage of our history: in the Westward expansion, in the migrations from small towns and rural areas to the cities and, more recently, to the suburbs, and once again in the current movement to the West Coast by millions of citizens. While not all Americans are nomads, the transient spirit affects many of us. Young people are prepared to move across the nation to take up an interesting job or simply to carry on with their education.

One consequence of this has been the weakening of family ties: whereas once all living generations of a family would reside close by one another, now first the children and then the grandchildren strike out to new communities and lives of their own. Each generation becomes virtually sufficient unto itself. Typical of mobile America are the mushrooming suburbs, where everyone is a newcomer. In many ways the busy social life of the suburbs is an attempt by uprooted individuals to create a community and a sense of belonging for themselves. So the modern premium on adjustment, on an easy tolerance in group relations, coincides with the tradition of equality.

So far as social mobility is concerned, it is a process whereby individuals enter new occupations and achieve higher status in the course of their own lifetimes. The number of Americans who actually go from rags to riches is not very great, but tens of millions have made modest progressions beyond the homes and surroundings in which they were raised. Men whose fathers were unskilled laborers are now salesmen and office workers; men whose fathers were small shopkeepers are now doctors, lawyers, and executives. While social barriers have existed in the United States and continue to exist, they have not been rigid. In particular, education—freer and more available in America than elsewhere in the world—is the key to advancement. And of those who manage to obtain a college diploma, most find that opportunities to rise are readily available.

Both kinds of mobility—horizontal and vertical—have their political implications. The geographical migration of so many over the land has a depressant effect; it disfranchises literally millions of citizens in the short run and inhibits their inclination for political activity in the long run. For political power tends to remain with the stay-at-homes, in community, state, and national party affairs. Transient Americans are often alienated from participation in party organizations. Indeed many of the attitudes displayed by our legislators are those of the people who stayed behind while others were moving on to other sections of the country.

An interesting illustration is in the growing suburbs. Those who commute to jobs in the central city are not particularly active in party politics. The parties in many suburban areas are more often than not dominated by the noncommuters—professionals and businessmen who intend to stay in the area and who actually work there. The commuting population, many of whom have moved in recently and who will move on in the course of time, find it difficult to build up an equity in the local party organization.

Moreover, vertical mobility tends to complicate political preferences and loyalties. Voters who are socially "on the way up" are subject to strong cross-pressures. Do they stay with the party of their working-class parents? Do they continue to identify themselves with the ethnic group and church of their childhood? Or do they adopt the preferences of their fellows in the professional or occupational group to which they now belong? These conflicts account in many cases for the large number of independents, switch-voters in our elections. Often they result in the outright avoidance of political affairs.

THE PRAGMATIC PASSION

No account of the United States is complete without underscoring our special penchant for concentrating on matters of the moment and our preference for using technology to solve human and social problems. As a philosophy, pragmatism is not an American invention, but no other nation has elaborated its tenets so completely or embraced it so enthusiastically. "Does it work?" is the critical test for almost every national proposal, and the exponents of this experimental, testing approach to life—William James and John Dewey—are the most notable of popular American philosophers. As W. W. Rostow has written:

> At his best the American came to be knowledgeable and wise about the nature of the physical world and about how life was really conducted: but he remained close to the facts and processes with which he lived. As an intellectual, the American was an empiricist: as a philosopher, he was a rather liberal pragmatist, loosely generalizing the situations and experiences his round of life made real. . . . [He] tended to elevate "life, experience, process, growth, function" over "logic, abstraction, deduction, mathematics and mechanics." [3]

Moreover, our national pragmatism is distinctive in its heavy reliance on technology as a means for finding the *ad hoc* solutions to problems. Until the Second World War, American science was never first rate, but American en-

---

[3] W. W. Rostow, *The United States in the World Arena: An Essay in Recent History* (New York, 1960), p. 14.

gineering was. Eli Whitney, Samuel Morse, Alexander Bell, Thomas Edison, Henry Ford gained fame by means of inventions, not discoveries. Yankee ingenuity—but not Yankee wisdom—was early heralded around the world. As tinkers, gadget makers, masters of production and the assembly line, we practiced both rural and urban pragmatism, first mechanizing the farm, and later the city. In short, Americans by their technological skills capitalized on natural abundance to produce affluence in an unparalleled demonstration of human endeavor—"the ventures and struggles of the pioneer, the exertions of the workman, the ingenuity of the inventor, the drive of the enterpriser, and the economic efficiency of all kinds of Americans, who shared a notorious addiction to hard work." [4]

In politics, pragmatism and inventiveness—applying moderately radical innovation to essentially familiar problems, as Rostow puts it—have been evident throughout our history. Ever since the Declaration of Independence and the Constitution established our national goals in general and idealistic terms, we have been ingenious in our interpretation and reinterpretation of the intentions of the Founding Fathers. Neither rigid nor sophisticated philosophies of government have had broad appeal for the public or the intellectual community. Instead, under the cover of pronouncements of high purpose and morality, sometimes irritating to foreign observers, we have approached public issues on a piecemeal, experimental basis. The stubborn fact, the concrete situation, and not well-rounded theoretical arguments, have been the catalysts for major public programs.

THE UNITED STATES AS MELTING POT

Finally, no interpretation of the American style can be complete without taking into account the special mix of our population. The continent was not only settled anew, it was settled as well by a disparate agglomeration of nationalities and classes. Until well into the nineteenth century, immigration was predominantly Anglo-Saxon in character. Thereafter, as the tide of immigration reached flood proportions, Irish, Germans, Italians, Scandinavians, Eastern Europeans came in increasing numbers, and English and Scottish immigration declined.

But the new arrivals did not overrun the institutions, processes, customs, and life styles established earlier. The children of the great waves of immigrants began to adjust themselves to the main currents of American life, and their grandchildren and great-grandchildren have all but completed the process. And the pattern to which they adjusted themselves was, more than anything, the "Anglo-Saxon" pattern of the past. Put another way, the immigrants had less impact on America than America had on them. And this is the first major characteristic of American pluralism.

There were reasons for this. One was that the Anglo-Saxons, having arrived first, controlled many of the dominant institutions of the society: they directed the citadels of finance and higher education, and the higher reaches of business and the national government. Any immigrant who wished to succeed in his adopted country would have to adapt himself to

---

[4] David M. Potter, *People of Plenty: Economic Abundance and the American Character* (Chicago, 1954), p. 89.

the standards already laid down, or at least compete according to the accepted rules. Moreover, the immigrants never actually outnumbered the old Americans. And even as successive waves arrived, those who had been in earlier waves were beginning to identify with the prevailing patterns. Thus German-Americans, already well established by 1900, looked on the Eastern European arrivals who came between 1900 and 1910 in much the same way that those of British stock did. The most important factor making for assimilation, however, was the sharp drop in immigration after 1920. With hardly any new materials, the melting pot could then set to work amalgamating whatever undigested elements were left.

The 1960 Census is revealing on this score. The total count for that year was just short of 180 million. Of this total population only 9.7 million people were born outside this country. In other words, about 170 million of us— approximately 95 percent—are native-born Americans. Furthermore only 24.3 million Americans had parents either one or both of whom were born outside the United States. This means that more than 80 percent of the 1960 population was not only born in this country but also had parents who were born here. The great majority of Americans, in short, are at least third-generation. While many of them still have distinctively "foreign" names and memories of upbringings in ethnic enclaves, most are in appearance well on the way to being completely Americanized.

Yet the common bond of being together in a strange country permitted and encouraged the continuation of subcultures, whether in city neighborhoods or rural settlements. Pockets of distinctive living styles remain—in Jewish apartment houses, or Italian streets, or Amish farms.

To the pluralism of nationality has been added the pluralism born of a specialized industrial society covering a large territory. This version is best indicated by the extraordinary number and variety of organizations and associations throughout the United States, all representative of one or another of the different roles in life most Americans play. They range from the National Association of Manufacturers to the Little League, from the Congress on Racial Equality to the Women's Christian Temperance Union, from the Teamsters' Union to the National Education Association. Not only do millions of Americans join some group, but many have memberships in more than one. They join because they have interests to protect and promote, information to share, and activities of mutual enjoyment and concern. Most of these organizations are voluntary. Indeed about the only exceptions are a few where membership is necessary if one is to pursue a particular occupation. And it is the voluntary character of American associational life that gives it its distinction.

All societies, of course—traditional and modern, democratic and totalitarian—are "pluralistic" in the sense that they contain groups. In traditional societies, however, such groups are organic units with deep roots and long histories: guilds, estates, established churches. And in totalitarian societies groups are firmly attached to the state apparatus and must act as arms of official policy. In the United States, in contrast, group life is shifting and transitory. Associations are formed and dissolved every year, and members come and go as interest rises and declines. Moreover most American associations, most of the time, have little to do with politics, and those that do are

Thomas Nast in *Harper's Weekly*

"This Is A White Man's Government"

Once secure in American society, immigrant groups characteristically were reluctant to extend equal freedom to Negroes or to newer arrivals. This strongly anti-Democratic cartoon was drawn by Nast in 1868.

not so much appended to the government as they are nongovernmental agencies trying to influence the shape and direction of public policy.

Yet even nonpolitical organizations such as the Little League or the American Bowling Congress have a political impact. For Americans, in adhering to a variety of associations, develop a plurality of loyalties. They have not simply a single allegiance to the government, but rather various points of identification in society. And plural loyalties are, in an important sense, symptomatic of personal freedom. For they signify a society's willingness to allow each citizen to pursue his own interests, and they are also centers of power from which individuals can limit the power of government.

An appreciation both of pluralism of migration and of speciality in role and function is essential to a proper understanding of the workings of American government. The still-lingering ethnic loyalties come to the surface in politics. A third-generation American of European background is eager to have one of his "own kind" in the Senate or in the Cabinet as a demonstration that people of immigrant origin have been accepted in the higher councils of the nation's life. The desire for such symbolic representation continues to run deep among those who feel that they do not yet have unobstructed entry to positions of power and prestige.

Today there are signs that the practice of "ticket balancing" in choosing electoral candidates is being framed more on religious than on national lines. Many sociologists have concluded that identifications today are more in terms of a person's religion—being a Protestant or a Catholic or a Jew—than in terms of the country from which his forebears hailed. One cause of this shift is related to the fact of mobility discussed earlier. Neighborhood Roman Catholic churches, for example, used to be "Irish" or "Italian" or "Polish" or "German," depending on the complexion of the parishes they served. Now, as their parishioners move up and out to other parts of the city, to the suburbs, or across the country, they join a new church that has no ethnic designation.

As for the political life of economic, social, and fraternal associations, not only are associations prepared to apply pressure to government agencies, but those agencies regard such intervention as entirely legitimate. One political scientist has summarized the role of groups in the governmental process as follows:

> The behaviors that constitute the process of government cannot be adequately understood apart from the groups, especially the organized and potential interest groups, which are operative at any point in time. . . . Collections of individuals interacting on the basis of shared attitudes and exerting claims upon other groups in the society usually find in the institutions of government an important means of achieving their objectives. That is, most interest groups become politicized on a continuing or intermittent basis. In this respect, therefore, such organized groups are as clearly a part of the governmental institution as are the political parties or the branches formally established by law or constitution.[5]

The political activities of groups are an important phase of the representative process. A physician, for example, may cast his ballot in a Congressional election along with his fellow citizens. But once his Congressman reaches Washington that doctor will continue to be concerned over legislation that affects the practice of medicine. The American Medical Association, speaking on behalf of its members, will be in constant contact with Congressmen, and it will make clear that the doctors' views on impending laws will be heard. Representation in American politics, then, is not simply something

---

[5] David Truman, *The Governmental Process* (New York, 1951), p. 502.

that is achieved by electing public officials by majority vote. It is a continuing process, going on between elections, and organized groups play one of the most vital roles in ensuring that the opinions of interested citizens are transmitted to the various agencies of government.

Dilemmas of the American Style

The characteristics that distinguish a people do not always fit easily together either within individual personalities or within the society considered as a whole. Not all the qualities reinforce or supplement one another to produce a coherent and consistent pattern of behavior—and not all are in accord with the facts of life.

At the center of American tensions, perhaps, is the commitment to equality born of our fresh beginning. Politically, as Hartz has emphasized, outside the ante bellum South, the United States has never had an aristocracy. Hence, it has never produced a genuine, successful, conservative movement, intent on preserving the established order. Instead two strands of liberalism —committed in varying degrees to individuality, equality, and change—have vied with one another throughout our history. Hartz calls these national "impulses"—one toward democracy and the other toward capitalism—and traces their tortuous paths in American political and intellectual history. Theoretically, the impulses can be brought together under the notion of democratic capitalism. In practice, the desire to applaud and encourage Horatio Alger's characters in their climb to success, and the desire to assist the more unfortunate who are left behind, can contradict one another, especially in public policy. So the slogans "human rights" and "property rights" often confront one another as equally persuasive, but not infrequently contradictory, guides to common action.

Thus one of the most persistent problems of the American creed is how to account for failure in terms other than individual moral defects in character. Americans are taught to believe that ambition and hard work will be rewarded. Yet many find that this promise is not fulfilled, that the expected opportunities never emerge. One result is that people tend to create a series of fictions about themselves and about society that will explain away their failure. "The greater the emphasis in a society upon the availability of 'equal opportunity for all,'" a political scientist concluded, "the greater the need for members of that society to develop an acceptable rationalization for their own social status." [6]

The rationale provided by the "capitalist impulse" emphasizes individual responsibility. The presumption runs that jobs are always available and that the unemployed ought to be out looking for work instead of expecting a handout. There is the sentiment that those who do not like living in slums should better themselves so that they can afford the move to a nicer neighborhood. There is the view that the aged should have put aside savings for their retirement or at least that children should accept the responsibility of caring for their parents.

---

[6] Robert Lane, "The Fear of Equality," *American Political Science Review* (March, 1959), Vol. LIII, p. 50.

The "democratic impulse" takes a different tack, holding that in a complex industrial society, the luckless individual may be more an innocent victim of impersonal forces—automation, the business cycle, structural unemployment—than personally incompetent or immoral. Over the years, spurred on by economic crisis, advocates of this view have created the social security and unemployment compensation programs, labor laws and low-cost housing, and expanded health services that exist today. In general they have worked to build a floor of minimum public assistance below which no individual can fall.

But the fact remains that not everyone has shared in our general affluence. The last Census recorded that one out of five families earned less than $3,000 per year, and it is quite plain that many Americans live in poverty despite the general rise in living standards characterizing the nation as a whole. Among them are the aged: old and retired people with no savings and only minimal pensions or none at all. There are also the unskilled who have jobs, but jobs which pay wages as low as $40 or $50 per week—laundry workers, restaurant employees, farm laborers, and the like. There are fatherless households, with a mother attempting to bring up the children by herself. And there are those in depressed areas where there is no work at all and men have given up looking for work (these people are not even counted as "unemployed," for to be so counted you must be "actively looking" for work). Preponderantly represented among the poor are those without education and those without white skins. The greatest victims of these groups are the children: who grow up without schooling, without incentives, and who frequently are destined to live at the margin of society, as have their parents.

Even with the recently heralded war on poverty, American society has difficulty in coming to grips with the problem. As one commentator observes:

> The United States contains an underdeveloped nation, a culture of poverty. Its inhabitants do not suffer the extreme privation of the peasants of Asia or the tribesmen of Africa, yet the mechanism of the misery is similar. They are beyond history, beyond progress, sunk in a paralyzing, maiming routine. This country seems to be caught in a paradox. Because its poverty is not so deadly, because so many are enjoying a decent standard of life, there are indifference and blindness to the plight of the poor. There are even those who deny that the culture of poverty exists.[7]

A second national paradox that arises from our simultaneous emphasis on equality and individuality is more political than economic. This is the problem of tolerance, proclaimed as an inevitable by-product of the individuality that open society promotes, but always threatened by the pressures for conformity that the impulse of equality has set loose. De Tocqueville is instructive in making plain how historically persistent this dilemma has been.

> As the conditions of men become equal amongst a people, individuals seem of less and society of greater importance. Or rather, every citi-

---

[7] Michael Harrington, *The Other America* (New York, 1962), p. 158.

"The Delinquency Problem Must Be Faced—We've Got To Build More Jails."

A liberal critique of the lack of education and of job training that keeps many people economically handicapped.

From *Straight Herblock,* Simon & Schuster, 1964

zen, being assimilated to all the rest, is lost in the crowd, and nothing stands conspicuous but the great and imposing image of the people at large. This naturally gives the men of democratic periods a lofty opinion of the privileges of society, and a very humble notion of the rights of individuals. . . . The public has a singular power. It does not persuade to certain opinions, but it enforces them and infuses them into the intellect by a sort of enormous pressure of the minds of all upon the reason of each.[8]

So alongside of our cherished value of individuality is our frequent preference for group endeavors, committees, team operations, our search for harmony, and distrust for the deviant and the dissenter.

The problem of tolerance is especially complex in the United States for it involves historically both civil liberties and civil rights. Our diverse heritage of many nationalities is compounded by the legacy of slavery. The Civil War compelled white Americans to grant equal ideological status to all races, but equivalent legal, social, and political standings have been slow and difficult in coming. Simultaneously, each wave of immigration has struggled for acceptability, and frequently the immigrants of one-generation standing have been the most hostile to the latest arrivals. The protest demonstrations, riots, and acts of violence of today attest to our chronic national difficulty in making equality a fact of American political life and shaking off the ingrained habits and customs of three hundred years of distinguishing, in various ways, men on the basis of color, creed, and nationality.

---

[8] De Tocqueville, *op. cit.,* pp. 307, 311.

"It May Not Bother You, But I'm Not Happy About Not Getting My Share Of The Affluent Society!"

An ironic comment on the "affluent society."

Interlandi in the Los Angeles *Times*

Simultaneously, the position of the dissenter in America is recurrently perilous. Individuals who wish to discourse on what they think to be the merits of Communism, atheism, or—in some parts of the country—racial integration discover that there are many who would prefer that such utterances not be made. The right of such individuals to express their ideas is juxtaposed with the security of the nation, the moral development of our youth, or more generally our society's way of life. And with such juxtapositions it is usually suggested that the individual should give way to the greater good that will ensue from his silence.

According to recent opinion polls, the great majority of our citizens—from 63 to 87 percent—believe "radical" books should be removed from public libraries, atheists barred from teaching, Communists prevented from speaking or holding a job. The Know-Nothing party of the nineteenth century, the "red scares" of the twentieth are examples of a temptation to define patriotism in narrow and parochial terms, of what has been called "our inveterate tending to judge others by the extent to which they contrive to be like ourselves." [9]

The problem of tolerance, then, is partly political and partly social. It is political in that government agencies—especially state legislatures—are often quite zealous in establishing rules that penalize those who deviate from established patterns. Needless to say, such laws and regulations are usually in response to public sentiment. Yet the problem is largely social in that popular feeling is frequently antagonistic to individuals and ideas that

---

[9] George Kennan, *American Diplomacy, 1900–1950* (Chicago, 1951), p. 135.

"You Read Books, Eh?"

A liberal view of the failure by "anti-subversive" hunters to respect academic inquiry and dissent.

From *The Herblock Book*, Beacon Press, 1952

appear to run counter to custom. Even if there were no political disabilities for dissenters, society would still make life difficult for them.

The American Political Approach

How do the distinctive national characteristics just outlined and the paradoxes they present influence the operation of the American political system? Clearly, as we have seen, they help set the agenda of public affairs, provoking conflicts such as those over civil rights and civil liberties that do not arise with such intensity in other cultures. Moreover, as we have also seen, they establish goals and objectives—levels of expectation—that the political system must strive to meet. Most important of all, however, the deeply ingrained habits and attitudes shared by most citizens "spill over" into American political processes and practices. They determine the responses as well as the challenges, the techniques by which we undertake to resolve the persistent tensions between conflict and order, stability and change, authority and agreement. Several of these practices have already been identified, but at least five deserve to be singled out as distinctively belonging to our political culture.

Popular government

Given the absence of an established order, the commitment to equality, and the practice of mobility, there is no question that our government is rooted in the consent of the governed. Aberrations and deviations from this principle have persisted throughout our history and continue today: special privileges accorded property owners, the long-time exclusion of women,

"*. . . And When The Enemies Of Peace Come Along, Wham, You Bash 'Em Like That. You Can Tell . . . They'll Be Carrying Clubs!"

Interlandi in the Los Angeles *Times*

Negroes, and others from the polls. But the political history of the United States can be read as an inexorable reduction of these barriers and a continuing expansion of the rights of political participation. De Tocqueville again:

> In America, the principle of the sovereignty of the people is neither barren nor concealed, as it is with some other nations. It is recognized by the customs and proclaimed by the laws. It spreads freely, and arrives without impediment at its most remote consequences.[10]

This does not mean that all Americans are actively involved in politics—or that minority rule does not occur. Machines, bosses, elites, courthouse rings are part of our history, and here, unlike other free nations, the number of political activists is small. Our voting turnout, for example, is among the lowest of the democracies in the world today. Our parties cannot manage to recruit more than a small fraction of the citizen body to work in campaigns, and even interest groups rely more on salaried lobbyists than on their members at the grass roots.

Yet it may well be that this apathy is a good sign: that Americans are not unduly excited about what goes on politically, that they feel no great need to join a party or even show up at the polls. With the exception of the rural South, our parties are "open" institutions and welcome virtually anyone willing to work with them. The fact that so few show willingness to do so may be a sign that they are fundamentally content with the way in which they are being governed.

So to date, totalitarian movements have been fringe movements in America. Extreme positions are continually being modified to become ac-

---

[10] De Tocqueville, *op. cit.*, Vol. I, p. 57.

ceptable to center groups of the public. Even the most cynical of politicians is intently concerned with capturing the attention and affection of the voter, by whatever stratagem or tactic.

Limited government

If we are democratic people, we are by no means prepared to let democratic government assume responsibility for the majority of social and economic functions. Alongside our commitment to a popular polity is our conviction that the public sphere should be a sharply demarcated one—excluded from many collective as well as private endeavors. This conviction, as we indicated earlier, stems not only from colonial experience and seventeenth-century philosophy but also from our success in achieving affluence through private efforts and organizations. Capitalism, property rights, individualism combine to maintain the large and flourishing private realm of activity. Moreover, there are explicit American convictions that lead to skepticism about public action—not the least being a fear of political power per se.

The signs of our wholehearted commitment to Lord Acton's famous "law" of politics (that power tends to corrupt and absolute power to corrupt absolutely) are all about us. Few Americans are interested in assuming public office, and most parents would be upset were their children to embark on political careers. The notions that corruption, personal ambition, and compromise with principles mark the political life are commonplace. Most of all, there is the continuing expression of distrust of government, the anxiety lest political power become concentrated and coercive. On the one hand, there is the belief that we ought to be governed by disinterested "statesmen"; on the other, the conviction that power should be fragmented and diffused because those who handle it cannot be trusted. The American attitude toward government is, it has been suggested, a reflection and extension of a more general attitude toward human nature:

> Traditional attitudes toward human nature, power, and government have been modified little during the last century and one-half. The suspicion of power and government is based on a suspicion of human nature. The popular view of human nature has reflected the Calvinist doctrine of original sin, and Americans have sought or anticipated evidence of human frailty and weakness in politics. Much of our politics has been based on the assumption that human nature is base nature and that the political man embodies human nature writ large.[11]

In modern circumstances, this suspicion of assigning authority to public offices places special constraints on the conduct of government and possibly even on the effective function of the entire economy. The expenditures that an individual and a business make for themselves are entirely legitimate. Those made by government agencies are to be looked upon with distrust in the American view. One economist has analyzed the "certain mystique attributed to the satisfaction of privately supplied wants":

---

[11] Arnold Rogow and Harold Lasswell, *Power, Corruption, and Rectitude* (Englewood Cliffs, 1963), p. 30.

A community decision to have a new school means that the individual surrenders the necessary amount, willy-nilly, in his taxes. But if he is left with that income, he is a free man. He can decide between a better car or a television set. The difficulty is that this argument leaves the community with no way of preferring the school. All private wants, where the individual can choose, are inherently superior to all public desires which must be paid for by taxation and with an inevitable component of compulsion.[12]

Political innocence

A corollary to popular and limited government, at once calling for popular support but not attracting great and continuing attention, is the relatively uninformed and uninterested views with which many citizens approach political affairs.

> The discharge of political duties appears to Americans to be a troublesome impediment, which diverts them from their occupation and business. These people think they are following the principle of self-interest, but the idea they entertain of that principle is a very crude one. . . .[13]

Americans are quite prepared to talk politics, but often their talk is unrealistic and illogical. When they are uninformed, their attitude to political matters is often tinged with a disillusionment that to some observers is close to a feeling of alienation. Commentators have suggested that many citizens feel ineffective in politics because they have concluded that it is impossible to dislodge entrenched machines and organization candidates. Some believe that the political structure is outdated, unable to cope with complex contemporary problems; in consequence, many wonder whether there are political solutions for their great anxieties. It is not clear to them that the underlying tensions between the races are susceptible to political amelioration, nor can it be conclusively demonstrated to them that our political institutions are equipped to deal with the technological revolutions going on in our midst.

Thus, Americans have frequently been prone to accept the "devil theory" explanation of political crisis and disaster. If a depression occurs, Wall Street is to blame. If a country falls into the hands of a foreign power, a small group of diplomats has sold out. If a new state tax is voted, legislators have been bought. If the nation is second best in defense or in space exploits, spies have been at work.

So the gap between the political knowledgeables and the ordinary citizen about actual problems at hand and realistic solutions is often quite sizable. Consequently the burdens and difficulties of those in positions of authority and accountable to the public are increased. Executives, legislators, and judges frequently must stand against popular conceptions of the problems at hand if they are to fulfill the duties of their office or provide reasonable solutions to public controversies. The Supreme Court, the President, and the Senate in particular, all in turn take action on such matters as school prayers,

---

[12] John K. Galbraith, *The Affluent Society* (Boston, 1958), p. 267.
[13] De Tocqueville, *op. cit.*, Vol. I, p. 253.

trading with adversaries, and public finances that the majority of citizens neither understand nor approve. People in positions of power—community leaders, elected officials, heads of associations—are thus usually more moderate, more tolerant, and more sensitive to the complexities of modern life than those they represent. And they have a crucial and difficult task of leadership.

The distinction between nation and government

The cynicism and lack of information about politics that many Americans display fosters another political tendency—the sharp distinction we often draw between the character of our civilization and our polity. Partly, this distinction results, as Rostow has pointed out, from the problem of "American rhetoric." [14] Since the Revolution, we have adopted a set of idealized, vaguely expressed, and highly moral national goals, filled with implicit philosophic ambiguities.

These high purposes served the function of unifying a diverse and divided society, and provided a cover of articulation under which practical compromise and adjustment could occur. But they also compounded the disillusionment of the public as it observed specific deviations from the norms, and they encouraged sharply differing judgments as to the vitality and integrity of the nation and that of the government. Our patriotism is usually more social than political, emphasizing the superiority of the general quality of our life, the healthy atmosphere of freedom and equality, the independence of the citizen. "Americanism" becomes a deep and abiding faith in the rhetoric of our timeless purposes, rather than confidence in our capacity to meet concrete situations that call for public action.

This distinction between country and state is made in many cultures, of course. But Americans seem to emphasize the distinction more than members of older societies do, professing greater loyalty to their nation. And this is a consequence of the characteristics of mobility and the swift tempo that have characterized the American experience:

> The United States is a country which has undergone rapid changes; it is loose in its attachment to most traditions except those of individual freedom and reverence for the Constitution. Americans are relatively unbound by professional and occupational ties and by local loyalties. When men's loyalties are loosely anchored to particular places and institutions, they sometimes feel the need to be loyal to their nation more urgently than do those persons and societies which are firmly established in traditional loyalties. The very looseness of local loyalties, which on the one hand is a condition of freedom, makes on the other hand for more sensitivity about national loyalty.[15]

Emphasis on process

The major features of the American political approach sketched so far may seem inadequate and unsatisfactory ones for the world's most powerful nation. An unshakable commitment to democracy is coupled with a disincli-

---

[14] Rostow, op. cit., p. 480.
[15] Edward Shils, The Torment of Secrecy (Glencoe, 1956), p. 78.

nation to permit democratic government to fulfill the demands placed upon it. The public whose consent to being governed is essential appears uninterested, uninformed, and often unskilled in the role it must assume. It reserves its admiration and loyalty for symbolic and ritualistic articulation of moral purposes and not for the officials and machinery assigned the task of realizing the national destiny.

Yet, a series of subtle and sensitive factors is at work to make our system operative. Essentially these are bound up in the American attention to *process:* to the extraordinary weight placed on the ways and means in which we work out our unarticulated compromises while continuing our grander rhetoric. Checks, balances, procedures, rules, regulations are all shrewdly built into the governmental structure, to modify the more general and grandiose expressions of our style. This concentration on process rather than philosophy arises almost inevitably from the main components of our national character and the conditions of our environment.

These are the ways that emphasis on process sustains the American political system. First, since popular government is demanded, formal machinery is required for elections, and informal organization becomes a prerequisite for effective campaigning and the presentation of popular grievances. As the years have passed, considerable ingenuity and skill have gone into the development of elaborate procedures to ensure peaceable, honest, and regular expressions of the public will. Moreover, despite the wishes of the Founding Fathers, the rise of the two-party system has encouraged the enforcement of these procedures, as each party watches the practices of the other.

Second, the concept of limited government requires special institutions and methods. Our celebrated separation of powers among executive, legislative, and judicial branches and among levels of our federal structure is not, as we shall learn, an accurate picture of political reality. All sorts of blendings of power have evolved over the years. But the fact that the structure is present and expressed in the form of a written constitution means that majorities of the moment can be frustrated by procedural devices, and minorities in command of one institution must come to terms with those of another. In short, compromise, adjustment, negotiation, and bargaining are prerequisites for political action, no matter how popular a cause may be.

Moreover, the existence of a flourishing private sector and of three echelons of government means that still other machinery and processes must be called into play to legitimize public action. Hence, the importance of laws, lawyers, and courts in our system and the development of the extraordinarily complex legal terminology for rendering decisions and making judgments about appropriate spheres of action. The unique role the United States Supreme Court plays, in contrast to judicial systems in other Western nations, and the constant recourse to legal solutions of complex policy issues are both reflections of our search for boundary lines in the use of power and restraints on arbitrary action by public or individual centers of power.

Finally, and perhaps most fundamentally, the commitment to process is a substitute for the bonds of family, class, and station that stabilize more traditional cultures. Precisely because our view of society is an atomistic rather than a corporate one, and our goals so vague and our rhetoric so general, respect for ways and means is the only foundation for broad agreement. Since we exist more as individuals in loose association than as members of a balanced, structured corporate whole with collective goals, consensus on the process of ordering our public relations is almost a minimal condition for orderly community existence. No other bonds exist to promise stability. Hence the appeal to law rings out in any major conflict, such as civil rights, in contrast to efforts to settle the issue on its substantive merits.

It is this commitment to explicit process that in general sets democracy apart from other systems and in particular often marks the difference between American and other open societies. It is this commitment that is also the prerequisite for the successful operation of the world's largest freely constituted government. Our superstructure of political philosophy offers few real guidelines on policy matters of the day. Our diverse groups have actually no great public program in common. Our belief in individualism and self-assertiveness precludes total commitment to an overarching and universal set of aspirations. We find order not in universal agreement or in suppressing disagreement and conflict, but in ordering the give-and-take of continuing struggle by explicit rules of the game. Process coupled with leadership skilled in making the process work and a public continually disposed to accept the decisions that so emerge are the necessities of American government.

So the chapters that follow do not examine the American political system by emphasizing the declarations of scholars and statesmen about what the nation ought to be, or by concentrating on the formal properties of institutions and law. Instead, they focus on the process directly: how issues are raised, campaigns won, and decisions made within the structure of rules, procedures, and constraints of the national environment. This approach makes the American system, we believe, understandable, predictable, and, in the end, defensible, as an extraordinary achievement in the free assembly and use of political power.

3 / Building the Political Foundations of a Nation

A n informed observer has said that one "cannot fail to be impressed with the amazing, the unique, continuity of American history and, in sharp contrast, the *dis*continuity of European history." [1] The Revolution itself in America, says another observer, appears "so exceptional as to approach the unique," and this uniqueness lies in "the continuity of its political and constitutional aspects with the experience and institutions of the past." [2]

The two political and constitutional aspects which have been dominant in American evolution are the rule of law and the principle of self-government. The period from 1776 to 1787 was one of the most creative periods and certainly the most constructive short period in the modern history of political institutions, but the inventiveness and adaptations of the period conformed with these two aspects, which were rooted in the experience of the past.

In the 180 years between the establishment of the Virginia colony in 1607 and the framing of the Constitution in 1787, a pattern of government evolved for a new nation. In the evolution since—another 180 years in 1967—material adaptations have been made in the system, but the continuity has remained unbroken. This chapter gives the story of the evolution in the first 180 years and shows the institutional system and political ideas that evolved; the next chapter will sketch developments in the second period, which completed the American political system as it is today.

The English Contribution

The logical source for American ideas and practices is of course England. In fact, English thinkers and writers and English traditions are responsible for many, if not most, of what we like to think of as American innovations. These contributions were made in four major areas.

PHILOSOPHY

In 1690, in the second of his *Two Treatises on Government,* John Locke synthesized the doctrines of natural right and social contract that had

---

[1] Daniel Boorstin, *The Genius of American Politics* (Chicago, 1953), p. 30 (Boorstin's italics).
[2] Benjamin Fletcher Wright, "Consensus and Continuity, 1776–1787," *Boston University Law Review* (Winter, 1958), Vol. XXXVIII, pp. 1, 50.

developed in Western Europe in a philosophy that was to be the foundation for the declaration of American principles in 1776. He stated that man's rights came to him from nature and included life, liberty, and property. Man needed government because he needed a legislature to define these rights and an executive to enforce them. In present-day language, this means that government was instrumental and that its purpose was to protect the rights of persons. To meet the needs for a legislature and an executive, man entered into a contract with his fellows to establish government. This idea of contract meant that government rested on the consent of men, not upon the divine ordination of kings. Moreover, said Locke, whenever government acted arbitrarily or abused its trust, it was legally dissolved and the people were free to establish a new government. Locke wrote to justify and explain the English Revolution of 1688; in doing so he prepared a philosophy for another revolution in 1776.

Locke also declared that government should act through known general rules. Another Englishman, James Harrington—whose *Commonwealth of Oceana* (1656) was read in America, argued for an "empire of laws and not of men." This idea, too, was to have an influence on Americans as they sought to safeguard liberty through constitutional law.

Locke gave to America a concept of limited government—government limited by its purpose and by its methods. He differed from other seventeenth- and eighteenth-century philosophers—Hobbes, who argued for absolute power in kings, and Rousseau, who argued for absolute power in the will of the people. He presented a conservative liberalism, combining the liberal philosophy of rights and contract with the British traditions of rule of law and, as we shall now see, of divided government.

STRUCTURE

It has been said that the Constitution of the United States branched off from the British constitution as it was in 1701. At that time English laws were made by the "king in Parliament," which meant by the assent of the House of Commons representing those who had voting rights, the House of Lords representing the aristocracy, and the king. The king had the power of veto, which he last used in 1706. The power to execute the laws was in the king and his ministers. In the Act of Settlement in 1701 it was decreed that the Crown could not remove judges, thus confirming the independence of the judiciary, for which Sir Edward Coke, the great English judge, had contended 100 years earlier. If one substitutes an elected executive for the king and an elected house for the Lords, and makes the veto power conditional (subject to overriding by another vote of the houses) instead of absolute, one finds that the structure is the same as that adopted for the United States in 1787. Even lesser details were transmitted: revenue bills could originate only in the House of Commons, and ministers of the king (though not the king himself) could be impeached through charges brought in the Commons and tried in the Lords.

Explanations of the British system were given to Americans primarily by two men—John Locke and the Baron de Montesquieu. Locke, in his second treatise, said that the British system was one of separation of powers. He saw three powers: the legislative, which was in the Commons, Lords, and

CHART 3–1 / Two Views of British Government

Locke's View of British Government (1690)
Separation of Powers

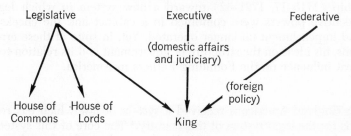

Legislative   Executive   Federative

(domestic affairs
and judiciary)

(foreign
policy)

House of   House of
Commons   Lords   King

Montesquieu's View of British Government (1748)
Checks and Balances

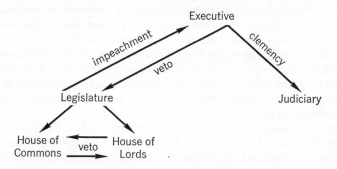

Executive

impeachment   clemency

veto

Legislature   Judiciary

House of   ◄—— veto   House of
Commons   ——►   Lords

king; the executive, which was maintenance of domestic peace and included the judiciary, and was in the king; and the federative, which encompassed relations with other states and was also in the king. Montesquieu, writing in 1748, modified Locke's listing of powers for he was writing after the Act of Settlement and could see the judiciary as a separate power. He was the first person in the modern world to define the chief powers of government as legislative, executive, and judicial. He went, however, beyond distinction of powers: he argued that there could be no liberty if any two of the three powers were united in the same persons or body of magistrates. Still further, he argued for checks within government and praised the British example: "The legislative body being composed of two parts, they check one another by the privilege of rejecting";[3] he claimed that the legislature would become despotic if not checked by a rejecting power in the executive; that the executive could moderate the dangers in the judiciary by mitigating sentences; and that the legislature could restrain through the power of impeachment. Americans found in the writings of Montesquieu the idea that liberty was safeguarded in England by separation of powers and by checks and balances.

---

[3] Baron de Montesquieu, *The Spirit of the Laws* (New York, 1949), Book II, Chapter 6, p. 160.

Montesquieu's interpretation of the British constitution can validly be criticized. He overlooked some safeguards for liberty in England, such as jury trial, the common law, and the participation of the people in local government. He did not see that the English had moved under Walpole's leadership (1715–17, 1721–42) toward a new system in which legislative and executive powers were combined in a cabinet and the checks of the veto and impeachment no longer operated. Yet, in spite of these errors and omissions, his ideas on the structure of government and its relation to liberty had great influence on the Founding Fathers in America.

LAW

From England Americans received a system of law which has remained the basis for the legal system of this country.[4] The core of this system is the common law—an accumulation of judicial precedents that have been evolving since the eleventh century. Common law defines the rights and obligations of men in contracts, damages to persons and property, and other everyday matters. It also defines relations of citizens to government, as in the rule that officers of government are answerable to the citizens for damages caused by illegal actions. Supplementing the common law is a second system, the judge-made law called equity, which contains additional remedies for rights—such as the writ of injunction, by which a court orders a party to do or to refrain from doing specified acts. Embodied in the law of England also were some great procedural pegs for freedom, such as the right of habeas corpus and the right of trial by jury.

Lawyers in America learned their law at first out of Sir Edward Coke's *Institutes,* then out of Sir William Blackstone's four-volume *Commentaries on the Laws of England.* Blackstone's *Commentaries,* published from 1765 to 1769, sold nearly as many copies in America before the Revolution as in England and became the bible of American lawyers for generations. While Locke's second treatise provided a philosophy to justify a revolution, Blackstone's *Commentaries* supplied continuity between the common law in England and the legal thinking of Americans.

RIGHTS

Last, but certainly not of less significance, the British handed their children wherever they went a heritage of rights developed over the centuries. British history is lined with great documents of freedom. Consider, for example, Magna Charta (1215), with its principle that men's rights should be determined by the law of the land and the judgment of one's peers; the Confirmation of Charters (1295), with its declaration that no new taxes should be levied without the consent of the people; the Habeas Corpus Act (1678), setting up more effective procedure for guarantee of the fundamental right that a person shall not be imprisoned without legal basis; and the Bill of Rights (1689), affirming such liberties as the right of petition, the right to bear arms for defense, and the right of the members of Parliament to liberty of debate. Much of the heritage of rights became embedded in

---

[4] Except in the state courts of Louisiana, where the legal system came from France.

the procedural and substantive safeguards of the common law and was summarized in Blackstone's *Commentaries.* Americans were to differ with the British over some claims of right, and they were to move to new plateaus in the assertion of freedom, but they were to retain, on achieving their independence, the most valuable bundle of civil rights ever possessed by a people to that date. The American Revolution itself was a struggle of Americans for what they regarded as the rights of Englishmen.

The Colonial Period and Its Institutional Development

Anchored off the coast of New England in 1620, the Pilgrim Fathers subscribed their names to the Mayflower Compact, declaring that we "doe by these presents solemnly and mutually in the presence of God, and one of another, covenant and combine our selves togeather into a civill body politick. . . ." Although they had just acknowledged loyalty to King James, "by the grace of God" their king, they were asserting in the Compact that government was formed by a social contract, which, differently stated, was the doctrine that political power rose from the consent of the governed. Although men would at other times combine the assertions of power descending from above and ascending from below, this idea that men could forge their own institutions was to be basic in the New World and ultimately was to shatter the traditions of the Old.

One year earlier at Jamestown, Virginia, another group of colonists had met in the first representative assembly in America. Representative government already existed in the parliaments of Europe, but if there was nothing new in the meeting at Jamestown, it was nonetheless a symbol that man had and was using a method of building government by consent. In America the practice of representative government would become traditional.

Nineteen years after the Compact a group of emigrants from Massachusetts to Connecticut framed and decreed the Fundamental Orders of Connecticut, which established the institutions of government for a new colony. They formed the first written constitution in America, indeed the first in the modern world. While governments in the Old World had evolved over a period of time, the Americans began the practice of establishing them by positive acts of people assembled in conventions. Like representative government, a constitution was a method of popular assent. The colonists had, moreover, used the word "fundamental." Thus the ideas of popular consent, a written constitution, and fundamental law were all embodied in the action of the political planners of Connecticut.

Three years later the legislative assembly (General Court) of Massachusetts enacted the Massachusetts Body of Liberties. They declared an intention "to collect and expresse . . . freedomes" and "to ratify them with our solemn consent." The idea of declaring rights, embodied in the great English documents, was being nurtured until the day that such declarations would become "bills of rights" in constitutions.

These more or less isolated episodes foretold the general tendencies of American political thought and experience: freedoms solemnly declared and guaranteed, popular sovereignty, representative government, fundamental law, a written constitution. Of these only the idea of a written constitution was novel, but the combination of these several ideas in the American setting was to produce a political system distinct from any that had existed in the Old World.

Other solid foundations for political practice were developed in the institutions of the colonies. Although the details varied, by the eighteenth century there was much uniformity in the major features of government in the colonies. In each colony there was a charter setting forth the main elements of structure—in the eight royal colonies a charter granted by the king, in the three proprietary colonies a charter granted by the proprietor, and in Rhode Island and Connecticut a charter framed by the colonists and approved by the king. Irrespective of their origin, these documents, along with the compacts of the colonists and the guarantees of right in the English law, came to be regarded as basic law. This idea of fundamental law was strengthened by the right of appeal from the highest court of a colony to the Judicial Committee of the Privy Council in England, which could set aside legislation of the colonies that contravened the charters or English law. However, since few cases were appealed to the Privy Council, the appeal of the colonists to the charters in their struggles with the governors was probably the strongest factor in the development of the colonial idea that these documents contained the higher, controlling law.

The structure of colonial governments came to bear close resemblance to that in England in 1701. Each colony had a governor. He was selected by the assembly in Rhode Island and Connecticut, by the proprietor in the three proprietary colonies, and by the king in the royal colonies. In this last group, the most numerous, the governor exercised the prerogatives of the king: appointment of executive and judicial officials, command of the armed forces, summoning and proroguing the assembly, absolute veto of legislation. In the proprietary colonies he exercised similar powers as representative of the proprietor. In each colony there was an elected assembly, which gained the right to raise taxes, appropriate money, and initiate and vote on legislation. In all except Pennsylvania there was a second house, which, in addition to its legislative function, was ordinarily an advisory cabinet for the governor and a court of appeal (as was the House of Lords in England). Normally the king or the proprietor appointed persons recommended by the governor to be members of the second house; it usually included higher administrative and judicial officials and select persons among the wealthier colonists. Usually the judges were appointed by the governor, but in the eighteenth century the courts came to be independent in practice from executive control. Though there was much confusion of powers in the councils, there was in this system a separation of powers similar to that in England.[5] Moreover, there was a frequent tug of war between the governor, who had executive powers, and the assemblies, which had the power of the purse—a real check and balance between the legislature and the governor. It is appropriate, therefore, "to regard Montes-

---

[5] See Benjamin Fletcher Wright, "The Origins of the Separation of Powers in America," *Economica* (May, 1933), Vol. VIII, pp. 169–85.

quieu's doctrines as a confirmation of something in which Americans had been conditioned for a century or more." [6]

These systems were not democratic in the modern sense. Ownership of land was a qualification for voting in most colonies, though in some ownership of personal property also qualified one for voting. Even higher qualifications were common for office-holding. Recent historical studies indicate, however, that the diffusion of property was sufficient in some parts of the country to allow a majority—in some places, even most—of the male citizens to vote. In any event, as Rossiter has shown, this was "seedtime" for constitutionalism and popular government. Regard for constitutions and the rights of men under law fixed the spirit of constitutionalism in the colonial mind. [7] In addition, local governments throughout the colonies operated with substantial autonomy and popular control. Except for the South, where local government was appointive and aristocratic, these governments served as excellent training grounds for self-government, particularly in New England, where the town meeting and unpaid officers prevailed. Moreover, there was everywhere a more democratic social structure than existed in the Old World, for there was no titled aristocracy, and there was freehold ownership of property as well as greater opportunity to acquire land or rise in the social scale than in older, more developed countries.

The Revolution

Although continuity with the English tradition was not severed, the Revolution in America produced consequences so monumental as to make it one of the moments of great change in the history of the world. The Revolution did much more than break connections with a mother country; it had additional economic, social, and political effects.

ECONOMIC INDEPENDENCE

One consequence of the Revolution was to bring an end to the economic dependence of colonialism, which was part of the system of mercantilism. Theoretically in such a system economic affairs were conducted for state purposes; actually, they were conducted for the benefit of those groups that were in a position to control the government of the colonizing country. In England the system of representation at the time gave this control to a landlord and merchant class in the mother country. These men could argue that the taxes on Americans were fair levies for their defense and that the regulations of trade were for their benefit; but the fact was that these acts of government were being imposed by one set of economic interests, represented in government, over another set, not represented.

The House of Commons did not represent all geographical areas, for new manufacturing cities like Manchester and Birmingham had no members,

---

[6] Alfred H. Kelly and Winfred A. Harbison, *The American Constitution: Its Origins and Development* (New York, 1948), p. 35.
[7] Clinton Rossiter, *Seedtime of the Republic: The Origin of the American Tradition of Political Liberty* (New York, 1953).

Poor Old England

An eighteenth-century cartoon shows Father England having trouble restraining his American children.

while seats were still allotted to areas having virtually no population. Arguments were made in England that Manchester, Birmingham, and the colonies were all "virtually represented" because the House of Commons represented the people of the realm, but this argument was unacceptable to the colonies. Through experience with their assemblies—in spite of some inequalities in representation—the colonies had become accustomed to representation of each geographical area.

Could any peaceful answer have been found for the problem of government which would have allowed the free development of the economy of the New World? The Americans by 1774 had come to demand complete autonomy on "taxation and internal polity," but they assented "from the necessity of the case" to regulations of "external commerce." [8] For American interests to have been protected by such regulations, a federal arrangement would have been necessary with American representation in an imperial parliament. This was, as Burke noted, rendered impossible by the ocean alone; there would have been additional difficulties because of the differences in economic interests, different stages of political development, incompatibilities of temper, and general lack of knowledge about federal systems of government. A more radical answer was contained in the claim of Samuel Adams that Parliament had no authority over the colonies, their relationship being only with the Crown. This solution to the problem of government, similar to that in the British Commonwealth of Nations of

[8] *Declaration of Rights and Resolves of the First Continental Congress.*

the twentieth century (in which there is full political and economic independence but symbolic allegiance to the monarch), was far too drastic for the eighteenth century.

Inability to resolve the problem of imperial government meant either colonial dependence or independence. Independence had the effect of allowing the economy of the New World to develop in response to the interests of the people in the area and without dependence upon regulations imposed from abroad—that is, it meant freedom for independent economic development. Thus economic freedom was the result of the political actions which brought independence.

DEVELOPMENT OF PHILOSOPHY

The second effect of the Revolution was that the philosophical doctrines of Locke came out of the library and the rival contentions of philosophers and worked their way into the minds of the masses of men. Henceforth, the natural rights of men and popular consent were to be familiar themes in the political doctrine of this nation.

The Declaration of Independence would summarize the themes, but the way had been prepared by the fifteen years of discussion begun in 1761 with James Otis' speech in Boston against the writs of assistance.[9] "Then and there," said John Adams, "the child independence was born." At first, however, it took only the form of a protest and an appeal to the rights of Englishmen. Until 1774 Americans rested their case primarily on their rights as English citizens. The writs, said Otis, were an infringement on an Englishman's right of "House," and a few years later "taxation without representation" was asserted to be violation of the English constitution. Otis did use the words "natural equity" in 1761, but the English constitution was presumed to embody natural equity. Thus, the house of representatives of Massachusetts in 1765 resolved "That there are certain essential rights of the British Constitution of government, which are founded in the law of God and nature, and are the common rights of mankind. . . ."[10] By 1774, however, the colonists were prepared to separate the two claims. In the Declaration and Resolves of the First Continental Congress they declared that they had rights "by the immutable laws of nature, the principles of the English constitution, and the several charters or compacts." By 1776 they were ready to make the ultimate appeal to a higher law of morality which men make when they decide that their condition is no longer tolerable.

It is generally agreed that Tom Paine was the man who stirred the Americans to this step. In a pamphlet called *Common Sense*, printed in January, 1776, he assailed monarchy: "Of more worth is one honest man to society, and in the sight of God, than all the crowned ruffians that ever lived"; attacked the English constitution: "so exceedingly complex, that the nation may suffer for years together without being able to discover in

---

[9] "Writs of assistance" were general search warrants allowing officers to search homes and other premises at will. For a fuller summary of the events see Andrew C. McLaughlin, *A Constitutional History of the United States* (New York and London, 1935), Chapters 1–9.

[10] Quoted in *ibid.*, p. 42.

which part the fault lies"; appealed for independence: "Oh ye that love mankind! Ye that dare oppose, not only the tyranny, but the tyrant, stand forth!" This was mass appeal, and the pamphlet got mass distribution. Its significance was that it "rallied the undecided and the wavering, and proved a trumpet call to the radicals." [11] On June 7 Congress resolved that "these united colonies are and of right ought to be free and independent states" and appointed a committee with Jefferson as chairman to draft a document proclaiming the revolution.

The Declaration of Independence is in two parts. The second states the grievances of the colonies and imputes the long line of abuses and violations of rights to the King. The first part is a statement of principles. In 110 words Jefferson capsules Lockian philosophy in phrases so well known that their conciseness, beauty, force, and import are easily overlooked. The opening is confident: "We hold these truths to be self-evident." There are five "truths":

1. ". . . that all men are created equal." This is more than Locke wrote. The meaning is ambiguous, but the brevity that produces ambiguity gives new force in new situations. It is not absurd, as some have claimed, for it does not refer to physical or mental equality, nor to the actual conditions of human existence, but to moral fact. Jefferson was asserting it as such. And he was asserting it as a test of government. It seems to mean that all men must be equal in rights; beyond that general statement the connotations of the phrase, like those of "equal protection of the law," are left for the moral conscience of the generations.

2. ". . . that they are endowed by their Creator with certain unalienable Rights, that among these are Life, Liberty and the pursuit of Happiness." The Declaration gives divine sanction to natural rights. Man has rights by virtue of his existence, and not even his own acts can alienate them. This is not inconsistent with the claim of civil right, but is assertion that there is a moral law higher than civil law. Jefferson did not, as Locke did, list property as one of the natural rights. Some might say it is included in the "pursuit of Happiness," and certainly most Americans of the time would have agreed that protection of property was a chief—indeed, a few said, *the* chief—end of government. On the other hand, some stated during the Revolutionary period that property was a right based solely on convention, and Jefferson himself wrote that the rights of property could be so far extended as to violate natural right.[12]

3. "That to secure these rights, Governments are instituted among Men." This is pure Lockian doctrine. It states a single purpose for government. It overlooks the fact that rights may have to be compromised to accommodate other men's claims of right, and the further fact that the objective of some men in instituting government is to obtain power over others. The statement was, however, one of a principle which should govern the purpose of government.

---

[11] Samuel Eliot Morison and Henry Steele Commager, *The Growth of the American Republic*, 4th ed. (New York, 1950), p. 194.

[12] Letter to the Reverend James Madison, October 28, 1795, *The Writings of Thomas Jefferson*, Ford ed. (New York, 1896), Vol. VII, p. 36.

4. ". . . deriving their just Powers from the consent of the governed." This is the principle of popular sovereignty and is opposed to claims of divine right or prescriptive right. The Declaration is silent on the possibility of conflict between popular sovereignty and natural right, that is, on actions of the people which infringe "unalienable" rights. It is silent about how the "consent of the governed" is to be provided in the organization and process of government and particularly on how factions among the governed, arising because of their various interests and ideas, are to be controlled. These were to be the central problems for those who prepared constitutions.

5. "That, whenever any form of Government becomes destructive of these ends, it is the Right of the People to alter or to abolish it. . . ." This too is pure Lockian doctrine. It asserts that revolution is, under certain conditions, a right. The Declaration adds immediately a note of caution: "Prudence, indeed, will dictate that Governments long established should not be changed for light and transient causes. . . ."

These were philosophical doctrines of the Revolution. Their significance was great not only in 1776 but for future generations. Yet the equalitarianism, which is announced in the first clause and implied in those that follow, did not herald a full-scale social revolution. The temper of the Revolution can be understood only if the balance between social change and continuity that characterized the period is now described.

CHANGE AND CONTINUITY

A third consequence of the Revolution was the beginning of a period of economic, social, and religious change. The power of the aristocratic elements in society was diminished by the exodus of the Tories, confiscation of much of their property, and the destruction of the governments through which their power was exerted. New groups of men who were not as committed to tradition rose to positions of influence. Landownership broadened as royal limitations on free settlement were swept away and as confiscated properties were distributed. The provisions in the laws of some of the states which favored the concentration of land ownership were repealed. "Within ten years 'every state had abolished entails except two, and those were two in which entails were rare. In fifteen years every state without exception abolished primogeniture'—all save four placing daughters on an equality with sons in distribution of landed inheritances." [13] Laws were passed for the benefit of debtors—the Revolution being the first period of debtor ascendancy in the politics of America. There was a trend toward disestablishment of churches and extension of religious freedom. Slavery was abolished, or the slave trade prohibited, in some states. Legal systems were reformed to remove the severities of the criminal law and of punishment for its violation.

The striking fact about these changes, in view of their "revolutionary" context, is their moderateness. The laws in favor of debtors are an exception,

---

[13] Charles and Mary Beard, *The Rise of American Civilization* (New York, 1930), p. 294, quoting J. Franklin Jameson, *The American Revolution Considered as a Social Movement* (Princeton, 1926).

but this tendency in legislation was to be corrected by prohibitions on the states in the Constitution of 1787. Some historians have found in these events evidence of a great difference between the Spirit of 1776 and the Spirit of 1787, the former being characterized as a period of populism, the latter as one of reaction. The difference between the two, however, will be grossly exaggerated if account is not taken of the moderate nature of the social changes generally, following 1776, and the temperate nature of the Framers, in 1787.

The American Revolution differed from both the French Revolution of 1789 and the Russian Revolution of 1917. The French sought elimination of their feudal inheritance and proclaimed rights that lacked foundation in a precedent constitution or tradition. The Americans, as Louis Hartz has said, skipped the feudal stage of history and hence had no economic and social inheritance to liquidate; they sought, in the main, preservation of their existing institutions. The Russians—who, again according to Hartz, skipped the liberal stage of history—tore up the roots of society in a complete social revolution; the Americans sought principally a political rather than a social change. In fact, Hartz argues that throughout American history the lack of a feudalism to liquidate has militated against socialist doctrine; thus American conflicts between the political "right" and the political "left" have been narrower than in Europe, where broader social antagonisms existed.[14] He refers us to a thesis of De Tocqueville:

> The great advantage of the Americans is, that they have arrived at a state of democracy without having to endure a democratic revolution; and that they are born equal, instead of becoming so.[15]

As for the American Revolution itself, Daniel Boorstin has even written about its "conservatism," and in comparison with the French and Russian revolutions, it is conservative indeed. It was primarily a political revolution that, in Boorstin's words, sought to sever "imperial legal relations" and preserve "a legacy of institutions." The nature of the Revolution is reflected not only in the first 110 words of the Declaration of Independence but also in its technical and legalistic description of historical rights that Americans said had been violated and that they desired to preserve.[16]

The First State Governments

The fourth consequence of the Revolution was the formation of state governments. In emphasis of this aspect of the Revolution, it has been said that ". . . the political ideas of the American Revolution, the Spirit of '76, is not accurately represented by Tom Paine nor adequately by the Declaration of Independence. For that spirit is also to be found in the state constitutions of 1776, of 1777, and of 1780, constitutions which were in many instances written by the men who wrote and signed the Declaration of Independence."[17] These constitutions repeated the principles of the Decla-

---

[14] Louis Hartz, *The Liberal Tradition in America* (New York, 1955), Chapter 1.
[15] Alexis de Tocqueville, *Democracy in America* (New York, 1954), Vol. II, p. 108.
[16] See Boorstin, *op. cit.*, pp. 80 ff.
[17] Wright, "Consensus and Continuity," p. 17.

ration but at the same time limited majority rule by the rule of law—now in written constitutions, by separation of powers and checks and balances, and by continued limitations on suffrage.

In 1775, as fighting occurred and as royal governors and other officials fled, governments began to pass into the hands of revolutionary assemblies. In 1776 new governments were given a constitutional foundation. Now came the eleven-year period (1776–87) of constitution-making, in which men, freed of old governments but familiar with history and doctrine, were given the opportunity to create new forms of government to implement the doctrines of rule of law and popular consent. There was much variation in the details of these governments; yet long-run trends for the nation—roots for giant trunks of practice and principle—were being set by the time of the adoption of the Massachusetts constitution of 1780.

WRITTEN CONSTITUTIONS

The first step was to base state governments on written constitutions. These were initially drafted and put into effect in ways that today would appear irregular. In Connecticut and Rhode Island the old charters were continued in effect without vote of the people. In some states constitutions were framed in revolutionary assemblies and put into operation without any approval by voters. But there was some protest: Jefferson said that the Virginia convention had usurped the "natural right" of the people, and a Massachusetts constitution was rejected by voters in 1778 mainly on the ground that a legislature had no right to draft a constitution. There was special authorization in some states and informal submission in some. It was left, however, to Massachusetts in 1780 to develop the procedure that conjoined in practice the principles of popular sovereignty and fundamental law and would be typical of American practice in the future: the legislature submitted to the people the question of whether they wanted to elect delegates to a constitutional convention; after affirmative vote, the people elected delegates to a convention; the constitution that emerged was ratified by popular vote.

BILLS OF RIGHTS

Prominent in some of these constitutions were bills of rights. The rights enumerated were mainly those in the English common law, such as trial by jury, or those in the great English documents. Yet some went beyond these, as in a precedent-setting provision in the Virginia bill of rights (1776) guaranteeing religious freedom. Mixed with the guarantees of rights were statements of principle. One principle was the rule of law: "to the end it may be a government of laws and not of men," as the Massachusetts constitution of 1780 declared. That constitution also affirmed that a separation of powers in government was the means of obtaining a government of law.

SEPARATION OF POWERS

The principle of separation of powers was stated in many of the constitutions. Thus the Maryland constitution declared that "the legislative, executive and judicial powers of government ought to be forever separate and distinct from each other." Nevertheless, the first governments established showed a marked concentration of powers in the legislatures. Reacting against strong executives as a result of colonial experience, the framers of state constitutions created governments of legislative supremacy. Two features of the constitutions created this supremacy. The first was the failure to provide for independent selection and tenure of the officers in the three departments of government. In most of the states the governor was elected by the legislature. This was also the usual method of selecting judges. Accompanying provisions set short terms and limitations on reelection. The second was the failure to provide for such intermingling of powers among the branches as to provide checks on the legislature. Thus in Rhode Island and Connecticut, where the governor was elected by the people, he possessed no participation in the legislative power through a power of veto. Yet this feature, as did adoption of constitutions, encountered protest. Jefferson declared with respect to the Virginia constitution of 1776 that "one hundred and seventy-three despots" (the number of members of the legislature) "would surely be as oppressive as one." And, as was the case with adoption of constitutions, the pattern for the future was to be set by 1780. The New York constitution of 1777 was the first to point toward the independence of the three departments and the combination of separation of powers and checks and balances which was to prevail in American governments. The governor was elected by the people for three years, the appointed judges were to serve during good behavior, the governor and the judges of the highest court had a power of veto or revision on legislation (subject to repassage by a two-thirds vote of the legislature), and an impeachment process was provided as a check upon executive and judicial officials. Yet the governor was still weak, for the power of appointment of executive officers was divided between a legislative council and the governor.[18]

The constitution of Massachusetts set the real pattern of the future. Just as the Massachusetts constitution of 1780 joined the principles of popular sovereignty and of fundamental law limiting government to a written constitution emanating from the people, so it joined the twin principles of separation of powers and checks and balances with the idea of liberty under law. This constitution, as did all but three state constitutions, provided for a two-house legislature. The legislature could appoint some executive officers, and the lower house could bring impeachment charges for trial in the upper house. The governor was elected by the people. He could appoint most executive and all judicial officers with the consent of a council predominantly legislative in composition, could veto legislation (subject to repassage by two-thirds vote of the houses of the legislature), and could pardon criminal offenses with the consent of the council. Judges would hold office during good behavior except for removal by the governor with the consent of the council upon request of the legislature. Their salaries could not be diminished during their terms of office. Judges of the supreme court could give advisory opinions to the legislature (still true in Massachusetts). Here then was a distribution of powers in which some legislative power was

---

[18] See Leslie Lipson, *The American Governor from Figurehead to Leader* (Chicago, 1938), Chapter 2.

vested in the executive and the judiciary, some judicial power in the legis-lature and the governor, and some executive power in the legislature. It was true separation of powers, qualified and thus made effective by checks and balances.

Still another development which was to increase the checks and balances in the system of government was judicial review. In the beginning there were several devices for maintaining the supremacy of the constitution. New York had a veto power in its council, composed of the governor and judges, against "laws inconsistent with the spirit" of the constitution; Massachusetts had an advisory power on legislation in the supreme court; Pennsylvania and Vermont had a council of censors which was to be elected every seventh year to check on whether the constitution had been preserved inviolate. But the state courts soon began to assert that they had the power to hold acts of the legislature unconstitutional; this was to be the primary role of the judiciary in the system of checks and balances.

MEN AND PROPERTY

How were these mechanical arrangements for government related to the social constitution of society? Who among the people could participate, and what protections were given to the different interests in the society? The qualifications for voting varied widely. In Virginia, according to Jefferson, less than one half of the taxpayers could vote. In Massachusetts, according to a recent study, most adult men could vote.[19] Suffrage reforms in the period of constitution-framing "advanced democratic practices and principles considerably." [20] In some states the requirement only that one be a taxpayer led virtually to white manhood suffrage. Yet the movement for extension of the suffrage was irregular and not always successful.[21] In addition to limitations on the suffrage for the lower house, other limitations existed for the protection of property interests. A larger amount of property was required in some states for voting for the upper house than for the lower one. Also, high property qualifications were required in some states for holding elective office. For example, under the Massachusetts constitution of 1780 a member of the house of representatives was required to possess a freehold worth one hundred pounds or any estate worth two hundred, a senator to have a freehold worth three hundred pounds or any estate worth six hundred, and the governor a freehold worth one thousand pounds. The various qualifications for voting and holding office in the several states show that those who possessed power believed that it should be retained in the hands of those who had some stake in society, and that ownership of property was the safest proof of such a stake. Yet the possession of property was so widespread, and the qualifications for voting often so easy to meet, that the popular base for government was in many parts of the country quite broad.

---

[19] See Robert E. Brown, *Middle-Class Democracy and the Revolution in Massachusetts, 1691–1780* (Ithaca, 1955).
[20] Chilton Williamson, *American Suffrage: From Property to Democracy, 1760–1860* (Princeton, 1960), p. 136.
[21] See Elisha P. Douglass, *Rebels and Democrats: The Struggle for Equal Political Rights and Majority Rule during the American Revolution* (Chapel Hill, 1955).

The United States of America and the Articles of Confederation

⑤ The fifth result of the War of Independence was the creation of the United States of America. When the resolution for independence was introduced in Congress on June 7, 1776, it was accompanied by a resolution on steps to be taken to form a confederation.

Union had been discussed on earlier occasions. There was once a New England Confederation. In 1754 an Albany Congress, composed of representatives of several colonies, considered a plan proposed by Benjamin Franklin for a federal union. The beginnings of union lay, however, in the cooperation that developed among the colonies in the conflict with England. Beginning in 1772, local committees of correspondence arose to keep in touch with similar groups. In 1773 Virginia suggested intercolonial committees of correspondence, and in 1774 a group representing extralegal groups in the colonies met in the First Continental Congress. It drew up a declaration of principles, commended resistance in Massachusetts, and resolved to stop importation of British goods. In 1775 the Second Continental Congress met. For six years it was the extralegal central government. It declared independence, selected a commander in chief, conducted negotiations with friendly nations, and sought support for Washington's armies.

The Continental Congress also selected a committee to draft a constitution, and debated, approved, and submitted one to the states. Ratification of the document, the Articles of Confederation, was delayed until a conflict between the states that owned Western lands and those that did not appeared to be settled. The Articles, the first constitution of the United States, went into effect on March 1, 1781.

The first article officially created the name "The United States of America." The union created was a confederation, that is, it was a union of states rather than of people, similar to the United Nations today. It was declared to be a "perpetual union," but this was not consistent with the provision that "Each state retains its sovereignty, freedom, and independence." Every power not "expressly delegated" was reserved to the states. The powers given to the Confederation were vested in a Congress. Each state could be represented by from two to five members but would have only one vote. On a long list of important matters the Congress could act only through the concurrence of nine states. Congress could appoint a Committee of States and other committees "for managing the general affairs of the United States," and a President to serve as presiding officer.

The lasting contributions of the Articles to the solutions of the problems of federal union have generally been overlooked. First, many of the powers to be vested in Congress by the Constitution of 1787 were enumerated in the Articles as "sole and exclusive" powers of Congress: to negotiate peace and declare war, enter into treaties and alliances, regulate the value of coins, fix standards of weights and measures, regulate trade with the Indians, establish post offices, build and equip a navy, and borrow money on its own authority. Second, basic rules of interstate comity and cooperation were included. (1) "The free inhabitants of each of these states . . . shall be entitled to all privileges and immunities of free citizens in the several states." This was accompanied by a statement of the specific rights

Generally considered the first political cartoon in America, this call to the colonies to unite against the coming French and Indian War was published by Benjamin Franklin in 1754.

of free ingress and regress to every state and of trade and commerce on the same conditions with inhabitants of the state. (2) It was required that fugitives from justice be returned. (3) "Full faith and credit shall be given in each of these states to the records, acts and judicial proceedings of the courts and magistrates in every other state."

There were, nevertheless, fundamental defects in the Articles of Confederation. First, two important powers—to tax and to regulate commerce—were not granted. Second, no provision was made for an executive, other than committees of Congress, or for a judiciary, except such courts as Congress might establish for trial of piracy and felony on the high seas and for hearing appeals in all cases of prize capture. Third, no important decisions could be made without the concurrence of nine states. Fourth, there was excessive dependence upon the states. In the absence of power to tax, Congress' means of obtaining funds was to requisition the states. To raise an army it had to requisition each state for its quota of troops. There was no enforcement power in the new government, through either executive officials or judges. Finally, the Articles could be strengthened only by amendments proposed by Congress and ratified by the legislatures of every state. The defect of this procedure was revealed by the failure of two amendments proposed by Congress because only twelve states ratified them.

The "vices of the political system," as Madison put it, were soon to be revealed. Foremost among the practical difficulties encountered was the failure of the states to honor requisitions upon them and to abide by treaty obligations. The provision in the Articles that "every state shall abide by the determinations of the united states in Congress assembled" on questions within its province proved to be admonition only. Added difficulties were the encroachments of the states upon each other's commerce and the inability of Congress to make treaty arrangements concerning commerce. In addition, Madison noted the "multiplicity," "mutability," and "injustice" of the laws of the states. The states not only had engaged in commercial competition with each other but had issued their own paper money and had loosened the obligations of contract by allowing payment of debts in depreciated currency.

These conditions led naturally to dissatisfaction among financial and commercial groups. The activities of the business community were seriously impaired by the lack of a single monetary system, the multiple regulations of the states on commerce, the inability to conclude and enforce trade treaties, and the lack of power to levy duties to protect infant manufactures. The conditions led also to much pessimism among statesmen of the day. Some were confirmed in their distrust of popular government. Typical of this group was John Jay, who said in 1786 that "the mass of men are neither wise nor good" and that the people considered "liberty and licentiousness" as the same thing. Even Washington in the same year declared that "mankind, when left to themselves, are unfit for their own government."

Other statements, however, indicated belief that the difficulties might be less fundamental—that the defect could be in institutions and that these might be reformed. Washington noted the states' jealousies of Congress and of one another and saw that they had made the federal establishment "a half-starved, limping government that appears to be always limping on crutches and tottering at every step." To a plea that he use his influence, he responded, "*Influence* is no *government*. Let us have one by which our lives, liberties, and properties will be secured, or let us know the worst at once. . . ." [22]

It was this hope rising above pessimism that led to plans for a strong national government. Even as early as 1780 and 1781, Hamilton, Madison, and others made proposals for a stronger government for the union. In succeeding years Congress proposed amendments, state legislatures suggested changes, and leading figures corresponded about the needs for governmental reform. Many proposals related to commerce, indicating the truth of Madison's statement that "most of our political evils can be traced to our commercial ones."

A dispute over commerce on the Potomac between Virginia and Maryland precipitated the series of events leading to a new constitution. Virginia, in 1786, invited all the states to send commissioners to a meeting to consider "the trade of the United States." This invitation resulted in commissioners from five states meeting at Annapolis in September, 1786. The group reported its conviction that discussion should be extended "to other objects, than those of commerce," and suggested to the states that they send delegates to Philadelphia "on the second Monday in May next" "to devise such further provisions as shall appear to them necessary to render the constitution of the federal government adequate to the exigencies of the union." Copies of this report to the states were transmitted to the Congress, which on February 21, 1787, issued its own call for the meeting in Philadelphia "for the sole and express purpose of revising the Articles of Con-

---

[22] The quotations from Jay and Washington are given with their sources in Albert J. Beveridge, *The Life of John Marshall* (Boston and New York, 1929), Vol. I, pp. 300–01, 308.

federation." Already six states had selected delegates for the Convention, and it met at the appointed place in May, 1787.

A Constitution for the Union [23]

Seeing the list of delegates to the Convention, Jefferson in Paris wrote to John Adams in London that "it really is an assembly of demi-gods." Robert Morris, delegate from Pensylvania, said after the Constitution was framed that it was "the work of plain, honest men." Though Jefferson's praise was extravagant, Morris' judgment was too restrained.

PERSONNEL

The Convention contained many men of distinction and superior talents who were eminently qualified for the task before them. They were the sort of men one would expect to be sent to a convention of this kind—lawyers and judges, businessmen, and a few doctors, college presidents, college professors, and gentlemen of leisure. They were men of education and of experience in public affairs. Of the fifty-five delegates who attended, thirty-one had college educations, thirty-nine had been members of Congress, seven had been state governors, and eight had served in constitutional conventions.[24] They reflected such a wide diversity of opinions and interests that quotations can be made from their speeches to represent conflicting views on nationalism and states' rights, populism and conservatism, and other matters. Farrand has said that they "took their work seriously." [25] Indeed, some of them would have agreed with Madison's statement in the Convention that they "were now to decide for ever the fate of republican government."

The member who made the greatest contribution to the success of the Convention was James Madison, who has been called "the Father of the Constitution." Thirty-six years of age, experienced in state government and as a member of Congress, he—in the words of a fellow delegate—blended "together the profound politician with the scholar" and was "a most agreeable, eloquent and convincing speaker." [26] He had made a thorough study of man's experience with confederations, had corresponded with others about the problems of union, and was apparently regarded as the leader of the group in the Convention favoring a strong national government.

Though all the leaders cannot be mentioned, a few cannot be overlooked. James Wilson of Pennsylvania, forty-five, immigrant from Scotland, able lawyer, signer of the Declaration of Independence, several times member of Congress, was a democratic nationalist in the sense that he believed that a strong national union could be achieved only through basing its government on the people. As draftsman in the committee of detail he had an

---

[23] The material on the following two pages was drawn substantially from Max Farrand, *The Framing of the Constitution* (New Haven, 1913), Chapter 2.

[24] Charles Warren, *The Making of the Constitution* (Boston, 1928), Vol. I, pp. 55–56.

[25] Farrand, *op. cit.*, p. 61.

[26] Quoted from *Notes of Major William Pierce* [Georgia] *in the Federal Convention of 1787*, in *Documents Illustrative of the Formation of the Union of the American States* (Washington, 1927).

unusual opportunity to influence the content of the Constitution. Washington's influence on the members must have been great, and it was given in support of the plan for a strong national government. Gouverneur Morris, brilliant member of the Philadelphia delegation, also supported a strong government and as a member of the committee on style and arrangement did much to put the Constitution in its final form and language. Alexander Hamilton, only thirty years of age, was one of the ablest members, but his views toward strong government went beyond those of his colleagues, and he left early, to return only for the purpose of signing the finished document.

METHODS OF WORK

It was Friday, the twenty-fifth of May, eleven days after the appointed date, before delegates had arrived from seven states and the Convention could be organized. It selected Washington as president and resolved to meet in secret and to allow each state one vote in the proceedings. By the twenty-ninth, delegates had arrived from ten states, and ultimately all states except Rhode Island were represented. On the twenty-ninth the Virginia Plan, no doubt primarily the work of Madison, was introduced by Governor Randolph and became the first subject of Convention discussions. Except for a two-day adjournment for the Fourth of July and one for ten days to allow a committee to prepare a report, the Convention was in continuous session until September 17. Late in the sessions it referred the resolutions it had passed to a committee of detail of five members and near the end to a committee on style and arrangement.

Although the Convention selected a secretary from outside its membership, the Convention records that are most useful for study come to us from Madison. He placed himself at the front of the room and took as copious notes as he could, sitting up at night to complete the record. Madison's notes summarize the speeches of the delegates, list the votes on motions, and in general provide a day-to-day account of the proceedings.[27]

Forty-two delegates were present at the end. All signed the Constitution except three—Governor Edmund Randolph and George Mason of Virginia and Elbridge Gerry of Massachusetts. Madison reports that as the last members were signing, Benjamin Franklin, then eighty-two years old, "looking toward the President's chair, at the back of which a rising sun had been painted, observed to a few members near him, that painters had found it difficult to distinguish in their art a rising from a setting sun. I have, said he, often and often in the course of the session . . . looked at that behind the President without being able to tell whether it was rising or setting: But now at length I have the happiness to know that it is a rising and not a setting sun."

A NATIONAL GOVERNMENT

The most important decision of the convention was made on the first day of its deliberations. It adopted a resolution by Randolph, seconded by Gouverneur Morris, "that a *national* government ought to be established

---

[27] Madison's notes are also printed in *ibid.*

consisting of a *supreme* legislative, executive, and judiciary." [28] They understood the purport of this momentous resolution. Gouverneur Morris said
that a "national, supreme government" would be a "*compulsive* operation."
Mason said that a government was needed that "could operate directly on
individuals," and General Pinkney expressed doubt whether their instructions allowed them to go this far. The resolution passed with six ayes,
New York divided, Connecticut opposed.

This was a bold decision. It took genius to adapt it to the coexistence of
thirteen states of varying size. The genius was a collective genius, born out
of debate, conflict, compromise, and consciousness of realities. The adaptation of the principle of a national government to the coexistence of the
states created something theretofore unknown—a federal system of government, different both from a confederation of states and from a consolidation of powers in a single government. This new entity was complicated by
many details, and only the major decisions can or need to be noted here.

One problem was that of the extent and method of delegation of powers
to the national government. The Virginia Plan proposed that the national
legislature should have, in addition to the powers vested in the Congress
of the Confederation, the power "to legislate in all cases to which the
separate states are incompetent, or in which the harmony of the United
States may be interrupted by the exercise of individual legislation." This
general statement on scope of powers was adopted, but with Randolph
"disclaiming any intention to give indefinite powers," and Madison expressing "a strong bias in favor of an enumeration and definition," though
doubting "its practicability." The delegates did find later that enumeration
was practicable, thereby establishing a national government with stated
powers.

Another problem was one which has been referred to as "the problem of
coercion." How could the powers of the national government be enforced?
The Virginia Plan proposed that the national legislature have the power
"to negative all laws passed by the several states, contravening in the
opinion of the national legislature the articles of union" and the further
power "to call forth the force of the union" against states failing to fulfill
their duties. It is fortunate that these solutions were not adopted, for the
first would have brought conflict between national and state *governments*
and the second would have created civil war between the union and resisting states. A combination of the Virginia Plan and the plan submitted later
by the New Jersey delegation proved to be a better solution. The Virginia
Plan called for a government which operated through executive and judicial organs *on people* rather than on states; the New Jersey Plan included
a provision that acts of Congress in pursuance of powers granted and treaties made under the authority of the United States should be *supreme law*
and the *judges of the states bound thereby*. These were not by themselves
complete answers, for they did not contain provision for appeal of state
court decisions to federal courts. But the Convention had provided for a
Supreme Court, and the Judiciary Act of 1789 was to provide for appeal

---

[28] The emphases appear in Madison's notes.

from the highest state court to the Supreme Court of any case where a claim was made under the Constitution or laws of the United States and denied by the state court.

The basic answers to the problem of national-state conflict were these: (1) enumeration of national powers; (2) enforcement of national law on individuals, not states; (3) resolution of issues of national and state power by the courts acting under the injunction to uphold the supreme law on cases arising between individuals; and (4) a federal judiciary with jurisdiction in the enforcement of national law and with appellate jurisdiction over state judiciaries to decide issues affecting national power. Thus the problem of coercion of states was solved by avoiding the necessity. Only in the Civil War and in the struggles over desegregation has "the force of the union" been used against the states. Except for these occurrences it has been possible to have both national and state governments operating in the same territory without shows of force between the two.

The third problem was that of representation. This is always a difficult problem in forming a union of unequal states. In the Convention the large-small state cleavage was quickly unmasked. It threatened to wreck the Convention. The feelings were so intense on one occasion that Franklin suggested prayer, to which Hamilton—the first American isolationist—is reported to have replied that the Convention had no need for "foreign aid." Gouverneur Morris was to say later that "the fate of America was suspended by a hair." The Virginia Plan proposed two houses, with representation in both apportioned among the states on the basis of "quotas of contribution" or of number of free inhabitants. A fight ensued and the large states won a temporary victory, first in a decision to apportion seats in the first house on the basis of population, and then in a vote for proportional representation also in the second house. The Convention now received the report from the committee of the whole, which had been deliberating on the Virginia Plan, but New Jersey brought forth an alternative plan. The two plans were now both referred to the committee of the whole for consideration. The New Jersey Plan proposed a revision of the Articles, retaining a one-house congress with equal state representation but granting it additional powers— including the powers to levy import duties and to regulate commerce, and providing for an executive and a judiciary. This plan would have continued the need to requisition funds from the states. After debate the Convention confirmed the important decision made earlier to base its deliberations on the Virginia Plan. But it was now brought perilously close to adjournment without agreement on the crucial issue of representation. The Great Compromise which solved the problem was itself a narrow decision, made by 5 yeas and 4 nays (Massachusetts divided, New York delegates absent). It is probably the most significant single-vote majority in American history. A few men of compromise saved the Convention. The heart of the compromise was equal representation in the Senate, proportional representation in the House of Representatives. Other features were, with the adjustments made later in the Convention, the counting of a slave as three fifths of a person in the enumeration of population, the apportionment of direct taxes on the same basis as representation in the House of Representatives, and the requirement that revenue bills originate in the House.

The result of the solution to these problems—delegation, coercion, representation—was to create a unique system of government. It was unique in that a constitution provided for two governments, each possessing substantial powers and substantial independence and both operating on the same individuals. It was unique in that, by the Great Compromise and other provisions of the Constitution, features characteristic of a confederacy (participation of states) and those characteristic of a national or unitary system (representation of people) were combined. This unique system is called federalism and will be further described, both as it existed originally and as it has evolved, in later chapters, especially Chapters 4 and 29.

CONFLICT, COMPROMISE, AND PROBLEM

It is instructive to contemplate the spirit of the Convention and the factors that made it a successful decision-making assembly. It was a forum in which all the major conflicts of interest and opinion in the nation were brought into focus: large versus small states, North versus South, East versus West, nationalists versus states'-righters, support for popular government versus suspicion of it. It has been customary to call the Constitution a "bundle of compromises" and to say that the Convention was dominated by a spirit of compromise. This is only a half-truth. There was indeed a great deal of conscious and unconscious compromising. At the same time, there was much concurrency—indeed unanimity—of opinion. The delegates were agreed on the seriousness of the evils of the existing system and impelled to remain at their task even when they seemed to be making little progress. They were agreed that they were seeking to establish a viable republican government—and they would have agreed that this meant a nonmonarchical system—one in which, as Madison was to say later, the government "derives all its powers directly or indirectly from the great body of the people." [29] They were agreed that the government should be one of separation of powers and checks and balances, that the Constitution of the union should be "the supreme law," and that restraints should be erected against state invasions of property rights.[30] In addition to compromise there was serious groping for workable solutions—a problem-solving attitude among the members. For example, we have seen that they wanted an enumeration of powers if it was feasible, and also a way to resolve national-state conflicts. Finally, there was a willingness to deliberate. Difficult problems or those on which there was division were postponed, brought up for reconsideration, and then patiently reanalyzed in the light of decisions made in the interim.

There were many compromises, a number of them between the North and the South. Already the differences in interest between an agricultural, exporting, slave-holding South and a manufacturing, commercial North were apparent. Madison said "the great danger to our general government is the great southern and northern interests of the continent, being opposed to each other." In one compromise the Southern delegates accepted the regula-

---

29 *The Federalist,* No. 39.
30 For fuller discussion see Carl J. Friedrich and Robert G. McCloskey, *From the Declaration of Independence to the Constitution: The Roots of American Constitutionalism* (New York, 1954), pp. xlvi–liv.

tion of commerce desired by the commercial interest with the proviso that there should be no taxation of exports; in another South and North agreed on the three-fifths ratio in counting slaves for determining representation in the House of Representatives; in still another the South obtained a provision that there should be no limitation of the importation of slaves before 1808.

The difficult search for answers to problems is perhaps best exemplified in the choice of a method for selecting the President. After the matter had had some discussion in the Convention Wilson said, "It is in truth the most difficult we have had to decide." Both the Virginia and the New Jersey plans provided for election by the national legislature, and five times the delegates voted for this method.[31] Yet these objections were repeatedly pressed: It would be the subject of intrigues in the legislature; the executive would not be independent, and the strength of the office would be impaired; "usurpation and tyranny on the part of the legislature will be the consequence." Though Roger Sherman argued that the executive ought to be "accountable to the legislature," Madison said it was "a fundamental principle of free government" that the three powers of government should be "independently exercised." Wilson and Gouverneur Morris favored election by the people, and Madison agreed that this was "the fittest in itself." But Wilson admitted many would think it "chimerical," and this was indeed a correct assessment of the sentiment of the delegates. They doubted the practicality of a popular election over such a large area. Madison noted, too, the difficulty in popular election because of great variations in suffrage qualifications among the states. There were proposals for selection of the executive by the state legislatures or governors, but it was seen that this scheme would weaken the national government. Of selection by governors, Randolph said, "They will not cherish the great oak which is to reduce them to paltry shrubs." Choice by electors chosen by the people in districts was proposed early by Wilson, when he was asked to "digest" the method of election by the people into "form." The final selection of election by electors was a result of a groping for a method that would avoid the defects of all other suggested methods.

PROPERTY AND MEN

In interpreting the work of the Convention many writers have emphasized that it reflected a conservative reaction against the populism of the Revolutionary period. There is danger that this interpretation, though substantially accurate, may overshadow the recognition of other elements in a complex matrix.

There were indeed many expressions of fear and distrust of the people, and some members undoubtedly agreed with Gerry (who did not sign the Constitution) that "the evils we experience flow from the excess of democracy." Others, however, would not have agreed with Gerry. Thus, when Madison predicted that in the future the majority of the people would have no property and argued that "the freeholders of society would be the safest depositories of republican liberty," Franklin responded "that we should not

---

[31] Clinton Rossiter, *The American Presidency*, 2nd ed. (New York, 1960), p. 77.

depress the virtue and public spirit of our common people." Though it is difficult to assess the temper of a body of men, some feeling of the lines of opinion may be gained from the views of some of the leaders. One may note, first, the simple national democracy of James Wilson. He desired a national government with strength, and to achieve this he argued for a government based on the people rather than on the states. He favored popular election of both houses of Congress and of the President, and annual election of members of the lower house. He "could not agree that property was the sole or the primary object of government and society"; he believed that the "majority of people wherever found ought in all questions to govern the minority"; and he feared that arrangements contemplated for the executive would have a "dangerous tendency toward aristocracy." The President should be a "man of the people." There was the more complex thought of Gouverneur Morris—scornful of democracy but nonetheless showing some strains of democratic thought. He asserted that men "unite in society for the protection of property" and fought vigorously for a freehold qualification for suffrage, fearing that the people who have no property would sell their votes "to the rich who will be able to buy them." Yet he favored election of the President by the people, arguing first that "if the people should elect, they will never fail to prefer some man of distinguished character, or services," and second that the President "should be the guardian of the people, even of the lower classes, against legislative tyranny, against the great and the wealthy who in the course of things will necessarily compose the legislative body. . . ." Then there was the qualified democracy of James Madison. Government, he said, "ought to secure the permanent interests [i.e., of property] of the country against innovation." There was danger that majorities "might under sudden impulses be tempted to commit injustice on the minority." This danger should, however, be "guarded against on republican principles." This could be done by dividing "the trust between different bodies of men, who might watch and check each other," by "refining the popular appointments" through indirect election of Senators, President, and judges, and particularly by making the Senate, through appointment for a long term, a check on democracy. This was government by the people but with the people checked and restrained against excesses.

There were many provisions in the Constitution to protect property rights. There was the Senate, which represented state legislatures, which in turn were presumed to be more favorable to property rights than the people; there were prohibitions against states coining money, issuing paper money, or impairing the obligation of contracts; there were compromises to protect the economic interests of the sections; there was even—and this was inevitable at the time—acceptance of property rights in human beings. Yet the Convention on some issues of vast importance left open the doors to social change. It left the determination of voting rights to the states; and though it was doubtless impracticable to do anything else because of the differences among the states in suffrage requirements, the delegates could see that liberal suffrage provisions would prevail. It left to Congress the right to admit new states with the same rules of representation as for the original states, disregarding the argument of some, particularly Gouverneur Morris, that "the rule of representation ought to be so fixed as to secure to the

Atlantic states a prevalence in the national councils." Their experience had enabled them already to foresee the democratic tendencies of the Western frontier, and yet they did not place barriers against equality for the people of the West.

When time brought veneration to the Convention, historians attributed to its members lofty moral motivations. Then, in contrast, Charles A. Beard in 1913 wrote *An Economic Interpretation of the Constitution*. Beard argued that the Convention was called because certain economic interests were adversely affected by existing conditions. These included those people who held depreciated government bonds and desired a government which could pay their face value; those engaged in manufacturing and commerce who wanted a protective tariff and relief from state interferences with commerce; those having investments in Western land who wanted a government which could protect these; and those having money to invest who wanted to be rid of state paper money and laws impairing contracts. According to Beard, the members of the Convention represented these interests and framed a Constitution to protect them. These conclusions have aroused heated discussions about the motivations of the Framers.[32]

It would be no reflection on the Framers to conclude that they saw the adverse effects of the governmental system on important economic interests and sought to correct the causes. This would only be acknowledging that they were realistic men with knowledge of the problems of their day. It would be no reflection on human nature to recognize that men seek through government to protect their economic interests, for there is an economic foundation to human welfare. It would be a reflection on the Framers if it could be substantiated that they were moved by narrow motives of self-protection which prevented them from establishing a government in which the interests of all classes and groups of men were protected. Beard himself, though criticized by many scholars for alleged overemphasis on economic influences, did not intend to draw this conclusion. Whatever else may be said, it is clear that statesmanship of an unusually high quality ruled the deliberations of the Convention. The glory of the Convention was in its handiwork, and the great attribute of this was that it did not foreclose the future but created a system of government under which, save only for the Civil War, there could be peaceful processes of struggle, compromise, and consensus among widely disparate interests and opinions within a large and growing nation.

Ratification

The Convention resolved to submit the new Constitution to conventions in the separate states for ratification and to provide that it go into effect when nine state conventions ratified it. There were several reasons for submitting the Constitution to conventions. First, as Rufus King said, the state

---

[32] Among these discussions, reference may be made to Robert E. Brown, *Charles Beard and the Constitution: A Critical Analysis of "An Economic Interpretation of the Constitution"* (Princeton, 1956) and Forrest McDonald, *We the People: The Economic Origins of the Constitution* (Chicago, 1958).

legislatures, "being to lose power, will be most likely to raise objections." Second, as Madison put it, a national constitution ought to be a source of authority "paramount to the respective constitutions of the states," which would not be true if it rested on sanction by the legislatures only. Third, again in Madison's words, "the new constitution should be ratified in the most unexceptional form, and by the supreme authority of the people themselves."

LEGAL OR POLITICAL ACT?

The Convention began by violating its instructions to revise the Articles; it closed by submitting a Constitution in violation of the amending clause of the Articles. Technically, the method of ratification was illegal in that it was to go to state conventions rather than state legislatures and in that it was to go into effect on approval of nine states. The latter provision was more than violation of an amending process; it could be construed as violation of a treaty which had established a "perpetual union" of thirteen states.

The framing and ratification of the Constitution was therefore not a legal act, but a political act establishing a new government. The Declaration of Independence, the framing of state constitutions, and the adoption of the Articles had been political rather than legal acts; and the framing and ratification of the Constitution was another step in the series. This one, however, like the Massachusetts constitution, was grounded on popular approval. This, under the theory of popular sovereignty, was the only theoretically sound basis for a supreme political act.

A CONTEST AND ITS AFTERMATH

The battle over ratification was a bitter one, and the Constitution squeezed to victory by a narrow margin. Rumors about the content of the Constitution spread, and a suspicion arose that popular liberties were being threatened. Hostility developed among diverse economic groups: small farmers who feared government by financial and commercial interests; men of property who were concerned about new taxing powers; and sectional groups who thought too much had been granted to other sections. In Virginia Patrick Henry and George Mason, in New York Governor George Clinton, and in Massachusetts Elbridge Gerry fought vigorously, sometimes viciously, against ratification. The deciding factor, however, was the superior leadership among the forces seeking ratification. Men held in high esteem by their fellows used influence, strategy, argument, and persuasion to win narrow victories in four pivotal states. In Pennsylvania they dragged in a quorum from the inns and steam-rollered a resolution through the legislature for a convention to be held only five weeks later, thus preventing the organization of effective inland opposition. In Massachusetts they beguiled John Hancock into support and won Samuel Adams by promising amendments; with the support of these powerful men ratification was achieved by a vote of 187 to 168. In Virginia the first step was to convert the influential Governor Randolph; the second was to align a great list of speakers—Randolph, Edmund Pendleton, George Wythe, "Light Horse Harry" Lee, John Marshall, Madison, and others; and the third was to agree to submit to Congress amendments containing guarantees of rights. In New York the strategy included a set of papers in exposition of the Constitution. When these four big states and seven others had ratified, arrangements were pushed to put the Constitution into effect. Two states—North Carolina and Rhode Island—ratified only after the new government was established.

Three aspects of the struggle over ratification are worthy of special note. First, Patrick Henry's pointed question early in the debates in the Virginia ratifying convention on why the Framers should have started the preamble with "We, the people" instead of "We, the states" not only reflected the opposition to a strong national union among the opponents of ratification, but presaged a continuing political conflict. Within a few years states' rights joined with populism and agrarianism in a political movement under Jefferson's leadership.[33] From then on, the struggle between nationalism and states' rights, which had been so violent in the ratification contest, would continue to be reflected in differences in interpretation of the Constitution and would itself reflect the conflicts of interests in the nation.

Second, the positive contribution of the opponents of ratification was a bill of rights for the national Constitution. The lack of a bill of rights was regarded as crucial by Mason, author of the Virginia bill of rights, who refused to sign the Constitution and opposed its ratification. He voiced the fears of many who opposed ratification. The proponents of ratification answered that there was no need for a bill of rights in a government that had only delegated powers. This reply did not satisfy the opponents, and the use and expansion of national powers has shown the defect in the proponents' argument. Their agreement to propose amendments was kept promptly, and a bill of rights was added as the first ten amendments.

Third, the struggle for ratification in New York led to the writing of *The Federalist*—a forceful argument for ratification of the Constitution, an able exposition of the principles of the Constitution, and a notable treatise on political science. This unusual group of eighty-five articles was written by Hamilton, Madison, and Jay (who composed only five of them) under the pen name "Publius." The essays were printed in New York newspapers at the rate of three or four a week during the struggle for ratification in New York. The effect of these profound, precise analyses on the members of the New York convention is uncertain, but they were a great repository of constitutional exposition and political wisdom for succeeding generations.

Conclusion

The acquired political wisdom of the Americans of 1787 included the following ideas:

RIGHTS

Man's rights are derived from a higher source than government (natural law), and may be protected in society by limitations on government (bills of rights), internal curbs within government (separation of powers and checks and balances), and operation of government through legal processes (government of laws).

---

[33] See Friedrich and McCloskey, *op. cit.*, p. lvii.

Governments derive their just powers from the consent of the governed (popular sovereignty), whose will is reflected in constitutions (constitutionalism) and through the representation of the people directly or indirectly in the offices of government (republicanism).

CONSTITUTIONALISM

The proper foundation of government is a written constitution which is the paramount law and hence should emanate directly from decisions of the people.

STRUCTURE OF GOVERNMENT

The power of government should be separated among three independent branches (separation of powers), and each should be subject to the check of the others (checks and balances).

FEDERALISM

The exigencies of economic and political life in the United States require a strong national government under a national constitution which is supreme, but the coexistence of state governments is also desirable.

Most of these ideas had European foundations. The idea of a written constitution—though not unknown in England—had flowered in this country, and federalism was an invention of the Philadelphia Convention. Also unique were the foundation of a government on this combination of ideas and the evolution of techniques (for example, constitutional conventions and declarations of rights limiting all branches of government) for putting the ideas in practice. The year 1780 for state government and 1787 for national government were times both of inventiveness and of consummation of experience.

These were also moments of beginning. Conflicts of interest and opinion, first revealed in the period of framing the Constitution, survived in the politics of the nation. Great changes in society raised new issues and worked transformations in political life. The institutions created in the eighteenth century were skeletons to which flesh and blood were added by new generations striving for new ends and for resolution of conflicts and problems. The story of these developments through a second period of evolution is told summarily in the chapter that follows and more fully through the rest of the book.

4 / Constitutional Change and the Federal System

When the delegates to the Convention of 1787 had finished their work and news of the draft Constitution swept through Philadelphia, a woman was said to have stopped Benjamin Franklin on the street and to have asked him, "Doctor Franklin, what kind of government have you given us?" "A republic, madam," Franklin replied, "if you can keep it." Today, in an era of computers, social security laws, and civil rights demonstrations, the fact that Americans manage the Republic under the same document of government written almost 180 years ago at the crest of the Age of Enlightenment is a remarkable achievement in Western political history. Even the most casual student of the American political system finds himself asking whether we really live under the same Constitution that Franklin signed, and, if so, what accounts for the permanency of our constitutional blueprint? To note that we have the oldest written constitution in effect anywhere in the world and one with far fewer amendments than those of even our closest competitors only deepens the question, Why?

Some commentators have explained this by viewing the federal Constitution as a masterful self-correcting mechanism, a realization in political form of the legendary perpetual motion machine. According to this view, our division of authority between states and nation under a federal system and our separation of powers and functions among three branches of the national government provided a series of institutional rivalries and internal checks which prevented any part of the system from breaking down or running too fast. While there is much to be said for a study of the United States Constitution as an exercise in political equilibrium, other nations, such as many Latin-American countries, followed our Constitution faithfully but had no success in making it work. Within a decade or two, sometimes within a few years of adopting the "American model," governments have collapsed, constitutions have been scrapped, and various forms of dictatorial rule have been imposed on the peoples. Thus if there is political magic in writing down the basic rules, installing a federal structure, and separating powers in the national government, there must be further ingredients in the American constitutional system that are also essential to the enterprise.

This has led other commentators to focus on two additional factors: the favorable physical and social conditions of the American nation and the special political qualities of the American people. Obviously, the rich continent Americans were able to exploit and develop, the skills that many immigrants from England and Europe brought to the New World, the underpopulation of our territories, the European investments that nurtured our infant industries, the favorable markets overseas for American raw materials and manufactured goods, the existence at our national birth of a sizable middle class, one predominant language, religion, race, and legal system, the lack of powerful nations along our borders, and our general isolation in time and space behind the oceans all combined to give the young Republic remarkably favorable conditions for national unification, economic development, and political stability. One has only to compare our situation with that of the new nations that have won independence since the Second World War—most of them facing resource shortages, unskilled labor forces, overpopulation, inadequate capital and foreign investments, crowded world markets, little or no middle-class base, mixed racial, tribal, or religious elements, competing and jealous neighbors, and Cold War military operations in their corners of the world—to appreciate what a superb environment the American nation had in which to work out its "manifest destiny." Whether the United States would have been able to grow and prosper under the Constitution of 1787 if we had been a new republic located in the middle of Western Europe during the era of the Napoleonic Wars has seemed doubtful to some students of our national history. Thus, objective conditions gave us a crucial fifty to seventy-five years of sheltered growth in which to achieve national unity and develop national power, both of which Americans tend to associate with the "magic" presence of the federal Constitution.

The second additional factor cited as underlying our constitutional stability is an apparent special talent of the American people for institutional development. Americans have had what one expert has called an "instinct for practical, workable government." While we began by viewing the Constitution as fundamental law, embodying a higher claim to obedience and moral respect than the day-to-day rules made by legislators and executives, we have also tended to approach the problem of adapting the Constitution to new conditions and crisis developments with a highly pragmatic perspective. Ideas and institutions have been stretched to fit; there has been no thought of scrapping the 1787 draft and starting over, even though this process of adaptation has often produced inconsistency and a "Rube Goldberg" style of political arrangements.

This so-called talent may stem, in part, from our British colonial heritage. The British capacity for evolutionary change, sometimes called "muddling through," left its imprint on the men at Philadelphia and on those who managed our constitutional machinery in the first generations of the Republic. However, Americans added to the somewhat aristocratic British tradition of evolutionary change an additional strand of pragmatic flexibility that was produced by the necessities of life along the Western frontier. Some nations are founded once, then governed thereafter. But Americans from the thirteen original states moved westward and southward to found new states all during the nineteenth and twentieth centuries. Each time, the principles of the Constitution were brought to new lands and strange conditions, and for a century Americans developed the valuable skills needed to adapt the Philadelphia Constitution to life in the Floridas, Kansas, California, Texas, Arizona, Alaska, and Hawaii. Only once, when the slavery issue cracked the nation apart and we fought a civil war, did the American capacity for political compromise and flexibility collapse. Thus this instinct for managing well has, according to some observers, helped to support our tradition of constitutional stability and gradual adaptation.

To speak of factors such as these, however, only sets the background of analysis. For a full understanding of American governmental development we must turn to a discussion of our processes of constitutional change and the growth of the federal system.

Constitutional Change in the American System

Changes in the operative Constitution of the United States have taken place through formal and informal means, sometimes in barely perceptible evolutionary growths and sometimes in painfully visible reactions to crises such as civil war, world war, depression, or racial conflict. We can identify five major processes of change that have filled in the empty spaces in the constitutional structure or have altered fundamentally some of the original architecture. These processes are formal constitutional amendment, judicial interpretation, statutory development, governmental custom and practice, and political developments.

CHANGE THROUGH FORMAL CONSTITUTIONAL AMENDMENTS

When the Framers completed their draft of the Constitution in 1787, they provided in Article V a process for amending the Constitution if this should become necessary. The amending process was divided into two steps. First, amendments must be proposed, by either a two-thirds majority of both houses of Congress or a national convention called by Congress on the petition of two thirds of the states. Second, proposed amendments must be ratified, either by the legislatures of three fourths of the states or at conventions called for ratification purposes in three fourths of the states. Congress can set a time limit for ratification; otherwise, there is no legal cutoff date for state ratification. Since the 1920s, by Congressional practice, each new proposal has contained a clause providing that valid ratification must be accomplished within seven years of presentation to the states.

Two limitations were written into the amendment clause, both considered essential to safeguard the political compromises of the Constitution. These provided (1) that no amendment prior to 1808 should affect the constitutional provisions barring federal interference with the slave trade or forbidding direct taxes not apportioned among the states according to population, and (2) that no amendment should deprive a state of its equal representation in the Senate, unless the state consented. These provisions can really be regarded as moral charges on future generations, since the idea of an unamendable clause preventing later amendment is more metaphysical than legal. It could itself be eliminated by the regular amendment process.

Since 1787, twenty-four amendments have been added to the Constitution, all proposed by Congress. In twenty-three of these, ratification was by

In Safe Waters At Last

The sixteenth amendment was finally ratified in 1913, eighteen years after the Supreme Court's decision that an income tax was unconstitutional.

Tom Bee in the Baltimore *Evening Sun*

state legislatures; only once, in 1933, when Prohibition was repealed, was ratification carried out by state conventions. Proposal of amendments by a national convention called via the petition of the states has never been used since 1787, though this has been used often by the states for amendment of their own constitutions, usually producing complete overhauls. At the national level the pattern has been for "single-shot" reform.

To understand the ideological and political realities of this formal process, we turn first to the amendments that have been adopted and then to those that were major contenders for adoption but were eventually defeated.

Looking closely at the amendments that have been adopted, three main periods of constitutional reform can be clearly identified. The first period, 1789–1804, producing twelve amendments, was an era in which the Constitution drafted at Philadelphia was brought into line with the power realities and ideological consensus of the new Republic. The first ten amendments, proposed in 1789 and promulgated in 1791, can really be regarded as part of the Constitution itself. They were the price that the anti-Federalists demanded for ratification of the Constitution, despite Federalist explanations that these provisions were unnecessary since no power to abuse such rights had been given to the new federal government. The Eleventh Amendment in 1798 overturned a Supreme Court ruling of 1793 that had allowed states to be sued in federal courts by citizens of another state; the action reflected the powerful states' rights currents that were instantly ready to reassert the original constitutional understanding that such suits were not to be maintained directly against the "sovereign" states. The last amendment in this period, the Twelfth, was adopted in 1804 because of the unforeseen rise of political parties. The Framers had expected the best man to receive a majority of state electoral votes and thus become President, while the runner-up would be Vice-President. In 1800, with party-line

A 1918 cartoon showed John Barleycorn "seeing stars" as state after state ratified the Eighteenth Amendment forbidding sales of alcoholic beverages.

Hammond in the Wichita *Eagle*

voting, the two Republican nominees, Jefferson and Burr, each received the same number of electoral votes, and a choice between them had to be made in the House of Representatives. The Twelfth Amendment solved this breakdown of the system by requiring state electors to vote for different persons for President and Vice-President.

In one sense, 109 years passed before the next "peacetime" amendment. This is because the second era was the five-year period, 1865–70, which saw the swift addition of three amendments that wrote the practical results of the Civil War and emancipation into the formal Constitution. All slaves were freed, and slavery was forbidden (Thirteenth Amendment); federal citizenship was extended to former slaves, and states were forbidden to deny persons equal protection of the laws or due process of law (Fourteenth Amendment); and states were forbidden to deny the right to vote on the basis of race, color, or previous condition of servitude (Fifteenth Amendment).

The third period, from 1913 to the present, has seen nine constitutional amendments added, four of them intended to democratize national governmental processes. Thus direct election of Senators was instituted in 1913; women's suffrage was provided in 1920; the District of Columbia was allowed to vote in Presidential elections (1961); and a ban on poll taxes for federal elections was ratified in 1964. The five remaining amendments did not fit this pattern. The Sixteenth Amendment in 1913 instituted the federal income tax. The prohibition of liquor by the Eighteenth Amendment in 1919 culminated a half-century crusade against the "evils of drink,"

TABLE 4–1 / Amendments to the Federal Constitution, 1789–1964

Amendment number	Year promulgated	Subject treated	Responsive to	Date proposed	Date ratified	Time elapsed yrs.	mos.
1–10	1791	Bill of Rights	Failure to include civil liberty guarantees in Constitution	Sept., 1789	Dec., 1791	2	2
11	1798	Immunity of state from suit in federal courts by citizen of another state	Supreme Court decision, *Chisholm v. Georgia* (1793)	Mar., 1794	Feb., 1795	0	11
12	1804	Separate election of President and Vice-President	Tie vote for President and Vice-President in 1800 election	Dec., 1803	July, 1804	0	7
13	1865	Outlawing of slavery	Civil War; slavery issue	Feb., 1865	Dec., 1865	0	10
14	1868	Federal citizenship, privileges and immunities; limit on state interference with equal protection and due process; and other provisions	Civil War; Supreme Court decision in *Dred Scott* case (1857)	June, 1866	July, 1868	2	0
15	1870	Right to vote regardless of race, color, or prior slavery	Civil War; Reconstruction conditions	Feb., 1869	Feb., 1870	0	11
16	1913	Federal power to tax individual incomes	Supreme Court decision, *Pollock v. Farmer's Loan* (1895)	July, 1909	Feb., 1913	3	6
17	1913	Direct election of U.S. Senators	"Popular election" movement; government reform	May, 1912	Apr., 1913	0	10
18	1919	Prohibition of liquor	Prohibition movement	Dec., 1917	Jan., 1919	1	1
19	1920	Women's suffrage	Women's suffrage movement; Supreme Court decision, *Minor v. Happersett* (1875)	June, 1919	Aug., 1920	1	2
20	1933	Elimination of "Lame Duck" session of Congress	Government reform; progressive movement	Mar., 1932	Jan., 1933	0	10
21	1933	Repeal of Prohibition	Failure of Prohibition; "wet" movement	Feb., 1933	Dec., 1933	0	9
22	1951	Two-term limit on Presidential tenure	Anti-F. D. Roosevelt sentiment following fourth term; Republican party pressure	Mar., 1947	Feb., 1951	3	11
23	1961	Right to vote in Presidential elections for District of Columbia residents	General public support for D.C. voters; Democratic party pressure	June, 1960	Mar., 1961	0	10
24	1964	Forbidding poll tax for voting in federal elections	Civil rights movement	Aug., 1962	Feb., 1964	1	5

while the Twenty-first Amendment in 1933 repealed the "great experiment" after its failure had become apparent. The Twentieth, in 1933, changed the dates of the inauguration of the President and the convening of Congress. The Twenty-second Amendment, in 1951, limited Presidential tenure to two terms; its sponsorship by conservatives and the limits it installed on the electorate's power to continue a President for a third term place it outside the "democratization of government" stream of amendments.

Five amendments were proposed by Congress but were never ratified by the states. Two of these, one dealing with apportioning seats in the House of Representatives and the other setting a special procedure for changing Congressional salaries, were submitted to the states in 1789, along with the ten amendments that became the Bill of Rights. A third proposal, in 1810, would have removed the citizenship of any person accepting a foreign title. The fourth, in 1861, would have forbidden constitutional amendments interfering with slavery in the states. The last unsuccessful proposal, in 1924, would have empowered Congress to regulate child labor.

In addition, many changes in the Constitution have been urged vigorously in sustained campaigns since 1789 but have never been adopted by Congress. Among the serious contenders have been proposals to change the Electoral College, lengthen the term of Congressmen to four years, require a popular referendum before declaring war, provide for executive authority during Presidential disability, limit the Supreme Court's power to declare acts of Congress unconstitutional, increase Congress' power to regulate agriculture and labor relations, and require Senate approval of executive agreements with foreign nations.

Looking over this record of successful and unsuccessful amendments, four main observations can be made about the amending process and its operation.

First, most of the amendments have played a major role in the adaptation of American governmental institutions to social change. The income tax amendment altered fundamentally the fiscal balance of power between the national and state governments. The democratization of government amendments brought aristocratic features of the eighteenth-century Constitution into harmony with twentieth-century ideas about popular government. The Fourteenth Amendment, with its broad clauses guaranteeing American citizens protection against state violations of their life, liberty, and property; due process of law; and equal protection of the laws, has set basic federal standards for the treatment by states of corporations, labor unions, religious groups, Negroes, and many other groups. In short, no chronicle of basic changes in the American political system could be written that did not treat the sources, passage, and application of the major constitutional amendments.

Second, it is Congress that has been the critical battleground for proposed amendments, not the states. Since 1789, some 4,500 resolutions calling for amendments have been introduced in Congress by the members of the two houses. Of these, only twenty-nine were adopted and sent to the states. In only thirty-five to forty instances did one house pass the resolution and the other fail to approve. Thus, while it is common for individual Senators and Congressmen to please constituents and register their own political convictions by filing amendment resolutions on every conceivable subject, Congressional committees have seen to it that only a tiny trickle of these resolutions ever reaches the floor for debate. Once Congress adopts a proposed amendment, however, ratification has followed in twenty-four of the twenty-nine instances. Approval by the states has been prompt, with an average of eighteen months between Congressional submission to the states and ratification. Since 1933, three of the five successful amendments have been ratified in less than one year.

Third, there has been a close connection between leading Supreme Court decisions and the amendment process. Three amendments, the Eleventh, Fourteenth, and Sixteenth, were directly prompted by Supreme Court rulings, the first taking away a federal jurisdiction approved by the Justices and the other two giving Congress powers that had been denied it by judicial decision. The Nineteenth Amendment overturned a Supreme Court ruling that had read the Constitution as *not* guaranteeing women the right to vote. What is equally significant is that quite a few of the unsuccessful but politically influential campaigns for amendments have been set in motion by assertive Supreme Court decisions, such as restrictive rulings on Congressional power over labor relations, agriculture, child labor, trusts, and so on; rulings expanding Presidential authority in foreign affairs and military power, or approving new Congressional taxing and spending powers; or rulings limiting the authority of the states in areas such as internal security, censorship, public religious observances, police practices, legislative apportionment, labor relations, and segregation. The primary reason for the small number of such reversals (there have been none since 1913) is that when the pressure for amendment begins to reflect a dominant consensus in the nation, changes in the Court's personnel or its majority philosophy have often led to modification of the judicial position. Such was the case, for example, in the 1930s over Congressional New Deal legislation; if the Court had not reversed itself, it is very likely that constitutional amendments would have been adopted to overturn the restrictive judicial rulings.

Fourth, whether the amendment process has been sufficiently responsive to popular will and changing national needs remains a matter of active debate among political scientists and civic leaders. It was the style during the nineteenth century to deplore the total inertia of the amendment process in the Congressional proposal stage. Woodrow Wilson lamented in 1885 that nothing short of "the impulse of self-preservation" and "the force of revolution" (as in the Civil War) would "move the cumbrous machinery of Article V." The fact that, apart from the three post-Civil War amendments, the Constitution was left unamended for more than a century (1804–1913) was cited by critics as proof that formal amendment seemed impossible as a matter of political practice. The addition of four major amendments in the period between 1913 and 1920, however, and the ratification of five more since then has led critics to soften or abandon the charge of total freeze, and to focus now on whether the pace of amendment is dangerously slow or merely properly careful.

Debates over the ratification process have followed a different path of argument. As early as 1788, Patrick Henry warned that one twentieth of the American people could block amendments. Modern critics update this charge by noting that the fourteen smallest states, with only 2 percent of the national population, could defeat ratification; the thirty-seven least populous states could ratify an amendment opposed by the thirteen largest states, with about 50 percent of the national population. As a leading student of the amendment process has noted, though, these are "parlor tricks, not political science." The record of ratification fights throughout our history shows that there has never been a division of states according to population size. States divide according to sectional allegiances, economic organization and resources, urban-rural factors, racial and religious composition, party position, and similar factors. In the amendment process (as in our politics as a whole), there has never been a Vermont-Delaware-Arkansas-Wyoming axis. Proposals to adopt at the federal level the system used by countries such as Switzerland or by American states such as Massachusetts, which places approval of proposed amendments before the voters in a general referendum, have never moved far in Congress nor have they had substantial public opinion behind them.

Probably the most pertinent answer to the debate over flexibility versus rigidity is to say that the amendment process cannot be assessed in such abstract form, apart from a consideration of the other processes by which the Constitution is changed and adapted. The foremost of these other techniques, in fact the main way in which our Constitution has been amended down through the years, has been by judicial interpretation. For we have really had two Constitutional Conventions in America, the one which sat for four months in Philadelphia in 1787 and the "continuing constitutional convention" made up of the Justices of the Supreme Court, who have been sitting constantly for over 175 years.

CONSTITUTIONAL CHANGE BY JUDICIAL INTERPRETATION

Whenever a litigant in state or federal court properly raises the claim that someone has acted in violation of the federal Constitution, the judges hearing that case must construe the meaning of the constitutional provision that has been called into issue. If this is an instance in which the Framers saw a specific problem, faced it squarely, adopted a clear policy, and expressed this in unequivocal language, the judge has the relatively easy task of applying a constitutional command to the facts before him. Thus, if federal agents slipped in through a basement window to search a man's home for counterfeit money, if no search warrant had been obtained from a judge before the entry and there were no special circumstances to justify the failure to get a warrant, a federal judge would have little trouble in ruling that this was an "unreasonable search" forbidden by the Fourth Amendment to the Constitution. The Framers, reacting to the British practice of searching the colonists' homes at will, had declared in the Fourth Amendment that "The right of the people to be secure in their persons, houses, papers, and effects, against unreasonable searches and seizures, shall not be violated. . . ." The basement entry was exactly what the Framers prohibited unless the police first obtained a warrant from a judicial official, by describing, under oath, the place to be searched, the suspected crime for which the search was required, and the specific things that were sought.

While we often assume that our constitutional conflicts in the Cold War era are as fresh as atomic power, the first fact to observe about judicial interpretation is that many of these issues (like the police search without a warrant) are substantially the same sociopolitical problems that the Framers considered in the Convention and provided for in the Constitution or the Bill of Rights. Such a catalog of continuing situations would include, among other things, separation of church and state, government censorship of the press, state interference with interstate commerce, the privilege against self-incrimination, or the definition of acts of treason. While the setting of these issues is obviously different from that in Washington's day, it is remarkable how similar are the collisions of values then and now, and how directly relevant are the Framers' constitutional choices among those values.

Even where the Framers expressed a clear constitutional policy on a given issue, however, the development of new social and economic conditions, new technology, and changes in public and social values may present the courts with subtle and difficult problems of application. For example:

1. In the late 1920s, state police wire-tapped the telephone conversations of a leading whisky smuggler. The wire-tap transcripts were used to convict the defendant, who carried his case to the Supreme Court with the complaint that the taps had been made without warrants and that telephone tapping was so sweeping a procedure that it would be an "unreasonable search and seizure" even if a warrant were obtained. By a 5-to-4 decision that is still the law of the land, the Supreme Court held in 1928 that telephone tapping was not forbidden by the Fourth Amendment and warrants were not required.[1] The Court reasoned that there was no physical entry into the home or office; that nothing tangible was taken away; and that persons speaking on the telephone had consciously and voluntarily projected their voices outside the protected boundaries of the home or office. The dissenting Justices attacked this reasoning as an overliteral reading of the Fourth Amendment and a failure to adapt its basic principle to the new technological means of invading privacy. If the Framers could have foreseen electronic eavesdropping, the dissenters argued, they would have wanted this means of police surveillance forbidden every bit as much as the policeman who slipped through a window.

2. In 1963, the Supreme Court reviewed the conviction of a man charged with illegal breaking and entering. The defendant had lacked funds to pay a lawyer to represent him, and the state in which he was tried, Florida, did not furnish a court-appointed lawyer for indigents unless a death-penalty case was involved. Ever since 1942, the Supreme Court had held that an indigent defendant had a right to have counsel provided by the state as a requirement of "due process of law." But this right was binding on the states only in death-penalty cases or where special factors were present (such as the defendant's being a minor, an illiterate, or feeble-minded). In the 1963 case, none of the special factors were present. Nevertheless, the Court ruled here that in all serious criminal trials, states are required constitutionally to furnish a lawyer to indigent defendants.[2] Clearly, the Consti-

---

[1] *Olmstead* v. *United States*, 277 U.S. 438 (1928).
[2] *Gideon* v. *Wainwright*, 372 U.S. 335 (1963).

tution had not changed since the Supreme Court ruling in 1942, nor had the objective disadvantages of not having a lawyer in a criminal case. What had changed was the dominant attitude of American society toward the fairness of trials in which government lawyers pressed the prosecution but a poor defendant without legal training had to fend for himself.

Hundreds of cases could be listed in which the Supreme Court has adapted constitutional provisions in this manner to new social and economic conditions, new technology, and changing social values. Congress' power to regulate interstate commerce, for example, has been read to authorize Congress to regulate railroads, television, and airplanes; to punish interstate automobile theft; to set standards for the purity of foods and drugs; to forbid racial segregation on interstate buses or at interstate terminals; and to set up collective bargaining machinery for labor and management in order to avoid strikes that would affect interstate commerce.

From the standpoint of our constitutional system, the central question raised in each of these judicial responses to changed conditions or values is whether the judiciary is justified in adapting what the Framers said in eighteenth-century clauses to modern situations, or whether judicial "adaptation" would do such violence to the Framers' intentions (or their silence) that constitutional amendment, not judicial change, is called for.

The *strict constructionist* view is that constitutional amendment should be used whenever basic changes in policy are required. As Chief Justice Roger Taney said for the Court in 1856:

> [The Constitution] speaks not only in the same words, but with the same meaning and intent with which it spoke when it came from the hands of its framers, and was voted on and adopted by the people of the United States. Any other rule of construction would abrogate the judicial character of this court, and make it the mere reflex of the popular opinion or passion of the day.[3]

Strict constructionist positions have been advanced to support both conservative and liberal economic and political doctrines. For example, Justice George Sutherland protested in the late 1930s against Supreme Court rulings interpreting the commerce clause to sustain Congressional power over labor-management relations, agriculture, and industrial conditions. "The meaning of the Constitution does not change with the ebb and flow of economic events," Justice Sutherland argued; Americans—and the Court—must respect constitutional provisions "when they pinch as well as when they comfort"; the proper role of the judiciary "does not include the power of amendment under the guise of interpretation." On other occasions, however, strict construction has been invoked by liberals to oppose judicial doctrines that were believed to be "interpreting away" the "precious safeguards of civil liberty." Justice Hugo Black, for example, has argued that the provisions of the Bill of Rights, especially the First Amendment, are "absolutes," not subject to relaxation or suspension by the Court's belief that we live "in times of emergency and stress." The Framers knew the risks involved

---

[3] *Dred Scott* v. *Sandford,* 19 How. 393 (1857).

when they adopted the Bill of Rights, said Black, and "its policy should not be changed without constitutional amendments by the people. . . ." [4]

The competing approach, *flexible construction*, usually starts by invoking Chief Justice John Marshall's famous remark in 1819, delivered in an opinion upholding as "necessary and proper" Congress' power to charter a national bank. "We must never forget," said Marshall, "that it is a constitution we are expounding . . . a constitution intended to endure for ages to come, and, consequently, to be adapted to the various crises of human affairs." [5] Flexible construction is thus seen as a technique for recognizing the growth of some constitutional principles through changing conditions, governmental experience, and social values, and acknowledging the contraction of other clauses through the same evolutionary processes. This is the "gloss which life has written" on constitutional clauses, Justice Felix Frankfurter remarked, and the court that is true to its function must try to reflect that gloss of history by balancing in its rulings the origin, formulation, and growth of a constitutional mandate, and its relevance to modern issues. If the Supreme Court does not fulfill this role, carefully and with the necessary self-restraint but nevertheless creatively, the flexible constructionists point out that dozens, even hundreds, of constitutional amendments would be necessary each generation.

As with strict construction, the flexible approach has been used by both conservative and liberal spokesmen. Liberals have supported expanded interpretations of clauses dealing with the commerce and taxing powers of Congress or with the President's authority as Chief Executive, when these interpretations were needed to support federal regulation of the economy, welfare laws, and internationalist measures. Conservatives have spoken of the need for flexibility when dealing with internal security measures or Congressional investigatory powers, arguing that the new setting of subversive activities and total Cold War requires modification of the seemingly absolute commands of the First Amendment.

Of course, in many vital areas of the Constitution, the Framers did not give us a clear record at all. Sometimes they had to write with deliberate ambiguity in order to win general approval from disputing factions within the Convention. Sometimes the Framers and the ratifying conventions made conflicting statements about what was done or intended. Finally, many contemporary problems were wholly unforeseen by the Framers, and a constitutional "policy" must be drawn from related clauses surrounding the issue in question or what is felt to be a parallel decision by the Framers.

It is remarkable how many important and heavily debated parts of the Constitution are ambiguous. The power of the Supreme Court to declare acts of Congress unconstitutional, the scope of the President's inherent executive power, and Congress' power to spend for the general welfare are major examples of ambiguous grants of affirmative power to government or to one of its branches, as in the executive power. The meaning of the First Amendment's ban on the establishment of religion, or the intention of the

---

[4] Hugo Black, "The Bill of Rights," in Alan F. Westin, ed., *An Autobiography of the Supreme Court* (New York, 1963), p. 397.
[5] *McCulloch* v. *Maryland*, 4 Wheat. 316 (1819).

"Can You See Me Now?"

This cartoon portrays the Supreme Court's power of judicial review as protecting the Constitutional rights of individuals as "intended" by the Framers.

From *Herblock's Special for Today,* Simon & Schuster, 1958

Fourteenth Amendment's Framers with regard to racial segregation in schools are illustrations of ambiguity in restrictive provisions.

In these situations, as Justice Robert Jackson once remarked frankly, the self-conscious judge must admit that he is forced to interpret the Constitution without much "really useful and unambiguous authority" about the Framers' exact intentions.

> Just what our forefathers did envision, or would have envisioned had they foreseen modern conditions, must be divined from materials almost as enigmatic as the dreams Joseph was called upon to interpret for Pharaoh. A century and a half of partisan debate and scholarly speculation yields no net result but only supplies more or less apt quotations from respected sources on each side of any question. They largely cancel each other.[6]

Thus judges cannot call up the ghosts of the Framers to secure a better record or force a majority vote on matters the Framers felt it either necessary or wise to pass on to future generations. And, despite predictable protests from segments of the population adversely affected by such judicial rulings, public opinion in America from John Marshall's day to the present has supported a consciously adaptive and creative style of judicial review by the Supreme Court. Thus the debate over strict and flexible construction tends to produce statements of equally valid and compelling general principles; choices between them in any given case will depend on the specific situation, the state of the historical record, the degree of adaptation attempted, and the attitude of dominant national opinion on the matter.

Before leaving the area of judicial interpretation, we should note that this process leaves untouched large areas of the Constitution and many vital

---

[6] *Youngstown Sheet and Tube Co.* v. *Sawyer,* 343 U.S. 579, 634–35 (1952).

constitutional disputes in each era. For reasons we discuss later when treating judicial review, the courts will not rule on many disputes because they are "political" questions entrusted to the elected branches of government (particularly foreign policy matters) or because the complaining party does not have a sufficient direct interest in the issue to bring the lawsuit to court. Thus the courts are not available to test *every* matter of constitutional change, and other processes must be relied on in many situations.

CHANGE THROUGH STATUTORY DEVELOPMENT

Constitutional amendments and leading Supreme Court cases on the Constitution are rare events; they command excited attention because of their comparative novelty. Yet every year, the Government Printing Office issues a major source of institutional and structural change in the American system —in the form of certain bills enacted by Congress and approved by the President. These *statutory sources* of governmental development can be placed under three main headings.

First are the statutes which shape or alter the operating structure of the national government. The Constitution speaks of the "executive departments" but does not specify them. Thus it is by legislation that we have developed our present structure of Departments; from the "old-line" Departments such as State and Treasury to new additions such as Health, Education and Welfare, or freshly reorganized Departments, such as Defense. It is by legislation that the federal independent regulatory agencies have been created, such as the Federal Trade Commission and the National Labor Relations Board; moreover, Congress must pass upon any changes or reorganizations in both the executive Departments and regulatory agencies, and Congressional approval is far from automatic, especially when political or ideological conflicts arise. In 1962, for example, President Kennedy sought to establish a new Cabinet-level Department for urban affairs, to deal with a variety of problems such as housing, transportation, juvenile delinquency, race relations, and others that have clustered around American city growth. It was generally assumed that the first Secretary of the Department (and the first Negro Cabinet member) would be Robert Weaver, a distinguished expert in urban problems then serving as director of the Federal Housing Administration. In a legislative fight that saw Southern Democrats joining conservative Republicans to oppose the new Department, the proposal was defeated, and no Department of Urban Affairs was created.

Statutes have also provided for the organization and jurisdiction of the federal court system. Apart from the Supreme Court of the United States, all other federal courts are creations of Congress. Statutes beginning with the famous Judiciary Act of 1789 define what cases the courts hear, how many judges are assigned to each tribunal, how many clerks, secretaries, or marshals will be provided, or how much money must be at stake before a citizen of one state can sue a citizen of another in the federal courts ($10,000). Through statutes, special courts for customs and patent appeals and for military appeals have been created. In this sense, the form and functions of the federal judiciary are essentially the product of Congressional design over the past 170 years, sometimes in harmony with the suggestions of the judges and at other times in conflict with them.

A second main function of statutory development has been to provide
2-those socioeconomic guarantees that are stated as constitutional rights in
such nations as France, Israel, Italy, or India. These guarantees include the
right to work, the right to a decent standard of living, the right to rest and
leisure, the right to security in old age, the right of labor to bargain freely
and to strike, and many other similar socioeconomic rights. Historically,
these were the responsibilities that Western governments took on in the
late nineteenth and twentieth centuries, when capitalist systems accepted
welfare and industrial-mediation functions, and other societies turned to
social-democratic or socialist theories of the rights to which citizens were
entitled in a just system. Since our Constitution was written at the high
point of eighteenth-century ideas of private responsibility in these spheres,
no such provisions were adopted in 1789 and none have been added by
amendment.

Instead, the guarantees have been added by Congressional acts dealing
with unemployment payments, minimum wages, social security, collective
bargaining, and so on, begun largely by the New Deal in the 1930s and
continuing in force through succeeding decades. The National Labor Relations Act, the Social Security Act, the Fair Labor Standards Act, the Agricultural Adjustment Act, and the basic Anti-Trust Laws are leading examples of what can be called "semiconstitutional" socioeconomic legislation.
Legally, any of these measures could be abolished tomorrow. But as right-
wing ideologues in the Republican party learned after Dwight Eisenhower's
election in 1952, far from abolishing social security or ending federally
supervised bargaining between employers and unions, the Republican
Administration continued to extend the coverage of social security and
added only marginal amendments to the national labor relations system.
Another aspect of these statutes that justifies the use of the term "semiconstitutional" in describing them is that their basic operative clauses resemble constitutional provisions in their majestic vagueness and their deliberate
policy of passing definition of specific policy to administrative agencies and
the courts. Thus anti-trust laws forbid acts that "substantially lessen competition" or "restrain trade," while the National Labor Relations Act forbids
"unfair labor practices." What substantially lessens or is unfair has been
developed in case-by-case adjudication in the agencies and courts. However,
unlike judicial construction of the Constitution, interpretations of the "semiconstitutional" laws can be changed at will by Congress. Any statute can
be amended or a particular provision repealed, which makes these laws that
deal with very specific situations and that must be adjusted to rapidly
changing events far more flexible than constitutional clauses, responding
sometimes to waves of national public opinion but even more often to the
steady pressure of special interest groups in the regulated areas.

A third role of statutory development (both at the state and federal levels)
is the adjustment of the boundaries between the public and private sectors
of American life. Given the heavy emphasis on private rights and limited
government in colonial and frontier America, this has tended historically
to be a one-way process—through which governmental functions have been
slowly expanded and exclusively private authority has been steadily diminished or regulated as problems have grown too large or too complex

to be effectively solved by private decisions. The laws passed to provide unemployment insurance, workmen's compensation for employees injured at work, public hospitalization, and old-age insurance benefits are leading examples of the entry by federal or state governments into fields that once were in the hands of private charity or local (usually town) authorities. State and federal legislation governing the relations of employers and employees is another major example of the shift to government supervision and standards in an area that once was exclusively the concern of the parties themselves. Because so much of the debate over these boundary-shifting legislative enactments has centered, in the past, on court tests of their constitutionality, it is often forgotten that most of this legislation falls clearly within the powers of the federal or state government, either before or after court pronouncements, and the basic ideological and interest-group debate is merely over the *wisdom* of giving the government full or shared responsibility in the new area. Yet this role of legislation is one of the most influential forces for change in the American governmental system, whether viewed narrowly as a product of ideological and socioeconomic changes or more broadly as potentially creative legislative response to changed conditions.

CHANGES THROUGH GOVERNMENTAL CUSTOM AND PRACTICE

Not all the developments and changes in the American governmental system are made through the formal processes of amendment, judicial decision, or legislation. Many significant rules of the game in American government have been made through governmental practices that were followed long enough to become customary and accepted procedures. The committee system of Congress is a good example. While there have been important pieces of legislation that set out the basic format of the committee system, the key operating rules of the committee system are not set down in statutes. This process of operating according to tradition is typified by the seniority system, which provides that the chairman of each standing committee is to be the member who has been longest on the committee from the party having the majority in Congress. He may be wholly hostile to the majority party's philosophy, have ideas that could not command anything close to a majority vote within his own committee, openly declare his intention of sabotaging the platform promises of the President, and be so superannuated that he cannot run committee meetings at all effectively. Yet the iron law of seniority, installed as a bipartisan rule of the game to avoid bitter power struggles over chairmanships at the start of each Congressional session, will determine who wields the gavel in such citadels of Congressional power as the House Ways and Means Committee, the Senate Foreign Relations Committee, and the Senate Judiciary Committee. The seniority system is a useful example of custom in American governmental development because unlike many other rules of Congress, the seniority system is not a general practice of parliamentary procedure inherited from Britain or from the philosophy of continental writers such as Montesquieu. Neither in the eighteenth century nor today are committee chairmen in the British, French, or other continental legislatures selected by seniority. It is an American innovation. Another example of governmental custom in Congress is the requirement that a candidate for Congress reside in the district in which he seeks election; this is not required by the Constitution or by any statute and is contrary to the British practice, yet it has become a rule of the game in our political process.

A different kind of governmental practice is interpretation of institutional authority built up by the operating agencies of government when the courts have not yet ruled on precise questions concerning them. These interpretations may be actions taken by Presidents or executive officials; they are often given full-dress accompanying justifications in "state documents," such as Presidential messages to Congress, veto messages, opinions of the Attorney General, and the like. A leading example was President Jackson's withdrawal of federal deposits from the National Bank in 1833, accompanied by his famous message on Presidential power. Or they may be committee reports, floor debates, or official preambles to legislation passed by Congress. An example of this was the "legislative history" carefully made in committee and on the floor during passage of the Taft-Hartley Act of 1947. In both the executive and legislative situations, the elected branches have made interpretations in response to concrete problems—from Indian raids on Western settlements or strikes affecting the movement of the United States mails in 1894 to sale of overage destroyers to Great Britain in 1940 or the failure of a state governor to provide police protection to Negro children seeking to enter desegregated schools under federal court order. Sometimes the actions taken are tested in the courts, and the judges weigh seriously the patterns of governmental practice that have been followed for many years or have been necessary in successive crises across a long time span. While these practices are significant precedents, they do not bind the courts, of course. The federal government had imposed a tax on incomes in the 1790s and again during the Civil War, yet the Supreme Court declared such a tax imposed in 1894 to be unconstitutional when the issue came before the Justices in 1895. However, many issues do not reach the courts, for the reasons already discussed in this chapter, and governmental practices in these areas represent rules of the game that have shaped our governmental system in significant fashion since the 1790s.

CHANGE THROUGH POLITICAL DEVELOPMENTS

Even after studying all of the evolutionary processes we have discussed, an observer of American institutions from abroad might well be unable to explain some of the most profound changes in our governmental system since 1790 and some of the key realities of our politics today. The missing elements are a variety of factors that can be grouped under the heading of political developments. The three most important to cite here are the rise of political parties, the expansion of suffrage, and the growth of organized interest groups.

When the Constitution was drafted, the United States had no political parties, only the colonists who supported the Crown and those who supported the Revolution. There were local factions in state politics after independence but no national parties that united common interests throughout the country and systematically pursued office to gain advantages for them. The idea of permanent parties was antithetical to the whole idea of republican government as the Framers saw it. By the 1790s, though, everyone could see that two distinct factions had evolved, the Federalist group led by Adams, Hamilton, and Jay, and the anti-Federalist group, captained by Jefferson and Madison. The Federalist faction, envisaging sea power as a key to future American greatness, favored the merchant class, looked toward amity with Britain (the major naval power of the era), and sought to enlarge national power. The anti-Federalist, or Republican, faction spoke for the Southern planters and small farmers of the North and West and defended states' rights against "centralization" in Washington. Believing that westward continental expansion would be the cornerstone of American power, this faction admired and sought the friendship of France (which controlled the Mississippi Valley area west of the United States) and championed her revolution. In the election of 1800, the Republicans ousted the Federalists from the Presidency. When the transfer of power was accomplished peacefully, the concept of a loyal opposition party was verified, and the United States found itself a nation with a two-party system recruited broadly in the population among diverse interests and not tied to single interests or single sections.

Rather than spelling the doom of the Republic, of course, political parties have proved to be a vital lubricant for the constitutional machine. They draw together the interests and principles of diverse groups in the nation and offer broad policies to deal with issues on which the public is divided. It is through party conventions and party primaries that individual candidates are selected. The parties have been a key instrument for adjusting conflicts between federal and state governments, since national leaders pressing for their policies can never forget that in the nomination and election phases of the great struggle for the Presidency, the parties are not under national control but function on a system of local power.

The second major political development—the expansion of the suffrage—is an omnibus trend that has been brought about by changing ideas of political justice, constitutional amendments, federal and state legislation, and court decisions. Because it spans so many of these other modes of change, and is itself a change of profound importance, we consider it under this heading.

When the decade of the 1780s opened, there were about two million free Americans in the thirteen states. Of these only 120,000 were voters. State qualifications restricted the suffrage to males over twenty-one years of age, residing in the voting district, and owning either a minimum amount of land or a considerable income from invested property. Religious restrictions in most states had either been dropped by the 1780s or went unenforced until they were formally repealed later. The effect of these suffrage qualifications in the young Republic was usually to lodge the power to choose public officials in the hands of a relatively small body of property-holders.

From 1780 to the present, our national history has been marked by a series of successive reform-waves in voting qualifications. Between 1780 and 1800, under the Jeffersonian impulse, the economic qualification was either eliminated completely or limited to payment of taxes in many of the states. From the 1820s to the 1850s, Jacksonian ideas of popular government —"one man, one vote"—were so widely adopted by the original and new states that property-holding qualifications were entirely eliminated. Suffrage was open to white males over twenty-one, whatever their economic position in society, with powerful effects on our party system, Presidential politics, and the substantive agenda of legislative affairs.

Following the Civil War, the Fifteenth Amendment prohibited states from denying the right to vote on the basis of race, color, or previous condition of servitude, and from 1870 until the triumph of white-supremacy regimes in the South in the 1890s, Negroes voted in substantial numbers throughout the Southern and border states, as well as in the North and West. Widespread legal and terrorist measures almost totally disfranchised Southern Negroes from 1900 to the late 1930s. However, judicial decisions in the 1940s outlawing the white primary, Congressional civil rights statutes in 1957 and 1960, enforcement campaigns by the Department of Justice in the 1950s and the 1960s, and voter registration campaigns by pro-civil rights groups, have brought Negro voting to substantial numbers in the South once again, and this is bound to continue. Of course, the Nineteenth Amendment (in 1920), forbidding states to deny the right to vote on account of sex, finally granting women's suffrage, completed the enfranchisement of all major classes of citizens in the United States.

The effect of these successive waves of suffrage enlargement has been to transform our politics and our legislative processes from an elite-based electoral foundation to a literate, over-twenty-one, taxpaying basis; in short, to open our political process to the full play of democratic forces.

The third political development of major importance has been the growth of organized interest groups. The literature on the "group basis" of American politics is very large and often conflicting in its estimates of influence. The subtleties of interest-group behavior are treated fully in Chapter 7. The point to make here is that early in the life of the Republic, Americans developed a pattern of organizing private associations of every conceivable kind to promote the common interests and principles of the members. Economic groups of a broad type were formed to advance the general positions of farmers, businessmen, professionals, and workers, and more specialized groups exist now to further the needs of Midwestern wheat growers, electrical appliance manufacturers, cost accountants, and truck drivers. Religious, racial, nationality, and ethnic groups speak in behalf of the Presbyterians, Negroes, Italian-Americans, and American Indians. There are ideological groups to promote liberalism, conservatism, one-worldism, capitalism, socialism, or John Birch-ism. There are single-shot groups formed to protect the vanishing buffalo, keep the tariff on German bicycles high, abolish the House Committee on Un-American Activities, or impeach Chief Justice Earl Warren. These and many other types of interest groups communicate to their members governmental policies that affect their members' interests, publicize the group's views and the facts they collect to the general public, lobby directly with legislators and administrators, mount legislative campaigns, and seek to influence the administration of laws once they are adopted.

While there is an important debate over how much the leaders of particular interest groups really speak for their members and how much the groups can deliver the membership's votes, there is little doubt that interest groups serve the functions of nominating issues for the agenda of public debate and legislative action and of helping public officials to gauge and structure public attitudes on leading issues. On the issue of broad federal aid to education, for example, the debates over the Kennedy Administration proposals in 1961–63 saw two coalition camps of interest groups drawn up on opposing sides of the President's program. In favor of broad aid were the National Education Association, the AFL–CIO, the National Farmers Union, Americans for Democratic Action, the National Congress of Parents and Teachers, and many others. Opposed to broad federal aid were the United States Chamber of Commerce, the Farm Bureau, the American Legion, the Daughters of the American Revolution, and like-minded groups. Generally in favor but deeply divided over specific aspects of the proposed legislation were the National Council of Churches of Christ, the National Catholic Welfare Conference, the American Jewish Congress, the National Association for the Advancement of Colored People, and other similar bodies; when the issues of aid to parochial schools or aid to schools refusing to desegregate arose, these groups made their basic presentations to Congress and the public. Congressmen, executive officials, and party leaders watch the positions of these interest groups carefully, and many legislative decisions are reached as a result of the persuasion and/or pressure that skilled interest-group representation brings to bear.

Thus the actions and interactions of interest groups, which are nowhere mentioned in the Constitution or provided for by law, provide a network of connective circuits that ties together the party system and legislative process in America with the sector of the population interested in public affairs. The more of a mass, urbanized, industrial nation we have become, many commentators would assert, the more the continued vitality of our democracy has rested upon this linkage function of interest groups.

Changes and Constants in the Federal System

So far, we have explored how well Americans have "kept the Republic," by tracing the changes brought about through constitutional amendment, judicial interpretation, statutory development, governmental custom and practice, and political-institutional growth. Another way of exploring this question—while focusing on a vital aspect of the American governmental process that we have deliberately failed to mention so far—is to look at what has happened to the *federal system* since it was created by the men at Philadelphia in 1787. Then, ours was the only federal system in existence. Today, the United States shares the title of a federal state with nations as diverse as Switzerland, Canada, Mexico, India, the Soviet Union, and the West German Republic. Like them, we place the individual citizen under two separate layers of authority, a central or national government on the one hand, and constituent or state governments on the other. Beyond this common characteristic, though, what Americans mean by federalism in theory and practice remains almost as unique in the 1960s as it was in the eighteenth century. Yet our own system would hardly be recognizable to Franklin if he could observe the way American federalism operates today.

FEDERALISM AND THE FOUNDING FATHERS: BLUEPRINT AND REALITY, 1789–1861

Fresh from experiencing the weaknesses and failures of the American Confederation of 1781 yet still strongly loyal to the states and hostile to the unitary national authority wielded by European kings, the Framers devised in 1787 an intermediate political form between these poles of loose league and centralized control. The federal union they constructed had three primary characteristics: (1) by an "organic act of all the people"—the Constitution—major governmental functions were allotted between two separate and independent authorities, the nation and the states, each of which was to be supreme in its own sphere of jurisdiction; (2) both the nation and the states were allowed to enforce their laws through their own officials and courts directly on individuals; and (3) the Supreme Court of the United States was installed (consciously or by fairly strong implication) as general umpire of federal-state conflicts, so that neither Congress nor any single state or group of states could determine conclusively for itself whose authority was legitimate in a disputed area.

The blueprint of the federal union met this objective in three primary ways—by specifying what functions and authority were given to the national government (delegated powers); by listing what functions and powers were denied to the national government or to the states (prohibited powers); and by stating the standard for settlement of national-state conflicts (national supremacy).

First, certain powers were delegated to the national government. Although some were stated in other parts of the Constitution, most of them are in Article I, Section 8, which lists eighteen grants of power to Congress. The first seventeen of these are express powers. They include authority over matters of war and foreign affairs, such as the power to declare war, raise armies, equip navies, establish uniform rules of naturalization, and so on. Other government powers relate to regulation and service of the economy, such as the power to coin money and to control its value, and to regulate foreign and interstate commerce. The national power to tax was given in broad terms: to pay the debts of the United States and provide for the "common defense" and "general welfare" of the United States. Miscellaneous powers delegated to the national government included authority to grant copyrights and patents, establish post offices and post roads, make laws on bankruptcy, and so on. After these seventeen grants of express power came the grant to Congress of implied power—"To make all laws which shall be necessary and proper for carrying into execution the foregoing powers, and all other powers vested by this Constitution in the government of the United States, or in any department or officer thereof."

Second, certain powers were denied by the Constitution. Some things were forbidden to both national and state governments, usually as interferences with the civil liberties of the citizen. These include prohibitions against making an act a crime retroactively (ex post facto laws) or punishing individuals by legislative act rather than by general laws and judicial trials (bills of attainder). Some powers were prohibited only to the states, either to safeguard the national unity sought by the Constitution or to protect individual rights, or both. These included powers absolutely denied the states, such as authority to coin money, enter into treaties with foreign powers, or interfere with the obligations of contracts, or denied to the states unless Congress gave its consent, as in the laying of duties on imports or exports, entering into compacts with other states, or keeping troops and warships in peacetime. Both the original Constitution and the first eight amendments applied many prohibitions to the national government, especially those safeguarding individual rights such as freedom of speech, press, religion, assembly, and fair trial.

In the third part of the blueprint, the national supremacy clause stated:

> This Constitution, and the laws of the United States which shall be made in pursuance thereof; and all treaties made, or which shall be made, under the authority of the United States, shall be the supreme law of the land. . . .

Judges "in every State" were to uphold this supreme law, "any thing in the Constitution or laws of any State to the contrary notwithstanding." Some powers, as we have noted, were denied to the national government specifically; on the other hand, however, national authority might—or might not—be implied as necessary to carry out expressly given powers. There was thus a foreseeable conflict over what national acts were "in pursuance" or treaties were "under the authority." While the standard of national supremacy was clearly stated, the Constitution created no explicit machinery for determining such issues.

Despite the broad grants of power to the national government, much authority over the economic, social, and political lives of the citizens remained with the states. In the state domain were regulation of the ownership, use, and transmission of property; the definition of offenses against persons and property (criminal law and torts); rules for marriage and divorce; control of local business, labor, farming, trades, and professions; provisions for education; welfare and correctional activities, including hospitals, children's homes, etc.; roads, canals, and other public works; taxation for these and other purposes; and the organization and control of local governmental units.

Although the national and state governments each had some spheres of exclusive power, there were many areas in which the Constitution expected both governments to exercise authority over the same affairs. Under these concurrent powers, both national and state governments could levy taxes, take private property upon payment of just compensation, pass criminal laws on the same matter (when the illegal activity affected both federal and state property or interests), and spend money for the general welfare.

This blueprint of the Constitution was affirmed rather than altered by the passage of the Tenth Amendment in 1791. This provides:

> The powers not delegated to the United States by the Constitution, nor prohibited by it to the States, are reserved to the States respectively, or to the people.

Frequently, the Tenth Amendment is misquoted by inserting the word "expressly" before the word "delegated"—as Governor George Wallace of Alabama did in 1963 when he tried to obstruct entry of a Negro student to the University of Alabama. Such misquotation tries to sidestep the plain fact that the Constitution gave Congress implied as well as express powers, and that this has been a major source for federal authority from the earliest years of the Republic to the present.

In addition to the three main features of the blueprint on national-state relations, there are various rules for relations among the states of the union. Each state was required to respect and enforce in its courts the laws and judicial decisions "of every other State" (the "full faith and credit" clause); to give citizens of other states all the privileges and immunities given to its own citizens; and to "deliver up" on the request of the state executive authorities persons charged with crime in another state. Fugitive slaves from other states were to be turned over to their owners upon proper claim. The states were required to secure the consent of Congress before entering into "any agreement or compact" with each other. New states were to be admitted into the union by Congress, but no state could be created within the boundaries of an existing state or from parts of several states without the consent of their state legislatures. The national government was charged with the obligation to guarantee every state "a republican form of government," protect states against invasion, and control "domestic violence" when invited into the state by its legislature (or executive when the legislature "cannot be convened").

This system of federal union had superb political and practical advantages for the new American nation. Its compromises between central and local powers persuaded all thirteen original states to form one government; strengthened the nation in its vital dealings with foreign powers; created a "free trade zone" throughout the country for the goods of every state; fostered mobility by permitting free migration of people from state to state; provided for the admission of new territories and states into the union; preserved the political and cultural diversity of states and sections; and attempted to allocate authority to the governmental unit best suited in size, resources, and political responsibility to perform that particular function.

This was the carefully constructed political mechanism devised by the Framers. But the real meaning of the structural and functional arrangements of federalism would have to be tested in the heat of political conflict over the jurisdictional lines between states and nation, and registered in the authoritative statements given by the Supreme Court. It was during the long period that Chief Justice John Marshall presided over the Supreme Court (1801–35), spanning the terms of five Presidents and major political and economic changes in our national life, that the basic constitutional rules of American federalism were given their classic statement. Marshall and the Court he headed gave enduring vitality to three basic rules of the American federal system:

First, the Court made the implied powers clause the most significant of the constitutional grants of power to Congress. Congress had in 1791 established a United States Bank to serve as a depository for national money and to facilitate federal borrowing. The bank's constitutionality was vigorously debated at that time, with Alexander Hamilton arguing that the bank was a proper means of exercising the fiscal powers delegated expressly to the national government and Thomas Jefferson contending that Congress could not establish a bank because the legislature could use only those means that were "indispensably necessary" to carry out its delegated functions. The first was a liberal, the latter a strict, construction of the implied powers clause. When Maryland levied a tax on the bank and the United States Bank refused to pay it, the issue of constitutionality came before the Supreme Court. There, in 1819, the Hamiltonian version of the clause was accepted. "Let the end be legitimate," Marshall wrote in *McCulloch* v. *Maryland*, "let it be within the scope of the Constitution, and all means which are appropriate, which are plainly adapted to that end, which are not prohibited, but consist with the letter and the spirit of the Constitution, are constitutional." [7] The *McCulloch* case established firmly the rule that the implied powers clause gives Congress the right to choose any appropriate means for carrying out the powers of the national government. Through the choice of means, it has been able to adopt new measures and new techniques when confronted with new situations, and hence the implied powers clause has come to be called the "elastic" clause. Thus to raise and support armies Congress may draft men and ration scarce commodities. Under its fiscal and currency powers—to tax, coin money and regulate its value, and borrow money—Congress has been able to establish a national banking system, to give currency control functions to the Federal Reserve System, and to limit private possession of gold.

Second, the Marshall Court made clear the crucial importance of the national supremacy clause in the American federal system. When the Marshall Court held Maryland's tax on the national bank to be unconstitutional in the *McCulloch* case, it established the principle that when a state law interferes with a national activity being carried out "in pursuance of the Constitution," the state law will be declared unconstitutional by the federal courts. From Marshall's time to the present, the national supremacy clause has been both a valuable tool and a source of controversy for the federal union. In contemporary times, it has been the basis of rulings striking down state taxes on interstate business, state racial segregation of interstate bus passengers, state registration systems for aliens, state labor laws interfering with national labor policies, and many other state regulations or programs that conflict with the programs and authority of the national government.

Third, the federal union, as the Marshall Court made clear in a series of leading cases, was a compact of all the people of the United States, not of the individual states as sovereigns. The union was permanent, no state could refuse to obey valid national measures, and there was no right of "interposition," "nullification," or "secession" against the union. This was easier to declare in judicial decisions than to enforce against resisting states, but the principle, announced by the Marshall Court and proved by the Civil War, as we will note shortly, became a fundamental tenet of the federal system.

These were the basic constitutional rules as confirmed in the constitutional

---

[7] *Op. cit.*

theory of the Supreme Court. Meanwhile, the practical workings of American federalism were set in the period from 1789 to 1861. Although the national government ran its postal system, maintained a navy, conducted wars, and had its own court system, it was already assisting the states and seeking their cooperation. It set aside land in the Western territories for education—the first grant-in-aid by the national government. It used state courts for trial of cases in federal jurisdiction, though with a right of appeal to the United States Supreme Court. It relied for its federal land forces on the state militia, which the Constitution had provided should be maintained by the states, subject to regulations of Congress and the right of the national government to call forth the militia to execute national laws, suppress insurrections, and repel invasions. In short, the idea that there were "good old days" when the two governments—national and state—operated in two entirely separate compartments is mostly fiction. At the same period, practical guidelines were developed for accommodating local and national exercises of concurrent powers. When Pennsylvania set up an elaborate system of control over pilots in the port of Philadelphia, a ship owner holding a federal coastal license claimed that the state regulations were illegal when applied to ships operating in interstate or foreign commerce. In the famous case of *Cooley* v. *Board of Wardens*,[8] the Supreme Court asserted that when a matter was local in its nature, when Congress had not acted directly on it, and when the state action did not burden or interfere with commerce, then the state law could stand even though it was incidentally a regulation of interstate or foreign commerce. Thus, under the "Cooley doctrine" states were later allowed to exclude aliens with communicable diseases, regulate headlights on interstate trains, or set interstate shipping rates unless Congress passed laws on these subjects or the Court found the state regulations to burden national functions.

Also established in this period was the political tradition of using "states' rights" as a weapon to serve the concrete interests of economic groups and political movements. Groups and parties could and did rally to the cause of "states' rights" when this served their immediate uses and could and did later completely reverse their position and defend national authority against parochialism and "states' wrongs" when that position advanced their claims more effectively. For example, the Northern mercantile interests that made up the backbone of the Federalist party supported national power against the "states' rights" position of the agrarian Southwestern Republicans in the 1790s; they condemned bitterly the claim of state power to disobey national sedition laws as put forward by the Virginia and Kentucky Resolutions of 1798. But when President Madison's conduct of the War of 1812 with Britain hurt Northern commercial interests heavily, the Federalists rushed to endorse, as crucial states' rights in our system, a similar principle of "lawful resistance" to national actions.

Still another basic element of federalism that began to develop in this first period (though it would be more important later) was the "rule of public demand." This means simply that when the American people want

[8] 12 How. 299 (1851).

something done for them by government, the failure of the local governments to do this will cause the larger units to enter the field with public approval and provide the services. Government aid to canals, railroads, and manufactures during this period followed such a pattern, as did public land development.

Finally, the role of the Supreme Court as umpire of the federal system and referee of nation-state conflicts was established. The Court would rule on whether Congress could charter a national bank or not and whether a state could tax it; whether regulation of ship pilots was under federal or state authority; or what constituted navigable streams which the nation could regulate. The constitutional battlegrounds that were marked off in this era—the commerce clause, the "national supremacy" clause, the taxing power, the "necessary and proper" clause, the Tenth Amendment—have remained the major terrain of federalism disputes ever since.

CIVIL WAR AND THE RISE OF THE ORGANIC UNION, 1861–1913

The "irrepressible conflict" of 1861–65 settled the basic question that had created political storms in 1798 over national sedition laws, in 1812–15 over the war with Britain, in 1832 over national tariff policy, and in the 1850s over fugitive slaves: Did any State have the right to oppose national law to the point of secession from the union as its final remedy? When the cannons were silenced in 1865, war had established what the Supreme Court had not been able to make stick before the fighting but could say with certitude in 1869: that ours was "an indestructible union, composed of indestructible states."

Between 1861 and 1913, American federalism underwent significant changes. While identification with state and locality did not vanish, the post-Civil War generations came increasingly to think of themselves fundamentally as Americans, and this flood of nationalistic sentiment marked the end of any taint of illegitimacy or secondary status for the national government. Major federal subsidies were awarded to the states, if they adopted programs urged by Congress, giving leverage to the national government to persuade by donation where it could not command. In this period, federal subsidies primarily took the form of lands and public works, as with the Morrill Act in 1862 awarding huge tracts of federal lands to states that would establish agricultural and mechanical arts colleges and creating state agricultural experiment stations. During this second era, the basic pressures that would reshape our federal system into its present form began to be felt: the rise of large-scale industry crossing state lines and forming national units; the development of a national transportation and marketing system; the increasing frequency and severity of national business depressions; the rise of labor-management conflicts directly affecting interstate commerce; large-scale immigration by Eastern and Southern European groups and their concentration in growing urban centers; the appearance of interstate crime and nationwide criminal operations; the intensification of minority-group pressures for greater social, economic, and political opportunities; and the entry of the United States into world politics and international wars.

These challenges were not met creatively by American federalism in the

1865–1913 era. It was a time of aggressive business expansion and consolidation, of low prestige for government, of ideas about "survival of the fittest," and of deep antilabor, antiforeign, antiminority sentiment.

These dominant interests were reflected in decisions of the Supreme Court. For example, in its 1895–96 term, the Justices struck down the federal income tax as unconstitutional; ruled that the Federal Anti-Trust Act of 1890 could not be applied against a 98 percent monopoly of sugar refining in the United States (on the ground that this was "local manufacture" and not "commerce"); and, when national power *was* upheld, it was to justify federal intervention in the Pullman railroad strike and the conviction of union leader Eugene Debs for conspiracy to interfere with interstate commerce and the mails. At the same time that national powers were strictly construed in cases such as the Sugar Trust decision, the states were also barred from legislating on many of the new problems of industrial capitalism, on the ground that the due process clause of the Fourteenth Amendment forbade state regulations that impaired rights of private contract and property. Accompanying these rulings were Supreme Court doctrines that denied the federal government authority to protect Negroes from discrimination by owners of public accommodation facilities and accepted as constitutional state racial segregation systems as long as the "separate" facilities were formally "equal." This period was also characterized by widespread corruption and inefficiency in state and local governments, with a wealth of links between corrupt politicians and business that led progressives to write such volumes of protest as Lincoln Steffens' famous *The Shame of the Cities* and *The Struggle for Self-Government.*

To some, the fact that American capitalism made its "great leap forward" in this era is proof that our system functions best when federal authority to tax incomes, regulate business, and aid farmers and workers is closely limited, and when the welfare function of the states is also closely circumscribed. To others, the so-called "golden age" of McKinley reflects a breakdown of government responsibility and flexible federalism, in which the human costs of industrialization were far higher than they needed to be.

THE NEW FEDERALISM, 1913 TO THE PRESENT: NATIONAL SUPREMACY AND NATIONAL CRISIS

Many commentators choose the date 1913, when the national government was given, by constitutional amendment, the power to tax incomes directly, as the symbolic year for the opening of a new era of national supremacy in the federal system. Potentially, this shifted the financial balance of power from the states to Washington. The potential was realized first when the Wilson Administration initiated grants for highway construction as well as loan programs for agriculture in 1916, and successfully financed a war in 1917–18. It was further realized in the vast extension of government credit institutions in the Hoover and Roosevelt Administrations (by 1958 loans outstanding for business, agriculture, housing, and other purposes in fifty-one government programs totaled over $76 billion); in the extension of grants-in-aid to states in the Social Security Act, housing act, and numerous other acts since the New Deal was inaugurated; and in the ability to finance the Second World War and the present-day defense establishment. Some states' righters who have recognized the effects of the income tax amendment have proposed that the maximum rate be set by amendment at 25 percent, but former President Eisenhower strongly opposed this proposal during his Administration as a threat to the maintenance of our national defenses, and others have opposed it then and since, feeling that it would destroy the national government's basic welfare programs.

Another change has been the establishment of extensive national controls over the economy, subject to the Supreme Court's ultimate confirmation. Also beginning in 1913, this time with the Federal Reserve Act giving the national government authority over the monetary system, there occurred the strengthening of antitrust legislation (in 1914 and many times later); national support for and regulation of agriculture; similar support and regulation of labor; and regulation of many industries operating in interstate commerce, such as radio communications, shipping, stockyards, interstate power utilities, motor carriers, airlines, and securities exchanges. Freedom under the constitutional system for trade across state lines and the economies of industrialism built an economy of interstate businesses, and this produced demands for regulation from the only government whose jurisdiction was coextensive with the interstate operations to be regulated. For a time the Supreme Court placed obstacles in the way of the development and created a "crisis" in American federalism. In 1918, in a 5-to-4 decision holding that Congress could not prohibit child labor in manufacturing establishments (because this was not itself commerce), the Court seemed to say that production of goods—agriculture, manufacturing, and labor—was outside the reach of the national government, except under such traditionally established controls as the antitrust laws. Again, in the *Schechter* decision in 1935, in which it held unconstitutional the New Deal program of industrial and labor codes created in the National Industrial Recovery Act, and in the *Butler* decision in 1936, in which it held unconstitutional the government's agricultural controls program, the Supreme Court seemed to be saying that the powers to regulate commerce and to tax could not be used to reach productive enterprise, only the conditions of interstate shipment. Many commentators noted that the Supreme Court's interpretation of the constitutional division of powers between the national government and the states had created a no man's land in which no government would have effective powers. The national government lacked the constitutional power and the states lacked the actual power, since, acting separately, they were powerless to deal with the complex interstate issues presented. This denial of power accorded with the older laissez-faire notions that it was inappropriate for government to regulate business, but it was out of harmony with rising public demands that government soften the harsh side-effects of industrialization and protect the minimum health, safety, and welfare of its citizens. Ultimately, the Court yielded. It recognized the right of state governments to regulate in decisions such as those upholding state power to set prices in virtually all industries (1934) and to fix minimum wages (1937). The Court also ratified the extensive powers of the national government over production, agriculture, and labor relations, whenever these affected interstate commerce, building on the classic Marshall doctrines that many thought should have been invoked all along. Between 1937, when the National Labor

Justus in the Minneapolis *Star*

"20th-Century Tug of War"

According to the liberal view, "states' rights" spokesmen are voices from the past.

Relations Act was upheld, and 1941, when a national law was upheld setting maximum hours and minimum wages and forbidding child labor, the Supreme Court confirmed fully Congress' power to regulate the economy in all its interstate aspects. What was reserved to the states in the area of economic regulation after this constitutional redefinition in the late 1930s was less a sphere of exclusive state power protected by the Tenth Amendment than it was an area that Congress chose not to regulate itself but to leave to state controls.

Yet the tension between national and state authority has remained as new issues have arisen. Today, the arguments often take the form of debates over "federal preemption," the question raised in federal court cases whether Congress intended by its legislation in a particular field to preclude the states from exercising concurrent powers over this subject. Where Congress clearly says that its laws are meant to be exclusive, or stipulates that the states may regulate alongside the federal acts, there is rarely an issue. But, for example, when Congress passes laws punishing the advocacy of overthrow of the United States Government by force and violence (the Smith Act), can the states pass "little Smith Acts" making such advocacy a state crime as well? Or, when Congress gives the National Labor Relations Board jurisdiction over labor disputes affecting interstate commerce, can state labor boards exercise control over labor disputes that have interstate aspects as long as the NLRB has not specifically ruled on such cases? In these controversies, the Supreme Court must apply the *Cooley* doctrine and determine whether the subject matter is essentially national in character, whether the state regulation interferes with the federal policy enacted, or whether the silence of Congress on the subject of parallel state action implies consent or hostility to such action in the particular instance. Since the Supreme Court has used the "federal preemption" doctrine to strike down more than a dozen major types of state laws in the fields of internal security, taxation, and economic regulation in the post-1945 era, some conservatives have sponsored legislation to require the federal courts to assume that Congress intended to allow state legislation in areas of concurrent jurisdiction unless the Congressional act expressly declares that the states may not do so. These proposals have been opposed on the ground that they would upset the existing balances between federal and state authority and would limit the creative role of the courts in adjusting the concurrent-power border lines. The conservatives' proposals were defeated throughout the late 1950s and 1960s, leaving the decision of federal preemption questions with the courts.

In addition, the tremendous rise in the importance of foreign policy to the American nation had its impact on the theory and practice of the federal system in these decades. From the explosion of the First World War through the Second World War, the Korean War, and the Cold War, the federal government has had to spend vast sums of money for national defense and to apply sweeping regulatory programs to support war and defense efforts. Reflecting these serious international conditions, the Supreme Court has steadily upheld broad power for the national government in the field of foreign affairs, often over the complaints of states'-rights protesters. This has taken three main forms. First, the Supreme Court has upheld national legislation enacted to carry out treaty obligations of the United States even though such laws would not have been within national power except for the treaty. The Court has held that treaties are constitutional according to "the authority of the United States" (as stated in the "national supremacy" clause of the Constitution) when made by the President and Senate and not found to be violative of constitutional prohibitions. The leading example was federal legislation to protect migratory birds from destructive hunting practices. This an area once held to be under *state* jurisdiction only, but when the United States made a treaty with Canada pledging both powers to protect such birds, federal power was affirmed. The Court held that the Tenth Amendment, with its principle of reserved powers, does not limit the government's treaty-making power.

Second, the Supreme Court declared in *United States* v. *Curtiss-Wright Export Corporation* [9] that the national government had inherent powers in foreign relations. The Court said that with respect to such matters the federal government's powers "did not depend upon the affirmative grants of the Constitution." These powers passed directly from the British Crown "to the colonies in their collective and corporate capacity as the United States of America" and "are equal to the right and power of the other members of the international family." This doctrine of inherent powers validated such past exercises of national power as acquisition of territory by discovery and occupation, expulsion of undesirable aliens, and executive agreements of the President—all powers that were not specifically delegated to the federal government in the Constitution. The doctrine, moreover, removed the necessity of justifying international policies as "pursuant to" the Constitution.

---

[9] 299 U.S. 304 (1936).

Third, the Supreme Court has particularly upheld the power of the President, as chief negotiator and spokesman of the nation in foreign relations, to conclude "executive agreements" with other nations, such as President Franklin Roosevelt's "destroyers for bases" exchange with Great Britain just before we entered the Second World War. Such executive agreements do not require ratification by the Senate, and thus the degree of control that is politically available to the states through their representation in the Senate cannot be used in these instances.

Conservatives in the late 1950s tried, in the "Bricker Amendment," to require Senate approval of executive agreements and to prevent treaties from enlarging Presidential power, but these efforts were defeated when the Eisenhower Administration stressed the need for both Presidential freedom of action and the existing check of Senate ratification against treaties that might infringe upon constitutional guarantees of individual rights.

Of course, all the forces that began in the second period—the rise of giant industry, economic cycles and depressions, foreign policy and war pressures —were accelerated from the First World War to the present. Moreover, public demands for welfare services such as social security, unemployment compensation, and the like, which the states were financially and politically unable to meet by themselves in the 1930s, have pulled the national government into areas that were once primarily local and state responsibilities. The net result of these forces has been to increase national responsibility and authority. While "Washington" cannot do it alone, the national government is the prime agency able to plan for total international competition and conflict, to watch the crucial checks and balances of industrial capitalism, and to offer a publicly oriented power to counter the pressures from big business, big labor, big agriculture, and even big crime.

THE INSTRUMENTS OF THE NEW FEDERALISM

Sketching the overall shift in power from the states to the national government across the years gives a gross picture of the unfolding Union, but it may not do justice to several important factors: the political limits that still control national authority; the cooperative quality of much national action; and the continued vitality of the state and local governments.

A few people still call the behemoth in Washington an unlimited autocrat, but such a view would cause federal officials to either laugh wildly or cry in remembered frustration. The national government itself still lies under strong state controls, through the election system which distributes Presidential electoral votes by states, chooses Senators from each state, and apportions Representatives by election districts within states; through the weapon of Senate confirmation of Presidential appointees, and the factor of "Senatorial courtesy," which (in effect) gives state and local officials veto power over many "federal" appointments; through the party system, which has its strongest roots in the state and local party organizations; through the influence of locally based interest groups on national policy-making; and through other powerful relationships and arrangements that make Washington far from a free agent in its dealings with matters that touch the prerogatives of state and local units and their constituencies. Thus, national programs for general federal aid to education, medical care plans for the

Independence Day

A conservative view of the increased power of the national government.

Knox in the Nashville *Banner*

aged, a department of urban affairs, and many other measures proposed by Presidents have been recently defeated in Congress because of the powerful and varied forces opposing national entry into these areas.

The fact that our federalist techniques are not simply shifts from state to national power is well illustrated by Washington's tendency to enter an area but actually to allow it to be administered by the states. One example of this basic tendency is the federal cash grant-in-aid programs. Beginning on a large scale with the grants for highway construction in 1916, these programs have provided the states with funds to do a wide variety of things—build hospitals and health centers, pay old-age pensions, institute vocational education programs, provide maternal care and child health service, fight venereal disease, renew urban areas, and so on. The cooperative aspect of the grant programs is that while the federal government chooses the program to support, dangles the inviting cash before the state governments to win their "voluntary" participation, and sets certain standards of administration (such as civil service employees on public welfare programs or certain accounting methods for highway fund disposals), the states do the actual administering, contribute anywhere from 10 percent to 50 percent of the funds themselves, and have important leeway in shaping the actual policy impact of these programs on local residents. Another example of cooperative federalism is the Tennessee Valley Authority, instituted in 1933 to coordinate development of the resources of the Tennessee Valley area, which takes in seven states. The Tennessee Valley Corporation, in close collaboration with the cities and states in the area, and with regional administration of many of the specific programs, operates TVA very much as a

CHART 4–1 / The American System: Limited, Divided, and Shared Powers

Controlling Principle: National Supremacy

1. U.S. Constitution
2. Laws made to implement Constitution
3. Treaties made under U.S. authority

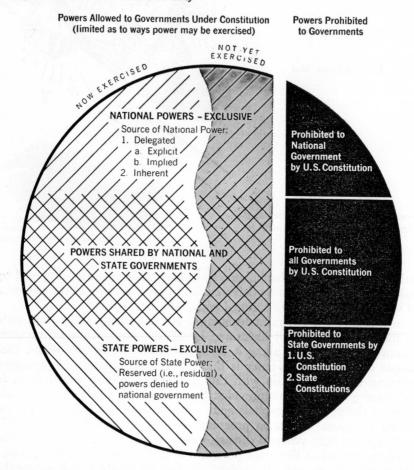

Powers Allowed to Governments Under Constitution
(limited as to ways power may be exercised)

Powers Prohibited
to Governments

NOT YET EXERCISED

NOW EXERCISED

NATIONAL POWERS – EXCLUSIVE
Source of National Power:
1. Delegated
   a. Explicit
   b. Implied
2. Inherent

Prohibited to National Government by U.S. Constitution

POWERS SHARED BY NATIONAL AND STATE GOVERNMENTS

Prohibited to all Governments by U.S. Constitution

STATE POWERS – EXCLUSIVE
Source of State Power:
Reserved (i.e., residual) powers denied to national government

Prohibited to State Governments by
1. U.S. Constitution
2. State Constitutions

resource department would if the United States were divided not into states but into five or six primary economic regions.

Actually, although grants-in-aid are the most conspicuous example, the instances of cooperative federalism are numerous. Thus when a person steals a car or kidnaps a baby and moves it across state lines, both state and national laws are violated, and the governments cooperate in the search for the guilty party; in addition, state and local police officers are often trained in national police schools. Of a different nature is the cooperation in economic matters: national and state agencies regulating utilities have worked out common requirements on accounting data to be kept by utility corporations; state banks are offered the opportunity to become members of the

Federal Reserve System and the Federal Deposit Insurance system; co-operative arrangements have been established between the national and states authorities which must approve sales of securities. In conservation of resources, foods and drugs regulation, and protection of health, national and state agencies are in constant contact with each other. Adjustment of responsibilities and cooperation, rather than separate enterprise and incessant conflict, are the normal, day-to-day characteristics of modern federalism.

In addition, there has been an important growth in direct relationships between the federal government and local communities such as towns, cities, and counties, often bypassing state controls. The federal government now subsidizes the building of municipal and county airports; awards large sums for local housing and slum clearance under federal urban renewal programs; grants funds for local experiments and community services in fields such as health, juvenile delinquency, and so on; and awards billions of dollars in defense contracts to ship-building yards or factories that spell jobs and prosperity for local areas. This leads to direct negotiations between mayors, city planning boards, local chambers of commerce, and union leaders on the one hand and federal agencies charged with awarding funds under the various national programs on the other, often with the Congressman from the locality or the United States Senators serving as key intermediaries. The implications of this growing local-federal relationship are many and will be discussed in later chapters, but the rise of new lines of lobbying and power relationships and the creation of alternatives to a rigid federal-state bargaining status in intergovernmental relations can be noted here.

The continued vitality of the states and the vast scope of the demands upon their attention are frequently overlooked by concentration on discussions of national power. Anyone who looks at the bills introduced and the statutes passed in regular sessions of state legislatures will see a wider span of domestic problems dealt with than in the legislation in Congress during the same period. Although the state measures are confined to "local" regulations, they must still deal with far-reaching issues of labor, public utilities, and agriculture, and they still are the only centers of licensing and other forms of regulation for the professions and service trades. Some large industries are still subject to state regulation—insurance (delegated by national statute), state banking, and oil, for example, and the states still charter new corporations and enact the general rules for existing corporations in their jurisdiction. Furthermore, while the national government sets standards when it grants money, the states still have much discretion in legislation about health, welfare, roads, and other matters for which federal money is received. Education, hospitals, correctional institutions, juvenile delinquency, property law, crimes, smog, local government, election law, and innumerable other items remain primarily on the state agenda. What now seems characteristic of American government is that most domestic problems of urgency and significance cannot be approached with hope of successful solution without the cooperation of two, or all three, levels of government.[10]

Another example of the continued vitality of the states is illustrated by the development of new forms by which the states can cope with the spillage

---

[10] For a complete discussion of intergovernmental cooperation, see Chapter 29.

of issues over the formal boundaries of one state. Chief among these is the interstate compact, by which two or more states (with the permission of Congress, as required in the Constitution) enter into an arrangement to apportion or govern something that affects all of their interests. The Colorado River Compact in 1928 governing the amount of water to be withdrawn by each state through which the Colorado River flows, the eight-state Ohio River Valley Compact in 1948 on sanitation control, or the Port of New York Authority created by a 1921 compact between New York and New Jersey to run the bus, train, water, and air systems serving the metropolitan New York area are leading examples of this development. Compacts have included regulation of soil resources, fisheries, paroled prisoners, and many other subjects. Despite the ingenuity and cooperation illustrated by many such interstate compacts, however, it is fair to say that a great bundle of multistate issues that groups of states should cope with are *not* being placed within the compact process, partly because it is difficult to arrange agreements among several states and partly because of the difficulty of making satisfactory arrangements for continuous and flexible administration through compacts.

A BALANCE SHEET ON THE NEW FEDERALISM

Two groups of arguments are typically set out to describe the case for stronger national power and the case for greater state authority, or, as these are sometimes called, the case for centralization versus decentralization. National-power advocates cite the need for overall national planning and programs to deal with urban blight, transportation decay, civil rights, and similar critical issues. State actions in these areas are often fiscally inadequate, piecemeal in planning, and highly inefficient in formulation and administration because of the lower levels of skill available in state governments as a whole. The national government, which is much more responsive to the will of the national majority, can act forcefully where the needs and demands are clear and can arrange compromises among warring minority groups when necessary. Moreover, fusing such domestic problems as civil rights, educational facilities, and scientific development, all needing day-to-day management, to the use of the nation's resources for national defense and foreign policy makes central guidance more vital than ever. Finally, the national-power advocate dismisses the idea that local control is *necessarily* a greater protection of the citizen's freedom than national responsibility; the Negroes and whites in Little Rock who wanted high school integration accepted peacefully were coerced by the state of Arkansas, and the person convicted of crime on the basis of a confession obtained through the use of force by the policeman in a Massachusetts town will usually find the national Supreme Court his most reliable defender.

On the other hand, the case for state authority and decentralization starts by questioning whether the national public really wants Washington to take on more and more programs in areas of education, labor, civil rights and the like. It is argued that such matters need the diverse programs and approaches of local jurisdictions in order to reflect faithfully the diversity in local conditions and local attitudes toward these issues. National programs are said to compel a dangerous uniformity, especially in a society as heterogeneous as ours. Further, the states and local communities are portrayed as being closer to the people and closer to the voters, so that programs here respond quickly to public will. Washington is distant, it is claimed—it is hard to influence, much more heavily bureaucratic, and preoccupied with the bigger issues. Finally, the states are described as little laboratories in which different laws and programs can be experimented with, to the overall benefit of other states and even the national government, which has based some of its most important programs on models developed by the states.

This debate, with "swift, uniform, positive responses to public needs" urged on the one hand (the national trend) and "varied, locally controlled, and less total solutions" advocated on the other (more state responsibility) has been a central aspect of our national politics throughout the past decades. It touches the question of minimum federal standards applied to state police practices, state power over labor relations and subversive activities, Presidential authority to conclude executive agreements with foreign nations, and existing federal grants-in-aid programs. The most significant thing to note is that every effort in recent decades to "bring government back home" (as the National Association of Manufacturers urged) or to "decentralize by [federal] order" (as a leading student of federalism put it) have come to naught. The two Hoover Commissions on reorganization of the federal government or the President's Federal-State Action Committee, all created during the 1940s and 1950s in the expectation that *some* functions could be turned back to the states, came up with no proposals for decentralization that were acceptable to Congress. This is not because of any centralizer's hypnotic influence on both Democratic and Republican executives and legislators but because the developing responsibilities of the national government satisfy three basic criteria for survival:

1. They meet strongly felt public needs and expectations.

2. They build up interest-group and local elements who strongly support their continuation.

3. The states offer no credible alternative programs or solutions.

The basic truth about the federal system, then, is that it is a nondoctrinaire, pragmatic arrangement, responsive to political and constitutional limits and opportunities. It distributes functions among American governments to produce not a layer cake of governmental authority, local, state, and national, but a "marble cake"—"Wherever you slice through it you reveal an inseparable mixture of differently colored ingredients . . . and in some places there are unexpected whirls and an imperceptible merging of colors. . . ." [11]

Summary: Constitutional Change and Federalism in the Nuclear Age

Through amendments, court interpretation, statutory development, custom, and political-institutional growth, the Philadelphia Constitution of

---

[11] Morton Grodzins, "Centralization and Decentralization in the American Federal System," in Robert A. Goldwin, ed., *A Nation of States* (Chicago, 1963), pp. 3–4.

1787 and the federal system have been modernized and retooled to confront the problems of running a continental, industrial nation in an age of clashing world empires and weapons of total destruction. Whether our instruments for adaptation delude us into retaining an eighteenth-century charter and an archaic division of authority when we should reorganize our society to cope with life-or-death issues is a meaningful question. Is separation of powers a valid system for running a national government that must act speedily and decisively in matters of labor disputes, defense policy, or civil rights? Is our system of elections one which really captures the attention of the citizenry, brings the best men into competition for office, and provides national leaders with the mandate to govern firmly? Is Congress organized to function properly as a representative body? Do we need intergovernmental agencies to administer regional plans for urban and suburban development, replacing the "formalistic" boundaries of city, county, and state? One common reply is to say that inertia and vested interests make any total revision of our system unlikely, short of a total national reorganization after atomic war. Another comment is that our past successes counsel us to hold fast to what has worked well before, rather than to fly to strange experiments that are not grounded in our distinctive history, ideology, and institutions.

To attempt answers to such questions at this point would be premature. In the major sections of the text that follow, there appear full discussions of the institutions, processes, personalities, and functions of the American governmental system. With this background, students will be able to react to the problem of reform or fundamental change and, in a real sense, this is what will be at the heart of their civic participation as voters and citizens in the years to come.

PART II
THE POLITICAL PROCESS

5 / Functions and Development of American Political Parties

Organizations styling themselves political parties have traveled under many names. There have been fascist, Communist, and vegetarian parties. There have been monarchist, socialist, and anarcho-syndicalist parties. These names stand for all sorts of groups—from small collections of cranks to highly disciplined paramilitary cadres. The history of the United States itself has seen the coming and going of the Greenback, Know-Nothing, Locofoco, and Prohibition parties. Yet the dominant experience of American politics has been with a "two-party" system in which the major parties, taken together, have usually been able to attract the votes of most of the electorate.

One reason why only two parties have been able to embrace the bulk of voting Americans is that the parties themselves have been loose coalitions formed to attract sufficient votes to gain control of government—not vehicles for propagating ideologies. By "ideology" is meant here a doctrine or a view of the world, specific in its particulars, that must either be completely accepted or completely rejected. It is rare for an ideological party to command majority support (outside the artificial totalitarian setting) if for no other reason than the extreme difficulty of getting any very large group of people to agree on questions of first principles and ultimate ends. Neither the Democrats nor the Republicans are ideological parties. However, Americans, whether they are Democrats or Republicans or uncommitted, accept as normal and desirable certain basic institutions and practices. Considering how much politics has to do with the distribution of wealth, it is important to note that the basic outlines of capitalism and economic individualism have seldom been questioned by the major actors in the political arena:

> The fierceness of the political struggles has often been misleading; for the range of vision embraced by the primary contestants in the major parties has always been bounded by the horizons of property and enterprise. However much at odds on specific issues, the major political traditions have shared a belief in the rights of property, the philosophy of economic individualism, the value of competition; they have accepted the economic virtues of capitalist culture as necessary qualities of man. . . . The sanctity of private property, the right of the individual to dispose of and invest it, the value of opportunity, and the natural evolution of self-interest and self-assertion, within

broad legal limits, into a beneficent social order have been staple tenets of the central faith in American political ideologies.[1]

Whether the struggle has been between Federalists and Jeffersonians, between Jacksonians and Whigs, or between Democrats and Republicans, the actual range of opinion and the actual collision of interests have been limited. Partisan contention has taken place within the bounds of a very general consensus, and the only occasion on which that consensus was ruptured—the Civil War—was not the result of a party battle. Indeed, more often than not the most interesting and significant controversies have taken place *within* the ranks of the major parties rather than between them. Smaller parties, enlisting only one economic class or sect or region, might afford the luxury of possessing a wholly consistent doctrine acceptable to a handful of true believers. But American parties have been nationwide structures—mosaics made up of widely varying groups and interests. Thus the United States has had no "confessional" party (made up of one religious group) and no party of "revolution" playing a major historical role, for such parties have never been able to meet the acid test of our pragmatic and low-temperature politics—offering to voters the reasonable expectation of early victory at the polls. Put another way, there simply have not been enough revolutionaries or religious zealots to make doctrinaire parties "pay" in the ultimate political coin—power. On the contrary, those who want to change society and those who wish to preserve the status quo have been able to find homes in *both* major parties and have also discovered that they must compromise their differences with their fellow partisans if they are to achieve political success and access to governmental power. American politicians quickly acquire an instinct for survival—they know that what counts are the votes cast for their candidates, that a good showing on Election Day is more important than the purity of one's principles.

The federal Constitution (and the various state constitutions which were revised after its adoption) established the single-member district as the standard American electoral unit. Under such an arrangement the "winner takes all," and small parties in the "district" have no chance of elevating anyone to power. In an election within a state assembly district, within a state for the governorship, or within the fifty states for the Presidency, there are no prizes reserved for second or third finishers. A party must demonstrate that it can quickly climb to the top of the heap, or its supporters begin to feel that their votes are being wasted and had better be switched to a party with a future. American electoral forms encourage big, diffuse parties— in direct contrast to the varying systems of proportional representation employed, for instance, in France, West Germany, and Italy, whereby seats in the legislatures are spread among the parties according to the percentage of the total vote which they receive. There a small party with a fairly constant following can be assured of some voice in the councils of state, election after election. In this country, to remain viable, a party must be a contender for majority status. The few exceptions to this rule are small local parties which trade on holding the balance of power between the

---

[1] Richard Hofstadter, *The American Political Tradition* (New York, 1948), p. viii.

Democrats and the Republicans—the foremost example of this being the Liberal party in New York.

The Functions of American Parties

Some parties exist to expound a particular parochial position. Some parties, as in the Soviet Union or Nazi Germany, have been employed for purposes of social control and mobilizing mass acceptance of the regime in power. In the American setting, the parties serve to align the various interest groups roughly in holding companies which allow government to be organized in a fairly orderly way and provide a mechanism for deciding who is to rule (hold office) and who is not. The time and attention of the voter is limited—he could not hope to choose meaningfully between dozens of contending candidates on Election Day. The major parties (if they are functioning properly) perform the necessary job of limiting that choice and rendering it comprehensible.

We say of the American system of government that the "people rule," and yet in any literal sense such a statement is absurd. What is intended by this expression is the notion that the leaders of political society—those who exert power over their fellow citizens—are ultimately dependent on the consent of the community for their continuance in power. But if the system is to work there must be machinery for selecting from the many the few who are to stand for the jobs—something in addition to the effective and structured opportunity to dispense with the "rascals" in power that is provided by elections. The people cannot *choose* their officials in elections (except in the town meeting situation which is fast becoming a curiosity of American politics); they *take their pick* among a limited number of alternatives which are posed for them. If the choice were not narrowed—if a great deal of selecting had not already been accomplished—the election would be a meaningless exercise. Straw votes on university campuses, in which candidates proliferate because numerous friendship groups must push their favorites, are harmless examples of what happens when an election is used to do the job of selecting from scratch. It is this preliminary selecting and narrowing that our parties do for us. They "recruit" aspirants to office, and in the healthy situation provide a series of political apprenticeships through which the prospective leader must pass on the way to the top.

Even if it were possible to elect officials without the mediation of parties, organizing government afterward would be terribly difficult. Party discipline among elected leaders in America (as will be seen in a later chapter) is not nearly so high as, for instance, among members of Parliament in the British House of Commons, yet it is a cohesive factor. It provides some minimal common loyalty and identification which allows us to speak of legislative majorities and which ties members of Congress to the White House when its occupant is of "their" party. With a governmental structure in which power is as divided as it is in the American case (between Congress and the Executive, between governors and legislatures), to have no common allegiances among the men who occupy these various positions would make the system even more difficult to operate than constitutionally it is.

All this does not mean that the parties are identical instruments, without distinctive characters, which simply exist in response to the needs of the system. It does not mean, for instance, that there is "no difference" between the Democratic and the Republican parties. In recent years, for instance, because of differences in the makeup of the two coalitions, the Democratic party has taken a more optimistic attitude toward the use of governmental power for social change than has the Republican party. It should simply be remembered that, above and beyond the approaches taken by the parties toward particular issues and problems, they perform certain vital neutral functions in the operation of the political process.

So long as governments exist, with their mandate to make policy and to allocate values, men will seek to discover ways and means of reaching public office. If there are any "laws" of politics and society, this is surely one of the first. Governments are neither independent nor impartial, and individuals with interests to promote cannot be prevented from calculating how to capture the reins of official power. It was inevitable, even before the ratification of the Constitution, that America would have political parties in one form or another. There were interests to be promoted, values to be secured, ambitions to be satisfied—and these ends sought by individuals and groups could only be attained where access was established to the seats of government. But experience was lacking at the birth of the Republic, and while it may have been naïve to assume that the problem of staffing government could be removed from partisan considerations, the fact remains that only gradually was a series of precedents inaugurated that made parties and popular elections an integral element in the governmental process. But before surveying this development, an examination of the term "party" is in order.

Parties are many things at one time, and party activity is to be found in a variety of settings. Rather than attempt at this juncture to give a definitive characterization of a political party, it would be best simply to indicate the various forms that party institutions and practices can take: (1) *The party-in-the-electorate:* When we speak of "the Democrats" or "the Republicans" here we are referring to the millions of ordinary citizens who tend to identify with and vote for the candidates of one party or another. (2) *The party organizations:* Here the "party" is actually those individuals who staff the committees, conventions, and elected or appointive positions within the national, state, and local organizations. These are the politicians, professional or semiprofessional, whose chief concern is to fill the offices of government with people bearing their own party's label. (3) *The party-in-government:* "The Democrats" or "the Republicans" in this instance are the men and women holding public office and who, by their actions, make a record (or fail to make one) on the basis of which party accomplishments will be judged. Thus we may have a "Democratic Congress" at one time or a "Republican Administration" at another. Any discussion of political parties will inevitably move from one to another of these meanings, often without stopping for breath. It is clear that the party organization often makes direct appeals to the electorate. But this is not the entirety of organized party activity, and the organizations have lives of their own that

Periodicals
... familiar w/ pts of view
... Cong Record
... Congressional Digest
Public Affairs Index

Pol. Sci. 303- American National Government
Mr. Zuccarello

This course is primarily an introduction to American National Government. It is intended to acquaint the student with the operation of the institutions of the central government and also with the operation of the American political process. During the course, the student will be expected to familiarize himself with the tools and the methods of research used by the modern political scientist.

REQUIRED TEXTS

Redford, Truman et al. Politics and Government in the United States. (National, State and Local edition). Harcourt, Brace and World. 1965.

Scott and Wallace. Politics U. S. A. 2 ed. Macmillan. 1965.

John C. Murray S. J. We Hold These Truths. Image. 1964 ed.

OUTLINE

X Sept 16- 21. Intro. to Pol. Sci. Building the Nation. The Constitution. Redford, Part I- Scott- #0, 7, 9, 11

23- Oct. 7. The Presidency, Congress. Redford, ch. 10 to 14. Scott. #'s 32 to 49.

Oct. 10- 24. The Political Process; Parties, Interest Groups. Voting Behavior. Redford, Part II, Scott- #'s 19 to 31.

Nov. 9-11 Law, Society and Politics. Redford, Ch. 15

18 The Pen of Justice— Redford, Ch. 17
Nov. 21— Dec. 2— Civil Liberty and Civil Rights— Redford, Ch. 18, 19
                    Scott— 13 to 18

Dec. 5   Govt. and the Economy, Redford, ch. 20, Scott, #'s 55 to 59.
7- 9   Govt. and Welfare. Redford, ch. 22.
12-14   Govt. and Money. Redford, ch. 23.
Jan. 4-6 Defense and Foreign Policy. #4/ Redford, ch. 24
          Scott— #'s 60-63
9-11   Making of Defense and Foreign Policy, Redford, ch. 25
13   Science, Technology and Natural Resources, Redford, ch. 21
          Scott, #9

Required:
1. A formal research paper on a topic of present day political importance.
9- 12 typewritten pages. Topic must be approved by the instructor.
It would be most desireable /77/the student use the interview
                                 that
technique of research as one of his tools. Paper is due no later
than January 9. Papers submitted late or on topics not approved by
the instructor will not be accepted.

2. Student report on Murray's book, due November 23. A question sheet
will be distributed on November 18.

- lect
- readings Scott
- class lectures

<u>Types</u>

- mult ch
- identify
- short essays
- long essay

should to application
"of principles
"valid pol decision"
advice you would give
valid

are frequently carried on apart from the public. And while those in government office may have been originally nominated by a party organization, their relation to the politicians back home can be a tenuous one. At all events, throughout any general discussion of party history and development it is a good idea to stop every so often to ask just which of the "three" parties—electoral, organizational, governmental—is being considered and how it relates to the other two.

The Development of American Parties: 1792–1860

The search for a "history" of our parties, for some strands of political continuity, can be extremely baffling. Not only have American parties undergone changes in name and turnover in membership, but it is difficult to detect straight lines of development from Revolutionary times to the current day. It might be satisfying, for example, if we could say that the same sorts of Americans first supported the new Constitution, then voted Federalist, then rallied behind the Whigs, and ultimately joined the Republicans. By the same token party history would fit a neat pattern if those who opposed the new Constitution were the people who comprised the Jeffersonian Republicans, the Jacksonian Democrats, and who now belong to the modern Democratic party. Unfortunately the shifting of populations and the shifting of interests and issues render any genealogy a bit artificial. To take one example, the Jeffersonian party was a pragmatic coalition of both men who had supported and men who had opposed the 1787 Constitution. Or, as another illustration, the modern Republican party recruited its initial members from both the Whigs and the Jacksonians. Here, once again, continuity of political outlook is far less important than organizational development in the context of the rise of new groups and social interests in the electorate.

The section that follows is the history of the party coalitions from the first Administration of George Washington to the eve of the Civil War. In seeking to understand the nature of today's American political institutions the historical approach is not always ideal—past politics do not automatically illuminate contemporary process. Yet because our political parties grew up through custom and usage outside of the constitutional framework, and because the party coalitions of today are so directly a product of those that went before, a historical survey is useful for getting at the nature—the internal structure—of American parties, and in particular, the process by which they change over time.

THE CONSTITUTIONAL VACUUM

The Constitution went into no little detail in outlining the role and responsibilities of the Congress. It had less to say on the Presidency, and it expended a minimum of words on the Supreme Court. However, on political parties it said nothing at all. The reason for this silence, quitely simply, was that in 1787 political parties (in the sense outlined above) did not exist. Throughout the colonial and confederation period a wide array of factions, cliques, and transitory coalitions of interests had been part of the political scene. But these were not "parties" so much as they were ephemeral alliances of individual politicos who came together to support particular candidates for particular offices at particular elections—and, as often as not, disbanded as soon as the ballots were counted. Nor could the early Americans look to their mother country for a model of a party system. The Whigs and Tories of England were really no more than parliamentary factions, not parties in the modern sense by that time. They were shifting combinations of great families and their allies which maneuvered for power and preferment. In England, moreover, the electorate was restricted to less than 5 percent of the adult male population, with the consequence that politics was an aristocratic pursuit. Indeed, national parties had yet to emerge anywhere in the world; the initial seeds were to be sown in American soil.

EARLY FACTIONAL POLITICS

The Framers of the Constitution naturally thought in terms of "factions." These were groups of individuals who rallied around a single leader to promote a certain interest or issue or candidate. Factions of this sort had no permanent structure, and they would form and disband with remarkable ease. Political observers of the time did use the term "party" on occasion, but it was merely a synonym for factional groupings. The consensus among the men who founded the Republic was a realistic one, for they acknowledged that factions would always exist whenever men were permitted to associate together for political purposes. At the same time the Framers sought to ensure that no single group or combination of groups would dominate the new government. James Madison expressed this sentiment in *The Federalist,* No. 10:

> The latent causes of faction . . . are sown in the nature of man; and we see them everywhere brought into different degrees of activity, according to the different circumstances of civil society. A zeal for different opinions, concerning religion, concerning government, and many other points, as well of speculation as of practice; an attachment to different leaders ambitiously contending for pre-eminence and power; or to persons of other descriptions whose fortunes have been interesting to the human passions, have, in turn, divided mankind into parties, inflamed them with mutual animosity, and rendered them much more disposed to vex and oppress each other than to cooperate for their common good.

This is a harsh indictment, and it was shared by Alexander Hamilton, Thomas Jefferson, and George Washington. A decade later, in his Farewell Address, Washington would speak of "baneful effects of the spirit of party"—a spirit tending "to distract the public councils and enfeeble the public administration." The prevailing assumptions were that a series of goals called the "common good" did indeed exist; that these goals and the means to achieving them would be known to the men who held public office; and that the stridently voiced claims of the self-interested could only confuse the public and debilitate the administration. There was, furthermore, the fear that there might grow up a huge "have-not" faction composed of those with little or no wealth or property. There were anxieties lest the emergence

LOOK ON THIS PICTURE,   AND ON THIS.

An early anti-Jefferson cartoon shows that personalities have always dominated American politics—even, as here, before the growth of parties.

of such a "faction" endanger not only the rights of property but other liberties and minority rights as well. If politics could not be left to the cool deliberations of gentlemen, at least governmental forms could be so engineered that a "party" of debtors could not easily gain control.

THE RULING CLASS

American politics, between the close of the War for Independence and the ratification of the Constitution, had been chiefly state politics. And within the thirteen states the reins of government had been in the hands of relatively small circles of individuals. To be sure, the franchise was gradually being extended by reducing the property qualifications for voting. No less important, a democratic atmosphere was growing, and the conviction was becoming widespread that simple men of little means had the right to participate in the political process. Nevertheless, throughout the eighteenth century citizens and voters had had the habit of placing power in the hands of the wellborn and the well-to-do. To be sure, there were occasional class frictions. The best-known example was Shays' Rebellion, when the debt-ridden farmers of Western Massachusetts rose against a state government dominated by the Boston financial and commercial interests. But generally speaking, the Framers were confident that ordinary citizens would vote for their social superiors. Hamilton, also writing in *The Federalist*, No. 38, predicted that "mechanics and manufacturers"—that is, skilled and unskilled workers—would have the good sense and indeed the humility to elect businessmen to public office rather than seek to elevate people from their own station in life:

> Mechanics and manufacturers will always be inclined, with few exceptions, to give their votes to merchants in preference to persons of their own professions or trades. . . . They are sensible that their habits in life have not been such as to give them those acquired endowments, without which in a deliberative assembly, the greatest natural abilities are for the most part useless.

The habit of deference on the part of the man in the street was counted upon to remove factional considerations from elections in particular and from politics in general.

Section 1 of Article II of the new Constitution illustrated the presumption that parties would not figure in selecting the President and Vice-President. An Electoral College was charged with filling these offices, and it was assumed that the balloting would be for individuals rather than for the standard-bearers of one or another party. Thus the man receiving a majority of the electoral votes was to be President and the runner-up would join his administration as Vice-President. Quite clearly the Framers did not contemplate the eventuality that the major contestants for the Presidency would be partisan opponents, for they provided that *both* front-runners would have a place in the government. The first election, it so happened, satisfied their expectations. Each member of the Electoral College had two votes, and the 138 ballots were cast as follows: 69 for George Washington, 34 for John Adams, and 35 distributed among ten other candidates. Washington and Adams had not run on a "ticket," and it is plain that no more than half of the electors cast a Washington-Adams pair of votes. Moreover, the fact that there was a total field of twelve contenders showed that there was no conscious attempt to narrow down the contest along partisan or any other lines.

Washington's Administration—its policies, its strategy, and its general tenor—was more than anything else the handiwork of Alexander Hamilton. The brilliant young Secretary of the Treasury was possessed of a vision of the great country that the new seaboard nation might become. He was a warm admirer of Great Britain, and he hoped that the American government would emulate the aristocratic style of politics then prevailing at Westminster. At the same time he realized that the United States would have to establish itself on a sound financial footing to win the confidence of investors both at home and abroad. For only with infusions of capital would commerce and industry grow, thus strengthening the entire society. Government, Hamilton was convinced, had to be both centralized in structure and energetic in practice if all of these ends were to be accomplished. His appeal, quite understandably, was not to the general public but rather to the constituency consisting of those who had done well financially or who expected to do so.

Hamilton's program and proposals are of course familiar: the federal government's assuming responsibility for the debts of the states; the establishment of the Bank of the United States; the Report on Manufactures; the inauguration of protective tariffs and excise taxes. In addition he established a position as a leader of Congress, constantly in touch with that branch and always available to help pilot through his measures. Far from being bound to his desk, he found time to accompany federal troops as they marched into Western Pennsylvania to put down the local farmers who refused to pay taxes on the whisky they distilled. Amid all this activity he was also weaving together a coalition of political supporters. Not yet a party, the Federalists were a network of notables up and down the Atlantic seaboard. Hamilton met and corresponded with merchants and planters, Congregational ministers and former army officers, financial speculators and shipbuilders. He helped into being newspapers in Boston, New York, and Philadelphia that would echo and explain the policies he was advancing. To ensure continuing support for his program, Hamilton was forced to create organizational links between government and a wider public. Hamilton was no democrat, but he acknowledged that Americans had at least to be persuaded of the correctness of their government's politics. The Federalist network was essentially the prototype of a national political party, although Hamilton did not at the time realize this. The Federalists did not organize effectively at the local level (the cause of their eventual undoing), but they were prepared, at least, to make an appeal for votes and support.

There was, during Washington's Administration, no "loyal opposition" to the group of men who held power. Thomas Jefferson was in the Cabinet as Secretary of State until 1793, although by 1791 he was growing restive over the tendencies toward centralization that Hamilton was encouraging. James Madison, the acknowledged "Father of the Constitution," was in the Congress and was willing for a time to go along with policies such as federal assumption of the states' debts. But while Madison had coauthored the *Federalist* with Hamilton, he was less strongly committed to the principle of an energetic executive branch and not at all enamored of the vision of an industrial America entertained by his one-time colleague. Thus he found himself, by stages, in the position of leading a Congressional "opposition" to the Administration. Legislators from New York and Pennsylvania joined with colleagues from North Carolina and Virginia to oppose both Hamilton and his programs. Madison and his fellow Virginians led the way, causing one Federalist to complain: "Virginia moves in a solid column, and the discipline of party is as severe as the Prussian. Deserters are not spared. Madison is become a desperate party leader."

THE RISE OF OPPOSITION

An anti-Federalist "party"? It was, at this time, really little more than a Congressional faction. However, opposition sentiment ranged at least from New York to North Carolina, and it was clear that antipathy to the Hamiltonian direction was a common ground on which many citizens could unite. In 1793 and 1794 almost three dozen "Democratic Societies" or "Republican Societies" came into being throughout the Union. There were ten in Pennsylvania, seventeen throughout the South, and others scattered in most of the remaining states. The Societies were not coordinated into a single national party, and most had very short histories. However, Republicans eventually went much further in organizing a party-in-the-electorate than had the Federalists. More important, they educated the public to the notion that opposition could take place within the framework of the Constitution. There are good reasons for believing that the tentative way in which opposition feeling began to grow was itself of importance:

> It was perhaps fortunate as well as inevitable that the Federalists, with their emphasis on stability and consolidation, came first on the scene and held power first; that the Republicans appeared later and were slower to gain the strength that made them contenders for public power; and that both formations still reached only limited numbers of voters, instead of achieving immediately the full mobilization of popular masses in party competition. If the new polity had begun its political life with two full-blown parties, both stirring broad mass action in their behalf, the frictions of party combat might have proved unmanageable.[2]

The Republicans did not elect their first President, Thomas Jefferson, until 1800. In 1796 John Adams, a strong Federalist, was chosen to succeed Washington. Yet in many ways the 1796 contest was a Republican victory and the first party victory, for that election coalesced anti-Administration opinion up and down the country and expressed opposition sentiment in the form of electoral support of an agreed-upon candidate. Indeed it is organized and coordinated agreement of citizens to enter and back a candidate which turns a vague movement into a coherent party.

Working from their Philadelphia headquarters, Republicans spread out their lines of communication to every state and to numberless communities. Most important, perhaps, men who were serving as legislators and local officeholders began to think of themselves as, and to act as, party politicians. Their loyalty was increasingly to a national organization made up of men who thought much as they did and to a national leader—Thomas Jefferson. The Republican party, moreover, had a broad base and enlisted into its ranks a large troop of ordinary citizens in contrast to the Federalists, whose leaders worked to rally popular support but were at the same time loath to allow a great deal of lower-level participation in the making of party policies.

The election of 1796 became a contest between Federalists and Republicans, not simply a choice between Adams and Jefferson. The two candidates did not actually campaign themselves; instead they allowed their *parties* to work on their behalf. In half of the states members of the Electoral College were already being chosen by popular vote, and many of the candidates for those seats announced beforehand that they were "Adams men" or "Jefferson men." What emerged, as much by accident as by design, were two "tickets." Each elector had two votes to cast, and a substantial proportion of them had decided to support a pair of candidates on party lines

---

[2] William N. Chambers, *Political Parties in a New Nation: The American Experience, 1776–1809* (New York, 1963), p. 66.

with the hope that one would be elected President and the other Vice-President. Thus there was a Federalist Adams-Pinckney ticket and a Jefferson-Burr ticket. What happened of course was that a Federalist President was chosen along with a Republican Vice-President:

John Adams (Federalist)	71
Thomas Jefferson (Republican)	68
Thomas Pinckney (Federalist)	59
Aaron Burr (Republican)	30
Others	48

Jefferson's near-miss marked the beginning of the end of the Federalist era. The "party of notables" had assumed that its aristocratic leaders would be able to maintain the unquestioning support of the less educated and less affluent elements of the community. Had not Hamilton said that the common people are "sensible that their habits in life have not been such as to give them those acquired endowments" that the political life requires? The Republican appeal, on the other hand, was a direct one to the public, and it spoke the language of democracy in unabashed terms. The result was that the Federalists held their own in New England, New York, and New Jersey, but they lost to Jeffersonian electors in Pennsylvania and throughout the South. To be sure, partisan patterns had yet to suffuse every part of the country. Aaron Burr was Jefferson's "running mate" only in selected states, as his low vote testified, and there continued to be scattered support for such local favorites as John Jay, Samuel Adams, and George Clinton. But compared with the previous two ballotings, the election of 1796 was a party contest.

THE FEDERALIST REACTION

The close call that Adams experienced was not without its effects on his party. The United States had been caught up in the struggle between Britain and France beyond the Atlantic, and the country continued divided in its sympathies for one or the other of the European powers. Madison spoke of the Federalists as "the British party," while Hamilton wondered aloud about the "Gallic faction" that to his eyes dominated the Republicans. But the Federalists had the power, in the Congress as well as in the Presidency, and they were becoming increasingly concerned over the legitimacy of the opposition they had been encountering in the country. Exactly how loyal were their Republican challengers? Were not some of their opponents working to subvert the legality and security of the nation itself? It is one thing to vie for office in a free and fair election; it is another to advance views and plan measures that will destroy the system itself. Under pressure the Federalists began to view partisan opposition as internal subversion.

The result was the Alien and Sedition Acts of 1798. They were of course aimed at the more extreme or exposed Republicans, the "determined and rancorous Jacobins," as one Federalist called them. There were about twenty sedition prosecutions, principally directed against Republican newspaper editors. When a Vermont journal published a letter suggesting that Congress incarcerate President Adams in a lunatic asylum, the editor was given a fine of $1,000 under the new statutes and then imprisoned. There were similar actions against the opposition press in New London, Boston, New York, and Richmond. The key question was how the general public would react to these repressive acts. If the man in the street had looked upon the victims as a handful of subversives who clearly deserved a spell in jail, then the Federalist legislation would have been accepted as a necessary means for safeguarding the nation in time of peril, and the development of a two-party system would have stopped in its tracks. Had this been public opinion, then the limits of permissible opposition would have been severely circumscribed; the party in power would have been able to dictate to its challengers just what they could and could not say and do. Carried further, the party in office might even ban the opposition as presenting a clear and present threat to the security of the nation—the "guided democracy" which is seen in some new nations today.

THE LEGITIMACY OF OPPOSITION

Public reaction was, however, in a different direction. More than a few people cried out against the Alien and Sedition prosecutions. Not all, of course, did so on grounds of constitutional principle or out of compassion for convicted journalists. The restrictions that the laws placed on aliens roused many recent immigrants, no small number of whom were clustered in Federalist strongholds in the Northern cities. There was also criticism of new taxes that the government had levied to make defense preparations for a possible war with France. And the most respected of Republican leaders, Jefferson and Madison, prepared resolutions which were passed by the Kentucky and Virginia legislatures condemning the laws as unwarranted uses of national authority. All this activity had its effect, and it was clear that the Federalists' zeal to legislate loyalty was not commanding unanimous agreement in the country. For example, John Marshall, who was elected as a Federalist Congressman in 1798, pledged to support repeal of the acts. That mid-term election did not produce a Republican sweep, and the Congressional lineup was much as it had been before, but change was taking place.

The emerging party system had weathered a storm and was now on a regular course. The system grew in the context of an expanding suffrage where electoral appeals had to be made to the mass of the people. The Federalist organization, limited to the well-to-do and the wellborn, was increasingly vulnerable. In 1800 Adams lost to Jefferson by 65 electoral votes to 73, and four years later, when Jefferson ran for reelection, his Federalist opponent received only 14 votes out of the 176 that were cast.

THE TWELFTH AMENDMENT

The fact that Jefferson and Burr had each received 73 votes in the year 1800—that is, that each had been supported on the two ballots of the 73 Republican electors—meant of course that both were equally eligible for the Presidency. When the decision went to the House of Representatives, Burr refused to announce that he was interested only in the office of Vice-President. As it happened, Hamilton's influence in Congress was the decisive factor, and although he thought Jefferson "a contemptible hypocrite" he preferred the Virginian to Burr. It was this patronizing nod from Hamilton that gave Jefferson the Presidency.

Obviously constitutional reform was needed to cope with this partisan process of Presidential selection. Thus in 1803 Jefferson asked the Congress to initiate an amendment requiring that members of the Electoral College "name in their ballots the person voted for as President, and in distinct ballots the person voted for as Vice-President." The amendment was sent to the states and ratified in time for the 1804 election. Henceforward each party would have to pick its two-man slate before the campaign, with the Vice-Presidential candidate knowing in advance that he was definitely the second man on the ticket. Democracy was also having its effect within the parties themselves, most particularly amid the Republican ranks. Statewide committees were set up to coordinate local activities, and the career of full-time politician (as opposed to gentleman politician) was taking form. One Massachusetts activist set down his myriad duties as follows:

> To communicate with the Central Committee of the State, and town or subcommittees—to watch over the Republican interest both in state and national governments especially as to elections and appointments—convey intelligence—confute false rumors—confirm the wavering in right principles—prevent delusion of weak brethren—and fight that most formidable enemy of civilized man, political ignorance. . . .[3]

And the country itself had come to accept the idea of a two-party system. If originally Hamilton, Madison, and Jefferson had worried about the damaging consequences of factional strife, by the turn of the century the last two were committed to the notion of elections along partisan lines. The need for an Electoral College majority had helped to limit the contending parties to two, as had the single-member districts. There was also the simple need for an "out" party—a need first filled by the Republicans—to challenge the "in" party. Fortunately American society at the time was relatively homogeneous, and hence the differences between the two camps were not glaring, despite the fears and suspicions of some of the Federalists to the contrary. If Republican farmers tended to resent the wealth and power concentrated in the cities, it must be remembered that these yeomen were themselves landowners and had an interest in preserving private property. Jefferson, in a letter written in 1798, expressed the growing feeling about the new institution of party and its place in political life:

> In every free and deliberating society there must, from the nature of man, be opposite parties and violent dissensions and discords; and one of these must for the most part prevail over the other for a longer or shorter time. Perhaps this party division is necessary to induce each to watch and relate to the people the proceedings of the other.[4]

THE JEFFERSONIAN PARTY

The "Virginian Dynasty"—Jefferson himself, then James Madison, and ultimately James Monroe—was to hold the White House for a total of six

---

[3] Quoted in *ibid.*, p. 165.
[4] Quoted in *ibid.*, p. 149.

terms or for almost a quarter of a century. In only one of the elections after 1800 did the Federalists give the Republicans more than token opposition. Thus if one of the functions of a two-party system is for the "out" party to criticize policies and procedures of the "in" party, the fact is that Federalist criticism less and less moved the public to repudiate the succession of Republican administrations. The aristocratic party could not gear itself to the new electorate and soon collapsed into cliques of bitter men. The Republicans, in contrast, had welded a national organization composed of state parties that were willing to stand together in support of a common Presidential candidate. It is worth pondering the meaning of this accomplishment. The consequence was that urban artisans in New York and slaveholders in Virginia were willing to forget their economic and social differences and to join in a common front in the arena of national politics. Such a national party was a product of leadership, organization, and communication; and it was sustained by a willingness at the top to engage in continual consultation and compromise. The Jeffersonian party was, in a sense, the model for all that followed.

Yet it might be said that Jefferson was *too* successful. The long years without serious challenge saw strains develop within Republican ranks. Prior to 1796 there had been factions instead of parties; after Jefferson stepped down in 1809 there began to emerge *intraparty* factions. Congressional elections brought to Washington new and younger Republicans who were increasingly at odds with Republican Presidents. These lawmakers included such commanding personalities as Henry Clay and John C. Calhoun. The War of 1812, the second Bank of the United States, tariffs, and proposed internal improvements (federal turnpikes and rivers and harbors projects) all saw a variety of Republican defections and combinations as the rolls were called. There developed a "Congressional party" and the "Presidential party" within the Republican ranks. There grew up the notion that Congressmen of a particular party were not necessarily obliged to follow the leadership of their President. This was a departure from the executive-legislative liaison that both Hamilton and Jefferson had carefully established, and since Madison's time tensions between the two major branches—even if controlled by the same party—have been a common feature of American government. This was probably inevitable. By the early 1820s the country's population had reached 10 million, more than double what it had been at the turn of the century. Any party attempting to embrace a vast majority of voters within such a burgeoning and differentiated nation would inevitably have difficulty holding the giant coalition together. Sheer size—the price of success—made for strain and often for stalemate. The 1824 election brought matters to a head. For two terms James Monroe had seemed the virtually unopposed and unanimous choice of the entire electorate. Yet beneath this smooth surface the Republican party had splintered into a congeries of warring factions.

The party was unable to agree on a single candidate for President, and thus no less than four Republicans were found running for that office in 1824. John Quincy Adams, Andrew Jackson, William H. Crawford, and Henry Clay—all members of the same party—presented themselves to the voters. In this election, furthermore, eighteen of the twenty-four states provided that electors were to be selected by popular vote, and hence the total popular vote that each candidate received was a matter of public record. This was a matter of grave consequence as the results were:

	Popular votes	Electoral votes
Andrew Jackson	153,544	99
John Quincy Adams	108,740	84
William H. Crawford	46,618	41
Henry Clay	47,136	37
	356,038	261

The problem, of course, was that none of the candidates received the required Electoral College majority and the choice had therefore to be made by the House of Representatives. But it was, of course, the old House, the one that had been elected two years previously, and after a good deal of maneuvering it selected Adams. To be sure, Jackson had not secured a popular majority. However, the choice of Adams was clearly made with little regard for the tide of public sentiment. Jackson's day, nevertheless, was not long in coming, and it marked a new stage in the development of party politics.

THE EXPANDING ELECTORATE

In state after state throughout the 1820s constitutional conventions had met to revise the state constitutions. The purpose of these sessions, more than anything else, was to abolish property qualifications for voting and to extend the suffrage to virtually everyone who was male, white, and adult. The work of the conventions proceeded apace largely because there was little opposition to the new egalitarian sentiment. The Federalist party had disintegrated by 1820, and there were few spokesmen for the old aristocratic view. To be sure, such voices occasionally found their way into the record. Chancellor James Kent warned the 1821 convention in New York that it stood "on the very edge of the precipice." Great cities were coming into being and with them, so it was said, a propertyless rabble. This populace, it was feared, would soon begin "to covet and to share the plunder of the rich." A monolithic majority would "tyrannize over the minority." Indeed, it would be the tendency of the "indolent and profligate to cast the whole burdens of society upon the industrious and the virtuous."

Such sentiments, heard at the Philadelphia Convention of 1787, had led to the indirect election of the President and the Senate, and the further presumption that voting for the House of Representatives would be limited by state legislation. All this was undone at the state conventions of the 1820s. Chancellor Kent proposed in New York that $250 in freehold property be required of voters for the state senate. He was voted down by a 5-to-1 margin on even that limited hedge against popular democracy. The story was much the same in the other states. In this altered political context the old Republican party shattered, and two new parties began to develop out of the pieces, each one attempting, more or less, to heed the Jeffersonian lessons of nationwide organization at the local level. The party which formed around Jackson was generally states' rights in orientation, while that which formed around Adams and Clay looked with favor on internal improvements and government action to expand the economy.

As has been indicated, in 1824 over a third of a million Americans went to the polls. Four years later the turnout was 1,155,350. Part of this rise is to be accounted for by the fact that the population increased by about 10 percent during the four-year interval, and partly it was the result of four more states joining the group that chose electors by popular vote. Even so, the chief cause of the multiplied size of the electorate lay in the abolition of property qualifications for voting. With Jackson running on

TABLE 5–1 / Percentage of Popular Vote of Elected Presidential Candidates

	Year	Candidate and party	Percentage of popular vote
1	1964	Lyndon B. Johnson (D)	61.0
2	1936	Franklin D. Roosevelt (D)	60.8
3	1920	Warren G. Harding (R)	60.4
4	1928	Herbert C. Hoover (R)	58.2
5	1956	Dwight D. Eisenhower (R)	57.6
6	1932	Franklin D. Roosevelt (D)	57.4
7	1904	Theodore Roosevelt (R)	57.4
8	1828	Andrew Jackson (D)	56.0
9	1872	Ulysses S. Grant (R)	55.6
10	1952	Dwight D. Eisenhower (R)	55.1
11	1864	Abraham Lincoln (R)	55.0
12	1832	Andrew Jackson (D)	55.0
13	1940	Franklin D. Roosevelt (D)	54.8
14	1924	Calvin Coolidge (R)	54.0
15	1944	Franklin D. Roosevelt (D)	53.5
16	1840	William Henry Harrison (Whig)	53.1
17	1868	Ulysses S. Grant (R)	52.7
18	1900	William McKinley (R)	51.7
19	1908	William Howard Taft (R)	51.6
20	1896	William McKinley (R)	51.1
21	1836	Martin Van Buren (D)	50.9
22	1852	Franklin Pierce (D)	50.9
23	1960	John F. Kennedy (D)	49.9
24	1844	James K. Polk (D)	49.6
25	1948	Harry S. Truman (D)	49.5
26	1916	Woodrow Wilson (D)	49.4
27	1880	James A. Garfield (R)	48.5
28	1884	Grover Cleveland (D)	48.5
29	1876	Rutherford B. Hayes (R)	48.0
30	1888	Benjamin Harrison (R)	47.9
31	1848	Zachary Taylor (Whig)	47.4
32	1892	Grover Cleveland (D)	46.1
33	1856	James Buchanan (D)	45.3
34	1912	Woodrow Wilson (D)	41.9
35	1860	Abraham Lincoln (R)	39.8

what would henceforward be known as the "Democratic" ticket and with John Quincy Adams running for reelection as a "National Republican," the results were as follows:

	Popular votes	Electoral votes
Andrew Jackson	647,286	178
John Quincy Adams	508,064	83
	1,155,350	261

Quite plainly the newly enfranchised voters supported both candidates, since Jackson received no more than 56 percent of the popular vote. While the period of his Presidency and the years immediately following is often called "the Age of Jackson," neither he nor any of his successors in the nineteenth century ever surpassed that percentage of the vote. What was beginning to emerge at that early juncture in the country's political history was a tendency toward a *fairly even* partisan balance within the electorate. In no Presidential election from 1828 to 1964 did the winner ever secure more than 62 percent of the popular vote, and only three of the thirty-five victors secured more than 60 percent of it. Indeed, in over a third of the elections the winner came to occupy the White House with only a plurality.

Whatever reasons there may be for fearing a "tyranny of the majority," it would appear that landslides are the exception rather than the rule even in Presidential contests. This is worth emphasizing because in subsequent "ages" and "eras" analysis of the voting figures reveals that what were often thought of as nationwide trends were actually supported by slender majorities at the polls.

WHO WERE THE JACKSONIANS?

Most history textbooks treat the Jacksonian period in terms of class conflict, suggesting that the political struggle expressed deep-seated economic tensions. There is a tendency to stress the newly enfranchised poor rising against the propertied class, which supported the National Republicans, or the Whigs, as that party came to call itself. However, too much emphasis on radical groups like the city-based Locofocos and the rural Barnburners can be misleading: an exaggeration of the amount of "left-wing," have-not sentiment at the time. Too much attention may also be given to the utterances of the Jacksonians themselves. Martin Van Buren, Jackson's successor in the White House and the leader of his forces in New York, saw the political division as between "those who live by the sweat of their brow and those who live by their wits." He placed the farmers and workers in the Jacksonian camp; he saw the opposing Whig side as composed of the "commercial, manufacturing, and trading classes," the "money power," and those in "possession of special and, in some cases, of exclusive privileges." But this lineup was far too neat to fit reality.

Recent research on voting during the Jacksonian period has done much to discredit previously held stereotypes of that era. Perhaps the most searching analysis has been of politics in New York, a state that was still largely agricultural and in many ways representative of the nation as a whole. In the elections between 1828 and 1852, the Democrats and Whigs were very

A Political Game Of Brag Or The Best Hand Out Of Four.

This 1831 anti-Democratic cartoon shows a noble Henry Clay (left), the National Republican (Whig) candidate; Vice-President Calhoun, with his back turned; William Wirt, candidate of the Anti-Masons (the first organized third party); and President Jackson, holding the cards of Intrigue, Corruption, and Imbecility. Jackson was reelected in 1832.

evenly matched in New York. And the issues in these elections—if they can be called "issues" at all—had very little to do with democracy versus aristocracy or the masses versus the classes. There is no evidence, first of all, that the poor supported the Jacksonian candidates and that the voters who were better off rallied around the Whigs. Many wealthy New York bankers, for example, voted for Jackson because he opposed the Bank of the United States and the concentration of financial power in Philadelphia. Nor was there a rural-urban split. Both parties secured electoral support in both the cities and the countryside. In addition to this, many of the so-called "issues"—such as the annexation of Texas—had little or no impact on voting decisions.

The reasons why New York voters supported the Democrats or the Whigs were somewhat more subtle. The highest concentration of Jacksonian support, for example, was found in a county with a large proportion of Dutch farmers. They were resentful of what they felt to be Yankee domination of the state and their own status as second-class citizens. When a New York turnpike was being constructed earlier in the century, an advertisement for workers explicitly stated, "No Dutchman need apply unless he is pretty well Yankeyfied." There was, furthermore, a strong traditionalist strain in the Jacksonian coalition. The Whigs, especially if Henry Clay was thought of as their leader, were seen as a party of innovation. Clay's "American System," with its emphasis on internal improvements and encouragement of a virtual revolution in the transportation facilities of the nation, threatened the traditional structure of society. Hence those who liked things as they were, who were fearful of change and innovation, looked to Jackson to restore the institutions and climate of former times.

One of the chief characteristics of American political parties is that various groups will simultaneously support the same candidate for quite different reasons. This has been a pronounced trait of the Democrats, and it had its origins in the Jacksonian period. Thus, along with the Dutch farmers, recent Irish immigrants to the United States were mobilized into the Democratic party, where they were able to give vent to their hostility toward anything British—and targets were easily found among the Whigs. This burst of ethnic antipathy was returned in kind. Commenting on one election, a Whig newspaper complained: "Everything in the shape of an Irishman was drummed to the polls and their votes made to pass . . . It was emphatically an Irish triumph." But the urban Democratic machine, welcoming new arrivals as they got off the boat, was already becoming well entrenched. Attempts to restrict the franchise were of no avail, and one of the chief contributions of the Jacksonian party was to help in assimilating immigrants by encouraging their political participation.

In New York, at least, the Democratic-Whig struggle was also marked by opposing positions on the question of racial equality. In 1846 there was a referendum on whether free Negroes should be given the vote. The ballot was then exclusively in the hands of white citizens, and they were called upon to decide whether nonwhites could join them at the polls. It was a clear party division, with the Whigs calling for passage of the referendum, and in Rockland County, strong Jackson territory, the vote was 96.4 percent against allowing Negroes to vote. The result was not far different in New York City, where the Irish were concerned. The New York *Tribune* lamented: "It was mournful to see hundreds who have not been six years in the country earnestly and abusively clamorous for the disenfranchisement of men whose fathers' fathers were born here, and many of them shed their blood for the defense of our liberties in the war of the Revolution." Quite plainly the number of Negroes was extremely small, but their having the vote was seen as a threatening symbol by many if not most of the Jacksonian adherents. The issue was not an economic one but had rather to do with social status and psychological security. Leading New York Whigs (of British stock) were sufficiently well established in the community to feel no fears over the granting of equal voting rights to Negroes. The forces at work in the referendum of 1846 have been recurrent in American party politics, and they deserve analysis no less than do the more obvious economic factors.

THE WHIG OPPOSITION

It is almost impossible to find a common denominator for the Whigs, so heterogeneous were the recruits who filled their ranks. There were the aristocratic elements of the Northeast who still adhered to the Federalist mood, and there were rising capitalists who favored tariffs and government protection. There were antislavery forces of New England, and there were Southern Whigs who owned the great cotton and sugar plantations. There were the Westerners who followed Henry Clay and wanted more roads, and there were the Anti-Masons who believed that a "secret society" was plotting to take over the nation. The Whig coalition was able to win the Presidency in 1840 and 1848, but on both occasions the men they managed to elect died in office. Despite the high incidence of propertied elements in Whig ranks, the party was both willing and able to make a broad-based appeal for votes. In the 1840 election in particular, the depression and unemployment of that year were blamed on the Democratic Administration. A frank attempt was made to get voters to cross party lines. "We have also many recruits in our ranks from the pressure of the times," William Henry Harrison said. "Most of them however will not be Whigs, but will vote for me . . . on the same grounds as they supported General Jackson." The flamboyant "Tippecanoe and Tyler too" campaign of 1840 was a nationwide drive, heavily laced with hard liquor and hearty music. Yet, once elected, the Whig Presidents found it impossible to satisfy the diverse interests that had placed them in office. By 1850 their Southern wing (the great planters) was going over to the Democrats, where it was to stay, and 1852 was the last election the party contested.

Despite the brevity of their career the Whigs made a vital contribution to the American party system. They were, for all their heterogeneity, a national party, and their Presidential candidates put up strong fights in every state of the union. At one time or another between 1828 and 1852 the Whigs won a majority of the votes in such diverse states as Louisiana and Michigan, Vermont and Indiana, Ohio and Florida, New Jersey and Kentucky. In all, twenty-one of the thirty states went Whig at least once during a Presidential year. "The great service of the Whig coalition in the development of the American political system was its contribution to the firm establishment of the two-party system," [5] one commentator has stated. The party may have "made a virtue of opposition for opposition's sake," but there is reason to believe that such a stance was not only necessary at the time but even desirable, considering the coalition character of the party and the impossibility of reaching an agreement on a program, let alone a doctrine.

THE FULLY DEVELOPED COALITION PATTERN

The pragmatic character of both the Whig and the Democratic parties was to become the pattern of future American politics. The Federalists and the Republicans (while never really ideological parties in the European sense) had disagreed on rather fundamental principles concerning the nature of the federal system. The division between Hamiltonians and Jeffersonians may not have been as sharp as some commentators have made it out to be, but it was nevertheless greater than that dividing any subsequent parties. For this reason party battles from the Jacksonian period on have been unstimulating to ears accustomed to European political dialogue. Alexis de Tocqueville, visiting America during Jackson's first Administration, reacted in this way:

---

[5] Wilfred E. Binkley, *American Political Parties* (New York, 1958).

America has had great parties, but has them no longer; and if her happiness is thereby considerably increased, her morality has suffered . . . . Great political parties, then, are not to be met within the United States at the present time . . . , and public opinion is divided into a thousand minute shades of differences upon questions of detail.

There is no religious animosity, because all religion is respected and no sect is predominant. There is no jealousy of rank, because the people are everything and none can contest their authority. Lastly, there is no public misery to serve as a means of agitation because the physical position of the country opens so wide a field to industry that man only needs to be let alone to accomplish prodigies. . . .

To a stranger all the domestic controversies of the Americans at first appear to be incomprehensible or puerile, and he is at a loss whether to pity a people who take such arrant trifles in good earnest or to envy that happiness which enables a community to discuss them.[6]

The Jacksonian experience showed that two national parties need not divide along religious, class, or economic lines. Both parties could find strength in all sections of the country, with not a little shifting back and forth from camp to camp on the part of voters. In such a political setting there would be little or no ideological conflict, and it would often appear that "issues" almost had to be invented in order to strike up interest in an election. Yet, as De Tocqueville noted, the absence of sharp party divisions was a sign that the society itself had no crucial problems that had to be settled by electoral means. The debates during campaign time might not be at an elevated level, but that intellectual loss might well be compensated for by the fact that the society itself was stable and agreed on the basic principles governing its way of life.

The vote, a small but important measure of power bestowed on each citizen, was coming to reflect a variety of motives. In the election of 1852, for example, the Whigs favored protective tariffs, and the Democrats opposed them. These, at least, were the official positions among the higher reaches of the party leadership and in Congressional circles. However, there is little reason to believe that discussions over the merits of issues such as the tariff were common among rank-and-file voters. Citizens were beginning to support one party or the other out of habit, custom, and prejudice; and the "reasons" they gave for their partisan preferences expressed deep-seated sentiments that transcended issues of the day. Thus in 1852 a Whig editor pointed out that in terms of sheer logic factory workers ought to have voted for Winfield Scott, for he and his fellow Whigs were committed to protecting domestic manufactures from foreign competition. Yet in a typical workshop, Horace Greeley sadly acknowledged, the votes were going for the Jacksonians:

> The very shop wherein fifteen out of every twenty workmen would be with us on the tariff issue fairly made and fully considered will often give a majority against us in the absence of such discussion.
>
> Jones hates the Whigs because Esq. Simpson is a leading Whig, and feels too big to speak to common people.

---

[6] Alexis de Tocqueville, *Democracy in America*, Phillips Bradley, ed. (New York, 1945), Vol. I, pp. 182–85.

Marks has been trained to believe that the Whigs were Tories in the Revolution and starved his father in the Jersey prisonship. So he is bound to hit them again at each election.

Smithers is for a Tariff himself, but his father before him was a Democrat, and he isn't going to turn his coat.

Smolker don't object to anything his Whig shopmates propose. But he is a foreigner and thinks the Whigs hate foreigners, so he feels bound to go against them.

Pitkin is a heretic in religion, and most of the leading Whigs he knows are Orthodox. And he can't stand Orthodoxy anyhow you fix it.

And so, for one or another of a hundred reasons, equally frivolous or irrelevant, voters are piled up against us, not for anything we as a party affirm or propose, but because of considerations . . . foreign from the real issues.[7]

This five-man "sample" of over a century ago shows how large a role negative thinking plays in voting behavior. Greeley's hypothetical Jones, Smolker, and Pitkin opposed the Whigs because they reacted strongly against what they felt to be the snobbishness or the religious prejudices of leading Whigs they had encountered. Marks also voted against the Whigs, not because of what they were in 1852 but because of their alleged record back in 1776—three quarters of a century before. And Smithers' filial loyalty was apparently paramount when it came time to cast his ballot. What was happening, of course, was that each of these men was projecting his personal history and his social sensibilities upon the major parties. That these men voted more against the Whigs than for the Democrats suggests that an important function of voting is to serve as an outlet for grievances that lie buried beneath the surface.

THE PRESIDENTIAL NOMINATING PROCESS— CAUCUSES AND CONVENTIONS

From 1800 to 1820 the Congressional caucus had been the principal mechanism for nominating Presidential candidates. This was especially the case with the Republican party, whose Senators and Representatives met in private sessions to decide on Jefferson, Madison, and Monroe at successive intervals. The Congressional caucus was, in effect, the party's executive committee. The question was how long the Congressional party would be able to represent and accommodate all of the factions and viewpoints within the Republican ranks. The system finally failed in 1824. A caucus did meet that year, and it nominated William Crawford of Georgia. However, as was noted earlier, other non-Congressional groups of "Republicans" met elsewhere and put up three additional candidates. As no one of them could secure an Electoral College majority the choice had to be made by the House of Representatives—which picked John Quincy Adams even though he had received fewer popular votes than had Andrew Jackson.

Having been defeated in Congress twice in a single year, the Jacksonians bent every effort to sever Congress from the nominating process. Jackson's

---

[7] Quoted in Lee Benson, *The Concept of Jacksonian Democracy* (New York, 1964), p. 280.

name was put up for the 1828 contest by the Tennessee legislature, as a sort of stopgap measure. And at the time Martin Van Buren, Jackson's New York ally, proposed that henceforward the Presidential candidate be selected by a national nominating convention. Such a convention did take place for the first time in 1831, setting a precedent that was watched at the time and emulated in the future. This first convention was actually organized by the Anti-Masonic party, a splinter group consisting chiefly of New York and Massachusetts farmers who were opposed to Jackson. Their public nominating session, attended by more than 100 delegates, met in Baltimore to name candidates for the Presidency and Vice-Presidency—who, ultimately, received less than 30,000 popular votes and only seven electoral votes in 1832. Yet this convention, fruitless as were its own efforts, had its impact on the more successful parties. For the Anti-Masons had taken the trouble to set up convention rules of procedure that were destined to last for more than a century in their major outlines. One such rule was that the party organizations within the various states would have the authority to pick their delegates by whatever means they saw fit. A second was that each delegation was to be proportionate in size to the state's electoral vote. In addition, a two-thirds majority within the convention was required to nominate a candidate.

The Democrats held their first convention in 1832, when Andrew Jackson was renominated by acclamation. Yet this national meeting was faced with the problem of selecting Jackson's running mate, the chief contenders being Van Buren and Calhoun. The Northerner was chosen over the Southerner by a margin of 208 to 75, the first successful application of the "two-thirds rule." The Democrats met again in 1835, and the Whigs convened for the first time on a national basis in 1839. For better or for worse, Congressional caucus nominations had passed into history. The doom of "King Caucus" was sealed because the Senators and Representatives of a party were too removed from the feelings of state party organizations when it came to selecting Presidential candidates. No less important, a successful nominee would have to carry a national appeal, attracting the votes not only of the party loyalists but of uncommitted citizens as well. Hence the chairman of an early Democratic convention remarked that "the democracy of the Union have been forced to look to a national convention as the best means of concentrating the popular will and giving it effect in the approaching election." The caucus was not a microcosm of the party at large.

THE GENESIS OF THE REPUBLICAN PARTY

By 1860 the party system had, for all practical purposes, taken the form it holds at the present time. Congress passed a law in 1845 decreeing that the first Tuesday following the first Monday of November was to be the national Election Day. Prior to 1845 each state had its own polling date, with the consequence that the results in some parts of the country would be known before others had voted. In 1848 the Democrats set up a national committee to make plans for and to speak on behalf of the party between conventions. This institution, having one member from each state, was copied by the Whigs four years later. In 1852, also, both parties drafted platforms—not so much to pledge action on specific policies as to rally their own adherents by adumbrating those general principles on which there was hopefully a consensus and "recognizing" each element of the party coalition with an appropriate plank. The deep divisions in each party on the issue of slavery were bridged by the 1852 platforms—a political exercise that has been the rule ever since.

The Whig party broke up after the election of 1852 because it could not, despite the elasticity of its platform, contain both its Southern and Northern wings. The issue of slavery's extension into the territories was simply too divisive. The Southern Whigs gravitated to the Democratic fold, and many Whigs in the North, joined by some dissident (free soil) Democrats, transferred their loyalty to the new Republican party, which was pledged to hold the line against the extension of the "peculiar institution." What is most important about the new Republicans is the speed with which they managed to establish themselves on the national political scene. They held their first organizing meeting in 1854, nominated Fremont as their first candidate in 1856, and elected Lincoln—albeit with only 39.8 percent of the vote— as their first President in 1860. The Republicans were not a "third party"; they came on the scene with the Whig organization in ruins and simply replaced that party in a political system which was by that time geared to the existence of two contending coalitions. There have been many changes in the coalitions over the past century, but the Democratic and Republican parties of today are the lineal descendents of the parties of 1860.

Continuity and Change: Democratic and Republican Coalitions, 1864–1964

In attempting to analyze and understand the evolution of party coalitions since the Civil War, some political scientists have developed a theory of "critical elections," a theory which identifies (in terms of Presidential elections) the years in which the composition of one or the other of the two party coalitions shifted in such a way as to produce a major realignment of the electorate, and a new majority in the country. This analysis seeks to explain these shifts in party predominance in terms of sociological, economic, and situational variables—that is, to show what developments in the American environment caused one coalition (or both) to break up and reform along new lines. If one examines closely the election results for the past century, taking care to compare results from specific geographic areas over several elections, three critical elections can be quickly identified: 1864, 1896, and 1928. Scholars who find the theory of critical elections useful do not contend that these are the only important elections or even the most important elections—simply that these were the years in which it became clear that a significant change was affecting the coalitions as they had operated up to that time. By many canons of historical consequence, 1932 is more important than 1928—yet it was in 1928, as we shall see, that realignment of the electorate, which was to make the Democratic victory of 1932 possible, first became apparent. In surveying the evolution of party coalitions up to the present time, we shall focus particularly on these critical years.

The Civil War had far less impact on the party system than it did on certain aspects of the nation's economy and social structure. Despite the secession of the South, George B. McClellan, the Democratic candidate, was able to make a good race against Lincoln in 1864. This close balance between the coalitions which emerged in 1864 was to persist down to 1896. While it is true that the Republicans held the White House from 1864 to 1884, no postwar Democratic candidate received less than 43 percent of the popular votes cast in those years. Indeed in the disputed Hayes-Tilden election of 1876, Tilden, the Democrat, received 250,000 more votes than Hayes, although the Republican was ultimately decreed to have carried the Electoral College. In 1884, and again in 1892, Grover Cleveland, the Democratic standard-bearer, was elected President.

The Republicans did have an "edge" during the 1870s and 1880s because the Democrats labored under the handicap of being associated with the defeated South. The Republicans not only enjoyed the advantage of running as saviors of the Union, but also had a record of accomplishment that cemented their electoral coalition:

> The inner strength of Republicanism did not rest on sentiment alone. Sentiment clothed bonds of substance. To the old soldiers—old Union soldiers—went pensions. To the manufacturers of the Northeast went tariffs. To the farmers of the Northwest went free land under the Homestead Act. To railroad promoters went land grants for the construction of railroads that tied together the West and the North—and assured that the flow of commerce would bypass the South. The synthesis of self-interest and glory formed a cohesive combination. The G.O.P. represented a wonderfully effective contrivance, not only for preserving the Union but for holding together East and West, magnate and factory worker, homesteader and banker, in the great enterprise of continental unification, development, and exploitation.[8]

Nonetheless, the Democrats were still a strong second party during this period. The election of 1896, however, upset this competitive situation by establishing a clear Republican national majority that survived (despite Wilson's victories) until 1932. The Democrats in 1892 had not only won the Presidency with Cleveland but had also gained control of both houses of Congress. This was an opportunity not simply to govern the nation but to build up the party's popularity among new groups throughout the country. Neither Cleveland nor the Congress, however, rose to the challenge. The President used troops to break the Pullman strike in 1894 and thus alienated a large portion of the urban working class. He also supported the gold standard, with the result that debt-ridden farmers in the West withdrew their support from him. In other particulars Cleveland seemed to side with the interests and attitudes of the Republican opposition. Even on the tariff question—traditionally an area where Democrats and Republicans parted company—he hedged, not taking a low tariff position. His negotiation of a gold-purchase loan with the House of Morgan caused many Democrats to wonder who was indeed presiding over the fortunes of the Republic. And, to cap it all, the 1893 depression caused unemployment and business failures for which the Democratic party was held accountable by many voters.

---

[8] V. O. Key, Jr., *Politics, Parties, and Pressure Groups,* 5th ed. (New York, 1964), p. 168.

An 1864 Republican cartoon depicting Lincoln as the giant Gulliver and his political opponents as Lilliputians.

The 1896 election was significant not simply because the Republicans turned the Democrats out of office—that had happened before. Its importance lay in the fact that the Republicans made deep inroads into social groups that had previously voted predominantly Democratic. The campaign of that year generated the deep emotions which can change individuals in their party identification. The Democratic convention nominated the young William Jennings Bryan after he had shattered the rafters with his famous "Cross of Gold" speech. It is the one time of which it can be truly said that the keynote speech stampeded the delegates into nominating the orator. Bryan was a Westerner, antagonistic to the "Eastern interests"; he was a simple man, deeply religious, and not at all an intellectual; but above all he was committed to the cause of "free silver" and mortally opposed to the gold standard. His nomination caused many conservative Democrats, including Cleveland himself, to desert the party. If Bryan was to win he would have to rally the nation's "have-nots" to his banner. And even before that he would have to convince them that they were in fact being exploited by Wall Street finance and its political minions.

Yet Bryan's approach to the electorate was a curious one. He was not a radical preaching thoroughgoing social and economic reform. The Democratic platform was by no means severely critical of the capitalist system, and it did not call for great increases in the regulatory powers of the federal government. Indeed, Bryan often affirmed his acceptance of existing arrangements. "Our campaign has not for its object the reconstruction of society," he declared in his acceptance speech. "Property is and will remain the

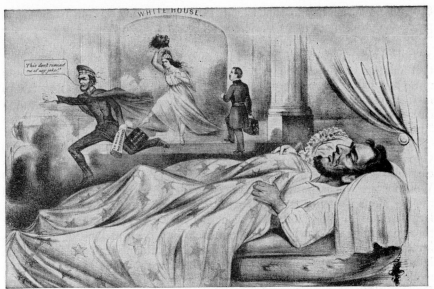

New-York Historical Society

"Coming Events Cast Their Shadows Before."

A pro-Democratic cartoon of 1864: Lincoln dreams of leaving the White House as McClellan, the Democratic candidate, enters.

stimulus to endeavor and the compensation for toil." Moreover, despite the scars of the Pullman strike, he was uninterested in labor legislation and talked vaguely of leaving such matters to the states. There was, in fact, only one issue in his mind, and this he felt to be the key to victory at the polls. That issue was free silver. If the campaign of 1896 resounded with the rhetoric of class struggle and capitalist exploitation, Bryan invariably framed his arguments in terms of the metallic basis of the currency. "Of all the instrumentalities which have been conceived by the mind of man for transferring the bread which one man earns to another man who does not earn it," he said in a speech at Hartford, "I believe the Gold Standard is the greatest." The free coinage of silver, he believed, would augment the supply of money, create more purchasing power, and bring prosperity to the masses of Americans. Bryan's campaign was, one historian has commented, "the only time in the history of the Republic when a candidate ran for the Presidency on the strength of a monomania." [9] Mark Hanna, the Republican campaign manager, observed of Bryan: "He's talking Silver all the time, and that's where we've got him."

Bryan had the personality, the lungs, and the moral convictions, but the Republicans had the votes in 1896. That the Republican party was the party of business could scarcely be hidden. Their strategy, therefore, was to persuade the voters that what was good for business was good for the country as a whole and for each citizen individually. Mark Hanna raised

---

[9] Richard Hofstadter, *American Political Tradition* (New York, 1948), p. 189.

$10 million in campaign funds from his wealthy fellow industrialists and proceeded to announce to the electorate that William McKinley was the "advance agent of prosperity" and that a Republican victory would bring a "full dinner pail" to all. The gold standard was defended on the ground that inflation would reduce wages, and there were hints that factories would grind to a halt if Bryan were to achieve his misguided ends. The Republican message was beamed to urban America, employees and employers alike, and cast the Democrats as the voice of agrarian radicalism. Bryan, with his "funny money," was "strong in the South and the Desert."

The result was a McKinley landslide: Bryan was defeated by over 600,000 votes. Of the forty-five states that then comprised the Union, the Democrats carried eleven in the South and another eleven in the sparsely populated West. Of greatest importance was not the fact that the Republicans carried the populous East but that they won in the major urban centers. The ten largest cities in the country all went for McKinley, despite the fact that these had been areas where the Democrats had been making good records for themselves since Jackson's time. The 1896 Republican success in the industrial cities, moreover, was not confined to any one class. Voters in working-class, middle-class, and upper-class neighborhoods who had voted Democratic in the previous election shifted to the Republicans. This chipping away of Democratic strength at its most strategic points was accomplished by a Republican effort to play down antagonisms between classes, to minimize rural versus urban tensions, and to ignore differences between immigrants and native Americans. There was, so their story went, room for everyone in the Republican party. The contrast between 1892 and 1896 voting in the New England states is instructive here:

> While the election of 1896 is often pictured as a last-ditch fight between the haves and the have-nots, that understanding of the contest was evidently restricted to the planes of leadership and oratory. It did not extend to the voting actions of the electorate. . . . In 1896 the industrial cities, in their aggregate vote at least, moved toward the Republicans in about the same degree as did the rural farming communities. . . . The Republicans gained in the working-class wards, just as they did in the silk-stocking wards, over their 1892 vote. They were able to place the blame for unemployment upon the Democrats and to propagate successfully the doctrine that the Republican party was the party of prosperity and the "full dinner pail." On the whole, the effect was apparently to reduce the degree of coincidence of class affiliation and partisan inclination. Nor was the election of 1896, in New England at least, a matter of heightened tension between city and country. Both city and country voters moved in the same direction. . . . Instead of a sharpening of class cleavages within New England, the voting apparently reflected a more sectional antagonism and anxiety, shared by all classes, expressed in opposition to the dangers supposed to be threatening from the West.[10]

The Democrats, having nominated Bryan, found themselves tied to a single issue. But that issue was a sectional issue. Bryan, committed to free

---

[10] V. O. Key, Jr., "A Theory of Critical Elections," *Journal of Politics* (February, 1955), Vol. XVII, pp. 13–15.

TABLE 5–2 / Democratic Proportion of the Major-Party Vote

Year	Candidate	Percentage
1892	Grover Cleveland	52.3
1896	William Jennings Bryan	47.8
1900	William Jennings Bryan	46.9
1904	Alton Parker	40.0
1908	William Jennings Bryan	45.5
1912	Woodrow Wilson	45.3*
1916	Woodrow Wilson	51.7
1920	James M. Cox	36.2
1924	John W. Davis	34.8
1928	Alfred E. Smith	41.3
1932	Franklin D. Roosevelt	59.1

* Percentage of three-party vote.

silver as a solution, was unable to enlist the sympathies of urban workers. Currency reform had no meaning for them, and they rightly sensed that he failed to comprehend the problems of industrial America. The Democrats knew that they needed urban votes to defeat McKinley. However the Great Commoner from Nebraska did not speak their language. "There was a deep irony in Bryan's attempt at an urban appeal," it has been pointed out. "He was no more able to understand immigrant ways or the city machine than the most naïve reformer." [11] The Democratic campaign of 1896, then, was oriented to rural America in general and to Western rural America in particular. It was conservative in that it rejected industrial capitalism and preferred to think of a nation of homesteaders. But the Census reports told a different story: by 1890 there were more Americans working in manufacturing, transportation, and related areas than there were in farming. The Republicans capitalized their politics on this new demography.

The 1896 election realigned the parties, giving the Republicans a majority that cut across class, occupational, and ethnic ties. The large industrial states of North and Midwest were firmly in their grasp. The Republican coalition continued to dominate American politics until 1928. After 1892 the Democratic candidate for the Presidency was to receive a majority of the major-party vote in only one out of the nine succeeding elections. The Democratic record between 1896 and 1932 was a story of decline, broken only once, by Wilson's reelection in 1916.

Bryan did even more poorly in his 1900 and 1908 races than he had in 1896; in 1904 Alton Parker, an Easterner, secured even fewer votes than Bryan had managed to do. Woodrow Wilson was elected in 1912 only because of the split in Republican ranks between Taft and Theodore Roosevelt; and his second-term victory was primarily owing to the temporary support given to any incumbent who seems to be doing well in a crisis situation (in his case, the approach of war). The legacy of Bryan was to

---

[11] William N. Chambers, *The Democrats: 1789–1964* (Princeton, 1964), p. 62.

continue to hamper the Democrats through 1924. They were a sectional party incapable of reconstituting a nationwide coalition—unable to comply with the first rule of success in American party politics.

AL SMITH AND THE 1928 ELECTION

The 1920s were Republican years again, after the aberrations of the Bull Moose Revolt and the First World War. Warren G. Harding, Calvin Coolidge, and Herbert Hoover were successively elected to the Presidency by impressive majorities. Their seemingly effortless victories appeared to testify that the Republican party was retaining its hold on voters of diverse classes, regions, and backgrounds. Even as late as 1924 the Democrats were still the party of the South and the party of Bryan. Their disastrous convention of that year exposed all of their weaknesses. The international ideals of Woodrow Wilson were tossed overboard when the delegates refused to include support for the League of Nations in the platform. Even more divisive was the issue of the Ku Klux Klan. The party's shrunken Northern wing wanted the platform to contain a plank that specifically repudiated the Klan by name. There was great opposition to this move—and not only from the South; even the seemingly immortal William Jennings Bryan arose to speak against too open a chastising of those who wore white sheets and set crosses aflame. To one observer, the eventual vote, rejecting a condemnation of the Klan, revealed where the Democratic center of power lay in 1924:

> It seemed to say, above all, that to many of the men who then set the style for the Democratic party, the only Americans worthy of the name were those who were Protestant, white, Anglo-Saxon in origin, who lived in rural districts and small towns, and whose forebears came to America before the Civil War. Those who did not meet all these specifications presumably were to be viewed as aliens—and perhaps as enemy aliens—in their own homeland.[12]

The Northern, urban elements within the party rallied to place in nomination the name of Alfred E. Smith. A product of the Lower East Side of New York who rose to become governor of his state, Irish in origin and Catholic in religion, Smith was known both for his record of legislative accomplishment (especially in the social welfare field) and for his support by the urban machines (especially New York's Tammany Hall). Ranged against him was William Gibbs McAdoo of California, son-in-law of Woodrow Wilson, who had the support of the Bryan wing of the party. It took a two-thirds majority to choose a candidate, with the result that each camp had an effective veto over the other and used it to full advantage. The 1924 convention ran on for 103 ballots, neither side giving way. Ultimately both groups gave up, and the proverbial smoke-filled room produced not so much a "compromise" candidate as someone willing to run in the party's name that November. John W. Davis, a Wall Street corporation lawyer, ran after a fashion and polled less than 30 percent of the popular vote. In fact, his total was only slightly over half that received by Coolidge and less than

---

[12] Jacob K. Javits, *Order of Battle* (New York, 1964), p. 18.

double the vote cast for Robert M. La Follette, a third (Progressive) party candidate.

The Democrats were completely demoralized by the 1924 defeat; Bryan died shortly thereafter, and the party's leadership went to Smith by default. Delegates to the convention of 1928 really despaired of displacing the Republicans that year; if the New York governor wanted to be a sacrificial lamb there were few left to object to his receiving the nomination. The campaign centered openly on Smith's "wet" position on Prohibition, and (on the level of whispers) it focused on his background—in particular, on his religion. A Catholic, so the argument ran, could not accept the separation of church and state enjoined by the Constitution. And Smith did lose. Indeed five states of the solid Democratic South—Florida, North Carolina, Virginia, Texas, and Tennessee—for the first time in history bolted to support a Republican because of Smith's Catholicism, his immigrant-urban background, and his stand on prohibition. Yet despite all this, Smith raised his party's share of the popular vote by 7 percent. And it is important to note where these gains came from.

Smith succeeded in winning over 120 *Northern* counties that had previously been in the Republican column; and the Democratic vote went up in every state lying east of the Mississippi and north of Ohio. Most significantly he secured a net plurality in the twelve largest cities of the nation: New York, Chicago, Philadelphia, Pittsburgh, Detroit, Cleveland, Baltimore, St. Louis, Boston, Milwaukee, San Francisco, and Los Angeles. In 1920 and 1924 the Republican aggregate plurality in these urban, industrial centers had been well over a million votes. Smith reversed that trend, giving the Democrats a plurality in those dozen cities taken together, and he started the Democrats on the way from minority to majority status. "The Republican hold on the cities was broken not by Roosevelt but by Alfred E. Smith," one commentator has written. "Before the Roosevelt Revolution there was an Al Smith Revolution."[13] Another analyst, speaking of the 1928 results in the New England states, substantiates this view:

> When one probes below the surface of the gross election figures it becomes apparent that a sharp and durable realignment occurred within the electorate, a fact reflective of the activation by the Democratic candidate of low-income, Catholic, urban voters of recent immigrant stock. In New England, at least, the Roosevelt revolution of 1932 was in large measure an Al Smith revolution of 1928.[14]

Smith's coming on the scene symbolized the heightened aspirations and expanding expectations of immigrant America. At the turn of the century such sentiments could not be roused, let alone mobilized. In 1900, for example, fourteen out of fifteen people ended their education at the elementary level. But three decades later the proportion of Americans in high school had increased sevenfold. The Democratic party's advances here were aided by an influx of academic and professional people who, despite their middle-class incomes and occupations, were discomfited by the business

---

[13] Samuel Lubell, *The Future of American Politics* (New York, 1951), p. 35.
[14] V. O. Key, Jr., "A Theory of Critical Elections," p. 4.

"Come Along, We're Going To The Trans-Lux To Hiss Roosevelt."

One of the most famous cartoons of the "Roosevelt years."

Drawing by Peter Arno
© 1936, 1964 The New Yorker Magazine, Inc.

orientation of the Republicans. These individuals had an influence on the economic and social thinking of the Democrats far out of proportion to their numbers. Their entry into politics caused Herbert Hoover to note that in 1928 "the growing left-wing movement, embracing many of the 'intelligentsia,' flocked to Governor Smith's support." For the Democratic party, even before the Depression, was becoming the haven of intellectuals no less than of the urban immigrant. The party that had, under Bryan, failed to mobilize a national coalition was once again forming its ranks.

The figures on voting turnout underline this development. In 1920, 44.2 percent of the eligible electorate showed up at the polls; and in 1924 the figure was almost identical: 44.3 percent. However in 1928 the proportion jumped to 52.3 percent. To be sure, part of this new element in the voting constituency consisted of women, who were just getting the habit of casting a ballot. But many of the new voters, both men and women, were citizens who had never before "participated" in politics and who now found reason for doing so. In 1928 Smith had been unable to hold the South and West— he was "wet" in a "dry" year, a Democrat in a Republican boom year. But what the Democrats had accomplished, under Smith's leadership, was to bring upon the national political scene a new group that would underpin their party up to the present day. The Democrats were not yet the majority party in 1928. But they were, for the first time since 1892, ready to become one again.

"Foreman John Q. Voter Gives The Verdict."

Roosevelt easily won a fourth term in 1944.

Berryman in the Washington *Evening Star*

FDR AND THE DURABLE MAJORITY

Who cared about the morality of Prohibition when the banks were closed? Economic circumstance, which had ensured Hoover's victory in 1928, encouraged a realignment of the electorate in 1932, which left the Democrats (in terms of registered voters and positive identifiers) the majority party in the country. Under the impact of the Depression, Smith's urban Democrats and Bryan's rural Democrats found there was room enough for both in the same coalition—especially since that coalition was headed by Franklin D. Roosevelt. Roosevelt appealed to the "little man," and the salaried workers and pensioners responded with a loyalty which has persisted to the present. Roosevelt, a superb manager of the city machine bosses, was also at home with the leaders of organized labor, emerging as a major political force by the end of his first term. Most important of all, Roosevelt had the confidence of the political leadership of the South—both the Populist leaders in the Bryan tradition (such as Senator "Cotton Ed" Smith of South Carolina) and the patricians such as Cordell Hull and Senator Walter George. The year 1932 saw the formation of the coalition, and 1936 saw its perfection. Of course not all the groups involved were pleased with the performance of the Administration all of the time. There were defections—both Al Smith and John W. Davis became opponents of Roosevelt, and the Administration's support of Britain, after the outbreak of war in Europe, cost the Democrats votes among German-Americans in the Midwest and Irish-Americans in the East. Yet on the whole FDR's majority wore amazingly well; neither the economic reverses of 1937–38, nor the third-term issue in 1940, nor the war in 1941 could put a serious crack in it.

While Roosevelt still headed the Democratic ticket it was possible to argue that the majority he commanded was a personal coalition—that many of the voters who pulled levers for the Democrats were not deeply committed Democrats at all, but were only attracted to the personality of the candidate or were voting for him out of a simple desire for a "way out" of the Depression. But for anyone who doubted that a Democratic majority existed, the 1948 election was the irrefutable answer. All the external signs (the stuff of which most newspaper columns are made) pointed to a victory for the Republican nominee, Governor Thomas E. Dewey of New York. The war was over and the "khaki" election of 1946 had resulted in a Republican-controlled Congress for the first time since 1932. Surely, it was said, this indicated that with Roosevelt and the Depression and Hitler gone, the country was returning to its pre-1932 Republican ways. The public opinion polls indicated that the popular estimate of the job President Truman was doing showed a progressive decline from the high he had enjoyed upon succeeding to the office. The Administration had also been embarrassed through late 1947 and early 1948 by a series of petty and sordid scandals—the telltale sign that the generally creative development of the Truman years had not been without spots of moral laxity. The Republican challenge was summed up in the confident question which became their campaign slogan: "Had Enough?" All the privations of the war years were associated with Democrats in power, and very few political observers saw any way the party could save itself from being turned out to make way for the party which had acceded to office after the First World War, pledging a return to "normalcy."

Much has been written to the effect that the scrappy and dramatic campaign waged by Truman was responsible for the Democratic victory in 1948. (Truman waged the last true whistle-stop campaign across country by train. Today candidates only do it for a few hundred miles as a change of pace from airliners.) Although the impact of Harry's "Give 'em hell" type cannot totally be discounted, the unromantic truth is that the electorate responded according to its basic structure. Up to the week before Election Day the Gallup poll showed Dewey ahead of Truman but with a rather large percentage of the sample undecided. The pollsters hypothesized that the undecided would split between the contenders in about the same way as those who stated their preference—an error which it took them years to live down. In fact, the undecided voted overwhelmingly for Truman; and they did so because they had, over the years, identified themselves with the Democratic party. The important point is that the majority Democratic coalition held up *despite* the Dixiecrat insurrection (Strom Thurmond of South Carolina stood for President on this regional, segregationist ticket and won the electoral vote of four states: South Carolina, Mississippi, Alabama, and Louisiana) and the candidacy of Henry Wallace on the Progressive ticket, which threatened to draw off the "left" of the Democratic party.

THE EISENHOWER VICTORIES:
REALIGNMENT OR ABERRATION?

Did the election of 1952 represent the breakup of the coalition which had held even through the adversity of 1948? Did the victory of the Republican candidate indicate a realignment of the electorate, similar to that of 1928, which would provide the GOP with a relatively stable majority? These were the questions raised by the comfortable margins by which Dwight Eisenhower defeated Adlai Stevenson in 1952 and 1956. It was obvious from a glance at voter registration figures that there were more people calling themselves Democrats in 1952 than there were Republicans. It was equally obvious that many of these "Democrats" voted for General Eisenhower and that many new voters (children from "Democratic families") cast a Republican ballot. There was little doubt that the crucial factor in the behavior of these thinly committed Democrats (Eisenhower Democrats as they came popularly to be called) was the personality and reputation of the candidate —they were moved from their normal party identification to vote not as Republicans, but for *Eisenhower*. But what would be the significance of this action for the voter's future behavior? Would the Eisenhower Democrats, once (or twice) having voted for the Republican nominee, begin to identify themselves as Republicans, or would they, once Eisenhower was removed from the political equation, revert back to Democratic allegiance?

As the 1960 election approached, this became the crucial operational question for political strategists on both sides. Without Eisenhower on the ticket the true configuration of the electorate should be revealed—either the old Democratic majority of 1948, or a newly structured Republican coalition. Unfortunately for those political scientists and historians who like their answers to be clear-cut, there was another factor—a somewhat slippery one—at work in the 1960 election which threw the election into a virtual dead heat and made analysis of the true alignment of the voters a very delicate matter. John F. Kennedy, the Democratic candidate, was a Roman Catholic.

Much has been said about the influence of the religious issue in the 1960 Presidential race. It has been argued both that Kennedy won because of his Catholicism and that he almost lost because of it. The most reliable body of research on 1960 voting is that accomplished at the Survey Research Center at the University of Michigan under the general direction of Angus Campbell. Its investigations indicate that there was a significant movement of Eisenhower Democrats back to the party but that this movement was canceled out by the number of traditional Democrats who cast ballots for Richard Nixon because they could not bring themselves to vote for a Catholic. The truth seems to be, based on the best statistical evidence available, that Kennedy lost many more votes than he gained because of his religion, and that the election would have seen the "reconstitution" of a clear Democratic majority except for the inability of many regular Democrats, especially provincial Democrats, to adjust to the idea of a Catholic President. Thus 1960 failed to answer definitively the question of the continued viability of the Roosevelt coalition.

1964: ANOTHER CRITICAL ELECTION?

It will be some time before political scientists and their batteries of computers have sorted out the constellation of variables that produced the Democratic Presidential landslide of 1964. By midnight on election night, however, it was apparent that there had been startling departures from the established patterns of party identification. The Republican candidate, reaping a harvest of segregationist votes in heavily Negro black-belt counties, was to sweep the five states of the deep South. Elsewhere in the country, there were dramatically heavy defections to the Democratic ticket among traditionally Republican groups. GOP suburban strongholds such as New York's Westchester County (including such affluent bedroom towns as Scarsdale, Mount Vernon, and Rye) were counted for Lyndon Johnson, with Republican candidates for Congress and local office barely holding on or actually losing to Democrats. Across the plains states (traditionally the Republican heartland) Johnson ran surprisingly well. Kansas, Nebraska, Iowa, the Dakotas—all delivered their electoral votes for Johnson, and he carried the mountain states and upper New England as well. President Johnson swept industrial America and was supported strongly by all elements of the Roosevelt-Truman-Kennedy Democratic majority except the voters of the Old South. He ran ahead of Kennedy in Negro and Jewish wards, better among trade union members, and almost as well among Catholics. He even brought back into the Democratic column such "Presidentially Republican" Southern states as Virginia and Florida.

Across the nation, regional loyalties to party, firm since the Civil War, were overturned. Class-status loyalties snapped as upper income groups showed marked Democratic propensities, and marginal farmers of the deep South—heirs to the Populist tradition of Bryan and his Dixie disciples—switched to the party they hoped was committed against using federal power to enforce Negro civil rights. It was an election which seemed to shout that the old order was passing away, and yet there were enough aberrant factors at work in 1964 to deter students from generalizing as quickly and broadly about partisan regroupment as the results first seemed to invite. Briefly, the analytical problem revolves around determining how much of the huge Democratic margin represents a permanent new Democratic electoral coalition, and how much resulted from the singular nature of the Goldwater candidacy.

Senator Goldwater's nomination and campaign violated so many of the rules of American politics that to catalog them in detail would require a chapter in itself. First, the Goldwater organization which won the nomination at San Francisco was ideological, dogmatic, and sectarian rather than pragmatic and concerned with maximizing its appeal. Second, it was concerned with purging the party and punishing opponents, consciously turning their backs on fence-mending and coalition-building. Third, the candidate chose to make his appeal in terms of such volatile and unfamiliar issues as race relations and military strategy. In short, the Goldwater team behaved as if it were running a "third" or "protest" party rather than putting together a Republican Presidential majority. In 1964, these tactics at least partially accounted for the creation of what Richard Rovere, in a thoughtful post-election article, dubbed the "one-and-a-half party system." "It is doubtful," Rovere noted,

> whether any one man in our history has ever attracted as much institutional censure as Goldwater, and as little institutional support. He ran without the endorsement or encouragement of any recognized power bloc or special interest, with the exceptions—if they can be

counted in that category—of the rightist propaganda organizations, certain oil and cattle interests in the Southwest, and certain military lobbies. Against him were ranged the most influential sections of the press, all of organized labor, most of organized religion, a considerable part of the business community, all but a handful of the intellectual and educational communities, most farm organizations, Negro groups without exception, and other ethnic groups almost without exception.[15]

Given the alienating and disruptive nature of the Senator's leadership, how solid are the startling gains made by the Democrats? Undoubtedly not all will prove lasting, yet even at this early stage there are several general observations which seem justified.

1. On the whole, regional identifications appear to have less political saliency than in the past. The exception to this trend, of course, is the deep South, but here race and regionalism have become so intermingled as to make it a deviant case—an exception to all rules.

2. The Democrats are unquestionably established as the party of the ethnic minorities and the deprived, with the Negro (whose political participation increases monthly) an important and loyal contributor of votes and demands.

3. The linkage between affluence and Republicanism, long a feature of our partisan landscape, has been weakened. Although many of the Scarsdale Johnsonites of 1964 will probably return to the GOP fold, potent taboos have been violated, and it is doubtful whether upper income groups will ever revert to their previous political homogeneity.

Conclusion: Our Shifting Political Topography

Most political scientists would probably accept the 1964 results as evidence that the Democrats continue to command a stable majority but would wonder if economic and sociological change is not altering the Democratic coalition to the point where it is no longer the old Roosevelt coalition at all but a new mutation. The increased participation of Negroes in politics has added a new dimension to the party, and the winds of political change which have been rising in the South during the past years have produced a highly unstable pattern of partisan allegiance. Vast new suburban rings gird our cities, and the laws governing their political behavior are yet to be learned. The face of America has changed greatly over the last two decades, and it seems probable that the political maps will have to be redrawn. It can be argued that 1964 saw a "critical election" in the sense of a visibly new alignment of the electorate but without a shift in majority between Democrats and Republicans.

---

[15] Richard H. Rovere, "Letter from Washington," *New Yorker*, November 14, 1964, p. 243.

6 / Party Organization and the Choosing of Leaders

A large business corporation—say, one of the major automobile companies—is a model of hierarchical organization. Top management will decide that the time has come to produce a new kind of car. Plans will be formulated, and the various divisions will begin work. Executives will give orders to department heads and these orders will be carried out. Branch managers at factories in a dozen or more states will be told to manufacture parts according to rigid specifications, and they will do just this. Each of a hundred thousand employees will be assigned a particular task, and each will perform the job allocated to him. The result is that as each new car rolls off the assembly line it actually works: it starts up; it moves; it is ready to be shipped to a salesroom. All this marvelously integrated activity is possible because a corporation is organized in accordance with the principles of discipline and responsibility. Each member of the organization knows that he is expected to follow the rules laid down by his immediate superior. Only by adherence to such patterns of discipline and responsibility does a car actually get put together. Moreover anyone who wishes to understand how companies like Ford and General Motors work would be well advised to begin their studies at the top. This is because decisions are made and orders are transmitted from the top down. While there are friendly consultations with those at lower levels, the fact remains either every employee does what his boss tells him to do, or he is replaced by someone who will. There is a great disparity in power between those at top and those at the bottom.

In American politics, on the other hand, the people who are supposed to be "on top" organizationally almost always have "subordinates" with considerable independent power. The disparities of power in the business corporation are virtually unknown to politics. In the American system, at least, power is dispersed too widely to allow for rigid party discipline. A national political party, *in theory*, is organized hierarchically. If rendered graphically this organization appears pyramid-shaped, consisting of layers representing the committees and personnel responsible for operations at each geographic level:

CHART 6–1 / Political Party Organization

But a political party has, in its essentials, very little similarity to a corporation, where executive and assembly-line workers depend for their livelihoods on remaining on the payroll. While political parties, through patronage, can command a measure of obedience, the power that one level has over its subordinate levels is far more tenuous and is based much more on consent than on discipline.

In a sense, each committee is an independent organ with its special constituency and problems. Depending on personalities and circumstances there may be either strong or weak ties between one "layer" of the pyramid and the ones directly above and below it. In a few states, for example, the state party chairman is a powerful figure who exercises great influence with his county chairmen; he may even be able to ensure that some county committees select as spokesman only someone handpicked by him. In other states, in contrast, the state chairman is a figurehead; the county committees in these states are island sovereignties that make and break alliances with each other as and when they see fit. Similarly, the national committee has no means of disciplining state committees that decide to disregard national policies. And very often ward and precinct leaders owe only the most formal fealty to their county chairmen.

The degree of disciplined organization that exists in a given state seems to be related to the extent of competition in that state *between parties.* The late V. O. Key noted that when two-party competition existed, the party organizations seemed to function in a more integrated fashion than in one-party situations where, as in much of the South, there was really no statewide party organization—only a collection of feuding baronies and personal machines. If the party must mobilize to win state offices, local organizations are inclined to surrender some of their autonomy; but where the party is unopposed, the political battle shifts to within the single party. The result is constant disarray. The powerful local organizations ("machines" controlling county, ward, and precinct committees) cannot be welded into an effective statewide network.

Thus if we are to examine the workings of the Democratic and the

Republican parties it is best to begin at the bottom of the pyramid rather than at the top. For unlike Ford and General Motors, the lower reaches of the parties have real autonomy and it is there that the bulk of "citizen contact" takes place.

Local Parties: The "Machine" and the "Organization"

When we think of local politics, the mind instantly fastens on certain emotion-charged terms: "the boss," "the machine," and "the courthouse gang." Certainly for a period of a hundred years, from the time of Jackson to the advent of the New Deal, this was a good way to describe the party system at its lower (city and county) levels. Tens of thousands of local wards and precincts were—and many still are—controlled by "captains" who delivered the votes for the machine, rewarded their constituents, and served as mediators between ordinary citizens and impersonal government. The importance of the machine captain was described in plain words by a Baltimore newspaperman in the 1920s:

> No clear idea of a party organization can be had unless you start from the bottom.
> To discuss Presidential politics without understanding precinct politics is an absurdity. It is like trying to solve a problem in trigonometry without having studied arithmetic.
> The election precinct is the smallest political division. . . . So is the precinct executive the smallest unit in the party machine. While he is the smallest he is also, by long odds, the most vital. . . . He is the bone and sinew of the machine. He is its foundation and the real source of its strength. If he does not function, the machine decays. If he quits, the machine dies.
> He is the actual connecting link between the people and the organization, and he is the only connecting link—the only man in the machine who has any point of direct contact with the voters, who knows anything about them, who has any real influence with them. All that the boss has in the way of power comes from the precinct executives. All that the machine has in the way of substance and solidity, he gives it. Without him there is no machine. He is the indispensable cog in the wheel.[1]

Machine control of city politics was in part the result of rapid urban growth. Throughout the nineteenth century there was a constant stream of people leaving the countryside to add to the growing populations of the cities. And alongside these native migrants from the rural areas came successive waves of immigrants from the various nations of Europe. All of these Americans were "uprooted" in the sense that they were newcomers to the cities and inexperienced in urban ways. They needed jobs, homes, and a welcome. Local politicians came forward to meet these needs. And in introducing the newcomers to urban life, they also enlisted them in party politics.

From the vantage point of the 1960s it is easy enough to see that the

---

[1] Frank R. Kent, *The Great Game of Politics* (New York, 1923), pp. 1–2.

Nast in *Harper's Weekly*

The Tweed Ring "Passes The Buck"

One of Thomas Nast's famous cartoons exposing the corrupt Tweed Ring.

people were being exploited by their friends, the political bosses. Instead of being grateful for favors handed down by the machine, they ought to have realized that the jobs and handouts trickling forth to them amounted to only a fraction of the governmental outlays they might rightfully have claimed. But such a realization would have taken information, political sophistication, and communication that had not yet begun to develop. The notion of the welfare state, indeed the notion of governmental responsibilities as opposed to favors, is a fairly recent conception. The boss was, in his way, a feudal lord and his followers were too "green" to conceive of an alternative to his authority.

Thus the precinct captains shepherded their flocks, and in return for performance on Election Day they accepted their due in jobs and graft from the city boss (or county boss; New York, for example, has had a machine for each borough or county). The bosses, men like Hague of Jersey City, Flynn of the Bronx, or Crump of Memphis, sometimes held elective office themselves (William Marcy Tweed was both mayor of New York and leader of Tammany Hall), but even if they did not, they had a great deal to say about who did. More important, they spoke for their city in the councils of the national party, and their ability to mobilize or refrain from mobilizing their organizations gave them considerable leverage. It is only in recent years that national candidates have occasionally attempted to bypass entrenched local bosses and set up citywide volunteer organizations to attempt to get out the vote. Even today, and even when the bypassed machine is weakened or internally split, this is very risky.

Bosses and machines, of course, have not been restricted to the cities. Rural counties have been as firmly controlled by small coteries, and delivered votes have been as common in the Jeffersonian countryside as in the urban areas. The difference between the two types of machines—rural and urban—has been one of style and nomenclature. In rural areas and small towns the political "bosses" (the "courthouse gang") do not issue their orders from a dingy clubhouse above the grocery store. On the contrary the rural boss is usually a member in good standing of the local social and economic elite. He is often a prominent banker or lawyer or merchant or wealthy farmer. Yet these men run the county organization (and committee) with a firm hand and have the economic means of recruiting the necessary votes to maintain their control. Some rural bosses also have tended to rely on a primitive level of political consciousness among their followings and have manipulated various potent community symbols—states' rights, white supremacy, or fiscal frugality—to deflect attention from their own oligarchical power. In the large cities, in contrast, there has tended to be a dissociation between the political bosses and the economic elite, and acceptance has been based more on favors and "service" than on symbol manipulation. Hence those with political power in urban areas have been looked down upon as somewhat disreputable whereas their rural counterparts are often considered pillars of the community.

FROM "MACHINE" TO "ORGANIZATION"

Commentators frequently remark that the day of the old-time boss has passed and that we now ought to speak instead of the "political leader." There is some truth in this, but not nearly so much as many people would like to believe. The old "machine" and the new "organization" are at least cousins. It is true that with federal and state welfare services, individuals need no longer go to their neighborhood precinct captain for a basket of groceries. And it is also true that fewer people are in need of the other kinds of help that the bosses used to provide. Moreover the rewards of patronage are skimpier than they once were, with civil service examinations covering most governmental jobs nowadays. Yet a survey conducted among more than a hundred local politicians in an Eastern state a few years ago revealed that precinct leaders are still active mediators in the political system. These were the most frequently cited tasks that precinct politicians in a New Jersey county said they performed for their constituents:

1. Help poorer people get work.
2. Help deserving people get public jobs on a highway crew, in the fire department or police force, or in state positions.
3. Show people how to get their social security benefits, welfare, and unemployment compensation.
4. Help citizens with problems like rent gouging, unfair labor practices, zoning, or unfair assessments.
5. Help one's precinct to get a needed traffic light, more parking space, or more policemen.

6. Run clambakes and other get-togethers for interested people even though no political campaign is involved.
7. Help citizens who are in difficulties with the law.
8. Help newcomers to this country to get adjusted and get places to live and work.
9. Work with some of the other party's people to reduce friction and keep the campaign from getting too rough.
10. Help boys with military service problems and advise on the best way to serve.[2]

What emerges is that even in the 1960s party activists still serve as intermediaries between a complex governmental structure and ordinary citizens who are bewildered by the bureaucratic maze. The local party does not dispense social security or unemployment checks, but local politicians can give expert advice on how to go about getting those benefits. They may no longer be able to place someone in the fire department on a strictly patronage basis, but they know when the examinations are given and where the openings are. And if they cannot provide a zoning variance they know whom to call and how to cut through the red tape. While it is true that all these services are available to the general population and may be legitimately claimed by any individual, the fact remains that governmental agencies often seem unapproachable to the average person. The intervention of the politician is often a necessary convenience, and it continues to earn him the gratitude of many "regulars" in his precinct.

The precinct leader still gains his power, his access to government, and his ability to hand out rewards by delivering the vote. He must still know his neighborhood and the people in it, and he must implant in them a loyalty to him as an individual or he will be supplanted. The hardworking captains can count on the continuing gratitude of a small nucleus of voters. These people have received or expect to receive favors and are therefore willing to turn out at the polls and vote as the organization wants them to. It does not take many such loyalists to carry a precinct, especially in a primary election, where the turnout may be relatively small. A local politician will have many personal friends and perhaps most of his relatives living in the immediate area. He selects the polling place (for which a rental is paid) and several pollwatchers (who get modest fees) and this patronage is bread cast upon the waters if the families of the beneficiaries are counted in. Then there are those holding government jobs, receiving welfare payments, or doing business with the city or county. The total will probably be fewer than 200 sure votes but quality—measured chiefly by regularity of voting in party primaries—makes up for quantity.

THE PRIMARY: TEST OF AN ORGANIZATION

Neither machines nor bosses can be expected to determine the outcome of general elections in November. Organization support is always important to national and statewide candidates, but the boss does not have the control

---

[2] Richard T. Frost, "Stability and Change in Local Party Politics," *Public Opinion Quarterly* (Summer, 1961), Vol. XXV, pp. 231–32.

over the results that he has in the primary where the vote is light. A large turnout at the polls can render an uncontrolled and unpredictable result. If a Democratic leader can carry his precinct for the Democratic candidate, so much the better. However the bloc of votes that the professional politicians control is but a small fraction of the total electorate. Ward and precinct chairmen and committeemen can weave a web of favors and obligations encompassing only so many people. After that point, their control—if not their influence—diminishes quite quickly. There is a sense of realism in party circles about just how much the precinct politician can reasonably be expected to do. And he is expected to deliver at the primary elections:

> His standing in politics, his place in the organization, and, in most cases, his job at the City Hall or Courthouse, depend upon his ability to carry his precinct in the primaries for the machine candidates. He can afford to lose the precinct in the general election. That will not hurt him much. It may not be his fault. He may be a Democrat in a Republican stronghold and the most he is expected to do is to make a good showing. But there is no excuse for him to lose in the primaries. He must deliver the goods there. If he cannot carry his precinct in the primaries he loses his position as precinct executive, he loses his political pull, and, in all probability, his political place. All hope of promotion in the machine is gone from him.[3]

Of course, if the organization operates in an area with two-party competition—that is, one containing only a potential majority (rather than a safe one) of voters who identify with the organization's party—the precinct captains are extremely valuable in getting out this larger vote. They cannot, however, hope to decide general elections solely with their deliverable vote.

The importance of the primary reveals a good deal about the internal structure of the parties. There are, first of all, two kinds of primary contests. On one hand the voter is asked to decide which individuals he wants to see as his party's candidates in the general election to be held in November. This primary, in other words, decides who is to have the nomination for a *public* office. On the other hand there are primary contests for *party* positions. These involve electing delegates to a state convention or precinct or ward committeemen. Sometimes the two sets of contests are related, if particular aspirants for party posts have announced their support for particular individuals seeking nominations for public positions, but there need not be such a connection. The importance of primaries is that they bring to a head the factional and personality conflicts that mark the internal life of the parties.

There are constant struggles for position and power within the ranks of the party. In theory the precinct leader loyally supports his ward leader, who in turn supports the county leader, who in turn supports the state chairman. In practice there are frequent defections and intraparty contests The party organization in the Fourth Ward, to use a hypothetical example, is counted upon to produce the votes in the primary to elect county committeemen who will support the county chairman. The leader of the Fourth Ward understands this and usually delivers enough votes to ensure that the

---

[3] Kent, *op. cit.*, pp. 2–3.

organization candidate wins. In return he is allowed to dispense county patronage and related services in his neighborhood. However sooner or later a group within the Fourth Ward will become dissatisfied with both the county chairman and the subservient ward leader. They will put up an "antiorganization" slate at the next primary and will run their own candidates for the county committee. The county organization will expect the "regular" ward leader to defeat these insurgents, and he will try his best, as his tenure in party office depends on his controlling the primary vote. The insurgents will make the most of their claim that they are opposing "the machine," and they will try to increase the primary turnout by appealing to party supporters who do not normally vote in the primaries. It is not easy for the opposition group to recruit enough support to overwhelm the loyalists who are prepared to line up behind the regular organization. Nevertheless insurgents often do win, usually because they persuade some precinct leaders to join their camp and bring their followings with them. In 1963, for example, every district leader in New York County was a man who got his position by bolting from the regular organization at one time in his career and running against the prevailing leader. Most insurgents are not "reformers" in the sense that they intend to abolish "machine" politics. What they want, usually, is to displace those ahead of them and to have more control themselves in the party structure—to become the organization themselves. The primaries are indeed exercises in internal party democracy, for they determine who is to hold power at the various levels of the party pyramid. To be sure these contests rage more over personalities than over issues and center on such matters as ethnic recognition rather than policy questions. What must be said, however, is that the struggle for control within a party—at the precinct, ward, county, or state level—is a relatively open one. It is usually possible for rebellious elements within the organization to take it over and alter its character and personnel; it is usually possible for an outside group to displace the organization altogether. Thus, in the sense that it is always possible to organize to "turn the rascals out," local party politics are pluralist and democratic.

THE RISE OF THE "AMATEURS"

American local politics has a long history of participation by groups of concerned citizens who are outraged over political corruption and inefficiency. Such groups can mobilize public resentment and get enough voters to the polls to win an important primary contest. After all, it may only take a handful of votes in each precinct to carry a primary. If an energetic "reform committee" can rouse out several thousand normally apathetic people it may outvote the party regulars who cast their ballots at the bosses' bidding.

This is precisely what happened, for example, in the Twenty-third Congressional District of the Bronx in 1964. The district had been, for thirty years, the personal base of Representative Charles A. Buckley, leader and product of the Bronx organization. While he was occasionally challenged in primary contests, his precinct captains always managed to deliver enough votes for his renomination in that safe Democratic district. However Buckley was often not in Washington for roll call votes in the House of Representatives, and he loaded his Congressional payroll with party workers who remained in the Bronx. In the eyes of many New Yorkers he was a highly visible political delinquent. Finally, in 1964, a true "reformer" arose to contest Buckley's hegemony. Jonathan Bingham hardly looked like a Bronx politician: he was Anglo-Saxon in origin, Ivy League in education, and not even—at the outset of the campaign—a resident of the Bronx. Buckley and his followers laughed off this Don Quixote, as they had laughed off others in the past. The party regulars assumed that ethnic loyalties (in this case, Irish), machine voting, and low turnout would all keep Bingham well down in second place.

Nevertheless the "reformer" won the June primary. The most interesting lesson of his victory lies in the voting statistics. There were approximately 250,000 adults in the Twenty-third Congressional District, virtually all of them eligible to vote. Yet less than 20 percent bothered to vote in the primary. Buckley's precinct workers brought in about 22,000 voters, in a "normal" year quite enough to win the day for him. However Bingham and his amateur helpers were able, by diligent doorbell ringing, to rouse an additional 26,000 Democrats to the polls—citizens who usually would have, for the most part, simply sat out a primary contest. In other words, the machine could deliver only 22,000 ground troops in a district covering a large part of the Bronx. The "reformers" had only to top this fraction of the electorate by several thousand to win.

There is reason to believe that the machines are a lot less stable and a good deal softer than most people think. "The fiction prevails," one commentator remarked, "that while party leaders may not always manage the public service well they are wizards in the conduct of party business." [4] Local machines are vulnerable on several counts. One of them is that while patronage is still available to be handed out, few party leaders conduct a periodic audit to determine whether the jobholders are actually serving the organization with the necessary zeal:

> Ties of friendship, blood, and community militate against the political discipline essential to the administration of patronage. The resulting lax and ineffective use of political jobs, the failure to appoint jobholders and supervise their activities with only the welfare of the party in mind, points to the possibility that one may very well need more of the arts of public administration to run a patronage than a civil service system. [5]

And related to this is the fact that precinct workers in sociologically changing areas tend to sit back on their laurels, assuming that their customary delivery of a hundred or so voters is all that is required. In particular, many are not enthusiastic about canvassing newcomers to their neighborhoods—especially arrivals of unfamiliar ethnic origins or economic status:

> Relatively few precinct workers canvass their areas vigorously or frequently. Once they acquire a patronage job and become a member in good standing of the local political club or ward headquarters, they

---

[4] V. O. Key, Jr., *Politics, Parties, and Pressure Groups*, 4th ed. (New York, 1958), p. 403.
[5] Frank J. Sorauf, "Patronage and Party," *Midwest Journal of Political Science* (May, 1959), Vol. III, pp. 117–18.

often concern themselves more with the social and fraternal advantages of membership (getting away from the wife a few nights a week, playing cards with "the boys," and swapping political yarns). . . . Precinct workers canvass principally their friends and a small group of voters who are well known and who can be relied upon. This renders most city machines very vulnerable to demographic changes which break up established contacts and introduce new elements into the neighborhood.[6]

In ignoring this cardinal operating principle of their trade they invite disaster for the machine and create a situation in which insurgents can gain control of precinct, ward, and county committees.

But are "reformers" willing and able to consolidate their gains after a one-shot victory over the machine? For many well-meaning enthusiasts, a single hard-fought campaign is exhilarating but not the sort of thing they want to repeat every year. Regular organization workers may be cut down to size by a primary defeat, but they are not necessarily out for good; sometimes they can marshal their resources against the reformers a year or two later and resume control of the local party organs. Political amateurs, moreover, may find it difficult to devote the time and energy necessary for serving constituents on a year-round basis. Many of them, for example, work at nine-to-five jobs in another part of the city, and they are not always readily available for intervening on behalf of a voter who has a problem with some public agency. Nevertheless amateurs have shown surprising success in many parts of the country. Most notable are the 5,000 clubs in California that comprise the "Democratic Council," an organization that enters and endorses candidates in the primaries alongside the regular party hierarchy. In California there is also an analogous "Republican Assembly" representing voter sentiment not always heard in established party councils. These groups have made headway because many Californians are newcomers to the state and have neither ethnic nor economic ties to the party organizations. Thus neither the Republicans nor the Democrats have entrenched machines based on long-standing loyalties. Much the same condition prevails in many new suburban communities all over the country—the influx of amateurs into the county has overwhelmed the old courthouse professionals. It remains to be seen, however, whether the "amateurization" of politics will develop into a significant national trend. Most large cities and the rural areas still have organizations of the conventional type. Serious questions can also be raised about the long-range effects of amateurs who can defeat a "regular" organization (perhaps beyond the possibility of a comeback), but who lack the staying power to create a stable organization to take its place. In brief, an organizational vacuum, especially in a one-party area, can easily be filled by a demagogue. Whatever the faults of the traditional machine or organization, it at least performed the most important function of a political party by providing for the orderly choice of leaders and recruiting professionals to run for office. The "cult of the personality," typified at the local level by Congressman Adam Clayton Powell

---

[6] James Q. Wilson, "The Economy of Patronage," *Journal of Political Economy* (August, 1961), Vol. LXIX, p. 377n.

of Harlem, is quite different. In such cases there is no organization based on services rendered to the voters. The relationship is the direct one of leader to mass following. The leader excites the follower who responds emotionally and immediately to *him*. As long as this personality identification exists, there is no need for organization—only for publicity.

State Parties: Poverty of Power

State parties vary widely in their composition and effectiveness, and it is virtually impossible to draw any generalizations that apply accurately in every part of the Union. Yet on the whole there is one common feature characterizing the Democratic parties of both New York and Georgia and the Republican parties of both New Jersey and Utah. This is the lack of effective statewide control and coordination of the local organizations.

> The most apparent, and perhaps the fundamental, incapacity of state parties lies in the frequency with which the leadership corps is fractionalized and lacking in both capacity and organization for action. Some state party organizations, to be sure, have an evident vitality as well as a fairly high degree of coherence. Yet a more common situation is the almost complete absence of a functioning statewide organization. There may be informal cliques that operate by and large in the background. There may be local organizations that exert power. Yet organizations prepared to cope responsibly with statewide matters with a statewide view are the exception.[7]

Local party machines may have efficient and well-led organizations on the city, county, and district levels. But only in a handful of states do these local leaders and their followings submit to the authority of the state chairman or even the governor. This, then, is one of the critical breaks in the party hierarchy. The state party is not so much an organized body as it is a temporary coalition of county and city leaders that may—and often does—fly apart at a moment's notice.

Certainly the primary system has contributed to the debilitation of state party leadership. Under the old convention method of making nominations for statewide office, the conclave may have been "run" by the bosses, but at least those who participated were party professionals who were skilled in matters of brokerage and compromise. By the end of such closed conventions the county and state leaders had agreed on a common slate and they could present a common front to the voters. In many states there were of course outside interests present—in body or in spirit—at the conventions. Railroads, banks, utilities, and mining companies might exert an informal yet influential presence over the delegates to ensure that the candidates who were named were "safe." Yet if there were occasional bribery and corruption, there were also discipline, leadership, and a structured system of apprenticeships through which men rose to the top. State parties at the turn of the century were often led by imposing men; such have rarely come in recent decades to the post of state chairman.

With the advent of the primary, any politician who wished to be gover-

---

[7] V. O. Key, Jr., *American State Politics* (New York, 1956), p. 271.

nor, Senator, lieutenant governor, or state auditor could develop a small group of supporters and place his name "before the people." If he had an engaging personality, some financial backing, and the temporary support of politicians in several other counties he might well secure enough votes for the nomination. If such candidates are victorious they owe their allegiance only to those factions that backed them. They are not linked to a party organization but to a personal clique of insiders. Added to this is the fact, indicated earlier, that in most parts of the country only a fraction of the eligible electorate turns out for the primaries. These voters are not usually a cross-section of the potential electorate for whom the party label has meaning; they often vote to promote special interests symbolized by one or another of the candidates. The consequence is that the state party organization finds itself undermined by the primary system:

> The unrepresentative block of participants in the primary, by nomi-nating candidates in their own image, seriously handicap the party in carrying the battle to the opposition in the general election. . . . Statewide party hierarchies . . . cannot thrive under repeatedly suc-cessful assaults upon their proposals by those who, on the basis of some special or parochial appeal, can manage to win nominations through the primary.[8]

The primaries, therefore, have weakened the state parties. By doing away with the closed convention and disciplined leadership, however, they have not so much returned the nominating power to "the people" as they have fragmented it among factional groups led by ambitious politicians. The old system was probably overorganized—the state leadership was too often oblivious to rank-and-file sentiment. The present system goes to the other extreme and is underorganized. The rank-and-file is bewildered by a series of candidates unknown to them and generally absents itself altogether from the nominating process.

One measure of the lack of discipline in the state parties can be found in the behavior of the delegations they send to the Presidential nominating conventions. While about a third of the states have primary contests for delegates, all but a handful of these primaries are "advisory"—that is, they do not bind the delegations to support any particular candidate. Hence it might be thought that each state's delegation would present a united front for one or another of the Presidential aspirants. Yet of the fifty state dele-gations at the 1960 Democratic Convention no more than twenty-eight agreed within themselves on a candidate. And at the 1952 Republican Con-vention, forty of the forty-eight delegations split their votes among the various contenders.

DISCIPLINE AND DISORDER IN MASSACHUSETTS

Illustrative of the contrasts among state party organizations is a com-parison of the Democratic and the Republican organizations in the Bay State. Throughout the late nineteenth and early twentieth century the stronghold of an aristocratic Republicanism based on and led by old Yankee

---

[8] *Ibid.*, pp. 166–67.

stock, Massachusetts experienced earlier than any other New England state the rise of an aggressive Democratic opposition based on and led by newer immigrant stock—most notably the Irish. The "new" Democrats were well established in Massachusetts before the critical election of 1928, but it was in that year that the political alignment was set in the form which—despite the rapid growth of the suburbs—survives today. The Democrats possess a clear majority within the electorate, but they are split both regionally (between Boston and the larger towns of the western part of the state) and ethnically (between the Irish and the Italian leadership). Although a continuing minority, the Republicans, with strength in the small towns and the suburbs, have managed to capitalize remarkably well on Democratic divisions; they have held the governorship for eight of the fourteen years since 1952. Relative Republican success has been partly due to the unsavory reputations and behavior of many local Democratic candidates and incumbents; however, the party's success is certainly also due in part to its superior organization and discipline. As one leading student of New England politics has put it:

> The Democratic organization in fact seems at times to be nothing at all. Something called the Jefferson-Jackson Day Committee often has more money and apparently more power than the state committee itself. Personal organizations are numerous and various strong men often go their own way without regard for other candidates in a campaign. In a good many areas, particularly in the small Republican towns, there is no Democratic organization of any kind. In some smaller urban centers where there are Democratic majorities, the party organization may practically give way to labor groups who do most of the work of campaigning.[9]

The Democratic state chairman has not been a powerful figure in the party, and real leadership has come from established figures such as the legendary James Michael Curley of Boston, and more recently, from John F. and Edward M. Kennedy. There has been a rapid turnover in Democratic chairmen, and heated factional battles have marked changes of incumbents. These struggles within the Democratic party have been open and loud, advertising to the public the divisions within the party. The Republicans have managed to do their fighting and choosing behind closed doors, and their chairman has had a great deal of influence in matters of organization, finance, and campaign strategy.

> A dispatch to the *New York Times* illustrated the differences of approach. It noted that the Democrats had allowed the reporters in to hear their showdown on replacing their chairman; it then went on to describe the Republican methods: "Following a brief exchange of statements in the newspapers, a characteristic hush fell over the Republican headquarters. It has been the experience of political reporters in Massachusetts for years that the Republicans promote publicity, and hire press agents to carry out the program so long as it is favorable. Anything unfavorable is carefully thrashed out behind the closed doors of private social and dining clubs. The participants then walk

---

[9] Duane Lockard, *New England State Politics* (Princeton, 1959), p. 125.

TABLE 6–1 / The Candidate and the Organization:
Reported Campaign Expenditures in 1954

	Amount reported to secretary of state
Democratic state committee	$ 15,200
Murphy-for-governor committee	232,600
Furcolo-for-Senator committee	49,600
Republican state committee	623,200
Saltonstall-for-Senator committee	71,600
Herter-for-governor committee	85,400

SOURCE: League of Women Voters of Massachusetts, *Massachusetts State Government* (Cambridge, 1956), p. 331.

out smiling at each other, each trying to ignore political knife handles protruding from their backs." [10]

One other measurable indication of the superior organization of Massachusetts Republicans is the manner in which party finance is handled. The state committee is, for the GOP, a central collection agency for funds and a conduit of these funds to the local organizations. The city and county leaders thus depend financially on the state leadership, and the integration of the party is furthered greatly by this control of the purse strings. The Democrats, on the other hand, do not control money centrally. What is collected by the local or personal organization is spent at that level, and no funds are funneled downward or upward. In Table 6–1, figures taken from the 1954 campaign reflect the difference clearly.

ATTEMPTED PROCEDURAL REFORM

One proposal aimed at strengthening the state parties has been the "pre-primary convention." This technique has been tried with mixed results in such divergent states as Massachusetts, Utah, and New Mexico. Its purpose is straightforward: to have one candidate for each office singled out as the "official" party nominee. Anyone in the state is allowed to circulate petitions and get his name entered on the primary ballot. Before the primary is held, however, a convention consisting of delegates from the various counties is called to endorse the candidate for each office that it feels best represents the statewide interests of the party. The assumption is that most citizens who adhere to a party do want to know who the "official" candidate is and who the challengers are. Many primary voters, for a mixture of motives, do desire this information. If the convention is sufficiently unified to put forward a candidate who attracts wide support from many sectors of the state party, the chances are good that he will overcome his opposition in the primary easily, and the state party leadership will be strengthened. However, if the state organization is very badly split, for instance, as the Democrats have been in Massachusetts, then the pre-primary convention does

[10] *Ibid.*, pp. 138–39.

TABLE 6–2 / Contests in Democratic and Republican Primaries for Statewide Offices in Massachusetts, 1950–56

OFFICE	DEMOCRATS Number of candidates				REPUBLICANS Number of candidates			
	1950	1952	1954	1956	1950	1952	1954	1956
Governor	1*	1*	2	2	6	1	1*	1
Lieutenant governor	5*	6*	1	3	5	1	1*	1
Secretary of state	8*	1*	1*	2*	7	1	1	1
Treasurer	1*	7*	3	5*	2	2	1	1
Auditor	1*	1*	1*	1*	2	1	1	1
Attorney general	4*	4*	1	2	5	1	1*	1*
U.S. Senator	–	1	3	–	–	1*	1*	–

* Races where incumbents were involved.
SOURCE: Duane Lockard, *New England State Politics* (Princeton, 1959), p. 133.

no more than to exacerbate the pattern of conflict. Table 6–2 indicates the failure of the pre-primary convention to return nominating power to the Democratic organization in Massachusetts, and its relative success for the Republicans. (The Massachusetts pre-primary convention law went into effect between the 1950 and 1952 elections.)

This Democratic dilemma received national attention in 1962, when Edward McCormack, state attorney general and nephew of House Speaker John McCormack, waged a bitter, though unsuccessful, primary campaign against Edward Kennedy, the choice of the pre-primary convention.

Whatever their possibilities, however, pre-primary conventions are still the exception rather than the rule, and fragmented state party leadership— or no leadership at all—continues to prevail in most sections of the country.

As mentioned earlier, there are indications that close two-party competition or the prospect of it in a state helps to close the leadership ranks. If a party's candidates will be seriously challenged in the November elections, where the number of voters is large and their behavior unpredictable, then they are motivated to work as a team and to enlist the support of party workers at the local level throughout the state. Just how many of our fifty states have viable two-party systems is not easy to determine. One approach is to ask whether candidates from both parties have, at one time or another, won statewide elections. Between 1946 and 1962, for example, candidates of *both* parties were successful in statewide contests in forty of the forty-eight states. (See Table 6–3. Alaska and Hawaii are omitted, since they have only been states since 1958 and 1959.) The meaning of this fact should not be underestimated. In a state like Texas it used to be assumed that to become a United States Senator all you had to do was to finish at the top of the Democratic primary. But John Tower showed in 1961 that a Republican could win a statewide contest in Texas, and this means that the Democrats may be driven to unify their forces in the midst of growing two-party competition. Similarly, Oklahoma elected a Republican governor in 1962, alerting the Democrats to the fact that their job was just half over once the primary dust had settled. Until recently, also, states such as Vermont, New

TABLE 6–3 / Statewide Senatorial and Gubernatorial Elections, 1946–64

State	Number of elections	Democrats elected	Republicans elected
Arkansas	16	16	0
North Carolina	14	14	0
Tennessee	14	15	0
Alabama	12	12	0
Georgia	12	12	0
South Carolina	12	12	0
Florida	12	14	0
Louisiana	11	12	0
Mississippi	12	12	0
Virginia	12	12	0
Texas	18	18	1
Rhode Island	17	16	2
Oklahoma	12	11	1
Missouri	12	12	1
West Virginia	13	12	2
New Mexico	16	13	4
Washington	11	8	4
Michigan	16	11	6
Nevada	13	9	4
Montana	11	7	4
Colorado	14	8	6
Kentucky	13	7	6
Ohio	16	8	8
Minnesota	16	9	7
Arizona	16	9	8
Illinois	11	6	5
Massachusetts	11	6	6
Wyoming	11	6	5
Connecticut	15	7	8
Delaware	11	5	7
Indiana	11	6	6
Wisconsin	17	7	11
Oregon	13	5	8
Maryland	12	4	8
Pennsylvania	11	3	9
Iowa	16	5	11
New York	13	4	9
California	13	3	10
Idaho	14	3	11
Maine	16	4	12
New Jersey	11	3	8
Nebraska	18	4	15
North Dakota	18	5	14
South Dakota	16	2	14
Kansas	17	2	15
New Hampshire	18	3	15
Utah	11	3	9
Vermont	16	2	15
	622	340	282

States are ranked in descending order according to the ratio of Democrats to Republicans elected within the state. Because no trend can be noted, Alaska and Hawaii are not included.

Hampshire, Kansas, and North Dakota were virtual one-party Republican strongholds. But since 1956 the voters in those states have elected Democratic Senators and governors. This is not to say that there is a strong Republican state party already formed in Oklahoma or a strong Democratic organization at work in Vermont. It has usually been the popularity of the candidate rather than an organized party that has broken the historic single-party monopolies. Competition, nonetheless, often has a direct impact on the organization of the dominant party in a state: presented with a series of challengers for important statewide offices it is prompted to put its own disorganized house in order.

The Nominating Process

Local party organizations (as opposed to state party organizations) are most effective in those areas—wards, precincts, cities, and counties—where a single party dominates the scene. For the local organization's strength lies in its ability to deliver the votes needed to win in a party primary, and it must work on the assumption that the candidate who emerges victorious in the primary will win without trouble at the general election. Moreover the machine is viable only when its own men hold city and county governmental offices—this allows precinct leaders to secure favors and services for their constituents. And the condition of one-party domination at the local level is the rule rather than the exception in most sections of the United States. The great majority of counties and legislative districts are either Republican or Democratic territories. When elections are held in these areas the opposition party seldom wins and frequently does not even bother to contest some of the offices. One survey, taken in 1955, pointed up the scarcity of effective local two-party competition:

> Three out of every four state legislative bodies or congressional delegations were so completely dominated by a single political party that that party controlled more than 66 percent of the members of the group. Excluding the 15 Border and Southern states, fully half of the remaining 33 state legislatures were controlled by one party holding at least two out of every three seats; in only six states was the controlling margin below 55 percent. Within the same group of non-Border, non-Southern states, 25 of the 33 congressional delegations were dominated by one party controlling two-thirds or more of the delegation members; only four delegations were so evenly divided as to give the majority party less than 55 percent of the members.[11]

The degree of one-party control may also be measured by reference to the number of seats in the Congress that change hands over a period of time. A Congressional district is competitive if the opposition candidate is able to defeat the incumbent at least occasionally. Yet in a majority of the 435 Congressional districts, Democrats and Republicans do not rotate in office. In the five elections for the House of Representatives held between 1952 and 1960, only ninety-five—or less than a quarter—of the seats actually

---

[11] Warren E. Miller, "One-Party Politics and the Voter," *American Political Science Review* (September, 1956), Vol. L, p. 707.

switched partisan hands. In other words out of the 435 seats no less than 340 remained in a single party's control through the elections of 1952, 1954, 1956, 1958, and 1960. And this situation is not confined to the solidly Democratic South. Even in the thirty-nine Northern states, seven out of every ten districts were held by one party throughout the decade.

The chief result of one-party control in an area is to give heightened importance to the process for nominating candidates. In some parts of the country the man who secures the nomination of the dominant party is given a virtual guarantee of victory, for he will receive only nominal opposition at the general election. In other sections history and custom will give one candidate a long lead over his opponent even before the election campaign begins.

Such nominations, to begin with, are completely in the hands of the state and local organizations. "The most extreme decentralization prevails, for each state and each congressional district exercises complete autonomy in the designation of nominees for Senate and House," V. O. Key has written. "No national party office, either Democratic or Republican, asserts the right to control nominations made by the party subsidiaries in the states or districts." [12] That is, state and local parties do not need the approval of any national party committee before they give their nomination to a particular individual. On the other hand the President, as party leader, may encourage someone to seek a candidacy within a state and let it be known that that person has White House support. Thus Dwight D. Eisenhower persuaded John Sherman Cooper, his Ambassador to India, to seek the Republican Senatorial nomination in Kentucky in 1956; and that same year he gave his blessing to Douglas McKay, his Secretary of the Interior, who sought to run for the Senate in Oregon. In both cases the President's men won the nominations, although McKay had to win a primary fight to do so. But generally speaking the President does not intervene. Franklin D. Roosevelt tried to unseat several anti-Administration Congressmen in the Democratic primaries in 1938. The result was a real slap in the face for the Chief Executive when most of these Senators and Representatives were renominated by their local constituents. This led James Farley, Roosevelt's national chairman, to conclude that "voters naturally and rightfully resent the unwarranted invasion of outsiders." [13] And counted among such "outsiders" is presumably the President himself.

In most states the nomination for governor, Senator, and Representative is by party primary. In a few states—notably New York, Connecticut, and Indiana—the decisions on statewide nominations are in the hands of a convention. But even in Connecticut an aspirant for the nomination for governor or Senator can demand that a primary be held if he receives 25 percent or more of the convention vote. Needless to say, delegates attending state conventions are party stalwarts who owe their chief allegiance to one or another of the factional leaders within the organization. Delegates to such conventions are elected in many cases, but they are usually chosen at primaries where the turnout is low and public interest is slight. Attention

---

[12] V. O. Key, Jr., *Politics, Parties, and Pressure Groups*, p. 476.
[13] James A. Farley, *Jim Farley's Story: The Roosevelt Years* (New York, 1948), p. 147.

should therefore be directed to the primaries, for it is under this system that the vast majority of nominations are made.

Since approximately three-quarters of the seats of the House of Representatives are safely in the hands of one party or the other, voters must be allowed to select between candidates for the dominant party's nomination in safe districts if they are to have a real choice as to who is to represent them. Yet the remarkable fact is that only about half the primaries in safe districts are contested. In the other half there is a single name on the primary ballot—usually that of the incumbent—and he wins the nomination simply because he lacks opposition.

The consequence is that the individual who secures a nomination for Congress in a safe one-party district will probably continue to be renominated and reelected for as long as he pleases. There are of course exceptions—often important ones—to this rule. A long-time incumbent will sometimes be challenged by a younger man within his own party, who out of personal ambition or issue orientation will seek to supplant him. This occasionally happens in areas where the composition of the population is undergoing changes. Thus the patrician Senator Walter F. George of Georgia was forced to step down in 1956 when it became clear that the Democrats of his state wanted to be represented by a more overt segregationist, Herman Talmadge. And in Westchester County, a conservative incumbent was defeated in the 1962 Republican Congressional primary by a young millionaire, Ogden Reid of the New York *Herald Tribune* family, who reflected the more moderate Republicanism of this New York suburb. Nevertheless the incumbent in a safe district is usually well entrenched with both the party organization and with a majority of the voters, and attempts to depose him in a primary contest are seldom successful. In 1960, for example, only five incumbent members of the House of Representatives failed to secure renomination because they were defeated in primaries. In 1962 the number was twelve; but this was unusually high because in five contests two districts had been thrown together due to reapportionment, and in those cases two incumbent Congressmen had to run against each other in a primary.

The curious result is that in one-party areas voters only have a choice between candidates when the incumbent retires and there is a race among various contenders for his mantle. Given the long life and good health of many Congressmen the interval between such contests can be as much as twenty or more years. All in all it is best to accept the conclusion that "the primary is not a successful alternative to two-party competition in most parts of the United States." [14]

Related to this is the fact that most citizens do not vote in primaries. Except for well-publicized contests for Presidential delegates in a few states every four years, the majority of Americans do not bother with the intraparty elections preceding the November general elections. In more than half of the 176 gubernatorial primaries held in fifteen Northern states between 1926 and 1952, fewer than 30 percent of the eligible electorate

---

[14] Julius Turner, "Primary Elections as the Alternative to Party Competition in Safe Districts," *Journal of Politics* (May, 1953), Vol. XV, p. 209.

bothered to go to the polls. Indeed in 145 of these 176 primaries for the man who might be their state's chief executive, less than four out of ten of the qualified voters were sufficiently interested to cast a ballot. Primaries were intended to take the nominating power out of the hands of the party bosses. Their purpose is to permit rank-and-file supporters of a party to select the candidates who will represent them at the general election. The case for the primary was forcefully put over a half-century ago by Robert M. La Follette of Wisconsin:

> Under our form of government the entire structure rests upon the nomination of candidates for office. This is the foundation of the representative system. If bad men control the nominations we cannot have good government. Let us start right. The life principle of representative government is that those chosen to govern shall faithfully represent the governed.
>
> To accomplish this we must abolish the caucus and the convention by law . . . and make all nominations by direct vote at a primary election.
>
> With the nominations of all candidates absolutely in the control of the people, under a system that gives every member of a party equal voice in making that nomination, the public official who desires renomination will not dare to seek it if he has served the machine and the lobby and betrayed the public trust. But under a primary election the public official who has kept faith with the public can appeal to that public for its approval with confidence.[15]

Clearly Senator La Follette's dream has not been realized. Most of "the people" fail to participate in the primaries, and they stay at home more because they are apathetic than because of any procedural difficulties they might encounter at the polls. What can be said is that at the lower levels of the party pyramid, where organizations are well established, the "regular" organization candidate is likely to win, because the precinct captains are able to round up enough voters to secure the needed majority for the candidate endorsed by the organization. Most organizations, however, do not extend their authority beyond a county's boundaries. In other words, there are few that effectively embrace all of a state. Indeed, for reasons mentioned above, most state party organizations are weak and faction-ridden. Because of this, systematic recruitment and nomination are the exception at the state level. Intraparty warfare between candidates of rival local organizations is the rule.

The National Committee

In theory at least there is a summit to the national pyramid of each party. This is the national committee, a body intended to supervise party activities in the four years intervening between the Presidential nominating conventions. In fact these committees meet infrequently and have no policy-making powers or functions. They are, to begin with, far too large to gather

---

15 *The Political Philosophy of Robert M. La Follette as Revealed in His Speeches and Writings* (Madison, 1920), pp. 29–31.

around a table. The Democratic National Committee has 100 members, one man and one woman from each state. The Republican National Committee is even bigger, for in addition to two members from each state it allows a place to the state chairman from every state having a Republican governor or a majority of whose Congressmen are Republicans or that cast a majority of its votes for the last Republican Presidential candidate. Both national committees are really honorary bodies, and the people who sit on them are not usually the important state leaders but middle-rank workers thought deserving of a symbolic reward.

It should not be surprising that the national committees as such have little to do. They have no authority over either Congressmen or the state parties, and at all events it is doubtful whether the 100 or more people on them could agree on a coherent line of party policy. The one person who can and does exercise some influence is the national chairman. He is not, in most cases, a member of the national committee and he is not usually elected by its members. Most of the time he is appointed by the party's Presidential candidate immediately after the national convention is adjourned. Probably the most famous national chairman was Mark Hanna, who was in effect manager of the Republican party between 1896 and 1904. A wealthy industrialist himself, he was able to raise money from and gain the support of the national business community for his party. But since his time the office has been less managerial and more concerned with public relations. During the 1920s and '30s the party in power often gave its chairmanship to the Postmaster General, on the theory that the conjunction of these two positions provided a focal point for coordinating patronage operations. But with the progressive decline of federal patronage even that custom has passed. Just how far a chairman will attempt to "speak for" his party depends on his own personality and his evaluation of his job. The Republican party has tended to give its chairmanship to individuals who take a limited view of their role, and on occasion they have bestowed it on members of Congress who are already well occupied with legislative duties. Probably the best-known chairman in recent years was Paul Butler, who served the Democrats between 1955 and 1959. He was a tireless speaker, traveling back and forth across the nation during Eisenhower's second term. Yet Butler's fault, in the eyes of many Democrats, was that he was *too specific* in his description of his party's supposed program and that he had no warrant to commit the party to these ideas. For Butler was a liberal Democrat—a Stevenson man and later a Kennedy man. His interpretation of his party's principles gave much discomfort to the many conservatives, particularly Southerners, in his camp. Their retort was that what the party needed most was a "silent Butler." This seems to reflect the general consensus on what a national party chairman should be.

The national chairman heads the party headquarters in Washington. These are quite modest operations, each having year-round staffs of about eighty to ninety employees. The headquarters maintain research departments, speakers' bureaus, and divisions dealing with sectors of the electorate such as women, young people, and minority groups. Newsletters and magazines are occasionally published, but the party headquarters is generally too small an enterprise to do much public relations work. Its audience

"I'll Save Him—
No, I'll Save Him!"

Bitter leadership quarrels arose
within the Republican party after
its overwhelming defeat in the
1964 election.

Canfield in the Newark *News*

for the most part consists of the state committeemen and county chairmen
who receive its bulletins and are thus informed about what the national
committee is doing. The chief between-election activity of the headquarters
is to raise money to pay off the deficit incurred at the last campaign. This
may amount to over a million dollars, and the finance division must discover
donors whose enthusiasm for their party continues on in the dark months
of winter and even in times of defeat. Hence the Jefferson, Jackson, and
Lincoln Day Dinners, where the birthdays of party patron saints happily
coincide with the due dates of loans owed by the party committees.

Financing Party Operations

The real problem concerning money in politics is that we do not know
enough about it. We know little about how much is spent or where it comes
from; we have only foggy notions about how much effect it has on the outcome of elections; and we do not even know whether all our fears and misgivings about suspected corrupt practices are justified.

Federal law regulating campaign contributions and expenses is generally
observed. However the laws are so filled with loopholes that they are unable to prevent anyone who so desires from giving as much money as he
wants to a candidate. The chief stipulations on financing campaigns, incorporated into the Corrupt Practices Act of 1925 and the Hatch Act of
1940, are as follows:

1. A candidate for the House of Representatives may spend no more than $5,000 on his campaign, and a Senatorial candidate may spend no more than $25,000. *However* these figures do not include the candidate's personal travel expenses, the printing and distribution of circulars, or telephone bills. More important, supporters of candidates can set up separate committees that can spend far in excess of $5,000 or $25,000. Thus with the receipts of such auxiliary committees added in, one candidate for the House of Representatives in 1960 reported expenditures of $62,228; a Senate candidate that same year had a total of $103,734 spent on his behalf.

2. National political committees are not permitted to spend or receive over $3 million in any one year. Thus for 1960 the Democratic National Committee reported a turnover of $2,991,706.61 and the Republican National Committee squeezed under the line with $2,994,865.77. *However* these are by no means the only committees to which one can contribute. If, in 1960, the Democratic National Committee had reached its $3 million ceiling a donor could always make his check out to the National Committee of Arts, Letters, and Science for John F. Kennedy for President. And an oversubscribed Republican National Committee could direct contributors to any of the following bodies:

> Conservative Floridians for Nixon-Lodge
> Committee for "The Real Nixon"
> National Federation of Republican Women
> National Nixon-Lodge Club
> Restaurant Voters for Nixon Committee
> Vote-Getters for Nixon-Lodge
> Metropolitan St. Louis Volunteers for Nixon-Lodge
> Young Republican National Federation

Thus the total Republican receipts came to $13,040,263 in 1960, and the Democratic total was $8,074,311. Forty-three Republican and twenty-nine Democratic committees reported financial activities in 1960. In effect, the $3 million limit per committee appears only to encourage the proliferation of new committees.

3. In any given year individual citizens are not allowed to contribute more than $5,000 to a candidate or to a committee. Donors can, however, give up to $5,000 to as many separate candidates and committees as they please. Thus in 1960 Laurance S. Rockefeller gave $3,000 to the Republican National Senatorial Committee, $3,000 to the United Republican Finance Committee, $3,000 to the Republican National Committee, $1,000 to the Television Committee of the Republican Campaign Dinners, and $975 to Volunteers for Nixon-Lodge—a total of $10,975. And Mr. and Mrs. Bart Lytton of Los Angeles managed, between them, to give $27,000 to five different Democratic committees.

4. Corporations and labor unions may not make direct contributions to candidates. However corporation executives, as individuals, may give as much as they like to various candidates and committees. Thus Frederick R. Kappel, the president of the American Telephone and Telegraph Company, gave $3,000 to three Republican groups in 1960; Frederic G. Donner, chair-

Putting The Screw On Him

A 1904 cartoon showed Teddy Roosevelt's campaign manager squeezing money out of the big corporations.

Keppler in *Puck*

man of the board of General Motors, gave the Republicans $2,000; and Crawford H. Greenewalt, the head of Du Pont, gave the same party $6,000 via several committees. Nevertheless these gifts, while very generous, are personal and are not "company money" except in a very indirect sense. Labor leaders tend to receive smaller salaries than corporation executives do (a union president may receive a salary of $40,000 a year, whereas a corporation president may receive $300,000), and therefore the former make less sizable personal contributions to political parties. Labor unions, however, have other means of directing money into political channels. First, union dues money—cash already in the regular union treasury—may be spent on the "political education" of the union's own members. So long as these funds are not devoted to campaigning among the general public they can be freely used to persuade union members to support particular candidates. Articles in union newspapers, for example, can quite legitimately exhort members to vote for or against a certain Congressman. Unions can also make voluntary collections among members and then pass these funds along to candidates. How voluntary are these "voluntary" collections? In the 1960 national campaign sixty labor committees managed to come up with a total of only $2,154,244 (all of which went to the Democratic party). This comes to less than twenty cents per union member throughout the country. Union money is active in politics, but the role it plays should not be exaggerated. It is, on the whole, easily outweighed by the gifts to the other side made by corporation executives and several wealthy families.

While figures for campaign contributions and expenditures may seem high the fact is that the costs of politics are really quite modest when compared with analogous activities. A reliable estimate of the entire cost of the 1960 primaries and elections for all national, state, and local offices is about $175 million.[16] (Since the total expenditures reported under federal law came to only $33 million that year, this estimate necessarily involves some guesswork about unreported contributions.) Nevertheless the figure of $175 million comes to about $2.50 per voter and is hardly a heavy investment, considering that a Presidential-year campaign is one of this country's heaviest exercises in advertising, public relations, and promotion. Indeed, as a nation we spend over $3 *billion* a year on commercial advertising—or more than fifteen times as much as we do on "selling" candidates to the electorate.

Moreover while the amount of money spent on campaigns rises year by year, so does the amount of money spent on other things. "The real costs of political campaigning have not soared steadily upward," one commentator has concluded. "Despite recent spurts caused by the use of television in some types of elections, the long-run dollar increase appears no greater than rises in the price level and national income." [17] Thus if the Republican war chest in 1896 contained $3.5 million, that party's reported spending of $13 million sixty years later is not a relative increase but merely a reflection of inflation and an expanded national income.

What can be said, however, is that the great bulk of campaign contributions continue to come from a wealthy minority. The majority of the funds received for Presidential campaigns comes in checks of $500 or over. In 1952, for example, only 19 percent of the money received by the Democrats and 12 percent of that received by the Republicans consisted of gifts of under $100. In 1960 the members of only eighteen families—most notably the Rockefellers, the Pews, and the Du Ponts—gave over a half-million dollars to the Republicans. The Democrats too have their share of wealthy contributors, although a lesser share. In a period of several weeks in the fall of 1963 four Democratic Senators—from Minnesota, Wyoming, Utah, and Wisconsin—paid visits to New York City and were able to secure substantial contributions from well-wishers many miles from their home territories.

Why do people contribute? Members of the Rockefeller and Du Pont families invest in the election of a Republican President because they sense that if that party takes over the White House their interests will gain more sympathetic attention. To be sure they sincerely believe that a Republican President will be good for the country as a whole, and few among the very rich have specific favors they want to ask of politicians once they are elected. But at a lower level, say in the case of a businessman who gives $1,000 to a Senator's campaign, a contribution may well be a means of subsequently gaining entry to that lawmaker's office. "The central objective of contribu-

---

[16] "1960 Political Campaign Contributions and Expenditures," *Congressional Quarterly Special Report* (June 30, 1961), p. 1058.
[17] Alexander Heard, *The Costs of Democracy* (Chapel Hill, 1960), p. 375.

"What Are You, Some
Kind Of A Fresh Air Nut?"

From *Straight Herblock*, Simon & Schuster, 1964

tions is access to the power of the elected officials." [18] The result is that those who help out a politician in his time of need can receive favored treatment when they have problems of their own. What is ironic is how inexpensive such an investment can be. For a gift of a few hundred dollars an individual may gain, in return, the intercession of a Congressman that will get him a government contract or a tariff provision that will ultimately net him or his business tens of thousands of dollars. One reason why such rewards exist is that so few citizens contribute at all. Except for the President most elected officeholders are beholden to a small list of donors and must be willing to give their time and attention generously to that select group.

This is one reason why proposals have advocated a broader base for contributions. It is assumed that the dominant access to lawmakers of a few wealthy contributors results largely from the apathy of millions of voters who could contribute to the political parties but do not. Theoretically, if lawmakers were less dependent on a small circle of wealthy donors they could give more adequate representation to their rank-and-file constituents. In fact, however, rank-and-file contributions are rarely large enough, even when large numbers of people participate, to balance the far more generous donations of a few very wealthy contributors. In 1959, for example, the Democrats inaugurated a "Dollars for Democrats" drive in which they attempted to raise small contributions by door-to-door appeals. In financial terms the project was a disappointment. Slightly over $100,000 was eventu-

---

[18] David B. Truman, *The Governmental Process* (New York, 1951), p. 309. Truman adds the qualification, "except when a donation is purely a matter of personal friendship."

ally raised and handed over to the Democratic National Committee. By comparison the Democrats collected over $400,000 that year from a few dozen contributors who each wrote out checks for $1,000 or more. Ordinary Americans simply do not have the habit of political giving. They make annual donations to their churches and community chests, but very few send money to their local party committees or to candidates. At the same time, however, parties find grass-roots fund drives profitable as a means of working up political enthusiasm. "If you can get someone to give you a dollar, he becomes a stockholder and will often be a more diligent supporter of your candidate," one Republican national chairman remarked. "Without exception, wherever campaign workers went after the individual donation and got it, that is where our vote increased." [19]

Just how much of a problem money in politics is remains an open question. One important aspect has to do with recruiting candidates. If two men in a party organization are seeking the nomination, and if one has the resources to pay his own campaign bills whereas the other has not, the odds are good that the wealthier aspirant will win out. This is especially the case in primary contests, for donors are frequently unwilling to commit themselves at this stage. The rise of more and more millionaires in politics is partly due to their ability to pay their own campaign bills, or at least a large share of them, in the early stages of their drive for office.

Party Personnel

Beyond voting, the test of political involvement is working with a political party. Just how many such workers there are is difficult to discover. A Gallup study of the 1954 Congressional campaign uncovered 2,160,000 Republicans and 3,020,000 Democrats who claimed that they had helped their party during the election. A survey taken by the Roper organization four years earlier found 11 percent of the sample maintaining that they had done such things as distribute leaflets, make speeches, or call on voters. These responses, however, are probably more an expression of good intentions or guilty consciences than they are signs of actual labors in the political vineyard. A University of Michigan poll revealed that only 10 percent of the voters had been personally contacted by party workers during a campaign. It is difficult to see how, if 11 percent of the people are supposedly hard at work, only 10 percent of the voters ever came in contact with these campaigners. Generally speaking, then, the vast majority of citizens are political spectators rather than performers.

Among the small minority that can properly be called "politicians" there are of course many gradations. Perhaps the best idea of the size of the base of this pyramid can be gained by saying that there are almost 250,000 precinct, ward, county, and state committee posts in the Democratic and Republican parties taken together. Between 20 percent and 40 percent of these positions may be unfilled at any given time, thus reducing the number of year-round activists to between 150,000 and 200,000.

---

[19] Leonard Hall, "An Old Pro Describes How U.S. Politics Have Changed," *Life* (April 25, 1960), p. 140.

OCCUPATION

A politician requires not only spare time but a sufficiently flexible schedule to be able to devote that time when it is needed. One afternoon he will have to be at the city hall to see about a job or a zoning variance for someone in his ward. Another morning he may have to attend a meeting of a county board, of which he happens to be a member. On still another occasion he will take off three days to attend a party conference at the state capital. Such activities are difficult, if not impossible, for someone who works for someone else and is tied to a desk or workbench from 9:00 to 5:00. This is one reason why self-employed lawyers and businessmen are so evident in political circles. Table 6–4 gives the occupational breakdown of the fifty-seven elected county chairmen in New Jersey, a fairly typical state in this respect. Along with the lawyers and businessmen are a large group of full-time elected and appointed government officeholders. These people are, of course, not permanent civil servants but rather officials who hold public positions due to their party connections. Indeed it is appropriate to point out that many people enter politics because their occupational interests are closely tied to the benefits forthcoming from public life. Lawyers are not permitted to advertise, but being active in politics helps them to become better known and thus builds up their practices. Furthermore a lawyer who works with a party may be rewarded with trusteeships, guardianships, and perhaps even a judgeship in the course of time. Businessmen and professionals such as real estate agents, undertakers, and chiropractors are interested in maintaining or adjusting local rules and legislation that affect their livelihoods. The material rewards of politics are thus one motivation for entering politics.

Insofar as efforts have been made to get more citizens active in party politics, one of the chief stumbling blocks has been that an increasing sector of the population no longer has a direct occupational interest in political involvement. The lawyer who works for himself may find that party work increases his practice; but the attorney who is employed by a large firm, as so many are nowadays, cannot see how political activity will aid his career. The self-employed businessman knows that being a political insider can help his bank account in many ways; this is not at all clear to the junior executive working for a large corporation. There is substantial evidence that politics is much more the province of the "old middle class" that is self-

TABLE 6–4 / Occupations of New Jersey County Chairmen

Lawyers	37.0%
Full-time government officials	19.5%
Businessmen	19.0%
Other professionals	12.0%
Housewives	7.0%
Others or unknown	5.5%
	100.0%

SOURCE: Richard T. Frost, "Stability and Change in Local Party Politics," *Public Opinion Quarterly* (Summer, 1961), Vol. XXV, p. 224.

employed than it is of the "new middle class," the members of which are salaried employees.

RESIDENTIAL STATUS

One role of the politician is that of broker—to reconcile or minimize differences among competing factions within the party or community. Thus an asset in political work—indeed, almost a prerequisite—is long-time residence in the community, and the network of long-standing personal relationships that this implies. This factor also tends to favor lawyers and businessmen who have returned to practice or run businesses in the communities in which they grew up or went to school. A study of 410 precinct committeemen in King County (Seattle), Washington, revealed that 71 percent had lived in the county for over twenty years, and more than half had resided in the Seattle area for at least thirty years.[20] Except in suburbs where everyone is a relative newcomer, it is not easy for a new arrival to the community to break into politics—especially via the dominant party. This premium on long-time residence prevents the parties from using the talents of millions of transient Americans; metropolitan Republicans, for example, have found themselves at odds with party organizations that are inhospitable to new recruits and new approaches. It is questionable as to whether newcomers can establish themselves in local party politics. For a party, no less than a corporation or a university, is a social system that is dependent on a durable intermeshing of personal relationships. And for a politician, even more than for a businessman or professor, an enduring core of personal constituents is a necessity for keeping his party in power in his area.

ISSUE ORIENTATION

Politicians do not live by their pocketbooks alone. Those who embark upon political careers, whether part time or full time, have an interest in public issues and are usually prepared to state their opinions on them. To be sure, a county chairman will be more concerned with the pros and cons of a road-building program than he will with economic aid to Southeast Asia. And it is also true that many politicians are mainly interested in personalities and positions rather than with what is done once their man is in power. However neither ideas nor issues can be avoided in the political arena, even if much of what is said is vague rhetoric rather than studied analysis. The question to be considered here is whether politicians reflect the views of rank-and-file voters for their party.

The delegates to the Presidential nominating conventions are certainly politicians. The 6,848 delegates and alternates who gathered at the two 1956 conventions came from state and county parties across the country and were probably representative of those back home who are year-round party workers. These delegates were polled in an attempt to ascertain their opinions on contemporary policy issues. At the same time a poll was conducted of ordinary citizens who identified themselves as either Democrats or Republicans, asking them the same questions that were put to the delegates. Some of the results of this study are given in the accompanying

---

[20] Hugh A. Bone, *Grassroots Party Leadership* (Seattle, 1952), p. 12.

TABLE 6–5 / Politicians and the Public

Should there be an increase in the following?	Percentage of Democratic delegates favoring increase	Percentage of Democratic voters favoring increase	Percentage of Republican delegates favoring increase	Percentage of Republican voters favoring increase
Government regulation of business	20.2	18.6	0.6	7.4
Federal aid to education	66.2	74.9	22.3	64.8
Public ownership of natural resources	57.5	35.3	12.9	31.1
Defense spending	20.7	50.5	13.6	45.7
Enforcement of integration	43.8	41.9	25.5	40.8

SOURCE: Herbert McClosky, *et al.*, "Issue Conflict and Consensus Among Party Leaders and Followers," *American Political Science Review* (June, 1960), Vol. LIV, pp. 411–15.

table. Two kinds of differences emerge. First, Republican delegates tend to be a much more highly integrated group, with a more cohesive set of political ideas, than the Democratic delegates. The Democrats have a much more diffuse, heterogeneous group of delegates (rural Southerners versus urban Northerners, for example), with a wider range of political viewpoints. Republican stands on all five issues in the table are quite one-sided; Democratic stands, on the other hand, show a substantially more even split among the delegates on almost every issue.

The second kind of difference appears between the stands of party delegates and those of rank-and-file voters of that party. The disparity is much more marked among the Republicans: delegates were uniformly more conservative than their followers. Republican delegates strongly opposed increased government activity in all five areas, whereas Republican voters were more tolerant of an expansion of the government's role. The gulf between Democratic delegates and voters was, on the whole, narrower than in the Republican camp. Moreover, Democratic disparities showed no clear-cut pattern: voters were more tolerant than delegates about increased government spending for education and defense; they were *less* tolerant about public ownership of natural resources. These tendencies seem to stem from the difference discussed above between Republican and Democratic delegates. Since Republican delegates tend to be drawn from the party's more provincial, doctrine-conscious wing, their views part noticeably from those of the rank-and-file voters, who tend to be more pragmatic in outlook. Since the Democratic delegates represent a wider range of viewpoints, their stands more closely resemble those of Democratic voters. The relative pragmatism of voters of either party is borne out by the relative similarity between the outlooks of Democratic and Republican voters—the only significant split was on the issue of government regulation of business.

It has already been indicated, in discussing the composition of the Democratic party, that citizens of recent immigrant origin were traditionally welcomed under that party's banner. Irish-Americans still play an important part in leading the Democrats, as do Italian- and Polish-Americans in areas where those groups are populous. Their original reason for entering politics was that many businesses and professions were closed to them, and rising in the party became a means to wealth and status in the community. Individuals with these ethnic backgrounds have now found opportunities outside the political realm. Indeed, third- and fourth-generation Americans experience little of the discrimination that their grandparents encountered. This process is still continuing. For example, positions at the lower levels of urban party organizations will probably be filled increasingly by Negroes in the coming years. For like other groups who have encountered difficulties in pursuing alternative careers, Negroes may well take advantage of the fact that local party organizational work is relatively open to minority groups. One clue as to whether this trend is beginning is the degree to which Negroes participate in campaign work, voting, and other forms of political activity. Voting turnouts among Negroes have traditionally been low, partly because of administrative roadblocks and partly because of lack of education, poverty, and low social status. One study, however, conducted in New Haven by Robert Dahl, indicates that in urban areas where Negroes are not discouraged from voting by legal barriers, this trend may be changing. Dahl found that 44 percent of the Negroes in New Haven had participated in political activity, whereas only 20 percent of the whites had done so. Dahl concluded:

> In contrast to the situation the Negro faces in the private socio-economic sphere, in local politics and government the barriers are comparatively slight. There is no discrimination against Negroes who wish to vote; they have participated in elections for generations. Though they are a relatively small minority, both parties compete vigorously for their support. . . . In comparison with whites, therefore, Negroes find no greater obstacles to achieving their goals through political action but very much greater obstacles in the sphere of private socio-economic activity. Consequently, it is reasonable to expect that Negroes will employ their resources to a greater extent in political action than the average white person does.[21]

These findings are, of course, not typical at present; Negroes are only beginning to assume positions in party organizations, and then only in selected urban areas of the country.

Election Procedures and Electoral Results

One seemingly minor but nevertheless vital concern of the parties is the way in which the machinery of elections is arranged. The history of American election laws (which are promulgated by state and local governments)

---

[21] Robert A. Dahl, "Who Participates in Local Politics and Why," *Science* (October 27, 1961), Vol. CXXXIV, pp. 1345–46.

has been a history of attempts by parties or factions to shape the procedures so as to help keep themselves in power or keep someone else out.

REGISTRATION

The size of the turnout for an election may well favor one party over another (or in primaries one faction over another). There are a number of districts in which those in power depend on the fact that the percentage turnout of the electorate is low, or in which a group that has managed to gain office after a particularly well-publicized campaign knows it can only stay there if it can get out a big vote in future elections. Many things, of course, influence turnout—for instance the weather on Election Day. However, one important factor over which interested partisans often have some control is the district's system of voter registration.

The officials at the polling place must have a list of those registered to vote so they can be identified and checked off as they cast their ballots. The harder the requirements for registration, the more likely that the voting turnout will be light, and vice versa. A cumbersome administrative process for registration discriminates against certain classes of prospective voters. The less educated (often the economically disadvantaged and those least able to take a morning off from work to register) are more likely to forget the whole thing than are a lawyer and his wife. If literacy tests are involved (a device by no means restricted to the South), the selective effect (especially on non-English-speaking minorities) is clear. Thus a seemingly neutral procedure can be manipulated to advantage in the party battle.

THE BALLOT

Experience has shown that the way in which the ballot appears will influence the outcome of the election. The chief reason for this is that there are many names on the ballot and in most instances the average voter is unfamiliar with all but a few of them. He appreciates some help in voting in the various contests, and the arrangement of the ballot may give him such aid. The "Indiana Ballot," used in about half the states, arranges all the candidates in vertical party columns. Most states using this form allow the voter to support a "straight ticket" for all offices simply by making a mark or pulling a lever at the top of the party column. Even if such a one-for-all vote is not allowed, the Indiana Ballot nevertheless makes it easy for a voter to run his pencil down a party column to vote a straight ticket. The Indiana Ballot, therefore, encourages party-line voting. In particular it strengthens the dominant party by exploiting the habitual loyalties of a majority of the electorate. Candidates for lower offices like state auditor or children's court judge may not be widely known but they can ride in on the coattails of those at the head of the party column. Most voters, we know, like to vote in all contests; they hate to leave the polling booth with some boxes still unmarked or some levers unpulled. The Indiana Ballot says, in effect, "When in doubt, vote a straight party line."

The "Massachusetts Ballot" attempts to have each contest and each set of candidates considered on their own merits. Thus each office has the candidates running for it listed in alphabetical order. If there are five contests, the voter must make five separate decisions. In 1960 in Massachusetts, for

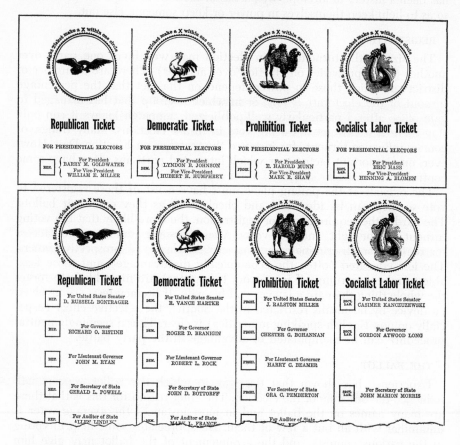

example, someone who wanted to vote a straight Republican ticket would have had to mark the fourth line in the Presidential contest, the first line in the race for governor, and the second line in the election of the lieutenant governor. Such hopping around encourages voters to split their tickets and to consider candidates as individuals rather than as the bearers of party standards. Candidates of the weaker party, especially if they have strong personalities, naturally prefer the Massachusetts Ballot. Research into voting behavior shows that the ballot form influences the outcome of elections:

> This simple difference in the rules governing the marking of the ballot has a substantial effect on the way the voter casts his vote. We find, in the states which make it relatively easy for the voter to mark a straight ticket, that the number of straight tickets marked is some 20 percent higher than in those states where the ballot requires a series of separate decisions among the candidates for each of the various offices.[22]

---

[22] Angus Campbell, "Recent Developments in Survey Studies of Political Behavior," Austin Ranney, ed., *Essays on the Behavioral Study of Politics* (Urbana, 1962), pp. 32–33.

	To vote for a Person, mark a Cross **X** in the Square at the right of the Party Name or Political Designation. **X**
ELECTORS OF **PRESIDENT** **AND** **VICE PRESIDENT.**	**GOVERNOR** Vote for ONE JOHN A. VOLPE – of Winchester~~~~~~Republican | JOSEPH D. WARD – of Fitchburg~~~~~~Democratic | HENNING A. BLOMEN – of Somerville~~~~Socialist Labor | GUY S. WILLIAMS – of Worcester~~~~~~Prohibition |
To vote for Electors of President and Vice President under any one of the following Party Names or Political Designations, mark a Cross **X** in the Square at the right of such Party Name or Political Designation. **X**	**LIEUTENANT GOVERNOR** Vote for ONE EDWARD F. McLAUGHLIN, Jr. – of Boston~~~~Democratic | AUGUSTUS G. MEANS – of Essex~~~~~~Republican | THOMAS MARATEA – of Greenfield~~~~~~Prohibition | FRANCIS A. VOTANO – of Lynn~~~~~~Socialist Labor |
Vote for ONE	
DECKER and **MUNN**~~~~~~Prohibition	**SECRETARY** Vote for ONE EDWARD W. BROOKE – of Boston~~~~~~Republican | KEVIN H. WHITE – of Boston~~~~~~Democratic |
HASS and **COZZINI**~~~~Socialist Labor	FRED M. INGERSOLL – of Lynn~~~~~~Socialist Labor | JULIA B. KOHLER – of Boston~~~~~~Prohibition |
KENNEDY and **JOHNSON**~~~~Democratic	**ATTORNEY GENERAL** Vote for ONE EDWARD J. McCORMACK, Jr. – of Boston~~~~Democratic | Candidate for Re-election
NIXON and **LODGE**~~~~~~Republican	GEORGE MICHAELS – of Newton~~~~~~Republican | AUGUST O. JOHNSON – of Medford~~~~~~Socialist Labor | WILLIAM D. ROSS – of Brookline~~~~~~Prohibition |
To vote for a Person, mark a Cross **X** in the Square at the right of the Party Name or Political Designation. **X**	
SENATOR IN CONGRESS Vote for ONE	**TREASURER** Vote for ONE
LEVERETT SALTONSTALL – of Dover~~Republican Candidate for Re-election	JOHN THOMAS DRISCOLL – of Boston~~~~~~Democratic | WALTER J. TRYBULSKI – of Chicopee~~~~~~Republican |
THOMAS J. O'CONNOR, Jr. of Springfield~~~	WARREN C. CARRERO of~~~~~~Prohibition

What are the political effects of straight-ticket voting versus ticket splitting? Ticket splitting may indicate increased political sophistication among voters—that they are evaluating candidates on their merits, giving more attention to issues than to party labels, and not allowing their choices to be dictated by party machines. Ticket splitting, however, can produce a Republican President and a Democratic Congress, or at the state level, a Democratic governor with Republicans in surrounding executive positions or a Republican legislature. Divided rule and stalemate may result. Straight-ticket voting makes it more likely that the winning administration will be partisan and that the victorious party can be held responsible for the conduct of government. On the other hand, bipartisan administrations produced by ticket splitting protect the interests of the minority by giving them a powerful opposition to the dominant party and by preventing highly partisan programs from being instituted.

THE TIMING OF ELECTIONS

The dates for choosing Presidential electors, United States Senators, and Congressmen are fixed by federal law. Every two years, on the first Tuesday after the first Monday in November, there is a "federal" election. States and localities, however, are not obliged to elect their officials at the same times as the federal offices are filled. In many cases, state and local elections are keyed to the national dates, but in some instances they are not—for good political reasons. Local candidates cannot help but be affected by the national races. Popular candidates for federal office can exercise considerable "coattail" effect—pulling up the vote for the whole party ticket. Local allegiances and issues tend to be submerged. The turnout is large because of the interest in national offices, and the local organization leaders have to contend with big, relatively unstable electorates rather than the smaller and more predictable electorates that a purely local election would bring to the polls. For these reasons a few states such as Virginia and New Jersey have established "off-year elections" for their governorships, and numerous mayors, sheriffs, and so on are purposely elected out of phase.

Conclusion: American Parties and Dispersed Power

As formal governmental power is dispersed by constitutional arrangement, informal political power is also dispersed within our loose and localized party structure. Because of this, the official and the unofficial political institutions reinforce one another. If political parties were truly disciplined and hierarchical—if policy were made at the top and executed by obedient troops in the field—then the federal system would in fact be a legal fiction, and "separation of powers" between executives and legislatures would be meaningless. It is often suggested that American political life would be elevated by reform of the parties along the lines of the British model—with clear party "positions" and a national leadership capable of commanding obedience to decisions made at the top (at least until replacement of the personnel at the top). Proponents of this position, however, fail to take account of the impact of their "improved" parties on our constitutional structures. It is all very well to say that if the party were disciplined, then leaders would be responsible for what the party did and for implementing the program for which the party stood. This is attractive until one realizes that the price paid would be the loss of effective political power (that is, the ability to say "no") by all levels and divisions of government except the judiciary and perhaps certain administrative agencies exercising quasi-judicial power. All legislators, governors, and perhaps even mayors and aldermen would be expected to comply with the party whips—any bolting of the party position on an important issue would endanger political life. The party leadership, presumably, would control the party label and decide who would be a candidate and who was no longer useful.

Thus, political systems are not machines with interchangeable parts. As a distinguished British politician once put it, "they are not for export." To argue that innovation and improvement in American party organization and procedure is unnecessary would be fatuous. Yet whatever the shortcomings in this state or that city, the party system is one which fleshes out our constitutional forms and which grew in response to the needs of our diversified society. It is so woven into the fabric of our political system that to contemplate its drastic alteration is to contemplate the remaking of the whole.

7 / Interest Groups and the Political Process

While individual citizens possess the constitutionally guaranteed opportunity to participate in the political process in elections, this is only *one* way in which those who do not rule influence the behavior of those who do. Groups and associations play a major role in articulating the interests of various segments of the "public." The public, in fact, is a patchwork of special groups and special interests—and if these are to achieve political expression this can best be done through the medium of a formally or informally organized group.

This is not to say that an individual cannot exert some measure of influence himself above and beyond his vote. He can write to his Congressman expressing his views on impending legislation. He can send a letter to his local newspaper in the hope of rallying others to his way of thinking (in effect, this is really an attempt to create a group). He can even go to the expense and trouble of initiating a test case in the courts, with the intention of evoking a Supreme Court decision that will affect the entire nation. Nevertheless most citizens, if they are to make their weight felt in the political world, must join forces with other citizens having similar interests to promote. There is political power in numbers. To the eyes of a city councilman a group with 500 members is a bloc of 500 potential voters. He will be likely to give respectful attention to their spokesmen, for few politicians are anxious to alienate whole groups of constituents. Americans have traditionally combined to improve their exercise of power. Alexis de Tocqueville, the French commentator, observed this tendency over a century ago:

> In no country in the world has the principle of association been more successfully used, or applied to a greater multitude of objects, than in America. In the United States, associations are established to promote the public safety, commerce, industry, morality, and religion. There is no end which the human will despairs of attaining through the combined power of individuals united in a society.[1]

The power of groups has been a central part of political discussion since the early days of the Republic. Factions were the building blocks of political

---

[1] Alexis de Tocqueville, *Democracy in America*, Phillips Bradley, ed. (New York, 1945), Vol. I, pp. 198–99.

Keppler in *Puck*

None But Millionaires Need Apply—
The Coming Style Of The Presidential Election

An 1890 cartoon showing business groups bidding for the Presidential chair.

parties. During the late nineteenth and early twentieth century there was much concern about the evil influences of the "interests" (meaning powerful business groups); during the 1930s and '40s there was deprecation of "pressure groups" that beguiled officials away from the "public interest." Today, there is more sympathy toward the role interest groups play in the political process. Such groups are recognized as agents of representation and as channels of communication, transmitting the views and sentiments of their members to the centers of power.

The Politics of Countervailing Power

If the power of government is to be limited in scope and responsive to those who are governed, then countervailing power must be located in social organizations that stand apart from and are unconnected with the state. Totalitarian societies require that all organized activity promote official lines of policy. A free society, in contrast, welcomes groups because they represent the diverse and conflicting interests found among its citizens.

Many groups, including political parties, can act as buffers against the growth of the power of national government and serve as agencies by which public sentiment is articulated. These organizations can be business, professional, racial, religious, fraternal, or civic in character. The interpreters of the Constitution have always respected freedom of association, regarding organizations as natural extensions of each individual's rights of expression. "Effective advocacy of both public and private points of view, particularly

controversial ones, is undeniably enhanced by group associations . . . ,"
Justice Harlan remarked in a decision supporting the activities of the
National Association for the Advancement of Colored People. "Freedom to
engage in association for the advancement of beliefs and ideas is an insep-
arable aspect of the 'liberty' assured by the due process clause of the
Fourteenth Amendment."[2]

WHAT DO WE MEAN BY "MEMBERSHIP"?

It would be absurd to say that all citizens are formal members of several
groups and that life is a constant round of meetings for most people.
Virtually everyone, however, has his interests protected or at least expressed
by one group or another, although he may not be a dues-paying member.
Americans are represented not only by the men they elect to office but also
by organizations that apply pressure on behalf of their members and by the
wider constituency which shares the group's interest. It must be recognized
that *participating group members* (as opposed to identifiers or fellow travelers) are not equally distributed within society. Association members tend
to be those with higher incomes and levels of education. And the number
of people who are formal members of two or more groups is relatively small.
Self-employed businessmen and professionals tend to be organizational activists. Doctors, dentists, funeral directors, hotel owners, and home builders
have concrete interests and will join associations as a matter of course.
So will lawyers, social workers, and highway engineers. Needless to say,
citizens with low income, education, and status are less involved in politics
and fewer of them become formal members of organized groups, with labor
union membership and religious and ethnic identifications being the most
important group-commitments. If a person owns his own hotel, he is more
likely to identify the prosperity of the hotel industry with his own well-
being than would a salaried assistant cashier, working for the Hilton chain.
The hotel owner has good reasons for joining the American Hotel Association. The cashier at the Pittsburgh-Hilton has a more tenuous identification
with the industry as a whole, and his status as a disabled veteran (whether
or not he is actually a member of the Disabled American Veterans organization) may be much more politically salient.

Many of the groups to which Americans belong have little, superficially,
to do with politics. Millions of middle-class citizens belong to bowling
leagues, parent-teacher associations, community improvement associations,
and charitable organizations. These groups, however, may be "political"
when they become concerned with the uses and distribution of power at the
local and even national levels. From time to time even the most apolitical
social and civic associations have to "lobby" lawmakers or to act as "pressure
groups." It should be added that Americans are not a very "political" people,
and it is not surprising that their "social" affiliations outnumber their more
direct political commitments. This order of priorities, of course, has important consequences for the stability of the system. Political concern is not
generalized; Americans participate politically in order to obtain specific,
pragmatic goals.

---

[2] *NAACP* v. *State of Alabama*, 78 S. Ct. 1171 (1958).

All citizens possess interests, but they do not feel them with equal intensity nor are they always able to define them in a precise way. One test of intensity of feeling is whether an individual will join an association to promote and protect an interest. It has, for example, been estimated that more than 10 million Americans are stamp collectors. However only 200,000—about 2 percent—have joined the local philatelic societies that are affiliated with the National Federation of Stamp Clubs. The fact that the vast majority of collectors are unorganized suggests that this pastime does not loom sufficiently large in the lives of collectors to impel them to join an interest group. On the other hand, out of 100,000 dentists in the United States, almost 95 percent have become members of the American Dental Association. A dentist's interest in the status of his profession is both economic and social, and his career occupies the major part of his waking hours. This interest, furthermore, is specific: a dentist has a fairly clear idea about what kind of legislation will help or harm his profession. Not all interests can be defined so clearly. A mother with a son of military age has an interest in world peace; a white-collar worker has an interest in maintaining a respectable social status for himself; a retired person living on a fixed pension has an interest in stable prices. But these interests tend to be vague and diffuse. It may be difficult for persons harboring such feelings to see group activity as relevant to their needs—difficult, indeed, to see political activity as potentially satisfying to their desires. Groups with limited, specific ends have the advantage in attracting participation and in pressing for legislative and administrative consideration. The soybean growers concentrate their efforts on seeing that particular sections of a particular bill are written in a particular way. Associations dedicated to grandiose ends, however worthy, find that the policy-making process is not well suited to their aspirations.

WHAT DO WE MEAN BY "GROUP"?

Any discussion of groups must acknowledge the distinction between aggregates of citizens and organized, coherent associations having a headquarters, officers, and articulated programs. Indeed much of our discourse on the "group basis" of American politics refers in fact to the heterogeneous character of the national population. Thus society is fragmented into numberless groups with varying degrees of political self-consciousness. Here is one list selected at random:

Suburbanites	Divorcees
Basketball fans	Farmers
Mexican-Americans	Moviegoers
Left-handed people	Teen-agers
Tall people	Midwesterners
Stamp collectors	Mothers with sons of draft age
Diabetics	Cat lovers
Veterans	

The key question is what role these "aggregate" or unorganized groups play in the political process. Left-handed people and divorcees, for example, are scattered throughout the country and have no particular sense of themselves as belonging to a group with a common political interest. Such Americans may suffer from minor social discrimination and may at times resent it, but neither left-handed people nor divorcees have organized in order to change this situation. People with these traits are "groups" in the sense that they share common attitudes, yet because there is no communication that recognizes the shared interest as politically relevant, these "groups" stand outside the effective political arena.

On the other hand, there are many unorganized groups that attract the attention of the politicians. In one area the parties will be concerned about winning what they think of as the "Mexican-American vote." In another district the focus may be on wooing what is regarded as the "veterans' vote," or at least not alienating those citizens who fit in that category. Yet officeholders and party officials are never sure whether such bloc votes actually exist. An animal lover may be annoyed because his Congressman fails to support an antivivisection bill. Yet interest in the welfare of animals is only one of many concerns and allegiances in the voter's life, and it is doubtful that he will vote against the Congressman simply because of this one bill. But who knows? A marginal party identifier, undecided between the two candidates, might be swayed by the incumbent's stand on vivisection. Factors such as these make politicians eager to please (or at least not to offend) the many groups, organized and unorganized, in their constituencies.

In addition to association and aggregate groups there have emerged on the American scene what may be called "corporate" groups. These are not associations of individual citizens but rather organizational complexes having political interests and the power to promote them. Theories of group politics have traditionally centered on associations such as the American Medical Association, the American Legion, the American Farm Bureau Federation, and the National Funeral Directors Association. In these cases it could be assumed that doctors, veterans, farmers, or undertakers came together voluntarily to promote their common interests. Moreover, it could be said that such organizations were democratic, at least in theory, in that officials were elected and that policies had the tacit or express consent of the members. Corporate groups such as the Natural Gas and Oil Resources Committee, the Association of American Railroads, the Committee for Economic Development, and the Iron and Steel Institute, on the other hand, have as members corporations rather than individuals. Some corporations are active in politics on their own. Companies like American Airlines, Atlantic Refining, Du Pont, Ford, General Motors, Radio Corporation of America, Standard Oil of New Jersey, and Westinghouse have registered as lobbyists. General Electric, for example, actually took a company stand on a "right-to-work" proposal up for referendum in California several years ago. It spent over $30,000 supporting its position by means of advertisements and related activities.

Whom do corporate groups represent? To some extent, these groups represent the corporation's stockholders. For the most part, however, stockholders are not consulted on the political stands that companies take, for the decisions in this area rest with top management. And although stockholders can vote at an annual meeting, ballots are cast on a basis of one vote per share and not per individual. Furthermore many of the major stockholders in corporate groups are other corporate groups such as insurance companies, banks, investment houses, pension funds, and foundations. It is difficult to characterize corporate groups and the role they should legitimately play in pressure politics. It is not difficult to grant that a group comprised of dentists has a right to spend money in an attempt to influence legislation. But whether a group of steel companies has an identical right is a disturbing and as yet unanswered question.

"INTERNAL DEMOCRACY" IN INTEREST GROUPS

One of the frequent criticisms of pressure groups is that the political stands they take do not, in fact, represent the sentiments of their rank-and-file members. It is claimed that national associations are run by full-time salaried bureaucracies and that policies are made by an elite minority within the organization. While it may be granted that a group's officers are elected by and accountable to the membership, in reality this theory masks apathy at the bottom and autocracy at the top. This question of the representative character of group leadership becomes important when voluntary associations participate in the political process. When the official of an organization testifies before a Congressional committee he will usually imply that he is expressing not his own views but those of the 100,000 or 500,000 or 1 million citizens who belong to his group. Whether he is actually echoing rank-and-file opinion, and whether the ordinary members of his organization in fact have opinions on specific bills, are questions that are seldom asked and even less frequently answered satisfactorily.

Most national associations are federal in structure. At the lowest level there is usually a county group, or a district group covering several counties, to which local members belong. The county or district groups hold regular meetings, usually once a month but sometimes only twice a year, depending on the degree of interest shown by the membership. A county medical society, for example, will have well-attended monthly gatherings, but a district society of funeral directors may meet less frequently and with a smaller turnout. The county or district group elects a delegate who becomes its spokesman at the state level. And the state meeting, generally once or twice a year, in turn selects delegates to represent it at the national level. Individual members are able to cast their ballots only at the county or district level. This means that if they want their points of view to be acted upon, they must gain the support first of the local society, and then of the state association; finally they must secure the votes of a majority in the governing body of the national organization. Expressions of rank-and-file opinion can be outvoted, shelved, or watered down at any of these stages. This arduous process makes it difficult for dissenting members at the bottom of the pyramid to have their resolutions translated into action by those at the top.

But this condition does not trouble local association members as much as one might think. For most individuals join groups for social and professional as well as political reasons. While county or district groups pick delegates to the association's state committee, these representatives are not usually instructed on how they should vote once they get there. And when they return from the state meeting their reports are usually perfunctory. Member knowledge of and interest in the affairs of the national association may be quite minimal. For many dentists, attendance at the national ADA conventions represents a combined vacation and business trip. The vast majority do not show up for the sessions where political policy is discussed. "You can't really do much as it's a select group that runs the show," one dentist has observed.[3] And even the delegates elected by the state groups to the national committee may have to be content with a titular role. The board of directors of the American Hotel Association, for example, has sixty members. This is far too unwieldy a body for discussion and policy determination. Moreover this board meets only twice a year, and there is a rapid turnover among its members. The result is that power gravitates to the AHA's eighteen-man executive committee and the salaried staff.

If power tends to be concentrated at the top in most associations, great emphasis is placed on establishing downward communication with rank-and-file members. Periodic magazines and newsletters discuss the group's problems and outline political means for solving them. The American Hotel Association, for example, has devoted articles in its journal to the state of legislation dealing with billboards on federal highways. On one occasion it listed the Senators who voted against a measure the AHA favored, the repeal of the cabaret tax, suggesting that its members remember those erring lawmakers on Election Day. However these communications lose much of their force as they travel from the national headquarters to the local member's mailbox. Few members can identify the bills their association is supporting and even fewer join pressure campaigns. A member of the National Association of Home Builders recalled: "I get a couple of letters now and then. They're always pushing for something." But he, like others, cannot ordinarily rouse himself to come to the aid of his association. There are indications that the efforts of doctors acting as individuals against federal medical programs are the exception rather than the rule.

In the light of such rank-and-file apathy and such concentrated power in the hands of association officials it might be concluded that groups are marked by rampant misrepresentation and sham democracy. National headquarters, it would appear, take positions in the names of their members; yet those members have neither participated in drawing up policies nor do they know much about the stands their associations have taken. But this is only one side of the story. One home builder, explaining his indifference to political matters, said: "We have some pretty big boys up there who take care of that." A member of the National Funeral Directors Association commented that the organization's Washington office "knows what is good for us and what isn't." Moreover members seldom feel the need to discuss political issues at their meetings or to transmit their ideas upward in the hierarchy. "You almost always find that the national association has already taken care of it," another home builder explained.

The power of national associations, therefore, seems to be based on the tacit consensus of local members. Most organizations are democratic in form —that is, top officials are elected for specified terms. But there are few contested elections and little rank-and-file participation in policy-making. Yet most members feel that they are being represented, and they have an un-

---

[3] This quotation and those in the following paragraphs are from interviews conducted with association members in the upstate New York area.

critical faith in their national leaders. To the extent that their own internal structures are representative in character, pressure groups are a legitimate part of the democratic political process.

THE SOURCES OF GROUP POWER

Of course all interest groups are not equally powerful. At the same time, however, there is no way of measuring the precise amount of power (defined as influence over the behavior of others) that each organization possesses. Little is to be gained by asking group spokesmen to assess their associations' influence. Most officials have a distorted view of their actual status in the political process, either overrating their power (when reporting their achievements to their own members) or minimizing their influence (when speaking to a suspicious public). Thus trade union leaders will claim that they are powerless in the face of business domination in Washington or the state capitals, and businessmen will ruefully attest that labor is running (and ruining) the country. A preferable approach is to sum up the resources that a group has at its disposal. Some of these are as follows:

1. The *number* of members a group has, and the number of nonmembers that identify themselves with the group's interests.

2. The *economic* and *social* resources a group has at its disposal. First, how much money does a group have at its disposal to spend on campaigns of persuasion? Second, what is the social prestige of those who belong to a group and the social acceptability of the aims the group is pursuing?

3. The degree of *involvement* that members feel with their group and the extent of their willingness to work for the organization's goals.

4. The quality of a group's *leadership*. This can be a matter partly of accident and partly of design. Some groups are successful because they produce talented leaders who are able not only to mobilize the group's members but to make a persuasive appeal for sympathy to the general public. Other groups have the resources to hire experienced lobbyists who know how to gain access to key public officials and who are adept at engineering popular support for the group's goals.

5. The relative *conservatism* of a group's goals. The American political process has the effect of favoring groups with conservative goals—that is, a group trying to maintain the *status quo* in a given area has an inherent advantage over a group trying to overturn it. Our legislative, administrative, and judicial systems are based on an intricate network of checks and balances designed to protect minority interests and prevent hasty action. The procedural hurdles built into the processes for enacting legislation, bringing a test case up to the Supreme Court, or enforcing decisions by regulatory agencies give added leverage to a group taking defensive action—to block proposed legislation, or to evade the decisions of federal courts or administrative agencies.

Groups possess these resources in varying combinations. Numbers, for example, do not tell the whole story. The AFL–CIO has a fluctuating membership, currently estimated between 13 and 14 million. This is about sixty times the numerical strength of the American Medical Association, which has only 250,000 physicians on its rolls. Clearly the AFL–CIO is not sixty times as powerful as the AMA; indeed some observers would say that organized medicine is more powerful than organized labor. The chief reason is that the AMA makes up in economic and social resources what it lacks in numbers. Doctors contribute more money to further their association's political projects than trade union members do. Moreover doctors have a high level of social prestige in the community and are therefore able to enlist wide public sympathy for their point of view. In addition, doctors show a greater degree of cohesion and involvement with their association than do trade unionists. This is due, in part at least, to the fact that physicians are better educated and have a better-developed sense of how power is exercised in society. Finally, the AMA is an interest group that has often favored maintenance of the *status quo,* particularly with regard to private medical practice; it has been particularly successful in influencing the public to identify with its values on such issues as opposition to government medical care for the aged (discussed later in the chapter). Unions, by contrast, often find it difficult to recruit support outside their own membership.

Other groups with fairly modest memberships and minimal economic and social resources still manage to achieve impressive political victories because of the unrelenting energy of their supporters. Often the members of such groups are highly committed and are willing to sacrifice their time and careers for a cause they think important. Thus they will talk, write letters, attend meetings, picket, and even go to jail in an effort to secure ends in which they believe. Such groups have worked for votes for women, prohibition, civil rights, and nuclear disarmament.

The Negro civil rights organizations formed in the last decade—the Southern Christian Leadership Conference, the Congress of Racial Equality (CORE), and the Student Non-Violent Coordinating Committee (nicknamed "Snick")—are examples of groups whose strength rests largely on the dedication of their memberships. The trend toward massive participation in civil rights demonstrations began in 1955 when Negroes in Montgomery, Alabama, under the leadership of the Reverend Martin Luther King, walked miles to work or organized car pools in order to boycott segregated buses in Montgomery. During the 1960s, civil rights groups developed broader types of direct-action tactics: in 1960 they began sit-ins at segregated Southern lunch counters; in 1961 they conducted freedom rides, wade-ins, swim-ins, kneel-ins, and lie-ins on segregated buses and at beaches, pools, churches, and construction sites. These demonstrations often brought arrests, beatings, and some bloodshed. One official of CORE described the membership his group required: "We need people to take risks." The members of civil rights organizations have been willing to break existing laws in order to question their constitutionality and, ultimately, to gain full citizenship. Sometimes such groups can rouse popular sympathies for their objectives; sometimes they alienate large sectors of the public. But they do attract legislative and administrative attention, and not infrequently a small but highly involved group is able to have an effective influence on government decisions.

"The Idea Of A March On Washington Is Ridiculous. Masses Of People Can't Influence Legislation, Only Lobbyists Can!"

A cartoon presenting the liberal's hostile view of lobbyists and the hope that the Negro March on Washington in 1963 *would* have some impact.

Interlandi in the Los Angeles *Times*

The Arenas of Interest Group Activities

American society is a pluralist one, in which many groups seek political power in a continuing competition. There is no single all-encompassing group that controls all channels of access to government. The very nature of our governmental forms encourages group development and conflict. Power is separated and divided among different levels of government and among branches of government. Many targets are provided for the association seeking to advance its cause. Voluntary associations arise in *society* rather than as official organs of the *state*. Totalitarian nations, after all, have many groups and associations too. But these are all appendages of the state or party apparatus and exist, by and large, at the pleasure of the regime. Interest groups in a free society, on the other hand, are independent in the sense that citizens are at liberty to form associations and engage in group activities without having to apply for official approval. And once formed, such groups are at liberty to use their power to influence the very policies of government itself; they bargain and compromise with each other—and with government agencies—to promote their members' interests.

In thinking of the activity of interest groups, one most readily associates it with legislative "lobbying"—and, indeed, lobbying in the legislative sphere is one important way in which groups go about the job of getting governmental power to work in their favor. However, groups operate in all political arenas, with a range of approaches and techniques extending far beyond the stereotype of the well-heeled and well-fleshed lobbyist who always picks up the luncheon check. A brief categorization of the forms of group activity will be helpful.

GROUPS IN THE LEGISLATIVE PROCESS

The cartoon lobbyist is not very useful in illustrating the variety of ways in which groups seek to influence the legislative product. Some fairly crude exchanging of "favors" exists, but many more sophisticated techniques are available to the Washington office of a group with an interest in a particular problem. For instance, Congressmen and Senators possess very limited resources for conducting the extensive research that is increasingly necessary for writing a bill. This is a service that can be provided by the national headquarters of an interest group concerned with the subject—the group's facilities extend those of the legislator. Groups send representatives to testify before legislative committees, initiate letter-writing campaigns among their followers as "evidence" of grass-roots sentiment for or against particular measures, and may even try to bypass legislators by lobbying with influential constituents who are asked in turn to make appropriate representations to their member. In addition, if a group can present itself as being able to "deliver" the votes of a sizable number of members, it has leverage beyond what any number of dinners or cocktail parties could achieve. The success of such activity ultimately depends on the readiness of Congressmen to succumb to the blandishments of interest groups. After all, lawmakers are free agents and need not grant an attentive ear to spokesmen for any groups with an axe to grind. But in fact lobbyists roam freely through the corridors of Capitol Hill and have easy access to Congressional offices. Congressmen do take time out to listen to their proposals, and very often the lobbyists' efforts are successful. Ideally, a Congressman might argue that he is responsible only to his own conscience, and consequently group representatives have no claim on him or his vote. In fact, matters are not so clear-cut.

As has been suggested, the Congressman can have detailed knowledge in only a limited number of areas, yet he is called upon to vote on bills dealing with all sorts of complex policies. He may have become a specialist on cotton prices or flood control, but he is also obliged to pass judgment on legislation dealing with veterans' pensions and jurisdictional strikes. In many areas, therefore, he will welcome information and advice from people who have expert knowledge of a field. Lobbyists perform this function. They do not enter a Congressman's office brandishing a club. On the contrary they come prepared to discourse on facts and figures with an air of sweet reasonableness. Congressmen listen to these recitals because they can obtain information not otherwise available to them, and in some sense the voice speaking is the *vox populi*. At the same time lawmakers learn to select their informants with a good deal of care. One Congressman may rely on a National Association of Manufacturers expert for facts on jurisdictional strikes, whereas another will pay heed to a spokesman from the AFL–CIO. The selection of facts presented by each will undoubtedly differ. The predispositions of a legislator toward issues will, then, influence his perception of the universe of groups around him.

The influence of "legislative representatives" is evidenced by the fact that the parties in the Congress do not take official stands on all pending matters of legislation. A Republican Senator, for example, may find that there is no Republican "party line" on many of the bills that he votes on. The party leaders may ask for his support on certain occasions, but he is not obliged to honor these requests, and he will not be penalized if he votes with many of the Democrats. Not being strictly responsible to party leaders, Congressmen have a wide area of personal discretion—and it is this freedom of action that lobbyists seek to exploit. If the Congressional parties had binding legislative programs, and if the first loyalty of Congressmen were to their parties, legislative lobbying might be much less prominent than it now is, and the "national offices" of the parties would be the scene of greater interest group conflict. Through this welter of organizations the legislator must find his own way, denied the tactic of claiming a binding party commitment.

Perhaps the most important reason why Congressmen are susceptible to lobbying is that representatives who speak for interest groups may well be transmitting the views of a specific bloc of voters back in the constituency. A legislator can never be sure that a lobbyist is not echoing the sentiments of important groups "at home." Congressmen—at least those in competitive districts—have their eye on the next election, and the representations of pressure groups can be indicators of how the local winds are blowing. Suppose, for example, that a Congressman won his seat by a margin of 10,000 votes. He will want to be sure that at the next election he retains, and perhaps increases, his edge. Moreover his constituency may include approximately 5,000 farmers, 3,000 veterans, 2,000 trade union members, 2,000 Negroes, and 1,000 doctors and dentists. To be sure, there will be overlapping among these groups: there will be Negro farmers, doctors who are veterans, and so forth. Nevertheless the "farm vote," the "Negro vote," the "veterans' vote," the "union vote," and the "medical vote" all add up to a significant electoral bloc. If many of these voters feel that their Congressman is not giving them adequate representation they may cast their ballots for his opponent at the next election. The Congressman, aware of his slim margin of victory, will want to know how he can satisfy such groups. He will listen to the spokesmen from the American Farm Bureau Federation, the American Legion, the National Association for the Advancement of Colored People, the American Medical Association, and the American Dental Association. Theoretically, if he obtains the approval of these groups he may win the support of their members at the polls. There is, of course, no way of knowing the extent to which these associations actually represent the political sentiments of their members. Only a small percentage of the Negroes in his district may belong to local branches of the NAACP. But it may well be that the NAACP reflects the sentiments of many Negroes who are not members. On the other hand, quite a large proportion of the veterans in his district may be members of the American Legion. But they may have joined the group for social reasons and have only a negligible commitment to the political program championed by the Legion. Or pressure groups in the Congressman's district may have conflicting goals, as, for example, when the Chamber of Commerce opposed the proposal to establish a Cabinet-level post for urban affairs, supported by the AFL–CIO and the NAACP. In such cases, a Congressman runs the risk of alienating one group if he attempts to placate the others. There may be more farmers than trade union members and Negroes combined in the Congressman's district, but on the other hand, the trade unionists and Negroes may feel more strongly about the passage of the bill. These problems have no clear-cut solutions. Moreover, the pressures that converge on a lawmaker may not be an accurate reflection of constituency opinion. It is left to the Congressman's own judgment and intuition to evaluate the extent to which the balance of groups he encounters in the course of his legislative work represents the true balance of interests in his district or in the nation.

A dramatic instance of interest group deadlock on Capitol Hill was the foundering, in 1962, of the federal aid to education proposals put forward by the Kennedy Administration as a major item in its legislative program. The President had recommended to Congress a three-year plan of "general Federal assistance for public elementary and secondary classroom construction and teachers' salaries." He had also taken the position that the Constitution prohibited any allocation of funds for constructing church schools or paying the salaries of teachers at these institutions. The National Education Association served as the keystone of interest group support for the bill, and it was joined by liberal Congressmen and Senators and other organizations such as the AFL–CIO, which were traditionally well disposed toward federal welfare activity. Opposition came first from conservative groups such as the U.S. Chamber of Commerce, which reinforced the fears of states' righters in Congress that federal funds would bring federal domination and "indoctrination." Many Southerners also saw the proposals as a new lever to force racial integration of the schools. Potent opposition also came from the hierarchy of the Roman Catholic Church. Francis Cardinal Spellman led the attack with the declaration that he was "opposed to any program of Federal aid that would penalize a multitude of America's children" for their attendance at church-supported schools.

The savage crosscurrents of interest and the strategic location of states'-rights conservatives in the Congressional power structure made for a tangle which the Administration's legislative tacticians were unable to work out. One student of the Congressional process, Hugh Douglas Price, described the stalemate as follows:

> There were at least three discernible levels of disagreement. On the first level there were low-temperature disputes over detailed matters of program administration, state allocation formulas, and so forth that could be adjusted by normal bureaucratic and interest group bargaining. Such disputes would exist even if there were a clear national consensus in favor of federal aid.
>
> At an intermediate level was the more basic split over the desirability of such a program, typified by the opposing views of the National Education Association and the U.S. Chamber of Commerce. This sort of conflict can still be handled, although it becomes difficult if the issues are framed in symbolic terms ("federal aid" versus "federal control").
>
> At a third level, such high-temperature issues as segregation and

the role of parochial schools are generally beyond the ability of Congress to handle. Next to being shot up by Puerto Rican nationalists (as happened in 1954), there are few less appealing prospects, especially for the House, than a floor fight combining race, religion, and control of the schools.[4]

GROUPS IN THE ADMINISTRATIVE PROCESS

In contemporary America, administrative agencies (or bureaucracies) exercise power that directly affects many strongly held interests in society. Bureaucracies are not neutral and politically sterile constructs; bureaucracies at all levels of government develop functional "constituencies" of their own—groups whose interest in the matters being disposed of by the agency continues over time, whose staff closely monitors the work of the agency, and whose leaders have established channels of communication to the decision makers in the bureaucracy. Thus, since the organization of the Agricultural Extension Service in the first decade of this century, the American Farm Bureau Federation has enjoyed a close relationship with the Department of Agriculture. The Department depended on the local Farm Bureaus to support the work of its county agents, and the officials of the Federation are often brought into the councils of the Department when new initiatives are under consideration. Two other major farm organizations, the National Farmers Union and the Grange, also enjoy close contact with the Department, but they have never been able to disturb the preeminence of the Federation in the Department's constituency; the newest and most militant farm group, the National Farmers Organization, has been hostile in its approach to the Department. An agency, of course, cannot count on the automatic support of the groups with a principal interest in its work. In many instances an agency may have to take a step which will cost it group support. However, when the constituency can be rallied behind a new program or a stand taken by the agency, it is a powerful asset. Friendly defense supply groups, for instance, are irreplaceable allies of the Pentagon in battles with the Congress, with other agencies, or even with the President.

This bureaucratic lobbying and constituency building is not, of course, confined to federal agencies. Wallace Sayre and Herbert Kaufman, in their study of New York City government and politics, remarked:

> The high commands of the line agencies—the Commissioners, their deputies and assistants, and their bureau chiefs—are key figures in the governmental process. They possess the formal legal powers of their agencies—the power to promulgate rules and regulations having the force of law; to fix the level and quality of service; to set conditions for, or withhold, licenses and permits and to suspend or revoke them; to deploy work forces and set project priorities, and to intervene in individual cases handled by their agencies. In addition to their formal authority, they are often treated as experts in their particular areas of public policy. But perhaps most important of all is that many agency leaders have, or develop, powerful incentives to function actively and

---

[4] Hugh Douglas Price, "Race, Religion and the Rules Committee," in Alan F. Westin, ed., *The Uses of Power* (New York, 1961), p. 70.

aggressively in the performance of their tasks and in defense of their agencies. . . .

Public opinion is amorphous, ambiguous, and apparently capricious a good deal of the time. Hence, while it is a valuable implement for most agency heads, it is not entirely reliable. That is why most commissioners and bureau chiefs foster continuing and helpful relations with nongovernmental groups, and often call upon these allies to aid them in their battles against contractions of jurisdiction and curtailment of appropriations, and to back their struggles to expand their powers or expenditures.[5]

The interest groups (running the gamut from defense industries to professional organizations such as the National Education Association) have a great deal at stake in gaining continued entree to relevant agencies. What they offer the bureaucrat is not votes and not money and not their prestige. Rather, they offer support with those organs of government to which votes, money, and prestige matter greatly—legislatures, elected executives, and political parties.

The intensity of constituency-agency conflict was well demonstrated in an article by Elwood Quesada, in which this veteran aviator reflected on his experiences as first administrator of the Federal Aviation Agency. With the boom in the aircraft industry during the early 1950s, and the prospect of many more, even faster aircraft ahead, it had become apparent by 1957 that something was going to have to be done about policing the skies. In 1957, responsibility for the control of air traffic and for the setting of air safety regulations was divided between three federal agencies—the Civil Aeronautics Administration, the Civil Aeronautics Board, and the Department of Defense. Military flying was strictly supervised by the service establishments, but civilian aviation—both private and commercial, but especially commercial—had enjoyed great latitude in its operations. The industry participated in every phase of the decision-making process, and the end product almost invariably bore the stamp of its approval. In short, the natural group constituency had overwhelmed the CAA, and although the CAB (which was responsible for rate regulation, allocation of routes, and such commercial aspects of aviation) had managed to maintain a somewhat more independent posture, the regulated were becoming the regulators. The two bureaucracies were becoming governmental spokesmen for the sectors of society over which they were supposed to be the watchdogs.

In 1955 a Presidential commission was appointed to survey the dimensions of the air safety problem, and to recommend what action, to include new legislation, might be felt necessary. The commission's report was delivered to President Eisenhower in the spring of 1957, and its recommendations formed the basis of a bill sent to Capitol Hill by the Administration that same summer. Congress acted quickly, and the new Federal Aviation Act was on the books before the end of the year. Under this statute, the CAB retained basically the authority it had enjoyed previously, but the old CAA was eliminated. In its place was created the FAA, with a more powerful

---

[5] Wallace S. Sayre and Herbert Kaufman, *Governing New York City* (New York, 1960), pp. 249–50, 257–58.

statutory grant of authority. Quesada was named to head the agency, and trouble began almost at once. He remarked:

> From my first day in office the irresponsible pressure asserted itself. The agency was still an embryo when Max Karant, vice president of the Aircraft Owners and Pilots Association (AOPA)—which purports to represent the fliers of private planes—bitterly warned his members of "increasing military domination of the FAA" [Quesada was a retired Air Force general]. Not long afterward, I was visited by the same organization's president, Joseph Hartranft. His purpose was to protest against our new medical requirements for pilots licenses . . . I listened to him attentively and then told him our decision would stand. "This means war" he answered, his face flushed.[6]

Nor did Administrator Quesada's constituency troubles stop with the pilots of private planes. The Air Line Pilots Association (ALPA) was also restive and suspicious of FAA regulating and standard-setting. Said Quesada:

> One pilot sent us anonymously what we call the ALPA "Do-It-Yourself-Kit." This is a collection of mimeographed material designed to teach pilots how to write to congressmen in protest against the FAA. It includes lists of key committee members, helpful hints on style, outlines, a collection of "suggested tidbits," and miscellaneous advice on how to give letters the ring of originality. Many of the communications from pilots which congressmen refer to our agency have obviously been inspired in this way.

The Administrator ruefully concludes that even in an area as sensitive as aviation, where so many human lives quite literally hang in the balance, of the over forty interest groups which from time to time participated in the rule-making process "a number of them have managed to put stumbling blocks in our way. The agency's new devotion to duty—it appears—came as a great shock to them."

GROUPS IN THE JUDICIAL PROCESS

We often forget that in the American experience, courts have been very much a part of the political process. They exercise great influence in allocating values for the community as a whole, and choosing among the conflicting demands of individuals. The rulings of courts, as centers of political power, can have great political significance for the goals of interest groups. By bringing legal actions, groups not only can gain immediate ends (that is, favorable decisions in particular cases), but, through skillful management of lawsuits, can draw from appellate courts precedents with far broader impact on their areas of interest. For example, the American Civil Liberties Union financed the litigation of a case questioning the power of New York state to write a prayer for use in public school classrooms. The ruling by the United States Supreme Court that such exercises were unconstitutional represented a *political* victory for the ACLU just as substantial as defeating a bill in Congress or persuading the Department of Defense that it ought

---

[6] E. R. Quesada, "The Pressures Against Air Safety," *Harper's Magazine* (January, 1961), Vol. CCXXII, pp. 58–64.

to keep open a shipyard about to be shut down by the Secretary of the Navy.

It should also be noted that the judicial process offers advantages to particular types of groups. In terms of membership and of money there is great disparity between the AFL–CIO and the American Humanist Society. In the Congressional arena, for instance, this disparity would be maximized. The AFL–CIO possesses the kinds of resources readily translated into legislative leverage. In a court, however, the disparity between the two groups would be minimized. Limited sums of money are involved (it is not possible to spend your way to a Supreme Court decision), and the judges are rarely concerned with the latest membership figures for the organizations that are actively involved (as plaintiff or defendant) or that are financing and managing the strategy of the case for the individuals who are actually parties in it.

Small groups, poor groups, groups representing the interests of minorities, or groups advocating unpopular causes have found access to judicial power much easier to obtain than access to legislative or executive power. In its infancy, the Negro civil rights movement worked very effectively through the courts. It was the NAACP Legal and Educational Defense Fund (a tax-free partner of the NAACP) under the leadership of Thurgood Marshall that fought test cases all the way to the Supreme Court, winning landmark decisions outlawing white primaries, restrictive covenants, and, in *Brown* v. *Topeka Board of Education* (1954), school segregation. (These cases are discussed further in Chapter 19.) For interest groups as for individuals, courts are a great leveler. V. O. Key has remarked:

> The role of the American courts in the determination of public policy brings them within the range of agencies with which, under some circumstances, pressure organizations must concern themselves. The records of presidential appointees to the Supreme Court undergo a searching scrutiny by pressure organizations, which are quick to oppose the confirmation of individuals thought to be biased against group interests. Given the customs of judicial action it is not good form to attempt to pressure judges. Yet interest groups often play an active role in litigation to test the constitutionality of legislation; the existence of an organization incidentally permits a sharing of the costs of such cases. Beyond the realm of constitutional questions, in some areas the reality of law is fixed not so much by the initiative of public authority as by the vigor of private litigation to maintain rights.[7]

GROUPS AND PUBLIC OPINION

While all important interest groups maintain a staff of Washington representatives, many organizations are coming to realize that the most effective method of influencing political decisions takes a more indirect form. With "traditional" lobbying, only a few hundred legislators in Washington are the direct targets of influence. "Public opinion lobbying," on the other hand, aims at convincing the lawmakers' constituents *en masse* that particular policies are right, on the assumption that these viewpoints will ultimately reach the legislators themselves. A public relations specialist who

---

[7] V. O. Key, Jr., *Politics, Parties, and Pressure Groups,* 5th ed. (New York, 1964), p. 140.

directed the political campaigns of the American Medical Association declared: "Our conception of practical politics is that if you have a sound enough case to convince the folks back home, you don't have to buttonhole the Senator. He will hear from home, and he will respect very highly the opinions he gets from that quarter." [8] The result of this shift in emphasis, of course, is that pressure politics becomes more ambitious, more expensive, and—in a sense—more democratic.

One type of grass-roots influence is exerted through massive demonstrations that express the needs and desires of a particular interest group in an effort to mobilize sympathetic public opinion. Such strategies do not require sophisticated public relations campaigns or expensive advertisements in the mass media—in fact such approaches would not be the best way to influence the audiences these groups wish to persuade. These tactics are often used by groups seeking to influence the public not so much on a particular bill as on broader goals that would require changes in social attitudes and behavior at all levels. The direct-action tactics used by civil rights groups illustrate this type of grass-roots campaign. As already mentioned, through the early 1960s civil rights organizations dramatized the injustices of segregation in public facilities. In 1963, the Department of Justice recorded that no less than 1,400 racial demonstrations took place throughout the country. And on August 28 of that year, the five major civil rights organizations—the Southern Christian Leadership Conference, the NAACP, CORE, the National Urban League, and the Student Non-Violent Coordinating Committee—joined forces to stage the largest demonstration ever held in Washington. 200,000 Negroes and whites marched on Washington and assembled before the Lincoln Memorial to petition for the full rights and opportunities of American citizenship.

Interest groups also conduct more extensive public relations campaigns at the grass-roots level that seek to convince the public that a particular policy is not only right but in the public's own best interest as well. This "engineering of consent" on a nationwide scale, however, costs a great deal of money, and few organizations have the financial resources for such campaigns. Public relations budgets are extremely costly, partly because a wide range of techniques must be used if millions of citizens are to be reached and persuaded.

More subtle and even more indirect than mass persuasion is the conscious effort to affect the ideas of the opinion makers. Research into communication and opinion formation clearly suggests that for different subjects there exist different, special or attentive publics—networks of influential communicators. If a group can introduce new ideas into the particular "net" with which it is concerned, it can affect the whole climate of opinion on the subject—both among the public and among decision makers. Thus when dealing with the courts in attempting to trigger precedents that will alter the law in its favor, a group would be well advised to consider the attitudes of legal opinion makers toward the subject at issue. Judges do not decide cases

---

[8] Leone Baxter, "How the Story Was Presented to the People." Speech delivered before the Second Southern Public Relations Conference, New Orleans, Louisiana, May 8, 1951.

in a vacuum. They draw on many sources in their searches for legally sensible answers to vexing questions, and among these sources are the writings of legal scholars—the teachers in the large and influential "national" law schools. Thus, when a point of law is in contest over a period of years, groups may have a significant effect on the formation of law if they can manage to stimulate professors to speak out in favor of their point of view. Such group activity is really no more or less than an attempt by the group to alter the political culture (the context of attitudes in which political activity takes place) in its favor.

A particularly effective public relations campaign was conducted by the American Medical Association to influence public opinion—and through it the legislators in Washington—against medical-care legislation proposed by President Truman shortly after his upset victory of 1948. Scheduled for serious consideration during the Congressional session of 1949 were several bills dealing with medical care. The most important of these, the Wagner-Murray-Dingell bill, had strong backing from the Truman Administration. Many Congressmen were inclined to support this legislation, and it was gaining more recruits every day. In essence the plan called for a government-operated health insurance program. Each citizen and his employer would contribute a portion of his income to a public fund, just as was already being done for social security, and out of this fund would be paid individual medical bills. Doctors would not become public employees and they would even have the option of not participating in the plan. Nevertheless the patient would no longer have to pay his physician, for the doctor would receive his remuneration directly from the government insurance fund. The proponents of the plan called it "health insurance"; its opponents called it "socialized medicine."

The first group to raise its voice against the proposal, naturally enough, was the American Medical Association. To allow a third party—the government—to take over paying bills would admit general influence on the fee structure and might open the way, or so the leaders of organized medicine felt, to a vast program of medical standard setting that would alter the whole sociology of the profession. Yet a survey of leaders of 1,500 civic organizations pointed out that "national health insurance is regarded with favor by a majority of citizen organization leaders in the United States." [9] The AMA's task was to affect the thinking not only of several thousand community leaders but of a sizable segment of the American public. To achieve this the organization's leaders took two major steps. First, they wrote to all the physicians who were members of the AMA's constituent medical societies—it is a federation—and asked each of them to contribute $25 to a political war chest. While it was not clear whether professional sanctions would be imposed on AMA members who did not participate in the campaign, in the end 140,000 doctors wrote out checks. This gave the AMA $3.5 million with which to begin its work. The second step was to retain the California public relations firm of Whitaker and Baxter to direct the campaign for "free medicine." But this did not mean that the public relations firm intended to conduct the

---

[9] This quotation and the others in the section are from Stanley Kelley, *Professional Public Relations and Political Power* (Baltimore, 1956), pp. 67–106.

fight all by itself. On the contrary, it made clear to the AMA that its role was to be one of planning, and the great part of the campaign would have to be carried out by the doctors themselves. Whitaker and Baxter were given the job of defining the issues and drawing up the program for what was to be known as the "National Education Campaign." The battle lines were narrowed down to an issue which was both simple and appealing: free medicine versus state medicine. For example, Whitaker and Baxter had reproduced Sir Luke Fildes' famous painting of a doctor tending to a sick little girl, and all physicians were asked to post this in their waiting rooms. Underneath the picture ran the message:

KEEP POLITICS OUT OF THIS PICTURE!

> When the life—or health—of a loved one is at stake, hope lies in the devoted service of your Doctor. Would you change this picture? Compulsory health insurance is political medicine. It would bring a third party—a politician—between you and your Doctor. It would bind up your family's health in red tape. It would result in heavy payroll taxes—and inferior medical care for you and your family. Don't let that happen here!

At the same time Whitaker and Baxter advised that a totally negative approach would carry little weight. "We will offer a positive program," Whitaker said, "because we realize that you can't beat something with nothing." This positive program was to emphasize the availability, coverage, and moral virtues of private health insurance plans—such as Blue Cross and Blue Shield—already in existence. For their part Whitaker and Baxter enlisted not only the doctors but also the members of other conservative associations sharing the AMA's sentiments. By 1952 over 8,000 groups ranging from the American Farm Bureau Federation and the American Legion to the American Bar Association and the United States Chamber of Commerce had come out publicly against health legislation.

In addition the message was brought to the public. The AMA began by authorizing an advertising budget of over a million dollars, with half of that destined for newspapers. (This was before television had become a standard household item.) By the end of the campaign it was estimated that the AMA case ("When You're Sick Do You Want Doctors—or Clerks?" "Political Medicine Is Bad Medicine!") had been aired in newspapers with circulations of 115,630,487, in magazines reaching 55,202,080 people, and on radio stations with 108,205,034 listeners. There seems little doubt that the American people were made aware that health insurance was an important political issue.

The keystone of the campaign, however, was neither the support coming from other associations nor the advertising in the mass media. In his own community, the physician is a figure with high status and public respect. He is looked upon with deference and, on medical matters, is regarded as an authority. Whitaker and Baxter decided that the authoritative aura surrounding the medical profession should be used for political purposes. "Without doubt the most effective single mission doctors can perform," Whitaker said, "is a thorough-going letter-writing job, beamed to their patients—*personal* letters, signed by the doctor on his professional letter-

"Now, Has Everyone Got One Of These Little Figures And A Set Of Pins?"

A liberal comment on the AMA's fight against the Kennedy Medicare bills.

From *Straight Herblock*, Simon & Schuster, 1964

head, and mailed in his own envelopes." That the doctors were prepared to pitch in with this grass-roots campaign is now a matter of record. Many discussed the health insurance with their patients in their own offices; others gave talks to small groups in their community. One Florida physician got into his private plane and showered the countryside with AMA leaflets. The wives of doctors formed themselves into ladies' auxiliaries and carried the message even further. New York doctors sent out thousands of letters reading:

> My dear patient:
> I wonder if you know about the threat which exists today against the kind of care I have been able to give my patients. The National Administration has a plan for compulsory sickness insurance, which is the entering wedge of the socialized State. This would put politics into medicine and destroy the doctor-patient relationship so necessary to good medical care.

In the end almost 20,000 New York doctors and allied professionals participated in this program of personal contact, sending more than 2 million letters to patients. In other states there was a similar range of activity. Interestingly enough, the cost of the New York campaign was only $13,000. But the number of unpaid man-hours devoted to it was tremendous.

What was the objective of the AMA campaign? It was, first of all, to stop Congress from passing a health insurance bill. In this aim it was successful. Neither in 1950 nor for a decade after did the Senate or the House of Representatives consider or vote upon legislation of this character. In some states and Congressional districts the doctors worked for the defeat of legislators who had come out in favor of the bill. But more significant was the fact that most Congressmen who had been supporting the bill withdrew their sponsorship as Election Day approached, and those who had been uncommitted came down on the opposition side. In short, the AMA's campaign was a powerful instrument in helping the legislators to make up their minds. And this end was achieved not by trying to persuade the Congressmen directly but rather by taking the case to the voters and letting them convey their sentiments to their elected representatives. The AMA's campaign was a massive effort to persuade the Congress, *by indirect means,* that it should abandon any idea of passing a national health insurance program.

While the American Medical Association's continuing campaign against government medical programs is based partly on the financial interest of its membership, the AMA also sees the issue partly in terms of the freedom of a doctor to run his practice without government supervision. It would thus be an error to assume that interest groups work exclusively for economic stakes; as we have seen, groups also organize to raise their status in society and to defend their conceptions of justice.

The Dangers of Group Politics: Myths and Realities

Much of the early literature on interest groups (and not an inconsiderable part of the contemporary writing on the subject) is concerned with the evil effect on public policy of a group that is able to exercise influence out of all proportion to its membership and identifiers. Thus the "public interest" is seen as subverted when an interest group wages a successful campaign to stop a bill that the "people really want," or when the people are "sold a bill of goods" by a "slick Madison Avenue" advertising agency. Thus far we have spoken in terms of roughly democratic competition among groups and of countervailing power operating in a pluralist environment—but what happens when there is no countervailing power? What are the dangers of the group process breaking down to the point where consistent minority domination is possible, and what are the checks and hedges that exist or can be built against such breakdown?

WHO WATCHES THE LOBBYISTS?

It is no surprise that lobbying by interest groups, both in Washington and at the grass roots, has been viewed with suspicion and mistrust. Even those associations that take their case directly to the public also make sure that they have their representatives at work in the halls where the legislators sit. Even after grass-roots sentiment has been aroused by means of a public relations campaign, lobbyists must translate such opinion into specific legislative proposals. There have always been some who felt that the men who converged on Capitol Hill were up to no good. While it is seldom suggested that bribes are passed or campaign contributions proffered, the view prevails that there is too much secrecy and special pleading in the lobbies. In 1946 the Congress attempted to clean out its own antechambers by adding to the Legislative Reorganization Act a title that would regulate lobbies. A lobbyist is any "person"—that is, an individual, a partnership, a committee, an association, a corporation, or any other group—"who by himself, or through any agent or employee or other person in any manner whatsoever, directly or indirectly, solicits, collects, or receives money or any other thing of value to be used principally to aid, or the principal purpose of which person is to aid, in the accomplishment of any of the following purposes: (a) The passage or defeat of any legislation by the Congress of the United States. (b) To influence, directly or indirectly, the passage or defeat of any legislation by the Congress of the United States." [10] Persons who come under this heading are required by law to do two things. First, they must, upon beginning their lobbying activities, register their names with the clerk of the House of Representatives and the secretary of the Senate. Second, they are required, once every three months, to file a report naming the principal sources of their income and the individuals to whom they have made payments. The purpose of this Act is not so much to regulate lobbyists as to shed light on them. They are now names on public record rather than anonymous figures. And rather than rumors of astronomical sums for ulterior purposes there are now open reports of amounts received and expended. The theory, of course, is that if matters are open they will also be above board.

From September, 1946, to September, 1962, a total of 6,504 persons registered their names.[11] In the first year of the law's operation there were over 700 registrations, but since that time new listings have settled down to an annual figure of about 350. The groups that register range from established corporations such as the American Can Company and the Hilton Hotels Corporation to labor unions such as the American Federation of Musicians and the International Association of Fire Fighters. There are foreign organizations such as the Compagnie Aramayo de Mines en Bolivia, professional groups such as the International Chiropractors Association, and citizen bodies like the National Federation of Country Clubs. Most numerous are the trade associations, including the American Bottlers of Carbonated Beverages, the Copper and Brass Research Association, the Group of Importers of Japanese Oysters, and the National Crushed Limestone Institute. In 1961, under the provision for reports on income and expenditures, registered lobbies reported that they spent slightly under $4 million in promoting their legislative interests. This ranged from $139,919 for the AFL–CIO and $163,405 for the American Medical Association to $600 for the Southwest Peanut Shellers' Association and $32.02 for the Bulgarian Claims Committee.

However in most observers' minds the problem of lobbying has in no significant way been solved by the registration law. Part of this results from the fact that there is no real agreement on what the problem is. If what is needed is to shed the "pitiless glare of publicity" on the lobbyists, the problem is that the reports on registrations and expenses are so unexceptionable that the public is hardly excited or informed by them. They are duly printed in the *Congressional Record,* and hence the information is available to anyone who takes the trouble to go to a library. But few people do. And while

---

[10] Public Law 601, Section 307, Seventy-ninth Congress, Second Session.
[11] "Lobby Round-Up," *Congressional Quarterly Almanac 1962.*

some newspapers may occasionally give some space to the annual listings, there is no evidence that the ordinary citizen knows or cares more about lobbying than he did in 1946.

One of the chief reasons for the law's ineffectiveness is that it defines a lobby as a group whose "principal purpose" is to influence the passage of legislation. Very few important groups are organized for the principal purpose of lobbying. The AFL–CIO, the National Association of Manufacturers, and the American Farm Bureau Federation all have a variety of purposes, only one of which is applying political pressure. For a while there was the fear that many organizations would not register because they could honestly say that their primary activity was not lobbying. This fear has not been realized. Even respectable corporations have registered as "lobbies." However, groups that register report only those expenditures which relate directly and principally to influencing legislation in Washington itself. In one recent year, for example, the American Hotel Association reported spending no more than $9,075.44 and the American Dental Association reported $40,232.71. In the first case this came to little over $1 per hotel and in the second less than $.50 per dentist. Yet both of these groups spent a good deal more than this on internal communications—of a political nature—to their members, exhorting them to write their Congressmen and apply other pressures. Nevertheless, as the law defines lobbying it is limited to regulating only those activities that take place under the shadow of the Capitol dome.

Congress' authority to scrutinize lobbying activities has been reviewed by the courts, but not in a decisive way. A committee of the House of Representatives demanded that a Dr. Edward Rumely, the head of a Committee for Constitutional Government, hand over a list of his group's financial supporters. Dr. Rumely refused, stating that he never received donations but only sold books to interested citizens. And, second, he justified his silence by stating that he wanted to protect his readers from "the pressure of the labor bosses" and "the smear of the left-wingers." Congress cited him for contempt for his silence; he was convicted by a district court, but the conviction was reversed by the Court of Appeals, and the Supreme Court upheld that reversal.[12] However, the Justices, avoiding the constitutional issue, implied that Congress did have the power to investigate and regulate lobbying.

Should grass-roots lobbying be regulated as well? Any such attempt would raise a great deal of controversy. For it may be claimed that attempts by groups to persuade public opinion constitute an exercise of free speech and therefore cannot be abridged by an act of Congress. If an association is looked upon as an extension of its individual members then it possesses the right, guaranteed to all citizens, to speak its mind freely and without regulation. A law might constitutionally require an association to speak under its own name instead of creating front organizations, but once this requirement is followed a group cannot be prevented from having its say in the marketplace of political ideas. The problem that arises, however, is not only one of free speech but also has to do with concentrated power. The Natural Gas and Oil Resources Committee, for example, is not an association of

---

[12] *United States* v. *Rumely,* 345 U.S. 41 (1953).

"Man, We're Pressure-Cooking On All Burners."

Another liberal portrait of economic interest groups controlling politics, not vice-versa.

From *Straight Herblock*, Simon & Schuster, 1964

citizens but rather a group of wealthy corporations. It may legitimately be asked if corporations, when they join an association, are entitled to rights of expression in the same way that flesh-and-blood persons are. For groups with corporations as members have funds that permit them access to mass media, public relations firms, and—in the final analysis—the public's mind. Organizations with more modest resources are plainly in a less advantageous position.

Finally there is the question of whether the government may itself legitimately engage in grass-roots persuasion, perhaps in reply to its critics. The American Medical Association had a clear field in its fight against health insurance, and one of the reasons it has been victorious was that the federal government did not embark on a countercampaign. If it is assumed that the President represents the people who elected him and endorsed his platform, then it might be argued that federal money and personnel should be made available on an extensive scale to sell the public on the merits of administration programs.

Of course government officials do "lobby." Every government department, from the Pentagon on down, has a public relations office, and attempts are made to get favorable interpretations of its policies and activities published in the press. A good example was the Surgeon General's report linking cigarette smoking and cancer, issued late in 1963. The "official" government position was that smoking is unhealthy and that it ought to be discouraged. More important, the report was discussed at a press conference that, in its planning and execution, would have done credit to a

Madison Avenue public relations firm. The result was acres of newsprint detailing the government's case against cigarettes. In this sense an official agency did do a "grass-roots" selling job on the American people. Yet the fact remains that neither the Surgeon General's office nor any other department is allowed to buy advertising space in newspapers or time on television to reinforce its arguments. When the A & P published advertisements explaining to the public why it should not be prosecuted for antitrust violations, the Justice Department could not purchase space to reply in kind. Government "grass-roots" lobbying is virtually limited to the stories it can get into the news columns. And that depends not only on the newsworthiness of the story but also on the political biases of the editors.

A MANIPULATED PUBLIC?

How easily are the American people swayed by grass-roots lobbying? The AMA tried to "sell" the electorate an item of political merchandise—opposition to health legislation—and a large part of the public was prepared to "buy" the ideas. Is the nation, then, prey to any group with the resources to reach the public mind and manipulate its thinking? Studies of totalitarian brainwashing and a series of utopian novels have reinforced the view that techniques of persuasion exist that may render the individual citizen powerless.

It is tempting to paint a bleak picture, to see propaganda and public relations as new forms of political engineering that will produce consent to all manner of laws and policies. The answer is that people's minds are not empty buckets, simply waiting to be filled with any ideas that powerful groups happen to be promoting. "The main lesson to be drawn," one psychologist has written, "is how very resistant people are to messages that fail to fit into their own picture of the world and their own objective circumstances, how they deliberately (if unconsciously) seek out only those views which agree with their own." [13] It is, in other words, not possible to "sell" an idea that runs directly counter to an individual's own settled judgments. And this provides one potent defense against the tactics of pressure groups. During the New Deal years, for example, 80 percent of the newspapers tried editorially to persuade their readers to vote against Franklin D. Roosevelt. But sentiments favoring the Democratic party ran deep among a majority of the electorate, and it persisted in supporting Roosevelt—even while continuing to read Republican newspapers. It is highly unlikely that a public relations campaign would be able to convert the American people to communism, atheism, or any other viewpoint at variance with their established values. What "pictures" do people have in their heads, and where do they get them? The AMA campaign provides a good example.

Americans had an image of the cost and quality of the medical care they were receiving. Having no such mental "picture" of an alternative system, they were influenced by the one that the AMA conjured up for them. In this case it was an image of "political medicine," of government bureaucrats coming between the doctor and his patients. This "picture" was an unpleasant one, to say the least, and it was identified with what would transpire if a

---

[13] J. A. C. Brown, *Techniques of Persuasion* (London, 1963), p. 309.

health insurance bill were enacted. There are, in sum, important areas open to grass-roots lobbyists, but these are only the areas about which the majority of Americans have no settled ideas and no body of immediate experience to serve as a guide.

Conclusion: Group Conflict and the General Welfare

Are the policies resulting from the conflicts and compromises of the pluralist political process truly in the "national interest"? Some sanguine observers suggest that the political arena is also governed by something like the "invisible hand" that Adam Smith hypothesized for the free marketplace. This unseen regulator ensures that power is met with power so that no single group becomes dominant in society, at the same time providing that all citizens benefit through the process of group conflict, even when they are not directly represented by being members of formal associations. In addition it is pointed out that the freedom to petition the government and to join with others to protect shared interests is the hallmark of a democratic society. While government may regulate some aspects of group activity, the important condition is that legislative and administrative bodies be responsive to the expressed wishes of their constituents. The group struggle may at times look chaotic: it may often appear to consist of selfish demands by special interests, all of which are fighting for a larger share of the pie. But the very fact that groups are allowed to pursue their interests so rampantly is a sign that the politics of democracy are in a healthy state.

The opposing view was stated by Jean-Jacques Rousseau in *The Social Contract*. He argued that there exists in society something called the "general will," a spirit of social unity not only pervading the body politic but also residing deep inside each citizen. The general will is not the sum of particular interests in a society but is rather an entity greater than these parts added together. A citizen may have one or more special interests, but he also has an interest in belonging to a rational community. Rousseau's view is that the general will must take priority over the group struggle:

> The General Will alone can direct the State according to the object for which it was instituted, i.e. the common good: for if the clashing of particular interests made the establishment of societies necessary, the agreement of these very interests made it possible. The common element in these different interests is what forms the social tie; and, were there no point of agreement among them all, no society could exist. It is solely on the basis of this common interest that every society should be governed.[14]

Rousseau's argument suggests that doctors and veterans, gas companies and cat lovers, indeed all special interests, ought to acknowledge that there are basic principles on which a community must be founded. But assent to the general will cannot be left to chance. The common good will not proceed automatically from the haphazard interplay of whichever groups happen to enter the political arena. Rousseau and those who echo his senti-

---

[14] Jean-Jacques Rousseau, *The Social Contract*, G. D. H. Cole, trans. (London, 1913), p. 20.

ments go on to say that firm national leadership at the helm is necessary if groups are to become aware of society's overriding needs. Not only must the pursuit of special interests be subordinated to the national interest, but the government must have sufficient power to control the group process and ensure that it does not frustrate the general welfare. But who is to define this general will? Who is to tell the conflicting groups that make up society what they "really" want? Rousseau argues that it is the responsibility of leaders to force the people to be free (act in consonance with the general will), yet this is surely a disturbing thought for anyone who has witnessed the efforts of Communist regimes to force freedom.

It must be admitted that the politics of group conflict is, on the surface, an untidy way of deciding who gets what, when, where, and how in a large, highly differentiated society such as ours. It must also be admitted that the "invisible hand" that is supposed to keep the books balanced is often more than a little shaky. There are sectors of the American population that do not make out very well in the group struggle, and they are often the groups that most need the resources of the government employed on their behalf— racial minorities, the undereducated, the poor, and the old. Even among organized groups, long years of experience, money, social prestige, and greater cohesiveness give some pressure groups far more influence—particularly in the legislative sphere—than others have. Yet on the whole, as our national development demonstrates, pluralist politics has been a highly creative process; and in our own time we are seeing some of the imbalances redressed. The Negro struggle for political and social equality demonstrates that the techniques of group politics are available to those at the bottom of the social ladder. With all the inequities and imperfections of the system, its performance commands considerable respect. Until we come across some fine philosophers (or technicians) whom we are prepared to make into kings, a good case can be made for staying with political pluralism.

8 / Voting Behavior

Among the group of citizens who are legally eligible to vote, the largest single bloc of individuals do not cast ballots for either the Republican or the Democratic party candidates. For every November, the fact once again emerges that a surprisingly large number of Americans do not vote at all.

The Constitution, in its original and unamended form, laid down no federal requirements for the suffrage. Indeed, in the early days of the Republic there was little direct voting for federal officeholders. Senators were selected by the state legislatures, as were the members of the Electoral College who then forgathered to chose the President. Only the House of Representatives was to be directly elected "by the people of the several states." And in this case the franchise was only to be bestowed upon those who, in their various states, were qualified to vote for "the most numerous branch" of their state's legislature. This meant, then, that the decision concerning who could participate in elections was left to the states. And in many important respects the decision as to who can vote, even in federal elections, remains a matter of state discretion.

Extension of Suffrage

Various amendments to the Constitution have extended the suffrage, in theory if not always in practice. The Fifteenth Amendment (1870) proclaimed that neither the states nor the federal government could deny the vote to any citizen "on account of race, color, or previous condition of servitude." The Nineteenth Amendment (1920) declared that the right to vote might not be denied or abridged "on account of sex." The Twenty-third Amendment (1961) gave the vote in Presidential elections, hitherto denied, to residents of the District of Columbia; and the Twenty-fourth Amendment (ratified in 1964) forbids states to demand the payment of a poll tax as a requirement for participating in Presidential or Congressional elections.

Thus the Constitution, in effect, says to the states: "You must allow anyone to vote in federal elections whom you permit to vote for members of the lower house of your state legislature. If you set certain qualifications for voting you must test Negroes on precisely the same basis as you do white citizens, and you must allow women to vote on the same basis as you do men. In other words you cannot have a 'double standard' which makes access to the polls easier for some people because of their race or sex. Finally, if you levy a poll tax, no matter what other penalties you may mete out to those who fail to pay, you cannot deprive nonpayers of their vote."

The first great hurdle facing those who wished to expand the suffrage was the lowering of state requirements for participation in state legislative elections. This was accomplished in the 1820s, when one by one the states rewrote their constitutions to abolish property-holding requirements, thereby extending the franchise to virtually all adult white males. The United States was the first country in the world to allow universal suffrage for white male adult citizens regardless of wealth or education. Within a decade, moreover, Presidential electors were also being chosen by popular vote rather than indirectly by the state legislatures. Compared with the experience of other countries America's progress in extending the franchise to hitherto voteless groups has been relatively peaceful. While we have had our share of riots and demonstrations, these have never had to do exclusively with questions of suffrage. Rather the electorate has been gradually widened, and only in rare cases has it been because those on the outside were themselves vociferous in their demands to be permitted entrance:

> The struggle for the ballot was almost bloodless, almost completely peaceful and astonishingly easy. Indeed the bulk of the newly enfranchised, including Negroes and nearly all women, won battles they never fought. . . . Somewhere along the line the anti-democratic forces simply abandoned the field.[1]

The vast majority of women, for example, did not feel intensely about their denial of the ballot prior to 1920. What can be said is that the vote has been "given" to new groups rather than their having "taken"—let alone "seized"—it. Indeed, the move to extend the franchise has as often as not been initiated by party politicians who believed they would win the gratitude and support of those added to the rolls. "The parties, assisted by some excited minorities, were the entrepreneurs, took the initiative and got the law of the franchise liberalized." [2] This was the case in the 1820s when those who already had the ballot consented to extending this privilege to their less prosperous fellow citizens with modest property holdings. It has also been the case in the 1960s when Northern Congressmen of both parties have sought to secure the franchise for Southern Negroes.

Limitations on Suffrage

Each state has a vast panoply of rules and regulations indicating who may and may not vote. The effect of these laws is to limit the number of citizens who may legitimately cast ballots in elections. To begin with, most states set a minimum voting age of twenty-one. The exceptions are Georgia and Kentucky, which let eighteen-year-olds enter the polls, Alaska, which

---

[1] E. E. Schattschneider, *The Semi-sovereign People* (New York, 1961), p. 100.
[2] *Ibid.*, p. 101.

Off To The Polls.

A satirical cartoon on the 1920 election, the first after the passage of the Nineteenth Amendment.

A.B.FROST..

Frost in *Life*

allows voting at nineteen, and Hawaii, which puts the age at twenty. It might be argued that because the other forty-six states deny the franchise to individuals of college age they are discriminating against citizens who are entitled to vote. But as such laws discriminate indiscriminately against *all* minors in a state, none of them can claim that he has been singled out for unfair treatment. In other cases state laws do serve to make voting difficult for various groups.

RESIDENCE REQUIREMENTS

A state usually demands that a person have lived there for an entire year before he can vote. On top of this he is often required to have been a resident of the county for three months and of his precinct for thirty days. These rules militate against transient Americans, an increasing proportion of the citizenry. For example, between November, 1959, and November, 1960, approximately three and a half million adults moved from one state to another. Most of these were thereby ruled ineligible to vote in the 1960 Presidential election. In the three months' period before the 1960 election, moreover, almost a million adults moved from one county to another within the same state and were in most instances barred from voting. A few states do have reciprocity arrangements whereby a person who was a duly registered voter in his old state can be immediately enrolled in his new residence. But such agreements are the exception rather than the rule.

Apart from the fact that the movers are on the whole younger than the nonmovers, it is difficult to ascribe peculiar characteristics to mobile Americans. Those who move can be manual laborers or white-collar workers, employed or unemployed, Negro or white. One therefore cannot conclude, for example, that either political party benefits from prevailing residence requirements. However, there is reason to suspect that the established machines of both parties have an interest in preventing the admittance of an undigested influx of newcomers to the polls. For such voters can be unpredictable in their behavior and, having lived in the area a shorter time, are less apt to accept the authority of local party organizations.

ABSENTEE BALLOTS

Absentee ballots are usually quite difficult to obtain, as many college seniors have come to learn. Not a few students who have turned twenty-one during the previous spring or over the summer decide that they would like to vote in the November election. However they often come to this decision in late September or early October, once the campaign has begun. They write home to find out about casting an absentee ballot through the mails— and then they learn that such applications are no longer being accepted, that such requests should have been made several weeks or even months earlier. It has been estimated by the American Heritage Foundation that in 1960 over two and a half million citizens were away from home on Election Day and were unable to obtain absentee ballots. In addition there were approximately five million people who were sick at home or in hospitals and who, because they could not get to the polls in person, did not vote. And about half a million Americans who were abroad were voteless as well. In almost all states a citizen must know well in advance that he will be out of town on Election Day, and he must go in person to the Board of Elections to arrange for an absentee ballot. Very few people have this advance knowledge, and even fewer remember or care to take the trouble involved. Once again, the party organizations prefer things as they are, and they have no real desire to reform the complexity and inconvenience of prevailing procedures. Party workers regard those voters who want absentee ballots as not to be "trusted."

LITERACY TESTS

Twenty-five states require literacy tests for admission to the polls, although in some the applicant may instead produce a high school diploma, which is assumed to be evidence that he knows how to read. There are about 800,000 illiterates residing in the states demanding such tests, most of them older people, and they are barred from the electorate. Courts in some states have ruled that reading examinations must be given exclusively in English. Hence citizens in New York and California who can read Spanish but not English are still unable to vote. America, unlike Canada and Switzerland, has not been considered a multilingual society. The result, in any event, is to deprive of the vote individuals who are at the bottom of the social and economic scale. Most observers seem to agree, however, that the ability to read English should be a minimal requirement for voting.

INSTITUTIONALIZED CITIZENS

Institutionalized citizens, particularly those in prisons and mental hospitals, are not permitted to vote by state law. The adult prison population is in excess of 200,000 and at any given time about 500,000 Americans are in mental institutions. Presumably good reasons can be given for these exclusions from the franchise.

DISFRANCHISED CITIZENS

The total number of adult citizens who cannot obtain ballots because of their failure to meet formal state requirements comes to almost 20 million. To be sure, a good many of these citizens would not vote in Presidential elections even if legal barriers did not stand in their way, but some nonvoters are people who would like very much to vote. In addition to these disappointed nonvoters there are several million Negroes in the South who are theoretically qualified but who are denied the ballot because local registrars interpret the law with extreme stringency. In county after county, especially in those rural areas where whites are in the minority, Negroes are failed on grounds of illiteracy or inadequately prepared applications, whereas whites who make the same mistakes are registered with a wink of the eye. One Southern Senator, in the course of the 1964 civil rights debate in Congress, was candid in admitting this discrimination: "I am frank to say that in many instances the reason why voting rights were not . . . made possible is that the white people in those counties [where they] are in a minority are afraid they would be outvoted." [3]

Whether or not this fear is justified remains to be seen. According to the 1960 Census there were 136 Southern counties where more than half of the population was nonwhite. In none of these counties were more Negroes registered than whites. Attempts are being made to register Negroes in some of these areas, but the task has been a difficult one. The white minorities in these counties have the economic and political power, and they can use it to retaliate against those who are active in registration drives. Many Southern Negroes, especially the older ones, have been alienated from politics for so long that they are reluctant to enter the field at this late date. Having been taught to regard politics as "white man's business" they must, one by one, be talked out of their fears and misgivings. And, of course, many rural Negroes in the South have been poorly educated and would be apathetic even if no barriers to the vote stood in their way. Indeed some observers suspect that even if white registrars were to welcome all Negro applicants in such areas only a fraction of them would show up to vote. On the other hand, in a few counties in the South Negro candidates are emerging and their presence on the ballot may bring larger turnouts.

Voters and Nonvoters: Who Votes and Why

Even when the effects of state laws and racial disabilities are discounted the fact remains that there are millions of Americans who do not vote even

---

[3] *Congressional Quarterly Weekly Report* (June 26, 1964), p. 1274.

though they would have no trouble in gaining admittance to the polls. There are several ways to measure election turnouts. In recent Presidential years as much as 65 percent of the adult population has gone to the polls. Yet it can be argued that voting is an annual, not a quadrennial, affair and that a person who stays home three years out of four is hardly a committed citizen. Thus if the mid-term Congressional elections are taken as the standard, the turnout in recent years has ranged from 40 to 45 percent. Thus over half of the eligible electorate fails to make the trip to the polls in the "off-year" contests when all Representatives, one third of the Senators, and about half the governors are chosen. These figures present a less than happy contrast to those of other democracies. In recent elections the turnout has been 74 percent in Japan, 77 percent in Great Britain, 83 percent in Israel, 88 percent in West Germany, and 93 percent in Italy. Why is American voter participation relatively low? First, residence and registration requirements are stricter in this country. Second, major elections at the national level are more frequent in this country than in democracies abroad, and our federal system accentuates this difference because our local, state, and national elections often do not coincide. Third, and most important, Americans tend to be less "political" than citizens of other democracies; while there are often identifiable issues in campaigns, American elections, even at the national level, tend to be less issue-oriented than those abroad. Day-to-day concern with government affairs also seems to be lower in this country. Low voter participation may stem partly from the implied consensus underlying the American political system—that is, *the stakes are usually low* in elections, even at the national level. In multiparty democracies, where each party represents a distinct, relatively narrow group of interests, voter participation is higher because most voters want to help to victory the party that best represents their particular set of interests. But by tradition, the United States has remained a two-party democracy, and the function of these parties has been to create broad coalitions of interests under umbrellas of vaguely defined aspirations, rather than specific programs. In addition, both parties have tended to nominate candidates with moderate views. Pressure groups, rather than parties, have been the vehicles for expressing social and economic conflicts in this country.

Who are the nonvoters in this country, and what distinguishes them from the voters? The voting rate was, in fact, higher in the nineteenth century than it has been in more recent times. Beginning in 1896 and proceeding down through 1916 the Presidential turnout gradually declined from 80 percent of the eligible electorate to less than 65 percent. In 1920 all women in the country were suddenly allowed to vote. But only a fraction of them did at the early stages, thus depressing the percentage turnout even farther. In fact it took almost a generation for women to accustom themselves to voting, and even so they still go to the polls less frequently than do men. As matters now stand there has been very little "improvement" in voting rates. The adult population of the 1960s is better educated and more affluent than any in the past, yet the turnout in the current decade comes nowhere near rivaling that of 1896. It may well be that there were great issues at stake in our grandparents' and great-grandparents' time and that these drove people to the polls. Certainly there are many millions of Americans today who are unable to get excited over elections. Here are some responses of nonvoters to questions put to them in a nationwide survey:

> It doesn't make any difference to me. I'm not interested in stuff like that. I don't listen to nothing. I don't even read about politics in the paper. (Pittsburgh housewife)

> I suppose you'd say I don't care too much about which one gets in. I always say they're all gentlemen when they go in as President but rascals when they come out. . . . I don't vote myself. I leave that for menfolks. (Georgia housewife)

> Voting doesn't make that much difference. What can an individual do about it? He can't really do much. (New York salesman)

> I have never registered or voted because I believe that prayers will do more than votes in keeping this country on the right path. (Retired California minister) [4]

If a large proportion, even at times a majority, of adult Americans find elections meaningless the fault may lie partly with the political structure. "Mass non-voting in the United States makes sense if we think . . . about the organization of politics," one writer has remarked. "The vote can be vitiated as effectively by placing obstacles in the way of organizing the electorate as it can by a denial of the right to vote." [5] Thus if competing candidates take similar positions on issues or no positions at all, if irrelevant considerations of personality take the center of the campaign stage, if important problems are ignored once the election is over—it will be concluded by many citizens that the electoral system has little relation to their own interests and concerns.

At the same time it is true that many individuals do care about who is running for office, and they participate in elections because they want one candidate or the other to win. We know, for example, that people with more years of schooling are apt to vote more frequently than those with fewer years of formal education. Yet this does not mean that education somehow "teaches" a person how the political system is relevant to his personal needs. On the contrary it may simply signify that those who are better educated are on the whole better off and that wealthier groups in society are more likely to see election outcomes as bearing on their interests. Quite clearly many of those in the "lower turnout" categories (see Table 8-1) might stand to gain by governmental activity on their behalf. This is certainly true, for example, in the cases of Negroes and people with low incomes. The problem is that the social groups whose needs are most acute are unfortunately, out of ignorance or apathy, unable to recognize this potential. Nevertheless the system is remarkably "open" in its potentialities, and if a group is able to get its members to the polls in increasing numbers and in a disciplined

---

[4] V. O. Key, Jr., *Public Opinion and American Democracy* (New York, 1962), p. 189.
[5] Schattschneider, *op. cit.*, p. 102.

TABLE 8–1 / Social Characteristics Correlated with Voting Turnout

High turnout	Low turnout
High education	Low education
High income	Low income
Occupations:	Occupations:
Businessmen	Unskilled workers
White-collar employees	Servants
Government employees	Service workers
Commercial-crop farmers	Subsistence farmers
Whites	Negroes
Men	Women
Older people (over 35)	Younger people (under 35)
Married people	Single people
Older residents in community	Newcomers in community
Members of organizations	Isolated individuals

SOURCE: Seymour M. Lipset, *Political Man: The Social Bases of Politics* (New York, 1959), p. 189.

fashion then elected officials and agencies responsive to such officials will have to start taking account of its demands.

Various studies of voting have shown that simple generalizations about electoral behavior must undergo modification if they are to explain the actual facts. Take, for example, the propositions that younger people are less apt to vote than older people and that wage workers have a lower turnout than white-collar employees and businessmen. An intensive survey of a medium-sized city in New York State, however, revealed these results:

	PERCENTAGES VOTING	
	White-collar and	*Wage*
AGE	*businessmen*	*workers*
21–24	74	35
25–34	75	65
35–54	85	79
55 and over	80	82

Thus it emerges that young white-collar employees and businessmen *begin* voting at a relatively early age whereas wage workers do not start until they are appreciably older. In fact the turnout among wage workers eventually catches up and finally surpasses that of office workers. It is important, therefore, to see that *neither* age nor type of employment is, by itself, the determinate factor in measuring turnout; the two factors are interrelated.

Or take another example. Do country dwellers vote more or less frequently than their city cousins? The following are the turnout percentages in the 1960 Presidential election for several fairly typical states:

	ELECTORAL TURNOUT		RURAL POPULATION	
	Percentage	Rank	Percentage	Rank
Great Plains				
Idaho	80.8	1st	58.6	12th
North Dakota	79.0	4th	64.9	3rd
Northeast				
Pennsylvania	70.5	30th	34.4	38th
New York	67.6	31st	27.2	46th
South				
South Carolina	31.5	47th	65.7	2nd
Mississippi	25.6	50th	63.8	5th

The highest percentage turnout in the nation, in Idaho, was in a predominantly rural state; and the lowest was also in a state that is largely rural, Mississippi. And states that are chiefly urban, such as New York and Pennsylvania, fall in between in terms of the proportions of their eligible citizens going to the polls. If we try to use the extent of a state's or district's rural or urban population as our sole variable, the conclusion must be that both urban and rural sections seem to have their equal shares of nonvoting citizens. The real question, therefore, is what *kinds* of farmers are less apt to vote and what *kinds* of city dwellers are less likely to go to the polls. The answers will clearly have to revolve around factors other than simply one's residence in a city or in the countryside. A study of the relationship between voting turnout and social characteristics such as education, income, occupation, race, age, sex, etc., as in Table 8–1 on p. 240, provides a more accurate breakdown of rural and urban voters and nonvoters.

Finally: Do women vote less than men? Yes, they do. However their voting turnout seems to fluctuate according to the type of election. It has already been indicated that more people vote in Presidential elections than do in the "off-year" contests for Congressmen. Thus a state may have a 65 percent turnout in 1964 and have only had a 50 percent turnout in 1962. Yet the fact seems to be that the fluctuations between Presidential and Congressional years have become more accentuated since women joined the electorate: [6]

	AVERAGE PERCENTAGE DIFFERENCE IN PRESIDENTIAL AND CONGRESSIONAL TURNOUTS	
STATE	*1888–1918*	*1920–58*
Minnesota	8	12
Massachusetts	9	15
Pennsylvania	10	14
North Dakota	10	14
New York	10	17
Iowa	13	25
Ohio	14	18

[6] William N. McPhee and William A. Glaser, *Public Opinion and Congressional Elections* (New York, 1962), p. 192.

Hence the important question is why women are less interested than men in voting for Congressmen.

Each of these examples illustrates the point that a single social characteristic—age, type of occupation, place of residence, sex—is not a sufficient explanation of voting or nonvoting. Various factors must be taken together if an accurate and realistic portrayal is to be created. Voting is an exercise in human behavior, and any theory of voting must take account of the complexities and variations of the men and women who comprise the American electorate. Thus, whether one votes or not is a function of whether he can accommodate his set of roles and beliefs to his perception of the candidates and the issues. With many citizens there is little or no problem in deciding for whom to vote. A person who is a Roman Catholic, a trade union member, of Irish extraction, and habitually a Democrat will find it "natural" to vote for an Irish-Catholic candidate who supports legislation favorable to labor. Not everyone, however, is so happily situated. Not a few Americans find themselves subjected to a variety of "cross-pressures" when they are called upon to cast their ballots. Students of voting behavior found these conditions in one typical county.

> Many voters subject to cross-pressures tended to belittle the whole affair. They escaped from any real conflict by losing interest in the election. . . . Those with no cross-pressures showed most interest in the election; even one cross-pressure meant a substantial increase in the proportion of voters who felt less interested in the election. And as the number of cross-pressures increases the degree of interest shows a steady decline.[7]

The sorts of internal "conflicts" an individual may experience can be quite varied. A woman may, for example, be brought up in a Republican family but have married a Democratic husband. Wishing to avoid domestic disharmony she may simply direct her energies in other directions and avoid political participation altogether. Or another person may have a set of beliefs arising from various religious, moral, and temperamental influences. He may find that the candidate who has been put forward by the party he usually favors supports ideas that run counter to his personal notions of right and wrong. Not wishing to support the opposing candidate, such a citizen may simply stay at home on Election Day. Caught in the cross-pressures between his moral convictions and his party loyalty, he decides that voting would be a meaningless act. Indeed, a very large number of Americans appear to find the ballot irrelevant to their own needs and interests. To be sure, no one ought to expect that one or the other of the candidates will have a personality and a program that is tailor-made to the expectations of everyone in the electorate. At the same time there is reason to believe that not a few citizens do set such an unrealistic standard for the system. The result is that they become disillusioned ("Politics is just a racket") or apathetic ("What's the use of voting?") or both ("The same crowd always ends up running things, so why bother?"). But politics is the art of the possible, and every candidate will inevitably be imperfect in the

---

[7] Paul F. Lazarsfeld, et al., The People's Choice (New York, 1944), p. 62.

eyes of some segment of the electorate. Indeed, one criterion of political maturity may be a willingness to support a man despite areas of disagreement with him. The fact that enough Americans possess this sophisticated awareness is an important, and often unacknowledged, element in the maintenance of a democracy.

Time and again voices are raised lamenting the fact that not everyone votes. Frequently this concern is expressed by nonpartisan groups that simply feel that low turnouts symbolize an abandonment of civic responsibility. Sometimes, however, the feeling arises that low voting is symptomatic of conditions that are less than democratic. "The blunt truth," one political scientist has written, "is that politicians and officials are under no compulsion to pay much heed to classes and groups of citizens that do not vote."[8] As nonvoters tend to cluster at the bottoms of the income, occupational, and educational pyramids, low incidences of voting will usually result in public policies more favorable to those groups already possessing economic and social advantages.

There are occasional suggestions that turnouts are probably at the level where they ought to be, that to herd more people to the polls would be to open the floodgates of unpredictable consequences. This position sees a danger in too much participation. Voting turnout in most elections has undoubtedly been limited, for example, by the tendency of both major parties to nominate candidates with moderate views. This leads to nonparticipation by many voters who feel that there is no point in voting since there appears to be no real choice between the candidates, or who feel that *both* candidates are too liberal or too conservative for their tastes. Voting turnout among these nonvoters would undoubtedly be increased if one candidate had relatively extreme views. This greater participation, however, would also emphasize the conflicts in society and encourage dissatisfied groups to express their discontentment with the system. Too much participation may be a symptom of excessive strains in the political system:

> In a society in which only fifty per cent of the electorate participates it is clear that politics does satisfy in a way the desire of the mass of the individuals in the state. As the percentage of participation rises above, let us say, ninety per cent, it is apparent that the tensions of political struggle are stretching to the breaking point the will toward the constitutional.[9]

It may, of course, be questioned whether electoral apathy on the part of citizens expresses their satisfaction with the system. Nonvoting may also be expressive of resentments, frustrations, and cynicism about the efficacy of political action. Yet it is plain that the recent history of mass voting in other countries can give rise to some misgivings. Authoritarian leaders in particular seek to gain and maintain power by creating great waves of popular sentiment on their behalf. "The greater the changes in the structure of the society . . . that a governing group is attempting to introduce," one soci-

---

[8] V. O. Key, Jr., *Southern Politics in State and Nation* (New York, 1950), p. 527.
[9] F. W. Wilson in Seymour M. Lipset, *Political Man: The Social Bases of Politics* (New York, 1959), p. 227.

ologist has suggested, "the more likely the leadership is to desire and even require a high level of participation by its citizens. . . ." [10]

This argument is, in many ways, the old one of quantity versus quality, of whether sheer numbers are a measure of political well-being. The answer is that while low turnouts can lead to injustice or at least discriminatory treatment, high turnouts can threaten the stability of the system by supporting ideological movements that seek to alter the constitutional structure. For people who usually do not vote are more apt to be roused to participation by an oversimplified program and an irresponsible leader. One solution to this dilemma is to propose that once legal and social obstacles to voting are removed, no indiscriminate effort should be made to drive people to vote. The ballot, in other words, should be *available* to anyone who wishes to use it, but those who do not want to avail themselves of their vote can tend to their gardens on Election Day. And if nonvoters do eventually discover reasons why they should begin to support a candidate or a party, then they can be welcomed—but not pushed—into the active electorate.

While one party may predominate over the other over a few decades, few candidates in national elections win by popular landslides. (No candidate for President in the twentieth century, for example, has garnered over 62 percent of the popular vote.) This seems to indicate that both the Republican and Democratic parties have a sizable, stable core of supporters. Which groups tend to support Democratic candidates, and which ones favor Republicans?

Surveys of Voting Behavior

While use of Census statistics and voting figures can reveal some interesting correlations, most serious students of voting behavior have concluded that they need more detailed information before they can draw conclusions about why people vote as they do. For this reason heavy reliance has been placed on the sample survey. The individuals in such a sample can be asked all sorts of questions that the Census enumerators omitted. For the Census-takers ask only for *information:* years of schooling, income, occupation, national origin, and so on. Survey interviewers can ask about religion, party preference, party preference of parents, frequency of voting. Moreover, the analyst of a sample survey can draw *inferences* about the person he is questioning: he can assign him to a social class and assess the level at which he interprets the political process and the intensity of his various concerns. Finally, an interviewer can ask questions about *opinions:* he can elicit a voter's approval or disapproval of policies and politicians, and sentiments in a wide variety of areas can be uncovered. Information, inferences, and opinions of this sort can *only* be secured by means of a special survey. Needless to say, while the field interviewers should be trained observers and subtle interrogators, their reports must be collated and analyzed by the professional social scientists who initiated and supervised the research project. They are the ones who correlate the diverse facts, attitudes, and opinions, and then place them in a coherent explanatory framework.

---

[10] *Ibid.,* p. 184.

". . . When Asked If She Would Vote For The Candidate, If Nominated, Subject Was 'Undecided' . . . !"

Interlandi in the Los Angeles *Times*

Quite plainly an hour-long questionnaire cannot be administered to the more than a hundred million adult Americans who make up the potential electorate. Therefore a sample of manageable size must be drawn. There are two ways in which this is usually done. (1) The first is to select a *community* which is felt to be fairly typical of the country as a whole or at least of a section of the nation. Thus a city or a county with about 50,000 eligible voters might be chosen and then a random sample of 1,000 of its residents would be interviewed. Such a 2 percent sample, if carefully drawn, is considered to be very reliable. One advantage of a single-community survey is that the questions asked can be geared to specific candidates and issues in the locality. Thus conclusions might be drawn not only about who supports the Democratic and Republican parties but also about who voted for Smith and Jones, the two candidates for mayor. Moreover a survey of this kind can be analyzed in the context of the history and social structure characterizing the city in question. While such a project may tell us a great deal about voting behavior in Elmira (New York) or Erie County (Ohio), there remains the problem of whether these communities are representative of the entire United States.

(2) For this reason there have been several *nationwide* surveys. But a 2 percent sample of a hundred million adult citizens would require 2 million interviews and this is obviously impossible. While most laymen find it difficult to believe, statistical experts agree that a national sample of 1,500 to 3,000 can provide a reliable cross-section of the attitudes and characteristics of the country's population as a whole. In fact, the odds are extremely high that two samples of the national population, drawn independently and under entirely separate auspices, will come up with comparable responses

to identical or only similarly phrased questions. A good deal of information about voting necessarily rests on such nationwide surveys. Some of these, like the Gallup and Roper polls, try to tell us beforehand *who* is going to win the Presidential election. Others, usually conducted under academic auspices, seek to find out *why* people vote as they do.

Party Identification

Most voting is party voting. In actual practice what this means is that most voters have learned to think of themselves as being "Democrats" or "Republicans," in much the same way that they think of themselves as Methodists or Presbyterians. The consequence is that when deciding which of two candidates to support, the majority of citizens are first influenced by the party label that each of the contenders wears. Indeed, most election contests are basically contests between the two major parties. Democratic and Republican candidates both begin a campaign with a hard core of supporters who are willing to support their party's nominee no matter who or what he happens to be.

> Few factors are of greater importance for our national elections than the lasting attachment of tens of millions of Americans to one of the parties. These loyalties establish a basic division of electoral strength within which the competition of particular campaigns takes place. And they are an important factor in assuring the stability of the party system itself.[11]

One test of the party identification of voters is what they do when called upon to vote for an office where they know nothing about either of the candidates. Somewhere in the middle of most ballots will be contests for such offices as county auditor, city comptroller, or commissioner of deeds. The fact is that very few citizens, once in the polling booth, actually fail to vote in all contests. And when they mark their ballots for obscure offices or unknown candidates they are, in reality, reverting to their deep-seated propensity to vote on the basis of party identification.

Not all "Democrats" and "Republicans," however, display an equal attachment to their parties. Under the probing of survey interviewers, respondents reveal that their loyalty to a party and its candidates can vary in intensity. For this reason it has been found necessary to classify individuals as being "strong," "weak," or "independent" in their party identifications. A nationwide survey of American voters has been taken every two years from 1952 to the present by researchers at the University of Michigan. If their 1960 findings, based on a sample of more than 3,000, are extended to the entire voting-age population, the following partisan breakdown emerges:

Strong Republicans	15,100,000
Weak Republicans	14,100,000
Independent Republicans	7,600,000
	36,800,000

---

[11] Angus Campbell, *et al.*, *The American Voter* (New York, 1960), p. 121.

Strong Democrats	22,700,000
Weak Democrats	27,000,000
Independent Democrats	8,600,000
	58,300,000
Independents	13,000,000

In actual fact, therefore, less than 40 million adult Americans—about 15 million Republicans and 23 million Democrats—are "strong" partisans. If the Democrats are able to keep their weaker and more independent supporters in their camp, they are likely to win a national election. There is, however, one factor that helps the Republicans to combat the Democrats' numerical advantage. This is that more Democrats come from social groups that are less regular in their voting habits. For every 100 professed Republicans more voters actually turn out to the polls on Election Day than is the case from among 100 Democrats. Recent elections have, moreover, demonstrated the Republicans' ability to win over Democratic voters. The victories of President Eisenhower in 1952 and 1956, and Vice-President Nixon's near-miss in 1960, testify that an impressive candidate or a vigorous campaign can draw out defectors from the opposing camp. (Needless to say, both parties also attempt to win support from the "independent"—or nonpartisan—group.) But Democrats who crossed over to vote for a Republican should not thereby be stripped of their Democratic identification. If they defect, it is a temporary defection. Indeed their support of the Republican candidate for the Presidency is as often as not accompanied by a vote for the Democratic Congressional candidate in their district and for other Democrats lower down on the ballot.

FAMILY ORIENTATION

Just as most Americans carry on their parents' religion, so they adhere to the party identification that characterized the home in which they were raised. University of Michigan interviewers in 1958 asked the people in their sample not only for their own partisan preferences but also for those of their fathers and mothers.[12]

PARENTS' IDENTIFICATION	RESPONDENT'S IDENTIFICATION (percentage)		
	Democratic	Independent	Republican
Democratic	72	39	10
Mixed or Independent	19	38	25
Republican	9	23	65
	100	100	100
	N = 689	N = 268	N = 399

---

[12] The figures given are derived from *ibid.*, p. 147.

Of the respondents who identified themselves as Democrats, 72 percent came from families where both parents had been Democrats before them. The figure for the Republican respondents, about 65 percent, was slightly but not significantly lower. What is interesting is that not more than 10 percent of the sample actually deserted their parents' party to ally themselves with the other party. As many as 25 percent, however, entered the "independent" column. Whether such a shift was a prelude to a more permanent change cannot be determined at this time.

That anywhere from two thirds to three fourths of the offspring are carrying on their parents' party identifications is, of course, a stabilizing factor in the electoral system. Interview responses show that this intergenerational transmission of loyalties is accepted as a matter of course: [18]

> I was just raised a Republican. (California housewife)

> I'm a Democrat. That's what my folks are. No reason otherwise. (South Dakota dental technician)

> My father is a Democrat and I'm one by inheritance, sort of. I know nothing about politics but I like the Democratic party. . . . (New York housewife)

> My dad is a Republican and we are all hot Republicans. (New York laborer)

> Our forefathers have been Democrats and we have naturally stuck with the Democratic party. (Wife of Massachusetts lawyer)

> I just know my folks and family always voted Republican and so I vote Republican. (Wife of Minnesota salesman)

It might be suggested that party identification of this sort is unreflective, even irrational. To stick with a party just because of a choice made by one's "folks" or "dad" or "forefathers" seems hardly the best of reasons for giving one's support to particular candidates. On the other hand it may well be that most offspring enter approximately the same social class and income group and continue with the same ethnic background that their parents had before them. The amount of social mobility in this country must not be exaggerated. What can be said, and this is something that surveys do not often try to measure, is that while the children may carry on with their parents' party identification they are not necessarily the same *kinds* of Democrats and Republicans that their parents were.

CANDIDATE ORIENTATION

A "party identification" has little meaning so long as it is tucked in the back of a voter's mind. It is in the actual act of voting that his loyalty to his chosen party comes into play. Yet elections focus on living and breathing candidates, and at least some of the voter's attention will be directed to the personalities of the men who are running for office. Citizens are apt to conjure up an image of a candidate as "standing for" various issues and as representing various traits of character and moral postures. Thus a vote for

---

[18] V. O. Key, Jr., *Public Opinion*, pp. 297–98.

one contender may be thought of as a vote for a stiffer foreign policy; a vote for another may be seen as elevating a hitherto neglected religious group; a vote for still another will be looked on as inaugurating a new sense of purpose in national politics. Each voter creates his own images of the candidates—and it is not at all impossible for two voters to project quite contradictory images upon the same candidate. Many voters will see their party's candidate as simply "their party's man" and will support him exclusively for partisan reasons. But a significant section of the electorate is prepared to cross over, at least temporarily, to vote for the other party's candidate if he seems to be more attractive as a person.

This means that "party identification" must be juxtaposed against "candidate orientation." Voter behavior in the 1956 and 1960 elections provides an insight into this process. In 1956 Dwight D. Eisenhower, a Republican, was reelected, receiving 57.4 percent of the popular vote. In 1960 John F. Kennedy, a Democrat, was elected by 49.7 percent of the popular vote. Quite clearly many voters who supported Eisenhower were not willing to vote for Richard Nixon, Kennedy's Republican opponent, four years later. And it is equally plain that a large number of citizens who bypassed Adlai Stevenson, Eisenhower's Democratic opponent, returned to support Kennedy in 1960. The 1956 election can be considered more of a "personality" election than the 1960 contest, which was a more genuine "party" election. To be sure, Kennedy's "personality"—especially as it embodied his religion—figured in 1960; there were significant numbers of Catholic defectors from the Republican party as well as Protestant defectors from the Democratic party. In terms of votes, however, Kennedy's Catholicism was less crucial than Eisenhower's appeal.

ISSUE ORIENTATION

Much more difficult to evaluate is a third factor, "issue orientation." It can be assumed that some Democrats—especially in Mississippi, Louisiana, Georgia, and South Carolina—deserted their party to support Barry Goldwater in 1964. For them it was concern over the tempo of civil rights advances that caused them to downgrade their traditional "party identification" and to give heightened emphasis to a salient election issue. Here are the remarks of some citizens who had voted Democratic prior to 1964 and who switched their allegiance to the Republican candidate: [14]

> When Goldwater told those New Yorkers at the Republican convention that they could leave the Republican party if they didn't like his civil rights views, I knew that at last we had someone who will fight for us.
>
> That civil rights law takes away the white man's rights.
>
> I'm sick and tired of these Negroes telling me what to do. The white man should stand up for his rights.
>
> I've always voted Democratic before, but the Democrats just moved in on me with a wheelbarrow and took my party away.

---

[14] Samuel Lubell (United Features Syndicate, August 3, 1964).

"Billy Graham As A Presidential Candidate—Now That's What I Call A Clear Choice!"

A humorous view of issue orientation.

Interlandi in the Los Angeles *Times*

These voters felt that their own party had come down on the wrong side of the civil rights controversy. In many elections issues have played a role in the voting decisions of individuals. It may be that "issue" is the wrong term here, for we are often dealing more with a vague emotional mood than with a measured consideration of programs and policies. Voters often seek to interpret a candidate's remarks on an issue to coincide with their own preferences. Nevertheless it was impossible to avoid speaking of the "Catholic issue" or the "Quemoy-Matsu issue" in 1960, the Suez Crisis in 1956, the Korean War in 1952, or the "third-term issue" in 1940. Catholicism and Kennedy could not be separated from each other, nor could Franklin Roosevelt and his bid for a third term. And it is difficult to say just how far the existence of the Korean War and the Suez Crisis aided the election and reelection of Dwight D. Eisenhower. About all that can be said is that, in one way or another, issues do figure in voting behavior and must be taken into account. They are part of the image of reality that the voter creates for himself, the image of the political world that leads him to make up his mind as Election Day approaches.

Social Characteristics of Voting Behavior

Voting behavior can and should be analyzed in terms of the varied social characteristics of the citizens who cast the ballots. Table 8–2, derived from sample surveys, breaks down the Stevenson and Kennedy supporters by six classifications: education, occupation, union membership, residence, religion, and race. In Table 8–3 these groups are ranked in order of their percentage support for the Democratic candidates in 1956 and 1960. Several points must be made if this form of analysis is to be employed:

TABLE 8–2 / Democratic Percentage of Two-Party Vote: 1956 and 1960 (by social classifications)

Group	1956 (Stevenson)	1960 (Kennedy)	Democratic gain (1960 over 1956)
Education			
Grade school	41	56	15
High school	45	53	8
College	31	36	5
Occupation of family head			
Professional and managerial	32	45	14
Other white collar	38	45	7
Skilled and semiskilled	45	59	14
Unskilled	55	60	5
Farmers	46	33	−13
Union affiliation of family head			
Union member	52	64	12
Nonunion	35	44	9
Place of residence			
Metropolitan area	45	58	13
Towns and cities	35	47	12
Rural	43	47	4
Religion			
Protestant	36	37	1
Catholic	46	81	35
Race			
White	39	48	9
Negro	66	71	5

SOURCE: Adapted from Fred I. Greenstein, *The American Party System and the American People* (Englewood Cliffs, 1963), pp. 24–25.

(1) We are dealing, to begin with, with social categories and not with people. In a sense we are examining "pieces" of people rather than their entire personalities. A Catholic trade union member living in a large city, for example, in all likelihood voted Democratic in 1960. But a Catholic lawyer living in a small town might as easily have supported Nixon as Kennedy. (2) Members of all these groups do not vote with the same frequency. Thus while 71 percent of the Negroes who voted gave their support to Kennedy, actually only slightly more than half of the Negroes who were surveyed voted at all. Similarly only 68 percent of the unskilled workers went to the polls. On the other hand, almost 90 percent of the college-educated individuals voted, as did 85 percent of those with professional and managerial occupations. All in all, groups supporting Nixon turned out to the polls more heavily than did those backing Kennedy. (3) Interpretation of group voting behavior must take into account issues or attributes of candidates that shape an individual election and cause some

TABLE 8–3 / Democratic Percentages of Votes of Selected Groups

1956	1960
Highest Democratic Percentage of Group Votes	

Negroes	Catholics
Unskilled workers	Negroes
Union members	Union members
— 50% —	Unskilled workers
Catholics	Skilled and semiskilled workers
Farmers	Metropolitan-area residents
Skilled and semiskilled workers	Grade school graduates
Metropolitan-area residents	High school graduates
High school graduates	— 50% —
Grade school graduates	Whites
Whites	City and town residents
Other white-collar employees	Rural residents
Protestants	Professionals and managers
City and town residents	Other white-collar employees
Nonunion workers	Nonunion workers
Professionals and managers	Protestants
College graduates	College graduates
	Farmers

Lowest Democratic Percentage of Group Votes

groups to alter their customary voting habits. Religion, for example, was an identifiable issue in 1960, and therefore the voting behavior of Catholics and Protestants was atypical: Kennedy received 81 percent of the Catholic vote in 1960, and Catholics headed the list of Democratic supporters, although in 1956 Stevenson had received only 46 percent of the Catholic vote. Conversely, although Kennedy garnered more support from almost all groups than Stevenson did in 1956, he lost support from Protestants. Kennedy's markedly urban image also modified the traditional voting behavior of certain groups: he gained 13 percent over Stevenson in support from metropolitan-area residents and 12 percent from town and city residents, but Kennedy suffered a 13 percent loss in support from farmers compared with Stevenson (who was competing against an Eisenhower landslide).

INCOME

Income is one social factor that is clearly associated with support for the two parties. Citizens with lower incomes—for example, Negroes and unskilled workers—tend to vote Democratic. More affluent voters, such as office workers and people with college educations, are more apt to support a Republican. This ought not to be surprising, for when it comes to economic matters Democratic candidates tend to favor "redistributive" policies to a greater degree than do Republicans. At the same time *where* one earns one's living can be important. Rural residents outside the South (most of whom, by the way, are not farmers) still give a majority of their votes to the Republicans even though rural incomes are appreciably below urban earnings. And in the South, of course, the Democratic party is supported by rich and poor alike.

Yet income remains a critical determinant, and other factors explaining

CHART 8–1 / Republican Voting Related to Family Income, 1960 Presidential Election

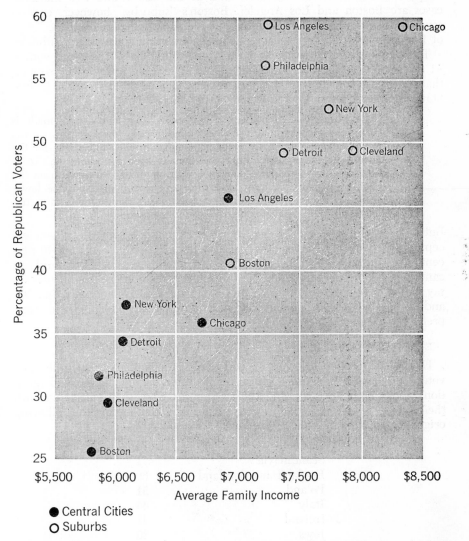

SOURCES: U.S. Bureau of the Census, *U.S. Census of Population: 1960. General Social and Economic Characteristics* (Washington, 1962), *passim.*

Republican National Committee, *The 1960 Elections: A Summary Report* (Washington, 1961), *passim.*

voting are often simply expressions of income. For example, it is often observed that while large cities are strongly Democratic, their suburbs tend to be more Republican. It is not suburban residence per se that makes people Republican; it is that moving to the suburbs is often the result of an increased income. As Chart 8–1 shows, there is an association between earnings and voting: the higher the income, the higher the Republican percentage. The incomes in the seven suburban complexes average $1,400 higher than those in the seven central cities, and Republican voting averaged 18 percent higher in the suburbs than in the cities. The two marginal cases are Boston and Los Angeles. Boston's "suburbs," however, contain several factory cities with substantial low-income population; and the "city" of Los Angeles is in large measure itself a sprawling collection of suburbs.

To focus on income is not to postulate a rigid "class" theory of voting. At the same time it would be a mistake to assume, in a dogmatic manner, that America is somehow a "classless" society. Classes do exist, in the United States as elsewhere, and much of our voting is class voting:

> On a world scale, the principal generalization which can be made is that parties are primarily based on either the lower classes or the middle and upper classes. This generalization even holds true for the American parties, which have traditionally been considered an exception to the class-cleavage pattern of Europe. The Democrats from the beginning of their history have drawn more support from the lower strata of the society, while the Federalist, Whig, and Republican parties have held the loyalties of the more privileged groups.[15]

But to be useful, this class theory must accommodate some important exceptions. As was seen, in the 1960 Presidential election no less than 40 percent of the unskilled workers who went to the polls voted for the Republican candidate, as did 36 percent of the trade union members. Thus all we can say is that people with lower incomes "tend to" vote Democratic, that "by and large" they support Democratic candidates, that "on the whole" they prefer the Democratic party.

ETHNIC BACKGROUND

Ethnic background also has a good deal to do with how an individual votes. Individuals interviewed in a 1952 sample survey were asked questions about their ancestry, and their responses were then correlated with their voting behavior. Thus the percentages of voters having the following origins cast their ballots for Eisenhower: [16]

Germany	74
Scandinavia	71
England and Scotland	69
Poland	51
Italy	44
Ireland	41
Jews	30
Negroes	21

---

[15] Lipset, op. cit., p. 230.
[16] Angus Campbell, et al., The Voter Decides (Evanston, 1954), p. 77.

It is interesting to examine these percentages with reference to the chronological "waves" of immigration from European countries to the United States; one would expect higher support for the Republican party to come from groups that arrived first in the United States, and vice versa. (All percentages, of course, would have to be reduced to arrive at "normal" ethnic voting percentages, because the 1952 election was an Eisenhower landslide.) A rough correlation appears between time of immigration and party voting allegiance; the exceptions to this pattern can be explained by special factors that offset this general tendency. The bulk of English and Scottish immigration, for example, took place before that of the Germans and Scandinavians— yet support for Eisenhower was greater from the latter groups. Three factors would explain this deviation: first, Eisenhower's parents were German immigrants. Second, the Scandinavians, traditionally conservative, tend to be concentrated in strongly conservative areas of the Midwest, where their leanings are reinforced by sectional tendencies. Third, many voters of British descent are Southerners who support the Democratic party to uphold the sectional tradition dating from the post-Civil War period. Another exception is provided by the Irish, who arrived relatively early (in the 1840s and '50s) but who gave disproportionately small support to the Republicans in 1952. Irish loyalty to the Democratic party may be partly due to the fact that soon after their arrival, Irish immigrants became active in local Democratic politics. Politicians of Irish descent have traditionally been powerful in the local Democratic machines in Northeastern cities (particularly in New England) that get out the vote on Election Day. The third exception is that although the arrival of Negroes to this country preceded that of all groups but the British, the Negro Republican vote was extremely small. Negro allegiance to the Democratic party, however, can be explained by the barriers that have been raised to maintain the minority status of Negroes, thus restricting improvement in their economic or social status.

In one sense discussing ethnic voting is another way of talking about income voting. Nationality groups that came to America in the earlier waves of immigration have had a longer time in which to establish themselves and to climb up the economic ladder. Those arriving more recently have yet to be fully accepted or assimilated and hence occupy lower-paying jobs. Thus we can generalize to a degree and say that German-Americans, whose forebears came in the 1840s, are apt to vote Republican; and we can suggest that Italian-Americans, whose parents or grandparents arrived in the first decade of this century, are likely to be Democrats. Yet we might discover, on further analysis, that we are not talking so much about "German-Americans" as opposed to "Italian-Americans" as we are about individuals who are earning $10,000 as opposed to those earning $5,000 a year. Where, then, does the economic element end and the ethnic emphasis begin?

Perhaps the best way to approach this question is to point to the important "deviant" cases. On the one hand there are millions of "poor white" Americans of Anglo-Saxon stock. In terms of time of arrival they should be sufficiently well settled in our national life to vote Republican. But in many instances economic status outweighs ethnic identification, and in consequence they vote Democratic because of the redistributive posture of that party.

On the other hand there are Jews, most of whom are of quite recent origin but who also have relatively high incomes. The vast majority of Jews vote Democratic even though this may result in their paying higher taxes for welfare services they do not themselves need. Jewish voting behavior ought certainly to be described as ethnic in character rather than economic.

Examination of Catholic voting demonstrates the conflicting pressures of ethnic or religious ties and income. Until around 1940, the Democrats traditionally received 65 to 70 percent of the Catholic vote. In the elections of 1940 and 1944, however, Roosevelt's percentage of the Catholic vote began to decline. Truman's election in 1948 brought Catholic defectors back to the Democratic fold. A study undertaken in 1948 concluded that high-income Catholics continued to vote Democratic despite their achievement of material success:

> No matter what demographic variable is controlled, the relationship between Catholic affiliation and party preference significantly remains. Not only that, but the religious affiliation—and the ethnic differences it represents—appears to be a stronger influence upon voting than any other single factor. For example, on each socio-economic status level about half as many Catholics vote Republican as Protestants. Catholics of high status vote more Democratic than do Protestants of low status. Thus Catholic affiliation is stronger than socio-economic status in determining voting.[17]

Yet in 1952, Stevenson received only 56 percent of the Catholic vote, and in 1956 his support dropped to 46 percent. Religious considerations were very strong, however, in the Kennedy election of 1960: he received 81 percent of the Catholic vote. Since the cross-pressures of religious ties and income appear to create vacillating voting patterns among groups moving up the economic scale, in most elections factors other than religion are decisive in determining how members of these groups will vote during these transition periods.

The grandchildren of the later immigrant waves are beginning to merge into the mainstream of American life. There is a good deal of intermarriage among various ethnic strains, and this is bound to weaken identifications with particular nationality groups. No less important, younger parents of immigrant stock are moving away from the ethnic ghettos where they were raised and are bringing up their own children in surroundings that harbor few reminders of the old country. Typical of this tendency is the rise of the suburb, which throws together Americans of varying backgrounds and accelerates the process of assimilation. There is reason to believe that ethnic voting, originally a product of the urban enclaves where people of similar backgrounds clustered together, is becoming less pronounced. But this does not necessarily mean that the Republican party will immediately be flooded by Democrats who are losing their ethnic ties. Party identifications can persist for long periods of time.

Some city dwellers who move to the suburbs carry their party loyalties with them. As one Boston suburbanite put it: "I own a nice home, have a new car, and am much better off than my parents were. I've been a Demo-

---

[17] Bernard Berelson, *et al.*, *Voting* (Chicago, 1954), p. 165.

crat all my life. Why should I change?" [18] On the other hand, many newly prosperous Americans are redefining their conceptions of themselves and with this shift in self-image comes a change in party affiliation. "As newcomers to the middle class enter suburbia, they must discard old values . . . ," one commentator has written. "People from big, urban Democratic wards tend to become Republican and, if anything, more conservative than those whose outlook they are unconsciously adopting." [19] Obviously the indications run both ways, and it is plain that the nation is in the midst of a significant political and social transition. Ethnic ties may be becoming weaker and economic conditions may be changing: these developments will clearly have consequences both for the political parties and for the voting behavior of individuals. But change, especially in the realm of party identification, is never rapid and seldom abrupt. Loyalties can persist long after the facts that created them have ceased to exist.

SECTIONALISM

"Everyone around here is a Republican" is the sort of response that interviewers frequently get when asking about party affiliation. The *section* of the country in which one lives has a good deal to do with how an individual votes. Indeed the hand of history weighs heavily in many areas, and people vote the same way despite the passage of time and changing political circumstances. "In some parts of Kentucky," it has been observed, "vote patterns are still determined by bitter battles over road construction which took place some seventy years ago." [20] In New England and the Midwest there are rural counties where the majority of voters, regardless of economic class or ethnic background, have been Republicans since the turn of the century. Sectional voting is particularly strong when a particular region sees itself beleaguered by other interests and areas:

> Sectionalism . . . contributes to the multiclass composition of each of the major parties, a characteristic bewildering to those who regard only a class politics as "natural." A politics that arrays the people of one section against those of another pulls into one party men of all social strata. A common interest bound the Southern banker, merchant, cotton farmers, and wage earner together. . . .[21]

It is not only in the South, but also in many parts of the North—especially in small towns and rural areas—that members of all social classes are found rallying under the same partisan standard in a joint effort to beat back urban-oriented candidates and legislation. Here, in fact, is a politics that welds classes together instead of dividing them. It might be asked what kinds of people think less of their economic status and give more emphasis to the historic party complexion of their area. One answer is that such voting patterns are most pronounced among citizens whose families and who themselves have resided in the same place over a prolonged period of

---

[18] Samuel Lubell, *The Future of American Politics* (New York, 1952), p. 60.

[19] William H. Whyte, Jr., *The Organization Man* (New York, 1956), pp. 331–32.

[20] Louis Harris, "Election Polling and Research," *Public Opinion Quarterly* (Spring, 1957), Vol. XXI, p. 111.

[21] V. O. Key, Jr., *Southern Politics in State and Nation*, p. 267.

time. To say that "everyone around here is a Republican" is often simply to say that "everyone" who is *still* living here is a Republican. (Those who have moved away may or may not take their Republicanism with them to their new homes, but the odds are good that they will adjust their political outlooks to their new settings.) Thus areas that experience few incursions of newcomers are apt to maintain stable partisan patterns. Political scientists have referred to the "more or less viscous pattern of traditional [voting] behavior" in these areas.[22] A study of Indiana, for example, revealed that of the twenty-two counties that voted most strongly Republican in the state in the 1900 Presidential election, sixteen were among the twenty-two counties going most heavily Republican in 1952. Most of these sixteen counties had lost rather than gained population in the fifty-two-year period. If there is an interclass consensus it can be suggested that the higher economic classes direct the terms of that consensus. However while the candidates of the dominant party are usually more sympathetic to the interests of the higher income groups, the fact remains that the votes of *all* groups go to such candidates. Marxian analysis would assert that in such situations those who are less well off had not yet achieved "class consciousness"—a rational perception of their own best interest. A more conservative assessment might be that "what's good for the bankers and the merchants is good for the whole community." The final answer depends, as it so frequently does, on one's own notion of what makes for "rational" voting.

THE GROUP CONTEXT OF VOTING

Whether the groups are more "political" than "social," or the other way around, most analysts place great emphasis on the *group* context of voting. "Voting is essentially a group experience," one of the pioneering voting studies concluded. "People who work or live or play together are likely to vote for the same candidates." [23] It has already been seen that hereditary voting is widespread, that children "learn" their party identification in the course of being raised by their parents. Of all the groups to which an individual belongs his family probably makes the deepest impression on him. "The family," one study of voting reported, "is a key reference group which transmits, indoctrinates, and sustains the political loyalties of its members." [24] Political talk, of necessity, takes place in groups, and exposure to such discussions helps individuals to make up their political minds. In addition to the family there are other groups with which a person will be affiliated: his companions at his place of work; people he knows through his church or fraternal organizations; his fellow bowlers at the Wednesday night league. We do know that, for most people, these group circles are overlapping rather than separated. This does not necessarily mean that the same companions are found in all groups. But it does mean that a person will discover that the values of one group to which he belongs will be reinforced

---

22 V. O. Key, Jr., and Frank Munger, "Social Determination and Electoral Decision: The Case of Indiana," *American Voting Behavior,* Eugene Burdick and Arthur Brodbeck, eds. (Glencoe, 1959), p. 288.

23 Lazarsfeld, *et al., op. cit.,* p. 161.

24 Herbert McClosky and Harold Dahlgren, "Primary Group Influence on Party Loyalty," *American Political Science Review* (September, 1959), Vol. LIII, p. 775.

rather than contradicted by his memberships in other groups. For this reason it is not surprising that "social groups imbue their individual members with the accepted political ideology of the group." [25] The American Legion post, the PTA, and the union local, however, must not be thought of as having some sinister influence over the minds of their members. Rather, people join a group because in a general way it articulates ideas which they already have in their heads. Hence if group memberships have an influence on voting, and they clearly do, it is not least because group discussions put into political focus the latent interests and aspirations of their members. "Most voters are anchored in a matrix of politically harmonious primary associations—a result, to some extent, of conscious selection and of the tendency for the social environment to bring together people of like views." [26]

Even in the most democratic of groups, some members are "more equal" than others. What this means is that within all formal and informal associations of individuals, there are always a few people who may be regarded as "opinion leaders." These persons are not necessarily those who hold high office, or indeed any office at all. "Opinion leaders are not identical with the socially prominent people in the community, or the richest people, or the civic leaders. They are found in all occupational groups." [27] Thus one opinion leader will be a more-articulate-than-average worker in a department of a factory; another will be a member of a country club who, for a variety of reasons, commands the respect of those around him. Opinion leaders, then, are scattered around the population at random, and every group regardless of where it is situated will probably contain at least one person to whom the others listen.

In many ways the opinion leader serves as a bridge between the mass media and the public. Newspapers, magazines, radio, and television all combine to present an image of political reality. But it is a swirling image, depicting a far-off world, and most people can make little sense out of it. However tens of thousands of opinion leaders, in small and informal group settings, interpret the messages of the mass media, pointing out in conversations with their friends and acquaintances the significance and relevance of reported political happenings. The very informality of such leadership, indeed, is what gives it its weight. For if we tend to approach the mass media with some suspicion, our defenses are down when we talk with our peers:

> If we read or tune in a speech, we usually have a definite mental set that tinges our receptiveness. Such purposive behavior is part of the broad area of our political experiences, to which we bring our convictions with a desire to test them and strengthen them by what is said. This mental set is armor against influence.
>
> On the other hand, people we meet for reasons other than political discussion are more likely to catch us unprepared, so to speak, if they make politics the topic. Politics gets through, especially to the indifferent, much more easily by personal contacts than in any other way,

[25] Lazarsfeld, et al., op. cit., p. 163.
[26] McCloskey and Dahlgren, op. cit., p. 775.
[27] Lazarsfeld, et al., op. cit., p. 165.

simply because it comes up unexpectedly as a side-line or marginal topic in a casual conversation.[28]

Concept Formation

But not all Americans perceive politics in the same way. Each citizen imparts a different meaning to what he sees—or to what he thinks he sees—going on in the political arena. In analyzing these differences students of voting behavior speak of "concept formation," by which they mean the level of generality at which an individual perceives and assesses the candidates and parties. Four such levels have been distinguished. The first level of concept formation is concerned with the application of political ideas to specific issues. Here a voter characterizes parties and candidates with reference to their location on one or another political spectrum. There are of course many such spectra, reflecting the interests and emphases of different groups in society. The most common ideological identifications are those running from "left" to "right" along the liberal-conservative continuum. Different voters stress different areas of public policy as criteria for measuring a candidate's ideological orientation. Some people evaluate candidates according to their stands on economic matters, some on civil rights, others on international affairs. A voter may well be "liberal" on civil rights and at the same time "conservative" about the government's role in social welfare. Very few Americans are consistently liberal or conservative on all questions. And even a voter who chooses a candidate on ideological grounds is unlikely to have a coherent philosophy that encompasses a comprehensive set of principles. He is more apt to have disparate, hazy sentiments about the tempo and direction of specific aspects of politics. For example a woman living in a Chicago suburb, when asked what she liked about the Republican party, replied:

> I think they're more middle-of-the-road, more conservative, not so subject to radical change. I like their foreign policy—and the segregation business, that's a middle-of-the-road policy. You can't push it too fast. You can instigate things, but you have to let them take their course slowly.[29]

Other voters judge candidates and the parties according to the benefits that particular *groups* will stand to gain if the election goes their way. Thus a New York City woman indicated why she liked the Democrats:

> My father is a Democrat and I'm one by inheritance, sort of. I know nothing about politics but I like the Democratic party because I know they are more for the poorer people.[30]

This woman thinks of the parties less in ideological terms—there is no allusion, for example, to the "liberalism" of the Democrats—than in terms of what each party will do for the group with which she identifies.

On a third level of concept formation, voters consider neither principles

---

[28] *Ibid.*, p. 166.
[29] Angus Campbell *et al., The American Voter*, pp. 228–29.
[30] *Ibid.*, p. 238.

nor policies but focus on *the nature of the times*. In these cases the "times" are usually seen as either good or bad, and parties and candidates are judged according to what they will do to preserve or ameliorate prevailing conditions. Thus a Philadelphia voter expressed a liking for Eisenhower in these terms:

> The only reason I would want to vote for him is that he is a former Army man and saw the horrors of war and therefore would want to keep the peace. That's the main concern of the world today.[31]

And finally there are the voters who cast their ballots with little reflection over ideology or issues, and who do not seem to relate elections to group benefits or to the problems of the day.

In fact only a very small number of voters appear to approach an election on an ideological, let alone a philosophical, level. Not many more than one in ten assess candidates and parties on the basis of their adherence to liberalism or conservatism or some similar generalized principle. About a third conceptualize in terms of group benefits; a quarter think mainly of the conditions of the times, and the remaining quarter have no issue content at all to their explanations.[32] The inevitable conclusion must be that the majority of the electorate reasons at a relatively "low" level of political sophistication. Whether this is good or bad is a vexing—and hardly new—question. In quantitative terms all votes are counted on an equal basis. The ballot cast by the most reflective professor of philosophy can be canceled out by the ballot of a prejudiced plumber. Yet "quality" is difficult to measure, and the philosopher may be stirred by nonrational considerations no less than the plumber. Just because the professor talks more coherently does not mean that his vote is devoid of emotional or temperamental content. Suppose that the question is asked, "Why are you voting for Candidate X rather than Candidate Y?" The articulated responses might be diagrammed as in Chart 8–2 on page 262.

But it may well be that the professor, for all his impressive array of "reasons," is simply voting for Candidate X because he is the professor's "kind of guy." For elections bring out the nonrational as well as the rational elements in all of us, and we all tend to impose upon our favored candidate our image of what we would like him to be. Indeed, the argument as to whether some votes are "qualitatively superior" to others may be based on premises that themselves need further examination.

Conclusions

American voting behavior is the focused expression of the citizen's participation in this nation's political system. The first fact to strike the observer is that the majority of votes seem to be cast on a hereditary, habitual, and unreflective basis. As we have discussed earlier, this is partly because both parties represent usually the same broad set of political ideas and tailor their programs and candidates to appeal to a wide spectrum of voters. Voters

---

[31] *Ibid.*, p. 242.
[32] *Ibid.*, p. 249.

CHART 8–2 / Voting Rationales

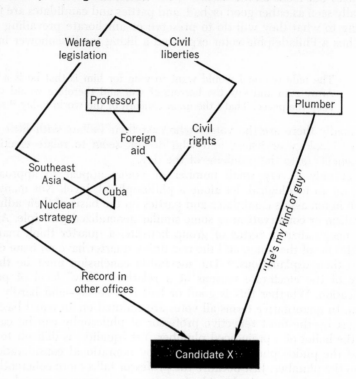

Welfare legislation

Civil liberties

Professor

Plumber

Foreign aid

Civil rights

Southeast Asia

Cuba

Nuclear strategy

Record in other offices

"He's my kind of guy"

Candidate X

are therefore less apt to feel that their vote will make a difference. Many people do not bother to vote at all; of those who do, many go through the mechanics of voting only to fulfill some vaguely defined civil obligation.

Voting behavior is strongly tied to the social system and to the social roles that individuals play. Religion, geographic locale, national origin, and primary groups all affect voting patterns. "Men act in a social frame of reference yielded by the groups of which they are a part," [33] one sociologist has remarked. And rich and poor, Protestants and Catholics, whites and Negroes, Southerners and Northerners—all try to ally with the parties and candidates that most closely represent their set of multiple interests, or conversely, that seem to oppose those of their antagonists.

Tens of millions of voters with prior party identifications project onto one candidate the attributes that they, as individual voters, would like to see their party embody. Parties and candidates are flexible enough to wear such projections and thus appear to exemplify the principles and characteristics that their adherents see in them.

---

[33] Robert K. Merton, *Social Theory and Social Structure* (Glencoe, 1957), p. 234.

9 / The Parties and the Presidency

M id-century political reality is, in all political systems, forcing more and more awesome responsibility onto the executive—the man at the top. It is true of American Presidents, British Prime Ministers and Soviet First Secretaries. This trend renders all the more crucial a continuing examination and understanding of how men on top get there. In this chapter, we shall discuss the route which must be travelled by an American Presidential candidate.

Richard Neustadt has observed:

> In the American political system the President sits in a unique seat and works within a unique frame of reference. The things he personally has to do are no respecters of the lines between "civil" and "military," or "foreign" and "domestic," or "legislative" and "executive," or "administrative" and "political." At his desk—and there alone —distinctions of these sort lose their last shred of meaning. The expectations centered in his person converge upon no other individual; nobody else . . . takes pressure in the consciousness that *he* has been elected "by the Nation." [1]

The entire population of the United States, almost 200 million Americans, is ultimately affected by the decisions which flow from the White House in Washington. If the power of the President is to be perceived as legitimate there must be evidence that the nation's Chief Executive governs with the consent of the citizen body. The American method of selecting a President— the intricate web of primaries, conventions, and campaigns—may at times appear unduly complex and often unnecessarily confusing. Yet this process is central to the theory and practice of democracy: the choosing of a single national leader who may rightly be said to have been endorsed by the majority.

The road to the Presidency is divided into two sections. The first is the path to the nomination. Here the would-be candidate must persuade the leadership of his party to make him its leader. The second half of the road is the campaign trail that leads to election night and the White House.

However, only a small fraction of the approximately 110 million eligible voters can participate in the intraparty Presidential nomination process. This is because only nineteen states (representing about 60 million voters)

---

[1] Richard E. Neustadt, *Presidential Power* (New York, 1960), p. 183.

have public primaries or preference polls that allow the public to choose delegates to the national party nominating conventions. And because many state party organizations offer the public one uncontested slate of convention delegates, only about 35 million voters can participate in primaries or polls offering real alternatives as to candidates. Moreover, only a small fraction of the eligible primary voters actually votes in these contests: in 1964, for example, only 12 million people took part in state primaries or polls. Finally, since only seven or eight states run meaningful primaries, even a candidate who won them all would not have enough votes to win the nomination. Candidates are usually listed in the primaries or polls in West Virginia, South Dakota, New Hampshire, Florida, California, Ohio, Oregon, and Wisconsin. These states usually supply only about 18 percent of the voting delegates to both the Republican and Democratic conventions. The choice of the Presidential nominee is ultimately decided by the convention delegates from nonprimary states.

Winning the Nomination

While everyone is familiar with the general outline of the classical Presidential campaign strategy (crisscrossing the country for hundreds of local appearances, making major speeches before important gatherings and groups, and concentrating on regions and sectors of the population which the candidate and his tacticians believe hold the key to a winning electoral coalition), the ways in which a man gets himself nominated are more obscure and less ritualized. In fact, there are multiple strategies which, depending on the prospective nominee's particular strengths and weaknesses, can be followed in making for a convention victory. The common denominator of these varied approaches, however, is the need for extensive and detailed knowledge on the part of the aspirant (or his managers) of the party whose highest prize he seeks. Theodore H. White, in his best-selling chronicle of the 1960 Presidential battle, vividly describes the scene in the living room of Robert Kennedy's Hyannisport summer home, on an October morning in 1959, when John F. Kennedy conducted the first full-scale briefing of a small group of aids who were to be his field commanders in his campaign for the Democratic Presidential nomination.

> John F. Kennedy opened the meeting . . . for three hours broken only occasionally by a bit of information he might request of the staff, [and] he proceeded, occasionally sitting, sometimes standing, to survey the entire country without map or notes. It was a tour of America, region by region, state by state, starting with New England, moving through the Atlantic states and the Midwest, through the farm states and the mountain states, down the Pacific Coast, through the Southwest and then the South. "What I remember," says [Lawrence F.] O'Brien, director of organization and keeper of the political ledgers, "was his remarkable knowledge of every state, not just the party leaders, not just the Senators in Washington, but he knew all the factions and the key people in all the factions."
> . . . Now and then Kennedy would pause, ask for comment on a local political situation where one or the other of his staff men had particular knowledge, invite corrections, then go on. By the time he

had finished and the group broke for lunch, the strategy had been clarified from the top down, as he saw it and meant to take it.[2]

Scattered throughout the United States are 3,000 very important people. These are the individuals, almost all of them active in state and local politics, who will eventually be the delegates to the national nominating conventions. In 1964 the Democratic Convention consisted of 2,318 voting delegates; the Republicans had 1,308. (The number is fairly flexible as the parties, especially the Republicans, add "bonus" delegates for states that have done well in the previous election.) Anyone who wants the nomination must cultivate this garden. A potential candidate must win as much favor as he can among the fifty-odd delegations to his party's convention. (The Republican Convention has delegates from the District of Columbia, Puerto Rico, and the Virgin Islands. The Democrats have delegates from these areas plus some from the Canal Zone.) In some cases the candidate for the nomination will have to state his case to delegations that have already been selected. In other instances he will have an opportunity to enter a primary and thus win delegates pledged to support him. But in all cases he must embark on this quest well before either the convention or the election. John Kennedy began to make the acquaintance of those local politicians who would probably go to the 1960 convention shortly after the close of the 1956 campaign. "Getting yourself known" is not simply a matter of making a reputation as a Senator or a governor; it also involves attending breakfasts in Trenton and dinners in Denver, showing the professionals that your smile is warm and that your politics are acceptable. Minds must be convinced, old loyalties must be broken, and competing candidates must be outdistanced.

PRIMARIES

Only fifteen states (and the District of Columbia) select their convention delegates by primaries. The primary system in each state is the result of state law, and hence the rules governing it apply equally to both parties. The systems used in the various states which hold primaries fall into four general categories:

1. In New York, Pennsylvania, Illinois, West Virginia, Alabama, Nebraska, and the District of Columbia the candidates for delegates' positions are not compelled to indicate which of the candidates for the Presidential nomination they would support if they were to be sent to the national convention. This means, for example, that voters in the New York primary are voting for someone who will be free to support whichever candidate he wants. Normally in New York, Pennsylvania, and Illinois there will be only one uncontested candidate for delegate on the primary ballot, who will have been selected by the official party organization. This means that he goes to the convention uncommitted or, more likely, prepared to follow the leaders of his state delegation.

2. In South Dakota, Massachusetts, and New Jersey the primary ballot may show a delegate's preference, but only if the candidate consents to

---

[2] Theodore H. White, *The Making of the President, 1960* (New York, 1961), pp. 65–66.

LAST CHANCE POLITICAL INN

NEUTRAL NIXON'S UNDERTAKING PARLOR

From *Straight Herblock*, Simon & Schuster, 1964

California

The 1964 California primary gave the moderate Republicans their "last chance" before the convention to stem the Goldwater movement. They failed, and the convention delegates overwhelmingly chose Goldwater as the candidate.

having his name entered. Delegates can also, and most often do, express no preference on candidates, simply running on an uncommitted basis. In these cases there is only a primary contest if two candidates decide to use the state as a battleground and lend their names to competing slates of delegates. This has happened in South Dakota, but almost never in Massachusetts and New Jersey where the party organizations prefer to keep control of the delegations.

3. In New Hampshire and Florida the ballot may indicate the Presidential preference of a candidate for delegate even if the Presidential candidate has not consented to having his name used. Thus an exuberant group of supporters can enter themselves as delegates on behalf of a candidate even if he himself would prefer to sit that one out. Hence Adlai Stevenson found himself running in the 1956 Florida primary simply because his well-wishers put him on the ballot.

4. In California, Ohio, Wisconsin, and Minnesota, uncommitted delegates are not allowed on the primary ballots. This means that would-be delegates must commit themselves to a candidate, gain his consent, and then run under his name. What usually happens is that to get at least one set of delegates on the ballot the governor of the state runs as a "favorite son." Thus in 1960 in California, Governor Edmund A. Brown's delegation was the only serious contender. Governor Brown was not a serious candidate for the Presidential nomination, but "outside" candidates, particularly Kennedy, were reluctant to come to California and challenge him on his home territory. On occasion, an outsider will enter a state to challenge the domain of a "favorite son." On other occasions the governor will step down and let

outsiders fight it out in his state's primary. In Wisconsin in 1960, for example, Governor Gaylord Nelson stood aside and watched Kennedy and Humphrey compete for the state's delegation.

In most of the states the primary is open only to the registered voters of a party. As registration takes place several months before the primary, it is usually impossible to shift parties simply in order to participate in the other party's primary. While registering with a party is not a sign of undying loyalty, and while it certainly does not commit one to support that party in the general election, it does confine the primary to those who have made a prior nominal commitment to one party's fortunes.

Two exceptions to this "closed primary" rule are Wisconsin and Minnesota. In these two states the primaries are "open": a voter need not register with one party or the other and he can participate in either the Republican or the Democratic contest. In Wisconsin in 1960 a total of 842,777 citizens turned out to vote in the Democratic primary. Were all of them Democrats? Estimates differed on how many Republicans were entering the enemy camp to choose between Kennedy and Humphrey. These Republicans had every incentive to infiltrate the opposition, as Nixon was running unopposed in their own primary. It can be noted that in the general election Kennedy got only 813,217 votes in Wisconsin—about thirty thousand less than the total Democratic primary turnout.

There are two theories about the motives of supporters of one party who cross over to vote in the other party's primary. The first view is that they tend to support the man they would mind least being elected if their own party's candidate were to be defeated. The second theory is that they support the man they think would be easiest for their own party's candidate to defeat in the election. According to the first theory a Wisconsin Democrat would cross over and vote for someone like Rockefeller in the Wisconsin Republican primary; according to the second he would vote for someone like Goldwater.

PREFERENCE POLLS

Ten states have, instead of or in addition to primaries, preference polls in which voters can express their preference for candidates directly. In states that have binding primary systems—New Hampshire, Massachusetts, New Jersey, Pennsylvania, West Virginia, Illinois, and Nebraska—these polls are simply advisory. This means that the delegates to the convention are asked to take note of the fact that various voters prefer particular aspirants. The difficulty with the preference polls—often called "popularity contests"— is that the names on the ballot are not always the significant contenders for the nomination. Generally speaking, delegations pay little or no attention to the results of these polls.

In the three states that have no primaries, however—Oregon, Maryland, and Indiana—preference polls are binding on the state delegates. Yet even this restriction is limited, since delegates are legally obliged to vote for the candidate favored by their state poll only on the first ballot; after that they are free to cast their votes according to personal preference. Oregon has the most interesting system. First of all, the party may only put up a single slate of uncommitted delegates. Then the state's secretary of state draws up a list for the preference poll consisting of the names of those people he considers to be important contenders for the nomination. He lists them on the basis of his own taste and judgment and does not try to find out if they themselves want to be entered in the contest. Thus in 1960 he placed only one name on the Republican ballot: Richard Nixon. On the Democratic poll he listed John Kennedy, Wayne Morse, Hubert Humphrey, Stuart Symington, and Lyndon Johnson. For reasons best known to himself he omitted Nelson Rockefeller, Barry Goldwater, and Adlai Stevenson—all of whom ultimately received some write-in votes. The winner of the poll is the candidate the delegates for each party must support when their convention opens.

THE PRIMARY CAMPAIGN

"My name is John Kennedy, I'm running for President in the primary," was the greeting that a bareheaded young man gave to anyone he could find on the streets of Phillips, Wisconsin (population: not quite 1,700), on a wintry March day in 1960. Like many candidates before him—and many who will come after—Kennedy was taking the primary road to the national convention. He had to. For only the most favored candidates can avoid entering their names in the primaries. An incumbent President who wants another term usually has no trouble securing renomination. A party that repudiated the Chief Executive it put in office four years before would seem so strife-torn that it could hardly win the confidence of the voters. On occasion the party has an heir apparent who has been all but promised the nomination. This is usually the case when a President declines to run again, making way for his handpicked successor, as Theodore Roosevelt did with William Howard Taft in 1908. While Dwight D. Eisenhower, in stepping down in 1960, never actually called on his party to nominate Richard Nixon, the general belief among Republicans was that Eisenhower wanted Nixon as his successor. No less important, the party professionals themselves wanted Nixon, and their near unanimity of opinion made primary contests superfluous for the Republicans in 1960. Candidates who are lucky enough to fall into these select categories are able to ignore the primaries, and when slates are entered on their behalf they are usually not contested.

There are other aspirants who bypass the primaries because, on the one hand, they sense they will not do well in them; and because, on the other, they know that if they have any chance for the nomination it is at the actual convention when the bright lights that sparkled at the primaries begin to fuse out on the second or third ballot. These reluctant contenders are the "dark horses," who hope for a deadlock so that they can emerge as a last-minute compromise choice. Chances for a dark-horse candidacy in the Democratic party were reduced in 1936, when the requirement for a two-thirds majority to choose a candidate was abolished, thus ending the informal Southern veto over Democratic candidates and reducing the chances of deadlock between two major contenders. The Republican party has not nominated a dark horse since Wendell Willkie in 1940.

Generally speaking, every four years at least one of the two parties has

"How Much Did This Enthusiastic Reception Cost Us?"

Interlandi in the Los Angeles *Times*

a serious primary contest. One reason for this is that the losing party's candidate from the previous election must often reestablish his leadership position by hitting the primary trail all over again. Thus Adlai Stevenson, the Democratic candidate in 1952, was compelled to enter several 1956 primaries just to demonstrate that his following was intact. Those who enter the Presidential arena for the first time usually have no choice but to enter the primary contests. This was the case even with Dwight D. Eisenhower in 1952, and John Kennedy had to take the same route eight years later. For neither of them had the status of national party leaders at the time, and both had to demonstrate that their claims to the Presidential candidacy were worth taking seriously.

Because of the expense of primary campaigns, few candidates are willing or able to enter every primary contest. The friendly handshake in Phillips, Wisconsin, must be augmented by numerous television appearances and advertisements over statewide stations. Primary campaign funds must be raised by the candidates and their well-wishers, because the national party committees necessarily reserve their blessings and resources for the men who are ultimately nominated. It has been estimated, for example, that the Eisenhower and Taft camps laid out $2.5 million each in their pre-convention campaigns of 1952. An aspirant with money and resources of his own has a great advantage in smoothing this part of the nomination path—in fact the financial resources of a candidate probably play their most critical role at the pre-convention stage. While money itself cannot guarantee success, lack of funds can bring a candidate's campaign to a standstill. One reason that Hubert Humphrey never became a really serious contender for the 1960 Democratic nomination was that he lacked the funds to make a newsworthy display. His defeat in West Virginia, for example, was partly due to lack of funds, and in turn, his defeat made it even more difficult to get further funds, thus effectively ending his campaign. While Humphrey waited in drafty airline terminals for delayed commercial flights, John Kennedy was able to hedgehop from town to town in his family's private plane. Similarly, Nelson Rockefeller was able to pave the way for his 1964 Republican primary contest in California by hiring a Los Angeles public relations firm to help organize grass-roots support. Clearly many qualified aspirants to the Presidency lack these resources. The disturbing suspicion is that the need for personal financial resources at the pre-convention stage may eliminate qualified candidates who lack personal fortunes or wealthy patrons.

Moreover, the primary campaigns necessarily become a candidate's full-time occupation from late winter through the convention. "I don't see how any officeholder can participate in a national primary campaign without neglecting the job the people elected him to do," Adlai Stevenson once remarked. Affairs are inevitably neglected in Albany or Springfield or on Capitol Hill as a governor or a senator pleads his case at the primary hustings.

WHAT DO THE PRIMARIES PROVE?

The major function of the primary is to present an opportunity for a Presidential aspirant to show that he is a vote-getter, a potential winner. No one really thinks that the voters of states like New Hampshire, West Virginia, and Oregon are exact samples of the American electorate. Yet when New Hampshire showed that it preferred Eisenhower to Senator Robert Taft in March of 1952, the word began to be spread that Eisenhower was a winner. Similarly Kennedy's primary victory in West Virginia, largely a Protestant state, went a long way toward persuading fence-sitting delegates in other parts of the country that religion had been overrated as an issue and that Kennedy had demonstrated that he was the man to back. Victory or defeat—particularly the former—may not be conclusive, however. One reason is because victory in a primary may be written off as the product of specific circumstances within a state and therefore not a significant indicator of national vote-getting power. Henry Cabot Lodge's write-in victory in the 1964 New Hampshire Republican primary was considered to reflect "favorite son" sentiment rather than national appeal. Similarly, Kennedy's victory over Hubert Humphrey in the 1960 Wisconsin Democratic primary was not considered conclusive because Kennedy won only 57 percent of the primary vote and only 20 of the 30 delegates pledged to him. Most important, his "victory" left unanswered the question of whether Kennedy could attract non-Catholic votes: he carried the 6 heavily Catholic districts of Wisconsin and lost the 4 predominantly Protestant ones. When asked what the Wisconsin result meant, Kennedy replied, "It means that we have to do it all over again. We have to go through and win every one of them—West Virginia and Maryland and Indiana and Oregon, all the way to the convention." Moreover, even a long string of victories in state primaries cannot guarantee the nomination. This was the sad experience of the late Estes Kefauver, who won more primaries than anyone else in 1952 but who nevertheless failed to muster enough delegates to give him a majority.

On the other hand, a poor showing in the primaries, while not conclusive, is more apt to be a portent of the candidate's ultimate reception at his party's convention. Wendell Willkie's bid for the Republican renomination in 1944 ground to a halt when the voters of Wisconsin turned him down. And Harold Stassen fell by the wayside in 1948 when he lost to Thomas Dewey in the Republican Oregon preference poll. Similarly Hubert Humphrey's defeat to John Kennedy in the 1960 West Virginia Democratic primary, following Humphrey's inconclusive defeat in Wisconsin, put him out of the race for the Democratic nomination. Barry Goldwater, however, who made poor showings throughout most of the 1964 primaries, still won the Republican nomination—basically because he had lined up the solid support of party organizations in nonprimary states.

It has been noted that a candidate can avoid the risks of a primary defeat in most states by withholding his name. To be sure, his zealous supporters can get together and run for delegates' positions in his name in New Hampshire and Florida without his permission. But both of these states have traditionally been considered one-party strongholds, and even a Democrat who is beaten in Florida can legitimately claim that his defeat stemmed from some local issue outside his control. The real pitfall is Oregon, where a candidate's name is placed on the preference poll if the newspapers mention him often enough. Its curious primary system may yet earn its name in history as the Graveyard of Presidential Aspirants.

There are, in addition, objections to the increasing emphasis on contesting primaries from the point of view of political resource allocation. As White remarks,

> Established leaders hate primaries for good reason. . . . Primaries suck up money from contributors who might better be tapped for the November finals; the charges and countercharges of primary civil war provide the enemy party with ammunition it can later use with blast effect against whichever primary contender emerges victorious; primary campaigns exhaust the candidate, use up his speech material, drain his vital energy, leave him limp before he clashes with the major enemy.[3]

PERSUADING THE POLITICIANS

As if wooing voters in Wisconsin, West Virginia, and Oregon were not enough, aspirants for their party's nomination must also make frequent but less publicized trips to other parts of the country. As we have mentioned, thirty-two states have no primaries or preference polls. In these states delegates are selected in a variety of ways—mainly by conventions, the representatives to which are chosen by local party members. Here the regular party stalwarts are the main participants, with the general public seldom bothering to find out what is going on. The consequence is that the delegations are usually appendages of the party organization, and the decision as to which candidate they will support rests with the state leadership. There-

---

[3] White, *op. cit.*, pp. 93–94.

fore a prospective candidate must confer with these leaders in their home territory, revealing not only his merits but hints of possible rewards if all goes well. The men in control of the delegations in such states often refuse to commit themselves one way or another. And they have good reason for their neutrality. Were they to declare for a candidate who subsequently failed at the convention they might later be denied a welcome at the White House when they needed favors. Sometimes these state party leaders are impressed with primary victories; all party politicians like a candidate who looks like a winner, although, as with Kefauver in 1952, they may feel that doing well in the primaries is not a valid indication of victory. These are the men who often turn the tide at the conventions. Candidates often make advance claims that they have the support of delegations representing non-primary states. But no one knows this for sure until the convention is actually balloting.

The Convention

It is not easy to conduct conventions with either solemnity or decorum (although the Republicans seem to be more successful at it than the Democrats). For many delegates, the convention is partly a holiday. Moreover the crowds are terrific. It is prudent to reward as many loyal party workers as possible with convention positions. In addition to the 1,300 to 1,500 delegates, there is an equal number of "alternate delegates," presumably to stand in for delegates who succumb to heat prostration. And then, to supply even more participants, many states enlarge their delegations by dividing their quota of votes among "half-delegates"—who may or may not be accompanied by "half-alternates." Thus the bona fide participants are easily raised to 3,000. Then there are the television commentators, the television interviewers, and the television technicians, and several hundred newspapermen, including every available correspondent from foreign periodicals.

The convention, however, is more than a gigantic pep rally. The bands, the demonstrations, and the banners are designed to arouse enthusiasm for the party among the delegates. Hopefully they will return to their states, wards, and precincts to communicate their fervor to party workers back home. Once every four years, the major political parties become truly "national" coalitions of state organizations, bound together by a common desire to control the White House. The nominating conventions represent the one physical embodiment of the parties as national decision-making bodies.

The convention preliminaries for both parties are similar. There is a Committee on Credentials that has to admit each delegation. On occasion a state will send two delegations—Alabama and Mississippi showed up with rival delegations at the 1964 Democratic Convention—and the Committee must decide which was selected legitimately. This can be a real test of power. The decision of the Credentials Committee, moreover, can be appealed to the convention floor, resulting in an early lineup of the competing factions. There is the Platform Committee. While the platforms themselves are, in Wendell Willkie's phrase, "fusions of ambiguity," the groups that draw them up nevertheless serve an important function. At the 1960

Democratic Convention the Platform Committee had no less than 108 members and sat for four full days listening to representatives of various interests plead their cases. Before it paraded seventy spokesmen who asked for planks on issues ranging from civil rights and farm supports to antivivisection legislation and statehood for Puerto Rico. The very act of listening to spokesmen from all of these organizations is important, even if only a vapid generality on the subject ends up in the platform. For the Platform Committee, with its public hearings, demonstrates that the party is not a closed corporation but an open forum ready to consider the ideas of all groups in the country. There are, to be sure, occasional fights over what is to go into the platform. The most dramatic splits have occurred between the Northern and Southern wings of the Democratic party over the civil rights plank. When a majority of the delegates at the 1948 Democratic Convention voted in favor of an amendment strengthening the civil rights plank of the party platform, Southern states walked out of the convention and formed the dissident Dixiecrat party for the 1948 election. Republican differences over their platforms have been less severe, although recently the more liberal elements in the party have pushed for a greater commitment to welfare legislation. Nelson Rockefeller, as spokesman for the liberal faction of the Republican party, was able to secure compromises on the 1960 platform from Richard Nixon to ensure a greater commitment to welfare spending, civil defense, etc. And in 1964 the Scranton-Rockefeller moderate Republican forces unsuccessfully battled the conservative-dominated platform committee and a majority of the delegates for a stronger civil rights plank, a greater commitment to welfare legislation, etc. Yet the ultimate writing and presentation of a platform serves to draw the various party factions together within a common ground. Their agreement to agree may be at a high level of generality, but no one expects a detailed spelling out of policies in a platform. And everyone realizes that time and circumstances may make the fulfillment even of specific promises impossible.

The actual convention opens with a keynote address. The formula for this speech is simple: extol one's own party and damn the opposition. Clare Boothe Luce, the Republican keynoter in 1948, was perhaps less than feminine in her excoriation of the opposition: "Democratic Presidents are always troubadors of trouble, crooners of catastrophe. They cannot win elections except in the climate of crisis. So the party, by its composition, has a vested interest in depression at home and war abroad." Or Governor Frank G. Clement of Tennessee, dilating on the first four years of the Eisenhower Administration at the Democratic Convention: "Your lands are studded with the white skulls and cross bones of broken Republican promises. How long, O America, shall these things endure? How long, O people of America, shall you permit the welfare of this democracy to be pounced on in the homeland and gambled on abroad?"

THE BALLOTING

The selection of a candidate takes one of three forms. First, there is nomination by acclamation; an incumbent President, an heir apparent, or the recognized party leader is thus chosen unanimously.

Second, there is the single-ballot convention. In 1952 Eisenhower received

595 votes on the first ballot, Taft got 500, and the remaining 101 were spread among three other candidates. Eisenhower had the most votes, though not a majority. But the bandwagon had started, and at the end of the balloting the chairmen of various Taft delegations stood up to say that their states were switching to Eisenhower. Thus the first ballot was recounted, with 841 for Eisenhower and 284 votes for Taft, with 81 for other candidates. Similarly, in the 1960 Democratic Convention Kennedy was nominated on the first ballot with 806 votes out of 1,521. He reached a majority only after the forty-ninth state had been polled, and after that the convention decided to nominate him unanimously. There is a certain prestige in being the state that puts the winner "over the top," and this is especially evident when delegation chairmen clamor to switch their first-ballot votes. At the 1964 Republican Convention in San Francisco, Senator Barry Goldwater won an easy first-ballot nomination. Despite his relatively poor showing in the primaries, Goldwater's organization had done a remarkable job of weighting delegations from nonprimary states with the Senator's supporters. With the Scranton-Rockefeller-Romney moderate forces in complete disarray, it became obvious before the first polling of the states was three quarters completed that Goldwater would be able to claim victory on the first ballot.

Third, and most interesting, is the multiballot convention, well illustrated by the Democratic Convention of 1952. Senator Estes Kefauver had made the rounds of the primaries, expecting that his victories would impress a substantial number of nonprimary delegates. But the leaders of these delegations were in no mood to be stampeded. Kefauver entered the convention with the largest number of votes, but he lacked the 616 needed for the nomination. There were three ballots that year:

	First	Second	Third
Kefauver	340	362½	275½
Russell	268	294	261
Stevenson	273	324½	617½
Harriman	123½	121	–
Others	224½	126½	74
	1229	1228½	1228

Kefauver led on the first ballot, and thus his fate depended on what happened to him on the second roll call. The problem for a first-ballot leader is that he must make a significant advance on the second ballot. That, and only that, is evidence that he is destined to be the winner. However Kefauver gained only 22½ votes on the second ballot, and delegates he was counting on began to look for a more auspicious bandwagon. Most of them switched to Stevenson by the third ballot, where the Illinois governor received just under the needed majority of votes. Utah switched 4½ votes to Stevenson, who then won the nomination.

In multiballot conventions, candidates and their emissaries rush from delegation to delegation between ballotings seeking votes. The majority of

"California's Governor Brown Would Make A Good Running Mate. Do You Think Americans Would Elect A Catholic For Vice-President?"

A satirical comment on "ticket balancing," even after the election of Kennedy, a Catholic, in 1960.

Interlandi in the Los Angeles *Times*

delegates are theoretically committed to favorite sons or other minor candidates, which means they are not committed at all. The frontrunners use every approach, from promises of office to threats of reprisal, to persuade the uncommitted delegations to hop on what is hopefully a bandwagon. Delegations themselves hold caucuses to decide what to do; and sometimes state groups will be split into one or more factions, each sympathetic to a different candidate. There are, somewhere in the convention hall or in the convention city, several dozen key delegation leaders who hold the power to put a man over the top. Every candidate wants to reach the ear of these men, and dragnets are laid and relaid incessantly. At the 1964 Republican Convention, Goldwater's staff workers were equipped with electronic devices so that they could report to and receive instructions from the central command post. Despite the myth about party bosses in "smoke-filled back rooms," nominees have been chosen this way relatively infrequently, and only when it appears clear that the convention is truly deadlocked and that a compromise candidate must be imposed upon it. This led to the nomination of Warren G. Harding on the tenth ballot at the 1920 Republican Convention and to John W. Davis, at the 1924 Democratic National Convention, after the forces of Alfred E. Smith and William McAdoo had been deadlocked for 102 ballots!

Vice-Presidential candidates are usually handpicked by the Presidential nominees. The Democrats, with less party discipline than the Republicans, have occasionally gotten into floor fights despite this custom. In 1956, Adlai Stevenson let the convention choose between Estes Kefauver and John Kennedy. In the past, in an effort to garner votes from a wide spectrum of voters, an important criterion for choosing Vice-Presidential candidates has often been that they possess attributes lacked by their Presidential running mates. The Democratic Convention of 1896 paired Presidential candidate William Jennings Bryan, an ardent Silverite from rural Nebraska, with Arthur Sewall, an Eastern banker and businessman. At the 1960 Democratic Convention, John F. Kennedy, a Catholic liberal from New England, chose as his running mate Lyndon Johnson, a more conservative Protestant from Texas. In 1964 Lyndon Johnson followed tradition and attempted to maximize the appeal of the ticket by his choice of Senator Hubert Humphrey, a Midwesterner, and a man identified with the "left" sector of the Democratic Party. Senator Goldwater, on the other hand, consciously ignored the conventional political wisdom in his choice as running mate of Representative William Miller, whose principal appeal was to the same sector of the Republican party represented by Goldwater himself. Goldwater apparently believed that homogeneity of opinion on the ticket would have more vote appeal than would balance. Two recent events may discourage this tradition of "ticket balancing": the Twenty-Second Amendment, ratified in 1951, provides that no President can serve more than two terms; this encourages Presidents, particularly when running for reelection, to choose running mates whom they can endorse—or even "groom"—as their successors. In addition, the assassination of President Kennedy in 1963 underscored the need to choose Vice-Presidential candidates who would best be qualified to fill the Presidency if necessary.

What kind of men are nominated for President by this curious amalgam of public primaries, private conferences, and national conventions? The Constitution stipulates only that eligible candidates be natural-born citizens of the United States, at least thirty-five years old, and residents of the United States for at least fourteen years. About 60 million Americans meet these criteria. Yet historical practice has placed more limiting stipulations on would-be candidates, although these unwritten criteria change over time. Until 1928, all nominees of major parties were male white Protestants, who generally represented the moderate forces in their parties and who had held prior state or national public office. In 1928, however, Al Smith became the first Catholic to be nominated by a major party. Apart from availability there are two other attributes a candidate must have: (1) he must be a good "party" man; (2) he must look like a winner. This is particularly a problem for the Republicans, who have been the minority party since 1932. Indeed they often have to make the painful decision as to whether to nominate a good party man or to select a potential winner. They have usually chosen the latter, much to the discomfort of the party regulars, who see principle sacrificed on the altar of success. Thus Robert Taft, a true Republican if there ever was one, was denied the nomination three times because it was thought he could not win. (As it happened, two of the three "winners" chosen in his place lost anyway.) In a departure from this tradition, the 1964 Republican Convention chose Barry Goldwater, representing the most conservative elements of the party, over several more moderate candidates. (Goldwater's success in winning the nomination may have been partly due to Republican doubt as to whether any Republican candidate would be able to defeat Lyndon Johnson in 1964.)

AN ALTERNATIVE: A NATIONAL PRIMARY?

Over the years there has been much harsh criticism of the nominating conventions: the atmosphere is too frivolous, the rituals are irrelevant, and the proceedings are too crowded for efficiency or comfort. On the one hand the deliberations are too much in the public eye, and on the other there are too many decisions arrived at in private rooms. Yet the convention remains the culmination of the nominating process not because of obscurantism or inertia but because there is no viable alternative to it. The only substitute plan that has been proposed—and until this time the proposal has yet to receive serious consideration in influential circles—is a national Presidential primary.

Instead of the various states deciding the dates and rules for their primary contests—or indeed whether they want to have primaries at all—there would be a single Primary Day throughout the country on a specified date. Prior to that date, probably in the late spring, both Democratic and Republican aspirants for their party's nomination would address campaigns to rank-and-file Democrats and Republicans throughout the country. And on Primary Day itself the supporters of each party would then cast their ballots for the man they want as leader of their own party. In this way every Democrat and Republican would have a chance to participate in selecting a candidate. Put another way, the opportunity now available to residents of Oregon, West Virginia, and a few other states would be given to everyone. Power would be taken from "the politicians" and bestowed on "the people."

A national primary would, of course, present several technical problems. First of all, which names would be listed on each party's ballot? Presumably each candidate would have to apply for listing, or at least give his consent if others proposed him. Yet this would eliminate from the start "reluctant" candidates, who do not wish to run in primaries yet who have been chosen in conventions after other contenders fell by the wayside. Even if such unwilling individuals were lost in the process there would remain the problem of sifting the less modest applicants to arrive at a slate of manageable size. While Oregon might leave this decision to its secretary of state it is difficult to imagine someone at the national level who might be given this awesome power. And then if each party's list of contenders were somehow narrowed to four names it would be likely that none of them would receive a popular majority. This would necessitate a runoff primary with bargaining and negotiations to determine how the supporters of the eliminated candidates would vote.

Clearly these "procedural" problems have their substantive aspect as well. A national primary would allow direct rather than indirect public participation in choosing party nominees. Since the real strength of the American political party system is located in the state organizations rather than at the national level, it seems unlikely that state party leaders would be willing (or could be forced) to give up their present influence over the nomination process via the convention system. Primaries tend to disintegrate parties, creating factional groups clustered around individuals rather than organizations. This disruptive process, now limited to internal factions within state organizations, would in a national primary tend to accentuate the regional

differences already weakening the national party coalitions of state organizations. A Democratic national primary, containing on the ballot a Southerner,
a Northeastern liberal, and an urban labor candidate, would make explicit
the rifts that are now compromised within the convention system. Furthermore, flamboyant party figures in the tradition of Huey Long or Joseph
McCarthy might win a national primary even though they could never carry
a convention. Finally, it is not necessarily advisable to ask every voter in the
country to commit himself to a party so as to be eligible to vote in a national
primary. Voters have a tendency to register with the stronger of the two
parties, and this can weaken the opposition party to the extent that effective
competition is impaired.

Another disadvantage of the national primary system is that it would
accentuate the advantage of the candidate with personal financial resources
in conducting a pre-convention campaign. Entering primaries in a handful
of states is expensive enough; candidates in a national primary would have
to glean financial support for their campaigns in all fifty states.

The Campaign

One premise of Presidential campaigns is that American society is best
viewed as a conglomeration of various social groups. There are farmers and
businessmen, city dwellers and suburbanites, and a wide variety of "hyphen-
ated-Americans." This is why there is so much talk of a "Catholic vote," a
"farm vote," a "Negro vote," and so on. Appeals are made to each of these
groups, particularly in underlining how they have been neglected (or provided for) in the past, and how the election of one (or the other) candidate
will secure their well-being in the future. This theory assumes that most
Americans think of themselves as members of one or another social group,
and that such a feeling of identification is an important motivation to their
voting behavior. Hence the parties set up special campaign committees to
make appeals to women, to minority groups, and even—in recent years—
to artists and intellectuals.

At the same time it is dangerous to presuppose that social groups constitute blocs that can be delivered to the party that makes the best deal with
their supposed leaders. Farmers, Catholics, businessmen, Jews, suburbanites,
and the rest are more sociological categories than they are organized and
coherently led groups in the community. There is no single association that
embraces each of these categories and no one recognized leader who voices
his followers' demands or is able to commit their votes to a party or a candidate. American society is much too informally put together for anything
like this to occur. If a Presidential aspirant wants to appeal to voters in
their group roles he must do this by reaching them as individuals. At best
he will hope to gain the open support of people who are known and respected by members of various groups, hoping that an awareness of these
endorsements will filter down. Even so, trade unionists have minds of their
own and have voted contrary to the suggestions of such labor leaders as
John L. Lewis, Walter Reuther, and James R. Hoffa. Negroes have not been
impressed with the political advice offered to them by Adam Clayton
Powell or Jackie Robinson, both of whom asked them at one time to vote

"Never Mind The Fine Print, Son—How Would You Like To Win That Girl?"

Goldwater's position on the civil rights issue during his campaign won him the votes of the traditionally Democratic "Solid South."

From *Straight Herblock*, Simon & Schuster, 1964

Republican; and farmers have sometimes been impervious to the partisan preferences expressed by those who head the major agriculture organizations. This independence of spirit leads to unpredictable voting behavior and continues to bedevil campaign strategists.

Thus voter behavior cannot be explained or influenced solely on the basis of group affiliations. Both political scientists and politicians know that the most enduring of all attitudes influencing voting is an individual's party identification. Most voters are predisposed to be either Democrats or Republicans and are inclined to support their own party's candidates. The difficulty is that it is on the national level, in a Presidential election, that voters are apt to forgo their party loyalty and to make their decisions on the basis of the candidates' personalities as they perceive them. For Presidential candidates are highly "visible": they are seen and heard on the mass media and are constant subjects of discussion for many months. Hence both parties must take account of party identification and candidate orientation.

Interestingly the two parties use different strategies here. The Democrats emphasize party identification more than the Republicans do. The Democrats know that they are the majority party, and that they will therefore win the election *so long as* their usual supporters turn out to vote and vote their customary line. This is why Democratic candidates stress the fact that they are Democrats. The Republican strategy, on the other hand, is to emphasize the candidate rather than the party. In 1960, for example, Richard Nixon seldom mentioned his Republicanism but rather made his appeal to all voters regardless of their prior allegiances. Eisenhower managed to win on this basis, and Nixon was successful in attracting some, but not enough,

Democrats to his side. In 1960 Nixon managed to attract 6 percent of voters who had cast their lot with Stevenson in 1956. Kennedy, on the other hand, attracted the vote of 17 percent of those who had voted for Eisenhower four years before.[4]

BEING SEEN BY THE PEOPLE

Television is the bane and blessing of campaign politics—bane because its expense can drive a party close to bankruptcy and blessing because it brings a close-up view of the candidates into virtually every household.

The 1960 campaign brought the innovation of televised debates: Kennedy and Nixon crossed swords four times, before audiences ranging from 60 to 75 million. Each candidate delivered a prepared statement on the topic for that debate, answered questions asked by a panel of journalists, and then briefly summed up his position. The debates gave the American public an opportunity to evaluate each candidate in juxtaposition with his opponent— to see how each man reacted under fire. Political commentators agree that Kennedy gained more than Nixon from the debates, though neither man won a clear-cut "victory." Nixon's wan appearance and apparent nervousness during the first debate, contrasted with Kennedy's seeming mastery of facts and self-confidence, helped to rebut Republican arguments that Kennedy was too young and inexperienced to be President. Moreover, the television confrontations emphasized the differences of opinion and approach between the two contenders and helped to bring campaign issues into clearer relief. In answer to a question on federal aid to education, for example, Nixon replied that he favored aid for school construction but not for teachers' salaries. Kennedy said he was for aid to both construction and salaries. On the offshore islands of Matsu and Quemoy, Nixon said their defense was vital whereas Kennedy thought they were probably dispensable.

THE EFFECT OF CAMPAIGNS ON VOTING BEHAVIOR

About two thirds of the electorate is habitually disposed to support one party or the other, and these citizens will vote for their party's candidate except in unusual circumstances. The Presidential campaign helps reactivate the convictions of these party supporters, many of whom have not been concerned with politics since the last Presidential election. This rallying of the faithful is no less important than making converts, since a strong core of supporters is a prerequisite to long-run party viability. The outcome of individual elections, however, ultimately hinges on the behavior of the mass of voters with only marginal or "thin" party identifications, and it is to this group that election campaigns are primarily aimed. The great problem for campaign strategists is to decide who the undecideds are, where they are, and what motivates them. There are two types of uncommitted voters. The first is generally relatively well educated, more concerned with issues than with party labels or personalities, and usually votes quite regularly. But there are only several million individuals in this category at most.

---

[4] Philip E. Converse, Angus Campbell, Warren E. Miller, and Donald E. Stokes, "Stability and Change in 1960: A Reinstating Election," *American Political Science Review* (June, 1961), Vol. LV, pp. 269–80.

The second type of uncommitted voter is quite nonpolitical, cares little about issues, and tends to stay home for most of the elections. This category —containing 30 to 40 million potential voters—gets much of the candidates' attention. One theory is that, being apolitical, this type of voter is primarily impressed with a candidate's personality. Another speculation is that he is negative in outlook—perhaps even "antipolitical"—and likes nothing better than a rousing attack on those responsible for the nation's problems. Campaigns do appear to affect the opinions of uncommitted voters, since voting studies show that appreciable segments of undecided voters who were undecided in September have made their decisions on candidates by the first week in November.

Thus committees are set up to woo the uncommitted vote, with titles like "Citizens for Johnson" and "Volunteers for Goldwater." Public opinion polls are used to persuade the uncommitted voters that one side or another is winning and that they ought to hop on the bandwagon. The chief targets are the undecided voters in the "key" states, those with large populations and hence substantial electoral votes. It may take only a few thousand voters to shift New York's forty-three or California's forty electoral votes into a candidate's camp. This is why the contenders usually concentrate their campaigns in states like New York, California, Pennsylvania, Ohio, and Illinois, or Texas, hoping to swing them into their column.

THE LEVEL OF CAMPAIGN DIALOGUE

"Ought a convicted adulteress and her paramour husband to be placed in the highest offices of this free and Christian land?" an anti-Jackson pamphlet asked during the 1828 campaign. Campaign rhetoric has been much more subdued in recent years. Personal attacks, irresponsible charges, and gross exaggerations seldom issue nowadays from Presidential candidates or their supporters. Some overzealous Republicans called the Democrats "the party of treason" in 1952. However while there was clearly a "Catholic issue" in the minds of many voters in 1960, no Republican political leader of national stature alluded to Kennedy's religion in disparaging terms. Indeed Kennedy himself discussed his Catholicism openly while Nixon was silent about it. The reason for the relatively recent shift in the direction of a higher level of campaign discourse is that Americans nowadays tend to be less indignant over their politics and place a higher premium on smooth social relations.

Of greater concern is the intellectual level of campaigning. The platforms, the speeches, and the pamphlets are models of vagueness and superficiality. The emphasis is on form rather than content, on how statements are made rather than what is said. There are several reasons for this tendency. Most Americans seldom engage in serious daily political discussions, and a Presidential campaign presents a fine opportunity to begin a public dialogue on major issues. The problem, however, is that a campaign is also a vote-getting enterprise. Its rhetoric is part of a grand strategy, the aim being not education but rather victory at the polls. In one sense an election is the worst possible time for rational political discussion. To make his points effectively a candidate must speak in caricatures: he must inflate his own party's achievements and puncture those of the opposition. Campaign time, then, is the time for black and white. If the truth is often gray, it must wait until after the votes are counted before it emerges again. These mild self-deceptions, however, serve the function of arousing interest and sharpening the issues in Presidential elections. People want to feel strongly that something important is at stake when they cast their ballots, that it does make some difference that one contender rather than the other reach the White House.

CAN CAMPAIGNING BE SCIENTIFIC?

Much of a campaign is tradition and ritual. The goals are of course well established: to get your messages across to as many people as possible, to influence their thinking, to win their votes. Yet the means by which these ends may be achieved are difficult to devise and even harder to validate. Is it really necessary to swing around long stretches of the country by train? What is added by making a conservation speech in Denver? How many votes are gained by a series of television spots? On these and other such questions one commentator—himself a candidate for office—has remarked: [5]

> Scientists refuse to accept an hypothesis until they have verified it by exhaustive examination of all available evidence which may prove or disprove it, and they continue to discard each successive hypothesis as it fails to meet their tests. By contrast, a politician must act on his hypotheses, which are tested only by looking backward on his acts. A candidate cannot even experiment. Because no one knows what works in a campaign, money is spent beyond the point of diminishing returns. To meet similar efforts of the opposition all advertising and propaganda devices are used—billboards, radio, TV, sound trucks, newspaper ads, letter-writing or telephone committee programs, handbills, bus cards. No one dares to omit any approach. Every cartridge must be fired because among the multitude of blanks one may be a bullet.

The natural reaction is to try every available technique, year in and year out. To cancel the conservation speech is to risk defeat at the polls. If a candidate wins the Presidency by an overwhelming majority, it may be possible to suggest that he didn't really *have* to visit Alaska, but those three electoral votes looked important in October. A campaign, then, is not a laboratory experiment. The stakes are real and the participants are in no mood to test the effectiveness of their methods. A campaign was effective if the candidate wins, and it was a failure if he loses. This test may not be scientific but there is no replacement for it.

In the final analysis, there are limits to any group's ability to persuade those who will not be persuaded. Frequently the major force at work in an election year is beyond the control of any party or candidate. There exists, at any period, a general "atmosphere" of public feeling about the state of the nation. If people are relatively contented with things as they are, they will be inclined to renew the term of the party holding the Presidency. If, on the other hand, they are unhappy about their own condition or that of the world, they will turn the incumbents out of office. This repudiation may

---

[5] Stimson Bullitt, *To Be a Politician* (Garden City, 1959), p. 90.

take place even if those holding power cannot logically be held accountable for the misfortunes that apparently beset society. Indeed one of the functions of parties in democratic politics is to provide visible, continuing institutions that can be held accountable for things going well or poorly. Elections give the average citizen the opportunity to pass judgment on those who seek to hold the reins of power in political life. The bases on which voters judge their rulers may occasionally be less than rational, but it is this check, this need for campaigns that appeal to the public, that compels governors to be responsive to the governed.

The Electoral College

The American people do not, of course, elect their President. The votes they cast in November are for electors, and the winning slate of electors of each state forgather in December to cast the official ballots that decide who is to occupy the White House for the coming four years. (It might be added that the entire Electoral College never meets as a single unit. The electors of each state come together at their respective state capitals and the results of their ballotings are formally transmitted to Washington. Under the provisions of the Twenty-third Amendment there will be three electors for the District of Columbia as well.)

Each state has as many electors as its combined number of Senators and Representatives. This arrangement benefits the states with smaller populations (and therefore fewer representatives) because they are assured of at least three electors. Thus Alaska, which according to population would have only one elector, has two additional electors to match its Senators. For California, on the other hand, which would be entitled to thirty-eight electors according to population, the additional two electors for its Senators is a much smaller gain proportionally.

On the other hand, the winner-take-all system of choosing electors favors the big two-party states. A Presidential candidate who wins a majority (or plurality) of popular votes within a state gets all its electoral votes. In 1960, for example, John Kennedy polled under 50.1 percent of the major-party vote in Illinois but nevertheless carried off all twenty-six of the state's electoral votes. The ability of big states to deliver large blocs of electoral votes gives these states great influence in the nominating process within both parties.

Given a combination of a candidate's overwhelming victories in some states and near-misses in others, it is altogether possible that he will win a popular majority in the nation as a whole and yet lose the election in the Electoral College. This occurred in 1876 when Samuel Tilden received 250,000 more popular votes than did Rutherford B. Hayes and yet lost in the Electoral College by a one-vote margin. In 1824 Jackson won more popular votes than John Quincy Adams but still lost the Presidency; and in 1888 Grover Cleveland was ahead at the polls but was far behind Benjamin Harrison in the Electoral College. (However in 1824 and 1888 Jackson and Cleveland had only popular pluralities, rather than majorities, because of the large votes going to minor candidates.)

Generally speaking, however, the candidate who wins a popular majority—

or even slightly under a majority, as did Truman in 1948 and Kennedy in 1960—receives a comfortable bonus of electoral votes. As Chart 9–1 shows, between 1920 and 1960 the electoral percentage was at least seven points higher and ran up to 36.6 points higher than the popular percentage.

In the past, even when the popular votes for the two candidates were close, the Democratic candidate did noticeably better in the Electoral College. The reason for this is that the electoral votes of the Southern states, which have traditionally been carried by Democratic candidates, represent a relatively small popular turnout (and thus it takes a smaller number of popular votes to yield a given number of electoral votes). In the 1960

CHART 9–1 / Popular Votes Versus Electoral Votes
Winning Candidates' Percentages of Total Vote: 1920–64

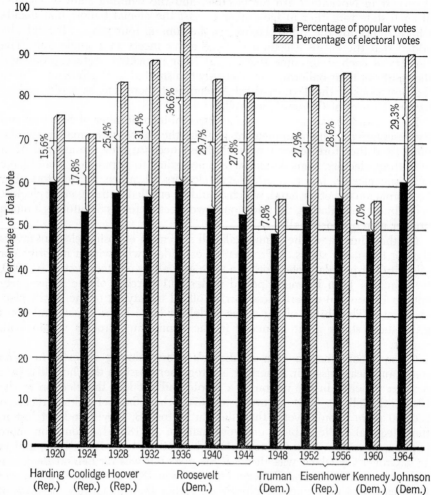

SOURCE: United States Bureau of the Census, *Statistical Abstract of the United States* (Washington).

election, for example, 928,825 Kansas voters went to the polls, and a majority of 561,474 gave Nixon the state's eight electoral votes. In South Carolina, however, only 386,688 voters went to the polls, and it took a majority of only 198,129 to put eight electoral votes in the Democratic column.

There is also the possibility that no candidate will win a majority of the electoral votes, thus throwing the decision to the House of Representatives —where each state, not each Representative, then has one vote in selecting the President. This could only happen, of course, if there were more than two candidates. Yet in 1948 the States' Rights party (the "Dixiecrats") ran a ticket and managed to carry four states with a total of thirty-nine electoral votes. Harry Truman had a popular margin of over 2 million votes, and he did win an electoral majority. However had there been a shift of 3,554 votes from Truman to Dewey in Ohio and a similar shift of 8,933 in California, Truman would not have had a majority in the Electoral College and the election would have been thrown to the House. In recent years several Southern states have tried to experiment with what is called the "free elector" plan. Under this arrangement the Democratic party's slate of electors is not pledged to support the Democratic Presidential candidate. They are, rather, free agents and can use their power as electors as they see fit. Thus in 1960 six of Alabama's electors, one of Oklahoma's, and all eight of Mississippi's cast their votes for Senator Harry Byrd of Virginia for President— even though they had given no indication during the campaign that Byrd would be their choice. The eventual intention of such a strategy is to support a third candidate, to deprive the two major contenders of electoral majorities, and thereby to throw the contest to the House of Representatives, where each state would have one vote—Alabama, Oklahoma, and Mississippi would thus have voting power equal to that of New York, California, and Illinois.

PROPOSED REFORMS

It would take an amendment to the Constitution to change the Electoral College system, and during the 1940s and 1950s Congress gave a good deal of attention to proposals for reform. At the outset suggestions for change came from individuals and groups who feared a repetition of 1888 and who wished to ensure that the Presidential candidate with the largest number of popular votes got safely to the White House. Their quite straightforward proposal was that the Electoral College be scrapped altogether and that popular votes be allowed to decide the Presidency. This plan may seem uncontroversial on the surface, but there were strong objections to it. Not least of the opposition came from those who saw the necessity for a "National Election Register" implicit in this reform. For if popular votes across the country were to elect the President then there would be pressure to make sure that all such votes were "equal"—that is, that requirements for Presidential registration, voting, counting of ballots, and recording of results were uniform. Such requirements would clearly give the federal government new powers of regulation over voting, a field now mainly belonging to the states. Important questions of both states' rights and civil rights arise here, which is probably why this reform has been greeted with so little enthusiasm among those who are empowered to amend the Constitution.

An alternative proposal, supported by entirely different groups, would retain electors for each state but would have each elector chosen by a Congressional district. In the 1960 election, for example, Nixon won a majority of the popular votes in Ohio and thus secured all twenty-five of that state's electoral votes. There are twenty-three Congressional districts in Ohio, and in 1960 seven of them elected Democratic Representatives. Under the proposed reform Ohio's electoral votes would have been reduced to twenty-three, with seven going to the Democratic candidate and sixteen to the Republican—assuming that Presidential voting corresponded to Congressional voting in each district.[6] One problem here is that Congressional districts would each have one elector even though such districts are not of equal size. Thus in 1960 the districts of Ohio ranged from one with a population of 726,156 down to one with 236,288. Congressional districts are drawn up by state legislatures, and the usual attempt is to favor rural areas as much as possible. If Presidential electors were tied to Congressional districts, the Presidency would of course tend to reflect the political outlook of the House of Representatives. The Democrats would therefore benefit as a party, but at the same time rural conservatives would gain over urban liberals.

A third proposal, called the Lodge-Gossett Amendment, was a compromise. Here the present allotment of electoral votes among the states would be retained, but those votes would be apportioned among the Presidential candidates in proportion to their popular votes within the state. Thus, to take Ohio again, in 1960 Kennedy received 1,944,248 votes to Nixon's 2,217,611. If the state's twenty-five electoral votes were split according to the popular vote ratio, Kennedy would have ended up with twelve of Ohio's electoral votes and Nixon would have had thirteen. With the Lodge-Gossett proposal each state would register its own voters under its own rules. The Senate did pass a resolution embodying the Lodge-Gossett reforms, but the House failed to act on it, and the proposed amendment was never sent to the states for ratification. Even if it had been it is doubtful if the required three-fourths of the legislatures would have supported it. For there appears to be a general willingness to go along with the Electoral College system as it now stands, and there is the feeling that any change will benefit some groups or interests and will harm others. This sentiment may change if at some future time the candidate with a popular majority fails to win an electoral majority and is thus barred from the White House. But just such a sacrifice, such a departure from the principle of majority rule, will probably be required before the country is roused to reform the Electoral College.

Conclusion: The Quiet Passage of Power

After the long months of pre-convention maneuvering, the sweating tumultuous press of the crowd in the hall at the moment of nomination, the weeks of madly paced speechmaking, the packed and howling sidewalks,

---

[6] This did happen to be the case in Ohio in 1960. However, not infrequently a majority of voters in a Congressional district will elect a Representative from one party and then turn around and support a Presidential candidate of the other party.

the hundreds of high school bands, Election Day is quiet. As Theodore White has put it, the passage of power is "invisible"—the sum of millions of isolated and secret acts.

> Between ten and midnight [on Election Night] the United States is politically leaderless—there is no center of information anywhere in the nation except in the New York headquarters of the great broadcasting companies and the two great wire services. No candidate and no party can afford the investment on election night to match the news-gathering resources of the mass media; and so, as every citizen sits in his home watching his TV set or listening to his radio, he is the equal of any other in knowledge. There is nothing that can be done in these hours, for no one can any longer direct the great strike for America's power; the polls have closed. Good or bad, whatever the decision, America will accept the decision—and cut down any man who goes against it, even though for millions it goes against their own votes. The general vote is an expression of national will, the only substitute for violence and blood. Its verdict is to be defended as one defends civilization itself.[7]

---

[7] White, *op. cit.*, p. 11.

PART III

THE PRESIDENT, CONGRESS, AND THE EXECUTIVE BRANCH

10 / The President: Mainspring of the System

In the conventional classification of governments, that of the United States is known as a Presidential system. This designation, though it ignores other governmental institutions such as federalism and the constitutional powers of the Supreme Court, emphasizes a crucial point: The most distinctive creation of the American system is the Presidency. Although this could have been apparent to only a few men in 1787, the development of the office in the intervening decades has made the fact inescapable in the mid-twentieth century.

The Eighteenth Century: The Era of the Legislature

The order of topics in the Constitution reveals the document's eighteenth-century origins. When the Founding Fathers dealt first with the Congress, second with the President, and third with the Judiciary, they were accurately reflecting the assumptions and philosophy of the time. Presumably they were guided in part by the patterns of the existing state constitutions and by the order of discussion in such influential and familiar commentaries as John Locke's *Second Treatise on Civil Government* (1690).

The members of the Philadelphia Convention of 1787 were also following, for the most part unconsciously, a logic that left them no sensible alternative. They were writing in the midst of what might be called, in the Anglo-American world at any rate, the era of the legislature. In Great Britain the Parliament was fast becoming the dominant governmental institution. Of course, the electoral base of the House of Commons was extremely narrow, and cabinet government in its modern sense had not fully developed. The language of the Declaration of Independence, which scarcely mentioned Parliament and charged George III personally with the grievances of the colonies, therefore accurately reflected the external form of the British regime. But it did not reflect the dominant trend in the government of Great Britain. Former London agents of the colonies, among them Benjamin Franklin, knew from direct experience that the center of power in British government was shifting increasingly toward the Parliament. "I was extremely busy," Franklin reported from London during the controversy over repeal of the Stamp Act in 1766, "attending members of both Houses, informing, explaining, consulting, disputing, in a continual hurry from morning to night." [1]

On this side of the Atlantic as revolutionary feeling mounted, the colonial assemblies were found to be a highly effective instrument against the Crown and its representatives. So strong was the sentiment against monarchy, against placing authority in the hands of any one person, that most of the post-revolutionary state constitutions established weak, multimember executives. Many of the individual delegates to the Philadelphia Convention wanted to create "a vigorous executive," but, knowing and reflecting the dominant sentiments in the country, they had more difficulty in agreeing upon this section of the Constitution than in adopting any other portion of the instrument. Both the temper of the times and considerations of political prudence required that the legislature should come first. Otherwise the proposed Constitution was unlikely to be accepted.

How, then, has the Presidency evolved from this situation into perhaps the most powerful single political position in the world today? The answers to the question are not mysterious, but they are complex; and to arrive at a full understanding of the changes in the Presidency, it is first necessary to understand the office as it now exists. The next section will attempt that analysis; later sections of the chapter will trace developments from the eighteenth-century atmosphere, which held so little promise of what was to come, through the many gradual changes of the nineteenth century, to the present.

The Twentieth Century: The Era of the President

The expectations growing out of contemporary domestic and international conditions have enormously extended the functions of the contemporary President. What are these functions? It is still useful to classify them under a limited number of constitutional and extraconstitutional headings, but in using such a list one must remember that its categories are largely conventional; that while the President's roles are *provided for* in the Constitution, they are only incompletely *specified;* and that they are continually being elaborated and modified by practice, statute, and necessity.

THE PRESIDENT AS CHIEF OF STATE

As Chief of State the President is the ceremonial head, not only of the government, but of the nation. He embodies, in William Howard Taft's phrase, the "dignity and majesty" of the American people, for other nations and for Americans themselves. When he goes abroad, he ranks with kings and above prime ministers, who are only heads of government, not heads of state. When he is at home he receives distinguished visitors as the country's chief host, and his dinners for the diplomatic corps or for visiting rulers are state dinners, not mere public banquets. In his performance of a wide variety of rituals, significant and trivial, he is acting as *the* representative of the American people. This is the common element present

---

[1] Quoted in Carl Van Doren, *Benjamin Franklin* (New York, 1938), p. 332.

when President Lyndon B. Johnson takes such varied actions as laying a wreath on the Tomb of the Unknowns, greeting the President of India at the airport and riding with him to the White House, decorating a military hero, issuing a Thanksgiving Proclamation, throwing out the first baseball of the season, dedicating a new dam, buying the first sheet of Christmas seals, congratulating the annual Peach Queen, awarding prizes to national 4-H Club champions, or lighting the nation's Christmas tree.

If one were to search for constitutional sources for this role, one might cite, at least in respect to the President's relations with foreign nations and dignitaries, the provisions that he "shall be commander in chief of the army and navy of the United States" and that "he shall receive ambassadors and other public ministers." But the fact of the matter is that the authority for this function is almost wholly conventional and extraconstitutional. A nation requires symbols of its unity, its power, and its virtues. If it lacks a royal family, it will create one. The President, the First Lady, and their children are our royal family pro tempore. We pick a President in a rough, partisan battle, but once he is elected we proclaim him President of all the people. He does not *exercise* all the power of the American nation, but he *represents* it all. In consequence, when he enters the White House as a successful candidate, he ceases even among his intimates (but not necessarily among headline writers and taxi drivers) to be "Ike" or "Jack" or "Lyndon" and becomes "Mr. President." It has been proposed, out of concern for efficiency or for the limits of one man's physical resources, that the functions of the President as Chief of State be reduced or dropped altogether as a wasteful use of the energies of an already overburdened man. Presidents, of course, do delegate the performance of many ceremonial duties to their Vice-Presidents and to members of the Cabinet, but they are wise to retain a good many of these responsibilities even if they are not, in fact, obliged to. For whatever contributes to the President's standing as the representative of the whole American people contributes also to the effectiveness with which he can perform his other roles. Thus if he appears in the eyes of a majority of the country to be speaking on a matter of import, not as the head of a particular administration but as the leader of the whole people, it may matter little that his opponents see his actions as motivated by considerations of partisan advantage. If he appears to be widely accepted as the moral spokesman of the American people, his opponents never can be sure that he is not. To avoid the risk themselves of appearing as enemies of the people, they are almost obliged, in public at any rate, to treat him on every occasion as if he were acting as Chief of State. They must respect the position even if they dislike the man, for attacks on the man may easily be interpreted as disparagement of the office.

Thus the role of Chief of State, with all its trivialities, is important to the Presidency. That it has no explicit statement in the Constitution makes it no less a Presidential function. That it carries with it no easily specified powers does not imply that it brings no power to the office. Cherished symbols are a source of power, defined or not, the more so if the symbol is a living one.

The function of Chief Executive rests more clearly on the Constitution, but the language of the relevant provisions is ambiguous in two senses. First, it appears to grant the President more power than in practice he actually has. Thus the opening sentence of Article II reads: "The executive power shall be vested in a President of the United States of America." This is apparently a sweeping assignment. But other provisions of the Constitution and various statutes give a considerable share of what might seem to be "executive power" especially to the Senate, but also to the Congress as a whole. On the other hand, the Constitution enumerates certain specific powers and duties of the President as Chief Executive that on the surface seem quite limited and even inconsequential:

> . . . he may require the opinion, in writing, of the principal officer in each of the executive departments, upon any subject relating to the duties of their respective offices . . . he shall nominate, and by and with the advice and consent of the Senate, shall appoint ambassadors, other public ministers and consuls, judges of the Supreme Court, and all other officers of the United States, whose appointments are not herein otherwise provided for, and which shall be established by law . . . he shall take care that the laws be faithfully executed . . .

But again, both by practice and by statute, around these apparently simple grants and directives has grown up virtually the whole structure of what the ordinary citizen would consider the executive power (not including the Commander in Chief function, which conventionally is treated separately).

The ordinary citizen's understandable assumption that the President is responsible for anything that happens, or fails to happen, in the executive branch therefore has considerable support in law and in practice. In any case the President cannot escape that responsibility. Yet the gap between the popular assumption and operating reality—to be explored further in later pages—may at times be quite wide. This gap, if it is to be filled at all, must be occupied by a President's *political* skills. Hence, somewhat ironically, the function of the Presidency that on first glance appears to be most *managerial,* to involve what some would describe as "mere administration," requires for its successful performance the highest degree of *political* dexterity.

Constitutionally the heart of the Chief Executive's function is in his duty to "take care that the laws be faithfully executed." Note that the President is not directed to execute the laws himself; rather he is instructed to see that others perform the execution faithfully. These others one would naturally describe, therefore, as his subordinates. But in varying degrees and for a variety of reasons that will be stated as this analysis proceeds, they may not in reality be his subordinates.

The execution of a law is rarely an automatic thing; almost invariably it involves some degree of discretion. Even the most familiar of administrative activities, those of traffic policemen, involve some determination of whether the momentary double-parking of an automobile warrants the issuance of a ticket. If the traffic ordinances of a city cannot be expected to foresee all the contingencies surrounding their enforcement, the far more complex and technical legislation of the federal government is no less likely to involve discretion in its execution. Thus with increasing frequency in recent decades, Congress has enacted statutes stating the conditions under which certain types of action may or shall be taken and authorizing the President or some subordinate executive to determine when those conditions have occurred and to issue rules, regulations, and orders necessary to give effect to the statutes. (These executive directives are referred to as "delegated legislation." They are published in the *Federal Register*.)

The President's duty to "take care that the laws be faithfully executed" must include supervision of the broad discretionary choices of his presumed subordinates, either in exercising authority granted to them by the Congress or in enforcing the laws through authority assigned to them by the President. The practice of "delegated legislation" thus has increased the President's *responsibilities* as Chief Executive, but his *authority* to discharge these responsibilities has not had any equally broad expansion. His formal means of controlling his nominal subordinates are limited in a number of ways, and his informal means are of varying reliability. We shall now examine some of these formal and informal means of control.

A President's formal control over his subordinates lies primarily in his powers of appointment and removal. To be able to pick one's subordinates and to replace them if they are not satisfactory would seem to be an elementary necessity for any executive. The vast majority of officials in the executive branch today, however, are recruited by the Civil Service Commission or related personnel agencies and appointed under the merit system. Of the remainder, amounting to approximately 10 percent of the more than 2 million civilian employees, most are appointed by the heads of agencies or by the President himself; but several thousand can be appointed only with "the advice and consent of the Senate." This constitutional power includes, in addition to commissioned officers in the armed forces—normally confirmed by the Senate as a matter of routine—a few thousand postmasters, and a roughly equal number of other civilian positions, perhaps a thousand of which involve significant policy-determining authority. In the last year of the Kennedy Administration (Eighty-seventh Congress, first session) nominations submitted to the Senate fell into the following classifications:

	Number	Percent
Commissioned officers in the armed forces	45,103	89
Postmasters	2,097	4
Other civilian positions, including judges	3,570	7
TOTAL	50,770	100

The limitations on the appointing power as an instrument of Presidential control of the executive branch are of three general types. First, the requirement of Senatorial confirmation puts into the Senate collectively—and into the individual hands of powerful Senators—bargaining power affecting some of the most important positions in the executive branch. In the case of Cabinet posts—the President's "official family"—the Senate normally confirms the President's nominations without difficulty, if only because in choosing men for these key positions Presidents avoid nominations expected to produce Senatorial opposition. Offering an acceptable nominee may be the price he pays for passage of an important bill, or for harmonious relations between Senators and the department concerned. The President need not *con*sult with Senators on such choices, but he will avoid offering them *in*sult. Second, with respect to positions in a Senator's own state that are subject to confirmation, the practice of "Senatorial courtesy" frequently takes the appointing power in reality out of executive hands. Under this custom, the Senate will refuse to confirm a nominee to a federal position in a Senator's state if the Senator declares the nominee "personally obnoxious" to him. (The complaining Senator normally must be of the President's party, and the party must be in the majority in the upper chamber.) In other words, where "Senatorial courtesy" operates, the President's nominee may, in fact, be a Senator's selection. The third type of limitation is an informal requirement. Whether the Senate's formal consent is necessary or not, an appointment in a Senator's state or sometimes one that is merely within the jurisdiction of an important Senate committee should not be made by the President or a department head until it has been cleared with the affected Senator. Failure to observe this practice, especially if the Senator offended thereby is of the President's party, may limit the nominee's usefulness in dealing with Congress, may affect the fortunes of the administration's legislative proposals, and may handicap the agency's appropriation requests.

The removal power of the President is subject to few formal limitations, but the informal constraints upon it are considerable. On the formal side, restrictions apply only in the case of those so-called independent agencies or multimember commissions, whose functions the Congress and the Supreme Court interpret as being quasi-legislative or quasi-judicial in character. A familiar example of these is the Interstate Commerce Commission. For all such positions the Congress may specify the causes for removal and the procedures that must be followed to effect it. Even if the Congress is silent about the grounds for removal, when the Court regards the agency's functions as being quasi-judicial it will not permit removal except for such causes as inefficiency, neglect of duty, or malfeasance in office.[2] On the informal side, Presidents may, of course, induce unwanted officials to resign. In some instances they have even demanded an undated letter of resignation as a condition of appointment. But if they do not employ these devices they are unable to prevent members of commissions classified as quasi-judicial from serving out their terms.

No formal restrictions inhibit the President's power to remove any official whose functions the Court regards as purely executive. This doctrine was not explicitly accepted by the Supreme Court until 1926, but it is now firmly established.[3] Removal of executive officials is subject to restriction in practice, however. This limitation may best be stated as follows: The President may remove any purely executive official *if he can afford the*

---

[2] *Humphrey's Executor* v. *U.S.*, 295 U.S. 602 (1935); *Wiener* v. *U.S.*, 357 U.S. 349 (1958).

[3] *Myers* v. *U.S.*, 272 U.S. 52 (1926). The court's opinion in this case, written by Chief Justice William Howard Taft, includes a historical account of the controversies over the removal power dating from 1789.

political costs. These costs arise from the circumstances of an official's appointment and of his continued performance. That is, if he enters upon his office with the support of friends, and, especially if he performs his assignments successfully, he acquires additional support among members of Congress, among his associates in the executive branch, and among interests concerned with the operations of his agency. If the President wishes to remove him for reasons of policy—and those are normally the ones that produce difficulty—the chances are that the official's views will be shared by various Senators, Representatives, and interest group leaders in a position to create difficulties for a President. They may, for example, be able to retaliate with costs in the form of opposition or reduced support in connection with other aspects of his program.

The prospect of these costs may seem too great to the President and thus prevent him from removing the official. Thus Franklin D. Roosevelt for several years kept Jesse Jones as head of the Reconstruction Finance Corporation and as Secretary of Commerce despite their policy differences and despite actions on Jones's part that had at least the appearance of disloyalty. Jones had a strong following on Capitol Hill and in the business community, so strong that only Roosevelt's certainty that Jones had worked secretly against him in the 1944 campaign finally persuaded the President to take the removal action. The harsh battle over Senate confirmation of Henry Wallace as Jones's successor was an index of the price Roosevelt paid. Not many cases are so dramatic, but an executive official need not be as formidable as Jesse Jones in order to make his removal appear to cost a President more than it is worth. This element of political cost is the principal justification for speaking of the officials of the executive branch as the President's "nominal subordinates."

Whether executive officials are in fact the President's subordinates depends on a variety of factors that will be explored more fully in Chapter 11. For the present, however, these can be summarized in the statement that the President's control depends upon his capacity to persuade officials in the executive branch. "Persuasion" here should be understood very broadly. It includes various forms of inducement, direct and through others. It extends not only to explicit rational argument but also—and more significantly—to the creation of a set of attitudes, an atmosphere in and outside the government, in which officials will feel that it is right or at least prudent to accede to the President's preferences. This element of persuasion, though conspicuous in the President's relations within the executive branch, permeates all of the Chief Executive's functions. As Professor Richard Neustadt briskly states, "Presidential *power* is the power to persuade." [4] The effectiveness of persuasion in one area, moreover, significantly determines its strength in another. Persuasion in this broad sense is thus the common denominator of all his functions. It ties together with a special intimacy his role as Chief Executive and his third major function, that of Chief Legislator.

---

[4] Richard E. Neustadt, *Presidential Power: The Politics of Leadership* (New York, 1960), p. 10.

Constitutionally the Presidential function usually referred to as Chief Legislator rests on three provisions. First, the Constitution requires that "He shall from time to time give to the Congress information of the state of the Union, and recommend to their consideration such measures as he shall judge necessary and expedient." This so-called "message power" extends not only to the annual Message on the State of the Union, which Presidents traditionally deliver at the opening of each session of Congress, but also to a large number of special messages—often a score or more in the course of a session. Most of these are sent to the Congress rather than delivered by the President in person. They may be fairly general in nature, but typically, except for the State of the Union message, they are quite specific. In recent years, moreover, they usually are accompanied by complete drafts of the legislation requested. Introduced formally by members of the House and Senate, these are usually known as "Administration bills." In composite they constitute the most important part of the legislative agenda.

Second, the Constitution gives the President a share in legislation by granting him the veto power. Under its most familiar form the veto is exercised by the President's returning to the house in which it originated—within ten days of receiving it—any bill to which he declines to give his signature. The returned bill must be accompanied by a message stating his objections. If two thirds of a quorum in each house votes to repass the bill, it becomes law despite the President's objections. A second form of the veto may occur if the Congress adjourns within ten days of the President's receipt of a bill. The President may then merely retain the bill unsigned—hence the term "pocket veto"—and the Congress has no opportunity to override. The President has a third option concerning a bill he disapproves, to allow it to become law without his signature by not signing it within the ten-day grace period, the Congress not having adjourned in the interim. This essentially weak type of protest is seldom used by contemporary Presidents.

In addition to the provision for overriding, two other factors restrict the scope of the veto power. In the first place, the President, unlike some state governors, must accept or reject a bill *in toto*. That is, he does not have the power of the "item veto," permitting rejection of undesirable provisions in otherwise acceptable legislation. Secondly, despite the directive in the Constitution that "Every order, resolution, or vote to which the concurrence of the Senate and the House of Representatives may be necessary (except on a question of adjournment) shall be presented to the President of the United States" and approved or disapproved by him as in the case of a bill, various legislative actions of consequence are not subject to any action by him. Thus it was decided early in the history of the Union that Congressional resolutions proposing amendments to the Constitution need not be submitted to the President.[5] Another type of resolution, the "concurrent" resolution, is also not submitted. Until fairly recently these were used primarily to express Congressional intent or preference and thus,

---

[5] *Hollingsworth* v. *Virginia*, 3 Dallas 378 (1798).

though requiring the "concurrence" of both houses, lacked the status of law. In recent years, however, the Congress has included in a number of statutes provisions for repeal or for overriding executive enforcement action by concurrent resolution—a kind of legislative veto. These resolutions presumably have the same status as other statutory actions, although their effect is negative. Their constitutionality has never been ruled upon by the Supreme Court.

Despite these limitations, the veto power is a formidable instrument. A single Presidential vote (the veto) can outweigh the votes of 289 Representatives and 66 Senators. More important, since it is rarely certain that a two-thirds majority of both houses will be forthcoming, the threat of a veto by the President or his spokesmen frequently produces amendments or other modifications in a bill which are expected to make it acceptable. The veto thus is not merely an instrument of negative influence; it has some positive utility for a President as well.

Third, the Constitution grants the President some power in connection with scheduling legislative sessions. He has the power "on extraordinary occasions" to call the Congress into special session. Today, when the legislature normally meets for eight or nine months of the year, this is of slight but occasional consequence. Among the most famous special sessions was that beginning in March, 1933, the so-called "Hundred Days," when the Congress rapidly enacted the early framework of Franklin Roosevelt's New Deal. The Constitution further provides that the President, when the houses of Congress are in disagreement over a time of adjournment, "may adjourn them to such time as he shall think proper." This power has never been exercised.

It would be inaccurate to assume that the function of Chief Legislator implies that the President necessarily has a high degree of control over the Congress. The Constitution, however, does make him a part of the legislative process, and expectations that the President act in most matters of national consequence have obliged him to take an increasingly active part in the enactment of important statutes. In the past quarter-century the Congress too has come to expect that the White House will be the chief source of its agenda, provider of grist for its committee mills and of topics for its debates. In no other way could it respond in orderly fashion to the demands that now focus upon the government. But the President needs a great deal more than his constitutional powers if he is to get what he considers essential from the legislature. This is where the politics of the Presidency appears once again.

For the label of Chief Legislator to have any substantial meaning a great deal of persuasion is required. A President can place some reliance on the ties of party, but, for reasons that will be discussed in more detail in the next section, these are often insufficient. He must, therefore, engage in a variety of activities—directly or through his staff—that will induce Congressional majorities, like executive subordinates, to feel that it is right or prudent to accept his minimum demands. Here he faces the threat of a vicious circle. If he fails conspicuously with Congress, his public image as Chief of State will not prevent losing support throughout the country, and his formal powers as Chief Executive will not guarantee the loyalty and zeal of his executive subordinates. If his support in the country declines, so will his fortunes in the Congress, and so on. In seeking to avoid this ominous prospect, the President both gains some help and adds some complications through his fourth major function, that of Party Leader.

THE PRESIDENT AS PARTY LEADER

Unlike the functions previously discussed, the role of Party Leader is wholly extraconstitutional. It does, however, reflect constitutional arrangements; that is, it rests on the circumstance that the Presidency (along with the Vice-Presidency) is the only elective office in the country requiring the successful candidate to have the support of a coalition of leaders in more than one state. In a sense, therefore, the "national party" of a successful Presidential candidate, while not his personal instrument, is indistinguishable from him; his fortunes in the electorate are essentially the party's fortunes. One of his and its chief concerns must be to keep this coalition intact and strong enough either to assure his reelection or to gain the nomination and election of a preferred successor. To do this his personal popularity in the country is, of course, crucial. In addition his use of patronage on state and local levels and his choice of policies to sponsor not only may influence the attitudes of members of Congress who are part of his coalition, but also may significantly affect the cohesion of supporting groups within the states. He is not completely free to choose with whom he will deal on patronage, of course, but his preference for one factional leader over another may have wide repercussions within a state as well as effects upon "his" party. Thus President Kennedy's decision in 1961 to bypass New York State Chairman Michael H. Prendergast and National Committeeman Carmine De Sapio contributed to the decline of the faction associated with them. In turn this decision gave prestige and strength to the rival faction led by Mayor Robert F. Wagner of New York City and former Governor Herbert Lehman. The President's choices among competing policies—for example, between public and private development of electric power resources, between vigorous and lip-service championship of racial integration in education and the like—will have similar if less obvious consequences.

In a sense, then, the President must be Party Leader just because he *is* President. He needs the party and the party needs him. This is the chief reason, of course, why a defeated Presidential candidate is no more than "titular" leader of his party. Even if he retains considerable popular following, he has little to give to the elements of the coalition that nominated him, many of whom are naturally likely to be looking for an alternative candidate who may perform more effectively in the next election.

Between the President's essentially electoral party and the party of the same name in the Congress important connections exist, but the two are not the same thing. The reasons for this separateness will be examined in more detail in Chapter 12; here it will be sufficient to note that the sanctions and rewards at the disposal of an incumbent President as Party Leader are rarely sufficient to control fully the electoral fortunes of candidates for the House and Senate. In particular, the President's influence tends to be weak at the crucial nominating stage, when it is decided who shall be the candidates for Congress from "his" party. Nevertheless, the electoral fortunes of a party's candidates, Congressional and Presidential, tend to fluctuate together. Thus only twice in more than a century and a quarter since the emergence of national political parties has the majority in the House not been of the same party as the President when both were chosen in the same election. In 1848 Zachary Taylor, a Whig, was elected President though the Whigs failed to gain a majority in the House; in 1956 Dwight D. Eisenhower was reelected, but the Democrats retained a majority of seats in the Congress. Whatever may occur in the processes of nomination, in general elections the preponderance of voters favor the Republicans as a whole or the Democrats as a whole, whatever the offices they seek. Especially in closely competitive areas, this can be a controlling factor.

The President stands out as the most prominent among his fellow partisans. A President discredited or repudiated is, therefore, a handicap to the whole ticket. Hence, in addition to personal ties and intangible loyalties to a common party—which are of real consequence—Representatives and Senators have a substantial incentive to respond to the wishes and policies of a President of their own party in a fashion that will present them both— the whole party—in the most favorable light. Even legislators from one-party states, among whom these incentives are likely to be least compelling, are not entirely indifferent to these common stakes. As Party Leader the President must attempt to exploit these *convergent* tendencies as fully as possible.

In a great many particular cases common party stakes are not sufficient, however, to assure a majority of votes in Congress for the President's plans. Consequently a President cannot rely wholly upon them. A Democratic President, for example, will need some Republican votes in Congress for certain of his measures. In particular, he will need them in the Senate for the two-thirds majority required by the Constitution for the acceptance of treaties; a Republican faces the same necessity. The President must, therefore, maintain relations of some cordiality with at least a fraction of the "opposition" in Congress, even if his party is nominally in the majority. Though he is a Party Leader, his partisanship must be limited. Given the expectation that as Chief of State the President will stand for the unity of the nation, his partisan behavior is further checked. The function of Party Leader, therefore, is essential and inescapable, but it must be performed within limits that may be severe even if they are not very precise.

THE PRESIDENT AS CHIEF DIPLOMAT

The fifth major function of the President is that of Chief Diplomat. In formal terms this derives from two items in the Constitution: first, that "He shall have power, by and with the advice and consent of the Senate, to make treaties, provided two thirds of the senators present concur"; and second, that "he shall receive ambassadors and other public ministers." In themselves these formal stipulations are of considerable consequence. As we have seen earlier, the "right of reception," as it is sometimes called, makes the President legally the sole means of communication between the government of the United States and all foreign powers. In addition, it confers the right, not seriously questioned since the early years of the

Constitution, to grant or to withhold recognition of a government by receiving or refusing to receive its diplomatic representative. Ambassadors of foreign governments are accredited to the President; though they necessarily maintain contacts informally throughout the government, in principle they are instruments of communication and negotiation between him and the foreign heads of state. Similarly, American ambassadors are not general representatives of this government but are specifically the President's emissaries.

To the extent that relations with other governments are restricted to communications between heads of state, the President's formal position is exclusive. These communications are important and extensive, but they do not include the full range of government actions in foreign affairs. Thus as soon as they include the making of a treaty the Senate must become involved. Early controversy over whether the Senate, as a body, had to give its consent to negotiation in its various stages has long since been settled in the negative. But Presidents, especially in recent decades, have found it prudent to work closely with Senators, especially the members of the Committee on Foreign Relations. Securing a two-thirds majority in the Senate is not easy at best; failure to consult with key Senators in the process of negotiations may produce two sorts of adverse effects. First, it may lead the Senate to reject the treaty outright. Second, the Senate may qualify its approval by attaching amendments or reservations that will require extensive renegotiation before the President can ratify the treaty. When the treaty involves several governments and the draft submitted to the Senate reflects a delicate balance of concessions among these governments, attempts at renegotiation to meet the Senate's reservations may be hopeless.

Thus Woodrow Wilson's decision not to include any Senator in the delegation to the peace conference at Versailles in 1919 is usually regarded as a blunder that led directly to Senate reservations to the treaty that were unacceptable to Wilson, with the result that the treaty was never ratified by the United States. Wilson would have had difficulty with the Versailles Treaty in any case, especially since it included adherence to the Covenant of the League of Nations, and even close collaboration with the Senate might not have saved it. Later Presidents have been careful to avoid placing themselves in his predicament.

Treaties are not the only form of contract between the United States and other governments, however. The Constitution clearly envisaged certain international alliances that were not to be subject to the kind of Senate action required for the ratification of treaties. (The provisions for such alliances are indirect, however. Article I, Section 10, provides that "No state shall enter into any treaty, alliance, or confederation"; a separate clause of the same section declares that "No state shall, without the consent of the Congress, . . . enter into any agreement or compact . . . with a foreign power. . . ." The implication is, therefore, that the United States may enter into a "compact" or "agreement" as well as a "treaty.")

These executive agreements, as they have come to be called, have a long history, and in recent years a large proportion of the arrangements with other governments have taken this form. In importance and effect they are often scarcely distinguishable from treaties. Thus the so-called "Hull-Lothian Agreement" of September, 1940, amounted to a virtual alliance between the United States and Britain. It exchanged fifty overage American destroyers for ninety-nine-year leases to a series of naval bases on British territory in the Western Atlantic. The crisis of British arms being what it was during the summer of 1940, the form of the executive agreement presumably was used as a device for saving valuable time, but its effects were as binding and permanent as those of a treaty. In some other circumstances where the form has been employed, more probably it was adopted as a means of bypassing a possible "veto" by a failure to get a two-thirds vote in the Senate. Not every administration has had the sort of experience that prompted John Hay, McKinley's Secretary of State, to observe:

> A treaty entering the Senate is like a bull going into the arena; no one can say just how or when the final blow will fall—But one thing is certain—it will never leave the arena alive.[6]

But the hazards have been great enough so that the executive agreement has become an increasingly frequent device, even when it has required for its effectiveness some later action by Congress, such as appropriation of money. A simple majority of the Senate and House in support of an appropriation request may be more readily forthcoming than a two-thirds majority of the Senate in support of a treaty.

A large number of executive agreements, moreover, are entered into on the basis of prior statutory authorization by the Congress. The most familiar, perhaps, are those negotiated under the authority of the series of Reciprocal Trade Agreements Acts, under which the President is authorized to agree to adjust tariff rates within limits set by law. The Lend-Lease Act, passed almost a year before our formal entrance into the Second World War, authorized the making of agreements under which tens of billions of dollars' worth of munitions and supplies were furnished to our allies. The various foreign aid statutes enacted since the late 1940s have carried similar provisions. Under less dramatic circumstances the United States has become a party to a wide range of international agreements governing postal services, patents, copyrights, trademarks, and participation in a variety of organizations.

Whether treaties or authorized executive agreements are involved, the important point is that both the Senate and the House share significantly in the formation of foreign policy. The President as Chief Diplomat can do a great many things under his own powers in this area, including making diplomatic maneuvers that make war inescapable and signing agreements that the Congress cannot refuse to implement without causing the country to appear ridiculous. But in a great many other matters appropriate majorities of the Senate or of both houses of Congress are essential. Especially in connection with policies where the chief instrument is not agreements but money—as in the foreign aid programs—a Presidential policy is meaningless without the support of the Congress.

The President's powers as Chief Diplomat, therefore, like those con-

---

[6] W. R. Taylor, *The Life and Letters of John Hay* (Boston, 1915), Vol. II, p. 393.

nected with his other functions, depend heavily upon his power to persuade. In the realm of foreign policy, moreover, the complexity of his responsibilities is increased by the necessity to reckon not only with the intricacies of the American system but also with the political circumstances of the countries with which he is negotiating. What meets the requirements of one may be unacceptable to the other. A President repudiated or under fire at home is not likely to be highly influential abroad; one whose initiatives on the foreign scene are consistently ineffectual will have trouble in persuading the Congress. He must be effective with both.

This necessity to lead—to be persuasive—both at home and abroad reflects the principal change in the President's function as Chief Diplomat since the Second World War. Before the end of that war it would have been conceivable for a President to say, as Warren G. Harding did in his inaugural address in 1921: "We seek no part in directing the destinies of the world." No President or serious aspirant for the White House since could have made such a statement unless he added, "But we have no choice." The United States, and therefore its President, inescapably must be the leader of the polyglot coalition loosely referred to as "the Free World." The President's once fairly restricted obligation to persuade thus has become global in about two decades. Upon his ability to discharge that obligation "the destinies of the world" may not solely depend, but to say so would not be to exaggerate very much.

THE PRESIDENT AS COMMANDER IN CHIEF

The President receives considerable assistance in the discharge of his diplomatic responsibilities from the powers associated with his sixth major function prescribed in the Constitution. He is "commander in chief of the army and navy of the United States, and of the militia of the several states, when called into the actual service of the United States." In fact, in a day when the weapons available to major powers are of such destructive proportions as to make "victory" a term of doubtful meaning, it is easy to think of military power primarily as a base from which diplomacy can proceed.

But military action is not confined to declared wars or to the use of thermonuclear bombs, and in less dramatic form the President's activities as Commander in Chief and as diplomat are essentially indistinguishable. Thus the movement of troops, ships, and aircraft into an area of international tension—the reinforcement of our garrisons in West Germany and Berlin, or the relocation of the Mediterranean Fleet—may be as essential a part of a diplomatic strategy as negotiation. Similarly, assigning military advisers and support groups to governments resisting invasion or insurrection—as President Truman did in Greece in 1947 or as President Kennedy did in South Vietnam in 1961—is an act of the Commander in Chief in aid of the President's diplomatic efforts. Also, the power of the President in times of nominal peace to assign American forces as he believes the exigencies of the international situation require may in some circumstances make essentially nominal the constitutional power of the Congress to declare war. Thus critics of Franklin Roosevelt charged that in the months before Pearl Harbor, by ordering American naval vessels to convoy supplies for Britain as far as Iceland, by directing American forces to destroy German submarines in the Western Atlantic on sight, and by similar acts, he was usurping the power of Congress to declare war.

The close connections between the President's diplomatic and military functions give an essentially modern significance to his role as Commander in Chief. The intention of the Founders was primarily to provide a device for subordinating the military establishment to ultimate civilian control by adding a civilian commander to the legislative and financial controls of the Congress—a President could even legally become the actual commander in the field. The invariable practice to the contrary, however, underscores the Founders' fundamental objective: to ensure that the military powers delegated to commanding officers would be subject to control by a civilian accountable to the electorate. This need is no less valid today, but the new American responsibilities in the world have added to the President's military role a new justification, no less cogent for its having been unforeseen in 1787. This is the necessity that the complex mixture of diplomatic and military planning and action that constitutes national security policy be coordinated and ultimately controlled by one man. The President could not direct the total foreign policy of the country without having at least formal control over each of its parts. With military resources and activities central to much of that policy, the President would have to be in a position to direct military action even if he were not formally entitled Commander.

The President's actions as Commander in Chief are of wider range than strictly military or diplomatic. In purely domestic matters he may use the military to enforce federal statutes and court orders, as President Kennedy did in 1962 when he sent troops into the University of Mississippi; he may employ the army to ensure the performance of necessary government functions, such as the movement of the mails; or, at the request of state authorities, he may direct the military to suppress and control riots and other disturbances. Some of these powers are authorized by acts of Congress. When the President proclaims a national emergency or the Congress declares war, moreover, a large number of other powers of domestic application, many of them relating to the military, may be invoked by the President. Thus after making a declaration of national emergency before our entry into the Second World War, Franklin Roosevelt invoked his discretionary powers as Commander in Chief to create a series of executive agencies that had no authority from the Congress except that implied in subsequent appropriations for their continuance. After Pearl Harbor the President as Commander in Chief issued the order which led to the evacuation from the West Coast states of more than one hundred thousand Japanese nationals and American citizens of Japanese parentage.

The President's function as Commander in Chief is thus a broad and inclusive one, but the restraints upon it are also considerable. The President's problems in his relations with his military subordinates are not very different from those he faces among his civilian executives. He has much the same need to persuade; he may support his requests with the power of reassignment and removal, but he can use the power only if he can afford the costs in controversy and loss of political support. When President

"Blame The Thing—I Can't Make It Work!"

President Cleveland labors over the keyboard of the Administration typewriter in an 1893 cartoon.

Truman in 1951 relieved General MacArthur of his command in the Far East because of the General's continued public criticism of the Administration's policies in the Korean War, he precipitated a storm of controversy and a full-dress Senate investigation. Most other Presidents have faced less dramatic but no less troublesome difficulties as Commander in Chief, for the ties of military executives with national or regional interest groups and with Congress and its committees are not essentially different from those of civilian executives.

In addition to its general powers of the purse, the Congress under the Constitution is granted the power "To declare war . . . To raise and support armies . . . To provide and maintain a navy . . . To make rules for the government and regulation of the land and naval forces." As we have seen, the meaning of these provisions in practice is not necessarily what it appears to be. At minimum, however, they help to make it inevitable that in the United States "military policy . . . exists in two worlds," the world of international politics and the world of domestic politics.[7] The latter is necessarily involved, since governmental decisions concerning military procurement, the recruitment, training, and pay of military personnel, and the location of military installations touch sensitive nerves within the body politic. Such decisions affect domestic politics as directly and as significantly as do proposals in the "civilian" sphere concerning the location

---

[7] Samuel P. Huntington, *The Common Defense: Strategic Programs in National Politics* (New York, 1961), p. 1.

"One At A Time, Dammit,
One At A Time!"

President Johnson as Chief Diplomat
in 1964.

Conrad in the Denver *Post*

of dams, the ownership of electric power resources, the allocation of highway aid funds, or the fixing of postal rates.

For the President the existence of military policy in "the world of
domestic politics" means that his power in fact is dependent upon his ability to persuade not only the military services, but sectors of the Congress
and their interest group allies as well. In these matters there may be little
of command in the function of Commander in Chief.

The American Presidency: Six Functions, One Man

A list of Presidential functions such as the one just discussed is a useful
way of looking at the variety of activities and powers that constitute the
office, but it can be misleading. It can give an inaccurate impression of
order and simplicity, whereas the reality of the Presidency contains complexity and strain, if not disorder. Any such list of functions, therefore, is
an analytical exercise, dividing reality into segments for purposes of description. But the Presidency remains a unit. The President—one man—performs
all six functions, and for all practical purposes he performs all of them
simultaneously. For, as the discussions of several of the functions have
suggested, what he does in any of his "chieftainships" materially affects
his success in each of the others.

This inseparability of functions is an inevitable consequence of the President's having become the mainspring of the governmental system. All of
those who look to his leadership—the Congress, executive officials, his party,
the voters, and the governments of other nations—in effect condition their

responses upon how he is doing with each of the other groups. His effectiveness as Chief Legislator and his influence as Chief Executive are interdependent; in turn they both reflect and mold his performance as Chief of State and Chief Diplomat; and so on. Foreign ministries around the globe watch American elections as barometers of Presidential influence; Congress and administrators respond to Presidential successes and failures in the world of diplomacy and in the affections of the electorate; the voters in turn react to, among other things, a President's apparent ability to get what he asks from his own and other governments. Thus it is scarcely an exaggeration to say that every action that a President takes affects his chances of success in every later action.

"Weak" Presidents and "Strong"

The pivotal character of the modern Presidency further means that the familiar and traditional distinction between "weak" and "strong" Presidents cannot mean quite what it has in the past. To be sure, Presidents may, for reasons of personality or skill or preference, be more or less aggressive in their relations with the Congress. They may exploit to the full or underutilize the sources of influence in their several functions. But no President today, however he may be inclined, can choose to be a Buchanan or a Franklin Pierce—two Presidents usually characterized as "weak" in their relations with the Congress and in the use of their initiatives. The modern President is the pivot whether he wants to be or not; he cannot escape the expectations that the system has created around his office. Truman and Eisenhower both entered the Presidency persuaded that the White House should not attempt to lead the Congress, and both were obliged in fact to attempt in some measure to do so.

On the other hand, a "strong" President, no matter how eager he may be to realize the potential influence of the office, is not in a position to command the system. He is expected to keep it moving in directions and at a rate acceptable to the country and to its allies, but he cannot guarantee this movement. He cannot compel from the Congress, the executive officials, or the party—to say nothing of the electorate or other governments—the responses that such movement may require. He is free to try to persuade; the country, in fact, is likely to suffer if he does not attempt to do so. For even if those who have a share in the performance of his various functions —members of Congress, his nominal subordinates in the executive, the voters, and even the governments of foreign countries—do not respond to his leadership as he would wish, they nonetheless rely upon that leadership. This is the essential meaning of the Presidency as the mainspring of the system: The President does not command its parts, but the system works inadequately if he does not try.

Shift to the Executive

How did the modern Presidency—with all the functions that we have just examined—get this way? How was the change made from the era of the legislature, at the time of the framing of the Constitution, to today's era of the President? It was not accomplished suddenly; as a matter of fact, it was not even accomplished by a series of overt, purposeful actions on the part of Presidents, Congress, or the electorate. Yet the Presidency has changed tremendously; if the text of the Constitution of the United States were to be rewritten in the predictable future, putting into constitutional language the practices actually followed today, the Presidency would come first. The new phrasing would allocate to the Congress the power to criticize, the power to approve, to disapprove, and to modify proposals laid before it, and the power to propose new lines of action in some areas of public policy. But an accurate statement of current practice would designate the President as the leader in most important matters of public policy; it would formally place in his office the most significant choices concerning foreign affairs and national security, subject to a variety of restrictions set by the Congress, by the Supreme Court, and by some officials of the executive branch. A twentieth-century statement of constitutional practice would reveal, as the document of 1787 does not, that in most matters the legislature is no longer first.

These changes in the working constitution are a result of the convergence of three factors: (1) the needs imposed by a rapidly changing society, which have created problems too complex to be treated primarily through legislative actions; (2) the requirements and opportunities produced by crises at home and abroad; and (3) the political talents of Presidents sensitive to these needs, requirements, and opportunities. The changes, moreover, have come about without distorting to any great degree the rather general terms in which the powers and duties of the President were stated in the second article of the Constitution.

THREE EXAMPLES OF PRESIDENTIAL GROWTH
IN THE NINETEENTH CENTURY

The potentialities for growth in the Presidency began to be evident as early as 1803. As President, Jefferson was presented with the opportunity to purchase the vast domain of French Louisiana for the United States as a result of the military and financial embarrassments of Napoleon. But, as a constitutional theorist and "strict constructionist," he was certain that the President lacked constitutional authority to acquire territory. He nevertheless agreed to the transaction, though he did seek the approval of Congress after the fact. His action was justified by Congress on the "new" ground that it was implicit in the President's power to make treaties. The acceptance of this justification also bears witness to another and perhaps more fundamental Jeffersonian innovation: his ability to draw power for the Presidency from a combination of support from his popular following in the nation and the skills of his lieutenants in the Congress. Since his day no President has succeeded in making the office effective without duplicating Jefferson's role as party leader.

In our second example, the successive crises of the Civil War, Abraham Lincoln was even less concerned than Jefferson had been about constitutional niceties. Lincoln took a series of executive actions, without prior Congressional authorization, which for a century have provided constitutional lawyers with material for debate. He spent federal funds, increased the size of the Army and Navy, established a military draft system, and suspended the writ of habeas corpus, to mention only a few. Several were ratified after the fact by the Congress, but not all of them. The Supreme Court, discredited by its pro-slavery decisions and loath to limit a President in wartime, did not declare any of the President's policies invalid during the war years.

Lincoln's actions were given *constitutional* justification, in his own words and in the works of some later scholars, by inference from his position as Commander in Chief and from his obligation to "take care that the laws be faithfully executed." One can reasonably assert, nevertheless, that at least some of his acts violated the Constitution. In *political* terms, however, the secession of the Southern states and the later crises of the war itself required vigorous leadership and speedy action. In the governmental system the most likely source for these was the Presidency. Emergency may not have compelled the President to act unconstitutionally, but it did compel him to act. The Constitution nowhere explicitly provided for the contingencies of secession and civil war; no constitutional document can provide for all possibilities. But it surely implied that in such circumstances the government would act, under leadership, and that this leadership would come from the Chief Executive. Putting the matter simply, one can say that Lincoln was *expected* to act.

The effect of such extraconstitutional expectations can be illustrated by a third event, during the first Administration of Theodore Roosevelt. In May of 1902, long-simmering unrest among the anthracite coal miners of Pennsylvania resulted in a strike of the United Mine Workers. The strike dragged on for five months, and by late summer the coal shortage became severe. The price of coal was rising rapidly. In early October, schools in New York City were closed for lack of coal. Republican leaders, including the President, were additionally worried about the effects of these conditions on the impending Congressional elections. Had the governor of Pennsylvania requested federal assistance to maintain order in the coal fields, the President legally could have sent in troops, but the strike remained relatively peaceful. No other constitutional or statutory basis for Presidential intervention existed. The Supreme Court's view of the federal government's control over commerce, which today would permit Congress to provide legislative authorization for dealing with such strikes, was then too narrow to permit a Presidential request for legislation.

The President nevertheless felt that he was expected to find a solution to the crisis. As he wrote to Senator Mark Hanna, "We have no earthly responsibility for it, but the public at large will visit upon our heads responsibility for the shortage in coal." [8] Working both directly and through various intermediaries, Roosevelt finally induced the union and the coal operators to resume operations and to agree to accept the terms recommended by a commission he would appoint.

Roosevelt's actions in the strike of 1902 set a precedent in the area of industrial relations by their recognition that when the effects of a labor dispute became widespread and critical the President was expected to do

---

[8] Quoted in Henry F. Pringle, *Theodore Roosevelt* (New York, 1956), p. 189.

something. Most of T. R.'s successors have responded to these expectations, sometimes with legal authorization and sometimes without. The requirements and needs of a changed society have, in effect, added such responsibility to the Presidential office.

CONDITIONS AND SOURCES OF CHANGE IN THE PRESIDENCY

Although the transition in the position of the Presidency has been constant, the rate at which this transition has taken place has not. Despite the isolated and dramatic examples of Jefferson and Lincoln, the development of the potential of the Presidency was gradual throughout the nineteenth century. With the advent of the twentieth, however, the significance of the Presidency expanded to its new dimensions at a faster rate than ever before. This tremendous increase in rate was again not a result of deliberate action on the part of the Presidents involved; rather it was the inevitable result of changing economic and social conditions, both domestic and international.

What were these conditions? And since these affect all departments of government, why should they have changed the relative importance of the President in the constitutional scheme? Can we point to factors that have been peculiarly Presidential? The establishment of the social security system in the 1930s, for example, added several thousand employees to the rolls of the executive branch, but their essentially clerical operations did not increase the power and importance of the President. Since the government's assumption of responsibility for a social security program is one of the items usually listed among indications of the government's—and by implication the President's—increased importance in the society, where does the President come in?

The answer is that the essential elements in the modern Presidency are the result of socioeconomic change and interdependence in the society, not the mere volume of federal government activities. When a society is subject to continual and rapid change and its structure is such that shifts in one part produce strains and frictions in another, its government must supply the means for speedy action. It must provide for effective negotiation of adjustments and for setting or at least proposing priorities among alternative lines of action. Thus it was the rapid development of the crisis of the Union that invited Lincoln's highhanded actions in 1861; it was the far-reaching effects of the strike in the anthracite coal fields in 1902, upon consumers and Republican candidates for Congress, that urged Theodore Roosevelt to assume the responsibility for finding a settlement.

Neither legislatures, nor courts, nor bureaucracies are the most likely sources of such action. It is possible for the Congress, especially through its leaders, to initiate some important governmental policies. For example, the civil rights legislation enacted during the second Eisenhower Administration owed more to Congressional than to Presidential efforts. As Democratic majority leader of the Senate in those years, moreover, Lyndon Johnson even went so far as to announce a series of formal legislative programs, as if he were competing with initiatives from the Republican-held White House. But these cases are exceptional. Legislative bodies rarely speak with one voice; an individual legislator, even a distinguished Senator, lacks the national standing of a President. As for the courts, they are inherently *reacting* institutions rather than initiating ones; they cannot speak until a dispute is brought before them, though interest group litigants supply endless opportunities for judicial intervention if the courts are so minded. And bureaucracies, though they are often more inventive than their critics recognize, lack the *political* authority essential to solving the demands emerging from crisis. The responses demanded by rapid change are to be expected, if they are to appear at all, from a source more capable of quick, decisive, and authoritative action. In the American scheme the Presidency is most likely to be that source. To return to our example of the social security system, it is not its routine operation that contributes to the importance of the President, as distinguished from the government. It is the fact that whenever the resources of the social security program appear inadequate to deal with a sharp rise in unemployment or the medical costs of the aged, the initiative for proposing remedial action to the nation is expected of the President. In the process he also is expected to suggest priorities between these and other uses of federal resources— housing, the military, foreign aid, and the rest. "What separates the major from the minor Presidents . . . ," a distinguished journalist has remarked, "is ability to perceive and seize initiative. For the laws of Congress cannot define, nor can custom anticipate, the unknown—and this is where the great Presidents must live, observant of the law yet beyond the law, Chief Executive and High Priest of American life at once." [9]

What kinds of domestic and international factors are most responsible for the increase in Presidential expectations? In a day when changes in the support price of wheat can produce reactions in foreign ministries around the globe, separation into domestic and foreign factors is more of a convenience than a strict division, but it will help to indicate the essential location of the pressure.

DOMESTIC FACTORS ENLARGING THE PRESIDENCY

On the domestic scene the most fundamental factor is the network of interdependencies created among producers, distributors, transporters, managers, workers, and consumers by a highly industrialized economy. This network normally exists in tolerable harmony, but it is not fully self-correcting. It involves a division of labor whose participants have yielded hope of self-sufficiency in return for the higher productivity that goes with specialization. But a consequence of this division is that disturbance or failure at any one point in the network affects the others in varying degrees, some immediately and some after an interval. If private parties directly involved in the disturbance cannot or do not take corrective action some of the parties—and the public—will expect the government to act, and the initiative for such action usually falls on the President.

Take the example of pricing policies by large corporations. One of the by-products of mass production has been the emergence in many industries of a few large corporations that account for the bulk of income and output in their spheres. These "giants" are generally able to control the prices

---

[9] Theodore H. White, *The Making of the President, 1960* (New York, 1961), p. 369.

at which their products will sell, since the companies' predominance over-comes the price-setting effects of market demand. (The precise degree of this control over prices and the means of achieving it may be debatable, but the fact of such price setting is generally accepted.) The price decisions of these corporations, especially in industries such as steel, rubber, petro-leum, and chemicals, whose output supplies the "raw" materials of many other industries, can have an important effect upon price levels throughout the economy.

As the effects of a price increase in one or more basic industries are felt or threatened in the cost of living (particularly in hardship for persons on fixed incomes), in declining exports, or in a variety of other activities of the society, demands and proposals for corrective action begin to appear. These may come from the business community, from labor organizations, from academicians, and a host of other sources; committees of the Congress may hold hearings on "administered pricing" or on "labor monopoly," and various bills may be introduced into the House and Senate; specialists in various executive agencies are likely to study the problem, to assess pro-posed solutions or to devise alternatives that may be added to the general discussion or merely circulated through governmental channels.

Any of these efforts may possibly result in actions—within or outside government—with which the President has no direct connection. The chances are, however, that if the problem persists he will be pressed to select and champion one or more proposals on which the executive branch and particularly the Congress can focus their attention. As the expectation grows that this is a matter for "the government," he will feel upon his head, as Theodore Roosevelt did in the 1902 strike, the responsibility for resolving the conflict. In particular, if his party depends heavily on certain groups in the electorate who show signs of party defection because of the continued conflict, the President will be called upon as Party Leader to formulate some corrective action.

A President's choices may not be those adopted, and the actions taken may be unsuccessful, but he cannot escape involvement. Change and inter-dependence in a complex society call for some central point in a govern-mental system at which alternative lines of action will be identified. The responsibility for setting the agenda of the society cannot be avoided, and the Presidency has become the most likely point for this function in the national government. In short, the President leads.

In a free society, not all of the corrective actions required are taken by the federal government or by any government. Some are managed by indi-viduals for themselves, some by corporations or other private groups, and some by the states and by local governments. But to insure that needs are not ignored which are beyond private means or beyond the public means of states and cities, many of these requirements for action converge upon Washington. Government action in one sphere may increase the problems in another.

As some of these functions of government and of the President become accepted, they may be formalized, at least in part, in continuing legislation. Thus in the Employment Act of 1946 the Congress accepted—hesitantly and somewhat reluctantly—a lesson of the Depression of the 1930s: that

Fischetti in the New York *Herald Tribune*

America The Beautiful

The President is now held responsible for all phases of the economy.

the federal government cannot escape concern with the state of the economy. The conditions of the Great Depression had produced, of course, an unprecedented increase in governmental activity in the economic realm and had added significantly to Presidential powers. But this was done as a matter of emergency, which many people hoped would be temporary. The Employment Act recognized that the government was obliged, as a continuing responsibility, to use its resources to foster maximum employment and economic growth and to avoid economic emergencies. The Act therefore directed the President, with the assistance of a Council of Economic Advisers, to report at least annually on the condition of the economy and to propose measures to achieve the objectives of the Act. Even without this legislation succeeding Presidents would probably have behaved in much the same way. Thus the chief significance of the Act is that it *institutionalized* and formally acknowledged the proposition that the government must assume some unspecified minimum degree of managerial responsibility for levels of employment and for rates of economic growth. It did formally what Theodore Roosevelt, in effect, did personally and informally in the coal strike of 1902. It identified the Presidency, moreover, as the point from which initiative for proposed programs appropriately should come.

As Presidential responsibility and initiative are accepted in such critical domestic matters as the stability and growth of the economy and as the office becomes increasingly pivotal in the political system, more and more groups turn to the President. Those specialists who want to do something about the deterioration of our major cities, those scientists who want to guide and protect the conduct and application of scientific research in the United States, and citizens who see some other problem that seems to call for coordinated action all feel that, if they can gain the President's involvement and support, the chances of achieving their solutions will be greatly enhanced.

The factors encouraging the focal character of the Presidency thus tend to be cumulative. As this occurs, moreover, an expansion takes place in the range of things on which the President may—if he chooses—assume leadership. No one in 1961 seems to have thought it improper for the President of the United States to direct his Secretary of Labor to attempt to settle a labor dispute between the Metropolitan Opera Company of New York and some of its employees. Imminent cancellation of the Metropolitan's season was regarded not merely as the loss of a means of entertainment in New York but, owing to the same forces of interdependence that have tied the country together in other respects, as a danger to a cultural resource of national importance. President Kennedy thus could intervene without risk of serious criticism. He had an option that would not have been open to his predecessors of a few decades earlier even if they had desired it.

INTERNATIONAL FACTORS

These domestic developments in the present century would be enough in themselves to explain the contemporary importance of the Presidency in the American system. They have been heavily supplemented, however, by forces flowing from the emergence of the United States as one of the superpowers in a world changed almost beyond recognition from the one dominated only a few decades ago by a handful of European nations. Change and interdependence on the domestic scene have placed increased responsibilities on the Presidency; the same factors in international politics have had an even stronger impact. For if the United States is to be effective in its foreign relations, it must, as nearly as possible, speak with one voice. That voice, by obvious necessity as well as by constitutional designation, is the Chief Executive's.

It is not quite the case that when questions of foreign policy have a relatively minor place in the problems confronting the country, the voice of the President is weak; on the other hand, it is very true that when external relations are of major consequence his voice is heard as is no other in the country. Looking at the situation of the United States in the 1830s, De Tocqueville saw in the insignificance of our foreign relations the chief cause of a relatively feeble executive power. "The policy of the Americans in relation to the whole world," he suggested, "is exceedingly simple; and it may almost be said that nobody stands in need of them, nor do they stand in need of anybody. Their independence is never threatened." Observing that in "a nation without neighbors" the Chief Executive gains little standing from his responsibility for the conduct of foreign relations, the perceptive Frenchman understood the effects that might be expected from a change in the nation's circumstances:

> If the existence of the Union were perpetually threatened, if its chief interests were in daily connection with those of other powerful nations,

the executive government would assume an increased importance in proportion to the measures expected of it and to those which it would execute.[10]

No one living in the latter half of the twentieth century need be told that the United States is no longer "a nation without neighbors," that our "chief interests" are indeed "in daily connection with those of other powerful nations," or that the existence of the Union is in fact daily threatened from beyond its borders.

These effects of the new international politics upon the Presidency are now so apparent, perhaps, that one is in danger of taking them for granted, of forgetting that they had their beginnings scarcely more than five short decades ago. As late as 1884 Woodrow Wilson, writing his classic study of the American system, *Congressional Government*, stated the proposition that "For all practical purposes the national government is supreme over the state governments." At that time he could not take an equally modern view of the Presidency. Rather, stating the thesis implied in the title of his book, he saw "Congress predominant over its so-called coordinate branches." The Presidency, he felt, was not a position of "recognized leadership in our politics"; it was "too silent and inactive, too little like a premiership and too much like a superintendency." In 1900, however, he felt obliged to prepare a new preface in which he corrected some matters of outdated detail but concerned himself primarily with the most important institutional consequence of "the plunge into international politics" associated with and following the war with Spain, namely, "the greatly increased power and opportunity for constructive statemanship given the President. . . ."

> The President of the United States is now, as of course, at the front of affairs, as no President, except Lincoln, has been since the first quarter of the nineteenth century, when the foreign relations of the new nation had first to be adjusted.

But Wilson knew that the effects of this enhanced Presidential position would not be confined to the office itself. Thus he anticipated that it might have "a very far-reaching effect upon our whole method of government," achieving "an integration" which he still found wanting in the operation of the system.[11] His anticipations were accurate, at least in their general tendency. The United States, despite illusions to the contrary that persisted at least until Pearl Harbor, would never again be as removed from events in the rest of the world as it had been through most of the nineteenth century. Never again would it be even approximately accurate to say of the Americans, as De Tocqueville did in the 1830s, that "nobody stands in need of them, nor do they stand in need of anybody." Never again would it be reasonable to say, as Wilson did in the 1880s, that "the business of the President, occasionally great, is usually not much above routine." [12]

The effects on the Presidency that Wilson anticipated have been per-

---

[10] Alexis de Tocqueville, *Democracy in America*, Phillips Bradley, ed. (New York, 1945), Vol. I, pp. 126 and 131.

[11] Woodrow Wilson, *Congressional Government* (Meridian edition, New York, 1956; first edition, Boston, 1885), pp. 22, 23, 52, and 141.

[12] *Ibid.*, p. 170.

sistent. They have been enormously stimulated, however, by American involvement in the two World Wars. The kind of total national effort that these conflicts required—full mobilization of the nation's manpower and its productive resources, plus centralized guidance of wages, prices, and civilian consumption—necessarily concentrated authority and leadership in the Chief Executive. The years since 1945 have seen relatively little shrinkage in the office. Not only do the statute books continue to carry authority for the President to act when he finds that overseas emergency conditions exist, but also the ordinary circumstances of our diplomatic relations—"ordinary" only by comparison with the more critical relations of war—have made Presidential actions and plans the focal point of both domestic and international politics.

The reasons why an increase in the importance of foreign relations augments the prominence of the Presidential office are not simple ones, to be explained merely by reference to "constitutional prescription" or to the efficiency implied in the nation's speaking with a single voice. These are valid factors, to be sure, but there are no obvious explanations for their validity. Since 1799 it has been a crime for anyone to encroach upon the President's exclusive right to negotiate with foreign powers. (This legislation, amended in 1909, is the so-called Logan Act, named after a Philadelphia Quaker who had undertaken private negotiation with France in 1798 in an attempt to avert war between that country and the United States.) The spirit of this prohibition is fairly frequently compromised, both by members of Congress and by private citizens. Yet its purpose is seldom actually violated. Why?

In the international sphere both the prospects of change and the implications of interdependence are quite different from what they are on the domestic scene. Political relations within a single nation rest on an assumption of ultimate agreement among contestants, on acceptance of some final legitimate authority, and on an expectation of nonviolent processes of settlement. They tend, in other words, toward stability. In the realm of international political relations these stabilizing factors either are missing or operate only to a moderate degree. While international relations are not wholly unstable, they resemble relations within a nation that is constantly on the verge of civil war. The "family of nations" includes no father. The commitments of nominal friends—even such close allies as Britain and the United States—cannot be complete or wholly reliable. Allies are always in part rivals and even potential opponents; the prospects of violent action are always present; and complete agreement tends to be a hope rather than an assumption. This is a kind of recipe for uncertainty and change, change of a sort from which "a nation without neighbors" is insulated.

A nation whose neighbors cover the globe is thus exposed to constant change. Given the tendency, in such an unstable set of relations, for any move to have far-reaching effects, such a nation must be able to act quickly and decisively. Given, further, the uncertainties in the international system and their close connection with possible military action, the nation must maintain a minimum degree of secrecy concerning its plans and intentions. This means that only a few people can participate in deciding matters of greatest import—those immediately associated with the office where quick and decisive action can best be taken. Given, finally, these two centralizing conditions, it clearly follows that information concerning the state of the international system and information concerning the prospects of change tend to converge upon the same point, the Presidency. The nature of the international system thus affords no acceptable alternative to Presidential responsibility and leadership. This is the fundamental basis for understanding Wilson's assertion:

> When foreign affairs play a prominent part in the politics and policy of a nation, its Executive must of necessity be its guide: must utter every initial judgment, take every first step of action, supply the information upon which it is to act, suggest and in large measure control its conduct.[13]

The particular conditions of diplomacy in the years since the Second World War have greatly augmented these tendencies in the Presidency of the United States. Four broad aspects of the new diplomacy can be identified. Each of these has increased the President's importance as the manager of the nation's affairs in the world.

First, through circumstances beyond its control, the nation has found itself at the head of one system of alliances in a bipolar world. As the trustee of that system it is obliged to be sensitive to changes within any member nation in the grouping, or between two members, because they may affect the structure of the system itself. For example, danger to Denmark need not immediately concern Italy or a developing dispute over Cyprus between Greece and Turkey need not directly affect Norway, but both may constitute threats to the stability of NATO, for which inescapably the United States and especially its President are chiefly responsible.

Second, since the Second World War there has been a huge increase in the importance of multilateral diplomacy, both within the principal alliance systems and, more important, within the United Nations. Multilateral negotiation, inherently more complex than bilateral, is further complicated when much of it must occur, as in the United Nations, in the light of full publicity. In this "new diplomacy" propaganda considerations become as important as secret negotiation. Policy thus must reckon not merely with the probable responses of the other party to a bilateral negotiation carried on in relative privacy, but also with the responses of all— both nations and individuals—who are witnesses to the public proceedings of the United Nations. This requirement obviously increases the need for central coordination by the President.

Third, this period has also produced significant changes in the number and character of the actors on the diplomatic scene. In little more than a decade, thanks to the rapid liquidation of the colonial system in Asia, the Middle East, and Africa, membership in the United Nations has risen from 50 to 113. At the same time power within the United Nations has gradually shifted from the Security Council, where the great powers can dominate, to the General Assembly, where all the new nations stand formally on an equal footing with the most powerful of the older powers. When one recalls

---

[13] *Ibid.*, p. 22.

that, in addition, many of these new nations, especially in Africa, are experiencing rapid internal change with consequent threats to their stability and to the stability of their commitments in the international system, the new complexities facing American diplomacy become apparent. Although managing these complexities requires an expanded roster of experts, it also demands strong direction from the President as the chief spokesman of the nation.

Fourth, the rivalry of Russia and the United States for the allegiance of the uncommitted countries plus the needs and demands of the "developing" nations have introduced essentially new instruments into diplomacy, chiefly economic aid in its various forms. Economic policy as an aspect of diplomatic relations is not in itself new, of course, but the scale and the stakes have so changed since the middle 1940s as to make the international politics of economic aid an essentially new phenomenon in the conduct of American foreign relations. In the process a new area for initiating and managing policy has been added to the Presidency.

Finally, the tasks and processes of our foreign policy have been enormously complicated, to say the least, by rapid changes in the character of military technology. Military power, of course, has always been the handmaiden of diplomacy, but until fairly recently the technology underlying such power was comparatively simple. More important, it changed relatively slowly. Before the Second World War a weapon system had a useful life of at least a generation. In a nuclear age of missiles and space vehicles, however, such systems may be obsolete within a few months of their production. Hence in a very real sense the frontiers of our military power and the limits of our diplomatic influence are set as much by the drawing boards of the engineers and the simulations of the computers as by the character of forces in being. This means, moreover, that a whole new set of considerations and a new set of actors—scientists and military technologists—must be involved in foreign policy. A decision for or against a program of nuclear testing, for example, involves simultaneously estimating the effects upon our structure of alliances, upon the attitudes of the uncommitted nations, upon the prospects of international arms control, and upon our position in the rapid and unending race for technological superiority. These new kinds of estimates ultimately can be made only by the occupant of the White House.

Thus the central importance of the Presidency has been fostered not only by the reemergence of foreign affairs as a main theme of our governmental concerns but by fundamental changes in the character of international politics and the increasingly complex interdependencies affecting our position in the world.

INTERDEPENDENCE OF FOREIGN AND DOMESTIC FACTORS

These foreign policy factors are in addition to the domestic forces discussed earlier in this chapter; but the two forces usually are closely interdependent. To take a welcome and not entirely fanciful example: Suppose that the two sides in the Cold War found it possible to reach an agreement on the reduction and control of armaments that would reduce by several billion dollars our expenditures for defense. This would involve no mere budgetary adjustment; it would jeopardize employment and earnings in wide sectors of American industry where resources are concentrated on defense production; it would threaten to affect the financial prospects of universities now receiving millions of dollars in defense-related research funds; it would, in other words, involve the kinds of dislocations created by demobilization after a war. Coordinated Presidential initiatives would be as necessary and as widely expected here as in a depression such as that of 1929.

This is an extreme example, but it could be repeated many times on a smaller scale. What connection can be seen, for instance, between the emergence of the new nations of Africa as important elements in international politics and Presidential initiatives concerning race relations in the United States? Between concern for the foreign policies of such countries and the price or wage decisions of American-owned corporations on which some underdeveloped economies are heavily dependent? Between a lowering of import restrictions on textiles and the international commitments of developing countries seeking through the textile trade to acquire needed foreign exchange? Between stable growth of the American economy and a policy of encouraging uncommitted countries to become trading partners of the West rather than of the Soviet bloc? The changes and interdependencies in each of these areas require that priorities be proposed, that coordinated action be taken, that initiatives be promptly forthcoming—the same requirements, in short, that have contributed to the emergence of the Presidency in spheres that may be regarded as purely domestic or purely international.

Mainspring or Caesar

The pivotal character of the modern Presidency in the American system has led some responsible observers to fear that, in Edward S. Corwin's words, ". . . the Presidency is a potential matrix of dictatorship. . . ." [14] For others the danger lies rather in the gap between the expectations that are focused on the President and the assured power that he may exercise. These latter fear that the necessity to initiate and the possibility that he may lack the capacity to persuade will converge in the weakening or failure of the system. Neither of these concerns altogether lacks substance. No guarantee can be found against the possibility that events will produce a shift toward an authoritarian form. Somewhat paradoxically, however, a narrowing of the gap between expectations and effective influence might well reduce the likelihood that events would foster a dictator in the White House. If that gap is so wide that persuasion cannot bridge it, the resulting ineffectiveness of the system could establish conditions in which authoritarian measures would be permitted or even welcomed. How wide the gap is in fact depends in considerable measure upon the quality of the President's instruments for persuasion. These instruments thus deserve a close analysis, which the next chapter will undertake.

---

[14] Edward S. Corwin, *The President: Office and Powers*, 3rd ed. (New York, 1948), p. 353.

11 / The Presidency and the Instruments of Leadership

To picture the Presidency as the mainspring of the American system is accurate, provided that the mechanical analogy is not carried too far. For a President to function in the manner suggested by the word "mainspring," more is necessary than the opportunity for leadership and initiative. " 'Powers' are no guarantee of power." [1] Why should this be so?

In the first place, a President, for reasons of preference or personality, may perhaps not take the lead. In such circumstances the system partially compensates by providing other sources of initiative, chiefly in the Congress. These alternative points of leadership, however, though they are continually in operation, lack the special resources of the Presidency, and rarely can do for the system as a whole what the modern Presidency can accomplish under favorable circumstances.

Secondly, and more characteristically, a President's efforts at persuasion may not be sufficient to close the gap between what the system requires—or at any rate what he attempts—and what in fact he can accomplish. A corollary of the proposition that a President simultaneously performs all six of the functions assigned to him by the Constitution and by tradition is that he must successfully persuade a motley assortment of individuals and groups whose consent or support is necessary for the accomplishment of his objectives. These others—including his nominal executive subordinates, a majority in the House and the Senate, the press, the electorate, and the governments of foreign nations—may not be susceptible to his attempts at persuasion. Their own objectives may be hopelessly contradictory; they may have reason to anticipate greater gain from rejecting Presidential suggestions than from acceding to them; or for other reasons they may be unwilling or unable to act as the President wishes. Reluctance or rebellion in one quarter, moreover, may spread rapidly to others, and the ever-threatening gap between expectation and performance, between attempt and accomplishment, may consequently be widened.

No procedural mechanism and no human effort may be able in any single instance to close this gap. How wide it becomes depends not only upon the inclinations and skills of the President as a person but also upon the

---

[1] Richard E. Neustadt, *Presidential Power: The Politics of Leadership* (New York, 1960), p. 10.

Don Hesse in the St. Louis *Globe-Democrat*

Overgrown

A conservative view of the growth of Executive leadership.

availability of appropriate instruments for his leadership. These would be necessary if only because a President's day contains too few hours for him unaided to keep in touch with all those whom he needs or who depend upon him—in and outside of the country—and to perform all of the acts of persuasion upon which the effectiveness of his efforts depends.

The devices that may serve as Presidential instruments are almost unlimited in number and are by no means confined to governmental agencies. The Secretary of State and the Director of the Bureau of the Budget obviously belong on a list of such instruments, but in appropriate circumstances either of these might be less important than a widely read newspaper columnist, an important friend in the business community, or one in the labor movement. These latter, however, are likely to be of less continuous importance than the official apparatus of the government. In this chapter, therefore, primary attention will be given to the official instruments that a President may use.

Broadly speaking, the usefulness to the President of any instrument of initiative depends upon two factors: first, the range and importance of the functions with which it is concerned and, second, the degree to which its political stakes approximate those of the President. The first factor is obvious enough. The second will be explained in detail later, but for the present it is sufficient to observe that agencies that can serve as vehicles of Presidential initiative may also rely, in varying degrees, upon sources other than (or in addition to) the President for their prestige, their influence, and their political survival. To the extent that these other sources of support are at odds with the President, the agencies they affect will be at similar odds with Presidential purposes. They even may perform in open

"Promise It Won't Rise
Any Higher?"

A liberal view: The need for increased
Executive leadership.

© 1961 by Bill Mauldin
From *What's Got Your Back Up?* Harper & Row

opposition to him. An agency's use to the President as an instrument of
leadership, therefore, depends strongly on the degree to which its goals
and his coincide. If conditions are favorable, the President may use the
instrument in one or both of two ways. First, it may be a channel through
which he acts, a means of carrying out his decisions; second, it may be a
source of advice to him from which he develops a line of action.

The Executive Office of the President

Although the name might suggest otherwise, the Executive Office of the
President is not a single governmental agency. It is rather the official
designation for a collection of organizations and individuals, each in principle charged with assisting the President in performing duties that are
distinctively Presidential. Created by executive order in 1939, the Executive Office now includes as its principal units the White House Office, the
Bureau of the Budget, the Council of Economic Advisers, and the National
Security Council. The agencies constituting the Executive Office employ
upwards of 2,500 people, a large proportion of whom are professional
specialists—lawyers, economists, statisticians, political scientists, journalists,
and many others. (If the employees of the Central Intelligence Agency,
organizationally subordinate to the National Security Council, were included, the total would be in the neighborhood of 12,000. The exact number is uncertain since CIA employees are not reported, for reasons of
national security.)

The heart of the White House Office—and of the entire Executive Office—is the President's personal staff, which numbers approximately twenty. The remaining 375 to 400 employees of the White House Office are principally clerical and custodial personnel; fifty or more are required just to handle the White House mail (which averages 4,000 to 5,000 incoming letters and telegrams each week, but may easily amount to several times that in a single day during a crisis or some other dramatic event). This personal staff is a comparatively recent phenomenon; its growth is one index of the increased importance of the modern Presidency. At the turn of the present century the President's immediate assistants were a secretary, a few clerks, and a messenger, all of whom were paid from the President's personal funds rather than as employees of the government. As recently as the Hoover Administration (1928–33) he still had fewer than half a dozen personal aides. When Franklin Roosevelt brought his "brain trust" to Washington in 1933 he was obliged to appoint most of these advisers to second-line positions in various departments, since the White House budget provided no place for them. One of the major recommendations of the Committee on Administrative Management, appointed by President Roosevelt in 1937, was an increase in the White House Staff. This Committee is itself an example of a temporary Presidential instrument, created by Roosevelt to recommend ways of strengthening the President's facilities for discharging his executive functions. The modern character of the White House Office, like the Executive Office of the President itself, thus dates from 1939.

A few members of the personal staff have obvious and sharply defined responsibilities, notably the Press Secretary and the Appointments Secretary. Recent Presidents also have designated one special assistant and one or more administrative assistants for liaison with members of Congress, discussing, negotiating, and soliciting support for the President's policies. Most of the President's assistants, however, are engaged on such assignments as he may make; they may have a particular specialty, but they are also generally equipped to perform, over a wide range of governmental problems, the anticipating, inquiring, investigating, and follow-up activities that constitute the heart of staff work.

In terms of the criteria suggested in the opening section of this chapter, the usefulness of the President's personal staff as a Presidential instrument is potentially very great. The range of its concerns is as broad as its members and the President are prepared to make it. Their proximity to him and their identification with his fortunes, especially if they have long been among his intimates, are likely to minimize divergence from his purposes.

The most important members of the President's personal staff often are men who have devoted themselves for years to the career of the man who appointed them. Nevertheless, in all essential respects members of the President's personal staff are not operating officials; what they can do for the President they do as his auxiliary eyes and ears, not as instruments with power of their own. Their influence depends upon recognition of their competence as individuals and upon the confidence that the President appears to place in them, especially the latter.

It is important, too, to recognize the hazards of the personal staff as well as the limitations. The chief hazard from the President's standpoint is that its members may move from being his *auxiliary* eyes and ears to doing most of his seeing and hearing—and thus his choosing—for him. Whether such a shift occurs is largely a matter of how the President himself uses his staff. If he delegates extensively and demands recommendations that reflect agreed staff positions, as was Eisenhower's practice throughout his Presidency, he is likely to lose touch with informative details and revealing conflicts. If that occurs, he is in danger of becoming a prisoner of his staff system rather than its master. A President concerned with maintaining an effective initiative cannot afford to relinquish the opportunity to make his own choices, for, as Neustadt aptly observes, "A President is so uniquely situated and his power so bound up with the uniqueness of his place, that he can count on no one else to be perceptive for him." [2] The White House Staff, in short, is indispensable to the Presidency, but it cannot be the President.

THE BUREAU OF THE BUDGET

The oldest and most significant institutional unit in the Executive Office is the Bureau of the Budget, created by the Budget and Accounting Act of 1921. (This act also established the General Accounting Office, an accounting and auditing agency headed by the Comptroller General, who is appointed by the President for a term of fifteen years but is responsible to the Congress.) Before the Bureau of the Budget was organized no one in the executive branch, not even the President, reviewed the financial requests of departments and independent agencies; they were merely collected by the Treasury Department and forwarded to the Congress for action. Few of those who favored the establishment of the "executive budget" in 1921 saw it as more than a housekeeping device, a means of promoting economy and financial efficiency in the executive branch—and for most of the first two decades of its existence it was in fact little more than that. Located in the Treasury Department—thus operationally as well as physically removed from the White House—it was nominally under the President's immediate direction; the intimacy that was expected to exist between the President and the Bureau is suggested by the Act's provision for the appointment of the Director by the President without the advice and consent of the Senate that is required for the appointment of Cabinet officers. But it was at most a minor means of Presidential initiative; the relatively static Administrations of Harding, Coolidge, and Hoover provided little opportunity for the Bureau to become a major Presidential instrument. A more significant role for the Bureau was symbolized in its transfer from the Treasury in 1939 to the Executive Office of the President when that agency was created.

The contemporary Bureau of the Budget has four chief functions. First is preparation and administration of the budget. This includes assisting the President in setting general budgetary policies, reviewing and approving, reducing, or (rarely) increasing the estimates submitted by the de-

---

[2] *Ibid.*, p. 179.

partments and agencies (subject to their appeal to the President). It also includes apportioning appropriations, which in effect involves controlling the rate at which appropriated funds may be spent. Second is legislative reference, which includes reviewing the requests of agencies for legislation, in order to determine whether such proposals are in conformity with the President's program, and reviewing legislation passed by the Congress and submitted to the President for his signature. (Legislative enactments at this stage, that is, awaiting the President's action, are known as "enrolled bills.") This latter duty means that the Bureau, after clearance with other interested executive agencies, recommends that the President either sign or veto a measure and, in the latter instance, prepares a draft of a proposed veto message. The third function is study of the organization and management practices of executive agencies. This study results not only in sponsorship of improvements in these matters but also in the preparation of major reorganization plans, which the President is authorized to put into effect if they are not disapproved by a Congressional "veto" by concurrent resolution.[3] The fourth function is improvement of financial management practices, in cooperation with the Treasury and the General Accounting Office, and review and coordination of the statistical services of the government.

Under appropriate circumstances the Bureau of the Budget can be enormously useful as an instrument of Presidential initiative. The heart of its potential value lies in the nature of the executive budget and in the process of budget administration. The budget need not be merely a device for economical administration, for relating expenditure plans to expected income, and for orderly accounting. A budget is also a program. Its construction permits the Bureau and the President to make a wide range of significant choices, not only as to the general level of expenditures in relation to the needs of the economy but also as to selecting the relative emphasis that should be given to competing demands for public funds—civil as opposed to military, one arm of the military or one proposed weapons system against another, increased educational subsidies rather than more funds for national parks, and so on. The execution of a budget after appropriations have been voted, moreover, can involve important opportunities for the control, even the alteration, of the program through regulating the rate of expenditure. And the performance of both of these duties—preparing the budget and executing it—necessarily gives to the Bureau an acquaintance with the problems and shortcomings of all other executive agencies that is unparalleled in scope and detail anywhere else in the government.

An agency chiefly concerned with these functions can be a major instrument for making nominal Presidential subordinates in the executive branch into something like actual subordinates, that is, subordinates willing or obliged to execute the President's wishes. In addition, its reach, while not as broad as the full range of a President's concerns, covers the whole of the executive branch and more. The proper execution of its functions also requires sensitivity to public demands, to the temper of the Congress, and

---

[3] On the "legislative veto," see Chapter 10, p. 299.

to the designs and desires of key Senators and Representatives in their relations with executive officials and with interest groups. A Bureau of the Budget functioning *in close alliance with the President* can become an unparalleled source of intragovernmental intelligence, of program advice, and of support for a President seeking to guide the governmental mechanism that he nominally heads. Insofar as it operates in this fashion, moreover, the Bureau of the Budget comes to be relied upon both by executive agencies and by the Congress, not for guidance in the strict sense but for a firm indication of Presidential preference and intent. Committee chairmen and other Congressional leaders as a matter of course may inquire of the Bureau—among others—the status of proposed legislation in relation to "the President's program," not necessarily because they will adhere to it but because they need to know Presidential intentions in setting their own agendas and in fixing their own priorities.

Whether the Bureau of the Budget reaches this level of usefulness depends both upon the President's own sensitivity to its potentialities and upon the type of leadership he selects for the Bureau. If his concern with his initiating function is slight and if in consequence his Director is preoccupied with housekeeping rather than with the policy aspects of its stated duties, the Bureau will still remain an essential element in the system—for the operation of the contemporary government without the executive budget is unimaginable—but it will become only marginally valuable as a Presidential instrument.

The two alternative possibilities for the Bureau as a Presidential instrument can be seen in the backgrounds and records of some of its Directors. The first, under Harding and Coolidge, was Charles G. Dawes, a Chicago banker who was interested almost entirely in economy and financial efficiency in the government and saw no disadvantage in the Bureau's isolated location in the Treasury. Harold D. Smith, Director during most of the Roosevelt period, was the first to make the Bureau a *Presidential* resource. Formerly a professor of political science, he responded to the innovating tendencies of Roosevelt and made himself and his staff indispensable in many of the President's actions and plans. Maurice H. Stans, Eisenhower's Director during most of his second Administration, was a certified public accountant who served as Deputy Postmaster General before taking over the Bureau of the Budget. Under his guidance the agency remained in the Presidential orbit, but it was less concerned with substantive programs and bore more resemblance to the Dawes than to the Smith period. A reemphasis on policy and substantive program occurred under President Kennedy's Directors, David E. Bell and Kermit Gordon, both of whom had backgrounds in government work as well as in the academic world. Their greater interest in policy is suggested by two facts: Bell left the Bureau of the Budget to become head of the foreign aid program (Agency for International Development or AID); Gordon, who stayed on during the first months of President Johnson's Administration, came to the Bureau after eighteen months as a member of the Council of Economic Advisers.

The political risks and political goals of the Bureau are compatible, but not identical, with those of the President. Its origin and its standard activities assure its survival and some measure of influence apart from Presidential support. As a part of the bureaucracy it has its own stakes, its own risks and goals, in its relations with other agencies and with the Congress. But programs and commitments that an agency develops in close association with the President can create joint stakes of greater magnitude. A Budget Director who knows he can speak for the President is not likely to misrepresent him, except by accident. Thus, while the Bureau of the Budget, like any other staff facility, cannot be a President's sole reliance, it can be an invaluable one, indispensable to his taking effective initiative.

THE COUNCIL OF ECONOMIC ADVISERS

The smallest and one of the youngest institutional staff units in the Executive Office is the Council of Economic Advisers. Created by statute in 1946, the Council is composed of three members, professional economists of high standing, appointed by the President with the consent of the Senate. The President designates one of their number as chairman. Five men have held this position since 1946: Edwin G. Nourse, at the time of his appointment an officer of the Brookings Institution; Leon H. Keyserling, one of the most influential government economists during the Roosevelt years; Arthur F. Burns and Raymond J. Saulnier, both professors of economics at Columbia University; and Walter W. Heller, professor of economics at the University of Minnesota.

As we have seen, the Employment Act of 1946, which established the Council, was an official acknowledgment of the chief lesson of the Great Depression—that the federal government had an inescapable responsibility for the level of income and employment in the economy. The Act aimed at achieving maximum employment and, by implication, stability of prices and healthy economic growth.

The functions of the Council in contributing to these objectives are to analyze trends in the economy, to appraise the adequacy of existing government programs in meeting the economic needs identified, and to recommend to the President policies necessary to achieve the goals of the law. In addition, the Council prepares for the President the "Economic Report" that the statute requires him to submit to the Congress at the beginning of each session. The preparation of this report, like the writing of the annual budget message, gives the President the occasion for a broad assessment of existing policies and for specifying the major guidelines for future governmental programs affecting the economy. The economy is of course always changing, and the Council is thus continually called upon to advise the President. But the requirement of an annual stock-taking provides what Neustadt calls a useful deadline, one compelling the President "to come to grips with those things he would want to make his own if he were free to interfere and pick and choose at will." [4] The regular advice of the Council can also give him critically important intelligence on executive-agency economic policies that are moving in directions inconsistent with his chosen guidelines.

---

[4] Neustadt, *op. cit.,* p. 156.

The Council also has limitations as a Presidential instrument. In the first place, its influence, with the President and elsewhere in the government including Congress, depends primarily upon its reputation for disinterested, professional competence. It may lose much of this if it appears to be tailoring its advice to fit the Administration's preconceptions. On the other hand, unless its members act before Congress and the country as spokesmen both for the President's economic program and for their own analyses, they may see these analyses ignored or misinterpreted. If they attempt to avoid both of these dangers, however, they may find themselves opposing the President's policies in questioning by committees of the Congress.

This problem caused considerable difficulty in the early years of the Council. Dr. Nourse took the position that the Advisers should not testify before Congress. For two years his colleagues, Leon Keyserling and John D. Clark, reluctantly conformed. The Council's relations with the Congress and even with the White House deteriorated. When Nourse somewhat inconsistently sought to protect his professional detachment by criticizing the President's policies in public speeches, a break with his colleagues and with the White House became inescapable. Nourse resigned in September, 1949. In subsequent years Council members normally have testified when requested to by Congress. They also have taken the position that they should resign if they felt obliged to dissent from the President's decisions. No such resignations have occurred.[5]

In the second place, economic considerations, despite their importance, are not the only factors relevant to Presidential policy choices. Thus while the President's confidence is essential to the Council, he cannot assume that the Council can or will take into account matters that lie beyond technical economic considerations. He also cannot assume that its stakes—in the long run professionally determined—are identical to his even when they are consistent with his. The more professional the Council's posture, therefore, the more it is limited to the specialized economic aspects of policy questions. In this respect the Council resembles the President's scientific advisers and differs from the generalists on the White House staff: The members of the Council give professional advice on technical questions, but "they are not across-the-board, general purpose counsellors and political intimates of the President."[6] The Council constitutes, in short, a Presidential instrument of potentially high utility, but not one of general-purpose range.

THE NATIONAL SECURITY COUNCIL

Significantly different from the other institutional staff units in the Executive Office but equally important, the National Security Council is composed of the President as chairman, the Vice-President, the Secretary of State, the Secretary of Defense, and the Director of the Office of Emergency Planning, itself a minor unit in the Executive Office. These members are provided for by statute, but in addition the President may appoint to

---

[5] Corinne Silverman, *The President's Economic Advisers* (New York, 1959).
[6] U.S. Senate, Committee on Government Operations, Subcommittee on National Policy Machinery, *Organizing for National Security* (Washington, 1961), Vol. III, p. 81.

it or invite to attend its meetings other officials, such as the Secretary of the Treasury, the Chairman of the Joint Chiefs of Staff, the Chairman of the Atomic Energy Commission, and the Director of the Central Intelligence Agency, which formally operates under the NSC.

The NSC thus bears a close resemblance to a Cabinet committee, although it was established by law. The National Security Act of 1947, which also took the first major step toward unification of the armed services under a Secretary of Defense, created the NSC as a body to advise the President on the coordination of foreign, military, and domestic policies.

The proceedings of the NSC are classified as top secret for security reasons; this secrecy may account in part for the many divergent estimates of its value to the government and to the President. It is argued, on the one hand, that since most of its members must represent the special viewpoints of their agencies, any agreements arrived at by the NSC are likely to be ambiguous compromises. On the other hand, it is asserted that the organization provides an essential arena in which the most critical military-diplomatic issues can be responsibly discussed. Probably both views are partly correct. The NSC normally operates by consideration of papers which, when approved by the President, become agreed policy. Particularly on documents dealing with broad strategic programs, such as the annual paper on "Basic National Security Policy," the NSC functions as what Samuel Huntington calls a "strategic legislature," with many of a regular legislature's characteristics of compromise and ambiguity.[7] It could hardly be otherwise, since on a matter of such broad import it would be unlikely that the President could ignore the determined views of the Secretary of State or the Secretary of Defense, even if they were in the minority. When, however, the NSC is concerned with specific action in a moment of crisis, such as a decision on whether to send troops into a threatened country of Southeast Asia, it more often acts in an advisory capacity, presenting the President with alternative views on proposed lines of action.

The NSC's concerns are obviously great, though by no means equal to those of the President. Its utility as an instrument of Presidential initiative, however, is undoubtedly limited, as in the case of the Cabinet itself, by the natural tendency of most of its members to represent the views and interests of their agencies. Nevertheless, if the President can know, either through Council discussions or through the efforts of his personal staff, the nature of these special concerns and what kinds of matters tend to be obscured in the agreements that are reached, he can gain some advantage. He needs a consensus among his key military and diplomatic subordinates, but he also needs to know what issues are being avoided or minimized in reaching and maintaining such consensus.

OTHER UNITS

Of less importance as Presidential instruments are two other units of the Executive Office. The Office of Emergency Planning was established as a successor to the Office of Civil and Defense Mobilization in 1961 when

---

[7] Samuel P. Huntington, *The Common Defense: Strategic Programs in National Politics* (New York, 1961), pp. 153 ff.

the operating responsibilities for civil defense were transferred from OCDM to the Department of Defense. It is charged with advising the President on the planning and coordination of policy concerning a wide variety of emergencies, both material disasters and the consequence of military action. Its concerns cover the emergency use of resources of all kinds, including manpower, materials, industry, transportation, and communication facilities. It plans for emergency government organization, for rehabilitation after an enemy attack, and for the stock-piling of strategic materials.

The Office of Science and Technology was created in 1962 to advise and assist the President in the effective use of science and scientists both in national security matters and in domestic areas of concern to the government. It studies and coordinates the programs of various federal agencies concerned with science and technology, maintains close relations with scientists throughout the country, and attempts to assure the vigor and effectiveness of scientific and technological work in and outside the government. It is headed by a leading scientist, since November, 1963, by Dr. Donald F. Hornig, formerly chairman of the chemistry department at Princeton University.

The Vice-President as an Executive

At a session of the Senate in the first Congress someone proposed that the Vice-President should be addressed as "His Superfluous Excellency." This characterization is overly harsh, but it points to the anomaly of a position that is close to power yet has little of its own. Lack of power plus the practices that usually have been followed in selecting candidates for the position are the basic reasons for the limited value of the Vice-Presidency as an executive instrument. This situation has little to do with the personal qualities of the incumbent; many Vice-Presidents have been men of great ability, but none has quite escaped the handicap of the absence of a substantial independent source of power.

In his capacity as President of the Senate the Vice-President, by long-established practice, is an outsider. Unlike the Speaker of the House, for reasons that will be explored in some detail in Chapter 13, he is not an important element in the internal power structure of the Senate. That is, he derives little or no influence from his position as such. A former Senator in the Vice-President's chair, especially one who is highly respected by his colleagues, like Alben Barkley (Vice-President from 1949 to 1953), may derive some influence from his personal associations. But a man as gifted as Lyndon Johnson, who as majority leader was without doubt the most powerful man in the Senate, did not, as he must have known when he agreed to run for Vice-President in 1960, retain more than a shadow of his former influence when he was that body's presiding officer. Counselor and adviser a Vice-President may be, and as such sometimes of value in aiding the President's legislative program, but at best his value is that of a respected alumnus rather than that of a Senate colleague or leader.

The Vice-President has few or no assured resources that can form the basis for effective influence. Even the political support he may have had at the nominating convention tends to dissipate as does that of a defeated candidate for the Presidency, and for much the same reasons. He is not in a position to help anyone else except as he can borrow influence from someone who has it. One likely source of influence, perhaps the most likely, is the President himself. The limitations on a President's ability and willingness to grant such support are substantial, though they may be declining, as we shall see shortly. Another possible source is in the Twenty-second Amendment, which limits a President to two terms and may, in consequence, make the Vice-Presidency a promising place from which to run for President. This is likely to require, however, a rather sharp departure from traditional practices in nominating men for the Vice-Presidency.

In the past, Vice-Presidential nominees characteristically have been chosen to appease the party supporters of a defeated rival for the Presidential nomination, as part of a deal by which a crucial bloc of convention votes was secured for the Presidential aspirant, or to balance the national ticket geographically and factionally. Thus in 1932 John Nance Garner of Texas was designated as Franklin Roosevelt's first running mate in return for the votes of the crucial Texas and California delegations at the Chicago convention. Wendell Willkie, a newcomer to national politics in 1940 and a New Yorker, was suitably matched by Charles McNary, a Senate professional, a Western (Oregon) progressive and a farm spokesman. In 1960 the astonishment of some "liberals" when Senator Kennedy—a liberal Catholic from Boston—chose Lyndon Johnson to run with him bore witness to the tactical advantages anticipated by party professionals from nominating a defeated rival who was a Southerner, a Protestant, and a moderate in domestic politics. But the choice also suggested a desire on Kennedy's part to choose a man of Presidential stature, able to be an effective President in case of the death or disability of the President. The assassination of President Kennedy is likely to reinforce such considerations in the minds of Presidential candidates as they indicate their preferred running mates.

Even if the traditional practices are changed, however, one cannot argue very forcibly that the old ones resulted in placing second-rate men in the post of heir apparent. Of the thirty men who have run for Vice-President on the tickets for the two major parties between 1900 and 1964, all but a handful have been men of competence, and some of them have been unusually gifted, such as Theodore Roosevelt (1900), Hiram W. Johnson (1912), Franklin D. Roosevelt (1920), and Earl Warren (1948).

Changed practice, however, will not fully answer the important questions of compatibility of person and viewpoint between the two candidates. Given almost inevitable differences in perspectives and goals, it is not likely that a President will regard a Vice-President as his alter ego. He may value his associate's political advice, especially one who is well acquainted in Congress, and he may make some use of him within the executive branch. Most recent Presidents have invited Vice-Presidents to attend Cabinet meetings. The Vice-President may also be appointed to some posts of secondary but not negligible importance. Thus Vice-President Nixon served as chairman of the President's Committee on Government Contracts. This agency was redesignated the President's Committee on Equal Employment Opportunity in 1961, and Vice-President Lyndon John-

"I Don't Know How *You* Feel,
But It's Making *Me* Nervous."

A comment on the absence of a Vice-President after Lyndon Johnson succeeded to the Presidency in 1963.

From *Straight Herblock*, Simon & Schuster, 1964

son was made its chairman. This position may have helped Johnson establish politically useful connections with the Negro community. Kennedy also made his Vice-President chairman of the National Aeronautics and Space Council, an advisory body in the Executive Office. Presidents in recent years have used their Vice-Presidents increasingly in a variety of ceremonial and quasi-diplomatic activities. Vice-President Lyndon Johnson's "good-will" trip to India in 1961 and his mission to Berlin during the crisis there in August of that year are examples. The Vice-President is by statute a member of the National Security Council, and recently it has become customary for him to preside in the President's absence. In all these positions, however, his influence is fairly limited, as he acts essentially for the President rather than on his own.

Whether these assignments of the Vice-President constitute a trend toward a substantial increase in the importance of the office is debatable. In view of the factors discussed above, it may seem doubtful, especially as there are other factors that may keep such tendencies within comparatively narrow limits. A President who delegated substantial authority to his Vice-President would be making the grant to a man not subject to his removal power. A President prepared to take that risk would, of course, be building up the political prospects of a possible successor. Most Presidents, especially in their second terms, facing the Twenty-second Amendment's ban on sharing Franklin Roosevelt's unique achievement of more than two terms, are likely to avoid as long as possible any indication of their chosen successor. To conserve their own presumably declining influence, they are likely to try to keep all the aspirants guessing as long as possible. A Vice-President who had been made into the obvious heir would thus be inconvenient.

Finally, it is sometimes argued that the Vice-President should become a sort of Assistant President, to relieve the President of some of his onerous burdens. In light of the discussion above, all that need be said of this view is that if the relief were substantial, it would weaken the Presidency, and if it were not substantial, it would not be much relief. The forces that make the Presidency the mainspring of the system, however, make it desirable that a man of ability be ready quickly to take the place of a dead or disabled President. Presidents are likely, therefore, in the future, as in the recent past, to keep their Vice-Presidents as fully apprised of current problems and policies as is compatible with maintaining the superordinate position of the Chief Executive. A Vice-President who takes office in an emergency, however great his talents, must be able, in today's setting of complexity and fast-moving crisis, to begin to discharge his new responsibilities with a minimum of delay and hesitation.

These same forces plus the lessons of the period following the assassination of John F. Kennedy are also likely to lead to a revision of the 1947 statute governing succession to the Presidency. That law provided that, after the Vice-President, the Speaker of the House and the President pro tempore of the Senate should succeed. Objections to this system include the view that these officials may not be of Presidential stature and may even be of a party in opposition to that of the late President. But the most weighty criticism is that both are likely, since seniority has much to do with their selection, to be too old to carry the burdens of the White House. When Lyndon Johnson was sworn in as President on November 22, 1963, John W. McCormack, the Speaker of the House, was nearly seventy-two, and Senator Carl Hayden, the President pro tempore, was eighty-six. Alternatives recently discussed include holding a special election, reassembling the members of the Electoral College to choose a Vice-President, returning to the old form of having the Cabinet officers—beginning with the Secretary of State—succeed, and having the former Vice-President designate a successor, with the consent of the Senate or of the whole Congress. One of these, or some variant, is likely before long to replace the present arrangements.

The Cabinet and Its Members

The President's Cabinet, as an institution and as a term, has been an accepted part of the American government since the 1790s. It is not mentioned in the Constitution, however, and it was not referred to in any statute until 1907. This quality of being an accepted institution with flexible status is symptomatic of the Cabinet's peculiarities. It is not a body whose members feel a strong collective responsibility and a mutual obligation; it is at best of limited usefulness to the President as a source of advice; yet Presidents have, with varying degrees of regularity, retained the Cabinet meeting as part of their busy operations. The Cabinet is thus less than one's preconceptions might suggest and more than its disillusioned critics would grant.

The persistence of the Cabinet is a reflection of certain needs of the Presidency itself. Its limitations derive from two factors: the considerations affecting the appointment of its members and their status as departmental executives.

THE PROCESS OF APPOINTMENT

Despite appearances to the contrary, a President does not in fact have complete discretion in selecting his Cabinet officers. In the first place, what may be called party considerations constitute a limitation. Not all of the selections must be drawn from the President's party, as we shall see. But almost all of them in fact are. In the course of the nomination and election campaigns obligations have been incurred—and sometimes promises have been given—that have to be recognized, if only for the sake of harmony in the President's coalition. The President may feel obligated to a man even if the qualities that made him valuable in the campaign are not pertinent to his usefulness as a member of the Cabinet. Thus the Connecticut Democratic organization played so invaluable a part in mounting Senator Kennedy's drive for the nomination in 1960 that it would have been unthinkable—or at least unwise—for President-elect Kennedy not to have found a place somewhere in the Administration for Governor Abraham Ribicoff if he desired one. It also may be prudent in the interests of party harmony to include an elder statesman of the party, as Wilson chose William Jennings Bryan for his first Secretary of State. But this device may have its limitations. Bryan's influence in the Democratic party made him an awkward instrument for Wilson's plans. Three times the party's nominee for President, Bryan had a strong following in the country and in the Congress. His views on domestic and external affairs were not identical with Wilson's. If overridden, he could "leak" his objections to Congress or to the press, and if he resigned he could create a storm of protest damaging to the President and his plans. (Both the advantages and the risks may have been in President Kennedy's mind when he named Adlai Stevenson Ambassador to the United Nations rather than Secretary of State in 1961.)

In the second place, some recognition must be given in the Cabinet to geographical balance and to the party organizations in the larger states. North, South, East, and West must all be represented. When a Department's activities are peculiarly concentrated in one section of the country, moreover, as those of Interior are in the West, its Secretary is expected to be either a resident of the area or at least publicly identified with it.

Third, several of the Departments, notably Agriculture, Commerce, Treasury, and Labor, are peculiarly identified with distinct segments of the society. Speaking for these segments, the relevant organized interest groups make every effort to assure conformity between their conceptions of a proper Secretary and the nominee's qualifications. Normally they cannot force the President's choice, and the man designated may not fit their specifications precisely, but he is not likely to be one who is clearly objectionable to them. This is an understandable circumstance, since, for example, a Secretary of the Treasury who was regarded with hostility by the financial and banking community would find it very nearly impossible to perform his statutory duties. This presumably was President Kennedy's reason for naming Douglas Dillon as Secretary of the Treasury. Though a Republican who had been Ambassador to France and Under Secretary of State in the Eisenhower Administration, Dillon was highly respected in financial circles. Without such confidence a Secretary of the Treasury would, at minimum, find rough going in his relations with Congress—where every Cabinet officer must earn his spurs. Relations between key committees in the House and Senate and related interest groups are in fact frequently so close that hostility toward a Cabinet officer from the one will almost certainly be reflected in a lack of friendliness from the other.

Fourth, real but unmeasurable obstacles are presented by the unwillingness or inability of some of the most desirable men to serve. Few Cabinets, in all probability, are composed entirely of a President's first choices; he may have been obliged to move fairly far down a preference list before he secured an acceptance. There are several possible reasons: considerations of health, problems of personal financial sacrifice, and, in the case of ambitious politicians, the fact that a Cabinet post normally does not further a public career but rather closes it—which may, for example, seriously restrict a President's ability to recruit able men from the Senate or the House.

Finally, a President must give some general consideration to the public impression that his Cabinet will make collectively. It may need balance in a socioeconomic sense or an appearance of youthful vigor or one of solid respectability, depending on the times and his sense of direction. An appearance of being "above" merely partisan considerations may be important. Thus when Franklin Roosevelt in 1940 appointed two prominent Republicans, Henry L. Stimson and Frank Knox, as Secretary of War and Secretary of the Navy respectively, he in effect announced a government of national unity (and incidentally reduced the chances of partisan criticism of his wartime Administration). Stimson had served Republican Presidents since Theodore Roosevelt and had been Taft's Secretary of War. Knox had been his party's candidate for Vice-President in 1936.

A President's freedom of choice is confined within these limits. But he may still be moving in the dark, even if the range of his personal acquaintance is broad. Franklin Roosevelt had met Harold Ickes for the first time only a few hours before he appointed him (a second choice) as Secretary of the Interior. And John F. Kennedy reportedly had seen Dean Rusk on only two occasions before inviting him to become Secretary of State, though he had been acquainted with Rusk's writings and with his reputation.

Given these features of their appointment, it is scarcely astonishing that the members of the Cabinet do not constitute a group of colleagues with a sense of mutual obligation. They come together as comparative strangers, chosen for varying and even contradictory reasons. They owe no obligation to each other—at most one to the President. Even to him their ties may not be controlling if they regard their appointments as rewards for services rendered, or if they look upon themselves as representatives of a particular clientele (which of course they tend to do as departmental executives).

DEPARTMENTAL EXECUTIVES AS COUNCILORS

The essence of the problem of the Cabinet member as a departmental executive is that, as Richard Neustadt expresses it, he has five masters: in addition to but not necessarily subordinate to the President, there are the Congress (especially its relevant committees); his departmental clients; his staff; and himself.[8] (The list appropriately does not include Cabinet colleagues.)

If a man cannot serve two masters without at least the appearance of disloyalty to one, his embarrassments with five would seem inescapable. Understanding the reasons for this situation will not only be a help in comprehending the limitations of the Cabinet but will also contribute to an understanding of some basic features of the government as a whole. A Department Secretary (or the administrator of any other agency) cannot be entirely his own master, since each of the other four masters controls power resources he is sure to need at one time or another. Serving their expectations and demands is the price he must pay for those resources. He has need of the President, to be sure: without Presidential endorsement and initiative his major proposals will be handicapped, and Presidential support when he comes under attack from in or outside the government may provide his margin of survival. But the President's resources also are limited. If defense of a member of his Cabinet might jeopardize a major part of his legislative program, for example, he may be obliged to withhold that defense. He cannot fight all of a Secretary's battles, and one who is in constant trouble becomes a burden to him. Thus the departmental executive is obliged to court his other masters. He must be prepared, if necessary, to "go it alone," that is, to do without assistance from the President. If he fails to do so, the Congress, especially through its relevant committees, can cut his authority as well as his appropriations and can enfeeble his efforts at initiating policy. His staff within the Department can withhold its support if they see him losing his influence with the Congress; without them, at least in the long run, he will be helpless. And client groups outside the government can give him trouble in the Congress, elsewhere in the executive branch, and in the press.

Thus, quite aside from any natural tendency for a man to identify with the goals and projects of the institution that he heads, a Cabinet officer cannot address the Chief Executive purely as a Presidential councilor on any matter that relates to his Department. Moreover, he is unlikely to have frequent occasion to advise the President on any matter of major consequence that does not relate to his Department.

THE CABINET AS COUNCIL

Cabinet officers not only have no reason to feel a strong sense of loyalty to each other, they are often quite literally rivals—in the inevitable jurisdictional conflicts that emerge in any government, in connection with budget allocations, and the like. Given this fact, they are not, left to themselves, disposed to bring before the entire Cabinet major matters concerning

---

[8] Neustadt, *op. cit.,* p. 39.

their Departments; they naturally prefer to get the President's attention alone. This circumstance, as Richard Fenno aptly puts it, "converts the meeting into a joint enterprise, in which 'joint' denotes a common determination to suppress vital issues and 'enterprise' consists in the great variety of devices for doing so." [9] Thus when the Cabinet members in effect set the agenda for meetings—as they often do when the customary pattern is followed of calling upon each member to raise matters of interest or allegedly common concern, beginning with the Secretary of State—almost inevitably they produce an agenda of trivialities, presented for discussion without advance notice. Little change seems to have resulted from the Eisenhower practice of having members submit in advance to a "Cabinet secretariat" any item they wished to have discussed. Some contribution toward a more orderly procedure was made by the Truman device—extended by Eisenhower and retained in part by his successors—of circulating an agenda in advance and of making a record of decisions. But these changes do not go to the heart of the problem of the Cabinet as a council.

Fundamentally the Cabinet is useful to a President—and to itself—only if its agenda is his. If he puts the questions to be discussed, he presumably can get a range of reactions that may be useful. The occasions when this suits his needs are not numerous. Hence the tendency is for most meetings to be of limited value. In addition, the President may be able in his conduct of the discussions to indicate fairly clearly the sorts of directions in which he wants the Administration to move and to give the discussion a kind of unity of purpose which Fenno calls "administrative coherence." [10] These two functions largely account for the persistence of the Cabinet council despite its other limitations. But they point to the basic fact that the Cabinet as a council can be only what the President chooses to make it. Its inherent limitations will always restrict its usefulness, but he can make use of it when such a situation suits his purposes and his preferences.

The Independent Agencies

By no means all of the administrative activities of concern to the President are contained within the ten executive Departments. The additional outside units, whose number fluctuates as legislation and executive reorganization plans create new offices and reassign or consolidate others, are collectively referred to as "independent agencies." They include from thirty to forty units of major consequence in the operations of the government. Some are headed by single administrators, while others, among them several of the most important, are headed by multimember commissions or boards.

From the viewpoint of their utility as instruments of Presidential leadership, however, it is important to divide them into two groups on the basis of what they are independent of. This distinction is basically a formal one, but, as later paragraphs will show, in this instance the form may carry with it considerable substance.

The first group, considerably the larger in number, contains agencies

---

[9] Richard F. Fenno, Jr., *The President's Cabinet* (Cambridge, 1959), p. 134.
[10] *Ibid.*, pp. 91 ff.

which are merely "independent of" the executive Departments. Except for the matter of rank, these agencies stand in the same relation to the President as do the Cabinet Departments; we shall refer to them as "executive agencies." The heads of some of them, in fact, are a good deal more intimately associated with the President than are some Department Secretaries. The Chairman of the Atomic Energy Commission normally is in closer and more frequent contact with him, for example, than is the Postmaster General.

The agencies in the second group, on the other hand, are in significant respects formally "independent of" the Chief Executive himself. There are eight of these, all headed by commissions or boards. Although they differ in important particulars from one another, they all have in common a regulatory function and may therefore be referred to collectively as "regulatory agencies." They include what are sometimes known as "the big six" commissions, reflecting the importance of their activities: the Interstate Commerce Commission, the Federal Trade Commission, the Federal Power Commission, the Federal Communications Commission, the Securities and Exchange Commission, and the National Labor Relations Board. The other two are the Civil Aeronautics Board and the Board of Governors of the Federal Reserve System. The activities of all but the last also include what the Supreme Court has designated as "quasi-judicial" functions.[11]

No agency in either of these groups, it should be noted, is "independent of" the Congress. Creatures of legislation and dependent on annual appropriations, they are neither formally nor informally beyond the reach of the Congress, its committees, or individual Senators and Representatives.

The important questions to ask concerning these two sets of agencies are: (1) Why are they independent? (2) What does "independent" mean in fact? (3) What difference does their "independence" make to the President's leadership and to the functioning of the government generally? The answers are often similar for both groups of agencies, but clarity may be served by discussing the two groups separately.

THE INDEPENDENT EXECUTIVE AGENCIES

Without attempting to be exhaustive, one can identify at least half a dozen reasons for the independence of this first group of agencies. All six reasons never apply to any one agency, but in some instances several of them are responsible. Except for mere matters of convenience, the reasons are fundamentally political: they reflect considerations of power, influence, and the conflict of interests in the governmental process.

(1) Flexibility—freedom of initiative—is the first characteristic reason for independent status, especially in the case of those agencies which in form are government corporations. The best-known example perhaps is the Tennessee Valley Authority, established in 1933 to develop the resources—in water, hydroelectric power, and agriculture—of a multistate region. Placing this function in one of the existing departments would have risked compelling conformity to its management and related procedures; this conformity might have inhibited flexible and imaginative operation and weakened its

---

[11] *Humphrey's Executor* v. *U.S.*, 295 U.S. 602 (1935).

efforts. Further, the TVA necessarily was obliged to work with the branches of various federal agencies in the region. Placing it in one Department, therefore, such as Interior, might have handicapped relations with others, such as Agriculture.

Flexibility also in large part accounts for the independent status of such agencies as the National Aeronautics and Space Administration (NASA), created in 1958. (A related consideration in this case was that the most likely departmental location would have been the Department of Defense, but locating it there would have placed an exclusively military stamp on the government's space research and exploration.) NASA was a major venture in the reestablishment of American prestige following the launching of the first Russian satellite in 1957. It was therefore freed from the presumably restricting effects of a departmental affiliation. It competes for budgetary support, for example, as a rival to, not as a part of, the Department of Defense; that is, appeals from the Budget Bureau's determinations concerning NASA go directly to the President rather than through a Cabinet Secretary. A similar example is the Housing and Home Finance Agency (HHFA), which carries on a wide variety of activities related to housing, including public housing construction and urban renewal programs. Although some of its units are fairly new, several of them, such as FHA (Federal Housing Administration) and Public Housing Administration, date from the New Deal days, when the need to act quickly and in novel ways argued against locating these activities in one of the "old line" Departments. The narrow border between "independent" and departmental status becomes visible if one recalls that the HHFA would have become the nucleus of a new Department of Urban Affairs if President Kennedy's proposals had been accepted by the Congress.

A second reason for independence, which we may call departmental incompatibility," can be seen in the history of an agency such as the Atomic Energy Commission. When the Atomic Energy Act was under consideration in 1945 and 1946, strong opposition to the only logical alternative to independence—control by the Defense Department—was expressed by groups of organized scientists and their allies in and outside of the government. This opposition reflected hostility to the exploitation of atomic energy exclusively for military purposes and fear that such assignment would doom any chances of a system of international control. It also, however, reflected an objection to giving the military domination over an energy resource which might eventually rival coal, oil, and electric power in commercial importance. (Under the Atomic Energy Act of 1946, subsequently modified to permit some private ownership, the government owned all fissionable materials, and private use of them could occur only under license.) The AEC by law maintains close liaison with the military—but formally, and as an equal.

Clientele relations in a somewhat different sense make up the third reason and largely account for the independent status of the Veterans Administration. In number of employees larger than any Department except Defense and Post Office, the VA since its creation in 1930 has been the governmental arm of the American Legion and other veterans' groups, for whose members —and nonmember veterans—it provides a wide range of services, including the largest system of socialized medicine outside of the military. Any transfer of the VA to one of the Departments would be politically impossible. None has been contemplated since the first Hoover Commission in 1949 proposed its consolidation with other agencies concerned with health and hospitalization. The storm produced by this logical proposal testified to the strength of the veterans' organizations and to their conviction that unless the VA is "independent" of all other executive agencies it will be insufficiently dependent upon the organized veterans.

The fourth example of a reason for independence—independence of political parties—is given by the Civil Service Commission, which is in one major respect unique. It could not constitutionally be made independent of the President, since to do so would encroach on his constitutional powers of appointment. Accordingly, the basic statute—the Pendleton Act of 1883 —explicitly subjected its members to his removal power. But the Act also specified that no more than two of the Commission's three members might be of the same party, and it directed the Commission to ignore recommendations from members of the Congress concerning appointments. The intent of the reformers responsible for the legislation thus was to make the Commission as independent as possible of the political parties and of the electoral organizations associated with Senators or Representatives or the President. The Civil Service Commission in effect occupies a kind of political no man's land between the assumed patronage demands of both the legislature and the President. The Congress authorizes its funds and its staff; the President promulgates its rules. But proposals—by the Brownlow Committee in 1937 and by some members of the first Hoover Commission in 1949—to replace the Commission with a single administrator, who would in effect become the President's director of personnel, have been received without enthusiasm in the Congress, in the Commission, and even within other segments of the executive establishment.

A fifth special kind of circumstance is illustrated by the United States Information Agency (USIA), which is responsible for American propaganda abroad. It has existed as an independent agency only since 1953; previously its activities had been conducted by the Department of State. Information or propaganda programs abroad are an important element of contemporary international politics and thus might be expected to be located in the Department chiefly responsible for foreign policy. The Department of State, however, is primarily concerned with the formulation of foreign policy and with the day-to-day conduct of diplomatic relations, and therefore its traditions and the inclinations of its career staff are inhospitable to large "operating" programs like that of the USIA. The latter's functions, however, could not reasonably be located in one of the other Departments, so independence became the only feasible alternative. USIA nevertheless operates under the policy guidance of the State Department and of the National Security Council.

Finally, a housekeeping agency such as the General Services Administration is independent principally because it is a service agency for the whole executive branch and thus cannot easily be located in any of the regular Departments. Created in 1949 by an act consolidating a number of separate activities, it procures and manages most government buildings, rental space, and various supplies and services. It also is responsible for such things as the management and preservation of government records, including the National Archives.

As instruments of Presidential initiative these agencies do not differ fundamentally from the executive Departments. Relations between their administrators and the President present the same characteristics and the same problems as do those between him and his Cabinet executives—and for essentially the same reasons.

THE INDEPENDENT REGULATORY AGENCIES

Most of the controversy concerning independent agencies has been concerned with the regulatory agencies, chiefly because of the importance of their activities in the operation of the government and in the functioning of the economy. This is best explained by the circumstances of their creation and the conditions of their operation. The form, procedure, and justification of these bodies are not the consequence of logic applied in advance but rather of accommodation to political circumstances plus a good deal of misleading rationalization and the inertia of tradition.

"Independence" is a relatively recent issue in connection with these commissions. The first of them, the Interstate Commerce Commission, was established in 1887 fundamentally in imitation of comparable bodies in the states. The latter were normally not subordinated to the state governors for two reasons: (1) the typical governor at that time was largely a figurehead, without control of the executive agencies, the heads of which typically were directly elected and thus in no way dependent on him; (2) the early state bodies were little more than substitutes for direct legislative regulation—principally of the railroads; thus independence was not an issue. The ICC, in fact, was administratively part of the Interior Department for the first two years of its existence. By the time the second regulatory commission was established—the Federal Trade Commission, in 1914—the ICC had become sufficiently respected to provide a pattern for imitation.

Two major factors accounting for this respect are significant, because basically they are almost precisely duplicated in the history of most of the other commissions. First, regulation, initially unwelcome to the affected groups in the economy, becomes accepted as manageable and as a defense against more objectionable actions. Most agitation for regulation in a new area springs out of a crisis or scandal—railroad malpractices in the 1870s and 1880s, the excesses of private exploitation of natural resources that lay behind the conservation movement in the first decades of this century, the conflicts in commercial air transport in the 1930s, the scandals associated with the stock market collapse of 1929, and the excesses of industry resistance to unionization until late in the 1930s. Characteristically the interests challenged by such agitation at first resist the threat. The affected industry may compromise on the commission device, however, on the well-grounded expectation that, once the agitation dies down, the commission, cut off from the main stream of political life—"independent" of the President and of any systematic supervision by the whole Congress—will be compelled to come to terms with the regulated interests. The industry will then criticize specific actions of the commission, as part of the disciplining process, but if outsiders

attack the commission or propose to place it in one of the "political" departments—its "independence" will be defended in terms of high principle. In
this way a commission tends to become a protection for the interests it was
established to regulate, guarding against glaring excesses but generally
doing little that is clearly unacceptable to the industry.

The second factor making for the acceptability of the ICC pattern is the
judicial nature of the commissions' procedures. All but one of them, the
Federal Reserve Board, employ procedures that are highly judicialized.
That is, although some of them may conduct investigations on their own
initiative, they tend to consider cases brought by complaining parties rather
than to initiate proceedings themselves; they handle cases in a formal adversary proceeding resembling a law suit, with the contending parties
producing most of the evidence; and they tend to make rules case by case,
in the manner of a common-law court. This judicialization is not an accident. The basic pattern was deliberately adopted by the ICC in its earliest
days as a defense against the tendencies of the courts and the bar to
restrict its jurisdiction and powers. It succeeded so well that it constituted
the accepted model for the five or more comparable agencies established
between 1914 and 1938. Debates on these subsequent regulatory measures,
in fact, frequently treated the ICC in the respectful terms usually reserved
for the Supreme Court. These terms, of course, implied a courtlike independence of the President, which has been the focus of controversy in the
last several decades.

The resulting basic pattern has become standard for the seven major
commissions: a multimember board whose members serve overlapping
terms of from five to seven years; bipartisan composition required by law
except for the NLRB; a highly judicialized mode of procedure; and exemption from the President's removal power except in cases of misconduct or
neglect of duty.

The heart of the issue of independence of the Chief Executive is these
commissions' "quasi-judicial" function. However the term "quasi-judicial"
may be understood—and it has never had precise definition by the Supreme
Court—it will not serve upon analysis as a logical justification of independence. If it means that these agencies have power to determine the
rights of citizens, as they do, the same may be said of many, if not most,
governmental agencies that enjoy no such independence. If it is understood
to mean the courtlike procedures of the commissions, it is clear that these
rest on convention rather than on necessity. More important, these same
kinds of functions for decades have been carried on within the executive
Departments without difficulty. For example, the Food and Drug Administration has operated as part of the departmental structure since 1907
(now in the Department of Health, Education and Welfare, but until 1940
in the Department of Agriculture). Shorn of the elements of rationalization,
the basis for independence becomes essentially political. Bias and favoritism
are no more likely inside than outside a regular Department. Regulatory
policies, however, may well be different in an agency directly responsive
to the policy-forming activities of the executive. The point is nicely illustrated in the history of the Federal Power Commission. It was created in
1920 after a long struggle between the advocates of conservation and the

private power companies and was at first an ex officio commission composed of the Secretaries of War, Interior, and Agriculture. Authorized to license all water-power exploitation of public lands and navigable streams, it was relatively inactive in the political circumstances of the 1920s. It was reconstituted as a five-man independent commission in 1930 and continued to pursue policies entirely acceptable to the industry. From the outset of the New Deal in 1933, however, President Roosevelt was able to invigorate the FPC. He replaced two of the commissioners with his own appointees, and he gave the Commission vigorous support and leadership—including sponsoring legislation greatly expanding its powers and jurisdiction. The vitality of the FPC did not last indefinitely, but in the period when it was most subject to Presidential leadership, it engaged in a program of actions not determined exclusively by the private interests subject to its control.

The real problem of independence, for Presidential leadership and for the operations of the government in general, lies in the effect of the commissions' policies on the government's ability to discharge its general economic responsibilities. "Separation from general economic policy is more difficult in an age when government underwrites a minimum standard of living and a commitment to high employment, and when it is deeply involved in the economy for reasons of national security and foreign policy." [12]

This point is nowhere better illustrated than in the Board of Governors of the Federal Reserve System (FRB), which differs in important respects from the other commissions. The FRB is composed of seven men appointed by the President with the advice and consent of the Senate for staggered terms of fourteen years, with a chairman designated by the President from among its members. It is essentially the governing board of a central banking system whose powers are granted by statute. The financial support of the FRB, however, comes not from appropriations but from payments made by banks that are members of the Federal Reserve System—all national banks and about one third of all the other banks in the country. The Board is normally classified as not performing quasi-judicial functions; that is, it does not for the most part directly determine the rights of individuals. But its powers over the money and credit supply can profoundly affect the state of the economy. At the time of its creation in 1913 and up until the Great Depression of the 1930s it was widely assumed that the FRB's control of interest rates and credit would alone eliminate the dangers of serious inflation or deflation. Today economists disagree over the efficacy of such controls, but no one doubts that FRB policies are important, that they significantly affect the government's fiscal policy, in particular its public debt management and its efforts at economic growth and stability.

The relations between the FRB, on the one hand, and the President, the Secretary of the Treasury, the Council of Economic Advisers, and related agencies, on the other, are thus a delicate matter. Disagreement could have major implications for the economy, but whether in such a contingency a President would claim a power of removal is highly conjectural—and whether

---

[12] Merle Fainsod, Lincoln Gordon, and Joseph C. Palamountain, Jr., *Government and the American Economy*, 3rd ed. (New York, 1959), p. 59.

he would be upheld by the Supreme Court is even more so. Woodrow Wilson once privately threatened to remove all the members of the FRB soon after its establishment, but no President has actually attempted such action.

Not all of the independent commissions have powers that are as significant for the economy as the FRB, but any of them may make policies that bear directly on the President's programs. They may be beyond the reach of his removal power, but the President has other partially effective means of control, and most recent Presidents have attempted in various ways to influence commission policies. The most readily available means of influence in the long run is the power of appointment, but the long run may be very long indeed, because of overlapping terms of considerable duration. Thus a President limited to eight years in the White House may not be able to get a commission majority sympathetic to his views before he himself is forced to retire. The appointing power, moreover, is subject to at least as severe limitations in connection with commissioners as with Cabinet appointments, in particular the restraints imposed by client groups. Some Presidents have been able to speed the process of replacement by securing the resignations of commissioners, and in one or two instances undated letters of resignation have been required as a condition of appointment, but this is not a common practice. Since 1950 the President has been empowered to designate the chairman for all but one of the commissions from among the commissioners. Since the chairman normally is the commission's chief executive, this power may be an important means of affecting policy. This may especially be the case if the President also makes a point of conferring with the chairmen, offering policy suggestions, and soliciting advice.

The exception to the President's power to designate the commission chairmen is in the ICC. In 1950, when this power was granted for all the other commissions under a series of reorganization plans submitted to Congress by President Truman, the ICC and its clients successfully fought the proposal on the ground that it jeopardized the Commission's "independence" and its responsibility to the Congress. The ICC in consequence continues its practice of electing a chairman from among its members, and the President cannot do to it what he can to the Supreme Court when he nominates a Chief Justice.

The President has a few additional formal powers affecting all the commissions. In particular he may request a commission study of any subject in its jurisdiction that he deems important. The request in most cases is not binding, but such a request is unlikely to be ignored entirely by any commission. Conformity both to these requests and to a President's views on general policy may be strengthened if a popular President with a strong Congressional following makes these views public, since no commission could long withstand open opposition from both the White House and a sizable segment of the Congress. In addition, the commissions' financial requests and operating procedures are subject to review by the Budget Bureau in the same fashion as are those of other agencies, and they are all in some measure dependent on the Department of Justice for the enforcement of their regulations.

The independent commissions are thus not completely independent of the President, and it can be argued that the problem of his relations with them differs only in degree from that encountered with his nominal subordinates in the executive branch. Degree can be important, however, especially as the notions of independence and bipartisanship reinforce a commission's tendencies to ignore a President's stake in its policies and actions. Whatever the formalities may be, he will be held responsible for the economic consequences of their policies. He may also suffer politically from revelations that exclusive dependence of a commission on its clientele has resulted in misconduct. It is not insignificant that both the Truman and the Eisenhower Administrations were seriously embarrassed by scandals that developed in the independent commissions.

A President therefore encounters difficult problems in employing the regulatory commissions as instruments of his initiative. Such is their importance to him and to his program, however, that an energetic President will feel impelled to use such sources of influence as he can acquire to induce them to accept his leadership. He may not be able to close the gap between what is expected of him by his larger constituency and what he can persuade these "independent" subordinates to do, but he can hardly escape the obligation to try.

Unofficial and Semiofficial Instruments of Leadership

It was stated at the beginning of this chapter that the instruments of Presidential leadership need not be part of the executive establishment nor even governmental in a formal sense. Such is the variety of these less obvious instruments that a complete catalog would be almost impossible to compile, but some understanding of the range involved can perhaps be gained by a discussion of a few examples.

THE "KITCHEN CABINET"

The growth of the White House Staff and the Executive Office of the President in the past two decades has so established the "institutionalized Presidency" that some observers have predicted the disappearance of the type of unofficial Presidential aide that has been a commonplace since at least the time of Jackson. In their never-ending search for a range of advice that is as disinterested as possible and for assistants whose attachment to their stake in office is as complete as can be, most Presidents, and especially forceful ones, have turned to persons in and outside the government who had no official place in the White House entourage. The term "kitchen cabinet" applied to such groups was first used contemptuously of the four men whom Andrew Jackson, ignoring his Cabinet, relied upon both for advice and for confidential assistance. All had at least some minor government connection, but their importance lay in the confidence placed in them by the President, for whose election in 1828 all four had worked assiduously. Lincoln had a similar group around him; so did Theodore Roosevelt, one of whose kitchen cabinet described its gatherings as ones in which "the President spoke without reserve on his executive problems, and read for our criticism and counsel his rough drafts of congressional messages, speeches, and notes to foreign governments." [13] Franklin Roosevelt's original "brain trust," none of whom had Cabinet rank, was a comparable group, and his use of men like Robert Sherwood and Judge Samuel Rosenman in the drafting of his speeches involved the same kind of relation. In a more specialized category, involving not only advice but also actions as Presidential agents, were the roles played by Colonel E. M. House in Wilson's Administration and by Harry Hopkins in the war years of Franklin Roosevelt's Presidency. John J. McCloy and Robert A. Lovett have played special advisory roles in every administration since the Second World War.

The likelihood of such relations continuing into the future is strong but does not lie primarily in the President's need for assistance as such. His more serious requirement is for advice or assistance that is unaffected by continuing connections within the government. Even the White House Staff, whose personal loyalties can be counted upon with considerable confidence, may in time become enmeshed in continuing relations among themselves and elsewhere within the government that may unwittingly influence their counsel. The increasingly "institutionalized Presidency," therefore, is unlikely entirely to do away with the phenomenon of the kitchen cabinet.

AD HOC COMMISSIONS

Presidents from the time of Washington have resorted, characteristically without statutory authorization, to the device of appointing *ad hoc* commissions to investigate some factual situation and, often, to recommend appropriate action. As recently as Theodore Roosevelt's day, however, this practice produced protests, usually from hostile elements in the Congress. They usually argued that without legal authorization such bodies were unconstitutional. In 1909, in fact, the Congress attempted, through a statute, to prevent Theodore Roosevelt from using the device. The President signed the measure in which the prohibition was included but announced his intention of ignoring it. Since that time the Presidential commission has become an accepted part of governmental operation.

Presidents may appoint these *ad hoc* commissions for a variety of reasons —as fact-finding instruments pure and simple, as devices for avoiding premature commitments on an insistent and troublesome problem, as harmless means of pacifying an insistent reform group, and the like. But the most interesting cases are those in which a commission is used to strengthen the President's capacity to impose a policy he regards as necessary, in short, those in which the *ad hoc* commission actually becomes an instrument of initiative. Ideally such a commission is composed of prominent citizens and technical experts of unimpeachable disinterestedness who are asked to study and make recommendations on a somewhat controversial problem but one for which detached men of intelligence are likely to agree on a certain solution—the one the President favors. Their report then

---

[13] Oscar Straus, *Under Four Administrations* (New York, 1922), pp. 206–07.

can have important news value. The President in turn can borrow the prestige of the commission's members to lend support to the policy he expected them to favor.

A good example is President Roosevelt's Committee to Investigate the Rubber Situation, appointed in 1942. The problem grew out of the critical shortage created by the Japanese seizure of the rubber-producing areas in the Far East at a time when facilities for making synthetic rubber in the United States were almost nonexistent. Expansion of synthetic manufacture involved active conflicts over patents and over petroleum versus grain alcohol as raw material. Such expansion, even if the competing interests could be reconciled, would require considerable time. A necessary immediate answer was the conservation of rubber, chiefly by the device of rationing gasoline, but this meant challenging the most powerful constellation of interests in modern America. This coalition speaks in the name of every citizen's God-given right to drive a car as much as he pleases and for any purpose he chooses. The President appointed a committee composed of Bernard Baruch, whose prestige as a counselor to Presidents was enormous, and Karl T. Compton and James B. Conant, both distinguished scientists and university presidents. The resulting report contained no surprises, but it received widespread publicity and helped materially in compelling the contending interests to accept a workable program of conservation, including gasoline rationing. Recent commissions that were set up to help the President with his legislative program have been the Clay commission on foreign aid (1963) and a commission on the question of government support for the construction of a supersonic jet transport, in competition with one being built jointly by France and Great Britain.

THE PRESS CONFERENCE AND THE PRESIDENTIAL PULPIT

The President's regular meetings with the White House correspondents are an illustration of an informal practice, developed in response to new conditions, which has become so completely a Presidential institution that he could not abolish it if he wished to. The press conference was begun as an informal arrangement by Theodore Roosevelt, who, when he described the White House as "a bully pulpit," revealed his own clear perception of the President as teacher to the nation. The conferences took on somewhat more formality as Washington and the White House became more important sources of news, but they only reached something like their contemporary form and importance under Franklin Roosevelt. In fact they may have reached the peak of their value to the President in those years. They were neither televised nor broadcast, and F. D. R. normally took a sizable portion of the allotted time to talk off the record and to give the background—as he saw it—for events and problems. This he could do with a candor and force possible only because his remarks were not for direct quotation. He was the master of the situation, whereas subsequent Presidents have been constantly in danger of becoming its victims. They have been compelled, especially with the advent of television, to make public shows of these meetings. An offhand, ill-considered response to an unexpected question can have serious political and diplomatic repercussions, and the way in which the President handles himself before the press and

"... So, In Keeping With Our Flexible Press Conference Format ..."

Recent Presidents have increased both the importance and the informality of the press conference.

Jim Berry—NEA

the cameras can help or handicap his standing with all the spectators in and out of Washington whom he needs to persuade.

Nevertheless, no contemporary President can afford to omit these conferences. An attempt to do so would earn him the hostility of the press, but, more important, it would mean foregoing an opportunity to make news, and no President prudently passes up an opportunity to dominate the headlines.

The chief danger of the institutionalized press conference, aside from the hazard of impulsive response, is that if it is held with too great regularity it may lose much of its public—as distinguished from its specialized—audience. Like any other television "show," it may lose its appeal. In this respect it has the same limitations as the too-frequent public address or the excess of Presidential commissions. These all depend for their public effect in part upon novelty and infrequency. For this reason President Kennedy wisely limited the occasions on which his press conferences could be carried "live" and did not hold them with unfailing regularity. Similarly, President Johnson had a series of unannounced, "spot" conferences for press people regularly attached to the White House before he had one of the full-dress sessions in the State Department auditorium. A President constantly "going to the people" is in danger of losing their attention and of merely blending into the unheard noise that is a constant accompaniment to modern life. His words will speak less loudly, in any case, than his deeds and the events with which he is associated, whether or not by his own choosing. He will be conserving such influence as his words may carry if through restraint he makes attention-getting events out of public utterances.

THE CONGRESSIONAL PARTY LEADERS

Presidents, even the most unenterprising ones, are obliged to maintain contact with the Congress, and they have devised a wide variety of means for doing so. Maintaining this contact is the chief function of one or more members of the White House Staff; the President's calendar of appointments regularly includes conferences with Senators and Representatives; and at critical stages in his legislative program the White House switchboard may be busy with his calls to wavering members of Congress. But as the Presidency has come to occupy a larger and larger place in the system, a kind of institution has grown up around the President's relations with the principal "elective" leaders of his Congressional party, especially the Speaker and majority leader in the House and the majority leader and chief whip in the Senate. Regular weekly conferences at the White House with these men on the status and prospects of the President's legislative program have become an established Washington institution in the past thirty years.

The Congressional leaders are not the President's agents on Capitol Hill, or not *merely* his agents. Even more than his nominal subordinates, the Cabinet officers, they have their own stakes—in their constituencies and in the Congress. But, for reasons that will be more closely examined in Chapter 13, they have *some* stake in his position and in their somewhat privileged relations with him. On the President's side these relations are of enormous, if not unlimited, value. (He cannot lead the Congress directly, partly because his days provide too few hours for such an engrossing activity.) The Congressional party leaders are points of persuasion and negotiation and are sources of valuable intelligence. To the degree that he can carry them with him, they are instruments of influence on Capitol Hill that are very nearly indispensable. The elective party leaders share some of these capacities with key committee chairmen and with the leaders of the opposition party, whom most Presidents find it useful to cultivate. But the range of the elective leaders' concerns more nearly approximates the President's than does that of any of these. The leaders are in a position to aid or facilitate the whole gamut of his legislative program.

An Overview of the Instruments of Leadership

Instruments of Presidential initiative that are ready-made and consistently reliable are, at best, few. The expectations that have made the Presidency the mainspring of the system are real, as are the problems, the needs, and the complex relationships from which these expectations have grown. But if the gap between what is expected from the President and what he is able to produce from the system is not to become intolerably wide, he is obliged to employ a sensitive ingenuity in manipulating and exploiting— rarely commanding—the variety of partially reliable devices available to him.

The gap, in some degree, will always be present. No set of formal procedures, no scheme of organization—certainly none that is in keeping with the spirit of our constitutional traditions—will assure closure. Attempts to eliminate the risks of Presidential leadership are doomed to failure. Equally well-intentioned efforts to reduce the admittedly enormous burdens of the office through institutional contrivances might also succeed in relieving it of much of its substance.

But this does not mean that organizational arrangements are of no consequence. Clearly the executive budget and the development of the Executive Office of the President are indispensable means of bringing Presidential— and governmental—performance into something like conformity with contemporary requirements. No less clearly, the relative independence of the major regulatory commissions at best increases the awkwardness of the President's situation and at worst may guarantee the frustration of his designs. But his problem of achieving effective leadership would only be reduced, not eliminated, if these functions were made a part of the executive. He would still need to persuade these new "subordinates" that their stakes were convergent with his.

Persistence of the gap in some degree, moreover, is not only inevitable, especially in the American system of "separated institutions sharing powers," [14] but to the extent that it stimulates political inventiveness and the search for formulas of adjustment, it is also an assurance of vitality—to say nothing of the freedom to dissent. In governing as in individual experience, creativeness emerges from the tensions between aspiration and possibility, provided that they are not so great as to produce only frustration.

Attempts to keep the President from narrowing the gap, by such conflicts over organization as the controversies concerning the independent commissions, are in part contests over the insulation of private interests from more inclusive public claims. They are also reflections of divergent views concerning the Presidency. In a far deeper sense they represent a continuing dispute over the range of responsibilities that shall be conceded to government as an institution. A society responding to change as rapid and extensive as the United States has experienced in the twentieth century can hardly be expected to avoid such divergences. Of necessity they are at the heart of the political contest. A President's search for and experiments with the instruments of initiative, therefore, are in a sense the central features of the society's search for means of dealing with the complexities of the contemporary world.

---

[14] Neustadt, *op. cit.*, p. 33.

12 / Presidents, Congresses, and Congressmen

The first Administration bill to reach the floor of the House of Representatives after President Kennedy was inaugurated in 1961 was a controversial measure to provide short-term relief to farmers producing grain for animal feed. The President faced the humiliating prospect that "his" initial legislative request would be defeated in the House. The key to success or failure lay not with Representatives from farm states but with a handful of New York City Democrats. They were indifferent to the bill as such, but they were angry at the Administration's handling of patronage appointments. Threatening until almost the last minute to oppose the feed bill, they ultimately did vote for it. But the narrow 209-to-202 margin by which the bill passed indicated clearly how close the President had come to embarrassment. "We want to show him," one of the group commented as the vote was about to be taken, "that we are bigger than he is." [1]

This episode illustrates a fundamental fact of the American system: The House and Senate share with the President many of the basic functions of governing, notably the enactment of legislation, but their stakes and their risks, even within the same party, may be sharply in conflict with his. This, in practice, is what "checks and balances" mean. It in general is what the Founding Fathers intended.

One of the characteristic tests of how well a President is performing is how well he gets along with Congress. Especially as the President's legislative program has come to be taken for granted as the principal agenda for the legislature, how much of it the Congress enacts becomes as much a popular measure of his performance as is a baseball player's batting average. Journalists easily cast Congressional treatment of a major Presidential proposal in the terms of victory and defeat. The assumption implicit in this attitude is that somehow a President ought to find ways of getting from the Congress what he thinks the country needs. That he may not, in fact, possess the means for such achievement is seldom taken into account.

The member of Congress also has his tests, and they may not be met by his consistent support of the President, even a President of his own party. He may have his own conceptions of appropriate public policy,

---

[1] Neil MacNeil, *Forge of Democracy: The House of Representatives* (New York, 1963), p. 251.

based possibly on long experience on a legislative committee; he may have his own distinctive ties to various interest groups; above all, he has his own political career to make or maintain, and that depends heavily on the "batting average" he has in his constituency. For, as veteran Representative Emanuel Celler suggested in the title of his autobiography, "You never leave Brooklyn." [2]

The Sources of Congressional-Presidential Conflict

The fundamental sources of this recurrent conflict are numerous, but they can be generally termed either constitutional or political. (The distinction cannot be pressed too far, as it is obvious that constitutional arrangements that fail reasonably to fit political realities, like the original plan for the indirect election of the President, are likely to be circumvented or ignored.)

CONSTITUTIONAL SOURCES

Perhaps the greatest ambiguity in the Constitution is the question of which takes precedence—the Chief Executive or the Congress. When the two are in conflict, which shall prevail? For reasons already mentioned in Chapter 10, most of the Founders naturally thought in terms of legislative supremacy, but they did establish an independently elected President and granted him powers that made him a participant in legislation. A "vigorous executive" was designed by the Convention and defended by the Constitution's proponents, but the legislature also was granted a series of nonlegislative functions, to be discussed shortly in more detail, which cast some doubt on the extent of that vigor. Of all the experiments that the Convention attempted, the one involving the relations of legislature and Chief Executive had the least promising outlook.

By a narrow vote the Convention decided to retain the prohibition against any person's simultaneously holding an office under the United States and being a member of either house of Congress. That decision virtually precluded the government's moving in the direction of ministerial responsibility to the legislature, as the British then were beginning to do. By the decision the Convention expressed an intention to separate the legislative and executive branches. A consequence of this decision, fully evident only in later years, was that the possibility of fusing the two branches by means of a system of political parties was made more uncertain—an obstacle that was strengthened by the arrangement of unequal terms—six years for Senators, four for the President, and two for Representatives—and by the provision that only one third of the Senate should be replaced at each biennial election. Legislative elections every two years assured the possibility that at the midpoint of each Presidential term the President and a majority in the House or in both chambers might be of opposing political parties. This has occurred no less than fifteen times—roughly one third of the midterm elections—in the course of our history. Conflicts between President and Congress have not always accompanied such party division, but the probabilities lie in that direction. To complicate matters, the one-

---

[2] Emanuel Celler, *You Never Leave Brooklyn* (New York, 1953).

third replacement restriction for the Senate may mean that popular support registered for a President in his own and in the House election may not immediately be reflected in the composition of the Senate.

POLITICAL SOURCES

The political sources of separatism derive fundamentally from a single fact: The forces—the organizations and the attitudes—responsible for the election and especially the nomination of members of Congress are not the same as those that put a President in the White House, even though in some instances they may seem to be fairly similar. In a general election the presence of the party label may make the results look harmonious, but in nominations—especially those made through the characteristic device of the direct primary—a variety of factors, often of a character wholly un-related to national or Presidential considerations, may account for the out-come. The effective electorate, moreover, those actually voting in midterm elections, is characteristically not a representative cross-section of the Presidential electorate either in a locality or in the country as a whole. Many more voters in Presidential elections are normally uninvolved in politics, loosely identified with a party, and likely to be swayed by the candidate's personal characteristics. In midterm Congressional elections more voters have the reverse of these characteristics and, in addition, are concerned with purely local issues. This means that the political risks of a President and a member of Congress, even one of the same party, are far from identical.

This basic political source of separatism is reinforced by aspects of the internal power structure in the Congress, to be discussed in more detail in Chapter 13.

Also working for separation is a factor that can best be described as "institutional patriotism," [3] which affects not only the relations between President and Congress but also those between the Senate and the House and between committees in the two chambers. Reflecting in part the different stakes already referred to, institutional patriotism represents the normal tendency of influential persons in an organization to identify with it, to accept its distinctive codes and outlooks, and to mistrust the behavior of adjacent, and in a sense rival, organizations. The phenomenon can be seen in the clashes between legislative committees within both the Senate and the House and in the thinly disguised resentments that members of the House on occasion feel toward the Senate, and vice versa. These are a combination of jurisdictional rivalries and of the suspicion that the other organization, whether it be another committee or the other house of Congress, is acting without sufficient awareness of the consequences for the viewer's group, that it is assuming undeserved credit for joint accomplishments, or that it is behaving with insufficient respect.

For example, for fifteen weeks—from mid-April until almost the end of July, 1962—no appropriation measures were enacted by the Congress. Money bills were passed by the House, to be sure. In turn they were amended in the Senate as usual. But they could not be enacted until the

---

[3] Donald M. Matthews, *U.S. Senators and Their World* (Chapel Hill, 1960), pp. 101–02.

"How Can You Be Napoleon
When I Am?"

Don Hesse in the St. Louis *Globe-Democrat*

differences between the two versions were ironed out in conference committees composed of members of the Appropriations Committees of both houses. (A conference committee of representatives, called "managers," from each house is appointed by their presiding officers to compromise differences in the terms of bills that both houses have passed. The results of such a conference must of course be approved by both houses.) The conference committees did not meet between April 10 and July 20 because the octogenarian chairmen of the two Appropriations Committees, Senator Carl Hayden of Arizona and Representative Clarence Cannon of Missouri, were feuding over where the meetings should be held and whether a Senator or Representative should chair them. By tradition all appropriation bills originate in the House; also by ancient tradition conference committees on such bills meet on the Senate side of the Capitol and are chaired by a Senator. In February of 1962 Cannon demanded that henceforth meeting places and chairmen should be alternated. Hayden and his committee agreed, provided that half the appropriation bills each year should originate in the Senate. Hence the stalemate.

Cannon's plan apparently was to try to block the practice in the Senate of restoring some of the more drastic appropriation cuts made in the House. He reasoned, presumably, that conference committees chaired by members of the House would make this more difficult. On the surface, therefore, the issue lay between "economy-minded" members of Congress and those disposed to more generous spending. But the reaction in the Senate was not along these lines. It was rather a bipartisan defense of Senate prerogatives. "The Senate refuses to become Cannon fodder," declared Everett Dirksen, the Republican leader. Among others who rose to support Hayden were

Senators Russell of Georgia, Robertson of Virginia, and Holland of Florida, all staunch fiscal conservatives. In the end Cannon and his committee dropped their demands.

As the New York *Times* commented, "The prestige at stake was institutional."[4] If this sort of thing can occur between the Senate and the House, it is clear that it can appear even more easily between the Congress and the President (plus others in the executive branch), whose stakes and circumstances are so markedly different.

The institutional patriotism that divides President and Congress also reflects a genuine legislative uneasiness in face of the twentieth-century shift of initiative in the government toward the President. Increased initiative from the White House does not, of course, narrow the range of things that the Congress *can* do. The constitutional powers have not formally been altered. But it does restrict what the Congress is *likely* to do. In consequence Congressional speeches for several decades have deplored the loss of legislative independence, have criticized Presidential encroachment, and have demanded a restoration of the Congress' "proper" role. Much of this is mere rhetoric; still more is a disguise for interest groups whose claims have been poorly received by the executive and who champion the legislature's "constitutional prerogatives" in the hope of improving their position. But much also reflects a genuine concern.

The initiative in legislative matters has not entirely shifted from the Congress. One must include among the political sources of separatism the substantial degree to which the Congress remains an alternative channel of initiative within the government. Frequently this alternative channel may compete with the Presidential one, as when, for example, an interest group unable to accomplish its purposes through the executive attempts to achieve them by way of Congress and its committees. Thus, in the spring of 1962 the President and the Secretary of Defense determined that the B-70 bomber, then in the development phase, should not go into production and that projected contracts should be terminated on the ground that the B-70 would be obsolete before it could become fully operational. The Chairman of the House Armed Services Committee, Carl Vinson of Georgia, was able to force a formal reconsideration of this decision and to gain a concession from the Administration—an agreement that a limited number of the planes would be produced for reconnaissance purposes. Vinson clearly spoke for that section of the Air Force committed to the manned bomber as a strategic weapon, but there was more than an implication that the manufacturers of the B-70 were also being represented.

Congress as an alternative channel of initiative may play a clearly constructive role. Thus in the late 1950s critics in the Congress persistently questioned the adequacy of the Administration's planned capacity for fighting a limited conventional war and eventually produced modifications in the policy.[5] Senators, whether or not members of the Foreign Relations Committee, have on more than one occasion suggested useful new depar-

---

[4] New York *Times,* July 21, 1962.
[5] Samuel P. Huntington, *The Common Defense: Strategic Programs in National Politics* (New York, 1961), pp. 145–46.

tures in foreign policy. And Congressional committees, such as the Subcommittee on National Policy Machinery of the Senate Committee on Government Operations in 1960 and 1961, have contributed significantly to the clarification of policy issues within the government.[6]

No member of the Congress, however, and none of its committees speaks from a position comparable to the President's. No leader in the Congress can commit both chambers to an agenda, to say nothing of committing them to a legislative program. Initiatives coming from Capitol Hill, therefore, lack the range and the resources of those from the White House. They may be sufficient to impose modifications in Presidential proposals, but if they are constructive initiatives of any breadth, their success is likely to depend on their being taken up by the President and incorporated in his program. The significant point is that the Congress can and does operate as an alternative channel of initiative—often quite successfully—and this continues the controversy over precedence between the two agencies that the Convention of 1787 left unresolved.

The Nonlegislative and Semilegislative Functions of Congress

The separatism between President and Congress is reinforced by the existence of a considerable number of Congressional activities that either are not legislative in nature at all or are really only extensions of the function of enacting statutes. Many of them are part of the scheme of "checks and balances" built into the Constitution.

AMENDING THE CONSTITUTION

By constitutional arrangement and by judicial interpretation, the Congress is the national agency that deals with amending the Constitution. The two methods of proposing amendments—by a two-thirds vote in each house (the only method actually employed thus far), or by calling a convention at the request of two thirds of the state legislatures—put the Congress at the center of things. Formally the President is out of the picture, as resolutions proposing amendments are not submitted for his signature. The White House may urge that an amendment be proposed, or express its dissatisfaction with one already proposed, or even actively attempt to defeat an amendment under consideration by the Congress, but the legislature is the constituent (constitution-making) agency at the national level. Even in connection with ratification, the Congress chooses whether the method shall be by action of three fourths of the state legislatures or by conventions in three fourths of the states called for the purpose.

ELECTING THE PRESIDENT AND VICE-PRESIDENT

The Congress and each of its houses have electoral functions. A formality, but one with symbolic importance, is the requirement that responsibility for counting the electoral votes for the two offices lies with the President of the Senate, "in the presence of the Senate and House of Representa-

---

[6] U.S. Senate, Committee on Government Operations, Subcommittee on National Policy Machinery, *Organizing for National Security* (3 vols., Washington, 1961).

tives." Somewhat more substantial are the powers—in case no candidate receives a majority of the electoral votes—of the House to elect the President and the Senate to choose the Vice-President. The choice of a President has not been thrown into the House since 1824. But the special position accorded the legislature by this requirement, especially to the House, is one of the subtle factors contributing to its collective self-regard.

IMPEACHING AND JUDGING

Similar consequence may be attributed to the judicial functions of the two chambers. The House has the sole power of impeachment and the Senate the sole power to try impeachment charges (the Chief Justice of the United States presiding when impeachment of the President is being tried). Only twelve impeachments have come to trial, all but three of them involving judges—President Andrew Johnson was impeached but acquitted in 1868. One can readily agree with Thomas Jefferson's judgment that impeachment is "the scarecrow of the Constitution," so infrequently is it used, but the mere existence of the power has relevance to the matter of separatism.

More important, the houses of Congress have the right, affirmed by the Supreme Court, to imprison for contempt a person who refuses to obey its legitimate demands—for example, to appear before it or one of its committees, to answer questions, or to supply evidence. Since the Court early held that such imprisonment could not extend beyond the adjournment of the house by which it was ordered,[7] Congress by statute has made this kind of contempt a criminal offense, enforceable in the regular courts and carrying sentences of varying lengths, but the presiding officer of the offended house still certifies the case to the Department of Justice without a vote by the chamber.

Finally, under the Constitution each house has an exclusive power not only to judge the elections by which its prospective members (persons certified to have won in the elections) have been chosen and to decide whether it will seat them, but also to punish a member for a breach of its rules, including what it may choose to regard as improper conduct, and it may censure or even expel one of its number. Challenges to election results— usually by the losing candidate—are fairly common, but the disciplining of sitting members by censure or expulsion is rare. The most recent and perhaps most dramatic case of the latter sort was the Senate's censure of the late Senator Joseph R. McCarthy of Wisconsin in 1954 for abuse of Senate committees. Such a vote is in effect a form of ostracism, which undermines a Senator's effectiveness, to say the least.

THE SENATE AND TREATIES

The making of treaties is a less significant aspect of foreign policy than it was several decades ago, because of such developments as the increased use of the executive agreement and the development of economic foreign policy under statutory authorization. It is not a minor matter, however. In 1961, for example, the Senate received ten Presidential requests for its

---

[7] *Anderson* v. *Dunn*, 6 Wheaton 204 (1821).

consent to ratification of treaties of various sorts. When one contemplates, moreover, the significance that the North Atlantic Treaty has had in the foreign relations of the United States for more than a decade or that the Nuclear Test Ban Treaty of 1963 may have, it is clear that treaties and the treaty power are still of considerable importance.

For present purposes, however, the Senate's executive functions in connection with treaties are peculiarly important for their secondary effects. They have resulted in a special, almost proprietary, interest in all phases of foreign policy on the part of the Senate, and especially its Committee on Foreign Relations. For years an assignment to the Committee on Foreign Relations has been one of the two or three most sought-after positions in the Senate, and its members are likely to be treated with special deference by the Secretary of State and others in the executive branch concerned with foreign policy. This state of affairs might be expected to result in a fusion and mutuality of concerns between the two groups, and in some instances it has. But probably at least as frequently it has had the opposite result. For this Committee, like most executive agencies, has two masters in addition to itself: first and foremost, the Senate as a whole, and secondarily the executive branch—the President and his Secretary of State. If the Committee is to be effective in the Senate, therefore, it cannot appear to be merely a tool of the executive. On occasion, at least, it must stand up to the executive and make this more than a matter of appearances. This it does, for example, when it cuts the requested foreign aid program. To retain its standing in the Senate unimpaired it must extract concessions from the executive on various matters, some of which—but by no means all—may be largely symbolic. Thus the intimate involvement of the Senate in the executive function of treaty-making may have the additional consequence of entangling general foreign policy questions with the institutional patriotism of the Senate.

THE SENATE AND PRESIDENTIAL APPOINTMENTS

The Senate's share in the essentially executive function of appointments has already been discussed briefly in Chapter 10.[8] Here it is examined as a factor contributing to the separatism of the President and Congress. The expectation of the Founders was that the Senate in performing this function would act as a council somewhat resembling that in several of the original states, scrutinizing Presidential selections in order to discourage favoritism and to keep out the unfit. But the supporters of the Constitution in the struggle for ratification also felt called upon to defend the arrangement against the charges that it would either give the President undue influence over the Senate or vice versa.[9] It has worked both ways, for reasons somewhat different from those anticipated. In addition, Senate confirmation has benefited a claimant unknown to the Founders: the state and local party organizations.

In the first place, Presidents may on occasion use appointments as the *quid pro quo* in bargaining for support of legislation, and on their side

---

[8] Chapter 10, pp. 295–96.
[9] See especially *The Federalist*, Nos. 76 and 77.

Senators may make a change in administration policy the price of support of a nomination. Second, as we noted in Chapter 10, the vast majority of nominations are confirmed routinely. But an appointment or two each year—to an ambassadorial post, to an independent commission, to a court, or even to the Cabinet—may stir up considerable controversy, in committee and on the Senate floor. Such controversy may have its source in party or factional rivalry. For committee hearings—in which outsiders and Representatives as well as Senators may testify—and floor debates on nominations both offer an opportunity for opponents to attack administration policies through challenges to nominees. The source of the hostility might also be an interest group. A group that is in an agency's clientele and fears that its influence with the President's nominee may be inadequate may persuade a friendly editor or member of Congress to oppose the nomination. Such a situation is especially likely if the President's intent in making the nomination is to alter some of the established policies of the affected agency.

The change of policy expected from an appointment may be more a matter of fear than of fact, especially in the case of judges. Predictions, based on previous attitudes and activities, of the kinds of positions that a judge will take, especially on major constitutional questions, are notoriously fallible. Thus Coolidge's nomination of Harlan Fiske Stone as a member of the Supreme Court was opposed by some Senate Progressives on the ground that his previous corporate practice would lead him to favor business. Yet he became one of the leaders of the "liberal" wing of the Court. But the reality of the threat is no gauge of the intensity of the dispute. Interest group biases may, of course, appear in the guise of charges of unfitness, especially if the group has established a claim to special competence in the area affected. Thus bar associations have demanded the right to pass on the fitness of judicial nominees, and recent Presidents have frequently granted some of their demands, sometimes at the insistence of Senators. Whether a reputation as a legal technician is the chief qualification for a judge, especially in the appellate courts, is of course debatable, and it may even occur that review by a bar association committee tends to discriminate against a nominee whose political views are unpopular with a majority of his professional colleagues.

Controversy over a nominee may also represent in some measure defense of the Senate's institutional patriotism. An example of this was the Senate's reaction to President Eisenhower's nomination of Lewis L. Strauss as Secretary of Commerce in 1958. As the Republican Chairman of the AEC from 1953 to 1958 Strauss had reduced the intimacy that had prevailed under his predecessor between the Commission and the Congressional Joint Committee on Atomic Energy. He had in particular acquired the personal resentment of Democratic Senator Clinton Anderson of New Mexico, who had become chairman of the Joint Committee in 1955. Anderson charged, among other things, that Strauss had not been candid in his relations with the Committee. The partisan element in the situation was closely allied to matters of interest group conflict, for Strauss had strongly supported the Administration's opposition to public development and ownership of atomic power installations. He also had been at the center of the Dixon-Yates affair in 1954 and 1955, which in its essentials was a phase in the continuing struggle between the TVA and the power companies over public versus private ownership of electric power facilities. The attack on Strauss was thus in part a challenge to the Administration and a skirmish in the long war over government ownership of power systems. Questioning and testimony in the Committee hearings dealt almost entirely with Strauss's past record and his alleged personal deficiencies; the problems of the Department of Commerce and questions concerning his ability to meet them were scarcely touched. The vote was against confirmation, 46 Senators supporting Strauss (15 Democrats and 31 Republicans) but 49 opposing him (47 Democrats and 2 Republicans). This vote by a narrow margin in effect registered a policy protest by the Democratic majority. More conspicuously it supported the charges of Anderson and other Senators that Strauss had failed to show a proper respect for Congress, and especially the Senate.

The institution of "Senatorial courtesy" is a third feature of the Senate's role in Presidential nominations, one not generally anticipated in 1787. John Adams, however, seems to have had a clear perception of what the Senate's power might lead to. In a letter written in July, 1789, he asked: "Will . . . [a Senator] not be under a temptation to use his influence with the president as well as his brother senators, to appoint persons . . . who will exert themselves in elections, to get out his enemies or opposers . . . and to get in his friends . . . ?" [10] The first precedent for the practice was established in 1789, when the Senate rejected Washington's nominee for Naval Officer for the Port of Savannah "apparently for no other reason than that the man was not acceptable to the faction in Georgia which her Senators chanced to represent." [11] Since then Presidents have rarely failed to clear with Senators of their own party nominations for positions in their states, although challenges do occur from time to time.

The persistence of the practice of Senatorial courtesy is significant in two connections. First, a Senator's concern over appointments in his state reflects the difference between his political stakes and the President's, and the consequent fact that he needs to be alert to the danger, whether intended or not, that the President may build up within the Senator's state an opposition to the party or factional organization with which the Senator is associated. Second, the practice itself testifies to and reinforces the Senate's institutional solidarity. Senators otherwise uncongenial, recognizing their common political circumstances, will grant this curious form of veto in order that they may on another occasion avail themselves of its protection. Each time it is used the institutional solidarity of the Senate is strengthened.

But the total significance of the Senate's role in nominations is not indicated by the frequency with which nominations are rejected or by the regularity with which Senators are consulted prior to the submission of

---

[10] Charles Francis Adams, ed., *The Works of John Adams* (Boston, 1850–56), Vol. VI, pp. 433–34.

[11] George H. Haynes, *The Senate of the United States* (Boston, 1938), Vol. II, pp. 736–37.

nominations. Some men decline a Presidential offer at the outset, out of reluctance to run the gantlet of the Senate's advice and consent. Not infrequently, moreover, Presidents withdraw a nomination after it has been made, usually at the formal request of the nominee, when it becomes evident that Senate resistance will be formidable. Even if confirmation is won after a vigorous conflict, the hostility revealed in the process may weaken the usefulness of an official whose duties require him to deal with the Congress. Controversy over confirmation is certain to put the official on notice that if he is to lead a reasonably successful political life he will be wise to give considerable respect to the views and desires of key Senators.

ADMINISTRATIVE SUPERVISION

The first lesson in legislative-executive protocol learned by an appointee in a confirmation struggle is in most cases amply reinforced in subsequent relations with key members of the House as well as the Senate, especially members of the subject-matter committees and the appropriations subcommittees with which he and his subordinates must deal. Checking on the actions of the executive branch and criticizing its policies are a normal part of the legislature's functions in all constitutional governments. The distinctive features of this activity under the American system result from the different risks of the elected executive and the elected legislators. Their fortunes do not necessarily rise or fall together.

In a formal sense the source of the problem lies in one of the great ambiguities of the Constitution. Article II clearly contemplated the creation of executive departments by law, that is, by acts of Congress. What the Congress may create, it may abolish or alter; what the Congress may alter or destroy, it may restrict and instruct. So essentially runs the argument. But what then becomes of the executive power that is "vested in a President" and of his duty to "take care that the laws be faithfully executed"? No executive subordinate can be entirely sure whether, in case of a difference of view, he is responsible to the President or to Congress.

No one would argue, therefore, that the legislature cannot legitimately inquire into the use of its grants of power and of funds. The usual view, in fact, is that the President and Congress "share" responsibility for administrative oversight. But when the stakes of power between President and Congress tend to diverge, the term "share" fails to express the likelihood of conflict. The prospect then may be that control may in fact lie in the legislature, in its committees, or in their chairmen.

Legislative domination of executive agencies normally increases with the length of time these agencies work with particular members of Congress. This period may be quite long. Take the case of Representative Carl Vinson of Georgia. Elected to Congress in 1914, the first midterm elections under Woodrow Wilson, he served continuously for fifty years. From 1931 to 1965, moreover, he was chairman or ranking minority member of the House Naval Affairs Committee and its successor after 1947, the Armed Services Committee. Small wonder if Vinson considered Presidents, Secretaries of Defense, and their immediate subordinates as recent arrivals and temporary occupants of executive positions, amateurs who had not been around long enough to know what they were doing.

Vinson's case is exceptional only in degree. He served longer than any other member of the House, to be sure, and few Representatives or Senators have dominated a major committee for quite so long. But as of 1965, more than half of the Representatives had served continuously in the House for ten years or more, and approximately the same proportion of Senators had served at least that long in the upper chamber.

The most fundamental source of the tendency for legislative supervision of administrative agencies to become close and detailed, and to threaten or displace Presidential influence, lies in the nature and location of the individual legislator's political risks. Executive officials, even when their freedom of action is formally rather narrow, are in a position to help or to hurt individuals or interest groups important in the constituency of a member of Congress. The awarding of a contract, a proposal to move or to eliminate a field office, a plan to enforce more vigorously the regulations under which an industry operates—such "routine" matters as this may threaten a Senator's or Congressman's constituents with hardship or disadvantage. Since the political reliance of a member of Congress is primarily upon individuals and groups in his constituency, he is almost compelled to try to influence such executive decisions in a way that will protect his position. He is compelled, not because he is necessarily incapable of taking a larger view, but because his failure to affect these decisions may cause him serious trouble. In the next election—especially in the primary—an opponent may successfully accuse him of neglecting or selling out the interests of his constituency. Against this prospective trouble the President, even one of his own party, can be of little personal help, except as the member can enlist the President to influence administrative decisions in the direction he desires. This he may be able to do. Since he cannot usually rely on Presidential aid, however, he is almost obliged to maintain such direct lines of influence in the executive branch as he can.

Congressional supervision of administration, largely because of its electoral implications, is not confined to the language of authorizing legislation or of appropriation acts. It is frequently the main theme of exchanges with executive officials in committee hearings; it is contained in the language of committee reports; it forms a large part of the less public stream of communications, by letter and by telephone, between members of Congress and executive agencies; and it supplies a major fraction of the content of speeches on the floor of both houses. Any administrator who ignores the intent of these expressions, especially when they come from an influential Representative or Senator, must be prepared with an effective defense.

INVESTIGATIVE FUNCTIONS

Whether the investigative activities of the Congress are regarded as legislative, nonlegislative, or semilegislative in character depends in large measure upon what investigations one examines, for the purposes that this kind of activity can serve are numerous. The classic functions of such investigations are and must be legislative. That is, the Congress understandably must be able to find its own facts on a given problem if it is to legislate concerning it. However restricted a view of its initiative one takes, one cannot reasonably expect the legislature to rely wholly on other sources for the information that it needs. Further, as we have just seen, the Congress hardly can be denied the means of finding out whether the laws are being enforced as they were intended and whether appropriations are being used properly. Finally, given the constitutional power of each house of the Congress to discipline its own members, investigations into the merits of charges against a member can hardly be regarded as outside of legislative prerogatives. These purposes incident to legislation are the chief reason why the courts have been reluctant to impose restrictions on Congressional investigations, since it would be difficult to limit excesses without handicapping the achievement of legitimate purposes.

Attacks on the administration

Probably most investigations, or some aspects of almost all of them, are directed more to persuading the electorate than to informing the legislature. This feature is often particularly noticeable when a partisan or interest group objective is served by an attack on the administration through an investigation. It is peculiarly likely to occur when the majority in one or both houses is not of the President's party. Thus the House investigation of the regulatory agencies in the late 1950s was sponsored by Democratic leaders with the expectation of gaining a partisan advantage—handsomely fulfilled when President Eisenhower's chief assistant, Sherman Adams, was obliged to resign following the revelation of some indiscreet behavior. But an opposition majority in Congress is not essential. If an investigation's sponsors can make charges so serious that refusal to investigate them might imply acknowledgment of guilt, a minority may be able to cause an administration acute embarrassment. This was the kind of circumstance that opened "the McCarthy period," when in 1950 the junior Senator from Wisconsin publicly charged the Secretary of State with having ignored evidence that 205 Communists were employed in the State Department. It was also part of the reason for Republican desires to prolong the 1964 investigation of the affairs of Robert G. Baker, secretary to the Senate Democrats before revelations of questionable business activities forced his resignation. Baker had been a protégé of Lyndon Johnson. Or if some dramatic event occurs that demands some public explanation, perhaps even a scapegoat, the President's party in Congress may be obliged to support an investigation. This was essentially the setting for the first Congressional investigation of the executive—the inquiry into the disastrous failure of the expedition led by General St. Clair against the Indians in the Western Reserve during Washington's first Administration. This sort of circumstance also was clearly the basis for the series of investigations following the debacle at Pearl Harbor on December 7, 1941.

Investigations aimed at embarrassing the administration have been the setting for a classic type of conflict with the executive: a Cabinet officer is called upon to testify or to supply documents to a committee, and the demand is rejected at the President's direction, on the ground that communications between him and his advisers are privileged or that disclosure

"And So, The Curtain Falls—
I said, 'And So, The Curtain
Falls!'"

From *Straight Herblock*, Simon & Schuster, 1964

When Congressional investigations turn to an examination of people closely connected with the Congress itself, the results are sometimes more embarrassing than originally intended.

would not in his judgment be in the public interest. Washington set the precedent in 1796 when he declined to supply the House with papers relating to Jay's Treaty. Most Presidents since then have had occasion to invoke "executive privilege" against the demands of Congressional investigations. (Even ex-Presidents have claimed the privilege. Thus Harry Truman soon after leaving the White House declined to comply with a request that he testify before the House Committee on Un-American Activities.) Congress has frequently challenged the claim of "executive privilege" but has found no way to enforce its protests.

Support of the administration

Congressional investigations need not be in opposition to the administration; the persuasive support they can give to pending legislation may be in aid of the President's program. The early New Deal legislation regulating stock exchanges and public utility holding companies gained invaluable support from the series of investigations conducted under Senate auspices from 1933 through 1935. Further, investigations that are potentially capable of strictly partisan results and of embarrassment to the administration need not have that result if they are handled with a different intention. A good example is Senator Harry S. Truman's Senate Committee to Investigate the National Defense Program during the Second

World War. This committee might have challenged President Roosevelt as Lincoln had been challenged by a Committee on the Conduct of the War created in 1861. Instead it operated essentially in support of the President's efforts to keep an eye on various procurement and production agencies. The potentially explosive Senate inquiry into Truman's dismissal of General MacArthur in 1951 is a related example. The care with which Senate leaders conducted these hearings avoided what might have been a free-for-all, damaging to the national security as well as to the President. A third example, slightly different, is the investigation carried on by the Senate Subcommittee on National Policy Machinery, chaired by Democratic Senator Henry M. Jackson and started during the Eisenhower Administration. Although it was at times critical of Eisenhower policies, its tone was that of a detached examination of crucial and difficult questions on which reasonable men could disagree.[12]

Publicizing the chairman

Not infrequently a legislative investigation may have as its chief result, if not its primary objective, promotion of the personal political fortunes of one of its members, usually the chairman. Any Senator or Representative may introduce a resolution establishing an investigating committee, and, by custom, if the resolution is adopted its sponsor is made chairman. If its hearings make the headlines—and the television screens—the member of Congress whose name the committee informally bears may suddenly become a major national figure. Thus the investigations of "interstate crime" under the chairmanship of Senator Estes Kefauver lifted him out of comparative obscurity and made him a popular aspirant for the Presidency in 1952 and 1956. Representative Richard Nixon's prominent part in the Alger Hiss case in 1948 as a member of the House Un-American Activities Committee contributed to his rapid rise in national politics.

Investigations and the rights of citizens

The Congressional investigations especially likely to provoke controversy and criticism are those aimed at influencing public opinion, particularly when they are also associated with "scapegoating" and achieving notoriety for the chairman. When these are the central purposes—whether or not legislation is expected to result from the investigation—the committee may easily sacrifice the privacy and even the legal rights of witnesses to the objective of making the members' view persuasive. They may also, in their efforts at "exposure," brand a witness as "guilty" of improper, if not illegal, behavior without his having the benefit of protections that would be available to him in a court of law. Although a committee in these circumstances pronounces no formal sentence of fine or imprisonment, permanent damage to the witness' reputation and even loss of his livelihood may occur. This tendency to punish by exposure lends support to the charge that investigating committees performing in this fashion are usurping a function that properly belongs only in the courts.

Although in recent years most instances in which committees have been

---

[12] See above, p. 357 and citation in footnote 6.

criticized for this sort of action have involved investigation of alleged subversive activities and associations, any investigation may be subject to such abuses regardless of its subject. Thus the Senate investigations in the early 1930s of stock exchange and investment banking practices were as abusive of privacy and the elements of fair play as any recent exposures. Unlike the latter, however, they did not destroy the careers of those whom they attacked.

The tendency toward such excesses is not peculiar to special or select committees set up for the purpose. Until 1947 investigations normally were conducted through such *ad hoc* committees. The Legislative Reorganization Act of 1946 attempted to confine the function to the regular standing committees, although in each session one or two special committees are still established. Even standing committees of the Senate must secure an appropriation for any substantial investigation, and most House committees in addition must be specifically granted the subpoena power. The only exceptions are the Committees on Appropriations, on Government Operations, and on Un-American Activities. The committees most widely criticized in recent years for invasion of private rights, however, have been standing committees or subcommittees: The House Committee on Un-American Activities, the Subcommittee on Internal Security of the Senate Judiciary Committee, and the Permanent Investigating Subcommittee of the Senate Committee on Government Operations.

For complicated reasons, the rights of a witness before such committees are limited. Every citizen, of course, has an obligation to supply any government agency with information that it may legitimately request, and the presumption is in favor of the Congress when a point is in dispute. There are, however, circumstances in which a witness may legitimately refuse to answer a committee's questions: First, he may decline to answer by invoking the Fifth Amendment's privilege against self-incrimination. Resort to this privilege means only that answering *might tend* to incriminate, but in the eyes of most ordinary citizens, unfortunately, it is often tantamount to an admission of guilt. Second, he may refuse to answer if the question is irrelevant to the authorized subject of the investigation.[13] The difficulty with this right, however, is that he must correctly anticipate what a court will regard as a pertinent question.[14] For, as when invoking the Fifth Amendment, a recalcitrant witness must be prepared to face an indictment for contempt of Congress and to justify his refusal to the satisfaction of the courts. Beyond these two, the witness essentially has no rights except those granted him by the committee.

Two important questions are suggested by this persistent conflict between the investigating function of Congress and private rights: First, why cannot the witness be guaranteed the safeguards he would have in court, such as the right to legal counsel and the right to cross-question others? Second, why cannot the Congress itself impose effective restraints on these committees or establish an alternative method of investigating that will be free of their deficiencies?

---

[13] *U.S.* v. *Rumely,* 345 U.S. 41 (1953); *Watkins* v. *U.S.,* 354 U.S. 178 (1957).
[14] *U.S.* v. *Barenblatt,* 360 U.S. 109 (1959).

On the first question, one must keep in mind that the purpose of a court trial is to determine whether it has been proved that a particular set of acts was committed and whether it has been established beyond reasonable doubt that the accused person committed them. Safeguards of the sort indicated were developed both to achieve these objectives and to protect the assumption, implicit in the notion that a man is innocent until he is proved guilty, that it is better for a guilty man to go free than for an innocent man to be punished. A legislative investigation to establish the need for a change in the statutes, however, need do no more than indicate that without such change certain undesirable results tend to occur. Thus, in the early 1930s it was not necessary for a Senate committee to prove that any one investment banker had behaved illegally or improperly in order to establish the desirability of increased regulation of trading in securities. If the absence of such regulation seemed to foster certain undesirable consequences, that was all that the investigation needed to show. To "judicialize" the committees by requiring them to observe courtlike procedures would delay and complicate their proceedings. Hence the reluctance of the courts to require additional restraints, lest the useful function of establishing the need for legislation be crippled by imposing a procedure designed for a wholly different function.

Concerning the question of Congress itself restraining the investigating committees, one frequently hears the suggestion that it is up to the Congress to use its powers of investigating more responsibly, as if that required merely an act of will. Unfortunately matters are not that simple. In the first place, authority in the Congress, about which we shall have more to say in Chapter 13, is not distributed in such a way as to permit the enforcement of such restraints except in the most extreme cases. For example, in the early 1940s a House investigation of the Federal Communications Commission was severely criticized both because of its tactics and because its chairman, Representative Eugene Cox of Georgia, clearly had initiated the inquiry to "punish" the FCC for referring to the Attorney General evidence of illegal activity by Cox. As criticism mounted, Speaker Sam Rayburn persuaded Cox to withdraw as chairman. Even the Speaker of the House could not *force* the withdrawal of Cox, himself a highly influential Representative. He could only *urge* it. Second, and more fundamental, both the weakness in the structure of authority and the casual acceptance in Congress of most of the vagaries of investigations reflect once again the localized character of a Congressman's political risks. Most Senators and Representatives look to the day when they can strengthen their political fortunes by heading an investigation of national importance. Even if they have no such ambition, they know that the threat to institute an investigation can be a means of protection against opponents in and out of the government. When an investigation is proposed by another member, they may suspect the motives of the sponsor, but they are unlikely to oppose it if doing so would establish a precedent that would hinder their own later efforts at political self-protection. Thus until the risks of the Senator or Representative are less decentralized than they are at present, the threat of abuse of the investigative function will be likely to persist.

Congressional Careers and Congressional Roles

The characteristic operations of Congress, especially its recurrent conflicts with the White House, are thus a composite of the arrangements of the Constitution, reinforced and supplemented by the decentralized, localized nature of the political risks faced by Representatives and Senators. These characteristics necessarily make the personal qualities of members of Congress important in the operation, since they allow more freedom of action to the individual member than does a more disciplined legislature such as the British Parliament. These personal qualities are in some measure influenced and constrained by the operating structures and traditions of the two chambers, as we shall see in Chapter 13, but they constitute nevertheless the "raw material" of the legislature.

Any institution, political or other, is affected by the characteristics of the people who are drawn into it. A college in which most of the students are only interested in having fun for a few years before going to work, in finding a marriage partner, and in making "good contacts" will differ sharply from one where the students' primary objectives are to equip themselves to understand the world they live in, to appreciate the fragile quality of the things that make a civilized man, and to prepare for a career that will be of some value to society. Similarly, a club whose members use it chiefly to gain recognition or advantage in other circles will be quite different from one whose members belong primarily because they enjoy the company of the others and are genuinely interested in its distinctive activities. The same can be said of churches, business firms, and most other institutions—including legislatures.

With respect to the House and Senate we can usefully ask two questions about these personal aspects of what is usually called the recruitment process: First, what variations exist in the qualities that are useful or necessary for getting elected? Second, what variations are there in the "uses" to which a Congressional position is put—in what the members expect to get out of it? What a Senator or Representative does and what kind of place the Congress is will depend heavily upon the answers to these two queries.

RECRUITMENT QUALIFICATIONS

All Senators and Representatives have certain formal qualifications necessary to their positions. Members of the House must be at least twenty-five years of age, Senators at least thirty; Representatives must have been citizens at least seven years, Senators at least nine years; both must be residents of the states from which they are chosen and, by tradition, most Representatives live in their districts. The typical member of Congress, in addition, has been resident in his state and locality for a major part of his life. He has, further, been actively involved in the organizational life of the community—its business, civic, religious, and fraternal organizations—and usually but not necessarily its political institutions. He characteristically has ambition, and his personal life is relatively free of what his locality would regard as scandalous moral behavior, although some variation may exist in the latter respect. Beyond these rather standard qualities we encounter considerable variation, but most of it seems to fall into two general areas: features of the social structure of the community or locality, and peculiarities of its party system.

The influence of social structure

Social structure as a factor in recruitment is important in several ways. In the first place, it will govern the range and character of the occupational alternatives open to a man of ability and aspiration. In a poor, relatively rural, nonindustrialized area these will be limited, and a political career—especially one that leads to Washington—is likely to be prized and respected. On the other hand, a prosperous, urban, industrial area will provide a wide variety of occupational channels for able and ambitious men; if the values of the area regard these channels as more desirable, the most talented men will not be attracted to a political career—even one in Congress. Thus the Southern states, most of which for many years and until quite recently fit the first of these descriptions, seem to have sent to the Congress a disproportionately large number of men with unusual political and parliamentary skills. These have been men who have chosen to remain in the South and have seen in politics a rewarding and respected outlet for their talents. In the North some of the most prosperous areas, perhaps especially suburbs like Westchester County, New York, often have been represented in the House by men whose talents by any criterion were considerably below those of many of their constituents and of their colleagues in the House. On the other hand, in an urban area containing sizable numbers of people of comparatively recent immigrant origin a career in politics may be more open to talented members of those groups than one in business or the other professions.

If the social structure of an area is relatively homogeneous in respect to occupation, incomes, and religious, racial, or nationality factors, the skills required of its representatives will be somewhat different from those of men elected from areas with greater diversity. The politically significant cleavages *within* such homogeneous areas are likely to be few. Usually they are, in fact, one-party areas. Thus as long as a man adequately reflects the dominant characteristics of the area, the qualities important to his political advancement may be peculiarly personal—his manner, "personality," family connections, and so on. The lack of diversity in the social structure, moreover, is sometimes less important than the homogeneity of the proportion of the population that actually votes. Thus in states of the South where, despite a good deal of diversity in the society, Negroes and a considerable portion of the lower income whites have not been part of the actual electorate, the characteristics needed by the member of Congress are, in addition to those dominant in the effective electorate, essentially personal. In such areas election results need turn on nothing more substantial than the voters' views of who is "the best man." In more heterogeneous districts, on the other hand, how the aspirants are identified on either side of the cleavages and resulting issues in the constituency may be the controlling factor. A member of Congress from the latter sort of area, therefore, will require more skill in recognizing and accommodating the claims of rival interests in his constituency than will one from a more homogeneous district.

In this respect there are fewer differences among Senators than among Representatives, since almost all statewide constituencies show a considerable degree of internal diversity. Take, for example, the division between urban and rural populations, a cleavage related to a wide range of political issues in the country, from farm price supports and urban renewal to foreign aid and minimum wages. Only eight of the 100 Senators in 1960 were from states that did not contain at least one standard metropolitan area—the Senators from the four states of Alaska, Idaho, Vermont, and Wyoming. (Briefly, a Standard Metropolitan Statistical Area, as defined by the Bureau of the Census, is a county or group of counties which contains at least one city of 50,000 inhabitants or more.) Although some of the remaining forty-six states had sizable populations outside the metropolitan areas, in most of them a Senator needed at least a minimum number of city votes to assure his election. By contrast, not only were many House districts not contained in metropolitan areas, but also approximately 15 percent of them did not even include a city larger than 25,000 in population.

One consequence of this rural-urban difference between the Senate and the House is that for the past thirty years the upper chamber has generally given far more support than the House to legislation attempting to deal with problems characteristic of our industrial society—public housing, urban renewal, social security, minimum wage standards. For essentially the same reason the House has been a good deal less ready than the Senate to accept the new position of the United States on the international scene and the politics that have grown from that position—participation in the United Nations and related agencies, support of "neutralist" nations, economic assistance to underdeveloped countries, cultural exchange programs, and the like. Homogeneous areas, especially rural ones, tend to be stable, relatively unaffected by changes in the society and in the world. To lead or to represent them requires skills different from those needed in areas directly experiencing change or highly responsive to it.

The influence of party systems

The qualities favored for entrance into the Congress are also affected by a series of factors associated with the party system. The character of the effective electorate—those who actually vote—has already been mentioned. In addition, variations in party structure, in party competition, and in party nominating processes can influence the kinds of skills the Congress will contain. An active and well-organized party at the state or local level can actively recruit, groom, and support candidates for public office, including the Congress. The qualities the party seeks are not uniform, of course, but they are likely to include the ability to work effectively as part of the organization. The candidate of such a party must make considerable personal effort to get himself elected—and most organizations will welcome a good vote-getter—but he is not completely on his own. He can rely on the organization and the pull of the party label to get out the vote in the general election. In a nomination contest—even one involving a direct primary—he can rely for assistance on a continuing organization.

Where no such organization or anything approximating it exists—as in most one-party areas, South and North—an aspirant for Congress is likely to need personal qualities and skills that will in some fashion substitute for those that a party organization might provide. His chief obstacles, almost by definition, will be in the primary, where the party label is now of no assistance. Unable to rely on a continuing organization, he is obliged either to contrive one of his own or—as not infrequently happens—to cultivate a slap-dash, hell-for-leather type of direct mass appeal that will in part substitute for organization. Demagogic types are to be found everywhere, but it is the party institutions that will largely determine whether the "skills" of the demagogue are an asset or a handicap in seeking public office. The Huey Longs, Gene Talmadges, and their ilk are not an accident on the political scene. Where party organization is weak or nonexistent, one can expect all sorts of extraneous factors—a flamboyant personality or popularity as a banjo-playing radio entertainer or fire-and-brimstone preacher—to be converted into a political career. A Senator Joseph McCarthy was more likely to be a product of Wisconsin politics with, until fairly recently, its weak parties than of the more disciplined system of a state like Pennsylvania. It is not astonishing if an area lacking in any kind of continuing party organization elects a Representative whose chief campaign slogan is "everything is made for love."

The party connections of Senators usually are different in kind from those of most Representatives because of the personal power of a Senator on the national scene. Being one of only two from a state, exercising influence upon executive appointments, and holding office for six years automatically make a Senator a factor to be reckoned with in a state's politics. In consequence Senatorial nominations—even in those states with weak party organizations—normally go to men who have achieved political prominence as governors, as occupants of some other statewide office, or as Representatives in Congress. In the latter case their "availability" may rest on a personal or demagogic base, but only a small proportion of Senators achieve the position without considerable prior political experience. And a well-organized state party is likely to regard a Senate nomination as one of the prize places on its ticket.

The degree of party competition in the constituency affects the attitudes, if not the personality characteristics, of members of Congress. In those constituencies where the margin of victory is slight—one third to one half of the House seats and a slightly smaller proportion in the Senate—an incumbent member of Congress approaches a reelection campaign acutely aware that his political survival easily may turn on how his party label currently appears in the eyes of the movable electorate. If he and the President are of the same party, the strength of the party label—especially in a year when a President also seeks reelection—will depend in part on these voters' responses to the President—his program, what he has done. In such circumstances the recruitment process is likely over the long run to turn up men whose views resemble those of Presidents. The problems that are most conspicuous in closely contested constituencies, therefore, are likely to be among the more acute national issues of domestic policy. Given the differences in Senate and House terms, this is a matter of more consequence to Representatives but it is relevant to both. These, then, are some of the informal prerequisites for a seat in Congress. They are chiefly a function of the social and political characteristics of the area from which the selection is made. Whether these factors will make a man a constructive representative in Washington is another matter. Certainly they will influence the kind of role that a man will play in the national legislature. The product of a vigorous state or local party is not likely to be the same sort of Representative—or Senator—as one whose career rests on being a one-man show.

THE USES OF CONGRESSIONAL OFFICE

The role that a man will play in Washington is also affected by his goals —by what he wants from his position. These objectives will, as suggested earlier, go a long way toward making the House or Senate what it is on the national scene. Here again we find a general difference between House and Senate. Despite the elaborate etiquette which requires that members of both House and Senate refer to their colleagues in the opposite wing of the Capitol as "the other body," the Senate is clearly the upper chamber. Its members, by and large, have "arrived," while the Representatives are more likely to be still "on the make." A Senator may desire to enter the federal judiciary; he may aspire to be his state's governor; he may be interested in a Cabinet post; and of course—if he comes from a large state —he may have Presidential ambitions; but for the most part the Senate is the capstone of a career, and most Senators enter with the idea of staying there. Those reconciled or contented with a Senate career may play a variety of roles reflecting personal and interest group commitments. Those from the South, for example, with only the remotest prospects of national elective office, are likely to become the core of the Senate's professionals, at least on the Democratic side of the aisle.

A Senator with Presidential aspirations—and more Senators entertain them than have a reasonable chance of being nominated—is likely to be an "outside man," what some Senators call a "show horse." That is, he will attempt to use the Senate to gain for himself the national reputation essential to approaching the object of his ambition. He may try to exploit the chairmanship of a dramatic investigating committee, as Senator Kefauver did in 1950, he may talk to the galleries on all manner of subjects, and he is likely to spend a good deal of his time about the country rather than in the Senate. In any case, he is likely to present a sharp contrast to the Senate careerist, the "work horse," carrying on the inconspicuous legislative drudgery which that role involves. The "show horse" is likely not to be highly influential within the Senate, though this is a price some Senators have been willing to pay if they thought it might lead to the White House.

Members of the House also may accept a position in that body as the peak of a career. Representatives elected by some party organizations in large cities may even be sent to the House as a place of semiretirement from the rigors of local politics. But a good many Representatives are "on the move." One indicator of this movement, though imperfect because it is a composite of all kinds of factors, is the House turnover rate. Each two years, from 15 to 25 percent of the Representatives are serving for the first time. A number of directions are taken by a Representative who moves on. The Senate may beckon. In recent years about one quarter of the Senators have come to the upper chamber directly from the House. (Movement the other way has occurred only rarely since John Quincy Adams entered the House in 1831.) Possibly other offices on the national level may seem attractive. But he also has a variety of possibilities in the states and cities. The effect of any of these alternatives upon his style of behavior in the House will depend primarily upon where he must appeal to gain his objective. In an extreme case this control on his future may lie in hands almost indifferent to his House performance. Thus in New York City for some years the most coveted party prizes have been the principal state and city judgeships, since they pay well, involve long tenure, and afford ample patronage to the party in the form of clerkships, bailiffs, and similar positions. For many—but not all—Representatives from New York City, mostly Democrats, the House becomes a waiting place where they serve until they get a chance at one of these court posts. They are part-time legislators with little interest in the House. This is true even though they may have considerable seniority. Thus at the end of the Eighty-seventh Congress (1962) nearly one half of New York City's twenty-two Representatives had served consecutively for ten years or more. But because they are generally uninterested in the business of the House, they usually are not influential in legislation, in the affairs of the committees, or in other activities affecting major national policy. Other cases are more characteristic, but whatever the aspiration of the Representative "on the move," the odds are that the influences controlling his prospects are predominantly in the state or locality.

Almost all Representatives, even if they seek only reelection, are engaged in a battle against obscurity. Few of their constituents know them and, unlike Senators and governors, they cannot hit the headlines almost at will. Most of them, therefore, and especially those seeking higher elective office, are hungry for opportunities to make a name. This eagerness, as Chapter 13 will indicate, makes them somewhat more ready to accept the preferences of the party leaders in the House; it also may tie the Representative fairly intimately to an incumbent Senator; and it may provide some leverage to the President, especially one in the same party. From such sources their reputations can be aided. But the net effect of the need to become better known is for the Representative to be drawn toward persons and activities in his locality that will enhance his reputation; his role in the House may thus become of limited national value.

The Question of Representation

Given this variety in the skills and backgrounds of the men who are recruited into the Congress, along with their diverse goals, one may well ask where the function of representation fits in all of this. A good deal of vagueness, even of meaningless nonsense, is popularly associated with this notion, yet in a system in which "the people's representatives" exercise significant powers it is not lacking in importance. At minimum the idea of representation implies that the government, and especially the legislature, will be so structured that no significant interest in the society will be excluded, in the sense of failing at least to get a hearing.

RESPONSIBILITY, RESPONSIVENESS, AND REPRESENTATION

Beyond this minimum the notion becomes complicated by the associated idea of self-government and what, if anything, it means. A moment's reflection will convince anyone that 180 million people or even 106 million voters cannot govern themselves. They cannot directly make the choices that are involved in setting public policy and enacting laws. Most of them, moreover, are sensible enough not to want to do these things. If they are able periodically to choose which of two or more sets of aspirants for public office seems likely to make the most acceptable kinds of decisions—or merely to throw out one set and take a chance that another will perform more satisfactorily—they are doing about all that they can or want to do outside of their personal and family preoccupations. Collectively, then, they designate elected officials to represent them.

But the inability of the people of a nation literally to govern themselves does not mean that a significant proportion of them have no firm views on any public questions, especially those questions bearing directly on their sources of livelihood and personal welfare. Since they designate "representatives" to make public choices for them, does this mean that on those questions where the voters hold fairly firm views the "representative" does or should choose precisely what those views indicate, assuming that he knows what they are? Almost by definition, one's opinions concerning matters directly affecting one's own welfare are basically selfish. Such opinions may not—and probably cannot—take into account conflicting preferences and long-term consequences. Must the representative reflect these "broader" factors in his choices and thus appear to "sell out" his constituents, or some of them? If so, in what sense can he be called a representative? (On the American national scene, of course, this question is especially complicated. Not only Representatives but also Senators and Presidents are chosen by the voters. When these disagree, who is in fact representative?)

A classic and frequently quoted statement of this problem was written two years before our Declaration of Independence by Edmund Burke, British statesman, philosopher, and, at the time, member of Parliament for Bristol. Burke conceded that a representative was obliged to keep in close touch with his constituents and to concern himself with their needs. But he argued that, as a member of a national legislature—"a deliberative assembly of one nation, with one interest, that of the whole"—he could not simply act as the voters' agent but had to exercise his judgment. If necessary he had to sacrifice his constituents' demands to what he viewed as the national interest. In turn his constituents, if they did not approve his actions, could vote him out at the next election. (They did.)

In actual fact members of the Congress are and must be both Burkeians and non-Burkeians, both agents and "governors"—on various matters and at various times. But a United States Senator or Representative today would be courting disaster if he took as outspoken a position as Burke's, though he often is applauded if he speaks in *general* terms of his high Burkeian duties. Given the high degree of localization of his political risks in connection with renomination and reelection, he may be or appear primarily an agent. His activities as agent and as governor, however, are mixed in various ways.

To a remarkable degree members of Congress are not only agents but errand boys for their constituents. Their offices are distributing centers for government publications, welcoming committees for groups of irate citizens or voyaging sightseers in Washington, and even informal employment agencies for federal job-seekers. They are expected to help get voters' sons out of (or into) the Navy, the Army, the Marines, or the Air Force. They must "open doors" in the executive establishment for constituents seeking a government contract or loan, or a favorable administrative ruling. They are obliged to look after the interests of local industries before legislative committees and administrative agencies, to contribute money and time to all manner of good causes in their districts, and to offer ceremonial congratulations to winning football teams, to high school graduating classes, and to successful garden clubs. Many Representatives require their staffs to scrutinize the "personal" news in all local papers and then send congratulatory notes. New parents also may receive a copy of the government's best-selling pamphlet on infant and child care.

Most Senators and Representatives also spend a good deal of their own time and that of their limited staff on constituent mail. Prompt and careful responses to communications from constituents are usually considered essential to maintaining one's place with the voters. This may be a relatively easy task for some, such as a number of representatives from the South whose constituents rarely write. For others the volume of mail can be very large, amounting to thousands of letters each day when a controversy is running. The problem of how to answer abusive mail may be tricky. One Representative is reported to deal with it in the following form: "Dear Sir: Today I received a letter from some crackpot who signed your name to it. I thought you ought to know about this before it went any further." [15] (The report does not say what happened next.)

Mail is one, but only one, of the many ways in which members of the Congress gain an impression of constituent opinion. Various other devices are employed as well. Local newspapers are read carefully and positions adopted by local groups are noted. Advice (rarely instructions) from close supporters in the local organization, party or personal, is sought and weighed. As frequently as possible visits to the home area are used to gain fresh impressions. Some Senators and Representatives even make an attempt to poll their constituents by mail ballot.

However the member of Congress may gauge opinion in his constituency, on some legislative matters he is likely to have—and likely to want—no choice. These are matters on which constituency opinion is so clear and so solid that he has no option, even if he wanted one. A Representative or Senator from a state of the deep South or the urban centers of the North

---

[15] MacNeil, *op. cit.*, p. 141.

needs no communications on a racial issue, and in all constituencies some policy matters are similarly devoid of the opportunity of choice.

Most legislative questions are not of this order, however. On many issues constituents haven't the remotest idea that the matter exists. Others are too narrowly technical to be covered by the kinds of communications the legislator receives. On still others constituency opinion is divided—or appears to be. On such matters the representative often has no choice but to be a Burke. Frequently these are questions of the greatest consequence—including many matters of foreign policy, such as the supplying of nuclear weapons to a multination organization—on which constituency guidance is slight. Others are issues like aid to church-sponsored schools, on which opinions and demands are so divided, even among supporters, that however he votes—or if he fails to vote—he may be in trouble. The results of his choices here may later produce reactions that threaten his survival, but he can only guess at them as best he can. On many of these issues—and on some where opinion seems fairly clear—he in fact acts like a governor, making the choices that in his judgment are best for the nation. (In all probability, if voting in Congress on foreign aid at any time since at least 1950 had scrupulously mirrored mass sentiment in the country, funds for that program would have been slight or might not have been voted at all.)

Thus in the actual working of the representative system—certainly as it operates in the Congress—the legislator is not completely an agent of his constituency because he cannot be. But on many matters he is responsive, often because he must be. He is responsive to a wide range of views, but chiefly to interests that can affect his political future. These interests characteristically are those held by organized groups, but they need not be. A representative looking into the future even a short way may anticipate the responses of various interests—and even the emergence of new groups. His judgment thus may be guided even more by what he expects future responses to be than by the current claims of various organized groups. Thus urban renewal may look like a good thing until property owners or tenants threatened by dispossession organize to defeat its supporters.

The importance of this element of personal judgment is an essential consequence of the second feature of the system—responsibility. Under generally free and open elections, conducted under conditions permitting remarkably full comment and discussion, representatives seeking reelection are responsible at the ballot box not only for their choices but for what the voters think those choices have been. The two may not be identical, for at times legislators may be the political victims of consequences completely beyond their individual control, as voters react against the condition of the economy and the state of the world. This sensitivity to electoral prospects and this exposure to the reactive whims of the electorate, however, seem to be inescapable costs of a system that seeks stability by attempting to assure at least a hearing for any politically relevant opinion in the society.

RESPONSIVENESS AND THE COMPOSITION OF CONGRESS

One indispensable component in the stability of a representative system is that a demand felt by any appreciable number of citizens must not go unheard or be compelled to seek undercover and subversive means of expression because it is denied spokesmen in the legislature—or elsewhere in the government.

This does not mean that the Congress must be so composed as to be an exact cross-section of the electorate. In fact its members are disproportionately drawn from certain sectors of the population. Thus the average age of the members of Congress—about fifty for Representatives and approximately sixty for Senators—is ten to twenty years higher than the average age of the voting population. The overwhelming majority of the Congress are men. In 1963 there were two women Senators and eleven women Representatives, but this obviously is a proportion far lower than in the electorate or in the total population. The members of Congress, moreover, have had much more formal education than the average citizen. Less than 10 percent of the population of voting age has had four years or more of college training, but most Representatives and Senators—well over 80 percent—have attended college, and approximately one half have earned advanced degrees of one sort or another. Ph.D.'s and members of Phi Beta Kappa are by no means a rarity in either house, and former college presidents and law school deans are included at present.

These differences from the population at large are of little or no consequence for the representative requirement suggested above. The politically relevant attitudes and demands of women are not different from those of men, and, with the possible exception of a few local situations, there is no such thing as a distinctive "women's vote." It is possible that the higher average age of members of Congress, as compared with the electorate, may make the legislature somewhat less receptive to innovation than a younger group might be, but this is highly debatable. Political cleavages along age or generational lines are not a feature of the society, though of course distributions of opinion among younger voters may differ from those among the older voters on various kinds of issues. Thus a study conducted in 1952 indicated that among adults over fifty-five more than twice the number of those under thirty-five thought that the government should do less than it was doing in social welfare. But in each set a sizable majority thought the present level of activity was satisfactory or that the government should do more.[16] Differences of education in themselves present no problem. In any group and in almost any social situation people tend to look to the most skilled—often but not always the most educated—for leadership and advice. Political skills—for example in speaking and organization—are likely to be associated with educational accomplishment.

Other respects in which the composition of Congress differs from the general population may be of somewhat more consequence, although the evidence is far from conclusive. Differences of viewpoint according to social class, however that troublesome concept may be defined, are by no means uncommon in the United States. Members of Congress, as one would expect from the figures on their educational attainments, are drawn over-

---

[16] V. O. Key, Jr., *Public Opinion and American Democracy* (New York, 1961), Table 10.3, p. 255.

whelmingly from the middle and upper strata of the society, judging by their occupations in private life. A considerable majority also come from families of comparable status. Thus the law, business, banking, and the other recognized professions account for the private occupations of most members. A small number, a little more than 10 percent, call themselves farmers. But wage-earners are few and far between, as are leaders of organized labor.

Undoubtedly this occupational or class bias creates some tendency to favor the political attitudes of the more fortunately situated strata in the society. The tendency is constrained to some extent, however, by the substantial fact that the overwhelming majority of these men are professional politicians. Whatever their private means of livelihood, they are men who have spent a substantial proportion of their lives in politics and in public office—and expect to spend more. This means that they cannot afford, and typically have no desire, to ignore the demands of any significant group of voters in their constituencies. Some irreducible minimum of class bias may remain, however. Farm laborers, sharecroppers, and various groups among the urban poor who do not vote, or cannot, are no threat to the elected legislator and have no means of being politically effective between elections. To the extent that their needs and wishes are distinctive and yet ignored, the system is biased against them.

Normally one can say that the "underrepresentation" of Catholics and Jews in the Congress, especially in the Senate, is of minor consequence. Most issues in American politics, especially at the national level, have not split the population into self-conscious religious groups. There are exceptions, however. Prohibition was primarily a fundamentalist Protestant movement. More recent and more critical are the controversies over whether a federal program of aid to primary and secondary schools should include church schools. Even here, however, the Catholic representatives—especially in the House—though fewer than the proportion of Catholics in the population, still have been numerous enough to block an aid program even if they have not succeeded in getting one to their own liking. Similarly, few consequences of any importance derive from the disproportionately large number of Representatives and Senators who are of "Yankee" stock or are descended from the old immigrant groups from Northwestern Europe.

This cannot quite be said of the matter of race. Negroes constitute more than 10 percent of the population, but there are no Negroes in the Senate —and never have been except briefly during Reconstruction—and recently they have accounted for less than 1 percent of the House membership, six Congressmen out of 435 in 1964–66. The reasons for this are complex, and by no means all of them directly reflect race. But fundamentally the underrepresentation of Negroes follows from two factors: first, the still quite general disfranchisement of Negroes in the South; and, second, the inescapable fact that few white voters anywhere in the country are yet willing to cast their ballots for a Negro running for a major office if a reasonably acceptable white is available as an alternative. This means that Negroes are elected to the House only from a few large cities containing Congressional districts whose voters are overwhelmingly of the Negro race. Many white members of Congress, of course, especially in the North, have sizable numbers of Negro voters in their constituencies. In consequence Negro claims have not gone unrepresented in the Congress, especially in the past decade.

The preference of Negro groups in recent years for gaining their objectives through the courts and the importance of the Negro vote in Presidential elections testify to their handicaps in the Congress. They indicate also that some parts of the political system may fairly well meet the criterion of representative responsiveness when the Congress alone does not. From the standpoint of the system's stability, the importance in Presidential elections of the Negro vote in such large states as New York, Illinois, and Michigan may well be great enough to compensate for the bias against Negroes in the composition of the Congress. This consideration should be borne in mind when one hears glib criticisms of the "power of minorities" under the present method of electing Presidents. If this so-called "power" were removed, the Negro might well be consigned to a kind of political ghetto, the explosive implications of which would resemble those evident in the declining years of most African colonies.

THE GERRYMANDER AND THE URBAN-RURAL CLEAVAGE

With the exception of some of the disabilities affecting Negroes, the important point about these "biases" in the composition of the Congress is that none of them is frozen into the system. If they should threaten the stability of the political system, they can be altered relatively easily. As changes occur in the prestige structure and the value system of the society, these patterns of Congressional membership can change; especially if new kinds of cleavage occur in the nation's politics, they can be modified almost imperceptibly and without official action.

This cannot be said of certain biases that derive from the distribution of Senate and House seats in relation to area and population. In the case of the Senate, of course, the factor is the constitutional guarantee of equal representation of all states, regardless of population—often described as the one unamendable provision of the Constitution. This means that in 1960 the two Senators from Alaska represented 226,000 people, the two from Nevada 285,000, and the two from Vermont 390,000, while New York's two Senators represented nearly 17,000,000, California's approximately the same number, and Pennsylvania's over 11,000,000. Or, if one likes to play with this sort of arithmetic, the "value" of a vote for a Senator in Alaska, with 124,000 citizens of voting age, was "worth" about eighty-seven times that of such a vote in New York, with 10,881,000 citizens twenty-one years of age or older.

Cleavages between small and large states as such, however, are not characteristic of American politics and rarely have been. Past divisions have normally been regional or sectional. To some extent they still are, but increasingly the sharpest divisions have been between sizable urban populations and those in small towns and rural areas. The assignment of seats in the Senate, because it favors the less populous states, also gives an advantage to the interests that are strongest in the rural and smaller urban areas. But, as explained earlier in the chapter, this bias is growing smaller as most states develop sizable urban-metropolitan concentrations of population whose demands Senators cannot ignore.

The situation in the House, however, is somewhat more serious, and not for constitutional reasons. To be sure, the Constitution provides that each state shall have at least one Representative. This meant in 1960 that each one of New York's forty-three districts contained more people—in some instances three or four times more—than the whole state of Alaska. But aside from this special provision, the seats in the House are apportioned among the states in proportion to population.

The technical steps in apportionment can be quickly summarized. The Constitution requires that after each decennial census the Congress by statute shall apportion seats among the states according to population. Through the Census of 1910, when the House reached its present size of 435, the conflicts over this decision were eased by increasing the number of seats. In 1920, following a tentative decision to create no additional seats, the Congress deadlocked and no reapportionment was made. In 1929, therefore, a statute provided that the number of seats should be fixed at 435 (temporarily increased to 437 in 1961 and 1962 after the admission of Alaska and Hawaii) and established a system of automatic reapportionment if Congress fails to act. Under this system the President after each census notifies the Congress of the number of Representatives each state would be entitled to under each of two complex methods of calculation (the method of "equal proportions" and the method of "major fractions"). If the Congress fails to act within sixty days, the reapportionment occurs automatically according to the method used after the previous census.

In 1842 the Congress required that members of the House be elected by districts, the boundaries of which are to be fixed by the state legislatures. Representation by district has remained the norm, though it is no longer required by law. It is the drawing of the district boundaries that produces the chief bias in House representation. The major means of discrimination is the gerrymander.

The gerrymander is a strictly American term (but not an exclusively American practice) derived from the name of Elbridge Gerry, governor of Massachusetts in 1814, who was responsible for the creation of a district in that state whose distorted shape was said to resemble a salamander. As a general term, "gerrymander" refers to the drawing of legislative district lines in such a way as to grant undue advantage to the party in control of the legislature that does the districting. Generally the advantage in its extreme form can be gained in one of two ways. The first of these is by gathering as many as possible of the minority party's voters into one district, so that in all the others they constitute a hopeless minority. This was the device used by the Republicans in California after the 1950 Census to create the Twenty-sixth District, heavily Democratic (by more than 60 percent even in 1956), which left six of the remaining eleven districts in Los Angeles County safely Republican. District boundaries throughout the state were so drawn that in 1954 Republicans won 63 percent of the state's House seats with only 48 percent of the statewide vote. After the 1960 Census a Democratic legislature turned the tables, so that in 1962 Democrats won 66 percent of the seats with 52 percent of the total vote.

The second way is to carve out of an area that strongly favors the opposition party one or more districts that can safely be counted on by the party controlling the legislature. An example is New York's Twelfth District, created by the Republican legislature after the 1950 Census by running a narrow district almost the whole distance across heavily Democratic Kings County (Brooklyn); the district voted Republican in four of the five subsequent elections.

A consequence that frequently but not invariably is associated with the gerrymander is that some districts in the same state contain huge populations while others are relatively small. Thus in 1960 the largest district in Texas, the Fifth (Dallas), contained over 950,000 people, more than four times as many as the smallest district in the state. Not surprisingly, the Dallas district was one of the two Republican districts in the state during the mid-1960s. Similarly, Michigan's Sixteenth Congressional District, in the heavily Democratic Detroit area, contained more than 800,000 people in 1960, while the Republican Twelfth District, in the thinly populated Upper Peninsula, had only 177,000 people. From time to time in the past the Congressional statutes apportioning Representatives among the states required that districts should be as nearly equal in population as possible and should be composed of compact and contiguous territory, but since 1911 none of these provisions has been specified in the law.

If the gerrymander were purely partisan, with the advantage in one state or at one time discounted by an opposite advantage in another state or at another time, it would be a relatively minor matter. But it has not been purely partisan, and the advantage—especially in more substantive terms than those of party—has not canceled out. The difficulty is that the state legislatures themselves have been unbalanced. State constitutional provisions, such as those in New York, have sometimes made it almost impossible for the Democrats (and the urban voters) to control the legislature. Thus during the Presidency of Franklin Roosevelt, when he easily carried the state four times and his party elected the governor, the Democrats were able to gain a majority in the state legislature for only one year. (In the 1964 elections, however, Lyndon Johnson's overwhelming plurality of over 2 million votes in New York state helped the Democrats capture control of both the state senate and assembly for the first time in three decades.) Malapportionment in state legislatures has also come from use of the gerrymander or from what is often called the "silent gerrymander"—the failure of a legislature to redistrict despite a state constitutional mandate. Thus the state of Tennessee had not redrawn its legislative districts from 1901 until the Supreme Court's 1962 decision in the case of *Baker* v. *Carr* opened the way to compelling conformity with the state's constitution.[17]

The immediate consequence of the imbalance in state legislatures is that they vastly overrepresent rural and small-town areas. Thus a recent study estimates that over the country as a whole counties with less than 25,000 population in 1960 had 171 percent of the representation to which they would have been entitled on a strictly proportional basis, while counties with 500,000 population or more had only 76 percent. The same

---

[17] *Baker* v. *Carr*, 369 U.S. 186 (1962).

study indicated, moreover, that this discrepancy had been widening steadily over the previous fifty years.[18] These state legislatures in turn are responsible, with the state governors, for drawing Congressional district boundaries.

The House of Representatives that has resulted from these imbalances thus has almost inevitably contained a bias in favor of rural and small-town areas. In a period in which the population movement has been from rural to urban (including suburban) areas, the silent gerrymander alone would have this effect—and it has not been alone. This means that the House of Representatives has been disproportionately composed of men from districts in which the most critical domestic issues of the day—urban renewal, race relations, social security, and the like—have little or no importance. Such areas of thin and declining population, moreover, are likely to be those least informed and least sensitive to the contemporary requirements of international as well as domestic affairs. Thus on almost the full range of major contemporary issues the representational bias of the House has been a potential threat to the adaptability of the political system.

The Supreme Court's decision in *Baker* v. *Carr* is important far beyond the borders of Tennessee, for it has opened the way to challenging malapportionment of state legislatures wherever it exists. In little more than a year after the Tennessee decision, suits challenging state legislative districting had been filed in three quarters of the states, and in a majority of these the existing apportionment in one or both houses had been declared unconstitutional.

The Court's decision in *Baker* v. *Carr* left unanswered a question that a number of citizens in states such as New York sought to have answered: Could a state constitution provide for representation in one house of the legislature on the basis of area—for example, a fixed number of legislators in each county regardless of its population—without violating the Constitution of the United States? In a series of cases decided in June, 1964, the Court answered this question in the negative and firmly endorsed the principle of representation by population in all state legislative bodies.[19]

Since every state except Nebraska has a bicameral legislature and since area has uniformly been the basis for representation in one of each state's houses, at least to some degree, these decisions promised to have very wide effects, making rural dominance even of one legislative chamber impossible. Constitutional amendments were at once introduced in Congress to permit representation in one house of a state legislature to be based on considerations other than population, and legislation was offered to postpone the effective date of the Court's decision. If these counteractions proved unsuccessful, it seemed likely that the state legislatures would cease to be biased against urban and suburban voters in the districting of the House of Representatives.

Baker v. *Carr* also opened the possibility that, especially if the state legislature did not correct the inequities among Congressional districts, the Supreme Court would abandon its previous refusal to act on them.[20] This

---

18 Paul T. David and Ralph Eisenberg, *Devaluation of the Urban and Suburban Vote* (Charlottesville, Va., 1961), p. 9.

19 *Reynolds* v. *Sims,* 377 U.S. 533 (1964).

20 *Colegrove* v. *Green,* 328 U.S. 549 (1946).

the Court did in February, 1964, in the case of *Wesberry* v. *Sanders*.[21] This case challenged the districting in Georgia, which favored the rural areas against the urban, especially the city of Atlanta. The Court, relying on *Baker* v. *Carr* as well as the inferred intent of the Constitution, stated that "as nearly as practicable," district boundaries should be so drawn that a vote in one district should carry as much weight as any in another—that district populations should approximate equality.

No precise measure of the disparities in population that would be constitutionally tolerable was set by the Court. If a difference of 100,000 between the largest and smallest districts were to be accepted, districts in thirty-seven states would be affected, as Mr. Justice Harlan pointed out in his dissent. If no district in a state were permitted to have more than twice the population of any other, fourteen states would be affected. If a more likely standard were adopted—that the population of no district should deviate by more than 20 percent from the average population of all districts in the state—twenty-eight states in 1964 would have failed to measure up.[22]

The immediate effect of the decision was to stimulate further Court cases challenging the arrangements in various states, to induce some state legislatures to redistrict before Court action compelled them, and to start hearings in the House Committee on the Judiciary on a proposed federal law setting standards consistent with the Court's judgment.

The long-run effects of the Court's action were two. First, the decision ① put into the hands of underrepresented sectors of the population a means of compelling the creation of a House of Representatives less biased against the areas of population growth and concentration within the states, a House less biased, therefore, against dealing with the issues characteristic of such areas. Depending on the standard adopted, a net shift in favor of the urban and suburban populations of perhaps no more than a dozen or fifteen seats seemed likely in the immediate wake of the decision, but a margin of this size might well have been sufficient in recent years to permit favorable action on a number of measures important to urban populations. Second, ② the decision made it almost certain that states showing increases or internal shifts in population after subsequent censuses would be obliged to redistrict. "Silent gerrymanders" would probably become extinct.

Neither the political nor the legal issues involved in the problem of representational bias have been finally settled. But the obstacles have been greatly reduced by the Supreme Court's actions.

Conclusions

Persistent tensions between President and Congress are a conspicuous feature of the American system. The sources of these strains are in part constitutional. In an equally fundamental sense, however, they are political.

---

[21] *Wesberry* v. *Sanders*, 376 U.S. 1 (1964).

[22] These states were Arizona, Arkansas, California, Colorado, Connecticut, Florida, Georgia, Idaho, Illinois, Indiana, Kansas, Kentucky, Louisiana, Maryland, Michigan, Mississippi, New Jersey, North Carolina, Ohio, Oregon, Oklahoma, Pennsylvania, South Dakota, Tennessee, Texas, Utah, Virginia, and Washington.

Doyle in the Philadelphia *Daily News*

"Now In Two Volumes."

Zschiesche in the Greensboro *Daily News*

Crossing The Potomac

Two views of the President's relationship to Congress.

Their origins frequently lie outside of the Congress and the government proper. That is, they reflect the local nature of the political risks to which a Senator or Representative is exposed. They also mirror the general tendency for the political stakes of the President and those of the member of Congress to be different. These differences in stakes are in some instances accentuated by the biases created by the system of representation. Such factors produce Senators and Representatives with a variety of skills and a diversity of goals, and this significantly affects the kinds of roles that members of Congress will choose to play and the responsiveness of the system as a whole.

The American scheme thus makes of the Congress an alternative channel of initiative within the government. The resulting difficulties are great both for most members of Congress and for the President. The Senator or Representative is almost obliged to exploit such opportunities as are available to him. The President, given the expectations focused on him in the country and in the Congress itself, cannot safely avoid trying in turn to persuade the Congress to accept his initiatives.

How these attempts turn out, of course, is dependent in considerable measure on the skills of these political actors. The outcome will also reflect, however, characteristics of the legislative process itself and of the power structure that may exist within the Congress. These matters the next chapter will examine.

13 / Congress: The Legislative Process

The machinery of the House and Senate is not a neutral registering device. Like the structure of any human institution, it favors some kinds of people, interests, or enterprises and hampers or excludes others. In short, the internal mechanisms of the Congress involve relations of power.

The Representative or Senator who enters the Congress confronts its internal structure of power and must come to some sort of terms with it. How effectively he is able to reflect the demands coming from his constituency and to meet his political risks will depend—as in the case of the President or any other official—on his capacity to get this structure to work on his behalf. As an individual, and especially as a new member of Congress, his resources are limited. Because he cannot dominate the structure, he finds that he must yield to the demands of those who do if he is to influence it in any degree. This is the chief source of leverage against him that is available to those leaders, including the President at least indirectly, who occupy key points in the legislative system.

Viewed as a whole, rather than from the standpoint of any one participant, the Congress is a remarkable, even an admirable, institution. It reflects the diverse goals and risks of its members and the variety of demands upon its attention from the White House, from the executive agencies, and from interest groups. Through a process of conflict, search, negotiation, and compromise it arrives at the legitimate rules that guide the country's complex affairs. The process is frequently bewildering, often frustrating, and occasionally even disturbing, yet it plays its part in governing the nation.

After the elements of this structure—its anatomy—are described in this chapter, it will be possible to indicate some of the varied ways in which the Congress operates.

The Structure of Power and Its Bases

The most characteristic comment on the political parties in the House and Senate is that they are undisciplined. A casual reading of the press reports of a Congressional session, moreover, will lend support to this view. On most votes in either house the majority and the losing side include some members of each party. Although there are some votes on which a *majority* of Republicans opposes a majority of Democrats, those on which *all* the members of one party oppose all members of the other normally occur only when the principal officers of each chamber are being chosen at the beginning of each Congress. (The votes referred to, of course, are ones on which the record shows how each member acted. These are the "yea-and-nay," or roll call, votes, on which each member casts his vote as his name is called. "Yea-and-nay" votes are constitutionally required only on motions to override a Presidential veto, but they may be demanded on other matters by one fifth of those present. On all other votes it is impossible to tell who favored which position. The House may successively use a voice vote, a division [in which those "for" stand and are counted and then those opposed], a teller vote [in which members are counted as they pass down one side or the other of the center aisle], as well as the yeas-and-nays. [It may also use ballots, but this practice has been in disuse for many years.] The Senate uses all but the teller vote and the ballot, but not successively.)

THE PARTISAN FRAME

Given the local nature of political risk in Congress, discussed in Chapter 12, this bipartisan voting should not be astonishing. But its extent can easily be exaggerated. The fact is that most members of Congress vote with the majority of their fellow partisans most of the time. Thus if one were compelled to predict the vote of a Senator or Representative and could have only one piece of information as a basis, the most useful information would be his party label. Both the records and the statements of Senators and Representatives show that they do not like to vote against a majority of their fellow partisans and particularly in opposition to their party leaders. Most legislators may do so on occasion, but many will go to considerable lengths—and sometimes even run heavy risks—to avoid doing so. (One way of avoiding such recorded opposition is to seek or to accept a "pair" with someone on the other side. Under a "pair" a member agrees not to vote if a member on the other side is obliged to be absent. Pairs are announced at the conclusion of roll calls, but they are not counted in determining the outcome of the vote.)

The basic reasons for this partisan predisposition are three. First is a ① simple sense of party loyalty and identification that is reinforced for most members by long experience in electoral contests and by a vague sense of party tradition. When Republican orators speak of "the party of Lincoln" or Democrats of "the party of Jefferson, Wilson, and Franklin D. Roosevelt," it means something. Nothing very precise, perhaps, and they would have as much trouble defining the sentiment as the fan of a professional baseball team would explaining his loyalty, but the feeling is none the less real. Second and a good deal more definite, the members of Con-② gress have some stake in the popular standing of the party label, as we have already seen. Even those from safe or one-party areas, moreover, have something to gain from their party's being "in control" of the government. Third ③ all manner of opportunities, favors, and advantages are at the disposal of the party's leaders, as later sections of this chapter will indicate, and in various ways these may be withheld from a member who too frequently votes "wrong."

Despite frequent evidence of what is called a lack of "party discipline," therefore, the partisan frame is real. It both reflects and reinforces the structure of power in the Congress.

"ELECTIVE" LEADERS AND "SENIORITY" LEADERS

It is valuable to distinguish two types of leaders within the Congress on the basis of the way their leadership position is determined. First are the "elective leaders," who are chosen by the members of the party caucus or conference in their respective houses or are designated by a leader who has been selected by that means. Second are the "seniority leaders," the chairmen and ranking minority members of the standing committees. A seniority leader reaches his position by virtue of having been continuously a member of a committee for longer than any other Senator or Representative of the same party.

Each leader, of whichever type, is an individual with his own style of operating, but one can identify certain broad differences between the two types. The elective leader, in the first place, is likely to stand toward the center on the spectrum of his party's attitudes. His influence depends heavily on persuasion and on the respect that his colleagues feel for him as a person. An extremist normally cannot establish these relations of confidence. If one does reach this sort of position, as occasionally happens, he is likely to be ineffective. The seniority leader, on the other hand, reaches his position by a route beyond control from within the chamber. Hence the accidents of elections, deaths, and resignations can often bring to seniority positions men who occupy an extreme position—usually conservative—in their parties. Second, the elective leader is a generalist, concerned with the total legislative product of his chamber and of the party, with overall strategy—including the President's—and with the political problems of most of his fellow partisans in the chamber. The seniority leader, however, is a specialist. He has reached his position by staying on a committee for years, and his influence in the house depends in considerable measure on his presumed expertness in the area of his committee's work. He is closely associated with the "clients" of his committee, among the interest groups and in the executive branch, and his world is likely to be confined to his committee, its jurisdiction, traditions, and prerogatives. Third, both types are likely to be skilled parliamentary tacticians, but the seniority leader within his bailiwick can more easily be something of a tyrant. His stock-in-trade conspicuously includes the power to stop things he opposes or to hold them up until his terms are met. The elective leader, on the other hand, more concerned with getting things done, must rely more heavily on positive inducements. His opportunities for dictation are relatively few.

The Speaker of the House

In the House the principal elective leader on the majority side is the Speaker. Although his is a constitutional position and he is thus formally elected by the whole House, in fact he is chosen by the majority caucus. Once nominated, he is automatically elected, since to fail to vote in the House for the caucus nominee is to declare oneself outside the party and to invite loss of the benefits that come from seniority within the party. The Speaker is a man of considerable seniority in the House, though not necessarily the most senior. Both parties in recent years have followed the practice of promoting their floor leader to Speaker when that post becomes vacant, a natural development for two reasons. First, the occupants of these two positions on the majority side must work in close harmony if either is to be effective. Thus for more than two decades the House Democratic leadership was the team of Sam Rayburn and John W. McCormack. Rayburn was the senior and more influential. But they were a team. Second, when a party drops from majority to minority status the former Speaker normally becomes minority floor leader, further helping to make the positions interchangeable.

The Speakership is, like most of the leadership posts in both houses, not just the sum of its formal powers. In the interest of clarity, however, it will be helpful to discuss these formal powers before analyzing the informal sources of influence available to the elective leaders generally.

The Speaker of the House is a distinctively American office. Like his counterpart in the British House of Commons, he presides over House sessions and is expected to enforce and interpret the rules with fairness to all sides. But, in contrast, he is a political official and is expected, within the rules, to aid the fortunes of his party. The situation has changed little since James G. Blaine, who became Speaker in 1869, said: "Chosen by the party representing the political majority in this House, the Speaker owes a faithful allegiance to the principles and policy of that party." [1] But most modern Speakers would agree with Joseph W. Martin's addition: "In order to retain his effectiveness, a Speaker has to be fair." [2] Next in line of succession to the White House following the Vice-President, the Speaker is a figure of genuine importance in Washington.

By a gradual process of development over the nineteenth century, the formal powers of the Speaker became formidable indeed. The major ones were three. He appointed all standing committees and their chairmen, but in the choosing he was expected to respect the claims of seniority. He was chairman of the powerful Committee on Rules, to be discussed more fully below. Finally, he had an almost unlimited power to recognize members on the floor of the House, but he was expected to use this power to grant a fair hearing to all sides and to reflect the views of a genuine majority. During the period from 1903 to 1910, when the Progressive Movement

---

[1] Mary Parker Follett, *The Speaker of the House of Representatives* (New York, 1896), p. 288.
[2] Joseph W. Martin, *My First Fifty Years in Politics* (New York, 1960), p. 181.

created cleavages in both parties but especially among the dominant Republicans, Speaker Joseph G. Cannon increasingly used these powers against the Progressives without regard for the powers' implied limitations. Understandably, a group of Progressive Republicans, led by George W. Norris of Nebraska, made common cause with the minority Democrats against "Cannonism." In the so-called "Revolution of 1910" the Speaker was removed from the Rules Committee, appointment of committees and their chairmen was taken from him and made elective, and the power of recognition was sharply restricted.

The centralization of power in the Speakership up to 1910, however, reflected the inescapable fact that a body as large as the House cannot function like the legendary town meeting with a fluid leadership under a neutral moderator. In consequence, largely by informal means which a skillful man can exploit, the Speakership has regained most of its former influence if not its formal powers. As a member of the House the Speaker (unlike the President of the Senate) can vote on any issue and can step down from the chair to participate in debate, privileges used sparingly by most Speakers when they desire to emphasize the party stakes in a particular legislative question. He still has significant powers of recognition; his decisions on the rules of debate—fairly closely limited by precedent— are rarely overridden; he refers bills to the standing committees, a matter of consequence when the precedents are unclear; he appoints all select and special committees and the House members (called "managers") of the Senate-House conference committees that iron out differences in the bills passed by the two chambers; and he appoints the chairman of the Committee of the Whole. The House uses the device of constituting itself a Committee of the Whole during what is usually the most critical phase of debate. In Committee the rules of debate are more informal, no roll call votes are taken, and 100 members rather than 218 are sufficient for a quorum. Since the chairman of the Committee of the Whole frequently must make decisions crucial for the fortunes of legislation, his appointment—usually for no longer than debate on a single bill—is of some consequence.

The floor leader in the House

The formal powers of the floor leader, a purely party post filled by caucus election, are few. As his title indicates, he is normally the chief strategist and tactician on the floor for his party. On the majority side the chief function of the floor leader is to set the schedule for debate. He shares this in varying degrees with others, notably the Speaker but also with the Rules Committee and to a lesser extent the minority leader. But his influence on the House timetable, crucial in any legislative body, is still considerable. Before 1910, when the Speaker appointed the majority floor leader, he typically was also chairman of the Ways and Means or Appropriations Committees, since these handled a large fraction of the House business. Now he normally holds no committee position, but on the majority side he still tends to be the Speaker's alter ego, and in the minority he is his party's prospective candidate for Speaker.

The whips and caucus chairmen

The whip is a name also taken over from the British system, where he is the chief instrument for imposing party discipline. In the House, however, he has no such function. The whip acts as assistant floor leader. Aided by fifteen to twenty assistant whips selected to work with members of the party from various regions, the whip sends out weekly notices of the legislative program, tries to see that members are on hand for key votes, and arranges "pairs." Most important, he and his assistants run "whip checks," polls of the party members, to estimate for the principal leaders the voting intentions of their "followers" on pending bills. Unlike their British counterparts, they do not attempt to impose a party position. The most that a whip, a floor leader, or even the Speaker is likely to do to "pressure" a party colleague is to say, "We really need your help on this one. I hope you can see your way clear." Of course, a freshman Representative soon learns that if he deserts the leaders too often he can expect no favors from them. Sam Rayburn used to advise new members, "If you want to get along, go along," but he did not mean that they should alienate important interests in their districts.

Each party also elects its caucus (or conference) chairman. Normally given to a relatively senior Representative, the position is not usually one of great significance. The relative unimportance of the caucus during most of the past forty years or so has made it secondary.

Party committees

Each party in the House has a number of committees of varying consequence which collectively are a part of the elective leadership. By all measures the most important of these are the two Committees on Committees. Established after the "Revolution of 1910" to nominate members of the standing committees, they in effect make the choices, since their slates are never rejected by the caucus or the House. By virtually unalterable convention the minority's Committee on Committees nominates for its positions on the standing committees—which by equally strong tradition are always bipartisan—although technically the majority's committee could choose both. Full committee slates are submitted soon after the opening of each Congress, but in fact the Committees on Committees make changes only when vacancies occur. The unwritten rule of seniority provides that a member cannot be removed from a committee except at his own request, and it is rarely violated. The members of the Republican Committee on Committees are elected by the delegations from the several states with Republican members. The Democrats since 1910 have followed the practice of using the Democratic members of the House Committee on Ways and Means as their Committee on Committees, a custom that makes Democratic membership on this already powerful standing committee a matter of even greater importance.

Getting the right committee assignment has enormous significance for a Representative's career in the House. Coveted committee posts are prizes of real value, therefore. Assigning these positions to "deserving" members and getting satisfactory committees—especially those handling the most important business of the House—is also of great consequence to the leadership. In both parties, therefore, the principal elective leaders play an active part in making the committee slates. That they must operate unofficially in this respect in no way reduces the role played by the leaders. In neither party can they have a completely free hand in appointments, but their "suggestions" are rarely ignored, and they have an effective veto on nominations from other sources. Joe Martin could have been speaking for his old friend Sam Rayburn and the Democrats as well as for himself and the Republicans when he said, "In the four years that I served as Speaker, no Republican went on an important committee without my approval." [3]

The Democratic and Republican Congressional Campaign Committees date back almost a century, when the turmoil associated with the impeachment of Andrew Johnson led to the creation of party committees in the Congress to manage election campaigns. In each party they are composed of one Representative from each state having a party member in the House, and they are usually chaired by a comparatively senior member from a safe district. They supply services and limited financial assistance to candidates of the party in elections, not in primaries. Both Committees are formally independent of the national party committees, but in recent years the Republicans have coordinated the financial aspects of the two. Supposed to operate with a fine impartiality, the Campaign Committees are rumored to favor deserving members who are in particularly good standing with the elective leadership.

Each party also now has in the House a Policy Committee. They are the most recent version of a series of party committees—earlier called Steering Committees—which in fact have done no steering and almost no policy-making. For the party out of "control" in both Congress and White House, the Policy Committee, like the caucus, may be a reasonably effective means of developing party positions. The chances are, however, that it either will function as the instrument of the principal elective leader or will become a dead letter. The latter is the more likely development on the majority side, since the Speaker and the floor leader, in collaboration with the President and the Rules Committee, make such party policy as is set and in any case will not welcome an alternative and less easily controlled instrument. The most general lesson to be learned from the history of steering committees, policy committees, and caucuses is that the sources of party disunity are not removed by creating forums for discussion and voting.

The House Committee on Rules

In a category by itself among the leadership elements in the House is the Committee on Rules. It is a standing committee of the House and thus technically is not part of the "elective" leadership. Its functions, however, are so critical to the operations of the majority's elective leaders and are

---

[3] *Ibid.*, p. 181.

"Come In—Come In"

A liberal view of the "grave-yard" role of the House Rules Committee.

From *The Herblock Book*, Beacon Press, 1952

so different from those of the other standing committees that it requires separate discussion.

If the duties of the Rules Committee were merely to propose from time to time alterations or codifications of the voluminous rules and precedents of the House, it would be a relatively unimportant body, like its counterpart in the Senate. It has the additional power, however, to propose to the House what are known as "special orders" or rules which in effect set both the *time* and the *terms* of debate on a bill.

A rule setting the time for consideration of a measure seems simple enough, but its importance is suggested by the fact that most major legislation is considered under the procedure of the special order. The alternative, generally speaking, is for a bill, once it is reported by a standing committee, to await its turn on one of the four House calendars, or lists of pending bills. (These calendars are: (1) the Union Calendar, for bills "of a public character" raising or appropriating money; (2) the House Calendar, for similar bills that do not raise or appropriate money; (3) the Private Calendar, for bills not of a public character; (4) the Consent Calendar, for noncontroversial bills proposed to be passed by unanimous consent. A fifth, the Discharge Calendar, is for motions to discharge a committee from further consideration of a bill.) The only exceptions to these procedures apply to certain committees in addition to Rules—notably Appropriations and Ways and Means—that have "leave to report at any time"; that is, the bills they report can be considered almost at once. But the power of the Rules Committee to set the terms of debate is of importance even for these committees. For the rule reported by the Committee not only may make a particular bill the order of business, it also may set a limit on the time for debate, specify what amendments may be considered, what votes may be taken, and what motions shall be in order. Any standing committee will prefer a special order that restricts or prohibits unwelcome amendments on the floor to the vicissitudes of ordinary procedure. (Rules allowing considerable time and opportunity for amendment are usually called "open" rules; those severely limiting members on these counts, "closed" or "gag" rules.)

The Rules Committee's power to grant rules also has its negative aspects, and these are the chief source of controversy over the Committee. That is, the Committee may refuse to grant a rule, thus usually preventing a bill's consideration; it may make its assent conditional on the sponsoring committee's agreement to change certain provisions of the bill; or it may report a rule that favors certain amendments unwelcome to the sponsors.

If the majority of the Rules Committee and the principal elective leaders of the majority party work in harmony—if the Speaker controls the Committee—the resulting control of the House agenda and the other standing committees is impressive. Normally such cooperation can be assumed, since the majority party always has twice the representation on Rules that is granted to the minority. The Democratic elective leaders, however, through the workings of the seniority rule and related factors, have been plagued by a frequent refusal of the nominal majority on the Committee to support them. Thus from the late 1930s until 1961, when the Democrats nominally controlled Rules with a membership of eight to four, two conservative Southerners on the Committee, voting with the four Republicans, were able to bottle up measures desired by Democratic Presidents and Congressional leaders or to force severe changes in them.

With the support of the Democratic elective leaders, two attempts in twelve years were made to chasten the Rules Committee. In 1949, with the help of Speaker Rayburn, a group of "Administration" Democrats were able to adopt the so-called "twenty-one-day rule." This provided that at certain specified times the chairman of a standing committee could call up a bill if the Rules Committee had not acted for twenty-one days after receiving a request for a special order. This device remained on the books for two years. Although it was quite effective, from the Speaker's viewpoint it was no substitute for a cooperative Rules Committee.

When the Democrats returned to the White House in 1961, the prospect of continued domination of the Rules Committee by a Republican–conservative Democratic coalition led to a second reform effort. This time the Speaker and his Democratic supporters chose to try to enlarge the Committee's membership from twelve to fifteen—two Democrats and one Republican—so that the leadership might count on a majority of eight to seven. After a vigorous battle, in which the President's resources as well as those of the Speaker were fully employed, the House adopted the proposal for a two-year period by a vote of 217 to 212. Members of the President's staff had worked vigorously on the issue, which found 195 Democrats and 22 Republicans opposing 148 Republicans and 64 Democrats (all Southerners), with President Kennedy's prestige as well as his program at stake. It is revealing, nevertheless, that the press described the vote as a "Kennedy victory." Two years later, again with the President's active support, the House made permanent the enlargement of the Committee. The 1963 vote was 235 to 196 (207 Democrats and 28 Republicans against 148 Republicans and 48 Democrats). A small majority of Southern Democrats this time supported the Administration.

The continued strength of the Rules Committee reflects a number of factors. First, the elective leaders of neither party wish to eliminate or seriously weaken it. Functioning cooperatively, it is too valuable an instrument of control. Second, given this leadership attitude, most rank-and-file members and even other committee chairmen have little inclination or incentive to buck Rules on a particular issue. This accounts for the infrequent resort to the "discharge petition," a device, requiring the signatures of a majority of the House or 218 members, to take a bill from a committee and bring it before the House. The elective leadership understandably dislikes this sort of repudiation of central control of the agenda, and the committee chairmen fear this kind of challenge to their prerogatives. Thus a member who sponsors or even signs a discharge petition is inviting leadership disapproval or even later retaliation. Finally, the Rules Committee, as a member of the House soon learns, can perform a very useful function as a whipping boy. That is, it can refuse to report a bill for which there may be intense interest group or even popular demand but which has provoked vigorous opposition. By refusing to grant a rule the Committee thus saves the House members from the pain of publicly choosing between opponents and critics of the measure. Thus at the time of the 1961 struggle "Judge" Howard W. Smith of Virginia, chairman of the Committee, threatened to embarrass members of the House by reporting out a bill requiring Congressmen to file public reports on their income and investments and another bill reducing the restrictions on trade with Communist nations. The protective function of the Rules Committee can also help the Speaker and is one reason why no one in his position is likely to assume membership on Rules. If he can get what he really wants from the Committee, he is delighted to escape some of the pressure that would come if the choice were clearly and invariably his.

THE SENATE

The President pro tempore of the Senate

Like the House, the Senate elects a presiding officer. Though the President pro tempore is a position provided for in the Constitution, though he follows the Speaker in line of succession to the Presidency, and though his election carries with it such perquisites as an official automobile, the occupant is not the equivalent of the Speaker of the House. Since he presides in the absence of the Vice-President, whose position is of no consequence in the Senate's power structure, he gains no significant powers from this role. Most critically, he has no control over the Senate's timetable. Such powers are lodged elsewhere or are controlled by the Senate rules, which are made to protect the chamber majority against a presiding officer of whom it disapproves or who may not even be of its partisan colors. He may have *personal* influence in the chamber, but leadership power must draw upon the resources of some continuing significant function. This the President pro tempore, like the Vice-President, lacks.

The floor leader

In both Senate parties the key elective leader is the floor leader (majority leader or minority leader). Necessarily the majority's floor leader is potentially the more influential, especially if the President is also of the same party, but his opposite number on the minority side may be of only slightly less consequence. In both parties the floor leader is elected by the caucus or the conference.

Compared with the Speaker and majority leader in the House, the Senate floor leader cannot be described by a statement of formal powers. By convention the principal function of the majority leader is to set the Senate's schedule, a function he performs in consultation with others, including the minority leader. The necessity for such consultation reflects two major facts. First, a Senator, in contrast to most Representatives, is a Washington figure in his own right. One of a relatively small and select group, his name is likely to be known both by constituents and by the Washington community. Only the more prominent and senior Representatives are likely to enjoy such personal repute. In consequence it is not inaccurate to say that Senators regard themselves as ambassadors of sovereign states, jealous of their equality of status. (Some, of course, are, in the George Orwell phrase, more equal than others, but the sense of individual importance is real and significant.) Second and equally important, the Senate, being a body less than one fourth the size of the House, operates much more informally and with far less dependence on its rules. The setting of the schedule and a great many other matters of less import are handled by "unanimous consent." This means that any Senator can block the majority leader's proposed schedule by objecting to his request for unanimous consent. Hence the minority leader—as well as other key Senators—must be privy to the majority leader's intentions, if not to his strategies. Since the rules and customs of the Senate practically prohibit any limitation on the *length* of a debate—except by unanimous consent—the Senate majority leader's scheduling function, unlike that in the House, is largely confined to fixing the *order* of consideration.

The majority leader is still the principal influence on the schedule. This is a crucial source of control in any legislative body. A majority leader interested in maximizing his power, therefore, will guard this prerogative carefully and exploit it to facilitate his objectives. He cannot indefinitely refuse to schedule a bill in which even a significant minority of the Senate is interested, but, as in the House, the time when he calls it up may affect its chances. This fact provides him with leverage, with the means of negotiating. It further implies that he is almost certain to be kept informed of the legislative projects, but not necessarily the strategies, of his colleagues, especially in his own party.

The majority leader's control of the schedule can be challenged, but these occasions are likely to be infrequent, especially from within his own party, because the floor leader has the means of retaliating against a challenger. For example, in March, 1959, during the course of a speech by Senator Proxmire of Wisconsin criticizing Majority Leader Lyndon Johnson's close control of the Senate program, the relatively junior Senator was asked why he had not exercised his right to object when Senator Johnson announced the schedule for a particular bill on the floor. The reply was, "This is the difficult position a Senator does not like to be put in. Nobody likes to be put in the position of objecting to unanimous consent agreements [between the majority and minority leaders] and causing trouble for other Senators." [4]

Largely because of the informality of the Senate's procedure, the floor leader, especially on the majority side, takes a more continuous and overt part in the management of affairs on the floor than does his opposite number in the House. Lacking both the close control that may be provided by the House Rules Committee and the collaboration of a presiding officer with the Speaker's power and influence, he is obliged to be on the floor most of the time. The majority leader's ability to function as floor manager is assured in part by the convention that whenever he rises from his seat in the first row on the right (Democratic) or left (Republican) side of the center aisle, the presiding officer will recognize him. He thus retains the parliamentary initiative.

Like their counterparts in the House, the principal elective leaders in the Senate have a variety of relatively informal means of influence which *in toto* can be impressive if they are skillfully exploited. In the first place, the floor leader has a substantial influence on committee assignments, which are quite as important to Senators as to Representatives. This influence the floor leader can use both to affect the composition of key committees and to create obligations to himself. Thus Lyndon Johnson, during whose tenure as majority leader the position reached a peak of importance, adopted the practice of assigning most freshman Senators to at least one major committee. This abandonment of the practice of making new men serve an apprenticeship on minor committees undoubtedly made these men grateful for his intervention. Similarly a floor leader can grant or withhold a wide variety of other favors, ranging from advice on a legislative problem or help in the constituency back home to the allocation of space in the Senate office buildings. Such favors can be converted, in the hands of an aggressive leader, into valuable support on the floor.

In recent decades the position of floor leader has undergone certain subtle changes. These have given a new character to the role, particularly that of the majority leader when he is also of the President's party. Until about 1920 the floor leaders in both parties typically were senior men, chairmen of major standing committees, which they frequently continued to chair while performing as floor leaders. Increasingly in recent years, however, both parties have picked junior men, often relatively young ones, who were not committee chairmen. Thus Lyndon Johnson in 1953 was made Democratic floor leader at the age of forty-four. He was in his first term as Senator. His successor, Michael J. Mansfield of Montana, was fifty-seven when he was designated in 1961 and was in his second Senate term.

---

[4] *Congressional Record,* Eighty-sixth Congress, First Session, March 9, 1959, p. 3181.

On the Republican side William F. Knowland of California became floor leader in 1953 at the age of forty-five, when he had been a Senator barely eight years. He was succeeded in 1959 by Everett McKinley Dirksen, who was sixty-three, slightly above the Senate average, but was only in his second term as Senator.

This tendency for the position to become an exclusive one is partly a consequence of the greatly increased volume of legislative business in Washington. (It is also reflected in the fact that modern Congresses are in almost continuous session throughout the year.) But the full-time character of the floor leader's role, especially if he is of the President's party, is clearly also a response to the shift of initiative toward the White House, which was discussed in Chapter 10. That is, he is not merely preoccupied with the volume of legislative business almost to the exclusion of personal responsibility on a standing committee; he is especially preoccupied with the *President's* legislative business.

If he is of the President's party, moreover, the floor leader has an inescapable stake in the President's program. This does not mean that he is a pliant Presidential tool. But it does mean that he must represent the President if he is to be leader of the Senate party. This point was dramatically underscored by Senator Knowland in February, 1954. Having decided to vote against President Eisenhower's position on an important issue of foreign policy, just before the final roll call he yielded his seat to Senator Saltonstall, the Republican whip, and in explanation of this unusual action explained to the Senate: "I have left the desk of the majority leader because I wish to make it very clear that what I say is not said as majority leader, but . . . in my capacity as an individual Senator. . . ." [5] The floor leader has his own political problems, both in his constituency and in the legislature, which may compel him to reject or modify the President's requests. When he does champion a Presidential proposal, he must rally Senate support largely by persuasion and negotiation, not by command. The negotiating requirement alone would oblige him to alter Presidential proposals in some measure. But in a subtle fashion his standing as floor leader, and thus his ability to solve his problems, depends on the progress of the President's program. In an earlier day the floor leader could be primarily the spokesman, sometimes the chief, of the key seniority leaders, of whom he usually was one. His contemporary stakes make him something of a rival of the seniority leaders, with problems which resemble those of the President.

This new character of the floor leader's role, even if he is not of the same party as the President, has given him a new degree of national prominence. He gets more attention in the press than most Senators or than all Representatives except the Speaker. National publicity being itself a source of influence, this in turn has contributed to the stature of the position. Finally, floor leaders, like other elective leaders of the President's party, can augment leverage with their colleagues through association with the President, as we shall see later in more detail.

The Senate floor leader's position can be played well, exploiting the full

---

[5] *Ibid.*, Eighty-third Congress, Second Session, February 26, 1954, p. 2371.

range of its possibilities, or it can be handled perfunctorily and minimally, if that is the occupant's disposition. Potentially, however, it is a position of enormous significance in the system.

The whip and the conference chairman

The position of the whips in the Senate basically corresponds to that in the House. The whip in both Senate parties normally is the second-ranking elective leader, whereas the House majority whip is in the third rank, after the Speaker and the floor leader. Nominally the whip, as in the House, performs the functions of checking voting intentions, getting members on the floor for key votes, and arranging pairs. In as small a body as the Senate no organization of assistant whips is necessary. The Senate whip also is normally the assistant floor leader, taking the leader's chair whenever the latter leaves the floor. Given the involvement of the floor leader in Senate floor activities, this assistant function adds to the whip's importance and normally makes him the floor leader's closest associate. In consequence the whip frequently is regarded as the most likely successor to the floor leader when that position becomes vacant.

The significance of the chairmanship of the conference (caucus) depends largely on the frequency of its meetings and particularly on the importance of the issues dealt with. Among the Democrats such meetings are rare. Republican meetings have been somewhat more frequent, especially when they have been in the minority (eighteen of the twenty-two years from 1933 through 1964), but their chairman normally has been more influential on personal grounds than because of his position.

Party committees

The two Committees on Committees perform the same functions as their House counterparts and they vary in size from eight to fifteen or more, depending on the size of the legislative party and the kinds of factional cleavages within it. As in the House, the principal elective leaders have a good deal of influence over the selections that are made.

The Senate parties also have their party Campaign Committees, and their functions are essentially the same as those in the House. They vary in size from five to eight members. They normally serve for two years—one election—and usually they are chosen from among Senators in whose states no Senatorial vacancy is scheduled to occur for at least two years.

The Policy Committees in the Senate parties are a good deal more important than those in the House. A major reason for this is that the Senate majority has no scheduling body like the House Rules Committee. The Majority Policy Committee is by no means the equivalent of the Rules Committee in the lower chamber, but, as a body of influential Senators, it is consulted by the floor leader in making his scheduling decisions. Second, in a chamber whose procedures depend so heavily on informal understandings the Policy Committee can be a valuable source of intelligence and advice to the leadership, whether majority or minority. These functions, plus the fact that the Committee, through the floor leader, is likely to be more quickly and completely informed concerning the President's legislative desires and intentions—especially, of course, if he is of the same party—account for the eagerness with which assignments to these Committees are sought.

The two parties differ in the ways in which they make up the Policy Committees. The Democratic Committee is appointed by the floor leader, who is its chairman, and usually includes—in addition to himself, the whip, and the secretary of the conference—six Senators who normally continue to serve as long as they remain in the Senate. The chairman of the Republican conference appoints its Policy Committee. In recent years it has had fifteen members. Republican rules limit the terms to four years for all except the ex officio members—chairman of the Policy Committee, chairman of the conference, floor leader, whip, secretary of the conference, and the President pro tempore if he is a Republican.

Whatever the differences in their composition, it is clear that the Policy Committees do not make "policy" in the substantive sense. A glance at the membership of recent Committees indicates why. A Committee containing such contrasting types as Leverett Saltonstall and Barry Goldwater or Hubert Humphrey and Richard Russell would scarcely be expected to agree on the substance of many matters of controversial character. On most roll call votes they are no more unified than their parties. But on the majority side they can discuss, influence, and even agree on matters of schedule. Southerners on the Democratic Committee may "go along" with a majority leader's decision to *call up* a civil rights bill, even though they *oppose* the measure on the floor. Members of the Majority Policy Committee rarely support attempts on the floor to upset the majority leader's decisions on the order in which bills shall be considered. The Majority Policy Committee thus performs a "policy" function but in the procedural rather than the substantive sense of the word.

The seniority leaders and the seniority "rule"

The chairmen and ranking minority members of the standing committees of the Congress are collectively referred to as "seniority leaders," as we have already explained. There are sixteen committees in the Senate and twenty in the House, not counting a few "select" committees and a number of joint committees of the two houses. Only one of these—the Joint Committee on Atomic Energy—has the power to report bills. The chairmen and ranking minority members reach their positions through the operation of the unwritten but almost inflexible "seniority rule." Once a man is on a committee, if he is consistently reelected and if he lives long enough, he will find himself at the top of the list and the committee's chairman when his party is in the majority. Nominally, of course, he is nominated as chairman by his party's Committee on Committees and elected by the chamber, but in practice the seniority rule settles the matter.

The "seniority rule" is one of the most criticized features of the Congress, and the arguments against it are impressive. These are primarily two. One relating to the personal capacities of the seniority leader and the other pertaining to the effects of the practice upon legislation. Briefly stated, the first objection is that the rule bears no relation to ability. Rather it merely rewards the capacity of a man to survive—physically and politically—regardless of his competence. The essential point of the second argu-

Fischetti in the New York *Herald Tribune*

"Happy Legislative Year—Bah, Humbug!"

ment is that the seniority rule makes it likely that the views and policies of committee chairmen will be out of step with sentiment in the country, particularly as reflected in Presidential elections. Since their powers are considerable, such committee chairmen can resist change and can impose upon the country policies that fall short of contemporary needs. Their disposition to do so is partly a reflection of the conservatism that is usually associated with age. More directly, it is a consequence of their necessarily representing constituencies—states or districts—that consistently and overwhelmingly favor one party. Thus among the forty House seniority leaders in the Eighty-seventh Congress (1961–62) nearly 70 percent had been reelected in 1960 by margins of 60 percent or more of the total vote. In the House as a whole, on the other hand, the proportion of safe seats is normally not much over 50 percent. Such "safe" constituencies in many cases are relatively untouched by the leading issues on the contemporary scene either because their populations literally have no experience with such problems or because the effective electorates within them are agreed on a particular view of them, one favoring maintenance of the *status quo*. In consequence, closely competitive constituencies, in which, it is argued, the major questions of the day are central to the attitudes of the electorate and hence are likely to be conspicuous features of Congressional campaigns, are discriminated against in the Congressional power structure. The obstructive inclinations of seniority leaders, it is argued, further bias Congressional action because safe constituencies are not evenly distributed over the country. Among the Republicans, they are concentrated primarily in the Middle West and among the Democrats primarily in the South, and the politically dominant attitudes in these areas are not representative of the country as a whole. Thus in 1962, ten of the chairmen of the twenty standing committees in the House came from the South and eleven of the ranking minority members from the Middle West; the proportions in the Senate were comparable. In the view of the critics these restrictive tendencies are encouraged because, once a man has been appointed to a committee, his succession to the chairmanship places him under no obligation to anyone in the Congress or in the government; he has no responsibility to anyone outside of those influences in his constituency that are responsible for his successive reelections.

The seniority rule, however, does not lack defenders, especially in the Congress, and their arguments have some substance. First, it is suggested that the obstructive tendencies of chairmen are exaggerated. Long experience in Washington can give them as broad a view of public policy as anyone in the government. Even if they lack such a view, they are not wholly free to indulge their preferences; for, despite their extensive power, they cannot indefinitely prevail in the committee and especially in the chamber against a determined majority that includes the elective leaders ready to use Presidential leverage. One reason for this is that the committee chairmen, even though their direct ties are primarily to their constituencies, may feel some stake in a party record; if the party in the next election is reduced to a minority, they will lose their chairmanships even if they retain their seats.

Second, defenders of the seniority rule point to the virtue that an automatic rule has for settling potentially explosive problems with a minimum of difficulty. This, of course, is why the seniority criterion is used for handling such matters in a wide variety of social groups. In institutions such as the Congress or its parties, where centralized authority is limited, the absence of some automatic arrangement would invite prolonged controversy in the opening weeks, or months, of a Congress, the bitterness of which might make cooperative enactment of a legislative program almost impossible. The defenders argue that until an alternative system is proposed which would work as smoothly as the seniority rule and which would have no equally objectionable consequences, no change is desirable. Open election in a party caucus would invite chaos, and its results could easily be as inequitable as the present ones. Thus it is doubtful that under such a system two Democratic chairmen in the House would be Negroes, but the seniority system has assured that result without controversy. The alternative of election by the committee members would be likely to increase the committees' independence of the elective leaders. The defenders react with equal skepticism to the suggestion that the majority party's Committee on Committees should choose chairmen strictly on the basis of "merit." Whose criteria of "merit" are to be controlling? And how is "merit" to be distinguished from mere preferences among alternative policies?

Fundamentally the persistence of the seniority rule reflects the familiar localized pattern of political risks in the Congress. Until Congressional careers—especially nominations—come to depend upon some central point, no authority within the Congress or within the government is likely to have the power to replace the seniority rule. It is well to remember that when Speakers had the authority to appoint House committees and their chairmen, they normally respected the claims of seniority and they often produced trouble on those occasions when they ignored seniority. A successful challenge to the seniority rule, after all, would be a threat to the authority of all seniority leaders, and in resisting it they would be supported by a large fraction of the Congress. The partial exceptions serve to confirm the rule. Thus in 1957 Senator John F. Kennedy was appointed to the Committee on Foreign Relations over Senator Estes Kefauver, who had a seniority advantage of four years. This would have been unlikely, however, if Kefauver had not for years been in the bad graces of influential Senators, especially the important Southern Democrats.

The committee, particularly if it is an important one, becomes for most members the means to a career *within* the Congress. This is especially the case in the House, where normally about two thirds of the members serve on only one standing committee. A second assignment, if one is made, is to a committee of minor importance. Senators serve on two committees, often two of major rank. Thus not only the seniority leaders but also most of those within striking distance of such a position would feel their prospects threatened by a direct challenge to the rule. Interests become vested and loyalties develop in a structure such as the standing committees, especially if they are the means to achieving personal goals.

THE POWER OF STANDING COMMITTEES

The seniority leaders, of course, would be of little consequence and the method of their selection a matter of indifference if the committees that they head were not of major consequence in the operation of Congress. The power of the standing committees depends upon four closely related facts.

Expertness

First, the committees are in an important sense composed of experts, notably the experienced members of the more significant committees. The Congress requires experts. The committee system, in fact, basically reflects the need for specialized counsel in any sizable legislative body dealing with a variety of complicated subjects. This counsel would not have to come exclusively from members of Congress. In a sense, as we shall see, it does not even today. In the early years of the Republic, Congress relied almost entirely upon advice directly from the executive, especially the Treasury. Standing committees—that is, permanent bodies continuing from one session to the next—were few. Reliance upon the executive branch diminished, however, as the vigor of the Presidency declined under Madison and Monroe. By the beginning of John Quincy Adams' Administration (1825) the essential features of the contemporary standing committee system were well established.

Committee expertise is developed not only from continuous experience with bills dealing with a given subject. It is also encouraged to some extent by the processes of selection for committee membership. Members of Congress frequently try to get appointments to committees whose subject matter is important to their constituencies or interests them for other reasons. Thus the members of the committees dealing with agriculture normally come from farm areas, and each is likely to be the spokesman for a major crop—wheat, corn, cotton, cattle, tobacco, dairy products, and so on. The Committees on Interior and Insular Affairs, especially in the Senate, are heavily weighted with men from the public lands states, with whose affairs these committees are primarily concerned. In turn the elective leaders and sometimes the committee chairmen, though they rarely have a free hand, screen the possibilities, particularly for the major committees. They try to designate men in whose judgment and willingness to work they have confidence and especially to prevent the appointment of men who for any of a number of reasons appear unreliable. Thus a man is unlikely to get on the Senate Finance Committee or the House Committee on Ways and Means, both of which deal primarily with taxation, if the leaders are doubtful of his judgment and "soundness," especially in financial matters. Thus "self-selection" and the leaders' choices tend to encourage the kind of commitment that fosters expertness.

Committees are expert in more than one way, however. They, or at least some of their members, know a good deal about the substance of what they consider. Yet they may be less well informed than some interest group representative or professional from the executive branch who appears before them. At their best, however, the committees show the expertness of the elected politician in judging the possible political effects of a proposal upon their constituencies and upon the country. This the "outside" specialists, except the President and a few of his associates, are not likely to have. For obvious reasons this kind of expertness is highly valued by their colleagues in the Congress.

Monopoly of the legislative routine

Second, the committees collectively almost completely monopolize the basic, routine steps in the legislative process. That is, with rare exceptions all legislation proposed to either house is considered in standing committee before the chamber itself takes any action concerning it. In any organization, to dominate recurrent, routine matters is to control a source of power. Such domination fosters expertness in the institution's machinery. More important, it affords control of the gateways to action. This control may not include the ability to prevent action, but it usually means that the speed and character of action can be influenced. The standing committees thus bear some resemblance to the "subordinate" units of the bureaucracy, with which in fact they have much in common.

Clientele relations

Third, the committees, with their jurisdictions relatively fixed, have relatively stable and close relations with their "clients" in the executive branch and among interest groups affected by their decisions. Other aspects of these relations will be discussed in the next chapter. Here it is sufficient to point out that these relations can constitute a firm "triple alliance," with each partner depending on the other for support. The executive agencies are scrupulously attentive to the wishes of "their" committees, and within the Congress these agencies are likely to be regarded as "belonging" to particular committees in a relation like that of subordinate to superior. Interest groups for their part are enormously concerned about appointments to the committees in which they are interested, and they sponsor and oppose candidacies before the elective leaders and the members of the Committees on Committees in order to assure the "right" sort of committee. They don't always succeed, of course, but they do often enough to make it inaccurate to think of group-committee relations as primarily a phenomenon of "pressure." Such groups don't need to use pressure; they tend to work with the committees as partners. Such clientele relations are a source of defense, frequently successful, against efforts to restrict a committee's prerogatives or to alter its decisions, whether the source is the White House, the elective leaders, or elsewhere.

Authority

Finally, the composite result of these three factors is the tendency in each house to respect the authority of its committees, to accept their actions—and inactions—without a challenge. Especially if the committee offers a unanimous recommendation—including both its Democratic and its Republican members—the natural disposition of most members is to say, in effect, "The committee members are the ones who looked into this question. They ought to know." This sort of thing occurs most easily and most frequently, of course, on bills of a fairly routine character, but even on matters of considerable controversy a bill that passes the House or Senate usually retains the essential form given it by the committee.

The standing committee *system* tends to be self-sustaining because each committee—and especially each chairman—tends to regard an attack on one as a threat to all. For example, there was substantial evidence that this was one reason for the Senate's 52-to-48 defeat of the Administration's bill for medical care for the aged through social security in 1962. The Finance Committee had not acted on the bill and seemed certain not to. The leadership consequently attempted the unusual maneuver of attaching it as an amendment to another measure. The negative votes of ten of the Senate's sixteen standing committee chairmen were not traceable simply to the lobbying activities of the American Medical Association. The threatened bypass of the Finance Committee was regarded as an attack on the prerogatives of all standing committees—and their chairmen.

COMMITTEE RANKINGS

Not all committees in the House and Senate are of equal importance or of equal power. In each chamber, in fact, a fairly definite and stable prestige ranking exists, reflecting the importance of the measures the committees handle and the range of their powers. The high-prestige committees are the ones to which appointment is most desired. Once a member achieves a place on a top committee he rarely changes. Hence the average seniority of the members of the more important committees normally is higher than the average for those lower in the prestige ranking. In the Senate, year in and year out, three committees stand at the top of the list: Foreign Relations, Appropriations, and Finance. The new Committee on Aeronautical and Space Sciences, created in 1958, also has ranked with these three in recent years. In 1962 the average years of service for these committees ranged from twelve to nearly fourteen. In contrast, the averages

From *Straight Herblock*, Simon & Schuster, 1964

"You See—First Women, Then Negroes, Now Congressmen And Senators."

The power of committees to regulate action on legislation is symbolized here.

for the Committees on the District of Columbia, on Interior and Insular Affairs, and on Public Works were between six and seven years. Such committees as these may be of great importance to particular Senators, but they are less generally attractive and thus tend to be made up of fewer men with high seniority. In between, their relative ranking shifting somewhat from year to year, are the other nine committees.

In the House three committees also are regularly at the top of the prestige ranking: Rules, Appropriations, and Ways and Means. In 1962 the members of these committees on the average had served continuously in the House for between fourteen and sixteen years. Lowest seniority was to be found on the Committees on Interior and Insular Affairs, on Post Office and Civil Service, and on Education and Labor, whose members averaged between six and eight years of continuous service. The remaining fourteen rank higher but none of them rivals the top three.

The chairman's power

Within the committee system the powers of the individual chairmen are formidable, although they vary somewhat from person to person and from committee to committee. The chairman usually calls committee meetings, largely sets the agenda, and rules on matters of order with an authority as firm as a Speaker's. The committee staff is primarily under his direction, except for the small fraction of the staff normally allocated to the minority —and therefore in effect to the ranking minority member. The chairman

"Throwing Out
The Brake Pedal"

A Southern view of the attempt to
overthrow conservative domination
of the House Rules Committee by
adding members.

Knox in the Nashville *Banner*

usually appoints all subcommittees. This is a matter of considerable consequence since a subcommittee and especially its chairmanship in a major
standing committee—such as House Appropriations—may be more important than any of a number of lesser standing committees of the chamber.
Standing committees tend to accept the determinations of subcommittees
in the same way that the House or Senate tends to accept committee
decisions. Thus Representative Otto E. Passman, first elected to the House
in 1946, has been chairman of the Appropriations subcommittee on foreign
operations for several years. He has carried the House with him in his
hostility to the foreign aid programs of Presidents Eisenhower, Kennedy,
and Johnson.

The chairman speaks for the committee in negotiations with the majority
elective leaders (and the ranking minority member with the leaders on his
side). He normally represents the committee on the floor, and when debate
is limited—as it usually is in the House—he and the ranking member in
opposition allocate the time among members wishing to speak. Once a bill
is passed he and the ranking minority member are usually appointed to
the conference committees which iron out differences between House and
Senate versions of a bill. Finally, these formal powers of the chairman
(and his minority colleague) are reinforced by such informal factors as
the experience and parliamentary "know-how" of a senior legislator normally will provide.

Even when a chairman cannot compel or induce his colleagues to take a positive action that he favors, he ordinarily can prevent committee action that he opposes. Revolts against chairmen do occur, but they are rare and usually require active support and leverage from "outside." For example, in 1953 the Eisenhower Administration called for a renewal of the excess profits tax. The Chairman of the House Ways and Means Committee, Representative Daniel Reed of New York, refused to hold a vote on the bill in committee. Considerable maneuvering was called for by the elective leaders, Speaker Joseph Martin and Majority Leader Charles Halleck, and by the Administration. This included inducing the Rules Committee to adopt a resolution which, if passed by the House, would have brought the bill to the floor despite inaction in Ways and Means. Under this threat, a majority of the Ways and Means members overrode Reed's ruling that a committee vote on the bill was out of order and reported it out favorably.

CONGRESSIONAL STAFF

The legislative branch employs approximately 23,000 people, who perform a variety of duties ranging from being pages on the Senate floor to highly responsible professional work. For an analysis of the influences upon Congressional decisions two sets of these are important—the personal staffs of the Representatives and Senators and the staffs of the standing committees.

Each member of Congress is granted an allowance for hiring a personal staff, whose number normally varies with the size of his constituency. Collectively this staff handles mail, assists with visitors and telephone calls, writes speeches, handles constituents' problems with the executive agencies, helps with committee work, supplies material during floor debates, and advises on political problems in the constituency. The key people in this group, however, are the one or two top aides to each member, usually called administrative assistants. Many of these, especially on the Senate side, are well-educated and able men with long experience on Capitol Hill or in the executive branch. Some, in fact, are relied upon heavily by their employers and carry considerable influence with them. In such cases it may be as important to "reach" an administrative assistant as to deal directly with his Senator.

Since the beginning of the twentieth century all standing committees of Congress have had clerical or professional staffs on a regular basis and some have enjoyed such assistance since the 1850s. For many years some of these "clerks" were highly qualified technicians who had made their careers with these committees, serving under a succession of chairmen. This tendency toward permanent, nonpartisan professional staffs was formalized in the Legislative Reorganization Act of 1946.[6] Under this statute standing committees were authorized to appoint such professional staffs, in addition to clerical help. An unlimited number was allotted to the Appropriations Committees and not more than four to the others. (In addition to these, the principal provisions of the Legislative Reorganization Act reduced the number of standing committees, redefined their jurisdictions, strengthened certain Congressional staff services, delegated the han-

---

[6] Public Law 601, Seventy-ninth Congress, Second Session; 60 *Stat.* 812.

dling of certain private claims against the government, set up a "legislative budget"—which became a dead letter almost at once, established the first general regulations on lobbying, raised Congressional salaries and allowances, and created a system of contributory pensions for members of the Congress.)

The professional staffs of the committees do not legally have permanent tenure, but continuity has become the practice. Partly because of this, many of the committees have attracted and retained highly competent people. These men carry on or commission research, plan hearings, draft bills, amendments, and reports, assist in floor action and on conference committees, and conduct inquiries in the executive agencies within their committees' jurisdictions. With contacts throughout the government and among relevant interest groups, these staff people are in a favorable position to supply committees with information, advice, and assistance. In addition, any committee or member of Congress can call upon the research facilities of the Legislative Reference Service in the Library of Congress and the bill-drafting skills of the lawyers in the offices of the House and Senate Legislative Counsel.

The problem of Congressional staff is essentially a question of how much. Without competent staff neither individual members nor committees could function effectively. With too much, especially too many experts, the danger would arise that the decisions of Congress were in fact made by staff rather than by elected representatives. Although that point has not been approached, the professional staff of Congress is an important and influential part of the structure.

TENSION AND LEVERAGE WITHIN THE POWER STRUCTURE

The most conspicuous feature of the Congressional structure of power is the absence of a clear and stable hierarchy. One can draw an organization chart of the House, for example, with the Speaker at the top, but it would describe the operation and the actual distribution of power even less accurately than most such charts. There is little that resembles a chain of command in either house, especially in the Senate, and, of course, neither house is consistently superior to the other one. As one might expect in a legislature that reflects the localization of risk characteristic of the party system, power is dispersed in several directions.

The chief centers of power in each house, however, are two: the principal elective leaders and the individual seniority leaders, especially the committee chairmen. In fact, it is accurate to say that, especially among the President's fellow partisans, these two tend to become competing, even contesting, centers of power. Symptoms of the conflict are easily seen. For example, on several occasions attempts have been made in the Senate, especially among the Republicans, to reconstitute the Policy Committee so as to have it include all the party's seniority leaders ex officio. In each case thus far these efforts have been successfully resisted by the elective leaders. If rivalry were not present, however, such attempts would be unlikely to occur.

With the growth of Presidential initiative, with the Administration increasingly fixing the major features of the Congressional agenda, the principal elective leaders of the majority or Presidential party almost inescapably develop stakes in the Chief Executive's program—at least in those parts of it that they choose to support. The seniority leaders, on the other hand, not only are involved in at most a segment of the President's program; they also would stand to lose in the long run by consistently taking Presidential proposals as offered, for they would encourage the expectation of subordination to the elected leaders and would gradually lose the capacity to bargain on behalf of their "clients." In short, their power would diminish.

This tendency toward bipolarity should not be exaggerated. Elective and seniority leaders both are figures in the inner "clubs" of their respective chambers; as old colleagues and friends they may easily have more in common as legislative politicians than they share with a President. This is an inclination, moreover, that is likely to be reinforced during periods when they are officially in opposition to the White House. Elective leaders belonging to the same party as the President, however, cannot be simply his spokesmen. They cannot effectively aid his enterprise unless they also remain in their own right respected members of the House or Senate. They must represent their chambers with the President as well as represent him in the halls of Congress. Finally, the precedence between elective and seniority leaders and the character and intensity of the competition between them depend heavily upon the skills and dispositions of the individuals involved. The powers of the elective leaders especially, even to a considerable degree those of the Speaker, are a composite of fragments of persuasion, obligation, and bargaining, as well as authority. An able and aggressive man can do much with them, but a maladroit or unassertive man can fail to exploit them without seriously risking loss of his post. Exceptions do occur. When Charles A. Halleck displaced Joseph W. Martin, Jr., as Republican floor leader in the House in 1959, much of Halleck's support from rank-and-file Republicans reflected twenty years of accumulated dissatisfaction with what they regarded as Martin's unaggressive leadership.

When the elective leaders and the appropriate seniority leaders are in agreement, the rank-and-file Representative or even Senator may have little option but to "go along." Even in the Senate, with its smaller size and its traditions of equality and unlimited debate, to oppose such a solid front may be futile. When a seniority leader and the elective leaders are opposed, however, the ordinary member's choices may be painful, for, whatever the demands from his constituency, he cannot achieve them in the long run unless he has acquired the standing necessary to make the Congressional machinery work for him. For this he usually needs help from both centers of power. Both sets of leaders, moreover, have means of influence upon him. With respect to members of his committee a chairman can grant or withhold all manner of favors, from favorable handling of a pet bill to assignment to a desired subcommittee. Especially in the House, where the majority of the members serve on only one committee, a chairman can make an enormous difference in a colleague's career. Chairmen of major committees with a broad jurisdiction, such as Appropriations or House Rules, can have in addition a reach well beyond the committees' membership. Failure to appropriate for a project important in one's constituency or refusal to grant a rule for a desired piece of legislation may be severe sanctions. Elective leaders, on the other hand, have their influence on committee assignments, their ability at times to put in a good word at the White House, and their control of the chamber's agenda. They can help to get a favored bill out of committee, in the House they can run interference with the Rules Committee, they can support or reject a request for suspension of the rules or unanimous consent, and they can grant or withhold a variety of means to enhance one's standing in his constituency.

No reliable generalization can be drawn concerning which set of leaders tends to predominate. In the first place, strength is often so nearly equal that the elective leader's relations with a committee and its chairman are ones of persuasion and behind-the-scenes bargaining. Especially with a committee chairman of high prestige and seniority, particularly in the Senate, a somewhat more junior floor leader may have to be more a petitioner than a bargainer. Second, the seniority leaders do not consult together and do not act collectively on matters of substantive policy, so that in a contest with a floor leader they tend to be isolated. But if the elective leaders' attempts imply an attack on the prerogatives of committees or their chairmen, the seniority leaders tend, as we have seen, to present a solid front. Third, the principal elective leaders in the party of the President, through their regular weekly sessions at the White House to review the legislative program and through their generally easy access to the President, gain a broad strategic advantage from their first-hand knowledge of his plans and preferences. Similarly, the White House legislative staff and the favors it can offer may operate as an effective complement to the elective leaders' efforts. But a committee chairman who rarely feels a need for Presidential assistance, such as Senator Byrd of Virginia, Chairman of the Finance Committee, may not readily be moved by these to recede from a decision not to act on an Administration bill, and his powers may be sufficient both to hold a majority of his committee in line and to prevail on the floor.

The Structure in Action: Legislative Procedure

TYPES OF LEGISLATIVE ACTION

In each house the formal actions taken through the power structure involve four different classes of proposals. Within each class the individual proposal bears an identifying number indicating the order in which it was introduced in the chamber, and each class has its distinctive designation. A *bill* is a general statutory proposal and is designated H. R. 1, H. R. 2 or S. 1, S. 2, depending on the house in which it is introduced. A *joint resolution*, designated H. J. Res. 1 or S. J. Res. 1, is normally a proposal on a limited matter rather than one of general application, but in substance it is often difficult to distinguish from a bill. It requires approval by the Senate, the House, and, except when it proposes an amendment to the Constitution, the President. With these approvals (or having been passed over a President's veto) a joint resolution becomes a law, as does an enacted bill. A *concurrent resolution,* labeled H. Con. Res. 1 or S. Con. Res. 1, requires only the concurrence of the other chamber. In principle it deals with matters wholly within the authority of the Congress rather than the government as a whole. In its most common form it is used to express a Congressional preference or to correct errors in bills passed by both houses and not yet signed by the President. Its most significant use, however, as pointed out in Chapter 10,[7] is provided for in various statutes which permit the Congress by concurrent resolution to disapprove Presidential reorganization plans and to terminate certain powers granted to the President by statute. In principle a concurrent resolution does not have the force of law, but when used in this way it constitutes a kind of legislative veto. Finally, a simple *resolution,* designated H. Res. 1 or S. Res. 1, deals with matters entirely within the competence of one house: its rules and orders, the establishment of a committee, authorization to print reports, and the like.

ORIGINS OF LEGISLATIVE PROPOSALS AND THEIR IMPLICATIONS

A legislative proposal, whatever its type, can be introduced into the Congress only by a Senator or Representative. The nature of its actual sponsorship, however, as distinguished from its formal origins, will make a great deal of difference in its chances for adoption. For in a given session several thousand bills and resolutions are introduced, while only a small fraction emerge from the committees, and a still smaller fraction are acted upon by the houses. A bill that is literally the project of an individual legislator, especially if it is controversial, is not a likely prospect for survival unless its sponsor is influential and has the strong support of legislators in both houses, of relevant interest groups, and of the affected executive agencies. Getting such support requires skillful and determined effort, in and outside of the Congress. It may take years of agitation, negotiation, drafting, and redrafting, in the light of new evidence and important attitudes. If the actual sponsor is a standing committee or its chairman, the chances are obviously better. This is one reason why committee assignments are of such importance to a member of Congress, for the likelihood that a committee will support a proposal is greater if he belongs to the committee than if he is an outsider. On the other hand, a sponsor who is able to get his proposal included among Administration measures has greatly increased the chances of action, since the President's program constitutes the heart of the agenda for the Congress and its committees. This applies whether the sponsor is an individual legislator, an interest group, an executive agency, or a combination of these. Without such support, in fact, a legislative project may never get out of the discussion stage. For example, a number of major items in the New Deal of the 1930s—the TVA, social security, and others—had been proposed and debated in the Congress for years without success until President Roosevelt made them a part of his program. Presidential endorsement does not guarantee passage,

---

[7] See Chapter 10, pp. 298–99.

of course, but it at least makes action more likely, especially if it comes when the time is *ripe* for action.

The sponsor of a bill (except tax legislation, which must originate in the House) must also choose carefully the chamber in which the bill is to be introduced; a favorable vote in the first chamber may assure quick passage by the second, whereas bitter debate or hostile committee treatment may damage its chances irreparably.

THE COMMITTEE STAGE

Review and report by a standing committee involves essentially the same procedures in both Senate and House. Most bills, of course, expire at the time of referral; they are pigeonholed. On many of those that survive, including most that involve any degree of controversy, public hearings are held, and the "staging" of these may be critical. What witnesses are invited, which ones are heard first and given most time, what competing "attractions" are running at the same time on Capitol Hill or elsewhere in Washington, what help the committee members give which witnesses in making their points effectively, and, last but far from least, how effective the press coverage of the hearings is—all these are matters on which the fate of a bill may turn. For hearings quite as often serve the functions of mobilizing and testing the support for a measure—or "demonstrating" opposition to it—as of informing the committee and the Congress. Interest groups do their most conspicuous work at the hearings, although this is not usually the point at which their influence with the committee is most important.

After hearings on a bill, if it goes any farther, it is usually taken up in a committee's "executive session," with outsiders, except professional staff, excluded. There it is discussed provision by provision, altered, amended, and voted upon. If no version can be worked out that a majority of the committee will support, at least for purposes of getting the bill out of committee, its progress is ended. In the committee at this stage a bill's supporters will make every effort to get a unanimous report or one supported by the largest possible majority, since a unanimous or nearly unanimous committee improves a bill's chances once it reaches the floor. Any legislator attempting to defeat a bill unanimously supported by a standing committee will, among other things, have to appear to his colleagues to be more of an "expert" on the substance of the measure than those who have examined it on behalf of the chamber.

The committee's intense and often conclusive work at this stage is one justification for the common assertion that the committees are "little legislatures." But a committee does not work in isolation, even in executive session. The elective leaders of both parties may try to persuade the committee—through the seniority leader or individual members or even the committee staff. Interest group representatives, executive officials, and members of the White House Staff may be similarly active, in collaboration and in opposition. The elective leaders are almost compelled to be active in this way, if only to get a bill of some sort to the floor. If a committee refuses to release a bill, devices exist, as we have seen, for discharging a committee from further consideration and for bringing a measure to the floor, but these are drastic devices, infrequently attempted and often unsuccessful.

GETTING TO THE FLOOR

A bill favorably reported to either chamber goes on the calendar. But that does not assure its going any farther. At this stage the problems are different in the two chambers. In the Senate, where things are simpler, at least on the surface, the rules provide during the first two hours of a legislative day for a call of the calendar of bills in the order in which they were reported. (In the Senate a "legislative day" is rarely the same as a calendar day, since the Senate frequently does not adjourn at the end of an afternoon, thus ending a legislative day, but merely recesses.) Only the most uncontroversial measures are handled in this way, however, for a bill usually is passed over at this stage if any Senator objects to its consideration. In most cases the majority leader, after the consultations discussed earlier in this chapter, moves the consideration of a bill. This is a powerful prerogative. For example, a controversial bill originating in the Senate that is not called up until late in a session is virtually doomed. Even if the Senate approves it, the chances of its going through the House before the session ends may be slight. Not only the majority leader but any Senator under the rules can call up any bill on the calendar, and this device sometimes succeeds over the majority leader's objections, but a Senator who attempts it invites retaliation from the leader.

In the House matters are more complicated. They revolve chiefly around the Rules Committee, as we have seen. When it operates in close cooperation with the Speaker and majority leader, their collective control of the timing of debate, of the moves that are in order on the floor, and even of the content of a bill reported to the House, is almost complete. When the elective leaders do not control the Rules Committee, however, it may be induced to act only after elaborate negotiation, if at all. There are other routes to the floor of the House, of course, but they are more hazardous.

Since 1909 the House rules have contained a provision for what is known as Calendar Wednesday. Originally a device for restricting the Speaker's control of the agenda, this procedure provides that every Wednesday is to be devoted to the standing committees, to be called in alphabetical order, whose chairmen may call up any bills reported by their committees. Such bills then become the business before the House. In recent years the House, on motion of the majority leader, usually has dispensed with Calendar Wednesday by unanimous consent. The frequency with which this happens attests to the effectiveness of the elective leaders' control of the agenda. On occasion Calendar Wednesday also may be used by the elective leaders to bypass the Rules Committee. Thus in 1950 the FEPC bill, which had been refused a special rule, got to the floor only by this means.

The House rules also provide other special occasions for getting a bill to the floor. From the viewpoint of the individual legislator, however, they are subject to severe limitations. Bills listed on the Unanimous Consent Calendar are in order on the first and third Mondays of the month and are called up for consideration in the order in which they have been filed.

But the Speaker may easily dispense with Consent Calendar day, and even if he does not, objection from the floor can prevent consideration of any such bill. The Private Calendar of bills benefiting particular persons is in order on the first and third Tuesday of each month. This calendar is less important than it was before passage of the Legislative Reorganization Act of 1946, which banned from consideration most monetary claims against the government and certain other private matters that once occupied a large fraction of the agenda. Most private bills today deal with exceptions to the immigration and naturalization laws. The elective leaders' control over this calendar is strong. Not only may it be dispensed with, but all bills under it are subject to the veto of official objectors designated by the majority and minority leaders. Finally, on two Mondays of each month and during the last six days of a session motions are in order "to suspend the rules and pass" any bill on the calendars. With respect to such motions, however, the Speaker's power of recognition is absolute, and even if he—by prearrangement—accepts the motion, a two-thirds vote is required and no amendments are in order. For a bill to succeed under suspension of the rules, therefore, not only the permission but the active support of the elective leaders are ordinarily required.

CONSIDERATION ON THE FLOOR

For the ordinary citizen the debates that occur once a bill becomes the pending business before the House or Senate may appear to be the most important phase of the legislative process. It is true that they provide a kind of climax to the proceedings, and the tactical maneuvers on and behind the scenes at this stage may set the fate of a bill. But the words spoken on the floor rarely determine any votes. On a measure of consequence, too much has occurred previously, too much has been said in hearings, in Capitol Hill offices, and in the press, for persuasion in debate to be critical. This does not mean that all minds are made up as debate begins. Often as the debate proceeds a great deal of behind-the-scenes maneuvering by the leaders, by White House staff, and by interest groups is concentrated on those members known or suspected to be uncertain.

Nor does this mean that debate is of no consequence, a mere ritual. For the great discussions in Congress, though they occur infrequently, are in a sense national debates. Members of the attentive public not only are an audience for them, but in an important sense are participants. The discussions that these debates precipitate are an essential part of the consensus-building function without which representative government is likely to be a feeble thing. They provide for the discerning administrator a kind of foretaste of the conflicts that he will inherit at the enforcement stage. For the sponsors of the bill, including the leaders, floor debates like committee reports are means of building the record which the courts will examine in determining "legislative intent." For the institution of judicial review means that legislators always work with the courts looking over their shoulders. For political leaders of all kinds the debates are part of the raw material with which personal and party "records" are built and issues are defined. Although what is said on the floor may be primarily "for the folks back home," in a representative system such communication is not a mere formality. Even within the House or Senate, moreover, what occurs in debate, especially what is said by the leaders, may be a most direct and efficient means of transmitting signals and instructions to the rank and file. Finally, the often drawn-out processes of debate can build up the tensions and suspense surrounding a pending decision and contribute subtly to the effectiveness of off-stage maneuvering.

Senate debate

The forms and conventions of debate differ sharply in the two chambers. In the Senate the custom of unlimited debate is distinctive. As we have already noted, it limits the majority leader's control of the agenda, for while he can usually set the *order* in which measures will come up, he can often not tell *how long* any of them will be discussed. Despite this peculiarity, the majority leader customarily is able to arrange a fixed time for voting on a bill or an amendment. Here his negotiations with the minority leader become critical. When he rises to ask unanimous consent to such a limitation, any Senator, on either side of the aisle, may still defeat the move by objecting. This can occur, but, as we have seen, the instruments of pressure in the floor leader's hands are substantial, and a tentative objection is frequently withdrawn after some persuasion—on or off the floor. Such informality and personal negotiation would be an impossibility in a body much larger than the Senate, and it may be unwarranted there. Its virtual absence today in the House is almost wholly a consequence of size, for what may be manageable in a chamber of 100 members becomes more than four and one-half times more difficult in one of 435.

Unlimited debate in the Senate, in the absence of unanimous consent, provides the means for what is called the filibuster, the attempt by one Senator or a minority group by prolonging debate to bring about the defeat of a measure or to prevent it from coming to a vote. Some of the most spectacular physical performances in American history have been provided by the one-man filibuster. One of the classic solo filibusterers was Senator Huey ("The Kingfish") Long of Louisiana, who in June, 1935, spoke for fifteen and one-half hours. His contemporaries in the Senate "found him impervious to sarcasm. No man could silence him." Long's 1935 record was broken by Senator Wayne Morse, who on April 24–25, 1953, spoke continuously for twenty-two hours and twenty-six minutes against an off-shore oil bill. More common and generally more effective are the filibusters planned and staged by a group of Senators.

In discussing the filibuster a distinction is sometimes made between an effort to *delay* a vote in order to "let the Senators hear from home" and one to *prevent* a vote because the filibusterers know that a majority of the Senate are prepared to pass the measure. In practice, however, it is rarely possible to tell the difference. Certainly the most characteristic use of the tactic is to hold up all other Senate business for so long—especially toward the end of a session when a great many essential measures are awaiting action—that the leaders will be forced to agree to drop the bill.

A filibuster can be defeated in various ways, none of them easy. Since an essential for maintaining one is that the filibusterers keep the right to the floor, any of a number of parliamentary missteps can occur which an alert opposition can exploit. Second, the filibusterers can be worn down physically if their opponents insist on keeping the Senate in continuous session, night and day, but this tactic is almost as hard on the other side, as Senators must remain on hand to answer a roll call or to act on some other parliamentary tactic that may suddenly be attempted by either side. Finally, the Senate rules provide for "cloture," a vote to limit the debate, but the requirements for its use are so severe that the maneuver is almost useless. A petition supporting a cloture motion must first be signed by one sixth of the members of the Senate. Two calendar days must elapse before it may be called up, and then two thirds of the members present must vote to bring debate to a close. But each Senator may still speak for an hour on the bill after cloture has been voted. Finally, cloture may not be applied to a debate on changing the Senate's rules, so that the chances of making it easier to invoke are not great. Since cloture was first adopted in 1917, it has been imposed only six times—in 1919, 1926, twice in 1927, and not again until 1962 and 1964. In August 1962, by a vote of 63 to 27, a bipartisan "conservative" majority imposed cloture on a group of "liberal" Democrats who had for fourteen days blocked a vote on the Administration's bill to set up a private corporation to construct and operate the "Telstar" communications satellite. The majority supporting cloture consisted of thirty-four Republicans and twenty-nine Democrats (including five Southerners); the minority opposing cloture consisted of two Republicans and twenty-seven Democrats (including fifteen Southerners as well as many of the most outspoken recent critics of the filibuster).

The sixth imposition of cloture took place on June 10, 1964, when the Senate broke a seventy-five day Southern filibuster against the 1964 Civil Rights Bill by a vote of 71 to 29. This represented the first time cloture had ever been successfully invoked to end a Southern filibuster against proposed civil rights legislation. The bipartisan majority consisted of forty-four Democrats and twenty-seven Republicans, led by Floor Leaders Michael Mansfield and Everett Dirksen. Only twenty-three Democrats (including twenty-one Southerners) and six Republicans (all from Western states) opposed cloture.

In recent years filibusters have been employed principally by Southerners opposing legislation on racial matters, but over the years they have been resorted to by Senators of all camps, on all manner of questions, and, one must add, from a wide variety of motives. The roster of great filibusterers of past and present includes such diverse figures as a Norris of Nebraska, a La Follette of Wisconsin, and a Thurmond of South Carolina, as well as a Morse of Oregon and a Huey Long of Louisiana. This suggests a major reason why getting a two-thirds vote for a cloture motion is difficult and rare. Senators of all persuasions are reluctant to establish a precedent weakening an instrument that they may wish at a later date to use for their own purposes. Despite this desire, criticism of the filibuster from within and outside the Senate has been increasingly severe. Proposals to amend the Senate rules so as to allow a majority a reasonable opportunity to restrict debate have been agitated in almost every session for the past three decades. They are not likely to disappear as long as the present obstacles to cloture remain substantially unmodified.

House debate

Dilatory tactics of various sorts are possible in the House but only within a limited range. For more than a hundred years, since the House reached approximately half its present size, it has been possible to close debate by a simple majority vote (on a motion for "the previous question"). More characteristically, however, the special orders adopted on the motion of the Rules Committee place in advance a limit on the length of debate. Most of the time of the House at this stage in the progress of a measure is spent in Committee of the Whole, where, as noted earlier, the procedural requirements are simpler and proceedings are more informal than in the House proper. Here all proposed amendments are debated, under a rule limiting speeches to five minutes each, and acted upon (without roll call votes). An amendment rejected in Committee of the Whole is lost. But when the Committee "rises" at the conclusion of the debate and "reports" to the House (the Speaker having resumed the chair), a roll call may be demanded on any amendment adopted in Committee of the Whole. Thus the House as such can—and not infrequently does—reject what the House as committee has tentatively accepted. Further debate, however, is normally not permitted under the rule, and usually only two more record votes are taken. One usually occurs on a motion to recommit the bill to the standing committee—with or without "instructions" to the committee. (If adopted, a recommittal motion in effect kills a bill for the session.) One may also occur on final passage of the bill.

USES OF THE VOTE

Determining the "meaning" of the votes in the House or Senate provides almost as much of an occupation for pundits and publicists as does the comparable interpretation of an election—and the pitfalls are equally great. Little reliability attaches, of course, to votes that cannot be identified with individual legislators, since except on "yea-and-nay" (roll call) votes one cannot tell even how the parties have divided, to say nothing of the choices of factions and individuals. Most citizens, of course, are unaware of how their Senators or Representatives vote, even on roll calls. But the politically active—including interest groups, party sponsors, and, especially, the aspiring primary or general-election opponents of the legislators—know.

Roll calls, therefore, are regarded with great respect by most members of Congress. One of the things that a majority leader is expected to do in announcing the weekly program is to indicate whether and when he anticipates that such record votes will be taken. This is not only to warn members to be present but to give them time to decide whether they will be present. For the issues on which a member of Congress does not vote may be more revealing of the conflicting demands upon him than the questions on which he is recorded. For example, an elective leader of the President's party, caught between Presidential preferences and constituency demands, may find it convenient to be off the floor when the question is decided.

Sponsors or opponents of a measure, including the leaders, may use the demand for a "yea-and-nay" vote as a tactical maneuver. Members subject to conflicting demands may be willing to vote one way if they are not individually recorded, but they may feel obliged to vote in the reverse direction on a roll call. Thus the demand for such a vote may in effect produce more sentiment in a particular direction than would be revealed by a more informal method. Roll call votes also may be used as delaying devices, especially in the House, where a record vote takes up to forty-five minutes to complete. (In the Senate such a vote can be taken in about ten minutes.) Finally, a record vote may be used when there is no question about the outcome but the sponsors desire a public indication of an over-whelming majority. Thus on a foreign policy question, for example, a nearly unanimous record vote is assumed to show the solidarity of the Congress on the matter.

How informative the roll call vote is to the outsider normally depends on the stage at which the vote is taken. A vote on final passage usually is less revealing than one taken earlier in the proceedings, since a member subject to conflicting demands may, for example, vote negatively on an amendment and, finding it certain that the measure is going to pass how-ever he decides, vote the other way on the final roll call. Or he may sup-port a bill on final passage only after its provisions have been drastically altered by a restrictive amendment for which he also voted.

CONFERENCE COMMITTEES

The Constitution makes no provision for handling disagreements between the two chambers on legislation, yet it is rare that a measure of any conse-quence passes each house in the same form. The joint conference com-mittees, appointed separately for each such bill, are provided for in the rules of each house. (The house in which a bill originated, of course, may simply vote to accept the amendments added in the other, thus making a committee of conference unnecessary.) No fixed number of members—actually "managers" on behalf of the House and Senate—is stipulated, be-cause the members from each house act as a unit, a majority of the "mana-gers" on each side determining what compromises shall be accepted. In consequence, though tradition requires that the Speaker of the House and the presiding officer (actually the floor leaders) in the Senate include among the "managers" the seniority leaders of the standing committees that have handled the bill, they may influence the outcome by appointing a large number of managers. Either house normally has from three to nine members.

The proceedings of conference committees are not public but they are often closely followed by those concerned, including the White House. Thus the leaders or sponsors may deliberately accept an unwelcome amend-ment at the debate stage in one house in the expectation that the con-ferees may be inclined or persuaded to drop it in conference. Under the rules conference committees are not supposed to deal with provisions of a bill that are not in dispute between the two houses. In practice, however, they may—on their own initiative or at the instance of others—alter agreed provisions, insert new material, or sometimes write a wholly new bill.

The reports of conference committees are submitted to the two cham-bers, where they must be accepted or rejected without amendment. Re-jection sends the bill back to conference, with or without instructions from the objecting house, and this sometimes happens. But the pressure to get some sort of bill passed is so heavy at this stage that the reports normally are accepted. Following such acceptance the measure, as an "enrolled bill," is signed by the Speaker of the House and the President of the Senate before it is sent to the White House.

THE PRESIDENT'S CHOICE

The formal options open to the President at this stage—signature, the two kinds of veto, and allowing it to become law without his signature—have already been discussed.[8] Four additional matters should be mentioned here. First, when a highly controversial bill has passed the Congress—even one the President has requested, if it appears to fall short of his requirements—pressures on the President to sign or veto can be enormous. Congressmen, executive officials, party leaders in the states, and interest groups all are likely directly or indirectly to try to persuade him. As in other aspects of his role, he is obliged to weigh the consequences, for the country and for his administration, as nearly as he can. If he reluctantly decides to sign a bill—or allow it to become law without his signature—he may issue a statement detailing his objections and calling for appropriate modifications at a later legislative session or through other means. A classic example of this occurred during 1943, when the Congress passed a major appropriation bill that contained an explicit prohibition against the continued employment of three named individuals in the executive branch. President Roosevelt might have vetoed the whole measure, but he chose rather to denounce the action. When the three later sued for their unpaid salaries, the Supreme Court upheld their claim, and the President's, by declaring the provision a bill of attainder and thus contrary to the Constitution.[9]

Such statements are related to a second important aspect of his choice, namely, the use of a veto message as a campaign document. Since the days of Jackson's battle over the Bank of the United States, Presidents often have directed their veto messages as much to the voters as to the Congress. Whether a veto is sustained or not, the message transmitting it—and the debate that usually follows in the Congress—often is an important part of the President's effort to maintain his initiative.

Third, the President on occasion may sign a measure but at the same time issue a statement giving his own interpretation of the meaning of an ambiguous provision. Such passages are not uncommon in legislation. Presidential interpretation of such a passage may not prevent enactment of a more explicitly objectionable provision at a later date, when the balance of forces in the Congress has changed, but it lends the weight of his prestige to the view he prefers and puts administrators, as well as legislators, on notice of his intentions.

Finally, if the President signs a bill that he wishes to have treated as a major element in the administration's record, he may turn the signing

---

[8] Chapter 10, p. 298; see also Chapter 11, p. 326, for the Budget Bureau's part in the President's action on legislation that has passed the Congress.
[9] *U.S.* v. *Lovett, et al.,* 328 U.S. 303 (1946).

ceremony into something like a victory celebration. Various guests will be invited to the ceremony, chiefly members of Congress who have played a major part in the enactment. As the news cameras click, the President, surrounded by these dignitaries, will sign the bill, using as many pens as possible, so that each of his more important guests may have one as a souvenir of the great occasion. Like the actions that we noted in Chapter 10 when talking of the President as Chief of State, these ceremonies are not inconsequential. They are among the flattering gestures that strengthen loyalty to him, and they illustrate the subtle ways in which the symbolism of the President as the central actor—even in legislation—is reinforced.

Assessment and Change

The warrant should now be clear for the suggestion at the outset of this chapter that the individual member of Congress, even if he merely tries to reflect demands from within his constituency, must reckon with the complex power relations in the legislative process. It should also be clear that these relations are so intricate, the number of points of leverage so numerous, as to make it often far easier to prevent action in the Congress than to take it.

Over the years, but with increasing frequency in recent decades, proposals have appeared whose principal intent has been to reduce this complexity and to make positive legislative action easier. The common tendency of all of these proposals is toward centralization of power and responsibility, although their sponsors are not always aware that this is the tenor of their suggestions. Some would attempt by various institutional contrivances to set up "programmatic" parties, complete with frequent conventions, platforms to which members of Congress would be committed by unspecified instruments of discipline, and the like. Others would provide means for strengthening the President's legislative role. But all look toward a greater degree of centralized leadership and control.

In the absence of some devastating crisis, such immediate, deliberate, and wholesale revisions in the structure of power that underlies the legislative process are unlikely to occur—whether by statute or by constitutional amendment. The more likely possibility is that these relations may undergo a gradual, unplanned modification, the results of which in time may involve far more centralization than prevails today. Tendencies in this direction may be seen not only in the marked Presidential involvement in legislation that has developed in recent decades. They are suggested also by the emergence of the elective leaders, especially in the President's party, from being the spokesmen for a coterie of committee chairmen to becoming partially rival leaders whose roles and sources of power are molded by their stakes in the President's agenda.

One should not forget, however, that the difficulty of change in the legislative process is not simply or even appreciably a matter of the weight of custom or the inability of unenlightened men to see what would be most efficient. The careers, goals, and powers of important men are at stake. Important interests in the country, moreover, some of them organized groups and some not, gain considerable advantage from things as

Congressional Pugilists

The legislative process has never been without conflict, as this cartoon from 1798 shows.

they are. For interests anxious to maintain the *status quo* have significant stakes in the complexities discussed in this chapter. These are not positions that would be apt to yield to direct assault, though they might be reduced through small increments of change.

Meanwhile it is equally clear that the Congress, with all its peculiarities, is neither moribund nor ineffective. We can assume that the basic functions of a representative legislature under a constitutional system are (1) to give its assent to changes in the legal rules of the society, (2) to give a fair hearing in the process to differing interests, so that the resulting rules may approximate as nearly as possible a consensus, and (3) to inform itself both of the need for new rules and of the effectiveness with which existing ones are administered. By these standards the Congress is probably the most effective legislative body in the world today. It may require changing, and yet out of its conflicts, its bewildering mixture of individual goals and loyalties, local demands, and national instruments, emerges a product of which a free people can be proud.

14 / Bureaucracy:
The Continuing Executive

The glamor of great election contests, the recurring conflicts between President and Congress, and the occasionally dramatic decisions of the Supreme Court tend to obscure a basic and important fact: the national government is much more than all of these. The Presidency, the Congress, and the Supreme Court are our principal instruments for making primary choices, for selecting among alternative actions in areas of major controversy, and for indicating in general terms what needs to be done. But only rarely do they actually carry out the things that they decide upon. They must almost always rely upon others for the identification of problems and the analysis of their elements as well as for the suggestion of alternative means of dealing with them. Within the government these "others" are the bureaucracy, the employees who carry on the day-to-day activities and much of the forward planning of the government. Collectively they constitute what we may call "the continuing executive."

For a number of reasons bureaucrats warrant separate treatment in a discussion of the national government. In the first place, their activities have significant consequences, whether they are seeing that the mail gets through, tracking down a nationwide ring of automobile thieves, keeping unwholesome food out of the channels of trade, conducting research on cancer, advising on a land-reform program in Iran, or reviewing your income-tax return. In the second place, the problems of these participants in the governmental process are often different from those that we have encountered in discussing the Presidency and the Congress. Third, because the powers they exercise are broad, the place of the bureaucracy in a representative system is a matter of major and continuing importance. As we noted in Chapter 12 in discussing the members of the Cabinet, the fact that they are "under" the Chief Executive on an organization chart or in a constitutional sense are nominally his subordinates may say very little about the influences to which they are in fact responsive or about the lines of responsibility that in fact affect their conduct.

The Nature of Bureaucracy

In ordinary parlance the term "bureaucracy" is one of abuse. Applied usually to government, it most frequently implies an organization encumbered with an excess of paper work and other red tape, manned by persons who are underworked if not overpaid, inefficient, and insensitive to the needs of those who are dependent on their services. As the word will be used here, a bureaucracy may have some or all of these characteristics, but it need not have any of them. Analytically "bureaucracy" is a neutral term, applying to a particular form of activity, like "transportation," which may be good or bad depending on who is transporting what, for what purposes.

In this neutral sense "bureaucracy" refers to the particular institutional form that legal authority tends to take in large organizations. Legal authority in turn is a right to command that is derived from general rules formulated through known and standardized processes. Distinguishable from, for example, authority based on tradition—as with the headman of a primitive tribe—or on the holder's personal qualities—as with the leader of a street-corner gang—legal authority is characteristic of large complex organizations. Hence it and its organizational form, bureaucracy, tend to be conspicuous features of modern industrialized societies, not only in their governments but in many corporations, universities, churches, foundations, and even professional baseball teams.

Bureaucracy, especially in government, has three basic characteristics. First, it involves a specialization of duties, subdivided and assigned to particular jurisdictions or offices that have a prescribed relationship, usually in the form of a hierarchy. A modern army, with its many activities arranged in units, each composing part of a larger one and all headed by a commander in chief, is an obvious example. Second, the behavior of the people occupying these various offices is guided by known, general rules, but this guidance ordinarily does not extend to every detail of conduct in the office. The rules, moreover, deal with the relations both of the parts of the organization to one another and of the organization to those outside of it; they can be changed only by legal authority. Third, the power that is legitimately exercised is an attribute of the office with its legally defined duties, not of the person who holds it. Thus when I am told to make a change in my income-tax return, my obedience is not to a certain dark-haired man named Samuel Jones, who lives in a California-style ranch house in the suburbs and grows those handsome begonias. It is to the Deputy Assistant District Director of Internal Revenue, enforcing the directives of the Regional Commissioner, the Commissioner of the Internal Revenue Service, and the Secretary of the Treasury.

This rather abstract discussion of bureaucracy is helpful for two reasons. First, it suggests the chief reasons why administrative action in a large organization like the executive branch tends to take the bureaucratic form. Without a standard arrangement of offices or jurisdictions and without the guidance of general rules—laws and regulations—subdivision of duties would produce only chaos. The behavior of the occupants of these offices would be unpredictable, not only to the outsider but also among themselves. The conduct of a large and complicated enterprise would be next to impossible. Second, an examination of the ways in which administration in the federal government follows or differs from this rather simple and abstract pattern and why will contribute to an understanding of the continuing executive and of the government as a whole.

Size and Composition of the Bureaucracy

The United States Government is by any standard much the largest employer in the country. The total number of civilian employees in the executive branch varies slightly from month to month and year to year, but for more than a decade it has been approximately 2,400,000. (Employees of the judicial and legislative branches, even though they include the staff of the General Accounting Office and of the Government Printing Office, would add a mere 28,000 more.) To this total the uniformed personnel of the military services can properly be added, since technically they are part of the bureaucracy. Including these—Army, Navy, Air Force, Marines, and Coast Guard—would more than double the civilian numbers, bringing the total to somewhat more than 5 million.

Since figures of this magnitude by themselves tend to lack meaning, a few comparisons will suggest some of their implications. The executive branch of the federal government has more employees, counting only the 2,400,000 civilians, than the combined total for the steel industry, the automobile industry, and the aircraft manufacturing industry (approximately 2,225,000). The entire population of the six smallest states in the Union in 1960 was nearly 100,000 less than the number of civilian bureaucrats in the executive branch. This population of employees is more than three times as large as the whole population of San Francisco in 1960, one and one-half times as large as that of Detroit, and nearly four times as large as that of New Orleans or Boston.

But these figures on the bureaucracy imply more than the mere size that is immediately suggested by such comparisons. They point, in the first place, to an enormous and continuing problem of organization. Further, since no one could comprehend the details of operation and management for more than a segment of this structure, they indicate the critical importance of means for communicating to the central points in the system the most significant problems of current administration. Third, they suggest that in a great many matters—perhaps most—initiative must be taken in positions organizationally far removed from the White House and from Capitol Hill. Finally, given the necessity for such dispersed initiative, these numbers indicate the importance of devices that may help to assure the responsibility of those bureaucrats who make significant choices—responsibility not only to superiors within the structure but also to the values and standards of the society.

These problems, although they are common to the whole bureaucracy, are concentrated in particular portions of it. Nearly half of the *civilians* in the executive branch (44 percent) are employed in the Department of Defense. Approximately another quarter (24 percent) are in the Post Office Department, and roughly 7 percent work for the Veterans Administration. These agencies, the three largest in the government, thus account for three quarters of all the civil servants in the executive branch. The other eight departments and several dozen independent agencies, which perform all the activities of the federal government not accounted for by these three giants, employ only about one quarter of the total. They range in size from over 90,000 in the Department of Agriculture and nearly 80,000 in the Treasury Department (the two next largest) to approximately a hundred in the National Science Foundation.

Although one tends to associate government and the bureaucracy with Washington, the vast majority of civil servants are scattered over the country and, in fact, over the globe. Only about 10 percent of the total are located in the District of Columbia and the surrounding parts of the Washington metropolitan area. Of the other 90 percent a good many probably have never been in the capital except as tourists. Approximately 165,000 employees, about 7 percent of the total, are even stationed outside the United States. Most of these are employed by the Department of Defense (almost two thirds) and the Department of State, about half of whose overseas personnel are in the foreign aid program.

The bureaucracy in general can be characterized, but to speak of a typical bureaucrat would be misleading. In the first place, by no means all civil servants are "white-collar" workers with clerical desk jobs. About 30 percent are "blue-collar" employees, the majority of them working in arsenals, shipyards, and other such establishments operated by the armed services. Included in the remainder, moreover, is an enormous variety of the most skilled personnel in the society: about 10,000 mathematicians and statisticians, nearly 50,000 professional medical people, several thousand chemists and physicists, psychologists, veterinarians, librarians, lawyers, economists, and engineers, to mention only some of the more numerous. Almost every recognized occupation in the society is represented, so that if one asks what bureaucrats do, one answer is that collectively they do about all the kinds of things that are to be done in the society.

Forms of Administrative Action

It is possible, however, to classify the activities of administrative *units* into four broad types. Any one unit may engage in several or even all four, and in each a wide variety of occupations may be involved. Thus the enforcement activities of the Food and Drug Administration require the services of chemists, biologists, physicians, lawyers, and accountants, among others. An examination of the principal forms of administration will simplify the task of analyzing the bureaucracy and the problems concerning its place in the governmental system.

LAW ENFORCEMENT

Perhaps the most familiar stereotype of government administration is the policeman, since the most elementary function of any government is the maintenance of peace and order within its jurisdiction. Thus the most ancient form of administrative or bureaucratic action is the detection, apprehension, and prosecution of those who have acted in violation of the laws. Of course, under our federal system most crimes against persons or property are the concerns of the states and the localities. But a considerable number

"Return Of The Snake Oil Man"

A caricature of the unscrupulous drug manufacturer—a target of bureaucratic enforcement agencies.

© 1959 by Bill Mauldin
From *What's Got Your Back Up?* Harper & Row

of federal statutes carry criminal and closely related penalties. Thus a conspiracy in restraint of trade involves criminal penalties under the anti-trust laws; deliberate failure to report taxable income is similarly punishable, as are the importation of narcotic drugs into the country without a permit and any number of attempts to defraud the government; violations of agricultural marketing quotas are subject to penalty, as is failure to pay employees the minimum hourly wage required of most types of business; and it is also a federal offense to transport a stolen motor vehicle across a state boundary or to sell certain types of dangerous drugs without a prescription.

The prosecution of alleged violations of federal law is chiefly the responsibility of the Department of Justice and its United States Attorneys. This Department, and especially the Federal Bureau of Investigation, also does much of the detection and apprehension work, particularly in connection with some of the more serious crimes such as kidnaping. But most other agencies in the executive branch that have enforcement responsibilities do their own detection and other work preceding prosecution. They frequently participate also in the prosecution phase.

The most important point to note in connection with enforcement—as with the other forms of administrative action—is that it inevitably involves choice. Partly because the staff and financial resources of any agency are limited, the administrators must choose which lines of enforcement to emphasize, which of many likely types of violation to investigate, which apparent violations are clear enough to be referred to the Department of Justice, which (in some situations) should be settled without formal prosecution, and so on. For example, the Internal Revenue Service obviously cannot examine in detail every one of the approximately 60 million individual and corporate income-tax returns filed each year. Some choice must be made among various ways of selecting the ones to be examined closely; when evidence of false reporting is found, a decision must be made on how many of the violator's previous returns should be reopened; when the investigation is complete, someone must decide whether the violations appear to have been deliberate, requiring criminal prosecution, or whether they were errors made in good faith, calling for only a financial settlement.

Such choices, inescapably involved in enforcement, necessarily set policy. Hence they inevitably lead to the questions of how and under what limitations the choices are made. They raise, in other words, the problems of organization, communication, and responsibility, which earlier in the chapter were described as the central problems of bureaucracy.

ADMINISTRATIVE LEGISLATION

Determining policy is a relatively obvious feature of the second form of administrative action, administrative legislation. This form derives chiefly from the increasingly common practice of Congress of enacting legislation which sets only broad policies, leaving to the executive branch the formulation of detailed rules and regulations for making such policies effective. Such quasi-legislative power has always been a feature of administration to some degree, but it has increased enormously as government has become involved in the highly complex, technical, and rapidly changing problems of contemporary society. Thus, in the years immediately following the Civil War, attempts by state legislatures to fix railroad rates by statute were a hopeless failure because such legislation could not take into account the varied circumstances of railroad operation and could not rapidly enough adapt to changes in those circumstances. Hence, first in the states and later in the national government the actual fixing of such rates was delegated to administrative agencies. The courts early declared, moreover, that such delegation of legislative power did not violate the constitutional separation of powers provided that the statutes contained appropriate standards to guide administrative discretion.[1]

This administrative power may take the form of "rules" or "regulations" applicable to a whole class of persons or situations, which is administrative legislation in the strict sense.[2] Or it may take the form of "orders" or "directives" applying to particular persons, organizations, or situations. The standards guiding these determinations may be fairly precise or, more characteristically, quite general. Thus standards of composition or purity may be set for drugs that may be sold in interstate commerce; a set of freight rates may be established for certain types of railroads; safety devices may

---

[1] *Grimand* v. *U.S.*, 220 U.S. 506 (1911). See also *Field* v. *Clark*, 143 U.S. 649 (1892) and *Hampton and Co.* v. *U.S.*, 276 U.S. 394 (1928). But compare *Schechter* v. *U.S.*, 295 U.S. 495 (1935). For further details on administrative legislation see Chapter 20, pp. 648–51.

[2] Since 1935 all such actions of general application have been published in the *Federal Register*, issued daily in Washington.

be prescribed for commercial aircraft; certain types of expenditures may be declared business expenses for income-tax purposes; bridges over navigable streams that "unreasonably obstruct" navigation may be removed or altered; railroad consolidations found to be "in the public interest" may be approved; aid may be granted to Iron Curtain countries if it is found to be in the "interests of national security"; and so on.

When the guiding standards are vague and the decisions to be made in issuing rules and orders are of major consequence to important interests in the society, administrative legislation may be highly controversial. It may therefore be conducted in circumstances of conflict different in form but not in intensity from those at the Congressional stage. For in a good many cases the decision in Congress may be, in effect, to pass on to the administrator unresolved and politically explosive conflicts thinly disguised by ambiguous verbal "standards." This shifting of the contest to the administrative arena may be an inescapable consequence of the technicality of the problems involved; it often may be the result of a compromise agreed on as the only way to create a majority enabling the legislation to pass. Whatever the reasons, however, the criteria that in fact guide administrative legislation are a matter of consequence for the functioning of the governmental system.

3 ADMINISTRATIVE ADJUDICATION

The quasi-judicial form of administrative action has already been introduced in Chapter 11, where the independent regulatory agencies were discussed.[3] It involves decisions on charges of law violation or in connection with disputes between individuals or organizations subject to the agencies' jurisdiction. Examples of the first type would be a charge by the Department of Agriculture that a licensee handling poultry in a regulated market had violated trading regulations or a dispute between an inventor and the Patent Office over denial of a patent. Examples of the second are disputes between unions and employers involving charges of unfair labor practices as defined in the labor relations statutes or disputes between rival claimants to a television channel.

The procedures involved in administrative adjudication, along with those of administrative legislation, have been matters of considerable controversy for more than two decades. Efforts have been made to make these actions conform to the procedures of the courts, to "judicialize" them, particularly in cases where the same agency issues the rules and also adjudicates disputes arising under them. Some of these we shall discuss later in connection with the Federal Administrative Procedure Act of 1946. Here the point of importance is that administrative adjudication frequently involves the making of choices of great consequence not only to the immediate parties but also to the society in general.

4 DIRECT OPERATIONS

No single term quite adequately covers the enormous range of enterprises and services performed by and for the federal government. Such

---

[3] Chapter 11, p. 343. Further details appear in Chapter 20, pp. 651–59.

direct operations, however, constitute a very large part of its administrative activity.

The Post Office service is the most obvious example, but the list also includes the operation of the national parks, national forests, and other public lands; the generation and sale of electric power by the Tennessee Valley Authority, the Bonneville Power Administration, and other agencies; the operation of the Panama Canal and various related businesses in the Canal Zone; the protection of bank deposits through the Federal Deposit Insurance Corporation; the provision of a wide range of loans, grants, and insurance programs for private and public housing, slum clearance, and urban renewal; the supply of hospital and medical services for veterans and their dependents; the operation of arsenals, shipyards, and atomic energy installations; the management of a pension system covering some 60 million people under social security; and the operation of a large number of research enterprises, including the most extensive medical research facilities in the country. With all these the list is still far from complete.

In addition one should include under direct government operations the very large volume of work that is performed by contract with private enterprises for supplies and services of various sorts. This represents several billion dollars spent annually for scientific research and development, most of it by contracts drawn by the Defense Department, the Atomic Energy Commission, and the National Aeronautics and Space Administration. It would also include far larger amounts in contracts for equipment and supplies, especially military items.

The making of policy through the exercise of choice is an inescapable part of the conduct of all such operations. In some instances the activities, especially old and established ones, are fairly removed from controversy, and the choices that are made by their administrators are therefore of limited consequence. Other choices, however, may affect the livelihood of individuals, corporations, and whole states. The economic dependencies that direct operation involves may create conditions in which it becomes difficult or impossible to take decisions that may otherwise be called for. Military requirements, for example, may in objective terms indicate the wisdom of eliminating further production of an aircraft or missile. If the economy of a whole area, such as Southern California, is heavily dependent upon such production, however, objective military requirements may not be the controlling factor in a decision.

Factors Affecting Bureaucratic Performance

Whatever the form of administrative action, the making of policy by the bureaucracy is a natural and inevitable accompaniment. The pattern of such choices and the forms of influence forces to which they respond hence become matters of importance and need to be understood.

ORGANIZATIONAL FORMS

The organization of the bureaucracy—the units into which a department is divided, the duties assigned them, and the way in which they are related to one another, both in form and in fact—is a fundamental determinant of its performance, of what kinds of choices are made and how. "Organization" has been usefully defined as "the structure of authoritative and habitual personal interrelations in an administrative system." [4] In Chapter 13 we have already seen some of the consequences that organization can have in a nonadministrative situation, the Congress. It is clear from the discussion there that the structure and distribution of authority in the two chambers, among committees, and among types of leaders make a difference in the kinds of choices or policies that the legislature produces. One form of "authoritative and habitual" relations emphasizes or encourages certain kinds of choices, certain criteria of selection, while another form fosters altogether different emphases and selections.

Take a familiar example of organization in another nonadministrative setting, student government. On most college campuses representatives on the governing body are chosen in one of three ways: by classes, by schools, or by social units (fraternities and sororities). The goals and perspectives in each of these types of unit are somewhat different. The content of the habitual relations that they involve differs. Hence the selection of one or another of these units of organization tends to give priority to a distinctive set of interests.

Organization and theories of organization are a large and complex area of study. This complexity reflects the recognition in recent years that "rules" and "principles" of organization necessarily rest on knowledge and assumptions about human behavior in general.[5] Nevertheless, in talking about administrative organization it has been customary to distinguish four alternative emphases in structuring units and their relationships to other units: (1) function or purpose, such as transporting and delivering the mail; (2) process, such as accounting or biological research; (3) clientele, such as veterans or exporters; and (4) place or geographic area, such as a multipurpose unit covering a river basin like the Missouri Valley. If the major divisions in an organization emphasize one of these criteria, their subdivisions will follow one or more of the others. Thus the *function* of handling the mail may be subdivided into the processes of finance, real estate management, transportation, and so on.

The major units of the federal bureaucracy are the Departments and the independent agencies. They have various bases of organization, usually that of function or clientele. (The criterion of place is comparatively rare as a primary basis of structure, since most departments and agencies are at least nominally nationwide organizations.) None of the ten Cabinet-level Departments can be neatly and completely classified by any one of the four listed criteria. They reflect the factors—essentially political factors, of course—responsible for their establishment and development.

The oldest (1789) is the Department of State (first known as the Department of Foreign Affairs), to whose major responsibility for the foreign policy function a number of purely domestic duties were added, most of which subsequently have been assigned elsewhere. The Department of the

---

[4] Dwight Waldo, *The Study of Public Administration* (New York, 1955), p. 6.
[5] Herbert A. Simon, *Administrative Behavior* (New York, 1947); James G. March and Herbert A. Simon, *Organizations* (New York, 1958).

Treasury (1789) is chiefly concerned with the function of managing the government's finances, but it also includes such activities as the Secret Service and (in peacetime) the Coast Guard. The Department of Defense (1947), the next to youngest, is basically a functional unit. Two of its three principal constituent units date from the early years of the Republic: the Department of the Navy (1798) and the Department of the Army (1789), which until the creation of the Department of the Air Force (1947) was called the Department of War. The continued designation of these three as "Departments" reflects resistances remaining from the efforts to unify the armed services after the Second World War, but the secretaries who head them are not members of the Cabinet.

The Department of Justice dates from 1870, although its head, the Attorney General, has sat in the Cabinet as the President's principal legal adviser since 1792. From the beginning it has been in effect the law office of the executive branch. It may be called in that respect a process unit, but it also operates the federal prisons and the Immigration and Naturalization Service and includes the Federal Bureau of Investigation among its activities.

The Post Office Department, primarily functional, was created in 1872, although the office of the Postmaster General dates from 1789 and its incumbent became a member of the Cabinet in Jackson's time.

The Department of the Interior (1849) has long been a kind of catchall for a variety of rather unrelated activities, but its growth from the General Land Office and the Office of Indian Affairs has continued to associate it primarily with problems, especially natural resource problems, west of the Mississippi. Broadly a functional unit, it comes closer than any other to specialization by geographic area.

The Department of Agriculture since its creation in 1862 has been primarily a clientele department, though it was not of Cabinet rank until 1889. Much the same can be said of the Department of Commerce (1913), although it is scarcely the sole spokesman for the business community in the executive branch and contains a number of activities only slightly connected with the affairs of its clients, notably the Weather Bureau, the Coast and Geodetic Survey (mapping and related functions), and the Bureau of Public Roads. The Department of Labor (1913) occupies a somewhat comparable position. Its political standing since the division of the Department of Commerce and Labor (1903–13) has been weak at times, reflecting in part the long struggle of the labor movement to gain legitimacy and acceptance. An indication that the Department still does not enjoy a secure and equal status is its size, approximately 7,000 employees. All of the other Departments have staffs of at least 30,000, and several contain bureaus almost as large as the whole Department of Labor.

Finally, the Department of Health, Education and Welfare not only is the youngest of the ten (1953) but also is the one which, even more than Interior, is a kind of holding company for several rather unrelated activities. As its long name suggests, it is basically a collection of functions. Its principal units are the Public Health Service, the Office of Education, the Social Security Administration, and the Food and Drug Administration.

No two of the Departments or independent agencies are organized identically, even in formal terms. Characteristically, however, they include three types of units: First, the secretary (or his equivalent in the independent establishments) and one or more undersecretaries and assistant secretaries, among whom nominal responsibility for supervising sectors of the Department's activities is distributed; second, a number of auxiliary or housekeeping activities affecting the whole Department, such as personnel, budgeting, accounting, and the like; third, the major operating units, usually known as bureaus but sometimes identified by such designations as office, service, or administration. In all agencies of the executive branch there are about 350 such units. They range in size from fewer than one hundred employees to more than 5,000.

AUTONOMY OF THE BUREAU

The bureau is the fundamental unit of the federal bureaucracy. It tends to be relatively indestructible and somewhat isolated from the remainder of the Department. Though its subunits—ordinarily called divisions—may occasionally show signs of some independence of the parent organization, these tendencies are slight in comparison with the weakness of Department-bureau relations.

Several reasons account for these characteristics of the bureau. First, they can be historical. The activities of much of the civil service have tended to grow from the recognition of a particular need and the recruitment, initially, of a small staff of specialists to deal with it. Sometimes this recognition has come from within the bureaucracy, sometimes from the Congress, and sometimes from outside the government; but characteristically it has come from a combination of all three. For example, soon after the export of livestock to Europe began in the 1870s the shippers encountered European import restrictions aimed at excluding certain diseases common among cattle in this country. State efforts at eradication of the diseases failed, and after considerable agitation in and outside the government to protect this export market the Congress in 1884 established by law a Bureau of Animal Industry, located this in the Department of Agriculture, and gave it authority—gradually expanded—to suppress livestock diseases. It continued as a bureau and under its original name from 1884 to 1953, when its functions were reassigned by the Secretary, acting under reorganizing authority granted by the Congress.

A second reason for these special characteristics can be found in the distinctive patterns of recruitment and promotion that contribute to a strong *esprit de corps* in a bureau. Thus, to return to the preceding example, the Bureau of Animal Industry became a major center for research in animal diseases, as well as a regulatory unit. It was a magnet for able and well-trained veterinary scientists all over the country. Another conspicuous and still current example is the Forest Service, which recruits most of its professional staff from the few leading schools of forestry in the country. The upper echelons of this bureau are composed of graduates of these schools who have spent their lives in forest management. Not unnaturally, they regard their location in the Department of Agriculture as merely a matter of housekeeping convenience.

Third, the chiefs of these bureaus often occupy their positions for a long time. Even if they are not appointed under civil service procedures—though about one third of them are—a good many are in fact career men in their bureaus. Compared with Secretaries and sub-Cabinet departmental officials appointed by the President, who continue in office on the average only two or three years, bureau chiefs tend to be "old hands." On the average they have had five years or more in their positions and fifteen or more in the federal service. Standing committees of the Congress, including appropriations subcommittees, tend to turn to these men when they have questions. Though committee members usually give polite attention to a Secretary and his immediate associates, they naturally regard the long-term man as the one who really knows the answers. This attitude is doubtless shared by the career men themselves. Their "superiors" are short-term amateurs, while they are the ones who have "been around" in Washington —in the bureaucracy and on the political scene—and are likely to remain through many changes of Secretaries.

Fourth, when both senior committee members and bureau officials continue in their positions for years, the tendency for long acquaintance to develop into "authoritative and habitual interrelations"—a kind of informal organization not normally shown on the charts—is predictable. If for no other reason than continued association between bureau chiefs and committees of Congress, the tendency for the bureau to act independently of its parent department is encouraged.

There are still other reasons. Each bureau also tends to acquire one or more clientele groups which establish customary relations with it. Given the tendency for Congressional committee jurisdictions to parallel those of executive agencies, moreover, similarly intimate relations develop between the committees and many of these outside groups, which are "clients" of the Senators and Representatives as well. This triangular relationship may be completely harmonious or it may, especially in the case of regulatory functions, involve strains of potential hostility. But, as the earlier discussion of the independent regulatory agencies pointed out, the relationship normally tends toward stability.[6] Especially in the face of a threat to bureau autonomy or to established practice—from the White House, from the Department, from another point within the Congress, or from outside the government—it may become an impressively strong "triple alliance."[7] The ability of the Interstate Commerce Commission and its client groups—particularly the railroads and the truckers—to influence Congress to deny the President authority to designate the Commission's chairman has its equivalent in the history of a number of bureaus.

The range of these client relations in the case of some bureaus may be very wide. Those of the Forest Service, for example, would include the leading schools of forestry, the professional organizations of foresters, sectors of the lumber industry, sportsmen and livestock raisers' groups whose members use the facilities of the national forests, and officials and organizations in communities economically dependent on the forests. Provided that

---

[6] Chapter 11, p. 342.
[7] The phrase is from Marver H. Bernstein, *The Job of the Federal Executive* (Washington, 1958), p. 86.

these clients maintain friendly relations with the bureau, they can be expected to make themselves heard, in Congress and elsewhere, in opposition to any effort to reduce the authority or the autonomy of the bureau.

Finally, these several factors both account for and reinforce the tendency in the Congress to "freeze" bureaus into the executive structure and to insulate them from other influences. Given the characteristic history noted above, it is not surprising that many bureaus are provided for by statute, which normally means, of course, that they cannot be abolished or their powers altered or transferred without subsequent statutory authority. Laws establishing bureaus also frequently grant various powers, not to the President or the Secretary, but quite explicitly to the bureaus and their chiefs. The more precisely these laws specify what a bureau chief shall do and how he shall do it, of course, the more meaningless is a Department head's power to "supervise" the bureau. An alternative arrangement would be for Congress to direct the President to set up an activity where and in the form that he deemed appropriate. In wartime, in fact, the President has been given such power with respect to emergency activities of a temporary character, but, except as his general reorganizing authority—to be discussed below—carries power something like this, it is far from normal practice. Another alternative would be to grant authority for an activity to a Department and its Secretary, allowing the latter to delegate and organize the authority as he saw fit. Historically, as we have seen, this has not been the normal practice, but in recent years the Secretaries of a number of Departments have been granted such powers. This has not, however, prevented the Congress from creating other bureaus by statute, and in some instances the power has been granted only with interesting and instructive exceptions.

For example, the Office of the Comptroller of the Currency is a bureau in the Department of the Treasury which was created by statute in 1863. It now has little to do with currency, since the national banks which it regulates no longer issue notes. The bureau does, however, control the establishment and consolidation of all national banks; it regulates their creation of branches; and, chiefly via examinations by its bank examiners, it supervises their overall operations. Like a regulatory commission, which it resembles, the Office of the Comptroller of the Currency over a century has developed a stable set of relations with its clients, the national banks and their trade associations. Anxiety for the autonomy and stability of these relations was aroused in 1950, when a Presidential reorganization plan proposed to give the Secretary of the Treasury general power to reorganize and to reallocate the Department's activities. As a result of this anxiety and the pressure it prompted, the Office of the Comptroller was specifically exempted from this authority.

PRESIDENTS, SECRETARIES, AND BUREAU CHIEFS

In the partial autonomy of the bureaus—and in the factors supporting it—lies a large part of the explanation for the inability of Cabinet members to function as disinterested Presidential counselors. As Chapter 11 indicated, a Secretary is dependent not only upon the President but also upon the Congress (especially through its standing committees), upon his Department's personnel, and upon his Department's client groups.[8] These ties of staff, Congressional committees, and clients, however, tend to be bureau ties because of the continuities and the concentrated experience to be encountered in the bureaus. A Cabinet officer freshly arrived on the scene and relatively inexperienced either in the ways of Washington or in the affairs of his department inevitably relies on the career people, especially the bureau chiefs. He really has little choice. If he wishes to make an impact in his position, he must draw on the substantive ideas of his staff or secure their guidance in formulating his strategies or persuade them to make his ideas and plans their own. Probably, he must do all three in varying combinations. If he has no such ambitions, he leaves things as they are.

A Cabinet officer must be able to go it alone, without appreciable Presidential help, in a contest with elements in the Congress and various interest groups. But he is likely soon to discover that the loyalties and commitments he needs to do so are in pawn to the various triple alliances in which the bureaus in his department are involved. They can only be redeemed by his joining one or more of them. For example, in the Department of Agriculture for years one of the strongest such alliances was that involving the state colleges of agriculture, the American Farm Bureau Federation, and the Department's Extension Service. Its roots date back as far as the 1860s, when the ties between the Department and the land-grant colleges developed, but they acquired particular strength after 1914 with the establishment of the cooperative educational extension service for farmers. This was a grant-in-aid program administered by a Department bureau (now known as the Federal Extension Service) in cooperation with the state agricultural colleges and the state and county units of the Farm Bureau. In the days when the Department was chiefly a research and promotional agency, extension was virtually the only channel of direct contact with the nation's farmers. The so-called "action" programs of the New Deal period—chiefly price supports and production controls—were a wholly new departure. They also called for direct contact with farmers, and the disposition of Secretary Henry A. Wallace and his associates was naturally to create new means for such contact. But despite the dissolving crisis of the Depression (and later the Second World War), no Secretary was able to conduct these and related programs without using the extension channel to the extent demanded by its sponsors—including members of the Congress.

A bureau chief—especially one in charge of a new or controversial undertaking—may have need of the Secretary, much as the latter may need the President. This is most likely to occur in connection with the jurisdictional rivalries that almost inevitably occur within—and particularly between—Departments. A classic case is the recurrent hostility between the Bureau of Reclamation in the Department of the Interior and the Corps of Engineers in the Department of the Army, both of which engage in dam construction and related projects for developing water resources. As the extended discussion in Chapter 22 will indicate,[9] they have come into

8 Chapter 11, p. 347.
9 Chapter 22, pp. 702–05.

conflict chiefly in the far West, where projects cannot be neatly separated into either irrigation (Reclamation) or flood control (Engineers). The Corps is the center of perhaps the strongest alliance on the Washington scene. The Bureau of Reclamation is less strongly fortified. Consequently Reclamation, in a dispute over whether a project is to be done by it or by the Engineers, almost inevitably depends on the Secretary of the Interior and through him on the President.

The chief of an established bureau, even if he encounters jurisdictional conflicts, has less need of a Secretary's assistance than the latter normally has of the President's or of his bureau chiefs'. To "go it alone" the chief of a bureau can draw on the kinds of established relations that make the bureau normally the key unit in the bureaucracy's structure. The Attorney General as head of the Department of Justice, on the other hand, is more likely to need to draw on the standing with Congress enjoyed by the Federal Bureau of Investigation and J. Edgar Hoover, its chief, than vice versa. A Secretary of Agriculture normally has more need of the "alliance" built around the Chief of the Forest Service than the latter has of either the Secretary's or the President's political resources.

THE POLITICS OF REORGANIZATION

There is no "one best" form of organization. Some discussions might lead one to believe that there is a perfect and eternal solution to the problem of organizing the bureaucracy, if only the powers-that-be in Washington had the wit to discover it and the courage to adopt it. Such a solution, however, is an illusion.

In an enterprise as complex and extensive as the federal government, it is imperative that the strains and demands upon the political system be handled as smoothly and as promptly as possible. The bureaucracy inevitably is a prime means for identifying as well as for handling these problems. Hence we can specify two broad criteria of good organization in a system that relies on Presidential initiative. First, the various activities in the bureaucracy should be so arranged in relation to one another that the most important problems will be easily identified and the insights required for dealing with them will be generated. Second, the units in the bureaucracy should be so located in the executive hierarchy that the issues most needing decision by the President will reach him easily and quickly. If these criteria are not met, the danger is not simply that important questions may be delayed or buried elsewhere in the structure; equally serious is the possibility that when problems finally reach the President they will arrive with essential choices obscured by prior compromises.

The criteria both imply that a fundamental influence on organization will be need-creating events in the world with which government deals. It follows that good organization should reflect the character of those needs at any given time. In a world of constant and rapid change what is an appropriate organization today may be inadequate a year from now. Organization thus tends to be a continuous process, not of pursuing a fixed, yet still undefined goal, but of adapting as effectively as possible to current and currently anticipated needs.

In the past three decades the Congress has acknowledged implicitly the validity of these premises concerning the organization of the executive branch. The explicit justifications for its actions usually have rested on such essentially secondary objectives as minimizing duplication and reducing expenditures. But it has granted to successive Chief Executives contingent powers of reorganization. Beginning in 1932 the Congress has passed a series of reorganization statutes authorizing the President to submit reorganization plans to the Congress, to go into effect in sixty days if not disapproved. Formally these statutes have varied in two respects: (1) in the number and character of the units specifically exempted by them from reorganization; (2) in the nature and difficulty of the method required to express Congressional disapproval. Some statutes have specifically exempted as many as seventeen agencies, both independent commissions and bureaus within Departments. Current legislation exempts only certain courts and the General Accounting Office and provides that no Department may be abolished, that the life of no temporary agency may be extended, and that no term of office may be increased. Congressional disapproval (the "legislative veto") has been expressed by concurrent resolution or, as at present, by the easier method of a simple resolution passed by either house.

Application of the first criterion of organization—fostering appropriate perspectives in agency relations—is illustrated by the transfer in 1940 of the Food and Drug Administration from the Department of Agriculture, where it had been placed from its beginnings in 1906, to the Federal Security Agency (predecessor of the Department of Health, Education and Welfare). When it was located in a Department and was controlled by Congressional committees that were closely identified with food producers and processors, the Food and Drug Administration's program tended to overemphasize such commercial matters as the adulteration of insecticides and fertilizers and to underemphasize the practices of food growers and processors that were potentially harmful to humans. Locating it in the Federal Security Agency, along with such units as the Public Health Service, and subjecting it to a different set of Congressional committees produced somewhat different characteristics in its programs.

An example of the application of the second criterion of organization—making critical units and issues easily accessible to the President—was the creation of the Federal Aviation Agency in 1958 as an "independent" unit directly responsible to the President. The FAA took over the function of the former Civil Aeronautics Authority, which had been located in the Department of Commerce. (Its duties include the enforcement of safety regulations and the development and operation of airways and airports.) Making it directly responsible to the President meant that its problems could reach him unaffected by the extraneous concerns of the Department of Commerce. It also meant that with direct access to the President the Agency could speak with greater authority in its complex dealings with the military, whose operations have to be reconciled with civilian use of the air lanes. A slightly different example of the second criterion was the transfer of the Bureau of the Budget from the Treasury Department to the Executive Office in 1939. This action not only recognized that budget choices may be crucial program choices. It also acknowledged that an effective Budget Bureau can itself help to attain this criterion of good organization. That is, its reach into departmental and bureau programs at all levels can be one means of raising issues to the White House level that might otherwise never get there.

The unwritten exemptions to a President's reorganization powers are extensive, however. As long as the Congress retains a legislative veto over such proposals—and that is likely to be a very long time—the alliance systems of a great many bureaus and agencies will be sufficient to jeopardize or to defeat any reorganization plan threatening the advantages gained from such relations. For example, even though it is not covered by statutory exemptions, the Federal Bureau of Investigation could prevent its being transferred to the Treasury Department and being made a division of the Secret Service; the Forest Service could still obstruct a transfer to Interior and the division of its functions between the Bureau of Land Management and the National Park Service; the Marines could thwart any attempt to combine them with the Army; the Corps of Engineers is amply equipped to prevent acceptance of the first Hoover Commission's recommendation that its civil functions be transferred out of the Army Department and into a new Water Development and Use Service along with the Bureau of Reclamation; and any of the "big six" independent regulatory commissions could resist transfer to one of the executive Departments.

The politics of reorganization are likely to be such, therefore, that these powers in the hands of the Chief Executive are not sufficient by themselves to permit full satisfaction of the two criteria of organization. If the necessary "authoritative and habitual relations" are to develop, they may also have to reflect the persuasion, bargaining, and maneuver which Chapter 10 identified as essential to executive leadership.

CIVIL SERVICE RECRUITMENT

The processes and patterns of recruitment significantly affect the values, perspectives, and goals that mold an institution. This should be evident from our discussion of Congressional careers in Chapter 12.[10] These processes and patterns are as important in the bureaucracy as they are elsewhere. In contrast with the relatively informal recruitment of members of Congress, however, entrance into the civil service is quite formal and institutionalized.

One informal factor of consequence does operate on the recruitment of civil servants. Government employment, whether federal, state, or local, carries with it less prestige than do occupations in industry or in other branches of the private sector of the society. As we noted in our discussion of Congress, the rewards and attractions of private employment, especially in the more industrialized sections of the country, seem to have been considerably greater than those in the government. This is far from the case in all societies, and it may be in the process of change in the United States. But the indications are still strong that the civil service, even in the federal government, does not get its full share of the ablest and most ambitious

---

[10] Chapter 12, p. 369.

young people in the country. Private bureaucracies, of course, including those in the business world, attract and retain ample numbers of inefficient and unimaginative timeservers, and the federal bureaucracy does include, as it has for decades, a large number of dedicated men and women whose ability would at least equal that of the best in any institution in the country. The proportion of the latter is undoubtedly lower, though, than it might be because of the relatively lower prestige of public employment. Salary differentials, which are appreciable only in the top positions, also have an effect, but they probably are a less fundamental factor in recruitment than the matter of general societal esteem.

Until about eighty years ago the federal bureaucracy was recruited almost exclusively on a partisan basis. Before the 1880s, that is, what was called the "spoils system" reigned effectively unchallenged. Every four years, or at least with every change of President, incumbent civil servants, often in fairly large numbers, were displaced by those of the President's party, those associated with his faction, and those associated with local party organizations or with members of Congress important in the President's entourage.

In the heyday of the spoils system and even until fairly recently many features of government operation were tolerably compatible with that mode of recruitment. In the first place, the government by modern standards was a small show. As recently as the turn of the century the total civilian employment in the executive branch was only about 230,000; all agencies, excluding the Post Office, employed fewer than 95,000 people. Even in 1933 total employment in the executive branch was less than 600,000, almost half of whom were in the Post Office. In the second place, technical specialization had not proceeded very far in modern terms, in keeping with the relatively uncomplicated, almost peripheral role of government in the society.

Third, the functions of the bureaucracy as a source of initiative, of policy proposals growing out of technical preoccupation with various features of a sensitively interdependent society, were relatively slight. Andrew Jackson's dictum that any intelligent man could perform any of the duties required in government office was not far from the mark. The spoils system did not mean, moreover, that competence was completely neglected in appointments. Ability was not always secured and not always sought, but it was by no means missing. Nor did the spoils system result in complete turnover with each change in administration. Many technical employees were retained and even gradually moved up into positions of considerable responsibility as the value of their experience and accumulated knowledge was recognized. But spoils and partisan attachments were by far the dominating recruitment factors.

The turn of the tide came in 1883 with the passage of the Pendleton Act, creating the Civil Service Commission and providing for, among other things, recruitment by open competitive examination. This legislation climaxed twenty years of agitation, during the course of which the spoils system was blamed for every evil, every failure, and every example of corruption in contemporary government operations. The efforts of the reformers were aided by the assassination in 1881 of President James A.

Garfield by a demented aspirant for a governmental post who held the President responsible for his failure to secure an appointment. But the inefficiencies of an unrestrained patronage system in a period of increasing governmental responsibility and complexity sooner or later would have made the change inevitable.

At the outset the competitive service covered only about 10 percent of the employees in the executive branch. Steady if somewhat spasmodic expansion by executive order and by statute over the intervening years has brought between 80 and 90 percent of federal employees under the competitive provisions of the Civil Service Act. If one includes such merit systems independent of the Civil Service Commission as the Foreign Service of the State Department, the FBI, the TVA, the Atomic Energy Commission, and the commissioned medical officers of the Public Health Service, the total is more than 90 percent. An appreciable fraction of the remainder is recruited outside of the competitive system because the positions are too specialized to be handled under the usual civil service procedures.

In the executive branch of the federal government, therefore, recruitment by patronage has disappeared except for a relatively small number of posts, including approximately 1,100 Cabinet, sub-Cabinet, and similar top-level positions. The effects on the character and operation of the bureaucracy have been considerable, and they have by no means been confined to increased technical competence, though that certainly has been one consequence.

PROBLEMS OF NEUTRALITY

One of the prime goals of the reformers who promoted the establishment and extension of the merit system was neutrality. If appointees to the government service, it was argued, could be selected on a basis of competence alone, through the device of open competitive examination, the civil service would become a politically neutral instrument. It would put its skills at the disposal of whichever political party had received the voters' mandate, loyally carrying out the policies arrived at by the political officers of the government. But it would have no partisan concerns and presumably it would take no part in the function of setting policies. Furthermore, recruitment through the competitive system would remove the partisan incentive to create government jobs whether they were needed or not. More important, it would do away with a situation in which appointees felt obligated not to their administrative superiors or even to the President but to their political sponsors in the Congress and in the local party organizations. Competence and neutrality were the central objectives.

These worthy objectives of the merit-system proponents have been approached, even if not completely attained, in the years since 1883 by extending the coverage of the competitive system and by additional devices aimed at insulating the bureaucracy from partisan politics. Conspicuously, the Hatch Act of 1939 extended the prohibitions of the 1883 legislation against political campaigning and assessing employees' salaries. For all practical purposes it prohibited all executive employees, whether under civil service or not, from engaging in any kind of partisan activity other than voting and discussions in the privacy of each employee's home. A second Hatch Act extended these limitations to state and local employees paid in whole or in part from federal funds.

Agency and professional politics

Partisan activity, however, is not the only form of politics. The units of the executive branch, as we have already seen, have inevitable ties with committees of the Congress and with interest groups; they are inescapably involved in the contests of influence between the President and his opponents in the Congress. Their stakes of personal and bureau survival are not tied to a political party—but they still exist. Paradoxically, greater technical competence and the virtual elimination of partisanship have increased the importance of different ties, of a professional and bureau nature.

Paralleling the unit-by-unit growth of the bureaus, as noted earlier, recruitment into the federal service has tended to occur along specialized professional lines—foresters into the Forest Service, chemists into the Food and Drug Administration, and so on. Efforts have also been made in the past three decades to recruit able young "generalists" with liberal arts educations directly from the colleges and universities and to make them the nucleus of the government-wide career service. Though these have been in part successful, the careers to which they provide an entrance are more likely to be bureau careers or at most Department ones, rather than government-wide ones. Given the importance of bureau units in the organizational structure, the manpower of the executive branch is for the most part not treated as a government-wide resource. Individuals with initiative can and do move from agency to agency, especially in Washington. For those who do not change agencies, however, advancement tends to depend on identification with the norms and objectives of the bureau or agency, including, of course, the norms of technical competence. Such identification, however, reinforces professional and agency politics—the politics of the "triple alliance" of bureau, client group, and Congressional committee.

These tendencies toward separatism and "agency self-government" are most conspicuous in the highly independent, professionalized status of several specialized corps in the executive branch. Thus the Foreign Service in the State Department has its own system of recruitment, promotion, and retirement. The Federal Bureau of Investigation is in essentially the same situation. The commissioned corps of the Public Health Service, in addition to conducting its own recruiting system, has succeeded in so arranging the statutes that the President, who appoints the Surgeon General ("chief" of the "bureau"), must choose him from among the personnel of the commissioned corps. The problems of such separatism are not fundamentally different from some of those involved in the question of civilian control of the military: the latter also are specialized corps in a separate segment of the total bureaucracy, and they present the possibility that without effective external controls the policies that they generate may reflect more the perspectives of just the corps itself than the values and needs of the political system as a whole.

Thus the pursuit of neutrality through the competitive system has created some new problems in the process of solving those stemming from partisan-ship. Neutrality toward political parties does not necessarily mean neutrality toward professional goals and agency politics. Agency goals may not be as broad and flexible as the needs of the governmental situation require. In a bureaucracy whose technical skills have made it a source of policy initiative, have given it influence within the Congress, and have granted it important delegated powers over the affairs of citizens, this narrowness may obstruct needed change. Like Congressional committee goals—and for some of the same reasons—agency goals may be parochial, unresponsive, and even irresponsible.

Neutrality and positive recruitment

The neutrality concept may also be at odds with the goal of high com-petence. Associated with the idea of neutrality is an essentially negative notion of the formal process of recruitment. At least implicit in the pro-gram of the civil service reformers was the assumption that vast numbers of people—and adequate numbers of able people—were eager to enter public employment. Thus the competitive examination, a screen to separate the competent from the incompetent regardless of party attachment, was the extent of what was required in recruitment. For reasons already dis-cussed, the assumption has seldom been correct. The system is clearly in-adequate in a virtually full-employment economy, in which industry and professional firms actively attempt to recruit the ablest young men and women in the country.

The efforts aimed at recruiting able young "generalists" for careers in the federal government have attempted to meet this problem in part. The latest version of these, functioning since 1955, is the Federal Service En-trance Examination, open to young people who have completed or are about to complete four years of college or the equivalent. The examinations are given regularly and are especially designed for students in the senior year of college study.

THE CONGRESS AND RECRUITMENT POLICY

Some of these disabilities of the recruitment system are, of course, trace-able to persistent attitudes within the Congress. These are symbolized in part by what in Chapter 11 was referred to as the political no man's land occupied by the Civil Service Commission, between the assumed patronage dispositions of both President and members of Congress. The latter, al-though they have gradually accepted the merit-system notion, have been nonetheless fearful that it might become a Presidential instrument. This fear is illustrated in the restrictions they placed on employee political ac-tivity in the 1939 Hatch Act. The chief motivation for these was the expectation that the employees of New Deal emergency agencies not under civil service might be used in electoral campaigns against members of Congress who opposed President Roosevelt. In keeping with this attitude and quite aside from the bureau-committee alliances discussed earlier, members of Congress usually expect civil servants to keep clear of a Presi-dent's shadow. (In particular cases, as our discussion of the "triple alliance" has shown, the bureaucrats may or may not do so, depending in part on a President's skill and standing.) Finally, and somewhat inconsistently, many members of Congress—partly because of the delegated powers that bureaucrats exercise—look with suspicion on civil servants. The suspicion further is mixed with some condescension toward people who have "never carried a precinct," and it may in some cases be accompanied by the feeling that improving the quality of the bureaucracy can only occur at the expense of Congressional power. This feeling also probably helps to hold down pay scales at the top bureaucratic level. It is a rare member of Congress who thinks any bureaucrat should be paid as much as himself, and Congressmen from small towns in which ordinary people have ordinary incomes are not disposed to give better rewards to "clerks" in the executive branch.

These attitudes foster and reinforce the negative features of recruitment. They also support a readiness in Congress to treat government employ-ment as a form of charity. Federal employment as a charitable award seems in part to underlie Congressional support for the institution of vet-erans' preference, which dates back at least to the Civil War. The Veterans Preference Act of 1944 grants extra points on examination scores to vet-erans, wives of disabled veterans, widows of deceased veterans if they have not remarried, and in some instances mothers of deceased or disabled veterans. It also requires that disabled veterans who pass examinations go to the head of eligible lists, and veterans are granted preference over non-veterans in similar employment when dismissals occur through personnel cuts. In consequence, about half of all executive-branch employees now have some form of veterans' preference.

RECRUITMENT AND THE LOYALTY PROGRAM

A critical and revealing problem that has affected, among other things, recruitment into the civil service is what is known as the federal loyalty and security program. Although it had its counterpart in the Second World War, it was primarily a product of the "Cold War." It began in 1947 when President Truman issued an executive order requiring that all pres-ent and prospective government employees submit to a loyalty check. Successive versions of this order under Truman and Eisenhower increased the severity of the criteria for clearance. At first they required, for dis-missal or refusal of appointment, "reasonable grounds . . . for the belief that the person . . . is disloyal." Then the burden of proof was shifted, so that clearance was denied if there was "reasonable doubt as to the loyalty" of the employee or applicant. The Congress entered the picture in 1950 with a statute authorizing Department heads to dismiss any em-ployee when they deemed it necessary in the interests of national security. Finally, in 1953 an Eisenhower order raised the requirements to a peak of severity by requiring that employment of any person must be "clearly consistent with the interests of national security."

No one would question the proposition that appointment to positions involving access to highly confidential information—sensitive positions—should be reserved for persons whose loyalty and reliability are above question. Spying and subversion are not illusions. They occur not only through the deliberately disloyal but also through the emotionally unstable

"That's The Kind We Want—
You Can See Just What He's
Not Thinking"

From *Herblock's Here and Now*, Simon & Schuster, 1955

The "loyalty-security" program, according to this view, has encouraged mediocrity in bureaucratic positions.

and those whose habits may make them vulnerable, for example, to blackmail. But to acknowledge this point is not to say that all governmental positions must be subject to the same precautions.

Hence the problems presented by a loyalty-security program are basically three: first, the matter of where the line is to be drawn between positions that are sensitive and those that are not; second, the question of standards, of how to define associations and actions to be deemed disloyal; and third, the procedure and the character of the evidence relied upon in loyalty-security actions.

The first of these seems simple, but in an atmosphere of semihysteria—such as prevailed in the "McCarthy years" of the late 1940s and early 1950s—it may not be. In the setting of the Alger Hiss case, of the widespread belief that the Soviet Union had secured the secrets of the atom bomb through espionage, and of the readiness by radical right-wing elements in the country and in Congress to see Communists on every hand, it was far from simple. Until the mid-1950s, in fact, no line was drawn. In 1956 the Supreme Court held that the 1950 statute limited the program to sensitive positions.[11] But as late as 1961 the Court permitted dismissal as a security risk of a short-order cook in a cafeteria concession located in a naval weapons factory.[12]

---

[11] *Cole* v. *Young*, 351 U.S. 536 (1956).
[12] *Cafeteria Workers* v. *McElroy*, 376 U.S. 886 (1961).

The second problem, standards, is at best troublesome. A man who in his mature years is a member of the Communist party may present a clear case, but what of the man who for a brief time in his college years was active in "radical" causes? Or what about the man who has publicly championed unpopular positions, such as the right of American Communists to hold public meetings? And how would one deal with the person whose sister or brother-in-law was a member of an organization that openly supported the foreign policy views of the Soviet Union? The standards of loyalty are not obvious ones, easily applied.

The third problem, procedure and evidence, is obviously complex. To require a formal hearing in all such cases would be cumbersome, to say the least. Yet discharge or failure to appoint as a "security risk" involves serious penalties, not the least of which is that the person may as a result subsequently be unable to secure employment even outside the government. It must be admitted that to permit a defendant to confront his accusers and to test the evidence against him might very well compromise the system of informants used, for example, by the FBI. But denial or restriction of this opportunity raises the nasty question of whether the constitutional rights of American citizens are not seriously jeopardized thereby. No one, of course, has a right to public employment, but what about the values of due process when a person is in effect publicly branded as a "security risk"?

The implications of these problems bear on the state of the bureaucracy as a whole and not merely on individuals. When sensitive positions are loosely defined and especially when safeguards concerning standards and evidence are weak, an atmosphere of mutual suspicion is fostered in the service itself. No certainty can exist that cranks or gossips are not threatening one's position, that a youthful indiscretion is not haunting one's mature years, or that an innocent and legitimate curiosity about the writings of left-wing radicals is not being used as a basis for suspicion. In such an atmosphere the initiative and imagination needed from the bureaucracy is discouraged. If a foreign service officer's 1943 report from China, arguing that support of the government of Chiang Kai-shek is a waste, is used in 1954 as an indication not of a realistic or even a mistaken or incomplete judgment but of subversive intent, what is the result? In such an atmosphere conformity carries a premium, and any prudent man will avoid sticking his neck out on any but the most mundane matters.

The effects on recruitment are equally serious. An atmosphere of suspicion and conformity is not one eagerly sought by inventive and able men. And a clearance program that turns on dubious or unvalidated evidence may deny to the government the services of an able and imaginative man who has acquired enemies in the course of his career.

No one can be certain how many genuinely disloyal or risky persons have been dismissed or denied employment under this program. It is clear, however, that the number is small, that the overwhelming majority of civil servants are loyal and responsible, and that the few disloyal cases have usually been discovered by ordinary police work rather than by loyalty-security checks.

With the close of the "McCarthy era" these matters have become less immediately insistent, but they remain as problems. How they are dealt with will have implications not only for civil liberties but also for the effectiveness of the bureaucracy.

TENURE AND TURNOVER

An almost inevitable accompaniment of recruitment by merit, as determined by competitive examination, is security of tenure. If arbitrary removal were possible, so the argument goes, partisan political preference could creep in through the back door though it was barred at the front. (This is, in fact, one of the threats implicit in a loosely administered loyalty-security policy.) Hence, under the civil service rules and statutes, after an employee has served for a probationary period of one year—during which he can be dropped without ceremony—he acquires civil service status. This means that, except in loyalty-security cases, he cannot be dismissed by his superiors without a rather long and complicated scheme of hearings and appeals. This system appears adequately to take care of eliminating obvious incompetents, but it may be too cumbersome to deal with the merely mediocre. Dismissals for cause do occur, but they are few, as one should expect; the annual rate is about one half of one percent.

Despite protections against arbitrary dismissal, however, and despite pay and fringe-benefit arrangements that make the lower grades of the civil service fairly comparable with private employment, security of employment may be less complete than in many private bureaucracies. The chief reason for this is that security in the job exists only as the job does, and the existence of the job depends not on the civil service rules and statutes but upon program authorizations and especially on appropriations. Here one encounters a consequence of the decentralized power of the Congressional committee system and of the relative power of different committees in the governmental structure. The committees that at least nominally deal with legislation governing general policies on recruitment, levels of pay, and conditions of work for the civil service proper and for the postal workers are the Committees on the Post Office and Civil Service. These committees normally give a sympathetic ear to the representatives of employee organizations, to the veterans' groups, and to the Civil Service Commission, in roughly that order. They tend to look favorably upon requested changes in pay levels and conditions of work, especially for the more numerous employees in the low grades. But these committees do not set the programs of the operating agencies and do not provide them with funds. Moreover, the substantive and program committees and especially the Committees on Appropriations, as we have seen, rank higher in the prestige and power structures of the House and Senate than do the Civil Service Committees. The former committees may control in detail the number and kinds of positions available to particular agencies and bureaus; yet the groups that are influential with the Civil Service Committees have limited access to them at best. The outlook of the Appropriations Committees in particular is characteristically one favoring the reduction of programs and the restriction of personnel. They not only may reduce funds but also, through the device of the "rider," may impose explicit limits on personnel levels, may restrict or eliminate certain kinds of jobs, and may even at times encroach on the jurisdiction of the Civil Service Committees by setting general rules for all executive employees.

The elimination of positions by the Congress is called a "reduction in force," a process that has produced in the jargon of Washington the verb "to rif," usually used in the passive voice, "to be riffed." When a reduction in force occurs, it is governed by a complex set of rules. Essentially it involves a kind of competition within the affected agency and among individuals with the same skills and occupying positions in the same pay class and grade. (Job classification is, along with recruitment by competitive examination, one of the key elements in the civil service system. It incorporates one of the key doctrines of the reform movement, equal pay for duties of equal difficulty and responsibility. Under the Classification Act of 1949 most positions in the civil service are assigned to one of eighteen pay classes, ranging from those with the most elementary and routine duties [G.S., for "general schedule," 1] to those carrying top responsibility, such as those of bureau chiefs [G.S. 18]. Rank in the civil service—as contrasted, for example, with the military—depends on the position, not on the person. Thus one has G.S. 15 rank only as long as one occupies a G.S. 15 position.)

When a reduction in force occurs, a displaced employee may accept demotion to a lower position in the same agency, thus displacing—"bumping" is the jargon term—someone without veteran status or with lower civil service rank. A slight reduction in force at the top of an agency, therefore, can have effects all along the line. In general, persons with civil service status displace those without, employees with veterans' preference are favored over those who lack it, and persons with greater seniority outrank those with fewer years of service. Persons released through a reduction in force are given reemployment preference over new recruits, so that a large proportion may remain in the service by shifting to another bureau or agency.

The common notion that no one who secures employment in the civil service is discharged or leaves for any other reason except death or retirement is thus wide of the mark. Turnover in the bureaucracy, for whatever reason, in fact occurs at an annual rate of 20 to 25 percent, representing between four and five hundred thousand persons per year. About half of this total represents voluntary withdrawals other than retirements. Some of these undoubtedly reflect the kinds of limitations on a career in the federal service, including the competition of private employers, that have been discussed here. Despite these limitations, however, many tens of thousands of able and dedicated people, realizing perhaps that the disadvantages of employment in a bureaucracy are not peculiar to government, find gratification and challenge in the civil service.

Recruitment and related practices in the personnel system thus have a variety of implications for the functioning of the bureaucracy. Most fundamentally, however, they reinforce the tendencies of the organizational structure to emphasize bureau and professional ties and in turn to foster alliances with Congressional committees. The "neutral" civil service has helped to make the bureaucracy a partially independent force in the governmental system, counted upon as a source of initiative by both President and Congress, dependent to some degree on both of these, and able at times to play one of them off against the other.

JUDICIALIZED RESTRAINTS

The choices made by bureaucrats normally have been subject to review in the courts. Relatively few such actions are in fact challenged, since the heart of administrative decision-making involves negotiation and informal settlement. Court review of bureaucratic actions, however, is available in most circumstances and is used from time to time.

Over the years the treatment of administrative decisions by the courts has varied, especially decisions by those agencies involved in administrative legislation and in the determination of private rights by "quasi-judicial" action of their own. The tendency of the courts until the mid-1930s was to regard many administrative determinations with suspicion, sometimes to ignore the findings of fact made by administrators and even to retry appealed cases *de novo*, that is, to hear them as if no other tribunal had previously taken jurisdiction of them. Gradually, however, the Supreme Court and the lower federal bench began to treat administrative determinations with more deference. Generally, review was confined to determining whether decisions had involved a fair hearing after proper advance notice to all parties and whether they were supported by "substantial evidence" consistent with statutory standards. The specific reasons for this change are complex and difficult to determine, but they rested on three general factors. One was the reduced prestige of judicial review resulting from the Court's rejection of Franklin Roosevelt's New Deal legislation between 1933 and 1937. A second undoubtedly was the sheer volume of administrative actions, greatly increased after 1933, which made court retrial of such actions almost literally impossible. Finally, as noted in Chapter 11, the courts gradually came to recognize that many administrative bodies already had in various ways "judicialized" their procedures, adopting courtlike practices as a defense against the hostile treatment the courts had tended to give them.

The courts have not been the only channel for imposing judicialized restraints upon the bureaucracy's actions, however. The Congress from time to time has passed procedural legislation applicable either to particular agencies or to the entire service. The most important example of the latter sort is the Administrative Procedure Act of 1946.

This legislation has an instructive history. It derived from agitation by the American Bar Association beginning in 1933. The motives behind its efforts were both altruistic and selfish—a normal combination in the political activities of organized professional groups, whether lawyers, physicians, undertakers, or any others. First was an undoubtedly warranted worry over the growth of administrative legislation and adjudication and over the sometimes careless handling of such matters in the emergency agencies created under the New Deal. Second was unquestionably a hostility to the substance and objectives of the new legislation. The organized bar in general and the American Bar Association in particular were among the chief opponents of the reforms under the New Deal; the objective of restricting these reforms procedurally was for many lawyers a substitute for defeating them politically. Third was a combination of an equally self-serving, but unexpressed, suspicion of a type of governing process that threatened to have less need of lawyers than did ordinary court procedures, and a familiar and understandable arrogance which views justice as impossible of achievement except through the complex and time-consuming procedures over whose mysteries the legal profession has a monopoly.

The Bar Association's public challenge viewed with alarm (1) the growth of administrative discretion; (2) the "mixture" of what they called quasi-legislative and quasi-judicial functions in the same hands, the usual charge being that the same unit served as both "prosecutor" and "judge" in administrative determinations; (3) what they regarded as the inadequacy of court review. The Congress, whose numerous lawyer members usually share the biases of their profession and thus give the organized bar an attentive ear, in response passed in 1940 a severely restrictive statute, the Walter-Logan bill, one of a succession of measures sponsored by the Bar Association. This bill, which President Roosevelt vetoed with a message of sharp rebuke, would have imposed a rigidly uniform procedure on all administrative rule-making and would have exposed almost all administrative determinations to a long series of judicial appeals *before* they could take effect.

The Administrative Procedure Act of 1946 was a much-modified version of the Walter-Logan bill. It had four major provisions: (1) to require notice and hearing before the issuance of rules of general application; (2) to require that orders to particular persons or organizations be issued only after decision through courtlike procedures specified in the Act; (3) to require the appointment, under the Civil Service Commission, of independent "hearing examiners" to conduct all preliminary proceedings in isolation from the rest of an agency; and (4) to grant the courts a broad power of judicial review.

Judgments of the effects of the Administrative Procedure Act differ. The weight of opinion, however, holds that it did little more than codify the practices previously followed in most administrative agencies. Since, for the reasons indicated, these already tended to be highly judicialized, the statute added very little to existing practice. More important, the courts, and especially the Supreme Court, have not been disposed as a result of the Act to modify materially the generally respectful view of administrative decision-making that they assumed after 1937.

Judicialized restraints, however, whether required by the courts or imposed by the Congress, are a real part of the setting of influences upon the actions of the "continuing executive."

Bureaucracy and the Problem of Choice: A Summary

The characteristics of the bureaucracy in the federal government thus differ in important respects from those specified in the simple model of bureaucracy sketched at the beginning of this chapter. Specialization of duties and of jurisdictions has proceeded far, but the element of hierarchy, despite the formalities of the organization chart, is not conspicuous. It

A "Board" In Place Of The Cornerstone

"Bureaucracy" is pictured in this conservative cartoon as a poor substitute for free enterprise.

Knox in the Nashville *Banner*

typically extends, that is, little beyond the bureau level. Authority is an attribute of the bureaucratic office rather than of the person of the occupant, and its exercise is constrained by public, general rules changeable and enforceable through established legal processes. But these rules only to a limited degree prescribe the relations among parts of the bureaucracy and the relations of any of its parts with the "outside" influences of the Presidency, the Congress, and interest groups.

Legal or politically effective controls over the bureaucracy lie in both the President and the Congress, and effective lines of control in any given case may run in either direction. Certain bureaus, for certain purposes or in particular circumstances, may operate in fact as Presidential or departmental subordinates. Others, differently situated, may look to the Congress and its committees for guidance. Between these alternatives, however, enough unpredictability may exist so that an agency may have considerable independence of both. The tendencies toward bureau autonomy, toward a collection of bureaucracies rather than a single bureaucratic structure, thus are strong.

The bureaucracy, especially in these quasi-autonomous units of the continuing executive, inevitably is involved in the making of policy. Partly in consequence of this semiautonomy and partly for other reasons, all the forms of administrative action involve choices among alternative policies. What can be said of the factors guiding and limiting these policy choices?

Both organizational forms and personnel practices, especially recruitment methods and the notion of civil service neutrality, make the principal criteria of choice professional, in two complementary senses. First, given the characteristic patterns of growth and staffing in the bureaucracy, there are the criteria drawn from the bureaucrat's technical or occupational specialty. Second, there are the criteria derived from identifications with the bureau and from professional managerial concern with the goals and the stable effectiveness of the bureau and its work. In the context of the separation of powers the latter preoccupation is especially strong. Given the varying and somewhat unpredictable relations among President, Congress, and interest groups, a search by career bureaucrats for contacts and support in all three that will minimize threats to a bureau program is not only natural but virtually inevitable. For most agencies relations with the judiciary are a secondary matter, but in the case of agencies whose actions are readily subject to court review, as we have seen, somewhat the same kind of search for protection is made in the direction of the judiciary.

The pattern of relations among a bureau and its executive-branch superiors, the Congress, and its interest clientele depends basically upon the size of the stakes that each feels in the bureau's functions. The President may almost be excluded from the affairs of an agency performing a routine set of activities. Such a bureau may be virtually an appendage of the Congress or a captive of its clientele or both. If the bureau program is or becomes a matter of consequence to the objectives of the President, however, he will be compelled to try to make the agency genuinely a Presidential instrument.

The need of a President from time to time to bring segments of the bureaucracy under his control underscores the point made in Chapter 10 that a President's roles are indivisible and that his successes or failures with any of those who look to him for leadership affect his prospects with all of the others.[13] Thus a President with effective influence in Congress will encounter less difficulty in persuading the bureaucrats; their preoccupations with stability and organizational survival will push them in his direction. Given the power structure in Congress and the strength of some of the alliances between committees and bureaus, such Presidential influence is not inevitably effective. Its prospects will be conditioned by what the President does in a variety of apparently unrelated arenas.

Despite the variety and complexity of the controls and influences upon bureaucratic choices, then, the continuing executive remains a distinctive sector of the governmental system. Its powers are formally dependent upon authorization from elsewhere in the structure, but the diffusion of initiative within that structure, the relations of rivalry and conflict among its parts, and the authority that derives from technical skill give the bureaucracy a degree of power and autonomy not evident from the formalities.

---

[13] Chapter 10, pp. 307–08.

PART IV

LIBERTY, JUSTICE, AND LAW

15 / Law, Society, and Politics

Ever since men came out of the caves, a system of justice has been at the heart of the governmental process. After constitutions are adopted and amended, after leaders are chosen and installed in office, and after legislation has set the basic lines of right and wrong, advantage and disadvantage, some machinery for the decision of disputes and the orderly adjustment of conflicts must be provided, and have sufficient prestige for its rulings to be accepted and obeyed.

In ancient times, high priests would stir through the entrails of chickens for signs from the gods about an act of state or an argument over land; today, austere judges dressed in black robes preside over richly paneled courtrooms to perform the same function. In either case, and in all the civilizations in between, the legal system is the point at which the ideals, conflicting interests, compromises with reality, and administrative talents of any society are applied to particular disputes and made into predictable rules of conduct for its citizens.

In this section of the text, we turn to the machinery of justice in America. In the first three chapters, we examine the relation of law in America to society, government, and politics; then we turn to the organization and procedures of courts and the American system of judicial review; and finally, we look at the lawyers, judges, and law-enforcement officials who operate the legal machinery. In the next two chapters, we explore the law and politics of constitutional rights in the United States, focusing on the central topics of property, liberty, fair procedure, and equality. With this road map at hand, we turn to the first topic, the role of law in American society, government, and politics.

The Web of Law in Modern Society

When the average college student thinks of law, his greatest difficulty is to put into some rational order the confusing mass of impressions about Congressional civil rights statutes, Nevada divorces, Supreme Court rulings on literary censorship, and Perry Mason trial tactics that tend to whirl around in his mind when "law" is mentioned. As it happens, defining and classifying law has also proved to be a troublesome problem for legal scholars and jurists. Just what forms of official action rise to the "dignity of law" and how to classify the different layers in the legal system have proved to be such complicated issues that law has been aptly described as a "seamless web" of rules, relationships, rights, and duties.

Despite the difficulty of framing a master definition, we can still identify the main divisions of law in the American legal system. *Constitutional law* is made up of the federal and state constitutions and court decisions interpreting these instruments. The function of constitutional law is to set up the structure of government in society, allocate power and jurisdiction to various agencies (or reserve rights to the people which government agencies cannot forbid), and define the formal rules of the "political game" (voting, tenure of office, amendments, and others). Thus the federal Constitution states in the Fifteenth Amendment that the right to vote is guaranteed without regard to race, color, or previous condition of servitude, and federal court decisions have interpreted this guarantee to mean that a party primary restricted to "whites only" is unconstitutional.

Statutory law is made up of the thousands of acts passed by federal and state legislatures and city councils. Such legislation can deal with major issues such as foreign aid, farm price supports, and state sales taxes, or with such minor matters as designating the state flower, defining a "wrestling exhibition," or authorizing a statue in a park in memory of a nineteenth-century Ukrainian hero. The key characteristics of statutory law are its experimental character, its detailed responses to the complexity of human affairs, its frequent revision to keep abreast of change, and its setting of general boundaries between legal and illegal conduct.

A third type of law, *administrative law,* is made up of the rules and regulations issued by administrative agencies as authorized by the constitutional and statutory provisions that control administrative decisions. The rules set by the Federal Communications Commission for awarding a television channel, President Harry Truman's Executive Order creating a loyalty program for federal employees, and the federal Administrative Procedure Act of 1946 illustrate administrative law.

A fourth type is *common law.* This is the body of principles developed by judges in deciding cases which are not directly controlled by constitutional, statutory, or administrative provisions. The judges apply previous legal precedents, the customs of the community, and changing conceptions of justice and fair play to find the rule to apply to new cases. When a person recovers $500 because his landlord installed a microphone in the apartment to "check for wild parties," this may be based on the common law "right to privacy" enforced by the courts in many states; and important parts of federal labor law (such as the definitions of "employee" and "independent contractor") have common law foundations.

Besides common law there is another branch of "judge-made" law, the law of *equity.* Developed originally because of the limited powers of the common law courts in England and the need for more flexibility in both procedures and remedies, equity provides special kinds of legal relief for persons whose rights are being or have been invaded. A man wanting to prevent his neighbor from cutting down a prize cherry tree that the neighbor claims is on his property line or the attempt by the nation's major steel companies to force President Harry Truman to release the firms he seized by executive order to avert a strike during the Korean War both illustrate proceedings in equity.

Since the United States is one of many nations in an international community, a final classification is *international law*. These are the principles established by treaties and other international agreements, or the customs built up by nations in their dealings with one another. When the United States seized assets within its borders owned by Fidel Castro's Cuban regime, the power of our government to do this was tested by international law principles (and the seizure was found to be improper in a 1964 decision of the United States Supreme Court). When the United States submits a dispute which it has with some other nation over territorial fishing rights or nationalization of American-owned assets to the decision of various international courts or special arbitration tribunals, international law is also at work.

This fivefold classification of American law identifies "law" primarily in terms of the source from which the rules come—the Constitution, legislatures, administrative agencies, courts, and international agreements. Law can also be viewed in terms of the subject matter that it governs. Thus *criminal law* refers to the body of rules defining illegal conduct and prescribing the trial of accused persons by the government, while *civil law* describes the rules governing property rights, family affairs, injuries done by negligence, and similar noncriminal matters. In still another perspective, *substantive law* is a term used to indicate the rules of law that define personal and property rights for individuals or organizations, while *procedural law* refers to the principles of evidence and the conduct of trials by which "substantive rights" are determined. Still another way of classifying law is according to the sovereign that promulgates it; *federal law*, *state law*, and *municipal law* illustrate the division by jurisdiction.

As all of these definitions and divisions suggest, what we call "law" is "made" at virtually every level of government and by almost every type of official. It can range from the most solemn declaration of American society's insistence upon fair trials or freedom of religion to special city ordinances reflecting the skilled lobbying of real estate groups, beauticians, and St. Patrick's Day paraders. To fit all of these uses into one coherent pattern, some observers have suggested that "law" is best understood in its relation to "politics" and "administration."[1]

> Politics is the play of human forces as individuals and groups struggle to get what they want within and from society. Administration is the process of wielding governmental organization according to the pattern agreed upon. Law is the area of agreement which the people, or the people in power, have reached about what will be done and how it will be done. Law represents the "settledness" of society. The content of law is determined through the processes of politics, it is carried into effect through the processes of administration, and disputes concerning its meaning are finally resolved through the judicial process.

---

[1] Carl Brent Swisher, *The Theory and Practice of American National Government* (Boston, 1951), p. 482.

In this sense, law is formed by and interacts with politics and administration, but has a greater prestige and a special set of symbols because it embodies popular agreement on what is a "just" rule for a particular problem.

The Functions of Law: Of Ford Cars, School Prayers, and Swiss Corporations

There is still another way to explore the meaning of law in American society and government, and that is by the functional approach. Putting aside the institutional source of laws or the formal subject-matter divisions of legal principles, what does law *do* and how does it fit into the ordering of human affairs in the second half of the twentieth century? In this perspective, American law can be divided into six main areas: regulator of property relations; regulator of family and social relations; assessor of private risks and liabilities; assessor of offenses against society; restraint on government and distributor of power; and regulator of the international community. Looking at law from these six vantage points provides an excellent insight into the way law develops, the needs it responds to, and the choice among conflicting values that lies at the heart of the legal process.

LAW AS REGULATOR OF PROPERTY AND THE MARKETPLACE

In Capital City, Louisiana, in 1954, a year of hot competition among auto dealers, the Capital City Ford Agency placed advertisements in the local newspaper announcing:

> Buy a Ford now and when the 1955 Fords come out, we'll trade even for your '54 Ford.

Mr. Johnson, a local resident who read this ad, bought a 1954 Ford from the agency, drove it happily until the 1955 models appeared, then presented his '54 for an "even trade." To his amazement and dismay, the manager of the agency refused to swap. He told Johnson that despite what might have been said in newspaper ads or during conversations with salesmen, the contract Johnson signed at the time of purchase had said nothing about trades in 1955. Johnson should have read the contract, the manager explained, since a written contract governs the obligations of seller and buyer. Johnson responded to this lecture on contract law by suing the agency for breach of agreement, in the Louisiana courts.

This is a typical problem for the law as regulator of private bargains and the marketplace, a role vital in all countries whether their economic arrangements are capitalist, socialist, or Communist. Here, the basic rule that contract law establishes is that the written agreement between two freely contracting, adult parties is the best proof of their intentions and defines the rights of the parties toward one another. The stability of business relations would be threatened by allowing buyers, on the basis of oral promises or general publicity by the seller, to alter the terms of a formal agreement read and signed by the parties. In addition, American contract law does not regard newspaper ads as legally binding offers to sell merchandise; the ads are directed really to the whole public, not any specific persons, and are only invitations to come in and offer to buy. Advertisers can then conclude the agreement by accepting the offer, or can refuse to make an agreement for many valid reasons, such as exhaustion of stock, a mistake in price in the advertisement, and the like.

On the other hand, what about Johnson's specific situation? The Capital City Ford Agency had not published a vague ad offering to sell Fords "at low, *low* prices" or to give "the best deal in town," statements that all sensible people know to be argumentative matters. Rather, the ad had made a very specific offer, to allow all purchasers of the 1954 model to trade it in, "even," for a 1955 car. Johnson was able to show that he had read the ad, had gone to the agency directly as a result of it, and had purchased the car with the understanding that the "even trade" arrangement was in force.

The decision of the Louisiana courts was for Johnson.[2] The judge's opinion noted that it would be an unfair enrichment of the car agency to let it lure buyers into making purchases by advertising promises that were deliberately left out of the agency's contracts.

Contract law—concerned with offers and acceptances, adequate consideration, conditions, and damages for breach of contract—is only one facet of law's role as regulator of property and the marketplace. Other "private law" aspects of this role include the rules governing the creation of estates in land, the use of property in trust, the laws of inheritance, and many other facets of commercial life. In addition, there is a "public law" side to property and marketplace jurisprudence: the business antitrust laws, labor-management laws, the laws regulating government contracts, the complex network of price, wage, and rationing controls in emergency periods, and the controls over rates, routes, subsidies, and licenses for the large part of industry that is subject to federal and state supervision through regulatory commissions. The "public law" sector embodies the need in modern societies to limit the private bargains and marketplace ethics of individuals, corporations, or labor unions in order to protect the public's basic interest in such values as industrial peace, fair competition, stable prices, shared resources in economic crisis, and open entry to industries under government licensing. Law here protects all the "Johnsons" and operates by public initiative rather than private lawsuit.

To illustrate the "public" sector of marketplace law, we can examine a case that parallels, on the public side, the Capital City Ford case. During the 1950s, the Colgate-Palmolive Company conducted a nationwide television advertising campaign for Rapid Shave, an aerated shaving cream product. The filmed commercial claimed that Rapid Shave had powerful "moisturizing" properties and, to prove this, the cream was shown being applied to what the announcer said was sandpaper. A razor swiftly shaved the paper clean of the "sand" particles, and the announcer told viewers that beards "as tough as sandpaper" would be shaved equally well if this shaving cream were used. Actually, sandpaper was not used in the commercial. Instead, a "Plexiglas mock-up" had been prepared by the company's

---

[2] *Johnson* v. *Capital City Ford Co.*, 85 So. 2d. 75 (La. App. 1955).

"It Turns Up In Some Of
The Jumbo, Giant, More-Colossal-
Than-Ever Cartons."

Control of misleading packaging
and labeling is part of the public
sector of marketplace law.

From *Straight Herblock*, Simon & Schuster, 1964

advertising agency for the television film. This looked like sandpaper, and its sand-substitute was easily removed by the razor.

In 1962, the Federal Trade Commission directed Colgate-Palmolive to stop showing its sandpaper commercials. The FTC acts under Congressional laws giving it power to prevent "unfair or deceptive" advertising, especially in the area of food, drug, and cosmetic products. The FTC claimed that Rapid Shave could not possibly shave real sandpaper in the manner and time shown by the commercials, nor could it shave a beard "as tough as sandpaper" as claimed. Demonstrations that do not demonstrate reality are deceptive and forbidden, said the FTC, and may not be used to induce the public to purchase a product.

Colgate-Palmolive and its advertising agency, Ted Bates & Co., had several answers to make. They argued that technical problems in television caused sandpaper not to look like sandpaper when it was photographed, thus requiring some type of simulation. Furthermore, the use of "simulated materials"—such as dry ice in chocolate syrup to depict steaming coffee—was a common practice in television. Finally, they argued that simulation was lawful, even if the public was shown something other than what the advertiser said it was, as long as nothing false was said about the product's properties.

The FTC was not persuaded. It ruled that advertisers must find ways to portray the qualities of their products that were true demonstrations. Such true demonstrations were not beyond the technical capacities of television photography, and use of falsehoods to sell a product were not justified by the product's genuine merits.

Under American law and under the specific provisions in the Congressional statute governing the Federal Trade Commission, the decisions of regulatory agencies can be appealed to the courts, which then consider the constitutionality of the legislative provisions, the fidelity of the agency's reading of the statutory law, and the presence of sufficient evidence to justify the agency's decision. In November of 1962, the FTC ruling in the "sandpaper" case was set aside by the United States Court of Appeals in Boston, Massachusetts,[3] on the ground that the FTC could forbid only demonstration techniques that constituted "material deception." Reviewing the facts, the Court did not find this to be present in the Plexiglas episode. As of 1964, the "sandpaper" case was pending in the United States Supreme Court.

LAW AS REGULATOR OF FAMILY AND SOCIAL RELATIONSHIPS

In 1947, a wealthy American woman was married in New York to Mr. W-D, a former Russian nobleman who had become an American citizen. During their courtship, Mr. W-D had stated that he was a prominent figure in European and American society circles; that he had always earned his own living and had never taken money from a woman; and that his purpose in marrying Mrs. W-D was to contribute to her happiness and to perform faithfully all his husbandly duties.

In 1949, Mrs. W-D sued in the New York courts to have the marriage annulled on the ground of fraud. According to Mrs. W-D, her husband's self-portrait had been wholly deceptive. He had been married previously and had been paid a large sum of money by his former wife as an "inducement" to give her an uncontested divorce; he was considered a fortune hunter and was not acceptable in European and American society; he had married Mrs. W-D primarily to get money to keep himself and his relatives in luxurious style without intending to work, and had done no work since the marriage; he had tried to get Mrs. W-D to give him money for a nonexistent business prospect and had attempted to collect commissions from the contractor who remodeled Mrs. W-D's house; and he had failed in his husbandly duties because he was, in Mrs. W-D's words, "a hypochondriac given to fits of uncontrollable temper and to periods of sexual impotency." Since Mr. W-D had secured her consent to the marriage by false representations, Mrs. W-D asked the court to dissolve the marriage as one that had never been validly contracted.

The trial court, after hearing the testimony of both parties, ruled that Mrs. W-D's allegations were all true and granted her an annulment. Mr. W-D carried the case to the Court of Appeals of New York, the highest tribunal in that state, where as we will see, the decision was reversed.

While regulation of the family was once exclusively under religious authority and was governed by church law and church tribunals, most family matters are now regulated by the statutory and court-made law of the state. In addition to questions of valid marriage, annulment, divorce,

---

[3] *Colgate-Palmolive Company* v. *FTC*, 310 F. 2d. 89 (1962).

and support after separation, domestic relations law deals with the legal and economic relations between husband and wife, and with relations between parent and child. The latter range from questions of legitimacy, adoption, and custody on separation to issues of parental responsibility for the contracts, torts, and crimes of the child. The family law of any society, sociologists suggest, portrays superbly the debates over changing morals and values of the system. Because this is very much the case, the debates among judges, legislators, religious leaders, and the public over the rules for such issues as marriage, divorce, or adoption are usually passionate and heated arguments. Should the state punish marriages between freely consenting members of different races? Should divorces be permitted for such grounds as mental cruelty or incompatibility, or should only such grave offenses as adultery be sufficient for divorce? Should the law require that a child given out for adoption be placed only with a family of the same religion as that of the child's parents, or as that of the mother if the parents were of different faiths? Should law make it easy or difficult for women to recover money damages for broken promises to marry? Where sincere religious belief directs that men have more than one wife, should the law punish such conduct on the ground that polygamy is forbidden by the laws of nature and the Judeo-Christian heritage?

In the W-D case, the New York Court of Appeals reversed the decision of the lower court and refused to permit Mrs. W-D to have the marriage annulled.[4] Annulment for fraud under New York law, the Court said, must be based on misrepresentations as to matters "vital to the marriage relationship." Such would be the pregnancy of the wife by a man other than the husband, undisclosed to the husband before the marriage, or the refusal of one party to fulfill a premarriage promise to follow a civil marriage with a religious ceremony deeply desired by the other party. But premarital falsehoods as to character, fortune, health, or "marrying for money" are not sufficient to void the marriage. Here, the Court ruled, W-D's falsehoods did not go to the "vital" matters. He never promised to "support" Mrs. W-D and this would have been unnecessary, given Mrs. W-D's wealth. He *had* earned his living before marriage, whatever might be said of how he had done it. While he falsely represented that he had never taken money from women, "premarital falsehoods much graver than that are insufficient for the judicial voiding of a marriage." As for his husbandly duties, there was no evidence that he refused to perform them, and the parties to a marriage must take one another, as the famous phrase goes, "in sickness and in health . . ." Thus, while the Court noted that Mr. W-D was "no model of chivalry or propriety" and emerged instead as a "fortune-hunter, a sluggard, [and] a hypochondriac," he had performed the "fundamental duties of the marriage relationship" and an annulment for fraud could not be granted.

LAW AS ASSESSOR OF PRIVATE RISKS AND LIABILITIES

While putting a new roof on an apartment house in Holyoke, Massachusetts, in 1941, the employees of a roofing company set up a "tar kettle"

---

[4] *Woronzoff-Daschkow* v. *Woronzoff-Daschkow*, 303 N.Y. 506 (1952).

in the backyard of the property. The kettle was made of heavy metal and stood about three feet high. A smaller pot containing tar was in the center of the kettle; around this pot, but still inside the kettle, was the fire that melted the tar and kept it hot.

On the day involved here, the roofers finished using the hot tar shortly before noon. They put out the fire, and covered the top of the kettle with a flat piece of sheet metal, held down by a slab of wood. At about three-thirty that afternoon, the six-year-old son of one of the tenants was playing on the flat roof of a low garage close to the spot where the tar kettle had been placed. One of the boy's playmates offered him a penny if he would jump on top of the tar kettle from the garage roof. The boy jumped, hit the cover on its side, and fell into the kettle. Though the fire was out, ten to twelve inches of tar in the inner pot was still hot enough to burn the boy severely, and he died soon afterward of these injuries. At the time of the accident, the workmen were all occupied on the roof of the apartment house.

The boy's father brought suit in the Massachusetts courts against the roofing company for damages, alleging that the child's death had been caused by the negligence of the company in not protecting the kettle more securely or having it guarded. Children were known to play in the yard, and anyone who sets up such a potentially dangerous instrument as a kettle of hot tar must exercise more care than was taken here. As the child's parent, the father asked the court to award damages for the suffering and death caused by the roofing company's creation of such a risk of harm.

This case shows the role of law in dealing with injuries done to persons and property in society. In earlier times, the boy's father might have killed the roofer, or even one of his children, in reprisal and vengeance. In modern days, law redresses injuries through two main channels: criminal prosecutions, where the government punishes those responsible for causing harm to another in a way forbidden by law; and "tort" actions, where the injured party brings a private suit for damages (or other special relief) when the injury was either unintentional or intentional but not criminal. Tort law protects not only property and the physical person but also the rights to privacy and reputation.

The issue of negligence, as involved in the tar kettle case, is at the heart of tort law. Negligence is not always required for an injured party to recover damages, for society can decide that a person who carries on dangerous activities, such as keeping wild animals or storing volatile explosives, must compensate anyone injured through these hazardous instrumentalities. Society can also leave injured parties to be compensated by means other than law suit against those causing the injury, as through private insurance or workmen's compensation programs.

For most injuries done in the daily business of living, recovery still depends on proving that there was negligence. In the tar kettle case, the Massachusetts courts were aware that if unreasonable requirements were imposed on roofers—or on automobile drivers, store owners, airlines, home owners, or newspapers—society would risk being frozen into a costly over-security. Tragic as injuries can be, the care required by law must take into account the need for social progress, reasonable precaution, unreasonable conduct by the injured party, the function of damages, and similar considerations.

In the tar kettle case, the Supreme Judicial Court of Massachusetts ultimately ruled in favor of the roofer.[5] His men had protected the kettle adequately against children playing on the ground, the Court said, and could not reasonably be expected "to anticipate or to guard against the bare possibility of injury to some child jumping through the cover into the pot from an adjoining roof. . . ." A final sentence in the Court's opinion, lamenting the "unfortunate occurrence," testified to the fact that distributing the risks and liabilities in a society, and doing justice between specific parties, is not without its pains for judges.

LAW AS ASSESSOR OF OFFENSES AGAINST SOCIETY

The Direct Sales Corporation of Buffalo, New York, a firm that sold drugs by mail at wholesale prices, was indicted in 1941 for conspiracy to violate the Federal Narcotics Act. The indictment charged that the wholesaler had sold morphine to a South Carolina doctor named Tate, over an extended period of time, in quantities so much greater than a doctor could prescribe in normal practice that the wholesaler must have known that Tate was distributing the morphine illegally. The government's evidence showed that the wholesaler pursued his sale of narcotic drugs aggressively through discount pricing and that he sold in huge lots despite government warnings to drug suppliers against such bulk sales. During 1939, the wholesaler sold Dr. Tate, a practitioner in a small rural community, between 5,000 and 6,000 morphine tablets a month; a doctor's average *yearly* supply was between 200 and 400 tablets. The government's evidence showed that Tate, among other shady medical customers of the wholesaler, was selling the morphine at high prices to addicts. (Tate was tried and convicted separately.)

At the trial and on appeal, the wholesaler's defense was that the sales were perfectly legal. Dr. Tate had ordered the drugs on the official blanks prescribed by federal law; no maximum amount to be sold to any one doctor at any one time, or even annually, was set by law. Since the wholesaler's sales were themselves legal, it was argued, there could be no conspiracy conviction just because Dr. Tate had used the morphine tablets illegally. The wholesaler's lawyers placed heavy reliance on a 1940 case in which the United States Supreme Court had reversed the conviction for conspiracy of a supplier who had sold sugar, yeast, and large cans to men specifically known by the supplier to engage in the illegal manufacture of alcohol. Such knowledge, the Court had said, was not enough to make the supplier part of a conspiracy, even though the supplies sold *were* used to manufacture whiskey illegally.

Criminal law, as Professor Herbert Wechsler of Columbia Law School has observed, "is the law on which men place their ultimate reliance for protection against all the deepest injuries that human conduct can inflict on individuals and institutions." Professor Wechsler continued:

---

[5] *Marengo v. Roy,* 318 Mass. 719 (1945)

By the same token, penal law governs the strongest force that we permit official agencies to bring to bear on individuals. Its promise as an instrument of safety is matched only by its power to destroy. If penal law is weak or ineffective, basic human interests are in jeopardy. If it is harsh or arbitrary in its impact, it works a gross injustice on those caught within its toils . . . . Nowhere in the entire legal field is more at stake for the community or for the individual.[6]

The major aspects of criminal law are (1) the definition of crimes (Is it murder for a doctor to shorten the life of an incurably ill patient at his request? Is it arson to burn down one's own house?); (2) the processes of investigation and trial by which guilt or innocence is established (Is telephone tapping a legitimate police method? What is the proper test for insanity? Should the government be allowed to comment to the jury on the failure of a defendant to testify at his trial?); and (3) the punishment that is imposed after conviction (What kind of punishment? How much? And for what purpose?).

In the drug wholesaler case, the basic issue was whether the defendant had a sufficient criminal intention and knowledge of the offense being committed by Tate to make him guilty of conspiracy with the doctor. Men must know that they are violating the law before they become guilty of a crime, though such knowledge can sometimes be assumed to go along automatically with commission of an act. Here, the jury found the wholesaler guilty and the United States Supreme Court affirmed the conviction in 1943.[7] The Justices distinguished the 1940 alcohol supplier's case by saying that there the goods sold were harmless in themselves and could have been used for purposes other than illegal distilling. But morphine was an inherently dangerous commodity whose distribution to doctors was regulated by law. This put the wholesaler on stricter notice that purchases in suspiciously large quantities would be for illegal purposes. The situation resembled that of selling hunting rifles and machine guns, the Court explained; both could conceivably be put to illegal use, but the intention of sellers must be judged by the obvious fact that the normal private customers for machine guns were "gangsters, not hunters." In the drug case, the normal customers for morphine distributed illegally were drug addicts, and the wholesaler's knowledge of Dr. Tate's excessive purchases constituted enough criminal intention to sustain the conspiracy conviction.

LAW AS RESTRAINT ON GOVERNMENT AND
DISTRIBUTOR OF POWER IN THE STATE

In 1951, the Board of Regents of New York, which supervises education throughout the state, composed a special prayer that was recommended to local school officials for recitation during the school day. The prayer read: "Almighty God, we acknowledge our dependence upon Thee, and we beg Thy blessings upon us, our parents, our teachers and our country."

[6] Herbert Wechsler, "The Challenge of a Model Penal Code," *Harvard Law Review* (1952), Volume LXV, pp. 1097–98.
[7] *Direct Sales Corporation* v. *U.S.*, 319 U.S. 703 (1943).

"I'll Get You In There If It Kills You."

A liberal view of attempts by critics of the school prayer decision to overturn the ruling by constitutional amendment.

From *Straight Herblock*, Simon & Schuster, 1964

In the community of New Hyde Park, a suburb of New York City, the local board of education directed in 1958 that each class say the prayer aloud at the beginning of school. Children could be excused from saying the prayer on the written request of their parents, and would either stand silently or leave the room during the recitation. School personnel were forbidden to comment on such nonparticipation.

A group of five parents—one Unitarian, two Jews, one Ethical Culturist, and one agnostic—brought suit in the New York courts, on behalf of their children in the New Hyde Park schools, challenging the Regents' Prayer as a violation of the United States Constitution. The First Amendment, they noted, forbids the federal government to make any law "respecting an establishment of religion or prohibiting the free exercise thereof"; this applies to the states also, as part of the "liberty" guaranteed against state interference by the Fourteenth Amendment. The protesting parents said that the use of government authority and public funds to institute an official prayer in the schools established a religion as forbidden by the Constitution. (Previous Supreme Court rulings had stated that it was an "establishment of religion" for the state to use its funds or official powers to teach religion in the public schools or compel observance of patriotic ceremonies there when these violated the religious principles of the school children.) Prayer was a matter for the home, the house of worship, and private organizations, not for the public schools, the complaining parents

"You Stay Out of Our Public Schools!"

A conservative interpretation of the Supreme Court's decision outlawing school prayers.

Knox in the Nashville *Banner*

argued. Furthermore, the introduction of an official prayer could only have divisive effects among children of different faiths, and would embarrass those, both believers and nonbelievers, who could not subscribe to the prayer. The New York courts, from the local court to the New York Court of Appeals, upheld the prayer as a valid nondenominational exercise of mixed patriotic and religious character. The parents then took their case to the Supreme Court of the United States, where it was considered and decided in 1962.

The New York school prayer case is a classic illustration of constitutional law in action. The federal Constitution and the constitutions of the fifty states grant certain specific powers to government and also place specific limits on government's authority to act. What government can and cannot do, and which branch of government can do it, is thus the heart of constitutional law. In the American system, the interpretation of the Constitution's meaning on these issues lies mainly with the courts, though each agency of government considers the constitutionality of its proposed actions before it undertakes them. In cases properly brought before the courts, the judges review the actions of Presidents, Congresses, Interstate Commerce Commissioners, governors, city councilmen, and police officers, and the idea that all of these elected and appointed officials can act lawfully only in pursuance of constitutional power is the basic assumption of our constitutional scheme of government. Since several chapters of this section deal in detail with American constitutional law and the role of judges in applying it, we can save an extended discussion of this phase of law until that point.

In the New York school prayer case, the Supreme Court had to decide whether the language of the "establishment clause," the discussions surrounding its adoption, its interpretation by previous Supreme Courts, governmental practice as to religious observances, and the specific facts of the New York prayer recitation made such a school prayer a valid public ceremony or an invalid establishment of religion. The majority of the Court held that the practice was unconstitutional.[8] The ceremony was clearly "a religious activity," wrote Justice Hugo Black for the majority; and "it is no part of the business of government to compose official prayers for any group of the American people to recite as part of a religious program carried on by government." Church and state are meant to be separate by the rule of the First Amendment, and this government prayer puts New York in the promulgation and enforcement of "religious activity." In addition, there is an "indirect coercive pressure upon religious minorities to conform" in such a situation. This does not mean that government must be hostile to religion and prayer, Justice Black noted, but that religion must be left "to the people themselves and to those the people choose to look to for religious guidance."

As often happens in law cases, especially in sensitive constitutional law cases, the Supreme Court was not unanimous. Justice Potter Stewart wrote a dissent that cited the long history of religious observances carried on in Congress, presided over by American Presidents, marking the daily opening of the Supreme Court, and capped by the addition in 1954 of the phrase "under God" to the nation's pledge of allegiance to the flag. He also mentioned the reference to God in the third stanza of the national anthem and on the nation's coins. These show, said Justice Stewart, that the United States has "highly cherished spiritual traditions," and the Regents' Prayer was only an attempt to have schoolchildren share that heritage. It is misapplying a "great constitutional principle" to hold that New York establishes an "official religion" when it lets "those who want to say a prayer say it."

At the heart of the case, as is so often true in civil liberty problems, was the conflict between the legislative or "popular" majority's desire to use public institutions for the observance of dominant ideas and opinions, and the desire of minority groups to keep compulsory practices or discriminatory situations out of the public sectors.

LAW AS REGULATOR IN THE INTERNATIONAL COMMUNITY

In 1942, shortly after the United States entered the Second World War, the federal government seized the assets of the General Aniline and Film Company, a chemical firm then worth about $40 million, incorporated in this country. General Aniline's shares, said the government, were owned by a Swiss holding company named Interhandel, which in turn was controlled by I. G. Farben of Germany. I. G. Farben's holdings were subject to seizure as enemy property under the Trading with the Enemy Act.

In 1946, with the war over, the United States signed an agreement with Switzerland under which Swiss assets frozen by law in the United States would be released, while the Swiss were to liquidate all German-owned properties in their country. "Final" determination as to which companies in Switzerland were German-controlled was to be made by a Swiss Authority of Review. If the United States disagreed with its determination, how-

---

[8] *Engel v. Vitale,* 370 U.S. 421 (1962).

ever, the 1946 agreement provided that the issue should go to international arbitration.

In 1948, the Swiss Authority of Review held that Interhandel had become free of Farben control in June, 1940, and was therefore a Swiss firm, not a German firm subject to liquidation. Shortly thereafter, the Swiss Government asked the United States to turn over the seized General Aniline assets to their owner, Interhandel.

The United States refused and the company's 8,000 employees and plants in eight states were continued under government management, through the Office of the Alien Property Custodian. The United States maintained that the determination of what were enemy assets in the United States was a matter for American authorities and did not fall under the 1946 agreement with Switzerland. Interhandel could make a claim to its property by suing in the American courts and proving its independence from Farben control in 1942. Interhandel brought such a suit in 1948.

By 1957, though, the case stood at an impasse. United States authorities insisted that Interhandel produce in the American courts certain documents relating to the question of German control; the Swiss bank-secrecy laws made it a crime for a Swiss company to disclose these to anyone. When the United States courts ordered Interhandel to produce the documents, the Swiss Government confiscated them before Interhandel could comply. Thereafter, Switzerland refused to provide the material for use in the federal courts.

While this impasse was developing, Switzerland continued to ask the United States to arbitrate the issue of Interhandel's character. When the United States declined, Switzerland sued the United States in 1957 before the International Court of Justice at The Hague, in Holland, seeking either an order directing the United States to arbitrate or else a decision by the International Court itself as to the status of Interhandel during the war period.

Public international law is the area of conflict between nations that is treated by legal procedures rather than dealt with by direct diplomacy or war. Since there is no international sovereign with power to compel obedience from all nation-states, as governments can within their own borders, international law at this stage of world development has a limited area of operations. It must often rest for its enforcement on the willingness of nations to abide by it, or to accept decisions of international tribunals expounding it, or to obey the resolutions of a body like the United Nations calling upon a member nation to adhere to a rule or principle of international law. The content of international law comes from the customary rules which nations have bound themselves to follow through treaties and conventions. Arbitration awards, diplomatic usages, and the rulings of the international courts are sometimes considered to "make" international law. As its ultimate goal, international law provides the vision of all nations settling their disputes by law and not force; in its immediate role, international law provides a means of resolving and adjusting those conflicts that are not regarded by powerful nations as issues of absolute national sovereignty.

The International Court of Justice, where the Swiss Government sued the United States in the Interhandel dispute, is the judicial arm of the United Nations and succeeded the World Court established under the League of Nations. It consists of fifteen judges elected for nine-year terms by the concurrent votes of the United Nations General Assembly and the Security Council. It hears, among other cases, the "contentious" disputes brought by nations against one another. The International Court's judgments bind nations that have accepted, either as a general matter in advance, or for the purposes of the particular case, the compulsory jurisdiction of the International Court. Both the United States and Switzerland had accepted in advance the compulsory jurisdiction of the Court, though the United States attached to its ratification of acceptance the so-called Connally Amendment, reserving the right to decide itself all issues "essentially within the domestic jurisdiction of the United States."

The decision of the International Court in the Interhandel case was handed down in 1959.[9] The Court rejected the contention of the United States that the issue was a matter for the "domestic jurisdiction" of the United States. It also rejected the American claim that the issue could not be decided by the International Court because the seizure took place before the International Court was created or because the dispute arose before both the United States and Switzerland had accepted the compulsory jurisdiction of the Court. However, the judges held that the Swiss suit could not be maintained in the International Court at that time because the Interhandel company had not carried to their conclusion the proceedings available in the American courts. Only when a final decision had been reached there could the case become subject to international law decision.

In 1962, Congress enacted a statute authorizing the government to sell General Aniline—now worth over $200 million—and use the proceeds to satisfy American war claims, with the Treasury Department holding the proceeds until determination of the suits over rightful ownership to the corporation. Interhandel filed a suit in the United States federal courts challenging the constitutionality of the 1962 sale act and forestalling the sale while the suit was pending. Then, in 1963, the Justice Department concluded an "agreement in principle" with Interhandel for sale of General Aniline to the highest bidder. The United States Government would get the first 11 percent of the sale price, then divide the remaining 89 percent equally with Interhandel, with $24 million of Interhandel's share paid to the United States to settle a tax claim against the company. As of early 1964, however, General Aniline had still not been sold, and most experts doubted whether the end of this law suit was in sight.

With the Interhandel case, we have now sampled six primary areas of American law in terms of the functions that law performs. The roles of constitutional provisions, legislative enactments, administrative decisions, court rulings, and international agreements have been portrayed by showing law at work in the peaceful resolution of basic and continuing conflicts of modern American society.

---

[9] *Interhandel Case* [1959], I.C.J. Rep. 266.

Basic Theories of Law

To stop with classification of law and a functional analysis would be to leave out one of the most important keys to understanding the American legal system and the judicial process. This key is the classic debate over the nature of law.

In democratic systems, law embodies two values that are in constant tension. On the one hand, law is the process that gives stability to the personal and property relations in a society, providing continuity with the past and permitting citizens to predict the probable legal consequences of their actions. Law is thus an instrument of the *status quo*. On the other hand, law must also provide for social change, not only through the statutes passed by elected organs of government but also, because constitutions and statutes can only be general guides, through the rulings of courts and administrative agencies in particular cases. Law must therefore be an instrument of transition, adjusting older rules to the changing power relations and shifting ideals of society.

In addition, there is another built-in tension to legal systems. The ideal of judging is that all those who come before the courts to assert their rights or defend their interests are entitled to equality of treatment under the existing rules. Law must be blind as between the rich and the poor, white and black, Gentile and Jew, liberal and conservative, pacifist and militarist, Northerner and Southerner. But to adhere to equality, especially in the public law sector, judges and other lawmakers must have some concept of justice that defines the relations of individuals, groups, society, and the state. By what standards is justice measured, and what happens when statute law or constitutional law conflicts with the judge's deep conviction that the law as enacted is unjust?

While the allegiances of party, economic interest group, religion, race, and class will affect the lawmaker's approach to these conflicts, he will also be guided by some basic approach to the legal system—a unifying idea about its nature, purposes, and possibilities. Men have debated about theories of law for thousands of years, understandably so because the legal theory of a state lies at the heart of managing empires, building civilizations, and cementing national loyalties. Over 600 years ago, the clash of theories was registered in a fourteenth-century law case reported in the English Year Books. After the trial had been completed in the royal court of Common Bench, one of the presiding judges asked, "Plaintiff, will you say anything else . . . ?" Thorpe, the plaintiff's lawyer, replied, "I think you will do as others have done in the same [type of] case, or else we do not know what the law is." One justice replied, "It is the will of the Justices." "No," interjected the Chief Justice, "law is that which is right." [10] More than 600 years later, the three views expressed by these men are still the main contending theories of law: "that which is right"—the *natural law* concept; "the will of the Justices"—the *positive law* concept; "as others have done"—the *sociological* or *developmental* concept. A basic statement

---

[10] *Langbridge's Case*, 19 Edw. III 375. Quoted in Harold Berman, *The Nature and Functions of Law* (Brooklyn, 1958), pp. 21–22.

of each of these, the problems each raises, and how they fit into the American legal system is what we turn to now.

"THAT WHICH IS RIGHT"—
THE NATURAL LAW TRADITION

The natural law tradition goes back as far as the Greek philosophers and is as modern as the Nuremberg trials of the Nazi leaders for "crimes against mankind." It assumes that there are fundamental and absolute concepts of law and justice that men can know and can apply to their political and social affairs. The validity of a legal system, and of every decision taken under it, rests on the harmony of its rules and regulations with the principles of natural law. One main school of natural law is religious in character and rests on man's presumed ability to discover fundamental, rational principles of right and wrong by which to test man-made laws. In this way, man participates in God's divine reason. Another school, sometimes called "rationalistic natural law," does not see natural law as flowing from divine origins but from a "rational universe" and man's self-developed moral codes. Whichever origin is assigned to the higher law standard, the natural law advocate would say that a constitutional clause that forbade anyone to practice anything but the national religion, or a systematic national program to destroy a racial or ethnic group, or the replacement of independent courts with a party-tribunal system of dealing out justice in particular cases would all violate natural law standards. The essential point is that a higher morality limits all powers of government.

"THE WILL OF THE JUSTICES"—
THE POSITIVE THEORY OF LAW

The second major theory of law, positivism, maintains that law is what the supreme political authority in the state commands and can enforce. (In our fourteenth-century case, the "will of the Justices" would ultimately have to be the will of the king who appointed the judges and in whose name they issued rulings.) While positivism sometimes cites a moral justification for its position—that it brings order out of the violent relations of men and protects property—the basic view of the positivist is that law must be separated from any standard of morality that is set by authorities other than the sovereign. This provides certainty as to what must be accepted as binding law, and provides stability by rejecting any outside test of validity. The role of judges under positivist theory is to apply the laws of the sovereign, not to substitute personal or religious notions of their own about what is wise.

The positivist theory can be used by almost any political system. In a theocratic state, positive law would be the command of the church authorities; in a monarchy, the will of a king; in a totalitarian system, the command of the leader; in a democracy, the acts of the elected government. Positive law can thus be reactionary in one circumstance, reformist in another, or even revolutionary. Its essential point is that human political institutions are the sole source and measure of law.

A third basic theory defines law not as a morally measured set of rules or as the applied will of a particular sovereign but as a gradual, organic growth of rules developed by men in specific societies and the processes used to adjust conflicting interests through a legal system. Law is viewed as growing out of family relations in primitive societies, then tribal customs, and developed stage by stage in response to changes in technology and the organization of society. The moral aspirations of the society as well as the particular policies of the sovereign are embodied in law.

In addition to its idea of evolutionary development, sociological theory also stresses the realistic analysis of how lawgivers and law-interpreters balance and adjust conflicting interests in society. When legislation is proposed to create a federal loyalty program, sociological theory sees legislators weighing the need of the state to protect itself from internal subversion against the equal need of the democratic state for freedom of expression and social criticism, and judges weighing the constitutionality of such measures are seen as engaged in the same balancing process.

Thus instead of discussing only the logic or the "right reason" of decisions, sociological theorists probe the economic, ideological, psychological, or class factors that influence judges and try to bring these into clear visibility so that society can see the factors at work and decide whether they are the desired criteria to be applied by the judges.

The essential point of sociological theory, therefore, is that it sees law as an organic growth of particular societies, by which conflicting interests of the day can be peaceably adjusted.

ANALYZING THE MAJOR THEORIES OF LAW

Each of the three theories is obviously more of an idealized statement than a description of what law actually was or is at any given time. In democratic societies, the three ideas tend to be blended inseparably in popular attitudes toward law. Positive law is seen as the normal foundation of statutory and administrative law, sociological analysis is used to describe realistically and criticize the decisions of the lawmakers and law-interpreters, and natural law is invoked as an ideal—especially in the courts—by those who believe their rights have been violated in a fundamental way by some decision. Positive law stresses stability, order, and legitimacy of authority unless changed by regular processes. Natural law stresses morality, reason, and restraint on the uses of power. Sociological theory expresses realism, criticism of law, and tries to accommodate both positive and higher law in terms of the adjustment of conflicting interests in light of the best historical and political experience of society.

THEORIES OF LAW AND THE AMERICAN LEGAL TRADITION

When we turn to the specific impact of these legal theories upon American constitutional and legal development, the most important fact to note is that American law has been shaped by each of the three schools as the Republic has moved from colonial times to the nuclear age. To describe this influence briefly:

Natural law ideas in the writings of John Locke, Thomas Jefferson, and Tom Paine, among many others, were an ingredient in America's revolutionary ideology. Statements that rulers could not abridge the "rights of mankind" and the laws of "Nature and Nature's God" permeated the major documents of our independence era. Once the colonists were established as a nation, the United States Supreme Court began to interpret many of the broad clauses of the Constitution protecting individual rights—"due process of law," "equal protection of the law," "deprivation of liberty," and "obligation of contracts"—as though these were shorthand terms for a body of natural law principles that the Founding Fathers had incorporated by reference into the Constitution and that the judges would apply to restrain offending government officials. At the same time, the idea that even the Constitution and the Supreme Court cannot justify violations of "higher law" has been another theme carried through American history by sizable bodies of public and political opinion. No free man need obey "a covenant with Hell," the antislavery leaders said of the Constitution after the *Dred Scott* decision in 1857 seemed to lock African slavery into permanent place on the American scene. Today, "freedom riders" and "sit-in" demonstrators against segregation often maintain that "unjust" laws need not be obeyed, and while they look to the Supreme Court to protect their rights, these demonstrators are prepared to violate segregation rules even if the Supreme Court does not uphold the right of Negroes to service by the side of white citizens.

The positivist tradition in the United States can be seen in the move, following the successful break with Great Britain, to limit the common law rules inherited from British law and applied by "aristocratic" judges. This was done through the adoption of codes by the state legislatures, a movement which swept American law in the middle of the nineteenth century. The codes spelled out rules for major legal issues of property and procedure and represented an attempt not only to rationalize the American legal system but also to protect the political and legal reforms of the Jacksonian movement from the hostile interpretations of conservative judges. Other positivist themes in American law can be seen in the constant assumption by many Americans that law can "legislate" morality in matters ranging from the drinking of liquor and respect for religion to the elimination of "dangerous" ideas about politics, economics, or society.

Finally, the sociological contribution to American law can be seen in the reaction against both natural law concepts and positivist doctrines that we associate with the ideas of Oliver Wendell Holmes, Jr., Roscoe Pound, Jerome Frank, and a steady stream of influential legal thinkers who changed the entire tone and outlook of American law between 1900 and the present. Their powerful analyses of how judges really decide cases, how flexible the Constitution really is and must be in the face of new crises facing the nation, and the basic role of legislation in adjusting conflicting group interests have become the common language of law taught in the law schools and understood broadly by the population.

Thus American law in its development over the past century and three quarters has registered all three main themes as to the nature and limits of law.

If we turn to the influence of legal theories on contemporary law in the United States, we can see these ideas at work in the day-to-day operations of lawmaking at the legislative level. In the consideration by a city council of a fair housing law, advocates of legal guarantees of racial equality in housing will clash with defenders of the individual's right to dispose of his house or to rent his apartments as he chooses, and the terms of the legislative debate will typically ring with appeals to "higher rights" or "fixed constitutional limits" or "balancing the interests." But the place in our society where the clash of legal theories is most dramatic and most influential for the whole governmental system is in the United States Supreme Court.

THE SUPREME COURT AND THE CLASH OF LEGAL THEORIES

We can illustrate the impact of legal theories within the contemporary United States Supreme Court by looking at one of the leading issues of constitutional law, the question of Supreme Court review of state actions affecting civil liberties. In 1833, the Supreme Court ruled that since the federal Bill of Rights had been written to place limits only on the federal government, a person who believed his fundamental rights had been invaded by *state* officials could not seek relief in the federal courts but had to rely on a law suit in the state courts under the civil liberty guarantees of the state constitution.[11] Following the Civil War, and reflecting the nationalist spirit produced by that conflict, the Thirteenth, Fourteenth, and Fifteenth Amendments wrote into the Constitution certain national guarantees of civil liberties that were made binding upon the states. The broadest of these was the famous clause in the Fourteenth Amendment declaring that "No State shall . . . deprive any person of life, liberty, or property, without due process of law. . . ."

The concept of "due process of law" dates back to the famous guarantees that the English barons won from the king in 1215 in Magna Charta and the due process clause had been written into the Fifth Amendment in 1791 as a limit to *federal* power. But the term had not been defined further in the Bill of Rights or the Fourteenth Amendment, and this produced a continuing debate in the Supreme Court after 1868 over two fundamental issues: (1) what specific rights are included in the guarantees of "life, liberty, or property," and (2) does the requirement of "due process of law" place on government only the requirement of orderly procedure and a fair hearing or does it impose limits on governmental measures which take away the substance of these rights even with fair procedures? While the Justices have approached these issues by tracing English constitutional history, the contemporaneous statements of the Framers of the Fourteenth Amendment, pre-1868 judicial precedents, and other paths of interpretation, the pivotal point reached by the Court again and again since 1868 has been one of constitutional philosophy, or, as we have called it earlier, legal theory.

A leading "due process" situation in which these theories have come into conflict involves state prosecutions for crime. In the Fourth through the

---

[11] *Barron* v. *Baltimore*, 7 Pet. 243 (1833).

Eighth Amendments to the federal Constitution, a series of procedural rights are spelled out as requirements for *federal* officials—guaranteeing security of the citizen from unreasonable searches and seizures, from excessive bail, and from cruel and unusual punishments; prescribing that trials shall be initiated only through indictment by grand jury and shall be decided by a petit jury; giving the accused a right to a speedy, public trial in which he can refuse to be a witness against himself; and many other important provisions for *federal* procedure. Before the adoption of the Fourteenth Amendment, however, the states could define for themselves the rights that would be given to accused persons in *state* criminal trials. After 1868, the Supreme Court began to examine departures by the states from the procedural arrangements of the Fourth through the Eighth Amendments to determine whether new methods of state police investigation or state court procedures deprived citizens of their national liberty or property rights without "due process."

In facing this problem, two conflicting positions developed within the Supreme Court and have continued from the 1880s to the present. The majority position within the Court, *selective incorporation,* allows the states to adopt procedures they think desirable "whether sanctioned by age or custom, or newly devised in the discretion of the legislature power, in furtherance of the general public good" as long as these do not violate "those fundamental principles of liberty and justice which lie at the base of all our civil and political institutions. . . ." [12] The Justices examine each challenged state practice to see whether what has been done interferes with rights that are "so rooted in the traditions and conscience of our people as to be ranked as fundamental," and represent "the very essence of a scheme of ordered liberty." [13] Under the rule of selective incorporation, states have been allowed to initiate prosecutions by a sworn statement of the district attorney passed on by a judge rather than by grand jury; to use fewer than twelve persons on a jury; to allow a prosecutor to comment to the jury on the failure of a defendant to take the witness stand; and to require persons to take "drunkometer" tests after auto accidents as a condition of keeping their driver's licenses. On the other hand, use of the "ordered liberty" standard has led the Court to outlaw such practices as pumping someone's stomach to recover morphine capsules swallowed to destroy evidence (as conduct that "shocks the conscience") or using in state courts evidence obtained by state police through unreasonable searches.

The second and minority position within the Supreme Court, *automatic incorporation,* contends that the due process clause of the Fourteenth Amendment made all of the specific provisions of the first eight amendments to the federal Constitution binding upon the states. These are incorporated exactly, and where the Fifth Amendment requires indictment by grand jury or the Seventh Amendment specifies jury trial in civil cases of $20 or more, that cannot be varied by the states. Furthermore, in judging the reasonableness of police searches or the applicability of the

---

[12] *Hurtado v. California,* 110 U.S. 516 (1884).
[13] *Palko v. Connecticut,* 302 U.S. 319 (1937).

self-incrimination and double jeopardy clauses, no distinction can be drawn from the federal-state system to allow greater latitude to Minnesota policemen or Kentucky criminal courts than to federal officials and tribunals.[14]

While there are complex questions of language construction and constitutional history involved in the debate over selective versus automatic incorporation, the clash of legal theories was central to the Court's debate. This is beautifully illustrated by the running debate during the 1940s and 1950s among the Justices, led by Justices Hugo Black and Felix Frankfurter, over "selective" or "automatic" incorporation of the first eight amendments in the due process clause. The Black-Frankfurter debate was strung out in a series of cases, but we will draw together the best of their comments into two integrated presentations of the two viewpoints.

Justice Hugo Black, attacking the selective position of the Court's majority, contended that the Bill of Rights was aimed at "the same kind of human evils that have emerged from century to century whenever excessive power is sought by the few at the expense of the many. . . ." It is beyond the proper role of the Justices to seek to "improve on the Bill of Rights by substituting natural-law concepts" for the provisions detailed there. The very idea that the Court "is endowed by the Constitution with boundless power under 'natural law' periodically to expand and contract constitutional standards to conform to the Court's conception of what at a particular time constitutes 'civilized decency' and 'fundamental liberty and justice' . . . should be abandoned as an incongruous excrescence on the Constitution." Such a policy violates "the great design of a written Constitution."

The majority position was defended by Justice Felix Frankfurter. The idea of due process employed by the Court, he said, "is not to be derided as a resort to a revival of 'natural law.' . . . In each case 'due process of law' requires an evaluation based on a disinterested inquiry pursued in the spirit of science, on a balanced order of facts exactly and fairly stated, on the detached consideration of conflicting claims, on a judgment not *ad hoc* and episodic but duly mindful of reconciling the needs both of continuity and change in a progressive society." Applying this spirit to the incorporation dispute, Frankfurter said, the Court should not hold the states to "narrow or provincial" procedural arrangements. Those provisions of the Bill of Rights that "are enduring reflections of experience with human nature" should be continued, but those that "express the restricted views of Eighteenth-Century England regarding the best methods for the ascertainment of facts" could be changed by the states. And, where automatic incorporation would freeze the due process clause to the abuses seen in 1791, selective application would allow progressive growth in constitutional guarantees.

Here the clash of theory was directly joined. Hugo Black, using the ammunition of the positive theory, insists upon applying the Constitution exactly as it was written and condemns the Court for setting itself up as a "higher judge" of civil liberty guarantees. Felix Frankfurter, though charged

---

[14] See the dissents in *Adamson* v. *California,* 332 U.S. 46 (1947); *Wolf* v. *Colorado,* 338 U.S. 25 (1949); and *Rochin* v. *California,* 342 U.S. 165 (1952).

with the natural law position, is really the sociological jurist, calling for judicial interpretation in light of changing conditions and the shifting consensus of American society as to the principles of fair procedure. Of course, a justice might adopt the selective approach, with its sociological perspectives, and interpret American attitudes and practice to require more (or less) incorporation than Justice Frankfurter did. And there are judges who have advocated having the best of both worlds. Justice Frank Murphy, for example, wrote a dissent in this stream of cases in which he urged the Court to incorporate literally the first eight amendments and also use the due process clause against any new practices that violated "ordered liberty" ideals.

The key point for our purposes is to see how the three fundamental ideas of natural law theory, positivist theory, and sociological theory are reflected and combined in American constitutional law, and to observe the place of "juristic philosophies" in the decisions of judges. Several limiting observations should be made at once about this process, however.

First, the great majority of American judges are obviously molded by their times in the choice of juristic theories. In an age when Nature and Nature's God were invoked to justify the American Revolution and the creation of a new governmental system, all factions within the Supreme Court talked in terms of judges who lacked individual will and applied the great principles of natural law that had been captured by the Founding Fathers in the liberty and property guarantees of the written Constitution. Today, when the process of judging is viewed by the informed public in a general climate of legal realism, judges must take account of the questions of subjectivity and judicial manipulation in the opinions justifying their constitutional decisions. Indeed, judges attack one another directly and forcibly for "judicial legislation." Thus, while a few judges may transcend their eras, looking either beyond or behind their times, the juristic theories of most judges reflect the dominant attitudes within society toward the role of law.

Second, some would say that "juristic theory" is the least relevant factor among those leading a judge to one result or another in great constitutional cases. The crucial determinants are said to be the judge's socioeconomic background, his ideological position, his relation to the factional divisions of the Court, his political ambitions, his attitude toward minority groups, his policy judgments on specific legislative programs being challenged, and similar factors that go to the judge's subjective beliefs. Juristic philosophies are seen as rationalizations of positions set off by more basic triggers of belief, and the ease with which juristic theories can be bent in specific cases to fit the judge's policy views is seen as proof that the theories are instruments, not foundations. There is little doubt that some judges fit this pattern all of the time, most judges fit it some of the time, and only a few rare spirits are able to govern themselves consistently by a general juristic theory. Nevertheless, it remains true that the concepts of self-control and disinterest, however difficult to achieve in practice, remain the ideal of our legal system and the standard of measurement for great judges. In this sense, even the most "realistic" analyst of judicial behavior comes to appreciate the influence of this ideal in the work of courts, and thus it is itself a "real" factor for judges in reaching decisions. (We return to this problem of judicial behavior in Chapters 16 and 17.)

Law and Politics: Is Law an Extension of Political Struggle by Other Means?

One final point needs to be discussed in examining the relation of law to society and government. Americans normally think of their legal system and the courts as the forum in which the rights and duties of individuals are adjudicated and the powers of government are delineated and enforced. In both "private law" matters of contracts and torts and "public law" matters of governmental action, the common assumption is that "politics" should and usually does halt at the courtroom's door.

In the sense that the rulings of the courts should be free from the dictation of political party leaders or of political favoritism, this is a correct assumption about the ideals of our system and, very largely, our practice. But there are legitimate ways in which law and the legal system are part of the larger political process in the nation, indeed, an inescapable part.

First, the courts should be seen as part of a continuous process of political decisions on public policy questions moving through time and space. New York passes a law on school prayer; school administrators for the state and local district apply the law. Then, some parents challenge it in court. The court, in our case, strikes down the particular law. The legislature and school districts react; a new version of a religious exercise may be drafted and instituted, such as singing "God Bless America"; an attempt may be made to secure a constitutional amendment rewriting the First Amendment; or a campaign may be launched in Congress to limit the appellate jurisdiction of the Supreme Court on school religious-practice cases. New measures will in turn be presented to the courts for review, and the courts' response to them will in turn produce new legislation, new administrative practices, and new political alignments and intergroup struggles. The same would be true if the public policy measures involved regulation of industry, labor relations, control of criminal activities, internal security, or any other matter on which powerful groups in society have interests that they will not hesitate to defend by political action. While this process of court rulings unfolding as stages in a continuum of political action operates even when the courts are passing on constitutional issues, it operates even more definitely in this manner when the courts are only interpreting statutes or executive regulations; then, the legislatures and executives can alter or overturn the courts' rulings simply by amending their own actions, and this makes the courts' role as participant and not ultimate arbiter of the political struggle even more clear.

Second, the way in which the courts affect the political process is a special matter, flowing from the special position of judges, the nature of case law and legal controversy, and the general operations of courts. Several major ways can be noted here. The courts can enlarge or narrow the arena of political decision. In matters of Negro civil rights, or labor union control, or antitrust laws, the courts often can decide whether the federal, state, or local government has primary jurisdiction to determine the rights and duties of groups and individuals. If Little Rock is supreme, Negroes may attend formerly all-white schools; if the State of Arkansas is supreme, the schools may remain segregated in fact; if the United States has primary authority, the schools will be desegregated. If the city of Miami Beach or the State of Florida can control the question of unionization of hotels, they may remain unorganized; if the National Labor Relations Board has jurisdiction, the hotels may be unionized overnight. The courts can thus define the arena of struggle, and this will have a direct effect on who wins, since the size of the arena will affect the relative power of business groups, civil rights groups, or labor groups in relation to the governing authorities.

Another way in which the courts affect the political process is by altering the timing of political struggle. By freezing political disputes for several years while they are considered in the courts, or by preventing elected officials from taking actions for several years while new statutes or constitutional amendments are secured to supply the authority denied by courts, the judges are able to affect the timing of political action in the nation. This may be a good thing in a given instance, requiring a reform movement or a repressive movement to go back to the electorate for a mandate or to redraft its key measures in more careful terms. It may also be a harmful factor, causing serious problems to go unsettled for dangerous lengths of time or hampering reform movements in their ability to achieve social progress while the public is attentive and enthusiastic about reform.

We will return to this point more specifically when we examine the development of judicial review in the United States and the role of groups in the judicial process. The essential point is that the courts are often customary and legitimate actors in the larger political process of the nation. The study of judicial behavior is therefore a study of decisions deeply affecting the political process in America, made under a special set of rules based on the traditions and institutions of the American legal system.

16 / Judicial Review and the Court System

The United States Supreme Court in the 1960s presents students of American government with a challenging paradox. On the one hand, some contemporary critics of the Supreme Court describe it as our most "archaic" and "aristocratic" political institution. Its proceedings open with a ceremonial crier calling out "Oyez, Oyez, Oyez," "admonishing" all persons having business before "the Honorable, the Supreme Court of the United States" to "draw near and give their attention," and invoking God's blessing on "the United States and this Honorable Court." The Justices preside on the bench in long black robes copied from the dress of British judges in medieval days. Lawyers arguing cases before the Justices are expected to use flowery phrases such as "If it please the Court," and to address the Justices as "Your Honors." The Court's opinions are filled with cobwebbed legal terms such as *mandamus, certiorari,* and *mens rea,* and decisions on urban renewal or Communist registration laws often rest on precedents from the time of George Washington or James K. Polk. The whole atmosphere of the Court seems more like that of a television play about eighteenth-century justice than a forum for conducting governmental affairs in the nuclear age.

Even more significant than the antique procedure, it is argued, is the fact that nine men—who were never elected to office, whose term extends until they die or retire voluntarily, and who can be removed only for "high crimes and misdemeanors" (and by the ponderous machinery of impeachment)—are authorized to declare unconstitutional the acts of popularly elected Presidents, Congresses, governors, state legislatures, and mayors. That a powerful industrial nation with a vigorous two-party system and a majoritarian ideology should continue to allow nine elderly lawyers to exercise such a veto power in the most sensitive areas of politics, economics, federalism, and group relations in contemporary America, subject to direct reversal only by formal constitutional amendment, is often portrayed as an incredible denial of American democratic principles.

Whenever this critique of the "archaic" and "aristocratic" Supreme Court was offered during the nineteenth and early twentieth centuries, students of American government would also receive what we might call the "classic rejoinder." They would be reminded that the American Republic was created by a written Constitution that deliberately limited the powers of

481

the national and state governments. This Constitution also guaranteed Americans certain fundamental rights of liberty, property, and equality that no elected officials or majority vote could take away. To enforce these limitations, the Framers set up an independent judiciary, whose particular function it was to articulate the ideals of limited government and constitutional rights and, when necessary to the decision of cases properly brought before them, to strike down governmental measures that violated the Constitution, thus keeping the majority within constitutional boundaries and protecting "minority rights." Therefore, the "classic rejoinder" concluded, if the Supreme Court's procedures were highly ceremonial, if the Justices tended to be older men than Congressional leaders or Cabinet officials, and if the world view of the Justices was generally that of the previous generation, these elements actually aided the "braking" and "conservative" function that the Supreme Court was created to perform in the American political system.

The difficulty with the "classic rejoinder" in the 1960s is that it simply does not describe the spirit or the influence of the contemporary Supreme Court. Today, the Justices give little comfort to most of the conservative and well-propertied groups in the nation. The Court's rulings on matters of antitrust law, industrial regulation, civil liberties, or civil rights have often been more "liberal" or "libertarian" in recent years than the positions espoused by the elected branches of state and national governments. Instead of exerting a negative influence in governmental affairs, the contemporary Supreme Court has actually prodded reluctant Congresses, Presidential administrations, and many states to take action on vital matters, such as desegregation, fair legislative districting, or separation of church and state, that were being ignored for a variety of political and institutional reasons.

Thus the debate over the Supreme Court and judicial review is no longer one between democratic critics and conservative defenders. It is a distinctly new and more subtle controversy, one brought into its sharpest focus by the basic question, "What is new since 1937 and what has remained constant in the role of the Supreme Court in American government?" The year 1937 is our pivotal point since this was when President Franklin Roosevelt led New Deal liberals in a full-scale attack on "the nine old men," culminating in the famous but unsuccessful "court-reform" proposals. It was also the year in which the Supreme Court majority, without the addition of any new Roosevelt appointees, changed its basic constitutional philosophy on the reach of federal and state legislative power over economic affairs, thereby upholding the New Deal economic program, and marking the beginning of a new era in both property rights and civil rights doctrines by the Supreme Court.

Before turning to this central question about the Supreme Court since 1937, however, there are four matters that should be described as a framework of analysis. These are (1) the ground rules of American judicial procedure; (2) the organization of the state and federal courts; (3) the jurisdiction and powers of the United States Supreme Court; and (4) the American theory of judicial review. Since these topics are quite complex, and their subtleties preoccupy law students for years and lawyers for their

Old Father Time Takes It In His Stride

A commentary on the "antiquated" methods of Supreme Court appointments.

Fitzpatrick in the St. Louis *Post-Dispatch*

whole careers, we treat them here only in the detail necessary to explain their basic aspects.

The Ground Rules of American Judicial Procedure

When the American judicial system deals with civil law suits and criminal prosecutions, its procedures are directed toward two different (though complementary) objectives. First, the judicial tribunal seeks to "find" what the facts are. This is not only the obvious matter of deciding whose version of an automobile accident, a political riot, or a sit-in demonstration to accept as accurate, but also of deciding which facts are legally "relevant" to this particular case, in the sense that they should have bearing on the result. For example, if Daphne Smith sues Philip Jones for $350 damages, alleging that Jones carelessly hit her motor scooter with his Caramba-35 sports car, there are a host of "facts" about Jones and his sports car that could be introduced into evidence. (1) Jones is 46, (2) thinning at the temples, (3) wears bifocals, (4) graduated from the University of California, (5) sells insurance, (6) is a Mason and a Presbyterian, (7) likes his martinis dry, (8) lives in a $35,000 ranch house, (9) had a toothache on the day of the accident, (10) was going to trade in the sports car at the end of the month, (11) hates motor scooters, (12) was thinking about a French movie he had seen recently while he was driving on the day of the accident, (13) is slightly neurotic and takes tranquilizers, (14) has had troublesome losses in the stock market lately, (15) votes Republican, (16) his sports car needed a motor tune-up, (17) he was driving 35 miles per hour in a 20-mile zone, and (18) his reflexes are a little slower than they used to be when he plays tennis with his oldest son. Some of these facts, such as 2, 6, 7, 8, and 15, the courts would probably exclude as evidence because they are irrelevant; some, such as 16 and 17, are crucial to the decision of the case; and some may or may not be relevant, depending on further development of their significance at the trial, such as 3, 9, 11, 12, 13, and 18. Fact-finding is thus a complicated and sophisticated problem even in "simple" cases, such as an automobile collision, and much more so when major antitrust suits, civil rights trials, or murder cases are involved.

The second function of the judicial tribunal is to determine what the law is. Again, this is not simply the obvious matter of looking up the constitutional, statutory, and case-law provisions that apply directly to the dispute at hand and applying them to the facts. Often, courts find that there are no laws or precedents that cover a new situation that comes before them, or that precedents are in basic conflict on a given point. In addition, one of the parties may claim that the statute or official action involved in the case violates the constitution of the state or federal government; this requires the court to rule on the meaning and scope of the constitutional clause that has been invoked and to determine whether the challenged act falls within the constitutional prohibition. Determining the law may also involve situations in which a court feels that the legal rule that has been established and followed by prior courts should be changed, either because the existing rule was arrived at originally through errors of judgment or history, or else because new socioeconomic conditions seem to require a different rule.

In the American court system, facts are generally supposed to be determined by a jury, composed of twelve men or women drawn from the local community and reflecting its knowledge and opinions. Questions of law, both as to legal rights and courtroom procedure, are the province of the judge. This division of functions has a variety of results. It lengthens trials, stresses emotional and dramatic appeals, forces the explanation of technical or legal matters in general terms, requires one continuous hearing in open court, and enables community sentiments to have a certain control over the legal rules (since a jury can simply find individual or group defendants with whom it sympathizes to be "innocent" even though they clearly committed the acts with which they were charged). Jury trials can sometimes be waived by defendants in criminal cases or by consent of both parties in civil cases. To ensure speed and avoid certain kinds of prejudice, the modern trend is to have many cases tried by the judge alone, who then rules on both the factual and legal issues. Out of 6,200 civil cases tried in the federal district courts in 1962, for example, 3,300 were heard by the judge alone and 2,900 with juries.

In the United States, fact-finding and law-determining by courts are reserved for what are known as "genuine cases and controversies." This phrase is shorthand for the requirement that before a dispute can be brought into court, it must be *a real contest between opposing parties over a controversy that is appropriate for judicial resolution and ready for judicial decision.* Since more than 300 years of legal evolution are capsuled in that definition, we should examine it carefully.

"A REAL CONTEST BETWEEN OPPOSING PARTIES"

In American courtroom trials, the opposing parties themselves determine which witnesses to call, which documents to offer in evidence, what questions to ask opposing witnesses, and what legal claims and supporting arguments to assert. The judge presides as an essentially neutral umpire. He does not make an independent investigation of the facts (as is done in many European countries). Except for an occasional question, he does not conduct examinations of the witnesses, nor does he introduce evidence, or control what goes into the lawyers' briefs. This system is known as the "adversary theory of justice," and rests on the assumption that the true facts and the real legal issues will emerge from the gladiatorial encounter of opposing parties and their trained lawyers in the open courtroom.

Since the judge (and the jury, if there is one in the case) depends on the dedication of each side to assure that both positions receive a strong presentation, a law suit in which both parties are really on the same side and are hoping to secure the same decision destroys the dynamic ingredient of the adversary system and could mislead courts into incorrect or unwise rulings. For example, suppose Congress passed a law requiring the Communist party to publish the names of its members in each city once a year in the local press, and the chairman of the party branch in Central City announced he did not intend to comply because the law was unconstitutional. Suppose also that the secretary of the Central City party branch, for tactical reasons, sued the chairman in federal district court to secure a court order directing him to comply and to conduct party affairs according to law. If such a law suit could be maintained, the district court would be deciding on the constitutionality of the Congressional act with one Communist party official arguing for the statute and another against it. The lack of a "real contest" and of truly "opposing parties" in such a trumped-up situation would be clear, and to avoid it, the rules of the American judicial process would require that the parties to a test of this Congressional statute be the United States Government and representatives of the Communist party. The same rules would apply if one officer of a corporation sued the president of the firm to prevent him from paying a federal tax or from following a state marketing regulation, on the ground that the measures were unconstitutional.[1]

"A CONTROVERSY APPROPRIATE FOR JUDICIAL RESOLUTION"

Most of the disputes that arise between individuals, groups, and government agencies can be brought into courts for adjudication if one of the parties desires a judicial ruling. It is clearly in the best interests of a demo-

---

[1] In a few states, such as Massachusetts, the courts are permitted by the state constitution to give the state legislature "advisory opinions" on the probable constitutionality of proposed legislation, without a real prosecution or test case under an existing law. This is not permitted in the federal courts.

cratic society to minimize tests of force and revolutions against government by providing ready access to the courts for the airing of grievances and the legal determination of rights. As a result of this liberal policy, American courts are jammed with all conceivable types of law suits—to force someone to stop driving his car across the plaintiff's lawn, to recover money damages from a newspaper because one of its columnists called the complaining party a "local Hitler," to have a town ordinance forbidding beer drinking on the beach declared unconstitutional as an invasion of the residents' liberty, or to decide whether the federal or state government—or no government—has the right to regulate the racial admission policies of Mrs. Murphy's boardinghouse. As these illustrations suggest, most law suits involve matters of money and property, reputation, constitutional rights, and distribution of power between governmental units in a federal system.

However, there are some disputes that courts will not decide, usually with the explanation that these are not "justiciable" questions. Sometimes, this is because the issues are really private and not governmental affairs. You cannot sue to make your neighbor stop frowning as you go by his yard or to compel him to let his children play with yours. You cannot sue the coach of a college football team to reinstate you as quarterback, on the ground that you are really a better player than the guy who was put in your place in the middle of the season. However, many situations that were once considered private and "nonjusticiable" have come to be issues for the courts as a result of legislation or changing court doctrines that grant new legal rights or impose new legal obligations, such as the hiring policies of employers or the admission policies of theater owners.

The other main area of "nonjusticiable" questions involves the powers and jurisdiction of governments. While the rules on "justiciability" in cases involving government power vary among the states and within the federal system, the principle that American courts generally accept is that they will not decide "political questions." In a 1962 decision,[2] the Supreme Court identified two kinds of "political questions." The first involve issues whose final judgment is committed by the Constitution or laws to a "coordinate political department"—the President or Congress in the federal system. The leading example is the field of foreign relations, where the court's lack of secret information, its lack of expertise in diplomatic affairs, and the grave consequences of interfering in delicate international negotiations or agreements all confirm the wisdom of rejecting law suits to halt foreign aid, force the recognition of Communist China, or prevent the signing of a test-ban treaty. Whether a state had properly ratified a proposed constitutional amendment or whether state governmental institutions constitute a "republican form of government" as guaranteed to citizens of every state by the federal Constitution are both instances in which Congress—by accepting the ratification or seating the Congressional delegation from the state—has final say.

The second category of political questions, the Supreme Court said, were

---

[2] *Baker* v. *Carr*, 369 U.S. 186 (1962).

those in which there was "a lack of judicially discoverable and manageable standards" for solving the problem. The leading example in this category used to be the drawing of boundaries by state legislatures for districts to elect state legislators or United States Congressmen. In a famous 1946 case,[3] the Supreme Court held that this was a "political thicket" which the federal courts should not enter, since there was no standard for determining the exact degree of equality required by the Constitution for a fairly apportioned system, and because the federal courts could not force districting on a fairer basis if the state legislature simply ignored the court's ruling. In 1962, however, the Supreme Court overturned this ruling and held that denial of the citizens' rights to equality in voting could be dealt with by the federal courts.[4] Between 1962 and 1964, apportionment systems in more than twelve states were declared unconstitutional, and five states themselves moved to reapportion their legislative districts to provide greater fairness in representation.

"A CONTROVERSY READY FOR JUDICIAL DECISION"

The final basic requirement for bringing a law suit in the American judicial system is that the case be ready, or "ripe," for courtroom adjudication. This means that everything has already been done to assert one's rights or to secure a decision from government agencies authorized to review the action that is being contested. A Negro teacher who wishes to sue the State of Mississippi for denying her the right to vote must first apply to the state voting registrar to be registered and be refused for an improper reason. Until she is refused officially (or the registrar deliberately evades seeing her and passing on her application), she has not "exhausted her administrative remedies" and is not ready to bring a law suit, either in the state or federal courts. A man who has been denied a permit from the city engineer to build a swimming pool in his backyard must first appeal to the board of zoning appeals or other administrative agency in the city before he can bring a law suit. The policy behind "ripening" controversies is to insure that all steps short of going-to-law have been followed between the parties in private disputes and that the regular procedures for hearing and appeal before government administrative bodies have been used to give government a chance to know and resolve the problem itself.

In discussing these three main requirements for bringing a law suit in American courts, it is important to distinguish the lack of a "genuine case and controversy" from the exercise of what is known as "judicial self-restraint." If there is no case and controversy, the court will not hear the dispute; it dismisses the complaint. When a court exercises "judicial self-restraint," it acknowledges that the rights of opposing parties in an appropriate and ripe controversy are at stake and hands down a decision on the "merits" of the dispute. But the court decides that the action taken in this matter by elected officials of government is not so unreasonable and arbitrary that courts should overturn it as unconstitutional.

---

[3] *Colegrove* v. *Green,* 328 U.S. 549 (1946).
[4] *Baker* v. *Carr.*

The Procedures for Trials and Appeals in the Judicial System

Assuming that a "genuine case or controversy" exists, a dispute can move through the American judicial process in two phases, the *trial* and the *appeal*. Here again, there is diversity among the states as to the steps, terms, and functions employed, but the description that follows is the basic pattern in most states.

A *trial*, as we have mentioned in passing, can either be a civil law suit or a criminal prosecution. In a civil law suit between John T. Anderson and the Running Waters Bubbler Company, arising because Anderson feels that the company sold him a defective water bubbler for his office, the case begins when Anderson—called the plaintiff—files a complaint in the proper state court describing the purchase of the bubbler, its defects, and the refusal of the company to repair or replace it, or take it back and refund his money. Anderson asks the court to award him $175, the original cost of the bubbler. The company will file an *answer* giving its version of the facts, or a *motion to dismiss*, which says that even if all the facts stated by Anderson are taken as true, he has no legal claim to recovery. (This might be because Anderson has had the bubbler for four months and the guarantee is only for three months.)

If the case is not dismissed, the lawyers for Anderson and the company will each make an *opening statement*. One judge will usually be presiding at the trial, and, depending on the type of case and whether it is waived by the parties, there may be a jury of twelve men and women (drawn from a larger panel of potential jurors called by law to "do jury duty"). If there is no jury, as we have noted, the judge rules on both the facts and the law in the case. After the opening statements, Anderson presents his case by introducing documentary evidence (the contract of sale for the bubbler, the inspection report of the repairman, and the like) and calling witnesses whose stories are obtained by direct questioning by Anderson's lawyer. The company lawyer has the right to cross-examine these witnesses to bring out conflicts in their stories, show their biases or mistakes in observation, and so on. After Anderson has presented his case, the company can again move to have the case dismissed, this time on the ground that all the plaintiff's evidence does not satisfy the "burden of proof" on the moving party to demonstrate his case sufficiently to justify a jury verdict in his favor. If the plaintiff has not done so, the judge will dismiss the case.

Assuming that the dismissal motion is denied, the Bubbler Company now calls its witnesses and presents its evidence, subject to cross-examination by Anderson's lawyer. Concluding its presentation, the defending party can move for a "directed verdict," on the ground that with both sides of the case presented, the jury could not reasonably find for the plaintiff.

If this motion is not granted, each side makes a closing argument to the jury, summing up the evidence and making its legal arguments. Then the judge delivers a "charge to the jury," which explains the legal rules (in this instance about contracts, warranties of good performance, standards of good performance, and the like) and the issues of fact raised by the testimony. Following the charge, the jury retires to the jury room, deliberates on the case, and brings in its verdict. It can find for either the plaintiff or the defendant in general terms, or in certain kinds of cases it can specify the amount of money that should be awarded ("$50,000 to the plumber whose arm was injured in the elevator crash"). In some states in civil cases the jury's verdict can be by majority vote. The losing party can then move for a new trial, on the ground that some error of procedure or of law was made during the trial, or for a "judgment notwithstanding the verdict," on the ground that the jury's verdict was against the evidence and the judge should enter an opposite verdict. If these motions fail, the judge fixes the judgment, and the losing party can then move to have the verdict reviewed by a higher court on appeal to correct substantial legal errors alleged to have been made in the trial court.

There are a few important differences between this format and procedures in the criminal prosecution. In the case of *The State of Illinois* v. *Leonard Lightfingers*, for shoplifting in violation of a state statute against petty larceny, the prosecution is usually initiated by the presentation of the facts by the district attorney to a grand jury (which returns an "indictment") or, in some states, to a judge (who issues an "information"), both bringing the defendant to trial. Once the case is begun, the stages are substantially the same throughout as in a civil case. However, the burden is on the government to prove the defendant's guilt "beyond a reasonable doubt," not simply to support a verdict that he "probably" did it. The jury's verdict must always be unanimous. If Lightfingers is found guilty, the sentence is usually set by the judge (though in some states the jury can do this) within the terms set by the petty larceny statute (which might read "two to five years in the state prison and/or $5,000 fine"). Although the defendant may appeal his conviction, federal and state constitutional prohibitions against putting a person twice into jeopardy for the same offense prevent the government from trying to reverse the acquittal on appeal. However, some states allow the government to appeal errors of law so that bad precedents are not set, but this will not affect the specific defendant's acquittal.

In both the state and federal judicial systems, the trial courts are packed with the drama and power of real life. Spectators often fill the courtroom, witnesses will pour out impassioned stories in their "own words," lawyers often conduct probing cross-examinations, stirring appeals are made to the jury or the judge to avenge society or strike blows for liberty or protect the security of investments, and days—even months—may be consumed in this turbulent trial process.

The *appellate courts* present a very different picture. If the appellate court grants a request for review, each side files a written brief with the court describing the facts of the case, the main points of the trial below, the legal issues being asserted on appeal, and the controlling legal precedents and policy considerations as each side sees them. The oral argument, which takes place before three or more judges in the appellate courts, rarely lasts more than from one to two hours for a case, even major constitutional cases. There are no witnesses, there is no jury, and fresh documentary evidence is usually not produced. Instead, the lawyers for the opposing parties present their legal positions in what is normally a calm and restrained atmosphere of intellectual analysis. The judges may sit back and let each lawyer state his case, but it is more typical for the judges to interrupt the lawyer often to ask probing questions about the precedents for his position and the public policy consequences of its adoption by the court.

After the oral argument, the judges retire to hold private conferences about the cases presented to them and to discuss (and debate) the issues. Their decision is reached by majority vote, and the majority usually issues a written opinion "for the Court" (written by one judge in the majority) stating their judgment and justifying their views. A judge who does not agree with the majority can record his opposing vote and write a dissenting opinion, while judges who agree with the result reached by the majority but not its exact line of reasoning can write a concurring opinion stating their positions. After the first appellate court in the state or federal judicial system has heard and decided an appeal, the losing party can try to carry the appeal to a higher appellate court. If the issues are of major importance and fit within certain categories set by state and federal law, the case can go to the highest court in that jurisdiction—state cases to the state supreme courts and federal cases to the United States Supreme Court. In addition, if a federal constitutional issue is involved, the decision of the state supreme court may be reviewable by the United States Supreme Court, as we will discuss shortly.

The conduct of trials and appeals, as described above, is the pattern followed in the two separate and independent court systems that exist side by side in the United States—the state judicial systems and the courts of the United States. How these courts are organized and the type of cases they decide is the topic we turn to next.

The Organization of State Courts

There are dozens of different types of courts in the fifty state judicial systems, and each state has developed its own way of dividing the business of initiating trials and hearing law suits, providing routes of appeals, and establishing a final court of review. Looking at the American state judicial systems as a whole, we find that most states have six types of courts, with varying names, forms, and combinations.

JUSTICES OF THE PEACE

Sometimes appointed but usually elected for short terms (from two to four years), the "J.P.'s" or "magistrates" decide minor civil cases (usually when the sum involved does not exceed a specified limit, such as $150 or $250) as well as minor criminal offenses (known as misdemeanors, such as speeding violations). "J.P.'s" usually do *not* have law degrees; their judicial functions are only part of their overall work and usually take in performing marriages and issuing fishing permits.

MUNICIPAL COURTS

Sometimes called city courts, police courts, or small claims courts, these are usually the first really judicial "courts" in the state system. They will usually hear civil cases where the sums involved are less than a specified limit, normally in the $500–$1000 range, and minor criminal offenses such as violations of city ordinances against littering the streets, disturbing the peace, or failing to provide proper fire exits in a theater. Judges from the municipal courts (and on up the state judicial ladder) generally have law degrees, and the procedures followed are the formal ones of a "court of record."

COUNTY COURTS

Sometimes called superior courts, these are the judicial bodies in which major civil cases and serious criminal offenses receive their initial hearing in the state judicial channel. Here trial by jury usually makes its appearance in state proceedings, and here the great bulge of cases is found. In most states judges are elected to the county or superior courts, with terms averaging from five to ten years. It has been estimated that 95 to 98 percent of the cases decided in the county courts are not appealed further.

COURTS OF SPECIAL JURISDICTION

The modern trend in judicial organization has been to create special courts to deal with problems such as domestic relations, juveniles, orphans, and probate (wills and estates), though county courts still handle these matters in some states. The new courts will often have more informal procedures than the county courts, the judges will usually have special training or experience in the problems treated, and special services will be attached to the court (such as counseling, psychiatric interviews, and the like) to supplement the formal hearings and decisions.

INTERMEDIATE COURTS OF APPEALS

Sometimes called the appellate division or the district court of appeals, these courts review appeals from cases decided by the municipal, county, and special courts, and sometimes from cases decided by state regulatory agencies. They will be geographically distributed through the state, in districts or regions, and judges at this level (whether elected or appointed) usually serve for relatively long terms, averaging from seven to twelve years.

STATE HIGH COURT

Generally called the Supreme Court, though sometimes known as the Court of Appeals (in New York and Maryland), and even called the Supreme Court of Errors (in Connecticut), this is the court of last resort, or final court, in the state judicial system. Review in this court is a matter of discretion with the judges, with only a few classes of cases giving a *right* to review in the state high court. Decisions of the high courts are final as to the meaning of the state constitution, construction of state statutes, state trial practice, and the like; the United States Supreme Court—as we shall see—will not review any of those matters unless substantial federal constitutional rights have been denied by the state law or its interpretation.

Some states elect and some appoint their highest judges, with most terms averaging from seven to fifteen years, and some running for life.

The Federal Judicial System

Beside the state courts stand the courts of the United States. Article III of the federal Constitution carefully spells out the cases which fall under federal jurisdiction. Only these may be brought to the federal courts for decision, and under rules that Congress enacts. Nine categories are specified, some involving interpretation of federal law, some covering disputes in which the parties are federal agents or diplomats accredited to the United States, some involving legal fields of special national character, and some to insure an impartial forum for disputes involving multistate interests. In summary form the nine types of cases that create federal jurisdiction are:

BY THE NATURE OF THE CASE

1. "arising under this Constitution, the laws of the United States, and treaties made . . . under their authority."
2. "admiralty and maritime jurisdiction."

BY THE NATURE OF THE PARTIES TO THE DISPUTE

3. "affecting ambassadors . . . ministers and consuls."
4. "to which the United States shall be a party."
5. "between two or more States."
6. "between a State and citizens of another State" (limited by the Eleventh Amendment in 1798 to cases in which a state is the plaintiff).
7. "between citizens of different States."
8. "between citizens of the same State claiming lands under grants of different States."
9. "between a State, or the citizens thereof, and foreign States, citizens or subjects."

From the time of the famous Judiciary Act of 1789 until the present period, Congress has exercised the power given to it by Article III to decide which courts in the federal system should hear cases in one or the other of these nine categories, and in which areas the state courts should be allowed to share or even to take over the hearing of these cases. The details of these Congressional acts and the rules for determining federal jurisdiction are not essential to our discussion here. Our primary interest is in *the structure and operations* of the federal courts.

The trial level in the federal system is made up of the federal district courts, eighty-six of which are distributed throughout the fifty states, with at least one in each.[5] From one to eighteen judges are assigned to each district court, according to the amount of legal work arising there. Generally,

---

[5] There are five additional district courts, one each in the District of Columbia, Puerto Rico, the Canal Zone, Guam, and the Virgin Islands.

a single district judge hears motions and presides at trials, unless a party challenges the constitutionality of a federal statute (and a few other special circumstances); in those situations, three judges will hear the case.

District court business divides into civil and criminal cases. *Civil cases* (about 58,000 in 1962) involve private disputes between citizens of different states involving $10,000 or more, or suits in which the federal government is a party. The major types of civil cases in the federal courts involve matters of *contract* (insurance claims, suits under defense contracts, and so on), *torts* (for injuries sustained on ships or airplanes, collisions with mail trucks, and the like); *real property* (involving leases or sales of federal land); and *statutory actions* (arising under federal statutes regulating antitrust, patents, taxes, civil rights, and the like). Miscellaneous civil matters that flood the district courts are passport applications, petitions for naturalization as American citizens, and petitions by individuals or business firms to be declared bankrupt.[6]

Criminal cases in the district courts (covering 33,000 defendants in 1962) involve prosecution of individuals or organizations for violation of federal laws. The four largest categories of federal prosecutions in the 1960s (with more than half of the total number of defendants) are embezzlement and fraud against the United States, liquor law violations, interstate auto theft, and larceny. Other numerically large categories include forgery, counterfeiting, narcotics, juvenile delinquency, and offenses under special statutes (obscene mailings, advocating overthrow of the government by force).

After a civil or criminal case has been determined by a federal district court, the losing party can take an appeal to the next level along the federal judicial avenue, the United States Court of Appeals. The United States is divided into eleven judicial circuits and each is assigned a court of appeals, composed of from three to nine judges and a chief judge. Here, cases are usually heard by a "panel" of three judges, though in particularly important cases, such as President Truman's seizure of the steel mills in 1952, all the judges in a court of appeals will sit *en banc*.

Cases come to the courts of appeals not only from the district courts but also from certain federal regulatory agencies, such as the National Labor Relations Board and the Federal Securities and Exchange Commission. The regulatory agency cases, by Congressional statute, go to the courts of appeals because the "facts" are supposed to have been determined already by the agencies, and the role of the courts of appeals is to see that no errors of law or procedure have occurred.

In 1962, the courts of appeals disposed of a little more than 4,000 cases. About 850 of these came from the regulatory agencies, slightly over 3,000 from the district courts, and ninety were cases that were started directly in the courts of appeals under special statutes. The 1962 figures show that less than 3 percent of the criminal cases and less than 6 percent of

---

[6] There is one special federal trial court, the Customs Court, with nine judges, that passes on disputes arising from the laws regulating the entry of goods into the United States from abroad, both by travelers returning and by commercial enterprises.

CHART 16-1 / The Federal Judicial System

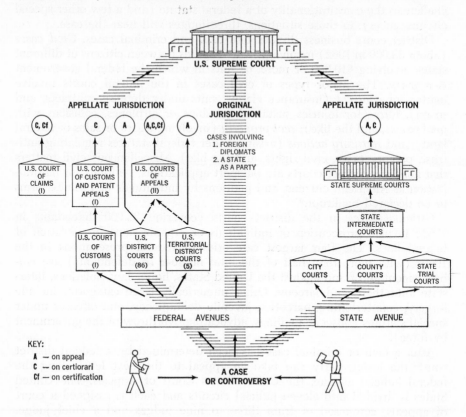

KEY:
A — on appeal
C — on certiorari
Cf — on certification

the civil cases determined in the district courts were carried into the courts of appeals.[7]

At the top of the federal judicial system is the United States Supreme Court, the final judicial authority on federal law and on disputes over the meaning of the United States Constitution. Since the organization, jurisdiction, and procedure of the Supreme Court are of such special importance in our governmental system, and for our discussion of changes in Supreme Court doctrine and influence since 1937, this topic is treated below as a separate section.

The Jurisdiction and Powers of the Supreme Court

"The judicial power of the United States," says Article III of the Constitution, "shall be vested in one Supreme Court, and in such inferior courts as the Congress may from time to time . . . establish." The number of Justices to be on the Supreme Court was not stated, and has therefore been a matter for regulation by Congress. Between 1789 and 1869, the Court's size

---

[7] There are two additional, special courts of appeals in the federal system, the Court of Customs and Patent Appeals, and the Court of Claims, each with five judges.

was varied from five to ten, Congress twice reducing the number and five times increasing it. Some of these changes were for practical purposes, such as adding Justices to preside at new judicial circuits created as the nation expanded to the Pacific. On other occasions, Congressional motives were frankly political, adding Justices to enable the President to affect the Court's balance of voting or cutting the Court's size to prevent the President from doing this. Since 1869, no change has been made in the provision for a nine-man court. In 1937, after Court decisions between the years 1935 and 1937 had struck down a series of major New Deal statutes, President Franklin Roosevelt sponsored legislation to provide "youth and energy" on the Court by giving the President authority to appoint a new Justice whenever an incumbent Justice reached the age of seventy and did not retire. This would have authorized a possible maximum of eighteen Justices. F. D. R.'s opponents attacked the plan as "Court-packing," and its resounding defeat in 1937 suggests that a nine-man Court has become established as a political tradition. (Roosevelt did have the satisfaction of seeing the Court reverse its 1933–36 position "under fire," however, and if the Court had not done so "voluntarily," the Court-reform plan might have been pressed successfully.)

The Supreme Court's jurisdiction is divided into two parts. In cases involving foreign diplomats or in those in which a state is a party, the Supreme Court has *original jurisdiction.* This means that the Justices get the dispute directly and hear it as a court of "first instance," finding what the facts are (through a lawyer, called a Special Master, appointed to hear the testimony) as well as determining the law. Only a trickle of cases today go directly to the Justices under their original jurisdiction. Between 1952 and 1962 no original cases were filed in four of these years, and the total filed in the decade was only sixteen. Despite their small number, these cases are often legally important and politically explosive pieces of litigation. Suits between states have been decided in recent years involving land boundaries, water rights, and taxing authority, with hundreds of millions of dollars resting on the conflict, for example, between Arizona and California as to water rights in the Colorado River. In the other major type of original case, litigation between the federal government and states, important disputes in the last three decades have included such matters as the fight between the federal and state governments for title to the rich oil deposits under the tideland waters off California, Texas, Louisiana, and Florida.

In all other cases, the Supreme Court has *appellate jurisdiction,* reviewing decisions that have already been made by trial courts and by "lower" appellate tribunals. As the chart on the opposite page indicates, there are two main avenues of appellate jurisdiction, one made up of cases from the federal district courts and courts of appeals, and the other of cases from the state courts. Since the Supreme Court is the final tribunal in the federal judicial system, its review of lower federal court cases is a logical and necessary situation, and has given rise to little dispute in our constitutional history. Review of state court decisions, on the other hand, has been a stormy sector from the days of Thomas Jefferson to the present. States' rights advocates contended in a series of famous cases during the first decades of the Republic that in a federal union with sovereign states and a limited national government, each state must have the final word on matters that lie within its territorial borders, such as land claims. The Supreme Court rejected this position and held instead that where a "substantial federal question" is determined by a state court, the need for protection of the citizen's federal constitutional rights and for uniformity of interpretation of the national Constitution throughout the Union required the United States Supreme Court to pass upon these questions. It was the nature of the case and not the court where it arose that governed federal review. The Court's view in this matter was supported not only by these policy considerations but by the language of the Constitution in Article VI, which provides that the Constitution, federal statutes, and treaties "shall be the supreme law of the land" and "Judges in every State shall be bound thereby, any thing in the Constitution or laws of any State to the contrary notwithstanding." The Supreme Court could therefore give effect only to the "supreme law," not state interpretations in cases involving claims of federal rights.

The Supreme Court's appellate jurisdiction was left by Article III to be set up "with such exceptions, and under such regulations as the Congress shall make." Under this Congressional power, successive Judiciary Acts since 1789 have defined the rules by which cases are brought to the Supreme Court, especially to give the Justices discretion to select those appeals that are truly important for developing a consistent and effective constitutional law for the nation, and to refuse to hear all others. Yet this Congressional power is also the lance with which Congress can thrust—or threaten to thrust—against the Court when the Justices hand down rulings that Congressmen bitterly oppose.

The only punitive exercise of this kind to date took place in 1868 and is something of an inconclusive incident. A Congressional statute, the Habeas Corpus Act of 1867, had authorized appeals to be made from military actions in the Southern states during Reconstruction directly to the Supreme Court, through filing a writ of habeas corpus. An editor named McCardle, who was being held by federal Army officers in Mississippi, filed such a writ in the Supreme Court, contending his imprisonment was improper because the Reconstruction Acts were unconstitutional. His case was argued in the Supreme Court and may even have been decided in the Court's conference, though the result was not announced and no opinions were written. While this was taking place, the Radical Republicans who controlled Congress became worried that the Supreme Court might declare the Reconstruction program unconstitutional. To prevent this—and warn the Court to take care—Congress repealed the jurisdiction of the Supreme Court under the Habeas Corpus Act of 1867 (overriding a veto of the repeal by President Andrew Johnson). After taking this action, the Court dismissed McCardle's case, stating that the removal of its jurisdiction was a valid exercise of Congress' authority under Article III.[8]

However, McCardle could still have brought his case to the Supreme Court by a regular appeal from a ruling of a federal circuit court on the

---

[8] *Ex parte McCardle,* 7 Wall. 506 (1869).

Our Overworked Supreme Court

An 1885 cartoon shows that the Supreme Court's calendar was crowded even then.

legality of his detention by the Army. Thus the Supreme Court did not say—and has never said—that Congress could shut off appellate review completely and leave the Court to its original jurisdiction, or could eliminate appeals from a given class of cases. The potential chaos that would be created by having fifty state supreme courts and eleven federal circuits all applying different rules of law suggests the policy against such a bar to Supreme Court review. Actually, the defeat in 1957–58 of attempts by Congressional critics of the "Warren Court" to eliminate its appellate jurisdiction in such areas as federal loyalty-security programs and state decisions on admission to the bar indicates that the Court's appellate jurisdiction, like its size, may have become protected by the force of political tradition, unless the Court were to act in total disregard of political realities.

The Supreme Court's appellate jurisdiction is made up of obligatory and discretionary cases. *Obligatory* cases come either on *appeal* from state or federal courts (where it is claimed that federal constitutional rights were violated) or by a little-used procedure called *certification,* by which a federal court of appeals certifies a new and difficult question directly to the Supreme Court for decision. *Discretionary* cases are presented by *petitions for certiorari,* which ask the Justices to call for the record of a state or federal court in a case and examine it for errors. The Court can simply refuse to grant certiorari (without having to give any reasons) if it thinks the claim has no merit or if it does not want to consider an issue at the time. In practice, the Justices can also dismiss cases that come to

TABLE 16–1 / The Supreme Court's Work: 1961 Term

Volume of Cases

Number of cases filed	2185
Number of cases remaining from previous term	385
(mostly pauper's writs from persons in prisons alleging	
that there were constitutional errors in their trials)	
Number of cases disposed of	2142
Number of cases carried over to next term	428
(mostly pauper's writs)	

Sources of Cases Disposed Of (2,142)

Federal courts		1050
Federal courts of appeals	973	
Federal district courts	39	
Special federal courts	38	
State courts		971
Pauper's writs from prisoners		121

Disposition of Cases (2,142)

Decided "on their merits"	171
(determining the issues)	
Denied review	2071

Cases Decided "on Their Merits" (171)

Decision of lower court affirmed	46
Decision of lower court reversed	125
Full opinions written by the Court	96
Orders or Memoranda	75

Breakdown of Cases Decided on Their Merits with Full Opinions (96)

Constitutional issues	29
Nonconstitutional matters	67
Civil cases	60
Criminal cases	36
From federal courts	65
From state courts	31
Unanimous decisions	37
Divided Court	59

Role of the United States Government in Supreme Court Litigation

Total number of cases in which U.S. participated		850/2142
Number of these cases decided on their merits		106
Decided in favor of Government's position	60	
Decided against Government's position	24	
Not classifiable as for or against	22	

them on *appeal* if the Court finds that they do not present a "substantial federal question," so that even the "obligatory" jurisdiction of the Court is "discretionary." This must be so if the Court is not to be so inundated with cases that it cannot give careful attention to the matters of crucial importance. In 1961–62, about 2,000 petitions for certiorari were filed and eighty-eight appeals (no certifications); the Court granted 7 percent of the certiorari petitions and heard 40 percent of the appeals. As Chief Justice Fred Vinson once explained, the Supreme Court does not sit to provide one last opportunity for litigants to re-try their cases; every case urged upon the Supreme Court has already been decided by one trial court and one or more appellate courts. The function of the Supreme Court is to interpret the Constitution of the United States, assure uniformity of judgments in the federal and state courts on these principles, and oversee the federal legal system.

The best way to illustrate the volume, sources, and disposition of the Supreme Court's work today is to take a tabular look at one term of the Supreme Court, from October, 1961, to June, 1962. (See page 498.)

As these figures indicate, a heavy tide of cases washes in on the nine Justices each year, and it is only through its discretionary powers to hear or deny these appeals that the Court is able to devote the time and care necessary to the important issues. The ninety-six cases that were decided with full opinions by the Court provide the primary "legal" and "educative" impact of the Justices, for here the Court explained why voters could challenge discriminatory boundaries in state legislative districts; [9] why a "disturbing the peace" conviction of eighteen "sit-in" demonstrators in New Orleans was unconstitutional; [10] why a merger between the Brown Shoe Company and the Kinney Shoe Company violated a federal law against substantially lessening competition; [11] why the contempt of Congress conviction of labor union leader Maurice Hutcheson was valid [12] but the conviction for contempt of nine witnesses called before the House Committee on Un-American Activities had to be reversed; [13] why an employer's action in suddenly providing wage increases and sick leave above the amount urged by the labor union representing the employees constituted an "unfair labor practice" under the Taft-Hartley Act; [14] and why New York's voluntary, "nondenominational" prayer for public school children violated the First Amendment's guarantee of separation between church and state.[15]

Since we will discuss in detail shortly the Court's philosophical positions, its procedures, and its internal divisions, we can turn now to one final item of basic description, the theory of judicial review.

---

[9] *Baker* v. *Carr.*
[10] *Garner* v. *Lousiana,* 368 U.S. 157 (1961).
[11] *Brown Shoe Co., Inc.* v. *United States,* 370 U.S. 294 (1962).
[12] *Hutcheson* v. *United States,* 369 U.S. 599 (1962).
[13] *Russell* v. *United States,* 369 U.S. 749 (1962).
[14] *N.L.R.B.* v. *Benne Katz,* 369 U.S. 736 (1962).
[15] *Engel* v. *Vitale,* 370 U.S. 421 (1962).

Judicial Review: The American Judge as Philosopher-King

The term "judicial review" refers to the power of a court to inquire whether a law, executive order, or other official action conflicts with the written constitution, and, if the court concludes that it does, to declare it unconstitutional and void. In analyzing this power, two quite separate situations must be distinguished: (1) the power of courts to pass on the acts of coordinate branches of the same government, such as federal courts judging acts of Congress or the Secretary of Defense, and the Illinois courts passing on the validity of Illinois statutes or orders of the governor; (2) the power of courts of the federal government to determine whether acts of a member-state in the federal system conflict with the federal Constitution.

Discussions of judicial review sometimes treat these as the same issue, but careful analysis makes it clear that they are not. In the first instance, judges are given special authority over the acts of elected branches in the same government. In the second, judges apply the law of all the people of all the states—the federal Constitution—to acts of a lesser sovereign, the member-state. A famous comment of Justice Oliver Wendell Holmes, Jr., explained the policy behind this difference in 1913: "I do not think the United States would come to an end if we lost our power to declare an Act of Congress void. I do think the Union would be imperilled if we could not make that declaration as to the laws of the several states."

Of course, some body other than the Supreme Court could conceivably pass on conflicts between the national Constitution and state acts, such as a special "Court of the Union," or such a power could be lodged in Congress. But, as we noted earlier, Article VI specified that the Constitution, federal laws, and treaties were to be "the supreme law of the land," and state judges were bound by this "law" regardless of what might appear in state laws or constitutions. It is from this clause that the Supreme Court has drawn its authority to apply the "supreme law of the land" when cases brought before it from the state courts on appeals contain assertions that federal rights have been denied by the state judges. Of course which powers are given to the national government and which are reserved to the states or whether there is any conflict between state acts and federal laws are questions of interpretation that stir passionate debates.

While federal judicial review of state court decisions is grounded on the explicit language of Article VI, nothing in the Constitution specifies that the Supreme Court has the power to declare acts of Congress or the President unconstitutional. Nor do any of the records of the Constitutional Convention indicate that the Framers clearly determined to give the Court such power and thought that they had done so by language employed in the document. Rather, the Constitution uses language that can be and was used to support judicial review as a "logical consequence" of our constitutional system. This suggestive language is found in the provision of Article VI that federal laws made "*in pursuance*" of the Constitution are the "supreme law of the land" and in the power given the Court by Article III to determine "all cases . . . arising under this Constitution. . . ."

On the first occasion when the Supreme Court claimed and exercised the power of judicial review of national acts, the famous case of *Marbury* v. *Madison* in 1803,[16] Chief Justice John Marshall's opinion for the Court relied on three key arguments: the principle that a written constitution is superior to all other acts of government made under it; the nature of our government as a system that was bound by law; and the sworn duty of federal judges to follow the Constitution, give effect only to constitutional laws, and determine which law prevails when there is a conflict.

Actually, Marshall's argument is not without its weak points, as critics in 1803 and today have been quick to point out. When there is a genuine disagreement between the elected branches of the federal government and the Court as to the constitutionality of a measure, why is the judge's oath more sacred than that of legislators and executives? Why shouldn't the judgment of each branch be final as to the constitutionality of measures under its own jurisdiction? Why should the expertness of judges in reading legal documents be assumed to make them expert in construing the special instrument that is a constitution, which represents both a framework of government and a division of power in a system? Most of Marshall's critics were willing to concede that legislative and executive acts affecting the judicial branch (as in *Marbury* v. *Madison*) could be resisted by the Court if found to be unconstitutional, but, as Senator Benjamin Wade of Ohio said in 1858, after the Supreme Court had held its second federal act invalid in the *Dred Scott* case: "I deny the doctrine that Judges have any right to decide the law of the land for every department of this Government."

From Marshall's day down to the present, the question whether the Framers really intended the Court to have this power has been warmly debated as a matter of constitutional history and political policy. The two most persuasive statements on the founding of judicial review—in the works of Professors Charles Beard and Edward S. Corwin—agree that judicial review is justified, but for different reasons. Beard searched through the records of the Constitutional Convention and some contemporaneous sources and concluded that twenty-five of the fifty-five men at the Convention, including the leaders at that meeting, "favored or at least accepted some form of judicial control." The idea was in close harmony with the dominant purpose of the Framers, which was to bring into operation a governmental system that would protect property interests and provide checks upon either monarchy or democracy. Corwin challenged Beard's characterization of the Convention proceedings, showed the highly ambiguous terms in which this was discussed and that the speakers often meant only review of state acts, and concluded that nothing in the Constitution represents the judgment of a Convention majority on what to do with the issue of judicial review of national legislation. Rather, Corwin felt, judicial review developed from the strong popular desire to check the abuses of legislative power by the state legislatures after 1787, and from the logical unfolding of the kind of government that the Constitution of 1787 had called into being.

Today, of course, the Supreme Court's power of judicial review has been

---

[16] 1 Cranch 137 (1803).

so long in use and the historical record has been so picked over that hardly any commentators seriously contend that the Court should give up a "usurped power." But the debate over the Court's having "seized" this authority has colored the argument over *how* the Court is using this far-reaching power at any given moment, with critics utilizing the claim of "bastard birth" to support demands for self-denial by the Justices. As for the Supreme Court, it refers to this power with majestic assurance in the present period. In 1958, when the Court (by its own count) struck down its eighty-second Congressional provision, in a case called *Trop* v. *Dulles*,[17] Chief Justice Earl Warren discussed the Court's authority in these tones:

> We are mindful of the gravity of the issue inevitably raised whenever the constitutionality of an Act of the National Legislature is challenged . . . . [But] we are oath-bound to defend the Constitution. This obligation requires that Congressional enactments be judged by the standards of the Constitution. The Judiciary has the duty of implementing the constitutional safeguards that protect individual rights . . . . The provisions of the Constitution are not time-worn adages or hollow shibboleths. They are vital, living principles that authorize and limit governmental powers in our Nation. They are the rules of government. When the constitutionality of an Act of Congress is challenged in this Court, we must apply those rules. If we do not, the words of the Constitution become little more than good advice . . . . We do well to approach the task cautiously, as all our predecessors have counseled. But the ordeal of judgment cannot be shirked.

Having described now the basic ground rules of American judicial procedure, the organization of state and federal courts, the jurisdiction and powers of the Supreme Court, and the American theory of judicial review, we are ready to consider the leading question posed at the start of this chapter: "What is new since 1937 and what has remained constant in the role of the Supreme Court in American government?" Is the Court since 1937, as some conservative critics have charged, a "runaway bench" that is substituting "sociology" for law, interfering in political concerns, forgetting judicial self-restraint, and ignoring institutional traditions, or is it the same kind of Court, fulfilling the same role and encountering the same kind of protest as the Justices have ever since the early 1800s?

The Supreme Court Since 1937

The simplest and most revealing way to analyze the contemporary role of the Supreme Court is to divide its operations and influences into two categories: factors that can be called "constant elements" since the Court's first meeting in Philadelphia in 1790 and "new aspects" that became ascendant within the Court or affected it from outside after 1937.

---

[17] 356 U.S. 86 (1958).

CONSTANT ELEMENTS IN THE SUPREME COURT'S RELATION
TO AMERICAN GOVERNMENT

1. *The Court always faces the most charged sociopolitical issues of the day.* A history of the constitutional decisions of the Supreme Court is a history of almost all the great political, socioeconomic, and intergroup conflicts in the domestic affairs of the American people. No sooner had a major issue arisen than the individuals or interest groups that lost the fight over it in the political arena rushed into court to seek vindication of "their rights" under the Constitution. If they were rebuffed by the courts, they usually kept trying again and again, creating monuments to the ingenuity of lawyers and clients in devising successful law suits. This "court-seeking psychology" of Americans can be explained in many ways. Some see it as a reflection of an "ideological split personality" between liberalism and conservatism in the American people; others as a filling of the policy vacuum created by our weak party system; others as a heritage of legalism and moralism from the Puritan tradition; and still others as the special (and one-sided) instrument by which conservatives defeated or deflected liberal legislative policies for more than a century, and which liberals now use with equal delight to thwart the will of anti-Communist or anticrime majorities in the state and federal legislatures.

Whatever the reasons, the Supreme Court has always been where the action was. Between 1790 and 1860, the Court issued key rulings on the charged issues of states' rights over commercial regulation and taxation; legislative regulation of property rights and contracts; and the status of slavery in the Union. Between 1865 and 1920, the Court dealt with Reconstruction and the rights of the newly freed Negro; the regulation of corporate enterprise in the formative period of American capitalism; the relations of labor and management; state and federal taxing powers; and civil liberties during wartime. Between 1920 and 1937, the Justices ruled on the central questions of industrial depression and recovery; social welfare; labor relations; agricultural policy; and the lines dividing state and federal power over economic affairs. Between 1937 and the present, the Court has issued important rulings in the areas of Cold War loyalty-security measures, segregation and racial discrimination, church-state relations, labor-management affairs, state procedure in criminal investigations and trials, and in many other areas.

Taken as a whole, the Court has pursued three basic concerns in its constitutional jurisprudence: balancing the parts of the federal Union; fostering a "sound" economic order; and protecting individual rights to property and liberty. In each era, the Court has assigned to the idea of "balance," "sound" economics, and individual "rights" its own reading of what the Constitution said and intended on these matters, adjusting the precedents to changed socioeconomic and technological conditions presented by the new cases. In concentrating on these three central themes, the Court has had to interpret and reinterpret certain constitutional clauses that have been the battleground of debate decade after decade. Before the Civil War, the two main provisions were the *commerce clause* (giving Congress the power "To regulate commerce with foreign nations, and among the several States, and with the Indian tribes") and the *contract clause* (forbidding the states to pass any law "impairing the obligation of contracts"). The commerce clause required the Justices to rule not only on what regulations of interstate sales of goods, transportation, and business firms Congress could make but also on what regulations of multi-state or intrastate commerce by the states would interfere with interstate freedom of movement. The contract clause brought the Court into judgment of legislative land grants and their revocation, debtor and creditor laws, and state regulation of chartered corporations.

Following the Civil War, the *commerce* and *contract* clauses continued to measure federal and state powers over commercial affairs but were joined on the Court's most active constitutional agenda by two powerfully radiating clauses put into the Fourteenth Amendment in 1868. These forbade states to deny any person "life, liberty, or property, without due process of law" or to "deny to any person . . . the equal protection of the laws." The *due process* clause was the primary standard for judging the "reasonableness" of state legislation governing labor conditions, welfare, taxation, and administrative regulation of industry. The *equal protection* clause also measured state action in these areas, as the Court struck down state actions that were said to discriminate unfairly against a particular business activity. While Negro civil rights, fairness in criminal procedure, and freedom of expression occasionally were considered under the due process and equal protection clauses before 1920, the occasions were rare and usually resulted in the Court finding that restrictive action of the state was constitutional; after 1920 until 1937, these clauses began to be used to place important limits on state action in the civil liberties field, though not in civil rights.

Looking at the post-1937 period, we can see that while the contract clause has become almost a dead letter in constitutional litigation, the commerce, due process, and equal protection clauses are still among the Court's handful of basic tools. The interpretations have changed—today the due process clause is used primarily to test state measures dealing with religion or free speech and to require states to provide high standards of fairness in criminal procedure; the equal protection clause now safeguards Negroes and other minority groups far more than it does corporations; and the commerce clause is used primarily to strike down state taxing and business regulation measures that seek to "Balkanize" the national economy. The essential point to note in this quick sketch of major clauses (and others such as the spending power, and the Tenth Amendment, could have been mentioned) is that the shifting policy issues of American society have been tested again and again by a handful of major constitutional clauses. These were drawn by the Framers in broad enough language and with sufficient sweep to them for each successive Court majority to be able to find in them the guidelines for adjusting constitutional standards to changing social conditions.

Of course, the fact that great issues are always *brought* to the Court, and that this is a constant element that has not changed since 1937, does not mean that the Court had to (or should) try to *settle* every explosive question. Some of the Court's severe "self-inflicted wounds," remarked Charles Evans Hughes in 1928 (after he had been on the Supreme Court for six years and had retired), were caused when the Justices failed to realize when to avoid, delay, or moderate judicial intervention in political conflicts. Hughes cited the Court's decisions supporting slavery in 1857, denying the legality of federal paper currency in 1870, and striking down the federal income tax in 1895—all holding federal measures unconstitutional—as the three most serious examples of a collapse of public confidence in the Court unnecessarily provoked by the Court's venturesomeness. Yet, despite such counsel, both within and outside the Court, the dominant tradition of the Court has been to accept and decide most of the explosive issues (though the Court's decisions, as we will discuss soon, are far from the "last word" on these matters). Nothing illustrates this reality better than the fact that when Hughes himself went back on the Supreme Court in 1930 as Chief Justice, it was during his tenure that the Court's vetoes of federal and state New Deal economic legislation led to the famous "Court-packing fight" of 1937. Thus the Supreme Court of the 1960s is squarely in the Court's historical pattern when it makes headlines with constitutional rulings on Communist-control measures, race relations, legislative districting, movie censorship, antitrust cases, and the like.

2. *The Court has always generated sharp controversy and "Court-curbing" campaigns.* Because it has dealt with the crucial issues of each major period in American history, and because its rulings have injured or thwarted powerful political, economic, and social movements, the Supreme Court has consistently been the target for passionate attacks and efforts to limit its powers. The presence of such a stream of controversy in every political generation (taking this to be from about twenty to twenty-five years) can be easily traced. Between 1800 and the 1820s, the United States witnessed harsh Jeffersonian protest over the "centralizing" decisions of the Marshall Court. Jeffersonians in Congress, in the Republican administrations, and in state courts and state bars, bitterly assailed the Court and urged withdrawal of the federal judiciary's claim to decide whether acts of Congress were constitutional or not, whether federal law was supreme over state law when this question arose in state courts and affected state property and state judicial procedure, or whether the President had exceeded his constitutional powers. Between 1830 and 1850, the nation saw the protests of the Jacksonians over Supreme Court interference with state regulation of commerce. There were also protests on slavery cases, both from the North (whenever the Supreme Court upheld the rights of slaveholders to go to federal court and secure their "chattels" back) and from the South (when the Supreme Court did not act as strongly as the Southerners wanted in enforcing slavery through the federal court system).

Between 1850 and 1875, a peak of controversy was reached with attacks on the *Dred Scott* decision on slavery in 1857 [18] and carried through the 1866–68 fight between the Radical Republicans in Congress and the Supreme Court Justices over the constitutionality of Reconstruction measures; we have already discussed Congressional action against the Court involving the *McCardle* case. The years from 1880 to 1900 featured the protests of farmers, Populists, and early labor movement leaders against what they called the "corporate bias" of the federal judiciary; 1896 was

---

[18] *Dred Scott* v. *Sandford*, 19 How. 393 (1857).

"I'll Have The Law On You"

A liberal defense of the Supreme Court against Congressional Court-curb proposals in 1958.

From Herblock's *Special for Today*, Simon & Schuster, 1958

the second time that the Supreme Court became a major issue in the Presidential campaign (the first such incident was 1860), and attacks upon the Court were a regular feature of the campaign's platform oratory.

In the period of 1900–25, the Progressives launched a full-scale attack on the Supreme Court's economic doctrines, challenging the "anti-Labor," "anti-Liberal" bias of the Justices. Both in 1912 and in 1924, Presidential third parties (the Bull Moose Movement in 1912 and the La Follette Progressive Movement in 1924) promised through their platforms and the speeches of their political leaders to provide checks against an overbearing Supreme Court if they were elected. Various proposals were advocated in Congress during this era to provide means for overturning decisions of the Supreme Court. Between 1925 and 1950 came the clash between the New Deal and the "nine old men," when the rulings of a majority on the Supreme Court erected a wall of constitutional doctrine against which most of the key New Deal measures rammed in vain before 1937.

Finally, 1950 to the present has been marked by a number of repeated crises about the United States Supreme Court's civil liberties and civil rights decisions. The most important of these protest movements, the so-called "Court-curbing attack of 1957–58," was a period in which Southern Congressmen, internal-security stalwarts, and some business groups challenged the Court's trend of decisions in areas of loyalty-security measures, Congressional investigations, desegregation, labor relations, antitrust, and so on.

To say then that the Supreme Court of the 1960s has generated angry reactions from interest groups and political movements and has made the

Court a "controversial agency" is to say that the Justices are running true to historical form.

3. *The Court has always had internal divisions and "splits" over constitutional questions.* When the Supreme Court in the 1960s divides 5–4 or 6–3 on major constitutional issues, and when the Justices exchange frank, passionate, and hard-hitting majority and minority opinions, this represents a continuation of tradition begun when Justice William Johnson, a Jeffersonian appointee, began in the 1810–20 period to dissent systematically and forcefully from several of the main doctrines of the Supreme Court majority led by Chief Justice John Marshall. Ever since then, "splits" within the Court on leading issues and on basic philosophy have been a regular feature of our constitutional system.

Some commentators in each of these eras have deplored these divisions, have criticized the formation of "cohesive blocs" within the Court, and have called for a show of constitutional "harmony" within the Court to reassure the public that constitutional law was above personal or ideological interests. While there can be a point at which personal bickering among the Justices and the lack of consistency of majority opinion can damage the Court's reputation, divisions are really a sign that the fiercely held views in the country at large on various sides of great questions are represented within the Court, and that the dialectic of debate is being transferred into constitutional terms that, hopefully, will lend themselves to resolution or compromise. To contend for a unanimous bench, in the 1960s or at any other time, is to confuse constitutional interpretation and adjudication with mathematics or religious good-fellowship.

4. *The Court's procedures and traditions for deciding cases have remained basically constant.* A fourth constant in the present situation of the Supreme Court is that its procedures for and outlook in deciding cases represent much the same ones that existed under Chief Justices Marshall, Fuller, and Hughes. Significant changes have been made in the discretion of the Court to hear certain types of cases, the Justices no longer have to saddle their horses and ride around the country hearing trial cases in the federal circuits, and the Court now has a superb marble temple to work in where once it had a room in the Senate basement. Yet the basic operations to decide cases have remained remarkably constant.

The Justices are still a small committee. They still function as a closed, corporate entity, steeped in the learning of the law, and operating through the still longer traditions of the Anglo-Saxon legal system. Even though the Justices now have two clerks each, and the Chief Justice has three, and even though they now have secretaries, elaborate suites, an effective Supreme Court Library, and the services of the Library of Congress to draw upon, most of the work of the Court is still as personal and as painfully slow as it has ever been. Each Justice, for example, still passes personally on every attempt to bring a case to the Supreme Court for decision. While the law clerks may write memoranda summarizing the cases which come by the thousands to the Court, each Justice considers personally whether to vote to accept or reject a case for consideration. Oral argument before the United States Supreme Court remains still the Socratic exchange so familiar in the courts of England and the United States throughout the formative years of this judicial system. While the briefs of counsel have grown longer, they are still about the same kind of appellate argument that Supreme Courts received in 1830 or 1890. The Justices still write their own opinions (aided by research and some drafting by law clerks).

Secrecy still surrounds the Court's deliberations, and neither the press nor Congress can probe into the internal processes of the Court's decision-making, as is done with executive and administrative agencies or Congressional procedures. Finally, the fact that the Justices have life tenure, with almost all of them seeing their Justiceship as the final stage of their political careers, creates a sense of independence from party pressures and a mood of dedication to principle which—while it does not guarantee either intellect or wisdom—does make the Court the most "long-range minded" of our national institutions in its approach to policy issues. This may give way to intense partisanship or ideological militancy in some Justices, and even in Court majorities (as in 1857 over slavery or in the 1930s on New Deal reforms), but the dominant tradition has been independence from party or factional positions.

5. *The types of Supreme Court Justices have been a constant element.* Even the Justices as individuals can be seen as a factor that has remained constant from 1790 to the present. No person who is not a lawyer has yet to sit on the Supreme Court, though there is no constitutional or statutory bar to appointing a political scientist or a constitutional historian. If one studies carefully the pre-Court professions of the Justices, the same basic types of the 1860s or 1920s are those that populate the Court today. There are the former members of the President's administration, drawn from Cabinet and executive officials. There are the powerful party figures, men who must be rewarded for service done to the President's party. There are the powerful members or immediately retired members of the Congress, some of whom are placed on the Court for party reasons and some in order to clear the way for the President's program. There are also prominent members of the bar and judges of the federal and state courts appointed to the Court, again usually following broad party and sectional lines. Occasionally, there have been law professors.

As these major categories indicate, the present Supreme Court, as a matter of occupational, career, and party lines, is a quite orthodox Court. Earl Warren was a Republican governor of California and the Republican Vice-Presidential nominee in 1948; his appointment as Chief Justice in 1953 derives from President Eisenhower's desire to reward him for his service. Hugo Black, a Democratic Senator from Alabama between 1928 and 1938, was appointed by President Franklin Roosevelt partly because of Black's yeoman's service in the Senate on behalf of New Deal measures, including Black's support of the President's Court-reform proposal of 1937, and partly because F. D. R. knew that Senatorial courtesy would prevent Black's nomination from encountering truly serious opposition in the Senate. William O. Douglas, though a law professor at Columbia and Yale in his early career, was a member and then chairman of the Securities and Exchange Commission during the New Deal, and is another instance of the executive official appointed to the Supreme Court. Tom Clark, the first of the Truman appointees, was a former United States Attorney General whose service to the Administration accounted for his nomination. The three Eisenhower appointees other than Chief Justice Warren represent no departure from tradition. John M. Harlan was a Wall Street lawyer and protégé of Republican party leader Thomas Dewey; Eisenhower had earlier appointed Harlan to the Federal Court of Appeals. William J. Brennan, Jr., was a judge of the Supreme Court of New Jersey, and as an Irish Catholic and a registered Democrat, represented a visibly political bid by Eisenhower before the 1956 election for the votes of Catholics and "Eisenhower Democrats." Potter Stewart was a Federal Court of Appeals judge and former practicing lawyer. The two Kennedy appointees, Justices Byron White and Arthur Goldberg, were both members of the President's executive family, White as Deputy Attorney General and Goldberg as Secretary of Labor.

A study of the ninety-one Supreme Court Justices between 1789 and 1957 showed that 96 percent of them were of English, Welsh, Scotch, Irish, or German origin.[19] In terms of religious affiliation, eighty-two of the ninety-one Justices were Protestants, six Roman Catholics, and three Jewish. As for political careers, ninety of the ninety-one had held political positions of some kind before nomination (federal, state, or local elective, appointive, judicial, or party posts). Viewed in terms of the kinds of lawyers they were before appointment, forty-nine were "primarily politicians" serving in elected office rather than devoting full time to law practice; twenty-four were primarily state or federal judges; eleven were primarily corporation lawyers; three were general practitioners of law; and four were primarily law professors. The author of this study, Professor John R. Schmidhauser, concluded from his examination of the recruitment of Justices that if the Supreme Court is, as Justice Felix Frankfurter once said, the "trustee of the conscience of the American system," "it is essentially the conscience of the American upper middle-class sharpened by the imperative of individual social responsibility and political activism, and conditioned by the conservative impact of legal training and professional legal attitudes and associations." This conclusion applies squarely to the Justices of the 1960s.

6. *The Court remains both a powerful and a highly vulnerable institution.* In the 1960s, with newspaper headlines and hour-long network television programs devoted to its major rulings, with Presidents, Congresses, governors, and state legislatures accepting (or being forced to accept) Supreme Court rulings on its powers, the Court seems to be an immensely powerful institution. And so it seemed to be when the Jeffersonians, Jacksonians, Populists, and New Dealers protested its immense effect on the economic and political issues of their day. Yet it is a continuing irony that the Supreme Court is a highly vulnerable institution, depending for its authority on the willingness of elected officials to carry out its orders and of the public to entrust such awesome policy decisions to the nine Justices.

To appreciate the Court's vulnerability, we need only note the direct

---

[19] John R. Schmidhauser, "The Justices of the Supreme Court: A Collective Portrait," *Midwest Journal of Political Science* (1959), Vol. III, pp. 1–49.

and indirect controls that the Justices are subject to in our system. Constitutional amendments can overturn unpopular rulings. Congressional statutes can reverse the Court's decision when these rest on interpretation of federal statutes. Congress' control over the Court's appellate jurisdiction can be used—or used as a threat—to cut off the Court's review of specific areas of controversy. Presidents are usually able to appoint new Justices and can deliberately seek to change the voting balances within the Court through these appointments. State and federal officials can mount embarrassingly effective resistance to the Court's orders, ranging from subtle inaction to open defiance, since the Justices must look to elected officials to enforce their orders. The bar and bench can raise influential protests against the Court's legal arguments and its professional competence. And every Supreme Court, finally, is acutely sensitive to continuous, widespread mistrust of its decisions by the general public.

Reflecting these realities, no Supreme Court in American history—before or after 1937—has ever defied for long the sustained will of "dominant opinion" in the nation. When the Court has met the determined will of these dominant forces—as it faced the Radical Republicans in 1866–68 or the New Deal in 1936–37—the existing Court majority has always modified its disputed doctrines to uphold the measure insisted upon by dominant opinion. The Court modified some of its civil liberty positions (or language) in 1959, following the "Court-curb" attack of 1957–58. As Thomas Reed Powell once said, the Court knows how to execute the "switch in time that saves nine." Here, too, the Justices of the 1960s are in the same ambiguous and challenging position as their predecessors. If they use the Court's symbols and authority wisely and with political skill, they can be a tremendous force in our national life; if they cross the invisible boundary lines and go too far, they risk swift and effective reprisals.

There are other constant elements that might have been discussed here, but the six mentioned above represent the main aspects of the contemporary Supreme Court's work that many journalists and uninformed critics point to as "new" and "revolutionary" innovations of the post-1937 or post-1957 Courts. Yet the Court since 1937 *has* been a new institution in several basic respects, and it is to these that we turn now.

NEW ASPECTS OF THE SUPREME COURT'S ROLE
IN AMERICAN GOVERNMENT AND POLITICS

1. *Basic changes in the Court's beneficiaries.* The first new element is that the beneficiaries of the Supreme Court's decisions have changed radically. Those who enjoyed the Court's protection before 1937 and those who enjoy the Court's protection today are quite different groups. Throughout the history of the Court down to the post-F. D. R. period, those who profited most from the Supreme Court's rulings on constitutional law were primarily New England businessmen, Western land speculators, Southern planters, slaveholders, the new industries that followed the Civil War (the railroads, manufacturing companies, and so on), the banking interests, the public utility holding companies—in short, the propertied elements in American economic life. We are not suggesting that the Supreme Court was a "kept" body, with the Justices simply hired by the masters of pro-

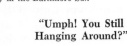

Duffy in the Baltimore *Sun*

"Umph! You Still Hanging Around?"

Seibel in the Richmond *Times-Dispatch*

At the beginning of the New Deal period, conservatives saw the Court as a proper check on the "unconstitutional" program, while liberals saw it as a threat to national economic recovery.

duction. What one can say is that the Supreme Court's definition of what property rights were guaranteed by the federal Constitution, as well as its concept of limited government, of states' rights, and of the idea of resort to the courts for determination of constitutionality rather than to the ultimate will of the elected branches, produced an ideal set of rules for those running a capitalist system. It provided the kind of fiscal stability, credit guarantees, protection of contracts, employer control over work conditions, and reliance upon private initiative and private welfare which served the business community and stood as a barrier to many revisionist efforts by farm, labor, and middle-class reform elements from 1800 to 1937.

Spokesmen for the business community understood that the Supreme Court was "their" institution in the nation's governmental structure, and defended it staunchly. During the 1840s, for example, Daniel Webster, the acknowledged dean of corporate counsel in the pre-Civil War era, commented that the nation's "chartered interests" knew that their "only security is to be found in this tribunal," with its checks upon the "unlimited despotism" of state governments and the "leveling ultraisms of anti-rentism or agrarianism. . . ." When American capitalism entered its eras of expansion and consolidation, and the Supreme Court—in one term, 1895—struck down the federal income tax, dismissed prosecutions against the sugar trust, and upheld the contempt conviction of American Railway Union President Eugene Debs—the business community did not try to contain its enthusiasm. J. Edward Simmons, president of the Fourth National Bank of New York, told an applauding audience of New York City commercial leaders: "I give you, gentlemen, the Supreme Court of the United States—guardian of the dollar, defender of private property, enemy of spoilation, sheet anchor of the Republic!"

In 1908, when the muckrakers were pressing for antimonopoly and pro-union reforms, the general counsel of the American Anti-Boycott Association told a convention of corporate delegates:

> In the wild storm that has been raging in the last four years, a storm that has threatened to drag our ship of state from its ancient and time-honored moorings, it has been the Constitution of the United States, as interpreted by the Supreme Court, that has been, thank God, all anchor and very little sail . . . . It was again that great Supreme Tribunal lifting its serene voice far above the angry factions of the hour, which has said that it is a fundamental right of every American whom he will employ and whom he will not employ.[20]

In 1911, when the Supreme Court cut sharply into the sweep of the Sherman Antitrust Laws, one of the Standard Oil executives capped the outpouring of corporate praise for the Court's decision by saying, "I am for the Supreme Court every time. For more than a hundred years it has been at work and it has never made a mistake . . . ." In 1936, the president of the Crucible Steel Corporation indicated business's appreciation of its great ally in the judiciary with the comment that: "The judiciary has again proved itself to be the bulwark of defense against the subtle and skillful manipulation of democratic processes to achieve unsanctioned theories."

Today, however, American business is saying very different things about the United States Supreme Court. In 1960, for example, a poll of the vice-presidents and general counsel of fifty of the nation's largest and most powerful corporations [21] asked them what they thought about the business decisions of the United States Supreme Court, as well as the civil liberty and equality decisions of the Court. The answers revealed that two thirds of the counsel were deeply hostile to the United States Supreme Court. A leading industrial manufacturing corporation's general counsel explained:

> I think the informed businessman is pretty well discouraged with the Warren Court. In matters affecting business, the Court has pretty well swept aside what was left of constitutional safeguards in the field of taxes and government regulation. The bloc of four with which the Chief Justice is usually found is quite beyond the pale of reason in the eyes of most of the men with whom I discuss these matters.[22]

Another representative comment came from the general counsel of a large food producing and marketing company:

> I feel, and I believe that most businessmen in large corporations feel, that in so-called civil liberties and civil rights decisions the Court by

---

[20] *Proceedings of the American Anti-Boycott Association* (1908), p. 21.
[21] Conducted by Alan F. Westin; replies in author's possession.
[22] *Ibid.*

and large has leaned over backward to a somewhat unusual degree in its attempt to sustain civil rights and liberties. Whereas, on the other hand, it has seemed not only unconcerned with but almost determined to ignore the rights of business.

As these comments indicate, most corporate spokesmen—although a small minority will defend the Court—speak of the United States Supreme Court today in the sad, sometimes sharp, tones of a man who sees his former mistress bestowing her favors on strangers. For its part, the post-1937 Supreme Court majority often treats the rigid property rights doctrines of the nineteenth- and early twentieth-century Justices as rather embarrassing reminders of an indiscreet liaison in its youth. The fact that there has been this rift in the classic love affair between business and the Supreme Court is one of the most significant aspects of the present Supreme Court's relation to the country and to public opinion.

Several things should be noted before leaving this point. What business is complaining about primarily is the absence of Supreme Court intervention to limit the power of the federal government to tax broadly, to regulate industry closely, and to supervise labor relations in detail. A close look at recent cases in the Supreme Court involving labor-management relations indicates that the decisions in these divide roughly fifty-fifty, with labor and management each winning about half each term. Even this, however, is too much for business, since the cases it loses are those usually in which it had hoped to see doctrines established in the Court that would turn back, or at least prevent, the further expansion of federal jurisdiction over the industry decisions, including those affecting labor relations.

On the other hand, a new set of beneficiaries have replaced business. Today, the new befriended include Negroes, persons claiming that their civil liberties have been infringed upon by the actions of elected majorities (Communists, syndicate leaders, balky college professors, loyalty-security risks, and so on), and spokesmen advocating that their right of religious freedom has been improperly limited in some fashion (such as Jews, Seventh Day Adventists, Unitarians, humanists, and atheists).

The groups which now defend the Supreme Court at legislative hearings and in the popular media are Americans for Democratic Action, the National Association for the Advancement of Colored People, the American Veterans Committee, the AFL–CIO, American Jewish Congress, American Civil Liberties Union, and similar groups in what is usually called the "Lib-Lab" coalition. Yet it should be marked that these groups are not defending *economic* interests (labor testimony on behalf of the Court has not been for its labor rulings but in defense of its civil rights and civil liberties decisions) but rather their *political* interests, in the larger sense of the word.

2. *Basic changes in the Court's areas of intervention.* Coupled with this change in the beneficiaries of the Court's rulings has been a change in the basic thrust of the Supreme Court's decisions. Prior to 1937, the bulk of the Court's politically sensitive, constitutional rulings were in the field of property controls—taxation, regulation of commerce, labor relations, antitrust, farm programs, etc. While there were always some cases involving criminal procedure (selection of juries, evidence rules, searches and sei-

zures, etc.), these were comparatively few in number and state criminal cases were generally left as the state supreme courts had decided them. In the 1960s, the Court decides few constitutional cases affecting property rights; its agenda is loaded with cases involving matters of liberty, equality, and fair procedure, so much so that almost half of the cases that the Supreme Court has decided with full opinions at its last two or three terms have been liberty, equality, and fair procedure cases.

There are a variety of connected reasons for this, some of which reflect choice by the Justices, while others reflect outside-the-Court factors. First, the Justices themselves washed the property cases out of their stream of constitutional decision by the basic doctrines adopted in 1937 and constantly adhered to since—that federal power to regulate the economy, under the commerce, tax, and general welfare clauses of the Constitution, is a broad power essential to managing an industrial economy and authorized by the Founding Fathers in their broad charter. This is not to be constricted by judge-made interpretations of what would be good for the nation. Thus, all of the doctrines about direct and indirect controls on commerce, power to regulate shipment of goods in interstate commerce but not production for commerce, federal power over manufacture but not agriculture—all of these and many more staples of the pre-1937 jurisprudence have been reduced to the simple inquiry: Did Congress use its broad power reasonably? So put, the Court has yet to find an unreasonable use of federal legislative power in property cases since 1937. It struck down a *Presidential* action as unconstitutional in 1952, of course, in the steel seizure case. And it came close to upsetting the federal statute requiring gamblers to pay a federal wagering tax (and thereby force them to register and declare themselves as bookies); but even here, the Court would not go behind the Congress' declaration that this was a revenue measure rather than an attempt to fight local crime (which has been held to be a matter of state rather than federal jurisdiction).

Another reason for the shift in agenda that traces to the Court's own volition is the way in which the majority of the Justices have enunciated constitutional doctrines which open up broad avenues of access to the Supreme Court for minority groups. Beginning with the *Gitlow* case in 1925, the Court ruled that the freedoms guaranteed in the First Amendment to the federal Constitution (freedom of speech, press, assembly, and religion, and the bar against religious establishment) were included in those rights to due process which the states could not infringe under the Fourteenth Amendment to the Constitution. This meant that the Court would now consider cases of state action alleged to violate First Amendment guarantees, something which had largely been a matter of final decision by state supreme courts before 1925. The *Gitlow* concept has been steadily widened, and the Court now polices a tremendous part of state governmental action under the Fourteenth Amendment, ranging from state use of hidden microphones and the fairness of state trials to the way in which states administer Sunday closing laws, set loyalty standards for their employees, conduct state legislative hearings, or separate the races. In addition, the Court virtually "invited" minority groups to litigate in the famous

Carolene Products case comment (1938) [23] that judicial intervention against legislative will was justified when the political process was unavailable for relief—as when Negroes and other racial minorities, or political radicals, or labor union organizers, were oppressed by hostile local majorities.

Turning from these factors which the Justices set in operation, we can see how other forces interacted with them to accentuate this trend. The new religious, racial, and liberal groups which sprang up on the American civic scene after the First World War (Jehovah's Witnesses, NAACP, ACLU, American Jewish Congress, and so on) have accepted the Court's invitation to litigate with alacrity. Many of these groups have perfected the techniques of the "test case" and are quite skillful in bringing to the Supreme Court cases which otherwise would probably never have been the subject of a Supreme Court ruling. Before 1937, it was largely businessmen, corporations, and business associations, such as the American Anti-Boycott League or the NAM, or some labor unions and groups like the Consumers League, which shaped the test cases. Now, it is the NAACP, ACLU, Protestants and Other Americans United for Separation of Church and State, the Anti-Defamation League, and many others which appear as the parties or as "friends of the Court" in the leading cases each term.

Another large factor affecting the agenda of the Court is that in economic affairs, the country is largely on a social-welfare capitalist plateau. There have been no radical departures from American economic organization and welfare laws since 1938. No nationalization of industry is in sight. Labor, management, and government do a kind of perpetual gavotte in collective bargaining, but without creating situations which produce constitutional tests. On the other hand, the major conflicts affecting our society domestically (foreign affairs have traditionally been something the Court left to the political branches) have been matters of *status*, not property. The problems of Communism, loyalty, and internal security that reached their peak in McCarthyism involved the definition of political deviation and the limits of liberty. The revolution in race relations since the Second World War and in religious interrelations probes our concepts of equality. And it is in this arena, of status, that the great constitutional debate of our generation has been raging.

3. *Basic changes in the public debate over the Court as an institution.* This major shift in the beneficiaries of judicial review and in the types of disputed constitutional cases has naturally created a dramatic difference in those who are defending the Court in the public arena and those who are attacking it. From the days of Marshall down through the late 1930s, as we noted earlier in tracing controversy over the Court, there was what could be called a tradition of *liberal* criticism of judicial review as an institution. The Jeffersonians, the Jacksonians, the Populists and Progressives, the New Dealers, all denounced the Supreme Court as a block to majority rule. In rational liberal theory, they argued that the Supreme Court was an insufferable restraint upon the right of elected agencies of

---

[23] *United States v. Carolene Products Co.*, 304 U.S. 144 (1938).

government to govern. In a democratic society, they argued, judges with life tenure had no right to substitute their notions of wise policy for the wishes of the people acting through Congress, the President, and the state governments. Yet, the liberal today is usually someone who defends the Supreme Court as a wise agency checking mass passions and protecting precious human rights from invasions by "populist sentiment" in state legislatures, Congress, and even the executive branch.

A similar reversal has taken place in the conservative camp. Formerly, when liberals attacked the Supreme Court, conservative and propertied groups would reply in rational conservative doctrine that the Supreme Court was a badly needed brake upon populist democracy. It was suggested that the Court provided a second sober look, a chance to reexamine actions taken in the heat of the day, and that some rights were higher and entitled to greater protection than were simple matters that were to be left to the give-and-take of majority rule. Yet today, it is exactly the key elements of the conservative camp—groups such as the American Legion, many leaders of the American Bar Association, state and local law-enforcement officers, Southern political leaders, conservative Republicans, and many businessmen—who cry that the Supreme Court is tampering with the wise conclusions of the people's representatives. These are the people who are now denouncing the notion that some doctrine of higher right gives the Court a license to intervene on behalf of Communists, Negroes, bohemians, radicals, and others who fall outside the conservative notion of truly useful Americans.

It is important to note, in observing this fascinating change of position, that this is the first conflict over the Court that does not present basically a party line division. Previously, Jefferson, Jackson, Lincoln, Bryan, and the two Roosevelts led the bulk of their party faithful against the disputed judicial doctrines, while the party dominated by property interests being protected by the Court defended the Justices—the Federalists, Whigs, and Republicans. Today, with property issues absent, there are no strict party positions. Congressional Republicans and Democrats are divided over the Court. Party leaders outside of Congress split along ideological rather than party positions.

Obviously, liberal and conservative spokesmen have not changed their positions; the explanation is that a majority of the Supreme Court has been handing down rulings ever since the late 1930s which have been more in accord with liberal notions of what the good society should be than with notions of the conservatives. Conservatives are opposing the Court because it has become "dangerously unsound" on constitutional and political matters. This demonstrates a classic adage of the political scientist. Whether a group approves or disapproves of a political institution is not a matter of long-range affiliation, loyalty, or abstract political theory but depends on whether that institution is serving the interests of the group at the moment. Since the major periods of dispute over judicial review in the past found the Court steadfastly devoted to conservative positions, the simple explanation of the first liberal switch toward judicial review is that liberals have had to wait from 1790 until the 1940s to find a set of Justices to whom they could attach their allegiance.

Three Is Growing Into A Crowd

A contemporary conservative view
of the Supreme Court's new role.

Jensen in the Chicago *Daily News*

Another point to be noted briefly is that the Supreme Court as an institution has changed on a sufficiently permanent basis so that the sense
of alienation of the conservatives has been constant ever since 1937. Many
conservatives, and much of the business community, expected that when
a Republican was restored to the White House his appointees to the Court
would wipe out the "socialist excesses" of F. D. R.'s Justices. When two of
Eisenhower's appointees, Chief Justice Warren and Justice Brennan, moved
into a position of broad agreement with Justices Black and Douglas, and
when Eisenhower's three other men, Harlan, Stewart, and Whittaker, went
no further toward turning back the clock than to accept the ideas of
Justice Frankfurter, then the business and conservative elements realized
that the Court would never be the same again.

This might have produced a sharp explosion, a move to change the
basis of judicial review, or to limit the Court's jurisdiction, or to change
the basis of appointing Justices. The reason why business has not been
openly hostile to the Court, in the sense of seeking such punitive measures
against it, and why most business leaders did not support the Jenner-
Butler Court-curbing bills of 1957–58, is that the Supreme Court's decisions
affecting property can be reached and affected by a more subtle mechanism, which we will call the "Congressional Court of Appeal."

We stated earlier that there are few *constitutional* decisions affecting
property with which the Supreme Court is concerned today. In no case
since 1937 has an act of Congress in the economic sphere been declared
unconstitutional. While there have been instances of state laws being de-

clared unconstitutional, primarily as burdens on interstate commerce, this has not been a central concern of the business community. The major areas of Supreme Court decisions that do affect business heavily today concern federal regulatory actions, federal tax laws, and federal regulation of labor relations. These turn largely on interpretation of federal statutes— the National Labor Relations Act, the Taft-Hartley Act, the Fair Labor Standards Act, the Social Security Act, wage and price statutes, and the basic enabling statutes of the major regulatory commissions, such as the Interstate Commerce Commission, the Federal Communications Commission, and the Civil Aeronautics Authority. Here, business soon discovered that when the Supreme Court handed down a decision which business did not like, it could go to Congress and ask that the statute be rewritten or even repealed, on the theory that a small band of "judicial legislators" had "misinterpreted" Congress's intention.

Between 1944 and 1960, there were fifty campaigns that could be called "reversal efforts," in which groups went before Congress seeking to have Congress overturn Supreme Court rulings. Seventy-five Supreme Court rulings were involved in these fifty instances. Of the fifty reversal efforts, thirty-four were successful, and some sixty Supreme Court rulings were either directly nullified or their doctrines were so limited that the action represented an overturning of the decision. Of the thirty-four successful efforts, twenty-four were brought by corporations, industry associations, or business interest groups, and accounted for revision of close to fifty Supreme Court cases. (Examples of these were revisions of the Social Security Act, the National Labor Relations Act, the Federal Power Act, and similar statutes.) This means that the business community has found a safety valve in the willingness of Congress to revise those legislative measures to which the Court has been giving a slightly more "antibusiness" interpretation than the existing Congressional mood would give. An anecdote in 1959 illustrates this well. At one Congressional hearing, Representative Wilbur Mills of Arkansas leaned across the witness table and commented to the president of Du Pont, Crawford Greenewalt, "It seems that it is becoming more and more almost a full-time job of the Congress to correct the Supreme Court's desire to legislate." Mr. Greenewalt nodded his approval, since he was seeking to have a major Supreme Court decision affecting Du Pont's ownership of General Motors stock softened, though not directly overturned.

Still another aspect that should be noted is that only two or three decisions affecting civil liberties have been overturned in Congress since 1944. One involved deportations, another a term in the federal law against sedition, and another a minor rewriting of the Supreme Court's decision in the *Jencks* case, involving the obligation of the government to produce statements made to the FBI by witnesses who then testify in federal court against a defendant. In all the other disputed civil liberties cases, involving loyalty criteria for admission to the state bar, anticensorship rulings, the federal loyalty-security program, federal passports, wire tapping, and a wide range of other issues, campaigns to have these decisions overturned in Congress have not been successful. Nor have the civil rights decisions of the Supreme Court been overturned, of course. No decision ordering states to desegregate in any facilities—schools, transportation, public accommodations, or public entertainment—has been cut back in any form by Congressional action. This suggests that the liberal allies of the Supreme Court are able to defend it fairly effectively against reprisals or reversals, at least in the setting of American politics and society since the late 1950s.

4. *Basic changes in the Court's doctrinal ethos.* Another element which is distinctly new in the present situation is what we could call the atmosphere and doctrinal ethos of the Supreme Court since 1937. This is a delicate point but one which is vitally important. Before the 1930s, the Supreme Court talked about constitutional law in highly traditionalist terms. As Justice Owen Roberts put it, the function of the United States Supreme Court was to lay a challenged statute or executive order beside the Constitution and see whether the former squared with the latter. This was a mechanistic notion of jurisprudence, even what could be called a slot-machine theory. One fed a statute into the machine and pulled the lever; if it came out two lemons and a cherry, it was not constitutional; if it came up three lemons or three cherries, it was constitutional. All the Justices did was to pull down the lever.

Today, it is not simply a few voices of dissent, as it was in the eras of dissenters such as Oliver Wendell Holmes, Jr., Louis D. Brandeis, Harlan Fiske Stone, or the first Justice John Marshall Harlan, who are talking in terms of legal realism. Ever since the late 1930s, a majority of the Supreme Court has been discussing the role of the Court, the meaning of the Constitution, and the principles of American constitutional order, in terms of sociological realism, of a jurisprudence which sees the role of the Supreme Court as part of the larger governmental process, not as a kind of separate "nocturnal council" in the Platonic sense. This means that several generations of legal debate have culminated in a Supreme Court which accepts a modern, liberal style of judicial review. Yet this also means that those who challenge the Supreme Court have as one of *their* primary weapons the fact of the new style—the discussion of economics, the references to political history, the use of sociological treatises, the absence of appeals to precedent as wholly controlling. For the techniques by which the Court does its work today do clash with the fundamentalist's notion of what the judiciary should do in our system. This is not just a matter of John Birch Society claims that the Court has become a Communist cell, or that Earl Warren should be impeached. Rather, it is a question of how widely accepted it is in America for the Court to say, in essence, "Look, we have no magic clothes on; we are not emperors, but simply lawyers transferred from legislative, political, practitioners', and professors' posts to try to apply the rules of the Constitution in a reflective and broad-gauged manner consistent with the intention of the Framers and the needs of modern public policy. We are not gods; neither are we men with as many pressures upon us as those who legislate. Our function is to uphold the great balances of American government—as Justice Robert Jackson put it, the balances between federal and state authority, liberty and order, human rights and property rights." One cannot read a contemporary Court decision and fail to realize how important this difference in tone and style is, as the Justices today explain their case to the public.

17 / The Men of Justice in America: Lawyers, Judges, and Law-Enforcers

In our country," a United States Congressman from Georgia remarked in 1814, "every man is presumed to carry the Constitution in his head or in his pocket, that he may at all times be ready to compare the acts of Government with the Constitution." There is much to support the view that the United States, then and now, is an unusually "law-minded" society. We tend to regard our Constitution as a kind of magic talisman; it ensures material success for the nation by releasing the energies of the citizenry while it guards the land from alien ideologies by the shield of republican principles. We give judges far-reaching authority to rule on issues of social and political policy that other systems do not leave to decision in law suits. Our lawyers play a role in civic, business, and political life far out of proportion to their numbers or wealth.

In addition, Americans insist upon "passing a law" to govern wide areas of personal and civic life, from the amount of flesh to be covered by a bathing suit to the political ideas that can be safely held by teachers. Our culture celebrates "law men" as authentic folk heroes, with television broadcasts about Matt Dillon, Lawrence Preston, and Perry Mason voicing the message that the rule of law is the basic ideal of our people, just as it was in 1780 when the Massachusetts Bill of Rights declared that ours was a "government of laws and not of men."

Yet beside this respect for law has been a conflicting theme of distrust for the restraints that fundamental law places on the execution of popular will. Throughout our history, there has also been a pattern of riot, vigilantism, and even lynching when "the law" did not "do its duty" in the view of local citizens. This impatience with "legal technicalities" (that is, constitutional and legal rules) continues today. Much of the public shows indifference to widely publicized illegal action by police and prosecutors, such as arrests solely on suspicion or telephone tapping. There is considerable resentment toward the legal profession as a whole, with lawyers regarded by many Americans as "tricky" and "immoral" men who twist the law to serve the interests of the rich and the "guilty." Finally, there is widespread public disregard of laws that American society insists upon enacting and then refuses to support, such as statutes against gambling, drinking, prostitution, or speeding on highways.

In this chapter, we examine the clash between the rule of law and dis-

520

trust for law in America by focusing on the men—lawyers, judges, and law-enforcers—whose primary task it is to administer and use the law once it has been defined by constitutions and legislatures.

Lawyers in America: The Bridge Between Government and Society

Lawyers play a unique role in the American governmental process, which explains why we discuss the activities of the legal profession but not those of doctors, engineers, accountants, or professors. Some of the reasons for the lawyers' unique role have been mentioned already—the special "law-mindedness" and legal language of American public life; the predominance of lawyers in our legislatures, executive agencies, and courts; the close relation of law practice to party politics and election campaigning; and the special importance of lawyers' organizations in public affairs. Viewed in a larger context, however, lawyers can be thought of as a "bridge" between the general citizenry and the huge impersonality of "government." Though many contacts between citizens and the government are carried on without a lawyer's counsel, the complexity of business and legal affairs makes a lawyer's expert advice so useful that the legal profession is found constantly performing a "middleman" function in the governmental process. How this function is carried on and what kind of a "recruitment reservoir" for government service the bar constitutes are the questions we turn to here.

Though lawyers make up less than 4 percent of the working force in the United States today, they have a total monopoly on judicial offices (above the justice-of-the-peace level) and also occupy more than 50 percent of the legislative and executive posts in our national, state, and city governments. Lawyers have maintained this weighted role ever since colonial days. Thirty-one of the fifty-five Framers of the Constitution were trained in law. In the years since national independence, about 66 percent of United States Senators, 55 percent of Congressmen, and 60 percent of state governors have been lawyers. (By contrast, a little over 10 percent of the members of the Supreme Soviet are lawyers, and about 50 percent of the members of the British House of Commons.)

Judgments about what lawyers bring to this public service tend to vary widely. In 1948, Supreme Court Justice Felix Frankfurter discussed the quality of lawyers in high federal offices and found this to be unusually high.[1] Listing the most "significant" Presidents of the United States—Washington, Jefferson, the two Adamses, Madison, Jackson, Polk, Lincoln, Cleveland, Wilson, and the two Roosevelts—Justice Frankfurter noted that with "the single exception of George Washington, they were all lawyers." He went through the roster of outstanding Secretaries of State and Secretaries of War, and listed a similar preponderance of lawyers among the acknowledged "greats" in these posts, men such as Henry Clay, Daniel Webster, Charles Evans Hughes, and Henry Stimson. A similar list, he said, could

---

[1] Felix Frankfurter, "Personal Ambitions of Judges," *American Bar Association Journal* (1948), Vol. XXXIV, p. 656.

undoubtedly be compiled for Congressmen, Senators, governors, and other holders of high office.

Justice Frankfurter explained the special role of lawyers in public affairs in two ways. First, the United States is what German jurists call a "law state," in which the division of authority between central and constituent governments inevitably throws up legal questions of power and tends to attract lawyers to the management of public affairs. Second, lawyers who are "true to their function" are "experts in relevance," trained to bring "intellectual disinterestedness" to bear on problems of public policy and to free their responses from "personal, class or partisan interests."

A contrasting judgment was expressed in lively terms over a hundred years before Justice Frankfurter's assessment, by a leading Jacksonian Democrat in the 1830s, Frederick Robinson.[2] Robinson denounced the "trades union of lawyers" in America for conspiring to fill the "whole government of the nation," with their colleagues in all the "principal officerships" of the country. The effect of this monopoly, he said, was wholly antidemocratic and self-serving. "The secret fraternity of the Bar," he argued, deliberately makes laws "as unintelligible as possible, since no one would pay them for advice concerning laws he himself could understand." Robinson advocated the election of sound laymen to public office who would adopt laws "written with the greatest simplicity and conciseness, alphabetically arranged in a single book, so that everyone could read and understand them for himself."

A modern counterpart to Robinson's attack is illustrated by the protest against lawyers and judges in 1937, when the bar and bench stood as principal antagonists of the New Deal program of President Franklin Roosevelt. In primitive societies, wrote I. F. Stone in *The Court Disposes*, the sacred rites were conducted by medicine men who muttered "abracadabra" and thereby ruled the people. Now, in the United States:

> The lawyer and the judge—our Medicine Men—explain to the worker whose salary has been cut that under the rule established by *Abercrombie* v. *Zilch*, 23 U.S. 318, 74 Sup. Ct. 62. 97 App. Div. 19, 34 Ct. Com. Pl. 712, unless he can obtain a writ of *certiorari* on a *fieri facias* the ancient maxim, *rebus in rem nihil obstat*, will leave him to feel the full effect of the due process clause, and the fee will be $25 (or $2500) sir, good morning, sir, and thank you.[3]

The *fact* of this disproportionate influence of lawyers in public life can be traced to several factors. First, it is easy for lawyers to run for public office or serve in government for a time and then reenter professional life, usually with enhanced career prospects. This contrasts with the generally sacrificial effect of such ventures in public service for businessmen, doctors, dentists, skilled workers, and others. Political campaigning itself serves as "free advertising" for young lawyers, even when they are not elected, and many members of the bar start running for local offices almost as soon as they hang up their shingles. Second, a large number of posts within the

---

[2] Quoted in Mark De Wolfe Howe, *Readings in American Legal History* (Cambridge, 1949), pp. 455–60.

[3] Isidor Feinstein (I. F. Stone), *The Court Disposes* (New York, 1937), p. 92.

legislatures, executive offices, and regulatory agencies have been viewed by American practice as requiring a legal background, since questions of constitutional law, statutory construction, and common law are central to expertise and decisions in those areas. Nonlawyers can and do serve here, often with distinction, but this is traditionally regarded as "exceptional." Third, there is a close tie between law and politics in our governmental system; this is the result not only of our "law-oriented" and "court-seeking" approach to public policy questions but also of the fact that political parties control two main sources of rewards sought by lawyers: the appointments to judgeships and the distribution of well-paid legal work for lawyers in private practice (such as executors of trusts and estates when no one has been named by the deceased, guardians of minors, referees in bankruptcy). To secure such appointments, it has been common for lawyers to start working early in their careers at the local party headquarters and to make party activity a regular part of their schedules. Finally, it is clear that many lawyers who have studied the legal system intensively in law school and then have struggled with the law's meaning and application in practice come to hunger for a primary rather than a secondary role in the lawmaking process. To be sure, they shape the law by the advocacy of clients' interests before judges and regulatory agencies, but the vision of drawing upon this experience to shape the law directly in legislatures, executive offices, or from the bench is virtually an occupational urge of the legal profession.

If factors such as these explain why lawyers gravitate toward public careers so heavily, and so successfully, the issue that remains is whether this has had, on the whole, a beneficial or harmful effect on our political life. As the comments by Justice Frankfurter and the Jacksonian-New Deal critics suggest, there are two warring schools of interpretation on this issue.

Critics of the lawyer as political participant portray the legal profession as inherently conservative or even reactionary, since training in the evolutionary growth of law and the importance of precedent make most lawyers suspicious of social reform and legislative experimentation. When they are in executive positions, lawyers usually adopt narrow, procedurally focused approaches, and too often prove unresponsive to the swift movement of domestic events or the subtleties of international relations. This criticism points to such "legalistic blunders" as Secretary of State Bryan's preoccupation on the eve of the First World War with signing arbitration treaties to make war "impossible," or Secretary of State Dulles' insistence in the 1950s on forcing Arab-Asian nations to join paper "defense pacts." In addition, the impact of the legal profession on the drafting of statutes in the legislature is seen as producing overcomplicated, legalistic, and unwieldy statutes, which often have the effect of smothering the substantive policies being fostered by the legislation.

On the other hand, supporters of the legal profession as a beneficial pool of public talent begin by asking what other professional or occupational group has had a better record than lawyers, in terms of integrity, creativeness, and dedication. Businessmen? Professors? Union leaders? Accountants? Farmers? If important criteria for public officials are respect for constitutional procedures, skill in drafting laws to express the meaning of their

William Sharp

A Fine Point Of Law.

A caricature of trial lawyers by William Sharp.

sponsors, concern for the peaceful adjustment of conflicting economic and social values, and high regard for fair play and due process—if these are key aspects of good public service in America—then lawyers have an unsurpassed record as an occupational group. As for rigidity and creativity, the mistakes of Bryan and Dulles were not the heritage of their lawyers' training, it is said, but a lack of realism and flexibility that is not usually the way of good lawyers, either in private practice or in public life. The careers of men such as Henry Stimson or Dean Acheson would be evidence that lawyer-diplomats can be superb negotiators and foreign policy leaders. Most important, opponents of the legal critics would note that the old patterns of archconservatism and isolationism that marked so much of the bar in the 1870–1930 period are no longer present. Today, many lawyers approach public service with a philosophy of sociological jurisprudence, a commitment to social welfare and internationalism, and a dedication to the cause of civil liberties and civil rights greater than that of most business and professional groups, believing these to be a special responsibility of lawyers in their capacity as guardians of the Constitution and the courts.

A Portrait of the American Legal Profession

Having examined the special role that lawyers play in our governmental and political processes, we turn now to a sketch of the legal profession itself—its size, rewards, and organization, as well as the main periods through which the bar has gone in our national history.

In 1963, the leading directory of lawyers in the United States, Martindale-Hubbell, listed about 250,000 members of the legal profession. While these lawyers are found in both small towns and major cities, the legal profession has tended to be concentrated in major urban centers of commerce and government. In 1959, clients paid more than $2.5 billion in fees for legal services.

When the 250,000 lawyers practicing in 1962 were surveyed to learn their professional status, it was found that: 78 percent were in private practice, about two thirds alone and one third in law firms; 10 percent were in government service; 8 percent were salaried employees in private industry; 3.5 percent were judges or court officers; and .05 percent were teachers in educational institutions. Within this division of the legal profession, some political scientists have speculated that there is a "shadowy" but important class stratification.

> The upper class, of course, is made up of the partners of the large firms, counsel for big corporations, and government lawyers at the Attorney General, Solicitor General, and Assistant Attorney General rank. The upper middle class might be viewed as composed of professors at Ivy League and other prestige law schools, government counsel just below the Assistant Attorney General rank, and partners in established and prosperous but not necessarily large urban firms. Country lawyers and professors at lesser-known law schools make up the lower middle class together with the highly mobile associates in the bigger offices. In the lowest class in the profession are those attorneys who specialize in criminal law, divorce cases, and personal injury suits. Members of this last group—men like Clarence Darrow, Melvin Belli, and Jerry Geisler—are frequently in the public spotlight. There is, however, a distinct tendency within the legal profession to look down on these lawyers, and . . . [their failure to become] Supreme Court Justices indicates that the bar has made its notions of social status felt.[4]

Whatever the exact pecking order among lawyers, the basic pattern of specialization indicated by the 1962 figures is a relatively new one, dating largely from the 1930s. Two very different historical patterns preceded this.

Between the founding of the American Republic and the close of the Civil War, the great bulk of lawyers were in individual and general private practice. Land titles and local commercial transactions were the main staples of law business, along with the bundle of personal and family affairs that inevitably required legal forms or proceedings. Six lawyers were considered a "giant" firm in the 1850s. In this era, the famous trial advocates, men such as Luther Martin, Daniel Webster, and Rufus Choate, argued all types of cases, and for whichever client hired their services first. Lawyers were usually active in political party affairs and it was largely from the party-centered but "independent bar" that judgeships were filled and executive appointments were made.

---

[4] Walter F. Murphy and C. Herman Pritchett, *Courts, Judges and Politics* (New York, 1961), pp. 122–23.

Between 1870 and 1930, profound changes took place in the bar, spurred by the expansion of manufacturing and commerce, the need for new legal forms to serve American capitalism in its growth period, and the rise of critical labor-management relations. In this era, top legal talent gravitated to large urban firms (often having fifty to seventy-five lawyers) devoted exclusively to servicing large corporate clients. Lawyers also joined the law departments of the corporations themselves, working up to the post of general counsel for railroads, banks, and steel companies. The leaders of this corporate bar, men such as Joseph Choate, Elihu Root, John W. Davis, and George Wharton Pepper, dominated the profession through the prestige of their association with business in an era of business hegemony in American life, and through leadership of the local, state, and national bar associations formed during this period. Judges at both the state and national levels were drawn heavily from the new corporate bar, and when corporate lawyers challenged in the courts various regulatory measures that affected their corporate clients, counsel found the bench highly responsive to the claim that our constitutional precepts forbade government intervention in business matters, or meddling with the marketplace and "free contracts" on behalf of the "underprivileged." While there were obviously many lawyers who did not become corporate specialists in this era, but remained general practitioners, the basic fact is that nothing approaching the size, talent, and resources of the corporate bar was available to support government, labor, farmers, or minority groups during this period from 1870 to 1930, and it was in these years that the legal profession became most closely identified with "big business" and strongly conservative positions.

It was during this period that the American Bar Association became the symbol of legal conservatism in America. Founded in 1878, the ABA began with 1,000 lawyers; by 1936, though it spoke in the name of the entire American legal profession, its membership was only 17 percent of the practicing bar. During these fifty years, ABA leaders were usually drawn from a coalition of Northern corporation lawyers and Southern lawyer politicians. Its political ideology can be suggested by its opposition to the federal Child Labor Amendment, support for injunctions against union picketing and strikes, opposition to regulatory agencies, campaigns to soften the antitrust laws, and approval of wide-ranging "antiradical" and loyalty-oath laws. Indifference within the ABA to serious shortcomings in the administration of justice in the courts forced leaders of the profession such as Roscoe Pound and James Wigmore to form the American Judicature Society in 1913, while ABA opposition to the New Deal in the 1930s led to the formation of the National Lawyers Guild in 1936 as a "liberal voice" within the profession. Both of the latter groups remained small organizations, however.

From the 1930s to the present, a new period for the bar has been developing, with important effects for the American governmental process. Most of the lawyers' fees still come from the business community, corporate law is still a leading specialty, and urban law firms have grown into even larger "law factories" (some with 150 lawyers). But more than

12,500 lawyers now work for the federal government and over 1,000 for the City of New York alone. The rise of "government lawyers" insures a continuing pool of talented counsel to defend "government's interests" in the courts and legislatures. More than thirty labor unions now have full-time law departments, and there are about 500 lawyers in firms or in individual practice who specialize in representing labor unions. (The appointment of Arthur Goldberg, formerly general counsel of the United Steelworkers of America and the AFL–CIO, to the United States Supreme Court in 1962 symbolizes the respectability of the "union lawyer" in the present period.)

Another new development within the legal profession has been the growth of legal staffs within civil liberty and minority-group organizations, providing a specialized group of lawyers who now bring test cases on behalf of liberty and equality claims as the corporate bar once did between 1870 and 1937 in behalf of property interests. Men such as Thurgood Marshall and Jack Greenberg of the NAACP, Leo Pfeffer and Will Maslow of the American Jewish Congress, Haydn Covington of Jehovah's Witnesses, and Osmund Fraenkel of the American Civil Liberties Union typify these "civil liberty" and "civil rights" advocates. Finally, the liberalizing role of law schools and of law professors has grown significantly in the past three decades. While there are still many conservative law professors, the attitudes of law teachers as a whole reflect the spread of legal realism and of the public policy responsibility of the law, and two generations of law students have already been shaped by the teaching and writing of the legal realists in law schools.

Organizations representing lawyers also underwent important changes after 1937. Through an energetic recruitment policy and the decision to base its House of Delegates on representatives from local and state bar associations, the American Bar Association grew until, in 1963, it had more than 114,000 members, about half of the active profession. Reflecting this new base and new attitudes within the bar, the ABA has grown increasingly less rigid and conservative in its policy positions during the 1950s and 1960s, admitting Negro lawyers to membership, opposing federal bills to "curb" the Supreme Court for its liberal civil liberty decisions, endorsing civil rights for all minority groups, and promoting a "World Peace Through Law" program that is strongly internationalist in approach. In 1963, the President of the ABA spoke out strongly for a renewed dedication in our schools and our communities to the "controversial" aspects of the Bill of Rights. While the National Lawyers Guild became a negligible organization (its membership is less than 1,000) as a result of internal conflicts over Communist leadership in the group, many of the bar's progressive attitudes are expressed by large and influential bar associations at the city and state levels. The associations in cities such as New York, Philadelphia, Chicago, and Houston play important roles in the legislative, judicial, and political life of their communities.

The Rule of Law or Rule by Lawyers

One problem that has remained rather constant for the bar as a whole and for the idea of a "rule of law" in practice has been the tendency for large numbers of the public to distrust lawyers. As one contributor to the *American Bar Association Journal* lamented in 1963,

> Ever since Christ equated lawyers with Pharisees and hypocrites, we have had our public relations problems. . . . The image of the friendly family lawyer has always succumbed to the more spectacular performance of the apparently merciless cross-examiner. The corporate lawyer is viewed by the public as the heartless gnome who worked out all the fine print with which the layman innocently became entangled in the course of a simple purchase of a refrigerator.[5]

Dean Roscoe Pound, surveying hostility to lawyers as a constant theme in American history, observed that every Utopia "has been designed to dispense with lawyers" and revolutionary movements such as the French in 1789 and the Soviets in 1917 hastened to outlaw the legal profession.[6] Yet, Pound remarked, we have no operating Utopias and the lawyers were reinstalled in both France and the Soviet Union. This suggests, he said, that public criticism does not really rest on the presence of an unusually large number of dishonest, predatory, or immoral men in the legal profession, as compared to other professions, but rather rests on several basic public attitudes, particularly in the United States: a general impatience with the restraints that law places on the will of the people; the constant gap in progress between public opinion and legal change; the inevitable tendency of law to become rigid, to some degree, despite the best efforts of sensitive judges and lawyers; public failure to appreciate the irreducible complexity of rule-making and rule-administration in large societies; public misunderstanding and distrust for the "game" aspects of the adversary process. On all of these subjects, Pound concluded, lawyers, political scientists, and public officials must educate the public, while working constantly to keep the legal system responsive to social needs and political change.

American Judges: Politics and the Robe

A second area that illustrates the classic tension between popular government and legal restraint in our society is the position of judges. Like most liberal societies, we regard judging as a special function and its custodians as a class apart from other governmental officers. Judges wear ceremonial robes; awe-inspiring formalities of architecture, decoration, and procedure are part of the judicial surroundings; men rise when judges enter the courtroom and all must use terms of dignity to "His Honor" when addressing judges. Whenever public confidence in the political process is shaken, it is traditional to call in judges to restore integrity and find the truth without favor; thus judges (and legislators) were used in the disputed Presidential election of 1876 to determine the victor, to investigate and clean up base-

---

[5] Letter, *American Bar Association Journal* (1963), Vol. XLIX, p. 136.
[6] Roscoe Pound, *The Lawyer from Antiquity to Modern Times* (Minneapolis, 1953), Chap. 1.

ball after the Black Sox scandal of 1919, to determine the cause of our devastating loss at Pearl Harbor in 1941, to prosecute on behalf of the nation in the Nuremberg War Crimes Trials in 1946, and to chair the commission set up in 1963 to investigate the assassination of President Kennedy.

Based on this civic ideal (some might call it a civic myth), judges are supposed to be "above politics." By this, it is meant that (1) they should be selected from the "best men available," without regard to political affiliation or prior party service; (2) "political" influences, whether of personal ideology, party, or interest groups, should not affect their decisions in specific cases; and (3) they should be immune from "political" reprisals based on unpopular rulings or controversial judicial philosophy (even though election and reelection of judges in many states runs somewhat counter to this ideal). In this section, we will examine American judges—primarily the federal judiciary—to see how our actual system of selecting, maintaining, and controlling judges conforms with the assumptions about a "nonpolitical" judiciary.

THE GENERAL PATTERN OF JUDICIAL SELECTION AND CONTROL IN THE UNITED STATES

Judges are part of the career civil service in most of the Western European democracies. A candidate for judicial office, after graduating from law school, presents himself for a special examination designed to measure qualities that are thought to produce good judges, as opposed to good lawyers. Once appointed by the executive, the young men begin as judicial officers and move upward from the lower to the higher courts, with promotions based primarily on evaluations by ministries of justice or judicial councils that do not rely heavily on political criteria. A judge on the Continent thus resembles an American career diplomat who enters the Foreign Service through examinations and then progresses, by internal selection processes of the Foreign Service, from second consul at Dar Es Salaam to ambassador in Buenos Aires. Judicial tenure is for life in Europe, with removal only for "misconduct."

This system flowed naturally from basic European political and legal traditions. Judges were once part of the royal household, and when the king's officers developed into the powerful bureaucracies of the nation-state era, the judges became part of this development also. In addition, the civil law system on the Continent, with its belief in precise codes applied scientifically by trained professionals, fostered the idea of the judge as a career specialist. Checked by aristocracies of birth, wealth, and military power, the legal profession in Europe was not able to exercise the influence that it did in the United States, and judgeships could not be preserved as special posts for practicing lawyers. Finally, the fact that European courts (with only a few exceptions) were not given the power of judicial review over the constitutionality of legislation gave credence to the concept of a "nonpolitical" judiciary and minimized party conflict over judicial appointments.

In the United States, ideas of government and law pointed us on a different path. Our common law tradition viewed judging as a creative

William Sharp

Order In The Court

A William Sharp caricature of lawyers consulting with a trial judge on a legal technicality.

art performed by men who mixed technical learning in the law with a "political" sense of the community's mores and needs; men drawn from community affairs were seen as best fitted for such a role. Furthermore, our experience in colonial years with judges who were considered "pliant tools" of the British Crown or royal governors determined the Framers of the American Constitution to free the judiciary from close reliance on the executive branch. When this fear was wedded to our concept of separation of powers, the notion of independence from either legislative or executive control became our ideal. Supporting all of these notions was the bar, with its belief in the practice of law as the prime requisite for judicial skills, and the general American distrust of "antidemocratic" professionalization of public offices.

Based on these influences, the United States developed a judicial system that recruits from the legal profession at large and rests upon two main (alternative) methods of selection. The "federal plan," used by the United States for all federal judges and by a few states (such as Connecticut, Delaware, Hawaii, Maryland, and New Jersey) for all or some of their judges, has the executive nominate judges and the upper house of the legislature confirm them. The "state election system," which is followed by two thirds of our states, provides for popular election of judges, sometimes with the judges running on party labels and sometimes on "nonpartisan" ballots. All federal judges are given life tenure on confirmation, but only two states (Massachusetts and Rhode Island) give life tenure on the first appointment. The other forty-eight states provide terms of office varying with the type of court and ranging from two to twenty-one years.

There are also a number of hybrid selection techniques employed by a few states, in which elements of executive nomination and popular election are mixed. We will mention these later when the federal and state election systems are compared. For the moment, however, we turn to a closer examination of the federal judiciary, to see what types of judges have been produced by this system in American history.

FEDERAL JUDGES: BLUEPRINT AND REALITY

The legal requirements for selecting and controlling federal judges have remained the same ever since the early days of the Republic. The Constitution provides that Justices of the Supreme Court shall be appointed by the President with the advice and consent of the Senate. Unlike the situation with Presidents and members of Congress, no requirements of age, citizenship, period of residence, or even legal training are specified. Constitutionally, a twenty-five-year-old French lady pediatrician without legal education could serve on the Supreme Court of the United States if nominated by a President and confirmed by the Senate. As for lower federal judges, Congressional statutes creating the federal district and circuit judgeships, beginning with the Judiciary Act of 1789, provided the same appointment system for these offices, as well as later for judges of special federal tribunals such as the Court of Claims.

The routine by which federal judicial appointments are made follows a classic pattern, though (as we will discuss) there are important differences in the power position of the various participants, depending on the level of federal court involved. When a federal judicial vacancy occurs, the President consults with a variety of persons (to a degree determined by his own inclinations and his sense of political prudence). These will typically include members of his official family (especially the Attorney General), leaders of his party, influential Senators, spokesmen for national and state bar associations, leaders of important interest groups, and, sometimes, individual members of the federal judiciary. Since the rise of the Cold War, FBI security checks are secured for leading prospects.

When the President has made his selection, the name of his nominee is sent to the Senate for confirmation. It is referred to the Senate Judiciary Committee, which appoints a subcommittee to hold hearings on the nomination. Sometimes, these are short, *pro forma* sessions; at others, where witnesses appear to contest the nomination, the critics, supporters, and (since 1925) even the nominee will testify. After the hearing stage, the subcommittee reports to the Judiciary Committee, which then votes on the nomination and sends its judgment to the Senate. If a majority of the Senators present and voting do not ballot to confirm, the nomination fails.

Two points should be discussed under the general heading of the federal selection and control process, before turning to specific courts. The first is that party affiliation is the single most conspicuous factor in federal judicial appointments. An average of about 90 percent of the federal judges chosen by Presidents from Washington to Johnson have come from the President's own party. Under a Republican such as Warren Harding (1921–23), 97.7 percent of the judges appointed were Republicans. Under a Democrat such as Woodrow Wilson (1912–20), 98.6 percent were

Democrats.[7] In fact, when the party average went down to the low eighties, as it did on several occasions, the explanation was not a spurt of bipartisanship but the cruel fact that Republican Presidents such as William H. Taft (1908–12) and Herbert Hoover (1928–32) could not find enough locally acceptable Republican lawyers to appoint to federal district judgeships in the deep South. Supreme Court appointments have been roughly in line with these averages for the federal judiciary as a whole, with 87.3 percent of the Justices between 1789 and 1963 coming from the President's own party. Although the party out of power in the White House often calls on the President to distribute federal judgeships more "equitably," especially when a large number of additional judgeships are created by Congress and will be filled all at once, Presidents have had a different idea of "equity." "More than enough good men for these judgeships can be found in our party," has been the prevailing philosophy. President Kennedy, for example, had sent eighty-two nominees to the Senate for judgeships by 1962; eighty-one were Democrats and the eighty-second was a member of the Liberal Party of New York (which supported Kennedy and the state Democratic ticket in the 1960 elections).

The primary effect of this partisan factor is that when the White House is occupied for long periods of time by one political party, the federal judiciary becomes solidly packed with its adherents. When Grover Cleveland, Woodrow Wilson, Franklin Roosevelt, and Dwight Eisenhower became Presidents, for example, each following more than a decade of White House control by the opposing party, they confronted a judiciary with from 80 to 90 percent of the judges from the opposing party. It is true, of course, that the broadness of the American party system can produce very liberal Republicans and very conservative Democrats, and the real socioeconomic views of Justices like Harlan Stone (a liberal Republican) or James McReynolds (a conservative Democrat) were what mattered in their decisions. But these tend to be the exceptional cases, and *most* judicial appointees reflect fairly closely the median positions of their party. In one sense, the Framers had such a prospect in mind when they conceived of the judiciary as a check upon a popular movement seizing control of the whole national government at one time. Seen from another perspective, however, this has meant that reformer Presidents such as Jefferson, Jackson, Lincoln, Wilson, and Franklin Roosevelt have had their programs harshly treated during the crucial first years of legislative innovation, at the hands of federal judges many of whose constitutional decisions were colored by party and ideological hostility to the reform measures.

The second general point about the national judiciary is that control of federal judges once they have been appointed has been minimal. Judges of the district courts, courts of appeals, and Supreme Court have life tenure. There is no compulsory retirement age. The presiding judges or senior judges of courts have no disciplinary powers over "junior" colleagues, nor can majority vote of judges on a court produce disciplinary action. Removal is solely by impeachment for "high crimes and misdemeanors,"

---

[7] See Ben R. Miller, "Federal Judicial Appointments," *American Bar Association Journal* (1955), Vol. XLI, p. 125.

initiated by majority vote of the House of Representatives and requiring a two-thirds vote of the Senate (after full trial) to convict. Of course, a federal judge who embezzles court funds could be prosecuted criminally by the federal government, or if he committed a violation of state law, such as drunken driving or manslaughter, could be tried by the state. Neither of these situations would result in automatic removal, however; only resignation or impeachment can produce that.

As a guarantee against punishing judges for unpopular decisions, this system has worked well and deserves continued support. Only one Supreme Court Justice has ever been impeached. Samuel Chase, a strong Federalist partisan, was accused by the Jeffersonians controlling Congress in 1805 of delivering political speeches from the bench and bullying defendants during sedition trials. Chase was narrowly acquitted. From then on, in Jefferson's words, impeachment was "not even a scarecrow" to frighten judges whose rulings offended Congress or the administration.[8] In recent years, some irate Congressmen have tried to have the entire Supreme Court impeached for the 1954 desegregation ruling or have demanded impeachment of individual Justices, such as Justice William O. Douglas for granting a stay of execution in 1953 to the convicted atomic-espionage defendants, Julius and Ethel Rosenberg. These threats were never taken seriously by the Justices, however, or by the majorities in Congress, and security from ideological reprisals through impeachment has had an important effect on the independence and venturesomeness of the federal judiciary.[9] Thus, the noisy campaign to "Impeach Earl Warren," led by extreme right-wing groups protesting against the Court's civil liberties and civil rights decisions in the past decade, is as futile an effort as can be mounted in American politics.

Once we move away from ideological matters, however, there is some question whether removal of federal judges has worked well or is sufficient today. As one recent commentator has noted:

> A Federal judge may suddenly become afflicted with a helpless insanity or blindness, deafness or senility; he may be convicted of murder, arson, or burglary; he may rend asunder the Canons of Judicial Ethics; or he may even be guilty of selling his justice.[10]

Yet only the awkward and complicated instrument of impeachment is available to remedy these situations if the judge refuses to resign.

The problem of judges staying on the bench after their physical or mental powers have failed has been met in part by providing for liberal pensions on voluntary retirement and partly through the informal pressures fellow judges usually bring to bear in such cases. These solutions are far from

---

[8] The only other "political" impeachment in American history was the conviction in 1862 of a Tennessee district court judge, West H. Humphrey, for supporting the Secession. In all, impeachment has been used twelve times for all federal officials. Nine instances involved judges, with four acquitted, four convicted, one resigning before a vote.

[9] Indirect controls on judicial behavior, such as campaigns to curtail a court's jurisdiction, reverse its decisions by constitutional amendment or legislation, etc., have been discussed in Chapter 16.

[10] Joseph Boykin, *The Corrupt Judge* (New York, 1963), p. 192.

The Ingenious Quarterback!

C. H. Berryman

A 1937 cartoon comments on Roosevelt's "Court-packing" plan, ostensibly designed to balance Justices past retirement age with "younger blood."

perfect, however, and willful but feeble-minded judges have plagued the federal bench on several occasions. Justice Stephen Field, for example, hung on at least two years longer than he was able to remain awake in the courtroom or follow issues sensibly in conference, but he was determined to stay on the Supreme Court longer than John Marshall; he did, to the enormous discomfort of his colleagues and the bar. This problem remains unsolved, but, many would say, is not serious enough to warrant new measures.

A more serious problem has been control of judicial misconduct and corruption. During our history, Congressional committees have held fifty-five full-dress investigations (for possible impeachment) into alleged misconduct by federal judges. Drunkenness and tyrannical behavior were involved in about a third, but almost two thirds involved corruption—misusing judicial powers over trusts, estates, and receiverships for personal gain or selling decisions in cases. In these fifty-five investigations, nine resulted in impeachments, eight produced official censure by the Congressional committee but not impeachment, sixteen saw judges resign from office to avoid impeachment, and twenty-two resulted in judges being absolved of charges. A leading student of corruption in the federal judiciary has noted that the thirty-three judges whose cases indicated corruption by no means exhaust the list.[11] Other federal judges—statistics are not available—resigned, after investigation but before official inquiries were begun, and were allowed to do so by Congress and the prosecuting authorities on the theory that this was a satisfactory remedy, given the need to

---

[11] *Ibid.*, p. 204.

preserve public confidence in the courts. Clearly, thirty-three plus is a tiny fraction of the federal judiciary in our history, and the standard of integrity and judicial propriety among federal judges has been high, probably far higher than at the local and state court level. But even a few tainted judges are too many, and those who feel impeachment is inadequate as a supervisory remedy have suggested several new techniques. One is that the House of Representatives continue to investigate cases as it now does in considering impeachment but that charges should be prosecuted by the Attorney General and be determined by an *ad hoc* court composed of three court of appeals judges appointed by the Chief Justice of the United States. Such a proposal passed the House of Representatives in 1937 and again in 1941, with support from the Roosevelt Administration and the American Bar Association. Critics argued that the potential threat to judicial independence and separation of powers was too great and that impeachment—or its threat—was sufficient. The resolutions never passed the Senate. Other proposals have been to give the Supreme Court authority to direct investigations through special referees, to require judges to file data on their financial dealings involving persons or companies involved in federal court matters, or to adopt at the federal level the plan used by Britain and in Massachusetts, New Jersey, Texas, and other states, which permits removal of judges by the executive, upon the recommendation of both houses of the legislature. Many of these proposals have come under discussion again following the disclosure in 1962 that a federal district judge in New York had accepted bribes to secure lighter sentences for defendants in fraud prosecutions.

Having looked at the partisan factor in federal judicial selection and the problem of removal, we turn now to a discussion of the three main layers of the national judicial system, since the judges at each layer require separate treatment.

NINE MEN AT THE TOP: WHAT MAKES A SUPREME COURT JUSTICE?

It is traditional for students of American government to say that the men appointed to the Supreme Court are, more than any other federal judicial nominees, the free choices of Presidents. The bonds that tie Presidents in appointing lower court judges will be explored shortly, but we can assess here how free the historical record shows Presidents to have been when they were selecting the men to preside at the top of the nation's judicial pyramid.

Two distinct periods can be identified in Presidential appointments to the Supreme Court. Between 1789 and 1894, eighty-four men were nominated to be Justices (excluding several who were nominated but declined to accept). Of these, twenty were not confirmed by the Senate, either by direct vote against confirmation or by deliberate failure of the Senate to act (causing appointments to lapse or forcing nominees to withdraw). This ratio of 23.8 percent rejections was higher than the ratio of rejections for any other judicial office, and far higher (by from two to four times) than the rejection rate for district or court of appeals judges. The basic pattern was set in the first action of this kind by the Senate, which refused in 1795 to confirm President Washington's promotion of John Rutledge from Associate Justice to Chief Justice. Rutledge, while a firm Federalist, had delivered a speech opposing the Jay Treaty, and for this, the Federalist majority in the Senate opposed his confirmation. This established the practice that the Senate would look into the nominee's views on constitutional and political questions, and if these were not regarded as "sound" by a Senate majority, would deny confirmation. Other rejections added further grounds, such as Senate opposition to a President and a desire to deny him important appointments; refusal to confirm appointments made close to a Presidential election in which the White House was likely to shift to the opposite party, which already had control of the Senate, thus giving the opposition the chance to name the Justice; vendettas over patronage between Presidents and powerful Senators when nominees came from a Senator's home state; and, on rare occasions, a belief that the nominee lacked ability as a lawyer and statesman. As this list of principal causes suggests, party issues and executive-legislative tensions were the dominant factors between 1789 and 1894, and Presidents seemed to be rather accustomed to having nominees to the Supreme Court turned down. At least, it was not an electrifying event to the country when such rejections took place.

Between 1895 and the present, forty-four men have been nominated to be Justices. Only one was rejected by the Senate. This was John J. Parker, a federal Court of Appeals judge named by President Herbert Hoover in 1930. Parker was opposed principally by three main groups. Negroes protested against anti-Negro sentiments he was supposed to have expressed while active in North Carolina politics before he became a judge. Labor union leaders were angered by several of his rulings on secondary boycotts, though these followed the prevailing rules laid down by the Supreme Court. Republican Progressives in the Senate thought Parker to be another economic conservative who would increase the majority opposed to any construction of the Constitution that limited property rights. Parker was defeated. (Ironically, Parker proved in his continued career as an appeals court judge to be a decidedly liberal jurist on labor, welfare, and civil rights issues, while Hoover's second nomination, the successful designation of Owen J. Roberts, put on the Supreme Court one of the men who voted solidly with the conservatives in the crucial period of 1933–36.)

While only one nominee was rejected in this second period, the Senate frequently held far-reaching committee hearings and general debates over the socioeconomic beliefs of nominees. Thus protests against Louis D. Brandeis' liberalism in 1916, Charles Evans Hughes' conservatism in 1930, John M. Harlan's internationalism in 1955, and William J. Brennan, Jr.'s attitudes on internal security issues in 1957 produced confirmation fights of varying degrees of intensity. All of the Presidents' men were confirmed, however.

The rejection of only one nominee since 1895 has led some commentators to suggest that a lessening of partisan responses in the Senate, coupled with somewhat greater Presidential concern with selecting men of at least minimum professional reputation, have combined to give Presidents in the twentieth century quite free rein in Supreme Court nominations. However, others suggest that Presidents have been prepackaging their nominations to fit known Senate moods and prejudices, so that avoidance of rejections has come largely from knowing what simply could not be done.

SUPREME COURT JUSTICES: A PROTOTYPE ANALYSIS

Of the ninety-seven men who have sat as Supreme Court Justices between 1789 and 1964, at least half can fairly be described as men of modest intellectual powers, without deep cores of self-consciousness, and not terribly troubled by the dilemma of exercising judicial review in a society valuing majority rule. These Justices were carried along by the dominant currents of opinion in their time, or by one of several main crosscurrents, and for them the process of judging usually appeared to be the application of rather clear precedents to specific problems. This may shock those who assume that the great majority of Supreme Court Justices have been giants, but it is both true and natural that the giants of the Court—Marshall, Story, Miller, Holmes, Brandeis, etc.—are matched in number by men such as Bushrod Washington, Thomas Todd, Nathan Clifford, Ward Hunt, William R. Day, Edward T. Sanford, or Harold Burton.

This leaves between thirty and forty Justices who were first- or second-level powers in the Courts on which they served. Some were powerful inside the Court, gathering colleagues into cohesive majorities or forming new majority coalitions. Some of these Justices were powerful in terms of their appeals outside the Court, usually in dissent, calling for new doctrines and criticizing the prevailing constitutional philosophy of the majority. Modern advertising would term these Justices the "influentials" in American constitutional history.

Looking at these influential Justices, one can see three main prototypes in terms of basic judicial philosophy. First have been the *True Believers*, who view the Constitution as setting forth certain rights that are entitled to absolute protection by the judiciary and who want the Supreme Court to exercise its powers fully to defend such rights whenever the elected branches of state or national government or private parties infringe upon them. The True Believer has sometimes been a liberal in his socioeconomic outlook, such as the first Justice John M. Harlan (1877–1911) or Justice Hugo Black, who joined the Court in 1937. Other True Believers have been ideological conservatives, such as Justices James Wilson (1789–98), Stephen Field (1863–99), or George Sutherland (1922–38). For these men, whatever their place on the ideological spectrum, the Supreme Court is a place where Truth is defended and Error lashed, where the Constitution embodies the American Way, and where the Court is at its finest when it commands Presidents and Congresses and governors to cease tampering with the fundamentals of the Republic.

The second prototype among the influential Justices has been the *Institutionalists*. Sometimes, these are men whose personal attitudes on social or economic questions would make them "liberals," such as Samuel Miller (1862–90), Louis D. Brandeis (1916–39), and Felix Frankfurter (1939–62), while others would be classified as "conservatives," such as Chief Justice Charles Evans Hughes (1930–41), Oliver Wendell Holmes (1902–32), and the second Justice John M. Harlan, who joined the Court in 1955. Their basic approach is that the Constitution created various powers and guaranteed various rights that often come into conflict under the actual pressures of governing, and that the Court ought to defer to the branches of government responsible to the electorate unless clearly defined constitutional rights have been directly violated. Such judicial conduct breeds responsibility among elected officials, avoids public overreliance on courts, and maximizes the authority of the judiciary when it does strike down popular acts as unconstitutional. Where the True Believer is likely to gird happily for showdowns between Court and Congress or Court and Presidents over assertive judicial rulings, the Institutionalists typically regard this as a disaster, possibly unavoidable in the extreme situation (like war in the international context), but to be entered into rarely.

Between the True Believers and the Institutionalists is a smaller number of Justices, the most individualistic (even quixotic) of all. These are the *Selective Interventionists,* who believe that the Court's basic role is to hold the crucial equilibrium in American government between majority rule and minority rights, national and state authority, and the public and private sectors, in the spirit that the Framers produced but adapted to the challenges of drastically different conditions. Both the judicial activism of True Believers and the judicial self-restraint of the Institutionalists are seen as overly rigid formulae by the Selective Interventionist, who decides in each of the momentous leading cases whether to wield the judicial veto or defer to elected authority. These questions are usually decided by weighing key imponderables: Can the political process correct itself? Will the Court's mandate be obeyed? Is this area one that is ready (especially in terms of leading public opinion) for constitutional change? Of the Selective Interventionists, Justices Joseph P. Bradley (1870–80), Benjamin N. Cardozo (1932–38), and Robert H. Jackson (1941–54) are leading examples.

SUPREME COURT JUSTICES: BACKGROUNDS, COMPOSITES, AND INDIVIDUALS

In the past decade, several studies have been made of the preappointment backgrounds of each Supreme Court Justice.[12] Taking the most significant categories of these studies (and updating them to 1963 unless otherwise noted), we have these facts:

Social origin

About 90 percent of the Justices came from families of "comfortable" to "wealthy" economic position, generally with accompanying social prestige and civic participation. Ten Justices came from what are usually called "humble origins."

Religious-racial stock

All the Justices have been white. Eighty-four were Protestants, six Catholic, and four Jewish. By national origins, eighty-eight came from Northern European countries; six from Southern, Central, or Eastern Europe. No Italian-American has served on the Court. Until Justice Goldberg, no one of Eastern European derivation had been appointed.

---

[12] John R. Schmidhauser, *The Supreme Court: Its Politics, Personalities, and Procedures* (New York, 1960); Henry J. Abraham, *The Judicial Process* (New York, 1962).

Careers

While all Supreme Court Justices have been lawyers, the major career specialties of the Justices through 1957 divided as follows: lawyers who were primarily politicians, forty-nine (53.9 percent); lawyers who were primarily state or federal judges, twenty-four (26.4 percent); eleven primarily corporation lawyers (12.1 percent, heavily concentrated between 1890 and 1930); three noncorporation lawyers (3.3 percent); and four lawyers primarily in academic life (4.4 percent). To this would be added the category of labor lawyer following Justice Goldberg's appointment in 1962.

Occupation at time of appointment

When appointed to the Supreme Court for the first time, the Justices came from the following positions: federal judge, nineteen; state judge, twenty; federal executive branch, twenty; private law practice, fourteen; United States Senator, eight; United States Representative, four; state governor, three; professor of law, two.

Party

As noted earlier in this chapter, 87.3 percent of the Justices came from the President's own party. Presidents crossed party lines on eleven occasions. The stated political affiliations of Justices from 1789 to 1963 have been: thirteen Federalists; one Whig; forty-six Democrats; thirty-six Republicans; and one Independent (Felix Frankfurter).

Section

Justices have been drawn rather evenly from the major regions of the country in each decade of our history. This does not mean that they have been evenly distributed by states. Partly because of concentration of legal talent and partly because of political importance, the five largest states in each decade have had about half the seats on the Court since 1789 (just as these states have produced most of our Presidents). Thus New York has had thirteen Justices, Ohio ten, Massachusetts eight, etc. In 1964, five of the Justices came from states in the top six in population: Warren from California, Harlan from New York, Goldberg from Illinois, Stewart from Ohio, and Clark from Texas. Twenty-one states, including Delaware, Florida, Missouri, and Wisconsin, have never been "represented" on the Supreme Court.

Using these data, one scholar has drawn the following "composite picture" of "the Supreme Court Justice." [13]

> White; generally Protestant . . . ; fifty to fifty-five years of age at the time of appointment; Anglo-Saxon ethnic stock . . . ; high social status; reared in an urban environment; member of a civic-minded, politically active, economically comfortable family; legal training; some type of public office; generally well-educated.

What this information about the Justices signifies is open to some debate. Those who have pioneered in these studies suggest that, while caution

---

[13] Abraham, *op. cit.*, p. 58.

must be exercised in assuming that background determines judicial philosophy, the selection process from 1789 to the present shows that the Supreme Court has been an institution dominated by the gentry class in our early history and by the "professionalized upper-middle classes" in recent times. Thus if the Court is the "keeper of the American conscience, it is essentially the conscience of the American upper-middle class," conditioned by the "conservative impact of legal training and professional legal attitudes and associations" and propelled by "individual social responsibility and political activism." [14]

Actually, if the figures are not viewed from 1789 to the present as a unit, but are broken down by period (as some studies have done), the "democratization" of the Supreme Court will be seen to be under way. In terms of religion, since 1895 four Jews and five Catholics have been appointed, almost one fourth of the Justices for that period. Where conservative corporation lawyers filled the Court heavily between 1890 and 1930, the 1930–63 period has seen active liberals who were Senators, governors, attorneys general, labor lawyers, and law professors appear on the Court.

Of course, the Supreme Court is not required to be a representative body, and its members need not register the religious, racial, sectional, class, or nationality percentages of the nation in each era. When Senator Richard Russell of Georgia called in 1962 for appointment of a Southerner and a "true conservative" because these groups were not "represented" on the present Court, his plea was not taken very seriously (and President Kennedy's next appointee was a Northern liberal, Arthur Goldberg). Yet the Court which enunciates the constitutional credo of the nation and is increasingly concerned with the questions of status in our rapidly changing society has the right aura about it and seems to grow out of our democratic traditions when it does include among its members persons whose backgrounds are varied as the nation is varied. Given the wide distribution of talent among minority groups, this need not produce the slightest drop in the quality of the bench. Several Negroes presently serving as federal judges or as law professors, for example, would add power and distinction to the Supreme Court, and could compete in legal knowledge and judicial temperament with the best the white community has to offer. To insist that a given seat be reserved for a Catholic, or an Italian, or a Negro, would be to weaken the dignity and independence of the Court and limit the President. But to consider this factor would be entirely appropriate for Presidents and their advisers, and the growing concern for the minimum representativeness (at least one Jew and one Catholic on the Court; soon perhaps, at least one Negro) has become part of the ethos of appointment policies.

DISTRICT COURT JUDGES AND THE GOVERNMENTAL PROCESS

For its sharp contrast with the Supreme Court selection process, we shift to the lowest level of the federal judiciary, the district court, to continue the discussion of federal judges. The authority of a district judge lies, as we saw in Chapter 16, wholly within the boundaries of a single state, and

---

[14] Schmidhauser, *op. cit.*, p. 49.

sometimes within a single county. Even though this judge applies federal law, and will be the final voice of federal law in over 90 percent of the cases brought before him, American practice by the 1840s had established the principle that district court appointments were primarily the "choices" of the party controlling the state, not of the President as nominal selector. This reflected the primacy of state political power in the American party system, and came to work as follows.

When one or both the United States Senators of a given state with a district court vacancy belong to the same party as the President, he must accept the nominee of the Senator or Senators. When both Senators belong to the opposition party, the President has to find someone acceptable to those Senators and the state leaders of the President's party. In practice, then, the Constitution's mandate of nomination by the President and confirmation by the Senate has been reversed; it is nomination by the local Senators and acquiescence (or limited negotiation) by the President.

This practice has been defended on several grounds. Local Senators are presumed to know better than a President or an Attorney General who are the best-qualified candidates for judicial office in their states. Furthermore, Senatorial choices would be sure to reflect the spirit of the local community and not be wholly out of tune with local attitudes, as might be the case if a President were to appoint a local maverick or short-term resident. Behind these explanations, of course, is that fact that federal judgeships pay quite well, are lifetime jobs, command enormous prestige, and are eagerly sought after by lawyers. This makes them one of the top rewards a local party can bestow on party contributors and workers, so that the local parties have fought tirelessly to retain control of them. Critics of Senatorial initiative in district court appointments maintain, on the other hand, that this process lowers the quality of federal judges by limiting Presidential choices, fosters patronage and payoff factors, and installs local prejudice often in the federal courthouse when it is exactly a more independent spirit than that found at city hall or the state house that is needed for equal federal justice.

The problems of Presidents over Senatorial control is illustrated nicely by two incidents. In 1929, President Herbert Hoover announced publicly that he would restore confidence in the federal judiciary (somewhat shaken by scandals in the Harding Administration) by refusing to appoint anyone as federal judge as a reward for party activity and that the recommendations of party organizations would be accepted only if nominees were "highly qualified." After several preliminary skirmishes, the showdown on Hoover's policy came in 1929. The senior Republican Senator from Pennsylvania, Daniel Reed, backed by the state organization, "nominated" Albert Watson, a state court judge from Scranton, for a district judgeship. Leaders of the state bar and even the senior judge of the federal circuit court protested informally to the White House that Watson was inferior material. Hoover delayed nominating Watson for several months. At this point, Senator Reed visited Hoover and told the President that if Watson's name was not sent to the Senate promptly, the Pennsylvania delegation in Congress would not support the President on key legislative matters.

Hoover sent Watson's name up, reluctantly, and Attorney General

Mitchell made a lukewarm endorsement of him as the "best available." The Judiciary Committee hearings disclosed that Watson's practice consisted primarily of uncontested divorce cases; that he had argued only six cases in court in twenty-six years at the bar; and that he was opposed by three fourths of the active lawyers in the district. The governor who had appointed him to his state judgeship wired opposition to the federal appointment. Several Progressive Republicans such as La Follette and Norris called on the Senate to reject the nomination and end local party dictation of district judges. Watson was confirmed, 53 to 22.

Another revealing instance took place in 1959. Early that year, President Dwight Eisenhower sent thirteen lower court nominations to the Senate. For most of the Congressional session, the Senate Judiciary Committee took no action on them. It turned out that the Senate Majority Leader, Lyndon Johnson of Texas, had his own candidate for a district court vacancy in Texas, but Eisenhower had nominated someone else. Even though Johnson was a Democrat and not entitled to "automatic nomination" power, his influence led the Judiciary Committee to keep Eisenhower's thirteen nominees waiting. Unable to break the deadlock, Eisenhower arranged to have his Texas nominee withdraw, and Senator Johnson's choice was named to the post. Three days later, the thirteen judges had been approved by the Senate Judiciary Committee and confirmed by the Senate.

As these two incidents suggest, district judgeships are not quite the patronage weapon for Presidents against Senators that they are often portrayed to be in the press. Rather, the appointments have become largely "Senatorial" prerogatives, for which Senators Reed and Johnson fought strongly and were supported by their Senate colleagues.

No studies have ever been made of the backgrounds of all or a significant sample of district judges. There have been distinguished men throughout the country and through our history who have served on the district bench, some for their whole careers and others on their way up to court of appeals and Supreme Court appointments. (Twenty percent of the Justices have come from the lower federal courts.) Furthermore, there has been no evidence that the party influence in selecting district judges has produced a system of party payoffs in return, either by favors in decisions or the kind of patronage that a judge controls through appointment of lawyers to be referees, receivers, trustees, and the like. Nevertheless, it is true that district judges rather naturally tend to be lawyers of local fame rather than statesmen with national reputations; that they make *Who's Who,* as one scholar noted, after rather than before their selection; and that local influences exert more pressure on district judges than on the upper courts, whose judges are not local residents anchored in the community. Yet it is important to note that in the charged cases involving racial discrimination in the South, most Southern district court judges have applied federal antidiscrimination laws and have done so despite the hostility from local political leaders toward such rulings.

COURT OF APPEALS JUDGES AND THE GOVERNMENTAL PROCESS

Since the jurisdiction of a court of appeals spreads over multi-state areas, the Senators of one state cannot control Presidential choices, as they can with district judges. A demonstration of this came in 1955, when President Eisenhower named the Solicitor General of the United States, Simon Sobeloff of Maryland, to the Court of Appeals for the Fourth Circuit. This circuit takes in Maryland, West Virginia, Virginia, North Carolina, and South Carolina. Since Sobeloff had presented the federal government's position calling for implementation of the school desegregation order and had defended the Supreme Court against charges of "judicial legislation," many Southern Senators opposed his confirmation. They managed to delay Judiciary Committee consideration of the nomination for a year. When Eisenhower and a bipartisan Senate group were able to force the nomination out of committee and onto the Senate floor, the Senators from North Carolina, South Carolina, and Virginia announced that Sobeloff—who would be sitting in "their" states—was "personally obnoxious" to them and should be rejected. Nevertheless, Sobeloff was confirmed. President Kennedy, by contrast, shifted Federal District Judge J. Skelly Wright, who had ordered desegregation of the New Orleans public schools, to the District of Columbia Court of Appeals when he wanted to promote him to Circuit Judge, since it would have been almost impossible to promote him to the Fifth Circuit (which includes Louisiana) because of Southern determination to "get" Wright.

What kind of men become court of appeals judges through this intermediate-stage selection process? A profile of the sixty-five judges occupying these judgeships in 1955 indicated that: [15]

Eighty percent were more than 60 years old. The youngest was forty-six and the oldest eighty-eight. A third had been more than sixty at the time of their appointments.

Fifty-five had some prior experience in state or national public office. The remaining ten had been practicing lawyers or law professors.

Thirty-eight had served as federal district judges or on state courts. Of these, twenty-seven had been district judges (federal), ten had served on both federal and state courts, and eleven had been state judges only.

Six had resigned from Congress to accept appeals court appointments, five from the Senate and one from the House.

Thirty-seven had served in the executive branch of state or nation, many as prosecutors earlier in their careers, and eight came from the United States Department of Justice.

The average tenure of the sitting judges was eleven years.

Comparing the appeals court and district judges, we find several important differences. District judges tend to come directly from law practice and to have had no prior experience in public office, though much in party service. Of those district court nominees who have had prior public service, more tend to have had state office than federal service. Court of appeals judges usually live in the cosmopolitan cities in their circuits and travel throughout the area; their social bonds often develop with the top elite of the law schools, federal executive, legal associations, and reform commissions. District judges tend to be closed in more by the influences of their

[15] Cortez A. M. Ewing, *American National Government* (New York, 1958), pp. 384–86.

old residences and old associations; ideological pressure from local editors, party leaders, and the informal power structure is greater; district judges presiding at complex criminal trials or antitrust suits become identified with *causes célèbres* more than appeals court judges, who share responsibility with other members of the court and have issues of law, primarily, to decide on appeal.

Looking at court of appeals judges as a group, therefore, we see that fairly broad Presidential freedom of choice, the high prestige of these courts among lawyers, and the relative immunity of these judges from community-tension atmospheres have produced a more independent and distinguished group than the district judges. This is also fostered by the promotion of the best of the district judges to court of appeals positions. Since few men leave the appeals court bench to seek other public office, and few are appointed to other posts, this becomes the "career" office of talented men in the closing decades of their lives. With tenure in office as long as it has been, the appeals court judges leave a clear imprint not only on the quality of federal justice in their regions, but often, in the case of men such as John J. Parker, Learned Hand, Jerome Frank, Calvert Magruder, and Charles Clark, on the development of federal law as a whole.

PROPOSED REFORMS OF THE FEDERAL JUDICIAL SELECTION PROCESS

Two main reforms have been proposed in recent years to "take the federal judiciary out of politics." The dominant groups behind these proposals have been the American Bar Association and conservative business and civic groups. The first reform would require that Justices of the Supreme Court have prior experience as judges of the state or national governments. The assumption here is that such prior service would indicate judicial temperament and would have prepared the nominee for his service on the nation's highest court. This idea has been subject to several criticisms— it would limit a President's choices by imposing the criteria for district court or state court selection upon him; judges acceptable to state parties and individual Senators would thus be the limited reservoir from which Supreme Court Justices would have to come. Overall, this would have a skewing effect on the ideology of Justices that would probably be quite conservative. In addition, no one has been able to show that prior judicial experience on trial courts or on intermediate appellate courts necessarily prepares a man for the special kind of constitutional decision-making and balancing-of-values process that is involved in Supreme Court adjudication. While some great Justices did have prior judicial experience, such as Oliver Wendell Holmes, Jr., on the Supreme Judicial Court of Massachusetts or Benjamin N. Cardozo on the Court of Appeals of New York, most of the great Justices had none—Marshall, Story, Curtis, Campbell, Miller, Bradley, Hughes, Brandeis, Frankfurter, Jackson, to name a few. Moreover, the Supreme Court in its best periods has had a mixture of careers in its members, each bringing a different perspective and different experience—some from Congress, some from the executive, some from the bar, some from state government, and so on.

The second proposal has been to urge that Presidents clear their nominees from district court to Supreme Court with the American Bar Association and the state bar association from the state where the nominee resides. Informal consultation with bar associations and bar leaders has been traditional, but in the 1950s, the American Bar Association pressed for formal submission of projected appointees to its Standing Committee on the Federal Judiciary. President Eisenhower began this as a general practice for the Attorney General's office in its preparation of appointment lists, but neither the Eisenhower nor Kennedy Administrations promised to abide automatically by the recommendations. Of eighty-five nominees that President Kennedy had sent to the Senate in 1962, for example, the American Bar Association had found fourteen exceptionally well qualified, forty-one well qualified, twenty-three qualified, and seven not qualified. Again, the issue at stake in the Bar Association rating is what criteria the Bar Association uses, the nature of the qualities that make a good Supreme Court Justice, and the problem of the ideological and policy representativeness of the Bar Association. Probably the system as it now works, of friendly liaison between the Department of Justice and bar associations but not a veto power, is the wise accommodation.

STATE COURT JUDGES: EXPERIMENTATION IN THE "LITTLE LABORATORIES"

While the state judiciary is discussed also in Chapter 27, under state and local government, it is useful here to compare the features of national judicial selection, tenure, and control with those of the states.

As we have noted, the dominant method of selection of judges in the states is popular election. Experimentation with election of judges went back as far as 1777 in Vermont, but it was the Jacksonian movement in the 1830s, with its belief in democratization of government and electoral control by the public, that spread this system throughout the states. Recapturing the judiciary from the conservative classes, from the aristocracy of the bar, and from the influences of special interest groups were the key objectives. Also part of the Jacksonian concept was limited tenure rather than life tenure for judges, to provide a means of keeping the judiciary "responsive" to dominant opinion and to avoid hardening of the judicial arteries. A majority of states in the mid-1840s still chose judges by gubernatorial appointment or legislative selection, but the Jacksonian reform was adopted by New York in 1846 and the tide ran strongly to election from then until the present. Today, two thirds of the states use election for most or all of their judges, sometimes on so-called "nonpartisan" ballots (no party label given) but more frequently on regular party ballots. The elective term for all state judges averages six years, but in many states life tenure or long terms (fourteen or twenty-one years) are provided for supreme court judges or judges at the intermediate appellate levels.

Several hybrid systems are used by a few states to attempt a mixture of the best features of the appointive and elective plans for judges. In 1934, California adopted a plan in which the governor presents one candidate for appellate court posts to a special commission composed of the chief justice of the state supreme court, the presiding justice of the district court of appeals for the area, and the state attorney general. If the commission approves the nominee, he is appointed for one year. At the end of that time, he runs for election on the statewide ballot for a twelve-year term. Only his name appears, without party label, and in this form: "Shall _____ be elected to the office of _____ for the term prescribed by law?" If he is defeated, the governor designates a new judge for one year until the next election.

A second major variation is the Missouri plan. Adopted by constitutional amendment in 1940, this provides that three candidates for all appellate courts and some trial courts in the state are nominated by special nominating commissions. The chief justice of the state supreme court, three lawyers elected by the state bar, and three nonlawyers appointed by the governor make up the leading commission for appellate court nominations, with members, unsalaried, serving for six-year terms. The governor must select one of the three persons nominated by the commission, and appoints him for one year. Following this year, the judge must be elected on a nonpartisan ballot, with a "Shall he be retained?" question as in California. Between 1940 and 1960, only one of forty-four appointments was rejected by the electorate, even though the state changed parties frequently at local and state levels. Variations of the Missouri plan have been adopted by Kansas, Alaska, and Iowa.

Comparisons of the appointive, elective, and hybrid systems for judicial selection and control in the states have concluded that, practically, they work much the same. That is, in both, it is the leaders of the political parties that are decisive in selecting the candidates who run for election or are appointed by governors. Furthermore, party competition is rare; usually, in two-party states, the parties get together and distribute judgeships according to the party ratios in the area, and then endorse one another's choices. Suggestions that bar associations should draw up a panel of names from which election or appointment would be made, it is said, would only transfer the political struggle to within the bar association, and the ideological and policy positions of the bar associations suggest that their ratings of judges would not be (as they have not been in the past) solely a matter of judicial temperament, legal wisdom, and probity.

Law-Enforcers: Of Crime and Punishment, and Federal Lawyers

The third group of men we deal with in this chapter are the law-enforcers. Strictly speaking, a law-enforcement agency is one that is charged with general peace-keeping duties, the investigation of crime, the prosecution of offenses, or the punishment of offenders. Since local, state, and federal governments each have authority to define crimes and punish offenders in their jurisdiction, the "police function" in American society has traditionally been a decentralized and overlapping process, scattered in hundreds of city police departments, county sheriffs' offices, state highway patrols, county and state prosecutors' offices, special port or transit authorities, state attorneys general, city jails and state penitentiaries, and federal investigative and enforcement bureaus.

Our focus in this discussion will be on federal law enforcement. This is primarily the responsibility of the United States Department of Justice, an omnibus agency with some 32,000 employees (about 2,000 of them lawyers), a $300 million annual budget, and an inscription on its walls that reads, "The United States wins its point whenever justice is done its citizens in the Courts." In addition to coordinating the peace-keeping, investigative, prosecutive, and corrective functions of federal law enforcement, the Department of Justice has two other major duties: to represent the United States in civil cases (in both the federal and state courts) and to give legal advice and services to the executive branch.

The Department of Justice was organized in 1870, when the beginnings of industrialization and centralization in post-Civil War America made clear the need for a full-scale agency to coordinate the legal and law-enforcement affairs of the federal government. Structurally, "Justice" is a typical federal executive department. Headed by the Attorney General of the United States (a Cabinet-rank official), it has accumulated since 1870 a mixture of three "offices," eight "divisions," two "bureaus," one "service," and two "boards," as the following organizational chart indicates:

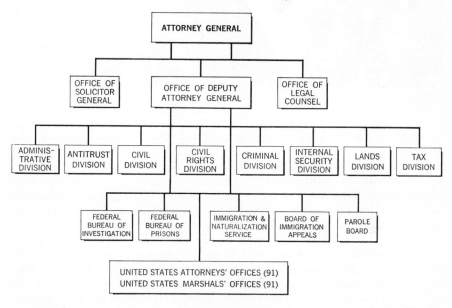

To understand the work of the Justice Department, we can start "in the field" and work back to the central offices in Washington. In each of the ninety-one federal judicial districts throughout the United States and its territories, there is a United States Attorney and a United States Marshal. The United States Attorney is in charge of prosecuting criminal cases in the federal district courts and bringing or defending civil actions involving the United States in either the federal or state courts. This gave rise to some 55,000 cases in 1962 and required staffs of almost 1,000 lawyers, plus clerks, secretaries, and professional specialists. More than $1.5 billion in claims against the United States is pending annually, but only from 5 to 10 percent of this amount is usually collected, and this is further

Stars Fell On Alabama

A liberal comment on the Attorney General's prompt action in sending federal marshals to Alabama after the "Freedom Rider" riots.

© 1961 by Bill Mauldin
From *What's Got Your Back Up?* Harper & Row

lessened by the $125 million the government wins in fines, penalties, and claims.

United States Attorneys are appointed by the President and confirmed by the Senate. In political reality, they represent the choices of the local Congressmen, Senators, and party organizations. While general policies as to the position of the United States Government in antitrust matters or civil rights or tax claims will be framed in Washington by the Attorney General or his assistant in charge of the particular division, and sometimes a specialist will be assigned from Washington to try a particularly complex case, the United States Attorney has broad discretion in affairs of his district, and decisions whether to prosecute a given suspect or not are usually in his hands. The United States Marshals, with their regular and special deputies, are in charge of taking prisoners into custody and transporting them to prisons, keeping order in federal courthouse buildings, and performing special duties such as restoring peace in Southern communities when riots have broken out in defiance of federal court orders desegregating schools or other public facilities. Also represented in the "field" are the district offices of the Federal Bureau of Investigation, which is charged with the investigation of all federal crimes that are not specifically lodged in other agencies (such as narcotics offenses and counterfeiting, which are under the jurisdiction of the Treasury Department).

These are the main components of federal law enforcement and legal representation in the field, organized, as we have seen, largely around the structure of the federal court system. In Washington, the central Department is set up as shown in the chart, with an operating division for each major area of law supervised by the Department and various offices and bureaus providing special services. At the top sits the Attorney General, often called the "principal law officer" of the federal government. His functions, blending the political and administrative with the executive and legal, present a sometimes conflicting set of tasks.

On the one hand, the Attorney General is a political adviser to the President and his administration, with strong party and patronage roles. He screens candidates for federal judgeships and United States Attorneys, serving as a liaison between local party leaders and the President. He advises the President on issues with constitutional or legal overtones, which run the gamut from treaty issues and defense production contracts to Negro voting rights and FBI wire-tapping practices. Though each President decides for himself how much to consult the Attorney General on such matters, and the President has his own Special Counsel whom he can use for legal-political advice, the Attorney General and Department of Justice aides have been at the center of most important legal controversies or programs involving recent administrations. Another political function is to present the Department's views to Congress on proposed legislation affecting legal affairs, which has found the Department in recent years playing a prominent role in such charged areas as internal security, civil rights, criminal control measures, and immigration. Finally, the decision whether to press prosecutions and appeals in the federal courts in tax, antitrust, criminal, or other cases will rest ultimately with the Attorney General, and this makes the Department a magnet for the pressures of powerful individuals and corporations, often with high party connections, who seek to "explain their views" and "receive a sympathetic hearing" from the Department. These and other aspects of the Department's work make it an agency with many political functions and party connections.

On the other hand, the Department's seal announces, *Qui pro domina justicia sequitur*, "Who prosecutes on behalf of Justice," and the public pledge of the Department is to provide executive enforcement of the law without fear or favor. Lawyers in the Department are all "officers of the Court," bound by the canons of legal ethics to respect "the Law" and to be faithful to the principles of the American Constitution beyond loyalty to party or election interests, at least where such a conflict becomes apparent. The police practices employed by the investigative arm of the Department, the FBI, are supposed always to be within the letter and spirit of the Bill of Rights, and the same applies to the conduct of federal marshals, prison guards, or immigration officers. When the Attorney General is charged by executive order with responsibility to compile a list of "subversive organizations" as a guide for the hiring and dismissal policies of federal agencies, the standards of judgment and the system for hearings and appeals should be models of respect for freedom of expression and association and procedural due process.

The fact that there have been celebrated scandals involving favoritism to defendants with high political connections, that some conduct by the FBI (such as its wire-tapping practices) is of the most doubtful legality, and that the loyalty-security record of the Justice Department has included a heavy portion of disrespect for civil liberties all indicate that there is a special tension between role and ideal in the Department that may represent a somewhat greater burden of public expectation than many other executive agencies have to shoulder. This is not because the other agencies are free to be naked instruments of party or political favoritism, but because the role of custodian of "the Law" places something of a higher standard upon "Justice."

The discharge of this obligation, in finest form, is illustrated by the Office of the Solicitor General. The Solicitor General, with only nine legal assistants, is the appellate lawyer of the United States Government, charged with presenting the position of the United States in cases before the Supreme Court. Solicitors General have included many of the finest lawyers in the nation's history, such as John W. Davis and Robert H. Jackson, and the tradition of independence from political pressure and of duty toward the Supreme Court is firmly embedded in the office. Our role, said the incumbent in 1964, a former government lawyer and Harvard Law School professor, Archibald Cox, is to see that "justice is served . . . . If we are wrong, we should confess our error. Our tone should be one of candor and restraint. The role of this office is to help the [Supreme] Court develop a system of justice." In pursuit of this role, the Solicitor General can refuse because of his view of the proper rule of law to present an appeal to the Supreme Court when a federal agency or a United States Attorney wants this pressed. If the general counsel of that agency or even the Attorney General does argue the case before the Justices (as can be done), the absence of the Solicitor General will ordinarily be two strikes against the government's case in the minds of the Justices. In 1955, for example, Solicitor General Simon Sobeloff declined to argue in behalf of the government in the case of *Peters* v. *Hobby,* involving the power of the Department of Health, Education and Welfare to dismiss a Yale professor of medicine from a consultant's post, on grounds of loyalty-security, without giving him a hearing at which he could confront the persons who had accused him. Attorney General Herbert Brownell signed the brief for the United States, but the Supreme Court overturned Professor Peters' dismissal (on a procedural ground). Many observers were convinced that the Solicitor General's withdrawal had damaged the government's moral position significantly, though it was not necessarily a crucial determinant.

Conclusion: The Men of Justice and the Rule of Law

Throughout this chapter, we have focused on the men charged with special responsibility to translate the rule-of-law ideal into practical reality for American government. The influence of lawyers, judges, and law-enforcers is probably greater in American government and politics than in any other political system and has been so from the birth of the Republic. Writing in 1830, the French social historian Alexis de Tocqueville observed:

> As most public men are or have been legal practitioners, they introduce the customs and technicalities of their profession into the management of public affairs. The jury extends this habit to all

classes. The language of the law thus becomes, in some measure, a [common] tongue; the spirit of the law, which is produced in the schools and courts of justice, gradually penetrates beyond their walls into the bosom of society, where it descends to the lowest classes, so that at last the whole people contract the habits and the tastes of the judicial magistrate.[16]

Historians and political scientists will argue strenuously about whether the special role of "law men" in America has been a progressive or reactionary force in any given era, or in our past as a whole, just as they will debate whether the "legalizing" of so many areas of American politics has been a good or a bad thing for the development of representative institutions, civic education, and democratic values. But few observers of American government will deny the men in the law their special place in our system. Thus the role of defense counsel and prosecutor, of the legal profession as a bridge between government and society, and of judges as a "special breed" of government official remain important topics for a discussion not only of the judicial system in the United States but our entire way of managing public affairs.

---

[16] Alexis de Tocqueville, *Democracy in America*, Phillips Bradley, ed. (New York, 1945), Vol. I, p. 290.

18 / Property, Liberty, and Justice in America: The Foundations of Civil Liberty

The founders of the American nation drew their conception of liberty and property from John Locke, who believed that the purpose of instituting governments among men was to secure effectively the individual's life, liberty, and property. These rights were considered to be interrelated and indivisible. Senator John Taylor of Virginia wrote in 1820, "The rights to life, liberty and property, are so intimately blended together, that neither can be lost in a state of society without losing all; or at least, neither can be impaired without wounding the others. Being indissolubly united, a principle which embraces either must embrace all. . . ."

The rights to liberty and property were regarded not only as natural rights but as essential conditions for the preservation of a free Republic. The man with property—wealth, land, or a prosperous business—could exercise his liberty to disagree with government or with dominant public opinion, since he did not risk his family's supper or his children's shoes by dissenting. Property was also believed to give men the incentive and the means, both in cash and in leisure, to develop themselves into better persons and better citizens. A final element in this propertied middle-class perspective was the belief that widespread ownership of property among the citizenry, especially ownership of land, would inhibit the rise of an urban proletariat or a peasantry that would seek centralized government or "leveling" of property.

On these concepts, the Founding Fathers were heartily united, and Americans have remained convinced of the basic importance of personal liberty and personal property to this day. Then and now, however, debate begins with the inescapable question, "How far may liberty or property be limited by government in the public interest, as defined by the elected branches of government?" When the government goes too far, we expect the courts to declare such measures unconstitutional. But what is "too far," when courts should intervene, and just what these rights encompass are issues that arouse passionate debates.

The Dual Tradition and Its Problems

Whether property or liberty is the most important constitutional right has been a constant theme in American history. It can be traced in the conflicts between John Adams and Thomas Jefferson, and its heritage is with us still, with only the costume and music changed. For example, the National Association of Manufacturers recently proclaimed that property rights must be restored to the privileged position they once occupied in our constitutional system. After all, the NAM argued, "the foundation of all freedom is the right to own and its corollary, the right to contract." [1]

> A mark of the unfree through the ages has been the legal incapacity to own property and make contracts. All of the other marks of freedom —free speech, a free press, freedom of religion and of peaceful assembly, and the suffrage—are either dependent on the right to own or are relatively meaningless without it. For example, what would free speech and a free press amount to if individuals were not permitted to own a piece of ground and the capital invested in a printing press? The right of peaceful assembly would be futile if the state owned all of the land on which people could assemble, for any meeting not approved by the government could not be held.

At the same time, the NAM has supported wide-ranging legislative investigations into "subversive activities," government loyalty-security programs, wire tapping for national security, outlawing of the Communist party, and many other measures that have been forcibly protested by the "liberty" spokesmen in the present period. Furthermore, the NAM has joined other business groups in protesting against a trend in Supreme Court doctrines since 1937 that has given greater protection to "liberty rights" and has left most decisions on "property rights" to the arena of legislative judgment.

The opposite view to the NAM's "property-first" outlook can be found in what is often called the "preferred position" concept of civil liberties, particularly in terms of the role of the courts in protecting this preferred status. Robert H. Jackson expressed this idea in terms that embody the fundamental principle of the "liberty-firsters" today. The Constitution meant to leave government free to regulate property and economic affairs, Jackson said, with only such ultimate restraints as "just compensation" and "due process" as boundary lines. This is because unwise economic laws "can be redressed by the processes of the ballot box or the pressures of opinion." Economic groups are powerful, well organized, and able to defend their interests.

However, when laws place restrictions on minority racial or religious groups, or curtail political meetings, or forbid picketing and leaflet distribution, then the Constitution intended the courts to step in to limit majority action.

> When the channels of opinion and of peaceful persuasion are corrupted or clogged, political correctives can no longer be relied on, and the democratic system is threatened at its most vital point. In that event, the Court, by intervening, restores the processes of democratic government; it does not disrupt them. [2]

To some extent, of course, the split between "liberty" and "property" rights is a matter of labels. Is freedom to be a lawyer, or schoolteacher, or plumber a liberty matter or a right of property? Is the right of a paro-

---

[1] National Association of Manufacturers, *Main Street vs. Washington, D.C.* (Washington, 1957).

[2] Robert H. Jackson, *The Struggle for Judicial Supremacy* (New York, 1941), p. 285.

chial school to teach in German, contrary to a state law requiring all instruction to be in English, a matter of the school's proprietary right or its liberty right? Before the 1930s, any sophisticated constitutional lawyer would have strained to place his client's case under the property label; since the late 1930s, the liberty label may be the preferred one in constitutional cases.

As we shall see, it is often a common allegiance to justice—to due process—that brings the "liberty-firsters" and "property-firsters" onto a common ground. Before exploring this theme, however, we turn to a specific discussion of liberty and property.

The Rights of Property

To avoid misunderstanding, we should define what is meant by "property" and its "rights." When people talk about property, they refer to the temporary possession or the full ownership of valuable things. These may be "tangibles," such as houses, horses, or Ford Thunderbirds, or "intangibles," such as stock in General Motors, patents for new atom-smashers, or franchises to drill for oil. To use these properties, and to provide a means of setting value on them, owners must have freedom to sell, exchange, and pledge their property, and have all these transactions protected by law. Property owners also seek the right to pass property on to their heirs, make gifts during their lifetimes, and engage in business ventures. Another element is the right to invoke the law to make the other party to a contract live up to the agreement. Property must also be held without fear of arbitrary government confiscation, if it is to be held securely.

All of these rights of property were well established and well protected by British common law in the American colonies long before the Constitution was written. It was also firmly established by the common law that property rights were not absolute. Property could not be used in ways that conflicted unduly with the rights of neighbors, with the rights of the public, or with the paramount rights of government. A man who whipped his horse cruelly could be fined for abusing his property. Law could forbid a man to burn rubber in his backyard because this created a nuisance in the neighborhood. Contracts to perform illegal acts, such as to pay gambling debts or commit an assault, could not be enforced in the courts, nor could contracts that took advantage of minors and the feeble-minded. Wills and trusts that gave property on terms that were "against public policy" ("To Genevieve, if she will remain a Protestant") were also unenforceable. In addition, contracts in restraint of trade were invalid, and making them could be punished by law. An owner's wish to keep his land or house had to give way when government needed that property to build a highway, erect a public building, or set up a military installation. Nor could property owners refuse to pay taxes when government needed to raise funds for public purposes. As we look at the present framework of property rights and at contemporary debates about their interpretation, two points must be kept in mind.

First, it must be realized that many public measures that affect property and wealth are viewed by the courts today as essentially administrative or legislative matters with which judges will not interfere. As long as the rates are not found to be "confiscatory" (and rates as high as 90 percent are not so considered), levels of income taxation cannot be challenged successfully in the courts; this is a matter for debate in Congress and for decision in the executive branch. Someone who deeply opposes spending billions of dollars of federal money for foreign aid to nations of Africa or Asia and believes this is taking his property for an improper purpose will not find the courts ready to consider the validity of such a policy; staunch anti-foreign aid spokesmen who have tried to withhold the portion of their federal income tax that foreign aid bears to the annual federal budget have had their claims dismissed in the federal courts. The degree of federal supervision of employer-employee relations in industries doing business in interstate commerce is another matter of legislative judgment, not a constitutional issue, under contemporary judicial doctrines.

Second, the growing need for positive government in a modern, interdependent, industrial society has led the courts to expand many of the powers of government to deal with property rights in ways that nineteenth-century Supreme Court majorities forbade. The revenue needs of government have brought more and more types of property and economic activity under taxation by federal and state authorities, and taxation carries with it the power to encourage, discourage, or even destroy a given activity or type of ownership. State police power in behalf of the health, safety, and welfare of its citizens and federal authority over interstate commerce, money, and defense have been the constitutional sources of extensive regulatory programs and welfare measures in recent decades. Despite these vast expansions of power, however, there remain vital constitutional limits beyond which the taxing and police powers may not go. There are also important constitutional rules as to how such valid measures must be framed and administered if they are to be upheld.

The Constitutional Structure of Property Rights

Looking at the federal Constitution, we can identify three basic sets of property guarantees that are still significant. First are the clauses inserted specifically to protect property rights against government invasion. These are the *contract clause* (Article I, Section 10) which says that "No State shall . . . pass any . . . law impairing the obligation of contracts," and the *just compensation* clause (in the Fifth Amendment) guaranteeing that "private property" shall not "be taken for public use, without just compensation."

Second are the provisions inserted to protect the sacred bundle of Lockian rights as a whole from arbitrary treatment by government authorities. The Fifth Amendment states that "No person shall . . . be deprived of life, liberty, or property, without *due process of law*. . . ." This restriction upon the federal government is matched by the provision in the Fourteenth Amendment limiting state power: "No State shall make or enforce any law which shall abridge the *privileges or immunities* of citizens of the United States; nor shall any State deprive any person of life, liberty, or property, without *due process of law*; nor deny to any person within its jurisdiction the *equal protection of the laws*."

Third are the③ clauses written primarily to protect individual liberty and fair procedure, which have also been applied over the decades to give important protections to holders of property. These would include the *freedom of speech and press* guarantees of the First Amendment, the protection against "*unreasonable searches and seizures*" in the Fourth Amendment, and the *privilege against self-incrimination in* the Fifth Amendment (forbidding any person to be compelled "to be a witness against himself . . .").

Property Rights and the "Incorporated"

We will examine the most important of these property rights guarantees in a moment. First, however, we must be aware that it often makes a legal difference whether an individual or a corporation seeks to assert these property rights. On some levels in American law, of course, individuals or corporations have been held to stand on the same plane. The courts and legislatures have made general the rights to contract, to engage in business, to hold property free from confiscation, and to be free from arbitrary regulation. Thus, despite heavy protests from critics in the late nineteenth century and some criticism even today, giant firms such as Bell Telephone and Standard Oil of New Jersey have been treated as individual "persons" under the contract clause, the due process clauses, the equal protection clause, and the just compensation clause. In these contexts, the corporation has been given "personal rights," perhaps on the theory that it represents flesh-and-blood persons who hold the stock; perhaps because giving the company "personality" makes the law of business obligations work more effectively. However, other constitutional rights have been held to apply only to individuals, either because we know this was the intention of the Framers or because such is the essential nature of the right. This is the case with the privileges and immunities clause of the Fourteenth Amendment and the self-incrimination clause of the Fifth Amendment. As the Supreme Court summarized the law as to self-incrimination in a 1957 case, for example: [3]

> It is settled that a corporation is not protected by the constitutional privilege against self-incrimination. A corporate officer may not withhold testimony or documents on the ground that his corporation would be incriminated. Nor may the custodian of corporate books or records withhold them on the ground that he personally might be incriminated by their production.

This statement indicates not only that the constitutional rights of individuals and corporations differ at several vital points, but also that an individual can lose some of his personal rights by becoming a corporate officer. This rule applies to officers of labor unions and voluntary associations as well as profit-making corporations. [4]

In addition, the courts will often apply a less sweeping standard of protection to business corporations than to individuals when corporations invoke some of the constitutional rights that do apply to them. As the

---

[3] *Curcio* v. *United States,* 354 U.S. 118 (1957).
[4] *Ibid.; United States* v. *Linen Service Council,* 141 F. Supp. 511 (1956).

Supreme Court said recently, corporations are entitled to protection against unreasonable searches and seizures (Fourth Amendment) but they can "claim no equality with individuals in the enjoyment of a right to privacy." [5] When corporations are chartered, the Court has explained, the state has reserved a "visitorial power" over records, books, and premises that would not be permissible where persons are involved, and this applies also to national authority "where the corporate activities are in the domain subject to the powers of Congress." The courts also have upheld more severe penalties for corporate violators of antitrust laws than for individuals committing the same offenses and have accepted means other than grand jury to indict corporations for crime in cases where grand juries would be required for indicting individuals. [6]

To discuss what rights of property are and are not upheld in concrete situations in modern America, let us consider several common situations that give rise to "property issues" and see how American law responds to them.

Boundary Lines in Property Regulation by Government

JUST COMPENSATION IN THE JET AGE

The home of Andrew Anguish is located within three blocks of the county airport. When jets started flying, Anguish's home vibrated at each take-off and landing. Ashtrays slid off tables, windows rattled, plaster cracked, conversation was impossible, and sleep—even with sleeping pills—was almost ended. Complaints by Anguish and his neighbors were met with the reply from the airport authorities that Congress had passed a law giving airports the right to use airspace leading into the fields and that all jet flights conformed to federal regulations as to noise control, flight patterns, and approach altitudes. The airport told Anguish to sue the airlines or the federal government.

Normally, when local, state, or federal governments exercise the sovereign's right of eminent domain to acquire private property for public projects, they pass a statute authorizing a specific program and appropriate money to compensate persons whose property will have to be taken to accomplish the project. Government appraisers then inspect the property and determine its fair market value at the time of taking. If an owner feels the government estimate is too low, he can challenge the appraisal in the courts and the judges will determine the reasonableness of the government's estimate.

Generally speaking, it is not likely that property owners will be able to retain their property by charging that the announced purpose is not really a "public" use as required by the Constitution. In addition to such clearly public uses as highways, schools, monuments, public buildings, and parks, the courts have held programs for flood control, reforestation, game refuges, and housing projects to be valid public uses, as well as beautification of cities through tree-plantings and pedestrian malls in downtown areas.

Luckily for our hypothetical Anguish, the United States Supreme Court

[5] *United States* v. *Morton Salt Co.*, 338 U.S. 632 (1950).
[6] See, for example, *United States* v. *White*, 137 F. 2d 24 (1943).

decided a case in 1961 that closely paralleled his.[7] Drawing on the basic concept that the just compensation clause was written to prevent a few persons from having to bear costs of public progress that should be charged to the entire citizenry, the majority held a county airport liable to pay compensation to home owners facing such jet noise and such damage to their use of property. In the majority opinion, Justice Douglas noted that air approaches were as necessary a part of an airport as landing strips and that a "taking" is accomplished whenever property is rendered "unusable" as here. The agency responsible to pay nearby owners was the authority that built the airport and operated it for public use.

THE CONTRACT CLAUSE AND THE SCHOOLTEACHER'S TENURE

Another important sector of property rights can be illustrated by considering the hypothetical dilemma of Charlotte Chalk, a biology teacher at Township High School. Under the State Teacher's Tenure Act, designed to keep good teachers by giving them job security, the state provided that any person teaching five successive years in any state school becomes a "permanent teacher" whose contract continues indefinitely and need not be renewed annually. It could be canceled by the state only for incompetency, insubordination, or neglect of duty, and only after notice and hearing for the employee.

Though Mrs. Chalk had become a permanent teacher, she was removed by the Township school board under a later statute that exempted Township schools from the Teacher's Tenure Act. Mrs. Chalk sued in state court for reinstatement, alleging that the second statute was forbidden by the clause in the federal Constitution prohibiting the states from interfering with the obligation of contracts.

In a 1938 decision resembling our hypothetical case, a 7–1 majority of the Court held the second state statute to be unconstitutional as an interference with the obligation of contract. Justice Owen Roberts' majority opinion stated that Indiana had voluntarily created a long-term contractual relationship with its permanent teachers and had bound itself not to revoke this contract except for stated causes. In the lone dissent, Justice Hugo Black said that Indiana lawmakers had never intended "to make contracts with a few citizens, that would take away from all the citizens, the constitutional power to alter the educational policy for the best interests of Indiana school children." By reading such a binding contract into the tenure act, Black said, the Supreme Court was presuming to run the Indiana school system.

Whether this case would still be followed in the 1960s might be open to some question; but it has never been overruled. However, most contract rights disputes today tend to be *nonconstitutional* problems, involving legislative decisions to limit the rights of people to make contracts. For example, federal antitrust laws will forbid a proposed merger of the Pennsylvania Railroad and the New York Central Railroad if the administrative agencies and courts find it tends "to lessen competition." Rate-setting bureaus of the nation's railroads or "dual rate conferences" of ocean shipping lines (which

---

[7] *Griggs* v. *Allegheny County,* 369 U.S. 84 (1962).

give a lower price to shippers who do all their business with members of a conference than to shippers who divide their business between conference members and nonconference water carriers) have been held by the Supreme Court to be contracts in violation of federal antitrust laws. (In both cases, Congress stepped in later to grant exemptions to the companies and legalize their practices.)

DUE PROCESS AND DRY CLEANERS

A final area of property rights protection can be illustrated by imagining a set of difficulties which fell on the Acme dry-cleaning business. First, the city council passed an ordinance forbidding any dry-cleaning plant to be located within the city limits, prompted by the councilmen's belief that such plants sent unpleasant fumes into residential neighborhoods. Second, the council required all owners to have their parking lots paved in concrete. (Acme's lot had been covered with asphalt blacktop.) Third, the city health department seized and destroyed 100 suits and dresses from Acme's plant after several persons were taken to the hospital with painful rashes caused by bodily contact with a residue left on clothing by a new dry-cleaning fluid. Finally, a state law specified that all outdoor advertising by retail stores was to be taken down and signs no larger than two by three feet were to be placed inside store windows. This was done as part of a campaign to beautify city streets and limit their gaudy commercial character.

Assuming all these things happened to one business, it would not take a lawyer long to realize that the firm's hope for redress in each of these situations would be the due process clause of the federal Fifth and Fourteenth Amendments or its counterpart in the state constitution.

Due process encompasses two ideas. *Substantive due process* requires that government action interfering with liberty and property rights must be based upon rational ways of achieving valid public purposes. *Procedural due process* requires that notice, fair hearing, and impartial appeal be given to all persons whose liberty or property rights are affected by government programs. What substantive due process means today under federal and state legal doctrines is the question raised by Acme's troubles.

1. Acme would probably have to sell its dry-cleaning plant. The Supreme Court has upheld the right of local governments under their police power to eliminate nuisances and bar undesirable business activity from the city areas, to protect the public and develop cities properly. In the absence of proof that the city had acted arbitrarily, or had discriminated against Acme individually, or was unreasonable in its judgment about fumes coming out of the plants, substantive due process would not help Acme. The city would not have to pay Acme for any loss in the sale.

2. Acme might be able to avoid having to repave its parking lot. In a 1960 case, an Ohio court held that where existing blacktop driveways were in good condition, a Cincinnati ordinance requiring concrete was "a clear and palpable abuse of power, worked an undue hardship on property owners . . . , was confiscatory, and constituted the taking of property without due process. . . ."[8] However, many state courts would reach the opposite

_____
[8] *Stueve* v. *Cincinnati*, 168 N.E. 574 (1960).

conclusion in this situation, and would criticize the Ohio judges for substituting their own notions of what was the strength, durability, and appearance of building materials for the more expert judgment of city specialists and city councilmen.

3. Acme could not recover from the city for the "contaminated" clothing destroyed. The courts uniformly uphold the government's power to destroy, without paying compensation or damages, property that is dangerous to public health, safety, or morals. These categories include such items of contraband as slot machines, heroin, bootleg liquor, and fraudulent weighing devices, as well as such "impure" objects as diseased cattle, blighted trees, cranberries with cancer-producing color additives, or milk with too high a bacteria count. Stray dogs and cats can be destroyed, and even an automobile carrying bootleg liquor can be confiscated as part of the enforcement program against illegal manufacture of alcohol.

4. Acme would probably win its final battle with the state. While broad state power to regulate billboards and display advertising has been sustained by the courts, American law has been sensitive to the need of businessmen to "advertise or perish," and the courts examine restrictive regulations in this area rather closely. For example, legislation requiring gasoline station owners to display their prices only in station windows and not on their gasoline pumps has been held unconstitutional under the due process clause, despite the government's argument that it was trying to minimize the effect of price wars.

PROCEDURAL DUE PROCESS AND PROPERTY RIGHTS

When a home owner finds that his house has been assessed by the city at a far higher value than he thinks proper, or a major airline wants to obtain permission from the Civil Aeronautics Board to fly the New York to Miami passenger run, or a drug manufacturer seeks to challenge the action of the Food and Drug Administration in seizing one of his products as impure, the key question for them will be what kind of hearing they can have to present their case to government officials. Partly as a matter of judicial definition (stemming from the constitutional guarantee that no person shall be deprived of property without "due process") and partly from state and federal legislative enactments (such as the federal Administrative Procedure Act of 1946), a general code of procedural rights has evolved to govern the regulation of property in the administrative process. Persons whose rights have been or will be affected must be given an opportunity to appear before the officials who have responsibility for making these decisions, to be represented by counsel, to introduce evidence in support of their case, and, usually, to know and be able to comment about the witnesses and evidence adverse to them. And, while the judiciary does not usually substitute its judgment about matters such as utility rates or television franchises for those of the regulatory agencies, as it constantly did before 1937, the basic right to appeal most final administrative decisions to the courts remains. Rulings overturning administrative decisions as unwarranted by the evidence, unjustified by the terms of the basic regulatory statute, or even based upon improper action by government agents are part of the yearly product of our courts and provide a major protection of property.

The Constitution protects the right to work at one's profession and trade as part of the citizen's basic liberty, and "free entry" is part of the American frontier free enterprise tradition. This self-selection has been growing steadily smaller in recent decades, however, as government protection of the public from fraud and mistreatment, the drive of groups to "professionalize" themselves and limit competition by securing state licensing controls, and a widening concept of businesses and professions "affected with a public interest" have all led to a growth in state and local government restrictions on the right to work. State licensing covers professions such as law, medicine, pharmacy, and accounting, "public utility" jobs such as driving a taxi, loading ships, and weighing produce in public markets, and a diverse list of occupations which have a history of improper conduct by many of their practitioners, such as boxing, running a pool hall, selling liquor, and being a "private eye." In most states, minimum levels of education, demonstration of skills through state examinations, and good moral character are required before a person can engage in any of these callings.

What constitutes proper government standards of "good moral character" has been a growing problem in recent decades. Past misconduct, if measured by previous convictions for serious crimes (especially those involving "moral turpitude"), is a common standard and one generally accepted. Loyalty oaths or non-Communist affidavits have been installed in many states for an astonishing list of callings, wrestlers in Indiana, bartenders in New Jersey, veterinarians in the state of Washington, piano-tuners in the District of Columbia, and pharmacists in Texas. Admission to the practice of law has been conditioned by many states on not being a Communist, not refusing to answer questions of a character committee as to Communist affiliations (past or present), and upon a willingness to bear arms in defense of the nation. (Loyalty oaths and standards for government employees, including public school teachers, raise a special issue since government acts here as the employer, not as licensing agent; these will be taken up later in our discussion of liberty). While religious or racial qualifications would be struck down if set by the states as conditions for entry into callings, the courts during the 1950s and 1960s have not struck down the ideological standards, despite arguments that the standards punish freedom of speech and press, penalize freedom of association, and "punish" persons without judicial trial. Only when past membership in an organization that was not illegal at the time of joining has been used by the states, in violation of the ex post facto principle, have the courts struck down the measures. In the future, however, it may be that courts will insist that the state show why it is necessary to have ideologically pure vets treat ailing cows, or fiercely loyal wrestlers groan before the fans in the local arena, before society allows ideological walls to be set around these lines of work.

New Problems of Property Rights

As types of property and their uses have changed in America, so have the problems over what "the rights of property" are. One example is the contemporary tension between "property rights" and "equality rights." What businesses are so public in character that government may require their owners to serve all orderly persons, regardless of factors such as race or religion? What types of commercial transactions (such as the sale by a private owner of his house to another private purchaser) may be placed under the restraints of nondiscrimination? What about private associations, ranging from labor unions and Community Chests to private schools, fraternities, tennis clubs, and veterans' groups? Furthermore, assuming "government" can regulate, *which* government—local, state, federal, or all three? Finally, what about sit-in, ride-in, and pray-in demonstrators who enter "private" businesses, clubs, or churches to protest racial discrimination? Do their arrests for trespass and state convictions represent enforcement of discriminatory policies by government in violation of the Fourteenth Amendment? These topics are fully treated in Chapter 19, but we outline them here to illustrate an important new context for the "property rights" debate.

Looking at the general position of property rights in the American system, one sees that compared to holders of property in most other countries of the world, the American is one of the most secure. Ideologically, the nation still accepts the "free enterprise" system, treasures the role of a propertied middle class in promoting political and economic stability, supports the usefulness of much corporate bigness to provide efficiency and progress in creating new products, and insists upon the requirement that government provide due process in executive agencies and the courts before affecting property rights.

Thus, while there would probably be no constitutional bar to nationalization of basic industry in our country—it could be done by application of the eminent domain power—this remains an unlikely possibility as long as the basic political and ideological commitment of the American people is to a mixed economy, featuring a primary private sector (regulated by the government) and a small but important publicly owned sector. It is on this basis that our present structure of property rights has been erected and continues to enjoy widespread public support.

Liberty Rights in America: The Dilemmas of Freedom

Justice Robert H. Jackson once characterized the American approach to liberty issues by noting: [9]

> Liberty is not the mere absence of restraint, it is not a spontaneous product of majority rule, it is not achieved merely by lifting underprivileged classes to power, nor is it the inevitable by-product of technological expansion. It is achieved only by a rule of law . . . in rationally and dispassionately devised rules which limit the majority's control over the individual and the minority. . . .

While the tensions between liberty and order are as old as government and have provided countless victories and defeats for freedom in American history, securing "liberty under law" in an age of nuclear warfare, subver-

---

[9] *The Supreme Court in the American System of Government* (Cambridge, 1955).

sive activities, racial tensions, industrial empires, densely packed cities, interstate crime syndicates, and huge government is an awesome task even for a nation that has struggled with liberty issues for almost two centuries.

When we deal with liberty issues, our "official" national philosophy is set by the First Amendment to the federal Constitution:

> Congress shall make no law respecting an establishment of religion, or prohibiting the free exercise thereof, or abridging the freedom of speech, or of the press; or the right of the people peaceably to assemble, and to petition the government for a redress of grievances.

There are other parts of the federal Constitution that contribute to our definition of liberty, of course, such as the narrow definition of treason (requiring an overt act rather than only words or advocacy, plus two witnesses to that act), or the prohibitions against bills of attainder (laws that impose punishment on a person or group of persons without giving them a judicial trial) and against ex post facto laws (making acts criminal offenses retroactively). But it is primarily the "first freedoms" of the First Amendment—religion, speech, press, and assembly—that constitute the "sacred bundle" of free expression and conscience. Justice Benjamin Cardozo called them "the indispensable condition of nearly every other form of freedom," and Justice Felix Frankfurter termed them "the well-spring of our civilization." They protect the right of individuals to hold, advocate, and publish their ideas freely, whether religious, political, social, or literary, and to conduct public meetings and organize groups of individuals to urge the acceptance of these ideas by government or society. As a corollary, the First Amendment denies Congress the power to impose an official set of religious, political, or social doctrines to which citizens must subscribe. "If there is one fixed star in our constitutional constellation," the Supreme Court said in 1943, "it is that no official, high or petty, can prescribe what shall be orthodox in politics, nationalism, religion, or other matters of opinion, or force citizens to confess by word or act their faith therein." [10] In addition to the rights of speech, press, religion, and assembly, two other liberty rights—freedom of association and the right of privacy—have come to be included in the bundle of liberties guaranteed by the First Amendment as necessary to expression and conscience, even though the terms "association" and "privacy" do not appear in the Constitution.

We should also note that the First Amendment's guarantee of free expression and conscience is a restraint not only on the *entire* federal government (the courts have included the executive and judicial branches as well as Congress under its coverage) but also on state governments. Since the 1920s, the federal courts have reviewed state actions affecting "first freedoms" as part of the "liberty" that the Fourteenth Amendment forbids the State to deprive its citizens of "without due process of law." Furthermore, every state constitution contains provisions similar to those of the First Amendment (though usually less absolute in phraseology), and these guarantees are applied in the state courts.

---

[10] *West Virginia Board of Education* v. *Barnette,* 319 U.S. 624 (1943).

In our analysis of liberty issues, we will deal first with the area of freedom of expression—speech, press, and association. We divide this discussion into two parts: those issues that do *not* involve loyalty-security matters and those that do. The Constitution makes no such distinction, of course, nor would the Supreme Court (except perhaps some of the liberal dissenters). Yet a close look at the cases shows this distinction to be a central factor in their results and perhaps the only sure pathway through the otherwise inexplicable maze of conflicting speech, press, and association rulings.

"LET TRUTH AND ERROR GRAPPLE"— FREE SPEECH AND ITS LIMITS

Speech ranges across a wide spectrum, from the conversations of a husband and wife in their living room to the political candidate's voice on a loud-speaker reaching thousands of persons packed into a city square. Society regulates all these speeches in some way, from forbidding the husband and wife to speak so loudly during an argument that they disturb the neighbors to punishing the political candidate if he incites his audience to march on opposition party headquarters and "smash it up a little." How much freedom of speech one can enjoy depends on what one says, where, when, and how, and even about whom.

In light of this reality, the Constitution's provision that "no law" shall be passed "abridging the freedom of speech" is stark in its absolutism. A few philosophers and judges, such as Professor Alexander Meiklejohn and Justice Hugo Black, have argued that the Founding Fathers really intended *all* speech to be immune from licensing, censorship, or penalty. The Supreme Court, however, has not accepted this view and has traditionally thrust some speech outside the warm shelter of the First Amendment, either by saying that some types of talking are not "speech" or that some laws regulating speech do not "abridge" it. As one of the Court's most fervent defenders of maximum free speech, Justice Frank Murphy, expressed this limiting principle for the Court's majority: [11]

> There are certain well-defined and narrowly limited classes of speech, the prevention and punishment of which have never been thought to raise any constitutional problem. These include the lewd and obscene, the profane, the libelous, and the insulting or "fighting" words—those which by their very utterance inflict injury or tend to an immediate breach of the peace. It has been well observed that such are no essential part of any exposition of ideas, and are of such slight social value as a step to truth that any benefit that may be derived from them is clearly outweighed by the social interest in order and morality.

The most effective way to understand the Court's approach to deciding whether something is "speech" or "nonspeech" is illustrated by the way it has placed cases on either side of the magic dividing line of permissibility in two areas: *"fighting words"* and *"incitement to riot."* In considering "fighting words," the Supreme Court *upheld* the conviction of a street orator

---

[11] *Chaplinsky* v. *New Hampshire,* 315 U.S. 568 (1942).

"Glad To Give You My Opinion. I'm For Disarmament, The Common Market, Foreign Aid, Federal Aid To Education, Medicare, The U.N.—Oh, Yes, And Aid To Teachers Who Get Fired For Expressing Their Opinions!"

for using offensive language in public when he called a policeman a "God damned racketeer" and "a damned fascist." [12] The Court *reversed* the conviction of a Jehovah's Witness who stopped two pedestrians on the street, secured their permission to play a phonograph record to them, and then cranked up a strongly anti-Catholic recording. When the pedestrians, both Catholics, told the Witness what they thought of his views, he stopped the record and walked on. No fight ensued and no crowd gathered.[13]

The Court's distinction between the two cases was that using abusive language about an individual to his face is not "communication of information or opinion" and therefore not "speech." Using strong and even vilifying language about a religion (or a party, a government, a foreign country, etc.) to passersby who consent to listen *is* communicating information and opinion, and will not be punishable unless public order is threatened in some direct way.

The other revealing instance concerns "incitement." On one side of the line, the Court placed the conviction of an ex-priest named Father Terminiello, whose record as an anti-Semite and racist led hundreds of citizens in Chicago to demonstrate outside a hall that he had hired for a speech.[14]

---

[12] *Ibid.*
[13] *Cantwell* v. *Connecticut,* 310 U.S. 296 (1940).
[14] *Terminiello* v. *Chicago,* 337 U.S. 1 (1949).

The demonstrators shouted opposition to Terminiello's views, tore at his followers when they entered the building, threw rocks in the windows, and tried to break into the hall *en masse,* but they were restrained by the police. Inside, Terminiello made a speech denouncing Jews as "slimy scum" and attacking the New Deal as a Jewish and Communist plot. These remarks stirred some people in the audience to shout "Kill the Jews" and prompted a few anti-Terminiello listeners to call the speaker a "God damned liar." Terminiello was arrested by Chicago police and convicted for breach of the peace; at the trial, the city judge instructed the jury that speech which "stirs the public to anger, invites dispute, brings about a condition of unrest, or creates a disturbance" warranted conviction. The Supreme Court reversed, holding that whatever might be the power to convict Terminiello under a statute for creating a riot, the judge's definition of illegitimate speech was far too broad to be constitutional. Three Justices described the riot situation in detail, likened it to the clash of opposing street factions of Nazi and Communist supporters in Europe, and dissented from the majority's ruling, warning that the Court's "doctrinaire logic" could "convert the constitutional Bill of Rights into a suicide pact."

In the contrasting case,[15] a Syracuse University student named Feiner made a speech on a street corner in which he called the mayor of Syracuse a "champagne-sipping bum," denounced the American Legion as a "Nazi Gestapo," and urged American Negroes to "rise up in arms and fight for their rights." A crowd gathered, blocking the sidewalk, and several persons in the audience protested to the police to get that "son of a bitch" off the box or they would. The police arrested Feiner when he refused to stop voluntarily and he was convicted of disorderly conduct. In this case, the Supreme Court upheld the conviction. It accepted the judgment of the jury and the state courts that the speaker's remarks were creating public disorder, and held the state empowered to avert that danger. Three Justices dissented, arguing that it was the duty of police to restrain unruly elements in the crowd, not to arrest the speaker to satisfy his critics. They also argued that the majority's refusal to weigh the evidence of disorder made it easy for police in the future to suppress speech simply by saying that trouble was brewing in the crowd. Obviously, the majority implied that a man who hires a hall and speaks to those who choose to come is entitled to greater protection against a hostile crowd than those who speak on street corners through loud-speakers and grab the ears of passersby. Also, the Feiner case arose under a valid disorderly conduct statute properly applied at the trial, while in the Terminiello case, the breach of the peace statute had been transformed, by the judge's charge to the jury, into a sweeping and improper limit on controversial speech. These are the kinds of distinctions that make the difference in the "speech" or "nonspeech" cases. Will future Courts insist that police at least make some effort to protect the speaker before they haul him down? Will a hostile audience in a park square set aside by the city for use by strollers and speakers be treated differently from a gathering on a city sidewalk with its traffic problem? These are the distinctions that may make the difference in future cases.

---

[15] *Feiner v. New York,* 340 U.S. 315 (1951).

In most free speech cases, however, the Supreme Court is not concerned with distinguishing "nonspeech" but with drawing the line between regulations of speech that "abridge" and regulations that do not. For example, licensing laws regulating use of the public parks and streets by speakers will "abridge" if they permit officials to pass on the content of the speaker's expression but not if they provide a carefully circumscribed system for apportioning use of the facilities without discriminating against particular speakers. Laws forbidding all picketing in labor disputes "abridge," but laws do not "abridge" when they regulate the manner and size of picketing to prevent it from becoming coercive, or outlaw picketing that seeks objectives forbidden by the state (such as picketing that calls for employers to violate the antitrust laws). Federal laws requiring "lobbyists" to register and disclose facts about their clients, funds, and activities do not "abridge" when they apply to persons communicating directly with Congressmen on matters of pending legislation, but the laws would "abridge" if applied to representatives of civic organizations that state their views on pending legislation and seek to influence the general public.

In deciding whether government measures abridge freedom of speech, a central question concerns the so-called "clear and present danger" test. In 1919, Justice Oliver Wendell Holmes, Jr., announced in an opinion for the Supreme Court that in prosecutions for illegal speech "the question in every case is whether the words used are used in such circumstances and are of such a nature as to create a clear and present danger that they will bring about the substantive evils that Congress has a right to prevent." [16] In non-loyalty-security cases, the clear and present danger test has been used on quite a few occasions to free defendants. For example, whether statements made outside the courtroom about the conduct of judges or judicial proceedings constitute "contempt of court" is governed by the clear and present danger test. In a 1962 case,[17] a judge in a Georgia community impaneled the grand jury to look into what was called "Negro bloc voting" in the county, on the assumption that corruption and bribery might be present. The county sheriff, in public statements and an open letter to the grand jury, said that the investigation was really an effort to intimidate Negro voters. The sheriff was convicted of contempt on the ground that his statement imputed lack of integrity to the judges and impeded the grand jury investigation. The Supreme Court reversed the conviction, holding that there was no showing that these expressions had impeded the jury or would create a clear and present danger of doing so. Against the bare possibility that they might, the Court said, we must place the importance to our society of allowing elected officials "freely to express themselves on matters of current importance."

FREEDOM OF THE PRESS: OF BURNING AND BANNING IN AMERICA

The "press" in America takes in everything from the smudgy mimeograph leaflet of a neighborhood "Save Our Schools" group to the New York *Times*, Doubleday Book Company, Columbia Broadcasting System, and Paramount

---

[16] *Schenck v. United States,* 249 U.S. 47 (1919).
[17] *Wood v. Georgia,* 370 U.S. 375 (1962).

Pictures. Each method of expression, the Supreme Court has said, is entitled to the guarantees of "liberty of expression," but these guarantees vary in meaning according to the type of communication involved, since "each method tends to present its own peculiar problems."

The courts have held that there is no constitutional bar to applying general business or welfare regulations to the press. The Court has upheld the power of the National Labor Relations Board to force the Associated Press to rehire a news editor improperly discharged for union activity, and rejected the Associated Press's contention that this interfered with control of editorial policy and freedom of the press.[18] The Sherman Antitrust Law and the Fair Labor Standards Act have also been applied to newspapers and press services. Of course, if regulatory measures discriminate against the press, that is a different matter. When the large newspapers in New Orleans opposed Huey Long in the 1930s, he had the Louisiana state legislature put a 2 percent advertising-license tax on the gross receipts of all newspapers selling more than 20,000 copies a week. It did not reach 120 weekly newspapers (almost all of which supported Long) but did apply to thirteen of the seventeen big dailies. The Supreme Court held the tax invalid as "a deliberate and calculated device in the guise of a tax to limit the circulation of information to which the public is entitled. . . ."[19]

The Supreme Court faces two central problems in free press cases: the banning, licensing, or censoring of publications before they appear and the punishment of authors or publishers for bad content after publication.

The basic rule as to prepublication restraints on the press was laid down by the Supreme Court in a famous 1931 case.[20] The State of Minnesota forbade, as a nuisance, the future publication of a weekly newspaper in Minneapolis that specialized in gaudy attacks on what it called "grafters," "corrupt" officials, and "Jewish gangsters" in that city. The Court overturned the injunction, stating that the press was constitutionally immune from "prior restraint" apart from "exceptional cases" such as in wartime, when the publication was obscene, or when it incited to violence. After publication, newspapers were liable to prosecution or private damage suit for what they published, but they could not be "censored" in advance as was done here.

In the matter of books, a 5-to-4 majority of the Court upheld, in 1957, a New York statute that permitted city officials to bring an injunction proceeding against persons selling "indecent" books or other materials.[21] Under the statute, the court trial was held within one day to decide the issue of whether the material was indecent; if the court upheld the complaint, the material would be destroyed. The Court's majority noted that this was seizing already published material, not enjoining future issues of a publication because of previous issues that were considered objectionable. The minority saw this as close to "book burning" and said that the law should be that the seller goes on trial, not the book.

The basic rule as to handbills and leaflets is that these are a useful means

---

[18] *Associated Press* v. *United States,* 326 U.S. 1 (1945).
[19] *Grosjean* v. *American Press Co.,* 297 U.S. 233 (1936).
[20] *Near* v. *Minnesota,* 283 U.S. 697 (1931).
[21] *Kingsley Books, Inc.* v. *Brown,* 354 U.S. 436 (1957).

"I Enjoyed Censoring The Movie So Much, One Of These Days I'd Like To Censor The Book."

From *Straight Herblock*, Simon & Schuster, 1964

of expression that may not be hindered by government when they are for political, religious, or civic purposes. Thus the Court struck down a city ordinance forbidding the distribution of any publications unless authorized by the city manager, in a case involving a Jehovah's Witness selling religious literature door-to-door.[22] To the city's argument that a "sanitary problem" was presented in cleaning up such literature, the Court held that pamphlets and leaflets "have been historic weapons in the defense of liberty, as the pamphlets of Thomas Paine and others in our own history abundantly attest," and their circulation may not be sacrificed to "sanitation." Ordinances limiting handbill distribution to certain parts of a city or requiring licenses to prevent fraudulent solicitation have also been struck down. However, *commercial* handbills can be regulated or their distribution licensed, though Jehovah's Witnesses' literature, which is sold, does not fall into the category of commercial matter. A supermarket that printed its Thursday specials on one side of a leaflet and a verse from Genesis on the other would not squeeze under the gate to immunity.

In the field of motion pictures, films are entitled to the protections of the First Amendment.[23] This has barred state censorship on grounds such as "sacrilege," "immorality," or "harmful to public order." Since 1952, the Supreme Court Justices have gathered in the Court's conference room for private showings of films such as "The Miracle," "M," "The Moon Is Blue," "Native Son," "La Ronde," and "Lady Chatterley's Lover," and have struck down state refusals to license all of these films. However, a 5-to-4 majority of the Court held in 1961 that the First Amendment did not forbid all

---

22 *Lovell* v. *Griffin*, 303 U.S. 444 (1938).
23 *Burstyn* v. *Wilson*, 343 U.S. 495 (1952).

motion picture licensing before exhibition.[24] The Court did not pass on the standards and procedures that would be required for such a licensing system to be valid, however; probably the only constitutional ground would be "obscenity." The proceedings for licensing would also have to afford full administrative due process.

One final aspect of prepublication restraint involves the United States Post Office. An 1872 federal law makes obscene or indecent publications "non-mailable," and postal authorities will reject all books, magazines, or other mail they consider obscene. In a 1962 case, the Supreme Court overturned a Post Office finding that certain magazines featuring pictures of "male nudes" and aimed primarily at homosexual readers were obscene publications.[25] Just what this means for Post Office censorship is not quite clear. Of the six-Justice majority, two Justices concluded that the magazines were not really obscene under Supreme Court standards; three said the federal law making obscene publications "non-mailable" did not authorize the Post Office to set up a system for sifting the mails to remove obscene material; one Justice voted against the Post Office but gave no reason for his vote. The Post Office also confiscates "questionable political literature" (primarily Communist publications) mailed to United States residents from abroad. A Congressional statute in 1962 provided statutory authority for such screening and seizure. This censoring of political matter or propaganda has yet to be tested in the Supreme Court, but most constitutional experts would not rate the Post Office's position as very secure when and if a test case gets to the Justices.

So far, the discussion of press issues has concerned restraints before publication or exhibition. The second major area of controversy involves restraint by punishment after publication. It is primarily in this area that the Court has struggled with the framing of constitutional standards for measuring "obscenity." In the leading cases, dating from the late 1950s, the Court has held that since obscenity is not "constitutionally protected speech," there is no need for proof that material alleged to be obscene will create a clear and present danger of antisocial conduct by its users. Instead, the standard is one of content: "Whether to the average person, applying contemporary community standards, the dominant theme of the material taken as a whole appeals to prurient interest." (Webster's Dictionary defines "prurient" as "itching; longing; of persons having lascivious longings; of desire, curiosity, or propensity; lewd.")

When this test was used by the courts in two cases involving state prosecution of a bookseller for knowingly selling obscene literature and a federal prosecution for using the mails to distribute obscene literature, the Court upheld both convictions without making an independent judgment as to the obscene character of the materials, as would be done in cases of movie censorship, for example.[26] The dissenters in these cases felt that the Court's opinion opened the door far too wide to censors. Furthermore, one dis-

---

[24] *Times Film Corporation* v. *Chicago,* 365 U.S. 43 (1961).

[25] *Manual Enterprises* v. *Day,* 370 U.S. 478 (1962).

[26] *Roth* v. *United States,* 354 U.S. 476 (1957); *Alberts* v. *California,* 354 U.S. 476 (1957).

senter, Justice John M. Harlan, would have struck down the federal conviction because the First Amendment should not allow national authorities to use the postal or commerce powers to impose a national ban on book distribution.

One other issue of postpublication restraints is the complicated problem of "group libel laws." In Chicago, Joseph Beauharnais, the leader of a racist group called the White Circle League, circulated leaflets denouncing Negroes for their "rapes, robberies, knives, guns, and marijuana," calling on the mayor and city council to stop further "invasions" by Negroes of white property and liberty, and rallying whites to band together to "prevent the white race from becoming mongrelized by the negro. . . ." The leaflet also invited readers to fill out a printed membership application and join the League. Illinois in the 1950s had a "group libel" law making it a crime for anyone to publish a writing or picture that portrays "depravity, criminality, unchastity, or lack of virtue of a class of citizens of any race, color, creed or religion . . . [or] exposes [them] to contempt, derision, or obloquy. . . ." This law was passed because an individual under American law, unless named personally, would not be able to bring a libel suit against someone who attacked his race or religion since the law assumes the individual had not been personally injured.

Beauharnais was convicted under the statute, and a 5-to-4 majority of the Court upheld the conviction.[27] The majority traced the background of this 1917 statute to race riots and tensions that had wracked Chicago, and reiterated that libelous matter was not "constitutionally protected speech." They felt that state law could extend the protection against libel to *groups* in the interests of protecting public peace and social relations. Three dissenters would have struck down the statute as an invasion of free speech and press. One additional dissenter would have applied the clear and present danger test to measure whether these leaflets were likely to produce the results the legislature was aiming to forbid. Very few states have group libel statutes, however, and even in these, they are rarely used.

Looking at the law of free press as a whole, it is clear that the public's attitude toward the scope of frank expression in matters of sex, morals, manners, and language has grown steadily more liberal since the Second World War. American movies (and foreign imports shown here) are much more daring than before the 1940s. Magazines sold by the millions at newsstands and drugstores feature four-color fold-outs of nude girls. Henry Miller's *Tropic of Cancer* now circulates freely in most communities, after thirty years of quarantine by Customs Officials, the Post Office, and state authorities. The theater—traditionally freer because it aimed at more adult audiences—is rarely bothered today no matter how avant-garde the themes it treats.

The Supreme Court has been both register and catalyst in this liberalizing process. Clearly, judicial action has opened avenues that would have remained closed because of local or state censorship, and the Court's rulings have enjoyed enough public support to withstand attempts to over-

---

[27] *Beauharnais v. Illinois,* 343 U.S. 250 (1952).

turn the judicial rules by constitutional amendment. The liberalizing trend has been hailed by many as a sign of American "maturity" and a victory for free expression over "Puritanism," while others have viewed with alarm the spread of "filth" and "obscenity" in the press, especially when this has as one of its main customer markets the youth of the nation. The major effect of judicial rulings has been to place this debate where it really belongs—in the realm of individual judgment, family control, and civic group influences—rather than to let it be a matter of general law, usually administered on a set of "lowest common denominator" standards by persons without appreciation of the creative literary and aesthetic functions.

FREEDOM OF ASSOCIATION IN A NATION OF "JOINERS"

In American society, private, voluntary groups of all kinds play a central role in the nation's politics. As a result, freedom of association—though not mentioned in the Constitution—has become a vital extension of the rights of free speech, press, and assembly. Yet American law has always recognized that group activity adds elements of size, power, and coordination that are not present when the same number of persons function separately. For better as well as for worse, groups have a "multiplier" effect.

The main constitutional problems involving free association (apart from loyalty-security) concern the authority of government to outlaw groups, to limit their activities, or to penalize membership in them directly or indirectly.

In a leading case on freedom of association, *NAACP v. Button*,[28] the Court struck down in 1963 a Virginia statute convicting the NAACP chapter in that state of violating several common law prohibitions on soliciting law cases and managing them for interests other than that of the specific client. The Court held this to violate the NAACP's right as a civic group to defend its interests and those of its members through the courts. Earlier, in 1958, the Court had refused to permit Alabama, under its registration laws for out-of-state corporations, to force the NAACP to produce the names and addresses of its members and agents within the state.[29] The Court said that "freedom to engage in association for the advocacy of belief and ideas is an inseparable aspect" of "liberty" and "state action which may have the effect of curtailing the freedom to associate is subject to the closest scrutiny." In both NAACP cases, the Court said that anonymity was vital to effective association, and the right to privacy in association of members of the NAACP could not be invaded on the basis of the interests asserted here by these states. (The Court distinguished a 1928 ruling which upheld New York's power to force the Ku Klux Klan to disclose its membership lists. There, the history of "unlawful intimidation and violence" by the Klan supported the state's intrusion, while no such history could be put forward in the NAACP cases.)

Another key aspect of associational freedom is the right to solicit members. In 1945, the Court struck down a Texas law requiring that all labor

---

[28] 371 U.S. 415 (1963).
[29] *National Association for the Advancement of Colored People v. Alabama*, 357 U.S. 449 (1958).

union organizers coming into the state to solicit members apply to the secretary of state for an organizer's card.[30] The organizer had to identify himself and show his credentials, after which the license had to be issued by the secretary. Thomas, a CIO organizer from Detroit, had deliberately addressed a meeting of refinery workers and invited them to join his union and had not applied for a card. The Court majority rejected the arguments that the Texas regulation was comparable to business registration, and that identification requirements were reasonable, by saying that freedom of speech and assembly rights cannot be subjected even to such limited licensing procedures. In a similar case in 1958, the Court struck down a municipal ordinance in Georgia that required a license for persons soliciting members for any dues-paying organization and gave the mayor and city council the right to approve the organization.[31] Here, it was the conviction of an organizer from the International Ladies Garment Workers Union that was reversed.

It should be noted, though, that federal and state labor relations statutes have been upheld in the many restrictions they place on what union representatives (as well as employers) may say and do in the course of organizing or collective bargaining. Also, laws forbidding unions to discriminate against prospective members because of race or to treat Negro members in discriminatory fashion have been upheld.

Freedom of Expression and the Loyalty-Security Context

At the beginning of this section, we said that the loyalty-security context usually made a difference in the outcome of free expression cases. By using the term "loyalty-security," we mean to highlight the fact that American public opinion and government policy have tended to merge the question of "loyalty"—which relates to the allegiance that a citizen must give his country by word or deed—and that of "security"—which involves concrete dangers to the nation, as in matters of espionage, sabotage, sedition, and planned penetration of government to manipulate policy-making. The characteristic response of American society in dealing with these matters has been to insist on strict "loyalty" tests and disloyalty penalties for persons who sharply challenge the dominant national consensus and to call this a *security* matter.

Perhaps the best way to explore this field is to summarize, in all their sweep, the network of loyalty-security measures that have been applied by government from 1940 to the present.

1. In 1940, Congress passed the "Smith Act," or Alien Registration Act, the first peacetime national sedition law since the short-lived Act of 1798. This forbids persons to advocate or teach the overthrow of any government in the United States by force or violence, or publish matter so advocating, or organize any group for that purpose, or become a member of any group that so advocates. Conspiracy to accomplish these purposes is also made criminal. Many states adopted "Little Smith Acts" in the 1940s.

---

[30] *Thomas* v. *Collins,* 323 U.S. 516 (1945).
[31] *Staub* v. *City of Baxley,* 355 U.S. 313 (1958).

2. Beginning in 1940, the federal government initiated various programs for testing the loyalty of federal employees. These programs have undergone changes under Presidents Truman, Eisenhower, Kennedy and Johnson, but the basic outline has been constant since 1947. The Attorney General has drawn up a list of subversive organizations to guide loyalty-security officials. Applicants for employment and existing employees list their associations, and field investigations are made by the FBI and Civil Service investigators into a person's life and associations. If "derogatory information" is turned up, a hearing is provided at which the employee hears the general charges against him and some of their specifics, and can give testimony and present that of other witnesses. He cannot get the investigation reports, learn who has said what about him, or cross-examine informants. Various higher appeal boards are available, with the Secretary of the Department or head of the agency in which the employee works having final judgment on the issue of loyalty-security. Loyalty-security programs are also in force for persons who work in corporations having government contracts that require classified information. An estimated million employees are covered here. Many states have set up parallel loyalty programs for all of their employees (including teachers), and loyalty oaths or tests are often employed in state licensing of professional groups.

3. The Taft-Hartley Labor Act of 1947 required all unions seeking to use the machinery of the National Labor Relations Act to have their officers execute an oath that they are not members of the Communist party and do not believe in the overthrow of the United States Government by illegal or unconstitutional means. (In 1959, this was amended to forbid anyone to serve as a union officer or a labor relations consultant who had been a member of the Communist party during the five years prior to the Act.)

4. The McCarran Internal Security Act of 1950, passed in reaction to the outbreak of the Korean War, is a long and involved measure, the central part of which requires that any organization found to be "Communist" by the Subversive Activities Control Board (after full hearings) must register with the Attorney General, disclose the names and addresses of its officers, account for its moneys and expenditures, and identify all of its mail and broadcasts as coming from "X, a Communist organization." Members of a registered organization are forbidden to hold nonelective federal posts, apply for or use a passport, or work in defense plants.

5. The Communist Control Act of 1954, sometimes termed the "liberal Congressman's answer to McCarthyism," states that it "outlaws" the Communist party and deprives it of the rights of "legal bodies" in the United States. Other sections provide that groups that are "Communist-infiltrated" must comply with the Internal Security Act, and Communist-infiltrated unions are deprived of access to the NLRB even though their officers may have signed the Taft-Hartley non-Communist oath. This has never been invoked or tested in court.

6. Provisions in the Nationality Act of 1940 and the Immigration and Nationality Act of 1952 prohibit aliens who are members of the Communist party from becoming naturalized citizens. Furthermore, a naturalized citizen can be "denaturalized" and deported if he had "mental reservations" (concealed beliefs in favor of the overthrow of the government by force)

when he took his oath of citizenship. If a naturalized citizen becomes a member of an organization advocating overthrow within five years of his naturalization, this is prima facie proof of mental reservation.

7. Both federal and state governments have enacted miscellaneous measures setting loyalty-security requirements for government benefits and penalizing Communists in various ways. For example, federal passport regulations and grants to college students have had loyalty provisions attached, and some states withhold welfare payments or social security benefits from Communists. Almost a third of the states bar the Communist party from the ballot.

8. The 1920s saw the beginning of widely publicized and far-ranging investigations of "subversive groups" and "subversive persons" by Congressional and state legislative investigating committees. These have been typified on the national scene by the House Committee on Un-American Activities and the Senate Permanent Investigating Committee (under Senator Joseph McCarthy) in the early 1950s, and in the states by the Lusk Committee in New York in the 1920s and the Broyles Committee (Illinois) and Tenney Committee (California) in the post-1945 era.

9. After the Second World War, there was a sweeping trend toward the installation of loyalty-security standards by private groups as a criterion for determining officership, membership, or employment status. Many business corporations, labor unions, educational institutions, the press and television, religious groups, and civic associations have come to consider "loyalty" as something to "check into" when hiring a new executive, choosing a baritone to sing the praises of the sponsor's shaving cream or razor blades, and deciding whether to expel a "left-wing" minister from the church.

This list contains the highlights of our national response to loyalty-security problems since the 1930s. It should be noted carefully that all these measures (or the parts of larger measures that are included here) are directed at the advocacy of *ideas* by speaking or writing or by joining organizations that are advocating those ideas by speaking and writing. What is affected is *expression*. We are not dealing in this discussion with the network of state and federal measures that punish *acts* against the safety and security of the nation, such as the laws forbidding treason, espionage, disclosure of atomic secrets, theft of government property, sabotage, perjury, acting for a foreign agent without registering, securing access to classified areas or secrets, inciting to violence, etc. The Supreme Court, like virtually all Americans, has no trouble in recognizing the need for such legislation; it is the loyalty-security measures restricting speech, press, and association that create the disagreements.

The first thing to observe about these loyalty-security measures is that in their origin and their application they have been directed almost entirely against the "left" in America, not equally against the extremes of left and right.

For example, there has been only a handful of dismissals from government employment because of membership in fascist or terroristic organizations. And while there have been important prosecutions of fascist agents or supporters for *acts* against the national security during the Second World War (under the treason and espionage laws), there have been very few trials under the loyalty-security statutes involving rightists. (One such example was the indictment in 1942 of twenty-eight alleged "pro-Nazis" for violating the Smith Act provisions against sedition. The trial ended in 1944 when the presiding judge died, and the case was never resumed.)

It has been against left-of-center organizations and spokesmen that the measures have been applied, ranging from genuine pro-labor, antidiscrimination, and peace groups that were improperly branded as "pro-Communist" or "Communist-controlled" to groups that were really Communist-controlled and to the Communist party itself, or offshoots of the Communist movement (such as the Trotskyites). This has naturally affected Supreme Court cases. Between 1920 and 1964, the Supreme Court decided almost 100 cases involving the validity of loyalty-security measures, ranging from prosecutions for speeches and writings criticizing the draft in the First World War to cases involving Smith Act prosecutions of Communist party leaders. All but a handful of these have involved the "left." The same is true of Congressional contempt citations in the political field. Some would say that the focus accurately reflects the fact that the United States has never had a significant fascist party threat, and that not even the German-American Bund in its heyday penetrated sectors of government and leading civic groups as the Communists did. This response leads us inevitably to an analysis of the nature of the Communist party and of American positions toward it.

COMMUNISM AND THE LIBERAL AMERICAN CONSENSUS

Behind the debates as to whether loyalty-security measures are necessary or whether any particular measure in this field is wise or dangerous, the basic question throughout the past four decades has been, "What is the Communist party and how should it be treated?" Along with this has gone a related question, "What about persons who are not members of the Communist party but stand in various stages of cooperation or sympathy with the Communist party and some of its particular aims?" Three main positions —representing the conditioning attitudes for our loyalty-security debates— have developed among Americans on these issues.

The first position, *No Rights for Revolutionaries*, sees the American Communist party as a dedicated, conspiratorial movement directly controlled by the Soviet Union to serve the interests of Soviet foreign policy. The Communist party works at underground tasks such as espionage and secret penetration of government and key civic groups; it maintains another part of the Communist "iceberg" above the water in the form of a political party and protest movement, in order to bring in recruits who will be used in the underground apparatus. In addition, the Communist party creates and manages a series of "front groups" or "progressive" coalitions, in which non-Communists are attracted to work by the side of Communists for such broad "common objectives" as "peace," "civil rights," and "labor." Ten such sympathizers are said to exist for every Party member. The result, it is said, is a core of determined and disciplined agents ready to topple the American system at a signal from Moscow.

With this picture of the American Communist party, the "no rights for revolutionaries" advocates assert that this country does not have to wait until the day of the *coup* or until a nuclear war breaks out. We should use all possible legal measures to punish and exert pressure on the Communists, through loyalty oaths, loyalty investigations, prosecutions of top leadership and local leaders, enactment of full disclosure laws and registration requirements, penetration by FBI agents, Congressional investigations, etc., all to harass the party, cost it money and time, and neutralize its potential for evil in our society. Another key reason for these measures is to keep weak-minded "dupes" and well-meaning "liberals" from being pulled into the Communist camp. When asked whether pursuit of such loyalty-security measures is not imitating the Communists themselves and curtailing freedom of expression and association, the supporters of this position would reply that the Communists state openly that they do not believe in democracy and do not believe in civil liberties; therefore, they cannot claim those rights in our country, since Communists would be the first ones to abolish all civil liberties if they came to power.

2. The second position supports *Freedom for the Thought We Hate.* Some of those holding it always believed the Communist party was a conspiratorial movement; others, especially during the 1920s and 1930s, saw the Soviet Union as an antifascist power building "socialism," and the American Communist party as a legitimate party of social protest here. Whichever estimate underlies this second position, its central thesis is that the American Communist party is a weak, wholly discredited movement in this country, and has been throughout the late 1940s, down to the present. The United States is a rich, stable, secure society, facing no internal crisis such as Russia faced in 1917 or Germany faced in the early 1930s. There is no analogy therefore to support the argument that a few thousand party members will topple the United States unless drastic loyalty-security measures are enacted.

Instead, this second position contends that FBI surveillance and the laws punishing *acts* against national security are fully adequate. We should apply the statutes on espionage, sabotage, and the like, but let the activities of the Communists that are above ground continue, as proof that ours is a free society and that we can meet *ideas* on the field of reason. Keep the ideological pressure on, but do not institute loyalty-testing oaths and forced-confession procedures whose inevitable effect will be to create a climate of fear and a stifling of free thought, not among the Communists themselves but among those whose genuinely independent thinking will be labeled as "Communist" and "disloyal." It is these persons who are usually caught in the net of loyalty machinery; spies and hidden party members are rarely turned up by federal employee loyalty-security programs. Furthermore, creating a vast loyalty-security apparatus, it is said, inevitably strengthens the hands of right-wing anti-Communists and reactionaries in America, who use the loyalty-security measures to discredit liberals, democratic socialists, pacifists, and others, as all being "tools of the Communists" and "disloyal." Loyalty-security machinery, it is contended, cannot be applied safely and carefully. By its very nature, it attempts to stifle belief and ideas, to compel persons to declare those beliefs publicly, and to punish those who will not conform or confess. Therefore, this second position concludes, we institute loyalty-security measures at a far greater peril to ourselves and our freedom than to the Communists, since they are delighted to pose as martyrs and point to the "class terror" and "persecution" of capitalistic societies.

③The third position, *Limited Loyalty-Security Measures for a Revolutionary Age*, rests on something of a middle ground between the views described above. It views the Communist party as partly a conspiratorial and partly a social protest movement, and wants to see the first aspect controlled while the second remains protected. It fears "witch-hunting" and knows the danger of official thought control. But advocates of this position do not believe that the machinery directed against *acts* of disloyalty is sufficient to protect the governmental and civic processes from Communist penetration. Communists must be barred from holding posts in government because they will use these posts to advance Soviet, not American, interests. And Communists must be kept also from certain key sectors of private life, such as defense industries, where national security is directly at stake.

Therefore, it is argued, *some* loyalty-security measures are necessary. The crucial factor is to limit these to the area of genuine security need; to draft precise and narrow legislation pinpointed in its effect to Communists and fascists; to provide full due process in the administration of this loyalty-security machinery; and to guard against overzealous crusaders seizing control of the machinery and employing it to punish dissent and discredit political opposition to the two major parties or the capitalist system. Under this third position, measures such as the Smith Act, the Communist Control Act of 1954, state antisedition laws, and denaturalization for "mental reservations" would be *illegitimate* loyalty-security measures because they do not really meet a security need and because their impact on free expression is too great. A limited federal loyalty-security program for employees in sensitive posts of government, on the other hand, would be proper. In this way, we respond effectively to the special character of the Communist party in a revolutionary age, but we protect both our reputation for freedom and our own precious rights by holding the loyalty-security apparatus to its proper sphere.

These three views reflect the main currents of thinking in the United States on the nature of the internal Communist challenge and how we should respond to it. We have swung between strong extremes on this question ever since the Russian Revolution. While the general population was always hostile to Communism as an ideology and to the American Communist party, we had the "Red scare" of the 1920s, relaxation during the 1930s, sharp tensions between 1946 and 1956, and then a return to relative relaxation between 1956 and the present. Today, while we still have the large network of loyalty-security measures described earlier and these are still being enforced—with varying degrees of diligence—the debate over the wisdom and necessity for these measures goes on.

COMMUNISM AND THE UNITED STATES SUPREME COURT

The cyclical pattern described above has been mirrored in the United States Supreme Court. During the tensions of the First World War and its aftermath, the Supreme Court had about a dozen cases involving prosecutions of persons for antiwar and antidraft statements that allegedly violated the federal espionage and sedition acts or for left-wing speeches that conflicted with state antisedition laws. In *every* case, the Court upheld the convictions and allowed persons such as Eugene Debs, Jacob Abrams, and

Benjamin Gitlow to go to jail.[32] Many important statements about free speech and its importance to a free society were made in these cases, sometimes in the opinions of the majority, sometimes in concurring and dissenting opinions (especially the formulation of the "clear and present danger" standard by Justices Oliver Wendell Holmes, Jr., and Louis D. Brandeis). But all of the defendants still went to jail for their speeches.

Between 1927 and 1940, in the climate of general relaxation on loyalty-security, the Court began to interpret loyalty-security needs more narrowly. In 1927, the Court threw out the conviction of an organizer for the Industrial Workers of the World, under a Kansas "criminal syndicalism" act. The Justices found no valid evidence that the IWW advocated violent change of government.[33] (Also, defendants such as Debs, Gitlow, and Whitney received executive pardons from Presidents and governors.) During the 1930s, the Court freed the defendants in cases involving state prosecutions for raising a red flag at a children's camp,[34] addressing a public meeting sponsored by the Communist party,[35] and possessing literature calling on Negroes to rise up against the Jim Crow system in the South.[36] In all of these cases, admitted Communist party members were the defendants, and in all the cases, the Court framed limits on state action or applied the "clear and present danger" test to free them. During the Second World War, apart from upholding the relocation of the Japanese-Americans on the West Coast [37] (see Chapter 19) and the treason-espionage convictions of German supporters,[38] the Court continued to free defendants in loyalty-security cases and to hold the government to tight constitutional limits. For example, the deportation of a top Communist leader was invalidated in 1943 on the ground that it had not been proved that the Communist party advocated violent overthrow of the government; [39] a Mississippi law forbidding speeches or literature "calculated to encourage disloyalty" was struck down in 1943; [40] a Congressional rider forbidding salaries to be paid to three specified "pro-Communist" federal employees was declared unconstitutional in 1946 as punishment without trial; [41] in 1944, in one of the few rightist cases, the Court voided the conviction of a man under the Espionage Act for distributing pro-Nazi and anti-Roosevelt literature because there was no proof that he intended to interfere with the armed services.[42] Many other instances in this period saw the Court acting vigorously to protect freedom of expression from restrictions in the name of loyalty-security necessities.

Between 1947 and 1955, however, the Court majority stopped freeing

---

[32] *Debs* v. *United States*, 249 U.S. 211 (1919); *Abrams* v. *United States*, 250 U.S. 616 (1919); *Gitlow* v. *New York*, 268 U.S. 652 (1925).
[33] *Fiske* v. *Kansas*, 274 U.S. 380 (1927).
[34] *Stromberg* v. *California*, 283 U.S. 359 (1931).
[35] *De Jonge* v. *Oregon*, 299 U.S. 353 (1937).
[36] *Herndon* v. *Lowry*, 301 U.S. 242 (1937).
[37] *Hirabayashi* v. *United States*, 320 U.S. 81 (1943).
[38] *Ex parte Quirin*, 317 U.S. 1 (1942).
[39] *Schneiderman* v. *United States*, 320 U.S. 118 (1943).
[40] *Taylor* v. *Mississippi*, 319 U.S. 583 (1943).
[41] *United States* v. *Lovett*, 328 U.S. 303 (1946).
[42] *Baumgartner* v. *United States*, 322 U.S. 665 (1944).

defendants and all but abandoned the clear and present danger test. This was the era of Alger Hiss's conviction for perjury in denying that he had given government secrets to a Communist agent. During this period, Harry Gold, David Greenglass, and Julius and Ethel Rosenberg were convicted for giving atomic secrets to the Soviet Union; the Cold War boiled up into the bloody "Korean police action" of 1950–52. High public hostility was registered against Communists and "pro-Communists." Loyalty prosecutions and charges of "softness on Communism" became part of the national climate of opinion.

In this eight-year period, the Court reflected loyalty-security concerns by upholding the Taft-Hartley non-Communist oath,[43] the Attorney General's list of subversive organizations,[44] the constitutionality of "conspiracy to advocate" trials of the Communist party's top officers under the Smith Act,[45] the deportation of naturalized citizens for membership in the Communist party in the 1920s and 1930s,[46] and state loyalty programs for employees and teachers.[47] The Court refused to hear cases in which witnesses had been convicted for refusing to answer the questions of legislative committees investigating loyalty and refused to interfere with the application of a loyalty program for federal employees.[48] In almost all of these loyalty-security cases between 1947 and 1955, the defendants went to jail. While there were strong debates within the Court on the constitutionality of many of these measures, the Court did not declare a single federal loyalty-security act or prosecution to be unconstitutional, and only a few state actions were held invalid, usually on procedural rather than lack-of-power grounds. Sometimes with fervor and sometimes with regret, the majority found the power in the elected branches of state and nation to install and use all of these loyalty-security mechanisms.

Between 1955 and the present, with the "phasing out" of Cold War tension, the ending of the Korean War, the official censuring of Senator Joseph McCarthy by his Senate colleagues (and his condemnation by most of the nation), the Republican party's assumption of responsibility for administering loyalty-security measures (thus softening party conflict over this issue) and similar developments, we entered a period of relative relaxation. During this time, the Supreme Court began to free defendants and strike down some loyalty-security laws or practices. For example, the convictions of several Communist party defendants under the Smith Act were thrown out because the judge at the trial did not instruct the jury that advocacy of the overthrow of the government as an "abstract idea" is lawful.[49] State sedition laws have been declared invalid as duplicating and conflicting with the federal Smith Act.[50] Federal employee loyalty programs

[43] *American Communications Association v. Douds,* 339 U.S. 382 (1950).
[44] *Joint Anti-Fascist Refugee Committee v. McGrath,* 341 U.S. 123 (1951).
[45] *Dennis v. United States,* 341 U.S. 494 (1951).
[46] *Harisiades v. Shaughnessy,* 342 U.S. 580 (1952); *Galvan v. Press,* 347 U.S. 522 (1954).
[47] *Adler v. Board of Education,* 342 U.S. 485 (1952).
[48] *Barsby v. United States,* 334 U.S. 843 (1948); *Lawson v. United States,* 339 U.S. 934 (1950); *Bailey v. Richardson,* 341 U.S. 918 (1951).
[49] *Yates v. United States,* 354 U.S. 298 (1957).
[50] *Pennsylvania v. Nelson,* 350 U.S. 497 (1956).

Traveling Papers

With the relaxation of the late 1950s, the federal courts began to strike down some of the loyalty restrictions of the earlier decade, here, refusals to issue passports on loyalty grounds without hearings.

From *Herblock's Here and Now*, Simon & Schuster, 1955

have been cut back sharply in coverage and held to increasingly strict requirements of procedural fairness.[51] Passport denials on the basis of alleged Communist affiliations, without hearings, were struck down.[52] A state requirement that tax-exempt organizations file loyalty oaths was declared unconstitutional.[53] A state oath for Florida teachers that they neither had nor would "lend aid, support, advice, counsel or influence to the Communist party" was held unconstitutionally vague.[54] A refusal to admit persons to the practice of law on the ground that their past Communist party membership proved lack of good character was overturned.[55] Convictions for contempt were reversed when the House Committee on Un-American Activities asked a witness such wide-ranging questions about his connections with Communist activities that the witness could not be sure just what the Committee was investigating, and thus could not know what he was risking if he refused to answer.[56]

At the same time, however, the period from 1955 to the present has been marked by some other Supreme Court decisions that have *upheld* loyalty-security laws and prosecutions. Prosecutions under the Smith Act for "know-

---

[51] *Peters* v. *Hobby,* 349 U.S. 331 (1955); *Cole* v. *Young,* 351 U.S. 536 (1956); *Vitarelli* v. *Seaton,* 359 U.S. 535 (1959); *Greene* v. *McElroy,* 360 U.S. 474 (1959).

[52] *Kent* v. *Dulles,* 357 U.S. 116 (1958); *Dayton* v. *Dulles,* 357 U.S. 144 (1958).

[53] *Speiser* v. *Randall,* 357 U.S. 513 (1958); *First Unitarian Church* v. *Los Angeles,* 357 U.S. 545 (1958).

[54] *Cramp* v. *Board,* 368 U.S. 278 (1961).

[55] *Schware* v. *New Mexico,* 353 U.S. 532 (1957).

[56] *Watkins* v. *United States,* 354 U.S. 178 (1957).

ing membership" in the Communist party have been upheld.[57] The constitutionality of the McCarran Internal Security Act's registration provisions for the Communist party was accepted in 1961.[58] Dismissals of teachers by the states for invoking the Fifth Amendment before Congressional committees probing loyalty have been affirmed.[59] Refusal by state bar committees to certify candidates for admission to the bar who refuse to answer questions about their political beliefs and associations has been upheld.[60] The Court has affirmed the power of the House Committee on Un-American Activities and of state investigators to compel witnesses either to answer questions or to rely solely on the privilege against self-incrimination, rejecting the argument that questions about what was "un-American" or questions "for the sake of exposure" were forbidden by the First Amendment.[61]

Thus, 1955 to the present has seen the Supreme Court majority make some thrusts for liberty, rejecting the "No Rights for Revolutionaries" position as well as the "Freedom for the Thought We Hate," in favor of the "Limited Loyalty-Security Measures" perspective. What we have had, then, is a majority position that has chipped away at the excesses of the 1946–54 loyalty-security programs but has not yet, and may never, challenge their basic constitutionality. As Professor John P. Frank has noted ruefully but realistically, "The dominant lesson of our history in the relation of the judiciary to repressions is that courts love liberty most when it is under pressure least."

THE RIGHT TO BE LEFT ALONE: PRIVACY AND THE CONSTITUTION

Like freedom of association, privacy is nowhere mentioned in the First Amendment. When most students of the Constitution think of privacy, they probably call to mind the Fourth Amendment to the Constitution, which provides that "persons, houses, papers, and effects" shall be secure from "unreasonable searches and seizures." In the conflicts over police use of wire-tapping and microphone devices against suspected criminals, or FBI surveillance by installing television-eye cameras to watch suspected subversives in their offices, it is the Fourth Amendment that generally predominates in the legal discussion.

Here, though, we are concerned with what might be called "personal and civic privacy." The Supreme Court has upheld ordinances that forbade "raucous" sound trucks from broadcasting through the city or through residential areas, and limitation of all sound trucks to certain hours would also be constitutional.[62] Again, the Court has upheld the right of home owners to post "No trespassing" or "No soliciting" signs and thereby exclude door-to-door advocates of religion and politics, as well as the Fuller brush man or the student working his way through college by selling magazine subscriptions.[63] In both of these cases, speech—what might be called active or

---

[57] *Scales* v. *United States*, 367 U.S. 203 (1961).
[58] *Communist Party* v. *Subversive Activities Control Board*, 367 U.S. 1 (1961).
[59] *Beilan* v. *Board of Education*, 357 U.S. 399 (1958).
[60] *Konigsberg* v. *State Bar of California*, 366 U.S. 36 (1961).
[61] *Barenblatt* v. *United States*, 360 U.S. 109 (1959).
[62] *Kovacs* v. *Cooper*, 336 U.S. 77 (1949).
[63] *Breard* v. *Alexandria*, 341 U.S. 623 (1951).

aggressive speech—was constitutionally limited because of the interest of society in repose, rest, and privacy within the home.

In another group of cases involving privacy, the Court has not found enough social utility to limit speech in the interests of repose. In the District of Columbia, the buses (a public utility) in the 1950s began to broadcast soft music and occasional commercial announcements during their rides. When a law suit was brought by passengers complaining that this made them a "captive audience" on a public utility and invaded their privacy interests in reading, thinking, or sight-seeing on the buses, a majority of the Court refused to recognize their claims.[64]

Though related to freedom of association, the right of members of civic organizations to exempt their membership lists from governmentally compelled disclosure, unless the state makes out a case for antisocial activities by the group, has recently been affirmed by the Supreme Court in a series of cases involving the NAACP in Southern states.[65] The Court spoke of a "right to privacy" and a "right of anonymity" in these cases that were protected by the First Amendment.

Viewed as a whole, what seems to be happening is that the idea of privacy as attached primarily to one's *property* rights (home, car, office, business secrets, reputation, papers, and the like), and of threats in terms of "trespass" to these rights, has increasingly been transferred by the courts in recent years to the area of *liberty*. This does not mean that privacy may never be invaded, of course, but that when the privacy of individuals and of civic groups is invaded, this interferes with a liberty right and may not be done without due process of law.

Such a development fits with the analysis of many political scientists that the equilibrium among privacy, publicity, and secrecy is one of the key relationships that must be maintained if a free, pluralistic society is to prosper. As Professor Edward Shils has put this, an important goal of a liberal society is to achieve "civility," which he defines as existing when there is "privacy" to nourish individual creativity and group expression; "publicity" of information to inform government and the public of the facts necessary to form the basis of wise judgment on public affairs; and certain areas of "secrecy" for government operations, to preserve integrity of internal policy-making. "Freedom," says Shils, "flourishes in the indifference of privacy." [66]

GOD AND CAESAR: RELIGIOUS ISSUES AND THE FIRST AMENDMENT

The First Amendment forbids both laws "prohibiting the free exercise of religion" and laws "respecting an establishment of religion." The two provisions interact, since establishing one religion as the official faith of the nation or a state would deny religious liberty to citizens of other faiths, or of no faith.

In the Supreme Court, the "free exercise" clause has primarily been the

---

[64] *Public Utilities Commission* v. *Pollak,* 343 U.S. 451 (1952).

[65] See, for example, *National Association for the Advancement of Colored People* v. *Alabama,* 357 U.S. 449 (1958); 360 U.S. 240 (1959).

[66] Edward Shils, *The Torment of Secrecy* (Glencoe, 1954).

shield of small sects and nonbelievers. Few recent cases upholding this right have involved direct denials of religious expression to Protestants, Catholics, and Jews. Those faiths can generally depend on their influential status as major, "recognized" religions to secure their freedom of operation. However, when Jewish groups and some Protestant denominations have tried to invoke the principle of their free religious exercise to challenge a *general* governmental regulation—as in the school prayer case, released-time systems for religious education, or Sunday closing laws—the Court has not accepted their position. Instead those issues have been fought out in the contemporary Court on the battleground of the nonestablishment clause. Here, the *four* great faiths of America—Protestants, Catholics, Jews, and secularists—have confronted one another in passionate debate over the boundary lines between religion and the state, and the preferment of one religious camp over another.

In defining "free exercise," the Court has held that "religious beliefs and opinions" are inviolate but religious "practices" may be regulated by federal and state police power. Laws outlawing practices such as polygamy, snake-handling, parades without a license, and sales of religious newspapers on the streets by children have all been upheld over the protests of Mormons, snake-worshippers, and Jehovah's Witnesses that these were exercises of religion.[67] To safeguard religious "belief," the Court has struck down laws requiring religious door-to-door solicitors to secure a police permit or taxing such activity;[68] invalidated requirements that children of Jehovah's Witnesses salute the flag in school despite their religious scruples against this ceremony;[69] and refused to permit the federal government to make it a requirement of naturalization that an alien swear he will defend the country by bearing arms when this violates his religious principles.[70] Furthermore, the Court threw out the mail fraud conviction of an offbeat cult called the "I Am" movement because the jury had to pass on the sincerity of the religious beliefs of the group's founder.[71] However, government officials do pass on the sincerity of *individuals* claiming draft exemption on the basis of religious convictions against war, with mixed results in the specific cases.[72]

Halfway between the guarantee of religious freedom and the ban on establishment lies the immunity of churches from government interference in their internal affairs. In cases ranging from the split between the Union and Confederate wings of the Presbyterian Church in the 1860s[73] to conflicts between the Moscow and American leadership of the Russian Orthodox Church,[74] the Court has held that government may not by statute or judicial decision determine which of two disputing factions within a church is en-

---

[67] *Reynolds* v. *United States,* 98 U.S. 145 (1879); *Prince* v. *Massachusetts,* 321 U.S. 158 (1944).
[68] *Murdock* v. *Pennsylvania,* 319 U.S. 105 (1943); *Follett* v. *McCormick,* 321 U.S. 573 (1944).
[69] *West Virginia State Board of Education* v. *Barnette.*
[70] *Girouard* v. *United States,* 328 U.S. 61 (1946).
[71] *United States* v. *Ballard,* 322 U.S. 78 (1944).
[72] See, for example, *Sicurella* v. *United States,* 348 U.S. 385 (1955); *Witmer* v. *United States,* 348 U.S. 375 (1955).
[73] *Watson* v. *Jones,* 13 Wall. 679 (1872).
[74] *Kedroff* v. *St. Nicholas Cathedral,* 344 U.S. 94 (1952).

titled to church property or to control over appointments and communicants. Those are matters for the church authorities to decide, not the government.

In the field of nonestablishment, the Supreme Court in 1947 laid down a classic definition of this constitutional rule: [75]

> Neither a state nor the Federal Government can set up a church. Neither can pass laws which aid one religion, aid all religions, or prefer one religion over another. Neither can force nor influence a person to go to or to remain away from church against his will or force him to profess a belief or disbelief in any religion. No person can be punished for entertaining or professing religious beliefs or disbeliefs, for church attendance or non-attendance. No tax in any amount, large or small, can be levied to support any religious activities or institutions, whatever they may be called, or whatever form they may adopt to teach or practice religion.

When faced with applying this rule to the varied and frequent church-state contacts that have characterized our national and local life, the Court since 1947 has run a rather zigzag course. The current law holds that the nonestablishment principle forbids such policies as sectarian instruction on school property during school hours,[76] officially composed prayers for school-children,[77] and an oath of belief in God as a requirement for becoming a notary public.[78] It does *not* forbid such activities as state subsidy of bus transportation of children to parochial schools (since this aids the child not the church),[79] or programs that allow those children requesting the privilege to leave school early for religious instruction, while keeping the other children in school.[80] Laws requiring that stores and business activities remain closed on Sunday have been upheld as general welfare regulations against the protest that these establish the Christian Sabbath and discriminate against groups such as Jews and Seventh Day Adventists, who refrain from labor on different days of the week and thus "pay a penalty" under the Sunday laws.[81]

As we noted earlier, many liberty questions do not get decided by the courts, either because the courts rule them to be political questions for the elected branches of government or because the technical rules of litigation make it almost impossible to get a test case before the Justices. This is particularly true of *federal* church-state issues. For example, Presidents Franklin Roosevelt and Harry S. Truman both sent a personal representative to Pope Pius XII, and President Truman nominated General Mark Clark to be a regular ambassador to the State of Vatican City, though the nomination was withdrawn and General Clark did not come up for Senate confirmation. Some Protestants, Jews, and secular groups objected to these practices as a "recognition of a church" forbidden by the nonestablishment clause. However, no one succeeded in getting a test of this policy before the courts

---

[75] *Everson v. Board of Education*, 330 U.S. 1 (1947).
[76] *McCollum v. Board of Education*, 333 U.S. 203 (1948).
[77] *Engel v. Vitale*, 370 U.S. 421 (1962).
[78] *Torcaso v. Watkins*, 367 U.S. 488 (1961).
[79] *Everson v. Board of Education.*
[80] *Zorach v. Clauson*, 343 U.S. 306 (1952).
[81] *Sunday Closing Law Cases*, 366 U.S. 420, 582, 599, 617 (1961).

between 1939 and 1950, or since; no one had "standing to sue" based on injury to himself, or to interests that the courts would let him assert. In many other matters, such as the presence of "In God We Trust" on our coins, or chaplains in the armed services, court rulings are also not likely. Whether a Congressional statute could authorize court suits to test the validity of federal funds for a parochial school is an unanswered question.

CONCLUSION: LIBERTY RIGHTS AND THE LAW

"My freedom to swing my arm," Justice Holmes once said, "stops where the other man's nose begins." This epigram describes many of the themes in this section on liberty. First, it suggests that the real testing time for liberty rights comes when their exercise collides with other values cherished by society—such as privacy, morality, public order, or internal security. Where all are lined up in a congenial circle swinging their arms more or less in rhythm—as usually happens when debates proceed within our two-party system by Democrats and Republicans—there is a fairly small risk of collisions. Liberty in this sector has been well secured in America, and while there are always bullies, bigots, censors, and the fearful to contend with, even here the law and community ethic of American society is usually on the side of liberty.

Second, it has been our dominant tradition that there is no denial of liberty *as a principle* in setting certain types of careful rules on those whose arm-swinging is consistently careless or deliberately aggressive. Limits on the expression of "fighting words," "libel," or "profanity" protect society's nose and its process of arm-swinging as well. As long as the rules are carefully pinpointed to the excesses and are administered with deep awareness of the social value in zealous free expression, our principles are secured, not betrayed.

Finally, there has been a continuing tension over the practice of American society in punishing those who swing their arms in unorthodox ways or with revolutionary ardor. This clash between our middle-class consensus and the radical dissenters is our special dilemma in liberty matters. As various studies of American public and group opinion demonstrate, most Americans do *not* have a belief in toleration which rests on faith in the social self-defense capabilities of a free society. Thus the nation has too often imposed standards of loyalty when all that was objectively needed were laws insuring security. On the other hand, the leading groups in the nation, and the courts, seem to understand better in the 1960s than they did in the 1950s that we *do* run risks every bit as great in muzzling free expression as in neglecting controls on subversive activities, and this suggests that important progress may have been made.

Justice: Due Process in a Free Society

When John Locke explained why men left a happy "state of nature" to form organized societies, the prime reason he cited was mankind's need for a "common judge" to arbitrate disputes over property and liberty matters. This system of justice, as we have already seen, involves the organization and selection of judges as well as the line to be drawn between judicial and political questions. (We have also observed how that line is blended in fact by American society.) A system of justice also depends on rules of procedure by which criminal cases are investigated and tried, civil cases are heard, and various semijudicial proceedings are conducted by executive and legislative agencies.

At first glance, the rules of procedure often seem to students to be technical or even obstructionist matters. At times, complex procedures are manipulated by clever lawyers to free "obviously guilty" racketeers, corrupt officials, racists, subversives, and the like. But as Justice Felix Frankfurter once observed, "The history of liberty is very largely the history of observance of fair procedure," and the procedure that protects one protects all in a free society. The English barons were seeking fair procedure when they extracted from King John the famous promise in Magna Charta that trials would be by "the law of the land." The protests of American colonists against general searches of their homes, arrests solely on suspicion, and detention of persons by the British authorities without speedy trial were major grievances in the revolutionary struggle of the 1760s and 1770s and led to important procedural guarantees in the federal and state constitutions, and their bills of rights. Throughout this struggle, it was understood that limited police practices, prompt and fair trials in public, and appeals to independent judges were crucial to the general security of property and the vigorous exercise of liberty. And so it remains today, whenever businessmen, taxpayers, Negro civil rights demonstrators, religious dissenters, and a host of other individuals and groups find themselves called before courts, legislative committees, or administrative agencies.

Most observers of American government realize that there is a locked-in tension between the due process rules and the freedom of government authorities to investigate, prosecute, and punish various antisocial activities, from gambling and petty theft to murder and espionage. How much a given "due process" limit on police or prosecutors "handcuffs law enforcement" and "threatens public safety" and whether the restriction is necessary are constant debates in this area.

What is not realized as often is that there can also be basic conflicts among the supporting justifications for due process rules. Three of these make up the "classic rationales." First is the belief that centuries of Anglo-American trial history show truth to be discovered best when due process rights are observed. The requirements of habeas corpus,[82] speedy trial, cross-examination of accusers, the privilege against self-incrimination, jury trial, and similar rights are vital to the exposure of falsehood, bias, mistake, coerced confessions, and government persecution, all of which impede the true determination of facts and motives, guilt or innocence. Due process is thus an essential ingredient in truth-seeking, wherever that truth may lead in its personal or political implications.

Second, due process represents a check on arbitrary government action. By forbidding police questioning of prisoners for days without rest or food, juries which exclude Negroes, or dismissal of government employees for

---

[82] Requiring the government to produce an arrested person in court and to specify the charge on which he is being held.

"disloyalty" without fair hearings, due process helps to maintain the balance of power between governmental might and the private sectors of society. The public's knowledge that government must follow the rules, cannot act arbitrarily, and can be brought to account if it does is essential to the confident exercise of free speech, free press, and political opposition, to the prevention of racial and religious discrimination, and the like. Due process is thus a roadblock to the police state.

The third basis of due process rights is their value in preserving and promoting individual dignity. Requiring accused persons to give testimony against themselves, secreting cameras in public bathrooms to catch sexual deviates, or allowing penniless defendants to stand trial in major criminal cases without lawyers are procedures that would display callous disregard for the dignity of individuals. Due process guarantees thus reflect a continuing sensitivity in American society to the moral unit of individualism and to the idea of fairness as a value in itself, even when the self-protection of society is involved.

In many instances, these three justifications for due process support one another harmoniously. Police third-degree treatment of suspects often produces false confessions (to stop the beatings); toleration of such police tactics would create widespread fear of government power; and mistreatment of a person held in custody clearly violates the human rights of persons, even those suspected of criminal conduct. In other situations, however, the three rationales may conflict, and society must decide which is the paramount consideration. For example, if truth-seeking is the prime goal, then a person who knows most about an event—the defendant or the prime witness—should be required to testify about it or else the jury should be able to draw unfavorable inferences about the silence and legislative committees should be able to cite for contempt the one balking an important inquiry. But if individual dignity and limiting government power are the primary considerations, then government should be required to make out a positive case or gather facts for legislation with its own witnesses and evidence, rather than forcing persons to incriminate themselves with their own testimony. Similarly, illegally obtained evidence—whether secured by hidden microphones in a bedroom, pumping the stomach of a suspect who swallowed morphine capsules when police apprehended him, hypnotizing a prisoner to tell what he really did, or searching a business office without first securing a warrant—should be excluded as court testimony. Here, when perfectly solid evidence of a real crime is barred from court—in order to deter police misconduct and protect individual dignity—"truth" is sacrificed to serve other due process values, and criminals may walk off scot-free.

Weighing a due process claim against a procedure government spokesmen consider necessary to public order, and setting priorities among the conflicting bases of due process rights are not the monopoly of any single branch of government in the federal and state systems. Legislatures have enacted important statutes setting rules for prisoner detention, electronic eavesdropping, reasonable bail, and so on, and executive agencies have promulgated important rules for regulatory agency hearings, passport applications, police practices, and other matters. But it is the courts that have traditionally been the most influential interpretive and "enforcement" agency in the due process field. Partly this is because due process so often involves the conduct of courts themselves, and of courtlike procedures; partly it stems from the fact that lawyers have been a powerful force in supporting due process values before the public and in bringing these issues to the courts; and partly the answer lies in the fact that the basic rules of due process are so often general constitutional guides requiring judicial elaboration and application to changing conditions. (What is an "unreasonable" search and seizure, for example, or "excessive" bail, an "impartial" jury, or "cruel" punishment?)

With these considerations as background, we can turn to the constitutional ground rules of contemporary due process. Since the federal government and the states each have their own constitutions, there are fifty-one "due process systems" in America, each setting rules for its own government procedures and each receiving authoritative interpretation from the highest court of the jurisdiction. Thus Illinois may have a different rule about jury votes having to be unanimous from that in Michigan, and both may be different from federal law. However, the Fourteenth Amendment to the federal Constitution, adopted in 1868 to ensure that all American citizens enjoyed certain basic national rights, includes a provision forbidding "any state" to "deprive any person of life, liberty, or property without due process of law. . . ." Under this standard, the United States Supreme Court reviews cases in which state procedures are alleged to violate due process, and if the Justices decide this is a matter requiring national uniformity, the Court will enforce "federal minimums" on every state, regardless of the state's own constitutional or judicial position on the issue.

As we saw in Chapter 15 (when we used the Fourteenth Amendment debates as an example of juristic philosophies), the majority rule of the Supreme Court is that Fourteenth Amendment "due process" comprises those rights in the first eight amendments to the federal Constitution that history, governmental practice, and our constitutional ideals show (to the Justices) to be basic to our system of "ordered liberty" in America. Of the procedural rights involved in the Fourth through Eighth Amendments, the Supreme Court has held that some do call for "federal minimums," such as security against unreasonable search and seizure, the right to counsel, and the ban against putting a person twice in jeopardy of life or limb for the same crime. Other provisions, such as the requirement that criminal trials be initiated only by an indictment by grand jury or the right to have trial by jury in all civil cases where more than $20 is involved, have not been held to be essential to "ordered liberty." As a result, these two provisions remain rules only for the federal government. States are free, if they wish, to start criminal trials by the motion of a district attorney heard by a magistrate, or to allow jury trials in civil cases only when more than $500 or $1,000 is at stake.

Thus the Supreme Court's role is not identical in federal and state due process cases. When federal action is involved, the Supreme Court rules on the basis of constitutional clauses setting specific procedures for federal officials. The Justices also act by virtue of the Supreme Court's position as the final authority in the federal judicial system responsible for "maintaining and establishing civilized standards of procedure and evidence," and seeing that "justice is done." When the Supreme Court reviews state action, however, the primary role in setting "civilized standards" lies with the political and judicial authorities of the state, and their acts are entitled to the respect due the separate sovereignty of states in a federal system of government. The United States Supreme Court intervenes to upset state procedures only when the state's action violates fundamental national ideas of fairness, just treatment, and ordered liberty.

While this remains the general theory, it is plain that the Supreme Court has broadened its due process review of state action enormously in the past three to four decades, bringing more and more state law-enforcement activity and hearing procedures under federal minimums. This reflects many factors, such as growing national uniformity and loss of state immunity generally in American society, increased public knowledge of, and concern over, local injustices in police practices and trial methods, and the expanded role of the Supreme Court in the whole civil liberties field.

With these constitutional ground rules in mind, we can divide the law of due process into two main areas: (1) issues relating to criminal control in the judicial arena, including law-enforcement practices that lead up to judicial trials; and (2) issues that relate to legislative and administrative proceedings, especially those we will call "semitrials." This division is made for clarity of analysis and because the different institutional setting usually produces different constitutional rules in the cases. Since bulky treatises have been written on these topics, and hundreds of United States Supreme Court cases have dealt with these problems (with continuing modification and changes of doctrine by the Court), we can only sample some of the basic rules and leading problems here.

DUE PROCESS AND CRIMINAL PROCEDURE

The control of crime by regular law enforcement and judicial trials can be viewed as moving through four consecutive stages: investigation; arrest and detention before trial; trial and appeal; and punishment. In each of these stages, the conflict over due process limits on government has some aspects that have carried over almost unchanged from the time of the Framers and others that are as new as laser-beam eavesdropping and psychiatry.

INVESTIGATION

As fans of "Naked City" and "87th Precinct" know so well, police investigation runs a wide gamut, from tedious week-long shadowing of subjects to spectrographic analysis of dried bloodstains by the police lab. Whenever such investigative activity is held to constitute a "search and seizure," the federal and state constitutions require that police go before a judge in a secret proceeding in advance (if there is time to do so), satisfy the judge that a crime has been or is about to be committed, and specify why a search of a specifically designated place or seizure of a particular thing is necessary to the solution of the crime.

Much police investigative activity has been held not to fall under the heading of "searches and seizures" at all, such as shadowing, looking through a window, photographing premises from outside, and planting informants within gangs or subversive organizations. All of these can be done without

Washington Is Trying To Arrange
Another "Hot Line."

A critical view of Justice Department
proposals to legalize federal wire tapping. The fact that Knox is a strong
conservative in his views underscores
the due process meeting ground of
liberals and conservatives.

Knox in the Nashville *Banner*

getting a warrant. In a 1928 ruling, the Supreme Court held that where
police did not enter the premises, tapping of telephone conversations through
connections farther along the lines did not seize anything tangible or search
in violation of the federal Constitution.[83] This rule has been extended in
recent decades to include listening to room conversations from outside by
sensitive microphone devices and "wiring up" a police agent or informant
with devices to record his conversations with suspects.[84] If police enter the
premises to install their listening or tapping equipment, however, or even
penetrate a wall with a long metal "spike-mike," this constitutes an "entry"
and will be an illegal search and seizure unless done by judicial warrant
under authorized state or federal procedures.[85] Although these rules mean
that there are no *constitutional* bans on electronic eavesdropping from outside, a Congressional statute has been interpreted to forbid the interception
and disclosure of telephone conversations in federal trials,[86] two states have
outlawed all police wire taps and banned wire-tap evidence in state courts,
and six states have placed police telephone tapping or room microphoning
under court-order controls.[87]

Even if an investigative activity is held to be a search and seizure, there
are some situations in which police can act without first obtaining a judicial

[83] *Olmstead* v. *United States,* 277 U.S. 438 (1928).
[84] *On Lee* v. *United States,* 343 U.S. 747 (1952).
[85] *Silverman* v. *United States,* 365 U.S. 505 (1961).
[86] *Nardone* v. *United States,* 302 U.S. 379 (1937).
[87] See Alan F. Westin, "Wiretapping: The Quiet Revolution," *Commentary* (1960), Vol.
XXIX, p. 333.

warrant. The main instances are when a person consents to a search by police, when evidence of crime comes into view of police during the regular patrols (marijuana on the back seat of a parked car), or when the search "is incident to a valid arrest." The last is illustrated at its simplest by police pursuit of bandits who have just held up a drugstore or a quick raid by police on a "floating crap game" in response to an informant's tip. In a 1963 decision, the Supreme Court explained that such searches "on the spot" were proper to prevent the use of weapons, escapes, and the destruction of evidence.[88]

The Supreme Court has also allowed search during arrest (even though a search warrant had not been obtained) when evidence was in plain view of the police or the premises were a one-room office.[89] However, searching a car of persons arrested for vagrancy has been held illegal, since there was time for police to get a search warrant and they neglected to do so.[90]

The reason this problem has given the state and federal courts such trouble (and has produced such conflicting rulings) lies primarily in the nature of police work and the mores of policemen. Partly for reasons of speed and secrecy, partly because they may not have enough facts yet to satisfy a judge as to the crime and to specify what they are seeking to find, and partly because of stubborn unwillingness to follow warrant procedures, many local and state police forces engage in searches without getting warrants. (This happens less often with federal agents, reflecting generally higher standards of professional and ethical conduct in federal law enforcement.) Such searching on suspicion only, bypassing the courts for reasons of convenience, and ignoring constitutional requirements are plainly illegal.

What to do about this continuing misconduct has presented courts with a troublesome dilemma. Decades of experience have shown that private law suits, administrative discipline, or criminal prosecutions of the police for such illegal action are hopeless remedies. Juries do not like to award damages to "criminals" against police officers, and district attorneys or attorneys general do not usually discipline or prosecute their own subordinates when this "overzealous" activity produces solutions to crimes and, often, public applause for catching criminals. Thus, beginning in 1914 for federal proceedings [91] and as a rule of due process for states since 1961,[92] the United States Supreme Court has held that evidence obtained by illegal search and seizure may not be used in criminal trials. Only in this way, the Justices decided, when the police know that they will lose cases resting upon illegally obtained evidence, will police officials be deterred from acting illegally, and police superiors be convinced to teach the constitutional rules to their officers. Letting "the criminal escape" because "the constable blundered" has been criticized by law-enforcement spokesmen as both dangerous and unnecessary, but the Supreme Court—and many students of law enforcement—remain

---

[88] *Ker v. California*, 374 U.S. 23 (1963).

[89] *United States v. Rabinowitz*, 339 U.S. 56 (1950).

[90] *Brinegar v. United States*, 338 U.S. 160 (1949); *Henry v. United States*, 361 U.S. 98 (1959).

[91] *Weeks v. United States*, 232 U.S. 383 (1914).

[92] *Mapp v. Ohio*, 367 U.S. 643 (1961).

convinced that this is the only way to control police misconduct and that the rule presents no serious bar to effective investigations.

DETENTION

Once persons are arrested by the police and "taken down to headquarters," two main issues of fair procedure arise, both growing out of the constitutional guarantee that persons need not give self-incriminating testimony. The first involves coercion of confessions by improper police methods. Use of drugs for narco-analysis or hypnotism of prisoners is forbidden, and lie-detector tests can be administered only with the prisoner's consent (and are not admissible as evidence). Extraction of confessions by any kind of force or threat of harm is outlawed, whether obtained through the crude thud of fist on face or more "subtle" techniques, such as warning a prisoner that the police cannot protect him from the mob outside unless he confesses at once. A 1963 case held it to be unconstitutional to tell a woman that her children would be taken from her by the state if she did not cooperate and confess in a marijuana case.[93] When it is found that confessions have been obtained "involuntarily," they are excluded from federal or state trials as a matter of due process, not only on unreliability grounds but because of the self-incrimination and human-dignity issues at stake. This usually means ordering a new trial when the confession was a central part of the conviction.

Just how much prolonged questioning of a detained prisoner, without any physical torture, will amount to coercion has given the courts difficult problems in boundary-setting. Questioning a man continuously for thirty-six hours by teams of officers has been held improper,[94] as have lesser periods when minors and persons of low mentality were involved.[95] How much time is given for sleep between questioning periods, whether the cell is freezing cold, whether food and cigarettes are provided at reasonable intervals, how long he is held before letting family or friends visit him, and what a prisoner is told about his constitutional rights during the interrogation are all relevant factors to the "total circumstances" affecting coerciveness. Ever since the 1940s, the Supreme Court has openly refused to accept the judgment of the trial jury and the state courts about the "facts" of coercion in state cases and has made an independent study of the trial record to determine "voluntariness" and due process.

The second main issue arising during detention is that of "timely arraignment." After a person is arrested, federal and state statutes generally provide that he must be brought "without unreasonable delay" before a judicial official, who holds a hearing on the probable cause for detention, informs the prisoner of his constitutional rights (primarily to remain silent and refuse to answer questions and to obtain a lawyer), and decides whether to return the prisoner to jail or release him on bail until the trial. Police feel that the hours of questioning before arraignment are vital to their investigative work; guilty persons are more likely to reveal inconsistencies, give

---

[93] *Lynumn* v. *Illinois,* 372 U.S. 528 (1963).
[94] *Ashcraft* v. *Tennessee,* 322 U.S. 143 (1942).
[95] *Fikes* v. *Alabama,* 352 U.S. 191 (1957).

leads, and make confessions before they appear at a judicial hearing than when they return to their cells, and the ability to question for a reasonable time before having to charge him formally often leads police to conclude that a detained suspect is not guilty and to let him go free. Critics of police delay in arraignment point out that most persons arrested for crime do not know of their constitutional rights to silence and counsel, and are deeply intimidated by the fact of detention and the physical presence of police interrogators; therefore, anything more than a few hours of questioning before arraignment becomes coercive. In a leading 1957 case,[96] the Supreme Court overturned the rape conviction of a District of Columbia Negro man who had been held and questioned for seven and one-half hours before the police attempted to go before a federal commissioner. The test is not any precise number of hours or minutes, said the Court, but the circumstances under which the police delay. If there are no special problems, such as locating a judge or checking out a readily ascertainable and key fact asserted by the prisoner, delays of the seven-and-one-half-hour variety will make confessions obtained by police during this period inadmissible. Federal legislation has been debated to define "reasonable delay," or to make confessions admissible in federal courts despite delay, but none had been passed by 1964. In some states, however, the late 1950s and early 1960s witnessed the passage of statutes prescribing a set number of hours for speedy arraignments unless special circumstances were present.

TRIAL AND APPEAL

Due process provides a code of working rules for virtually every aspect of criminal trials and appeals, from the way in which the trial is initiated (by indictment of a grand jury or on a finding of "probable cause" by a magistrate) to the procedures for asking a state supreme court or the United States Supreme Court to reconsider its "final" ruling once again. In brief outline, defendants in the federal and state courts enjoy the "due process rights" to have a definite charge lodged against them, a speedy and public trial, legal counsel for the defense, the right to be present at the trial, to compel witnesses to appear, to cross-examine hostile witnesses, to refuse to testify at all themselves, to be tried by an impartial jury and judge in a courtroom atmosphere free from intimidation or terror, to be presumed innocent until proved guilty beyond a reasonable doubt, and to appeal to higher courts to correct errors of fact-finding or law made at the trial. We can sample two of these basic "trial rights"—the assistance of counsel and an "impartial" jury—to observe the conflicting values involved and the judicial choices at work.

The right to counsel illustrates the capacity for growth in due process standards as American society has changed its notions of what constitutes fundamental fairness in criminal procedure. Before 1938, the Sixth Amendment's provision that the accused was entitled to "the assistance of counsel for his defense" had been held to require court appointment of a lawyer in federal trials for defendants without funds only in capital (death penalty) cases. In 1938, the Supreme Court held that counsel must be present

---

[96] *Mallory v. United States,* 354 U.S. 449 (1957).

(unless intelligently waived by the accused) "in all criminal proceedings" in the federal courts.[97] Before 1963, defense counsel was required in state trials (under Fourteenth Amendment due process) only when certain factors were present making counsel seem to the Justices to be essential to fairness, such as a capital case, where the defendant was young or illiterate, or where the legal issues were so complicated that a layman could not be expected to protect his interests intelligently.[98] This selective process was heavily criticized as inadequate in its understanding of what denial of counsel, for economic reasons, meant to any defendant in a criminal trial. Then, in 1963, the Supreme Court decided that counsel was constitutionally required for defendants in all state criminal cases.[99] "[R]eason and reflection require us to recognize," the Court's unanimous opinion explained, "that in our adversary system of criminal justice, any person hauled into court, who is too poor to hire a lawyer, cannot be assured a fair trial unless counsel is provided for him." Today, a combination of privately supported legal aid societies, "public defender" organizations, and court-appointed lawyers provide counsel for indigent defendants. There are proposals in Congress and many states, however, to make the provision of lawyers for indigent defendants a public responsibility paid for by public funds as part of the costs of providing justice.

What constitutes an "impartial" jury illustrates the problems of practicality and democratic theory raised by due process trial rules. Jury trial in the federal system requires a panel of twelve persons, supervision of the proceedings by a judge, and a unanimous verdict. These elements have not been held to be so vital to fundamental fairness that the states must duplicate them, as we have noted, and states are free to have less than twelve on a jury or to use majority verdicts in noncapital cases. While prospective jurors can be challenged for any actual bias they have, "impartiality" has not been held to be violated when employees of the government that is bringing the prosecution serve on the jury.[100] This ruling rejected the argument that federal employees in the District of Columbia, who make up most of the federal jurors, would not be free to acquit defendants in Communist trials because of the federal loyalty-security programs and fear of their job futures.

The most active due process issue in the jury area today involves the classic Anglo-American concept that the accused is entitled to be tried by a jury representing a "cross-section" of the community. Deliberate exclusion of women, manual workers, Negroes, or Mexican-Americans from the federal or state jury lists is clearly unconstitutional. But the Supreme Court has refused to say that strict proportional representation of groups in the community is constitutionally required. Under this doctrine, New York's "blue ribbon juries" which favor college graduates, businessmen, and club members in the selection process have been upheld over protests that

---

[97] *Johnson v. Zerbst,* 304 U.S. 458 (1938).
[98] See *Powell v. Alabama,* 287 U.S. 45 (1932); *Betts v. Brady,* 316 U.S. 455 (1942); *Crooker v. California,* 357 U.S. 433 (1958).
[99] *Gideon v. Wainwright,* 372 U.S. 335 (1963).
[100] *Dennis v. United States,* 339 U.S. 162 (1950).

"persons of the upper economic and social stratum" have a greater tendency to convict persons accused of crime than a truly cross-sectional jury.[101] In addition, the mere absence of Negroes or Catholics on a given jury in a community where that group makes up 10 or even 50 percent of the population does not make the conviction of a Negro or a Catholic defendant invalid.[102] Proof of an intention to exclude and of machinery to accomplish this purpose must be provided.

PUNISHMENT

The Constitution does not state the philosophical reason underlying punishment of criminals in America—whether deterrence, vengeance, rehabilitation, release of community tension, or some mixture of these elements. The Eighth Amendment does say that "cruel and unusual punishments" may not be inflicted, and this has been held to outlaw torture, the wearing of heavy chains on hands and feet during prison terms, and deliberately slow execution. Whipping of prisoners has never been held to be "cruel and unusual" by the Supreme Court, however, primarily because it was quite common when the Constitution was written; only one state, Delaware, still allows it. Execution by new methods such as gas or electrocution has been upheld, and the death penalty itself is constitutional, though it has been abolished by legislation in nine states. In one tragically bizarre case,[103] the Supreme Court allowed a second electrocution for a condemned prisoner after the first electrocution effort by the state had failed because of inadequate current; the second execution was held not to be a cruel and unusual punishment. Recently, the Supreme Court applied the cruel and unusual punishment standard to strike down a federal statute taking away the citizenship of military personnel convicted by court-martial of wartime desertion.[104] Denationalization, said the Court's opinion, constitutes "the total destruction of the individual's status in organized society. It is a form of punishment more primitive than torture, for it destroys for the individual the political existence that was centuries in the development."

The idea of punishment is also the dividing line between those governmental proceedings that must satisfy every command of due process and those that need not live up to such high standards.

DUE PROCESS AND SEMITRIALS

In criminal trials, determining the guilt or innocence of a defendant is the central purpose of the affair. As the titles of criminal cases indicate— *United States* v. *Leonard Lightfingers* or *The State of California* v. *Watery Cellars Construction Company*—these are clearly adversary proceedings, with "government" arrayed on one side and private parties on the other. The pace of trial and appeal is deliberately slow, in keeping with the official branding of persons as criminals and the infliction of punishment, and when the moment comes for final decision, presumptions of inno-

---

101 *Fay* v. *New York,* 332 U.S. 261 (1947).
102 *Brown* v. *Allen,* 344 U.S. 443 (1953).
103 *Louisiana ex. rel. Francis* v. *Resweber,* 329 U.S. 459 (1947).
104 *Trop* v. *Dulles,* 356 U.S. 86 (1958).

cence are deliberately placed on the defendant's side of the scale. In all of this, as noted already, the rules of due process are designed primarily to find truth, protect human dignity, and limit government power.

In what we call "semitrials"—certain types of proceedings conducted by executive and legislative agencies—most of the key characteristics of criminal proceedings are absent, or at least are greatly modified. The purposes will be of a general executive or legislative nature—to protect government secrets and policy-making processes from foreign agents (in employee loyalty-security hearings held by executive agencies), or to remove undesirable aliens from the country (in deportation hearings), or to collect, evaluate, and publicize facts that may require legislative action (in legislative committee hearings). When a state public service commission decides not to renew a bus company's franchise to serve a particular route, or the Federal Communications Commission does not renew a radio station's license because of "off-color" programming by its leading disc jockey, the protection of the public from faulty service or offensive broadcasting is the prime concern. Yet, to accomplish the governmental purposes involved in each of these examples, government agencies often find themselves having to probe "guilt" or "innocence"—secure the facts, examine motives, choose between conflicting accounts of witnesses, and make "findings" of responsibility in a procedure resembling the judicial trial. And when these executive and legislative agencies take action, the results are often quite severe for individuals or organizations—dismissing government employees with the stigma of "disloyalty" on their records, deporting persons who may have lived in the United States for many years and have businesses and families here, forcing witnesses (by subpoena) to testify at legislative investigations and expose their activities to widespread public view, or ending a franchise on which the holder may have spent great sums of money (and which may be worth millions of dollars).

Because semitrials do not formally determine "guilt" in the criminal sense, and do not impose the kind of punishment that the courts require to set the alarm bell of full due process ringing, the Supreme Court has held that semitrials need only be "fair" hearings. What constitutes "fairness" will vary with each type of situation.

Disputes have involved such due process types of problems as whether there must be a definite and supported "charge," whether there is the right to confront hostile witnesses and cross-examine them; what rules of permissible evidence will be followed; and whether there should be "presumptions of innocence" and "burdens of proof." How these rules of fairness have been applied in semitrials can be seen by sampling two leading areas of controversy: deportation proceedings and passport hearings.

In the leading Supreme Court case on deportation, an 1893 decision,[105] the Justices held that the federal government's right to expel foreigners living in the United States who had not become citizens through naturalization "is as absolute and unqualified as the right to prohibit . . . their entrance into the country." Deportation is "not a punishment for crime," however, and neither Congress' rules governing deportation nor the pro-

---

[105] *Fong Yue Ting* v. *United States*, 149 U.S. 698 (1893).

ceedings held by officers of the Immigration Service are subject to the due process limitations of criminal trials.[106] While the ex post facto clause forbids "punishment" in criminal trials based on activity that was lawful when done and had ended before the statute proscribed it, an alien who joined the Communist party in New York in 1922, when it was a lawful party and not mentioned in the immigration laws, can now be deported under a 1950 statute retroactively specifying such past membership as grounds for deportation.[107] In addition, while criminal due process requires that a person have "knowing" membership in an organization that is now held to be illegal or subversive, aliens can be deported even for "innocent" membership in the Communist party.[108] This applies to persons who joined without really knowing of the Communist party's doctrines about overthrowing the government and then left when they realized its policies. In addition, aliens may be held without bail throughout the hearings on deportation, in contrast to the "right to bail" that usually exists in criminal cases.[109] As for the hearings themselves, secret evidence from informers or government undercover agents can be relied on by the deportation examiners, and there is no right to cross-examine even the witnesses who appear openly.[110] The agency's decision does not have to be convincing "beyond a reasonable doubt," but only has to be based on "substantial evidence" in the record.[111]

However, the seriousness of deportations has led the Court to say that a "fair hearing" is required. This has been interpreted to mean that "hearsay" evidence may not be used and "vague" charges will not be tolerated.[112] The Immigration Service must follow its own rules of procedure, and failure to do so will violate the rights of the alien. And any person held for deportation who claims that he is really a citizen (through birth, marriage, naturalization, etc.) is entitled to a regular trial in the courts on this issue.[113]

As this capsule summary shows, aliens do not get full due process, but they receive what the courts hold to be elements of a fair hearing. In a 1952 decision,[114] the Supreme Court said that if the question of deportation's really being "punishment" were a new one, the issue might be decided differently. But on the basis of more than fifty years of court decisions, Congressional statutes, and executive branch practice, the Justices considered the issue too well settled to be reopened. There are signs that it may be reopened in the late 1960s, however, especially since the Supreme Court has just held the related act of denaturalization to be a cruel and unusual punishment that Congress could not impose without a judicial trial, even for wartime desertion by servicemen.[115]

Passport hearings provide a second illustration of fairness in semitrials.

---

106 *Ibid.*
107 *Harisiades* v. *Shaughnessy.*
108 *Galvan* v. *Press.*
109 *Carlson* v. *Landon,* 342 U.S. 524 (1952).
110 *Jay* v. *Boyd,* 351 U.S. 345 (1956).
111 *Carlson* v. *Landon.*
112 *Jordan* v. *DeGeorge,* 341 U.S. 223 (1951).
113 *Ng Fung Ho* v. *White,* 259 U.S. 276 (1922).
114 *Harisiades* v. *Shaughnessy.*
115 *Kennedy* v. *Martinez,* 372 U.S. 144 (1963).

Today, passports are checked as Americans leave the United States to travel abroad, and countries of destination generally refuse admission to persons who do not bear a valid passport from their "home" country. During the 1940s and 1950s, the Department of State, which has charge of issuing passports under Congressional statutes, refused passports to persons who were Communists, on the grounds that their travel would advance the Communist movement and be "prejudicial to the interests of the United States." Many persons who flatly denied that they were Communists had their passports held up or denied. No hearings were held, no specifications of charges were given, and the basis of the State Department's judgments was not disclosed to the applicants. Of course this meant no confrontation of accusers or cross-examination. After growing public criticism of this practice, the Supreme Court held in 1958 that Congress had not authorized denials of passports for anything other than unlawful conduct or lack of citizenship.[116] In so reading Congressional intent, the Court was guided by the desire not to impute unconstitutional acts to the Congress, since "the right to travel is a part of the 'liberty' of which the citizen cannot be deprived without the due process of law of the Fifth Amendment. . . ."

Having placed its decision striking down the State Department's pre–1958 practice on a lack of Congressional authorization, the Court did not have to say what kind of passport hearing *would* satisfy due process. But the State Department caught the warning message, and dropped from its passport application forms any questions about Communist party membership, present or past. In addition, passports were issued to persons such as Paul Robeson, Corliss Lamont, and Rockwell Kent, who had been consistently denied passports in earlier years because of alleged Communist connections. Following the Supreme Court decision in 1961 upholding the constitutionality of the McCarran Act,[117] which includes a provision making it a crime for a member of a party found to be Communist to apply for a passport, the State Department restored a question about present Communist party membership to its passport forms. Meanwhile, lower federal court rulings have held that before a passport can be denied, a "quasi-judicial" hearing is required, with notice and a full proceeding, and that undisclosed confidential information cannot be used as a basis for the examiner's judgment.[118] Whether all these lower court rulings will be accepted by the Supreme Court remains to be seen, but the requirement of clear standards and a full hearing are likely to be declared constitutional minimums for passport decisions if the Court does reach the issue soon.

DUE PROCESS IN THE NONGOVERNMENTAL SECTOR

So far, we have discussed due process solely in terms of the duties of government toward those affected by official action. However, procedural due process within the crucial "private governments" of American society has become an important issue of public concern in recent decades. Must

---

[116] *Kent v. Dulles.*

[117] *Communist Party v. Subversive Activities Control Board.*

[118] See *Bauer v. Acheson,* 106 F. Supp. 445 (1952); *Dulles v. Nathan,* 225 F. 2d. 29 (1955); *Boudin v. Dulles,* 136 F. Supp. 218 (1955).

Gusher Oil Company give a statement of charges, a hearing, and an appeal to an employee (whether clerk or executive) who is going to be fired or disciplined? If expulsion from the Metal Benders' Union for "opposing the best interest of the union" will mean that someone will lose his job with that company or in the whole industry, because there is a "closed shop" contract providing that only union members can work, must the union give notice, hearing, and appeal also? Under pressure from government investigations, from the corporate personnel and union members themselves; as a result of "good communication" theories within management and union bureaucracies; and to provide a benign "public image," there is a growing trend within companies and unions to install due process and make it meaningful. General Motors, for example, uses a retired federal judge to hear and decide all cases of appeals by GM dealers whose franchises have been terminated by the company for any reason, and the review-decision of the judge is binding upon the company. The United Automobile Workers created a Board of Public Review, composed of a group of outstanding civic and religious leaders, who provide a similar appeal process for disciplinary actions taken against any union member that the member feels to be unjust. While such systems have been initiated in quite a few companies and unions, there are many observers who feel that safeguards must be legislated if real due process is to be given. The Labor-Management Act of 1959 (known as the Landrum-Griffin Act) included in its "Bill of Rights" provisions for unions a complete system of appeals to government agencies and the courts against arbitrary union action against members. The "Dealer's Day in Court" Law of 1957 gave auto dealers a right to sue in federal court to test the reasonableness of franchise terminations. Increasingly, this area will occupy the attention of civic leaders as provision for fair hearings within private groups comes to be regarded as a critical issue for American democracy in the age of large organizations.

DUE PROCESS: THE MEETING GROUND
FOR LIBERALS AND CONSERVATIVES

Earlier in this chapter, in discussing the conflict between "liberty-firsters" and "property-firsters" over the primacy of Lockian principles, we said that due process, or justice, may well be the connecting point of agreement between the two warring camps. In studies of the development of due process concepts during the past decades, it is interesting to note that interest groups that usually agree on very little of substance often stand together in defending due process. When the Supreme Court has condemned illegal searches and seizures, the liberal weeklies and civil liberties organizations have been joined by the *Wall Street Journal* in their hurrahs for the Court. When more due process rights were held essential for federal loyalty-security hearings, conservatives from the American Bar Association stood beside leaders of Americans for Democratic Action and the American Civil Liberties Union in voicing approval. The basic reason is that the due process rules enunciated in "Communist cases" or "racketeer cases" are precedents for antitrust cases as well, and the procedures set for witnesses called before "anti-Communist" investigating committees will be guidelines for hearings on drug companies, missile manufacturers, labor unions, private foundations, civil rights groups, and university professors. Sometimes, of course, the deep commitment of liberals to "exposing the military-industrial complex" or of conservatives to "penetrating the labor conspiracy" or "the pro-Communists in government" will lead members of these groups to argue that full due process is not needed in "semitrials" or that the rules of due process should be softened in criminal proceedings. But the basic trend over time has been for due process to receive a fairly high bipartisan and bi-ideological support in America, despite occasional public hostility against the rules when these interfere with the speedy apprehension and conviction of especially detested offenders.

19 / Civil Rights: Equality and Citizenship in a Free Society

In the fourth century B.C., Aristotle concluded that the most important cause of revolutions in the state was the struggle over equality. Those held in inferior status press for treatment comparable to that of the privileged groups. Those in privileged positions defend their advantages on the basis of "superior qualities" or historical claims. Such equality struggles may involve the ultimate issue of slavery and freedom, or more "mediate" issues of economic, religious, racial, political, or sex equality. Sometimes the conflict may lie dormant, or smolder quietly; then, often unexpectedly, it can erupt and shake the state to its foundation.

When Americans wrote the Declaration of Independence in 1776, they proclaimed the new nation "dedicated to the proposition that all men are created equal. . . ." Throughout the nineteenth century, American egalitarianism was so complete and "radical" that it stood as the despair of European conservatives and a polestar for subject nationalities everywhere. Yet even then, the United States had allowed a double standard to penetrate its equality tradition—providing one law for whites and quite different laws for blacks—that had been noted by Alexis de Tocqueville in 1835, had been at the root of the American Civil War, and was to stain the law, politics, and social culture of the American nation down to the middle of the twentieth century. Only today, in our generation, has the double standard been repudiated and the promise of the Declaration of Independence redeemed.

To explore this central issue of American government and politics, we begin by noting briefly how equality issues become matters of government responsibility and action; then we trace the important lines of historical development of our equality rules and practices; and finally, we survey the key civil rights issues of the late 1960s.

Equality issues become matters of governmental action in two major ways. First, governments define in constitutional clauses, laws, administrative regulations, and court decisions those who are entitled to enjoy various rights and privileges within the nation or a state, and on what terms. Federal provisions specify, for example, who can be a citizen of the United States, who can serve on federal juries, who can be elected President or Congressman, who qualifies for a National Defense Education Act scholarship, or who can secure a passport to travel abroad. State provisions determine who can vote in Tennessee, be a judge in Wisconsin, practice pharmacy in Maine, or qualify for unemployment compensation in Oregon. All of these government acts involve matters of classification through law, the including and excluding of categories of people and the setting of various qualifications for the exercise of rights. Many other public laws involve equality judgments. Every taxing statute distinguishes between types of taxpayers in matters of rate structure, deductions, and exemptions. Every zoning law elevates one type of business activity, or building style, or civic use over competing interests. Eighteen-year-old males are called up for military service with the United States but seventeen-year-old boys are not, and the huskiest twenty-year-old girl will have to volunteer if she wants to be in the nation's armed forces. In these and countless other regulations, government sets up distinctions, and the equality issue raised in each instance is whether the classification is fair and reasonable or whether it embodies distinctions that are legally improper.

The second way that government enters the equality struggle is by setting minimum equality standards in the "private" sector. When powerful private groups engage in practices that have a direct effect on the public economic, social, or political well-being, government often steps in to mediate or even to control these activities. The hiring and promotion policies of corporations, the admission practices of labor unions, the selection standards of private colleges and universities, the practices of real estate brokers and rental agents, and the guest policies of public-service facilities such as railroads, restaurants, hotels, theaters, and buses are all illustrations of "private" activities that have come under government equality regulation because the policies of these private agencies affect public well-being. Local and state authorities traditionally intervene under their constitutional power to protect the health, safety, morals, and public order of their communities, and under their powers to set standards for corporations and associations chartered by the state. The federal government has drawn its primary authority in this area from the effect of private activities on interstate commerce, interstate travel, the national armed forces, federally financed or federally aided programs, and the specific provisions of the federal Constitution declaring citizen's rights.

Of course, equality problems may arise in the private sphere for which government has not, as yet, intervened to set equality minimums. The local tennis club, county medical society, garden club, sorority, businessman's luncheon club, and veterans' organization are examples of groups that typically set up membership standards which include some groups and exclude others. If those standards include racial and religious bars or quotas, these are often debated vigorously today, within such groups and in their communities, but government has not intervened here as with labor unions or theater owners. How quickly the policy of government "minimums" is pressing toward these remaining areas will be discussed in the last part of this chapter.

Equality in the American Tradition, 1781–1963: The Rise and Fall of the Double Standard

To trace the American tradition of equality in all its powerful achievements and "special exceptions," we will divide our national experience into three primary periods: 1781–1863, the era of white egalitarianism and Negro slavery; 1863–1941, the era when the double standard was grafted onto the American system despite universal freedom; and 1941–63, the era when the double standard for white and black was finally rejected by American law, politics, and civic opinion.[1] Throughout this survey, we will be contrasting American equality practices on matters of religion, nationality, sex, and sometimes property, with those that have dealt with race (which we use to include the term "color"). As we will see, some of the subject arenas of these equality conflicts arose early in the life of the American Republic and have persisted as prime battlefields, such as equality in citizenship, voting, public accommodations, and the administration of justice. Other equality issues arose later in our history, such as equality in the military services or in public education (largely a post-Civil War phenomenon, when public education systems were developed). Still other issues, such as equality in employment and housing, are even more recent additions to the equality agenda. Obviously, we should note, only the major developments in this 187-year history can be compressed into our survey of American equality practices, but only with such a survey of basic trends can the civil rights issues facing American government in the late 1960s be adequately understood.

EQUALITY IN THE YOUNG REPUBLIC: OF FREE MEN AND SLAVES, 1781–1863

The American people who made up the young Republic in 1781 were for the most part white, of English and Northwest European nationality and stock, and 90 percent Protestant in religious identification. Estimates are that, apart from Indians, there were three and a quarter million Americans in 1781, of whom two million were free persons, 600,000 Negro slaves, 300,000 indentured servants, 250,000 debtors and vagrants being held to "involuntary labor," and 50,000 convicts shipped to the colonies by Great Britain.

Based on this population, the leaders of the American states defined their ideas of equality in four major documents of national constitutionalism before the Civil War: the Declaration of Independence, the Articles of Confederation, the Federal Constitution, and the federal Bill of Rights, and in the various state constitutions and bills of rights as well.

---

[1] For excellent works on the equality theme in United States history, see Gunnar Myrdal, *An American Dilemma* (New York, 1944); C. Vann Woodward, *The Strange Career of Jim Crow* (New York, 1957); Robert J. Harris, *The Quest for Equality* (Baton Rouge, 1960); Dwight L. Dumond, *Antislavery: The Crusade for Freedom in America* (Ann Arbor, 1961); Horace Flack, *The Adoption of the Fourteenth Amendment* (Baltimore, 1908); John Hope Franklin, *From Slavery to Freedom: A History of American Negroes*, 2nd ed. (New York, 1956); Milton Konvitz, *A Century of Civil Rights* (New York, 1961).

The most famous and comprehensive statement of the American ideal of equality came in the Declaration of Independence. "We hold these truths to be self-evident," the colonists stated in 1776, "that all men are created equal, that they are endowed by their Creator with certain unalienable Rights, that among these are Life, Liberty, and the pursuit of Happiness. That to secure these rights Governments are instituted among Men, deriving their just powers from the consent of the governed." Drawn from a stream of political thought that flowed from the Greek Stoics, Roman law, Christianity, feudal institutions, English philosophers such as Richard Hooker and John Locke, colonial compacts, and the ideas of colonial leaders such as Roger Williams, George Mason, and Thomas Jefferson, the Declaration reflected two central aspects of the American tradition of equality: first, the equality of men in the sight of their Creator and the eyes of the law and, second, the duty of government to protect persons in their inalienable rights.

These principles were expressed in many of the state constitutions and bills of rights in the period between 1776 and the adoption of the Articles of Confederation in 1781. Virginia's Bill of Rights (1776) declared "That all men are by nature equally free and independent . . ." and the Massachusetts Declaration of Rights of 1780 used almost identical language. These declarations were made operative parts of the Virginia and Massachusetts constitutions, and in the famous *Quock Walker* case of 1783, the Supreme Judicial Court of Massachusetts held slavery to be illegal in that Commonwealth, on the basis of the equality guarantee. Chief Justice Cushing's opinion declared:

> [Slavery] has been a usage—a usage which took its origin from the practice of some of the European nations, and the regulations of British government respecting the then Colonies, for the benefit of trade and wealth. But whatever sentiments have formerly prevailed in this particular or slid in upon us by the example of others, a different idea has taken place with the people of America, more favorable to the natural rights of mankind, and to that natural, innate desire of Liberty, which with Heaven (without regard to color, complexion, or shape of noses-features) has inspired all the human race. And upon this ground or Constitution of Government, by which the people of this Commonwealth have solemnly bound themselves, sets out with declaring that all men are born free and equal—and that every subject is entitled to liberty, and to have it guarded by the laws, as well as life and property—and in short is totally repugnant to the idea of being born slaves. This being the case . . . there can be no such thing as perpetual servitude of a rational creature, unless his liberty is forfeited by some criminal conduct or given up by personal consent or contract . . . .[2]

This was not the interpretation that Virginia, with one third of the slaves in the new Republic, put on her declaration of equality. While many of

---

[2] The ruling was issued officially but was not published in 1783. An abstract of the text was incorporated in an opinion of the Supreme Judicial Court of Massachusetts in 1874 and can be found in Henry S. Commager, *Documents of American History*, 5th ed. (New York, 1949), p. 110.

the leading Virginians deplored slavery, among them Washington, Madison, and Jefferson, these emancipationists expected slavery to die out gradually as an uneconomical and illiberal system. Hopefully, this would be enforced by state law when the time was right, but as of the 1780s, none of the slaveholding states followed Massachusetts' example in the *Quock Walker* case.

When the national union was being constructed, through the Articles of Confederation and the federal Constitution, the issue of slavery was one that threatened to prevent agreement between South and North. The "solution" that saved the day was that the American Framers simply remained silent in our national charters about the standard of equality of the Declaration of Independence and the state bills of rights. Thus, the word "equality" does not appear in any reference to persons in the Articles, the Constitution, or the federal Bill of Rights. Instead, a clear distinction was enunciated between free persons and those not free. The Articles of Confederation provided that the privileges and immunities of "free citizenship" in each state were available to the "free inhabitants of each of these States, paupers, vagabonds, and fugitives from Justice excepted . . ." The federal Constitution provided a status in our law for "all other persons" not "free" in the three-fifths compromise for taxation and representation, in the clause barring federal interference with "importation of persons" before 1808, and in the requirement that persons "held to service or labour" must be "delivered up" if they escaped to other states.

Thus, the principles of equality of the "declaratory" Declaration of Independence were not carried into the three "operative charters" in the formative period of the new Republic; the antislavery spirit that many American leaders attached to the independence struggle was thus not registered in fundamental law. To see specifically how equality law in America divided into two separate streams, one for the white and one for the black, we turn to several main areas of equality conflict from 1781 to 1863.

Admission to citizenship in the young republic

Between 1781 and the 1860s, the population of the United States went from slightly over three million to more than thirty-one million. The federal Constitution provided that those who were granted citizenship by a state automatically became "citizens of the United States," and this meant, in practice, that all "free whites" in the new Republic became citizens. As for new immigrants, a Congressional act in 1790 provided that any "free white person" who resided in the United States for five years could become a "naturalized" citizen by asking to have citizenship status conferred on him by a proceeding in either the federal or state courts.

The single example of restriction of equality for white immigrants in this period was the Alien and Naturalization Acts of 1798. Passed by the Federalists out of hostility to the liberal French *émigrés* who fled to the United States during the 1790s and became leading (some would say "incendiary") Jeffersonian-Republicans, the Alien Act gave the President power to expel "undesirable aliens" by executive order, while the Naturalization Act increased from five to fourteen years the period required for residence before acquiring citizenship. President Adams never expelled any aliens, and the entire legislation was repealed in 1801 by the Jeffersonian-controlled Congress. Throughout the remainder of this period, no restrictions—political, religious, racial, country-of-origin, personal factors, or any others—were imposed on free immigration and naturalization.

The great controversy over citizenship in this period involved the status of the free Negro. By the early 1800s almost 100,000 Negroes had been freed by their owners, had purchased their freedom, or had simply escaped to the North and were living in Northern and Western communities. They paid taxes, were allowed to vote (at least for a time, as we will discuss later), and even held public offices in some Northern states. Whether they were citizens of the United States, however, was hotly argued by pro- and anti-Negro forces. The crucial test came in 1857, in the famous *Dred Scott* case.[3] Scott, a slave, had been taken by his owner from the slave state of Missouri into territory that had been declared to be free land by the Congressional act of 1820 known as the Missouri Compromise. Scott sued in federal district court, claiming that by his presence in free territory he had become a free man. In the part of its decision relevant to our discussion here, the Supreme Court held that Scott could not maintain his suit in federal court since no Negro, free or slave, could become a citizen of the United States. Chief Justice Roger Taney based this conclusion on the various clauses in the federal Constitution indicating that slavery was a lawful institution in those states approving it, and that Negroes were not intended to be citizens. Thus they "had no rights which the white man was bound to respect." After this decision, no state could constitutionally confer the status of national citizen on the Negro, unless, Taney noted, a constitutional amendment was enacted to alter the Constitution. One civil war later, this was exactly what the nation did.

Voting and equality

Out of two million free Americans in 1781, only 120,000 were voters. This small number was a result of the qualifications set for voting by the states under the prevailing theory that suffrage was not a right of citizenship but a privilege conferred on those persons who met certain high standards. Generally, these standards restricted the suffrage to males (though women had voted for a time in Massachusetts and New Jersey) over twenty-one years of age, residing in the voting district, and having certain property "minimums" to guarantee a "stake in society." The latter usually meant ownership of land or of a considerable income from property. Earlier restrictions on voting that many of the colonies had placed on Catholics, Jews, Quakers, debtors, and others were either dropped by the state constitutions in the 1780s or else became "dead letters" until formally repealed at later dates.

The first wave of suffrage reform came between 1780 and 1800, when six of the thirteen original states either abolished the economic qualification entirely or limited it to payment of taxes. By the 1820s, nine newly admitted states had no economic qualification and three others set only taxpaying requirements. Following the wave of "popular democracy" ideas

---

[3] *Dred Scott v. Sandford,* 60 U.S. 393 (1857).

spread by the Jacksonian movement, property-holding qualifications were wholly abandoned in the states (by 1852) and only seven states continued taxpaying requirements. By the late 1850s, the only "stake in society" required for voting by a white adult male residing in the state was enough concern with the problems of government to go to the polls on Election Day.

Again, the line between white and black was drawn sharply. When the number of free Negroes in Northern states was relatively few, Negroes were allowed to vote, and many did so in New York, Pennsylvania, Maryland, and North Carolina during the period from 1776 to the 1790s. In the period between 1800 and 1830, however, free Negroes were gradually denied the franchise by constitutional change in every state except the New England ones. In New York after 1823, for example, Negroes had to meet a special $250 property-ownership qualification and a three-year residence requirement that did not apply to whites. By the Civil War, America's 500,000 free Negroes were disfranchised in all but a few states.

Equal administration of justice

By the term "administration of justice," we mean the treatment that members of minority groups receive from the police and courts, as well as the protection public authorities give to minority group members who may be threatened by public violence. The years from 1825 to 1855 have been called the "time of the mob" in American history because of the widespread riots, whippings, tarrings and featherings, beatings, destruction of property, and expulsion from communities that crowds of the citizenry inflicted upon groups that incurred their ire. The chief victims of this mob action in communities throughout the nation were (1) Irish and German Catholics, who were feared as economic competitors by many "old-stock" working-men and were hated by some for their divergent religious and social mores; (2) the Mormons, who were viewed as dangerous because of their religious doctrines, their land-holding policies, and their antislavery sentiments; (3) the Masonic Order, which was denounced as a secret society plotting to overthrow the Republic; and (4) the Abolitionists, who were mistreated in the North as well as the South for their ideas about forcibly ending slavery. Many local elected authorities and small militia forces of this period were unable or unwilling to control mob action against groups that stood for principles repugnant to community morality; there were also major political movements in the 1840s (the Native-American party) and the 1850s (the Know-Nothings) that openly advocated both legal and "direct-action" measures against "aliens, Masons, Papists, and foreigners." In addition, mob violence was often taken against the communities of free Negroes living in the North and Middle Atlantic States, in actions ranging from burning of Negro churches and schools to expulsion of entire Negro populations from cities.

This widespread use of street fighting and violence, in direct disregard of the legal rights of victimized groups to hold their own views, underscores an important aspect of the problem of equality, that formal rights can be valueless if government does not use its authority to enforce legal guarantees against physical violence and threats by angry majorities.

(Unfortunately, the mob actions of 1825–55 have had a continuing history that stretches down to the present day.)

Looking back over the period of 1781–1863 as a whole, we see clearly the emergence of the two major trends that have marked the tradition of equality in the United States. First was a steadily widening practice of equal treatment for religious and nationality groups, and the abolition of economic and party distinctions in the enjoyment of citizenship rights. The second was a contrary tradition of unequal treatment and second-class citizenship for Negroes, not only by holding Negroes as slaves in the South but also by the treatment given them when they became free men and women in most of the Northern states. The double standard had been born, and a nation went to civil war with the crisis between slavery and freedom at the heart of the conflict.

THE DOUBLE STANDARD ENSHRINED, 1863–1941

The first two decades after the Civil War saw major expansions of the constitutional guarantees of equality in America. While the Emancipation Proclamation of 1863 declared slaves in the seceding states to be free, it was the Thirteenth Amendment in 1865, outlawing slavery anywhere in the United States, that guaranteed what the Supreme Court called "universal civil freedom" for every American. Outlawing slavery was only a beginning, however, and the antislavery Republican party leaders who held national authority after the Civil War went well beyond emancipation. The heart of their efforts was the Fourteenth Amendment, adopted in 1868. Section 1 of this Amendment declared:

> All persons born or naturalized in the United States, and subject to the jurisdiction thereof, are citizens of the United States and of the State wherein they reside. No state shall make or enforce any law which shall abridge the privileges or immunities of citizens of the United States; nor shall any State deprive any person of life, liberty, or property, without due process of law; nor deny to any person within its jurisdiction the equal protection of the laws.

In the minds of most of its Framers and of the state conventions that ratified it, this amendment was intended to work a major change in the relationship of national to state power. It clearly overturned the rule of the *Dred Scott* case, so that every person born in the United States, white or black, was entitled to exercise all the privileges and immunities of national citizenship equally with any other citizen. The guarantee that life, liberty, and property should not be taken from any person without due process of law was made a national rule binding on state governments. Finally, the Fourteenth Amendment gathered up the equality ideal of the Declaration of Independence and made "equal protection of the laws" a command for every state to obey. In a separate amendment, the Fifteenth, ratified in 1870, the Republicans completed their constitutional work by providing that the right to vote could not be abridged by either the federal or state governments "on account of race, color, or previous condition of servitude."

NEGROE KILLED.
SEYMOUR RATIFICATION
KKK

One Vote Less

A Nast cartoon of 1868 shows a murdered Negro in Richmond. Notice the "KKK" on the wall.

Thomas Nast in *Harper's Weekly*

Each of these Civil War Amendments provided that Congress should have power to enforce their provisions by appropriate legislation, and Congressional majorities in the late 1860s and 1870s did pass a series of civil rights statutes spelling out the rights of the new Negro freedman and providing penalties for denial of these rights. Two of the most important of these Congressional statutes punished private conspiracies which attempted to deny persons their constitutional rights (the "anti-Klan" act of 1871) and forbade owners of public accommodation facilities to deny persons service because of "race or color" (the Civil Rights Act of 1875).

Between 1865 and the early 1880s, the egalitarian spirit of the civil rights movement was reflected in widespread Negro voting throughout the South, the presence of Negroes in federal and state offices, judicial enforcement of citizenship rights for Negroes in the courts, steadily widening service of Negroes beside whites in theaters, restaurants, hotels, and public carriers from Maine to Florida, and active Negro civil rights organizations and protest movements. In the rural South and in some of the more exclusive Northern establishments, Negroes were still denied their equal rights by local authorities, or were refused entry to public accommodation facilities. But the clear national trend in these years was toward exercise of civil rights and white acceptance of Negro patronage, and no Southern state maintained, in law or fact, a Jim Crow society. Behind these advances, operating both as moral prod and legal shield, were the federal civil rights statutes, and the ultimate threat of federal force.

The entry of Negroes into full citizenship did not take place in a social and political vacuum, however, and the last quarter of the nineteenth century proved to be a disastrous milieu for experimentation in racial equality. The years of the 1880s through the 1920s were a period of expanding capitalism and a free enterprise philosophy that led middle-class Americans to distrust government intervention in "private affairs," especially by the federal government. It was also a period in which the Southern states were returned to full participation in national political life, with the removal of federal Reconstruction forces as part of the "compromise" that chose the Republican, Hayes, over the Democrat, Tilden, in the electoral photo-finish for the Presidency in 1876. As the 1880s and 1890s wore on, race relations were deeply affected by burgeoning elitist ideas in American life such as belief in Anglo-Saxon racial superiority, the Darwinian notion of the "survival of the fittest," the "white man's burden" to rule colonial peoples, anti-Semitism, and fears of mass emigration to the United States of "inferior" peoples from Eastern and Southern Europe and the Orient. Later, following the Spanish-American War, isolationist and antiforeign sentiments grew in the public mind.

The impact of these even stronger currents on racial equality was registered in the United States Supreme Court, and thus in our basic constitutional policies, in two distinct phases. Beginning in 1876 and culminating in the *Civil Rights Cases* of 1883,[4] the Supreme Court struck down as unconstitutional the key federal laws forbidding *private* denials of civil rights. The Justices did this by limiting sharply the "privileges and immunities" that went with national citizenship, and then reading the language "no State" in the Fourteenth and Fifteenth Amendments to mean literally the action of state governmental officials. The Court rejected arguments that it was "state action" when corporations and persons licensed by the states to serve all without discrimination used race as a criterion, as well as the view that inaction by the state in dealing with mob violence and intimidation of citizens required federal protection. Justice Joseph Bradley commented for the Court that there had to be a time when the Negro ceased to be "the special favorite of the law" and took on "the rank of a mere citizen." Only Justice John M. Harlan, a former slaveholder who had become a civil rights Republican in Kentucky, dissented in the *Civil Rights Cases* and supported the equal treatment law for public accommodations.

The *Civil Rights Cases,* while a not-unreasonable reading of the language (though not the spirit) of the Fourteenth Amendment, did two things to the condition of racial equality. First, this reading destroyed the delicate balance of federal guarantees, Negro protest movements, and private enlightenment that had produced peacefully integrated public facilities throughout the nation in the 1870s and early 1880s. Second, it affected national politics by denying Congress power to protect the Negro's right to equal treatment and wiping the civil rights issue from the Republican party's agenda of national legislative responsibility; at the same time, it affected Southern politics by making "anti-Negro" positions a promising avenue for those who saw rallying of "poor whites" to the standard of segregation as their best hope for electoral victories.

If the Supreme Court had stopped with the first phase of interpretation of the Civil War Amendments, the situation of Negroes would have been

---

[4] 109 U.S. 3 (1883).

bad but not impossible. Even in the South, there was no wholesale imposition of segregation in public accommodation facilities after the ruling of
1883. During the late 1880s, Negroes shared places beside whites in many
Southern restaurants, streetcars, public halls, and theaters. But increasingly,
Democratic and Populist leaders in the South found the Negro a prime
target. While there had been a few isolated segregation laws passed after
the Civil War, eight Southern states passed laws between 1887 and 1891
requiring railroads to maintain white and Negro passengers in separate cars
and then waited to see how these laws based on race would be received by
the United States Supreme Court.

In 1896, the Supreme Court upheld railroad segregation laws in the leading case of *Plessy* v. *Ferguson*.[5] While this was state action, the Court held,
it was not discriminatory against Negroes, since whites were separated
from Negroes just as much as Negroes were separated from whites. The
fact that race was made the basis for separation was not considered an
improper classification, the Court felt, and Justice Brown remarked that
if the act was deemed to "stamp the colored race with a badge of inferiority,"
it was "not by reason of anything found in the act, but solely because the
colored race choose to put that construction upon it." "If one race be
inferior to another socially," Justice Brown concluded, "the Constitution of
the United States cannot put them upon the same plane. . . ."

Again, Justice John Harlan was the sole dissenter. Pointing out that the
known purpose of the segregation laws was to force Negroes out of white
facilities, Harlan stated that compelling segregation violated the personal
liberty of white as well as Negro citizens and used race as an unreasonable
classification, denying equal protection of the laws. In reply to Justice
Brown's comment about racial inferiority, Harlan said:

> The white race deems itself to be the dominant race in this country.
> And so it is, in prestige, in achievements, in education, in wealth
> and in power. So, I doubt not, it will continue to be for all time,
> if it remains true to its great heritage and holds fast to the principles
> of constitutional liberty. But in view of the Constitution, in the eye
> of the law, there is in this country no superior, dominant, ruling class
> of citizens. There is no caste here. Our Constitution is color-blind,
> and neither knows nor tolerates classes among citizens. . . . The law
> regards man as man, and takes no account of his surroundings or of
> his color when his civil rights as guaranteed by the supreme law of
> the land are involved.

Harlan's justly famous dissent was only a dissent, however. In a 1906 case,
Berea College v. *Kentucky*,[6] the Supreme Court carried the "separate but
equal" doctrine to a final conclusion by upholding a state law that made
it a crime for the proprietors of a *private* school willingly to educate white
and Negro students together.

Under these narrow constitutional interpretations, the chalk line of rigid
racial segregation was methodically drawn by law, custom, and, where
necessary, by force throughout the Southern and border states, and by

---

[5] 163 U.S. 537 (1896).
[6] 211 U.S. 45 (1908).

more subtle (but still effective) social discrimination throughout most of the North. A brief description of the racial limits placed on the exercise of key citizenship rights in this era indicates how far the double standard was carried.

In *public accommodations*, racial segregation was required by law in the South for almost every form of contact between whites and Negroes except walking on the street; as one list of sample rules noted, Jim Crow was applied to "waiting rooms, theaters, boardinghouses, water fountains, ticket windows, streetcars, penitentiaries, county jails, convict camps, institutions for the blind and deaf, and hospitals for the insane." [7] Negro accommodations were invariably inferior, and Negroes had to pay "equal prices" for "unequal" facilities such as dirty "Jim Crow cars" on the railroads, the back "Jim Crow room" in restaurants, or the "Nigger gallery" at theaters. While eighteen states in the North had passed laws forbidding discrimination by public accommodation owners (in reaction to the *Civil Rights Cases* ruling that such matters lay with the states and not the federal authority), these laws quickly rusted with neglect during this era, and most leading Northern hotels, restaurants, and theaters refused with impunity to serve Negro customers. A symbol of how far segregation had become the national mode was that the Wilson Administration in 1912–14 instituted segregation in the lunchrooms, rest rooms, and shops maintained by the federal government itself for federal employees and visitors. Washington, D.C., thus became a completely "Jim Crow" capital in the first four decades of the twentieth century, inside the federal establishment and in the public accommodation facilities throughout the District.

In the field of *voting*, the Southern Negro was methodically pushed away from the polls by a combination of restrictive laws and official discrimination. The legal devices included requirements that prospective voters pay a poll tax or own land, or demonstrate reading and writing skills to the satisfaction of local (white) registrars, or be able to explain the state constitution to the satisfaction of these registrars. Though the Supreme Court did strike down Southern laws exempting persons from literacy tests and poll taxes if their grandfathers had voted in the state, since this could apply only to whites,[8] the nullification of this device did little to stem the disfranchisement drive. And, when the Supreme Court held unconstitutional state laws forbidding Negroes to vote in the Democratic primary,[9] Southern leaders overcame this ruling easily by having the Democratic party adopt a "whites only" rule as a "private association" free to set any conditions it pleased for participation in its "internal affairs." [10] By 1910, the boast of one leading Virginia political figure that the South would see to "the elimination of every Negro voter who can be gotten rid of" had come true. A study showed "virtually no" Negroes voting in the all-important Democratic

---

[7] *Freedom to the Free: A Report to the President by the United States Commission on Civil Rights* (1963), p. 61.
[8] *Guinn* v. *United States*, 238 U.S. 347 (1915). This case marked the first test suit brought to the Supreme Court by the NAACP.
[9] *Nixon* v. *Herndon*, 273 U.S. 536 (1927).
[10] This device was upheld by the Supreme Court in *Grovey* v. *Townsend*, 295 U.S. 45 (1935).

primary in the Southern states in the 1930s and only 100,000 Negroes in general elections.[11] In the North, however, Negroes did vote, and as whole wards or Congressional districts became populated primarily by Negroes, their interests received some attention and protection in Northern communities.

In the area of *housing*, the South created separate "Negro quarters" in this era through local ordinances forbidding mixed neighborhoods and by local zoning controls. As Negroes moved North, they found that economic and social pressures channeled them into urban Negro ghettos, such as New York City's Harlem and Chicago's South Side. Restrictive covenants signed by home owners forbidding the sale of property to Negroes limited Negro access to newer parts of Northern cities and the rising suburbs. The Federal Housing Administration (FHA) actively encouraged "homogeneous" neighborhoods and restrictive covenants in these years, and approved restrictive practices by banks and real estate agents.

Education in the public schools of the Southern and border states was divided into strictly separated white and Negro systems. Had these been truly "separate but equal," there might have been the period of educational progress and self-improvement that Negro leaders such as Booker T. Washington called for. But the undisputed facts are that Southern states starved Negro education in this era, providing generally older, dilapidated, and overcrowded school plants for Negroes, hand-me-down books, lower-paid Negro teachers, and "agricultural and mechanical colleges" for Negro higher education. "Too much learnin' spoils a good farm hand" was the dominant white attitude toward Negro education. And, in the North, residential segregation, when coupled with the prevailing concept of the "neighborhood school," produced a high degree of school segregation in Northern urban centers.

The *administration of justice* in the South saw Negroes excluded from service on grand juries and trial juries through the power of local sheriffs and judges to make up jury lists. This insured all-white juries to try cases involving not only Negro defendants or Negro civil rights claimants, but also white officials or private vigilantes who might be indicted for anti-Negro acts. Added to this was toleration by public officials and civic leaders of Ku Klux Klan terroristic activities and mob lynching throughout the South; lynchings averaged 100 per year in this period, the great majority of the victims being Negroes, with few convictions of those perpetrating the outrages. Newspaper stories and official surveys documented widespread police mistreatment of Negroes arrested on suspicion or accused of crimes, as well as to keep them "in their place." Most important psychologically was the etiquette of inferiority adopted by Southern public officials when dealing with Negro citizens. Negro men were called "Boy" or by their first names, and Negro women "Girl" or "Auntie," depending on their age, not only on the street but in public proceedings. Any notion that the law was impartial in result or process where Negroes were concerned in the South in this era is wholly mistaken, whatever individual acts of kindness

---

[11] U.S. Department of Justice, *Protection of the Rights of Individuals* (1952).

or paternalism the Negro may have encountered from white persons or government charities.

Racial discrimination permeated *employment* patterns, since Negroes were the group hardest hit by the agricultural depression of the 1920s and the industrial Depression of 1929–35. Since they were "last hired, first fired" in the factories, Negroes found themselves forced to work for lower wages than whites in the same jobs. When employment opportunities returned after the Depression, most "Negro" opportunities came in the "dirty and dangerous" specialties, and a combination of employer and union bars kept Negroes from most of the upward-moving industrial jobs. Some improvement came in the late 1930s as Negroes moved into auto production, machine tools, and similar industries. When it came to white-collar and technical posts in this period, most national corporations had a strict "no Negroes" policy, and complete bars were put on sales or executive positions.

Finally, in the national *military services*, Negroes during the First World War were segregated in the Army, Navy, and Coast Guard, with Negro units generally assigned to menial jobs such as mess duty and camp clean-up. As late as the eve of the Second World War, a government study found that Negroes were wholly excluded from the Army Air Corps, Marine Corps, and the Tank, Signal, Engineer, and Artillery Corps of the Army.[12]

Looking at the *occupational and social position* of Negro-American citizens between 1863 and 1941—men and women guaranteed equality before the law by the federal Constitution—one cannot call the record of the United States less than shameful. To be sure, some Negro-Americans achieved success in the arts, education, law, business, science, and sports despite total segregation in the South and ghetto boundaries in much of the North. And groups were formed in these years to press for civil rights and assist Negro self-development, such as the Urban League and the National Association for the Advancement of Colored People (NAACP). Also, there were many white Americans—in civic, educational, and political life—who fought beside Negro spokesmen in these organizations and opposed segregation, such as the Catholic Interracial Council, the American Jewish Committee, and the Congress of Industrial Organizations (CIO). But the twin promises of the Declaration of Independence and the Fourteenth Amendment—that Americans would be regarded as equal before the law and that government would protect these equality rights—not only were ignored, but were openly flouted by American law, politics, culture, and social thought in these years.

As we have observed earlier, the double standard followed lines of *color*, and other nonwhite groups also found the 1883–1941 era a hard time in America. American Indians were treated as "Negroes" and segregated in Southern and Southwestern states when they left the federal Indian reservations. Widespread discrimination against Chinese- and Japanese-Americans existed on the West Coast, and against Mexican-Americans in the Southwest. For any such "colored citizens," what came to be called "second-class status" was the rule.

---

[12] *Freedom to the Free*, p. 114.

The progress of minority religious and nationality groups in the 1863–1941 era provided a vital contrast. Compared with these "colored" citizens, Catholics and Jews among the "old stock" and the new immigrants from Southern and Eastern Europe faced no *legal* discrimination or bars, and only occasional hostility in the administration of law. As a result, with their basic self-respect preserved, with access to white schools, able to make the most of economic opportunities and allowed to develop strong self-help agencies, white minority groups as a whole prospered along with white Protestant Americans. They moved quickly into political and civic activity in the cities and learned to protect their interests when attacked.

It was *social* rather than legal discrimination that white minority groups encountered in this era, and in strong doses. With ideas of Anglo-Saxon racial supremacy, anti-Semitism, and anti-Catholicism spreading generally in majority culture, many public accommodation facilities began in the late nineteenth century to bar Catholics and Jews. "No Jews or Dogs Allowed" was a sign printed and sold in dime stories in this period and posted in those establishments that preferred open declarations to a quiet but equally strict policy. "No Catholics Need Apply" appeared in the newspaper ads and bulletin notices of many employers. Refusal to hire Catholics and Jews for white-collar, sales, and executive posts in local and national businesses was commonplace. Many leading professional schools, such as those for medicine, engineering, and architecture, established quotas for Jewish and Catholic applicants. Restrictive covenants binding home owners not to sell to "Negroes, Jews, Roman Catholics, Indians, Mongolians, or other Non-Caucasians" covered vast areas of the country. Most important of all, anti-Semitic and anti-Catholic sentiments were widely accepted "genteel" views in this era, held in many of the "best circles" and not just limited to the Klan, the German-American Bund, or Gerald L. K. Smith's Christian Nationalists. This was the era of the stereotype in America, with the "lazy drunkards" Pat and Mike or the "hook-nosed," "pushy" Abie and Ikie, or the "swarthy," "untrustworthy" Luigi—stock characters, along with Rastus and Mandy, in popular humor. Then as now, popular humor told much about the values of any society.

One major break-through in equality during these years came in the field of women's civil rights. The Supreme Court held in 1875 that nothing in the Fourteenth Amendment gave women the right to vote; that was up to each state. While a few states gave women the vote in the nineteenth century (especially in the progressive Western states, where women were in shorter supply), it took the militant Suffragette movement decades to win the ballot for women. Using street parades, publicity, lobbying, hunger strikes in jail, and even handcuffing themselves to legislators' desks and the doors of city halls, the Suffragettes finally won adoption of the Nineteenth Amendment, ratified in 1920. This forbade the federal government or the states to deny the vote to anyone "on account of sex."

THE FALL OF THE DOUBLE STANDARD:
AMERICAN EGALITARIANISM REDEEMED, 1941–63

Just as the larger national and international climate between 1890 and 1940 was not auspicious for the Negro in America, or for the social position of white minority groups, so that climate during 1941–63 was just the opposite—a milieu in which national and international influences of every kind exerted constant pressure *against* the double standard and strengthened those seeking full civil rights for every American. In the foreign arena, the Second World War demanded soldiers in the field and workers in the factories, and put a high premium on national unity; "racism" and "anti-Semitism" were part of the fascist ideology and practice we were fighting. Following the Second World War, colored peoples in Asia, the Middle East, and Africa won their independence; their achievements, their importance to our economic and political interests, and their unshakable hostility to anti-Negro practices within the United States affected American officials concerned with foreign policy and much of the American public as well. Furthermore, American racial policies were a weak spot in the post-1946 rivalry between the United States and the Soviet Union in Western Europe as well as in the new nations. On the domestic scene, migration of Negroes to Northern communities and the growing economic and political influence of white minority groups strengthened the political position of those opposed to segregation on moral and self-interest grounds. And the fight against discrimination once again began to interest white Protestant liberals whose attention had been caught up by economic recovery in the 1930s and the war in the 1940s; once again, justice for the Negro and eradication of religious prejudice began to attract the energies of the "old American" reformers as it had in the 1870s.

These broad forces were the background for four major trends of the 1941–63 era: (1) a shift in Supreme Court interpretations from acceptance of "separate but equal" to a total rejection of racial discrimination by law; (2) a shift in the role of the federal government and Northern state governments from passive roles to active protection of civil rights; (3) a significant growth in the militancy and organized protest activities of white minority groups and the Negro; and (4) a steady change in national white opinion toward the justice of the Negro's claim to full equality.

How these trends developed can best be seen by dividing our narrative into two phases, 1941–53 and 1954–63, and tracing the broad developments in civil rights law and practice in these periods.

1941–53: Chipping away at "separate but equal"

Between 1941 and 1953, the United States Supreme Court, the federal executive, and the Northern states began to approach official segregation and "social" discrimination in a newly critical fashion. In a series of important rulings, the Supreme Court outlawed racial discrimination in the Democratic white primary on the ground that it was an integral part of the official election process; [13] struck down segregation of passengers on interstate travel as a "burden on interstate commerce"; [14] held that enforcement of racially and religiously restrictive covenants in federal or state courts would violate the Constitution as "government action"; [15] and ruled

---

[13] *Smith* v. *Allwright*, 321 U.S. 649 (1944).
[14] *Morgan* v. *Virginia*, 328 U.S. 373 (1946).
[15] *Shelley* v. *Kraemer*, 334 U.S. 1 (1948).

that hereafter federal courts would demand genuine equality in the separate schools provided for Negroes.[16] How genuine this educational equality would have to be was indicated in the same case, which not only compared the newly created Negro law school with the physical plant, library, and faculty quality of the white University of Texas Law School, but also insisted on equality in the influence of the alumni and the reputation of the two schools in the community. It was clear that very few separate colleges and schools could stand such comparisons. Though none of these rulings challenged the *Plessy* v. *Ferguson* doctrine that separate facilities for Negroes were constitutional, the principle had been dealt a series of hammer blows that had it shaking.

Presidential action between 1941 and 1953 also broke with the passiveness of the White House in civil rights matters during previous decades. Under pressure of a threatened march on Washington by Negroes in 1941, President Franklin Roosevelt issued an executive order forbidding discrimination in defense industries or government employment and created a federal Fair Employment Practices Committee to deal with the problem through public hearings, inquiries into complaints, and recommendations to the parties.[17] (The Committee was abolished through Southern and conservative-Republican teamwork in Congress in 1946.) Also in 1946, President Harry Truman created the President's Committee on Civil Rights;[18] its report in 1947, *To Secure These Rights,* surveyed American civil rights practices and called for wide-scale remedial action to fulfill American ideals. Its proposals included federal laws to forbid lynching and discrimination in voting requirements, to create a permanent FEPC and a permanent Commission on Civil Rights, and to expand the small Civil Rights Section in the Department of Justice that had been set up in 1939. At considerable risk to his party position and his campaign for reelection, President Truman recommended these proposals for enactment by Congress, but no action was taken during the remaining years of the Truman Administration (1948–52).

With Congressional action blocked by Southern-conservative and Republican opposition to civil rights measures, and the ultimate control of the filibuster in the Senate, Presidential authority became the basis for several other important actions in this period. In 1948, President Truman issued an executive order ending "separate but equal" recruiting, training, and service in the United States Army.[19] Another executive order in 1948 declared that federal jobs were to be distributed without regard to "race, color, religion or national origin," and established a Fair Employment Board to oversee the policy.[20] In 1951, a Presidential order created the Committee on Government Contract Compliance, requiring businesses holding contracts with the federal government to pledge and provide fair employment policies.[21] In addition, executive agencies during the Truman Administration

---

[16] *Sweatt* v. *Painter,* 339 U.S. 629 (1950).
[17] Exec. Order 8802, *Federal Register,* Vol. VI (1941), p. 3109.
[18] Exec. Order 9808, *Federal Register,* Vol. XI (1946), p. 14153.
[19] Exec. Order 9981, *Federal Register,* Vol. XIII (1948), p. 4313.
[20] Exec. Order 9980, *Ibid.,* p. 4311.
[21] Exec. Order 10308, *Federal Register,* Vol. XVI (1951), p. 12303.

shared the civil rights action. The FHA, for example, ended in 1949 its long-standing policy of favoring "homogeneous" neighborhoods and began in 1950 a policy of refusing to insure home mortgages which had restrictive covenants.

When President Eisenhower took office in 1953, he continued the policy of using executive authority in key areas of civil rights. In 1953, he created the President's Committee on Government Contracts,[22] headed by Vice-President Nixon, with power to receive complaints about discrimination by government contractors; the agency placing the contract made the investigation of these complaints, and the possibility of cancellation of the contract was the sanction that stood in the background. Other executive agencies in 1953 added new measures. The Defense Department ordered an end to segregated schools on military bases, and the National Capital Housing Authority declared that "open occupancy" would be the rule for all public low-cost housing in the District of Columbia.

State and municipal governments outside the South became active as well in protecting civil rights. New York and New Jersey in 1945 passed fair employment laws, giving authority to state commissions to issue cease and desist orders enforceable in state courts against employers who were found to have engaged in discrimination. Most of the work of these commissions, however, was by conference, conciliation, and publicity. By 1953, six other Northern states had passed similar laws. Complaints of discrimination in the eighteen states with public accommodation antidiscrimination laws began to be pressed, heard, and remedied. Other state laws forbade discrimination by public educational institutions.

The great contrast to these developments, as we have noted, was in Congress. From 1946 to 1953, Congress refused to enact antilynching or anti-poll tax laws, to create a federal FEPC, or to enact any of the other measures recommended by the President and civil rights groups. It also refused to include an antidiscrimination rider in the Selective Service Act of 1948 (leading President Truman to do this by executive order). By 1953, it seemed that when the outer limits of executive authority were reached, federal progress would stop, and that nothing could be done about the all-pervasive system of Jim Crow in the South.

1954–63: THE GREAT BREAK-THROUGH

It was at this point that the break-through came. On May 17, 1954, the Supreme Court of the United States held in *Brown* v. *Board of Education*[23] that segregation in state public education was inherently discriminatory and unconstitutional. In a companion case, the Court struck down school segregation by federal authorities in the District of Columbia.[24] "Separate but equal" was now dead in public education, and it was clear that the logic of the Court's opinion would carry the principle to all other areas where a state required racial segregation.

Having issued this monumental ruling, which overnight transferred the

---

[22] Exec. Order 10479, *Federal Register,* Vol. XVIII (1953), p. 4899.
[23] 347 U.S. 483 (1954).
[24] *Bolling* v. *Sharpe,* 347 U.S. 497 (1954).

legal sanction and moral authority of the nation's basic law from the segregationist forces to the civil rights advocates, the Justices then had to face the question of implementing their decree in the twenty-one states and the District of Columbia with segregated public schools. Recognizing the complexity of the task, the Court took a year to hear arguments from the interested parties (Negro plaintiffs, Southern attorneys general, the United States Government, and various groups) and, in 1955, provided its blueprint for change. School authorities would not be required to make full and instant compliance but could work out, under the supervision of the local lower federal courts, transitional programs that led "with all deliberate speed" to desegregated school systems.[25]

For almost two years after the initial *Brown* ruling, it seemed as though desegregation might come peacefully to the nation. By the end of the 1956 school year, 699 school districts, principally in the border states of Delaware, Maryland, West Virginia, Kentucky, Missouri, and Oklahoma, and in a few "outer" Southern states such as Texas and Tennessee, had admitted Negro pupils to formerly all-white schools. Even more important, 690 of these had been integrated without the necessity of court injunction suit.

By 1956, though, the South had recovered its balance and had issued its challenge. "The Deep South Says Never" (as one magazine article put it) symbolized the determination of Southern public officials, private anti-integration groups such as the White Citizens Councils, and Southern white public opinion that the Supreme Court's mandate could be evaded. "Gradualism" would take them generations, and Senator Eastland of Mississippi said he could foresee "a hundred or even hundreds of years of litigation" before the South would be ready for integration. As the late 1950s unfolded, five primary forms of Southern intransigence had emerged as the segregationist strategy:

Closing of public schools

Some states by law and some by local school board decisions closed their public schools in 1955–57, either leasing the property to private groups for segregated "private" schools or selling the facilities outright. This tactic was met directly by a series of lower federal and state court rulings in 1958 and 1959 holding such closing to be in evasion of the *Brown* mandate and illegal.[26]

Delay because of threatened violence

As a means of intimidating Negro parents and students, and to provide a basis for saying that the situation was "too dangerous" for immediate integration, violent demonstrations were mounted by local segregationist groups against court-ordered integration. These demonstrations, complete with spitting at Negro children and hitting ministers who might accompany them to school, were often aided by "outside" demonstrators sent into the community by segregationist groups from other areas, and local police

---

25 *Brown* v. *Board of Education,* 349 U.S. 294 (1955).
26 *Aaron* v. *Cooper,* 261 F. 2d. 97 (8th Cir. 1958); *Harrison* v. *Day,* 106 S.E. 2d. 636 (Va. 1959).

**Poplarville, Mississippi,
U.S.A., 1959**

Racial violence in the South during
the 1950s led to the decisive events
of 1963.

From *Straight Herblock*, Simon & Schuster, 1964

sometimes encouraged the melee or did nothing to halt it. From 1956
through 1963, court-ordered desegregation was met each September by such
violence: in Clinton, Tennessee, in 1956; Little Rock, Arkansas, in 1957;
New Orleans, Louisiana, in 1960; and at the University of Mississippi at
Oxford in 1962, to mention the leading incidents. In Little Rock, President
Eisenhower had to send in federal troops when Governor Faubus ordered
the Arkansas National Guard to prevent Negro students from entering
Central High School; the Supreme Court upheld Eisenhower's authority to
use troops and refused to permit any delay in integration in Little Rock
because of the violence.[27] President Kennedy also had to use federal marshals, and then combat troops, in 1962 to secure the admission of James
Meredith to the University of Mississippi, after Governor Barnett failed
to provide adequate state police protection and wild riots erupted on the
Oxford campus.

3. Pupil-placement laws

More successful than school-closings and violence were laws enacted
throughout the South strengthening the authority of local school boards
to assign students to particular schools according to the board's own formula, and providing complex procedures for Negro parents seeking to
transfer their children to schools outside their neighborhood. This became
the backbone of "tokenism," the policy of allowing six or ten Negro students into a school of 2,000 whites and keeping the rest of the system
thoroughly segregated. While lower federal courts began in 1962–63 to

---

[27] *Cooper v. Aaron*, 358 U.S. 1 (1958).

criticize the use of pupil-placement laws to foster "token integration," the laws were not held to be unconstitutional per se, since they were reasonable administrative provisions on their face.[28] That their application would be scrutinized more closely in the middle 1960s began to be apparent, however.

Anti-Supreme Court campaigns

Viewing the United States Supreme Court as the wellspring of their present troubles, Southern segregationists mounted a steady campaign after 1954 to curb the Court and force reversal of its *Brown* ruling. Efforts were made to show that the Justices had "Communist affiliations" or that the legal and sociological authorities cited by the Court in the *Brown* case were "pro-Communists." Southern Congressional spokesmen called for impeachment of some or all of the Justices for violating their oath of office by "rewriting the Constitution by judicial fiat." Constitutional amendments were sponsored to return full control over public education to state authority, as well as bills to limit the appellate jurisdiction of the Supreme Court over school segregation cases. None of these efforts was successful, and the only time the Court was seriously threatened came in 1957–58, when Southern Senators found additional allies among right-wing Republicans and Northern Democrats angered by the Supreme Court's rulings on internal security cases during the 1956 term. (See Chapter 16.) The bills to "curb the Court" failed, however, largely through the tactical skill during the Senate fight exercised by then Majority Leader Lyndon B. Johnson.

Anti-NAACP measures

If the Supreme Court was the voice of forced change for the South, segregationists knew that it was the NAACP that had provided the occasions for those declarations with the test suits that NAACP lawyers and funds had made possible. Facing increased NAACP lawsuits to enforce and extend the *Brown* ruling, many Southern states moved to harass, or even to ban completely, the NAACP "presence" in their states. State legislative investigations into "Communist influence" in the NAACP were conducted, and witnesses who refused to provide the membership lists of state NAACP chapters were cited for contempt. Statutes against lawyers "soliciting" legal cases or "managing" litigation were invoked against the NAACP and criminal prosecutions were launched. Alabama required the NAACP to register under existing state laws governing out-of-state corporations, and then to furnish membership lists to qualify under the registration proceedings; when the NAACP did not comply, it was ordered to disband in Alabama. Each of these examples of harassment resulted in Supreme Court measures striking down the convictions as improper applications of legitimate state power, designed without justification to resist integration by punishing legitimate Negro organizational activity.[29] But the drain on NAACP funds and time, and the elimination of the NAACP wholly for years in some

---

[28] See *Bush* v. *Orleans Parish School Board*, 308 F. 2d. 491 (5th Cir. 1962).
[29] See *NAACP* v. *Alabama*, 357 U.S. 449 (1958).

states, made these tactics highly satisfactory for segregationist states even though they ultimately lost their cases in the Supreme Court.

In addition to its major ruling on segregated education, the Supreme Court carried the new equality standard into other cases brought to it in the 1954-63 period. Among these important rulings were cases striking down the use of racial standards in the drawing of legislative voting districts (to minimize Negro voters),[30] outlawing racial segregation in all interstate bus, railroad, or airport facilities;[31] applying the same rule to privately owned concessions housed within publicly owned facilities such as municipal garages, terminals, parks, etc.;[32] and upholding the constitutionality of the voting-protection provisions of the Civil Rights Act of 1957[33] (see below).

In this climate of "new law" and "new expectations" (as well as "massive resistance" in the South) set off by the Supreme Court's 1954-63 decisions, Presidential, Northern state and—finally—Congressional actions to insure civil rights were also accelerated. By 1957, the growing civil rights movements, the increasing importance of Negro voters in key Northern states, and pressure from world public opinion finally provided enough conditioning factors to compel Congress to take up and bring to a vote the civil rights proposals that President Eisenhower had been sending to Congress since 1953. Through bipartisan cooperation from Speaker Sam Rayburn and Senate Majority Leader Lyndon B. Johnson, the Eisenhower Administration put through the Civil Rights Act of 1957.[34] This did four major things: (1) authorized the federal government to sue directly in federal district court for a civil injunction where any person is deprived of his right to vote (previously, the individual had to sue for himself, bearing both the cost and the local pressure); (2) gave federal district courts jurisdiction over such civil proceedings without requiring that state administrative and judicial remedies be first "exhausted" (which had meant endless delays through the deliberately tortuous maze of procedures set up by Southern states for contesting voting rulings); (3) created the United States Commission on Civil Rights, a bipartisan body authorized to investigate reports of denials of voting rights, collect data on the progress of equal protection of the laws, and appraise federal policies to protect such equality; and (4) expanded the Civil Rights Section of the Department of Justice into a full Division, under an Assistant Attorney General for Civil Rights. Defeated in 1957, however, was the so-called "Title III" of the Administration bill, which would have permitted the Attorney General to seek injunctions in federal court when there had been denials of the civil rights of persons, apart from voting matters.

Between 1957 and 1963, the Civil Rights Commission held extensive hearings throughout the country, in the North and West as well as in the South;

---

[30] *Gomillion* v. *Lightfoot,* 364 U.S. 339 (1960).
[31] *Bailey* v. *Patterson,* 369 U.S. 31 (1962); *Turner* v. *Memphis,* 369 U.S. 350 (1962).
[32] *Burton* v. *Wilmington Parking Authority,* 365 U.S. 715 (1961).
[33] *U.S.* v. *Raines,* 362 U.S. 17 (1960).
[34] 71 Stat. 634 (1957).

published a series of thorough and revealing reports on both progress and lack of progress on civil rights in the fields of education, voting, public accommodations, justice, housing, etc.; and made a number of proposals for additional federal measures needed to insure full enjoyment of civil rights guaranteed by law. (Many of these proposals became part of the Civil Rights Acts of 1960 and 1964). The life and funds of the Commission were in most precarious conditions in these years, however, with Southern forces in Congress able to hold renewals of the Commission's life to one- or two-year periods, and to limit its financial resources closely.

The Department of Justice had used its authority under the Act of 1957 to bring thirty-three suits (by 1963) in various counties in Alabama, Georgia, Louisiana, Mississippi, and other Southern states where voting registrars had engaged in discriminatory practices or intimidation against Negro applicants for voting status. To meet various devices developed by Southern officials to evade the provisions of the Civil Rights Act of 1957, such as having the voting registrars brought to federal court resign while the case was pending, requiring fresh suits against successor officials and new evidence of discrimination, Congress passed in 1960 another "voting" Civil Rights Act.[35] This allowed federal district courts to appoint federal voting referees whenever the court found "a pattern or practice" of discrimination; the referee could receive applications for registration and certify those qualified to the federal court, which could then order the individual to be admitted to the voting rolls. Refusal to admit such individuals was subject to punishment as a contempt of court. The 1960 Act also required state officials to keep registration and voting records for twenty-two months after each election, gave federal authorities power to inspect these records, and allowed suit against the state directly when a voting registrar resigned during a proceeding under the 1957 Act.

Thus, the Acts of 1957 and 1960 put the legislative organ of the national government behind civil rights reform. Many civil rights supporters felt Congress had barely begun to do the things necessary, in both the number of subjects treated and the adequacy of the tools given to do the job even in the voting area. But a start had been made, and the seventy-year-old "veto power" of Southern segregationist forces in the Senate had been overcome.

Executive action in the 1954–63 period continued in significant fashion. A Committee on Government Employment Policy was created by the President in 1955 to hear individual complaints alleging racial or religious discrimination in hiring or promotion by federal agencies.[36] Over 1,500 such complaints were heard by 1963, most being settled by consultation with the agency involved, about a quarter resulting in adverse opinions, and fewer than 100 producing calls for corrective action by the specific agency. The Committee did not have power to direct compliance.

When the Kennedy Administration took office, it merged the Committee on Government Employment Policy and the Committee on Government Contracts into one, more powerful body, the Committee on Equal Employ-

---

[35] 74 Stat. 86 (1960).
[36] Exec. Order 10590, *Federal Register*, Vol. XX (1955), p. 409.

ment Opportunities,[37] with Vice-President Lyndon Johnson as its chairman. This body, for the first time, had power to investigate situations within federal agencies on its own initiative and to issue orders of compliance. The executive order also required all government contractors to include nondiscrimination clauses in their contracts with the United States and to submit regular reports on their compliance with fair employment policies, and gave the Committee power to investigate employer and union practices, with authority to cancel the contracts of noncomplying businesses.

In 1962, President Kennedy appointed a Committee on Equal Opportunity in the Armed Forces, to deal with the problem of discrimination encountered in Southern communities by Negro servicemen. These soldiers were often unable to find decent housing, had to send their children to segregated schools, and had no decent recreational facilities open to them on a nonsegregated (or often on any) basis. The Committee was directed to recommend ways to overcome these situations. Also in 1962, President Kennedy fulfilled a pledge he had made in the 1960 campaign, with a "stroke of the pen" signing Executive Order 11063, prohibiting discrimination in federally assisted housing.[38] Concern over the effect of such an order on the Kennedy legislative program in Congress and on the economic reaction of the housing industry had led the President to hold back for two years on the "stroke," just as it had led the Kennedy Administration not to propose any new civil rights bills to Congress between 1960 and 1963. The housing order covered sales or leases of housing operated by the federal government, housing built through federal grants or loans, and housing financed by federal urban renewal or slum clearance funds. A Committee on Equal Opportunity in Housing was created to supervise the program, with cancellation of grants or loans as the prime weapon to insure compliance.

State action outside the South between 1954 and 1963 also increased protection of civil rights. By 1963, twenty-one states had enacted enforceable fair employment practices laws; nineteen states and fifty-five cities had fair housing laws; and twenty-eight states had legislation forbidding discrimination in public accommodations. In all of these areas, the commissions and agencies set up to promote and enforce the policies were far more active and handled far more cases than had been processed in the early 1950s, indicating both more determination by citizens to enforce their rights and willingness of the agencies to follow the cases through to solutions.

Finally, no account of the 1954–63 period would be complete without mention of the voluntary actions of private business, labor, religious, and civic groups, either eliminating their own former practices of discrimination or giving financial and personal support to the Negro civil rights struggle as a cause. Some idea of the wide range of these actions may be obtained from the following items, just a few taken from a 48-page summary published by the American Jewish Committee:

---

[37] Exec. Order 10925, *Federal Register,* Vol. XXVI (1961), p. 1977.
[38] Exec. Order 11063, *Federal Register,* Vol. XXVII (1962), p. 11527.

1957	The AFL–CIO orders a Cleveland local of the International Brotherhood of Electrical Workers to end racial discrimination or have its charter revoked.
1957	The Louisville Methodist Church opens Kentucky Wesleyan College to Negro students.
1958	New York City newspapers agree to refuse all real estate advertising carrying racial specifications.
1959	The American Legion breaks with its affiliate, the "40 and 8 Society" over continued racial restrictions.
1959	Nine symphony orchestras, nine Broadway musicals, and thirteen television orchestras hire Negro musicians for the first time during the year.
1961	The International Association of Machinists dissolves its all-Negro locals.
1961	The Professional Golfers Association drops its "Caucasians Only" clause for membership.
1962	Catholic parochial schools in eleven Southern states now integrated.
1962	The influential Cosmos Club in Washington, D.C., votes to eliminate racial and religious policies for membership.
1962	Major movie theaters in Miami, Florida, drop color bars, as did Howard Johnson Restaurants in Florida, North Carolina, and Virginia.[39]

As we survey the procession of judicial, executive, and legislative actions by federal and state governments during 1954–63, and the voluntary antidiscrimination efforts of private groups, several basic conclusions are suggested. American constitutional law by 1963 had clearly and unequivocally outlawed all racial segregation by government or by private owners in publicly owned facilities. Both American national political parties stood pledged to secure civil rights for Negroes and other nonwhite groups. The injustice of racial discrimination had been denounced and was being fought by the governing authorities of all American religious bodies. Public opinion polls showed that national opinion supported the Negro's cause against both Southern segregationists and Northern discriminators. Talented Negroes had been appointed in ever-growing numbers to high federal posts during the 1950s and 1960s; had been elected to many local, state, and federal offices; and were being hired for influential jobs once closed to nonwhites in American industry.

Yet it was clear by 1963 that all of this did not provide the basis for resolution of a deepening racial conflict in the United States. One explanation was the familiar theory that a group long held in degrading and oppressed status becomes increasingly militant as its just claims are in the process of being met; having tasted freedom, they want it in full, not at the pace or in the dosage that former segregationists or discriminators wish to provide. But far more important than this reason was the reality of life that faced Negro-Americans in 1963. To examine that reality carefully is to understand what set off the now-famous civil rights upheavals

---

[39] American Jewish Committee, *The People Take the Lead: A Record of Progress in Civil Rights, 1954 to 1963* (New York, 1963).

of 1963 and marked the opening of a new era in the history of equality in the American Republic.

The 1963 Civil Rights Upheaval: New Ideals and Old Realities

During the "long hot summer" of 1963, Negro demonstrators were packed in American streets from Boston to Birmingham. Why they were there, why their leaders said over and over again that they had finally "lost faith in the white power structure" of America, can be explained by examining the status of the Negro in five prime areas in 1963.

1. Because of its symbolic importance, the first area of protest was continued segregation in education. By 1963, 51 percent of the Negro school population in the seven border states were attending school with white children.[40] But the percentage of increase had been dropping alarmingly year after year. Between 1962 and 1963, the increase was less than 1 percent; at that pace, it would be the twenty-first century before 90 percent integration was achieved in the "enlightened" areas of the border states.

The graver cause for unrest lay in the eleven states of the deep South. Here, glacial slowness was the rule, despite the "prestige" entry of a handful of Negroes in a few schools in such major cities as Atlanta, Dallas, Memphis, and others. The overall figures showed that in 1963, only four tenths of 1 percent of Negro school children in the deep South—12,868 out of a Negro school enrollment of 2,840,452—were in integrated classes. In Alabama, Mississippi, and South Carolina, not a single Negro child was in an integrated school. Arkansas had only 246 such children, Georgia 44, and Louisiana 107, clearly "token" contingents. Again, the rate of change was alarmingly slow. Between 1962 and 1963, only a few hundred additional Negro children entered white schools. The *law* might be on the side of the Negro seeking entry to integrated public schools in the South, but Southern resistance seemed to be triumphing, and Senator Eastland's pledge of "a hundred years" of litigation was no longer to be laughed off as hyperbole.

Moreover, Negro groups had grown increasingly pessimistic over *de facto* school segregation in Northern cities. In 1961, a test case in New Rochelle, New York, had led a federal district judge to hold that the school board had created a segregated-in-fact school system, and this denied Negroes their constitutional rights.[41] By 1962, actions had been started in forty-three Northern cities to compel redistricting from "all-Negro" or "90 percent" Negro schools to more balanced plants. Some Northern communities such as New York City and Detroit took affirmative action to even out racial balances in 1962–63, but increasingly dense Negro populations in the core of the Northern cities, the general movement of white families

---

[40] These figures, and those that follow for the deep South, come from the *Southern School News*.

[41] 191 F. Supp. 181 (S.D. N.Y. 1961).

"Those Alabama Stories Are Sickening. Why Can't They Be Like Us And Find Some Nice, Refined Way To Keep The Negroes Out?"

From *Straight Herblock*, Simon & Schuster, 1964

into suburbs, and resistance by some white parents to the "busing" and transfer measures needed to achieve integrated schools led to a *growth* rather than a decline in *de facto* segregation in Northern urban centers during the 1961–63 period.

2. Next to education in importance—and many might put it ahead of education—was the employment situation of Negroes. The rapid trend toward automation in American industry was hitting Negroes hardest, as the largest pool of unskilled and semiskilled workers most easily replaced by the machines. Statistics in early 1963 showed 12.7 percent of non-whites unemployed, but only 5.9 percent of whites. Broken down, these figures showed that 20.3 percent of Negro laborers were out of work, and 29.8 percent of Negro teen-agers seeking work. In a city like Detroit, 60 percent of the Negro population were unemployed, though Negroes made up only 20 percent of Detroit's total population.

Adding to the impact of automation on Negro unemployment was the presence of persistent racial bars set by many important labor unions (refusing to admit Negroes to membership, or to let them into the apprenticeship programs training union members for better-paying skilled jobs). Building trades unions, electrical workers, and railroads were notorious examples. And where the corporate job market was booming most—in secretarial and white-collar work, technical and professional posts, sales, and executive ranks—complete exclusion of Negroes or "tokenism" was still the rule in most of the nation's major corporations and large local businesses. This was the cold fact despite genuine fair employment policies by distinguished companies such as International Harvester, RCA, Inland Steel, Pitney-Bowes, or North American Aviation, and despite the achievements impelled by the President's Committee on Equal Employment Opportunities. Surveys of Negro employees above the assembly line in banking, steel, autos, utilities, airlines, communication, and other key industries showed small fractions of Negro employees, and little effort by company personnel officers to change this ratio when new men were hired.

3. The third area of the 1963 upheaval was housing. Despite the adoption of fair housing laws by nineteen states and fifty-five municipalities, and the President's executive order of 1962, Negroes were becoming *more*, not less, segregated in their residential situation in the North and West in the early 1960s. As mentioned earlier, white populations were moving out of the older core of the large cities. Between 1950 and 1960, the white population decreased 13 percent in Boston, 12.5 percent in St. Louis, and 9.7 percent in Detroit, for example. The Negro migration to these cities grew steadily as well, until by 1963, Negroes made up 20 to 53 percent of the population of eight major cities: Chicago, Philadelphia, Detroit, Washington, D.C., Baltimore, Cleveland, New Orleans, and Houston, and more than 13 percent in New York City and Los Angeles. Within the cities, high-cost new apartment buildings, and discriminatory policies against the few Negroes who could afford to pay these rents, kept Negroes from most of the fashionable "in-city" private projects. Meanwhile, the older parts of the city filled up with Negroes, and low-cost city housing tended to be "all-Negro" housing in one part of the city and "all-white" in others. "Urban renewal is Negro removal" complained many civil rights leaders who saw older integrated neighborhoods bulldozed for trade centers, shopping malls, art and concert centers, or convention halls, while displaced Negro families had to move into the remaining Negro concentrations of those cities.

What made the situation in the cities worse was the barrier Negroes found in many Northern suburbs. Under FHA and VA practices from the Second World War until the late 1950s, $117 billion had been given in housing loans under "homogeneous neighborhood" policies. The result had been the creation of all-white cities around many of the major urban centers of the nation, such as the Levittowns of Long Island, Pennsylvania, and New Jersey; Lakewood near Los Angeles; and Park Forest outside Chicago. Negroes had been systematically barred when these communities were built and sold. As for present practices, a combination of discriminatory practices by real estate agents, mortgage lending institutions, and many local home owners in the suburbs made the movement of any substantial number of Negroes into these communities very difficult.

The result of these developments was increasing "ghettoization" of Negroes in cities and creation of predominantly Negro suburbs, with all the segregation of schools, churches, civic groups, recreational facilities, and business life that such a condition brought with it.

4. A fourth area of Negro unrest concerned the continuing refusal of most public accommodation facilities in the Southern and border states to

A Northern view of the "private property" issue.

© 1963 by Bill Mauldin

serve Negro customers. Once across the Potomac into Maryland and Virginia, Negroes encountered "Whites Only" policies at hotels, motels, restaurants, amusement parks, beaches, theaters, food markets, barber shops, and many, many other establishments. Such policies were not forbidden by any Supreme Court decisions where the facilities were privately owned and not concessions on public grounds. Some victories had been won by voluntary action, negotiation, and boycotts (see below for accounts of sit-in campaigns and bus boycotts in this period), but the great majority of facilities remained closed to Negroes in the South of 1963. The human impact of this situation was pictured by Roy Wilkins of the NAACP. When Negroes traveled on business, governmental, military, or personal affairs into the South, they encountered daily a degrading "differential treatment" that no free white American would tolerate. A Negro had to worry: "Where can my family and I eat? Where can we use a rest room? . . . Will my children be denied a soft drink or an ice cream cone because they are not white?" Condemning Congress' continued failure to push legislation outlawing such practices, which clearly lay within Congress' authority over interstate travel, Wilkins noted that a Congressional act forbade railroads from "confining livestock for more than twenty-eight hours without unloading them into pens for at least five hours for rest, water, and feeding." "Are cows, hogs, and sheep more valuable than human beings" and are "their rest, water, and feeding a proper subject for congressional legislative action, [while] the rest and feeding of Negro Americans in hotels, restaurants, and other public places" cannot be dealt with?[42]

5. The final, and in many ways the most threatening, area of protest involved the violent harassment of civil rights workers and Negro spokesmen in the South in the early 1960s. In many Southern states as a whole, and in areas of other states, white law-enforcement officials and elected leaders either would not or could not protect Negro and white civil rights workers from beatings, bombings, and shootings. Sometimes, the violence came from the white police themselves. The reports of the United States Commission on Civil Rights for these years are filled with documented stories of such incidents. Two illustrations will serve here. In Birmingham, Alabama, there were fifty "unsolved" bombings against Negroes between 1947 and 1963. On Sunday morning, September 15, 1963, while Negroes in the Sixteenth Street Baptist Church heard their minister preach on Matthew 5, "The Love That Forgives," a bomb expertly planted in the church cellar and timed for the Sunday service exploded, killing four Negro girls, ages eleven to fourteen. As of 1964, no one had been arrested for the crime.

The other example involves the state of Mississippi, where anti-Negro violence was a steady diet in this period. In 1955, a fourteen-year-old Negro named Emmett Till was killed and his bound body thrown in the Tallahatchie River because he supposedly whistled at a white woman; his now self-confessed murderer was acquitted by a local all-white jury. In 1958, a white mob broke into the Pearl County jail and killed Mack Parker, a Negro being held on suspicion of raping a white woman. No one was convicted for this murder. In 1963, the state leader of the NAACP, Medgar Evers, was killed by a rifle shot from ambush as he entered his home.

After collecting and documenting many instances of police brutality and private violence in their state, the Mississippi State Advisory Committee of the United States Commission on Civil Rights reported in 1963 that "a responsible state government could take energetic steps" to punish such wrongdoing, but the white government of Mississippi "is not sufficiently concerned. . . ." Furthermore, the federal government had failed in its own duty to provide "the citizens of Mississippi the protection due them as American citizens," through a combination of belief that it lacked adequate statutory authority to intervene, inadequate funds and staff in the Department of Justice, and the hurdle of having to try cases before all-white juries with a record of acquitting Mississippi policemen of responsibility in civil rights violation cases.[43]

As these brief examples indicate, violence against civil rights workers in many Southern states, while they were exercising absolutely legal rights to seek voting registration, calling for an end to segregation, or demonstrating in peaceful and orderly fashion, led Negro leaders to believe that more federal force would have to be exerted or Negroes would start fighting back.

---

[42] Testimony of Roy Wilkins before the Senate Commerce Committee, reprinted in Alan F. Westin, ed., *Freedom Now! The Civil Rights Struggle in America* (New York, 1964), pp. 158–61.
[43] Report reprinted in *ibid.*, pp. 205–09.

1963 to the Present: A New Era of Conflict and Resolution in Civil Rights

Out of these developments just described—stalemate in school desegregation in the deep South, growing unemployment among Negro workers, increasing ghettoization of Negro communities, continued rejection of Negro customers by most public accommodation facilities in the South, and mounting private and police violence against civil rights workers—came the now-famous Negro protest of 1963. Just what triggered this movement and sent masses of Negroes into the streets both north and south of the Mason-Dixon line in the spring and summer of 1963 cannot be pinpointed exactly. In one sense, this was the "next logical step" in mounting "direct action" campaigns by Negroes and their white supporters in the civil rights cause. Building on the legal victories won by the NAACP and the successful negotiations with civic groups by the Urban League, the late 1950s and early 1960s had seen the rise of new tactics and new groups.

In 1955, for example, the local Negro community of Montgomery, Alabama, mounted a year-long boycott of the city buses when these continued to follow segregated seating practices, and a federal court injunction finally forbade discriminatory seating. Negroes who had formerly sat all their lives in the "Jim Crow rear" were willing to walk miles to work or wait hours in line for car pools. "My feets is tired," one seventy-two-year-old Negro woman told a reporter, "but my soul is rested." The boycott in Montgomery set a pattern for similar boycotts of dime stores, department stores, buses, and markets in other communities in the South, and led to the creation in 1956 of the Southern Christian Leadership Conference, a group of religious leaders and laymen committed to "nonviolent protest" and led by Dr. Martin Luther King, Jr.

Another new phase was marked in 1960, when Negro students from the North Carolina Agricultural and Technical College began a "sit-in" demonstration at the Woolworth lunch counter in Greensboro. Though subjected to insults, spitting, jostling, and even dousing with catsup, the students kept seated and asked to be served. Soon, sit-ins in restaurants, read-ins at libraries, pray-ins at white churches, and sleep-ins in hotel lobbies spread through the South, primarily by Negro students under Southern Christian Leadership guidance and following "nonviolent" techniques. The efforts sometimes led to changes in service policy, sometimes to arrests for "trespassing," sometimes to police-tolerated violence by local whites, and sometimes to forcible removal by police and arrest for resisting an officer.

The next major development was "Freedom Rides" into the South, sponsored by the Congress of Racial Equality (CORE), a group founded in 1943. These rides were designed to test—and expose—segregation practices in interstate travel and terminal facilities in the South, practices that were clearly illegal under Supreme Court rulings. As groups of Negro and white Freedom Riders entered Southern communities on interstate buses, they met refusals to be served food or be given haircuts in terminals in such places as Danville, Virginia, and Greensboro, North Carolina. Riders were arrested in Charlotte, North Carolina, for refusal to abide by segregated shoeshine policies. Then, riders were beaten in Rock Hill, South Carolina. In Montgomery, Alabama, mobs seriously injured twenty riders. Finally, local police inaction in Alabama led President Kennedy to send in 400 federal marshals to restore order. As the Freedom Riders moved into Mississippi, more than 300 were arrested and convicted, primarily for refusing to obey the orders of Mississippi police to separate into "white" and "Negro" waiting room facilities.

All of these campaigns and movements testified to growing Negro militancy and unwillingness to be passive under continuing segregation and discrimination. Yet none of these precedents gathered up Negro leaders and masses in communities throughout the country for a direct challenge to local public authorities and white civic leadership. What prompted this development was the confrontation in Birmingham, Alabama, in the spring of 1963. During early 1963, Dr. King had led Negro delegations and then had picketed to persuade Birmingham officials (in one of the most segregated and violent cities of the deep South) to pursue a "minimum program" of racial justice. This program consisted of a request for fair employment opportunities in the city, desegregation in downtown eating places, and formation of a biracial committee to work out gradual integration of the local schools. When this program was rejected totally and out of hand, Dr. King began leading several thousand Birmingham Negro residents, including Negro school children, in orderly street marches. The demonstrators were met, and swept off the streets, by high-pressure fire hoses, herded off the march routes by police dogs snapping at them, and shocked by electric "prods" used for handling cattle. Pictures of Birmingham Negroes being hit by streams of water, bitten by dogs, and given electric shocks were front-page news in every newspaper in the United States, and everywhere abroad. More than 2,500 demonstrators, including Dr. King and school children, were arrested and jailed for demonstrating.

Like an atomic chain reaction, Birmingham set off street demonstrations by masses of Negroes and white supporters in the North and by Negro masses in the South. Notice was served, civil rights leaders said with new bitterness, that "normal" business and civic affairs could not continue anywhere unless good-faith efforts were made by "local white power structures" and public officials to meet Negro demands for fair treatment and their legal rights. The symbol of this new protest spirit was the March on Washington held August 28, 1963. More than 200,000 Negroes and whites assembled in Washington to demand a strong, omnibus federal civil rights law and remedial action by local and state governments throughout the North. The March was endorsed by labor leaders, heads of Protestant, Catholic, and Jewish bodies, and dozens of civic groups. Before and after the Washington March, the press featured almost daily during the remaining months of 1963 accounts of new sit-ins and street demonstrations. In response, President Kennedy sent a strong civil rights bill to Congress, where a warm reception by Democratic and Republican leaders indicated that "the head of black steam" had been felt by the elected officials of the nation.

"Naturally The Southerners Will Object."

A Southern concept of the Civil Rights Act.

Brooks in the Birmingham *News*

Late in June of 1964, after a protracted fight against Southern filibuster efforts in the Senate, a bipartisan coalition produced the Civil Rights Act of 1964,[45] the most comprehensive federal civil rights law since the ill-fated experiments of the 1870s. The Act does the following:

1. Outlaws racial discrimination in hotels, restaurants, theaters, gas stations, and other public accommodations that affect interstate commerce, as well as in all publicly operated facilities;
2. Forbids racial discrimination either by employers or labor unions in businesses with more than 100 employees, with this minimum number reduced gradually to twenty-five by 1968; a Federal Fair Employment Practices Commission is created to administer this policy;
3. Permits the executive to halt federal aid funds to state or private programs in which racial discrimination is allowed to continue;
4. Prohibits voting registrars from applying different standards to white and Negro applicants, requires literacy tests to be in writing, and makes a sixth-grade education a "rebuttable presumption" of literacy;
5. Extends the life of the United States Commission on Civil Rights to 1968;
6. Establishes a Community Relations Service to help conciliate racial disputes;
7. Authorizes the Attorney General to bring enforcement suits against public accommodation owners who discriminate, and on behalf of persons whose constitutional rights have been violated in school segregation or other cases.

---

[44] Public Law 88–352 (1964).

"At Least I'll Be Some Company."

A Northern concept of the Civil Rights Act.

LePelley in the *Christian Science Monitor*

Acceptance of the Civil Rights Act of 1964 by those whose former policies were now outlawed varied in 1964-65. In the public accommodations area, for example, many formerly segregated hotels and restaurants in Birmingham, Savannah, Dallas, Memphis, Charleston, and Jackson opened their service to Negroes. Other owners chose to resist. Violence was used to drive Negroes from some restaurants in Atlanta, Albany (Georgia), Laurel (Mississippi), and other communities, with suits brought against the owners in several of these instances. Some owners, as in Jackson, Richmond, and Durham, chose to turn their hotels and restaurants into "private clubs" to avoid integration; how commercially feasible these policies would be and whether they would be upheld by the courts remained to be seen. In several areas, suits were brought by owners to have the public accommodation features of the Civil Rights Act of 1964 held unconstitutional, but the Supreme Court unanimously ruled this section of the Act to be constitutional in December of 1964. As a whole, voluntary compliance with the new public accommodation rules of nondiscrimination was remarkably good in the South (and in many areas in the North where owners had previously rejected Negro clientele and there had been no state law barring such conduct). Complying owners in the deep South could now explain to their fiercely segregationist friends or customers that they were only "obeying the law" by serving Negroes. How well the voting, employment, and other features of the Act would work would take more time to tell.

Civil Rights and American Government:
The Continuing Agenda

Few civil rights supporters—or opponents—were under any illusion that passage of the 1964 federal statute would insure "instant civil rights" for the American Negro or create a state of harmonious relations between all whites and Negroes throughout the country. Indeed, of the five problems indicated as areas of protest in the 1963 Negro upheaval, the Act of 1964 did not even deal with two—increasing segregation in Negro housing and violence against civil rights workers. As if to underscore this situation, during the first month after the Act was passed, three young civil rights workers, two whites and one Negro, disappeared in Mississippi and their station wagon was found burned in a swamp. They were later found to have been murdered. Furthermore, even those problems that the Act of 1964 did cope with in far-reaching fashion, such as the fair employment issue, might rest in their fundamental solution upon economic rather than civil rights measures; unless ways could be found to overcome the unemployment problem and increase the pool of jobs for all American workers, Negroes might win a "fair share" of "not enough to go around."

Given these realities, the best way to conclude this review and analysis of civil rights is to indicate some of the major remaining problems of legal, governmental, political, and civic policy on equality that are sure to preoccupy the nation in the late 1960s.

EQUAL OPPORTUNITY, PLANNED INTEGRATION, AND COMPENSATION

Even with "full equality" for the Negro accepted by American society—as justice owing to Negroes, as essential for the health of American community life, and as a long-needed implementation of the nation's basic egalitarian ideal—problems have arisen as to what "full equality" means and what measures must be taken to bring this condition into being.

One approach, probably the view that most white Americans have adopted as both the "right" and the "practical" method, is the policy of *equal opportunity*. Whatever may have been the practices and heritage of the past, entrance today into education, public and privately owned housing, public and private employment, labor union membership, and other sectors of national socioeconomic life should be strictly on "merit," paying no attention to race, color, religion, or nationality. What our goal should be, according to the "equal opportunity" position, is a "color-blind" society.

In fields such as voting, or access to public accommodation facilities, the "color-blind" approach obviously works well, for it puts Negroes instantly on a plane of true equality. Such is not the case, however, where past practices against Negroes have built up situations of "frozen discrimination," companies with few Negroes in skilled or white-collar posts; labor unions with no Negro members; government agencies with no Negro employees; or schools that have become 80 to 95 percent Negro because of earlier "neighborhood school" criteria. If a "color-blind" policy is now applied rigorously to such situations, it could take generations before the "frozen discrimination" melts and equality is achieved. Meanwhile, the existing masses of Negroes will face a continuation of segregated education and housing, and employment opportunities will be sharply limited.

Because of this condition, many Negro groups and white civil rights supporters have come to advocate other policies, the two most important of which are *planned integration* and *compensation.* Both rest on the assumption that a society seeking true racial justice and intergroup harmony should be *color-conscious,* not *color-blind.*

Planned integration is best illustrated by the issue of housing. When public housing authorities rent apartments or when private builders sell homes in large projects, should they adopt a "first-come, first-served" policy, or should they try to achieve integrated communities by setting rough quotas of racial groups? Proponents of the "benign (or pro-integration) quota" argue that unless such quotas are adopted, apartment houses and home projects that are opened on a nondiscriminatory basis are in grave danger of becoming "all-Negro" and defeating the purpose of integration. Past studies show that because decent housing has so often been denied to Negroes in cities and suburbs, good housing in the low and middle price ranges opened to all comers quickly attracts many Negro customers. When Negro occupancy is in the 10 to 40 percent range, integration has worked well. But when the Negro proportion becomes 45 to 60 percent, what has been called the "tipping point" is reached. White families begin to feel uneasy and tend to move out; before long, the project is 90 to 100 percent Negro. This tendency may be greatly deplored, but it has been such a fundamental fact of white behavior (whatever the religious or nationality backgrounds of the whites involved) that "benign quota" advocates say ignoring it is to court disaster in housing integration in the next decades. Setting quotas based on the racial percentages in the local community as a whole, or a "tipping point" boundary of 40 percent, is seen as the solution, for this generation, at least.

Critics of this planned integration approach reply that denial of an apartment or home to a Negro, someone already hard pressed to find decent housing, violates constitutional law when done by government agencies and fair housing laws in those states or municipalities having such measures. More fundamentally, it would pander to bigotry and perpetuate an inferior, "don't tip the white man's supremacy" role for Negroes. The solution is to enforce complete antidiscrimination policies throughout the community, and to let the natural desires for "own group" and "mixed group" clusters in housing work themselves out.

Recently, a third, middle-ground approach has been developed by some integration-minded builders and private "fair housing committees." This approach seeks to keep communities balanced interracially by helping Negroes find apartments and homes in formerly all-white sections and not just in a few concentrated areas, and by asking Negroes voluntarily to refrain from "filling up" Negro sections in the suburbs or renovated sections of cities. Whether such a voluntary program can spread Negro occupancy widely enough, or whether self-segregation is too deep a force to be met in this way, remains to be seen.

The other illustration of the conflict between "color-blind" and "color-conscious" policies involves so-called *compensation programs*. These programs call for special efforts by governmental and private employers to overcome existing employment imbalances by making extra efforts to hire qualified Negroes. These "extra efforts" include preferring Negro applicants over whites when qualifications are equal, and deciding on certain numbers of Negro employees to be added each year to the factory or office force. Advocates of compensation do not suggest this as a permanent policy but only as a temporary expedient, until this generation of Negroes that have been barred from full opportunity by the discrimination of this generation of whites have been brought into situations of opportunity. In pursuit of such compensation programs, some local and national Negro groups have conducted buyers' boycotts of companies whose proportion of Negro employees is not at least near the proportion of Negroes in the local community. Advocates of compensation urge many other measures to accompany such a policy—government antipoverty campaigns, retraining for workers displaced by automation, etc.—but they are convinced that if preferment is not adopted, Negroes will be the major casualties of the structural changes taking place in the American economy in the coming decade.

Critics of compensation programs attack this proposal because they feel it perpetuates racial standards, would deepen conflict between white and Negro work-competitors from assembly line to executive suite, would penalize whites today for what whites did fifty or twenty-five years ago, would operate against the interests of other economically disadvantaged nonwhite groups (such as Puerto Ricans, Mexican-Americans, etc.), and would create initiative-destroying expectations of paternalistic treatment among Negroes themselves. The solution here, it is argued, is a combination of total nondiscrimination; major governmental and private programs of education, training, and employment of job-seekers; and determined efforts by Negroes themselves to win recognition of their talents in the new equality ethos which provides the milieu for Negro self-respect and initiative.

TECHNIQUES OF CIVIL RIGHTS STRUGGLE: ON THE LIMITS OF CIVIL DISOBEDIENCE IN A FREE SOCIETY

One of the frontier problems facing American law and government in the coming decade in the equality area involves the techniques of protest used by Negroes and their white allies. Dr. Martin Luther King, Jr., expressed the view of most civil rights groups when he noted realistically in 1963 that only "pressure" had brought Negroes their recent gains in civil rights.

> History is the long and tragic story of the fact that privileged groups seldom give up their privileges voluntarily. Individuals may see the moral light and voluntarily give up their unjust posture; but as Reinhold Niebuhr has reminded us, groups are more immoral than individuals. We know through painful experience that freedom is

never voluntarily given by the oppressor; it must be demanded by the oppressed.[46]

In keeping with this view, the techniques of "demand" and "pressure" have gone through several distinct phases in the period from 1941 to the present. Between 1941 and 1953, successful Negro protests were primarily in the form of legal test suits sponsored by the NAACP; negotiation and bargaining with Northern white businessmen and government officials, primarily by the National Urban League; and local lobbying for civil rights legislation and executive action by Negro political and civic leaders in Northern communities. There were occasional picket lines, buyers' boycotts, rallies, and marches, but these rarely achieved major importance. Between 1954 and 1963, law suits continued, both to enforce the new constitutional rules and to defend arrested civil rights workers, as did negotiations and lobbying in the North. To these classic techniques were added new methods we have discussed earlier: sit-ins and other entries into segregated facilities; Freedom Rides; large-scale community boycotts; and large-scale street demonstrations (whether to picket, pray, or march). All of these were nonviolent, and what violence did ensue took the form of unanswered white attacks on the demonstrators. In most instances, the demonstrators were seeking to persuade Southern public officials to obey the supreme law of the land, and in most instances the means chosen—picketing, peaceful demonstrations, boycotts, etc.—were clearly legal means of protest under existing Supreme Court rulings. Only the sit-in technique, with its trespass on an owner's property and refusal to leave when told to, posed a question—the limits of permissible protest—on which the Supreme Court had not directly ruled as of 1964.

After 1963, even more "militant" techniques of "direct action" began to be used, especially by the newer civil rights groups such as the Congress of Racial Equality, the Student Non-Violent Coordinating Committee, and various local civil rights committees. One such tactic was harassment of general community life. This took the form of halting traffic on the Brooklyn Bridge at the height of the evening rush hour by lying across the roadway, dumping garbage collected from Negro slum areas in front of City Hall in New York, and deliberately stalling cars on highways leading to civic events such as baseball games. Other actions threatened by these activists included leaving the water faucets open all day in a city to create water shortages or jamming the telephone switchboards to city halls by mass telephone campaigns. Such harassment techniques have been defended as the only way to "break through community apathy" and "focus attention" on the socioeconomic and constitutional claims of Negroes.

Another example of the new techniques is to blockade public officials or private parties who refuse to take the action sought by civil rights groups. Pickets with arms locked have kept teachers and educational administrators from entering school offices, until police broke a path through; other activists have lain down in the path of bulldozers and chained themselves to entrance gates at construction sites where job dis-

---

[46] Quoted in Westin, *op. cit.*, p. vi.

crimination was alleged; and others have formed "human walls" across the driveways of restaurants and food markets where it was said that insufficient numbers of Negroes were employed. The militants argue that no one can be "neutral" and go on with "business as usual." To continue working on such projects or in such businesses is to commit an act against civil rights.

These techniques of harassment and blockade have raised the question of how far civil rights militants should go—legally and morally—in support of their claims. In the case of the Southern sit-ins and protest marches, civil rights leaders have pointed out that these techniques were directed against public officials and civic leaders who had flatly refused to obey the nation's laws or to negotiate on ways to end racial discrimination. The protests were pinpointed, nonviolent, affected those who were engaging in acts of discrimination, and created the basis for court cases that would rule on the legality of the acts complained against. But when harassment of general populations or blockades of facilities are carried on, and especially in Northern communities where the full processes of law, politics, and civic protest are open to Negroes, many legal experts and citizens feel the boundary line has been crossed into improper conduct. Setting out exactly the degrees of militant protest that are constitutionally protected free expression and those that are not will obviously be a major activity of the courts in the coming decade, and drawing the moral and tactically advantageous lines will account for a major part of the tension among Negro civil rights groups themselves.

These illustrations of major problems indicate that the journey to full equality by a heterogeneous society with a long heritage of racial discrimination will not be easy, especially when the problems are complicated by radical technological and socioeconomic changes in American life. The militants will be needed to press for the content and not just the forms of equality, and the moderates will be needed to find workable solutions and prevent the struggle from embittering the whole of American civic life. Perhaps the most important point to note, especially in light of the history of the American double standard, is that our era is now one in which the ideal and the reality of American life are being brought into as much harmony as human institutions, at their best, will allow.

PART V

GOVERNMENT

IN ACTION

20 / Government and the Economy: Politics, Process, and Substance

In *The Federalist*, James Madison set forth many reasons why men divided into contending groups in society, such as "zeal for different opinions concerning religion, concerning government, and many other points," and also "attachment to different leaders." He recognized, however, that the economic factor was crucial:

> But the most common and durable source of factions has been the various and unequal distribution of property. Those who hold and those who are without property have ever formed distinct interests in society. Those who are creditors, and those who are debtors, fall under a like discrimination. A landed interest, a manufacturing interest, a mercantile interest, a moneyed interest, with many lesser interests, grow up of necessity in civilized nations, and divide them into different classes, actuated by different sentiments and views.

"The regulation of these various and interfering interests," he added, "forms the principal task of modern legislation. . . ." [1]

Madison's contemporaries saw the possibilities for a more positive and selective role for government in the economy. Hamilton proposed that government should promote finance and manufacturing, while Jefferson desired that government advance the interests of agriculture "and of commerce as its handmaid."

The Constitution itself was an economic document. It reconciled sectional interests, as in the compromises on commerce. It contained many decisions favorable to property rights. It granted Congress the powers of regulation that Madison foresaw would be needed—to "regulate commerce," to "coin money" and "regulate the value thereof." It provided for facilities for commerce—for example, a common system of weights and measures, and patents and copyrights. Buttressed by Justice John Marshall's opinions, the Constitution would free the commerce of the nation from state restraints and thus open one great national market for goods. In short, it provided a basis for a national economy, with national protections for capital and commerce and power to regulate them.

There have been special reasons for the dominance of economic issues in the United States. Certain noneconomic issues which have split men

---

[1] *The Federalist*, No. 10.

into warring groups in other countries have been largely absent from the American political arena. The representative form of government and the separation of religion and government are matters on which there has been general consensus. Relations with foreign countries have raised fewer issues during most of our history than in other countries. The result has been that issues of politics naturally turned on economic policy. There has been, moreover, a general consensus in favor of the capitalistic system. Lines of policy development have thus followed durable patterns over time, and the contest among "the various and interfering interests" has been moderate and often obscured by the multiple institutions of government within which policy decisions were made.

Historic Trends in the Role of Government

The American consensus on the capitalistic system of production has been accompanied by an acceptance of certain traditional functions of government. Safeguards for property ownership and for private contracts have been embedded in the common law, in constitutions, and in legislation since the founding of the nation. Provisions for a monetary system, a postal system, and other facilities of commerce were, by 1789, established functions of government.

A study of the politics of the nation in the early years shows that even at that time men generally were willing to accept an even larger role of government, provided that it would advance their interests. Prior to the Civil War, sections and groups struggled for the support of their interests on four large economic issues: (1) tariffs for protection of home production; (2) development of the West—which involved internal improvements, sale of land in small portions or at low cost, and grants of land to homesteaders; (3) easy credit terms versus sound banking; (4) free labor versus slave labor.

Recent historical research has shown that at this period men also sought state legislation to advance their economic welfare. Legislatures provided "internal improvements"—roads, canals, and, for a period, railways—to advance agriculture, commerce, and industry. Also numerous laws were passed for the licensing of occupations, inspection of goods, protection of debtors, and other purposes, all of which involved detailed regulation of economic pursuits. Louis Hartz has concluded that in the early part of our history people saw no threat to their personal liberty in government legislation to promote their economic interests.[2]

In the course of the nineteenth century, however, two changes occurred—one political and the other economic. Political power was democratized; that is, the control of all branches of government, except the federal courts and some state courts, formally passed to the people directly. Giant corporations arose and economic power was concentrated in financial and industrial leaders. Political power, widely dispersed, and economic power, highly concentrated, came in conflict. The former was reflected in succes-

---

[2] Louis Hartz, *Economic Policy and Democratic Thought: Pennsylvania, 1776–1860* (Cambridge, Mass., 1948).

History Repeats Itself

An 1889 cartoon compared the robber barons of the Middle Ages with the robber barons of the day.

sive demands for government regulation—from members of the Grange, from the Populist and Progressive movements. Faced with this situation, those who suffered economically from the new regulations embraced, as a means of defense, the ideology of laissez faire. This ideology, which holds that government should not intervene in the economy, was widely proclaimed by a rising group of professional economists and was used by attorneys representing clients who were disappointed with the results of politics in legislative and administrative bodies.

The laissez-faire theorists did not want the elimination of all government regulation—they were not anarchists. They knew that government, in protecting property rights, also in effect "regulated" them—that is, it determined which property rights would be protected and to what extent, and what contracts would be enforced. What they desired was a line of protection against regulations that they thought were unreasonable. They believed, in effect, in selective laissez faire, and they sought to determine the principles that would—and should, in their view—fix the appropriate role of government in the economy.

In the United States those who were dissatisfied with regulatory laws had a peculiar opportunity. With judicial review of legislation established as a national tradition, they could turn to the courts, particularly to the Supreme Court. At first, the Supreme Court upheld regulatory statutes, declaring in 1876 that "for protection against abuses of legislatures the people must resort to the polls, not to the courts." [3] Attorneys representing

---

[3] *Munn* v. *Illinois*, 94 U.S. 113, 134 (1877).

the losers in legislative battles were, however, persistent, and, in a short time, successful. The Supreme Court became arbiter for a full half-century (from about 1887 to 1937) of conflicts over the proper function of government in economy. It limited the power of first the state legislatures and then Congress, which in the twentieth century began to pass legislation similar to that previously enacted by the states.

The Court was able to exercise this function through the due process clauses of the Fifth and Fourteenth Amendments. It interpreted these clauses to mean that the legislatures could not pass laws that would deprive people of acquired property rights or certain economic liberties except for proper purposes and by proper means. The Court elaborated a set of guiding principles for determining in specific cases what was proper, and hence constitutional. Thus liberty, according to the Court, included the right to engage in an occupation; this liberty could be legally infringed by license or certificate requirements for the practice of learned professions or for supplying utility services or by prohibition or regulation of some businesses, like liquor or prostitution, which could be regarded as inherently damaging to the community. On the other hand, the Court held that entry could not be restricted in businesses not falling within the categories of reasonable exceptions—anyone had the right to run an employment agency or an ice business. According to judicial doctrine, liberty of contract, which included the right to contract about wages, hours, and prices, was also guaranteed by due process. Exceptions could be made to this right by legislation if they were enacted for certain paramount public interests, such as protection of health. But exception could not be normally made on labor matters where the major purpose was to alter the positions of parties or merely to increase the economic benefit of one party. For example, in one famous case in 1905, the Court declared invalid a New York State statute that would limit bakery employees to a ten-hour day because of health hazards associated with flour dust. Said the Court,

> . . . we think that such a law as this, although passed in the assumed exercise of the police power, and as relating to the public health, or the health of the employees named, is not within that power, and is invalid. The act is not . . . a health law, but is an illegal interference with the rights of individuals, both employers and employees, to make contracts regarding labor upon such terms as they may think best. . . .[4]

The Court's writing of selective laissez faire into the Constitution under the rubric of due process and its erection of a set of doctrines for determining which exceptions were legitimate was criticized both within the Court itself and outside it. Informed observers could see that on the great economic confrontations of the day—labor versus capital, consumers versus utility monopolies—the Court's principles gave victory to one side against the other. Attacks within the Court began with the premise that the Court could not pass judgment on issues by reference to assumed abstract principles on the relation of the government to the economy. Justice Holmes,

---

[4] *Lochner v. New York*, 198 U.S. 45, 61 (1905).

who dissented in the Court decision that declared invalid the New York statute limiting the hours of bakery employees, argued as follows: "The Fourteenth Amendment does not enact Mr. Herbert Spencer's *Social Statics* [the leading polemical writing of the laissez-faire school of thought]. . . . A Constitution is not intended to embody a particular economic theory, whether of paternalism and the organic relation of the citizen to the state or of laissez faire." The more moderate attack came from men such as Justice Brandeis, who argued that the legitimacy of particular pieces of legislation should not be determined according to their conformity with ideological principles but, rather, empirically: Was the legislation in question a reasonable means of correcting an existing evil? Brandeis thought that much more deference should be given to the legislature's judgment on what was reasonable. The other line of attack went even further: If the Constitution did not embody one economic theory over another, then issues of economic policy were outside the jurisdiction of the courts altogether, and interests contending for economic policies on their behalf should appeal not to the courts but rather to the legislative or executive branches through the machinery provided by the Constitution.

The Great Depression, however, was the event that shattered the Court's edifice of constitutional principles. Not only labor and consumers, who had suffered judicial defeats in the past, but also investors—those in whose interests the court had voided laws—looked to government for remedial legislation. A change of view was presaged by a 1934 Supreme Court decision, announced by Justice Roberts, upholding a minimum price law for milk, although milk was not a product traditionally in the special category of public utilities. Said Justice Roberts,

> It is clear that there is no closed class or category of businesses affected with a public interest. . . . The phrase "affected with a public interest" can, in the nature of things, mean no more than that an industry, for adequate reason, is subject to control for the public good.[5]

Shortly thereafter, in 1937, the Court reversed the old opinion that government could not set minimum wages for women, and a little later it upheld the act by which Congress set maximum hours and minimum wages for both male and female employees.

The Court has now scrapped most of the limitations on regulatory power which it developed after 1880. There are still major limitations in favor of property, such as the Fifth Amendment's prohibition against appropriating property without just compensation, or the judicial rule that utility rates fixed by public agencies must be fair and reasonable. Yet the Court has substantially adopted the view of Justice Holmes that the Constitution does not embody any economic theory, and has thereby reverted to the view of 1876 that economic policy is to be determined by the political process rather than through the courts.

Today the issues of economic policy are viewed differently than they were in the judicial setting of 1887–1937. First, the Court, and indeed most

---

[5] *Nebbia* v. *New York,* 291 U.S. 502, 536 (1937).

commentators on public issues, used to posit only two interests, which were considered as being in complete opposition. As far back as the Charles River Bridge case in 1837 (in which the Court upheld a Massachusetts legislative action that overrode a bridge company's contractual claim), the Court has had to make decisions between large public interests and conflicting private interests. Today, however, it is recognized that there are many "various and interfering interests," as Madison said, and that regulatory legislation may be, in effect, a decision that advances some private interests at the expense of others. The meaningful protections for the various interests are rarely found in judicial doctrines, which prevent one interest from winning by voiding or upholding legislation favoring one group over another; protections do exist, however, in the legislative and administrative processes of government, where all interests can obtain a hearing and consideration of their demands for government action or inaction.

Second, a factor that Madison did not foresee is now recognized: that interests are interdependent and that particular interests are dependent on the successful performance of the economy as a whole. An executive's property values and opportunities for investment, a laborer's opportunity for a job—indeed, all men's opportunity to sustain their earnings—may be dependent upon forces beyond their control. Even a man's liberty is not safeguarded to him solely by the absence of government restraint; as President Johnson said in a commencement address at Swarthmore College, "The truth is, far from crushing the individual, government at its best liberates him from the enslaving forces of his environment."

Third, men do not view the contemporary problem as being one of separation of the political and economic orders, but as being the determination of the appropriate combination of economic forces and political action. It is no longer assumed that government can stay out of the economy completely. The questions are as follows: To what extent can economic forces be expected to operate beneficially? And in what ways can government effectively supplement or supplant them?

Finally, it is no longer assumed that issues of economic policy will be determined according to rational, universal principles of jurisprudence or morality. It is assumed instead that they will be determined through political processes in which the contending interests press for advantage within an institutional system in which committee members of Congress and their staff aides, the President and his staff aides, administrative bureaus or commissions, and outside consultants analyze which solutions to problems are desirable and workable. These processes will now be examined in some detail.

The Establishment of Programs

Legislation for the initiation of a new government activity is the result of the political processes we have just described. For example, railroad regulation began in this country because users of the railroads—farmers, merchants, and other groups—became indignant over what they felt were exorbitantly high rates and discrimination in charges among different types of shippers and among different shippers. This indignation led to the establishment of state commissions, beginning in Illinois in 1871, with authority to regulate rates, and establishment of the Interstate Commerce Commission in 1887 for the purpose of preventing unreasonable and discriminatory rates. Thus railroad regulation was the result of demands from groups outside and antagonistic to the railroad industry.

Licensing laws represent another source of demand for regulation. Though some licensing laws have resulted from demands of external groups (for example, in the field of foods and drugs), occupational groups themselves have often demanded government action to exclude from their ranks persons who did not meet desired standards. Lawyers, doctors, teachers, plumbers, beauticians, and many other groups have obtained licensing for their occupations.

When the conflict is among industry groups, the victory goes to the dominant groups. A good example is the establishment of production controls in the oil industry. In 1930 a wildcatter brought in the East Texas oil field—a strip some eight miles wide and forty miles long which began to yield oil in unanticipated quantities. The strip was occupied by small farmers, city lot-holders, and other owners of small tracts. Under the "rule of capture" of Texas law each had the right to capture the oil under his land by drilling wells. Many wells were quickly drilled, oil flowed in abundance—and the price of crude oil dropped from over one dollar to ten cents per barrel. The drilling had only started, and an industry was demoralized. Drilling contractors, new refinery companies in the area, many local interests, and a rapidly growing "independent" oil industry (that is, uncontrolled by the major companies) found quick returns in the situation, but the major oil industries and some independent interests found it intolerable. After special sessions of the legislature of Texas the latter interests, aided by the arguments that there was a public interest in prevention of wasted oil, won the victory; a system of restriction of oil production, called proration, was established.[6]

The conflict over legislation is often, as in the case of oil, among ownership groups. A different kind of conflict is indicated by legislation dealing with labor-management relations; here the conflict is between ownership and workers. Each side has pushed for legislation in its favor and each has tried to use the agencies of political struggle—the political parties, the press, the speaker's platform, group organization, and lobbying—to obtain the legislation it desired or to repeal that which it opposed. The result has been an increasingly intensive regulation of labor-management relations.

All groups demanding legislation try to show that there is a public need for doing what they demand. There may be real substance in such claims. The shipper's interest in transportation is obvious, and railroad transportation was a necessity for the development of the nation. It can be argued that the economics of overhead costs made it inevitable for the railroads to discriminate in rates in order to get big shippers' business and then to combine among themselves to avoid cutthroat competition; there appeared,

---

[6] See Warner E. Mills, Jr., *Martial Law in East Texas* (University, Ala., 1960).

therefore, to be a real public need for regulation. Licensing of doctors or even of beauticians may meet a real public need for protection of health (or ladies' beauty) against poorly trained practitioners. Oil proration may indeed have been one route to conservation of a scarce resource, particularly in view of the engineers' discovery in East Texas that uncontrolled drilling and production was reducing the water pressure which pushed the oil to the surface.

In some cases this need for public action is so clearly evident that the government acts without strong interest group pressure. An example is the allocation in the 1920s of wavelengths for radio services. The technology of radio communication called for prevention of interference among users, and clearly this need for regulation would become more urgent as more users, and new uses, of the electromagnetic spectrum created a shortage of wavelength bands. Similarly, an air traffic system, involving licensing of airmen and aircraft, and ultimately a large air traffic control system, was essential for safety of all who use the airways. Even earlier, the economics of public utility service made it generally obvious that utilities were "natural monopolies" and would need to be regulated for the public interests. For a large city any other system would be impossible, since a city must limit the rights granted by franchise to use and even repeatedly tear up its streets, and a large city like New York which places its utility facilities underground faces complex engineering problems.

Even when public needs are inherent in a situation, interest groups are influential during the period when programs of government control and service are being established. For example, there were groups eager to supply radio, air transportation, and utilities services for profit. The interests of these groups were made known to legislators and were influential in determining the scope and types of public legislative policy. Always then, new government activity is created in the crucible of politics.

Government programs, however, must do more than merely achieve compromises among interest groups. Legislators, executives, and staff aides also try to choose technically feasible and economically and socially satisfactory ways of attaining desired objectives. The experiences of the past will often help to reveal methods which can be used to meet a new situation. For example, when the National Labor Relations Act was passed in 1935 the draftsmen built on techniques of past legislation. Following the Federal Trade Commission Act of 1914, which prohibited "unfair methods of competition," this act prohibited "unfair labor practices." Just as the prohibition in the first act was to be enforced by cease and desist orders issued by a federal commission, so the new act would be enforced by the same kind of orders issued by the National Labor Relations Board. The system of elections to determine the representatives of employees for purposes of collective bargaining was borrowed, at least in part, from the 1934 amendments to the Railway Labor Act. Today a considerable body of technique and administrative experience is available to the legislator. Old models will not always serve, however. The framers of the Public Utility Holding Company Act of 1935 had to search for new concepts and new techniques. They found that public utility holding companies could be justified only if they were the means of attaining geographically and economically integrated utility systems, and they devised techniques through which the existing complicated systems, built by promoters to obtain extraordinary financial gains, could be simplified toward this primary objective.

In searching for new techniques of legislation and new means of enforcement, politicians must seek the aid of technical experts in establishing policies. Government programs thus represent responses both to dominant groups in politics and to informed judgments on what is workable. Although many students of government stress the development of policies as responses to interest group pressures, the contributions of the administrators and experts are vital. One observer has argued that objective study and scientific research have been the primary ingredients of public-policy development:

> . . . the development of public policy and of the methods of its administration owed less in the long run to the processes of conflict among political parties and social or economic pressure groups than to the more objective processes of research and discussion among professional groups.[7]

Only a rational policy that reflects both political pressures and professional expertness can blend conflicting interests to create a solution that is efficient and acceptable to the parties concerned.

The Administration of Programs

As discussed in Chapter 11, government programs, particularly economic ones, are generally administered by bureaus within Departments, independent executive agencies, or independent regulatory commissions. The Food and Drug Administration is in the Department of Health, Education and Welfare; the Packers and Stockyards Administration, agricultural stabilization functions, and many other regulatory functions are in the Department of Agriculture; and the Antitrust Division is in the Department of Justice. Other agencies, such as the Atomic Energy Commission and the Federal Aviation Agency, are independent executive establishments. In addition, the independent regulatory boards and commissions represent a unique feature of economic administration.

AGENCY OPERATIONS

A great effort has been made to ensure that these agencies operate in accordance with standards set forth in legislation. Although they are given wide discretion in the application of legal standards, they may be overruled by the courts or subjected to Congressional investigation. Administration by commissions has been defended as a means of providing expert consideration of policy and application of law. Staff members of these

---

[7] Don K. Price, *Government and Science: Their Dynamic Relation in American Democracy* (New York, 1954), p. v.

agencies, recruited on the basis of special competence and serving for long periods, become experts in their fields. Procedural requirements, many of which are in the Administrative Procedure Act, are designed to ensure fairness to affected parties, adequate attainment of statutory objectives, and efficient execution of agency work without unnecessary delays and expense to the government and private parties.

Since few agency decisions are reviewed in the courts, procedural agency processes have special importance. The process by which the Civil Aeronautics Board determines whether to grant a permit to an airline to institute service from one city to another may serve as an example of the work of the agencies that regulate industries (rail, motor, water, air transportation, radio and TV, and power). The application is docketed, and other related applications may be consolidated with it for consideration as a group. The docket may eventually contain numerous applications and relate to large areas of service; this was true, for example, of the Chicago–New York Service case decided in 1955, which examined the needs for service to two major cities. After decisions on consolidation the docketed case will be assigned to an examiner by a chief hearing examiner.

The examiner, similar to a trial judge, fills a position provided for in the Administrative Procedure Act. He is appointed from Civil Service Commission lists, his salary is determined by the Commission, and he can be removed only after a hearing by the Commission. In other words, he is substantially independent from agency control.

The examiner will usually call the parties together in a prehearing conference, as do judges in many court cases, to define the scope of the case and set forth ground rules for the proceedings. In accordance with these rules, written evidence and rebuttals will be submitted by the parties on prescribed dates. Next there will be an open hearing with cross-examination of witnesses on the evidence submitted and with oral arguments by the attorneys. The examiner will then make what is called an "initial decision," though the agencies sometimes, in accordance with discretion allowed by the Administrative Procedure Act, allow examiners to make only recommended decisions.

After the examiner's decision the parties may appeal to the Board. The case is then placed on the Board's dockets, briefs are received from attorneys, and oral argument presented to the Board. Since the Board is deluged with many items of business, it will be assisted by the General Counsel's office, and the individual members of the Board will be assisted by their attorney aides. After the Board's decision some parties will probably ask for reconsideration, and the Board will probably deny it. Thereafter, any party may appeal to a court of appeals, and thereafter, through application for a writ of certiorari, to the Supreme Court.

The foregoing is a simplified statement of a procedure which may become quite intricate and lengthy. Another simplified illustration of the work of a regulatory agency is the procedure of the Federal Trade Commission in handling a false-advertising case. The statute authorizes the Commission to issue a complaint when such action is in the "public interest," and to issue a cease and desist order if it finds there is a violation of the provision which prevents "unfair methods of competition and unfair and deceptive acts in commerce." The staff of the Commission handling enforcement cases is divided into three parts: preliminary investigation, prosecution, and hearing. Certain offices within the Commission consider complaints received by the Commission alleging violation of law, and on their own initiative they examine the advertising copy of newspapers, magazines, radio, and television. A company may learn that its advertising copy is under question and come to the Commission offices for a conference with the staff. It may adjust its copy to avoid a staff recommendation to the Commission that a complaint be issued. If the staff or the Commission itself does recommend that a complaint be issued, the companies may, without admitting guilt, sign a consent decree to cease and desist. In either event the case comes to an end. If neither action is taken, the case is docketed for hearing. It is assigned by the chief hearing examiner to a subordinate examiner who becomes the judge in the proceedings. The prosecution office within the Commission will assign one or more attorneys for prosecution. The Administrative Procedure Act requires complete separation of the prosecuting and adjudicatory staffs and prevents the examiner from consulting with either of the parties (the accused or the Commission attorneys) without giving notice to the other and the opportunity to participate. After taking testimony in open hearing, receiving briefs from attorneys, and hearing oral arguments, the examiner will take the case under advisement and in due time issue an initial decision. From this decision the parties may appeal to the Commission.

These are examples of judicialized procedures. In other cases, where rules are issued and the statute does not require decision on a record, the procedure will be legislative. The Administrative Procedure Act requires (with many exceptions) that unless the agency finds it "impracticable, unnecessary, or contrary to the public interest," notice of the intention to make a rule must be published and opportunity given to interested persons to present their views either in written or oral form. These provisions allow for agency flexibility. On the other hand, in some important types of rule-making proceedings, such as rate-making, statutes regularly provide for a decision based on a record made in a hearing.

In still other cases the procedure is administrative. An example is that of the Board of Governors of the Federal Reserve System in making decisions on open-market purchases of United States securities. Every three weeks the seven members of the Board of Governors and the twelve presidents of the Federal Reserve Banks meet in Washington to discuss open-market purchases; the members of the Board and five of the presidents selected for this purpose then determine the policy to be followed. This is neither an adjudicatory decision nor rule-making, but an operating decision to govern Federal Reserve purchases; many agency decisions fall into this category. They may be procedural decisions, such as the decision to consolidate several applications for airline service. Or they may be management decisions, such as that providing more personnel for a particular task. They may be decisions on what is called informal disposal of cases; that is, disposal without a hearing. This category may include a decision not to issue a complaint, or a decision to accept a party's agreement to desist from an alleged offense, or a decision to allow an interim rate increase pending the decision in a formal proceeding.

Similar tasks are handled by similar processes in different agencies, whether they are commissions, independent executive agencies, or Departments. Statutory provisions, judicial decisions, and agency practice have brought substantial uniformity in basic procedures, though there remain variations among agencies in details.

The ideal objectives of the administration agencies can never be fully attained, of course. The effort to provide fair procedure may result in lengthy, expensive proceedings: In a report to President-elect Kennedy in late 1960 James Landis attacked the "inordinate delays" and the cost of administrative proceedings. Fairness among parties may be prevented by the failure to develop standards according to which decisions can be made. The need for more adequate standards of decision has been vigorously argued by many professional observers. Agencies may be so loaded with decisions on particular applications and other matters that they have little time to consider emerging or long-standing policy problems. Expertness may suffer because of rapid turnover of agency heads or failure to obtain and retain a qualified staff.

It has been argued that economic regulation should be nonpolitical and hence that it should be undertaken by commissions composed of members from both parties, serving long, overlapping terms, and having substantial independence from the President. It has been shown in Chapter 11 that this effort may conflict with the need for Presidential leadership and co-ordination and is in conflict with the trends which have made the President "the mainspring" of the political system.

The effort to make regulation a nonpolitical process is only partially successful. Politics does not end when a regulatory statute is passed; it swirls thereafter around the regulatory agencies. Some of these have the power to grant certificates or licenses which may soon be worth millions of dollars—for example, a television license in a big city; some can determine rates of charge which will affect the profit and loss account of business concerns; the Federal Reserve Board and the Federal Home Loan Bank Board can influence interest rates; all can take types of action which determine how many dollars will go into which pockets. This creates politics at two levels: that of influence upon decisions in particular cases, and that of influence on longer-run policies.

INFLUENCE ON DECISION OF PARTICULAR CASES

In 1958 the shocking disclosures of a House subcommittee led to the resignation of two high-ranking public officials. Commissioner Richard A. Mack served on the Federal Communications Commission and cast his vote on which of four applicants would receive one of the juiciest awards ever given by the Commission: the Channel 10 television assignment for Miami, Florida. The testimony before the subcommittee showed that Mack had received substantial sums from companies in which he had invested no money, and that the arrangement for this was made by a friend who was at the same time expressing interest in behalf of the award of Channel

10 to one of the applicants; there were even rumors that Mack had pledged his vote. The other resignation was that of Sherman Adams, Assistant to the President of the United States, who had often been referred to as "Assistant President." Adams had intervened "off the record" with FTC in aid of Bernard Goldfine—whose exceedingly close friendship was evidenced in substantial personal gifts to Adams.

The resignation of these two officials concentrated attention on a problem that had previously received insufficient notice. No informed person believed that Mack's behavior was typical of commissioners. The significance of the Mack case was that the testimony before the subcommittee showed that various parties seeking Channel 10 had sought to find friends who could make friendly contacts with the commissioners, and that United States Senators communicated with commissioners on behalf of applicants. As one newspaper put it, the whole thing formed "a picture of county courthouse finagling at its unloveliest." [8] Combined with the revelations of the "off-the-record" visits and telephone calls of former New Deal official Thomas G. Corcoran to members of the Federal Power Commission in behalf of his client, the Midwestern Gas Transmission Co., the Mack case portrayed the existence of a system of ex parte (off-the-record) contacts with commissioners on cases which were required by law to be decided on the basis of a public record. The Adams case served to emphasize that communications to commissioners from highly placed political officials carried dangers of influence on decision. Such communications from the President's office were believed to be quite exceptional, and Adams' actions led to his resignation; but such communications from Congress were known to be a customary part of a Congressman's service to constituents and caused no resignations of Congressmen.

The aftermath of these revelations has been a search for a remedy. There has been agreement on the need but uncertainty as to what should be prohibited and what the methods of enforcement should be. One proposal came from President Kennedy, who sent a message to Congress in 1961 recommending

> legislation requiring each agency, within 120 days, to promulgate a code of behavior specifying the particular standard to be applied in each type of agency proceeding and containing an absolute prohibition against ex parte contact in all proceedings between private parties in which law or agency regulation requires that a decision be made solely on the record of a formal hearing.

Many believe that the only effective remedy is for the agencies to disclose all communications received by them on types of matters which should be determined without political influence. Others think that the problem of influence can be solved only by drastic surgery on regulatory commissions, which would take away their judicial functions and place these in specialized judicial tribunals.

---

[8] See Victor G. Rosenblum, "How to Get into TV: The Federal Communications Commission and Miami's Channel 10," in Alan F. Westin, ed., *The Uses of Power* (New York, 1962).

An example of a contest over policy will illustrate the continuing impact of politics on government regulation.[9] The case relates to natural gas and is chosen because it illustrates clearly many aspects of the struggle of groups to control regulatory policy.

The natural gas industry is regulated on three levels. Distribution to consumers is regulated by the state in which the gas is received. The physical acts of producing gas and gathering it at terminals are regulated by the state in which the gas is produced. The intermediate step, i.e., transportation and sale of gas at wholesale (to distributing companies) by pipeline companies, is regulated by the national government under the Natural Gas Act of 1938. This act provided for regulation of wholesale sales in interstate commerce; it exempted "the production and gathering" of gas. This exemption was the subject of the battle here summarized. When did "production and gathering" end—after or before sale to the pipeline company? If after sale, then producers' prices were exempt from regulation; if before sale, then they were subject to regulation under the law.

The Federal Power Commission is the agency of administration for the Natural Gas Act. It did not assert jurisdiction over sales of "independents" (that is, concerns which were not pipelines or subsidiaries of pipelines) to pipelines. Nevertheless, some of the phrasing used by the Commission, and the failure of the courts to declare a favorable interpretation, aroused the fears of the independents that they might be held to be subject to the rate-making powers of the Commission.

The significance of such a decision for the gas producer can be understood only if two other facts are kept in mind. First, the producer regards himself as being in a speculative venture, reaching for great gains but in danger of falling along the way. Second, the Federal Power Commission espoused the rule of fair return on actual legitimate investment. To the independent gas producer such a rule seemed like an absurd transfer of notions developed for monopolistic utility industries to a speculative mining industry. The "independents," some of which were large companies, decided to fight to prevent the threatened regulation.

The first round of the battle took place before the Congress. Although the FPC tried to allay fears that it would assert jurisdiction, bills reflecting the desires of the natural gas industry were introduced in both houses of Congress to restrict the jurisdiction of the Commission. Ultimately the bill considered was referred to as the Kerr bill, after Senator Kerr of Oklahoma, a gas-producing state. In 1948 and 1949 the bills passed the House by large majorities, but did not emerge from the Senate Committee on Interstate and Foreign Commerce. The first round thus ended indecisively. Then in 1949 the second round was fought in a contest over the renomination of Commissioner Leland Olds of the Federal Power Commission. Olds had been a member of the Commission for ten years and had been

[9] The summary is taken substantially from Emmette S. Redford, *American Government and the Economy* (New York, 1965), pp. 486–89. And see Joseph P. Harris, "The Senatorial Rejection of Leland Olds: A Case Study," *American Political Science Review* (September, 1951), Vol. XLV, pp. 674–92.

widely hailed as a leader in the development of the Commission's regulation of electric utilities and natural gas. By 1949 he had reached the conclusion that the Federal Power Commission did have jurisdiction over independent producers' rates and had opposed the enactment of the Kerr bill. For this reason the gas industry opposed his renomination, by charging, through a member of the House of Representatives from Texas (another gas state), that Olds in his early manhood had held Communist ideas. The battle was fought vigorously in the Senate committee considering the renomination and on the floor of the Senate, and in spite of President Truman's intervention to urge his confirmation, Olds's appointment was rejected by a 53-to-15 vote. Round two obviously went to the producers. The battle now moved into a third round, the Senate consideration of the Kerr bill in 1950. The Federal Power Commission was itself now divided on the issue of whether it had jurisdiction under the act of 1938, and it appeared that, in the absence of new legislation, the issue would be determined by the new chairman of the Commission. Under these conditions the decision on the Kerr bill was important. The debate was a hard-fought one between Senators from gas-producing states and those from consuming states. Senators representing producing states argued that regulation was unnecessary because of competition among producers and that regulation was dangerous because it would dampen the urge for exploration. The opposition denied both arguments. In the end the bill passed the Senate 44 to 38 and the House concurred in amendments and passed the bill by a vote of 176 to 174. President Truman vetoed it, and the veto stood. Round three restored the contest to a draw. The fourth round was fought inside the Commission. The issue was focused in the Phillips case, in which the Commission was to determine whether the Phillips Petroleum Company, a large independent, was subject to the act. The Commission held that it was not. Commissioner Draper, who voted with the majority, was confirmed by the Senate for a new term; Commissioner Buchanan, who voted with the minority for holding the company subject to the act, was not confirmed when his reappointment came up. Round four was another victory for producers. The fifth round of the battle was before the Supreme Court. The Phillips case went upward on appeal to the Court.[10] There it was decided by a 5-to-3 vote that the Commission had been wrong—that it did have jurisdiction over the Phillips Company's sales and hence over producers' sales generally. This decision, a victory for consumers, led to increased effort by legislators representing the gas-producing states. A sixth round was fought, this one again in the Congress, which passed a modified bill restricting jurisdiction. Then an unusual event tipped the scales to the other side. Senator Case of South Dakota announced that he had been offered a payment of $2,500 to influence his vote on the issue. President Eisenhower thereupon vetoed the bill, stating his approval of the purposes of the bill but abhorrence of the methods of some of its proponents.

This put the problem back on the doorsteps of the Commission, where round seven was to be fought. By Supreme Court decision the Commission

---

[10] *Phillips Petroleum Co.* v. *Wisconsin*, 347 U.S. 672 (1954).

now had the jurisdiction it had previously declined to take. It faced one of the thorniest problems ever handed to a regulatory agency: By what method should it determine the value of the gas sold by independents to pipelines? Should it set prices on the basis of costs of each producer-seller, thereby giving different prices to different sellers in the same gas field? Justice Jackson of the Supreme Court had argued in a decision in 1944 that this would be absurd.[11] He had said that utility pricing methods were unsuited to the gas-producing industry. He had proposed a uniform price for all producers in the gas field. Assuming that regulation could not be avoided, this made sense to the gas industry. It sought, in hearings before the FPC, for a relaxation of the cost-of-production principle and adoption of the looser field-price theory. The Commission, on its part, faced a practical problem of handling thousands of determinations if it set different prices for each well on a cost basis. It announced in 1960 that it would proceed on an area-pricing basis.[12] Here the matter stood in 1964, though other rounds may still be fought. In the meantime, policy rests in the center: the independents are subject to regulation, but it apparently will be on a looser basis than is attempted in utility regulation.

What conclusions are pointed out by this battle between producers, seeking to avoid regulation, and consumers, seeking to impose it? First, this example shows that policy issues on which there is deep disagreement among interest groups will protrude above commissions and courts into the political arena. Second, it shows that appointments to commissions may become political issues. Third, it shows that a dissatisfied or threatened economic interest will shop from one counter to another in government, seeking to obtain the best bargain in its behalf. Finally, it demonstrates that in the contest of politics the organs of the government themselves get aligned with interests. Madison's statement in *The Federalist* that regulation of "various and interfering interests forms the principal task of modern legislation" was followed in the same sentence by these words: "and involves the spirit of party and faction in the necessary and ordinary operations of the government." Members of Congress in both houses aligned themselves on the natural gas issue on the basis of the constituencies they represented; members of the Commission were drawn into a conflict where their decisions, on whatever basis they were made, put them on the side of one group of contestants or the other, and in so doing determined their own survival or nonsurvival in public position.

To present a correct view of the regulatory process it must be added that in many cases policy issues are determined within the regulatory agencies without the appeal to politics that occurred on the natural gas issue. Government could not carry its burden unless many of its problems of policy could be handled by administrative processes. Commissions and Departments do become instruments through which policy conflicts with lesser agitational effect are resolved. Thus, for example, the ICC has been quite successful in achieving a balance among the interests involved in

---

[11] *Federal Power Commission* v. *Hope Natural Gas Co.*, 320 U.S. 591 (1944).
[12] 35 P.U.R. 3d 199 (1960).

railroad and motor transportation; it has left important problems unsolved, but it has handled many policy issues without their eruption into the outer realms of politics. But the following question may be asked: When it resolves conflicts, when it achieves a "moving balance" among interests, is it not itself serving as a political instrument rather than, as some have said, as the Supreme Court of the Transportation World?

Five Major Roles of Government

Pressures for regulation and promotion of the "various and interfering" interests and for government action to promote the interdependent interests of men have led to a vast outpouring of laws, administrative regulations, and judicial decisions at national, state, and local levels of government. For the national government five major roles will be discussed in the remainder of this chapter: promoting the health of the economy; maintaining a competitive system; fostering labor-management accommodation (another role, the prescription by government of minimum labor benefits, is discussed in Chapter 22); regulating and promoting industries; and supplying service through government enterprises.

PROMOTING THE HEALTH OF THE ECONOMY

Madison, Hamilton, and Jefferson could not foresee the most important function of modern economic legislation. It is not the regulation and promotion of "various and interfering interests," but rather the maintenance of the welfare of the economy as a whole to ensure that interdependent interests of men are safeguarded. When the economy sank into a deep and continuing depression from 1929 to 1933, recovery became the prime objective of legislation; when the Second World War came, maximum production of essential commodities became the first objective; during this war and in the years following, the prevention of runaway inflation was also an objective; as the Cold War developed, continued growth of the economy became essential, not only for employment of men but for national defense; when the American dollar deficit to foreign countries became frightening in 1960 and the European Common Market moved forward in 1961, the maintenance of American exports became imperative for the stability of our domestic and foreign policy. These are some examples of policy objectives which, though realizable only by decisions affecting particular group interests, extend to the general well-being of the American economy.

Although campaigners for public office had long promised "a full dinner pail," "a chicken in every pot," and "two cars in every garage," it was not until the Great Depression that men became conscious of the large role government might play in the management of the economy. Still, the efforts of government were regarded as temporary, to be abandoned when recovery was sustained; in the same way the controls by government over the economy in the Second World War were reluctantly accepted as war emergency measures only. When, however, at the end of that war a postwar decline of employment and production of serious proportions was feared, Congress adopted a policy for the future. In the Employment Act

A 1953 cartoon depicts the traditional conflicts over foreign trade as a threat to the domestic economy.

From *Herblock's Here and Now,* Simon & Schuster, 1955

of 1946, it finally declared that "it is the continuing policy and responsibility of the federal government . . . to promote maximum employment, production, and purchasing power."

The wording of the Act was the result of many compromises. The Act itself was carefully framed to emphasize preservation of "free competitive enterprise"; to make explicit the sharing of responsibility among the federal government, industry, agriculture, labor, and state and local governments for attainment of the objectives of the Act; and to avoid any commitment to any particular method of attaining its objectives, such as expansion of public expenditures. Nevertheless, it was a charter of responsibility for the national government, and it was understood that fiscal measures would be among those considered.

To implement the policy the President is directed to submit an economic report to Congress each year in which, among other things, he sets forth a program for carrying out the policy of the Act. To assist him in this and other functions under the Act, Congress provided for a Council of Economic Advisers of three men, to serve in the Executive Office of the President. To focus attention of Congress on the policy problems, a Joint Economic Committee was created to study matters relating to the Economic Report and means of coordinating programs to attain the objectives of the Act.

The continuation of increases in price levels since the Second World War has led to a fear of inflation as well as a desire to avoid depression. There have been bills in Congress to amend the Employment Act to state specifically that stability of price levels is one objective of economic policy.

There has also been concern that the rate of growth in the American economy might not be sufficient. Consequently, there has been a tendency to redefine the objectives of national policy. The Joint Economic Committee in 1960 identified "the main objectives of public economic policy as a high and stable rate of employment, a high rate of growth in our national output and productive capacity, and a high degree of stability in the general level of prices." [13]

The government's control over the economy is so extensive that it has a substantial tool kit from which it can make choices in carrying out the policy of the Employment Act. The chief tools are fiscal and monetary in nature.

The fiscal tools are expenditures, taxes, and borrowing. When government desires to check a downturn in the economy it may increase its expenditures, lower its taxes, and obtain funds by borrowing from banks. Conversely, if it desires to check an inflationary trend it may decrease expenditures, raise taxes, and reduce its debt. This topic will be discussed more fully in Chapter 23.

The monetary tools are chiefly exercised through the Federal Reserve System. An increase in the supply of money without a corresponding increase in the supply of goods will have an inflationary tendency, that is, a tendency toward a rising price level. Conversely, a decrease in the supply of money has a deflationary tendency. The monetary supply is determined primarily by the amount of credit created by the commercial banks. The amount of credit is in turn affected by the amount and cost of funds available to the banks for loan. The Federal Reserve Board can affect these matters in several ways: (1) by raising or lowering the amount of reserves against demand deposits which must be maintained by commercial banks; (2) by raising or lowering the rediscount rate, that is, the rate charged the commercial banks by the Federal Reserve Banks on commercial paper accepted by them; (3) most frequently, by purchases or sales in the open market of government securities by the Federal Reserve Banks, which will increase or decrease the amount of deposits in banks and hence their credit funds. In addition to these monetary powers the Federal Reserve Board has the power to control speculation on the security markets by setting the margin requirements for purchases. In the Second World War and the Korean War the Board also had the power to impose certain controls over installment credit.

Another instrument exists through which the government can exert control: debt management. The government can, by selling short-term securities to banks, add to their credit supply. A shift to long-term securities or to sales to the general public will have the opposite effect.

Although these and other tools may be sufficient for a substantial curb on deflationary or inflationary trends, there are nevertheless reasons to doubt their complete effectiveness. First, there are practical difficulties to be faced. The national government may not find it feasible, in view of

---

[13] United States Senate, Joint Economic Committee, *Employment, Growth, and Price Levels,* Senate Report No. 1043 (Washington, 1961), Eighty-sixth Congress, Second Session, January 26, 1960.

national defense needs and welfare commitments, to diminish materially its expenditures in the face of the threat of inflation. Facing recession, on the other hand, it may find it difficult to increase expenditures quickly: It would take time to vote authorizations for public works expenditures, to let contracts, and to get building under way, and state and local co-operation with the national government would be impaired by debt limi-tations in their constitutions and charters. The national government might, therefore, as in the New Deal period, resort to make-work projects to pro-vide employment. Second, there is doubt as to what amount of effect monetary controls will have. Thus increasing the interest rate may not prevent industries and persons from borrowing; conversely, decreasing it may not materially spur investment if there is doubt about the future. Third, it is difficult to coordinate the various government programs and the several agencies responsible for these. For example, the Federal Re-serve Board may be interested in curbing credit while the Treasury may be interested in expanding it so as to obtain a low interest rate on govern-ment bonds. Moreover, coordinating national, state, and local expendi-tures is a well-nigh impossible task. Finally, and chiefly, these matters of taxes, expenditures, credit supply, and interest rate are among the most controversial of political issues. They affect so vitally and so differently the "various and interfering interests" that the issues concerning them are thrown into the maelstrom of politics, where conflict is more common than agreement and where compromise and shifts of direction are more to be expected than consistency and coordination in policy.

The conflicts of interest and opinion are among the most divisive in our society today. In 1963 when President Kennedy proposed a tax cut in order to stimulate the economy, Senator Byrd, chairman of the committee in the Senate which would have to report out the measure, held out because he wanted reductions in the budget. A reduction in expenditures equivalent to the tax cut would have taken as much money out of the economy as a tax cut put in it and thus negated, except for psychological effects, the effect of the latter on the economy. Yet President Johnson was able to win passage of the tax cut in 1964 only by convincing Senator Byrd that ex-penditures would be reduced. Thus, the President's objective of using fiscal powers of government to stimulate the economy was compromised by the Senator's desire to balance the budget.

Another conflict is over the level of interest rates. Raising interest rates is a damper on inflation, and is regarded with favor by those who regard inflation at the time as a serious danger, and by those who have money to lend. Those who want to expand their businesses may look with disfavor on the policy, and some think the method of control bears too heavily on the poor. Consistently over the years, Congressman Patman, from a stra-tegic committee chairmanship, has criticized the Federal Reserve Board's anti-inflationary steps.

There is the additional fact that inflation itself is regarded favorably by many. Some leading economists have expressed the view that a small amount of continuous inflation is favorable to economic growth. And there are enough groups in the population who profit immediately by some in-flation to make a strong program to counteract it appear politically dangerous. It is easier to obtain popular support for measures against recession than it is for measures against inflation.

The fact remains, nevertheless, that there is a large measure of agreement that government should exert its powers to check recession or to prevent a high rate of inflation. No political party in power in the future can escape the responsibility of using the government's tool kit to maintain growth and stability in the economy. Above the conflict of "various and interfering interests," and high on the agenda of government tasks is the maintenance, in cooperation with private interests, of economic growth and stability.

MAINTAINING A COMPETITIVE SYSTEM

The great corporate revolution, which has changed the nature of the American economy, started soon after the Civil War. While men were still pioneering on the frontier, huge organizations of capital were bringing the railroads and the major industries of the nation under their dominance. Although the full significance of this development could not then be understood, individualistic Americans were angered and demanded legislation to curb the activities of the corporate giants, commonly referred to as trusts; the new legislation was called antitrust legislation. Such legislation was passed almost simultaneously in many of the states and by the Congress. It still embodies the basic American policy toward business.

Antitrust legislation has as its purpose the maintenance of a competitive economy. It is a support for this kind of economy that laissez-faire economists desired. Yet in fact antitrust legislation represents a departure from laissez faire, for in order to preserve free competition, the government must restrict freedom of contract.

The function of preserving a competitive economy was initially assumed by the national government in the Sherman Antitrust Act of 1890. This act contained two provisions: Section 1 dealt with restraints of trade without respect to whether they produced monopoly; it prohibited "Every contract, combination, or conspiracy in restraint of trade." Section 2 prohibited monopolizing or attempting to monopolize. Both provisions were limited to interstate or foreign commerce.

Section 2 has a more limited significance than Section 1. Its scope is determined by the definition of monopoly. The most detailed was that given by a federal court in the Aluminum case in 1945; [14] it was said that 90 percent control would constitute a monopoly, 33 percent would not, and that it was doubtful whether 60 or 64 percent would. It was also said that if a company had a monopoly "thrust" upon it as a "passive beneficiary" it was not illegal, but that if it gained a monopoly by progressively embracing each new opportunity this would make it illegal even though it had been guilty of no unfair or coercive tactics toward competitors.

Section 1 was interpreted in the Standard Oil case of 1911 to apply only to unreasonable restraints of trade.[15] Under this interpretation some kinds of restraints are per se unreasonable. For example, price-fixing agreements

---

[14] *United States* v. *Aluminum Co. of America*, 148 F. 2d 416 (1945).
[15] *Standard Oil Co. of N.J.* v. *U.S.*, 221 U.S. 1 (1911).

are "conclusively presumed" to be illegal in all cases. On the other hand, most other types of agreement among competing companies will be held illegal only if there is proof of undue restraint on commerce. The proof ordinarily relates to the effect of the agreement or combination on competition.

Several major effects follow from the use of the rule of reason. It allows flexibility to the courts in interpretation of the Act. Some observers see an advantage in the courts' ability to make the decision in each case in response to the circumstances in the industry. Yet this flexibility brings with it uncertainty as to whether particular courses of action will be held illegal. Neither business nor the Department of Justice, which enforces the Act, has clear guidance. Moreover, the Department of Justice has the burden of proving that particular courses of action constitute "undue" restraints on commerce.

The Sherman Act can be enforced through suits brought by persons injured or through criminal or civil action brought by the Department of Justice. In practice, however, the Department usually combines the civil with the criminal action and seeks a civil remedy; it is primarily interested in corrective action rather than punishment. The civil remedies most frequently sought are decrees that illegal practices be discontinued or that a combination be dissolved.

There have been periods of strong and of weak enforcement of the Act. The first ten years after 1890 were a period of weak enforcement; but from 1901 to the First World War the Roosevelt, Taft, and Wilson Administrations vigorously pushed enforcement action against concerns in almost every major industry. From 1917 to 1937 there was another period of weak enforcement. Then a new Antitrust Division was created in the Department of Justice, increased appropriations were made for antitrust investigation and enforcement, and a second period of vigor in enforcement began.

Dissatisfaction with early results led the Republican, Democratic, and Progressive political parties to propose additional antitrust legislation in 1912, and in 1914 supplementary legislation was enacted. The Federal Trade Commission Act and the Clayton Act embodied the concept that competition should be fair as well as free. The Federal Trade Commission Act prohibited "unfair methods of competition." The Clayton Act contained four substantive provisions: Section 2 was designed to prevent tying contracts ("If you want to sell this one of our products you must also sell that one") and exclusive dealing contracts ("If you want to sell our product you must not sell anybody else's"); Section 3, to limit certain price discriminations; Section 7, to prevent intercorporate purchases of stock which would substantially lessen competition or tend to create a monopoly; and Section 8, to prevent interlocking directorates. The effects of the provisions were, however, substantially limited by qualifying phrases.

Several acts since 1914 have expanded the prohibitions imposed at that time. The Robinson-Patman Act of 1936 is a detailed and complicated statute which tries to protect small purchasers against price discriminations that favor large buyers. The Wheeler-Lea Act of 1938 amended the Federal Trade Commission Act in such a way as to prohibit "unfair methods of competition and unfair and deceptive acts in commerce." The effect of this was to reverse a Supreme Court decision that the "unfair methods of competition" prohibition was designed only to protect competitors, not consumers. The new act also strengthened the remedy of the Federal Trade Commission and imposed penalties for false advertising of foods, drugs, cosmetics, and mechanical devices (such as those to reduce weight) used to change the human figure. The Anti-Merger Act of 1950 amended Section 7 of the Clayton Act, which had contained the stock-purchases provision. This important amendment made the merger of two or more corporations illegal under the same conditions that an intercorporate stock purchase would be. Under Section 2 of the Sherman Act a merger was illegal only if it created a monopoly, but under the Act of 1950 a merger is illegal if it tends to lessen competition substantially or tends to create a monopoly.

Much interest has been concentrated recently on Section 7 cases. The government in 1957 won a major victory through a decision which held that Du Pont ownership of 23 percent of the stock of General Motors was illegal because Du Pont's sale of fabrics and finishes to General Motors tended substantially to lessen competition in such sales.[16] The Supreme Court made significant new findings: first, that Section 7 applied to a vertical combination (supplier and purchaser brought under one control) as well as to a horizontal one, and, second, that a stock purchase could become illegal even though it was not illegal at the time it was made. Du Pont's ownership at the time the suit was brought, said the Supreme Court, tended to lessen competition, though this was not true at the time of purchase thirty-two years earlier. More interest has centered, however, in the provisions of Section 7 limiting mergers. Both the Federal Trade Commission and the Antitrust Division are very active in the enforcement of the antimerger amendment to Section 7.

There have been many limitations on the effectiveness of antitrust policy, including the following:

1. Underlying all other difficulties is the fact that support for the antitrust policy is weak. The Judiciary and Small Business committees keep pressure on the enforcement agencies and make frequent investigations into antitrust policy and enforcement. But policies inconsistent with antitrust are considered by other Congressional committees. Not since the election of 1912 has antitrust been among the important issues in a Presidential election, and not since President Wilson has any President concentrated attention on antitrust as a major problem of the nation. The Supreme Court has been divided and has vacillated in its interpretation of the antitrust statutes, though in the past twenty years it has given them more force and consistency. There is no strong general public interest in antitrust policy. Finally, there is a lack of consensus among economists and publicists as to the extent to which government should intervene to maintain a competitive economy and the means by which such action could be made effective.

2. The policy has not been adequately underpinned and has even some-

---

[16] U.S. v. E. I. du Pont de Nemours, 353 U.S. 586 (1957).

times been undermined by other government policies. Protective tariffs have often set an umbrella on prices, protecting monopolistic combinations. Patents, by their nature, grant monopolies, and the antitrust laws have not always prevented patent pools and restrictions on use of patents which extended these monopolies even further. Purchase of patents and withholding them from use has been a means of protecting existing patent monopolies. Laxity in state incorporation laws and the absence of any national regulation of security issues until 1933 facilitated promoters' efforts to gain control of vast industrial empires with investment of small amounts of capital. Statutes providing for regulation of specific industries have allowed regulatory commissions to authorize action which otherwise would be in violation of antitrust laws. Exemptions have been made for special groups. Statutes passed by Congress also dilute the antitrust laws; for example, the fair trade law allows manufacturers of trademarked articles to insist that these products be sold by retailers at manufacturers' list prices in those states that legalize this practice.

3. There are many gaps and qualifications in the statutes. One can sometimes do legally by a contract of agency what he could not do by a contract of sale. Interlocking directorates among competing industrial firms are illegal under stated conditions, but interlocking directorates between financial and industrial firms escape from this provision of the Clayton Act. Qualifications, of which those cited are only examples, are frequently the result of compromises within Congress and indicate a lack of legislative consensus on the extent to which antitrust policy should be strengthened.

4. Antitrust sometimes becomes a weak weapon to meet new types of situations. Where a few concerns supply all or most of the market and their capital investments are large, price competition may cease to exist, and yet there may be no evidence of collusion or coercion or combination. The will not to disturb the existing price structure may be strong, and competition may move into other forms, such as advertising, product differentiation, or improved service. Some companies have a dominating position which enables them to set the price level that will be followed by others.

5. Enforcement difficulties are great. Small government staffs with limited appropriations struggle against great aggregations of capital with large staffs of attorneys and other experts. Proof of effects on competition, or of evil intent, or of unreasonable restraint, or of other matters may require months or years of effort. Appeals may prolong the struggle. It is often difficult even after obtaining a judgment to gain more than half a victory, for then the contest turns upon the question of which remedy shall be applied. Often it is difficult to find an appropriate remedy, particularly when there has been a merger of assets over a period of years. Yet there is no statutory requirement that concerns proposing to merge shall give notice to the government prior to merger—a requirement persistently advocated by the late Senator Kefauver.

Despite the difficulties of gathering proof of collusion in restraint of trade, the government achieved another antitrust victory in the 1961 case of price fixing in the electrical equipment industry. Notable among antitrust cases because of the prominence of the firms and individuals involved (executives of industrial giants like Westinghouse and General Electric),

"Good Gracious, You Mean To Say Something's Been Going On Here For Fifty Years?"

From *Straight Herblock*, Simon & Schuster, 1964

and because jail sentences were served by some of those convicted, this case became a major antitrust victory for the government because a few of the men involved, feeling that others were trying to hide behind them, decided to give evidence. Some were also motivated by another case shortly before in which a federal judge had sent an executive to jail, and these men hoped to avoid jail by cooperating with the Justice Department. The result was that the Department obtained detailed evidence of an extensive price-fixing conspiracy. When making bids on heavy electrical equipment, representatives of more than twenty firms got together to agree on a price, and to agree as to which company should submit the winning low bid on each project. Turns were taken, on a proportional sharing basis, according to the phases of the moon, with clandestine hotel meetings, secret telephone calls, and all the other appurtenances of television melodrama.[17]

The case illustrated another method of enforcement which may revolutionize antitrust enforcement. Following the electrical equipment decision hundreds of suits were brought by cities, states, and private parties for damages. It will take years to complete the trial or settlement of these suits, and the amount of the damages will be very large. Henceforth, every corporation which violates the antitrust laws, or risks violation, will shudder at the possibility of customer suits.

There have always been differences of opinion as to what function gov-

---

[17] For the fascinating details, see John G. Fuller, *The Gentlemen Conspirators* (New York, 1962), or John Herling, *The Great Price Conspiracy* (New York, 1962).

ernment should perform in maintaining competition. Theodore Roosevelt thought that there were good combinations and bad combinations; he favored an administrative agency to pass judgment upon combinations and supervise those which were accepted. Woodrow Wilson, on the other hand, wanted no "coming to terms" with the "trusts." Some judges, economists, and business leaders have thought that some forms of joint business action were natural economic developments and therefore should be accepted as legitimate; others have thought either that the combinations were in a large part the result of artificial advantages obtained from patents, access to financial markets, or ability to use unfair tactics, and hence illegal, or that even if they were a natural development they should nevertheless be restrained by law.

There has been general agreement that government should prevent unfair and coercive competitive tactics. There has also been substantial consensus that collusive arrangements among competitors that materially restrict competition should be prohibited. Some people have argued, however, that such arrangements should in certain instances be accepted, subject to government supervision, and this has been provided in regulatory statutes for a number of industries. The largest difference of opinion has been over the proper response of government to "bigness"—the attainment of size sufficient to permit market leadership or dominance.

Justice Brandeis expressed the views of many when he referred to "the curse of bigness." Those who hold this view see many dangers in bigness: (1) that excessive size may make for inefficiency; (2) that large concerns may be able to exercise market controls; (3) that such concerns may separately or as members of associations be able to exert a dangerous amount of political influence, or may even be able, through control of communications, to shape the thinking of the people; (4) that bigness will lead to abuses which will make government regulation necessary for additional industries.

On the other hand, David E. Lilienthal summarized the views of many in a recent defense of bigness as the basis of high productivity. "Size," he said, "is our greatest functional asset," and there is a "curse of smallness" in such industries as coal and lumber.[18]

There may be sound support for both views. By virtue of developments in the science, technology, and art of administration man's capacity for efficient conduct of large undertakings has been greatly increased. Size has proved to be a necessary asset for production for mass markets and for defense in the nuclear-missiles age. Yet questions remain: How large is too large? What are the consequences when units of private power are able to dominate markets? Will these units of power make decisions on price levels and production rates in the context of their own interests? Even though the decisions are made by men of conscience and public spirit, can the nation expect that their decisions will give adequate attention to the basic needs for economic growth and price stability?

There are recurring suggestions that the intervention of government will have to be expanded because of the existence of market power in private

---

[18] David E. Lilienthal, *Big Business: A New Era* (New York, 1952), pp. 33, 143.

groups. Recently, for example, bills have been introduced in Congress which would require notice from large corporations before price increases and would require hearings on proposed increases, either on a mandatory basis or within the discretion of the President. Others have proposed utility regulation for one or more industries in which there is a large degree of concentration. The difficulty of carrying out such measures successfully leads many to prefer effective antitrust legislation and enforcement. It appears that antitrust issues will remain on the public policy agenda.

FOSTERING LABOR-MANAGEMENT ACCOMMODATION

Although government sets minimum standards on conditions and benefits of employment, employers and employees negotiate terms of settlement above the minimum standards. Great emphasis has been placed in this country on the freedom of private parties to decide for themselves the hours, wages, and other terms of their contracts of employment. Both corporate and union officials treasure this process as a basic freedom.

Yet in no area is the accuracy of Madison's analysis of government as a mediator among "various and interfering interests" more clearly substantiated. Labor organizations desire protection for rights to unionize, bargain collectively, strike, boycott, and picket. Employers desire restrictions on these rights. Employer groups support use of the injunction in labor disputes; labor groups abhor the instrument. The balancing and regulation of the conflicting interests of labor and management has become one of the most difficult and persistent tasks of government.

Nevertheless, the Madisonian description only partly describes the task of government. There are community interests to be safeguarded in addition to the competing interests of labor and management. In the nineteenth century, the community interest was simply the maintenance of peace at the site of the labor conflict. Later, there was an additional interest in avoiding interruptions of essential transportation and production. Recently, there have been suggestions of a third interest—the prevention of settlements of labor disputes which might cause price inflation.

Prior to 1926, policies on labor-management relations were determined and applied almost exclusively in the courts. Since that time these policies have been made increasingly in the Congress and carried out by administrative agencies. Five important acts relating to labor-management relations have been passed.

The act that ushered in a new period of legislative and administrative control was the Railway Labor Act of 1926. This act was the culmination of a series of enactments beginning in 1888 with a view toward peaceful settlement of railway labor disputes. The Act of 1926 stated labor's right to organize without interference from employers. It provided for collective labor contracts and made it the duty of each party to try to reach agreement on a contract. It set up procedure for negotiation and peaceful settlement: (1) each party was required to give the other thirty days' notice of intention to change the terms of agreement; (2) it was the duty of the parties to confer with each other; (3) a National Mediation Board was to assist the parties in reaching an agreement through mediation or suggestion that they arbitrate the dispute, and (by amendments in 1934) to hold elections to determine which union was desired by employees as their representative; and (4) the President in case of national emergency could appoint a fact-finding board to analyze the issues in dispute and make recommendations for settlement.

Until the Second World War this machinery for settlement worked so well that its success was widely acclaimed. But the machinery of the Act was inadequate to prevent serious railroad strikes which broke out in 1946, 1948, and 1950. In all three cases the President—acting under special wartime powers which had not been rescinded—seized the railroads involved; even then, in the last two cases, labor leaders declined to call off strikes immediately, and the Department of Justice asked for injunctions. With special authority for seizure no longer delegated to the President the question arises: What shall government's policy be when the procedures of the Railway Labor Act fail? When a nationwide strike of railroad workers was imminent in 1963, Congress provided for compulsory settlement of the dispute by an *ad hoc* board. This was the first peacetime compulsory arbitration in our history. Even its efforts did not solve all issues in controversy, and to avoid a strike, President Johnson called the representatives of the roads and the workers to the White House, where, with the aid of government mediators, a settlement was reached. The President said he did not intend to "bury" collective bargaining, but for the fourth time since the war the continuation of railroad service depended on Presidential action.

The second act is the Norris-La Guardia, or Anti-Injunction, Act of 1932. The labor injunction, first issued by an American court in 1875, had become the chief weapon of the employer in his struggle with labor. It was inherently an effective weapon for breaking strikes, inasmuch as violation of a court injunction was contempt of court and hence punishable by prompt and summary action. It was even more potent because of abuses occurring in its application. It was often issued without a hearing; the terms of the injunction were often so broad as to cut off almost all union activity at the scene of conflict; the terms were sometimes so vague that union leaders did not know what actions could legally be taken.[19] The Act of 1932 regulated the use of the labor injunction in federal courts. After declaring the right of labor to self-organization without "interference, restraint, or coercion" by employers, it (1) made workers' agreements not to join unions as a condition of employment (called "yellow-dog contracts") unenforceable in national courts; (2) strictly regulated the procedure in labor injunction proceedings, requiring hearings, jury trial in contempt proceedings, and other safeguards; and (3) narrowly restricted the causes for issuance and the items which could be prohibited. The effect of this act was substantially to take national courts out of labor disputes; it represented the farthest extension of a "hands-off" policy by government. It substantially ended the period of judicial control of labor disputes.

The "hands-off" policy for the federal courts was quickly followed by legislative intervention. In a series of three labor acts Congress has sought to balance the rights of parties and to protect the interests of the public

---

[19] See Felix Frankfurter and Nathan Greene, *The Labor Injunction* (New York, 1930).

in labor relations in industry, as it attempted for railroads in the Railway Labor Act. These are the National Labor Relations Act of 1935, the Taft-Hartley Act of 1947, and the Labor Reform Act of 1959.

The National Labor Relations Act was the most notable achievement in behalf of the labor union movement in our history. Under its protection the number of union members increased from four million to seventeen million, although the Act applied only to industries engaged in or affecting interstate commerce. It declared the right of employees to self-organization and collective bargaining. It labeled as "unfair" such practices as (1) interference by an employer with his employees' choice of union representatives and (2) an employer's refusal to bargain collectively with the representatives of his employees. It set up a National Labor Relations Board with two functions: (1) to hold elections to determine which organization the employees desired to represent them, and (2) to issue complaints, hold hearings, and make decisions on alleged violations of the Act, issuing cease and desist orders against employers found to be in violation.

There was great employer dissatisfaction with the increase in the strength of organized labor under the Act, and in the Taft-Hartley Act the employer group won some redress against what it regarded as an imbalance in labor policy. In significant amendments to the National Labor Relations Act, some of the leverage that management had lost to unions in 1935 was restored. It was stated that employees had the right to self-organization or to refrain from self-organization. A new category of unfair labor practices was created—those which could be committed by a labor organization or its agents. The particular victories of the employers included the following provisions. (1) The Act prohibited the closed shop, that is, arrangements under which persons could not be hired unless they were already members of unions. This type of arrangement had been allowable under the preceding act. The new act allowed only the union shop, that is, employer-employee contracts providing that a person be required to join the union within a stated number of days of employment. (2) It prohibited secondary boycotts, that is, unions could not induce employees to strike or stop work to force their employer to cease doing business with another firm in which there was a labor dispute. (3) It granted permission to employers to express their views to employees on matters of unionization, provided no threats or promises were made. (4) It removed the protections of the earlier labor relations act for supervisory employees, and it prohibited certification (provided for under the NLRA) of unions that included company guards with other employees. (5) It prohibited the inclusion in the union of company professional employees with other employees unless a majority of the professionals voted for inclusion, and it similarly protected separate craft union members. (6) It required certified unions to bargain collectively with employers—an obligation which had previously been stipulated only for employers. (7) It required the Board to give priority to complaints on certain types of unfair labor practices committed by unions. In addition, the Taft-Hartley Act required unions to report organizational facts and financial data to the Secretary of Labor, and denied the protections of the Labor Relations Act to unions whose officers had not taken an anti-Communist oath. Another section of the Taft-

Hartley Act amended the Federal Corrupt Practices Act to prevent labor unions from contributing or expending funds in political campaigns for national office.

Other provisions of the Taft-Hartley Act represented the government's response to the new challenge of finding ways to protect the public interest in continuous production and transportation without undermining the process of collective bargaining. These provisions, designed to facilitate settlement of labor disputes and prevent commerce stoppage, were patterned after the Railway Labor Act, with significant modifications only in procedures during national emergencies. Both parties are required to give notice of intention to seek modification of a labor contract, both are obligated to bargain, and a new independent agency known as the Federal Mediation and Conciliation Service provides facilities for conciliation, mediation, and voluntary arbitration. In case a dispute imperils the national health or safety, the President can intervene by appointment of a board of inquiry. Upon report of a board, which can find facts but make no recommendations, the President may direct the Attorney General to petition a federal district court to issue an injunction against continuance of the strike or lockout; this injunction may remain in effect for eighty days. In the meantime the President reconvenes the board of inquiry, and if the dispute is still not settled it makes a report at the end of sixty days. Within the remaining twenty days of the injunction period the employees vote on the acceptance or rejection of the employer's last offer. If the dispute is still not settled after all these steps the President makes recommendations to Congress for appropriate action.

One big question for the future is whether the national government can avoid more intervention in labor disputes than is provided in the Taft-Hartley Act. The growth during recent years of national unions leads to the possibility of a tie-up of whole industries. Seizure and operation by the government is one possibility if an emergency develops. But there are disadvantages in seizure. If in effect it continues the *status quo* with respect to the issues in dispute, it may unduly favor the employer and remove his incentive to bargain. On the other hand, seizure puts pressure on the government to adjudicate the issues in controversy, which becomes compulsory settlement. Compulsory settlement, that is, determination of the issues by public authority, has its advocates, but arguments against it have prevailed: (1) it would be difficult, probably impossible, to state clear standards for judgment, such as could be applied in a judicial proceeding; (2) the Chief Executive, who would undoubtedly be the agent of intervention, would be drawn deeper into labor-management politics, increasing the burdens of his office; (3) there would be danger that over a period of time the frequency of government intervention would increase, thereby weakening the freedom and responsibility of the parties which exist in the system of collective bargaining; (4) there would be no assurance that decisions adverse to labor would be accepted by labor, and hence that strikes would be averted in all cases.

Neither labor nor management desires any form of compulsory settlement, and politicians and professional experts in labor-management relations strive persistently to find ways to avoid it. They place their hopes on government mediation, forced continuation of bargaining, and occasional Presidential intervention. They hope for continued improvement of mediation, and some professional experts even suggest regular participation of neutrals at the bargaining table. They hope for the continued success of Presidential intervention, but the President lacks statutory powers and must depend upon the backing of the public and his persuasion of the two sides, at the risk each time of failure and loss of prestige.

Recently, government's participation in labor matters was extended. President Kennedy announced noninflationary guides for settlement of labor disputes. Although these guides have influenced negotiations to some extent, influential persons on both sides in the labor-management conflict have condemned them as an encroachment on collective bargaining. Thus, the President, working toward one government objective—a healthy economy—came into conflict with another objective—freedom of the parties in labor-management negotiations.

The third act passed by Congress was the Labor Reform Act (Labor-Management Reporting and Disclosure Act) of 1959. This act grew out of a series of investigations of labor racketeering, beginning in 1957 and conducted by the Senate Select Committee on Improper Activities in the Labor or Management Field. These investigations had revealed misappropriation of union funds by union officials, collusion between company managers and union officers against the interests of employees, strong-arm tactics to maintain one-man rule in unions, gangster infiltration into unions, and other forms of corruption and coercive acts. Action on these matters became engulfed, however, in controversy over other changes in labor law. Labor organizations wanted some softening of certain Taft-Hartley prohibitions on labor, through provisions which opponents referred to as "sweeteners." Others wanted to take advantage of the interest aroused in labor malpractices to obtain amendments to Taft-Hartley which would further restrict labor. The result was a bitter fight, massive lobbying, and an omnibus act containing a detailed set of regulations.

In general, the Act does three things. First, it contains what is called a bill of rights for union members. Presumably such a bill of rights is adopted for the protection of union members; actually it appeals to employer groups because it tends to lessen the power of labor leaders. In the main this bill of rights emphasizes democracy and due process. It guarantees "equal rights and privileges" to members in union elections and meetings, and it bars unions from raising dues or initiation fees without a majority vote of members of local unions and a majority vote of the executive board or convention in national and international unions. It requires written charges and hearings before members are disciplined. It makes violation of these and other guarantees in the bill of rights a crime and also allows injured union members to file civil suits for relief. This section carries government deep into the internal administration of private associations and may set a precedent for deeper penetration into such matters in private corporations.

Second, the Act seeks to establish responsibility in union management. This it does by many provisions; for example, it prescribes the conduct of elections; it requires reporting to the Secretary of Labor on salaries and loans and "conflict of interest" payments to union officers and on other matters; and it defines new categories of federal offenses, such as stealing or misappropriating union funds and picketing for purposes of extortion.

Third, the Act in effect amends several Taft-Hartley provisions. It permits the states to assume jurisdiction over labor matters that the National Labor Relations Board refuses to handle. Since the Board has refused to handle complaints relating to smaller companies, this provision will have the effect of bringing these under state jurisdiction, where in many cases the laws on unions are more restrictive than those of the national government. In addition, the Act both tightened and extended the provisions of Taft-Hartley with respect to secondary boycotts and certain forms of picketing. It outlawed, with certain exceptions, the so-called "hot cargo" contracts, under which employers agree with unions not to do business with "unfair" or struck firms.

PROMOTING AND REGULATING INDUSTRIES

Policies of government to promote economic growth and stability, fair competition, and amicable labor-management relations affect the economy as a whole. In addition, national, state, and local governments promote and regulate particular industries.

Forms of activity

The forms of aid by government to industries are so varied that almost every economic group is aided directly or indirectly. Some receive subsidies in money, while others benefit from services. The regulatory activities of government fall generally into five main categories.[20] The oldest is safety and health regulation, usually enforced by inspection. For example, mines have long been subject to safety regulations for the protection of workers, and railroad, bus, truck, and air transportation have been governed by safety rules for the protection of workers and passengers. Healthy working conditions in factories have been a goal of legislation since the 1870s. The consumer is also the beneficiary of health regulations; these will be discussed in Chapter 22.

A second type of regulation, handled at the state level, is licensing, that is, any form of requirement for permission, whether through a permit, registration, license, approval, certificate of public convenience and necessity, or other form of consent. Restrictions on entry now exist for learned professions such as law, medicine, teaching; service occupations of various sorts, such as barbering, hairdressing, or plumbing; banking; insurance; creation of corporations; sale of utility service; taxi service; nursing homes; liquor stores, taverns, and pool halls; and miscellaneous other kinds of economic service. After entry additional forms of licensing may be required. Thus, companies supplying railroad transportation service and public utility service are usually required to obtain consent for expansion or contraction of their service, for sale of securities, and for merging with, buying stock of, or leasing the property of another company.

---

[20] Discussion summarized from Redford, *op. cit.*, Chapter 17.

Still another form of regulation is price regulation, often called rate regulation. Today the most familiar areas of price regulation are railroad, truck and bus, water, and air transportation; power, gas, and water utilities; interest charges; agricultural products. In some cases only maximum rates are set, the protection being for the consumer of the service; in other cases minimum prices are maintained, the objective being to stabilize prices for the producer of the commodity; in some cases both maximum and minimum prices are set.

A fourth type of regulation is production control. Limitation of entry or expansion by license is of course one form of control of production. Beyond this, a system of production control exists for two major industries. The national government, through its program of loans and marketing controls, indirectly regulates agricultural production. Texas and certain other states producing petroleum limit production and prorate the allowable production among oil fields and down to wells within fields.

A final type of regulation is control of finance. Banking and insurance are intimately and comprehensively regulated. The financial operations of utility industries are also subjected to regulation.

Air commerce

To illustrate the government's role in the promotion and regulation of various industries, we shall give a brief discussion of its functions in air commerce, where typical forms of government activity are revealed.

Government both promotes and regulates the air transport industry, the regulation being carried out under the Federal Aviation Act of 1958, which replaced the Civil Aeronautics Act of 1938. Both statutes declared the policy of promoting civil aviation to meet the needs of the postal system, commerce, and national defense. The system of promotion and regulation has four parts.

1. *Safety.* Safety on the airways is promoted by licensing, safety rules, and air-traffic management. Pilots must be licensed. Planes and their equipment are also licensed to ensure that only airworthy equipment is used. An elaborate system of safety rules governs all flying; in addition, all air traffic is subject to the traffic-management system. Under this system, controls are maintained in the traffic towers at airports over take-off, flying on the airways, and landing. This whole system of safety protection is now the responsibility of the Federal Aviation Agency, headed by an administrator appointed by the President with approval of the Senate. The Agency's authority extends, with certain limitations to protect military efficiency, to military as well as civil air traffic. The results can be seen in part in a remarkably good safety record on American commercial flights.

2. *Economic regulation of domestic commercial transportation.* In the Civil Aeronautics Act of 1938, Congress adopted a policy of regulated competition for the air transport industry. Neither monopoly nor unlimited entry was desired. The policy was borrowed from railroad regulation, and it was believed that regulated competition would ensure the development of air transportation by financially sound companies. The basic desire was to promote the development of air transportation, but the regulatory instru-

ments were those of utility regulation. A certificate of public convenience and necessity would be required for operation of commercial service to the public or for consolidation of companies rendering such service, and rates would be regulated. Supplementing these conventional forms of control was the authorization of subsidy payments to airline companies.

A Civil Aeronautics Board was created to administer the system of economic regulation.[21] The bulk of commercial passenger transportation is licensed in two parts: the trunk line companies supplying transportation between major transportation centers, and the local service airlines supplying service to smaller cities and connecting service to the trunk lines. In addition, limited service is allowed by the irregular or nonscheduled carriers.

The Board's chief task has been the management of competition. It determined in 1941 that there were enough trunk line carriers; the number of these has actually dwindled from nineteen to eleven. Competition among them has been restricted, and they also have been protected from the irregular carriers. Until 1955 the Board had a restrictive policy as to expansion of competition; in that year it made new grants of service rights to the trunk lines to expand competition; now it is under pressure to allow consolidations of lines because of the high expenses of jet transportation. On the other hand, for the local service lines, the Board has adopted the policy of area service by a single company. These are all under subsidy, and competition would increase subsidy costs. All trunk lines except one now operate without subsidy.

3. *International transportation.* The Civil Aeronautics Board also has jurisdiction over international air transport. It grants permits for foreign air transport and can influence rates of American companies. There are some peculiarities of this control. All decisions on permits for foreign service are subject to the approval or disapproval of the President. The Department of State also participates in the control over foreign air transportation. Rates and other matters relating to such transportation are governed by international agreement. Negotiations are conducted by the Department of State with representation and policy leadership from the Civil Aeronautics Board.

4. *Airport construction.* The national government, under the Federal Airport Act, grants money to political subdivisions for assistance in constructing airports, and this federal aid program is administered by the Federal Aviation Agency. Normally airports are constructed by cities with federal aid. Cities may recoup part of their cost through fees for airport use.

Air transportation illustrates the role of government in promoting and balancing interests. Safety is such a dominant interest of air travelers that huge sums are spent to achieve it, and complaints such as those of commercial air pilots against the rule requiring retirement at sixty are brushed aside. On the other hand, some compromises must be made, for a perfect safety system would impose too heavy a cost in electronic equipment on the various types of users of the airways. The Civil Aeronautics Board

---

[21] The Board until 1958 also had responsibilities in safety promotion. It now has only one such function, the investigation of the causes of accidents on commercial airlines.

seeks to meet the interest of communities in expanded air transport, but it seeks also to avoid increased subsidy costs. To strike a balance it has a general rule that there must be expectancy of at least five emplanements a day for a city to get service, but recently over five hundred cities were allowed service without that minimum. It mediates among the claims of rival airlines for service.

It also strikes balances between concepts of desirable public policy. For the trunk lines it accepts the concept of competition as a desirable objective, as well as the concept of sound financial condition of companies, and it limits competition to meet this objective. Regulation is thus the process of reaching judgment on opposed objectives.

Regulation for other industries

Many other American industries are subjected to comprehensive regulation—banking being the first of these. Private banks are almost unknown today. Banks are chartered by state or federal administrative agencies, which also examine them periodically. They are further regulated if they join the Federal Deposit Insurance Corporation or the Federal Reserve System, and all national banks must belong to both. To list some other industries, insurance is comprehensively regulated through license and supervision by the state governments. The housing industry is now substantially promoted and regulated through the requirements of the Federal Housing Administration for FHA loans, the chartering of savings and loan associations, and the support and regulation of the home loan market through the Federal Home Loan Banks. Railroads are comprehensively regulated by state and national authority, with regulation extending to safety, rates, expansion or contraction of service, consolidations, security issues, service, in fact, to almost every aspect of railroad management. The interstate aspects of the basic utilities—telephone, power, and gas—are regulated by the federal government, and their local business is regulated by most of the state governments. In some cases this regulation is as comprehensive as that for railroads. Radio and television communication is regulated by the Federal Communications Commission, chiefly through licensing requirements. Stock and commodity exchanges are regulated by federal agencies and security issuances by federal and state governments. Trucks and buses are also subject to regulation by federal and state governments if they operate in both interstate and intrastate commerce, and in any case are subject to the state's safety and load regulations. Maritime transportation is promoted and regulated by the federal government. Finally, the production and marketing of agricultural products is regulated in as complex a system of controls as exists for any industry.

There is no common purpose extending through all of these areas. Thus banking and insurance are regulated to ensure safety and adequacy of facilities; utilities, primarily to ensure good service at reasonable rates; radio and television, for the purpose of preventing confusion to the listener from duplicating use of airwaves. The regulation in each case is the empirical result of meeting each problem as it arises with the government action deemed appropriate.

A frequent subject of controversy is whether public enterprise, that is, public supply of a commodity or service, shall be chosen instead of regulation and promotion of private enterprise. In many other countries with free political institutions the choice has been made in favor of substantial use of public enterprise. Thus in England government has normally chosen state enterprise rather than regulation of major industries. Western nations generally have made extensive use of government enterprise, and such key industries as transportation and communication are government-owned and managed in most countries.

In this country there has been more choice in favor of regulated private enterprise. Nevertheless, there is a considerable amount of public enterprise. There are municipal enterprises, such as those for water, electricity, passenger transportation, and housing. In the states the main public enterprises are in the fields of power, liquor, insurance (unemployment and workmen's compensation), and transportation (roads and bridges primarily). At the national level the chief fields of public enterprise are communications, defense enterprises, credit, housing, insurance, and power. The largest public enterprise in the Western world is the United States Post Office, which carries the mail, distributes it through some 40,000 post offices and a system of home delivery, and operates a savings bank system for small depositors. Atomic energy is a tremendous government monopoly, though much of the operation is carried out through tightly supervised private manufacturers. Military arsenals and Navy construction yards are government undertakings, and during the Second World War the government financed construction of defense plants of various sorts. In the credit field government enterprise has been quite extensive. Beginning in 1916, a system of credit institutions evolved for agricultural producers. Though the capital for these is now predominantly private, they were developed with government capital and are still semipublic institutions. Loans are made by these enterprises for purchase of farms and equipment. Through another institution—the Commodity Credit Corporation—the government supports farm prices by commodity loans to farmers. In the 1930s business credit was extended by the giant Reconstruction Finance Corporation to companies suffering from the Depression. In the Second World War it financed the operation of several subsidiaries which sponsored production of essential commodities. It has now been liquidated, but a successor agency in the Department of Commerce makes loans to small business. It can be said, however, that in business credit, unlike agricultural credit, government activity has had small impact except in depression and wartime emergencies. An Export-Import Bank is an exception for a special purpose. Its primary function is to participate in or guarantee credits extended by United States exporters, commercial banks, and other financial institutions supporting foreign purchasers of exports from the United States, and also to make direct loans to finance United States exports. During the Great Depression a government corporation made loans to home owners to save their properties from foreclosure by mortgage holders, or to make repairs.

Today the government operates in diverse ways in the housing field, including maintenance of Home Loan Banks, which are credit reservoirs for private lending institutions; grants or loans to cities for public housing developments; and a system of insurance against loss on loans made by private lenders. The government also insures bank deposits, provides insurance for the aged and their survivors, and operates a number of other insurance programs. Insurance for private investors—primarily in housing and bank deposits—and for individuals against the hazards of life is a major type of public enterprise.

The most publicized enterprises of the national government have been the giant river development projects. These have multiple purposes, including flood control, irrigation, and soil conservation; but the most distinctive public enterprise feature is the generation and sale of electric power. The Boulder Canyon Project, the Tennessee Valley Authority, the Bonneville Power Administration (for the Columbia River Basin), and the New York Power Authority are the most notable of these public power undertakings.

Government enterprises are managed in two ways. Many of them are operated as departments or bureaus of departments. This is true, for example, of the United States Post Office and of many municipal water and electricity systems. Others are operated by government corporations or authorities. Examples are the Tennessee Valley Authority, the St. Lawrence Seaway Development Corporation, and the Port of New York Authority.

Government corporations have more freedom from the annual appropriation process than departments. They are usually authorized to borrow money up to stated limits and to reuse the revenues they obtain through sales or loan payments. They are separate legal entities which can sue and be sued in their own name. They may have almost complete autonomy or be supervised by political officials.

There are persuasive arguments both for and against the use of the corporate device in government management. On one hand, it is a means of escaping from traditional rules and practices unsuited to operation of a business enterprise, such as the archaic rule that a government cannot sue or be sued without its consent or such as the appropriation process through which funds are made available on an annual basis. This viewpoint was succinctly stated by President Roosevelt when he recommended that the Tennessee Valley Authority be set up in 1933 as "a corporation clothed with the power of government but possessed of the flexibility of a private enterprise."

On the other hand, many see weaknesses in the corporate device. They believe that arrangements should exist for coordination of the activities of corporations with the rest of the government. They believe that these agencies, being public agencies and existing for public purposes, should be subject to control by representatives of the people.

The contending views were compromised on the national level in the Government Corporation Act of 1945.[22] This act accepted the use of the corporate device, but only when authorized by Congress. It provided that the corporations should submit annual budgets to the Bureau of the Budget

---

[22] 59 *Stat.* 597.

but that the corporate budget should be a "business-type budget, or plan of operations, with due allowance given to the need for flexibility. . . ." It provided for commercial audits, that is, "in accordance with the principles and procedures applicable to commercial corporate transactions." It contemplated the floating of corporate bond issues, as authorized under separate acts, but it gave the Treasury Department control over issuances, including forms and denominations, maturities, interest rates, terms and conditions, and offering dates. By other acts, most corporations are subject to civil service laws and are located within a department.

Government enterprises are not always sustained fully by their own revenues. Many municipal transportation systems are subsidized out of general revenues, while some cities draw profits from their power systems into their general revenue funds. The Post Office operates with a large deficit, and the Rural Electrification Administration subsidizes rural cooperatives by lending them money at 2 percent, a rate lower than that at which the government obtains it. In multipurpose river projects, where flood control and power supply and other purposes are served, a complicated basis of allocating costs among the several purposes has been evolved, and that portion of costs attributable to power is recouped by revenues from sale of power. There is always argument, nevertheless, over whether the full costs are paid. Private power companies allege that the sums paid in lieu of taxes by TVA are incommensurate with taxes paid by similar private concerns. In most cases, of course, public enterprises are completely tax-exempt, and this may create problems for taxing jurisdictions other than the one that runs the enterprise.

Should the government operate the Post Office at a deficit, thus giving a subsidy for newspaper and magazine circulation and for other interests? Should it subsidize public housing projects for low-income families? Should it subsidize local transportation in order to maintain low rates of charge? Should it make a profit from municipal power systems? These questions of policy become political issues. Some people think that the corporate device should be so established as to emphasize the idea that a government corporation should stand on its own feet, but others hold that social benefits are of more importance than the financial record of the government enterprise and see no reason why a government corporation, or a government department operating a business enterprise, should not operate at a deficit if social benefits are thereby obtained.

Interpretation and Prospects

The insights of American political philosophers of the eighteenth century were more prophetic than those of the English economic philosopher Adam Smith, who published his *Wealth of Nations* in 1776. Smith argued that an unregulated economy would operate automatically for the public good and that state intervention would be inefficient and bungling. Madison, on the other hand, foresaw that men would divide into factions, each seeking the government's support, and that regulation of economic interests would be "the principal task of modern legislation." Hamilton and

Jefferson went even further: they anticipated a role for government in influencing the kind of economy the nation would have.

Neither the economic philosopher nor the political philosophers anticipated developments in nineteenth- and twentieth-century conditions. None foresaw corporate capitalism and the impact of rival interests created by it. None foretold the demands upon government arising from great convulsions in the economy created by depression and international conflict. None, therefore, could predict a political economy in which government was under constant pressure for positive action to protect and promote interdependent interests.

How can one characterize the substantive interventions of government in the economy in this country? Clearly these have been responses to politics and the needs of the time. Solutions have been sought for particular problems as they arose. Consequently, there are many inconsistencies in public policy. Yet there are general patterns in the evolution of the American framework of public policy: maintenance of free and fair competition, maintenance of collective bargaining in labor-management relations, a minimum base for working standards and compensation, a utility type of regulation for monopolies, regulated competition for transportation, aid to sick industries with large employment and importance for the nation, licensing for professions and occupations of various types, and monetary and fiscal controls to insure growth and stability in the economy.

Many basic government policies have as their purpose the support of private mechanisms. Antitrust policy aims toward maintenance of the market as the regulator of price and production, labor policy toward the maintenance of bargaining between employers and employees, and monetary and fiscal policy primarily toward growth and stability in private markets. Certain other policies, such as minimum labor standards and social security programs, raise cost levels in industry but still rely on the private entrepreneur to make such adjustments in his operations as are necessary to cover additional costs. On the other hand, in many situations government intervention supplants the operation of market forces to a great extent. This is true especially of programs of production control in agriculture and oil, price control in utilities and transportation, quotas and special tariff provisions in international trade regulation, and the sale of a commodity or service by government itself.

Prospects for the future include new problems and more politics. A change, which began with defense preparations in the Second World War, is the interlinking of the private and the public spheres of our society through the device of the government contract. In defense, atomic energy, and space and general scientific research, American business and research institutions are closely tied to the government through contracts. In effect, then, a partnership has developed between government and business. Public responsibilities are placed on private parties, public secrets are shared, security checks are made on private as well as on public employees, and a large amount of detailed government supervision is combined with private management. This development creates new problems for government—for example, protection of government secrets and a fight against

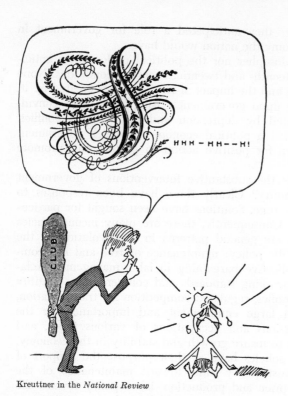

HHH–HH––H!

Conservatives opposed Kennedy's attempts to mollify business after he had intervened in the steel crisis of 1962.

Kreuttner in the *National Review*

excessive costs, particularly in contracts which provide for a margin of profit over costs. It also creates new interests, and a new phase in politics —cities, states, and business interests contending for government contracts.

The long-time trend toward concentration both in business and in labor raises questions about the adequacy of traditional policies. It has been noted that President Johnson was forced to intervene to avoid a railroad strike in 1964, as President Truman had been before. In 1962, President Kennedy, believing that a steel price rise would have dangerous inflationary effects, called upon the industry to rescind a price increase, characterizing the increase as "wholly unjustifiable and irresponsible defiance of the public interest." President Johnson's and President Kennedy's actions raise the following questions: Will collective bargaining succeed? Will antitrust alone protect the public from excessive prices? Will efforts to manage the economy through monetary and fiscal controls succeed without some direct control of prices? But does experience in regulation of industries provide basis for a hope that price control, or wage control, could succeed? One conclusion appears clear: the extent of success in present policies of collective bargaining, antitrust, and monetary and fiscal control will determine whether deeper penetration of government into the economy will occur in the future.

Another development is the increased importance of comprehensive perspectives and policies in a society of interdependent interests. Surface transportation, for example, has become a complex system with railroads,

"Hey, Look—There's LBJ!"

President Johnson was more successful in gaining the confidence of businessmen.

Hesse in the St. Louis *Globe-Democrat*

trucks and buses, ocean, lake, and river vessels, pipelines, and private automobiles as components, and with cities, states, and many national agencies—the Interstate Commerce Commission, the Civil Aeronautics Board, the Bureau of Public Roads, and others—handling aspects of the problem. To cite an even more important example, economic growth and stability have innumerable facets and are affected by the action of numerous government agencies.

In the latter instance Congress has created instruments—the Council of Economic Advisers and the Joint Economic Committee—to provide a comprehensive perspective. The Council of Economic Advisers was called by one Senator an "economic brain." It represents an effort to supply one of two components in a political system of decision-making—objective study on the ways of accommodating the conflicting and the interdependent interests of men. The other component is pluralistic politics—the struggle of these interests for the favor of government.

21 / Science, Technology, and Natural Resources

The mushroom cloud over Hiroshima, the torrents of water spilling over Grand Coulee Dam during a runoff, the forest of stubby derricks over a Texas oil field, the carefully maintained trails and cabins in Blue Ridge National Park—these depict vividly man's increasing mastery over nature for his own purposes. They are also important examples of government at work. America relies extensively on the free enterprise system for the development of natural resources: land, water, timber, energy, minerals, and chemicals. The scientific knowledge and technical skills necessary to discover and use these resources are produced in universities and in private industrial research laboratories, where the tradition of free inquiry is unchallenged. Yet, so important is the management of the country's resource base that inevitably the government must be heavily involved.

The Insatiable American Appetite

Our national security depends upon having the most advanced weapons systems possible, knowledge of the newest energy sources, the newest and best building materials, and the most recent communications advances. Continued national prosperity turns on our capacity to substitute a cheap abundant material like aluminum for an expensive scarce one like copper. Our capacity to support our rapidly expanding population is a function of "keeping up" in the supply of food, fuels, water, and materials.

These are no small tasks. In terms of sheer numbers, maintaining an adequate resource base is a massive undertaking. In the first half of the twentieth century, our insatiable American appetite required a fivefold increase in production output even though our population only doubled. By mid-century we took from the earth two and one half times more bituminous coal than we did in 1900; three times more copper; three and one-half times more iron ore; four times more zinc; twenty-six times more natural gas; and thirty times more crude oil. The average American consumes each year more than 14,000 pounds of fuel for heat and energy; 10,000 pounds of building materials; 1,600 pounds of food; and some 7,200 pounds of metallic and nonmetallic materials, for a grand total of eighteen tons per person per year. Under the pressure of an expanding economy, the supply of so-called "exhaustible" resources (ore and oil, for example,

"Boy, We Could Develop That Into Some Fine Stumps"

From *Herblock's Here and Now*, Simon & Schuster, 1955

which cannot be replaced within thousands of years) is being reduced at an ever accelerating rate. Between 1900 and 1950, 26 million tons of coal, 40 billion barrels of petroleum, 3 billion tons of iron ore, 22 million tons of lead, 26 million tons of zinc, and 33 million tons of copper were taken from the land. Every ten years, annual requirements for these resources double from their 1950 rate. Even the so-called "renewable" resources, such as timber, agricultural land, and water, are being drawn upon far more rapidly than they are being replaced. Our inventory of saw-timber, for example, is being used at a rate 40 percent faster than its annual growth rate. Water demand has increased eightfold since 1900, now exceeding 180 million gallons per day.[1]

In the never-ending search for new resources and in the conservation and replenishment of old ones, the key factor is the quality and size of our "scientific enterprise." In contrast to older views of resource management, where the aim seemed to be to "lock up" existing supplies, our policies now emphasize finding new materials. Though some naturalists still warn of a plundered planet, we no longer regard our resource base as a fixed supply of materials steadily diminishing in size and value. Instead, the base is looked upon as a constantly changing combination of the components of the earth's crust, the atmosphere, and the energy

---

[1] The most comprehensive study of United States national resources of this generation is the five-volume report of the President's Materials Policy Commission. The figures cited here were taken from Volume I, titled *Resources for Freedom: Foundations for Growth and Security* (Washington, 1952), Chapter 2.

forces of nature, which varies as our capacity to utilize new resources grows. Advances in science and technology constantly alter the materials available to us and our dependence on old stocks; at the same time they expand the base of *usable* resources. Sperm whales off Nantucket and buffalo on the Western plains were once vital resources for our ancestors. Yet the pools of petroleum under Texas, the iron ore of Minnesota, and the phosphate deposits of Florida were then of no value. Now the virtual disappearance of the buffalo may occasion nostalgic concern but no economic pain, while the existence or nonexistence of petroleum is a matter of national security.

The real problem of conservation and resource use, then, is how to acquire new materials in time to replace dwindling supplies of old ones, how to achieve fuller uses of known resources, how to make materials work harder and longer and to give them "second life," as in the case of recycling water or reclaiming scrap metal; the major concern is to prevent waste, not to hoard remaining stocks. Principal reliance is being placed on the accomplishments of research and development to tap new components of the resource base which have heretofore been unavailable, to find new processes for using old resources more extensively, and to reduce the costs of development. The nation and the world thus ultimately depend on science and technology to support population growth at rising standards of living.

Together with the support of the research and development process stand more traditional resource-management policies. It is important that the stock of timber be replenished through continual reforestation. It is desirable that worn-out farm and grazing lands be reclaimed and that by-products from oil and mineral extraction be put to use. Control of water pollution and soil erosion is necessary to reduce the pressure on finding new sources. For an increasingly urban population wildlife havens, forests, lakes, and rivers are important for recreation. All these conservation programs supplement and support our research efforts.

The government is thus involved in resource management for vital and compelling reasons, and in three principal ways. First, it underwrites the expansion of the existing base by extensive *research and development programs*—in such agencies as the National Science Foundation, the Atomic Energy Commission, the National Aeronautics and Space Administration, the National Institutes of Health, and the Department of Defense. Second, it is heavily involved in the *direct development, promotion, and management* of certain existing resources, most notably land and water, by public organizations like the Forest Service and the Departments of Interior and Agriculture. Third, both the nation and the states *regulate* many private resource-development activities, as in the case of oil, natural gas, many minerals, and a considerable portion of timber.[2]

---

[2] The government also *conditions* the resource environment indirectly, but in important ways: in its economic and monetary policies, in its foreign relations and national security programs designed to give us access to resources of other nations, and as a large purchaser of materials in its own right. But these are not primarily considered as resource policies.

How effectively government performs in its three major roles is a function of the politics of resource development and management. A complex set of political subsystems operates in shaping research and development policies and programs of conservation and regulation. Usually these systems consist of the "triple alliances" of government bureaus, private interest groups, and Congressional committees, though the extensive involvement of the states and even local government in conservation and regulation of policy often adds a fourth dimension to resource politics.

The relative positions and political power of the members of these triple alliances vary from program to program. Sometimes the private interest groups appear to prevail over government bureaus and to be in league with Congressional committees. Occasionally the competition among great federal agencies is the most distinctive feature. Whatever the combination, these subsystems and the programs they direct constitute our national resource management. Before we can judge how adequate our total resource program is for present and future needs, we have to know how the subsystems make their decisions, how they are related to one another, and how they are made responsible to the President, Congress, and the public.

Underwriting Innovation:
Government Support for Science and Technology

The most visible political subsystem at work in the resource field today is the one that manages our research process. In its present character and magnitude, this system is of recent origin, beginning in the Second World War; yet actually the tradition of government use and support of science and technology is as old as the nation itself.

Several of the Founding Fathers, particularly Benjamin Franklin and Thomas Jefferson, combined skill in politics with leadership in science. The establishment of the census, of specific standards for weights and measures, and of the provision for the patenting of inventions were the first signs of the new nation's respect for science and technology. In the early years of the Republic, the federal government sponsored expeditions to explore the coastal and inland resources of the country, considered the establishment of a national university, supported inventors, and accepted the bequest which made possible the Smithsonian institution.

These early efforts, however, were often abortive and always restricted. The rise of Jacksonian democracy created a climate of opinion essentially suspicious of the uncommon man in science as well as in any other pursuit. The prevailing doctrine of states' rights further limited federal capacity to advance scientific ventures. The outbreak of the Civil War, however, led to a major expansion in the federal government's relation to science. The war itself prompted the military to place extensive reliance on research for weapons and military equipment—the perfection of ironclad ships and new advances in food processing and ammunition manufacture. In 1863 Congress established the National Academy of Sciences, a self-perpetuating body of scientists, to investigate various fields of science at the request of the government. The greatest change took place in agricultural research, when the Morrill Act of 1862 gave grants of land for state colleges and created research bureaus on these campuses to investigate particular farm problems. For the next fifty years, this elaborate network of agricultural field stations was to demonstrate dramatically the value of systematic research by providing the most productive agriculture the world had ever witnessed.

National emergencies continued to provide the prime impetus for public support of science. During the First World War, the National Advisory Committee for Aeronautics was established; Thomas Edison headed a Naval Consulting Board for science, and President Wilson established the National Research Council as an offshoot of the National Academy of Sciences to work on specific research projects of interest to the government. During the Depression, President Franklin Roosevelt established a Presidential Scientific Advisory Board. His Administration also produced an important report, *Research—A National Resource*, that explored the potential of science in providing growth in a weak economy, for the first time.

But it was the Second World War that stimulated a major revolution in the government's attitude toward research. The Office of Scientific Research and Development (headed by Vannevar Bush, a distinguished engineer from MIT) was established to coordinate military research and development, and the accomplishments of science in the war—the atomic bomb, the proximity fuse, radar, blood plasma—showed clearly the vast potential of organized and directed research. By the time the war had ended, the research centers which the government had established, the new relationships forged between public agencies and universities, and the research programs under way in military departments had become a unified national enterprise.[3]

Bush laid the groundwork for a permanent alliance between science and government in his report to President Truman in 1945 entitled *Science, The Endless Frontier*. In this document he made clear that science was the chief avenue through which new materials, new products, and new resources would become available. He called for the support of basic science as capital to assure an economy of abundance. In rapid succession, the Atomic Energy Commission was established, the National Science Foundation was created, military research programs were reorganized and expanded, and the President's Science Advisory Committee and the Office of Science and Technology were formed within the Executive Office. New programs in medical research were instituted by the National Institutes of Health, and the National Aeronautics and Space Administration was launched in 1958 to plan the American space efforts. All of these signaled a basic national commitment to underwrite scientific progress. The revolution is most dramatically expressed in dollars. In 1939, the federal budget included some $50 million for research. In 1964 the federal government spent $15 *billion*—60 percent of the total national investment—for research and development, as contrasted to a 29 percent share by industry and 11 percent for academic and nonprofit research enterprises.

---

[3] A good historical account of scientists in the Second World War is found in J. P. Baxter, III, *Scientists Against Time* (New York, 1946).

The new public investment in science and technology has raised a host of public policy questions. Should research be carried on principally within government establishments or by support to private industries and universities? How much should be spent on research? What scientific fields should be emphasized? Who should decide where and how research activities will be carried on? What guarantees are necessary to insure that freedom of scientific inquiry will be preserved? How can discoveries and inventions made under public auspices be fed into the private sector?

Over the last twenty years these decisions have been increasingly important, and as policies have been hammered out a pattern of politics has emerged. Natural scientists, traditionally aloof from the political arena, have come to be influential in high councils of state. New industries have sprung up almost entirely dependent on government support and hence vitally interested in the ways government manages research and development. The new government scientific agencies have developed missions and objectives of their own. From them a political subsystem has emerged which may be far more influential in determining the structure of the American economy and the resource base on which it rests than those concerned with the conservation and development of existing land, water, mineral, and energy supplies. Indeed, President Eisenhower in his farewell address to the nation, warned that American society might be on the verge of domination by a "scientific-technological elite."

THE EMERGING STRUCTURE
FOR PUBLIC RESEARCH AND DEVELOPMENT

Some of the major policy questions raised by government entry into science have received at least tentative answers. One of the most important issues—where research and development activities will be lodged—has been resolved in favor of primary reliance on private enterprises and universities. Of the $8 billion authorized for research and development in 1960, over $6 billion was "extramural"—that is, spent outside government laboratories. Federal agencies rely principally on two legal devices—the contract and the grant—to forge a working partnership with business and academic organizations in executing research programs.

Both these devices have been used by government for a long time, but in scientific areas they have been substantially modified. It is often not possible to advertise for bids in the development of complex weapons-systems structures or satellites because it is impossible to specify a still unknown product, and relatively few firms have the skills and resources to engage in this complex work. Hence, most research and development contracts are negotiated with one of a small number of firms, and the government guarantees reimbursement of all costs plus a reasonable rate of return. Also, federal agencies use the contract method to support entire laboratories rather than specific research projects—as is the case with the Los Alamos Laboratory managed by the University of California or the Lincoln Laboratory of MIT. And a single contractor may be chosen to manage an entire weapons system and to subcontract specific phases of the program to other industries. This was the case in the production of the B-70 bomber, where North American Aviation was made the prime contractor for the design, development, and production of the complete weapon.[4]

Contracts are used most extensively in the defense and space fields, where time is of the utmost importance and technological innovation rather than basic research is required. The grant is the favored instrument in nondefense areas, and here new relationships between government and colleges and universities have emerged. The National Science Foundation, established in 1950, is the agency specifically charged with fostering basic research. Annually it awards some $200 million to individual scientists or laboratories to undertake specific research they propose, and to a limited extent it gives general-purpose grants to universities and other research institutions. The National Institutes of Health carry out a similar program in medicine, making grants to researchers, universities, and hospitals to support investigations in the conquest of cancer, heart disease, arthritis, allergy, and infectious and metabolic diseases, and research in dentistry and psychiatry. With appropriations which have grown from $10 to $300 million between 1947 and 1960, the Institutes currently support over 10,000 projects at 1,000 separate institutions annually.

As with the National Science Foundation, the Institutes operate by establishing panels of experts (some 1,700) in selected fields to review and evaluate applications submitted by individual scientists and to select certain fields as "targets" for concentrated research. Compared to research and development contracts, grant programs are designed to function with a minimum of red tape: there are few requirements for reporting, there is broad latitude in the conduct of the research, and the grantee is allowed to retain facilities and equipment purchased with the funds of his grant.

This heavy reliance on extramural research is the distinctive characteristic of publicly organized science in America. It reflects our traditional preference for private enterprise and independent scholarship. It also endows the national research effort with qualities of flexibility and a capacity for rapid expansion which are unique in the world. At the same time, however, the new partnership has raised some knotty problems. So far as contracts are concerned, the reliance on negotiated arrangements tends to reduce price competition and risk-taking, the essentials of the enterprise system. Administered prices and nonmarket controls blur the difference between the public and private sectors and substitute enterprises which defy precise description. Moreover, the need to assure high technological and managerial competence in defense projects has led to a high concentration of awards to a few large firms. Today, firms with over 5,000 employees perform over 70 percent of all research and development work in electronics, for example. Thus, by its scientific programs, the government may be encouraging monopolistic tendencies in the economy while the Justice Department still seeks to enforce the Sherman Antitrust Law. Finally, the staffs of government agencies themselves may fail to develop

---

[4] See J. Stefan Dupre and Sanford A. Lakoff, *Science and the Nation: Policy and Politics* (Englewood Cliffs, N.J., 1963).

the critical skills essential to direct and oversee research and development activities.

As for the grants, there has been a concentration of awards in high prestige universities similar to that of contracts to large firms. In 1962, 95 percent of the billion-plus federal dollars given to universities and colleges by twenty-eight different agencies went to fewer than 100 institutions. Twenty-six institutions accounted for 28 percent of the total, and twelve received at least $5 million each year. These universities and colleges are in a position further to strengthen their lead, for they thus have funds to support some 25,000 graduate students.[5] However, the acceptance of government-sponsored research on a campus complicates the university administration; it raises issues of academic freedom where classified projects are involved and investigators require loyalty and security clearances; it distorts emphasis from humanities to the sciences; and it places heavy (and nonreimbursed) indirect costs on general university facilities. Nevertheless, for both industry and university there is a growing tendency to become dependent on public support and unable to exist without it.

THE POLITICS OF PUBLIC RESEARCH

What is the decision-making process that sustains the elaborate web of contractual and grant relations binding together the national government, industry, and universities in extramural research and development activities? Who issues priorities in research fields and chooses between alternative grant applications?

In 1952 a Presidential commission reported that "the Government, up from almost nothing since the beginning of the century, is now the great force behind scientific and technical research in this country. . . . Yet this great force is headless. . . . When one looks for a coherent research policy directed toward materials or indeed to anything else equally specific, one does not find it. . . ."[6] A decade later, when federal research and development expenditures had multiplied many times, still no clear-cut policy for science had emerged to specify areas in which funds and manpower might most appropriately be applied. But those years did witness the appearance of new policy-making and advisory mechanisms to shape science policy as well as the rise of powerful interest groups concerned with the size and character of research and development.

Three interest groups in particular have sought to shape the modern national research enterprise along special lines. Spokesmen for the scientific community, military leaders and their industrial supporters, and highly placed civil servants in the top echelon of the national bureaucracy have succeeded in achieving spheres of influence in shaping scientific policy. Sometimes they have dramatically confronted one another.

The spokesmen for scientists constitute a new group of political activists on the national scene. Recruited during the Second World War on an

---

[5] Harold Orlans, *The Effects of Federal Programs on Higher Education* (Washington, 1962).

[6] President's Materials Policy Commission, *op. cit.*, p. 144.

emergency basis to turn technological break-throughs to defense purposes, many scientists had their first sustained working experience with the military profession, the government administrator, and the elected official in laboratories such as the Manhattan Project or the Radiation Laboratory at MIT. These scientists emerged with strong convictions about the proper organization of government-sponsored research and the need to assure that science would not become "politicized." In particular, they became convinced of the need to insure that atomic science would be used for international peace and not for "reactionary" or "adventurist" purposes.

The first venture of the "new scientists" into policy-making occurred during the enactment of legislation establishing the Atomic Energy Commission. Then the young atomic scientists successfully opposed a bill which would have continued the program under military auspices, and they displayed considerable skill lobbying for the creation of an independent agency under civilian direction. Similar controversies broke out in the establishment of the NSF and the reorganization of research and development in the military. In 1954, a crisis in science-government relations occurred when a special security-review board created by President Eisenhower denied clearance to Dr. Robert Oppenheimer (a distinguished physicist who had directed the Los Alamos Laboratory in the war) on the grounds that his personal associations and policy views raised reasonable doubts as to his loyalty and reliability. This move, which many scientists regarded as "official McCarthyism," alienated a number of leading scientists from further participation in government programs. Controversies among scientists over appropriate public policies in the development of the hydrogen bomb, nuclear testing, and disarmament further impaired the scientists' political influence in the mid-1950s.

But the Soviet launching of Sputnik in 1957 prompted the government to turn again to scientists for advice and counsel. In that year the post of Special Assistant to the President for Science and Technology was created. The Science Advisory Committee, which had not had direct access to the President since the Second World War, was reestablished at the White House level. In 1959 a Federal Council for Science and Technology was created to bring together representatives of policy rank from agencies with large scientific programs and thereby improve coordination among research activities. In 1962 the Office of Science and Technology was established in the Executive Office of the President, headed by the Special Assistant, who remained the President's personal adviser but directed a permanent staff to provide scientific counsel to other executive agencies and the Congress. Assistant Secretaries for research and development were placed in major Departments, and the positions were filled largely by professional engineers and scientists. Increased funds were provided to the National Science Foundation, whose panels were already drawn from members of the scientific community. Proposals for a Department of Science were seriously considered as a further institutionalization of the scientists in government. In the space of four years, a new advisory apparatus with direct access to the President appeared, to speak for science and to undertake to assure that the basic tenets of the scientific community—the pursuit of knowledge unfettered by immediate considerations of practical

"Dear Boy, Where Have You Been Keeping Yourself?"

The "loyalty-security" system with regard to scientists was reevaluated with the appearance of the first sputnik.

From *Herblock's Special for Today*, Simon & Schuster, 1958

utility, and support for scientific education and training—were respected. In 1963, Dr. Oppenheimer received the Fermi Award, for distinguished contributions to atomic research, from President Johnson—an event fittingly symbolic of the new rapport.

Yet the scientists are still by no means unchallenged either in the making of policy on matters that involve complex scientific and engineering considerations or in developing a basic approach to research support. One nonscientific group which has been highly influential in shaping administration and budgetary processes for government scientists has consisted of highly placed civil service generalists. These administrators often regard scientists as simply another species of experts, comparable to lawyers and accountants; that is, they should be kept "on tap but not on top." They succeeded in persuading President Truman not to establish the National Science Foundation until a single director was selected to replace the part-time board that scientists had preferred and until other special organizational features were eliminated. Generalists also opposed the elevation of the Scientific Advisory Committee to Presidential level and the establishment of a Department of Science. In general, they wish to maintain pre-eminence of regular budgetary and administrative procedures as against the desires of scientists for substantial professional independence.

Another group in addition to the scientists and civilian administrators has great influence in research and development policy. This consists of

"Yaaach! This Is One Morning I Wouldn't Mind Being Replaced By Automation—Walter Reuther Notwithstanding!"

Automation as a result of scientific research has become a major labor issue.

Interlandi in the Los Angeles *Times*

military leaders and the industrial concerns heavily involved in defense work. In the same speech in which Eisenhower identified the "scientific-technological elite" he warned of the "unwarranted influence" of "the military-industrial complex." As defense expenditures have spiraled and the bulk of research and development programs has come under the direction of the Pentagon, the rise of the "military lobby" has been viewed with alarm in some quarters. Critics fear not only its assumed vested interest in maintaining defense spending at high levels but also the pressure it may exert on scientific manpower and research activities by overemphasizing defense-related projects. In particular, the difficulty the Defense Department has found in abandoning weapons systems no longer considered the most effective or reliable, such as the B-70 bomber or the Skybolt missile, has led some to fear that objective research decisions, on the basis of the best technical advice, cannot be made.

It is not clear whether these fears are exaggerated, but certain facts have been established. First, a large number of retired military officers of high rank are employed by the large defense contractors, a point that raises questions as to their influence in military procurement and research and development operations. Second, defense companies often engage in advertising campaigns extolling the virtues of competing weapons systems, as in the cases of the Army's Nike-Hercules missile (acclaimed in magazines and newspapers by its prime contractor, the Western Electric Company) and the Air Force Bomarc missile (heralded by its prime contractor, Boeing Aircraft). Third, large potential political influence lies in the groups closely associated with the military. The Association of the United States

Army, the Navy League, the Air Force Association, the American Ordnance Association, the Aerospace Industries Association, and the National Security Industrial Association are large groups devoted "to informing and educating" the public. Though they stoutly deny any interest in specific defense projects, the general thrust of their activities seems oriented to the objectives of the services they support.[7]

Other considerations besides purely official ones clearly enter into research and development decisions. Congressmen seek expenditures in their own districts; small business claims special considerations; reserve and national guard units protest efforts to reduce their size and number on grounds of technological obsolescence. Thus, in the space and defense field, the location of new research centers, laboratories, and installations becomes of vital political concern. Services, contractors, and Congress provide one of the most dramatic examples of the "triple alliance" at work—one with great consequences for priorities in research and development and the overall research effort. Together with scientists and general administrators, these groups help shape the nation's long-run resource base.

The upshot of the tugs of war in research politics seems to be that where defense considerations loom large—and this is the case for over two thirds of the research and development expenditures—the Defense Department and its allies are decisive in orienting research to essentially military missions. Some spillover into pure research and civilian technology is achieved in these defense projects, but by and large they are essentially engineering in character. That is, they are concerned with improved application of existing scientific knowledge.

In the realm of basic research, though the total government support is much smaller, the scientific community seems more securely in command. The advisory panels of the National Science Foundation and the National Institutes of Health are composed of scientists drawn from academic circles, predominantly in the Northeast, California, and Chicago, and the allocation of funds depends primarily on their judgments. Whether these research awards are made on the "best" basis of innovative promise is hard to say, but they are determined by what distinguished and qualified scientists think is best.

Whatever the outcome of competing interests, the government is now involved permanently as the prime agent for generating technological progress. And the scientific advance presses forward at an ever accelerating rate. A generation ago, notions that man could fly faster than the speed of sound, probe the earth's upper atmosphere and portions of the universe, communicate by microwaves reflected from earth-circling satellites, construct great assembly lines operated by automation, or set out to create life, were the province of science fiction. Now they are accepted as everyday facts of life. Under these circumstances, it is not surprising that most scientists and most public officials alike have come to look upon their new relationship as a mutual alliance for the betterment of human life.

---

[7] Dupre and Lakoff, op. cit., Chapter 2, give an interesting account of the politics of defense research and development activities.

THE NATIONAL SPACE PROGRAM:
A CASE STUDY IN GOVERNMENT RESEARCH

Perhaps the most dramatic example of government science in action is the national space program, which has as its objective placing a man on the moon and returning him to earth before 1970. The initiation and expansion of this program illustrate both the capacity of the government to alter radically the components of our resource base and the workings of the research political system. From what will be at least a $30 billion investment in space exploration will flow new knowledge of the earth's atmosphere and the universe, new communications devices and procedures, new metals to replace old ones in short supply, new medical discoveries, new ways of disposing of human wastes, new and much smaller computer devices, and new systems of organizing and managing human effort. How great the "spinoff" into the civilian economy will be is still unpredictable, but it seems likely to be substantial. Similarly the second-order effects on educational institutions, the industrial complex, and our scientific manpower pool will be major. Our progress in space, as in atomic energy, will be—at least in the beginning—the result of efforts in the public, not the private, sector of the economy.

The space program also shows how research politics works when every element in the subsystem is actively engaged. Originally, our efforts to put a satellite into orbit were small ones carried on in the Navy's Project Vanguard with the assistance and support of private scientists involved in the International Geophysical Year of 1958. When the Russians' launching of Sputnik I in 1957 demonstrated at least temporary superiority in satellite and rocket thrust technology, a violent public and political reaction occurred in the United States. The Defense Department established a new Advanced Research Projects Agency and speeded up its missile program. Scientists called for a total reevaluation of American education in and support of the natural sciences. The Congress, under the leadership of Lyndon Johnson, then Democratic Majority Leader of the Senate, initiated a full-scale inquiry into our defense program. The Eisenhower Administration responded by creating the post of Special Assistant for Science and Technology and submitting legislation for the establishment of an independent civilian agency, the National Aeronautics and Space Administration.

The consideration of this legislation showed the parties-in-interest in sharp relief. The military services wanted the major space activities to remain in the Pentagon, though interservice rivalry led the Air Force ultimately to support a civilian establishment. Several existing scientific agencies indicated their suitability to assume the task. Many private scientists were more concerned with federal support for scientific education and research in general than with the new program in particular, and feared that undue concentration on space would distort our total scientific effort. Senators and Congressmen voiced alarm at the evidence of Soviet technical superiority and the post-Sputnik propaganda and prestige victories.

In the final outcome all the parties gained something. Both the military and the civilian space programs were substantially expanded, and the military was assured control over space projects deemed essential to its missions. Research budgets for the National Science Foundation and other agencies were rapidly increased, and funds were made available for graduate training in the sciences. A civilian agency was established with a broad program for investigation of outer space. At the insistence of Senator Lyndon Johnson, a National Space Council was established, consisting of top-level officials in the government and aimed at securing a comprehensive and highly visible space program. Subsequently, appropriations for NASA were increased spectacularly, from $700 million the first year to over $5 billion in 1963. When attached to a national emergency, science again proved to have irresistible political appeal.

Today both some eminent scientists and some public officials voice concern over the size of our space effort, pointing out that we have yet to achieve a balanced and comprehensive total science program. They question in particular the need for a manned flight to the moon, emphasizing that instrumented vehicles can probably gather the same scientific information, warning of the drain on scientific manpower involved, and pointing to the possibility that other important public programs may be neglected. They ask whether or not the same funds, devoted to foreign aid or other scientific research programs, might not more effectively enhance our international position and our national security. But the space program goes ahead, at once a testimony to American faith in technology as a way out of major public problems and an indication of the difficulty of developing public policy for our greatest resource, human creativity.

The Politics of Land Use:
The Local Interest Group at Work

While science continues to expand our resource base, other governmental programs focus on the preservation of existing supplies. The nation's first major conservation program was launched by President Theodore Roosevelt, alarmed at the reckless exploitation of timber, minerals, and grazing lands. Today, these programs continue, each directed by a more or less autonomous political subsystem.

The politics of land management is organized around one very simple fact: the federal government is the nation's biggest landowner. Except for the original thirteen colonies and Texas, all the territory the United States acquired in its continental expansion—some 1.4 billion acres—was once "public domain"—the property of the federal government. By sales to gain revenue, by grants to states, railroads, and other private parties, and by preemption homestead laws, which donated land to settlers, Washington has transferred over one billion acres to other ownership. Yet today, over 400 million acres are still in federal hands, a total area four times larger than California, and comprising 53 percent of all the land of the eleven Western states.[8] About 178 million acres of government land are used as grazing districts for cattle and sheep or are "unappropriated"—

---

[8] Charles A. Reich, *Bureaucracy and the Forests*, Occasional Paper of the Center for the Study of Democratic Institutions, Fund for the Republic, Inc. (New York, 1962).

that is, not used at all. The rest is set aside for national forests (167 million acres), reclamation areas (16 million acres), parks and historic sites (15 million acres), wildlife refuges (8 million acres), Indian and other institutional reservations (1.4 million acres), military uses (21.5 million acres).[9] In addition, states own some 8 million acres, again mostly in the West. The fact of government ownership generates a continuing set of political conflicts: how government should develop these areas, what regulatory policies it should have for private timber and mining operations on its land, and indeed whether it should continue to function as a landlord at all.

Two great federal agencies, the Department of the Interior and the Department of Agriculture, are responsible for the majority of public land activities. But the close relation between land and water means that other federal agencies, such as the Corps of Engineers and the Tennessee Valley Authority, as well as many state governments, play important roles in land management. Around them cluster important private interest groups who, while recognizing the value of conservation and resource replenishment, make their living off the public lands. These groups, especially in the West, and especially in land managed by the Department of Interior, tend to dominate policy-making on the public domain.

Established in 1849 as a general housekeeper for the federal government, the Department of Interior now views itself as the "custodian of natural resources" for the United States. Its Bureau of Land Management controls some 142 million acres (the so-called "federal range"), classifying land uses, issuing licenses, permits, and leases for mining and range activities, and regulating commercial forest operations on land under its jurisdiction. The basic law providing for the control and rehabilitation of the topsoil of the range is the Taylor Grazing Act of 1934, designed primarily to stop overgrazing and soil deterioration by establishing grazing districts in the Western states, by calculating their capacity to support livestock, and by then issuing permits for grazing to stockmen.

As for mining, laws dating back a hundred years provide a *location* system for metallic and a few nonmetallic ores, by which private individuals can acquire title to land on which they discover mineral deposits, and a *leasing* system for private extraction of oil, gas, coal, and phosphates. Private timber operations are authorized by competitive bidding and under supervision designed to assure sustained yield of publicly owned forest land (about one fourth of the total productive forests).

Other units within Interior emphasize recreational and wildlife preservation activities. The National Park Service maintains some 192 parks and installations on more than 15 million acres of land. The Fish and Wildlife Service has a comprehensive conservation program to assure sportsmen of continued stocks of fish and game. The Bureau of Outdoor Recreation, established in 1962, is a further effort to develop a national program with respect to the enjoyment of land and forest resources, placing special emphasis on the needs of our urban population. And units such as the Geological Survey, the Bureau of Mines, and the Office of Mineral Exploi-

---

[9] See United States Department of Agriculture, *Year Book of Agriculture*, for general analysis of changing public land uses and allocations.

tation undertake research and development activities designed to preserve and expand land resources.

In addition to the Interior programs are complementary and sometimes competitive activities of the Department of Agriculture. The Forest Service, established in 1905, manages the timber, mineral, and other resources of the 154 national forests covering 170 million acres in thirty-nine states and Puerto Rico, chiefly concentrated in Idaho, California, Oregon, and Montana. Its activities closely parallel those of the Bureau of Land Management for the rest of the public domain, but sharp differences in administrative philosophy and operating techniques exist between the two organizations. Indeed, so competitive have the operations of these agencies become on such matters as timber operations, mining leases, and sales of public land that tense confrontations have occurred. Forest and Park Service Rangers have engaged in pitched battles, with fists and sticks, to defend their respective services.

The Department of Agriculture also has major conservation programs for private land resources. Its Soil Conservation Service provides technical assistance to individual farmers in the conservation of their land and water, through grass-roots organization of 3,000 local districts throughout the nation. These districts, directed by boards composed of local farmers, include over 90 percent of existing American farms. Technical specialists from the Soil Conservation Service, making surveys of soil capacities, prepare a treatment plan for the farmer to follow, specifying the kind of fertilizers and crops most appropriate for particular holdings. In the same way the Forest Service provides technical assistance to small woodland owners and, in turn, state governments provide similar assistance. New York, for example, long a leader in the field, has over 3 million acres under state management in forest preserves such as the Adirondack and Catskill areas.[10] It buys abandoned farm lands to be used for wildlife and lumber operations and to provide "small-tract" reforestation.

Finally, federal and state governments work together in the land-use field through the century-old land-grant college system and the network of agricultural experimental stations and extension services it has produced. Established in 1862, when the Morrill Act granted some 11 million acres of land to the states for the support of colleges to teach agriculture, engineering, and home economics, the system has underwritten the development of many of the nation's state universities and has provided a continuing emphasis on agriculture and land-use policies. The extension services, aided by federal funds, and the experiment stations provide close, continued communication between farmers, governments, and educational centers. The result is a set of programs staffed by specialists from both levels of government but closely tied together at the local level by informal working arrangements.

The key institution in the politics of land is the special-purpose local district. This is the instrument through which private interests exercise continuing and heavy influence on the programs. By statute and administrative rule, federal and state agencies have placed the clientele they serve

---

[10] *Ibid.*

in positions of official responsibility within the programs.[11] In doing so, they provide the political basis for support of the agencies' activities, since satisfied customers in soil conservation, timber-management policies, and grazing are likely to be important members of Congressional constituencies, especially in the West. But the pattern of local districts and committees also makes for tension between national conservation groups intent on a more vigorous conservation practice, professional administrators within the agencies, and the users or direct beneficiaries of the program. In many instances, it appears that the real decision makers in land-management policies are the interest groups involved: the farmers, stockmen, and timbermen.

The presence and influence of the clientele working through the advisory system is the principal factor behind the continued division of federal responsibilities between Interior and Agriculture. Their operations are clearly visible in the grazing program of the Bureau of Land Management as it is applied on the public range. Here, the clientele and the Congressmen have made league against the bureaucrat, so that grazing policy under the Taylor Grazing Act is one shaped principally by a small minority of Western stockmen. In this instance, the district advisory boards established by the Bureau are typically composed of "the upper strata of a rural caste system." [12] Representatives of stockmen also make up the state and national boards and keep in close contact with Congressmen from the range states. These Congressmen serve on the committees and subcommittees overseeing the work of the Bureau of Land Management. Thus any radical changes in grazing policies, fees, or organization proposed by Bureau personnel are likely to meet opposition both from home and from Washington. The stockmen and Congressmen converge to keep regulation and supervision at a minimum and to assure that no powerful administrative agency threatens them. "The close collaboration and agreement between stockmen's associations, the advisory boards, certain Western congressmen and some administrators has at times been an invincible combination." [13]

The clientele-oriented character of land-management politics has concerned some students of government for at least a generation, especially those who advocate strengthening the supervisory and executive functions of the President. In 1937, the President's Committee on Administrative Management recommended the establishment of a Department of Conservation, consolidating all major land-management activities. The first Hoover Commission in 1949 proposed the establishment of an Agricultural Resources Conservation Service in the Department of Agriculture, to which the Bureau of Land Management would be transferred. Other suggestions have included placing the Forest Service in the Department of Interior, the creation of a Federal Land Corporation, and the creation of a Federal

---

[11] For an incisive political analysis of the operations of these local district committees in the Department of Agriculture, see Morton Grodzins, Separate Statement, *Review of the Farm Committee System*, United States Department of Agriculture, Study Committee (November, 1962) (mimeographed).

[12] Phillip O. Foss, *Politics and Grass: The Administration of Grazing on the Public Domain* (Seattle, 1960) provides the most recent political analysis of land politics on the range. The citation is from p. 196.

[13] *Ibid.*, p. 202.

Land Review Board. The two basic aims of all these proposals have been, first, to introduce some uniform policy criteria in the handling of the public domain and the providing of technical assistance to private land-holders and, second, to consolidate research, informational, and reporting services.

To date none of these proposals has been adopted. Understandably, land interest groups prefer a highly decentralized organization which assures them of many places of access and a strong voice in policy matters. As for the agencies, though their heads might prefer tighter control over field offices and greater policy discretion, they rarely favor the merger of their enterprises with those in other Departments. So they have joined forces with clients and Congressmen alike to preserve their separate iden-tities. As a consequence, a large number of separate public programs now go forward to preserve, restore, and increase the effectiveness of land. By and large, all are motivated by a broad common desire to prevent further damage to this basic resource and all express the same philosophy of modern resource management. But these programs are fashioned and executed on a highly individualistic basis, and their administrators are more likely to look to the clienteles they serve for guidance than to their official superiors.

Water Politics: Empire Building
in the Federal Executive

Like the land-management programs, the public activities devoted to assuring the nation of a sufficient water supply for household, industrial, and farm use may be viewed as the product of a special political sub-system involving users, federal and state bureaucrats, and legislators, all vying with one another and yet all united in opposing comprehensive executive direction. In the case of water, however, the bureaucracies pro-ceed from positions of much greater strength than their counterparts in land management. Not only is the sense of agency identity and profes-sionalization somewhat stronger and their relations with the Congress more harmonious, but also the interests with which they deal are more divided. Water, in an increasingly urban nation, has many simultaneous uses. Hence, in contrast to the case of the stockmen and the range, a number of groups with quite conflicting interests in water development are likely to cluster around a specific project with no single interest predominant. In such instances it often falls to the public agencies involved to reconcile different objectives in the development of water resources.

Concepts of appropriate water policy have changed radically in the twentieth century. Until thirty years ago, the development of water re-sources proceeded on a project-by-project basis with usually a single pre-dominant objective. Dams were built and reservoirs created for flood control purposes, or to supply water for canals, produce public power, or irrigate farm land. With the completion of the Hoover Dam in 1930, however, the concept of the multiple-purpose storage project was born. The act authorizing Hoover Dam included as its objectives the prevention of floods, the improvement of navigation, the generation of electricity, the reclamation of lands, and other beneficial purposes. It firmly established the principle of comparing costs to benefits and utilizing the resulting ratio as a measure for determining the desirability of a project.

In succeeding years new standards for "sound" water policy have emerged. One is the concept of basinwide development—a system of works, in place of a single project, to coordinate water use for an entire river basin—first applied to the Miami River of Ohio after a devastating flood in 1913, but taken up elsewhere only in the 1930s. Another is the integration of water development with land-use planning. There followed attempts to mesh (or "articulate," in the planners' language) land and water development programs and to provide for unified administration of these schemes—two concepts which are now favorites in the academic writings about the best water development programs.[14]

Like the multiple-purpose sustained-yield philosophy of land management, however, these concepts are more often acknowledged in principle than adopted in practice. The large multipurpose project is accepted doctrine for all public agencies in the field: almost 500 such dams have been built in the United States, twelve since 1946. But the realization of basinwide and regionwide programs relating land and water resources under unified management has been much more difficult.

The reasons for the lag between concepts and practice are found in the nature of water politics. Four great federal agencies now share responsibilities for water resources, each with different traditions, a different basis of political support, and different policy emphases. The conflicts among these agencies, and between them and the President and Congress, are among the most intense and dramatic in American political history.

The oldest agency concerned with water development is the Army Corps of Engineers. The Corps is both a civil and military engineering and construction agency, responsible since the early 1800s for national internal improvement programs and public works for harbors and navigable rivers. After the Mississippi flood of 1879, the Corps was given primary responsibility for flood-prevention programs on that river. The Flood Control Act of 1936 formally extended its civilian work to all of the United States. In carrying out flood-control work, the Corps tradition has established fewer requirements on local authorities than other water agencies. These liberal policies, plus the benefits which its program brought local areas, have resulted in strong Congressional, local government, civic, and business support for its activities. Since 1901, these interests have been organized as the National Rivers and Harbors Congress, working closely with the Corps in identifying and assigning priorities to appropriate policies.[15]

Because of the popularity of COE projects with local constituencies, Congressmen place special importance on the work of the Corps. Each year's Rivers and Harbors appropriation bill is the result of intensive logrolling among individual members seeking to secure their share from the pork barrel of suggested projects. For its part, the Corps has sought to

---

[14] A full description of these concepts is provided in Roscoe C. Martin, *River Basin Administration in the Delaware* (Syracuse, 1960).

[15] The most comprehensive study of the Corps of Engineers is Arthur Maass, *Muddy Waters, the Army Engineers and the Nation's Rivers* (Cambridge, Mass., 1951).

maintain close legislative relations, often referring to itself as "the engineer consultants to, and contractors for, the Congress of the United States."

The second major water resources agency is the Bureau of Reclamation in the Department of Interior. Established in 1902, its responsibility is conservation, development, and utilization of land and water resources in seventeen western states; hence, it focuses on irrigation, power, and other uses besides flood control. Further, it deals with separate Congressional committees in the authorization and appropriation for its projects.

Created in response to the political unrest of the small Western farmer, dedicated to making previously worthless lands valuable, and operating in areas where strong local pressure groups frequently did not exist, the Bureau has been more responsive to regional multipurpose approaches than has the Corps. It has also been prepared to impose more federal regulations and requirements on power and water users than has the Corps, and to use different formulas for the calculation of costs and benefits. The creation of the Bonneville, Southeastern, and Southwestern Power Administrations within the Department of Interior to market electricity produced by national dams and power stations in these areas tends further to distinguish Interior's resource approach from that of the Corps.

A more recent entry into the field is the Department of Agriculture. Since 1936, the Department has been authorized to investigate "watersheds and measures for runoff and waterflow retardation and soil erosion prevention in watersheds"—that is, to seek means for controlling and using water upstream near its sources. Since 1944, it has been empowered to make upstream installations for watershed protection—small reservoir projects, in contrast to the larger COE and Reclamation dams.

Finally, the Tennessee Valley Authority, created in 1933, represents the nation's one major experiment in comprehensive regional planning under unified administration. A public corporation, possessing considerable financial and organizational autonomy, the TVA is concerned with the general development of the entire Tennessee Valley area. Its operations cover 40,000 square miles in seven states and include some thirty-one dams and hydroelectric plants and 1,000 miles of navigable water. Flood control, navigation improvement, and electric power represent the initial major concerns, but through a network of agreements with state and local officials, the TVA has embraced a number of other programs. It operates the Muscle Shoals fertilizer and munitions plant (established as a First World War government installation) and has developed an active fertilizer research, experimentation, and demonstration program to improve regional farm practices. It has a large-scale forestry program, focused on improving practices of private timber operators. It has extensive recreational and health programs, and collaborates with state and local agencies in planning and development work. In short, the TVA program is the closest approximation to the concepts of a broad resource development program which the United States offers. Its supporters have hailed the Authority as America's best example of modern progressive democracy at work.[16] Its detractors have called its programs socialistic.

---

[16] The outstanding defense of the Authority is David E. Lilienthal, *TVA: Democracy on the March* (New York, 1944).

The existence of these four agencies, each with different policies for water development, has provoked continuing conflict over water use, plans, and projects. Although each has been engaged in multipurpose development for a generation, the Corps of Engineers and the Bureau of Reclamation often compete for the right to plan, design, and construct the same downstream project. Both are critical of the effectiveness of Agriculture's upstream program. All three are suspicious of TVA's program when it is presented as a model to be applied to the other major regions of the nation. In addition, state governments have powerful interest in water utilization plans because the development of large interstate rivers poses knotty problems of allocating the available water supply among the states involved. Accordingly, they have insisted on the right to be consulted in federal programs and to construct projects of their own.

Under these circumstances, it is not surprising that after the passage of the Flood Control Act of 1936, extending the Corps' jurisdiction and authorizing the participation of Agriculture, open warfare broke out. One of the most spectacular engagements took place on the Kings River in the Central Valley of California.[17] At the request of local interests in 1937, both the COE and the Bureau of Reclamation prepared multipurpose development plans, each stressing different uses and each calculating costs and benefits differently to demonstrate the superiority of its own plan. Local interests—irrigation districts, chambers of commerce, water users' associations—noting that the COE's plan offered maximum federal contributions with minimum federal controls over payments, land speculation, and private power development, lined up with the Engineers. President Roosevelt, however, chose the Bureau plan, identifying irrigation and power uses as the project's "dominant purpose," and so instructed the federal agencies. But the Corps disregarded the Presidential wishes and with Congressional support secured authorization for the project, a feat dramatically demonstrating the agency's political influence and skill.

Since the direct confrontation of the two agencies at Kings River, and the defiance of Presidential policy, a pattern of some interagency coordination has emerged. In 1944, the COE and the Bureau concluded a pact for the development of the Missouri Basin—the so-called Pick-Sloan Plan, named after the then Chief of the Engineers and the Commissioner of Reclamation, who met in a St. Louis hotel room to come to an agreement. In effect, the plan was a combination of projects and programs previously prepared separately by the two agencies. It included the Corps' proposals for flood control and navigational works on the main stem of the river and the Bureau's irrigation and power projects upstream.

Later characterized as no real plan at all, but "a division of projects, each agency agreeing to forgo the privilege of criticizing projects assigned by agreement to the other," the compact at least served to bring together seven federal organizations and ten states in continuous working relations to form the Missouri Basin Inter-Agency Committee.[18]

---

[17] Maass, *op. cit.*, presents a detailed study of this incident.
[18] Martin, *op. cit.*, Chapter 11.

Similar arrangements of voluntary interagency collaboration have been adopted in most other major river basins. None has resulted in programs which meet the criteria of comprehensive developmental planning. One recent effort, the Arkansas-White-Red Basins Interagency Committee, involved six federal agencies and eight states in five years of study and planning between 1950 and 1955. The Committee was unable to agree on mutual procedures for making studies; its members could not concur on the technical and engineering findings of their experts; procedures for the coordination of study assignments were unsatisfactory to participants; and the final report acknowledged "for the most part projects formulated prior to the AWR survey have been included in the plan with little change as a result of the survey."

Despite the limitations of the interagency approach, proposals for stronger, more unified administration have not been acceptable to the Congress. The TVA experiment, although widely praised in planning and conservation circles and politically popular within the Valley, has faced stiff opposition from private power companies, from those who view the Authority as a forerunner of socialism and centralized government in America, and from the other federal agencies and their supporters. Attempts to create other basin authorities or their equivalents have failed, as have efforts to combine the national programs of the major federal agencies. In 1949, the first Hoover Commission studying the overall organization of the federal government recommended that Corps and Reclamation activities be combined within the Interior Department or a New Department of Natural Resources. In 1950, the President's Water Resources Policy Commission recommended the establishment of interagency river basin commissions with authority to coordinate and direct agency functions in each region. In 1952, the Missouri Basin Survey Commission proposed a permanent commission for the Missouri Basin. None of these proposals has been accepted, nor have recommendations for a centralized review procedure within the Executive Office of the President found favor. The separate federal agencies thus continue their separate ways, each equipped with strong professional traditions, each supported by different interest groups and different Congressional committees, and each persuaded of the superiority of its particular approach. In these circumstances, the *modus vivendi* accomplished by the interagency committees is perhaps the best compromise which water politics can be expected to produce.

The Politics of Nonrenewable Resources: The Preeminence of the States

In land and water politics, federal activities are central to the public programs now in being. In the public controversies which involve so-called "nonrenewable resources"—especially the energy sources of oil, coal, and gas—the role of state government is more important. Though the federal government controls the extraction of minerals found under national public lands, engages in substantial research activities, enforces some interstate regulation, and makes international trade policies, its responsibilities are more limited here than in other areas. The conservation and use of metallic

"They Don't Like
To Be Disturbed"

Liberals felt the Eisenhower Administration refused to regulate the oil industry properly.

From *Herblock's Special for Today*, Simon & Schuster, 1958

and nonmetallic minerals and energy fuels are determined by the marketplace or are made the subject of state public policy.

At present, the most important and complex set of regulatory policies deals with the oil industry. Historically, the state of Texas has exercised predominance and influence in efforts to control oil production. Petroleum production involves two primary economic problems. Existing wells can always deliver quantities of oil many times larger than the demand for oil in a given year; this surplus, if not controlled, both wastes the commodity and leads to ruinous price competition. On the other hand, total known reserves are considerably less than the long-run future demand, so that the discovery of new oil pools is essential. Hence, if sound conservation practices and profitable operations are to be achieved, public policy must at the same time restrict the current flow of oil to market and assure that exploration for new wells continues.

In 1930–32, the discovery of the East Texas oil field placed 1 million barrels a day on a market already reeling from the Depression and the price of crude oil dropped precipitately from over one dollar to ten cents per barrel. The state of Texas made a futile attempt to invoke martial law to control the situation, but a unique regulatory system ultimately developed. With Texas, the major producer, taking the lead, most of the oil-producing states have enacted similar oil conservation laws to govern the proration of production from existing wells (assigning production quotas to individual wells) and the drilling of new wells over known oil pools. The states, with the consent of the Congress, have formed an Interstate Oil Compact Commission, which serves as an instrument for voluntary cooperation among the states. The federal government assists the states by forwarding to them regular estimates of market demand for oil from which production quotas can be determined. It has also made illegal the shipment of oil produced in violation of state orders. In addition, the federal government controls fuel imports, and as oil imports have become increasingly important, the federal role in determining the amount of oil which can be imported in effect controls total oil production in this country.

Critics of the present program argue that the state-dominated, industry-sponsored regulations, while effective in stabilizing prices in periods of lowering demand, neither assure the best long-run conservation practices nor protect the consumer in time of prosperity. They argue that the regulations now favor the large producers and do not adequately provide a continuing supply in times of national emergency. The net result, they suggest, is the creation of a "favored" industry rather than sound public policy. Moreover, they hold that the political influence of the oil industry is so great in many of the states that state taxes and royalties from oil have been kept at much lower levels than those applying to other business enterprises.

Proposals for a more active federal role and stricter conservation practices have met with little success, however. On the contrary, in the 1950s, the states enlarged their sphere of influence by assuming control over oil production in the so-called "tidelands" off the nation's coasts. Large oil deposits exist there on the continental shelf, and when technical advances made it possible to drill for them under the sea, the oil-producing states laid claim to lands three to twelve miles offshore. The Supreme Court ruled that the tidelands were part of the national domain, but Congress enacted legislation placing them in state hands, with prerogatives for royalties and regulations falling chiefly to Texas, California, and Louisiana. Thus the states remain the chosen instruments for the management of oil resources.

One finds neither the states nor the national government as heavily involved in the conservation and use of other minerals; exploration is not a major aspect of these industries, and there are relatively few problems of temporary overproduction. Both the federal government and the states, however, have regulated working and safety conditions in mines for many years (following a series of mine disasters in the late nineteenth century), and both levels engage in research activities. In 1952 a Presidential commission completed an exhaustive study of American materials policy with heavy emphasis on mineral-resource supply and demand. Stock-piling of critical materials for defense purposes has continued since the Second World War. But no comprehensive promotion or subsidy programs exist in this area. The conservation of nonrenewable resources except oil continues essentially as a responsibility for the private sector of the economy, except in times of industrial distress. Here the record indicates that the industries prefer to make arrangements at the state level, keeping regulators as close to home as possible.

Summary: The Endless Frontier

Neither the American program for scientific exploration nor those for resource conservation and management can be said to proceed from a national and comprehensive plan. Research, land, water, mineral, and energy policies are the result of continuing struggles among complex sets of interest groups, agencies, and executive and Congressional control bodies. None of them can be said to be entirely consistent, and all of them have been dependent on the continued expansion of the resource base through science and technology. So the United States has experienced a series of "conservation crises"—all relieved by the timely arrival of new innovation.

In 1870, when our forest reserves were being rapidly stripped and thousands of acres were left desolate, coal overtook wood as the prime energy source. By the Second World War, when easily available coal reserves seemed on the point of exhaustion, liquid and gaseous fuels displaced coal, handling two thirds of all energy requirements. While our waste of land through erosion and poor grazing and farming practices has been prodigious, research has so multiplied agricultural productivity that we possess large and continuing farm surpluses. Though occasional water shortages occur in rapidly growing urban areas or in semiarid regions, research in saline water conversion promises additional supplies. In short, the skills of the scientific and technological communities have continually functioned to tap new resource bases in the earth and its atmosphere just when old ones appeared inadequate.

Nevertheless, profound transformations in our resource policies have occurred. Originally, the material richness of the continent seemed so great that no one questioned our capacity to sustain a growing population and an expanding economy. Beginning in the twentieth century, however, we realized that our success in tapping our natural endowments had been so great that we faced the issue of proper resource conservation. Accordingly, we inaugurated broad programs in the better management of renewable resources and proper extraction of nonrenewable ones. Since the closing of the Western frontier, we have made great strides in adopting effective land, water, timber, and mineral conservation measures and in assuring an increasingly urban nation of access to nature for recreational purposes.

Yet such is the nature of our political system and our economic base that these programs have rarely achieved their stated goal of prudent use of existing materials to secure their long-run availability at low cost. Comprehensive promotional and regulatory policies and unified organizational arrangements have failed in the face of opposition of resource-users, government bureaus, and sympathetic Congressional committees. In the view of professional conservationists, resource politics still prevents the best applications of our natural wealth, and Americans remain profligate in their attitudes toward their portion of the earth and its bounty.

Nevertheless, the basic reason underlying our approach to resource management appears to be not so much the limited perspectives of interest groups active in these political subsystems as the fact that we continue to live on a frontier. The natural frontier of the West is closed, but the exploration of Vannevar Bush's endless frontier of science continues unabated and with increasing success. Government policy toward both natural and scientific resources exhibits many shortcomings and poses many problems. But in the minds of most Americans, technological ingenuity and scientific creativity remain the ultimate answer to the question of how we propose to support our civilization.

22 / Government and Welfare in the "Affluent Society"

In this country, the classic pattern of colonial America and the early Republic was one of individual and family self-reliance in economic affairs. An individual was expected to "stand on his own feet," except for special periods of dependency, such as childhood, old age, or physical infirmity; in these times, he relied largely on family aid. Yet even in these early years there was recognition of some public responsibility for the indigent. In Plymouth Colony, for example, a 1642 statute required that "Every township shall make competent provision for the maintenance of their poor according as they shall find most convenient and suitable for themselves by an order and general agreement in a public town meeting." [1] Town and county payments to the poor were almost everywhere niggardly, however, and the eligibility requirements for aid were harsh. Since pauperism was seen as the result of the individual's failure to follow the precepts of Poor Richard's Almanack, the politically dominant forces felt that government policy should not "encourage the lazy" by too much generosity to the poor. There was much debate over whether there should be "indoor" care in almshouses, work colonies to put indigents to profitable social use, or "farming out" of the indigent to individuals, even by auction. All in all, the lot of the poor in this classic era was miserable.

Special social conditions contributed to these attitudes toward the poor. The frontier and the lack of a highly developed technology kept open opportunities for self-employment and for simple living on one's own resources. Family cohesiveness gave the crippled, the blind, the lazy, and other unfortunates or misfits a source of minimum support. A social consciousness had not yet been aroused in the nation generally concerning the continued existence of the semifeudal institution of indentured labor, slave labor, and the appalling living conditions and dependence on the wage system in factory towns.

Expansion of Welfare Legislation

The first big break from personal and family responsibility in the United States was the development of the public school system in the nineteenth

---

[1] Robert Kelso, *History of Public Poor Relief in Massachusetts* (Boston, 1922), p. 92, quoting Plymouth Colony Records, Vol. XI, p. 41.

century. A child, however indigent his parents were, could finally have an opportunity for an education at the expense of those who were able to pay. Another step in the nineteenth century was the development of state institutions for care of orphans, the blind, deaf, and mute, and tubercular and mental patients; ultimately efforts would be made to conduct all of these institutions in conformity with the idea of the dignity of man. Meanwhile, there were the beginnings of modern types of legislation to protect the worker, and state and local programs for aid to the indigent continued to expand and improve.

In the twentieth century still broader objectives are discernible in welfare legislation. While the interests of the worker and the indigent have been given increased recognition, those of the people generally, and particularly of the middle class, are also promoted. Relief for unfortunates is still an objective, but opportunity and security for all, again including the middle class, are frequently stated. Adding these new objectives to the old ones has resulted in a constantly accelerated outpouring of legislation.

Several causes explain this steady trend toward expanded public welfare legislation. First, the nation has moved from self-employment in pioneer, rural conditions to the dependent employment relationships of an industrialized, urbanized society. Technology and entrepreneurial genius have brought large-scale enterprise, which by now has spread even to retailing and agriculture. In 1960 five out of every six dollars of personal income in this country came from salaries and wages. When employment opportunities in such a society contract, whether through recession, automation, or changes in the products of industry, unemployment and an earlier retirement date for millions are often the results. Even college graduates, most of whom are now salaried employees in organizations, have limited opportunities at middle age to transfer to new organizations or new types of employment. Urbanization, which takes people away from the resources of the land and makes them face regular payments for rent, utilities, and food, heightens still further the welfare problem. Increased mobility of the population has impaired reliance upon families and destroyed expectancy of aid from neighbors. And those who are chronically poor or have suffered most severely from job unavailability are likely to find that *their* families are faced with the same situation. All of these developments make the modern versions of frontier self-sufficiency—secure jobs, savings, and private insurance—unavailable for large segments of the population. Responsible government must act in this situation.

Second, attitudes toward the needy have changed. In the late nineteenth century, harsh factory conditions and exploitation of the poor set off a wave of humanitarian sentiment, which grew as industrial forces moved into the twentieth century. The experience of Jane Addams and her settlement house in Chicago led many to believe that poverty was often the result of unfavorable environmental conditions rather than shiftlessness. The courts also began at the same time to respond favorably to legislation designed to protect women and children. The Great Depression of 1929–33, which brought 10 million unemployed and 18 million on relief, expanded the view that men were not always responsible for their plight.

While churches, luncheon clubs, charitable organizations, and foundations continue to seek projects to aid needy people, the sheer size of the problem—in dollars and in organizational aspects—has led the public to expect the government to act.

Third, the American ideal of opportunity has required government action to keep the race open to all. While we retain our belief that this is a land in which economic opportunities exist for persons with initiative and talent, welfare legislation in fields such as education, health, and child protection has become part of the process of keeping these opportunities open.

Fourth, the fact that this is a "land of plenty"—that most Americans share the benefits of an "affluent society" [2]—contributes to a sense of moral responsibility for the areas of poverty that remain. In foods and textiles the nation's problem is surplus rather than scarcity. Some basic industries, such as steel, have a large unused capacity. Luxury items, from the third family car to the candied ants in the supermarket, have become the mark of American consumption. In such a society, the persistence of poverty makes a program of welfare both financially supportable and morally imperative.

A fifth cause lies in changing notions about the possibility of assuring personal security through government programs. Prudent men have always, of course, sought security for their families against violence, through law, police, and courts, and against need, through property accumulation for themselves and their heirs. In the modern period private insurance has provided an additional means of protection against need. Yet Americans learned in the Depression that property accumulation by individuals and private insurance could not provide, even for members of the middle class, adequate protection against such occurrences as unemployment, old age, and widowhood. They saw, too, in the Social Security Act of 1935 a demonstration of how government might provide everyone with minimum levels of protection against need.

The recently announced "war on poverty" of President Johnson reflects these several factors of social change and attitude. Tens of millions of people, perhaps as many as one fifth of the population, belong to what Michael Harrington has called "the other America." [3] They have found no secure place, or have lost their place, in an economy of job dependency. They share little of the affluence of society, and they lack opportunity and security. The President in January, 1964, announced the "war on poverty," and followed up the announcement with a special message to the Congress on March 16, 1964, detailing his "war plan." Calling for the Economic Opportunity Act of 1964, the President emphasized federal aid to local communities, a national service corps that would combine study and useful work for youths, and a work-study plan to aid poor youths through college. Said the President, "On similar occasions in the past we have often been called upon to wage war against foreign enemies which threatened our

---

[2] See David M. Potter, *People of Plenty: Economic Abundance and the American Character* (Chicago, 1954) and John K. Galbraith, *The Affluent Society* (Cambridge, Mass., 1958).

[3] Michael Harrington, *The Other America: Poverty in the United States* (New York, 1962).

Pratt in the Sacramento *Bee*

"There's This Other State Of The Union."

A liberal view of the "War on Poverty."

freedom. Today we are asked to declare war on a domestic enemy which threatens the strength of our nation and the welfare of our people."

The Federal Role in Expanding Welfare Functions

Except for veterans' assistance, aid for education in agriculture and mechanical arts, and some scattered enactments relative to health or other matters under the commerce power, the national government was not active in welfare programs until the twentieth century. Indeed, the great expansion of national legislation began with the New Deal. Today, however, welfare activities continuously engage the attention of Congress; their importance in national affairs was emphasized by the creation in 1953 of the Department of Health, Education and Welfare. This Department is, nevertheless, only one of the organizations through which national welfare legislation is administered.

The commerce power has provided the constitutional basis for some of the national legislation. Food and drug laws and minimum wage and maximum hour legislation are examples. More of the legislation is grounded on Congress' power to tax for "the general welfare of the United States." This power to tax was expanded tremendously by the income-tax amendment in 1913, which has enabled the national government to obtain vast sums for social purposes. The spending power that accompanies the taxing power extends broadly to "the general welfare." This provides the basis for national expenditures in many areas in which the Congress might lack the power to legislate extensively, if at all, under other provisions in the Constitution.

Although some welfare activities are exclusively national and some others exclusively on a local or state level, cooperation among two or all three levels of government is a characteristic feature of much welfare legislation and administration. This is one of the fields in which cooperative government has been most extended. In many fields—education, health, relief for

Hubenthal in the New York *Journal-American*

"Pass The Ammunition!"

A conservative view of the "War on Poverty."

the indigent—the state and local governments already had established programs and administrative agencies that could be expanded under the stimulus of national grants-in-aid.

Current Conflicts in Interests and Ideologies

There are many conflicts of interest over welfare legislation. Economic differences play a central role. Many people with comfortable economic positions in society are antagonistic to a "welfare state" and to the tax burdens it creates. Those without minimum economic resources will seek as much government aid as possible. Usually, the balance of power in these situations has been held by the American middle class, those with incomes today, for example, between $5,000 and $15,000. The largest advance in welfare legislation came with the Social Security Act of 1935; the middle class had suddenly become conscious of its insecurity and exerted its powerful political influence to support President Franklin Roosevelt's welfare proposal. Expenditures for education now generally have a strong appeal because public education—with the financial and social advances it promises to talented students—represents a basic goal of the middle class. To the extent that the middle class is affected, welfare programs are likely to be based on the insurance principle rather than tests of means. On the other hand, the middle class is often inattentive to the problems of the very poor, such as provision of new housing for the poor when slum areas are cleared. The movement toward a "welfare state" is checked also by the low level of participation in politics of the lower income groups.[4]

The rural-urban cleavage is also significant in welfare legislation. Urban populations have a greater consciousness of personal insecurity in an industrialized, urbanized society than does the rural population. The urban gain in representation as a result of *Baker* v. *Carr* [5] may be expected, therefore, to lead to more social legislation. Finally, the interests and attitudes of functional groups are involved in almost all proposals for welfare legislation. Thus, teachers are interested in more appropriations for education, social workers want more attention paid to problems of dependency, and many doctors want to avoid certain types of public medical programs. It will be evident, however, in the following discussion that the class, urban-rural, and functional cleavages in interest differ among the several fields in which legislation is enacted for the "general welfare."

These differences in interests and the strains between tradition and change lead to basic ideological conflicts over the way individual opportunity and security will be provided in the 1960s. Some people still express the view that responsibility for personal needs should be placed firmly on the individual and the family, even though this will mean less opportunity and less security for many. Others say that the opportunity and security of all is so important that the arrangements for these should be as complete and as certain as society can provide, even though this results in some decline in personal and family responsibility.

The issue of public responsibility differs for different subjects of legislation, and the balances struck between the contending philosophies often reflect the relative strength of the forces in a given field. In education, government has gone far toward providing an equal system for all, irrespective of ability to pay. This situation is accepted by most of those who would oppose extensive public responsibility on many other subjects of legislation. On the other hand, housing is an example of a field in which private responsibility has been historically dominant, and in which the conflict over the extent of public responsibility erupts in almost every session of Congress. In medicine the issue is sharply drawn, and the balances are yet to be determined. In most fields the government seeks to provide only minimum safeguards or guarantees, leaving the individual with responsibility for supplementing them.

A second ideological conflict is between local and state responsibility and that of the national government. Some believe that the responsibility for public welfare should rest in the main on local and state governments, while others believe that provision for public protection should be made uniform and adequate through national legislation. This conflict is related to the first one. Those who believe in placing responsibility on the individual argue for state and local action, and those who favor larger assump-

---

[4] See Paul Felix Lazarsfeld, Bernard Berelson, and Hazel Gaudet, *The People's Choice* (New York, 1944), p. 145, and E. E. Schattschneider, *The Semisovereign People: A Realist's View of Democracy in America* (New York, 1960), Chapter 2.
[5] See pages 382–84.

tion of public responsibility argue for national legislation, for it is recognized by both groups that the state and local governments cannot provide as extensive a system of welfare protection as the national government can.

With respect to this conflict also, public policy has followed a middle path. The forces that lead to the existence of the problems are reflected in local, state, and national legislation. The people living in a new world of dependency upon institutions exert influence on each level of government to meet those problems which it can feasibly deal with. The result is welfare legislation at all levels.

A third conflict is over methods of public action. Some people advocate aid to individuals only on the basis of need. This means some kind of "means" test, i.e., of a person's ability to take care of himself. It means check by an administrative staff—social workers usually—on the economic condition of those who solicit aid. Others advocate the use of the insurance principle. This means that payments are made, under stated conditions, on the basis of legal right. It means automatic payment to those in defined categories, such as the aged or the unemployed.

Both of these approaches have been used in American legislation, sometimes—as in payments to the aged—as complementary approaches in the solution of the same problem. Sometimes, however—as will be noted in the discussion of medical care for the aged—the conflict of views is reflected in opposed recommendations for legislation.

Education

The public school is this country's most distinctive and significant contribution to the modern role of government. Practice ran far ahead of philosophy, for while men were saying that "that government which governs least, governs best" and while they were talking about protection of rights *from* government, they were creating opportunity *through* government and were laying the basis for the belief that man's individual achievement depended upon positive action by government. While the courts preserved the ideal of equality under the law, and the governmental system rested substantially but passively on the ideal of political equality, and the economic system and the frontiers of land and technology provided abundant but individualized economic opportunity, the public school was the one positive instrument of government for giving effect to the idea of equality.

Nevertheless, American education reflects the pluralism of American civilization. The free public school has been paralleled by the freedom of parents to choose between private and public education. Private schools with emphases in their educational programs different from those of public schools have flourished.[6] The public school has, however, provided education for the bulk of students at the elementary and secondary levels. At

---

[6] The freedom of the private school from public dictation was safeguarded in the decision in *Meyer* v. *Nebraska*, 262 U.S. 390 (1923), in which restriction of the teaching of foreign languages was held unconstitutional insofar as it applied to private schools.

the college level the private school has met a larger proportion of the need for educational facilities, but even here the public institution has been the dominant facility outside the Northeastern part of the country.

The local school district has been the historical unit for administration of the primary and secondary school system, and the junior college system in some states. In recent years much of the responsibility for primary and secondary education has been shifted from local to state governments, and the states now provide a substantial portion of the funds. State supervision has helped to encourage or force school consolidation, to establish minimum standards of pay for teachers, to encourage specific curriculum developments, to certify teachers, to approve textbooks, and to take other steps to both limit and assist the local jurisdictions. The states have also established and operated, usually through state boards, senior colleges and universities, and have sponsored junior colleges.

Although education is often called a state and local function, the national government has participated in the function in numerous ways. It first supported education through grants of land. In arranging for the disposal of Western lands in 1785 Congress reserved one section (640 acres) of every township for the endowment of schools within the township. In a day when higher education was oriented toward law, the ministry, and teaching the classics, Congress stimulated practical and applied education by passing the Morrill Act of 1862, which provided for grants of land to each state for the establishment of colleges "to specialize in agriculture and mechanical arts."

When the land was gone the national government began to give monetary grants in aid of education. Before the end of the nineteenth century it initiated monetary aids to the agricultural and mechanical colleges, including grants to aid in the extension programs of these colleges. Through these grants the largest program of adult education in the history of this nation has been supported—a program carried out mainly through county agents and home demonstration agents. By the Smith-Hughes Act of 1917 Congress provided for grants-in-aid for vocational education in the public schools. More recently, grants-in-aid have been initiated for many special programs and purposes. Grants of money and food to support the school lunch program began in the Depression. Acts passed in 1950 provided for grants for construction, maintenance, and operation of schools in districts where federal activities have resulted in a substantial increase in school population. In the near-panic following the Russians' launching of Sputnik on October 4, 1957, Congress—with the National Defense Education Act of 1958—launched a big program of grants to states for improvement of educational programs in science, mathematics, and foreign languages. High unemployment rates led to the passage in 1961 of an act that provided for grants for training and retraining of unemployed youth and adults—an activity that has been expanded since President Johnson's program for a "war on poverty" was enacted. Higher education receives aid in the form of long-term loans for construction of dormitories and in the form of loans and grants for construction of classrooms, libraries, and other academic facilities.

In recent years there has also been a movement for general aid to edu-

Palmer in the Springfield, Mo., *Leader and Press*

"Mary Has A Little (?) Lamb."

Engelhardt in the St. Louis *Post-Dispatch*

"Here, Kid, Go Buy Yourself An
Education."

Some people considered President Kennedy's school aid proposal exorbitant; other observers pointed out that it represented only a small fraction of defense expenditures.

cation by the national government. In 1960 the Republican party platform called for national aid for school construction and the Democratic party platform for aid for both school construction and teachers' salaries. In the same year general school aid legislation passed both houses of Congress but failed because of differences on fundamental issues. The Democratic party platform of 1964 again called for aid to education generally, including both classroom construction and teachers' salaries.

General educational aid by the national government has run into opposition based upon fear of the expenditures that might be involved. More importantly, it has been caught in the crossfire between those who favor and those who oppose federal aid to parochial schools. Most legislation comes about because of a coalition of interests; general aid to education has not been successful in Congress because the potential coalition is split both by the religious issue and by the desegregation dispute, since any national government aid must be on an integrated basis.

Workers' Welfare

The soundest foundation for workers' welfare is the opportunity of each person of employment age to earn a living. It is certainly better to have employment than relief for the unemployed; wage structures that sustain those employed than wage supplements through relief payments; and education and training for employment than relief because of unemployability.

Maintenance of an economy that provides employment opportunities at living wages and of education that equips all for employment are therefore the most basic welfare programs for workers. These general policies are supplemented, however, by four special policies.

SAFETY AND HEALTH

The oldest of these special policies is that for the protection of safety and health of workers. Legislation to ensure safe and healthy working conditions came as a natural result of the Industrial Revolution and the introduction of machine technology. Although such legislation had been passed in the nineteenth century, twentieth-century revelations of horrible conditions led to more vigorous measures in the first decade of the century. Ultimately, many states came to have comprehensive codes of protective measures, often with administrative agencies to issue regulations under the codes and to inspect premises to ensure compliance.

In this area, as in many others, public and private efforts have supplemented each other. Private companies have developed safety engineering measures, moved undoubtedly by both humanitarian and cost-saving objectives. Labor unions keep a watchful eye on safety conditions and push for effective protective measures.

Early safety legislation is now supplemented by public efforts toward the vocational rehabilitation of those handicapped by disease, congenital defect, or accident. Congress enacted the Vocational Rehabilitation Act in 1920 and expanded the program in the Barden–La Follette Act of 1943. The program is administered in the Office of Vocational Rehabilitation in the Department of Health, Education and Welfare. The Office makes grants to the states, which usually administer their programs through an office of vocational rehabilitation in the state department of education. Such offices provide many services, including physical examination to determine work capacity; medical, surgical, psychiatric, and hospital treatment; artificial limbs and hearing aids; job training; maintenance during training; occupational tools; placement and adjustment aid after employment. Vocational services to those who are handicapped is also provided by the Veterans Administration and through the educational program of the public schools.

CHILD LABOR

A second policy for the protection of workers' welfare is embodied in child labor legislation. Such legislation is designed not only to protect the health and safety of children but also to protect adult employment by forbidding child labor competition. The states were the first to pass such legislation, giving attention primarily to hazardous and unhealthy occupational pursuits in areas such as mines or tenement factories. National efforts were stalemated for several decades. A national statute prohibiting the shipment in interstate commerce of goods made in factories which employed children was held unconstitutional in 1918,[7] and a follow-up statute attempting the same objective through a tax on child-produced goods met

---

[7] *Hammer* v. *Dagenhart*, 247 U.S. 251 (1918).

a similar fate in 1922.[8] A child labor amendment, submitted by Congress to the states in 1924 to authorize national legislation on the subject, has never been ratified. However, changing constitutional attitudes led the Supreme Court to uphold the Fair Labor Standards Act of 1938 [9] and reverse earlier bars on national action. The 1938 act forbids labor by persons under sixteen years of age, subject to the authority of the Secretary of Labor to raise the age to eighteen or lower it to fourteen in certain types of situations. The prohibition extends to labor in interstate commerce or in production of goods for commerce and also, since 1961, to labor in enterprises of the following types: retail or service establishments with annual sales of $1 million (if they receive $250,000 of merchandise from across state lines), local trolley or bus carriers with revenues of $1 million, construction companies with sales of $350,000, and gasoline service stations with sales of $250,000. Exempted are agricultural labor outside school hours, delivery of newspapers, acting in motion pictures or theatrical, radio, or television productions, and labor performed by children for parents except in manufacturing and mining or occupations brought under the Act by order of the Secretary.

More effective perhaps than direct legislation prohibiting child labor have been two other public policies. One of them is set forth in the compulsory school attendance laws. Although these laws have often allowed exceptions where children needed to help in family support, they have declared society's expectancy that children be in school, and they have been rigidly enforced. The other policy is that of public provision for family assistance in the aid to dependent children program and in the survivors' benefits of the social security program (see pages 724 and 726–27). These public payments reduce the pressure for child employment.

HOURS OF LABOR

The original objective in legislation limiting hours of labor was the protection of the health of the worker; the laws were passed when a work week of sixty or more hours was quite common and "keeping idle hands from mischief" was the moral defense of a "total" workday. The early legislation limited the hours that women could work in any capacity or that men could work in especially hazardous occupations. Later, the states passed laws generally limiting the hours of male workers. In the first quarter of this century, the forty-eight-hour week became standard in industry, with Congress adopting it for railroads in the Adamson Act of 1916. Then when the Great Depression threw one fourth to one third of the working population out of jobs a movement developed for a shorter week to spread employment around. Bills were introduced in Congress for a thirty-hour week.

The result was a provision for a forty-hour week in the Fair Labor Standards Act of 1938. The means of enforcement is the provision that time and a half must be paid for overtime, that is, beyond forty hours per week. There are special provisions relaxing or removing the overtime

---

[8] *Bailey* v. *Drexel Furniture Co.*, 259 U.S. 20 (1922).
[9] *United States* v. *Darby*, 312 U.S. 100 (1941).

requirement in seasonal or irregular employment and in companies which sign labor contracts limiting hours over a six-month or full year period. There were numerous exemptions from the maximum hour-overtime provisions prior to 1961. When some of these were removed in 1961, it was provided that the maximum hours for newly covered industries should be forty-four hours beginning in September, 1963, forty-two beginning the following year, and forty after September, 1965. The exemptions which remain now are similar to those from the minimum wage provisions and are discussed below.

Many labor contracts now provide for less than forty hours per week of work. In August, 1961, officials of the AFL–CIO called for a thirty-five-hour week, and this objective is now a major item in labor's legislative program.

MINIMUM WAGES

Statutes providing minimum wage levels were passed by states in the early part of this century. These statutes applied only to women, and their asserted justification was the protection of health and morals. In 1923 the Supreme Court by a 5-to-3 vote held a statute of Congress setting minimum wages for women in the District of Columbia to be a violation of the due process clause of the Fifth Amendment.[10] But in the Great Depression the ideas developed that those who cut wages below a minimum level were unfair competitors and that it was in the public interest to maintain the purchasing power of the lower income groups. The result was that in 1933 the National Recovery Administration (NRA) adopted the policy of including minimum wage provisions in codes of fair competition approved by it. These provisions applied to male and female employees, thus setting a new pattern for minimum wage legislation. The provisions expired when the NRA program was held unconstitutional in 1935.

States were in the meantime again enacting minimum wage laws for women, and the Supreme Court upheld such a statute in 1937.[11] Congress, picking up selected pieces of the old NRA program, included minimum wage provisions in the Fair Labor Standards Act of 1938. The minimum wages set were 25 cents per hour for the first year, 30 cents for the next six, and 40 cents after 1945. They have been raised steadily by amendments so that $1.25 became the effective minimum wage in September, 1963.

From 1959 to 1961 there was also a battle over exemptions from the minimum wage requirements. Exempted from both the hours and wages provisions of the 1938 Act were such large groups as employees in retail and service establishments, in agriculture, in local trolley and bus service, and in processing of fish and agricultural products. President Kennedy in 1961 recommended inclusion of about 4,300,000 additional workers; and although the Senate substantially accepted this recommendation, a rival bill supported by a Republican-Southern Democrat coalition—which in-

---

[10] *Adkins v. Children's Hospital,* 261 U.S. 525 (1923).
[11] *West Coast Hotel Co. v. Parrish,* 300 U.S. 379 (1937).

cluded only about 1,300,000 workers—passed the House. The big issue was over inclusion of retail and service workers. Restaurant workers were exempted from both bills, and laundry workers were excluded at the conference committee stage. Finally, the President and the Senate won a substantial victory, with the retail and service groups, referred to in the discussion of the 1961 child labor amendments, being included. The Act as amended still leaves millions of workers outside its coverage, such as, for example, employees in restaurants, laundries, agriculture, and many related occupations, small newspapers, and small retail and service establishments.

Conflicts over minimum wages may be expected to be on the agenda of Congress repeatedly in the future. One question will be whether existing exemptions shall be trimmed further. Another question will be whether the level of minimum wages shall be raised. (Both broadening of coverage and a $2 minimum hourly wage are included in the AFL–CIO legislative program for 1965.) Such questions will create deep conflicts of opinion, as indicated by the divisions in Congress on the issues presented between 1959 and 1961. There will be sectional cleavages, with representatives from older areas of industrialization having union wage scales tending to favor the legislation and with those from newer industrialized areas having a low unionization rate tending to oppose it. Representatives from Southern states with such industries as textile and tobacco production have been most strongly opposed to such legislation. There will be deep conflicts of interest over whether new groups of laborers shall be included. There will be differences of opinion on economic effects, and strong ideological differences. The arguments pro and con are both economic and social. Some persons argue that minimum wage standards increase unemployment, others that they increase purchasing power and thus stimulate employment. Some stress the social arguments rather than the economic—arguing that it is undesirable to have substandard wages and that the existence of such wages leads to the need for supplementing income for families through some form of public aid or subsidy.

Social Insurance

In the twentieth century governments have given increasing attention to some of the tragic hazards of life, such as the death of the wage-earner, sudden unemployment, old age, blindness, sickness, and injury in the course of employment.

Again the states first gave attention to these problems. By 1934 forty-five states had laws for aid to widowed mothers with children, twenty-four for aid to the blind, and twenty-five for old-age pensions. The application of the laws was generally dependent upon local action, however, and the amount of the payments was usually quite inadequate to meet the needs of those benefited.[12] In the first quarter of the century the states had passed

---

[12] See Grace Abbott, "Recent Trends in Mothers' Aid," *Social Service Review* (June, 1934), Vol. VIII, p. 194; Children's Bureau, *Mothers' Aid, 1931* (Washington,

"Two Chickens In Every Garage"

This 1932 cartoon comments ironically on the Great Depression and on President Hoover's optimistic predictions of "two cars in every garage" and "two chickens in every pot."

Rollin Kirby in the New York *World-Telegram*

laws establishing workmen's compensation (payments for injuries sustained in the course of employment), and in 1932 Wisconsin established an unemployment insurance program.

Again the Great Depression was the entry point into a new era. On June 8, 1934, President Roosevelt said in a message to Congress that the American people wanted "some safeguard against misfortunes which cannot be wholly eliminated in this man-made world of ours." He appointed a Committee on Economic Security whose recommendations formed the basis for the Social Security Act of 1935. With the National Labor Relations Act of the same year, this was one of the two most significant acts of the New Deal period. While the NLRA changed the balance of economic forces by increasing the power of unions (see page 670), the Social Security Act altered—more than any other statute has done—the relations of people to government. Two of the most important programs included with others in this omnibus legislation are social insurance for the unemployed and for retired persons.

UNEMPLOYMENT COMPENSATION

The Depression had made people aware of the shift to a time of job dependency in an industrialized society and of the threat to millions from technological or cyclical unemployment. Moreover, the experience of Eng-

---

1933); Bureau of Labor Statistics, "Public Provision for Pensions to the Blind in 1934," *Monthly Labor Review* (September, 1935), Vol. LXI, p. 484; Florence B. Parker, "Experience Under State Old-Age Pension Acts in 1934," *Monthly Labor Review* (August, 1935), Vol. XL, p. 303.

land with a national insurance program led to an opinion that, in addition to relieving the condition of the unemployed, insurance payments could be a built-in stabilizer for the economy—setting a base to a depression by sustaining purchasing power.

Wisconsin broke the ice on this form of insurance with a statute in 1932. Yet it was clear that states would be reluctant to place costs of insurance on industry in their states if they were not assured that other states competing for the same industries would do the same. The Social Security Act provided a direct answer for this reluctance. It imposed a national tax on employers of 3 percent of their payroll. However, in any state which adopted an approved unemployment compensation plan nine tenths of the tax would not be collected. Of course, under this provision all states promptly legislated for unemployment insurance. Under the existing system the states administer programs approved by the Department of Labor. The national government collects a tax (now .35 of 1 percent of the payroll) and with the funds so obtained grants money to the states for administration of the unemployment insurance plan. The states collect taxes for their programs. The states have all adopted merit-rating programs under which the amount of tax paid by the employer is dependent upon his own record in avoiding unemployment among his employees.

The general pattern of unemployment insurance is the payment to the unemployed person of a percentage of his wages for a certain number of weeks, or until he again becomes employed. Most states provide a waiting period, perhaps a week, before payments are made. To be eligible a person must be able to work and be available for work, and not be unemployed because of discharge for misconduct, leaving work without cause, or refusal to accept suitable employment. Also, state laws usually contain a prohibition or some restrictions on payment of benefits to those participating in a strike.

There are a number of problems in unemployment insurance. One of them is that many employed persons are not covered. The national statute requires only that employers of four or more persons shall make payments, but some states have decreased this and about one third have reduced the figure to one employee. National law allows other exclusions, and the states have commonly used this authority to exclude agricultural labor, domestic service, employment for state and local governments, and employment for nonprofit organizations. Second, the level of payments may not be large enough to maintain a reasonable amount of purchasing power. The maximum amount payable varies among the states, but a maximum of $35 to $40 per week is typical. This is a great help to low-paid employees but may be of small help to the person who has been making $200 to $500 per week. Legislatures have raised levels of payment but in many states these raises have not equaled cost of living increases. Third, periods of unemployment may be more prolonged than the periods allowed for payment. During a recent period (1961–62) when a considerable number of unemployed persons had exhausted their payments, Congress provided federal funds for extension of payments. Fourth, there are problems of preventing abuse of the system. Some persons try to avoid obtaining employment in order to remain on the rolls for unemployment compensation.

States try to prevent such malingering by restricting payments to a percentage of one's past wage and by maintaining close cooperation between the placement officers of the state employment services and the payment officers for unemployment insurance.

Today every state has a system of public employment offices to assist employers in locating employees and employees in locating jobs. A person desiring employment registers at the nearest employment office. Services are rendered without cost, and all persons receiving unemployment insurance must be registered at an employment office.

OLD AGE, SURVIVORS, AND DISABILITY INSURANCE (OASDI)

Income for the aged was the central issue of social security debate in 1935, and it still is. The causes for the concern are undisputed. A large percentage of the aged are unemployable. Many are dependent, with the Presidential Committee on Economic Security in 1935 finding that at least one half of the persons over sixty-five were in this category. Thirty-four percent of the aged in Connecticut, for example, were found to have no income whatsoever. Many, perhaps most, are in frequent need of medical care, and many reach the condition where they require constant specialized care. Aid from their children has become increasingly ineffective. Furthermore, the number of aged persons is increasing, with their percentage of the total population more than doubling from 1900 to 1960 (from 4.1 percent to over 9 percent).

The answer of Congress in 1935 was in two parts: public assistance to the needy aged, and retirement insurance for most of the population. The insurance program is one in which a person can participate with a sense of dignity, for his payments come to him as a statutory right without any check on his need. The method of financing is equal contribution by the employer and the employee, the employer deducting the employee's contribution from his wage payment. The administrative arrangements are simple and are carried out exclusively by the national government—through the Social Security Administration of the Department of Health, Education and Welfare. Employers make reports on wages paid to each person and transmit the tax payments. Every insured person is given a number, and a record of payments made on his wages is kept by name and number in a central office. Field offices of the Social Security Administration take claims from individuals for benefit payments and supply information on the program to those concerned.

While originally there were many exemptions from the retirement insurance plan, amendments to the Act have now made its coverage nearly complete. Self-employed persons, except doctors of medicine, can come under the program if they choose to. Employees of religious, charitable, and private educational organizations may be included by choice of the organization and the employees. Employees of state and local governments may be included by action of their governments. Domestic service for any employer who pays $50 per quarter or more, and farm labor for any employer who pays $150 cash or more annually or for whom twenty days' work is performed, are included. Railroad employees and civilian employees of the federal government are included under separate programs set up by national legislation. As a result of the amendments, voluntary action to come under the program by numerous public and private organizations and private persons, and parallel programs for railroad workers, military personnel, and public civilian personnel, it can be expected that before long most persons reaching retirement age will be eligible for some form of public retirement benefit.

In 1964 the benefits under the Act accrued more largely from a series of amendments than from the original act. Eligibility begins at the age of sixty-two, but with reduced benefits if retirement occurs before sixty-five. The amount of payment received depends on two factors: the retired person's wage record and whether he has family dependents. The minimum and maximum monthly payments for a person with no dependents who retires at the age of sixty-five or above are $40 and $127. Additional payments are made when the retired worker has an unmarried child under eighteen, a wife sixty-two or older (or at any age if there is a child under eighteen), or a dependent husband sixty-two or older.

A modified form of life insurance, called survivors' benefits, and a system of disability insurance have been added by amendments to the Act. Survivors' benefits are paid monthly for dependents under eighteen or above retirement age. Disability payments are made to any employee covered by the insurance plan who has a physical or mental disability that prevents substantial gainful employment over an indefinite period.

The social security system is not identical in all respects with private insurance. First, amendments to the Social Security Act have brought many people into the system to whom benefits will be paid long before any substantial funds are accumulated by taxes on their wages. Second, the amount of benefits to which anyone is entitled, though based on income, is not equated strictly with taxes paid on his wages. For example, a retired person whose average monthly income had been $200 would receive $84 per month, which is 66 percent of the $127 which would be received by a worker whose average income had been $400 per month. Third, a man has no absolute right to his payments upon retirement age, for the payments may be reduced or denied because of income from employment which a person chooses to engage in after reaching retirement age.

The American system is a compromise system. It is not like the pre-1961 British flat-rate system, under which everybody's contributions and benefits were substantially the same; such a system must lead to low benefits because of the inability of low-paid workers to pay for adequate benefits. It is not like private insurance in which variable benefits are adjusted neatly to variable contributions; such a system would lead to low benefits for those most in need of benefits. The American system builds this system of social payment based on need into the schedule of benefits. Fundamentally the whole system is designed to guarantee to most of the population a minimum level of protection, and to reduce thereby the need for payments under public assistance programs upon the basis of means tests.

WORKMEN'S COMPENSATION

Workmen's compensation was not a part of social security legislation. The states still legislate on this subject without any form of aid from the national government. The first act was passed in New York in 1910 and represented the first legislation in this country to spread the risks of this "man-made world" through a system of social insurance.[13]

Under the common law a worker who was injured in the course of employment could sue his employer, seeking payment for the injury, but the employer could avoid payment through several defenses: that the worker contributed to the accident through his negligence, or that "fellow servants" contributed to it, or that the worker assumed the risks in hazardous occupation by accepting his employment. The concept of the law was that the employer paid only when he was at fault. Although this seemed to be fair doctrine, investigations showed that the system produced a host of harmful effects to workers and society: delays in payments to workers due to court contests, loss of major portions of the recovery in attorney's fees, and inadequate compensation for the injured person or his survivors. At the beginning of the twentieth century, legislation was passed modifying the common law defenses. Congress in 1908 adopted such a statute, called the Federal Employers' Liability Act, which is still in force for railroad employees in interstate commerce. The states, however, adopted a new system which became known as workmen's compensation. Its features were: (1) removal of the employer's common law defenses, except for special contributing causes such as drunkenness of the injured employee; (2) limitation of the employer's liability to amounts stated in the statute; (3) hearing of cases by administrative tribunals; and (4) provision for insurance of the employer's liability. This system was deemed fair to both parties: the laborer had more security because of simplified and faster procedure and removal of the employer's defenses; the employer's liability was limited and could be insured. The Supreme Court of the United States upheld the system, as against claims that it deprived employers of due process of law, saying that the employer could include the costs in the prices charged the public, which should, said the Court, bear the total cost of employment.[14]

These statutes have been amended through the years. One type of amendment was to add provision for payments to employees who contracted diseases as the result of employment. Another was to reduce exemptions of types of employment, the most common remaining exemptions being farm employment, domestic employment, and employment in establishments with only a few workers.

Recently, the question has been raised as to whether the worker is faring adequately under these statutes. Today in automobile injury cases the amount awarded to a plaintiff is sometimes quite large, as much as $50,000 to $200,000. On the other hand, the payments provided under state workmen's compensation statutes often have not kept pace with inflation.[15]

---

[13] For the history of workmen's compensation see Walter F. Dodd, *Administration of Workmen's Compensation* (New York, 1936).

[14] Constitutionality was determined in three decisions in 1917: *White v. New York Central R.R. Co.*, 243 U.S. 188; *Hawkins v. Bleakley*, 243 U.S. 210; *Mountain Timber Co. v. Washington*, 243 U.S. 219.

[15] For a thorough analysis of present-day workmen's compensation laws see Herman

It may be expected that the amount and duration of payments to injured workers will be on the agenda for consideration in state legislatures in the future.

Public Assistance

In public assistance programs direct monetary grants are made to individuals on the basis of their need. Beginning with the Social Security Act, national grants-in-aid have been made to the states for assistance to special categories of needy persons: the aged, the blind, and dependent children. Amendments have authorized grants for disabled persons and for medical care for the aged. In addition to these five special programs there are in every state general assistance programs financed wholly by the state and local governments. A total of 6.8 million persons received aid in June, 1963, under the five federally supported assistance programs in the fifty states, the District of Columbia, Puerto Rico, Guam, and the Virgin Islands. Of the approximately $4 billion expended for the program in the year ending June 30, 1961, about 52 percent came from national funds, 35.9 percent from state funds, and 12.1 percent from local funds.[16] In other words only one out of every eight dollars for public assistance is now of strictly local origin. The national grants are administered by the Bureau of Family Services in the Department of Health, Education and Welfare, and in each state there is a single department of welfare. The national government requires each state to have a merit system for selection of employees as a condition for receiving aid, and in the main the program is administered by professional social workers, who evaluate the need of applicants for assistance.

At first the largest of the special programs was that for the needy aged. As was anticipated, however, the broadening of social security coverage has brought a decline in the percentage of the aged receiving public assistance. The decline was from 22.6 percent in 1950 to 13.5 percent in 1961. On the other hand, the level of payments under social security has not been sufficient to remove entirely the necessity for supplementary old-age assistance, for 31 percent of those receiving old-age assistance in 1961 were also recipients of retirement insurance under the social security program. The average payment per recipient in June, 1963, was $77.05, with the amount varying from $9 in Puerto Rico and $35 in Mississippi to $106 in California and $113 in the District of Columbia.

In terms of number of persons assisted, aid to families with dependent children (AFDC) is now the largest of the programs. The portion of the child population assisted has risen from 2 to almost 4 percent since 1940. Payments may be made to the mother or guardian because the father is dead, incapacitated, or absent because of estrangement from the family or other cause, and since 1961 because the father was unemployed. The average

---

Miles Somers and Anne Ramsay Somers, *Workmen's Compensation: Prevention, Insurance, and Rehabilitation of Occupational Disability* (New York and London, 1954).

[16] All statistics in this section are from United States Department of Health, Education and Welfare, *Annual Report, 1961*, pp. 53–56; and *Annual Report, 1963*, pp. 47–115.

AFDC family has four members (typically a mother with three children) and receives an average of $120 per month. Only one mother out of six has finished high school. Aid for dependent children is among the most difficult to operate of public welfare programs. On the one hand, providing sustenance and an opportunity to children in need should perhaps have the highest priority among people who place a high value on the individual; on the other hand, the welfare workers who administer this program find in many cases a need for rebuilding a sense of family responsibility. Actually, public payments for dependent children have been low in comparison with those for the aged, the blind, and the disabled; this may be due both to a lack of political pressure on behalf of the children and their parents and to the feeling of some citizens that dependency of parents should not be encouraged.

Two smaller programs are now well established. All states participate in a program for aid to the dependent blind, with the average monthly payment per recipient ranging in June, 1963, from $8 in Puerto Rico to $137 in Massachusetts. All states except two participated in 1963 in the program for permanent and totally disabled, with the average monthly payments ranging from less than $9 in Puerto Rico to $132 in Massachusetts.

A special program for medical care authorized in 1960 will be explained in the succeeding section.

Health

Health is not only a concern of the individual and of a diversified set of health industries; it has become one of the major functions of government. It is a local-state-national function, and in no other government function is there a more extensive system of cooperative relationships among levels of government. The health department is the customary agency of administration in local and state governments, and in the national government the Public Health Service of the Department of Health, Education and Welfare is the chief agency of administration. The Service now spends about $1.25 billion per year; about 70 percent of this goes as grants to states and local governments, universities, hospitals, and private institutions. The influence of the PHS radiates into almost all fields of health activity. Other national agencies with significant health functions are the Veterans Administration, the Food and Drug Administration, and the Bureau of Public Assistance.

Of the many types of public health activity three main categories deserve mention. The first is the maintenance of a physical environment conducive to good health. Long-established functions—such as quarantine, sewage disposal, water sanitation, and inspection of eating places—are constantly being supplemented by new ones. Thus, in recent years national, state and local governments have participated in development of programs for the avoidance of air pollution, and several administrative agencies in Washington have given attention to protection against radiation effects from nuclear fission. A second function is hospital service. State and local governments have provided most of the mental and tuberculosis hospitals and also have maintained general hospitals through which much charity care is provided. The national government operates veterans' hospitals and a number of special-purpose hospitals, such as those for care of lepers and narcotics addicts. To overcome a serious hospital shortage throughout the nation, Congress in 1946 passed the Hospital Survey and Construction (Hill-Burton) Act, making available through the states funds for construction of public and private hospitals and other health facilities—including now such things as nurses' residences and rehabilitation centers. In fourteen years nearly 6,000 hospital projects were assisted at a total cost of about $5 billion, about one third of which came from the national government.[17] A third function is research. The national government is now sponsoring about 40 per cent of the medical research in the country. In the five years ending in 1961 its expenditures for this purpose quintupled, and they have continued to rise at a slower pace.[18] The giant medical research program is conducted through a number of national institutes, which are the research arm of the Public Health Service and which operate their own laboratories and make grants to universities, hospitals, and other institutions for research.

MEDICAL CARE FOR THE AGED

Few persons seriously contend that medical care for the aged is not an acute problem. The high incidence of illness among the aged, combined with their low incomes and high medical costs, makes it difficult, or even impossible, for many aged persons to obtain the medical care they need without some form of insurance or assistance. It is estimated that more than one dollar out of every four now spent for medical care by the aged is from public funds.[19] The issue is how provision is to be made for adequate medical care for the aged in the future. There are four main methods. The first is private insurance. The hazards of illness have led about two thirds of the population to insure the risks in Blue Cross (hospital care), Blue Shield (physician care), or other private insurance organizations. It has been difficult for the aged to obtain or retain such insurance—at least for all types of illnesses, though the tendency now is toward liberalization of the policies of insurance companies on insurance for the aged. The insurance plans may not cover all types of illnesses, all types of medical care needed, or all expenses for any illness or type of care. In addition, the insurance fee may be higher than many among the aged can pay. One type of proposal has been government subsidy to the needy aged for payment of insurance premiums to private companies.

A second method is direct supply of personal medical care through government institutions. This is the method for supplying medical care to Army personnel and their families and to veterans who have service-connected disabilities or who state that they are unable to pay for medical

[17] *Annual Report, 1961*, p. 153.
[18] *Ibid.*, p. 208.
[19] United States Department of Health, Education and Welfare, *The Health Care of the Aged: Background Facts Relating to the Financing Problem* (Washington, 1962), p. 77.

care. The service is rendered in the main through government hospitals. In addition, free care is given in state mental and tuberculosis hospitals and to charity patients in many other state and local hospitals. The aged, of course, are included among the beneficiaries of institutional care, and as an increasing number of veterans reach old age the percentage of the aged population eligible for such care will increase. This is pure government medicine, or, stated differently, "socialized medicine" in a true sense.

A third method is benefit payments to the needy aged or payments directly to hospitals, nursing homes, and medical personnel for their care. State and local governments have sometimes made such payments as part of general assistance. With the passage of the Social Security Act the cost of medical care could be included in old-age assistance payments. Subsequently the Act was amended, first in 1950 to provide for direct payments by the states to institutions or persons supplying health services to needy aged, and in 1956 to provide for separate national matching of medical care payments above the regular cash assistance payment to the aged person. Then, in 1960, the Kerr-Mills Act raised the amount of payments allowable to old-age-assistance recipients for medical care. The Act also initiated a new program, called Medical Care for the Aged, under which the national government would participate in medical care payments by state and local governments to aged persons *who were not receiving old-age assistance payments.* The action of the states under these pieces of legislation has varied, both in the types of medical care for which payment would be made and in the amounts and conditions of payment. Many of the states have not been especially generous to the aged in the plans they adopted. This third method is payment on the basis of need, as determined by local or state personnel, and is comparable to the assistance programs set up in the Social Security Act of 1935.

The fourth method is social insurance. Under this system the aged would receive payments for medical expenses as a right if they were covered under the Old Age, Survivors, and Disability Insurance program. The proposed bills providing for this assistance have differed in details on what services would be covered: hospitalization, nursing home care, physicians' services, drugs, etc.; on the level of payments (for example, $10 per day for hospital care) or their duration; on whether the payments should cover only the initial period of illness or illnesses that had become chronic. In one plan (Senator Javits' bill) an individual could choose whether to come under a social security plan for short-term illnesses, a social security plan for long-term illnesses, or to have payments made by the government on his account to a private insurance company. Under all bills which have been considered the patient would have been free to choose his doctor, and doctors free to charge what fees they desired, though public payment would have been made only up to scheduled amounts.

A national compulsory health insurance program for the entire population of the country was recommended to Congress by President Truman. This aroused the vigorous opposition of the American Medical Association, which employed the public relations firm of Whittaker and Baxter and spent $4,678,000 in three and a half years on a "National Education Cam-

Someone's At The Door, Grandma!

A cartoon supporting the AMA's position on Medicare.

Knox in the Nashville *Banner*

paign." [20] In contrast, President Eisenhower proposed reinsurance of private health insurance organizations on some large risks. Neither Truman's nor Eisenhower's proposal got out of committee in Congress. President Kennedy revived the idea of government insurance for medical expenses but confined his proposal to the aged entitled to Old Age, Survivors, and Disability Insurance benefits. The American Medical Association fought this program as vigorously as it had fought President Truman's broader one. It created in 1961 an American Medical Political Action Committee to marshal attacks on what had now come to be called "Medicare."

In 1961 a bill embodying President Kennedy's recommendations was stymied in committee in both houses; in the Senate an attempt to tie the program to other legislation by amendment was defeated by a vote of 52 to 48. President Johnson has made the proposal for health insurance for the aged a part of his domestic program.

Housing

Local governments have long maintained some standards with respect to housing through their building codes and their sanitation and safety

[20] See Stanley Kelley, Jr., *Professional Public Relations and Political Power* (Baltimore, 1956), Chapter 3, for a description of the American Medical Association's National Education Campaign.

regulations. Once again, the depression year of 1932 marked the shift of leadership in public housing activity to the national government.

From that time on, the national government has encouraged the flow of private capital into housing construction. An early means of doing this was the creation in 1932 of the Federal Home Loan Bank system, providing a credit reservoir for the nation's savings and loan industry. At the top of the system is the Federal Home Loan Bank Board. Under the Board's supervision are eleven regional Home Loan Banks, which obtain funds from stock subscriptions, deposits of member institutions, and sale of bonds, and from such funds make loans to private lending institutions. In addition to its central banking functions the Federal Home Loan Bank Board charters and supervises federal savings and loan associations.

Another means of stimulating private investment in housing is through insurance of savings accounts up to $10,000 in federal savings and loan associations and approved state-chartered associations. This is done by the Federal Savings and Loan Corporation, which makes insurance assessments on member institutions. Still another means of facilitating investment is through the insurance of home mortgages. This is done through the Federal Housing Administration (FHA), which insures approved loans at one half of 1 percent of the unpaid principal. To support liquidity and price levels of mortgages the Federal National Mortgage Association (nicknamed "Fannie May") buys and sells FHA mortgages.

The effect of these several banking and insurance measures is to maintain a flow of low-interest, long-term loans for private housing. No other industries except agriculture and commercial banking have been so extensively supported by government. As a result of the arrangements for public and private collaboration over one half of the nonfarm homes of the country were owner-occupied by 1950, as compared with about one third sixty years earlier.[21]

A second type of national function in housing is assistance to state and local governments in slum clearance and urban redevelopment. This program was established by Title I of the Housing Act of 1949 and substantially expanded in the Housing Act of 1954. Under these acts national grants may be made to defray two thirds of the costs of urban renewal projects. The usual procedure is for a city to develop a plan, then to acquire the properties in an area, demolish the structures which cannot be rehabilitated, and either sell the land to private developers or erect a city housing project.

A third program is public housing. During the Depression the national government developed over fifty housing projects, primarily to provide employment. These were subsequently transferred to local governments. Then in 1937 Congress provided for loans and grants by the United States to state and local governments for construction of public housing. Such projects are usually constructed and managed by cities and maintained as low-rent housing with the national government contributing a capital grant or an annual subsidy.

---

[21] Housing and Home Finance Agency, *The 1950 Housing Situation in Charts* (Washington, October, 1951), pp. 20–21 (pamphlet).

Urban redevelopment, with or without public housing, is now an established and growing program among American cities. Thirteen years after
the 1949 act was passed, 1,210 projects had been approved for 636 participating cities.[22] Yet progress in the program is slow.[23] It takes years to
make plans, buy property, and to arrange for removal of residents and
for destruction of buildings. Moreover, completed private projects are
often luxury apartments for upper income groups, and new slum areas are
created by the shift of low-income population to residential areas where
rents are low and housing accommodations are declining. Urban renewal
may bring modernization and beautification of downtown areas, but it will
accomplish its objective only if it provides better housing for slum dwellers.
Some argue that public housing objectives can be attained only with
subsidization to low-income residents.

Yet there is vigorous opposition to public housing from private owners
and developers of rental property and from those who cherish the philosophy of self-help. Consequently, the number of public housing units to be
authorized is a recurrent subject of conflict in the Congress.

Slums and blighted areas are America's poorest exhibit and the central
city's major problem. The Housing Act of 1949 announced the goal of "a
decent home and a suitable living environment for every American family,"
but this goal is still far from being achieved. A Rockefeller Brothers Fund
study estimated a need for $4 to $7 billion expenditure annually for urban
renewal and rehousing by 1967 as compared with about $1 billion expended
in 1961.

Consumer Protection

Although all persons are consumers, the organization within our society
for promotion of consumer interests is weak. There is a Consumers Union,
with an educational program reaching hundreds of thousands of people
through its monthly bulletin, and support for consumer interests is given
by many women's organizations and by professional home economists.
Most people, however, are more aroused by government programs that
affect their earnings or taxes than those that affect their own spending.
Consequently, the interests of consumers are often neglected or overwhelmed by opposition from powerful producer interests.

Nevertheless, consumer interests obtain some measure of protection by
government. Sometimes laws are passed due to strong belief patterns or
obvious public needs, as in the case of regulation of rates of monopolistic
utilities. At other times legislation is due to revelations of gross threats to
public health or safety. Occasionally the efforts of a dedicated person or
group contribute materially to the result. And often the interests of consumers coincide with those of some producer groups with strength. Though
the laws may be mild and loaded with compromises which impair their

---

[22] Housing and Home Finance Agency, *Fourteenth Annual Report* (Washington, 1961),
p. 287. Only seventy-six projects had been completed by the end of 1962.
[23] On the problems and needs see Catherine Bauer Wurster, "Framework for an Urban
Society," in *Goals for America*, President's Commission on National Goals (New York,
1960), pp. 225–47.

effectiveness, they do set standards which elicit some voluntary compliance and are supported in some measure by administrative action. The laws usually establish centers of administration in which, despite outside resistance and inward adaptation to influences contrary to consumer interests, men struggle for the maintenance of the legal standards and for their improvement through further legislation. Also, those government agencies which are large purchasers keep a watchful eye on costs and quality and in this way act as virtual representatives of all consumers. Similarly, cities often initiate action before state and national utility commissions for protection of consumer interests.

It has sometimes been suggested that additional representation be provided in government for consumer interests through consumer advisory councils, consumer representatives in regulatory agencies, or a consumers' department in the executive branch. Consumer advisory councils have been used, notably by the National Recovery Administration from 1933 to 1935, and they may be of real value; but it is doubtful whether they can accomplish much before agencies whose programs are oriented by law to producer interests. The idea of appointing a consumers' counsel to initiate cases and represent consumer interests before regulatory agencies has much appeal, but so likewise does the argument that the appointment of such officials would diminish the sense of responsibility of the agencies themselves to protect consumer interests.[24] This latter argument also has some application to the suggestion for a consumers' department, for it is important that many departments and agencies of government should regard themselves as having a responsibility to consumers. There would be a problem, moreover, as to which agencies should be transferred to such a Department and a question as to whether real gain would be made by such transfers.

Despite the problems, there are signs of increased official efforts to organize the consumer interest. President Kennedy sent to Congress the first special message ever devoted solely to consumer protection, and since then President Johnson also has demonstrated interest in the consumer. In 1961, President Kennedy created a Consumer Advisory Council, and in 1964 President Johnson added a Special Assistant for Consumer Affairs to the White House staff.

Except perhaps for regulation of utility prices, the largest effort of government for consumer protection is directed toward safeguarding him from unhealthy foods and drugs. In 1906, after Upton Sinclair had published *The Jungle*, a blistering exposé of conditions in the Chicago stockyards, Congress enacted the Meat Inspection Act. This act provided for inspection of all meat which was to be shipped in interstate commerce. Today the housewife relies on the federal inspector's stamp on the meat package for assurance of safety and quality. In 1906 also—after an educational program by Dr. Harvey W. Wiley, chief chemist in the Department of Agriculture, on the danger of preservatives—Congress enacted the Food and Drug Act. It

---

[24] For disappointing results from a consumers' counsel in an agency established to promote producer interests, see Kathryn Arnow, *The Consumers' Counsel and the National Bituminous Coal Commission*, rev. ed. (University, Ala., 1950).

prohibited interstate commerce in adulterated or misbranded foods and drugs and is administered by the Food and Drug Administration, now in the Department of Health, Education and Welfare. Through the years the Food and Drug Administration, then in the Department of Agriculture and manned by dedicated specialists, struggled to give protection to the public under a weak statute, with inadequate appropriations, and against vigorous pressure from agricultural processors who could sometimes find support in the politically appointive, top administrative positions of the Department.[25]

In 1938, after more than one hundred deaths from a drug called "Elixir Sulfanilamide," Congress materially strengthened the Food and Drug Act. Among other things, the amendments expanded the Act's coverage to include cosmetics (excluding soap) and therapeutic devices, and increased the penalties for violation. Not included under the prohibitions of the Food and Drug Act is false advertising. This is within the jurisdiction of the Federal Trade Commission. It has been noted that the Federal Trade Commission Act was amended in 1938 to include protection of consumers as an objective. In addition, new sections were added which provided new remedies for false advertising of foods, drugs, and cosmetics, and of devices designed to affect the structure or function of the body or to prevent or treat disease. Henceforth, while a manufacturer who falsely advertised most products could have only a cease and desist order issued against him by the Federal Trade Commission, one who falsely advertised a drug, food, cosmetic, or body device was subject to a cease and desist order, a court injunction, and criminal penalties.

Triggered by discoveries of enormous profits of drug manufacturers on certain new and expensive drugs, a Senate subcommittee chaired by Senator Kefauver began an investigation of drug marketing in 1958. When the investigations revealed that laws did not give adequate protection to the consumer against untested drugs, Senator Kefauver, with the aid of a handful of Senators, labored doggedly for passage of amendments to add effective safeguards. This effort appeared to be stymied until the effects of the drug Thalidomide were revealed. Thalidomide, a sedative given to pregnant mothers, was alleged to have caused 3,500 to 5,000 deformed babies in Western Europe. It had not been marketed in this country only because an employee of the Food and Drug Administration—a physician, Dr. Frances O. Kelsey—had repeatedly called for more information about the drug. The law only allowed official certification of a drug to be withheld for sixty days, but by asking repeatedly for more information Dr. Kelsey had protected the American public. The Thalidomide revelations, like those of 1906 and 1938, led to enactment of many of the Kefauver proposals. Prior to 1962, drugs could only be denied certification by the Food and Drug Administration if they were proved to be unsafe; and certification was automatic if the administration had not acted within a prescribed time. The amendments in 1962 provided among other new safeguards that new drugs should not be certified without evaluation of their effectiveness as well as their

---

[25] See E. Pendleton Herring, *Public Administration and the Public Interest* (New York and London, 1936), Chapter 15.

safety; they also contained procedural changes designed to give the Food and Drug Administration opportunity to evaluate a drug before determining whether to certify it or to allow its automatic certification.

Certain special acts have been passed which protect the consumer of other products. The Wool Products Labeling Act of 1940 requires labeling of most wool products, the Fur Products Labeling Act of 1951 requires labeling of furs, and the Flammable Fabrics Act of 1953 forbade distribution of wearing apparel so flammable as to be dangerous to the wearer. Generally, however, the doctrine "Let the buyer beware" still applies to the consumer's choices in the United States, except for food and drugs.

Other Welfare Activities

The foregoing summary of activities in the major functional areas gives only a partial picture of the widely diversified welfare activities of government. There are a number of agencies performing functions, usually of varied types, for special clienteles referred to only incidentally, or not at all, in the preceding discussions. There is a Bureau of Indian Affairs, with health, educational, and other functions; a Children's Bureau, which conducts a number of programs related to health and welfare; a section of the Department of Labor which protects migrant workers from Mexico. The largest of the special agencies is the Veterans Administration. This mammoth agency has an annual appropriation of more than $5 billion and has about 150,000 employees in its medical care program alone. Among other things, it administers hospitals, makes pension and other benefit payments, guarantees loans for purchase of homes, conducts rehabilitation and training programs, and administers public insurance for veterans.

There are also many miscellaneous special activities, one of which is of sufficient size to deserve special mention—disaster relief. Public Law 875, passed in 1950, authorized national aid to state and local governments to alleviate suffering and damage resulting from major disasters, to repair essential public facilities damaged in such disasters, and to foster the development of state and local plans and organizations to cope with major disasters. The disaster relief program is coordinated on the national level by the Office of Emergency Planning, which operates through regional offices; these in turn maintain close relations with state governments. The states have developed organizations and plans for meeting disaster situations and have encouraged local governments to set up cooperating arrangements.

A "Welfare State"?

Is it correct to describe America as a "welfare state"? Two types of response may be given, one on the basis of responsibility, the other on the basis of success. In each case the response is a statement of opposite considerations.

If the term "welfare state" means only that government has assumed minimums of responsibility for opportunity, security, and physical protection, then the term may be appropriately used for the United States. If, on the other hand, the term implies that government carries the full, or even the main, responsibility for assuring personal welfare, then the American state is not a welfare state. What is clear about American society is that private and public actions are complementary. Just as in the economic aspect of society the market is the primary mechanism of social control and public intervention is correctional and supplementary, so in the aspect of personal welfare the basic responsibility is placed on the individual and the family, but responsibilities are also assumed collectively. Opportunity and security are provided through a mixture of private, quasi-public, and public activities.

On the criterion of success, it can be said that the standard of personal living of a large majority of Americans is very high in comparison with that of most other peoples now or in the past, and that much has been done to insure both the individual's opportunity and his protection against the hazards of life through the combination of private and public action. On the other hand, the conditions of life of slum dwellers, displaced farm workers, chronically unemployed urban workers, minority racial groups, and second- and third-generation relief recipients are such that one cannot contend that the welfare of all has been attained. Good opportunity is not universal, and protection against the hazards of life is incomplete.

The unfinished task of American society with respect to these two things will determine the welfare agenda of government in the future. Efforts will be made to achieve the American dream of opportunity for all. President Johnson's "war on poverty" must include an effort to avoid a forced retreat— the decline into poverty and helplessness of millions of people with no skills or the wrong skills for today's and tomorrow's needs—and a battle for the new goal of lifting other millions of people ("the other America," Michael Harrington has called it) from relief or near-relief status to competence, and in instances to desire for self-sustaining activity. Efforts will have to be made, also, to extend the protections against the hazards of life. These must include steps to remove exemptions from coverage of welfare legislation, to add new forms of protection, and to provide more liberal payments to some groups. These strivings toward opportunity and security will be reflected in the politics of the future.

Whether the United States is a "welfare state," or will ever become one, may be arguable; but, undoubtedly, welfare issues—arising from the conditions of the time, the aims and needs of people, and the political pressures exerted by them—will form a large part of the politics and problems of the nation.

23 / Government and Money

The typical American may carry, on a typical day, his children to a public school on a public street past a public hospital and a public housing project, or a public dam, and feel the jar of a public jet breaking the sound barrier overhead. The water he drinks, the cream in his coffee, the vitamins he has just taken, even the air he breathes, have all been matters of public regulation. The policeman at the intersection, the fire house on the corner, the public park and the city coliseum he is passing are all evidence that government's activity on his behalf stretches from his protection to his recreation.

On all this there is the dollar sign. Functions of government must be translated into figures. Decisions must be made on how much will be spent, how the money will be obtained, and how the flow of funds will be regulated through accounting procedures. This is the arena of public finance into which all politics and administration must ultimately move.

Some basic facts about public expenditures are essential for background to this chapter. The first fact is that the percentage of the nation's productive output being used for public programs has increased greatly in the last thirty-five years. In economist's language, the public sector of the economy has grown more rapidly than the private sector. Government statisticians now accumulate figures on the gross national product (GNP), meaning all goods and services produced in the nation, and on government purchases of goods and services.[1] Table 23–1 shows that just prior to the Great Depres-

---

[1] Inaccurate conclusions are often drawn from statistics on public finance because the method of their development is not understood.

1. There is an important distinction between total expenditures and the expenditures which take goods and services from the economy. Total expenditures include what are called transfer payments, such as pensions payments out of public funds and net interest payments. These two types of payments transfer money from one group of persons to another (those who pay taxes and those who receive payments), and thus have an effect on the distribution of income; but they do not extract from the economy any portion of its output for public uses. Without these payments, there is left government purchases of goods and services. These purchases represent the value of the nation's currently produced output bought directly by government. Quite obviously, this provides a more accurate estimate of the cost to society of the public sector of the economy than does the total expenditure figure.

2. Monetary figures may be given on a gross or a net basis. The Bureau of Census

TABLE 23–1 / Government Purchases in Selected Years, 1929–63

Year	Percentage of total economy	Year	Percentage of total economy
1929	8.16	1944	46.26
1930	9.98	1949	15.61
1934	15.26	1954	20.78
1939	14.79	1961	20.82
		1963	21.38

SOURCE: Percentages for 1929–54 derived from figures in *Economic Report of the President Transmitted to the Congress, January, 1962, Together with the Annual Report of the Council of Economic Advisers* (Washington, 1962), Appendix B, Table B-7, p. 217. Percentages for 1961 and 1963 derived from figures in the same report for January, 1964, Appendix C, Table C-1, p. 207. 1963 figure estimated.

sion of 1929 government purchases were less than 10 percent of the output of society. During the Depression a new plateau of about 15 percent was reached. In the Second World War and the Korean War the percentage temporarily went much higher. Then there was a leveling off at a new plateau of about 21 percent.

A second fact is that, due primarily to the increase in military purchases, the purchases of goods and services by the national government have now become larger than those of state and local governments combined. In 1929 state and local governments purchased goods and services in the amount of $7.2 billion as compared with $1.3 billion by the national government, and in 1939 the figure for state-local governments was $8.2 as compared with $5.2 for the national government. But 1950 was the last year in which state and local purchases were larger than those of the national government. In 1963 national purchases were $66.4 billion and state-local purchases $58.8 billion.

Nevertheless, the costs of government have been increasing at all three levels. It is not possible to present comparative data on *purchases* of goods and services by the three levels of government, but total *expenditures* can be compared. Chart 23–1 shows, without adjustments for changes in the value of the dollar, the growth in expenditures by the three levels of government. It shows that over a fifty-year span, from 1913 to 1963, local expenditures became about twenty-four times greater while state and national expenditures both became over 100 times greater. It also shows the

accumulates data on a gross basis, thereby including all receipts and expenditures of special funds and enterprises, while the Bureau of the Budget reports data on a net basis, including for an enterprise like the Post Office only the surplus or deficit carried into the budget.

3. Expenditures may be overstated by double inclusions such as would be the case if a grant of money from the national government to a state government, which then expended the funds, were counted as an expenditure of both governments. A more accurate statement would net out duplicate expenditures by counting expenditures only for the first government which disbursed the funds.

CHART 23–1 / Expenditures of National, State, and Local Governments (United States) for Selected Years from 1913 to 1963, in Billions of Dollars

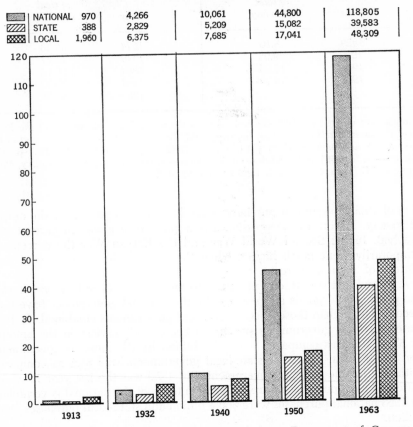

	NATIONAL	970	4,266	10,061	44,800	118,805
	STATE	388	2,829	5,209	15,082	39,583
	LOCAL	1,960	6,375	7,685	17,041	48,309

SOURCE: Figures for 1913–50 derived from United States Department of Commerce, Bureau of the Census, "Historical Summary of Governmental Finances in the United States," *1957 Census of Governments* (Washington, 1959), Vol. XIV, No. 3, pp. 16–17 (national government data), pp. 20–21 (state government data), and pp. 22–23 (local government data). Data for 1963 were derived from United States Department of Commerce, Bureau of the Census, *Governmental Finances in the United States, 1963* (Washington, 1964), p. 23. Intergovernmental revenues not deducted from expenditure figures.

startling fact that, in spite of national defense expenditures, state expenditures have grown at about the same rate as national expenditures, in the recent period of 1950 to 1963, and over the fifty-year period at five sixths of the national rate.

The bulk of the expenditures at each level of government goes to a few large functions. Chart 23–2 shows the allocation of the budget dollar in the President's budget for the fiscal year 1965. Since veterans' payments and at least the bulk of the interest payments are the result of past wars and defense preparations, it is apparent that close to 61 cents of the budget

740 / Government in Action

CHART 23–2 / Allocation of the Budget Dollar, 1965 (Estimate)

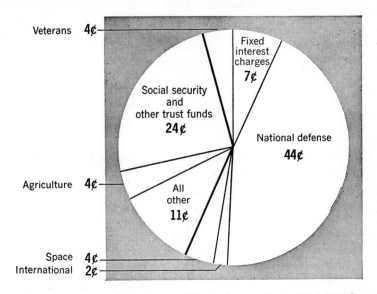

SOURCE: United States Bureau of the Budget, *The Budget in Brief, 1965* (Washington, 1964), front cover.

CHART 23–3 / State Government General Expenditures (United States), by Type of Function, 1963

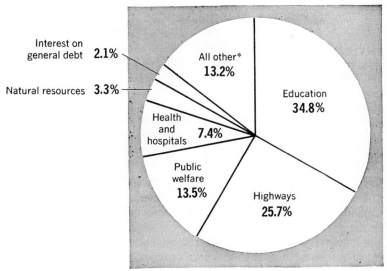

* Includes:

Housing and Urban Renewal	.1%
Air Transportation	.2%
Social Insurance Administration	1.2%
Miscellaneous	12.9%

SOURCE: United States Department of Commerce, Bureau of the Census, *Governmental Finances in the United States, 1963* (Washington, 1964), p. 24.

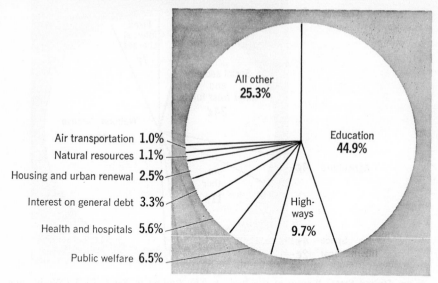

Air transportation **1.0%**
Natural resources **1.1%**
Housing and urban renewal **2.5%**
Interest on general debt **3.3%**
Health and hospitals **5.6%**
Public welfare **6.5%**

All other
25.3%

Education
44.9%

High-
ways
9.7%

* These data are estimates based on a sample of local governments and thus are subject to a degree of sampling variation. See source, pp. 14–15, for a fuller discussion of their reliability.

SOURCE: United States Department of Commerce, Bureau of the Census, *Governmental Finances in the United States, 1961* (Washington, 1962), p. 22.

dollar is spent on national defense, international, and space programs, and that only 39 cents goes to domestic programs.

Chart 23–3 shows that the bulk of state expenditures goes for four purposes—education, highways, public welfare, and public health; and Chart 23–4 shows that the largest volume of local expenditures is for these same purposes.

Decisions on the expenditure of public funds are crucial determinants of the role of government, the quantity and quality of its services, and the allocation of its benefits. Decisions on the means of raising the money determine the distribution of costs among groups of persons. In addition to immediate personal effects, both types of decision influence the health of the nation's economy. These processes of decision-making and the problems of public finance in present-day governments are among the most important in public affairs today.

The Budget

The budget has become a universal instrument of governments. The major characteristic of a budget is that it is a single plan for expenditures for a government (national, state, city, or other unit) as a whole. It is prepared in a central office and is an instrument for coordination and unified planning. In nearly all governments the chief executive is made responsible for the preparation of the budget; the budget office is either a staff unit in his office or is located in a department of finance responsible to him.

The budget is so familiar a feature of government today that its recent origins may be overlooked. In America it is a twentieth-century development. The movement for budgeting originated in the cities, following revelations of municipal corruption by the muckrakers at the turn of the century. The National Municipal League, formed in 1894, and the New York Bureau of Municipal Research, established in 1906, led the movement for the municipal budget, and by the end of the first quarter of this century the budget was solidly established in municipal governments generally. The movement spread quickly to the states, most of which set up budget systems of some sort in the decade between 1910 and 1920. In the national government the previously regular surpluses of customs revenues over expenditures became irregular after 1894; this naturally led to greater interest in economical use of funds. A report released in 1912 by President Taft's Commission on Economy and Efficiency favored a national budget and led to discussions which ended in the passage of the Budget and Accounting Act of 1921. This act made the President responsible for preparation and submission to Congress of a budget and created the Bureau of the Budget to assist him in the task.[2]

Three aspects of budgeting are significant today, the first two at all levels of government, the third particularly at the national level. First, the budget is an instrument of financial management. It is a means of looking at both the revenue and expenditure sides of the ledger sheet and determining what amount of money can or will be spent. The budget itself is a financial plan for an ensuing fiscal period. It is customarily accompanied by reports on revenues and expenditures, estimated or actual, for the current year and one or two past years. It provides an overall view of the financial operations of the government and provides an opportunity also to trim the fat from agency appropriation requests. This planning, reporting, and trimming is a major part of the business side of government.

This aspect of budgeting led to its quick adoption by governments generally. It was the central feature of the "Double-E" movement—the movement for economy and efficiency in government—in the first quarter of this century. All persons interested in good government could in good faith support a movement to substitute sound financial planning for laxity and corruption in government finances, and conservatives particularly could respond to an effort to obtain economy in government expenditures.

Second, the budget is a means of reaching decisions on program objectives. It is a means of appraising programs and making determinations on their scope and direction. In the process of budgeting most agencies develop their plans and make their choices among competing pressures for expansion. It is in the central budget office that the competing programs of agencies are measured in dollar terms and evaluated against the total sum which it is financially feasible and politically expedient to consider as the

---

[2] On these developments see Jesse Burkhead, *Government Budgeting* (New York and London, 1956), Chapter 1.

maximum for expenditure. It is through the budget recommendations of the chief executive that he is able to exercise continuous influence on the policies of agencies. Program decisions will often be made by other processes, but their implementation is usually uncertain until they have run the budget gantlet.

Third, the national budget is an instrument of economic planning. The term "economic planning" may be objectionable to many who fear any idea that the course of the economy should be materially influenced by centralized decision of government rather than determined by the decentralized decisions of the marketplace, but in fact there is an element of economic planning in any decision of government to use its tool kit of available authorities and influences to affect the course of the economy. The budget is the chief tool in this kit. Expenditures can be raised to stimulate the economy or they can be cut to dampen inflationary tendencies. Similarly, taxes can be cut or raised for the same effects. Only the national government, however, can play this game with any degree of effectiveness,[3] for the resources of the states and localities are limited and their constitutions or charters usually restrict their debt-creating and taxing authority.

The national government first used fiscal—that is, expenditure and taxing —policy for general economic promotion and regulation in the Depression of the thirties. In the same decade the English economist John Maynard Keynes advocated the positive use of fiscal policy to compensate for the slackening in investment and expenditure in the private economy. A little later, statisticians developed national income accounting, through which the aggregate level of production of goods and services in the economy could be estimated. Since then other statistical measures, such as the rate of annual economic growth, have been perfected. Thus, theory justifies and statistical measures make possible budgeting in terms of effects on the economy. In such budgeting consideration is given to aggregates—to the measures of growth and stability in the economy as a whole, and to the relation of government expenditures to these ends.

These matters are dealt with in the President's annual economic report but referred to only summarily in the President's actual budget. They give rise to some of the deepest conflicts in public opinion. Many people still regard the national budget as a matter of internal housekeeping, having the same function as a family budget. In their view the budget is an instrument of sound finance and decision on competing program claims, and it should be balanced, except for occasional emergencies. Others look at the national budget in terms of its effects upon economic growth and stability. To them the objective of an annually balanced national budget is nonsense. They claim that it should be unbalanced on the surplus side when there is threat of inflationary instability, and unbalanced on the deficit side when statistical indicators show the existence or threat of recession or the slowing of economic growth.

The tax reduction enacted by the Congress in 1964 illustrates both views of budgeting. It will go down in the history books as our first *purposeful* increase of an expected deficit in order to stimulate employment and eco-

---

[3] For limitations on this effectiveness see pp. 660–61.

"Idol Must Have Human
Sacrifice."

Despite modern economic theories,
the tradition of a balanced budget
lives on.

From *Straight Herblock*, Simon & Schuster, 1964

nomic growth; yet President Johnson felt it politically essential to call for an economy drive on government expenditures to diminish the evil effects of a larger deficit in the eyes of the balanced budget advocates. The President is the nation's Chief Budgeter, in one sense, but the chairmen of the Senate Finance and House Ways and Means Committees are coordinate policy makers for taxation, and Senator Harry F. Byrd required economy as the price for tax reduction. The issue of budget balancing is thus one that involves the size not just of the budget (that is, the expenditure estimates) but also of the projected income to the government. One's desire for a balanced budget may thus conflict with eagerness to accept the personal benefit of a reduced tax burden.

Furthermore, different ideas of what the budget is for are reflected in appointments to the Bureau of the Budget. The late President Kennedy appointed two men trained as economists to be successive Directors of the Bureau, emphasizing the economic impact of the budget. President Eisenhower, on the other hand, emphasized the concept of the budget as a device for achieving economy and efficiency, through appointments to the office of men with business management and accounting backgrounds.

THE BUDGET PROCESS

The budget process is one of "screening, filtering, and revising" at successive levels.[4] At some operating level—a department of physics in a univer-

---

[4] Verne B. Lewis, "Budgetary Administration in the Department of Agriculture," in John M. Gaus and Leon O. Wolcott, *Public Administration and the United States Department of Agriculture* (Chicago, 1940), p. 405.

sity, a bureau in the Department of Commerce, or a regional office in the Department of Health, Education and Welfare—men will prepare statements of their dollar needs for a future period. They will probably be operating under some instructions from above—"Hold the line," "Ask for increases only where the need is imperative," or "Achieve a reduction." This downward flow of communication almost always calls for economy. It is the first line of defense against mounting demands. Then from the operating level, where the detailed planning begins, the estimates of need flow upward through budget offices whose ears are turned to the executives whom they serve. From the top executive office government budgets go to legislatures, where they start moving through another hierarchical flow—from subcommittees to committees, to the houses, to conference committees, and back to the houses.

In this downward flow of instruction and upward flow of estimates a variety of roles are played by the people involved in the process. At the level where responsibility for programs is placed, men plan for the adequacy of the programs. The doctor who heads a public health service or the educator who supervises a public school sees ways in which the service rendered could be improved, if only there were more money. At the first level above him, where his claims compete with other claims, there will be a compromise of two roles: promotion of the claims of the services, and reduction of these to make them palatable at still later stages of the process. The higher the claims move, in their journey toward approval, the more will be their dilution in the face of pressure for economy. All the way up the channel the professional budget officials are motivated by the belief that operators ask for too much and by the knowledge that their function is to trim the fat and to get the totals down to the limits set by their instructions. There will be some exceptions for services favored by their political superiors, but generally the budgeters are trimmers.

Outside the governmental structure other roles will be played. Interest groups desiring to prevent higher taxes will have been cultivating a public attitude in favor of economy and will have lobbyists swarming around the key legislators. The government agencies will have been cultivating the groups which favor their programs and these groups will add to the swarm of lobbyists. Few citizens are aware of the multiple checks and balances resulting from the hierarchical process, the conflicting roles of actors, and the competition for public support in the complex and hectic process of budgeting.

It would be a mistake to think that all the programs of government are reevaluated each time a budget is prepared. Programs and activities already established are normally accepted without question. The budget maker's attention is focused on the points of expansion or contraction; and in a society where population is growing, inflation is normal, and demands for government service are increasing, it is usually on points of expansion. The point is that policy-making is incremental [5]—it is like a tree growing and

---

[5] See Charles E. Lindblom, "Policy Analysis," *American Economic Review* (June, 1958), Vol. XLVIII, pp. 298–312.

adding new branches.[6] Seldom does the budget maker consider whether to cut a tree down or even remove a branch; his problem is whether to add new branches or increase the foliage. For this reason, legislators reviewing budget estimates may take a close look at new activities. Thus Congressman Rooney observed, "This may be only $250 but this is the camel's nose. These things never get out of the budget. They manage to stay and grow." [7]

In addition, the budget maker is circumscribed in various ways. In the national government he finds it difficult to regulate the flow of expenditures into the economy at any given time, for two major reasons. First, many items of expenditure are of a continuing nature, unless a drastic overhaul of programs is made. And second, appropriations may authorize contracts in stated amounts within the fiscal year, but the money may not be completely spent until later years when the contracts are completed. In military and space programs this accumulation of obligations from prior years diminishes the opportunity of the government to reduce the rate of flow of expenditures promptly; similarly, the lag time between planning for expenditures and the actual expenditure reduces the opportunity to increase the flow of expenditures quickly.

Complexities of technology and foreign policy push the government increasingly toward long-range development projects whose initial costs are wasted unless completion costs are paid several years later, and which simply cannot be completed within the single-year budget span. Weapons systems provide one important example, and a major step in Defense Department budgeting has been the inauguration since 1961 of a process for projecting costs of each system for five years ahead, so that the full implications of a currently small expenditure may be analyzed and decisions made now that will determine part of the budget half a decade later. The manned space programs provide an even more dramatic illustration. From the time of President Kennedy's decision to press forward with the man-to-the-moon program to the first lunar landing will be at least eight or nine years, perhaps more. Twenty billion dollars are involved, perhaps more. The President's 1962 decision will circumscribe the budgeters for at least a decade in a very substantial way.

In state and local governments the budget maker is often limited by constitutional or legislative requirements that money derived from certain taxes be used for certain purposes, thus destroying the flexibility that would exist if appropriations could be made for various purposes, as desired, from one general fund. In the same way, legal restrictions may exist on the amount or on the kinds of taxes that can be levied, the amount of debt that may be incurred, or the amount of money that may be expended for stated purposes. Legal earmarking of funds for special purposes and legal restrictions on taxes, debts, and expenditures may greatly limit the freedom of the budget planner and the legislature in determining the amount of expenditures or the allocation of appropriations among different purposes.

---

[6] For discussion of the analogy, see Herbert A. Simon, *Administrative Behavior*, 2nd ed. (New York, 1957), pp. xxvii–xxxiii.
[7] Quoted from Aaron Wildavsky, *The Politics of the Budgetary Process* (Boston, 1964), p. 112.

Smaller decisions in the budget-making process can be made semiscientifically on the basis of cost analyses. Mountains of cost figures are accumulated and digested into summary statements by the operators of government services, and comparisons can sometimes be made with the costs of supplying the same services in other governments or in private jurisdictions. But budget-making is not wholly or even dominantly scientific. Quantitative comparisons of costs per student do not measure the quality of education, and cost figures alone do not determine decisions on whether to expand highway construction or public welfare expenditures. The large decisions on quality and on choice among competing claims will be influenced by value considerations and by the strength of the political pressures of organized groups and agencies representing their interests. Budget-making begins in administrative procedure but ends in politics.

The form in which the budget is prepared is important. Originally most budgets were built around objects of expenditure, such as salaries, travel costs, and capital expenditures. Nowadays efforts are made toward "performance" and "program" budgeting. In essence such budgeting centers on the functions and activities for which funds are required. A *performance* budget seeks to isolate units of activity, such as miles of road constructed or number of students educated, and to state the costs in terms of such units. Such performance estimates, based on past costs, can be aggregated into a *program* budget, which projects the plans of government in terms of results to be accomplished. Some writers use the terms performance budgeting and program budgeting interchangeably, while others distinguish them as two aspects of a process of measuring expenditures by performance units and aggregating these into program plans.[8] Either way, this type of budgeting gives the chief executive and the legislature a better picture of what government will do with its money than a budget which merely classifies expenditures by object. It is, however, often very difficult to build budgets around functions or activities, while it is easy to summarize expenditures by object.

All in all, the budget process is a compound of three elements: a push for enlargement, a counter push for economy, and compromises between these rival forces and among the competing claims of agencies.

BUDGET-MAKING IN THE NATIONAL GOVERNMENT

The fiscal year of the United States Government runs from July 1 to June 30 and is named for the later year. Thus, the fiscal year 1967 ends June 30, 1967. The planning for the budget cycle that ends on that date will have begun at least twenty-seven months earlier, that is, in the spring of 1965. Hence a budget cycle includes a prolonged period of planning and of expenditure and overlaps with other such budget cycles. Agencies in the spring of 1965 were executing the 1965 budget, arguing in Congress for the 1966 budget, and planning the 1967 budget.

---

[8] On the distinction see Burkhead, *op. cit.*, pp. 139–40; for full discussion of the subject see Burkhead, Chapters 6 and 7, and Frederick C. Mosher, *Program Budgeting: Theory and Practice with Particular Reference to the U.S. Department of the Army* (Chicago, 1954).

Tricky Plumbing

The conflict between enlargement and economy in preparing a budget is depicted here by a conservative commentator.

Hesse in the St. Louis *Globe-Democrat*

Executive planning of the budget is in three stages. First, prior to June, 1965, two kinds of planning will have been proceeding on the 1967 budget. The bureaus and then the departmental budget offices will have been working up estimates of their needs. The Bureau of the Budget will have been engaged in conversations with the Treasury Department and the Council of Economic Advisers on the anticipated levels of national income and of national tax yields, with major spending agencies on their probable requirements, and with the President on his response to these forecasts of revenue and statements of need. Then, probably in June, the Bureau will initiate the second stage by transmitting to the major spending agencies a policy letter which sets forth guidelines and probably defines "ceilings" which the agencies should regard as at least tentative limits on their planning. There will also be a "call for estimates" with deadlines and specific instructions on budget forms and other technical matters. Approximately three months will be spent by the agencies in getting their final estimates in shape. Departmental reviews, internal hearings, and adjustments in figures will be made before sending the agency budgets to the Bureau of the Budget by the end of September. This point marks the beginning of the third stage— that of top-level consideration of the estimates. In October and November the Bureau will conduct hearings at which each agency, sometimes for part of a day and sometimes for many days, will argue its case before Bureau officials. This hearing will be followed by the Director's review, in which the recommendations of the division chiefs of the Bureau and further pleas by the agencies will be evaluated by committees composed of the top officials of the Bureau. In the meantime, conferences will be held with the President, and the Bureau will be working on the President's Budget Message. In December this process of Bureau consideration merges into that of Presidential review and final decisions are made. In January the President's Budget Message and budget are transmitted to the Congress.

To understand Congressional action with respect to expenditures it is necessary to distinguish two parts of the process of legalizing the spending of money. The first is the passage of legislation which *authorizes* the expenditure. Such legislation goes to the program committees, such as the armed services committees and the committees on agriculture. These committees are usually composed of persons who, either at the time of their appointment or through long association with the functions with which they deal, have a sympathetic attitude toward the adequacy of governmental programs. Their responsiveness to group demands leads to legislation for activities which will require expenditure of money. In many cases, however, the program committees insert restrictive clauses which will limit expenditures, and in some cases they are the scenes of battles over the amount and timing of expenditures. Thus, for example, in 1962 when the President recommended authorization for the Alliance for Progress of $3 billion for four years with an appropriation of $600 million the first year, the Foreign Relations Committee of the Senate recommended authorization of $600 million the first year and $800 million each for the next three years, and the corresponding House committee recommended authorization of $600 million for each of the four years.

Whatever the authorizations voted by the houses, their effect is dependent upon *appropriations*, which of course will often fall short of the amount of the authorizations. When, for example, a State Department official sought in an appropriation hearing to rely on an authorization, Representative Rooney told him he should "never lose sight of the fact that the Appropriations Committees are the saucers that cool the legislative tea. Just because you have an authorization does not mean a thing to us. . . ." [9]

Conflicts between cost analysis and political criteria abound in budgeting. An example is the military program area, where multibillion-dollar weapons systems have loomed large in government expenditures in recent years. No sooner, for example, had Secretary of Defense Robert McNamara decided against nuclear power plants for some proposed aircraft carriers, on the basis of cost estimates made with the aid of mathematical analysis, than members of the Congressional Joint Committee on Atomic Energy protested vigorously and threatened a fight. The future of the manned bomber has similarly been a question on which cost-effectiveness analysis and the constituency pressures arising from companies and workers engaged in airplane manufacture have been at odds. Government budgets do not allocate funds just among government departments: the "hardware" decisions also allocate funds among competing firms, industries, states, and Congressional districts, and the affected elements are not bashful about pressing their claims.

Appropriations can, as a result of constitutional provision, be made for only one year. The annual consideration of budget estimates referred by the President is in the committees on appropriations: there is only one

---

[9] Quotation from Wildavsky, *op. cit.*, p. 100.

committee in each house, but each operates through subcommittees. The most thorough consideration is in the House subcommittees, and House action on appropriation bills always precedes Senate action. The Senate committee is a kind of appeal center for the agencies from cuts made in the House committee.

The House subcommittees are among the hardest working units of Congress.[10] So heavy is their load that the rules provide that a member of the Appropriations Committee may hold no other committee assignment. Months of hearings are held on appropriation requests, and the hearings are followed by executive sessions of the subcommittees. The subcommittee members, assisted by the committee staff, specialize on their respective parts of the budget. They occupy strategic positions of great power over bureaus, holding a whip hand which is often more threatening than any supervision from within the executive branch. With the program committees they constitute another line of supervision over agencies, thus contributing to the joint executive-legislative supervision of administration. They regard themselves as the watchdogs of the Treasury, and in performance of this function they may dig deeply into the minutiae of budget estimates. Beyond this, they will take an interest in the methods of administration, and even the policy, of agencies. Particularly strategic is the position of the subcommittee chairman, whose sympathy or antagonism will mean much to an agency.

The politically astute bureau chief or agency head will thus court the relevant appropriations subcommittee members, and will "check in" informally when he wishes to make some marginal adjustment in the use of funds. Much of Congressional influence over the executive rests upon the informal influence derived from financial power, rather than upon formal authority or formal investigations. People and money are, it has been said, the lifeblood of administration. The appropriations subcommittees not only control the money; through this they also shape the size of staff available to do the job and occasionally the types of employees to be used. In 1956, for example, a subcommittee, responding to the desires of a Congressional colleague of great prestige, threatened virtually to eliminate the appropriation for the Business and Defense Services Administration of the Department of Commerce unless that agency promised to terminate the use as division heads of businessmen who were still in the pay of their private employers while working for the government without compensation. The agency changed its personnel practices.

A spirit of reciprocity among the committee members and particularly the subcommittee chairmen gives much finality to subcommittee recommendations at the committee stage. Similarly, substantial amendment on the floor of the houses is infrequent. Moreover, the appropriations debates are likely to range over wider and more spectacular issues than the details of an appropriation. From the houses the appropriations bills will almost

---

[10] On Congressional consideration see Arthur W. Macmahon, "Congressional Oversight of Administration: The Power of the Purse," *Political Science Quarterly* (June and September, 1943), Vol. LVIII, pp. 161–90, 380–414; also, Richard F. Fenno, Jr., "The House Appropriations Committee as a Political System: The Problem of Integration," *American Political Science Review* (June, 1962), Vol. LVI, pp. 310–24.

always go to conference committees and, after agreement by the houses, to the President. Many aspects of this process are of crucial significance to a nation whose national budget has become one of the weightiest influences on national security, world peace, and public welfare. One question is the quality of analysis. Certainly, there is no question about the sufficiency of the number of considerations given to proposed budgets. But quality involves expertness and perspective; and expertness requires specialization. Budgeting has become a professionalized aspect of management, and much competence has been developed in the budget offices of the agencies. The Bureau of the Budget is a kind of magnet, drawing to it able young men who desire careers in management and who are challenged by the opportunity to work in a center having government-wide responsibilities. The House Committee on Appropriations is regarded as an attractive assignment by Congressmen, many of whom move there from other assignments. There they remain for extended periods, there they specialize in subcommittee work, and hence they become specialists—and in this respect experts. They are assisted by the largest committee staff in Congress. Yet the task is tremendous, and the difficulties of obtaining a grasp of even the incremental points in budget estimates appear insuperable. Perspective for viewing possible choices may be destroyed by the very process of specialization needed to understand details. In the Bureau of the Budget intercommunication and review procedures counteract the deleterious effects of specialization, without destroying its advantages. But in the Congressional committees, the socialization of members—their absorption into the work habits of the Congressional system—brings acceptance of reciprocity and finality to the work of subcommittees.[11] A government-wide perspective is prevented by the system of specialization, which is aggravated by the logrolling of members ("You support my project, I'll support yours") for inclusion of constituency projects dear to their hearts. While fat is trimmed from agency diets by the committees, some luxury pork for the districts of the nation is added.

Senator Hubert Humphrey expressed the plight of the legislator facing the multibillion-dollar budget in terms both succinct and plaintive:

> I serve on the Appropriations Committee. If I never served on anything else for the rest of my life, it would be ten jobs in one. How can any man know about a hundred billion dollars? All the Bureau of the Budget has to do is to accumulate and present that budget. [Editor's note: The Director of the Bureau may not entirely agree with this.] The Congress has to decide on it. The Budget Bureau has thousands of employees. There are less than a hundred on the staffs of the Appropriations Committees of both houses of Congress.[12]

Some committee members take pride in their watchdog function. One declared, "No subcommittee of which I have been a member has ever reported out a bill without a cut in the budget." Conversely, members often identify completely with agency programs, and back them staunchly. "To

---

[11] Fenno, *op. cit.*, pp. 316–18.
[12] Center for the Study of Democratic Institutions, *The Mazes of Modern Government* (Santa Barbara, Calif., 1964) (pamphlet).

me forestry has become a religion," said one. One investigator found that the House Appropriations Committee, considering thirty-seven bureau budgets from 1947 to 1959, did reduce estimates 77.2 percent of the time.[13]

Some effort has been made in the past, however, to focus attention on aggregates as well as specifics. The Legislative Reorganization Act of 1946 provided for a Joint Committee on the Legislative Budget, to be composed of all members of the House and Senate Appropriations Committees, the House Ways and Means Committee, and the Senate Finance Committee; its function was to prepare a concurrent resolution for the houses to set a ceiling on appropriations. In the 1947 session, the Senate amended the resolution recommended by the Committee and no agreement was reached in conference committee. In 1948 the houses approved a ceiling but exceeded it when appropriations were passed. In 1949 the procedure broke down, and it has not functioned since. In 1950 another kind of procedure was employed. The House Appropriations Committee reported, and the houses passed, an omnibus appropriation, containing in one bill all the year's appropriations. The procedure has not been followed since, for it is difficult to arbitrate and reduce the proposals coming from the separate subcommittees. The fragmentation and dispersal inherent in the subcommittee system, designed to provide specialization and attention to specifics, militates against action in the whole committee or in a joint committee. The ex officio membership on each subcommittee of the chairman and ranking minority members of the committee, together with the coordinating activity of committee staff do, to an extent, supplement the full committee's function; [14] but the fact remains that only in the Bureau of the Budget itself is there significant success in counteracting specialization with perspective.

Another problem is the lack of an effective executive check upon the excesses of Congressional committees in appropriation bills. They may pad such bills with funds for pet projects of Congressmen in behalf of their constituents; they may include details of administration which impair executive responsibility; and they may even attach legislative riders having little or no connection with the appropriation of money. The President is usually unable to consider a veto of an appropriation bill, because such an action would leave agencies without funds. In forty-one states the governor now has the power—which was also conferred on the President of the Confederate States—to veto single items in appropriation bills. This power has often been recommended for the President of the United States. Some fear, however, that the existence of the power would lead to some breakdown of Congressional caution and passing the buck to the President; others argue that it would provide a check against excessive expenditures, protection against Congressional encroachment on administration, and restoration of the President's veto power. Perhaps the decisive consideration has been political jealousy within the legislative branch. The members of Congress do not favor a step that would remove a (to them) useful leverage with the President, that would shift decision-making power from the Capitol to the

---

[13] Wildavsky, op. cit., pp. 47–48.
[14] George B. Galloway, *Congressional Reorganization Revisited* (College Park, Md., 1956), pp. 15 ff.

White House. The appropriations rider (an often extraneous addendum to an appropriations bill, used to get something that the Congressional sponsors know the President would veto if he could) is a time-honored, if otherwise deplored, device.

One rider that has been described in detail [15] provided that certain local military installations producing goods that could be purchased from private firms (a Navy Department rope factory in Boston that produced cables and hawsers was the particular focal point of controversy) could not be closed by the President—as part of an Eisenhower Administration drive to diminish governmental competition with private enterprise—without the specific permission of the Appropriations Committees. Perhaps the most famous rider of recent years was that by which Congress tried to force the ouster of three officials by citing their names and specifying that none of the funds in the bill should be used to pay their salaries. The Supreme Court voided this one as a bill of attainder.[16]

Other problems arise out of the time factors in the appropriation process. The process of planning must begin so early that many changes in conditions affecting needs for funds cannot be anticipated. One result is that supplementary estimates are sometimes sent in after the original requests have already been considered; another and more serious effect is that public programs may be impaired by a kind of straitjacket from the appropriation process. Also, the limit of annual appropriations, once regarded as so important a protection of the liberty of the citizen, may now prevent long-range planning. The Defense Department, for example, in breaking down estimates year by year, spends much time which might more efficiently be spent in long-range projections; and the Department of State finds itself limited in its arrangements with foreign countries by the inability to commit funds for longer than a year. Finally, Congress does not always pass the appropriation bills before the beginning of the fiscal year. This delay creates the necessity for special authorizations for short periods, usually for continuation of the same rate of expenditure. Such special authorizations do not, however, prevent losses in efficiency as agencies mark time and delay forward planning and commitments pending passage of the annual appropriation bills.

THE BUDGET PROCESS: EXECUTION AND AUDITING

It is commonly said that the budget cycle consists of four parts: preparation of a budget, usually an executive responsibility; appropriation of funds, always a legislative responsibility; execution of the budget, an executive process; and final accounting of expenditures, done by an auditor independent of executive authority.

Execution involves the expenditure of the money and the controls exercised thereover. A central problem is the amount of flexibility allowable to an agency in the execution. One form of appropriation is the "line-item," in which each item of expenditure is set down separately in the appropriation

---

[15] See Edith T. Carper, *The Defense Appropriations Rider* (University, Ala., 1960).
[16] *Lovett* v. *U.S.*, 328 U.S. 303 (1946).

act. This may be carried so far that each position to be occupied by a person is listed and the salary prescribed for that position. The opposite form is the "lump-sum" appropriation, in which the appropriation is made to the agency in a single sum or lumped in large categories of expenditure. A line-item appropriation has disadvantages: It allows legislative meddling in administrative detail and inhibits any flexibility in expenditures over the fiscal year. On the other hand, legislatures may be reluctant to go the whole way to a single lump-sum appropriation. They are likely to combine specific designation of many projects and amounts authorized therefor, lump-sum appropriations for defined categories of expenditure, and specific limitations on expenditures for stated purposes such as travel, publications, and administrative expense.

Sometimes legislatures provide for centralized executive controls over budget execution. One method is control over transfers. In Great Britain appropriations are made in items, which are in effect categories of expenditure; and transfers may be made from item to item with the consent of the Treasury. Allowance of transfers, with or without central approval, is uncommon in this country. Another method is to place emergency funds at the disposal of the chief executive. This has often been done in American states and the President is now customarily given blocks of money to be used for stated types of emergencies. Occasionally there has been grant of authority to chief executives to approve or disapprove specific types of expenditures.

The primary method of centralized control used by the United States Government is apportionment of funds. Apportionment means that maximum limits are fixed on the amount of money to be expended by an agency in each period (month or quarter) of the year. This is for the purpose of insuring that, except for unusual contingencies which justify a request for a supplementary appropriation before the year is over, the money appropriated will last through the fiscal period. The Bureau of the Budget has authority over apportionments, and in practice this means that agencies are required by it to divide the money appropriated into quarterly segments.

Money is appropriated to administering agencies. These are subject to legal and administrative requirements, of which those in the national government are typical. Accounts must be maintained as prescribed in a Joint Accounting Program developed cooperatively by the Comptroller General (the auditor), the Treasury, and the Bureau of the Budget. Within each agency allotments are made to component units, and these allotments determine the limits of their expenditures. Funds are set aside for the account of the agency on the books of the Treasury, and when an appropriate official in an agency certifies the legality of the expenditure to the chief disbursing officer of the Treasury checks are written for payment from the Treasury and debited to the agency accounts.

The effect of these and the auditing arrangements is to create a system of checks on funds disposal. A financial official in the agency certifies the legality of the expenditure, this is verified by a disbursing officer in the Department of the Treasury, the check is written in the office of the Treasurer, and finally an audit is made by the auditor.

In the national government the auditor is called the Comptroller General.[17] He heads the General Accounting Office and is conceived to be the agent of Congress. He is appointed by the President with the advice and consent of the Senate for a fifteen-year term and is removable only by a joint resolution of the houses of Congress.

Sources for Government Dollars

Most of the revenue of government comes from taxes, although the Post Office, public power projects, and many other activities of government are financed in whole or in part, indeed occasionally with a surplus, by the sale to the public of goods and services. Licenses and other activities may be financed by fees charged recipients, but the total of all these nontax revenues is relatively small.

Taxes arouse deep emotions, conflicting opinions, and much politics. Some persons accept taxes fatalistically, recognizing that part of the expenditure is for sheer survival and believing perhaps, as Justice Holmes did, that when one pays taxes he "buys civilization." A few may even have concluded that the proportion of the income of society which taxes can, and do, divert to public purposes is an index of the advance of its culture, provided the diversions are used for beneficent purposes. On the other hand, many people regard taxes as an onerous, even unjust, personal deprivation or as an encumbrance on the private economy. They believe that government should limit its services in order to reduce or prevent further advances in taxes, and they may believe that government is wasteful in its use of taxes.

In addition to these differences of opinion over services and taxes, there are profound conflicts over the apportionment of taxes among the different groups in the population. Some people believe strongly in the principle of taxation according to ability to pay, while others believe that costs should be distributed more in accordance with benefits received. With respect to this conflict of opinion, taxes may be classified in three categories: proportional taxes, where the rate remains constant as the base on which the tax is levied increases; progressive taxes, where the rate rises as the base increases; and regressive taxes, where the rate decreases as the base increases. The differences in point of view about whether taxes should be proportional, progressive, or regressive are paralleled by differences on the economic effect of taxes. Some stress the fact that high taxes on low-bracket income earners reduce their purchasing power and argue that this restricts the expansion of production and sales for a mass market. Others emphasize the effect of high taxes on high-bracket incomes in reducing savings and reason that this prevents the investment necessary for an expanding economy.

The philosophical positions will usually reflect differences of interest among those who argue on the plane of theory. Those who have much and those who have little will divide in their attitudes toward parties, candi-

---

[17] The authoritative discussion of the development of this office is Harvey C. Mansfield's *The Comptroller General: A Study in the Law and Practice of Financial Administration* (New Haven, 1939); see also Mansfield's later chapter in Fritz Morstein Marx, ed., *Elements of Public Administration*, 2nd ed. (Englewood Cliffs, N.J., 1959), Chapter 25.

dates, public policy, and government itself. Thus, in the states there are recurring, and often bitter, battles over whether to raise money by sales taxes, which have a regressive effect, or by income taxes, which usually have a progressive effect. Thus, also, in the Congress, every tax bill brings some conflict between those who want to get the money from those with good incomes and those who want to avoid this by "broadening the tax base."

The decision makers in government find therefore that getting the money is a thankless, difficult, but necessary endeavor. Unavoidably, their judgments will be influenced by a variety of considerations, one of which is fairness. As already noted, one standard is taxation according to benefit received. This standard is sometimes followed, as when a special district is created to supply water to users and the charge is made on the basis of the amount of water used. But normally today there is some redistribution of income in the taxing and spending policies of government. Some people pay more, others less, than the cost of their benefits, indicating a tendency toward taxation according to ability to pay. As we have noted, some will believe that there is moral or economic justification for placing the burden of government costs on the financially well off; others may not consider it to be fair or economic but accept it because of sheer necessity. A second consideration is adequacy of government revenues. Government must be supported, and one test of a good tax is whether it will produce the needed money without producing intolerable burdens on particular groups of persons. More and more the three levels of government, taken together, are reaching for all the available sources of revenue that can be tapped without undue hardship. A third factor is whether the tax can be efficiently administered. The costs of collection and the opportunities for evasion or unequal treatment become tests of the appropriateness of a tax. A final consideration is the effect of a tax on the economy. Decision makers at local and state levels may be especially interested in avoiding taxes which deter location of industry in their areas. Those at the national level may be interested in whether the tax contains a built-in flexibility so that it bears less heavily on persons and industry in recessions and raises more money in prosperous times, thus having the effect of softening recession and checking inflation. At the national level the test of adequacy, strongly dominant in governments generally, may yield to considerations of economic effect, and lead perhaps to deficit financing.

Trends in Taxation

The necessities of government, conflicts of interest, and different views of public policy have yielded variety in the tax patterns of governments. Nevertheless, certain trends are discernible. Local governments have depended largely on the property tax. In 1962 cities obtained 73.3 percent of their tax revenue from this tax, only 17 percent coming from sales and gross receipts taxes, and 9.7 percent from license fees and miscellaneous taxes. School districts and counties have obtained even more of their tax revenues from the property tax, for they have had less opportunity than cities to use other forms of taxes.

Until recent decades, state governments also relied mainly on the property tax. They faced a special problem in use of the tax: under the system of local assessment, the rates of assessment differed in various parts of a state and this produced much geographical inequality among taxpayers. Some states have tried to solve this problem by creating state boards for territorial equalization or by providing for state assessment of some types of property. The larger trend, however, has been toward release of the property tax to local jurisdictions. The chief tax sources for the states are now general and selective sales taxes and gross receipts taxes. General sales and gross receipts taxes yielded nearly one fourth of state taxes in 1963, even though the taxes were used in only thirty-seven states. Selective sales taxes on such things as tobacco, alcoholic beverages, and motor fuel raised the yield of sales and gross receipts taxes to nearly three fifths of all state taxes. States also levy individual income taxes and corporate income taxes, thirty-three having the former and thirty-eight the latter in 1964.[18] Finally, motor vehicle licenses are a major source of revenue, and natural resources taxes, and death and gift taxes, add to the list.

The tax sources of the national government have been affected by constitutional provisions. The Constitution placed some significant limitations on the taxing power of the national government. First, it cannot tax exports. Second, indirect taxes, that is, duties, imposts, and excises, must be geographically uniform. This does not mean that different rates cannot be set on different articles. Also, the Supreme Court has held that it is constitutional to allow reduced federal estate-tax rates in states that levy such taxes.[19] Third, direct taxes must be apportioned among the states according to their population. Poll taxes and land taxes have been held to be direct taxes. A land tax apportioned according to population would be inequitable, even absurd; and hence the property tax is eliminated as a source of national revenue. The Supreme Court in 1895 held that an income-tax law which included levies on income from property was a direct tax,[20] and this eliminated this tax source until the passage of the Sixteenth Amendment. Fourth, there is a judicial rule that the national government cannot lay taxes on state functions in such a way as to impair state sovereignty. The precise line of limitation is a technical one. Finally, in 1936 the Supreme Court declared that a tax must be for national rather than local welfare,[21] but this limitation has not since 1936 resulted in any tax being held unconstitutional.

The Constitution opened the way for levy of import duties, and until the adoption of the Sixteenth Amendment in 1913 customs duties were the chief regular source of national revenue. The adoption of the Sixteenth Amendment was a watershed in national financing, for the income tax is now the largest revenue producer. In the federal budget for 1965 it was estimated that the budget dollar would come from: individual income

---

[18] Council of State Governments, *The Book of the States, 1964–1965* (Chicago, 1964), pp. 235–36.
[19] *Florida* v. *Mellon*, 273 U.S. 12 (1927).
[20] *Pollock* v. *Farmers' Loan & Trust Co.*, 157 U.S. 429 (1895).
[21] *United States* v. *Butler*, 297 U.S. 1 (1936).

Source	Millions of dollars	Percentage of total general revenue
Total [2]	40,483	
Total general revenue	35,899	
Intergovernmental revenue	10,904	30.4
From federal government	719	2.0
From states	10,185	28.4
Revenue from own sources	29,579	
General revenue from own sources	24,995	69.7
Taxes	19,804	55.2
Property	17,370	48.4
Individual income	258	.72
Corporate income [3]		
Sales, gross receipts	1,432	4.0
Motor vehicle and operators' licenses	113	.31
All other	631	1.76
Charges, miscellaneous general revenue	5,192	14.5
Utility	3,856 [4]	
Liquor store revenue	141	.42
Insurance trust revenue	587	1.63

[1] Duplicative transactions between levels of government were excluded in arriving at aggregates.
[2] Includes general revenue and utility, liquor store, and insurance trust revenues.
[3] Minor amount included in individual income tax figure.
[4] Utility expenditures (including capital outlay) exceeded utility revenues (total expenditure for utilities was 4,531).

SOURCE: Percentages are derived from United States Department of Commerce, Bureau of the Census, *Governmental Finances in the United States, 1961* (Washington, 1962), p. 20.

taxes—40 cents, corporation income taxes—21 cents, excise taxes—12 cents, employment taxes—14 cents, all others (estate, gift, customs duties, etc.)— 11 cents, and borrowing—2 cents.

Intergovernmental Finance

The largest trend in the financing of governments is the shift of costs from local to state and from state to national jurisdictions. In part this is the result of the politics of groups which find it easier to obtain their ends through an act of a single government that will then force other governments to cooperate to supply a desired level of service. In part it comes from the relative disadvantages of local and state governments in comparison with the national government as taxing jurisdictions.

Many local governments find the property tax to be an overly lean source of revenue. Owners of tangible personal property (i.e., furniture, automobiles, office equipment, and all other tangible property except real estate) generally escape the tax through failure to assess their property; the same

TABLE 23–3 / State Revenue, by Source (United States), 1961

Source	Millions of dollars	Percentage of total general revenue
Total [1]	34,603	
Total general revenue	28,693	
Intergovernmental revenue	6,782	23.6
From federal government	6,412	22.3
From local government	370	1.3
Revenue from own sources	27,821	
General revenue from own sources	21,911	76.4
Taxes	19,057	66.4
Property	631	2.2
Individual income	2,355	8.2
Corporate income	1,266	4.4
Sales, gross receipts	11,031	38.4
Motor vehicle and operators' licenses	1,641	5.7
Death and gift	501	1.7
All other	1,632	5.7
Charges and miscellaneous general revenue	2,854	9.9
Liquor store revenue	1,119	3.9
Insurance trust revenue	4,791	16.7

[1] Includes liquor store and insurance trust revenues.

SOURCE: Percentages are derived from United States Department of Commerce, Bureau of the Census, *Governmental Finances in the United States, 1961* (Washington, 1962), p. 20.

is true of holders of intangible property (stocks, bonds, and other securities) where the tax is a general property tax, i.e., at the same rate on all types of property, as it most generally is. The result is that the tax yield is largely limited to what can be imposed on real property and on business inventories. Yet there is resistance to increasing the rate from those who hold these kinds of property—the real estate interests, home owners, and business enterprises with real property and large inventories.

The problems of local governments are further aggravated by limitations—in constitutions, statutes, or charters—on the amount of the tax. Limitations on the maximum percentage of the levy are customary, and often, also, on the purposes for which the taxes are to be used.

The problems of local finance are not serious in many suburban areas with high property values and low population density. They are especially serious in central cities in metropolitan areas where population density is great, poverty is extensive, and the costs of city services are high. The divergences between population density and governmental costs, on the one hand, and property values, on the other, among the cities in a metropolitan cluster create great diversities in ability to finance government through the property tax.

How can local governments meet the problems presented? First, they may seek improvement in the administration of the property tax, try to obtain relief from legal limitations, and urge state and federal governments owning property within their borders to make payments in lieu of taxes. In all of these endeavors, however, they may face hard, perhaps insuperable, obstacles. Second, they may look for other local revenue sources. Yet the fear of driving businesses or residents from the city limits the effort to raise money by sales or income taxes. Third, they may support moves for special districts for particular purposes as a means of escaping from tax limitations, taking the evils as well as the advantages of such action. Fourth, they may try to get the state or the national government to assume certain types of expenditure, such as buying right-of-way for highways, or to take over some functions, as in health and welfare. Finally—and this is the main method through which the problems of local finance are being met—they may obtain revenues from the state and federal governments. In 1962, 30.4 percent of the general revenue of local governments came from state and national governments, primarily the state government, as compared with 6.5 percent in 1902. (See Table 23–4.)

The states also have faced new problems in financing government. They have been more successful than local government in finding productive new taxes. Yet the same demands for new and improved services which place strains on the localities impose burdens on the states. In 1962 the payments of the states to local governments totaled $10.9 billion and took more than one dollar out of three from state budgets. This even does not include all the means of state assistance, as for example, the assumption by the state

TABLE 23–4 / Intergovernmental Revenue of Local Governments in the United States for Selected Years from 1902 to 1962

Year	From federal government	From state government	Percentage of total general revenue
	(millions of dollars)	(millions of dollars)	
1962	750	10,929	30.4
1957	343	7,196	29.7
1950	211	4,217	31.6
1942	56	1,780	25.8
1936	229	1,417	26.6
1934	83	1,318	24.1
1932	10	801	14.2
1902	4	52	6.5

SOURCE: Percentages for 1902–57 were derived from data taken from United States Department of Commerce, Bureau of the Census and Social Science Research Council, *Historical Statistics of the United States, Colonial Times to 1957* (Washington, 1960), p. 729. Percentages for 1961 were derived from data taken from United States Department of Commerce, Bureau of the Census, *Governmental Finances in the United States, 1962* (Washington, 1963), p. 20.

of North Carolina of direct maintenance of a nine-month school system, or the allowance of retention by localities of a portion of state-imposed but locally collected taxes. Meanwhile, the states were expanding expenditures for the services rendered directly by them. Also, state debt, like local debt, was increasing. Between 1954 and 1963 state and local debt more than doubled, from $38.9 billion to $86.4 billion—at a time when the national debt (so much discussed) increased only 13 percent and actually declined on a per capita basis. Finally, it should be noted that there are great differences in the average per capita income in the states, creating substantial differences in the capacity to support public services.

The financial problem of the states, like that of the localities, has been met in part by intergovernmental revenue. In 1962 the national government gave $7.8 billion in grants-in-aid to state and local (mainly state) governments, and the amount given the states was approximately one fourth of their budgets.

The grant-in-aid—bringing to the state one fourth of its budget and taking from it one third of its funds—has been the most significant development in the twentieth century in the reallocation of costs of services among the three levels of government. It has been said that "the grant has become a fully matured device of cooperative government." [22] It results in a sharing of costs for specific services between two levels of governments or even among three, for much of the grant-in-aid money received by the states from the national government is passed on to localities. The grants are customarily made for specific programs and usually with some conditions as to the use of the money.

The biggest problem in the use of this method of cooperative government is the determination of the formula for distribution. Sometimes the grantor government merely offers to pay a stated percentage of the number of dollars expended on a service. National grants initially were frequently on a 50 percent basis. More generally now the grant is made on some more specific test of need, for example, for highways the miles of road actually constructed, or for education the school-age population or number of children enrolled. In some cases, an equalization element is included in the formula for distribution; that is, more money is given to financially poor areas than to richer ones. Just the opposite effect may be produced by provisions for a minimum amount to each area. Obviously, there will be conflicts of interests over these matters: between poor states and rich states, and between those individuals who place great emphasis on a minimum standard of service for the nation as a whole and those who desire equal opportunity to improve existing services.

National Revenue Problems

The national government has had two advantages in financing its functions in this century. First, it has been able to resort to deficit financing.

---

[22] Commission on Intergovernmental Relations, *Report to the President for Transmittal to the Congress* (Washington, 1955), p. 120.

From 1940 to 1945 the national debt was increased by approximately $216 billion. It was less than $17 billion in 1929 and is expected to be $317 billion in 1965. The burden of such a debt on the people and the economy may be reduced by increase in national income—by increased production, by inflation, or both. In fact, the percentage of the government's debt to national income decreased from 143 in 1945 to 106 in 1950, 83 in 1955, and 65 in 1963. Obviously, this source of revenue can be large if national income expands. Obviously, also, deficit financing carries the danger of inflation and the attitudes of the people on this danger will affect the extent of its use.

The other advantage is the availability of the individual and corporate income tax—the result of the Sixteenth Amendment. Yet two aspects of this revenue source are noteworthy. One is the erosion of the tax through a mass of special provisions. The purchase of retirement annuities for employees or officers of corporations and other organizations defers payment of tax until annuities are paid, at which time the tax rate on the individual receiving the annuity is expected to be lower than when the money is set aside. Capital gains are taxed at lower rates than other forms of income, providing an escape valve for persons with large incomes. Business expense deductions provide other opportunities for evasion of tax. A depletion allowance allows oil companies and individuals a total exemption from tax on the first 27.5 percent of gross income, or on half of the net profit, whichever is less, from oil production; lesser exemptions are allowed to producers of certain other natural resource products. These examples illustrate the complexity of the income-tax laws and the many special interests which are built into the law.

Because some types of income are taxed at lower rates than others (the maximum on long-term capital gains is 25 percent) and some are not taxed at all (interest received from municipal bonds), one may have a very substantial income, yet pay little or no tax. The author of a recent book on the tax system tells us that in 1959 seventeen Americans had incomes of $1 million or more, yet had to pay no federal income tax. One man earned $20 million, yet owed no tax.[23]

The 1964 tax legislation reduced the maximum formal rate from 91 percent to 70 percent. In fact, however, probably no one will pay even the new, lower maximum, for those with very high incomes are most often able to use capital gains and other legal means of reducing taxable income.

An additional factor which affects the yield of the tax is the condition of the economy itself. As recession sets in, the tax yield declines; as recovery ensues, the yield grows. For this instability of the revenue yield there is a compensating advantage. The tax is a built-in stabilizer of the economy. The economy is less weighted with taxes when recovery is needed and most weighted when inflation is threatened. This automatic effect may be accentuated by positive decisions of government, as when taxes were reduced in 1964 to stimulate economic growth.

At the national level of government the tax system—both the types of taxes and the level of taxes—is, like the budget, thought of today as a tool

---

[23] Philip M. Stern, *The Great Treasury Raid* (New York, 1964), p. 4.

Fischetti in the New York *Herald Tribune*

"Now Get Out There And Spend!"

One consumer's reaction to the tax cut.

of general economic stabilization as well as a way of financing government. Its utility for counter-cyclical purposes, however, is diminished by its rigidity. Tax level changes were made by the Congress in 1964, and some economists argue that legislative delays brought the latest tax cut into being about a year later than when most needed for its stimulating effects.

In 1961, a high-level voluntary study group, the Commission on Money and Credit, advocated that the President should be granted discretionary authority to change the basic rate up or down, within a 5-point range, for limited periods of time to increase the flexibility of the income-tax system. If a recession threatened, for example, the rates could thus be quickly reduced to increase purchasing power as a stimulant. President Kennedy included this proposal in his 1962 Economic Report but did not push it when Congress showed antagonism. Once again, economic policy ran into separation-of-powers jealousies, and there is nothing about which the legislators are more zealous to maintain their prerogatives than the field of taxation. Legislators, of course, are conscious of the sensitivity of their constituents on issues of taxation. They know, also, that issues of taxation are mixed with the other issues they confront.

Although public finance in an academic institution generally resides in the department of economics, in the "real world" it is as much a subject of politics. He who wants extensive action programs by government will be more inclined to accept a higher level of taxation than the man who would like to see governmental activities (and therefore expenditures) reduced. It sometimes appears to happen that objections to one side of the coin are in truth aimed at the other side. For example, to say that a certain costly

Jack Be Nimble—Jack Be Quick

A conservative reaction to the tax cut proposal.

Hesse in the St. Louis *Globe-Democrat*

program is unnecessary may cloak an objection based primarily on implications for the tax level. And of course we would all like to have our cake while eating: reduce taxes but maintain expenditure on all worthy programs. Politics, as we have tried to show in these pages, unites the two sides of the coin: expenditures and taxation.

24 / America in the World: Defense and Foreign Policy

In a single generation we have witnessed a revolution in the priorities of government. Although our relations with other countries have always been important to the nation and of concern to our leaders, it is only in the mid-twentieth century that the problems of foreign affairs and defense have come to cast a shadow over all else. They dominate the headlines, preempt the attention of statesmen, consume two thirds of our annual federal budget, and affect significantly the course of domestic politics. Even the ancient fears of depression, of poverty, and of want in old age no longer cloud the future as does the fear of nuclear devastation. The United States Government must today respond to a host of problems presented by expansionist Communist totalitarianism and by the rise of the newly independent nonwhite nations. On the nature of these responses depends our physical survival, not to mention that of our free society.

It is difficult to date precisely the beginning of this ascendance of foreign affairs. The collapse of the European balance of power in the conflagration of 1914 destroyed forever the conditions which had allowed America to go its isolated way protected by great barrier oceans policed by the British Navy. During the 1920s and 1930s the advancing technology of war made it impossible for Americans to be sure they could remain untouched by any sizable conflict. The Second World War catapulted the United States into the position of leader of the free world, and permanent American involvement in world politics became the central fact of life of the postwar period. Since 1945 new conditions beyond the nation's control have driven it to greater and greater commitments around the globe. These far-flung responsibilities have brought awesome complexity in decision-making for defense and foreign affairs and are placing great strains on our democratic political institutions. The magnitude of these developments can only be appreciated against the backdrop of what had gone before.

Prelude to Power: Defense and Foreign Policy Before 1914

In order to make sense of the history of America's external affairs from 1789 to 1914, it is necessary to understand the difference between neutrality and isolation. Neutrality is a *policy* which is followed when a state is involved in a particular international situation. Isolation is simply the

Ch. Nelan

"The Concert Of Europe"

A cartoon of 1898 shows the nations of Europe wooing the isolated United States while Uncle Sam watches distrustfully.

condition or *circumstance* of not being involved. During the debates over American entry into the two World Wars these concepts were blurred and run together. Many people in the 1930s advocated neutrality as a policy which would somehow restore isolation, but it is clear that the two are not one and the same. Thus in the early years of our national existence our government chose a policy of neutrality in the power struggles of Europe precisely because the new United States was not isolated from the Continent and its politics. We developed a military policy, based on state militias, which was geared to the threatening European "presence" in the New World. The course enjoined by President George Washington in his Neutrality Proclamation ("pursue a conduct friendly and impartial towards the belligerents") was not dictated by the irrelevance of Europe's struggles to the new nation, but was rather a calculated plan to preserve American independence at a time when the Old World powers were still active in the Americas. Washington was telling his countrymen to trade with everyone and take sides with no one or the United States was likely to be crushed between superior conflicting forces. The policy of neutrality enjoyed remarkable success despite our being drawn into the War of 1812, and the existence of the young country was preserved.

Isolation, of course, was something devoutly desired by the statesmen of the formative period. Jefferson wished the United States "to stand with respect to Europe precisely on the footing of China." Within three decades the wish was granted and isolation was actually achieved. Europe's overseas influence progressively declined, and the Monroe Doctrine, enunciated in 1823, represents not so much a program as a simple announcement of the fact that the Continental power was no longer decisive in the New World. America had become, in De Tocqueville's phrase, "a nation without neighbors"; the policy of neutrality was no longer needed because of the condition of isolation. Yet there was more to the Monroe Doctrine than the pronouncement of Europe's exile from the hemisphere and America's lack of interest in Europe. The fledgling Republic was also confidently asserting the moral and political superiority of the New World to the Old. The decadent politics of Europe led to war, the Doctrine implied; the democratic system of the United States was seen naturally productive of peace. This sense of the superiority of the American polity to the old orders beyond the Atlantic was to color the whole conduct of our foreign relations during the nineteenth and early twentieth centuries, and in somewhat vulgarized form is very much alive today.

The Monroe Doctrine stated an American policy for Europe: ". . . in wars of European powers in matters relating to themselves we have never taken any part, nor does it comport with our policy so to do. We would be concerned only when our rights are invaded or seriously menaced." Our forefathers were encouraged in such aloof sentiments by a set of fortuitous circumstances which created its isolation: our oceans separated us from powerful nations; the British Navy maintained the freedom of the seas desired by America; and a Pax Britannica prevailed over the world. Not until the rise to power of a newly unified Germany was this Pax Britannica threatened, and by this time America was stepping out in the world. The United States was launched into the Spanish-American War and was declaring an Open Door policy for China. Toward the end of the nineteenth century, American interests were expanding at the same time that the hegemony of Great Britain was declining—the back of the old international system was about to be broken. America was to be "involved" once more.

The Latin-American policy of the nation was distinctly different. Again the United States' position was stated in the Monroe Doctrine. Though the rights of European powers with respect to existing colonies were recognized, the Doctrine stated the United States would consider any attempt of the European powers "to extend their system to any portion of this hemisphere as dangerous to our peace and safety." A serious challenge was presented to the policy in 1861 when Napoleon III sent armies into Mexico, but the threat dissolved when American troops were moved to the Rio Grande in 1865. At the turn of the century, Presidents Cleveland and Roosevelt stiffened the Doctrine by demanding in 1895 that Great Britain arbitrate a boundary dispute with Venezuela and in 1902 that Germany and other powers arbitrate monetary claims against Venezuela. Both demands were successful, and the threatened interventions of European powers in a Latin-American country were avoided.

At the same time that the United States was busy excluding Europe from Latin America, however, this nation was intervening there almost at will. Said Secretary of State Richard Olney in 1895:

Today the United States is practically sovereign on this continent, and its fiat is law upon the subjects to which it confines its interposition. Why? . . . It is because, in addition to all other grounds, its infinite resources combined with its isolated position render it master of the situation . . . .[1]

In 1902 we exploited a revolutionary situation in order to obtain the Panama Canal Zone. In 1904 President Roosevelt declared that "chronic wrong-doing" might, in Latin America, "require intervention by some civilized nation, and in the Western Hemisphere, the adherence of the United States to the Monroe Doctrine may force the United States however reluctantly, in flagrant cases of such wrongdoing or impotence, to the exercise of an international police power." Giant American concerns like the United Fruit Company came almost to own some Latin-American countries (hence the derisive term "Banana Republics"), and Americans came to manifest a proprietary feeling toward the territories and peoples to the south. "Speak softly," said the first Roosevelt, "but carry a big stick"; and an American-named receiver administered the financial affairs of the Dominican Republic under protection of the United States Navy. The United States in 1915 landed Marines in Haiti and assumed financial supervision and administrative control over Haitian affairs, and to protect United States citizens and property kept Marines in Nicaragua from 1911 to 1925. Such exercise of power led to Latin-American charges of American imperialism and fostered a smoldering resentment of the "Yankee," which has burst into flame in our own time. In the meantime there was developing a third element in American policy. This was the Pan-American movement, which had as its object the strengthening of economic, social, and political relations among Latin-American countries. As early as 1889 a first Pan-American conference was held, and in the fourth such conference in 1910 the Pan American Union, with headquarters in Washington, was established. After the First World War, and building upon the heritage of the Pan-American movement, the United States sought to alter its interventionist posture toward Latin America and embarked on a "Good Neighbor" policy. This policy was formally initiated in the Hoover Administration and carried forward enthusiastically by President Roosevelt and his first Secretary of State, Cordell Hull. At the Montevideo Conference of 1933 the United States and the Latin-American countries pledged nonintervention in each other's affairs, and in Buenos Aires in 1936 they agreed on the principle of consultation of all American countries in the event of a threat to the security of the hemisphere.

The most important problems of foreign relations for the United States during its first century were those that involved the expansion of its borders. It was the "Manifest Destiny" of America to grow. Expansionism was the inevitable "policy" of the nation. There were claims to Western lands, Indian wars, the purchase of the Louisiana Territory and of Florida, Northeastern boundary disputes, the annexation of Texas, the Mexican War, the Gadsden purchase, and for the Oregon Territory the slogan was "Fifty-four forty or

---

[1] Letter from Richard Olney to Thomas Bayard, July 20, 1895, *Foreign Relations, 1895,* Volume I, p. 558.

fight." Alaska was added by a diplomatic deal, Hawaii by a treaty of annexation, the Philippines and Puerto Rico by a war with Spain. Expansion was accomplished by diplomacy, migration of people, and the use of naked force. Military policy became a function of the drive to acquire and hold new real estate.

In the Northwest Ordinance of 1784 Congress announced the principle that territories should be ultimately admitted to the Union as states. This principle has been followed for all continental territory, including Alaska, and has been extended to Hawaii. Independence was given to Cuba and, much later, to the Philippines. Commonwealth status was eventually accorded to Puerto Rico. There were those who feared that acquisition of noncontiguous territory with different racial groups and a low level of economic development would lead to an American colonialism, and to a certain extent these fears were justified. The United States had to put down a revolt to keep the Philippines, and we kept them for almost half a century. Hawaii and Puerto Rico were maintained as unincorporated territories for what, in retrospect, seem embarrassingly long times. On the whole, however, the American record was good, and the subsequent development of Cuba and the Philippines suggests, perhaps, a rethinking of the relative merits of immediate independence as opposed to a transitional period of colonial administration.

As to economic relations with other nations, American policy showed the results of conflicting domestic interests. On the one hand, this was an exporting nation, particularly of grain and cotton. In the twentieth century it would also become a nation of investors, notably in Latin America. On the other hand, there was development of manufacturing and much agrarian discontent, leading to demands for protection of the home market for American industry. The demands of interests led to both promotive and restrictive policies. Supporting trade and investment meant supporting bold policies like freedom of the seas, opening of trade with Japan, the Open Door policy in China, and intervention in Latin America. Restrictive policies varied with the fluctuations of the tariff rates. From a moderately protective position in the beginning, the nation moved after 1812 to greater protectionism, then from 1833 into a period of declining protectionism, then after the middle of the nineteenth century into a forty-year period of peace on the tariff issue, then to revival of the contest: with higher protectionism after the Wilson Act of 1894, lower after the Underwood Act of 1913, higher after the Fordney-McCumber and Smoot-Hawley Acts of 1922 and 1930, respectively, and downward after the enactment of the Reciprocal Trade Act of 1934.

In summary, during the first century and a half of our independence, the American nation became committed to certain broad principles of international conduct. We asserted the rights of neutrals in war, and the concomitant freedom of the seas. We struggled against exclusive rights for any nation and for equal rights for the United States in areas (such as China and Japan) newly opened to commerce. Although we annexed certain developing Western lands and intervened repeatedly in Latin America, we supported the principle of nonintervention in internal affairs of nations and the right of self-determination of peoples (as long as they weren't Indians).

Until well into the twentieth century we offered a haven for the poor and dissatisfied from all nations. We advocated submitting disputes to arbitration, supported international law, and flirted with the idea of outlawing war. The nation thought that peace and order were normal conditions of international relations, that morality could govern in the affairs of nations, that military power was an evil to be avoided, and that America's duty to itself and its role in the world was merely to demonstrate the viability of domestic institutions built on freedom and democracy.

1914 to 1937: The End of Isolation and the Retreat from Involvement

The shots at Sarajevo signaled the collapse of an intricately balanced and organized world order, and rang up the curtain on what the French political scientist Raymond Aron has called "the century of total war." For the United States it was to be the century of total involvement, but one would never have guessed it from the detachment with which most Americans viewed the eruption across the Atlantic. German-Americans and ardent Anglophiles aside, most people were prepared to regard the war as the regrettable but inevitable consequence of political intrigue in the "European Cockpit." Had a public opinion sample been taken, it would certainly have shown dominant pro-Allied sentiment, but the overriding desire was to stay out. "I didn't raise my boy to be a soldier," sang American mothers.

It should be noted, however, that the United States was not quite as unprepared to play the game of big-power international politics by 1914 as it had been twenty years before. Through most of the nineteenth century (with the exception of the Civil War period) the Army had been pushing the Indians westward, rather than making itself useful as an instrument of foreign policy. The War Department had been badly organized, and there was no general staff system in effect for preparing plans and directing operations. The chiefs of the various branches of the Army reported directly to the Secretary of War. In like manner, the Navy had left much to be desired. It had been charged with responsibility for keeping open the shipping lanes—a job which the Royal Navy was doing anyway. The Department of State, below the Secretary, had been little more than a covey of clerks keeping track of America's ambassadors and consuls in the field. Beginning in the 1890s, under vigorous Secretaries like Richard Olney and John Hay, the State Department was expanded and improved. A foundation was laid for the creation—in 1924—of a career Foreign Service to represent the United States abroad. In the War Department, under Secretary Elihu Root, a general staff was set up in 1903, and unity of command was achieved under a single chief of staff to whom all other commanders reported. As for the Navy, it underwent a real renaissance in the last decade of the nineteenth century. With the publication in 1890 of Admiral Alfred Thayer Mahan's monumental study, *The Influence of Sea Power upon History, 1660–1783*, and the increasing commercial activity in the Western Pacific, there was a growing appreciation of the influence a nation could wield if possessed of an adequate fleet. The Caribbean had become an "American Lake," and leaders like Teddy Roosevelt hoped to make the same true of the Pacific. The Navy came to be looked upon as a continuing guarantor of isolation—it was the "first line" of the nation's defense. Although this newly refurbished sea force had a strong orientation toward the Pacific, it was a twentieth-century type of fighting machine which entitled America to a somewhat greater voice in the world at large.

In short, the *fin de siècle* interlude of commercial adventures in Asia and imperialistic adventures in the Caribbean occasioned some improvements in the instruments of American external policy. It did little, however, to prepare the nation intellectually for full involvement in world affairs. We faced the future with perfect faith in our moral superiority, our strategic invulnerability, and our power to do just about anything.

The President led the nation up the hill to international involvement and then watched it go down. As the pressures of the world situation mounted through 1915 and 1916, as the outrages of unrestricted submarine warfare multiplied, Woodrow Wilson spoke of a people "too proud to fight." When at last the President who had "kept us out of war" was forced by events to commit America to the struggle, he justified the move on millennial moral grounds—it was to be "a war to end all wars." America the Superior would gain the victory and lead the squabbling powers of Europe to a lasting peace based on a rejection of the old diplomacy and statecraft. "Open covenants, openly arrived at" would insure the rights of all peoples (however they were to be defined) to self-determination. The First World War was oversold to the nation, and as is inevitable with any oversell, there came a proportionately bitter disillusionment. Peace, many believed, was something concomitant with military victory. They did not understand that the continued application of American power was needed to stabilize the international environment. A wave of disillusionment helped to sweep the United States away from the League of Nations—and Wilson to his death. America had tested the burden of power and sought isolation once more. The machinery of warfare was disassembled, and political leaders promised that Johnny would never go away again.

But the world was not the same. The old international system from which America had benefited for so long simply could not be "put back together." There was no "normalcy," as the tortured Wilson's successor put it, nor was there any hiding behind the fleet. The scientific revolution which had made the Great War so devastating was accelerating, not slowing down. The Italian strategist Douhet was developing a theory of how to fight a war from the air, and American Army Colonel Billy Mitchell was busy proving its workability on capital ships from the Navy's mothball fleet. The country managed to ignore all this, however, and the standard historical interpretation of the 1920s and 1930s as an inward-looking period is certainly correct. The nation was preoccupied with domestic crises, and our government responded to crises abroad first with treaties renouncing force (the Kellogg-Briand Pact of 1927), and then with Neutrality Acts (in 1935, 1936, and 1937). But while neutrality had been a rational and successful policy for the new and weak America (as it seems to be for new and weak nations today), it was neither rational nor successful for the economically mature America of the late thirties. The United States was a great power in fact; it had behaved like one in 1917. With the threat of expansionist regimes in both Europe and the Far East, it had, sooner or later, to begin acting like one again.

All this was quite apparent to Franklin Roosevelt as his attention shifted from domestic to foreign concerns after 1937. It would be his job to lead the nation up the hill, and to make sure that this time there would be no going down.

The Second World War and the Acceptance of Free World Leadership

In October of 1937, the President delivered a speech in Chicago in which he declared:

> It seems unfortunately true that the epidemic of world lawlessness is spreading. When an epidemic of physical disease starts to spread, the community approves and joins in a quarantine of the patients in order to protect the health of the community against the spread of the disease.

The public and press reaction to this "Quarantine Speech" was so negative that Roosevelt was forced to proceed with great caution in preparing America, morally and physically, to engage Germany and Japan. Even the fall of France before Hitler's *Blitzkrieg* in the spring of 1940 did not bring domestic opinion around to accepting the necessity of involvement. Roosevelt, not an insensitive judge of the country's thinking, felt impelled to declare in a campaign speech in Boston in October of 1940, "I shall say it again and again and again. Your boys are not going to be sent into any foreign wars." Great Britain was to be shored up by "all aid short of war." Congress did accept the nation's first peacetime draft in 1940, and after three months of agonizing politicking, the Lend-Lease program was approved in early 1941. Under this arrangement a steady stream of sustaining war materiel was pumped into England. Thanks only to the men of England's RAF's Fighter Command, which denied Goering's *Luftwaffe* control of the skies over the Channel during the summer and fall of 1940, this aid sufficed to avert complete disaster for the democracies.

The shock of Pearl Harbor altered everything overnight. Although there was much less tumult and shouting than when the troops sailed for France in 1917, there was the same sense of absolute commitment to a moral crusade—and the same naïve faith in military victory, the single all-demanding goal. "The American people in their righteous might will win through to absolute victory," said the President. Thus it was that the single test of any proposal, any program, any initiative, became "How will it bring unconditional surrender any faster?" This policy of putting purely military goals before all other considerations (called by H. Bradford Westerfield the policy of "total war and limited diplomacy") was perhaps supportive of morale, but it often resulted in gross distortion of the options among which our leaders chose. Nowhere was this clearer than in our relations with the Soviet Union. On many occasions the United States gave way to Stalin for fear that to do otherwise would cause a reduction of Russia's war effort.

This concentration on victory at the price of larger political considerations did not, however, altogether retard official thinking about America's role in keeping the eventual peace. Roosevelt and his advisers were determined that Wilson's fate would not be theirs—that this time there would be no American withdrawal from responsibility. From the beginning the United States took a leading part in creating the United Nations. This signified its readiness to participate in world affairs, even as the rejection of the League of Nations had signified its desire to remain uncommitted. The change was later symbolized by United States representation at the United Nations for eight years (1953–61) by the grandson of Senator Henry Cabot Lodge, who had been so influential in defeating Wilson on the issue of membership in the League.

In the conduct of the war, America had the experience of 1917–18 to fall back on. Once before in the century we had organized for mobilization, allocated scarce resources, and sent Army divisions into battle in consort with European allies. The Army had been on something less than half rations during the twenties and thirties, but no budget cuts could alter the experience which the officers of the regular service had had in thinking in terms of joint global operations. The Navy had suffered lean years, but nonetheless was ready with a two-ocean capacity—even after the disaster to the Pacific Fleet. The rapid rise of the military to great influence in the councils of state was dramatized by the move of the service bureaucracies early in the war from cramped quarters in the old Munitions Building on Constitution Avenue to the gleaming and strange new Pentagon Building across the Potomac. The organizational machinery by which the war was administered reflected very much the style of the President. Although new agencies (Office of Defense Mobilization, Bureau of Economic Warfare, Office of Price Administration, etc.) sprang up overnight, the establishment around Roosevelt, where the great decisions were made, was characteristically casual. Roosevelt worked well with Army Chief of Staff George Marshall and with Admiral King, the Chief of Naval Operations. With them and a few handpicked personal advisers (such as Harry Hopkins, Admiral Leahy, Sumner Welles, and James Byrnes), the President felt he had all the immediate organization he needed to shape the policies of the Grand Alliance.

The war ended with victorious American forces spread across the globe, and the United States possessed, alone among the nations, a superweapon which added a whole terrifying new dimension to international conflict. America was also, without immediately realizing it, already face to face in Eurasia with an expansionist Communist system—and the policies pursued to bring the war to a quick close served us badly in our confrontation with this new, insufficiently appreciated, adversary. We failed, perhaps most importantly, to occupy as much of defeated Germany as possible, and the consequences of this failure haunt us today in the shape of the Communist German Democratic Republic. As one analyst has put it:

> The original decision not to do so [push on as far to the East in Europe as possible in order to increase our bargaining power with the Rus-

sians] was made with tragically little scrutiny on the part of top officials either in Britain or the United States. In Washington, the policymakers were even influenced by a positive desire to minimize American occupation responsibilities in Germany so that more troops could be moved to the Far East. Thus, the narrow military emphasis of United States policy, which hastened the Anglo-American conquest of Germany and thereby provided rich though unpremeditated political opportunities, also tended to dissipate those opportunities in advance by accelerating a technically efficient reconcentration of forces against Japan.[2]

The nation emerged from the struggle with a new orientation toward the world, in the sense that commitment to the continuing job of keeping the peace was new. But the country wanted the troops home and the rationing system abolished at a stroke, and that was an old story. The burden of involvement had been heavy from 1941 to 1945, and while Americans were resigned to the fact that they could not put it down as they had attempted to do after 1918, they did feel that it ought to get a lot lighter with the fall of Hitler and the Mikado. The reverse, however, proved true.

The Changing Conditions of Survival

Britain, France, and Italy were weakened, Russia was consolidating her gains in Eastern Europe, China was in a civil war, and desperate human needs existed around the globe. New roles in relief and world reconstruction were thrust upon a nation which less than a decade before was almost exclusively absorbed in its own domestic problems. Technological change had created new powers of destruction and was shrinking the globe. Atomic power and jet engines were part of the new language of a new age.

A revolution was under way in the underdeveloped areas of the world, a revolution with two dimensions. One was political: the movement for national independence. The sentiment of nationalism which stirred the European continent through the nineteenth century and the early part of the twentieth, and which animated the struggle for independence in Latin America in the nineteenth, had now burst into Africa and Asia. The postwar period has been one of liquidation of Western colonialism and rise of new nations. Peoples who only yesterday had been dependent colonials were clamoring for admission to the family of nations. The second dimension of the revolution was social. The peoples in the underdeveloped areas of the world, some of whom had been educated abroad and others of whom had seen evidences of Western wealth, were looking for a new life. They desired to move their countries swiftly into the twentieth century. Most of these peoples were interested in avoiding alignment in the struggle of big powers, for in the forefront of their thinking were their domestic objectives of independence and economic advancement. They were preparing their own "neutrality proclamations."

Finally, there was the Soviet Union and what was soon to become known

---

[2] H. Bradford Westerfield, *The Instruments of America's Foreign Policy* (New York, 1963), p. 91.

as the Cold War. In early 1946, speaking at Westminster College in Fulton, Missouri, Winston Churchill denounced the Soviet Union as an expansionist state, and declared to the American people:

> From Stettin in the Baltic to Trieste in the Adriatic, an iron curtain has descended across the Continent. Behind that line lie all the capitals of the ancient states of Central and Eastern Europe. Warsaw, Berlin, Prague, Vienna, Budapest, Belgrade, Bucharest, and Sofia, all the famous cities and the populations around them lie in the Soviet sphere and all are subject in one form or another, not only to Soviet influence but to a very high and increasing control from Moscow.

During the war years it had been the hope of American leaders that after the victory, the Soviet Union would conduct herself as a responsible member of the community of nations, and the very structure of the United Nations was conceived as dependent on "great-power unity." It was considered imperative that the two nations get along, and it was with great reluctance that our leaders came to ask whether the nature of the Soviet system made such normal relations simply impossible. Presidential adviser Harry Hopkins had said after the Big Three conference at Yalta:

> We really believed in our hearts that this was the dawn of the new day. . . . The Russians had proved that they could be reasonable and far-seeing, and there wasn't any doubt in the minds of the President or any of us that we could live with them and get along with them peacefully for as far into the future as any of us could imagine.[3]

These hopes died hard. And it took many months for the men who made American foreign policy to accept the hard reality of Russian aggression and intransigence. The United States was heading into another conflict—a frustrating and protracted conflict.

The difficulty which our policy-makers experienced in coming to terms with the Soviet threat was compounded by another difficulty which severely limited the capacity of the United States in the immediate postwar period to exercise its power effectively. Our armed forces had been powerful and widely deployed in the fall of 1945, but demobilization proceeded at such a rate that by the end of 1946 the great war machine was decimated. In the words of W. W. Rostow, now Chairman of the State Department's Policy Planning Council:

> By 1947 the Navy and Air Force were cut to about one-seventh of wartime peak strength, the Army to one-sixteenth. Over-all total military personnel were reduced by mid-1947 to 13 per cent of the mid-1945 peak. But figures alone do not adequately convey the impact of demobilization. Due to the discharge of key trained men, a lack of volunteers, and the need to maintain overhead establishments and noncombat units, the number of combat divisions at readiness was pitifully low. The Air Force reported in December 1946 only two and in June 1947 only 11 groups at combat effectiveness, out of the 52 groups provided as peacetime establishment. The Navy, perhaps less

---

[3] Robert E. Sherwood, *Roosevelt and Hopkins: An Intimate History* (New York, 1948), p. 870.

drastically affected than the other two services, was nevertheless stretched thin by a more rapid demobilization of personnel than of base units, which resulted in nominally active units being immobilized for lack of crews.[4]

We did, of course, enjoy a monopoly of the new atomic weapons, but our stock pile was very small, and their use would have exposed all of Western Europe to Soviet occupation, which we lacked the ground forces to prevent.

This, then, was the environment in which the United States had to act, and the limitations which operated on its action. For President Truman and his aides the problems of defense and keeping the peace had become problems of survival.

The Policy of Containment: Moments of Decision

On March 17, 1948, one month after the Communists seized control of Czechoslovakia, President Truman in a message to Congress identified the Soviet Union as the "one nation" blocking peace. In the years since that statement was made, the United States has painfully evolved a policy toward the Communist world which has come to be called "containment." We have pursued this policy with modifications and a few divergences down to the present. An influential ideologist of containment was the career diplomat George Kennan, who, under the *nom de plume* of "Mr. X," published an article in the July, 1947, issue of the influential periodical *Foreign Affairs*, entitled "The Sources of Soviet Conduct." Kennan wrote that "the main element in any United States policy toward the Soviet Union must be that of a long-term, patient but firm and vigilant containment of Russian expansive tendencies." As a policy attitude, containment, of course, antedated Kennan's writing by some months, and it was only given real substance later by the action of our government in certain testing situations in which we responded to crises involving the Soviet Union and ourselves.

The first of these was the decision to aid Greece and Turkey, accompanied by the announcement of the Truman Doctrine. On the afternoon of February 21, 1947, a representative of the British Embassy delivered at the Department of State two notes which reviewed the dire economic and military positions of Greece and Turkey and the inability of Britain to continue to support them even in the face of the threat of their falling under Russian control. At this moment Great Britain "handed the job of world leadership, with all its burdens and all its glory, to the United States." [5] America took it. On March 12, President Truman, addressing Congress, said, "I believe that we must assist free peoples to work out their own destiny in their own way." Congress responded, and the United States gave Greece and Turkey economic and financial aid and removed the immediate threat that the Russians might dominate the Mediterranean and through it the Middle East and Southern Europe.

A second decision was foretold in a speech by Secretary of State Marshall at Harvard's commencement exercises on June 5, 1947. He told of the im-

[4] W. W. Rostow, *The United States in the World Arena* (New York, 1960), p. 172.
[5] Joseph M. Jones, *The Fifteen Weeks* (New York, 1955), p. 7.

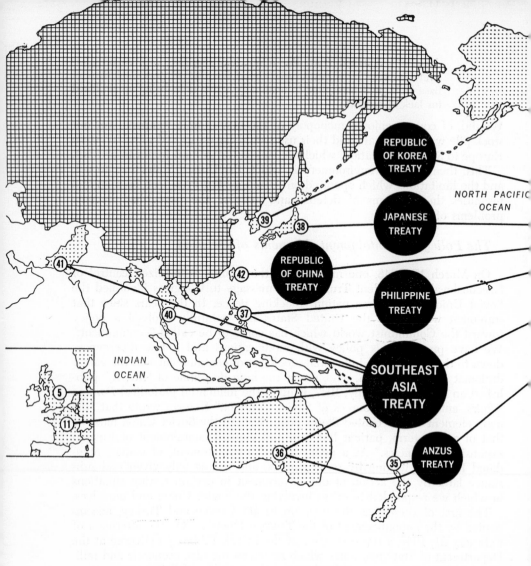

NORTH ATLANTIC TREATY (15 NATIONS) A treaty signed April 4, 1949, by which "the parties agree that an armed attack against one or more of them in Europe or North America shall be considered an attack against them all; and . . . each of them . . . will assist the . . . attacked by taking forthwith, individually and in concert with the other parties, such action as it deems necessary including the use of armed force . . . ."   **1 United States.   2 Canada.   3 Iceland.   4 Norway.   5 United Kingdom.   6 Netherlands.   7 Denmark.   8 Belgium.   9 Luxembourg.   10 Portugal.   11 France. 12 Italy.   13 Greece.   14 Turkey.   15 Federal Republic of Germany.**

RIO TREATY (21 NATIONS) A treaty signed September 2, 1947, which provides that an armed attack against any American State "shall be considered as an attack against all the American States and . . . each one . . . undertakes to assist in meeting the attack . . . ."   **1 United States. 16 Mexico.   17 Haiti.   18 Dominican Republic.   19 Honduras.   20 Guatemala.   21 El Salvador. 22 Nicaragua.   23 Costa Rica.   24 Panama.   25 Colombia.   26 Venezuela.   27 Ecuador.   28 Peru. 29 Brazil.   30 Bolivia.   31 Paraguay.   32 Chile.   33 Argentina.   34 Uruguay.**

ANZUS (Australia–New Zealand–United States) TREATY (3 NATIONS) A treaty signed September 1, 1951, whereby each of the parties "recognizes that an armed attack in the Pacific Area on any of the parties would be dangerous to its own peace and safety and declares that it would act to meet the common danger in accordance with its constitutional processes."   **1 United States.   35 New Zealand.   36 Australia.**

PHILIPPINE TREATY (BILATERAL) A treaty signed August 30, 1951, by which the parties recognize "that an armed attack in the Pacific Area on either of the parties would be dangerous to its own peace and safety" and each party agrees that it will act "to meet the common dangers in accordance with its constitutional processes."   **1 United States.   37 Philippines.**

FIGURE 24–1   /   United States Collective Defense Arrangements

NORTH ATLANTIC TREATY

RIO TREATY

Washington

NORTH ATLANTIC OCEAN

PACIFIC OCEAN

SOUTH ATLANTIC OCEAN

U.S. and countries with which it has mutual defense treaties

Communist bloc

JAPANESE TREATY (BILATERAL) A treaty signed January 19, 1960, whereby each party "recognizes that an armed attack against either party in the territories under the administration of Japan would be dangerous to its own peace and safety and declares that it would act to meet the common danger in accordance with its constitutional provisions and processes." The treaty replaced the security treaty signed September 8, 1951. **1 United States. 38 Japan.**

REPUBLIC OF KOREA (South Korea) TREATY (BILATERAL) A treaty signed October 1, 1953, whereby each party "recognizes that an armed attack in the Pacific Area on either of the parties . . . would be dangerous to its own peace and safety" and that each party "would act to meet the common danger in accordance with its constitutional processes." **1 United States. 39 Republic of Korea.**

SOUTHEAST ASIA TREATY (8 NATIONS) A treaty signed September 8, 1954, whereby each party "recognizes that aggression by means of armed attack in the treaty area against any of the parties . . . would endanger its own peace and safety" and each will "in that event act to meet the common danger in accordance with its constitutional processes." **1 United States. 5 United Kingdom. 11 France. 35 New Zealand. 36 Australia. 37 Philippines. 40 Thailand. 41 Pakistan.**

REPUBLIC OF CHINA (Formosa) TREATY (BILATERAL) A treaty signed December 2, 1954, whereby each of the parties "recognizes that an armed attack in the West Pacific Area directed against the territories of either of the parties would be dangerous to its own peace and safety," and that each "would act to meet the common danger in accordance with its constitutional processes." The territory of the Republic of China is defined as "Taiwan (Formosa) and the Pescadores." **1 United States. 42 Republic of China (Formosa).**

minent collapse of Western Europe unless aid came promptly and declared, "It is logical that the United States should do whatever it is able to assist in the return of normal economic health in the world, without which there can be no political stabilization or assured peace." This was the Marshall Plan. The announced enemy was "hunger, poverty, desperation, and chaos," and assistance by other nations was invited. Russia adamantly refused to participate. The multibillion-dollar economic aid given by the United States at this time restored the economies of Western Europe and in so doing removed the threat of Communist takeover.

After preliminary obstructions to Western commerce with Berlin, the Soviet Union on June 24, 1948, stopped all rail and road traffic between Western Europe and the western sector of Berlin. The United States broke this Berlin blockade by the Berlin airlift, the flying of food and other necessities to Berlin. Already on June 11 the Senate had passed the Vandenberg Resolution calling for American military support to regional alliances under Article 51 of the United Nations Charter, and on April 4, 1949, the treaty for the North Atlantic Treaty Organization (NATO) was signed. This was the first peacetime military alliance entered into by the United States since the eighteenth century, and its significance as a counter to Soviet expansion can hardly be overstressed. The member states agreed that an attack on one would be an attack on all and further agreed "to unite their efforts for collective defense and for the preservation of peace and security." In line with this commitment a complex organization has been established including, among other things, a joint command system. For the United States it is an alliance to which we have committed troops and bombs. America established a "forward" defense line in the West at the Elbe River.

NATo

Other decisions were to follow on foreign aid. On the one hand, a Mutual Defense Assistance Act in 1949 authorized the President to furnish "military assistance" to parties to the North Atlantic Alliance. Military aid was thus added to economic assistance. On the other hand, President Truman had earlier in the same year stressed a so-called Point Four Program (point four in his Inaugural Address) in which he called for technical aid to underdeveloped areas. The American program came to include military, economic, and technical assistance.

The test of containment came suddenly, on the Korean Peninsula, on June 24, 1950. The last American fighting forces had been withdrawn from this divided country almost a year before (the United States had only about 500 advisory personnel in Korea at the time of the attack), and the Republic of Korea must have looked to the Communist leaders like a plum ripe for plucking. Truman was faced with an awesome decision which he had to make alone and at once—there was no time to ask Congress, no time to let a popular consensus take shape, not even time to wait for United Nations action. As the Republic of Korea forces reeled back before the initial thrust of the invasion, the President of the United States committed our armed forces to the struggle. Within hours, American combat aircraft were flying operational missions in the Korean War. We fought this "nasty little war," along with our UN allies, until the truce was signed at Panmunjon on July 27, 1953. The struggle cost 23,300 American lives, and our UN allies lost 14,000. Critics of the Truman Administration argued that simply repulsing an invasion was too little a victory for so much blood. The debate still rages as to whether the fighting should have been carried into China (after the latter's intervention in the conflict), and Korean unification thus achieved. Looking back, however, it is possible to see three "results" of the war which affected the whole course of the Cold War.

First, the United States demonstrated that, in the face of naked Communist aggression, it was willing to put its troops and treasure on the line.

Second, the Korean War rearmed America. During the early years of the policy of containment, as we have noted, our military machine was sadly inadequate. We had lacked a defense policy geared to support our foreign policy. Under the lash of the Korean War, Congress appropriated the money to create a realistic defense establishment. The armed forces grew from 1.5 to 3.5 million men, and the annual defense budget grew from $12 billion to $41 billion.

Third, America had demonstrated to itself that it was capable of fighting a limited war. The calls for a crusade, for absolute victory, for unconditional surrender, for a holy war to the death were all heard. But these calls were not heeded to the exclusion of such pragmatic considerations as matching limited objectives with the limited applications of force. "The subordination of the military point of view to the political," the nineteenth-century strategist Karl von Clausewitz had stated, "is . . . the only thing that is rationally possible." Americans were learning this lesson.

The Truman Doctrine, the Marshall Plan, the breaking of the Berlin blockade, the establishment of NATO, and the fighting of the Korean War— these American responses to the changed conditions of survival gave bone and muscle to containment, and they are basic to an understanding of the contemporary debates over defense and foreign policy.

Continuing Problems of Defense and Foreign Policy

Although it is difficult to group all the diverse complexities of present-day external policy under any small number of headings, some such effort must be made if we are not to find ourselves intellectually paralyzed before the welter of problems. Involvement around the globe has thrown up certain distinct *clusters* of issues which our decision makers must face, and which we can seek to analyze.

THE SEARCH FOR THE "FLEXIBLE RESPONSE"

The Soviet Union possesses thermonuclear weapons and the capacity to deliver them. This is the great difference between 1950 and today. When America began to rearm during 1950 and 1951, it set about creating a military establishment which was to have *one* purpose—to contain the expansion of the Communist bloc. With the Soviet Air Force now in a position to devastate the continental United States, American military policy has developed two objectives: first, ensuring that the Soviet Union never finds that it is in its national interest to launch a nuclear attack against the United States; second, containing the expansion of the Communist bloc. To do these separate jobs a balance of nuclear and conventional forces is obviously necessary; the "great debates" over defense in the late fifties and early sixties have revolved around the proper nature of this balance and how much the country could afford to pay for it.

In 1953 a new national administration took power, committed to reduce the expenditures of the federal government. Although the American monopoly of nuclear striking power was fast becoming a thing of the past, it was determined that principal reliance could be placed on atomic weapons for halting Communist aggression. Ground troops are expensive to keep—putting the money into the Strategic Air Command would, it was suggested, give "more bang for the buck." If the Soviet leaders started trouble anywhere in the world, we would simply order them to desist or be subjected to "massive retaliation." The difficulty with this strategy was that the Soviet Union was becoming able to get considerable "rubble for the ruble." As Soviet strategic power grew, the "credibility" of massive retaliation began to be less persuasive. It was obvious that the United States would not use nuclear weapons against Moscow to punish a limited Soviet thrust (like the closing off of the autobahn to Berlin), when the Soviet Union was in a position to level American cities in return. An overnuclearized American military establishment was in danger of becoming musclebound.

Thus, in the later years of the Eisenhower Administration and the first years of the Kennedy Administration, there was a reexamination of our ability to wage war with conventional arms. It was the aim of the "Kennedy men" to put the United States in a position where it could respond to any situation with a *proportional* application of force. Thus the President would have some range of *options* in dealing with an aggression; he would not be limited to launching a nuclear attack or backing down. Since this buildup of conventional forces took place *in addition* to the perfecting of our nuclear arsenal (always our ultimate protection against Soviet "nuclear blackmail"), its cost was considerable. The Kennedy defense budgets ran approximately $10 billion per year over the amount the Eisenhower Administration had spent in its last year.

A further problem has recently arisen, one not easily solved by adding more dollars to the budget. This is the question of how to act effectively against irregular insurgent forces operating in the less developed parts of the world—the question of how to fight guerrilla warfare. The answer may seem simple at first glance. The streamlined American Army, backed up by the most efficient tactical air support, ought to be able to take care of ragtag bands living off the land and equipped only with small arms. Unfortunately it does not work that way. For one thing, the United States rarely finds itself in a position of fighting the battle directly; in most cases (as in South Vietnam) the fighting must be carried on by local forces—a whole new field manual must be written for conducting a war in which our participation is not stated to be more than "advisory." Secondly, Starfire jets and homing Sidewinder rockets are of precious little help in raising living standards in an Asian village or in persuading peasants that the established government is interested in their welfare. In short, a guerrilla war is won by effective political action at the grass roots—or not at all. The American military officer is busy learning a new role as leader of a civic action team.

In succeeding years we will see these issues and problems debated again and again in the search for a military policy and defense establishment responsive to rapidly changing political reality, in the search, that is, for the flexible response.

ARMS CONTROL AND DISARMAMENT

Disarmament has been under public discussion and been the subject of innumerable conferences since 1946. In 1961 the United States Arms Control and Disarmament Agency was created to deal with the problem. There are two kinds of pressures creating interest in the subject. First is the increasing cost of armament, which puts strain on the economy and diverts the resources of the nation from social welfare to military programs. Second is the concern that a nuclear war might be touched off by accident, and this concern is accompanied by recognition that such a danger will be enhanced as the "nuclear club" is enlarged to include France, China, and then other nations. Yet the problems are so difficult and national interests so deeply involved that agreement, even among the few powers now having nuclear weapons, has been difficult to achieve.

It has been said, "Much East-West 'negotiation' has been in fact diplomatic shadow-boxing, thoroughly overladen with propaganda." [6] There have also been periods of renewed hope, however, and the seriousness of the problem and the public interest in it have kept alive the discussions. The United States started in 1946 with the Baruch Plan, specifying United Nations ownership, management, and/or licensing of all atomic materials and facilities. In recent years the United States position has called for limited measures of "arms control" (as opposed to complete disarmament), coupled with an insistence on effective inspection. We have held that there can be no limitation of nuclear stock piles or cessation of production unless a system of inspection and control is agreed to beforehand which will prevent a complying nation from being duped by a noncomplying one. The Soviet Union has advocated broad programs of general and complete disarmament (extending to both conventional and nuclear armaments) but has been unwilling to agree in advance to inspection and control of the demilitarizing process. This difference in positions has brought most conferences to a stalemate and leaves mankind under the continuing threat of a nuclear holocaust. In the meantime citizens are perplexed and divided in their views, some fearing that disarmament will bring a depression or allow the nation to be tricked into lowering its defenses; others believing that disarmament is a high-priority objective but that only minimal "arms control" agreements are practical until the Russians become less obstinate. A small percentage believing in such radical steps as unilateral disarmament have been very vocal in urging immediate United States action to bring about disarmament.

The one step toward "breaking" the arms race was taken in a treaty signed by the United States, the Soviet Union, and a number of other na-

---

[6] Louis Henkin, ed., *Arms Control: Issues for the Public* (Englewood Cliffs, N.J., 1961), p. 19.

Big Fuss About A Drop In The Bucket

A pessimistic appraisal of the value of the test ban treaty. Other observers have been more hopeful.

Hesse in the St. Louis *Globe-Democrat*

tions—not including Communist China and France—in 1963. The treaty provides for cessation of above-ground testing of nuclear weapons, subject to the reservation that a nation may resume testing on notice to other parties to the treaty. The immediate effect of this limited test ban is to stop the pollution of the atmosphere and the resulting dangers of genetic damage to the world's population. The treaty may mark the beginning of real progress toward meaningful arms control.

FOREIGN AID

Assistance from strong to weak nations is a settled feature of twentieth-century international relations. The United States has rendered economic and military aid: through the Lend-Lease program, which supplied materials to England and Russia for the prosecution of the war against Germany; through a number of agencies which administered relief after the war; to Greece and Turkey, and then to Western Europe under the Marshall Plan; and through a series of postwar programs of assistance. Today the Soviet Union carries on a program of economic and military aid, and a competitive factor has been added to the granting of aid. The recipient nation can threaten one power by the suggestion that it might turn to the other. Western European nations in addition now participate in aiding less developed countries.

There have been many changes in the American aid program since the Second World War. The Marshall Plan provided for aid to rebuild previously developed economies. After 1949 there was an increased emphasis on military aid. Recently another shift has taken place. President Kennedy stressed the objective of stimulating economic development. There have been institutional and programmatic innovations, notably the Alliance for Progress, an emphasis on capital loans, and the establishment of the Peace Corps.

Our aid effort is continually under criticism and subject to Congressional scrutiny. The President has great difficulty each year in preventing drastic cuts in appropriations for the program. The doubts are directed at many real problems in the administration of aid. It is charged that there is waste (the famous roads that lead to nowhere), and undoubtedly there is a constant problem of fighting waste. It is alleged that often the money does not reach the people of a nation but is drained off by local bureaucracies and politicians, with accompanying corruption. There is indeed a problem of avoiding this without at the same time interfering too much with the affairs of the receiving countries. There is the implication (as in the novel *The Ugly American*) [7] that Americans abroad live in luxury and do not come to grips with the real problems of the people; yet it has been difficult to get Americans to go abroad without high compensation. There has been violent criticism of aid to Communist countries like Poland and Yugoslavia when the government has been seeking to help such countries toward independence from Soviet control or influence. There is restiveness about aid to neutral countries which often criticize the United States, but it is neither possible nor desirable to purchase full agreement with United States policies by allocations of money. There is difficulty in achieving economic development in countries having a large population growth, lack of capital resources, entrenchment of aristocracies, and absence of viable political institutions; yet the alternative to making an effort may be Communist takeover. One basic difficulty is the confusion of objectives. Many Americans have a genuine interest in helping other peoples to attain higher living standards and to achieve viable economic and political systems. Others, thinking of this as charity, argue that it should begin at home or should be no part of the business of government. Both of these groups often overlook considerations of political strategy in the choice of nations to receive aid and in the type of aid to be given them.

THE UNITED NATIONS

One of the continuing problems of United States foreign policy is participation in the United Nations. The United States was a chief sponsor of the United Nations and has given it support since its charter was signed in 1945. The United Nations is not a world government or a superstate. Its deliberations are conducted and votes are cast by delegates of states rather than by representatives of peoples. These delegates are in fact diplomatic representatives operating under instructions from their home governments. The United Nations depends for funds and military units upon the action of states.

The Charter provides for two main organs. The General Assembly represents the states equally, each being allowed as many as five delegates but only one vote. The Security Council is composed of eleven members, five of which—the United States, the Soviet Union, the United Kingdom, France,

---

[7] William J. Lederer and Eugene Burdick, *The Ugly American* (New York, 1958).

and Nationalist China—are permanent members and six of which are elected by the General Assembly for two-year terms. In the General Assembly passage of the most important matters requires a two-thirds vote, others a majority vote. In the Security Council procedural matters are decided by vote of seven members, other matters by vote of seven members including all of the permanent members. Thus any permanent member of the Council has a veto over any substantive decision.

The General Assembly is an organ of discussion and of loose supervision over the many parts of the United Nations system. The most important functions were delegated in the Charter to the Security Council. The Charter states as the first purpose of the United Nations "to maintain international peace and security" and, it confers "on the Security Council primary responsibility" for this important task. It may investigate disputes or situations leading to international friction and make recommendations to the parties on pacific settlement; it may call upon member states to interrupt economic relations, communications, or diplomatic relations with offenders; it may decide to use armed forces and call upon member states for contingents of these.

Although it has suffered many reverses, the United Nations in its operations has shown a flexibility somewhat comparable to that of the United States under its Constitution. Several major developments have occurred. First, the Council has deteriorated. The high hopes that some had for security in the world at the end of the Second World War rested on the expectation that the victors would form a concert of great powers. Instead of a concert there developed an open East-West conflict. The relative unanimity hoped for among the big five on the Security Council gave way to a succession of vetoes—the Soviet Union having used the veto for the hundredth time in June, 1962. As a result, the Council cannot function as an organ of peace and security on matters in dispute between the major powers. Second, the Assembly has grown in influence. Article 14 of the Charter gives it authority to "recommend measures for the peaceful adjustment of any situation." This gives the Assembly an anchor point, and it has done more than the Charter provision specifically authorized it to do. It decided in 1950, at the time of the Korean invasion, that when the Security Council was deadlocked or failed to act the Assembly could call upon states for collective measures; it brought into being a United Nations Emergency Force with contingents from ten states in the Suez dispute in 1956; and it supported the Secretary General in measures to restore peace in the Congo in 1961 and in Cyprus in 1964. It has, in addition, been a useful forum for the discussion of global issues, as was anticipated by the framers of the Charter. Third, as the Assembly has grown in strength and as new nations of Asia and Africa have become independent and been admitted to the United Nations, the influence of small nations has increased. The balance of power between large and small nations provided in the Charter is dependent upon the existence of a strong Council, and this has disappeared. With a strong Assembly and a weak Council small nations are in a commanding position. The Assembly has become, therefore, a forum for the airing of the views of neutrals in the Cold War and of the grievances and the hopes of the underdeveloped nations. Fourth, the three Secretaries General have demonstrated the possibilities for strong leadership at the top, and this leadership accounted in no small part for the effectiveness of the United Nations in a number of situations where peace was threatened. The Soviet Union, regarding itself as the loser in the Congo in 1961, sought to obtain a plural Secretariat, representing the neutrals and the two sides in the Cold War, but this attempt was defeated when U Thant of Burma was named to succeed Dag Hammarskjold. It remains to be seen whether the same forces which have destroyed the effectiveness of the Council will destroy the opportunities for leadership in the executive Secretariat. Fifth, despite its weaknesses the United Nations has found ways of responding to a number of treacherous situations. On the Israeli border, in Korea, in the Suez, in the Congo, and in Cyprus, and in some less spectacular situations it has responded effectively. Sixth, the auxiliary and affiliated units of the United Nations have had a vigorous life. The Economic and Social Council has made studies and recommendations and operated relief and rehabilitation programs. It has spawned a number of its own subsidiaries, which are active on a wide variety of fronts. The International Bank for Reconstruction and Development has made loans to members, and the United Nations has conducted a program of technical assistance. The United Nations Educational, Scientific and Cultural Organization has promoted cooperation among scholars and cultural groups and given new impulse to educational developments of many forms in the nations of the world.

The future holds large questions for the United States with respect to its relations to the United Nations. In 1964 there was a critical problem over the failure of Russia and France to pay their portion of U.N. costs. In addition, decisions of the world organization may, given the new influence of small nations, go against the United States more frequently. This will lead to new demands from groups within this country for us to restrict our participation. In any case, our policy-makers will be forced with difficult decisions as to what problems should and what problems should *not* be "taken to the United Nations."

FOREIGN TRADE

Trade policy involves the accommodation of foreign and domestic considerations. It is, on the one hand, a part of foreign policy by which friends are won or kept, enemies are penalized, and the substantive aims of America are achieved. It is, on the other hand, an instrument for promoting internal economic prosperity. In the postwar period the President, whether Democrat or Republican, has been more sensitive than Congress to the international effects of trade policy, while the Congress has been more sensitive to its effects upon sectional domestic interests. Until 1951 the Congressional division on trade policy was substantially a party division, with the Democrats favoring a liberal (low-tariff) trade policy and the Republicans opposing it. From 1951 onward there has been substantial defection from the party position by Democrats from Southern textile manufacturing areas, followed by other Democrats distressed over oil and coal imports. Similarly, Republican unity has been broken by belief in Midwestern and Eastern

"If You Like It, Spread The Word Around."

© 1964 by Bill Mauldin

Trade with Communist satellite countries has been considered one way of breaking down the Iron Curtain.

states that farm interests and mass production industries would be assisted by expansion of export markets. In the fifties these sectional interests formed bipartisan coalitions for and against liberalizing trade policy.[8]

After the war the United States participated in framing a charter for an International Trade Organization, but the President dropped the proposal after its unfavorable reception by Congress. In place of this, a more limited instrument called the General Agreement on Tariffs and Trade (GATT) was drafted. The United States has participated in GATT, though it has never been endorsed by Congress. It serves as a forum for negotiation among the nations of the world on tariff reduction.

The authority of the President to negotiate reductions has come to him through extensions of the Trade Agreements Act of 1934. Congress renewed the Act eight times between 1945 and 1958. On the occasion of each renewal opportunity was provided to amend the Act, and from 1948 the tendency was toward restriction of the power delegated to the President to reduce tariffs.[9]

Three phases in postwar trade policy may be noted. Following the war the United States adopted a liberal trade policy in order to assist in the restoration of Western Europe, the development of Japanese industry, and the economic growth of the underdeveloped nations. Gradually, however,

---

[8] See Joe R. Wilkinson, *Politics and Trade Policy* (Washington, 1960).
[9] For summary see William Siebold, Jr., "Trade Policies Since World War II," *Current History* (June, 1962), Vol. XLII, pp. 356–61.

the government moved into a policy of preventing competitive threats to American industries from "low-wage countries." Congress put restrictions on Presidential reduction of tariffs below "peril points" and enacted an "escape clause" through which reductions, once effected, could be withdrawn. Congress expanded "buy American" legislation, which required government agencies to give preference to domestic suppliers. Quota restrictions were imposed on imports of oil, textiles, and some agricultural products receiving price support at home. A third phase began with the Trade Expansion Act of 1962. This act gave the President larger tariff-cutting authority than had ever been granted by Congress to a President. He was also given authority to give "Trade Adjustment Assistance" to industry and labor injured by tariff reductions. Loans, loan guarantees, technical assistance, and special tax reductions could be made for industry, and retraining and relocation allowances and other benefits could be given to labor. Thus, a new means was found for combining "no serious injury" to domestic interests with liberal international trade policy.

In addition, the Act granted special authority for eliminating tariffs on categories of goods where the United States and the European Common Market countries [10] accounted for 80 percent of free-world trade. The significance of this provision was, of course, diminished by Britain's exclusion from the Common Market. Hope remains high, however, that the new trade policy can be made to serve the United States' international interest without damaging its domestic economy.

LATIN-AMERICAN RELATIONS

Since the Second World War the United States' relations with Latin America have been beset with difficulties. On the one hand, a relatively sophisticated machinery for protecting hemispheric security has been developed. On the other hand, there has been an erosion of the good feeling that had resulted from the Good Neighbor policy of the 1930s. At the "Rio Conference" of 1947 a treaty was signed through which regional security arrangements, which had been developing over the years, were perfected, and reconciled with Article 51 of the United Nations Charter (as was done later in NATO for Western Europe). At Bogotá the following year, the formal machinery for execution of the Rio Treaty was established—the Organization of American States. The Organization operates through three agencies: a conference intended to meet every five years, "meetings of consultation" whenever there is a threat to American security, and the Pan American Union, which serves as the secretariat and acts for the OAS pending meetings of consultation. Each member of the Organization is committed to cooperate in resisting threats to peace and security, and a two-thirds vote on methods of resistance binds all members except when the use of force is involved. This regional security system was successful in handling

---

[10] By the 1957 Treaty of Rome, France, West Germany, Italy, and the "Benelux" countries agreed to an arrangement for merging their national economies (over a period of time) into a single European economy. In its first year of operation this European Economic Community, or Common Market, proved successful. The United States economy will be increasingly taxed to compete with this new Europe. Only if we reduce tariffs on Europe's goods will we retain access to Europe's markets.

Fischetti in the New York *Herald Tribune*

"War On Poverty? Heavens, Didn't You Know I'm A Pacifist?!!!"

The success of the Alliance for Progress depends on internal reforms in Latin America.

a Nicaragua-Costa Rica dispute in 1955 but has experienced only partial success in dealing with the more serious threat of Castro's Cuba.

The deterioration of our Latin-American relations was spotlighted by a series of events in the late fifties, notably anti-American demonstrations during a good-will tour by Vice-President Nixon in 1958. There were many causes for Latin-American distrust, even resentment, of the United States. Among these was the feeling that the United States, in its economic aid programs, had been far less concerned about its Latin-American neighbors than about European and Asian nations. In its closing years the Eisenhower Administration initiated steps to make larger sums available for Latin-American development through international banking organizations. The Kennedy Administration initiated a sizable program of development aid called the Alliance for Progress. The concept of the Alliance is that American aid will be given for projects geared to economic and social reforms approved by both the United States and the recipient country. It is still too early to tell whether the Alliance will contribute materially to Latin-American economic development, whether effective programs of social reform will be undertaken, and whether this new effort of the United States can overcome the many tensions that plague our relations with the nations to our south.

Since the rise to power of a Communist regime in Cuba, the search for a viable policy toward Latin America has become a top concern of Washington planners. To the restive poor in many Latin countries "Fidelismo" appears the "wave of the future," new hope for improving their lot, and an outlet for their anguished resentment of the United States. We are paying a heavy price for the decades during which the United States was "practically sovereign" in the Western Hemisphere.

NATO AND THE NEW EUROPE

The North Atlantic Alliance was forged out of the fear that Soviet armies might overrun a Western Europe weakened by the war. As long as this fear was strong (as long as Europe was palpably unable to defend itself), it cemented the Alliance. SHAPE, with its American commanders (Eisenhower, Gruenther, Norstad, and Lemnitzer), and its American-controlled nuclear weapons, was staunchly supported by the chancelleries of the Continent. Two things have changed in the last several years. First, the likelihood of massive Soviet aggression has seemed to diminish, but second, and more importantly, European economic power has been reborn. Every casual newspaper reader is familiar with the vocabulary of European confidence— "Economic Miracle," "Third Force," "Common Market." Frenchmen, West Germans, and Italians are demanding more of a voice in determining the policy of the Alliance and are feeling less and less compulsion to integrate sizable portions of their armed forces into the NATO establishment. The French, proving particularly restive, have initiated a costly program of nuclear weapons development in an effort to achieve "independence" from the United States. More moderate European opinion asks, "If we must rely on the American 'deterrent' for our safety, shouldn't we have some say about the conditions of its use?" It seems inevitable that as time goes on control over certain types of nuclear arms will be shared by a number of strong nations of the free world. The Kennedy Administration responded to these new pressures with the suggestion of a "multilateral force" of nuclear-equipped surface ships, manned by mixed crews. The enthusiasm generated by this idea in Europe has been less than overwhelming.

The United States can expect division of interest and opinion among nations which have hitherto followed its leadership, and in a very direct way the new difficulties are a result of past foreign policy successes. The strains within the Alliance are a product of its having done its job, and the booming economies are a tribute to the wisdom behind the Marshall Plan.

THE CHANGING NATURE OF THE COLD WAR

In order to formulate policy in a rational fashion, it is necessary to understand the precise nature of the problem—or the threat—to which you are seeking to respond. The nature of the Cold War (or the nature of the Communist threat) has changed over the past fifteen years and the pace of change is accelerating. Policy (including military strategy) must constantly be involved in keeping up. In the late forties we spoke of Stalin's Russia, in the mid-fifties we spoke of the Soviet Bloc, today we resort to vague phrases such as "Communist world" to denote the group of countries ruled by Marxist-Leninist regimes.

What did we mean by the term Cold War when we first began using it— during the period 1945–50? Basically, we meant a struggle against the rather unambiguous challenge of Soviet Communist expansionism. Lenin had written that "As long as capitalism and socialism exist, we cannot live in peace; in the end, one or the other will triumph—a funeral dirge will be sung over the Soviet Republic or over world capitalism." Soviet theoreticians held that war to the bitter end with capitalist states was inevitable and that violent revolution was the principal means by which the proletariat of a country could gain power. This challenge was met, as has been seen, with a policy of containment. In the election campaign of 1952 some Republican spokesmen attacked this policy as inadequate and argued for a program of "rolling back" the Iron Curtain. Confronted, however, with the Hungarian Revolt in 1956, the Republican Administration shrank back from precipitating what might have become a world conflict, and containment remained the root of our policy. We created a military strategy to support the policy, and have stuck with it to "the brink of war" in Berlin and Cuba. All this is fairly clear: America against Russia, West against East.

In recent years, however, there have been increasing divisions and divergences between Communist governments. The split between China and the Soviet Union is, in the opinion of many experts, irreparable. Tiny Albania denounced Khrushchev's Russia, and the Russian satellites have sought more freedom from Moscow. In the place of a monolithic bloc, we find a collection of "national Communisms." While the Chinese Communists have continued to argue the inevitability of world conflict, in the Soviet Union there has appeared a revisionist argument that only insurgent "wars of national liberation" are justified. The Soviet leadership, worried by the rise of China and interested in solidifying and extending economic progress at home, seems less militant in pursuing revolution. The Chinese, in their turn, have become the main agent of Communist expansionism. The issue is thus no longer a simple one of the United States versus the Soviet Union. For America this means changes in policy—means quite basic adjustments in the methods by which the Cold War has, up to now, been carried on.

The Cold War has been fought by many methods. In the forefront is diplomacy, through which the American position is defined and efforts are made to win support of other nations, to negotiate with the Soviet Union, and to deal with instances of conflict. In the background is the American military "system." This includes, in addition to our own forces, a series of defensive alliances ringing the rim of the Communist world. These represent American commitments to the defense of nations around the globe. Military bases have been established by agreement with friendly nations. Military aid to many such nations is given in the form of money for the purchase of equipment, for delivery of American equipment, and for training of armed forces personnel. To diplomacy and military arrangements is added the battle against poverty—the seedbed of Communism—through economic aid and a propaganda effort carried on by the United States Information Agency. Each of these methods may face alteration in response to the changes within the Communist camp. Asia (and perhaps Latin America) is replacing Europe as the critical locus of conflict.

The difficulties facing the United States in the conduct of the Cold War are tremendous. First, the Soviet Union has certain advantages in psychological warfare. Its doctrine is dramatic and simple: capitalism, and its corollary of the past—imperialism—are responsible for the troubles of the world; Communism offers a means of salvation; the victory of Communism is inevitable. Western "liberalism" is a more complex body of ideas, and hence more difficult to present in street-corner oratory. In fact, one common aspect of the liberal creed is the desirability of dissent, which creates diversity of opinion. Second, the enemy is supremely pragmatic and follows the Communist doctrine that "action programs" should change as conditions change. Direct assault may be suspended, but infiltration and propaganda continue. Flexibility is the chief characteristic of Communist strategy, and any means which ultimately advance the cause of Communism are moral. Third, the necessary conditions for growth of Western political and economic institutions do not exist in many underdeveloped countries. Democracy has proved viable in countries with a large middle class, high literacy, and experience in operation of local self-government. Capitalism has thrived in countries with surplus private savings; and "welfare capitalism," with few exceptions, has flourished in countries with democratic institutions. Every step forward depends on other steps being taken, and the process of development on the Western model is very slow—as witnessed by the experience of India. The Communists, by contrast, offer glib promises of quick progress. Fourth, there is often difficulty for the United States in responding to Communist efforts to subvert a non-Communist government. Are we, or are we not, justified in intervening in the domestic political life of the "target" nation? We desire to avoid the spread of Communism but we also favor self-determination, and may sometimes have to make difficult choices— in Cuba, Laos, and other places. *Finally,* at home some find the expediencies of the Cold War hard to understand, the costs and strains difficult to endure, and the frustrations difficult to reconcile with the "habit of victory" of the past. These things lead to confusion in policies and opinion and to difficulties in maintaining rational and consistent policy. In part, the problem of the Cold War is internal: it is the problem of adjustment in thinking to the conditions and frustrations of a prolonged struggle and even more to the complexities of world involvement and leadership.

Myths and Foreign Policy: Underlying American Attitudes

In a healthy democratic system leaders should sometimes move in advance of popular opinion—but never too far in advance. For the making of our foreign policy this simple ground rule produces a problem. When the town mayor proposes a new sewerage system, his constituents have some basis in their own experience for evaluating what he has to say. Most of these same citizens have no such capacity for evaluating the progress of the war in South Vietnam. They do, however, have opinions on the subject, and these opinions are largely a function of certain basic attitudes or assumptions about the nature of the external world and the potential of United States power, combined with what sketchy information is provided by news media. These broadly shared attitudes (or mental "sets") are of crucial significance, for (in the form of "public opinion") they operate as limiting factors on decision makers—restricting and constricting the range of policy choices open to those in power. We have already noted, for instance, how President Franklin Roosevelt was forced to draw back from a commitment to oppose the dictators by the icy reception accorded his

Quarantine Speech. He had challenged the then current assumption that the European and Asian power balances were none of America's business.

Of course all democrats agree that leaders are quite properly partial prisoners of their constituents' beliefs. At the same time, however, democrats recognize the responsibility of leaders to inform the public on policies deemed by them to be desirable. In a sense, the central problem of carrying on foreign relations is creating understanding of the issues and consensus on responses among those "opinion leaders" who influence public opinion. In turn, these leaders—the President, others in official positions, news commentators, editors of the press, and scholars in universities—must lead the nation in intelligent discourse.

The problem is only partially one of conveying facts on strange and remote situations. (Radio and television commentators find it necessary to describe where Zanzibar *is* each time it is mentioned on the air.) It is, in addition, that of getting people to correlate their attitudes and expectations with the realities of world affairs.

In many ways history has left the American people ill-prepared for the Cold War struggle and world-wide involvement. Certain "myths" or prejudices—Walter Lippmann called them "stereotypes"—survive from the past and condition the effectiveness of national leaders in reaching viable positions on foreign affairs issues. A full summary of American vestigial notions is not possible here, but a few of these can be examined.

SIMPLICITY AND CONSPIRACY

It is difficult to grasp the complexities of a single foreign policy situation, and it is impossible to comprehend them for all situations which force American attention. Hence, if things go wrong for the United States, it is charged that this is because stupid or wicked leaders are making silly mistakes. World history is seen as something "made in U.S.A.," and if it comes out badly someone is just not doing his job. This view shows little appreciation of the events and processes over which the United States has no control and very limited capacity to influence. "Who lost China?" thundered critics of the State Department in 1949 and 1950. Their question, though they did not realize it, rested on the assumption that the State Department (or the President, or somebody) *had* China. Thus, complicated patterns of events, involving agonizing choices between competing evils, are reduced to the level of a Western movie—the only problem is thus to find the bandits who are poisoning the waterhole. Assuming that the normal condition in the world is harmony and peace, some Americans see discord as the work of conspirators—Wall Street, the British, the State Department, Harvard, International Jewry, or Mao Tse-tung. "Someone" is responsible for it all.

It is, of course, evident that only a minority of Americans really believe all of this, but the ideas persist sufficiently to allow politicians and commentators to activate them in particular situations, presenting difficulties for responsible leaders who seek to lead the nation in intelligent discourse.

DEMAND FOR SOLUTIONS

As a people, we have tended to assume that with sufficient application of American initiative and resources anything could be "fixed" and in a very short period of time. The results of the Marshall Plan were very satisfying because they were speedy and tangible, but few of the problems to which the United States must respond in the sixties are so tractable. In many areas (such as aid to developing countries), expensive programs, running over many years, produce unspectacular (if important) results. This means that often programs must be oversold to the American people in order to achieve their adoption by Congress—with the accompanying inevitable disillusionment. The Alliance for Progress, for instance, was presented to Congress amid such optimistic predictions that one reporter remarked that it seemed as though all of Latin America would look like Miami Beach by 1965. The backlash of disappointment over the slow progress of the Alliance program was partly responsible for the "foreign aid" revolt which saw Presidential appropriations requests cut almost in half in late 1963.

VICTORY, NOT COMPROMISE

Americans have been accustomed to victory. They have never lost a war and they had their way with Indians and their neighbors on the frontiers. They have believed that the New World was superior to the Old, and hence that it was right that America should prevail. Hence, it is difficult to accept something less than complete victory. There was disillusionment over Korea because there was no victory over the Chinese. There is frustration over Cuba because American interests do not prevail. It is hard to accept the idea that the other Latin-American countries, the American allies across the seas, even the Russians and Cubans, now have stakes in Cuba, and that complete victory may be forestalled by these stakes. The consciousness that politics is the adjustment of conflicting interests has only recently been realized in domestic affairs, but it is more essential in the poker game of international affairs where many players sit around the table. The realization that an American card play must itself be determined by anticipation of effects on other situations and other actors, and that the poker game will never be finally concluded with 100 percent realization of American aims, may itself lead to a spirit of frustration, to a desire to withdraw from the game, or to a demand for desperate and rash plays.

IDEALISM AND REALISM

Historically, American thinking about international relations has been idealistic. Americans have believed that moral principles should govern international policies and have proudly proclaimed that their nation was one which had stood for right and justice. They have abhorred the doctrines that might makes right and that the end justifies the means. They fought one war to make "the world safe for democracy" and another to crush fascist dictatorship; they have since proclaimed the cause of freedom against Communist dictatorship; they have favored self-determination of peoples, protection of the rights of the weak, maintenance of international law, and a world of peace and good will.

Americans have generally either refused to recognize, or recognized with apology or shame, actions which seemed to be at variance with the goal of peaceful pursuit of righteous aims. Gunboat diplomacy, the "Big Stick" (especially when American economic interests were at stake), callousness toward Indians, are regarded as exceptional and out of accord with the American spirit. Of greater significance than these episodic events is the abhorrence of power in the American tradition. Our moralism has made the use of power suspect—we have gone to war not merely as a way of employing military power to obtain some politically desirable end, but rather as a means of *ending* the necessity of having to use power.

The realization, therefore, that the existence of power, and its use as an instrument of national diplomacy, is essential for success comes as a shock to many Americans. American soldiers are sent to Korea and Vietnam not with any purpose of ending the use of force but to support American diplomatic aims abroad. The appropriate justification for such actions, and for a costly military apparatus which accounts for more than half of the abhorred national tax burden, must be given by national leaders. Their task is, however, complicated by the strain on the American conscience resulting from the conflict between its views on how nations *should* act and how nations *do* act. On the one hand, Americans continue to treasure the idea that conditions which have characterized social advance can come to prevail in world affairs: law and the means of enforcing it, machinery for adjustment of differences among men, trade and communication, and the freedom and peace that results only after these developments. On the other hand, they realize that the contest among national states is an unending struggle for power. The combination of idealism (without the utopianism which has sometimes characterized it) with realism that accepts the necessity of power without making it an end, is no easy challenge for Americans to meet.

Conclusion: Adjusting to the "Twilight Struggle"

What has been said here about American attitudes toward foreign affairs and about the problems of prosecuting the Cold War should not lead to pessimism, but to an awareness of the magnitude and novelty of the challenge which our country faces in this half-century. We have not been used to protracted conflicts, and historically have sought quick and simple solutions to our problems, and yet we have carried the burdens of free-world leadership and defense without any giving up for two decades. There is still great appeal in the suggestion that we just get busy and "win the Cold War" (thereafter to enjoy, one supposes, a return to normalcy). Yet it is increasingly apparent that living with the possibility of nuclear obliteration has "aged" the American consciousness very rapidly. No one today much cares to contemplate a war to end all wars. America for the first time fights a dreary, continuing conflict. It would be well for us all to ponder Winston Churchill's advice on the subject of living with both thermonuclear weapons and aggressive Communism:

> The day may dawn when . . . tormented generations [will] march forth serene and triumphant from the hideous epoch in which we have to dwell. Meanwhile, never flinch, never weary, never despair.[11]

---

[11] Quoted in Westerfield, *op. cit.*, p. 519.

25 / The Making of Defense and Foreign Policy: Institutions and Processes

In the preceding chapter we examined the outlines of American defense and foreign policy as they had developed up to our time, noted certain major problem areas which will require the attention of our decision makers in the coming years, and analyzed some characteristic American attitudes toward foreign affairs which retain sufficient potency to influence the shape of future policy. We now turn to a consideration of the ways in which defense and foreign policy decisions are made in the United States today; to a look at the institutions involved in the process, and the "politics" of this process. We have seen in general terms *what* the decisions have been, but *who* makes them and *how?*

The making of foreign and defense policy in the United States today is probably as complex a task as ever confronted man. Policy makers face a kaleidoscopic kind of world. A Russian move in Berlin, an Egyptian step in Suez, or a revolution in Cuba call for immediate new analyses and extensive revision of United States positions. Nor can American policy be made unilaterally as in domestic affairs; it must be made with consideration of the reactions of enemies, neutrals, and allies. A move in Cuba must be weighed in relation to Latin-American reactions, and a decision on intervention in Southeast Asia be made with respect to our alliances, our ability to succeed, and our reserve capacity for other situations. In addition to external complications, there are difficulties in coordinating the actions of agencies within our own government. One writer has suggested that we "imagine a polygon of numerous sides of uneven length that indicate the involvement in foreign affairs of nearly every part of the government and of the aspects of society to which they are linked." [1] Robert A. Lovett, onetime Secretary of Defense, and a man with long experience in defense and foreign affairs, has referred to this arrangement as "the foul-up factor."

> This is really a method of requiring power to be shared—even though responsibility may not be—and of introducing rival claimants from another department with a different mission into the policy-making or decision-taking process.
>
> This is the "foul-up factor" in our methods. . . .
>
> Whether or not this itch to get in the act is a form of status seeking,

[1] Arthur W. Macmahon, *Administration in Foreign Affairs* (University, Ala., 1953), p. 4.

"What's Our Firm, Unswerving
Asia Policy This Week?"

From *Herblock's Here and Now,* Simon & Schuster, 1955

the idea seems to have got around that just because some decision
may affect your activities, you automatically have a right to take part
in making it . . . there is some reason to feel that the doctrine may
be getting out of hand and that what was designed to act as a policeman may, in fact, become a jailor.[2]

If one scans the pages of the *U.S. Government Organization Manual,* or
examines organizational charts showing the formal, legal relationship of
one agency to another, it is difficult to see how such conflicts with so many
participants develop. The charts seem to make clear who is responsible to
whom, and how power and responsibility are located within the system.
The reality of power is infinitely more complex and indeterminate. As we
shall presently see, the Central Intelligence Agency is formally located
within the Executive Office of the President, but there are ten miles between the White House and Langley, Virginia. In fact, CIA stands in
relation to the President on about the same plane as, say, the United States
Information Agency—an "independent" agency whose director is supposed
to be governed by policy guidance from the Secretary of State. The Joint
Chiefs of Staff enjoy a particularly ambiguous position—they are the "principal" planning staff for both the President and the Secretary of Defense.
Although it is clear that the chain of command for military operations extends from the President to the Secretary of Defense to the Joint Chiefs
and thence to certain combat commands, a strong chairman of the Joint
Chiefs can be a formidable competitor for any civilian Secretary. An organi-

[2] Robert A. Lovett, Statement before the Senate Subcommittee on National Policy
Machinery, February 23, 1960.

zation chart, however, shows the Joint Chiefs tucked neatly away in a box "under" the Secretary of Defense. It is necessary to know not only the formal position of the bureaucracies involved in defense and foreign policy but also the interrelationships in the process of decision. In the following pages we describe the governmental "actors" in defense and foreign policy-making, and then examine the processes in which they are involved.

The President and His Personal Establishment

At the vortex of the policy-making process is the President. He is the "mainspring" of the system; he must propose, coordinate, integrate, and decide. He must also struggle to keep himself from becoming a captive of the bureaucracies which are designed to help him. Both the Constitution and the nature of his electorate (nationwide) place this staggering responsibility on him—"Advisers," as President Kennedy once said, "can always go on to other advice, but the President must act." In Chapter 11, the White House Office Staff was examined in some detail. Within this group the President has a tiny but significant "personal establishment" which serves to give the "man at the top" extra eyes and ears—to extend his power and influence over the making of foreign policy. In hour-to-hour contact with the President, these few men can provide him with information (intelligence is, perhaps, a better term) which he might not otherwise get, or might get only in diluted form. Finished position papers, coming from the executive departments, sometimes gloss over differences of opinion within these departments which it is very much in the President's interest to know about.

Key man among these personal aides is the Special Assistant to the President for National Security Affairs. The position was created in 1953; however, Presidents in the past had co-opted into their official family trusted persons who served as personal advisers on matters of defense and foreign affairs. Thus Woodrow Wilson made use of Colonel Edward House, and Franklin Roosevelt of Harry Hopkins. (Nor does the existence of a formal position now hinder the President from drawing on persons not on the White House payroll and employing them as personal agents in the policy-making process. Attorney General Robert Kennedy was often used this way by his brother—notably in the review of Central Intelligence Agency operations which took place after the abortive Bay of Pigs landings in Cuba in the spring of 1961.) The duties of the security assistant include directing the small secretariat of the National Security Council (which prepares materials for discussion at NSC meetings), but the incumbent's main job, under Eisenhower, Kennedy, and Johnson, has been to keep the President informed—to get him "up" on topics which he must discuss easily if he is to exercise his powers effectively. During crises, this function may take on critical significance. In October of 1962 it was McGeorge Bundy, President Kennedy's security assistant, who was the first man in the White House Office to receive word that aerial photography revealed the presence of offensive missiles in Cuba. This information precipitated the crisis in which the United States made clear its intention to employ any increment of force necessary to effect the removal of the Soviet weapons, and which ended after eleven tension-charged days with Khrushchev's agreement to withdraw all IRBM and MRBM weapons. Bundy was awakened by Pentagon officials with the news of the first sightings at about three o'clock on the morning of Wednesday, October 16. Faced with the decision of whether to wake the President or hold off informing him until breakfast time, Bundy chose not to disturb his Chief's rest on the pragmatic grounds that there was little that the President could do anyway in those early hours before the first findings had even been checked and confirmed. President Kennedy later endorsed Bundy's decision. Throughout the "missile crisis" Bundy acted as coordinator of the so-called "Executive Committee" of the National Security Council, which President Kennedy called together to help him in analysis and decision. Thus the security assistant became, for a brief but crucial period, a secretary to an American council of war.

The security assistant has, from the point of view of a President, certain assets possessed neither by departmental officials (secretaries, assistant secretaries, bureau chiefs, etc.), nor by persons holding no official position. The security assistant has no departmental constituency which might impair his absolute loyalty to the "Boss," and yet he is *there* at all times, working in the West Wing of the White House. At the President's elbow, he has immediate access to intelligence estimates, "country surveys," and other things the President may want to know about on fifteen minutes notice. Different Presidents have different styles of operation, and they organize and utilize their personal staffs in different ways. This makes it difficult to predict how the job of security assistant will develop. It is clear, however, that he has now become important to the President. A 1963 Senate staff study of our foreign and defense policy-making machinery concluded that:

> The needs of a President and the needs of the departments and agencies are not identical—and herein lies a source of administrative difficulties and misunderstanding.
>
> What does a President need to do his job?
>
> Essentially he wants to keep control of the situation—to get early warning of items for his agenda before his options are foreclosed, to pick his issues and lift these out of normal channels, to obtain priority attention from key officials on the issues he pulls to his desk, to get prompt support for his initiatives, and to keep other matters on a smooth course, with his lines of information open, so that he can intervene if a need arises.[3]

The security assistant and the few other personal aides of the White House Office help the President do this.

The Department of State

The Secretary of the Department of State is the senior adviser to the President on foreign affairs. This office has not recently been a path to

---

[3] United States Senate, Committee on Government Operations, Subcommittee on National Security Staffing and Operations, *Administration of National Security* (Washington, 1963), pp. 2–3.

political advancement, as it was for four of our first six Presidents. It is, nevertheless, generally considered the office second in importance within the government. In postwar years it has been held by men like Marshall, Acheson, and Dulles, who have left their imprints on American policy. Dean Acheson has described the intimate working relations of the Secretary with the President. He saw "the President on business almost every day, and rarely less than four times a week," and sent a constant stream of communications to the President.[4] At times in the past, Presidents have seemed to ignore Secretaries of State (as Franklin Roosevelt sometimes ignored Edward Stettinius), but in our day the Secretary is becoming more and more essential to the President.

Behind the Secretary is the Department with its Washington headquarters and its field stations. The Washington office is organized in part along geographical, and in part along functional, lines. The primary organization is geographical, with separate bureaus existing for each of the major areas of the world. This is a historic pattern dating back to 1833. Within the geographical bureaus are the "country desks," a term which originated when there was a single man keeping track of each foreign country. The secondary organization is functional. Such major functions as economic affairs, cultural relations, and intelligence are organized in separate offices. The functional organization has grown rapidly in recent years as multilateral has tended to replace bilateral diplomacy and as problems must be approached on a world-wide or regional basis. The two patterns of organization existing side by side result in specialization both by area and by function. There is inevitably some struggle, often deep conflict, between those dealing with geographical areas and those dealing with functional problems which are global in scope. Both points of view must be brought into focus in foreign policy-making.

At the top of the Department are policy and managerial aides for the Secretary. Included here is a Policy Planning Council, created in 1947 as a flexible body for long-range study and planning. It assists the Secretary in evaluating the adequacy of current policy and weighs the advisability of new initiatives. Another important top-level unit is the Secretariat, which coordinates the flow of paper inward to the Secretary and assures the implementation of his decisions through the Department. There are also two Under Secretaries of State, performing indispensable functions in the areas of policy-making and departmental administration, respectively. Though the Department is always "reorganized" when new Secretaries come to office, these basic arrangements remain.

In the field, there are diplomatic and consular representatives. The latter look after the property, business, and personal interests of Americans; the former conduct our political relations with other governments. A diplomatic mission is headed by an ambassador or minister serving in the capital city of a nation recognized by the United States. Other departments and agencies of our government also operate abroad, perhaps as many as fifteen in a single capital. The ambassador is the head of the "country team" and faces the problem of coordinating and supervising practically all the representa-

---

[4] Don K. Price, ed., *The Secretary of State* (Englewood Cliffs, N.J., 1960), pp. 45–46.

tives of the United States in "his" country. The 1963 Senate staff study previously referred to comments that:

> . . . in the field, as in Washington, the task of coordination has grown more complex as the instruments of national policy have multiplied. The major elements of the modern diplomatic mission are State, AID, USIS, the service attachés (Army, Navy, and Air Force), military assistance advisory groups (MAAGS), and CIA. Often there is also an area military commander.
>
> Although all members of the country team acknowledge the ambassador's position, respect his precedence as chief of mission, tell him about their work, show him their cables, and invite his comments, their dependence on him and their desire to be coordinated by him differ greatly. As a general rule, their readiness to accept his right of decision varies with the degree to which they are involved in operational matters, such as the conduct of aid programs, and have their own reporting lines to Washington.
>
> The political counselors and other old-line members of the diplomatic staff are most dependent on the ambassador and have the greatest interest in supporting him. They have no line of reporting except through the ambassador—and informal letters to colleagues in Washington. At the other end of the spectrum is the MAAG. Its work is highly operational, it has its own lines to the Pentagon, and it tends to take a restricted view of the ambassador's right to interpose himself between it and the Pentagon on budgetary, programing, and operational decisions. The other groups fall somewhere between these positions. CIA is closer to the MAAG model, while USIS falls closer to the diplomatic model and AID somewhere in the middle.[5]

In addition to its "national" ambassadors, United States representation now includes ambassadors or similar officials at such important posts as the United Nations, NATO, and the Coal and Steel Community in Western Europe. Paris, to take the extreme case, is graced by no fewer than *four* United States ambassadors.

The Department has its own peculiar personnel problems. In Washington the permanent "home" staff is a part of the classified civil service. Abroad, the United States has been represented by Foreign Service officers, who, under the Rogers Act of 1924, form a separate corps. They are "generalists," recruited at an early age, tested primarily in such subjects as history and languages, and usually sent abroad, with only brief assignments at home. In spite of their ability there have been criticisms: (1) that they were a separate Ivy-League-educated "caste"—somewhat detached from American life and separate in thought from the civil service at home; (2) that there was need for recruitment of specialists in such fields as science, economics, and cultural affairs; and (3) that the Foreign Service had not expanded sufficiently to meet current needs, its members constituting in the immediate postwar period only about 11 percent of employees abroad. To correct these deficiencies a number of changes were made after the Second World War. First, in 1946 Congress provided for addition to the Foreign Service by

---

[5] *Administration of National Security,* pp. 10–11.

creating two new classes of officers: (1) the Foreign Service reserve corps, composed of about 700 persons having specialized skills and serving for periods of no more than five years; (2) the Foreign Service staff, a career service with two groups—about 1,200 officers ineligible for the Foreign Service, and persons for stenographic, clerical, technical, and custodial work. Second, the examinations for Foreign Service officers have been altered to allow entry of specialists. Third, the Foreign Service and the home service have been "Wristonized." As a result of a report to Secretary Dulles by Henry Wriston, then President of Brown University, there has been a substantial integration of the two services. Nowadays the Foreign Service totals about 4,000 persons including, in addition to the old corps, many persons who held important positions in the Department of State; there is also provision for alternation between the home and Foreign services.

Another personnel problem has been the appointment of heads of missions abroad. There has been an increasing trend toward promotion of Foreign Service officers to the post of ambassador or minister. About two thirds of these positions are now held by career officers. But some of the most important posts go to political appointees. There are two main reasons for this: The posts carry honor and prestige and are valuable political capital; and they are too expensive for any but extremely wealthy persons to hold. Although some political appointees have been among the nation's ablest, many believe that the "treatment of embassies as political patronage is an unalloyed evil." [6] Congress, it is suggested, could make an important contribution to the effectiveness of our Foreign Service by increasing the expense allowances for our large embassies so that the President could choose first-rate men without regard to inherited fortunes or campaign contributions.

As principal agent for the President, the State Department today is engaged in a range of activities which would have been unthinkable a few decades ago, and it has had to adapt itself internally to considerable strain. Secretary Rusk, testifying recently before a Senate committee, put it this way:

> You see, today, sir, because of the pace of business, relatively junior officers in the Department of State are sending out telegrams on matters which before World War II might well have gone to the Secretary himself. Our business could not be handled in any other way. We have to give broad policy guidance, but we also have to let our junior colleagues act because not to act itself is a decision. A deputy director of an office is, as I indicated earlier, sending out telegrams. If he has a responsibility, which we accept in the Department of State, for insuring that the interests of the other departments are fully taken into account, then he must be in direct touch with his colleagues in the other departments. That means that there is a range of contact which I think is inevitable and essential.[7]

---

[6] Henry M. Wriston in Price, op. cit., p. 95.
[7] United States Senate, Committee on Government Operations, Subcommittee on National Policy Machinery, Organizing for National Security, Eighty-seventh Congress, First Session, August 24, 1961.

The United States Information Agency

The mission of the USIA is to make American policies understood (sympathetically) abroad. The Agency's program is geared to persuading people that there is a harmony between their interests and objectives in the world and the policy of the United States. This mission also extends to "exposing" the fatuity of opposing positions, and refuting criticisms of American decisions. The USIA grew out of several smaller organizations which had experimented with the techniques of "psychological warfare," and whose efforts had come to little because of their tendency to separate programs of persuasion (propaganda) from actual foreign policy decisions. To put out "sell America" material without reference to what our government is actually doing in the target country is useless, and the USIA, notably under the directorship of Edward R. Murrow from 1961 to 1963, has attempted to avoid this mistake.

The USIA was set up under an executive reorganization plan in 1953. It is organizationally independent of the State Department, although the director is enjoined to receive guidance on policy matters from the Secretary of State. It is geographically organized around area assistant directors for Latin America, Europe, the Far East, the Near East, South Asia, and Africa. In addition there are functionalized "services" for such things as broadcasting, motion pictures, and publications. An Office of Plans, located in USIA headquarters in Washington, maintains liaison with "State," "Defense," the National Security Council, and the White House Office, but the operations of the Agency are carried on through several hundred field offices around the world. Since the Agency is charged with the responsibility of interpreting United States moves for overseas audiences, it has an obvious interest in participating in decisions which affect our foreign relations. In addition, the Agency has developed a reputation for expertise in "public relations," and it is often felt that USIA advice must be sought before any initiative is attempted. Thus, during the Cuban missile crisis of October, 1962, President Kennedy sought the counsel of Edward R. Murrow as to what United States actions would receive popular support in what countries. After his accession to the Presidency, Lyndon Johnson asked the incumbent USIA director, Carl Rowan, to attend meetings of the National Security Council.

The Agency for International Development

Since the Second World War, American foreign aid has been administered through a succession of organizations (all referred to by initials). Marshall Plan aid was administered through the Economic Cooperation Agency (ECA), and President Truman's Point Four program was implemented by the Technical Cooperation Administration (TCA). With the increased emphasis on military assistance in the early fifties, there came the Mutual Security Agency (MSA)—which subsumed the activities of the old ECA and combined economic and military aid. In the latter years of the Eisenhower Administration, the pendulum swung again toward nonmilitary assistance, and the MSA gave way to the International Cooperation Administration (ICA) and the Development Loan Fund (DLF). With the coming of the Kennedy Administration in 1961, all the economic aid activities were consolidated in a single new agency which was attached to the State Department—the Agency for International Development (AID). Military assistance became the responsibility of the Assistant Secretary of Defense for international security affairs.

AID has had a difficult institutional life. It has no great domestic constituency to support it, and its activities (spending taxpayers' dollars abroad) are always attractive targets for Congressional sharpshooting. AID operates programs of development loans, grants, and investment guarantees. It carries on research into the problems of economic growth and development and operates the Alliance for Progress program. In addition, AID exercises control over the famous "Contingency Fund," which allows the United States to respond to rapidly developing situations with offers of assistance. Unlike the USIA, AID is not independent of the State Department, but is "semiautonomous" within it. The administrator of the Agency "reports directly" to both the Secretary of State and the President. Despite the annual agonies of the appropriations battle, economic assistance has become a principal instrument of American foreign policy, and the importance attached to the operations of AID was symbolized by the move of Budget Director David Bell to the administratorship of the Agency in 1963.

The United States Arms Control and Disarmament Agency

By 1961 concern over the delicate "balance of terror" which insured "peace" between the Soviet Union and the United States, combined with apprehension about the perils of nuclear dispersion, gave rise to a specialized agency of government to deal with the very complicated and intractable problems involved in controlling the proliferation of weapons. Although United States policy was (and is) directed primarily toward achieving some measure of arms control, the new organization was also mandated to examine the possibilities of eventual disarmament. In the three years preceding the Disarmament Agency's creation, the pace of international discussions of arms control had increased to the extent that a considerable bureaucracy was needed to ensure that when the American delegation left for the next round of talks at Geneva it was properly prepared and supported.

The headquarters of the Disarmament Agency is on the fifth floor of the State Department Building, and like the administrator of AID its director serves as "principal adviser" to both the President and the Secretary of State on matters falling within his ambit of concern. The Agency is charged with research directed toward solving problems of arms control (how many seismic stations would be needed to detect blasts of a specified kilotonnage), with preparing position papers for consideration by the National Security Council, and with the actual conduct of disarmament and arms control negotiations.

William C. Foster, the Agency's present director, heads the American delegation at Geneva, and it seems clear (especially since the successful negotiation of the limited test ban in 1963) that the Disarmament Agency will have an increasing voice in the making of security policy.

The Department of Defense

The constitutional responsibility for the common defense rests with the President as Commander in Chief, but the day-to-day job of protecting us is the business of the Department of Defense and its civilian Secretary. America began its national history with federal military power unified under a single Secretary of War. This unity of control proved quite transitory. The small United States Navy managed to "win independence" from the War Department in 1798. From that year until 1947, the military establishment was bifurcated between "War" and "Navy." The officers of the two services believed that any centralized command, at a level below the President himself, could only impair their respective effectiveness, and civilian Secretaries also accepted this view. The Army and Navy went their separate ways through the nineteenth century, each developing its own definition of its mission, its own strategic concepts and tactical doctrine. As late as the first Administration of Woodrow Wilson, a Secretary of War could say to the Secretary of the Navy: "I don't care a damn about the Navy, and you don't care a damn about the Army. You run your machine, and I'll run mine." [8] The separatist tendencies of each service and its civilian partisans are not just good-natured rivalries of the sort paraded each November at Army-Navy football games; they are deeply rooted in a history of separation and elaborate justifications for separation.

In 1903 a first attempt at achieving coordination below Presidential level was made with the creation of the Army-Navy Joint Board (a forerunner of the Joint Chiefs of Staff). This group sought to work out, for the first time in our history, war plans based on various international contingencies. It was during this same period that the services themselves were going through the throes of reorganization. Before, there had been little coordination *within* the two Departments below the level of the Secretaries. In 1900 the Navy established a general board to integrate the planning of the various bureaus on the naval establishment. In 1903 the Army general staff system was worked out, and the position of chief of staff was created. But in spite of this, the Joint Board was unable to overcome the habits of a hundred years of autarchy, and it proved impossible to reconcile the planning of the two services. Little real use was ever made of the Board.

The American experience with global war in 1916–18 rekindled interest in coordinating, even unifying, the activities of "War" and "Navy." There was much study of the problems, but little action. As one student of defense organization has observed: "Between 1919 and 1939, reorganization of the defense establishment was considered by nineteen boards or government study groups." [9] In the light of contemporary realities, there is a quaint side to much of this pre-Second World War discussion. Thus the 1925 Morrow Board observed in its official report that:

> If the two present service organizations were consolidated under a single secretary, it would at once become necessary to create a super

---

[8] Quoted in Harry Howe Ransom, *Can American Democracy Survive Cold War?* (Garden City, N.Y., 1963), pp. 5–6.
[9] *Ibid.*, p. 6.

staff. No secretary of national defense could operate the two organizations without subsecretaries or technical advisers. This super general staff, which would be in addition to the present service staffs, would necessarily comprise Army and Navy advisers who had been educated not only in their own particular schools but who would be required to have taken courses in schools of the service to which they did not belong. It is difficult to see how any such superorganization would make for economy in time of peace or efficiency in time of war.[10]

It took the Second World War (along with increased use of aviation in warfare) to provide the necessary conditions for institutional innovation.

In 1943 the War Department, reversing its historical position, took a strong stand for the consolidation of the Army and Navy within a single department and under a single secretary. Army leaders such as Henry Stimson, George Marshall, and Dwight Eisenhower, faced with organizing vast allied campaigns, were forced to the conclusion that new machinery for coordination was needed. The Navy leadership, however, remained unpersuaded. Secretary Knox, Under Secretary Forrestal, and Admiral King, the principal Navy Department spokesmen, feared that in any superservice department the role of sea power in warfare would be insufficiently appreciated and that in such a centralized establishment it would be easy for the Air Force to claim a monopoly of air power. The air commanders, for their part, were interested in getting out from under Army control—reorganization would provide an opportunity for this and hence the airmen favored reorganization. During the war a step toward coordination was taken in the creation of a Joint Chiefs of Staff (very similar to our present JCS), which became a unified planning center directly under the Commander in Chief, with representation from the Army and Navy Departments and from the Army Air Corps.

With the coming of peace in 1945 newly felt pressures forced greater integration of the services, first loosely, then more tightly. The greatest pressure in the beginning was the desire of the Air Corps for a separate status, which could most easily be achieved in a single new military department. Also, there was increased need immediately after the war for more effective machinery for settlement of conflicting claims of the services. In 1945 and 1946 there was uncertainty over the strategy for future war, and intense interservice competition developed as each establishment sought to stake out claims to particular missions and to push particular programs. The Army supported universal military training as a means of maintaining ground forces it thought essential; the Air Corps came forward with a demand for seventy regular Air Force groups supported by national guard and reserve units; the Navy had a concrete plan for large facilities, including long-range aircraft. Some order *had* to be brought to this situation, and after several extensive studies of the problem, President Truman sent to Capitol Hill proposals for consolidation upon which Congress eventually acted. There were still many in high places who doubted the wisdom of a single defense department. Secretary of the Navy Forrestal, in hearings on the bill which was to become the National Security Act of 1947, argued,

---

[10] *Ibid.*, p. 8.

. . . the business of the Navy is 28 billion. The business of the Army is in the order of 70 billion. There is no human being capable, in my judgment, of sitting on top of all that and assuring that you have the fine integration and efficiency which it is presumed would result from . . . consolidation.[11]

Forrestal was later selected to do the job of which he had held "no human being capable."

Unification, however, came in stages. By the National Security Act of 1947 a third department, that of the Air Force, was created. Each department was to be independently administered by its own secretary. Created also was a Secretary of Defense. His function was only general direction and coordination of the "military establishment," and he had only a small staff to aid him. His most significant power was to "supervise and coordinate" the budget estimates of the three Departments. In 1949 the "military establishment" was elevated to the status of an executive department. The Secretary was given a Deputy Secretary and three Assistant Secretaries to work with him; the three services were downgraded from "executive" to "military" departments and their secretaries left off the new National Security Council. Provisions were made for strong financial controls by the Department of Defense over the services by the establishment of a comptroller, who has become one of the most powerful budget officers in government. President Eisenhower in 1953 further strengthened the Department by creating new aides with responsibilities in such fields as manpower and personnel, and supply and logistics. Then by act of Congress in 1958 the Secretary of Defense was given direct authority over unified commands (such as the North American Air Defense Command) and authority to provide centralized direction of research and development through a director of research and engineering. He also gained the power to transfer weapons systems from one service to another. These and the agency of the comptroller, along with a civilian staff of about 2,000, have finally provided the basis for a central direction of the defense system.

However, the job of running this Department has been difficult—as Forrestal predicted. In the fall of 1949, after two years at the post, Forrestal himself resigned, suffering from "operational fatigue." A few weeks later he leaped to his death from an eighteenth-story window of the Bethesda Naval Hospital. Several of his successors have had great difficulty in making their views prevail over those of the service Secretaries and uniformed leaders. There is still a kind of "legalized insubordination" authorized by the National Security Act—with service Secretaries authorized, under certain circumstances, to take problems directly to the President. The secretary who would really *run* the Department of Defense is bound to bruise many feelings. The rivalries of course remain. The services are backed by established national associations, such as the Air Force Association and the Navy League, and have linked themselves with industrial concerns producing their weapons. They have also carefully developed their liaison with Congress, and a service can marshal considerable support when one of its projects is threatened. In

---

[11] Quoted in Arnold A. Rogow, *James Forrestal* (New York, 1964), p. 213.

"Not In The Corridors, Dammit!"

A comment on inter-service rivalry during the Eisenhower Administration.

From *Herblock's Special for Today*, Simon & Schuster, 1958

national defense, as in other fields of government activity, the interrelations of public and private persons form a whirlpool of defensive and aggressive activity. These multiple centers of power when converging toward Congressional action can limit the strength of the integrated power in the Secretary of Defense and the President himself. As the strategic questions are being settled, new ones emerge, and rivalry has continued over such things as "who would build the missiles, who would operate them, and how much would be spent on one missile system against another." [12]

There have been additional, though less dramatic, factors which have led toward an increase of pressure on the Secretary of Defense. One is the need for some civilian intermediary between the Joint Chiefs of Staff and the President so as to relieve the load of strategic planning which has rested on the President since the creation of the Joint Chiefs during the war. Thus the Defense Secretary has gradually come to be a sort of second-in-command to the President—not just the administrator of the defense bureaucracy. As the nature of weaponry has changed, it has been necessary to reorganize the services, with many resulting tensions. [13] Finally, as coordination with the Department of State, the Bureau of the Budget, and other agencies became a dominant requirement in the making of national policy, the need for a single office representing the defense establishment in these relations grew

[12] Samuel P. Huntington, "Interservice Competition and the Political Roles of the Armed Services," *American Political Science Review* (March, 1961), Vol. LV, p. 50.
[13] See Gene M. Lyons, "The New Civil-Military Relations," *American Political Science Review* (March, 1961), Vol. LV, pp. 53–63.

in importance. Necessity has thrust more and more duties upon the Secretaries, who have in recent years tended to exercise them strongly, but the legacy of separation remains.

The structure of military forces maintained and administered from the Pentagon Building is as impressive in totality as it is secret in detail. Before the outbreak of the Korean War, the defense budgets had been running about $12 billion per year. The National Security Council had approved a plan for sweeping rearmament (stressing the importance of conventional capabilities), but until the Communist world supplied the incentive, there had been little prospect of getting Congress to appropriate the necessary funds. With the exception of the severe cutback on ground forces in the mid-fifties, post-Korean development has been toward a more versatile, harder-hitting, larger, and more expensive apparatus of violence.

The instruments of violence controlled from the Pentagon today can be grouped under four broad headings: [14]

1. *Strategic retaliatory forces.* These are forces designed to deter any Soviet nuclear attack upon the United States. They consist of intercontinental ballistic missiles in hardened (protected) sites, certain older unprotected missiles, the seagoing Polaris system (intermediate range missiles fired from beneath the surface), and about 400 manned bombers.

2. *Continental air and missile defense forces.* These forces consist of an integrated system of early warning radar (one network for manned bombers and another for missiles), interceptor aircraft, and interceptor missiles. At present, the interceptor missiles are effective only against aircraft, but new systems, designed to destroy incoming missiles, are under development.

3. *Reconnaissance forces.* U-2 aircraft and SAMOS "spy" satellites provide the Defense Department and the President with "hard" photographic intelligence of Soviet and "Bloc" capabilities. More sophisticated systems based on sound and infrared light are projected.

4. *General-purpose forces.* Eighteen Army and three Marine divisions, supported by aircraft of the Tactical Air Command and the two Marine Air Wings, are the heart of our conventional war forces. Their employment around the globe depends on the sealift capacity of the Navy and on the Air Force's Military Air Transport Command. Increasing emphasis is being placed on grouping these forces in functional commands (tailored to do a certain job) that can be moved rapidly by air to anywhere trouble breaks out.

THE JOINT CHIEFS OF STAFF

Although a Joint Chiefs organization existed during the Second World War, the JCS in its present form is another creation of the National Security Act of 1947. The staff itself is composed of a chairman (drawn from the Army, Navy, or Air Force), the Chief of Staff of the Army, the Chief of Staff of the Air Force, and the Chief of Naval Operations. The Commandant of the Marine Corps (which is under the Navy Department) sits as "co-equal" of the other members when matters concerning the Marines are

---

[14] These categories are suggested by Roswell L. Gilpatric, "Our Defense Needs," *Foreign Affairs* (April, 1964), Vol. XLII, p. 366.

**TABLE 25–1 / Defense Budgets as a Percentage of the American
Gross National Product**

Calendar year	Gross national product (billions of dollars)	National defense spending (billions of dollars)	Percentage
1944	211.4	88.6	41.9
1945	213.6	75.9	35.5
1946	210.7	18.8	8.9
1947	234.3	11.4	4.9
1948	259.4	11.6	4.5
1949	258.1	13.6	5.3
1950	284.6	14.3	5.0
1951	329.0	33.9	10.3
1952	347.0	46.4	13.4
1953	365.4	49.3	13.5
1954	363.1	41.2	11.3
1955	397.5	39.1	9.8
1956	419.2	40.3	9.6
1957	442.8	44.4	10.0
1958	444.2	44.8	10.1
1959	482.1	46.0	9.5
1960	503.2	45.1	9.0

SOURCE: Samuel P. Huntington, *The Common Defense* (New York, 1961), p. 282.

under discussion. The chairman is appointed by the President with the advice and consent of the Senate, and automatically becomes the ranking officer of the military establishment. During the first decade of the staff's existence under the National Security Act (which established the chairmanship), it was assumed that the position would be rotated among the three services. Thus the Army's Omar Bradley became the first chairman, Navy Admiral Arthur Radford the second, and General Nathan Twining of the Air Force the third. Army General Lyman Lemnitzer was the fourth incumbent, but with the expiration of his three-year term (a limitation recently fixed by Congress) in 1962, President Kennedy ended the "tradition" by appointing General Maxwell Taylor to the post. Taylor was succeeded by yet another Army General, Earle G. Wheeler, when the former resigned the chairmanship to become ambassador to South Vietnam in June of 1964.

The Chiefs have two functions—planning for all possible military contingencies, and, on behalf of the Secretary of Defense, exercising operational control over certain joint and specified commands (such as the joint STRIKE Command—an air, sea, ground command prepared at a moment's notice to "tailor" a force to fit a particular situation). In carrying out their planning mission the Chiefs are assisted by a joint staff of about 400 officers drawn from all services. This group is headed by a director, appointed by the JCS chairman, who is occupied with preparing and screening material to be considered by the Chiefs. Various sections of the Joint Staff examine problems of operations, logistics, personnel, and intelligence. In addition, specialized groups apply themselves to long-range forecasting of the military situation and to "programing" requirements for years to come.

There has been heated debate over the proper role of the JCS, and its growing influence has been resented by some senior officers of each of the services, who seem to feel, alternately, that the JCS are doing too much, or that they do too much talking and too little acting. This latter criticism has found expression in the often quoted quip of a senior naval officer that "the Congress *debates,* the Supreme Court *deliberates,* but for some reason or other the Joint Chiefs of Staff just bicker." [15] It is important to remember that the Chiefs do not have operational control over all the armed forces but only over certain commands and that each of the services has a planning apparatus of its own. The JCS play an important part in making defense policy, but they by no means make it alone; the individual services, through their secretaries, can still exert influence on the Secretary of Defense, and through him, on the President.

The Executive Office of the President

The Executive Office must not be confused with the White House Office—the "personal establishment" of the President. The Executive Office (see Chapter 11) is a *collection* of very disparate and dissimilar agencies which, in theory, work directly in support of the Chief Executive. In some cases, however, agencies within this "holding company" enjoy no closer relation to the President than organizations located elsewhere in the bureaucratic structure. Several of them do play major roles in making defense and foreign policy.

THE NATIONAL SECURITY COUNCIL

How do we achieve a marriage between foreign policy and the military policy which is necessary to make it effective? If the structure of policy and the structure of forces are not aligned, the nation cannot act effectively in the world, and yet, throughout most of our history no mechanism existed for effecting such coordination other than the President himself. In 1919, Franklin Roosevelt, then Assistant Secretary of the Navy, took note of this deficiency:

> The foreign policy of a government depends for its acceptance by other nations upon the naval and military force that is behind it.
>
> Hence . . . in the framing of our policies, it is necessary to know how much they [the policies] will cost to maintain by force, in order to assign them their relative importance.
>
> Conversely, it is necessary for the [military establishment] to know what policies it may be called upon to uphold by force, in order to formulate plans. . . .[16]

---

[15] Quoted in Samuel P. Huntington, *The Common Defense* (New York, 1961), p. 170.
[16] Quoted in Ransom, *op. cit.,* pp. 15–16.

We have seen the difficulty that was involved in achieving coordination between the service establishments—there was equal trouble in achieving coordination between the defense bureaucracy and the foreign policy bureaucracy.

During the Second World War, Roosevelt, feeling the lack he noted years before, improvised an instrument of coordination in the form of an informal "War Cabinet" of picked advisers. Roosevelt largely bypassed the Secretaries of State, War, and Navy. Through intermediaries such as Admiral Leahy, Harry Hopkins, and James F. Byrnes, the President dealt with the second- and third-level bureaucrats in order to achieve integration of effort around the war aims of his Administration. Though in some respects this informal arrangement served Roosevelt well, the international political aspects of the war kept getting lost from sight. With the passage of the National Security Act, an effort was made to provide a mechanism which would help the President with what Samuel P. Huntington has called the "great equation"—matching foreign policy with military policy with what resources the nation can afford.

The NSC (see Chapter 11) is composed of fixed statutory members (the Secretaries of State and Defense, the director of the Office of Emergency Planning, the Vice-President, and the President). It is customary for the director of the Central Intelligence Agency and the chairman of the Joint Chiefs to attend. Other officials may be included at the pleasure of the President. The NSC has a forty-person secretariat headed by an executive secretary, and the Special Assistant to the President for National Security Affairs coordinates the work of this group with the interests and requirements of the Council. In short, the drafters of the Security Act envisaged the NSC as the mechanism where all the pieces of intelligence, resources, and priorities would be put together.

Different Presidents, however, have used the Council in different ways. Truman was concerned about a possible usurpation of his own powers by the NSC. He felt that it was *his* Council and possessed no authority in its own right as did the British War Cabinet, after which the NSC was modeled. He found it valuable as an advisory body.

Eisenhower, on the other hand, regarded the NSC as an institution in its own right—as *the* Council. His first Assistant for National Security Affairs, Robert Cutler, worked hard to institutionalize the Council—to turn it into an organ which would present unified recommendations to the President and then monitor the implementation of the decisions which the President took.

President Kennedy, during his first months in office, made little use of the Council, but following the debacle at the Bay of Pigs in April, 1961, he began to make more use of it. In the Cuban crisis of October, 1962, Kennedy put together a sort of super-NSC, made up of regular NSC participants plus selected outsiders whose counsel the President valued. This executive committee of the NSC represents a kind of blending of the formalism of the National Security Act machinery with the informal, *ad hoc* approach of Franklin Roosevelt.

During his first year in office President Johnson showed every indication of being comfortable with a "tailored" or "augmented" NSC, and indicated

no desire to institutionalize the Council or make it an overseer of administration of defense and foreign policy.[17]

THE CENTRAL INTELLIGENCE AGENCY

Because so little is known about the Central Intelligence Agency, much
nonsense is said about it. A few contemporary writers seem to have
singled it out as the "invisible government"—a sinister elite which "really"
manages all America's external relations—which "really" calls the turn in
defense policy. The publicized CIA role in the 1961 Cuban adventure has
lent some credence to these stories. Certainly the existence of a secret and
expensive operation of this sort (the appropriations for the Agency are
hidden in the executive budget, but estimates range around $2 billion per
year) poses a problem for an "open society," but before it can reasonably
be discussed, some effort must be made to put the CIA's role in perspective.

Before the Second World War the United States, incredible as it may
seem, possessed almost no machinery for covert intelligence gathering. The
prevailing view was represented by the statement attributed to Hoover's
Secretary of State, Henry L. Stimson, upon his discovery that a small office
had been established within his Department for the purpose of breaking
codes. "Gentlemen," said the Secretary, "do not read each other's mail."
During the war an apparatus was set up for gathering intelligence by
espionage, and for carrying out clandestine operations, often of a paramilitary nature, in foreign countries. This Office of Strategic Services (OSS)
was dismantled after 1945; but it was soon apparent that if the United
States was to contain the Soviet Union, it must have detailed knowledge on
which to act. The Security Act of 1947 provided for the establishment of
the CIA, and the Agency developed three main functions: the collection of
raw intelligence or information; the study and interpretation of this material;
and the conduct of clandestine political operations overseas—a functional
hangover from the OSS.

In recent years it has been very easy to spot instances of CIA failure.
(In 1961 the United States backed the rightist Laotian General Phoumi
Nosavan at the very moment that his influence had declined to the vanishing
point and his army was melting away.) It has been much more difficult to
identify the Agency's successes. (To what extent was President Kennedy's
handling of the Cuban missile crisis a function of the intelligence he received
from the CIA?) Almost no one would challenge the appropriateness of gathering intelligence in the modern age, even if this must be done by covert
means. There is even general agreement that the process by which this is
accomplished must be kept secret from the American people. There is
widespread doubt, however, of the desirability of the CIA getting involved
with operations (even military adventures) by which foreign governments
are subverted or propped up. Today almost nothing except a natural disaster
can happen anywhere in the world without rumors spreading that "big CIA
money" was spent to make it happen or prevent it from happening.

The CIA, of course, is not the only intelligence-gathering unit of the

---

[17] For an extended examination of this, see Ransom, *op. cit.*, pp. 28–55.

"We're Being Tailed."

This cartoon comments on the 1961
investigation of the CIA.

government. While it has a monopoly on "operations," it pools its information
with that drawn from such agencies as the State Department's Bureau of
Intelligence and Research, the National Security Agency (which makes
codes and breaks them), and the Defense Intelligence Agency (which draws
on the intelligence-gathering agencies of the uniformed services). The
director of the CIA serves as chairman of the United States Intelligence
Board (composed of the heads of some nine intelligence-collecting organizations), which seeks to integrate efforts within this "intelligence community."
The end products of all this effort are the intelligence estimates submitted
to the National Security Council and the President.

The priorities and command decisions of American intelligence-gathering
and clandestine operations are made by a special group consisting of the
President, the Secretary of Defense, the Secretary of State, and the director
of the CIA. Within this small circle reposes the only complete knowledge
and control of CIA and other intelligence activities. Proposals have been
made that a joint committee of Congress (similar to the Joint Committee
on Atomic Energy) be created to share the knowledge and thus be able to
criticize the decisions and review requests for appropriations. The special
Presidential team, headed by General Maxwell Taylor and including Attorney
General Robert Kennedy, which surveyed CIA activities after the Bay of
Pigs fiasco, rejected this innovation as impractical. It was held that such
information as would be necessary for effective operation of a committee
could not safely be dispersed beyond the President and a few of his closest

advisers. There is thus a subtle irony in the inscription chiseled above the main entrance to the CIA's gleaming new headquarters in suburban Virginia, "Ye shall know the truth and the truth shall make you free."

THE BUREAU OF THE BUDGET

The President must make crucial choices between agencies and programs in making up his executive budget for the coming fiscal year. In a very real sense, the budget *is* the policy of the United States on any given issue— expressed in the ultimate vocabulary of dollars and cents. The Bureau of the Budget (described in Chapters 11 and 23) assists the President in deciding what he must scrap for a particular year, and what he should spend. Through this agency come the budget requests of State, Defense, USIA, AID, and (by a process the particulars of which are secret) CIA. The Bureau now includes an International Division and a Military Division. Its influence in deciding what can safely be spent ensures it a role in the shaping of security policy.

THE OFFICE OF EMERGENCY PLANNING

What is the domestic capacity of the nation for dealing with crisis situations? The answer to this question at any particular time will obviously have some bearing on what the President will commit the nation to do in the world. The National Security Act created a National Security Resources Board to prepare these "internal intelligence estimates," and the Office of Emergency Planning is the direct successor of this Board. Various divisions of the Office deal with manpower, communications, natural resources, and transportation facilities. The director of the OEP is a statutory member of the National Security Council, and as adviser to the President on what the country has in readiness and can do in an emergency, he can affect the decisional process in foreign policy and defense.

The Congress

In foreign affairs and national defense, as in other functions of government, the Constitution provided for "a sharing of powers" between the President and Congress. To Congress was delegated the power to declare war, raise and maintain armed forces, appropriate money, and to the Senate the power to confirm appointments of ambassadors and to give "advice and consent" on treaties by two-thirds vote. It was shown in Chapter 10 that the President has become the mainspring in international as well as domestic matters. In fact, necessity for strength and unity in defense and foreign policy has made for greater concentration of power in these fields than in domestic policy. The President supplies the initiative and direction for national policy. Nevertheless, the Congress still exercises real power and influence.

In national defense, Congress has determined the organization of the defense establishment, determining such things since the Second World War as the creation of the Department of the Air Force and the Department of Defense, the powers to be exercised by the Secretary of Defense, and the positions of the Joint Chiefs. Congress has increasingly become an "overseer" of the administration of the Pentagon—requiring even that certain decisions be cleared with the Armed Services Committees of Congress. Questions of pure military strategy rarely come before the Congress; it does consider questions of the structure of forces which are to implement strategy. Rarely do the lawmakers make any major cuts in the defense budget (no Senator or Congressman wants it on his head that he denied the military a weapon or resource which might "save American lives"), but Congress has great concern about whether the Air Force or another service is liberally treated, which company will build a plane, and what military bases will be located where. Since 1950 Congress has voted just about what was asked, and has exercised power by making micro-adjustments in the ways the monies for defense were spent.[18]

Congressional involvement is much greater in the making of foreign policy. It has in recent years regularly reduced the appropriation for foreign aid requested by the President, and it has, either by specific restrictions or by manifest attitudes, limited the President in use of funds for aid to particular countries. It has determined in legislation the foreign trade policy of the nation. Through enactments on such matters as immigration and naturalization it has affected relations with other countries. These are but leading examples of the effects of legislation and appropriations, which are supplemented by the continuous discussion, investigation, criticism, and suggestion from within the Congress. Every schoolboy knows that the Senatorial veto power prevented American entrance into the League of Nations and hangs as a constant threat against the treaty-making power of the President.

It is apparent that although the President initiates, Congress must be reckoned with in defense and foreign policy. Since Congress conducts much of its business in committees, certain groups (the Foreign Affairs and Foreign Relations Committees of the House and Senate, respectively, the Armed Services Committees, the Military Appropriations Subcommittees, and the Joint Committee on Atomic Energy) are particularly crucial from the point of view of an administration with a program it wants to implement. The chairmen of crucial committees—such men as Senator Fulbright (Democrat from Arkansas), chairman of the Senate Foreign Relations Committee; Senator Russell (Democrat from Georgia), chairman of the Senate Armed Services Committee; Representative Vinson (Democrat from Georgia), chairman until his retirement in 1965 of the House Armed Services Committee; and Representative Mahon (Democrat from Texas), chairman of the House Appropriations Committee—and the ranking minority members, along with the majority and minority leaders of the houses, must be informed, courted, and often coaxed by the President if he is to be able to pursue the policies he desires.

Some persons have desired to enlarge the checks and balances in foreign policy-making. This purpose was reflected, for example, in the Bricker Amendment, which failed by one vote to obtain a two-thirds majority in the Senate. This amendment proposed that Congress have power "to regulate all executive and other agreements with any foreign power or international

---

[18] See Huntington, *op. cit.*, pp. 123–66.

organization." On the other hand, many have been concerned over the effects of the constitutional provision which gives a minority (one third and one) of the Senate the power to block treaties, and over the threats to unity and strength in the sharing of powers. It may, however, be noted that the flexible interpretation of the Constitution has allowed Congress to delegate powers to the President—on trade, foreign aid, and other matters—which have strengthened the President, and that at the same time Congress has retained checks for itself by giving authorizations for short periods and by retaining its powers of appropriation, investigation, and discussion. The bridge between the President, seeking to provide a vigorous foreign policy, and a Congress reflecting the divisions of a pluralistic society and suspicious of executive power can only be maintained through the executive's making as much factual information available to Congress as will be useful to it and not hazardous to national security, through willingness of both to seek accommodation, and through the ability of the President to persuade the Congress of the correctness of his policies.

Other Agencies

Almost every department or agency of government becomes involved from time to time in the politics of national security. The Council of Economic Advisers and the Secretary of the Treasury advise the President on the impact of appropriation requests on the economy. The Peace Corps also plans and administers a program of "foreign aid" and is "attached" to the Department of State. The National Aeronautics and Space Administration fixes responsibilities of agencies in aeronautical and space development and advises the President on plans for such development. The Departments of Commerce and Agriculture, though serving primarily for domestic purposes, have extensive responsibilities with respect to international commercial matters. If the Department of State is engaged in international trade negotiations, its position can be determined only after conferences with representatives of the Departments of government established to protect the economic interests involved (Agriculture, Commerce, Labor), and these Departments will be represented in every stage of the negotiations. Each governmental institution will come to a given problem with a particular perspective, and each will have its own particular stakes to protect, its own particular programs to advance.

It should not be assumed that perfect integration is possible. No provisions for coordination will ever work perfectly when a multitude of different activities are carried on, when technological change is rapid, when the situations to be dealt with are constantly changing, and when the agencies are beset with pressures and attacks from Congress, private groups, and communication media. There will always be failures of coordination, and the struggle to achieve better machinery and techniques will go on.

Parties, Pressure Groups, and National Policy

It would be a great mistake to assume that because questions of defense and foreign policy are so complex, or that because most of the important

"Well, It Takes All Kinds. . . ."

© 1961 by Bill Mauldin
From *What's Got Your Back Up?* Harper & Row

decisions are taken within the bureaucracy of the executive branch, non-governmental political actors—parties and interest groups—do not become involved in the decisional process. There are a few decisions which are taken in an atmosphere so rarefied that they may be said to be outside the domestic political universe (at least at the moment they are taken) but only a very few. Truman's Korea decision and Kennedy's Cuban missile decisions are examples of this type.

It cannot normally be expected that the party in opposition will forego its obligation to uncover weaknesses in the President's policies and the administration thereof, or that it will ignore foreign policy issues in campaigns and in the political dialogue between campaigns. In the difficult period when Cold War policies were being developed after the Second World War, while the President and the Congressional majority represented different parties, bipartisan cooperation developed between President Truman and Senator Vandenberg, chairman of the powerful Senate Foreign Relations Committee. A readiness of the President to consult and to share facts (accompanied by the expectation of Republican victory in the coming Presidential election) led opposition leaders to contribute constructively to the search for solutions. In the years since 1948, it has become clear that politics will not stop "at the water's edge"; yet it is still expected that the President will consult with the opposition and that a certain minimal bipartisan support may be developed for the outlines of policy.

Not only parties, but interest groups, become involved in shaping policy. Throughout most of our history, American foreign policy has been affected by the feelings of ethnic groupings within our derivative population. Thus, during the nineteenth century, it would not do to appear too friendly with Great Britain, or the "Irish vote" would be lost. During the tense months leading up to our declaration of war against Germany in 1917, various German-American associations lobbied intensively against United States intervention. The involvement of economic groups (especially in the area of trade policy) in decision-making has been even more pronounced. When the question is one of opening the American market to the importation of Japanese cotton goods, organized management and organized labor within the textile industry form a united front in demanding that Congress patch up the tariff walls (even if this would mean the Japanese seeking a market for their goods in Communist China—an obvious setback for United States policy in Asia).

Extragovernmental groups also are participants in the struggles over defense policy. We have already noted the powerful service associations (staffed by retired and reserve officers) which serve as civilian constituencies to the Air Force, Army, and Navy. Recognition should also be given to the various industrial groups which supply the materiel of modern war and have vast amounts of capital committed to defense production. These supplier groups, of course, compete among themselves, and their loyalties are divided among the armed services according to what types of weapons they produce; yet their influence was great enough for President Eisenhower, in his last official public statement, to warn of a "military-industrial complex" which had the capacity to influence policy-making at all levels of government. In addition, defense installations in the United States create around themselves whole civilian communities whose existence is dependent on the operations of a local base or the continuation of a program which brings large numbers of federal employees to their areas. Any hint that the Navy Department might be reevaluating the usefulness of the Brooklyn Navy Yard is sure to bring to the Pentagon an irate New York City Congressional delegation (reinforced by both Senators) demanding to know how such folly as closing down the "Yard" could possibly be contemplated.

Many Americans are affected in their views on the importation of Arabian oil by the interests they hold in domestic companies, and others are affected by their sympathy for or their antagonism to the development of the state of Israel. Or, using another example, it is difficult to get Southerners to accept adjustments in racial relations on the ground that this will enhance the government's ability to deal with the developing nonwhite world. Thus the varied regional and group attitudes of Americans have a great effect upon what can be undertaken or accomplished in foreign affairs.

Studies in the Process of Policy-making

Thus far, we have examined individually various institutions and groups which interact to make those decisions about defense and foreign affairs which we refer to as "American policy." As one newspaperman who covers the State Department recently remarked:

> Foreign policy is not really made at all, only managed, on an *ad hoc* basis at best. It is buffeted by the colliding visions, gripes, talents,

fights, fears, errors, powers, and pressures of hundreds of people and dozens of institutions, of politicians and scholars, businessmen and newspapermen, foreign and domestic.[19]

In Chapter 24, looking back over our history, we could see patterns in American decisions which could unhesitatingly be called "policies." But the operating officials who must act and react day in, day out (often on the basis of much less information than they would like), cannot function in terms of grand designs alone. We say that the American foreign policy toward the Communist world is "containment"; yet to the man on the spot the important question is, "What, in the light of the consensus on 'containment,' should I recommend on two problems about which I must brief my Secretary at four-thirty this afternoon?" Policy is something which grows out of a multiplicity of past decisions, and comes to influence future decisions.

Different kinds of decisions are taken in characteristically different ways. In order to develop an understanding of the way policy is "managed," let us examine the American response to four specific issues which are roughly typical of four general categories of foreign and defense policy issues. In each case we shall be concerned to see *who* is involved in decision-making (the range of actors), and the *conditions* under which the decision is taken (openly or in secret, tentatively or irreversibly).

THE TRADITIONAL DIPLOMATIC ISSUE

In 1903 the United States Government signed a treaty with the Republic of Panama which fixed the conditions under which the new Panama Canal was to operate. The treaty accorded the United States the right to run the Canal, and to exercise control over the Canal Zone—the narrow strips of land along each side of the passageway. In 1903 Panamanian leaders felt they were fortunate in obtaining such an arrangement; by 1964 they had changed their minds. Nationalism and resentment of the United States had welled up as dominating emotions in Latin America in recent decades, and the Panamanians, by the early sixties, had come to resent bitterly the existence of an American enclave within their national territory. This resentment was enhanced by the superior economic status of the Americans who lived within the Zone and "ran" the Canal. In 1962 Panamanian President Roberto Chiari asked President Kennedy to consider revision of the treaty in a way to give Panama greater control of the waterway. Kennedy responded favorably to the overture, but officials of the State Department cautioned against hasty action, and nothing significant was accomplished. Throughout 1962 and 1963 the government of Panama continued to warn the United States that popular feeling in its country was running high on the issue of the Canal. On January 9, 1964, rioting broke out when American high school students within the Zone hauled down the Panamanian flag which flew in front of their school (under an arrangement agreed to a year before by Kennedy and Chiari) and ran up the Stars and Stripes. Panamanian crowds crossed into the Canal Zone, and the American military commander, seeing the problem as one of protecting a strategic defense

---

[19] Max Frankel, the New York *Times*, June 29, 1964.

installation, met the crowds with combat troops and tear gas. Within forty-eight hours Panama broke off diplomatic relations with the United States, and our "Panamanian policy" was a shambles.

The United States ambassadorship to Panama was vacant when the rioting broke out, but President Johnson quickly appointed Edwin Martin, former Assistant Secretary of State for Latin-American Affairs, to act as chief United States negotiator in attempting to effect restoration of relations, and to begin discussion on the differences that separated the countries. President Johnson himself talked by telephone with President Chiari. The Organization of American States, with the blessings of the State Department, set up a peace committee through which Martin could communicate with Panama's foreign minister, Galileo Solís. The discussions revolved around Panama's demand that the United States agree to a revision of the 1903 treaty as a condition of the resumption of normal relations. The United States was willing to entertain the question of treaty revision, but was unwilling to *agree in advance,* and under pressure, to renegotiate the pact. To do so, Washington (meaning the President, Secretary of State Rusk, and newly appointed Assistant Secretary for Latin America Thomas Mann) felt, would set a bad precedent, and expose the Administration to the Republican charge that it had knuckled under to a form of international blackmail. Somehow, a verbal formula had to be found which would allow both governments to come off gracefully in the eyes of their own people and open the way for discussions of the substantive problem of the Canal. There followed intense, and often seemingly petty, diplomatic-semantic wrangles over whether the United States was agreeing to "discussions" or *"negociaciones formales."* Several times talks broke up with exchanges of recrimination. The Johnson Administration sought to make maximum use of the machinery of the OAS, and when Panama invoked the Rio Treaty of 1947 (which provided for an OAS determination of whether aggression had taken place), the United States went along with the move. Through the patient application of traditional diplomatic skills (bargaining) and the agency of established machinery of international adjustment (the OAS), a cooling-off period was agreed to. During this period Panamanian national elections were held, and President Chiari's party preserved itself in power. After this victory, a face-saving phraseology was quickly worked out, and first steps toward a new treaty (expected by both sides anyway) were taken.

In responding to a traditional diplomatic issue of this sort, the principal decision makers were the President, the Secretary of State, and the geographic section of the State Department directly concerned. Since the whole effort was conducted rather openly (the actual cables exchanged during the crisis were secret, of course, but the press was kept almost up to the minute on the course of the talks), Congress and the "public" became involved in the process—to the extent that immediate Congressional and popular reactions had to be taken into account before each decision or proposal was made. None of the decisions taken during the crisis were really final—all were subject to reversal. (It is easy enough to withdraw a proposed draft communiqué in the light of changing circumstances.)

This same pattern of relatively "open" politics is duplicated in, for example, negotiations with the countries of the Common Market on tariff reductions. In this case the involvement of economic interest groups widens, somewhat, the range of actors. Within the government, the primacy of the Secretary of State as adviser to the President goes almost unquestioned in such matters.

THE ISSUE OF COLD WAR POLITICS

On August 13, 1961, East Germany walled itself off from West Berlin. By fall, the Soviet Union had stepped up its harassment of American transportation (ground and air) moving into West Berlin. It was felt in Washington that this action represented a serious attempt by the Soviet Union to alter the status of West Berlin and to abrogate the rights of the other Allies (Britain, France, and the United States) which were guaranteed by four-power accords drawn up in 1945 for the governance of the city. To President Kennedy, and his aides throughout the government, it appeared that the "heat was really on." The United States had tolerated the construction of the Wall, and it now seemed that the Soviets sought to exploit the momentum of events in order to gain their long-standing objective of moving the "imperialists" back behind the Elbe. The Soviet Union possessed a superiority of conventional forces in Berlin, and for American leaders the central problem was one of convincing the Soviets of our firm intention to defend Berlin with any increment of force required.

In regard to an issue such as this, the State Department and the President did not work out decisions bilaterally. The Defense Department, the Joint Chiefs of Staff, and the CIA all had a part in shaping the American response. President Kennedy made little use of the machinery of the NSC in the "Berlin buildup of 1961"; instead he brought the principals to his office individually or in small groups to hear their reports and recommendations. The first Administration countermeasure was to dispatch to Berlin retired Army General Lucius Clay—who, as military governor during the Berlin blockade of 1948–49, had become a symbol of American determination to preserve the freedom of West Berlin. Clay, as the President's personal representative, insisted on the maintenance of Allied rights in the city to the extent of sending military police patrols into the Soviet sector with United States tanks positioned to ensure that the patrol car was not held up at the Soviet check point. In addition, President Kennedy announced a buildup of the United States Army (two new divisions) and called thousands of reservists to active duty.

Since part of the American strategy was to keep the Soviet Union guessing as to exactly what its next move would be (all the while making it clear that there would be *some* next move if the Soviets did not desist), there was a veil of secrecy thrown around the decision-making process. Only certain selected pieces of information were released, and only some United States actions were announced publicly. Congressional and public reactions could not be discounted—whatever course the Administration took; and no matter how secret its deliberations were kept, the confrontation on the streets of Berlin was quite visible. Yet the policy-making process is much more "closed" when the issue is one of Cold War politics than when one of adjusting our relationship to another country where Cold War politics are not involved. The Administration realized full well that a disaster in Berlin would bring eventual punishment at the polls, but secrecy gave it room to decide without weighing immediate public and Congressional reactions quite as heavily as would be necessary in a traditional diplomatic issue. In addition, the decisions taken in respect to Berlin had about them a quality of finality missing from the conventional diplomatic situation. When you make it plain to a nation with nuclear weapons that you will shoot at its military personnel if they do certain things, you are no longer dealing with wordings that can be retracted at the next session of the talks, or turned down by the Senate. Thus while the intraexecutive involvement is greater with the Cold War issue than with the traditional diplomatic issue, the extraexecutive involvement is greatly diminished.

THE CRISIS ISSUE

The Berlin buildup as a response to a Soviet probing took weeks to decide upon and months to execute. There is another sort of Cold War situation in which our leaders are called upon to act—an ultimate Cold War issue in which the question becomes one of committing ourselves, within a matter of days or hours, to use nuclear weapons against the Soviet Union if certain Soviet behavior is not halted or undertaken. It is a bit difficult to generalize about decision-making in such situations since, fortunately, there are few cases to work from. The nature of these crisis issues, however, makes it imperative that we attempt some understanding of how a United States response is fashioned. We have already touched on the first few hours of the Cuban missile crisis of October, 1962, the "classic case" of nuclear decision-making, and its lessons are of preeminent importance.

Intelligence was the key to "Cuba II." It was the trigger of the confrontation, and it was finally the instrument which allowed the United States to "settle" the affair with something less than an invasion of Cuba. Before the beginning of the Soviet buildup in Cuba in the summer of 1962, U-2's flown by civilian CIA pilots had carried out photo missions over the island. The introduction of surface-to-air missiles into Cuba prompted a switch to Air Force planes and pilots. It was one of these planes, making the first reconnaissance over the western half of Cuba since early September, which on the morning of October 14 photographed mobile medium-range missiles near San Cristobal. This "hard intelligence" was relayed to Washington, and after analysis, passed to McGeorge Bundy. Bundy informed the President at eight o'clock on the morning of October 16. Kennedy at once summoned to the White House a group of selected advisers, which, with certain additions, came to be known during the next two weeks as the Executive Committee of the National Security Council (Excom). This ad hoc team consisted of McGeorge Bundy, Attorney General Robert Kennedy, Vice-President Lyndon Johnson, Secretary of State Dean Rusk, Secretary of Defense Robert McNamara, his deputy Roswell Gilpatric, General Maxwell Taylor, Major General Marshall Carter, deputy director of the CIA (Director John McCone was out of town), Presidential adviser Theodore Sorensen, Secretary of the Treasury Douglas Dillon, Under Secretary of State George Ball, and Edwin Martin, Assistant Secretary of State for Latin America. Adlai Stevenson, American ambassador to the UN, and McCone joined the group later that day, and former Secretary of State Dean Acheson

"Don't See Anything Disturbing"

An anti-Administration view of the official attitude toward the second Cuban crisis.

Hesse in The St. Louis *Globe-Democrat*

and former Secretary of Defense Robert Lovett were co-opted later in the week.

No decisions were reached quickly; various possible courses of action (invade, bomb the sites, try to bargain with Khrushchev, naval blockade) were suggested and talked out. By Friday, October 19, a "rolling" consensus was achieved on blockade coupled with the promise of further action if the missiles were not removed. On Friday the decision was actually made. It was not until Monday evening, however, that the public or the leaders of Congress were informed of what was occurring. In the meantime, a massive land and sea buildup was in progress in Florida and on the Caribbean. The President, during his televised address to the nation, committed the United States to stopping Soviet ships on the high seas and escalating the crisis to any level the Soviet Union felt it could afford. The decision-making process had been completely closed and the decision was in a real sense final. There was always the possibility of not actually stopping the Soviet ships, but Kennedy was very close to the kind of decision which is truly irreversible. We had announced to the Soviet Union exactly what we intended to do, and to back down from such a posture would have been disastrous. The Soviet Union would then have had good reason to believe that it could behave as it wished anywhere in the world without United States force being used against it.

Of the three issues and responses examined thus far, the Panamanian example reflects the most open decisional process and the least expensive in terms of the immediate stakes involved. The Cuban missile crisis represents a closed arena of choice and almost absolute stakes. The Berlin confrontation of 1961 is the case in between.

American policy must be geared to the power which we can exert in the world, and decisions as to what we shall spend on what military programs are a crucial aspect of national policy. In this area the President, the Secretary of Defense, the Joint Chiefs, the Bureau of the Budget, and the Secretary of State are involved. (State has a great deal to say about what our foreign policy needs in the way of supporting military forces, and its recommendations carry great weight.) In addition, the individual services (as potential competitors) become involved, as does the intelligence community (in defining what opposing forces we must be prepared to counter in what areas of the world). The range of actors is widened still more by the intrusion of defense contractors into the policy process. To cite one recent example, in the two weeks in the summer of 1963 before President Kennedy announced the scrapping of the Skybolt missile system (an aircraft-borne medium-range missile), North American Aviation—prime contractor for the system—ran full-page advertisements in national magazines touting the effectiveness of "their" weapon (which had consistently failed to perform under test conditions).

There is also Congressional involvement in struggles over defense programs, and each service can count upon certain partisans among the Congressmen and Senators at appropriations time. In spite of this, little real public scrutiny or participation with respect to issues of resource allocation is possible. The facts needed to evaluate competing options are so highly classified and so highly complex that only a small circle of people in the executive branch, the Congress, and the defense industry are "literate" in such matters.

In late 1963 and early 1964, an issue of resource allocation developed with the Army and Air Force on one side and the Navy on the other. The issue was the relative emphasis (in dollars and cents) to be given seapower and airlift capacities. In the fall of 1963, the Army and Air Force had conducted a dramatic joint exercise ("Big Lift") in which the personnel of an entire Army division was airlifted to Europe in the course of three days. The military policy implications of the effort were painfully obvious to both the Navy and our European allies. By using air transport to deploy troops directly from the continental United States, it would be possible to bring home certain forces garrisoned abroad (with a favorable effect on the nagging balance of payments problem) and to cut down on the Navy fleets and task forces, with their organic complements of Marines, which have thus far provided the United States with its only capacity to apply power swiftly to varied locations around the world. As a result of the Big Lift's success, Army leaders argued that military forces should henceforth be organized in functional, tailored commands to be deployed by air at the onset of trouble.

In December, 1963, the Army won an important victory for functionalism and airlift when responsibility for defense of the Middle East (to include the Indian subcontinent) and of Africa south of the Sahara was shifted from naval commanders to the commander of the United States STRIKE Command (the headquarters of this organization is at McDill Air Force Base on the outskirts of Tampa, Florida). The equipment that provides the sealift capacity of the Navy is rapidly becoming overaged, and unless the emphasis on airlift is soon reversed, the United States will have made a very final kind of commitment to a particular military structure—for augmenting our sealift capacity overnight would not be easy even for American technology and industry. The process by which this decision is being made is invisible to the public; and even if it were not invisible it would be difficult to comprehend. Certain issues of resource allocation can be transmuted into public questions (as in the "missile gap" debates of the 1960 Presidential campaign), but the great part of these very significant decisions will be fought over in "restricted areas" of the security bureaucracy.

Conclusions: Can American Democracy Survive the Cold War?

Will the instruments and processes which we have developed to protect ourselves in the last twenty years alter the nature of our democratic political system and libertarian political ethics to the extent that we lose the very thing we seek to preserve? One student of national security has recently warned that:

> America's defense and democracy are threatened partly because we may fail to recognize and to cope adequately with what I shall call the problem of organizational lead-time. Our governmental system resists rapid structural change. My greatest concern is that in periods of obsessive fear or true national emergency, radical changes will occur in our institutions—in the name of national security—which will severely damage the democratic framework.[20]

There are certainly some characteristics of the defense and foreign policy-making process (the new "security politics") which should be carefully watched.

SECRECY

"Burn before reading." This old joke captures something of the environment within which our planners operate. There are several elements in the problem. First, is the difficulty of judging the performance of our leaders, since we do not know the details of the problems with which they are grappling. Second, is the temptation, now constantly before officials, to cover up mistakes and unpleasant facts by stamping them TOP SECRET. In politics, information is power, and the elaborate security systems which have been introduced into government within the last two decades provide many opportunities for monopolizing information.

THE NEW AMERICAN MILITARY

In the list of abuses recorded in the Declaration of Independence are these two: "He has kept among us in times of peace, standing armies, without the consent of our legislatures. He has affected to render the military independent of and superior to the civil power." Hamilton found it necessary to write a Federalist paper to answer the objection "that proper pro-

---

[20] Ransom, *op. cit.*, p. xi.

vision has not been made against the existence of standing armies in time of peace." [21] The nation quickly developed a navy and a standing army. Yet the standing military force was at a minimal level, main reliance was on the militia, and expanded armed forces were cut back quickly after each war. Now with the advent of continuous readiness and with the enormous increase in the size of the military defense system, new aspects of the old problem of civilian control are presented.

There are a multitude of structural arrangements through which civilian control can be exerted: the Congress, the President, the Secretary of Defense and the Secretaries of the three services, the Bureau of the Budget and the comptrollers (budget officers) in the military departments, the Atomic Energy Commission and National Aeronautics and Space Administration, the Federal Aviation Agency, and the National Security Council are but some of the centers through which civilian personnel can exert control. The military is dependent upon science and money, and this means dependence upon civilian aid and control. It is hedged in by the large corps of professional civilian employees in the defense establishment and by the scientists, budget makers, and policy determiners outside. On the other hand, military officers or ex-military officers are often appointed to top civilian positions. Moreover, military personnel serve on coordinating committees and are assigned to service in other agencies. These arrangements result in hand-in-glove activity at successive levels up the administrative hierarchy. Policy must be made with the participation of new civilian bureaucracies in science and budgeting, new military leadership interested in weapons technology and foreign and economic policies,[22] and a political leadership forced to reconcile, limit, and set priorities.

It is, of course, the political leadership which has the right to make decisions. This was the meaning of the Truman-MacArthur conflict. In a disagreement between a military leader looking at military possibilities and a President seeking international objectives, the former must either yield or be relieved. In conflicts over the right of military officers to make speeches, they, like other public officials, have been required to submit to restraints. Yet the military will have numerous opportunities within the executive branch, before Congress, and through its affiliated organizations to make its influence felt on public policy.

One episode in postwar history will show some of the problems. In 1945 Congress began consideration of an organization for the control of atomic energy. A bill prepared in the War Department was introduced and reported by the House Military Affairs Committee. It was criticized for giving the military excessive control. In the Senate a special committee under the chairmanship of Senator McMahon was created to consider the problem. The result of this consideration (and of President Truman's insistence that the entire program be under civilian control) was a bill which provided for a full-time, five-man, all-civilian Atomic Energy Commission. The military services objected to this complete civilian control. After the Senate had passed the bill, a bitter struggle ensued in the House. The House Military

---

[21] *The Federalist*, No. 24.

[22] See Lyons, *op. cit.*

Affairs Committee proposed that one member of the Commission be a military man, but the bill as passed contained only a provision for the assignment of a military officer to administer one of the divisions under the Commission. The settlement provided for civilian direction with military participation, and served as a model for organizational arrangements in the fields where both civilian and military are involved. Over the years the Atomic Energy Commission has been attentive to military needs, preserving atomic secrets and occasionally prodding the military into new weapons developments.

PRIMACY OF THE PRESIDENT

Protection of American security and national interest requires prompt decision and strong leadership. These are qualities obtainable only through a single official with strength and power to decide and act; in the American system this official is the President. At the same time, the American tradition of government presumes leadership to be tempered and limited by the sharing of governmental power, by the contest of parties for control of the government, and by active discussion within, and representation of, the "public." A balance between integration of power, forced by necessity, and pluralistic democracy, embodied in our tradition, can be difficult to strike in a period when emergencies arise frequently and a single decision, or a failure to decide, may set off an irreversible chain of consequences.

The Constitution, framed in a day when the urgencies of decision in international relations and national defense were not as apparent as now, dispersed power throughout the government. Congress was vested with power to declare war, raise and maintain armed forces, and appropriate money, and the Senate was to give "advice and consent" on treaties by two-thirds vote. Yet the foregoing has shown the primacy of the executive branch in international affairs. This problem cannot be resolved by minor institutional tinkering. The Congress will continue to reflect the divisions of a large and pluralistic society and a restiveness over executive strength. Yet necessity will continue to require vigorous executive leadership. As concluded earlier, the "bridge" between the two can only be maintained by the executive making as much information available to Congress as will be useful to it without endangering national security; by a willingness of the Congressional leadership to seek means of accommodation with the White House; and by the ability of the President to persuade the Congress that his way of managing defense and foreign policy is what the country wants and needs.

PART VI
THE STATES AND
COMMUNITIES

26 / The Political Heritage of the Grass Roots

When an American thinks of politics, he usually thinks of national and international affairs. The decisions of the President, the maneuverings within the Congress, the pronouncements of the Supreme Court, the intrigues of foreign governments, and the crises in the United Nations cover most of the front pages in most of the metropolitan dailies across the country. The topics of inflation, farm surpluses, missile bases, NATO, aid to underdeveloped countries, and satellites make up our common political table talk. At least in this century, the dramatic, the spectacular, and the significant matters of state seem increasingly to center in Washington, D.C.

Yet despite the glamour of national events, the work horses in American politics are state and local governments. These lower echelons of the American federal system carry out the greatest volume of public business, settle the greatest number of political conflicts, make the majority of public decisions, and direct the bulk of public programs. State and local governments have the major responsibility for maintaining domestic law and order, for educating the nation's children, and for caring for the chronically sick and the mentally ill. They also share in the regulation of our great private insurance and banking establishments; help supervise the provision of water, gas, electric, and other public utilities; oversee the use of land; and review the sale and transfer of property. Their courts settle by far the greatest number of civil and criminal judicial controversies.

These state and local governments, then, are by no means puny systems. Compared with the *domestic* agencies of the federal government (that is, excluding military defense and foreign aid), all state and local agencies together have two and one-half times as many employees. Moreover, state and local governments are expanding their activities at a much faster rate than the national government is expanding its own. Between 1950 and 1962, their general expenditures increased by 160 percent; during the same period, federal expenditures rose by only 135 percent. As a proportion of the gross national product, state and local expenditures for goods and services rose 45 percent between 1952 and 1962 while similar federal expenditures declined 26 percent. Little wonder that Alan Campbell has called state and local activities "the most dynamic sector" of the American economy. Their growth rates outstrip those of all other parts of our economic system.

Most observers expect these trends to continue. As the federal government continues to be occupied with defense and foreign affairs, it is states, cities, counties, highway boards, transit authorities, school boards, water, sewerage, and irrigation districts that build the welfare state. "It is no longer true," in Peter F. Drucker's words, "as it was in the New Deal years, that the federal government is the only government that really matters. But most people still talk as if it were." [1]

Thus while the survival of the United States as a nation depends on how wisely decisions are made in Washington, the public necessities and amenities we enjoy and the intelligent use of many of our material and human resources turn to a large extent on the collective performance of thousands of separate governments. The quality of American life thus rests in the decisions of state and local public officials.

Subsystems in the American Political Process

We can study state and local politics in the United States in several different ways. One method is to think of the units below the national level separately, each as a formal legal entity with a specific geographical jurisdiction and substantial powers of its own. By these standards, in 1962, there were 91,235 such governments in existence, as states, counties, cities, towns, boroughs, villages, special districts, and public authorities. By law the states are the key units, endowed with all governmental powers not vested specifically in the national government by the Constitution, or reserved to the people. The other jurisdictions are subdivisions or creatures of the state. [2]

From this perspective, the sheer number of separate units is the most dramatic characteristic of state and local politics. Though the 1962 figure of 91,235 represents a decrease of 11,000 units since 1957 and 25,000 since 1952 (mostly due to the consolidation of school districts), the multiplicity of government units is still impressive. Within the total, the several categories of units have fluctuated in number, as Table 26–1 shows. Counties, for instance, have remained almost constant in number but have gradually assumed more and more programs formerly carried out by smaller local units. In the South and West especially, reform of urban county government structures and expansion of their activities have occurred so frequently since the Second World War that these units scarcely resemble their rural counterparts.

Within counties, there are on the average twenty-nine smaller jurisdictions. Their number has *decreased* steadily in recent years: a reduction of 12 percent since 1957 and 24 percent since 1952. One third of all counties contain less than ten units each; 115 (mostly in large urban areas) contain 100 units or more. The number of municipalities (incorporated cities or boroughs) has increased across the country, almost 5 percent since 1957. The number of townships (units with a variety of functions found primarily in the twenty northeastern and north-central states) has remained about the same.

---

[1] Peter F. Drucker, "Breakdown of Government," *Harper's* (January, 1959), p. 31.
[2] United States Department of Commerce, Bureau of the Census, *Governmental Organization*, in *Census of Governments, 1962* (Washington, 1963).

TABLE 26–1 / Governments of the United States

Type of government	1962	1957 *	1952 *	1942
Total	91,236	102,392	116,807	155,116
U.S. government	1	1	1	1
States	50	50	50	48
Local governments	91,185	102,341	116,756	155,067
Counties	3,043	3,050	3,052	3,050
Municipalities	17,997	17,215	16,807	16,220
Townships	17,144	17,198	17,202	18,919
School districts	34,678	50,454	67,355	108,579
Special districts	18,323	14,424	12,340	8,299

* Adjusted to include units in Alaska and Hawaii, which were reported separately prior to adoption of statehood for these areas in 1959.

SOURCE: United States Department of Commerce, Bureau of the Census, *Governmental Organization,* in *Census of Governments, 1962* (Washington, 1963), p. 2.

So far as special-purpose governments are concerned, the number of school districts has declined by 30 percent between 1957 and 1962, but other special districts have proliferated, increasing by 15 percent between 1957 and 1962. These districts are usually created to provide a single governmental service. One third are located in rural areas, engaged in soil and water conservation activities; about one fifth offer fire protection; and the remainder carry out such urban programs as water supply and housing. Given this variety, simply keeping tabs on the number and duties of different types of American government—and trying to account for the fluctuations in trends—can be a complicated undertaking.

In addition to considering state and local governments as separate entities with distinctive legal form, we may look at them from another perspective as parts of a seamless web of government. These units are, in fact, bound to the national government by the Constitution, financial grants and loans from one unit to another, a common body of law, and national political parties and pressure groups that deal simultaneously with all levels of government. So all of American politics can appear closely knit together; we speak of a "cooperative" federal system, joint public programs, and a single political "career" ladder where the politically ambitious begin on the low rungs of the local precinct captaincy to climb to the national Presidency. Looked at this way, state and local levels of government and politics form the broad base of a pyramid that constitutes a single structure of political activity—one nation, indivisible. The activities of these units can be studied as special aspects of executive, legislative, and judicial behavior or of public administration, party, and interest group politics. Either way, they can be incorporated in one general theory of American government.

Yet neither an image of state and local governments as a jumble of separate legal jurisdictions nor one that considers them as a monolithic political order is an accurate picture of political behavior at these levels. The thousands of jurisdictions are not piled helter-skelter on top of one another, doing only and precisely what the law says they must do. Instead, each structure serves a distinct function in relation to a larger political system and maintains purposeful and continuing relations with other jurisdictions. On the other hand, they are not merely cogs in a single American system either. For all the blurring of official responsibilities among governments brought about by grants-in-aid, informal cooperation among public health specialists, engineers, and other civil servants at all levels of government, and the emergence of national parties, each unit on a given level still presides over a domain of public affairs in which its decisions are predominant. Though technically the local governments are creatures of the state (established by state law or constitution) two systems—state and local—actually coexist below the national government. Separate systems that link different levels of government can also be usefully distinguished—those found in grant-in-aid programs or in law enforcement, for example.

What are the properties of state and local political systems that set them apart from the national system and each other? Essentially they are systematic variations that can be detected in their structure and functions—marginal differences, by and large, but, when taken together, differences that produce distinctive patterns of political behavior. Like all political systems, those at the state and local levels are more or less consciously designed to fulfill specific political purposes. To give two examples: local public schools play a vital role in conditioning the public to obey laws and participate in elections, a process we call political socialization; state political parties recruit individuals to run for public office. Both systems are concerned with settling the conflicts which arise among interest groups and individuals. And both record the resolution of those conflicts in laws, programs, expenditures, and regulations.

Four specific differences distinguish the structure and functions of American state and local subsystems from the national government and from subnational systems in other countries, (1) the *scope* of their authority and activity; (2) the *participants* who seek to influence that authority and direct that activity; (3) the special *objectives* which these participants have; and (4) the *roles, rules,* and *instruments* through which the participants work.

By the *scope* of the systems, we mean the activities with which the systems are principally concerned—and which their decisions govern and direct. We imply also the boundaries of these activities in relation to other political systems. We do *not* mean the geographical jurisdiction involved—the size of Montana or the continental location of St. Louis. For a long time, for example, the proper concern of local government was held to be providing a necessary "bundle of services" for organized community life—law enforcement, education, certain public utilities—which private enterprise for one reason or another could not or would not carry out. Similarly, the attention of state government has traditionally been fixed on the development and management of natural resources and the encouragement of transportation and communication facilities to speed economic development, either by underwriting private efforts or by direct action.

Sometimes, of course, dissatisfaction with state and local performance in these matters has resulted in their reassignment to the national government, as happened, for example, when the breakdown of local welfare programs during the Great Depression led to a national relief program. Moreover, each generation finds each level grappling with a new set of problems which require public decisions. Thus the advent of the automobile caused a revolution in traditional transportation programs. Nonetheless, for each system there is a continuing body of decisions concerning certain public activities which provide a focal point for examining the system's operations. Year in and year out, education, welfare, public works, public safety, and transportation comprise the major products of the state and local systems.

The *participants* in the two systems are often the counterparts of those we have already observed on the national level. Each level has its specified elective offices to be filled—governors, legislators, mayors, aldermen, sometimes judges—each its appointed administrators and permanent personnel, each its party officers and workers. Then there is a host of actors almost identical with those in Washington. Veterans' organizations, farmers, small businessmen, labor organizations, and the Chamber of Commerce maintain state as well as national headquarters; they testify before, and try to influence, county boards and city councils as well as Congress. Newspapers, television stations, and other media often play important roles in state and local politics.

But the character of state and local decisions encourages new groups, organizations, and individuals to become active in politics—sheriffs' associations, groups of local merchants, intrastate industrial associations—and results in a different cast of characters. Groups which have particular prominence on the national scene, for example, the Americans for Democratic Action and the National Air Force Association, may be less influential or inactive at the lower levels. Interests scarcely noticed in Washington—citrus growers in Florida and nursing homes in Massachusetts—have new prominence.

One obvious and major difference in the mix of political activists in state and local governments is that the number of participants tends to be fewer than at the federal level. Also, the smaller the area a government encompasses, the more likely it is that a single political party holds a continuing large majority and that a few groups are consistently influential. It is not unusual therefore to find oilmen in Texas and stockmen in Montana playing a more decisive part in their local affairs than at the national levels.

The *objectives* which the participants seek may also parallel those of their counterparts in Washington. Yet usually the character of the decisions involved, the traditions of the system, and the composition of the rest of the participants give rise to a different set of goals. State and local politics are less likely, for example, to have the ideological flavor of national politics. They are more likely to be particularist, with political groups focusing their campaigns on the work of special agencies or advocating specialized pieces of legislation, instead of being concerned with advancing a general and comprehensive platform. Moreover, a great deal of attention is given to the issue of honesty and competence in state and local governments. Partly this is because of the spectacular legacy of bossism and corruption which these governments must combat, partly because controversy regarding programs

"You Have The Liberty Of Voting For Anyone You Please; But We Have The Liberty Of Counting . . ."

The corrupt local "machine politics" depicted in this Nast cartoon has largely disappeared.

revolves not so much over the purpose of an activity as the efficiency with which it is carried out.

Finally, state and local systems are distinguished by the *roles* the participants assume, the *rules* under which the political game is played, and the *instruments* used to settle conflicts and to achieve compromise. Though in legal form all states but Nebraska parallel the nation in having a bicameral legislature, an independently elected executive, and a separate judiciary, and all states but Louisiana rely on English common law as the foundation of their legal system, differences in the powers and prerogatives, structure, and organization of the three branches are substantial. As a general rule, the chief executives of American states do not have power and influence paralleling that of the American President, and the scope and impact of state judicial action may be quite different from what it is nationally. As for the informal mechanisms of party organizations, scarcely one half of the states can be said to have strong two-party competitive situations comparable to the national one. In many states widespread use of primaries, recalls, and referendums in elections tends to dilute party discipline. In others, political organizations built around personalities are much more important than the Republican and Democratic State Committees.

At the local level, many municipalities have dispensed with the doctrine of the separation of powers and have installed new forms of government which give prominence to the executive, most notably the city-manager and the strong-mayor organizations. Most also have rid themselves of the political "machines" of the nineteenth and early twentieth centuries. The formal officeholder is now more independent of the "boss" in the back room. The supervision of elections is vastly more effective than two generations ago when slogans such as "vote early and often" were common in Boston, New York, and Philadelphia.

Within this broad framework of republican forms of government, popular elections, some degree of partisan identification, and a commitment to legal procedures and practices, a wide variety of habits and institutions exists. Generally, however, the customs and mores of state and local politics put more emphasis on personality than on party discipline, attach more importance to legislative than to executive action, give more leeway to independent centers of power in the state and municipal departments and agencies, and concentrate more on material than ideological rewards and benefits for the participants.

This chapter will examine the historical origins of these political systems, the forces that support their independent existence today, and the kinds of decisions they now make. Later chapters will deal with the relation of the systems and their decisions to the social and economic environment of modern American life, focusing on the problems of adjustment which confront old governments in new surroundings. They will also provide more details about the roles, rules, and institutions which channel the systems' decisions and about the characteristics of the participants and the consequences of their decisions. Our first task, however, is to understand how and why the systems exist and the public problems that they try to resolve.

The Foundations of the System

Why does the American governmental structure, in company with those of Australia, Canada, New Zealand, and Switzerland, have three more or less independent systems of politics? What factors account for the continued existence of state and local governments today—in an age of mass culture and mass media that bind together all the regions in the country?

Historically, the two systems owe their existence in America to the special pattern of settlement and the course of colonial development on the North American continent. The first commercial and royal expeditions to the New World of necessity established colonies that were small in size and physically isolated from one another. The founders of St. Augustine, Plymouth, and Jamestown all received separate grants of authority from European rulers. Their inhabitants came from different backgrounds and religions, and had crossed the Atlantic for different reasons. Nothing was more natural than for each community to exhibit an independence of political action and a degree of self-sufficiency made necessary by the wilderness environment. In contrast to the European city or English borough, where the influence of the central government represented by the high sheriff or justice of the peace had been evident for centuries, local governments in America early took on an autonomy born of "common sense combined with the circumstance of the place." The seaports and frontier villages of early America operated as independent governments because there was literally no other way to organize community life.[3]

A different set of circumstances accounts for the existence of the American states. Established originally by broad charters from European and English Crowns and encompassing areas deemed of sufficient size to permit profitable gold mining, fur trapping, and other resource exploitations, the boundaries of the original colonies began to assume increasing significance by the end of the seventeenth century. Though the local governments remained the actual executors of public laws—collecting the taxes, overseeing the construction of the roads, establishing the schools, and caring for the poor—the colonial governments became the legal repositories of superior political authority granted by the mother country, personified by the royal governor, and exercised in the control of foreign trade and commerce.[4]

In addition to being the settlers' links to the civilized world and therefore their imperial policy makers, the colonies came to take on distinctive styles of life. The ex-prisoners who settled Georgia, the Catholics in Maryland, the Dutch of New Amsterdam, the gentry of Virginia—all responded in different ways to their different environments. Soon the Southern plantation system, the seafaring life of New England, the orderly farm and town existence of the Middle Atlantic states gave rise to distinctive sets of loyalties, colloquialisms in speech and manner, and regional attitudes and prejudices.

As military action against the Indians and among the colonial powers themselves became more frequent and better organized, the colonies also found themselves of convenient size for the assembly of militia and the supply and direction of campaigns suitable to the technology of the day. By the time of the Revolution, therefore, the forerunners of the American states were cultural and social entities, having some experience in the conduct of foreign and military affairs and possessing institutions of government that already represented the advance guard of democratic institutions. Their existence made a federal system after the Revolution almost inevitable.

Historical conditions of early settlement may account for the establishment of the federal structure, but they do not explain its vigor and strength today. When we ask why the structure persists, a different set of forces becomes relevant: the heritage of American political ideology, the inherent complexities which still remain in governing an entire continent, and the survival instinct of any set of institutions involving human beings. Because their home-grown institutions seemed to solve problems successfully, because there appear to be continuing and useful tasks for the systems to carry out, and because it is natural to value any heritage which survives, Americans have believed they should continue the old structures through

---

[3] Carl Bridenbaugh, *Cities in the Wilderness: The First Century of Urban Life in America, 1625–1742* (New York, 1938).

[4] Victoria Schuck, "The Massachusetts Governor: Hamstrung by History?" Robert R. Robbins, ed., *State Government and Public Responsibility, 1961: The Role of the Governor in Massachusetts* (papers of 1961 Tufts Assembly on Massachusetts Government, Medford, Mass., 1961).

the nineteenth and twentieth centuries. Indeed, so strong has been the support of the systems that the constitutional supremacy of the national system had ultimately to be imposed by force in the Civil War. Since then, too, neither economic disaster nor military emergency has substantially changed the mixed emotions with which most Americans regard expanding activities of the federal government. The popular view, recorded at the ballot box and by public opinion poll, is that to the greatest possible extent public programs should be carried out at the lowest level of government. Even in the heyday of the New Deal, proposals for the radical reorganization of the states into large regional complexes were dismissed immediately. Since the Second World War as urban problems have multiplied, plans for the reorganization of local governments have been consistently rejected.

The rationale for this basic conviction comes in two parts. Many of us believe that the smaller the government, the more sensitive it will be to popular will. Many of us also believe that governments of limited size are more likely to be better managed than larger governments. These beliefs may not always be in accord with the facts—some of the most striking recorded examples both of autocratic rule and of mismanagement come from the local and state levels. But they are an important part of our political ideology—what we think government should be, whether or not our conceptions are always realistic. The political potency in the call for "grassroots democracy" and the sentimental nostalgia evoked by the remaining examples of town meeting government in New England are still strong.

Pragmatically, of course, in time of physical disaster, depression, or war, we look to the federal government for assistance or reform, and we have accepted a number of changes in the respective position of the three levels of government since 1789. But the ideology has altered little since the days when Jefferson called the New England towns "the wisest inventions ever devised by the wit of man for the perfect exercise of self government" and De Tocqueville hailed "provincial" institutions as the best protection against both despotism and democratic excesses. "How," he inquired, "can a populace unaccustomed to freedom in small concerns, learn to use it temperately in great affairs?" [5] Today their sentiments are echoed by scholars who believe that small governments provide the "roots of civilization" and by laymen like the resident of Tarrytown, New York, who in protesting the consolidation of his local school district wrote, "I would feel that I had surrendered some of my manhood if I gave to the politicians in White Plains the legal right to control in the slightest degree the education of my children." [6] True or false, then, these belief patterns fulfill powerful needs of identity and personality. In a complex industrial society, the small town and small government have the special appeal of contrast and individuality.

The ideological foundation of state and local politics is powerfully reinforced by the provisions of the Constitution and the philosophy which underlies them. Though broad interpretations by the Supreme Court of the general welfare and commerce clauses of the Constitution have ex-

---

[5] Alexis de Tocqueville, *Democracy in America* (New York, 1900), p. 66.
[6] Victor Jones, *Metropolitan Government* (Chicago, 1942), p. 297.

panded the range of permissible national activities, the legal presumption that the state is the basic unit of government is essentially unchallenged. Thus whenever a new problem appears that seems to require public action, the legal disposition is to assign it to state or local governments; and in this instance the theory of the law is supported by public sentiment. The safest way to avoid entanglement and delay is to pay homage to states' rights and prerogatives.

In addition to the legal preferences that support state and local governments, certain practical considerations—among them maintaining political consensus and governing a nation across an entire continent—commend the use of the lower levels of government. Even when a program may seem clearly national in character, its political appeal and operating effectiveness will frequently be enhanced by providing opportunities for state and local participation. Many national welfare, highway, and agricultural programs include elaborate arrangements to "bring in" the other levels of government, thus assuring their concurrence and making possible regional adjustments in the program. For example, the states have assumed a great part of the job of carrying out the national welfare program, and the cities engage in active partnership with Washington in the expanding urban renewal effort.

Beside the support which our political ideology, our legal structure, and our continental size give to the continued operations of state and local governments, there is still another force: the tendency of any going concern to perpetuate itself. Nothing is more natural than for individuals and institutions to believe that their work is important, if not vital, to the well-being of the society to which they belong. After three centuries of evolution, American states and municipalities have acquired the traditions and the sanctions of survival. Understandably, the men and women who hold public office at these levels believe that their jobs are required in the best interests of the nation, that the programs they carry out are essential, and that the institutions in which they serve represent the best possible way of organizing a continental democracy. Even if it could be demonstrated to an objective observer that complete control by the national government or some entirely new system of regional or community politics was more democratic and efficient, it is unlikely that the present participants would agree. And the system has its friends and supporters in the national government: Congressmen seeking improvements for their home districts; Senators as representatives of the states; Cabinet members selected to provide regional viewpoints on Presidential matters; the Electoral College itself—all act as built-in restraints against the expansion of national power. The fact that the state and local systems have been in operation a long time is a good reason for supposing that they will continue.

Historical practices and innovations of the past now crystallized into doctrine and beliefs; experience and customs specified in constitutions and statutes; ancient loyalties transformed gradually into grass-roots ideology and supported by individuals and groups who stand to gain by the perpetuation of the institutions—these are the foundations of modern state and local governments. But granted the persistence and permanence of the systems, just what do they do today?

The Present Organization of the Systems:
(1) The Concerns of the States

In terms of the activities of state and local political systems today, past behavior is no reliable guide to present performance. The participants they involve, the programs they carry out, the decisions they make no more resemble those of their predecessors than space rockets look like balloons. Today, the mercantilist enterprises of the seventeenth and eighteenth centuries, and the limited programs of the nineteenth, are gone. In their place are highly organized institutions committed to a doctrine of positive social services, making decisions that involve the spending of billions of dollars each year and that influence the development of the national economy and the character of national life in significant ways.

Table 26–2 shows in broad outline the main tasks of the two systems and suggests the kinds of decisions involved and the types of participants likely to be active. Column 1 summarizes the characteristics of all fifty American states according to the program areas in which major decisions are made, ranked in terms of expenditures. These figures indicate where taxes, manpower, and executive direction are being applied and give us clues as to what decisions are likely to be of the greatest political concern. They also enable us to judge how universal the major programs and decisions are for all the state systems. Column 2 summarizes the programs of local governments in much the same way. Column 3 shows per capita expenditures for state and local expenditures combined.

The figures suggest first the variety and subtle distinctions among states and among local governments. Although six programs predominate, their range in level of financial support, the size of the bureaucracy involved, and the magnitude of the operation in relation to the population served is very wide. These differences suggest differences in the kinds and interests of the participants, the strategies and tactics involved, the attitudes of the electorate, and the role of particular institutions and rules. A welfare program in Louisiana is not planned on the same basis of calculations that would be employed in Montana. The priorities assigned by the people of Rhode Island for schools and highways do not parallel those of Minnesotans.

Yet the table does emphasize some common properties, making interstate and intermunicipal differences mostly those of degree. For each system today the kinds of decisions that the state and local systems consider appropriate for their consideration are much the same. So far as the states are concerned, there are now three major arenas for decisions: *transportation, education,* and *welfare.* Since the Great Depression and the Second World War, state political systems have taken over from the localities the responsibility for deciding what kind of transportation facilities will serve the American public, what kind of public assistance will be given the indigent, the aged, the infirm, and the mentally sick, and what personnel and curriculum standards should guide the public schools.

The state systems make by no means *all* the decisions for these substantive fields. The broad outlines of the welfare programs in the United States are determined by the federal government, and so are many of the design

	STATE			LOCAL	
Function	Total expenditures 1961 (millions of dollars)	Percentage of total	Function	Total expenditures 1961 (millions of dollars)	Percentage of total
Total	19,004	100	Total	37,197.3	100
Highways	6,229.5	33	Education	16,781.7	45
Education	3,792	20	Highways	3,613.8	10
Welfare	2,311.2	12	Public safety	2,842.1	8
Health, hospitals	2,059.1	11	Welfare	2,408.8	6
Administration	725.5	4	Health, hospitals	2,028.0	5
Interest on general debt	583.8	3	Sewerage and sanitation	1,774.4	5
Police	260.9	1	Administration	1,508.6	4
			Interest on general debt	1,240.0	3
			Local parks	857.1	2

SOURCE: Adapted from United States Department of Commerce, Bureau of the Census, *Governmental Finances in 1961* (Washington, 1962).

and location features of the national highway program. More than half the cost of both programs is paid by federal funds. To be sure, local governments are still involved in health and hospital programs, and they are the actual operators of the public schools. But it is in these areas that the states make their most important decisions, and in each area there are wide choices. Hence, in each one conflicts build up among groups which will be affected by the decisions, coalitions are formed among them, compromises and agreements result according to the rules and institutions involved, and programs are finally authorized. In short, politics is at work.

TRANSPORTATION

Measured in terms of dollars spent each year, the largest program the state systems direct is transportation—more particularly, highways. By a combination of historical precedent and technological change (which frequently propels a government into a new field of endeavor), the states now have the responsibility of providing running space for the American automobile. It is national policy that we have an interstate highway system which includes a network of urban expressways as well as intercity and rural roads; the federal government has supplied 90 percent of the funds spent for interstate highways in the United States in the last ten years. Municipalities still maintain local streets, and counties build some roads within their borders. But the direct responsibility for construction and main-

STATE AND LOCAL EXPENDITURES PER CAPITA

Function	Low	Average	High
Education	75.16	112.40	175.21
Highways	34.22	53.78	143.20
Welfare	10.62	25.79	51.32
Health, hospitals	9.71	22.33	57.16
Administration	2.93	6.11	14.81
Interest on general debt	2.46	9.96	18.12
Police	4.56	11.02	26.41

tenance of the highway is today principally that of the state government—and to much of the public, the state and the quality and quantity of its highways are synonymous. Within the limits set by federal standards, and subject to federal supervision, the state political system—or more precisely, a segment of it—determines precise routes for new highways, selects the particular features of highway design to be used, employs consultants, sets the limit of highway expenditures, and awards contracts for actual construction.[7]

Each of these decisions affects the interest of a certain number of participants in the state political system. So far as highways are concerned, most candidates for a state elective office have not unreasonably equated the auto-user and the voter. They interpret the electorate's attitude as one which rewards an efficient road builder with votes. In this interpretation, they are encouraged by such groups as the automobile makers in Detroit (who have sponsored contests to find ways for spending more tax money on roads) and the American Automobile Association.

Therefore, since the twenties, a major plank in gubernatorial platforms across the country has been "Good Roads," and almost every legislator devotes large parts of his campaign speeches to pledging that if he is elected, "our district will get its share of highways." One of the most prominent state executive officials below the governor is the Highway Commissioner

[7] For a comprehensive analysis of the role of the states in the national highway program, see Lyle C. Fitch, *et al., Urban Transportation and Public Policy* (San Francisco, 1964).

or Chairman of the Road Board. The State Highway Department itself is usually the largest state agency. Its permanent staff is engaged in impressive problems of design and construction that attract able professional career employees, active and energetic in the development of their programs.

But "highway politics" has more participants than either the car-owning, car-driving public, or the elected officials and administrators eager to meet the public's demands. The commercial highway users have a vital stake in the roads, and truck and bus companies and trade associates work diligently for their improvement. Moreover, road building involves the taking of private property by eminent domain; the letting of contracts for earth removal and road construction; the purchase of building materials in vast quantities; and the selection and purchase of equipment from the highway-building industry. It requires the hiring of a large number of permanent employees and many more temporary employees at peak times of construction or snow removal.

In the process, each of these activities attracts groups and individuals interested in the outcome of particular decisions. Land-taking may offer the opportunity for a private interest with advance knowledge of the location of a new route to purchase the land along the right-of-way, force up its price, and reap a high profit when the state takes title. The award of contracts may mark the beginning of a construction empire for the successful bidder or the bankruptcy of the firm that failed to get a share of the work. The selection of a particular piece of equipment, or the specification of asphalt instead of cement paving, may affect the fortunes of an entire industry. The hiring of a few dozen employees recommended by a particular legislator may influence the outcome of a highway appropriation bill and simultaneously help the reelection of the legislator.

The field of transportation, however, is not restricted to highways. The provision of harbor and airport facilities is frequently a state concern, although again federal and local agencies are almost always involved in these programs to some extent. State regulatory agencies share, in company with the federal Interstate Commerce Commission, important powers in fixing the rates and conditions of service of private railroads, buses, and trucks; occasionally, states manage rapid transit agencies. At the present time, when transportation technology is changing rapidly and private railroads are withdrawing from the passenger-carrier field, this arena of decision-making can be especially turbulent. Many railroads seek to abandon passenger service while union representatives and commuter organizations work vigorously to expand rail traffic. According to the outcome in particular states, the pressures upon the highway system increase or decline.

In the field of modern transportation the state political system chooses among the various modes of transportation, and after the balance is struck makes decisions concerning the programs to be authorized, the resources to be used, and the persons to be benefited in the process of development and maintenance. Under such circumstances it is small wonder that the development of our modern highway system appears to be politics at its most elemental level: where the prizes are obvious, the contestants are active, and the conflict rages without quarter.

"After Many Delays, We Finally Begin Our Five-Week Special Course To Define The Nature Of Communism For High School Students—With 'Conditional Assent,' Of Course . . . !"

Local interest groups often act as vigilantes over the choice and content of educational curricula.

Interlandi in the Los Angeles *Times*

EDUCATION

Compared with the politics of transportation, the decisions that states make in the field of education may seem at first glance to be noncontroversial, dignified, and sedate. There are relatively few charges of corruption and wrongdoing in state departments of education, such as misappropriation of funds, padding of accounts, or favoritism in the awarding of building contracts by state superintendents. More than most public decisions, those in education tend to be made in a "nonpolitical" atmosphere, involving only professional educators, "explaining," "guiding," or "recommending" noncontroversial measures to be taken by lay public officials.

Yet, as a matter of fact, education policy bubbles with political controversy. There are questions of what should be taught: the three R's or techniques of life adjustment. There are issues of the decorum and behavior of schoolteachers; the design and quality of school buildings; the content of history and civilization courses. Broad constitutional questions concerning the separation of church and state become school issues when the question of classroom prayers is raised. In a technological age, the nation's security may literally depend on the kind and level of its education—as Sputnik I dramatically demonstrated in the late 1950s. Even more basic, the capacity of a democratic nation to govern itself and the opportunities available to each of its citizens to develop his or her innate talents to the fullest depend on public education. In this sense, the American schools are the most thoroughly political institutions in the country.

Despite or because of these continuing important responsibilities, public education is kept apart from other government agencies. It often operates at both the state and the local level as a separate political system, with its own tax revenue, elected officials, and institutions. Moreover, to a degree excep-

tional at any level of American government, the expert and the administrator make major choices affecting the extent and quality of public education. School needs, methods of financing, courses of study, and the details
of architecture and school building construction are by and large shaped
by professional criteria. A highly trained corps of career public servants,
advancing by a series of steps prescribed by graduate schools of education,
and following well-articulated and detailed philosophies of instruction,
directs what has now become the largest bureaucracy in the United States.
Occasionally the public may protest the program of the educators, objecting to its costs or its philosophy, and demand a return to the essentials of
schooling without frills—but these revolts are rarely effective. In the long
run the public supports the aims of professional education.

The role of the state political system in this field is confined to a limited
number of decisions, which are nonetheless highly important to the functioning of the schools. Since 1945 the states have increasingly undertaken
to provide financial support to local school districts, so that 40 percent of
the average school budget is derived from state revenues, and the degree
of contribution in twenty-six states exceeds 40 percent.[8]

In providing these funds, more and more states have taken into account
differences in needs and wealth among local districts. Through so-called
"minimum foundation programs," most states now allocate their contributions in some direct relation to the number of children to be educated, and
in some inverse relation to the tax resources of the local communities. In
effect, the states have been the principal vehicle by which certain bedrock
standards held by educators as essential to an adequate public education
have been installed on a nearly universal basis.

It is not just educational administrators, however, who are active in school
affairs at the state level. As an employee group the classroom teachers in
the American states form a cohesive and powerful political force. Operating
through state chapters of the National Educational Association on professional matters, and as the American Federation of Teachers union on the
bread-and-butter issues of higher pay and better working conditions, the
more than one and one-half million teachers in the United States agitate
for specific benefits at the state level. In most states, they have succeeded
in assuring that the state department of education controls entry into the
profession by the process of "certifying" prescribed training standards for
teachers, accredits local schools, and sets salary schedules and work conditions which local school districts must follow. One Florida legislator dubbed
the teachers' organizations and their lay disciples, the Parent-Teacher Associations, "The Lobby of the Good" as he watched a new hundred-million-
dollar financial support formula pass through the Senate with scarcely any
debate and without a dissenting vote. "I can no more vote against these
people," he said, "than I can vote against Americanism. They are mother-
hood, orphans, veterans all rolled into one."

In addition to providing funds and setting personnel standards, the state

---

[8] The most comprehensive recent examination of the public education system in America
is found in the twelve monographs included in Jesse Burkhead, director, *The Economics
and Politics of Public Education Series* (Syracuse, 1962–63).

political systems have other important duties. In many states they select textbooks and provide special visual aids and technical advice to local school administrators. They encourage by a variety of financial and legal incentives the consolidation of school districts which appear too small to be efficient. Each of these activities has political as well as educational overtones. The selection of textbooks does not only involve considerations of civil liberties and problems of censorship. It also is a multimillion-dollar business, for state adoption of a text can provide sizable returns for author and publisher alike.

In its role as a major educational enterprise, the state is more than a standard setter and money raiser. In higher education the states are the direct operators of one quarter of the nation's colleges and universities. Counting teachers and junior colleges, one finds that by mid-century state governments were spending over $5 billion in support of higher education.[9] As in the case of highways, public expectations have figured prominently in expansion. The promise of equal access to a college degree for the voter's sons and daughters has often replaced the pledge of two cars in every garage as an effective campaign slogan.

More than the influence of the public at large is involved in higher education, however. The alumni of the great state universities, organized and active, are suitable material from which political organizations can be fashioned. When called to aid their alma mater, they often combine schoolboy fervor with adult know-how and influence and present a formidable political front. University and college presidents frequently become skilled witnesses before legislative committees, eloquent spokesmen for more funds at gubernatorial budget hearings, and persuasive orators on public occasions. Finally, the heavy capital requirements which universities make—in dormitories, football stadiums, libraries, laboratories, and classrooms—represent contracts and jobs for architects, engineers, and construction companies.

In both public schools and higher education the states are today deeply committed to supporting an educational program from kindergarten to the Ph.D.—and in shaping the state's role the professional educator predominates. With most departments of education operating in a quasi-independent manner in fact, if not by law, and with the state universities asserting their autonomy as a matter of academic freedom, elected public officials in state politics often somewhat wistfully feel that in their direction of educational affairs they have a tiger by the tail. Committed to an extensive program of state support, they are also committed to a process of decision-making in which professional control and direction are at least as advanced as in any other state activity, and show little sign of diminishing.

WELFARE

Compared to the central involvement of the state political system in transportation and education, the role of the states in public welfare on first inspection appears less important and more routine. In the traditional direct welfare activities—assistance to the aged, to the blind, to dependent

---

[9] See Council of State Governments, *The Book of the States* (Chicago, annually) for basic data respecting operations and financing of state government.

children, and to the physically incapacitated—the New Deal grants-in-aid programs enacted in the 1930s seem to have put Washington squarely in charge, and the states have appeared as mere conduits for the transfer of funds from the national to the local levels: "governments that spend money they do not raise and raise money they do not spend," in V. O. Key's classic phrase.[10]

Yet appearances can be deceiving. Though the federal government provides the modern counterpart of the "outdoor" relief system of a hundred years ago, through its assistance payments and more decisively through the national social security insurance program, the states remain heavily involved. For one thing, they contribute a substantial share of the cost of the federally sponsored programs, and they determine the maximum limits of payments. They also provide the administrative structure, the supervisory personnel, and the caseworkers required for the actual operations of a program. As the aged population of the United States has increased, many states have sponsored separate relief programs of their own. Governors and legislatures find that old-age pensions have a political attraction approaching that of highways, and the national network of Golden Age clubs is recognized as a potent political force.

Even more dramatic than the states' development of fringe pension plans in the last generation has been their provision of comprehensive institutional care for selected categories of the needy. Shaking off the old tradition of treating the indigent and mentally ill as criminals, the states have rapidly expanded and upgraded institutional care for these individuals. Beginning with tuberculosis sanitoria and now extending to mental hospitals, the facilities provided by state governments have come to emphasize treatment rather than custodial care. State farms for retarded children, state hospitals and special schools for children afflicted with cerebral palsy and other diseases, and state hospitals for the insane, for the care of chronic diseases, for the handling of terminal cases, now are commonplace. Currently almost $1 billion a year is appropriated for public health activities alone at the state level.

These decisions to supplement federal funds and to invest heavily in "indoor" relief facilities attract their own special proponents and opponents. Beside each of the classic adversaries—for example, the aged who want more care versus the taxpayers' groups who want to reduce public expenditures generally—particular interest groups take their stand. Psychologists and psychiatrists, for example, now regard the state institutions as the principal postgraduate training ground for their professions and indeed as a major avenue for career advancement. Social work is now a professional career rather than a charitable occupation. Hence professional welfare and medical organizations work for higher salary levels, better working conditions, and more comprehensive health and welfare programs. The professions are also concerned with their relative status in the state administrative structure, comparative salary schedules, and the allotment of executive positions. Sporadically psychiatrists, psychologists, and social workers engage in intra-

---

[10] V. O. Key, Jr., *American State Politics: An Introduction* (New York, 1956), p. 8.

mural warfare against one another—before uniting in defense of a larger budget request.

Moreover, since the institutions are usually semiautonomous, self-sufficient enterprises, in isolated locations, their staffs become small communities. Employees, professional and nonprofessional, their families, and friends form articulate and skillful coalitions, working for the continued improvement of the facilities. These institutional interests in recent years have been joined by important lay groups. New advocates of expanded programs have appeared, especially in the field of mental health, where modern drugs now offer promise of relatively rapid and complete cures in place of permanent confinement. Mental health associations, exceptional children associations, and hospital associations are now organized in every state in the union and are nationally federated. These provide a new look to welfare politics, for the services are no longer used by only a few groups in the population. They are available to, and may eventually be required by, almost every member of society.

The job of expanding welfare programs is not always an easy one. Institutional care raises more issues than that of increased expenditures. As public hospitals increase in number, they provide stiff competition for private hospitals and nursing homes offering the same care. These private facilities often take the persuasive position that the states are needlessly duplicating existing institutions, providing services at a greater expense than is possible under private management, and engaging in practices injurious to the free-enterprise system. This final complaint carries ideological punch in budget hearings and legislative debate, for though the welfare state is a matter of fact in America it has yet to find its way into our political folklore. The spirit of the frontier had little tolerance for the incapacitated individual who could not pull his own oar, and though the frontier has been closed for some seventy years, many conservative citizens still equate disability with incompetence or immorality.

A final participant in the welfare debate is the press, though the influence of newspapers and other media tends to swing from one side of the controversy to another. Welfare institutions are ready-made locations for the production of the "human side of the news." Depending on the objectives and attitudes of the reporter, a mental hospital, a county farm, or a children's home can always produce a headline. If conditions of neglect, cruelty, and inattention cannot be discovered, then certainly the opposite charge of "coddling" inmates without respect for public safety can be made. So the possibility of sporadic publicity adds a dash of excitement and intrigue to a program which otherwise is not the daily concern of the world at large.

The Present Organization of the Systems:
(2) Local Responsibilities

While the states devote most of their financial resources and manpower to transportation, education, and welfare, the local political systems have their own public decisions to make. Their primary concern is with a separate phase of the public school process and with two other major programs.

Local governments have prime responsibility for law and order in American society except in times of extraordinary emergency. They also have the obligation to provide the community facilities and services necessary to support private community development. Water and sewerage systems, electric plants and lines, playgrounds and neighborhood parks, hospitals, streets, lighting, and incinerators—the capital investment commonly called public works—result from public decisions made at the local level. These programs consume the largest share of the local budgets and manpower and represent the bedrock jobs which all localities everywhere, in some way or other, are expected to carry out.

THE LOCAL PUBLIC SCHOOL

While state educational decisions concern finances and setting of professional standards, the local decisions are those of actual operation and management. The community political process wrestles with questions of detail and specifics. How much will this year's school budget be? What courses should be taught? What schedule of bus arrivals and departures should be established? Should the high school band have new uniforms? How many children represent the optimum class size? What architectural design should be adopted for the new school? Should controversial speakers on religion or politics be allowed to use school property for public meetings? The net result of the answers to all these questions is the establishment of the particular quality of education which a locality decides is satisfactory. While the state provides minimum financing and standards, local money and local personnel practices establish the conditions which actually prevail in our schoolhouses.

The governing of local education is for the most part carried on in a separate political structure. Partly, this condition is the result of historical accident when school districts were first established within walking radius of the schoolhouse and hence became more numerous than other local jurisdictions. Partly, the importance of education as "the carrier of democracy" seems to justify special arrangements. During the nineteenth century, when cities fell under the domination of bosses and machines, the importance of having independent school management was underscored. Finally, the professional educator quite understandably prefers his separate institution.

For all these reasons, the political autonomy of public education is almost universal at the local level. Except in large cities and in parts of New England, school politics are separated from local politics by the establishment of special school districts, each authorized to raise revenues of its own and each directed by a board or commission, which is usually elected. The districts range in size from those as large as counties to those smaller than a town or hamlet. In recent years, the number of districts has been greatly reduced by consolidation, especially in rural areas, to accommodate new forms of transportation and new educational concepts of the best size of schools. They retain their independence, however, and education remains a "unique function" in American government, and some 35,000 school districts prove it.

Within the school districts, once again the professional educator emerges

"Well, Rip Van Winkle?"

Some local communities have drawn
criticism for lagging behind federal
and state education programs.

Brooks in the Birmingham *News*

as the key participant. In the person of the local school superintendent, the educator holds the key executive position in the local school program. He shapes the budget, hires and fires teachers, appoints principals, establishes faculty committees to pass on matters of curriculum and school organization, oversees the letting of contracts, and makes the arrangements for school transportation.

To carry out his policies, the superintendent must be supported by an elected (occasionally appointed) board of citizens known variously as the Board of Education, District School Board, or School Committee in different parts of the country. Legally, these bodies are the governors and managers of local schools formally empowered to "make school policy." In practice they more often serve as friendly allies of the superintendent, working, in the words of one observer, to "defend the schools against public criticism, and persuade the people to open their pocketbooks." In addition to the school boards, the local Parent-Teacher Associations, local chapters of the state's educational association, and the local Federation of Teachers can usually be counted on to be active. They mobilize the public support for additional funds and manpower, under the slogan "Better Schools Make Better Communities."

Although the "pro-school" forces are impressive in number and activity, they by no means have matters entirely their own way. Depending on the size and type of community involved (an old city or a new suburb, for example, a manufacturing town or a residential one, a large metropolis or a farm village), strong and occasionally violent opposition may be evident. There are always residents who simply want taxes kept down and

The Political Heritage of the Grass Roots / 853

residents who have no children. There are also political opponents of what the schools teach. Closely allied with them may be the "anti-frills and fads" movement—the citizens who inquire why each high school has its own auditorium or why two- or three-story schools are no longer fashionable among school architects. There are groups, too, prepared to accuse particular superintendents, teachers, and textbooks of teaching un-American doctrines. At times these movements have succeeded in disrupting a number of school administrations across the continent. Finally, there are the usual interests which congregate whenever public buildings are to be erected, public supplies and equipment furnished, public meals prepared—architects, contractors, school furniture companies, school bus companies, caterers, and the like.

To this more or less usual range of decisions at the local level may be added the complex problems of management raised by the United States Supreme Court ruling of 1954 requiring racial integration "with all deliberate speed." Since that time, legislatures have debated whether or not to allow schools to operate under integrated conditions in some states, and governors have interfered with the process in others. In the end, however, the states have no meaningful choices in this major conflict among levels of government. The local level makes the real decisions of how rapidly, with how many children, at what grades, in which schools, and by which formulas integration shall proceed. It is these questions of quantity and detail that crop up in local school administration to tax the ingenuity of school boards and superintendents alike and to bring new participants into the arena of local politics.

PUBLIC SAFETY

Local school operations represent the most expensive local programs and certainly, in many areas, the set of decisions receiving the greatest popular attention. In other places, however, especially in the older and larger cities, debates over conditions in the schools are no more intense than those over the protection of life and property. More than any other activity, the responsibility for public safety, for enforcing the law and maintaining reasonable conditions of community protection, falls upon local governments. To be sure, federal enforcement agencies—the Secret Service, the FBI, and the Customs Office—have jurisdiction over a limited number of crimes, such as kidnaping, bank robbery, and espionage. State police or patrols have in recent years become well-trained, well-organized forces. Other state facilities are available to help in fire prevention activities, the inspection of private buildings for compliance with health and safety regulations, and juvenile delinquency work. But the municipal police force continues to be the principal instrument on which we rely to restrain a traditionally unruly people from systematic and insupportable violence. And local fire departments and local building and sanitary code inspectors are the prime operating agencies in maintaining our national inventory of housing and facilities in good condition.

One way to indicate the dimensions of the public safety job is by statistics. Annually, the Federal Bureau of Investigation reports some 8,000 murders, 14,000 rapes, and 600,000 burglaries. There were 25,000 fires (in cities of over 1 million) in the United States for which alarms for fire equipment were sounded. There were over 9 million dilapidated dwelling units in American municipalities—a fair index to the need for sanitary, health, and fire inspections of buildings. In response to these needs over a quarter of a million policemen are employed by local governments in the United States, and there are almost a quarter of a million firemen. This is an average of 1.43 policemen and 1.32 firemen for every 1,000 residents in cities over 10,000.[11]

The direction and supervision of these enforcement agencies are by no means routine tasks. They involve the local political process in major, often controversial, decisions. Public safety agencies require special discipline and performance on the part of their personnel, approaching those of military organizations. But these conditions do not prevent politics. On the contrary, firemen and policemen have some of the best-organized employee associations in government; these are capable of wielding considerable political influence in active pursuit of improved pay and working conditions. But complicating matters further, fire and police levels of compensation often serve as pace setters for other municipal employees and thus are a decisive force in fixing the size of the budget and the tax rate. In dealing with public safety agencies, then, a mayor or a council may find that every major managerial issue for the entire government is raised by his police and fire department and must be settled there.

Public safety involves other and even more explosive issues. A series of small crimes or one dangerous criminal on the loose can always, if the local newspapers choose, become a "crime wave." If the general public feels that its police or fire department is ineffective, the next election is likely to sweep every incumbent out of office. On the other hand, in the matter of traffic enforcement the very efficiency of the police can trigger off similar waves of public antagonism. Given the American ambivalence toward the law, either too lax or too strict enforcement can spell political trouble.

Even more sensitive than issues of police efficiency are issues of police corruption, ever-present swords of Damocles, especially for mayors of large cities. Corruption charges toward police and inspection officers are often hurled irresponsibly and are frequently highly exaggerated. Yet the fact that corruption is an actual and continuing problem has been documented in one Congressional investigation after another.

The nature of police work invites corruption. Since the police have the lawful monopoly on physical violence, it is often vital to some interests to influence that power. In the United States, the temptation is intensified by the public's desire to "write all their moral yearnings in the statute books" and then make other arrangements to make sure the law is not rigorously enforced. An expert on American police practices for over a quarter of a century has pointed out that the United States arrest and conviction record for crimes which the public abhors—murder, rape, kidnaping—exceeds 90 percent. It is the publicly "inoffensive" crimes—off-track betting on horse

---

[11] See International Association of City Managers, *The Municipal Yearbook* (Chicago, annually), a reference book paralleling *The Book of the States* in covering local government activities.

racing, other forms of gaming, violation of the so-called "blue laws," traffic violations—that encourage bribery, payoffs, and the fix. Police departments that rigorously prohibit these activities find little public support.

Moreover, in the case of gambling, extremely profitable businesses are involved, and the offenders will pay large sums to be allowed to operate enterprises which few find objectionable. To be sure, these "less" offensive activities may lead to far more serious ones—prostitution, narcotics, and internecine gang warfare. But the opening wedge to persuade an individual officer or a police department to overlook a violation is usually a comparatively small one.

Fire departments are less exposed to these temptations in their main work. But in their inspection activities, as in the case of sanitary, health, and housing inspections, property owners may believe it is less expensive to bribe the inspector than to remove the violation. Again, large investments become critically dependent on nonenforcement of the law.

Finally, there are philosophical issues along with questions about the effectiveness and honesty of enforcement programs. These decisions involve the handling of juvenile delinquents, whether "soft" or "hard" attitudes are most effective, the role of the psychologist or of the youth worker versus that of the policeman on the beat. Civil liberties are also at stake—the propriety of interrogation methods, for example. Humanitarian concerns also arise—the living conditions in jails and detention homes. All these decisions which govern the behavior of enforcement personnel combine to make public safety politics among the most turbulent in America.

PUBLIC WORKS

In contrast to the decisions about education and public safety which a local political system must make, questions concerning the installation of water lines, sewerage systems, and street lights, sometimes the generation of electric power and the regulation of private gas, electric, and transit utilities, may seem mundane and commonplace. Once again, however, controversial decisions of consequence are at hand. The public works program which a municipality or a special district furnishes or regulates determines in no small measure the pattern of residential, private, commercial, and industrial settlement in a community. It also provides opportunities for "contract politics"—the coalitions between private businesses and public officials which tend to arise whenever government is engaged in large-scale procurement and construction.

Historically, the first modern public utilities were privately owned and operated, subject to public regulation by the granting of local franchises and later by the regulation of rates and service schedules. This process of public supervision proved ineffective in the nineteenth century as the private utilities often openly and blatantly moved to "charge what the traffic would bear." Inflated building costs, inaccurate accounting for investments, dummy interest payments, and complicated arrangements for interlocking ownership among companies pushed up the prices of the basic utilities and resulted in profits which were exorbitant even in the heyday of laissez faire. Since utilities are natural or technological monopolies, so structured as to make competition impossible, the consumers had no choice but to pay the high prices.

But even when thoughtfully administered, local regulation proved difficult—for problems of determining the actual costs of installations, a fair rate of return, and true value of property proved exceedingly complex, particularly when the utility covered a much larger territory than the municipality. Subsequently federal and state regulation and a changing perspective on the part of private management substantially improved conditions and telephone, gas, and, to a lesser extent, electric utilities remained in private hands. But in other fields, the nineteenth-century experience led more and more local governments to own and operate utilities directly. These facilities now make up the bulk of their public works investment.

Today, three quarters of all municipalities with a population of over 5,000 own their own water distribution system. Almost all own their sewerage systems and over one half own their treatment plants. Municipal airports are the rule rather than the exception; so are auditoriums and incinerators. Municipal parking buildings are rapidly appearing and fifty-eight municipalities (with populations over 5,000) own and operate transit or bus lines. Charged with responsibility for not only these but streets, sidewalks, traffic direction, parks, and playgrounds, the average municipal government now presides over an extensive enterprise of public works.

In the construction and operation of this wide array of facilities, two kinds of politics are usually involved. The first is the now familiar variety—the decisions of where and when to provide service, which arise whenever a public body is engaged in an enterprise involving a substantial amount of construction work: the selection of architect and contractor, the setting of quality standards, the determination of the conditions for borrowing the necessary funds, the supervision of the work, and the purchase of material. In these respects, public works politics parallels that of transportation, except that it is usually more routine and regular.

Unlike highway costs, most public works expenses can be charged directly to the actual users; this condition makes it possible for utility agencies to follow the practices of private enterprise in obtaining revenue, making investments, and controlling operations. Moreover, while public works investments have risen sharply in the last few years, they have not proceeded in the atmosphere of emergency and revolutionary changes in construction techniques which have characterized the highway program. Hence well-established local public works and utility agencies with experienced engineering and supervisory personnel have carried out the program. Finally, there is little public disagreement involved in deciding when and where utilities are required. Needs for public works can usually be calculated on the basis of the size of the population to be served and objective standards exist for making new investment. All these conditions make for more routine public decisions than in the other local programs, though the decisions are no less important.

A second kind of politics involving public works arouses more conflict and controversy. As urban populations have grown in number and spilled over central-city boundary lines to suburbs, the provision of utilities has not

"Let's Not Play Bridge This After-noon—Let's Write Nasty Letters To Editors!"

Local controversy over public works may involve emotional and unin-formed arguments.

CATERLANDI© 1964, LOS ANGELES TIMES
Interlandi in the Los Angeles *Times*

always kept up with the increase and movement of the residents. Rapidly growing municipalities have found it more and more difficult to secure new water reservoirs or to locate new airports without protests from neighboring jurisdictions, and older cities use existing facilities less efficiently as their populations decline. As the new suburban communities have faced the need for expensive capital investment in public works, questions of intermunici-pality collaboration have arisen—the tapping of central-city water lines and sewerage systems by suburbs, and the joint use of incinerators, auditoriums, and libraries. Fifty years ago, negotiations over such matters often led to the annexation of fringe communities to the mother city. Now they usually result in the establishment of special water, sewerage, or street-lighting districts independent of the central or suburban governments, or to con-tractual arrangements among cities for the mutual purchase or exchange of services. Whatever the form, the added pressure for community facilities by a growing population gives rise to a form of politics perhaps best charac-terized as intermunicipal diplomacy. As the problems of servicing the new settlements grow in intensity, and questions of relative cost and benefits continue to arise, decisions in this realm may approach the controversies evident in education and public safety.

Finally, a "surprise" conflict in recent years has concerned the fluoridation of public water supplies. Although the chemical treatment of drinking water with fluoride to prevent tooth decay has been approved by dental and medical associations and subjected to extensive testing, its application has provoked violent controversy. Groups protesting that their civil rights are being infringed or that the water is being poisoned have defeated fluorida-tion programs in many communities across the country.

State and Local Governments as Going Concerns

Not all the expenditures, personnel, and political attention of our lower echelons are devoted to the six main activities outlined above. There are important decisions made at the state level in the operation of the court system and correctional institutions, in agriculture, conservation, and a dozen other fields. In the localities, public health, licensing, recreation, and the recording of property deeds and transfers consume attention and resources. We shall discuss some of these activities later on.

Nonetheless the six programs—transportation, education, welfare, public schools, safety, and public works—represent the major arenas in which political conflicts develop and are resolved at the present time and the important issues which the state and local systems decide. They cover the bulk of the actions—of local politicians, public officials, pressure groups, lobbyists, bureaucrats, and individual citizens, newspaper reporters, editors, and publishers—that shape public decisions. The decisions that the participants in the systems make are at times heavily influenced by decisions made at other levels. Yet a substantial degree of autonomy remains for each system, and the influence of state and local units in intergovernmental programs involving the national government is substantial. In short, state and local political systems are going concerns, with the legal authority, money, manpower, policies, and programs to qualify as distinct and independent powers resolving issues in their own ways.

The remaining chapters in this section will analyze the processes by which the state and local systems manage conflicts, resolve disputes, and make decisions on their own and in collaboration with each other or with Washington. They explore how influence is acquired and distributed among the principal participants in state and local politics; how issues are raised and resolved; and how political stability is maintained.

Once the principal properties of local, state, and intergovernmental politics are identified, the relation of the systems to their changing environments is examined, and the impact on the governments of powerful modern economic and social forces—most notably industrialization and urbanization—is noted. And here, the question of how the systems deal with "new" American communities—the interstate region and the metropolitan area—becomes critically important.

27 / The Performance of the States

By almost every test of political significance, the key units in American subnational political affairs are the fifty state governments. They are the only such components endowed with constitutional autonomy. They determine the powers, duties, revenues, and forms of local governments, including those of the largest cities in the nation. They are the basis on which our national political parties are organized and our national elections conducted. So the responses made by the multitude of local institutions to their changing environments—and indeed the actual execution of many national domestic programs—depend to a great degree on the decisions of the states.

The way the states conduct their affairs and make their decisions is also a matter of considerable controversy. Their continued vitality is considered by many to be fundamental to the American way of life. To some commentators, they guarantee "territorial democracy" in America; states' rights are imperative to prevent "despotism and enervating centralization." [1] To others, "state government is the tawdriest, most incompetent and most stultifying unit of the nation's political structure." [2]

One thing is certain. Until very recently, the states have been extraordinarily impervious to change in their formal structure, constitutions, election procedures, and decision-making processes. While they have rapidly expanded the size of their bureaucracies, added new programs, and acquired new revenues, they have not radically modified their institutions and procedures. So political systems originally designed to handle political conflicts of a rural, relatively homogeneous, and widely diffused society are employed today to produce decisions and programs of an entirely different order. It is this paradox of old forms and new tasks, of critical but controversial roles in the federal system, that makes an accurate appraisal of state governments today both a complicated and an important undertaking.

---

[1] Russell Kirk, "The Prospects for Territorial Democracy in America," Robert A. Goldwin, ed., *A Nation of States: Essays on the American Federal System* (Chicago, 1963), p. 42.
[2] Robert A. Allen, ed., *The Sovereign States* (New York, 1949), p. 11.

The Revolutionary Prototype: State Government in the Age of Reason

American state political institutions emerged from the traditions of the thirteen colonies shaped both by the pragmatic experiences of settling a new continent and by principles of highly abstract political philosophy. The original settlements on the eastern seaboard were designed not expressly for democratic purposes and indeed only incidentally for public purposes. Instead, their governing bodies were often conceived principally as instruments by which the investors in the trading companies were able to maintain and supervise their operations. Community conditions soon led to major modifications in the original company charters, as the early governors and their assistants acceded to demands for town representation by the freemen among the settlers. The great and general courts in Massachusetts, for example, gradually became bodies with distinct and independent responsibilities apart from company management. As the conflicts between royal governors and colonists intensified, the behavior of legislative bodies became increasingly independent. Separation of governmental powers was an established fact years before the Revolution, and the colonial assemblies became the prime instruments for rebellion.[3]

After the Revolution, the political philosophy of the day was able to justify the native institutions. In England and on the Continent the power of parliaments was growing, and the "contract" theory of government—with its emphasis on the division and restraint of governmental powers and on checks and balances—was being favorably received by politically influential people of the day. In the Constitutional Convention the founders of the new national government gave explicit recognition to these concepts by providing for the separation of executive, legislative, and judicial powers. The first Congress added the further restraint of a bill of rights. At the state level, the same doctrines took the form of much longer documents, which provided for the three separate branches of government, drastically curtailed the powers of the executive branch, which had for so long represented the Crown, and incorporated similar or identical bills of rights.

To a greater extent than in the case of the national government, state constitutions proclaimed the primacy of the legislature. That branch was typically charged with the specific rights to initiate policy and to raise revenue. Frequently, it was empowered to appoint governors and judges and often the chief executive was forbidden to veto legislation. Sweeping authority for impeachment of executive and judicial officials was granted. When the detailed state constitutions did not prescribe how particular matters of public policy were to be handled, the presumption was that the decision lay with the legislative branch.

---

[3] See Allan R. Richards, "The Traditions of Government in Our States," *The Forty-Eight States: Their Tasks as Policy Makers and Administrators* (New York, 1955); see also Victoria Schuck, "The Massachusetts Governor: Hamstrung by History," Robert R. Robbins, ed., *State Government and Public Responsibility, 1961: The Role of the Governor in Massachusetts* (papers of 1961 Tufts Assembly on Massachusetts Government, Medford, Mass., 1961).

Not only were the new states legislatively oriented, they were usually more representative of established economic elites than of the "common man." The ruling class of merchants, plantation owners, and professional men continued to dominate the direction of public affairs, as it had done prior to the Declaration of Independence. To be sure, "the people" were granted inalienable rights and all power was officially vested in them, but political practice did not always follow principle. Most of the states, for example, established both religious and property qualifications for voting, and state legislatures were typically bicameral to represent both the common wealth and aristocratic wealth. Although the new constitutions were framed by Revolutionary conventions or existing legislatures, except for Massachusetts and New Hampshire, they were not popularly ratified. The town fathers of old—the rich, the able, and the wellborn, as John Adams called them—remained securely in command of the public domain, though constrained and challenged by the democratic ideology that had been set loose in the fervor of the Revolution. Exceptions existed. In the new states of Tennessee and Kentucky a spirit of frontier democracy was at work, but the original colonies, by and large, remained dominated by the few.[4]

Finally, in the early years of the American Republic the states were typically at the center of public affairs. The powers of the national government were limited and specific, and it would take generations of court interpretations to expand the application of the interstate commerce and general welfare clauses of the Constitution. Local governments were creatures of the state, and though they exercised considerable autonomy in practice their subordinate legal status was never in doubt. The bulk of the armed forces of the United States was the militia of the states. Responsibility for internal improvements, welfare, highways, and education was theirs, and the federal government often employed state administration structures to carry out its duties as well. The state judicial system was responsible for the adjudication of most controversies. In short, in terms of basic powers and operating programs, the government "that mattered" to citizens in the late eighteenth and early nineteenth centuries was the government in the state house.

The States' Line of Development

With their emphasis on legislative supremacy and their sensitivity to the demands of the ruling class, most of the new states' governments followed a path of evolution different from that of the national establishment. The Founding Fathers in Philadelphia had not provided for as vigorous a Chief Executive as some of the Convention's delegates had wished, and they left the determination of suffrage qualifications and the conduct of elections to the state. Nonetheless, the short and relatively simple federal Constitution provided substantial room for the expansion of Presidential powers, and skilled incumbents soon learned to use its authority, as we have seen in Chapter 10. Moreover, the Congress was necessarily representative of a far more diverse constituency than were the legislatures, and as it dealt with

---

[4] Richards, *op. cit.*, p. 42.

broad and visible issues, it proved to be a more responsive instrument to popular sentiment.

In the late 1700s and early 1800s, modifications in state government practice did take place. Revisions in state constitutions produced some limitations on legislative authority after land frauds in Georgia and a rash of bank scandals in several states were exposed. Some control was placed on the already prevalent custom of special acts for special interests in place of general lawmaking. There was some liberalization of the suffrage requirements, as exemplified by Tennessee's first constitution. State judiciaries established the principle of the judicial review. In several states the powers of the governor over the legislature were strengthened by longer terms, direct popular election, greater appointive powers, and the right to veto legislative bills.

As the Jacksonian philosophy swept the land, with its faith in the common man, broader franchise, and partisan politics, new state constitutions limited the time and frequency of legislative sessions and the amount of indebtedness state legislatures could authorize; they also placed limitations on tax rates and incorporation laws. More executive officials and judges were popularly elected, and more power was placed in their hands. Yet throughout the nineteenth century, while Jackson, Lincoln, and Cleveland were asserting the primacy of the Presidency, the legislature remained the key instrument of state policy-making. In 1831, De Tocqueville wrote, "In America the legislature of each state is supreme; nothing can impede its authority." Seventy years later another distinguished foreign observer of American politics, Lord Bryce, concluded, "The legislature . . . is so much the strongest force in the several States that we may almost call it the Government and ignore all other authorities." [5]

Although legislatures continued as the focal points of state governments, the major tasks and functions of the governments themselves became increasingly obscure. The Civil War did more than settle the moral issue of slavery and the constitutional issue of secession. Once the doctrine of national supremacy was established, the precise role the states should play in the American political system became uncertain. By the latter part of the nineteenth century, at least in the eyes of the voter, the duties and responsibilities of the "middle tier" of American governments had become blurred, in contrast with the activities that national and local governments were expected to undertake.[6] Other forces contributed to the "fuzziness" of the states' image: most notably, industrialization and urbanization. The increasing nationalization of the economy made the federal establishment the most natural agent to carry out economic development policy. Local communities had the immediate responsibility of dealing with the problems of urban growth. The states fell somewhere in between, and although some of them undertook positive programs of economic reform and assistance to the new cities, their laws were often struck down by courts then intent on protecting private property rights.

---

[5] Quoted by Richards, op. cit., pp. 43, 51.
[6] See Paul S. Reinsch, American Legislatures and Legislative Methods (New York, 1907), Chapter 4.

When measured by dollars spent or employees hired, recent trends expanding the magnitude of state activity have done little to clarify the question of the state's role in American life. Increased grants-in-aid from Washington have been aimed at increasing the effectiveness of particular programs in health, highways, or welfare; they have been made on a piecemeal basis and have rarely served to support the general institution of state government. Often it has been difficult to distinguish state activities from federal ones. In place of the pre-Civil War doctrine of dual federalism, in which the states and the nation were presumed to have distinct and separate spheres of activity, the modern concept of cooperative federalism emerged to emphasize the inseparability of the domestic concerns of both levels and to blend duties and responsibilities.

By the middle of the twentieth century, then, states had become characterized as "conduits" through which federal funds passed for distribution to local governments, giving rise to such observations as "The American people are not boiling with concern about the workings of their state governments." [7] Or as another commentator has observed, "Probably not one percent of the voters have read their state constitutions or know the name of any state official except the governor. It is also probably safe to assume that, since most newspapers find the greatest news value in the scandals, crimes, and other misdeeds in state politics they omit or give little space to what is well and honestly accomplished. Accordingly, the pictures of state affairs the voters have in their heads are mostly of strife and struggle among a lot of fools and crooks." [8]

Legislative Government in the States Today

How do today's state governments, commanding little public understanding or respect, make decisions about public issues today? Obviously, given fifty separate states, each with different constitutions, customs, and constituencies, no single answer is possible. The patterns of decision-making in New York and in South Dakota, for example, differ greatly in terms of the issues that are considered important, the predominant political party in control of the government, the size of the electorate, and a number of other characteristics. But the greatest common denominator, given the historical background of state politics, remains the general importance of the legislative bodies. Their long dominance in directing state public affairs suggests that an understanding of their behavior is the key to explaining how most state governments perform.

The formal structure and processes of state legislative bodies parallel in broad respects those of the United States Congress. Their decision-making is a collective process involving fifty groups of between 43 and 424 men and women who consider from 30 to 8,000 bills annually and enact into law from 10 to 2,000 of them each year. Highly stylized procedures of committee hearings, debates, and votes, again similar to those of the Congress, winnow

---

[7] V. O. Key, Jr., *American State Politics: An Introduction* (New York, 1956), p. 3.
[8] Dayton D. McKean, "The Politics of the States," *The Forty-Eight States: Their Tasks as Policy Makers and Administrators* (New York, 1955), p. 66.

**Capitol Hill—
Legislative Mountain**

This cartoon shows some of the problems facing a state legislature at the beginning of a session.

Knox in the Nashville *Banner*

the number of bills seriously considered, in order to make the work load manageable. Four principal factors, however, operate beneath the formal procedure to determine which bills eventually receive consideration; which among these are judged to be important and controversial; and which are eventually passed. They are: (1) the basis of representation established for the legislature; (2) the pattern of party alignment and the degree of party cohesion; (3) the character of interest group activity in the state; (4) the legislators' personalities and individual perceptions of their duties. These factors vary in importance from state to state, and they exist in a multitude of combinations. But certain broad trends are visible for each factor in almost all states and their study is of real help in understanding legislative behavior. We shall therefore consider each one briefly.[9]

THE BASIS OF REPRESENTATION

Legislators represent constituencies; and constituencies in a highly urbanized society distinguishable along class, occupational, ethnic, and geographical lines have different public needs and different perceptions of the public interest. One obvious explanation of legislative behavior, therefore, is found

---

[9] An excellent recent empirical analysis of the variables involved in legislative behavior is Thomas A. Flinn, *Party Responsibility in the States: Some Causal Factors* (paper delivered at 1963 annual meeting of American Political Science Association). A sizable literature, mostly in periodicals, investigates legislative decisions on roll call votes and is broadly supportive of Flinn's analysis.

in the varying composition of the different constituencies electing the legislators. But an even more vital factor is the "filter" imposed on these views by the designs of legislative districts. These designs prevent a strong one-to-one correlation between divisions in constituency attitudes and legislative attitudes. They sharply modify the cardinal principle of the simplistic version of democratic theory, "one man, one vote," even though the United States system now explicitly subscribes to the doctrine. This theory states that, whenever possible, every citizen ought to participate directly in governmental deliberations. When this is not possible, he should be represented in a manner which makes his influence equivalent to that of every other citizen. In the American states, although the doctrine is accepted in principle and in law, its practice is still far from universal.

Chief among the limitations influencing the composition of our state legislatures are the restrictions on suffrage—the right of an individual to vote. Although religious and property qualifications have been abandoned, women have been granted the vote, and restrictions on race have been formally revoked, other limitations persist. These deal with age (except for four states, a voter must be over twenty-one); residence in the state, county, and voting district (usually one year for the first, between one and six months for the second, less than three months for the third); citizenship; and literacy. The apparently innocuous residence requirement is of increasing importance in a nation where one fifth of the population moves each year (the upper middle class is especially mobile). The literacy requirement established in eighteen states is often used in the South to prevent Negro voting. The severity of the tests ranges from Alaska's standard that the voter be able to read or speak English to that of Mississippi, where a voter must be able to read and write any section of the state constitution and give a "reasonable" interpretation of it. Other disqualifications apply to criminals in stated categories, the insane, and those who have not paid poll taxes. For certain local elections involving finances, property qualifications are still in force.[10]

The general intent of these limitations is to ensure that voters have the maturity and intellectual capacity to exercise the vote. But when combined with requirements for registration and absentee voting and the complicated form of some ballots, they also result in discrimination against minority groups and make more difficult the participation of all voters. Overall, the result is to favor legislators representative of a constituency with different characteristics—older, with established residences and some education—than those of the total population.

Another limitation on direct representation is the fact that considerations other than population often shape the composition of legislatures, with different considerations applying to senates and houses of representatives. One finds that of the ninety-nine houses in American state legislatures (Nebraska has a unicameral legislature), thirty-two use population or some definition of qualified voters as the basis; eight use population but with "weighted" ratios, which means that some groups of voters have greater representation than others; forty-five employ a combination of population

---

[10] Council of State Governments, *The Book of the States* (Chicago, 1960), pp. 20–21.

and area; eight allocate representatives according to political units; five allocate by a fixed constitutional formula; and one allocates by taxation. "Weighted ratios" are obtained by dividing the total population of a state by the number of legislative seats and then granting representation to legislative districts whose population totals only a *fraction* of the quotient. Districts with only one half of the quotient in Alaska, Hawaii, Michigan, or Oregon, for example, are guaranteed representation and more populous districts have their number of legislators automatically reduced. So in Oregon, the population of senatorial districts varies from 67,000 to 26,000.[11]

Area is combined with population in three ways: by limiting the number of legislators from any one political unit; by guaranteeing minimum representation for all units; or by imposing both maximum and minimum representation. So Alabama allows no more than one senator from each county, Kansas grants one seat in the lower house to each of its 105 counties, and California both limits counties to not more than one senator and provides that not more than three counties can be joined in a single senatorial district. So far as representation by political unit is concerned, each town in Vermont, regardless of size, sends one representative to the lower house; and Arizona, Connecticut, Delaware, and New Jersey by constitution or statute provide for fixed apportionment on a unit basis.

An additional limitation to the "one man, one vote" principle is the manner in which districts are laid out geographically and the number of representatives chosen from each district. Though constitutions usually prescribe that districts are to be compact and contiguous, they are in fact often "gerrymandered." That is, they are drawn in odd shapes or sizes to provide roughly equal populations but at the same time to ensure that one party, group, or class is in the predominant majority. Further, though in American political thought single-member districts are preferable to those in which several legislators are elected simultaneously (because a single representative is considered more visible and accountable to his constituency), nearly half of all members in the lower houses of state legislatures are chosen from multimember districts. Thus, citizens of Denver select fifteen members of the legislature; those in Cuyahoga County (Cleveland), Ohio, choose eighteen state representatives and six state senators. In these instances, one party with 51 percent of the total vote may systematically take all the seats, whereas if the districts were broken up, a different composition by party preferences would appear. Thus the preferences of voters who represent a substantial minority opinion may be heavily discounted.

Finally, the population basis of representation can get sadly out of date through the failure of state legislatures to take into account population changes by reapportioning available seats among established election districts. As Americans leave the farms to go into cities and suburbs, the number of representatives allotted to urban areas is slow to change. Thirty-seven state constitutions place the responsibility for reapportionment solely in the hands of the legislature—and its members are not easily disposed to vote

---

[11] The best general discussion of these and other factors is Malcolm H. Jewell, *The State Legislature* (New York, 1962). The comparisons and contrasts of various state requirements are taken from his tables and discussions.

themselves out of their positions. Under these circumstances, it is not surprising that only seventeen states reapportioned after the 1950 census and that some of the results were negligible.

The failure of states to act in the face of the snowballing shifts in populations within states led the United States Supreme Court in *Baker* v. *Carr* to declare in 1962 that the population imbalance among representative districts was so great that the federal courts could require reapportionment and redistricting. This ruling, directed originally to Tennessee, held that if no response from state governments was forthcoming, the courts themselves could prepare and apply reapportionment plans of their own. An indication of the latent pressure for change released by the Court decision against "arbitrary and capricious representation" was the fact that only six months after the case four states had adopted new bases for legislative representation, and in twenty-five other states, court decisions were pending or legislative action was being taken.

The Court decision implies that radical adjustments are likely to be forthcoming in the basis of representation, moving more closely to the "one man, one vote" rule. It is probable that the drastic examples of discrimination against urban areas will disappear: conditions like those that prevail in California, for example, where Los Angeles County, with almost 40 percent of the state's total population, elects only one of the forty state senators; or in Vermont, where members of the house represent towns and cities varying in population from 49 to 35,531. However rapidly changes occur, the achievement of "ideal" allocations is some years away.

The combination of all these limitations has shaped most American legislatures to give rural and small-town populations political influence disproportionate to their number. For our purposes, they indicate that legislators give careful attention to nonurban matters, adjust statewide laws to give special allowances to nonurban areas—notably in cases of highways and aid to education—and tend to discount the importance of urban problems. The "upstate" vote in New York historically stands against New York City; the "pork-chop boys" from rural northern and western counties in Florida outvote delegations from Miami, Jacksonville, and the Tampa–St. Petersburg area; downstate rural Illinois representatives outnumber those from the Chicago metropolitan area. Today, at least, acres as well as people shape the political attitudes and decisions of most state legislatures.

There are other consequences of the formulas for representation aside from the way heads are counted; they affect the functioning of the other three prime factors. By providing for overrepresentation of rural areas in the legislature, many state constitutions increase the probability of divided party rule in their governments. A majority of voters balloting on a statewide basis may elect a governor from one party, but find that their majority is so concentrated in a few areas that the legislature, elected on the basis of many separate districts, may be in the hands of the opposition party because the majority votes have been "wasted" in a few districts. This situation is not unknown in Washington, of course, as earlier chapters have indicated. In the states, however, "divided" government is a greater probability than in the United States, especially when the Democrats control the executive. Thus, Michigan had Democratic governors continuously between 1948

"Great Scott!
We've Lost Our Vote!"

A humorous comment on rural overrepresentation and the 1962 Supreme
Court decision.

Sanders in the Kansas City *Star*

and 1962, elected by margins as high as 56 percent of the total vote, but Republicans maintained a majority in both legislative houses throughout that period. Illinois, Ohio, and New Jersey provide similar if less striking examples.[12]

The basis of legislative representation also often weakens the internal operations of minority parties. In many election districts where one party has been long in power, the opposition finds it difficult to find strong candidates and contest elections. Especially in multimember districts where the winning party is likely to sweep all the seats, opposition may be nominal or nonexistent. Even in Illinois, where a cumulative voting system was recently in effect for the house of representatives (under this system a voter may give his three votes in a three-seat district to one candidate, or divide them equally, or give two to one), and one minority representative is almost guaranteed, the minority party was likely to nominate only the candidate it could elect. In single-member district states, where one party is dominant, it is not uncommon for 60 percent of the seats to go by default.

For both parties, the distorted representative base often encourages factionalism—a division within the major parties—either by emphasizing the importance of primaries for the majority party or by dividing the minority party between "safe-seaters" and those in contested districts. In the first instance, as minority opposition in elections declines, intraparty primary contests increase. Thus in Louisiana there is a thirty-year history of Long and anti-Long factions; in Virginia, the Byrd organization fends off attacks from the anti-Byrd faction; in Kentucky there have been Chandler and anti-Chandler forces—all within a nominally Democratic party. As for the inter-

---

[12] *Ibid.*

"Change The Legislature? Let's Change The U.S. Constitution!"

Rural resistance to reapportionment programs has been strong.

Canfield in the Newark *Evening News*

nal division within a minority party, Rhode Island provides a good example: Small-town Republicans still frequently hold the majority in the state senate, but they typically poll a minority vote in statewide elections. Republicans in urban areas complain that the action of the senate frequently diminishes the attractiveness of their party to the city and suburban voter.

The bias toward ruralism also tends to affect the role of interest groups and individual members of the legislature—enhancing the influence of farm organizations and small business groups at the expense of labor and large industries and increasing the power of rural legislators from safe districts in important committee and leadership assignments within the legislature. All in all, the basis of representation is a significant influence on almost every aspect of legislative behavior. In all likelihood, few recent decisions of the Supreme Court will work such a fundamental change in the American political system as the "reapportionment decision" of 1962 and subsequent rulings.

THE IMPACT OF PARTY

Superimposed on the geographical constituency that a state legislator represents is his party allegiance. What this allegiance represents in terms of ideology, public policy positions, and regularity in voting behavior varies enormously from state to state. But in almost every state, a party designation is affixed next to a candidate's name on the ballot in the general election, and in some states this affiliation carries with it the tacit obligation to support his party's candidates for leadership positions in the legislature and his party's positions on major public issues.

The partisan environment of the fifty states ranges from the tight one-party domination where the minority has never captured either the governorship or over 20 percent of the representatives in either house since the Second World War (a situation in ten Southern states) to the vigorous two-party competition where control of legislative and executive branches has shifted recurrently (as represented in nine states, mostly in the far West). Four states have usually been dominated by one party in addition to the ten of the deep South—but minority legislative representation has exceeded 20 percent. Nine others have tended to one-party dominance by always having one party in legislative control but occasionally producing a governor from the opposition. Eight can be designated as "limited" two-party states, where the governorship has been captured by one party at least half the time and the legislature most of the time. And there are other versions of limited two-party competition, where one party customarily controls the executive and the other the legislature (two states) or where different parties are in command in the two houses of the legislature (four states).[13] Obviously, the party impact within each of these categories is different. In one-party states it may mean little more than a ritualistic method for organizing legislative business; in two-party states it may be a decisive factor.

To the legislators of "in-between" states, the relative strength of each party has several implications. If the executive is of the opposite party, a condition existing in thirty-two states at some time in the postwar period, the traditional tension between executive and legislature may be heightened. Between 1930 and 1950 there were Republican legislatures facing Democratic governors 51 percent of the time as against 18 percent of the time for Democratic legislatures encountering Republican governors. Since 1952, GOP chief executives have encountered opposition control more frequently—39 percent of the Republican state administrations have been so situated as against 55 percent of the Democratic.

Party allegiance is most likely to count where legislative membership is closely divided between Republicans and Democrats. Positions taken in party caucuses—meetings where Democratic and Republican legislators gather informally to discuss and consider pending legislation—may have the effect of binding individual members. Or the signals may be passed directly by party leaders without pausing for caucus deliberations.

The importance of party can usually be determined by analyzing voting behavior on roll call votes where the majority of Democrats vote against a majority of Republicans. The technique is known as the index of cohesion (if all Democrats vote one way, the index is 100; if they are equally divided, 0; if three fourths vote the same, the index is 50). Indices above 60 percent are considered significant, and states like New York, Pennsylvania, Rhode Island, Massachusetts, and Connecticut typically display greater party regularity than the United States Congress does.

Indices of cohesion are not always reliable, however. Sometimes issues are decided on a party basis at the committee level or through interhouse consultation of the leadership. Sometimes roll calls are not taken even when the bill is a matter of party controversy. And party discipline is not always a function of party competition; often the preferences of legislative leaders and interest groups are more important. Small minority parties may exhibit close cohesion because of similarity of views and ease of communication

---

[13] Hawaii and Alaska are excluded from this count, as their history as states is too short to show a definite trend.

even when they stand little or no chance of winning. Nevertheless, the results of quantitative and qualitative studies indicate that in a few states party alignments are the decisive factor in legislative voting and in many states, on many occasions, an important one.

Where among the two-party oriented states is the party influence most likely to be strong? First, where the urban and rural conflict is great: Democrats tend to represent urban constituencies and Republicans rural, rich suburban, and small-town ones. Here the influence of party and the representative base reinforce each other. Second, where class and ethnic differences are pronounced: The Democratic party tends to speak for Catholics, descendants of Irish and European immigrants, Negroes, labor, and low-income groups, and the Republican party is oriented to Protestant, Anglo-Saxon, and business constituencies. These differences tend to make the parties a product of something more than historical accident; to produce different points of view about the proper role of government; to lead to different program and policy stands; and to submerge the importance of personality and geographical location. Conversely, when both parties draw their strength from the same type of constituencies—rural or urban, religious, ethnic, or occupational—programmatic differences are minimized, and the issues between parties are likely to be those which the party activists regard as important so far as organizational political strength is concerned but with which the public is not heavily involved.

In states tending toward one-partyism, factionalism within the dominant party may replace party-line splits. Here, the measure of cohesion is applied to blocs of legislators who recurrently take similar positions on major legislation. The blocs may be a function of ideological conviction, as the liberal and conservative wings of the New Hampshire Republican party seem to represent. They may divide according to loyalty and support for the governor or for a dominant state political figure, as was true of Virginia and the Georgia of Herman Talmadge's day. They may be multiple in number, representing several political personalities and their followings. Compared to party divisions, factional allegiances are likely to be far less permanent, and members may enter and withdraw to recoalesce in new groups as issues change. Thus the impact of factionalism is usually less potent and less predictable than that of party influence where the latter exists in any strong measure.

INTEREST GROUPS

In addition to geographical and party considerations, state legislators are often swayed, as are Congressmen, by the appeals of interest groups usually concerned with only a limited number of issues, generally economic in character. Thus, legislative antechambers are crowded with lobbyists for race tracks, railroads, truckers, insurance companies, labor unions, professions regulated by the state—doctors, hairdressers, accountants, and the like—businesses with close governmental ties, such as nursing homes, highway contractors, and farm bureaus. By personal contact, by mail, through the use of intermediaries, and by claiming public support, voting strength, rightness of position, political influence within the parties, and monetary rewards, the spokesmen for these groups undertake to persuade legislators to vote "their way." [14]

Other interest groups take a broader view of public policy. Thus, major labor organizations like the AFL–CIO, the United States Chamber of Commerce, and the Farm Bureau take positions on many issues besides those which directly affect their obvious economic interests. Church groups, the League of Women Voters, and members of taxpayers' associations are active on a wide front in pursuit of what they conceive to be "better government." Public agencies and public personnel, most notably public school teachers, school boards and administrators, highway departments, and health officials, often join these groups to display persuasive legislative influence.

The particular "mix" of interest group legislative activity varies from state to state and from legislative session to legislative session. But in every state a group of professional lobbyists exists, usually lawyers and ex-legislators, which represents "clients" interested in the legislation of the moment. One lobbyist may have a range of clients from liquor dealers to church groups; he works to make their views known to the members of both houses. He may concentrate on dealing with the leadership or key committee members; he may buttonhole individual legislators in the corridors; he may provide assistance in drafting highly technical legislation to protect his clients. Or, he may also testify at committee hearings, organize mail campaigns, see that newspapers are informed of the issue, or arrange for television coverage, or contribute to the campaign funds of selected legislators. The professional lobbyist is a highly skilled and experienced figure in state legislatures today. His income may be large and his influence substantial, especially on matters where parties have taken no stand and the public is not well informed or particularly concerned. Especially in matters of business regulation, government procurement, and detailed provisions of tax legislation, he may be the most important influence in decision-making.

The function of the lobbyist should not be viewed as an exclusively self-seeking and negative influence. As with many other political figures that the public often considers immoral and selfish, the representative of "special interests" plays so crucial a role in the operations of representative government that if he did not exist, he or a substitute would have to be created. State legislators, more than Congressmen, tend to be part-time politicians, many of them unversed in the problems and operations of their governments. Compared to the members of Congress, they are not well supported by technical staffs who can study and advise on new legislation. In many states they do not even have offices or secretaries of their own. Increasingly they face complex technical problems of public policy, without the means to gain the knowledge essential for intelligent stands on issues.

The experienced lobbyist often makes up for this lack of research and advice. To be sure, his point of view is a biased one. But the information

---

[14] An excellent case study of pressure group politics at the state level is the analysis of the Pennsylvania Railroad controversy in Andrew Hacker, "Pressure Politics in Pennsylvania: The Truckers vs. the Railroads," Alan F. Westin, ed., *The Uses of Power* (New York, 1962).

he gathers, the issues he presents, and the focus his presentation places on a policy question are often indispensable in helping a legislator make up his mind. The more experienced lobbyist, representing more broadly based pressure groups, often conducts studies and provides information that approach objectivity. And where many interest groups are ably represented, the legislator is exposed to conflicting points of view that are a fair approximation of the desires of the fragmented constituency he represents.

LEGISLATIVE PERSONALITIES

The fourth factor of great importance in determining state legislative behavior consists of the strategic positions of individual legislators and the various ways in which they view their duties—the roles they assume.

In most state legislatures the holders of strategic positions—the presiding officer of the senate, the speaker of the lower house, the chairmen of important standing committees, particularly those dealing with finance—have authority equal to and frequently greater than their counterparts in Congress. The presiding officers of state legislatures have special opportunities for influence: they control appointments to committees under circumstances where rules of seniority, geographical distribution, and party representation are frequently less well established than in Congress. They operate in parliamentary circumstances where use of the written record is less extensive than in the national legislature, where press coverage is more spotty, and where the opportunity for technical maneuvers is greater. They generally have greater flexibility in assigning bills to committees and in establishing orders of procedures. Thus many states have "iron dukes" in the chairs of speaker and the president of the senate, and these presiding positions are often highly coveted and vigorously contested.

The position of a few key committees and their chairmen is also likely to be important. Rules committees do not generally control the order in which bills reach the floor for debate in state legislatures, as they do in the Congress, but they are important in governing general procedures. In many state legislatures there are also party steering and policy committees which determine party strategy, later to be endorsed by party caucuses. In at least twenty states legislative councils operating with research staffs between sessions play an important role in planning programs for coming sessions and shaping key policy issues. These committees are likely to be far more important than the other standing committees dealing with substantive matters such as health, welfare, and labor.[15]

Yet a few legislative leaders of long standing can easily overshadow the committees. For one thing, a rapid turnover in committee membership prevents the committees from assuming the importance of their counterparts in Congress. For another, few committees possess a staff for independent work. Finally, the great discretion granted the leaders allows them to "pack" committees with members of their own persuasion or otherwise to assure their loyalty and support. Though committees' recommendations may exercise great weight in general debate (in some states their work is extremely

---

[15] See Karl A. Bosworth, "Lawmaking in State Governments," *The Forty-Eight States: Their Tasks as Policy Makers and Administrators.*

significant in modifying the character of proposed legislation), state legislatures are generally organized to place predominant power in the hands of a relatively few experienced and energetic members in positions of leadership.

Underlying both the general behavior of the legislative leaders and the ways they achieve status and support from their colleagues are the conceptions of the legislative role which the representatives and senators bring to their jobs—and their personal reasons for seeking office. Recent research has shed considerable light on these phenomena.

One study of four state legislatures classifies legislators according to how they approach the job of determining what bills are important and how they should vote on them.[16] Four types are identified: The "Ritualists" are preoccupied with the technical operations of the legislative body, with their eyes fixed on calendars, process, and procedure, so that the way legislative work is done—rather than its substance—is the focus of their attention. Then there are "Tribunes," committed to the proposition of the direct representation of their constituencies' views whatever they may be, and dedicated to constant soundings of public opinion. Third, there are "Inventors," persuaded that their task is to exercise independent judgments based on their special knowledge and expertness in fields of public policy, actively searching for solutions to important public policies. Finally, there are "Brokers," who consider themselves mediators and arbitrators between competing interest groups and constituencies and view a day well spent when some realistic compromise has been achieved on an issue of importance.

A second study has focused more on motivations and objectives than on the role perceptions of legislators. James Barber, investigating the Connecticut legislature, classifies members, according to their personal needs and adaptations, as "Spectators," "Advertisers," "Reluctants," or "Lawmakers." [17] The first are passive observers of the scene, finding satisfaction in the spectacle, compensating for feelings of social inferiority, and content to follow the leaders. The second are more concerned with receiving individual publicity to advance personal and professional aims than in considering the substance of the legislative calendar. "Reluctants" appear on the stage as a result of moral compulsions expressed in the form of civic duty—often exercising considerable influence but receiving little satisfaction from their work. Thus the relatively few "Lawmakers," active and happy in their task, are the only real energizers of the legislative process and the innovators of public policy.

Clearly, the composition of legislatures in terms of either the ways their members view their jobs or their reasons for participation varies from state to state. Clearly, too, cross-pressures arise between these perceptions and the forces of constituencies, parties, and interest groups. So the Inventors and the Lawmakers face the Brokers and the Advertisers in competition for legislative leadership—and the output of a legislative session may well depend on the predominant class of leaders. The inner politics of each

---

[16] John C. Wahlke, Heinz Eulau, William Buchanan, and LeRoy C. Ferguson, *The Legislative System: Explorations in Legislative Behavior* (New York, 1955).

[17] James D. Barber, *Lawmaker: A Study of Political Adaptation* (New Haven, 1962).

house—admission to the small circle of leadership, the mix of different types of personalities, the skill of a legislator in acquiring status and respect—contain crucial variables in determining legislative behavior; accordingly, no two state legislatures are the same. The probes into roles and personal needs, moreover, underline the strategic importance of a few key figures holding posts of high authority in each body. Where this pattern does not exist, legislative performance is likely to be erratic, low in volume, and unsuccessful in making decisions on important but controversial matters.

THE PATTERN OF LEGISLATIVE BEHAVIOR

What findings stem from this study of the four major bases for legislative decision-making, aside from the fact that they exist in different combinations across the country? One safe generalization is that until the 1962 Court decision, the most important influence was the manner in which representation was determined. Almost every state in the 1950s exhibited a strong bias for assuring that rural and small-town voters had a greater influence than urban city voters (though this does not necessarily mean that their attitudes on some major issues directly conflict). And whether a legislator's constituency is rural or urban, he is generally excused from party or other allegiances if he determines his position on "what his people want." The link with the home town is probably the strongest determinant of legislative behavior—and it reinforces a pattern of legislative personalities where Ritualists and Reluctants predominate.

But that link, strong as it is in such small home towns, is reinforced by the other factors to make legislative decisions more frequently minority decisions than majority ones. Where party discipline is strong, the legislative party in power is frequently distinct from the majority party of the state—even from the general party leadership. That is, the legislative members, Democratic or Republican, are likely to have a "club" which stands apart from the state committee of the party. Where party discipline is weak, factionalism tends to put power in the hands of an even smaller group. On highly complex and technical issues, the influence of special interest groups representing highly organized minorities and led by skilled lobbyists often increases the persuasiveness of minority opinion. Finally, the important role of legislative leadership means that within the legislatures a few members have the reins of power securely in their hands. Thus, most state legislatures today make their record on the basis of how their leadership judges the strength of geographical, party, and interest group pressures. Accordingly, legislative priority tends to emphasize rural, minority party, and special-interest legislation, with little latitude given the Inventor and Lawmaker. Problems of the emerging urban communities thus are handled in an inhospitable framework.

The Role of the Governor

The disposition of state legislatures to deal with public issues from a minority perspective has led to a continued decline in their popular prestige in this century. Strong reform movements for reconstituting these bodies presently exist in many states. But the effects of growing dissatisfaction have gone even beyond pressures for changing legislative behavior. A steady rise in the position and eminence of the executive branch has accompanied the decline in legislative status. Though no state chief executive rivals the President in power, governors have, over the last forty years, expanded their influence and activity.

Some growth in the powers and prerogatives of the governor occurred in the nineteenth century, as a result of early legislative scandals and the increasing importance of administrative matters. But it was not until the close of the First World War that revisions in state constitutions began to provide the executive branches with instruments by which they could exercise important influence on state policy-making. In 1917, Illinois undertook a major administrative reorganization of its state institutions, consolidating a hundred offices, boards, and agencies into nine departments directly responsible to the governor. By 1919, New Jersey, Massachusetts, and Nebraska had followed suit, to be joined by twenty-six other states by 1937.[18] After the Second World War nearly three quarters of the states followed the example of governmental reorganization in Washington by creating "Baby Hoover Commissions," named after the special federal commission chaired by former President Herbert Hoover.

The prime objective of both the prewar and postwar reforms was to improve governmental efficiency and economy. The recommendations of the reorganization movement almost invariably included strengthening the governor's control over the preparation and presentation of the budget; expanding his staff facilities; increasing his appointment and removal powers over state department heads; lengthening his term of office; and extending his power to veto legislation.[19]

As a consequence of these reforms, the present-day governor has new advantages: the chances are better than two to one that he will serve a four-year term of office, and a little better than fifty-fifty that he can constitutionally continue in office indefinitely if he can be reelected. Four out of five governors receive a salary exceeding $10,000 a year and ten are paid more than $25,000. Better than four out of five governors possess the item veto—which enables them to disapprove individual appropriations in general revenue bills. With or without senatorial consent, more than half of the governors appoint the states' chief budget officers, tax officers, and heads of the principal departments of labor, health, welfare, insurance, highways, conservation.[20]

State executive power is by no means monolithic, however. A number of other executive offices—notably the treasurer, auditor, attorney general, and the commissioners of education and agriculture—are likely to be independently elected. This competition among executives contrasts sharply with the President's situation. Nevertheless, compared to the governor's position

---

[18] See Leslie Lipson, *The American Governor from Figurehead to Leader* (Chicago, 1939).

[19] Robert C. Wood, "The Metropolitan Governor" (unpublished Ph.D. dissertation, Harvard University, 1949).

[20] Council of State Governments, *op. cit.*, Section IV.

of two generations ago, his command of the executive establishment and his bargaining position vis-à-vis the legislature have been substantially enlarged.

What specific political resources is the contemporary governor likely to possess in the arena of state politics aside from his legal prerogatives and powers? Essentially there are five sources of influence available to him: (1) his role as representative of "the whole state"—a single symbol of the public intent; (2) his powers to bargain on the basis of either constitutional or statutory authority with the legislature; (3) his use of the party instrument to gain consent and support for his views in the legislature; (4) the powers that flow from his administrative and executive authority; and (5) his personal capacity for persuasion—charm, articulateness, character, or acumen. Each of these sources consists of an amalgam of formal and informal powers and each governor uses them in different combinations. Let us examine each one briefly.

REPRESENTATIVE OF THE "PUBLIC GOOD"

The governor is the most visible public figure in state politics, frequently overshadowing in prominence the state's senators. Moreover, he is far more likely to be more sensitive than they are to the demands of urban voters. Elected on a statewide basis, he must shape his political strategy by calculations quite different from the state legislator's, for his constituency in all but the most sparsely populated Western and Southern states is bound to be heterogeneous, with sharply different political attitudes and aspirations. Moreover, as ceremonial chief of state, the governor has a ritualistic role to play comparable to the President's role as Chief of State: in ribbon-cutting ceremonies, in the reception of foreign visitors, in appeals for charity, as economic "ambassador" to promote the state's economic development, as speechmaker at brotherhood banquets, and a dozen other similar activities. These characteristics of visibility, responsiveness to an urban-oriented constituency, and symbolism of authority cast the chief executive in a role which is larger than a partisan or an executive one. They tend to make the governor the chief "problem-solver" in state politics, the official the public looks to for rational (or rationalized) answers to major problems on criteria ostensibly based on the interests of "all the people." To the degree a governor can effectively symbolize the public interest in a generalized sense and tap the wellsprings of whatever political consensus exists within his state, he has a political resource available to no other public figure.

Governors rise above politics in various ways: by calling on distinguished citizens for unselfish public service; by using objective studies, experts, and impartial committees to settle controversial issues; by high-level speeches and strategic appearances before nonpartisan groups; by quelling public disorder through the use of the state militia. In New York, in recent years, Governor Rockefeller's intervention in educational and labor disputes in New York City has been on the ground of representing the higher public interest (though at the same time it brought undoubted political advantages to his party). Across the continent two decades ago, Governor Earl Warren of California enjoyed unprecedented success by adopting a nonpartisan, statesmanlike approach toward the majority of issues facing him. In Florida during the 1950s, Governor LeRoy Collins proceeded along the same course.

In essence, the strength of these men was that in a nation and time when highly partisan political activity was unpopular, they displayed the image of statesmen.

THE GOVERNOR AS LEGISLATIVE LEADER

State chief executives are often able to exercise substantial influence over legislative behavior. Part of this power rests in the governor's formal authority, especially in those states where major reorganizational changes have been accomplished. If a governor possesses budget-making powers (that is, if he has the duty to prepare and submit a budget which the legislature must consider), if he is equipped with staff resources for research and study of major issues, if he has the item veto, and if few other constitutionally elected executive officers vie with him for popular and legislative favor, he can almost always take the leadership in shaping the major legislative program. Even in states where the governor does not possess these tools, his constitutional duty to deliver messages to the legislature, to veto entire bills, and to call special sessions are important resources for bargaining with legislatures and their leaders. The number and effectiveness of these resources vary greatly from state to state, but all governors have some means for legislative negotiation.

Supplementing the executive's formal powers with respect to legislation are a series of other resources available from his administrative, judicial, and political responsibilities. When a governor makes an administrative appointment at the suggestion of a legislator, authorizes the construction of a new highway in a legislator's district, grants a pardon for a legislator's constituent, or speaks in support of a candidate for legislative office, he is likely to increase his legislative influence. (On the other hand, he may lose ground with other legislators if he does not distribute these favors systematically or with due regard to the relative influence of individual members.)

There are other informal ways for persuasion and negotiation: conferences with individual legislators before key bills are voted on; "open houses" and other social events where politicking can go on in an atmosphere of conviviality; instructions through party caucuses; and regular meetings with leadership in both houses. If a governor has been a legislator earlier in his career, the simple fact of "belonging to the club" and being familiar with legislative folkways may be of enormous importance. The essential point in gubernatorial-legislative relations is that the use of formal powers by governors can be increased or decreased by the use of informal exchanges of benefits between the two components of the system.

THE PARTY AS A MEANS FOR INFLUENCE

Most governors are at least titular heads of their state political parties. The amount of political influence that results from this position varies in direct proportion to the strength, cohesion, and discipline of the state parties. For example, though Governor G. Mennen Williams of Michigan was elected to an unprecedented six consecutive terms of office, and the Michigan State Democratic Committee during this period was vigorous, disciplined, and effective, Republicans remained in control of the legislature. *All* of the executive powers, formal and informal, proved insufficient to resolve financial and taxation issues in this instance. In Rhode Island, after the Second World War the senate remained in Republican hands and the party strength of two Democratic governors had to be supplemented by other sources of influence.

Finally, there are states in which the party mechanism is not of use to the governor in any major way. In states of one-party domination, as in the South and Midwest, the governors have to rely on factions responsive to them personally—and often these are fragile organizations. Even in two-party states, where competition might be expected to encourage discipline and cohesion within a party, the party label may be only a façade covering a host of bitterly contending factions. In Massachusetts, the Democratic party has been wracked with internal warfare for years and until recently was organized largely on the basis of personalities. In that state, governors have lost influence by attempting to work through party channels in campaigning or in handling patronage. At best, the party has been a marginal resource, sometimes convenient for securing funds but with little relevance so far as elections, legislative maneuvering, or executive staffing were concerned.

THE GOVERNOR AS CHIEF EXECUTIVE

A basic source of political strength for a governor is the substance of the office formally established by the state constitution. Every such constitution contains some version of the provision that the executive take care to see that the laws are faithfully executed. More popularly, he is expected to preserve "law and order." This assignment means that all governors have some authority over a sizable bureaucracy and some discretion in exercising ordinance-making and enforcement powers.

Supervision of the state bureaucracy means that the chief executive has access to expert specialized information that is superior to that of the legislature. He can have detailed knowledge of highway location alternatives, the conditions of state institutions, and the level of welfare programs—knowledge only sporadically available to the public or to other political figures. He can receive counsel as to how to resolve certain issues, and he can deploy trained personnel to document policy positions. The governor's administrative role also equips him with appointment and removal powers that vary considerably from state to state but that allow for exchanges with legislators and party officials. Finally, the governor's administrative responsibilities allow him, if he chooses, to emphasize the solution of public issues by modern management techniques and to establish a record as an honest, skilled, efficient, and economical administrator capably directing a large and complex enterprise.

The governor's constitutional executive powers provide another means for exercising influence. In his authority to prescribe rules and regulations necessary for the execution of general legislation, the state chief executive can determine priorities among various state programs, set the terms and conditions of their administration, and choose to accelerate or retard the execution of particular laws—acts which may have important political consequences. Thus Abraham Ribicoff of Connecticut established himself as an important political figure by making a highway safety program the principal effort of his first administration, and many other chief executives have followed suit.

Another obvious choice for all governors is the degree to which they choose to employ state police for the enforcement of gambling and nuisance laws. Most governors also face sometime in their administration the decision as to the use of the executive power under emergency conditions: to call out the national guard in time of strike, disaster, or public disorder; to seize industries threatened by labor disorder in order to keep services available to the public; or to declare a general state of emergency and assume special powers. These acts can have an important effect on a governor's popularity and status among both voters and other politicians. Yet they require no legislation and little real administrative ability. They are simply decisions to use explicit or inherent constitutional powers.

The executive role of the governor can, however, be overemphasized. In about four fifths of the states he shares power with other constitutionally elected officers: the secretary of state, the attorney general, and the treasurer, each of whom can be regarded as a present or potential political competitor. Frequently, his power to appoint other major department and agency heads is limited or nonexistent and often his removal powers are subject to challenge. Especially in recent years, the creation of independent state agencies, boards, and commissions that have been equipped with their own fiscal and spending powers—turnpike authorities and resource development corporations, for example—has served to limit the governor's supervisory responsibilities.

Even with the agencies which the governor supervises directly, the opportunity for real direction and control may be limited. The size of present state bureaucracies, their rapid expansion, and the technical nature of many of their tasks all make continuous supervision extraordinarily difficult. The governor is also limited in personnel matters. Civil service regulations determine conditions of employment for the vast majority of jobs in many states and career administrators are likely to be independent in behavior, used to seeing governors come and go while their departmental operations go on unchanged. Even for positions where a governor can appoint a person of his own choosing, considerations of party and legislative relations restrict his choices.

Though governors are the formal chief executives of our states and are thus theoretically most concerned with administrative matters, in actuality their constitutional authority is less likely to increase their political influence and power than are any of their other sources of strength. Therefore few governors devote the bulk of their time to administrative matters, and few believe that a record as a skilled administrator really improves their chances for reelection.

EXECUTIVE CHARISMA

A final gubernatorial resource is the executive's own personality. This is a source of power potentially available to all state political activists. But the governor's office provides an exceptional stage for an individual who is disposed to use emotional and dramatic techniques to gain support for his programs. The mass media are prepared to cover his activities; indeed, they can hardly avoid doing so. His ceremonial activities afford ample opportunity for exposure. His acts command attention and make news. It is not surprising, then, that the ranks of American governors past and present include some of the most colorful figures in our political life: "Kissing Jim" Folsom of Alabama, Herman Talmadge of Georgia, Huey "The Kingfish" Long of Louisiana, "Alfalfa" Bill Murray of Oklahoma, James Michael Curley of Massachusetts, "Happy" Chandler of Kentucky. These executives may not be entered in our history books as the greatest governors, but they enjoyed widespread and intense support during their turbulent careers, and the secret of their successes lay less in what they did or how they proceeded in administrative, executive, or legislative roles than in how they were perceived by the public at large. Today, with an increasingly middle-class and white-collar electorate, there are fewer governors of flamboyant style. But the cultivation of the proper "image" through appropriate public relations techniques remains a major preoccupation of the states' chief executives.

THE PATTERN OF GUBERNATORIAL BEHAVIOR

By virtue of these political resources, the modern state governor emerges as a figure of considerable and growing consequence in state politics. He has overthrown many of the restraints that Revolutionary tradition and antiquated constitutions imposed on his office. In a few states like New Jersey, New York, and California he occupies a clearly predominant position of power. It is still a mistake, however, to view him in most states and at most times as the unchallenged leader in public policy-making or as master of his own executive branch. No governor possesses powers comparable to that of the President. Instead, he appears principally as a bargainer coexisting and competing with legislative leadership, other constitutional executive officers, independent agency heads, and party figures. He is preoccupied with mustering the political resources sufficient to persuade the other activists "to go along with the Governor." He may be active or passive in his performance, liberal or strict in the interpretation of the powers of his office. But in most states, and for most chief executives, legislative action finally determines the main course of public affairs.

The Separate Way of the Courts

Earlier chapters have already examined the state court systems as specialized agencies for law enforcement and described their work in settling disputes between private persons, and between private persons and the state, according to criteria established by custom, usage, or reasoning (common law and equity), or by statutory or constitutional interpretation. In addition to their prime judicial function, the courts play an important role in general decision-making in the states, both formally and informally. According to the doctrine of judicial review, state judiciaries, as well as federal courts, can nullify decisions of the legislature and the executive on the ground that they violate constitutional provisions or are not in accord with "due process of law," a phrase by which the courts consider the reasonableness of action. In nine states, the highest courts can also render advisory opinions as to whether the action a legislature or executive is considering is permissible—thus engaging in the anticipation of policy decisions. State courts also exercise administrative responsibilities, including in some states the appointment and supervision of certain public officials, control over elections, issuing of business licenses, and the management of estates of deceased persons or those declared in bankruptcy.

The process of judicial review offers the courts an opportunity to intervene directly and formally in the state decision-making process, especially when legislatures are unable to achieve any solution. A state's administrative activities often place its courts in the mainstream of politics, since the probating of wills, the selection of officials, and the supervision of elections are matters of direct concern to political activists. And because judges are elected, or are appointed by the governor (in lower courts by mayors or other officials), their personal careers are likely to have involved considerable political activity.

In most states the formal powers of judicial review have grown over the years since the case of *Holmes* v. *Walton* was recorded in New Jersey in 1780. On grounds that statutes violate constitutional protections of either personal or property rights, go against due process, exceed authority vested in legislative or executive branches, conflict with the constitutional distribution of powers, or contravene revenue provisions (along with assorted other miscellaneous determinations), courts have struck down major legislative acts in every state. One study reported 144 such decisions in Illinois between 1870 and 1941 and another seventy-six for New York in the twenty-three-year period between 1914 and 1937. In recent years, the willingness of courts to accept new concepts of state activity in taxation, health, urban renewal, and public transportation as being part of the police or "eminent domain" power of the state has been of major importance in the evolution of new state and local roles. Now, under the federal mandate to reapportion legislatures, courts are busy with the most delicate and influential political task in state governments today: reshaping the pattern of legislative behavior. In these decisions, the judicial role in general policymaking is that of an umpire between competing forces.

In their administrative decisions (as distinct from their policy decisions), the courts assume a different role, which affects the political positions of legislators, governors, and party leaders. From a political point of view, judges often possess valuable resources. The appointment of guardians and executors of estates, referees in foreclosures, commissioners in incompetency hearings, court employees, and other public officers can reward one party at the expense of another, move aspiring young lawyers up career ladders, and ease the household budgets of legally trained political activists. Because the links between political parties and the legal profession are traditionally strong, almost any act that tends to put one law firm or another in a favorable position is likely to enhance or detract from the prestige and support of a particular political organization. Hence judges enjoy a position of influence which extends beyond the interpretation of rules and procedures. In the normal course of their business they are in a position to offer other political activists benefits which are strongly desired.[21]

This potential influence is, however, subject to certain conditions. Where judges are elected, as they are in most states, they need political support and loyalty. Where they are appointed, they may well recognize some obligation to their benefactor. Indeed, according to Curtis Bok's definition, "A state judge is a lawyer who once knew a governor." Because a judgeship is so coveted a professional goal of so many lawyers, its occupancy is likely to be an object of considerable competition. Thus, governors, party leaders, and legislators have their own resources for influencing the judiciary.

The pressure that can be applied to the courts is limited. The special cast of the legal profession, the important role of bar associations in the selection of judges in many states, the detailed proscriptions for conducting trials, arriving at decisions, and administering decrees often serve to insulate the judicial process from the most overt kinds of influence. Outside intervention in the settlement of individual cases is rare. Moreover, judges once securely on the bench have a reputation for becoming independent. Nevertheless, in assisting an aspiring lawyer to become a judge, party professionals can obtain compensatory benefits: party allegiance, sometimes party contributions, sensitivity to the party's patronage needs, and often the use of the incumbent's prestige and influence in nonjudicial circumstances. Thus courts remain sensitive to the legislative and executive behavior through the party medium.

The informal political resources of the courts and the restraints upon them rarely focus on matters of policy, as they do with formal judicial review. They deal essentially with personnel and procedure, and in that sense the courts as influencers of the bulk of political decisions play a negligible role. Nonetheless, by serving as the third member of the triangle which also includes the executive and the legislature, the courts often act as the intermediary through which accommodations among the other two are found. A judicial favor instigated by a governor may placate or persuade a legislator. Alternatively, by appointing a recalcitrant opponent—or his law partner—to the bench, or by using the bench to reward past services or to remove a dangerous competitor in a future campaign, governors gain influence. Thus, the judicial organization often becomes a field on which contests of executive and legislative supremacy are waged.

In short, state judiciaries are important in state decision-making in two ways. First, in their exercise of judicial review, the courts play "Nature" in the political game; that is, they represent a force powerful enough to change the rules without notice. They impose new interpretations of the constitutions and statutes. They decide contests in ways that are not always reflections of the respective influence that legislators and governors command. Second, through the media of political parties and the legal profession they offer opportunities for the other participants in the political arena to increase their bargaining position, and in the interplay they are in a position to

---

[21] See Wallace S. Sayre and Herbert Kaufman, *Governing New York City* (New York, 1960), pp. 522–44. This is an excellent contemporary analysis of courts and politics.

affect the distribution of influence among institutions and parties within each state.

The Rise of the Bureaucracies

In formal constitutional terms, the administrative agencies, departments, boards, and commissions of state governments are organizations that exist to carry out decisions determined by legislators, governors, and courts. In actuality, however, these organizations, like their federal counterparts, possess political influence of their own, and often initiate policies or modify decisions by their legal superiors. In all probability, the role of state administrative agencies in determining the decision output of the state political system is greater than that of the federal establishments, since few governors possess the President's power for administrative supervision and management.

Moreover, the state agencies not only strike alliances with private interest groups affected by their activities, but also have developed systematic liaisons with federal agencies through the mechanism of the grants-in-aid device. Thus the last thirty years have witnessed the emergence of the so-called "functional specialists" in highways, health, welfare, education, and resource development, who technically occupy nonpolicy positions, but who with companion specialists in Washington and their private clienteles play an important part in general decision-making.

The political activity of the functional specialist usually follows a predictable route. Initially trained in a particular profession, charged with the responsibility of carrying out a public program in his area of competence, the administrator of any agency comes early to believe that his program is the most important in the state. He also feels that the money and talent at his disposal are woefully inadequate. Thus he presses for a larger budget and more personnel through the regular budgetary channels to the governor. Simultaneously he is likely to employ other means for persuading the top decision makers. One is to activate his clientele to work as individual citizens, in groups or through lobbyists, to expand the program. He may also try to interest the federal agencies and departments in providing grants and technical assistance. In effect, he presents a united front with his fellow professional specialists at the federal and local levels, and through professional associations, continuous working contacts, and joint programs presses forward to help achieve their common program goals.

At the state level, the specialist points out to governors and legislative committees that increases in his budget will automatically result in larger federal contributions, because national grants are usually provided on a matching basis. At the federal level the President and the Congress are enjoined to increase appropriations, because the states will then be encouraged to expand their financing. So budget makers at both levels are effectively cross-pressured.

This push-pull pattern in functional programs is evident in almost every one of the states' major activities. For highways, the state highway and public works department and the United States Bureau of Public Roads join forces through the agency of the Association of State Highway Commissioners to plan and construct the interstate highway system and primary and secondary state roads. In welfare, the federal programs of assistance to the aged, the blind, the handicapped, and dependent children receive additional state money and are administered by state agencies subject to minimum federal regulation. In health, state departments look to the Surgeon General in Washington for a variety of grants in hospital construction, research, and community health programs. Only the state education program has remained largely outside the area of federal cooperation and control.

Because education is still principally a state and local concern, this area offers the best example of the state specialist "going it alone" in exercising political influence. Since the Second World War, all states except Nebraska have adopted state aid programs for local public schools, usually to ensure a minimum level of expenditures for every district in the state and often seeking to equalize the proportion of local tax sources devoted to education—that is, to make the "tax effort" for schools roughly the same for poor localities as for rich ones. A recent study of how these school-aid laws were adopted in eight states in the Northeast demonstrates how important a role professional schoolmen play in legislative and executive action.

In the Northeast, the push for more state aid typically began in the academic halls of the great schools of education at Columbia and Harvard, where professors devised the principles of the programs and developed the framework of the new laws. Then state departments of education, in consultation with the professors, organized grass-roots support from professional teachers' associations, superintendents and local school boards, Parent-Teacher Associations, school betterment councils, Leagues of Women Voters, and other civic organizations. Usually they sought to join these groups in a permanent organization, such as the New York State Educational Conference Board. The schoolmen then undertook to persuade the governors and key legislators to adopt the program as their own. They worked as lobbyists in legislative sessions, stirred up public support, and made alliances with tax and business groups that wanted local tax relief. Thus they built a coalition sufficient to pass the new legislation.

The strategy and tactics of the schoolmen varied from state to state. Sometimes they worked through the majority political party, with the state board of education taking the lead, as in Rhode Island. Sometimes, as in New York, the private associations in the Conference Board were most influential. Some ad hoc organizations worked for a year and then disbanded, as in Massachusetts. Sometimes, as in Maine, the governor and legislative leadership were the decisive factors. But in all instances, the professional specialists in education, in universities, and in bureaucracies as well as their lay disciples started their states on the road to programs of new magnitude.

Like all other key decision makers, the specialists work under many constraints. First, according to the folklore of American government, they are not supposed to be active in policy-making, and much of their influence needs to be exerted quietly and cautiously. Second, our folklore does not cast the bureaucrat in a hero's role; consequently he rarely has a favorable public image. Third, the demands among competing specialists—for schools, health, highways, and welfare—tend to cancel one another out and trigger off exhausting and time-consuming interagency squabbles. Finally, in states organized according to modern management principles, the influence of the specialist in operating agencies is counterbalanced by that of the staff specialists supporting the governor and legislatures who work to regularize the allocation of resources among the agencies. A central budget agency, a central purchasing and personnel system, or an active legislative reference bureau can force line agencies to use formal channels of program proposals, can review the effectiveness of their operations, and can discourage the use of outside means of influence. Their work tends to substitute rationalized methods of determining priorities among programs in place of a catch-as-catch-can set of appeals in the midst of a legislative session and to enhance the influence of the elected officials.

Nevertheless, as program-proposers and agitators, the functional specialists, especially those endowed with federal grants, often possess the greatest resources of indirect influence. Governors and legislators can establish over-all ceilings under which all departments must exist; they can on occasion cut back programs across the board; they can threaten disciplinary action. Legislators can investigate, denounce, expose, and rebel. But the professional administrator, learned in the ways of the state house, is likely to know the ways and possess the means to protect his program and to propose new laws that are politically popular. At the end of a legislative session in most American states, the governor may have had his way on a half dozen of major issues; the legislature or its leadership may have achieved some of its principal goals, and the courts may have struck down some important laws. But most of the decisions on what money is spent for what purposes will have been the result in large measure of the proposals and pressures generated by the administrators.

The States Today: Structures Without a General Function

A summary of the most important political actors and institutions in our fifty states establishes American state governments as familiar examples of the Western form of government established some two hundred years ago. In basic design, the states are democratically based and republican in organization—that is, organized to divide power and recognize elements other than population in their representative base. As in other Western governments, state decision-making is activated by a number of special groups in the public constituency—that is, it is pluralistic—and it proceeds by highly developed and stylized rules.

What differentiates state governments from the national government and from other free governments is principally the path and speed of their evolution. The operation of state political systems has not resulted in as rapid a rise in executive responsibility as in other systems, and in most states the role of party as a basis for organizing public sentiment, selecting political activists, or directing their action is much weaker than elsewhere. Legislatures remain the dominant institutions, still structured to emphasize minority points of view and to deal only indirectly with the political issues which concern most of their constituencies. The governors tend to be less influential than their counterparts in other systems; the administrators who

"The Mean Old Federal Courts Are Trying To Impose Their Will On Others"

Sometimes state and local governments disagree, as shown by this cartoon commenting on the controversy generated by the closing of some public schools in Virginia in 1956.

HERBLOCK
COPR. THE WASHINGTON POST CO.

From *Herblock's Special For Today*, Simon & Schuster, 1958

are professionally oriented more influential. Most of all, public decisions are likely to be the result of particularized action of particularized interests, constantly forming and re-forming, and major decisions are rarely related to one another or to part of a general program, executive or legislative. The output of the system in laws, programs, money, and activity is thus a potpourri of responses to an assortment of different stimuli. Major conflicts respecting far-ranging economic and social development are fought out in other political arenas—the national or the local.

These differences in political behavior in the state systems are then principally differences in degree, not in kind, of structure or process. They seem to have arisen because in the transition of the country from a rural isolated nation to an urban internationally oriented one, the separate identity of individual state societies, their economic base, the customs, attitudes, and styles, have steadily weakened, but corresponding changes in political structure have not occurred. As Professor York Willbern has pointed out, states have lost their sense of community and no longer seem an effective basis for organizing important aspects of human activity.[22] They command less attention, less loyalty, and less respect from the public and therefore seem without a general purpose.

This is not to say that the systems do not work or perform the important functions spelled out at the beginning of this chapter. They are the key units in the American federal system, the basis of our party organization, the overseers of local government. Nonetheless, by and large, the state sys-

[22] York Willbern, "The States as Components in an Areal Division of Powers," Arthur Maass, ed., *Area and Power* (Glencoe, 1959).

tems remain artificial mechanisms in the sense that they are detached from other important societal systems. As going concerns they continue to maintain a political identity, and as organizations they preserve themselves and expand by virtue of the links with the nation and the locality. But only recently, in the reapportionment forced on the legislatures by the federal courts and in the gradual spread of two-party patterns of competition, have the states shown signs of adjusting their structures to accommodate the new functions and workloads they now carry. Not until they come to deal directly with urban and regional issues are they likely to regain the status, importance, and independent purpose they enjoyed when the Republic was first established.

28 / The Pattern of Local Government

Town-making will perhaps be the final battleground between the East and the West. In an affluent society, the quantitative competition is going to become less and less important. The final battle will be fought on quality." [1]

In the American effort to endow our modern communities with quality and to make everyday living pleasant and manageable for almost 200 million Americans, local governments play a critical role. They are, in the words of the Municipal Manpower Commission, a "growth industry," busily engaged in providing public facilities and services for expanding populations, planning new land uses, building new cities and rebuilding old ones, and resolving the conflicts that arise in an increasingly urban and complex environment. Every time a new home is built in a metropolitan area, a public investment of $18,500 is required—for streets, sewers, schools, police and fire stations, water, gas, and electricity—for public services provided to the new family, and new services are required at a value of $1,000 each year. The demands on the local government growth industry are enormous—and the need for foresight, skill, and enterprise in making decisions at the local level is obvious.

Yet, to many observers, American local governments are ill prepared to meet the challenge. Government machinery looks obsolete, fragmented among hundreds of local units, characterized by central-city–suburban rivalry, plagued at once with problems of explosive growth in metropolitan areas and rapid decline in small towns and rural areas. Shortages abound— of skilled personnel, administrators, engineers, physicians, nurses, librarians, and social workers. Vigorous leadership often seems lacking. Even a basic understanding of the role of local government is lacking. "Too many people think of local government as composed of trash collectors, police, and firemen and fail to realize the range of tasks to be done and of human talents needed." [2]

Despite the obvious challenges to local units in the modern world, the wholesale indictment of present local institutions that many critics express does not seem justifiable. For one thing, in terms of providing more

---

[1] Bruno Zevi, quoted in Municipal Manpower Commission, *Governmental Manpower for Tomorrow's Cities* (New York, 1962), p. 11.
[2] *Ibid.*, p. 5.

890

and better community facilities and services, the record of the grass roots in the last twenty years is impressive. For another, the performance of local governments varies enormously across the country and within metropolitan areas. Before we can accurately gauge the gap between challenge and response, we need to know how local political systems actually function today and the process of evolution they have recently been experiencing.

The first property of local governments that must be understood is that they are legally creatures of the states. Cities, the local governments that carry out most of the programs and deal with most of the conflicts in urban areas, are legally established as *municipalities* chartered by either general or special act of the state legislature. Smaller units such as boroughs, villages, and towns (outside New England, New York, and Wisconsin) are also classified as *municipalities*. Municipal charters usually take the form of an incorporation document endowing the cities with a legal personality comparable to that possessed by a business corporation. They specify the duties, powers, and financial resources of the municipality in great detail. For many years, the so-called "Home Rule" movement has argued that municipalities ought to frame their own charters, but the basic state right of supervision and oversight remains essentially unchanged.

Counties are legal subdivisions of the state originally established for purposes of administrative and judicial convenience. They exist in all states except Rhode Island (though Connecticut has to all intents and purposes eliminated the county) and Louisiana, where the *parish* is a comparable unit. Their powers, as well as their internal organization, vary greatly from state to state, but generally they are even more subject to state control than municipalities.

Townships are organized local governments, legally distinct from municipalities, that exist in twenty-two states. They are termed "towns" in the six New England states, as well as "plantations" in Maine and "locations" in New Hampshire. Outside the Northeast, they usually have limited powers and are active chiefly in rural areas. Again they are creatures of the states.

School districts are established by twenty-nine state governments as entities independent from other local units; in four states other governments administer the schools; in seventeen a mixed system exists. *Special districts*, most usually concerned with fire protection, drainage, and conservation but covering a variety of functions, exist in every state.

According to standard terminology, to qualify as a local government all these units must possess the characteristics of (1) existence as an "organized entity," (2) governmental character (i.e., officials who are in some way publicly accountable), and (3) substantial autonomy, defined as "considerable" fiscal and administrative independence.[3] The fact remains, however, that the power to establish and abolish units, to define their authority—both financial and operative—and to shape their structure rests in the last analysis with the state.

Two other key characteristics of local governments are their number and diversity. These properties derive from the nation's size and the states'

[3] United States Department of Commerce, Bureau of the Census, *Governmental Organization*, in *Census of Governments, 1962* (Washington, 1963), p. 15.

varied, pragmatic approach in establishing governments. The last official census count (in 1962) reported 91,236 units of government in existence in the United States; federal and state governments excluded, this resulted in 17,997 municipalities, 3,043 counties, 17,144 township governments, 34,678 school districts, and 18,323 special districts.[4] When variations in terms of forms of internal management, specific powers and duties, character of political recruitment to office, and political style are considered, it is obvious that our local units form a mosaic of structures unparalleled in the world. New York City, with a budget second only to that of the federal government, is a municipality. So are Sulphur Springs, Texas, and Rice Lake, Wisconsin. Obviously, the three face different issues, deal with different conflicts, and operate different programs.

Finally, though local governments are not legally independent enterprises and though they vary enormously in type and activity, a common public ideology surrounds them. As indicated in Chapter 26, the American belief that the best governments are the governments closest to home is of long standing. A great deal of the vigor of this belief was lost when the local government came to preside over large cities and took the form of the municipality. Then the figure of the city boss and his machine took the place of the respected town father and the town meeting, and local politics became tarnished by elements of corruption and mediocrity. Nevertheless, the public still expects the local governments to respond to their demands over a wide range of activities and looks to them to provide the facilities and services necessary for orderly community existence, even though they often legally lack the authority to do so.

These major characteristics of local government suggest that we study these units in a different way than we have analyzed national or state politics. The large number of units requires that we employ a comparative technique. The 90,000 separate units need to be classified initially according to some *typology* which relates them to the characteristics of the communities in which they operate. Then within each major category, differences in structure and responsibilities will have to be identified. Next, we need to know something about how interests are articulated and combined and what pattern of influence results. And finally, we need to explore differences in "outputs"—the issues, decisions, and programs that preoccupy the local political systems. The next sections of the chapter, then, divide types of general-purpose local government according to their urban, suburban, and rural settings and under each summarize their characteristic structure, distribution of political resources, and major political issues.

Urban Government: The Big City and Its Satellites

The local governments spending the most money and employing the most people are the 219 municipalities that serve as general governments of the central cities in standard metropolitan areas. These units preside over the most densely populated and heterogeneous communities with the most

---

[4] *Ibid.,* p. 1.

varied land use in the United States. Of these the most visible and—in terms of magnitude of operations—the most important are the twenty-two cities with populations exceeding 500,000 each. Their expenditures in 1960 accounted for more than one third of all municipal spending and total municipal employment.

Because of the size, density, and complexity of their communities, big-city municipalities also embrace more functions than most local governments. They frequently manage the public schools directly, and they provide recreational and cultural programs which no other municipalities undertake. New York City, for example, maintains municipal colleges with an enrollment of some 80,000; conducts research in geriatrics, cancer, and mental health; offers free psychiatric sessions in an effort to curb juvenile delinquency; and supports puppet shows, Shakespeare workshops, and jazz concerts.[5]

The structure of big-city governments was originally patterned after English prototypes: a council composed of aldermen and councilmen (the latter being the only elected officials) held both executive and legislative powers, and the mayor was chiefly a ceremonial figure. After the Revolution, cities experienced successive waves of new forms of organization. First came the division of the council into a bicameral body, patterned after the federal Congress. Then, the Jacksonian practice of electing almost every official, legislative and executive alike, became popular. Subsequently, cities experimented with commission forms of government (i.e., a small body combining executive and legislative powers) in the early part of the twentieth century and with the strong-mayor—council and city-manager forms.

Today, sixteen of the twenty largest municipalities function under some version of the strong-mayor—council plan.[6] In theory, the plan is designed to make the mayor the undisputed master of the executive agencies and to give him substantial legislative powers in the form of budget-making, the veto, and the right to propose legislation. But only Boston and Cleveland among the largest cities make the mayor the sole elected official among the chief administrative officers, and in several cities the mayor shares budgetary and administrative powers. In New York, the eight-member Board of Estimate (mayor, council president, comptroller, and five borough presidents) is considered "the center of gravity" in the city's political process. In Chicago, a council committee prepares the budget. Detroit's strong-mayor government is cluttered with advisory committees to check mayoralty action.

Nonetheless, except for Cincinnati with its manager-council form, Washington, D.C., operating under a special commission appointed by the President of the United States, Minneapolis, and Milwaukee, large American cities provide their chief executives with substantial formal powers. In recent years, several cities have augmented the mayor's position by providing

---

[5] See Robert C. Wood, *1400 Governments: The Political Economy of the New York Metropolitan Region* (Cambridge, Mass., 1960), Chapter 1.
[6] The summary figures used in discussion of municipal forms of government are drawn from International Association of City Managers, *The Municipal Yearbook* (annually).

him with a chief administrative officer to discharge the important staff administrative duties of supervising line departments and providing central management services.

Below the 500,000 population mark the frequency of strong-mayor–council forms drops off rapidly. As the size of the city decreases, the city-manager plan gains in popularity. Forty percent of the cities between 250,000 and 500,000 have manager forms; 49 percent of the cities between 100,000 and 250,000; and over 50 percent of those between 50,000 and 100,000.

The principal feature of the council-manager form, as it is called formally, is that all "policy-making" responsibility is vested in a council of elected laymen, while "policy execution" is assigned to a nonelected professional administrator known as a manager. The plan's rationale is that the essential task of a municipal government is to provide an array of services—an infrastructure of social capital—necessary to support social and economic life in the city. Further, the character and level of these services—utilities, streets, fire and police protection, health, welfare, some recreational facilities—is considered to be almost self-evident. Hence, it is presumed that fewer conflicts over political jurisdiction occur at the city level than at the state or national ones.

Given these assumptions, the council is considered to be an adequate mirror for the views of the city electorate on issues and to be able to resolve them. The manager, usually trained as an engineer or executive, has the duty of seeing that the government's day-to-day operations are carried out in a businesslike manner. First established in two small cities at the turn of the century, the council-manager plan is now especially popular in the Midwest and West, in such municipalities as Kansas City, Dallas, San Diego, Rochester, and Toledo.[7]

The other structures for municipal government—the commission and weak-mayor forms—are on the decline in large and medium-sized cities. The commission form vests legislative and executive powers in a small body, usually of five members. Experience demonstrated, however, that it failed to fix responsibility and encouraged development of separate spheres of influence among commissioners, each charged with the supervision of a separate set of departments. Memphis, Portland (Oregon), Birmingham, St. Paul, Omaha, and Jersey City are the principal cities that still operate under this plan.

The weak-mayor plan, with many executive and administrative officers directly elected or appointed by large councils reserving budget-making and supervisory powers to themselves, has similarly proved unsatisfactory in most large cities. Providence, Atlanta, and Los Angeles are the principal municipalities operating under this form. Chicago, with its large council, retains some of the structural characteristics of the plan.

The two principal forms of big-city government—strong mayor and city

---

[7] For a clear exposition of the plan, see Richard S. Childs, *Civic Victories* (New York, 1952). For an analysis of the plan in action, see Gladys Kammerer, *et al.*, *City Managers in Politics: An Analysis of Manager Tenure and Termination* (Gainesville, 1962).

manager—have sharply divergent implications for the exercise of executive and legislative powers. In the first, the mayor is the key political figure, with public attention fixed upon his activity and with the initiative for decision-making in his power. In the second, executive action is reduced at least in the public view to administrative and technical matters and the council emerges as the principal focus of popular attention. City managers often acquire substantial influence in their own right and come to lead and direct the council. But they do so without a mandate gained from direct election, and they frequently split with the council on matters of public policy. In the first instance, city politics revolves around the chief executive, while the council performs chiefly as his critic and reviewer. In the other instance, council decisions, including the appointment and discharge of city managers (occurring at reasonably frequent intervals), provide the political fireworks.

THE DISTRIBUTION OF POLITICAL INFLUENCE IN LARGE CITIES

Structural differences are only one of the variations in urban political systems. The number of informal power centers and the patterning of their relations represent a second difference.

Two popular tenets of American political folklore are that political decisions in large-city municipalities are concentrated in the hands of a few people and that, since the Civil War, this group has been principally motivated by private gain. That is, behind the mayor and the council—or opposed to the desires of the professional city manager—an elite, a boss, or a machine "runs things" for personal benefit.

The reality of modern big-city politics is much more complex than this simplistic notion. Indeed, in many cities, as the following sections indicate, it is more accurate to say that nobody "runs things," in so far as having control over all the major decisions that the political system produces is concerned. The "boss" ideology is left over from the political myths of past generations.

Oligarchic rule: first families and machines

It is true that in different historical periods, in different cities, for different reasons, urban political power has been tightly organized. In the sizable seaport towns of colonial and Revolutionary times, the management of public affairs was originally in the hands of a few town fathers. Town officials were recruited from the clergy and merchant class; the severe suffrage restrictions barred women, landless people, and indentured servants from participation in public affairs. Robert Dahl in his study of New Haven dubbed the early years of politics in that city—from 1784 to 1842— "rule by the patricians." Every mayor in those years was drawn from the "Standing Order" and possessed both wealth and social position. Dahl estimates that in the early 1800s, when New Haven's population exceeded 5,000, the top elite was not over 100. In 1811, of 600 adult males, 343 were qualified to vote and only 249 elected the mayor.[8]

---

[8] Robert Dahl, *Who Governs?* (New Haven, 1963).

The rising tide of industrialism swept over the Standing Order, as men without social prestige acquired wealth as business entrepreneurs. In New Haven and most other American cities, the "ex-plebes" became political influentials, both as representatives of the new economic class and as professional politicians. Their rise laid the foundation for the political machine which flourished in the late nineteenth and early twentieth centuries.

The machine, and its leader, the boss, emerged coincidentally with the flood of European immigrants. Its first function was to do battle on behalf of the newcomers against the old patricians. It was a political mechanism designed to assimilate the wave after wave of Irish, Italian, German, Scandinavian, and Balkan people dumped into the big cities on the eastern seaboard—and recruit them into American political and social life. Often, the newcomers arrived without jobs, money, or command of the language, and sometimes sick and weary. Frequently the man of the house was unable to support his family, and the wife worked as a domestic servant to a patrician family. The household took up residence in cellars, attics, or other mean quarters. Employment in established businesses and professions was difficult.[9]

In this context the boss assumed the role of protector of the poor, providing shelter, jobs, food, recreation—in short, offering both a rudimentary welfare service and instruction in the process of adaptation to a new culture. In return, he asked political loyalty expressed in votes. To immigrants born in societies where ties of kinship and friendship were strong, representative government was unknown, and personal obligations were more meaningful than abstract legal ones, these requests did not seem unreasonable. So, as the immigrant minorities grew in size, they provided the votes by which the boss dominated the formal machinery of city government.

Once secure in city hall, the boss increased his influence in three ways. He made alliances with elements of the commercial, financial, and industrial communities doing business in the city, exchanging licenses, public utility franchises, and construction contracts for money and support. He also discovered that the expanding public programs which city governments undertook to accommodate the growing population could be more than vehicles for personal favors in the form of jobs and contracts: they could be vote-getters by themselves. So after the First World War, bosses began to make records as "builders" and "doers"—constructing hospitals, parks, and civic centers in such numbers and with such speed as to show up the conservative management of the town fathers. Finally, the boss became a master of campaign strategies. He offered balanced tickets representing different ethnic groups. He rigged elections by the use of "repeaters" (voters who went from poll to poll using names of other voters who had moved away or even died—the so-called graveyard vote), by stuffing ballot boxes, or by fraudulent tallies. In this second stage of the machine, the boss moved from his "protector" role to become the dispenser of bread and circuses. It is important to note, however, that even in his heyday, the boss was usually challenged by other political groups and that his sphere of influence was limited, since local government powers and payrolls were small compared to those of the private sector.

[9] See Arthur M. Schlesinger, Sr., *The Rise of the City, 1878–1896* (New York, 1933).

The decentralization of political influence

Neither first families nor bosses form centers of political influence in large cities today. Here and there strong political organizations exist—the Democratic organization in Chicago directed by Mayor Daley in the late 1950s or that led by Congressman Green in Philadelphia in the early 1960s. But most machines built on the classic model have disappeared. Those that remain are modified in behavior and limited in scope of activity. Especially since the Second World War, urban politics has been characterized by a steady diffusion of the old pattern of relatively concentrated, unified political influence.

Fewer and fewer large cities possess a cohesive, "efficiently" operating political system with only a few major activists, easily identified, with closely knit relationships, and with rapid and frequent communications. Now the more typical urban system is composed of many more discrete arenas, with separate sets of participants making separate sets of political decisions. A number of power centers exist in many large cities, relatively independent of one another and preoccupied with a narrow range of decisions. Typically, there are political activists who make campaigns and elections their principal concern; others who focus on public finance; still others interested primarily in economic and land development; and some concentrating on law enforcement and organized crime. Each of these separate groups is likely to exhibit quite different characteristics in the way it arrives at decisions.[10]

Several factors account for diffusion of political influence. First, the continued assimilation of the descendants of the European immigrants into American economic and social life has made more Americans independent of politics as a means for satisfying personal and family needs. Citizens of foreign descent are now established in business or the professions. Favors from machines and bosses are no longer required or wanted by groups who used to provide their voting strength. Instead, these voters have adopted middle-class Anglo-Saxon values, which make political involvement less desirable and acceptable as a way of acquiring status.

Second, the big-city voters who are not members of the middle class socially and economically have new and very specialized political interests. They divide into quite different groups: Negroes who seek better schools and housing accommodations; welfare families; citizens who live in the exclusive wealthy downtown neighborhoods; professional city employees. Bloc voting in great numbers rarely exists, and city politicians today build coalitions from such diverse groups that they cannot make many important public decisions without some loss of popularity from one sector or another. As we will see later on, the rising Negro minority in large cities makes political decision-making especially complex.

Third, the low-income minority groups who still need political help may see politics in a different light than their predecessors did. Their attitudes

---

[10] Two principal models of the present pattern of big-city politics are presented by Dahl, *op. cit.*, and Edward C. Banfield, *Political Influence* (Glencoe, 1961). See also Edward C. Banfield and James Q. Wilson, *City Politics* (Cambridge, Mass., 1963).

toward politicians seem to have shifted from one of loyalty and rapport to that of distrust, or, as some analysts have called it, "alienation." [11] That is, many low-status citizens no longer believe city politicians sincerely want to help solve their personal problems. Instead, they think they are tools for the rich business community or are concerned with lining their own pockets.

Finally, the professional big-city bureaucracy has taken over many of the welfare functions the machine used to provide informally. It has also undergone a face-lifting in terms of its own performance. Civil service regulations now sharply restrict opportunities for patronage. Municipal administrators have achieved professional status and have acquired independent influence in programs in the fields of health, urban renewal, and education. Below the top management level, white-collar and blue-collar city employees have organized themselves in civil service associations or labor unions in order to make their own demands upon political leaders. Thus, the city enterprise which used to furnish the machine with so many of its political resources by providing jobs, contracts, and special privileges has grown increasingly independent.

The municipal reform movement

Accelerating and capitalizing on these basic forces working for diffusion of power has been a group of political activists variously dubbed muckrakers, mugwumps, and reformers. After the boss first rose to power, he faced opposition from the ranks of the old town fathers, new citizens wishing to symbolize their arrival in the middle class, and the immigrants who came not from Europe but off the American family farm. Originally, the political aim of these groups was little more than "to throw the rascals out." Thus three generations ago the Massachusetts Reform Club, the City Club of New York, the Municipal League of Philadelphia, and the Baltimore Reform League expressed outrage at boss rule and municipal corruption.[12]

The limits of this early evangelism quickly became clear. Reformers sometimes captured public office in the latter part of the nineteenth century and the early part of the twentieth, but they were usually overthrown in the next election. The reform movement came to emphasize new procedures and institutions as well as new men for city government. Reformers urged stricter enforcement of registration and balloting requirements in voting. They advocated direct popular action through the initiative, recall, and referendum (in general, the use of a petition signed by a relatively small number of voters calling for a general vote to decide an issue or to dismiss an official from office). They worked for proportional representation, a method of election by which a voter can express the intensity of his preference for one candidate and thus increase the electoral power of cohesive minority groups. The greatest innovation of the institution-minded reformers was the city-manager form of government, designed, as we have seen, to reduce to a minimum the scope of old-style politics and to pattern

---

[11] See Murray Levin, *The Alienated Voter* (New York, 1960).
[12] See Frank M. Stewart, *A Half Century of Municipal Reform: The History of the National Municipal League* (Los Angeles, 1950).

public decision-making along the lines of private business. The manager plan fitted especially well with the middle-class values of the reformers by emphasizing honesty, efficiency, and professional skill and minimizing the political conflicts which might exist in a city's constituency.

In recent years, reform movements have stressed still other aims. They have worked to create new organizations that participate directly in politics. One type is the "watchdog" group, established to look over the shoulders of public officials in their activities, study budgets and tax rates, and evaluate new civic projects. Sometimes, this type takes the form of municipal research bureaus, taxpayers' associations, citizens' leagues. Occasionally, the organization is a local political party, such as the Cambridge Civic Association in Massachusetts, the Citizens' Association of Kansas City, and the Cincinnati Charter Committee, endorsing candidates for office and working directly to mobilize the vote. More frequently, however, it concentrates on specific issues and attempts to influence officials through attendance at public hearings, newspaper releases, analysis of proposals, and private conversations.

A second contemporary reform strategy has been to change the composition and leadership of existing political parties, in effect infiltrating the old machines. So-called blue ribbon party reform took place in Philadelphia in the 1950s when Joseph Clark and Richardson Dilworth changed the face of the Democratic organization for a time. The California Democratic Clubs represent a similar infusion of new party members (amateurs in the view of the professional politician) in cities across that state. In New York, the founding of the Lexington Democratic Club in 1949 began a movement culminating in the overthrow in 1960 of Carmine De Sapio as head of Tammany and the emergence of the New York Committee for Democratic Voters (led by former Senator Lehman, Mrs. Eleanor Roosevelt, and Thomas Finletter) as the headquarters of some thirty reform clubs. In contrast to earlier generations of reformers, the intraparty ones are likely to be young, more liberal in outlook, and more oriented toward issues. They are not against politics; they seek to change its emphasis from personal to policy objectives and to make internal party organization more democratic.

The machine today

Over the years, then, the basic forces that raised the standard of living in American cities, assimilated the newcomers, and infused their descendants with middle-class values found their political expression in successive waves of reformers. They have reduced the power of town fathers and bosses alike. The former have largely withdrawn from politics except to serve on advisory committees or to head up civic projects, providing "symbols of legitimacy" for political decisions made by others. The latter have seen their scope of influence progressively reduced as welfare and assistance programs have been placed in the hands of the professional bureaucrats and as civil service and tighter management practices have reduced the opportunities for patronage and business favors which were key resources for the machine. Today the "organization" is threatened even in its stronghold of nomination and election decisions by the intraparty reformists. In most large cities where party politics is important, some kind of inner circle is still in command: Chicago, New York, and Philadelphia provide the best examples. But in these cases the machine has had to change its image: disavow old practices of gaining loyalty, improve municipal operations, admit new-style politicians to leadership, and talk increasingly in terms of middle-class values.

One other remnant of bossism is still evident in the connection between city politics and organized crime. Often treated in sensational terms, the activities of organized crime, especially gambling, affect the fortunes of political organizations in important ways. Because they are illegal, these operations function successfully only as long as the police choose not to investigate their activities. Hence, the need for criminals to assure a "fix." Second, because organized crime is such a sizable profitable investment, the motivation for securing the "fix" is high, and the motivation for removing any competing syndicate equally high. Thus, strong compulsions exist to link at least part of the political process to the so-called underworld.

Sometimes the link takes the form of corruption in a city's police department and other enforcement agencies and in judicial proceedings. In this instance it may be regularized to the point where only lower echelon political activists and bureaucracies are involved and elected officials are free from any association. This appears to have been the case in the Chicago and Denver police scandals in the late 1950s and early 1960s. Sometimes, protection is provided for organized crime in exchange for campaign contributions to high-placed officials. In instances such as these, the pattern of involvement, as the Senate investigations led by Senator Estes Kefauver in the 1950s indicated, is likely to cover a wider band of political activity.

In both cases, however, the role of organized crime in politics is usually restricted and negative today. That is, the syndicate rarely concerns itself directly with the nomination and election processes except to supply financing and is not often involved with major decisions about programs or political conflicts which city government makes. Further, organized crime rarely seeks any specific positive actions on the part of bureaucracies or politicians. Indeed, as Senator Paul Douglas has said, contributions from "shady" sources often leave a candidate freer to exercise his own judgment on matters of high policy than support from "respectable" sources. Moreover, there is rarely widespread, continuing public pressure to eliminate these connections. The public rarely regards bookmaking, for example, as a serious crime (although church and welfare groups may take an opposite view).

Nevertheless, the continuing association of syndicates and law enforcers has long-run effects on local government operations. Payoffs and bribes to secure protection undermine professional standards and the general integrity of local political institutions. It is not what police and public officials do as a consequence of the fix, but the impact on morale of the rank-and-file and the attitudes of cynicism and disrespect which the public comes to adopt toward politics that are the principal implications. All these effects contribute to an overall—but indirect—loss of status and prestige for city government, reinforcing the deep-seated American belief that the city is the center for immorality in national life.

With such exceptions noted, then, few large cities today are directed by a comprehensive, tightly organized, and monolithic political system. Typically, separate power centers concerned with separate kinds of decisions exist, each strong enough to maintain independence in its own sphere but unable to extend the scope of its influence. In these separate centers making decisions about schools, welfare, taxation, police, renewal, housing, the formally elected officials, not persons behind the scenes, are most likely to wield the greatest influence. In the largest cities, the office of the mayor is the key power center, with incumbents who are professional career politicians. Daley of Chicago, Collins of Boston, Clark and Dilworth of Philadelphia, Tucker of St. Louis, Lawrence of Pittsburgh, West of Nashville, and Lee of New Haven represent in the post-Second World War years the new breed of visible, strong, and often spectacular city leaders who have chosen politics as their lifetime work.

Despite their power and capacities, the new mayors are severely limited. They adopt a posture of vigorous, energetic leadership more frequently than they establish an actual record of sustained accomplishment. In their actual decisions they often appear to move cautiously, constrained by the separate centers of influence which surround them. As Edward Banfield has demonstrated in the instance of Chicago, Robert Dahl for New Haven, and Wallace Sayre and Herbert Kaufman for New York,[13] the mayor's preferred strategy is to wait until the political activists in one area have arrived at some agreement among themselves and then to ratify the decision by the sanction of his office. Most mayors engage in an elaborate process of "checking out" new proposals, organizing civic committees to serve as weather vanes and lightning rods for new plans, and testing public reaction through the press and established civic organizations.

In the present circumstances, there is little else that the mayors can do as they work to reconcile the demands of widely different numbers of interest groups—professional bureaucracies, old business reform groups, new liberal reform groups, the remnants of old machines, the press, labor, and Negro minority interests. The upshot is that announcements about decisions, plans, and programs in big cities usually outstrip actual accomplishments, and the impression of activity is often politically more important than its substance.

ISSUES IN THE LARGE CITIES

What decisions is the modern urban political system called upon to make? Oliver Williams has suggested that they fall into four broad categories and that the relative emphasis a system chooses to place among these categories is expressive of the role and philosophy of the government within the city. On the basis of Williams' classification the system makes (1) *caretaker decisions*—those concerned with the administration of traditional municipal services; (2) *amenities decisions*—those concerned with fringe services or the quality and level of accepted services; (3) *development decisions*—those when the government chooses to act as an instrument for community

---

13 Dahl, *op. cit.*; Banfield, *op. cit.*; Wallace S. Sayre and Herbert Kaufman, *Governing New York City* (New York, 1960).

growth; and (4) *conflict decisions*—those when it serves as the arbiter be-tween sharply opposed interests in the city population on matters which only incidentally affect city programs.[14]

In the caretaker role, the urban system makes decisions concerned with efficiency and economy of routine services, management and personnel practices, the replacement and expansion of the municipal plant—school buildings, waterworks, streets, and sewers. The issue of the greatest con-tinuing concern is likely to be that of law enforcement: the maintenance of order under complex and difficult circumstances and the professionalization of the police force. But the provision of fire protection, the enforcement of sanitary and health codes, the regulation or production of public utilities, the administration of the welfare program can all become visible, important decisions with significant political implications. Usually, they are handled without fanfare by the professional administrators in the system. They only become visible at the time the city's budget is prepared, when a scandal breaks, or when an emergency occurs.

Issues concerned with amenities are usually cast in spending and taxing terms. They are concerned with the quantity and quality of services the municipality should offer. For big cities the provision of specialized school facilities or improved instruction to provide "higher horizons," the estab-lishment of parks, playgrounds, mental health clinics, and the sponsorship of art festivals and other cultural enterprises are issues to be weighed against the tax rate. Here the division of interest groups appears along economic lines: the big taxpayer seeks to hold the line against new levies, while spender groups representing parents, art lovers, health enthusiasts advocate more and better services. Since established programs are represented by established bureaucracies, the job of maintaining relatively constant tax levels turns on the capacity of taxpayers' groups to restrain the city's impulse for new services.

In the present situation, when the increase in the taxable property within the large cities is at a much slower rate than in the suburbs, and in some instances is nonexistent, the battles over amenities and their financing are recurrent and taken seriously by the politicians.

Caretaker and amenities decisions, though recurrent, are not the major issues in urban politics today. Today the focus of big-city politics falls in-creasingly on the developmental and arbiter roles of the governments. As for the first, the mounting financial pressures on the municipality stimulate local policy makers to find ways and means for ensuring future growth. Bold plans for changing the city appear, and they affect many groups within the population in different ways. Developmental activities of local govern-ment often intensify conflict and hostilities among groups and classes who coexisted with reasonable success in earlier times when the city government played only the caretaker and amenities roles. Development decisions, in turn, force cities into the position of arbiter—as is presently the case in the civil rights protest movements of urban Negroes.

---

[14] Oliver P. Williams, "A Topology for Comparative Local Government," *Midwest Journal of Political Science* (May, 1961), Vol. V, pp. 150–65. See also Banfield and Wilson, *op. cit.*, Chapter 1.

Developmental and conflict-arbitration decisions include such diverse matters as planning and zoning ordinances, promotional programs to attract new industry, public housing projects, intercession in labor-management disputes, and fluoridation controversies. At the present time, however, three issues seem to be most crucial to the reputation and influence of the top activists in urban politics: urban renewal, transportation, and the accommodation of the newest of the city's immigrant groups, the Negroes.

Urban renewal

The most important developmental program in most large cities today is that aimed at the rehabilitation of old commercial, industrial, and residential areas. Technological and economic forces in the private sector of the city's activities have for a generation encouraged the migration of people and jobs out of the core to the hinterland of the metropolitan area. Faced with a loss of population and, in some cities, falling property values, many city officials believe that only large programs to reclaim economic activities now locating in the suburbs or to discover new economic functions can preserve the core city. Urban renewal is the major public effort that undertakes this change in the pattern of urban land use.

Urban renewal is a joint program of the cities and the federal government, originating in the slum-clearance measures of the 1930s. It has existed in its present form, with some modifications, since 1949. Under the program, federal funds are provided to match local money to acquire or rehabilitate blighted land, clear off or modernize obsolete or dilapidated structures, and make sites available for new uses. When the sites are physically cleared of old structures, two thirds of the difference between the costs of acquisition and clearance and the resale to private developers—called the "write-down" cost—is paid by the federal government. The city also uses its powers of eminent domain in order to assemble the many separately owned tracts of land and ensure an economically feasible new investment.[15]

Originally, urban renewal projects were almost always "total clearance" ones. They proceeded on an individual basis, wherever a particular neighborhood seemed suitable for redevelopment and funds and plans were available. By 1954 considerable opposition had developed to the piecemeal "bulldozer" approach, and new amendments to the federal legislation emphasized conservation and betterment of existing structures whenever possible. These amendments authorized redevelopment for commercial and industrial as well as residential use. They also tried to place each project in a general development plan by requiring cities to put them in the framework of a "workable program." As a prerequisite to federal aid, cities were asked to demonstrate that they had adequate building and health codes, a proper administrative structure for renewal, sufficient local financing and public support, and had or were preparing a comprehensive plan of development with provisions for relocating displaced persons, and a structural analysis of the extent of neighborhood deterioration.

In the first ten years of the program, some 500 communities participated

---

15 See Peter H. Rossi and Robert A. Rentler, *The Politics of Urban Renewal* (New York, 1961).

in urban renewal, including nearly every large city in the United States, and some 100 projects were completed by the end of 1961. Since then, the size of the program has expanded rapidly. In relation to the total amount of obsolete urban real estate, however (there were some 4 million substandard units, in run-down condition and lacking basic sanitary facilities, in metropolitan areas in 1961), the impact of renewal remains small. In New York, where the largest program in the nation has rehabilitated some 500 acres of land, 5,000 acres of slums remain. Philadelphia has certified some 9,000 acres as suitable for redevelopment. In Boston nearly 20 percent of the city's residential area has been classified as substandard. The total cost for removing urban blight has been estimated as between $125 billion and $1 trillion, yet during the 1950s an average of only $300 million a year was committed by the federal government to the program.

More than lack of funds has impeded urban renewal. Though the program has obvious political appeal to mayors seeking to expand the municipal tax base, businessmen wishing to preserve downtown investments, and families in search of better houses, it also provokes political opposition. Especially when renewal takes the form of clearance of existing homes, present residents often bitterly object to being moved. Landlords who control slum property face the prospect of losing one of the most lucrative sources of income in the real estate business. Minority groups often fear that they will be forced back into neighborhood ghettos that they have only recently left. When the project takes the form of a commercial or industrial development, other members of the downtown business community—retail merchants, owners of older office buildings and apartments—face competition from modern stores and buildings. City agencies that have to assume the responsibility of carrying out the workable program object to new duties and methods of operations. And the kind of new project chosen, its architectural style, the selection of the private sponsors, are frequent sources of administrative and political dissension.

With such widespread repercussions throughout the political system, then, renewal programs have generated a special subspecies of urban politics. Many mayors make their reputations as vigorous proponents for progress by advocating large-scale renewal activities. The urban renewal administrator (the professional in charge of a city's program) has emerged as an important political actor in his own right. Where mayors and renewal administrators are alert, they have built up sizable public support from the press, families wishing to rehabilitate their homes or find better ones, bankers, and neighborhood associations. But they have also had to deal with the sources of opposition while simultaneously executing a program of great complexity.

These obstacles have made the politics of renewal dangerous for many officials. One needs a rare combination of skill and know-how to develop renewal projects that make both political and economic sense. Although renewal programs are an important municipal activity, after more than a decade of experimentation, they proceed slowly and uncertainly, depending on the particular mix of supporters and opponents. Only mayors with considerable influence and energy, supported by skillful administrators, are likely to move as rapidly as the originators of the program first expected.

Even with federal assistance, renewal remains an unsettled issue in many cities instead of a routinized activity, constantly triggering off major political controversies.

Transportation

In purely legal terms urban political systems have few major decisions to make about transportation. Although most of them maintain their network of streets, occasionally adding new ones, and some operate or supervise mass transportation systems, state and federal governments determine most urban transportation policy. Under the Federal Highway Act of 1956, the United States is responsible for the 41,000-mile Interstate Highway System, which serves 65 percent of the nation's urban population, and assumes 90 percent of its costs. State highway departments plan, construct, and maintain secondary and tertiary roads, and in a few states they handle city streets as well. Federal and state regulatory commissions oversee the commuting services of the railroads and most bus and transit companies, and the federal government underwrites the largest share of municipal airport construction. In all these matters, city officials have few direct responsibilities except traffic management.[16]

Yet the design and character of the urban transportation system vitally affects the course of urban development. The automobile and the highways it demanded are a major factor in America's rapid suburban growth. The accessibility of downtown stores and industries is a major determinant of their property value. City offices depend on commuter rail facilities, and factories on trucking, for their existence. Thus the decisions made at state and federal levels about transportation vitally affect the land use, economic vitality, and future of the large central cities—and the popularity of the political systems which govern them.

Since the Second World War, mayors, councilmen, and city interest groups have tried to influence these decisions indirectly. They seek ways and means to guide the planning of an expressway through a downtown area, the proposed abandonment of a commuter train by an interstate railway, or the possible extension of rapid transit or bus lines. Sometimes their interests are specific in nature: a fear that the expressway will destroy a neighborhood or lead to drastic losses in property values. Sometimes they are general: the anxiety of merchants that the lack of parking facilities will discourage shoppers or that new routes will encourage the rise of new shopping centers, causing the central business district to be bypassed. In all these instances, the city's political activists find themselves in the position of representing their constituencies in state and federal arenas.

Los Angeles represents the extreme example of how a city may spread geographically and politically as the preference for automobile travel grows. Abandoning a rapid transit system which was fairly well developed in the 1930s, the city by 1960 possessed the most extensive express highway network in the world. But it also discovered that over half of the land of the central business district was devoted to the highways, their ramps, cloverleafs, and parking lots. Thus the Los Angeles metropolitan area has become

---

16 See Wilfred Owen, *The Metropolitan Transportation Problem* (Washington, 1956).

Hubenthal in the Los Angeles *Herald Examiner*

"Less Than The Time
To The Airport"

The construction of superhighways has not solved the urban transportation problem.

geographically the largest in the nation, with one of the lowest population densities. Further, the provision of public services has evolved toward a contract system whereby many small suburban municipalities arrange with the county and city for police, fire protection, utilities, trash collection, and street maintenance. The possibility of either integrated transportation planning or political decision-making has correspondingly declined.

In reaction to the Los Angeles example of "diffusion," many city mayors have become enthusiasts for mass transportation, seeking state and federal aid to bolster subway and bus systems hard hit by dwindling revenues and fewer riders. In San Francisco, Pittsburgh, Chicago, Philadelphia, and Washington major studies of new transportation networks have been completed analyzing the impact of alternate kinds of transportation on city land uses, and federal assistance has been authorized for loans and grants to improve existing transportation services. Generally, the city's policy makers have contended that mass transportation is more efficient for moving large numbers of people in terms of total investment in facilities and would require a smaller outlay of public funds. The opposing argument held by state highway commissioners defines efficiency in terms of convenience to individual motorists and, by various calculations, estimates that in portal-to-portal travel, the automobile is more convenient and cheaper.

Whatever position city politicians take on transportation, and whether the issues are large (i.e., what type of transportation) or small (i.e., the exact route for a new highway), city leaders find themselves in strategically weak positions in any major conflict. Highway enthusiasts have a strong political coalition in most states: farmers, land developers, motorists,

This Is Progress?

© 1959 by Bill Mauldin
From *What's Got Your Back Up?* Harper & Row

automobile manufacturers, and road contractors possess both numbers and money as political resources. Governors and legislators frequently make their records on highway progress. And turnpike and development authorities have a tradition of independent behavior.

In contrast, the supporters of mass transportation represent the depressed industries of rail- and transit-equipment builders, with no history of access to federal support, with only the commuter minority of the public on their side, and with only the professional planners and students of urban affairs their principal spokesmen. Moreover, city politicians have had to work through their legislative delegations to exercise what influence they possess. Not only are these delegations outnumbered in the legislatures but also they are frequently political competitors of the local officials. They have little desire, therefore, to build the reputations or enhance the prestige of municipal officeholders who may campaign against them in coming years.

Under these circumstances, it is not surprising that highway politics has usually gone against the interests of the city politicians and that independent authorities and state transportation programs represent threats to their positions. Though in recent years some cities like Philadelphia and Boston have been able to reinvigorate mass transportation, and the federal government has moved to give greater consideration to broad transportation planning in metropolitan areas, it is unlikely that urban public policy which de-emphasizes the highway will soon be effected. In the meantime, the city political systems content themselves with striving to accommodate the new expressways, providing parking facilities, and negotiating for routes that disturb the smallest number of the most influential of their constituency. Thus in the public decisions which will have the greatest impact on the future of the cities, the urban political activists will probably have had the least to say.

The Negro immigrant

If urban renewal and transportation represent the key developmental decisions that now concern the great cities, the accommodation of the Southern, rural Negro poses the greatest potential conflict that city government will have to arbitrate. Like the other two issues, this one carries with it sizable hazards for the urban political system and results from forces which are not susceptible to control by the system.

Between 1950 and 1960, about 1.5 million Negroes migrated to the large metropolitan areas of the Northeast, Midwest, and Far West. If present trends continue, 79 percent of the 26 million Negroes expected to be living in the United States by 1975 will be located in urban areas, and most of them will be in the large central cities. In 1960, the nonwhite population of cities over 500,000 averaged 17 percent. By 1975, it is expected to average 28 percent. In Washington, D.C., it is already close to 60 percent.[17]

The Negro migration raises many of the same problems posed by the earlier migrations of Europeans. Although it occurs at a time when housing accommodations are comparatively better and population densities lower, the Negro pattern of settlement has nonetheless been in the form of low-cost, often substandard housing in neighborhoods already predominantly Negro in composition. Moreover, the problems that the earlier newcomers faced of moving from a rural to an urban culture, finding employment, acquiring new skills, and obtaining governmental assistance in their first years are present in this migration.

Yet there are special characteristics with special political significance in the process of accommodation today. The Negro is an American, already a citizen, and capable of exercising political power at once. Moreover, his political activity has as a major purpose the achieving of an effective civil rights program. At the same time, however, the Negro's different skin color means that the process of entry into new neighborhoods is more clearly and immediately identifiable. Thus, the Negro at once both possesses more potential influence than other immigrants and faces greater problems of accommodation.[18]

One political resource of the Negroes is their growing numbers. The continued migration provides the city Negro population with the same opportunities for cohesive political action as the Irish, Italian, Polish, German, and Scandinavian once possessed. Organized by wards and precincts, as in Chicago, Cleveland, and St. Louis, Negroes become an important voting bloc that can provide the basis for a semblance of old-style political organization. A second resource lies in the Negroes' rights as citizens and the powerful support given them by the federal courts. This means that the Negro has

---

[17] David McEntire, *Residence and Race* (Berkeley, 1960).
[18] See James Q. Wilson, *Negro Politics: The Search for Leadership* (Glencoe, 1960).

access to the judicial process for securing many of his special goals to a degree the earlier minorities did not.

These two avenues for influence sometimes divide Negro political leadership. Some concentrate on the time-honored process of using their political position to meet the personal needs of constituents: finding housing and jobs, and handling welfare problems. In these instances, the Negro politician is likely to be a regular member of the existing political organization. Others, however, are more concerned with the effective exercise of civil rights and more prone to use the courts and formal government antidiscrimination programs to secure these rights by judicial enforcement of fair practices in housing, schools, and employment. These leaders are more independent of the regular organization and likely to be critical of those who "go along."

Both types of influence, however, have combined to modify the behavior of the city political system. Mayors, councilors, and political leaders are aware that the Negroes now form an important voting bloc and shape their campaign strategy accordingly. They are also in the forefront in supporting state laws against discriminatory practices, they are prepared to make new arrangements to assure that schools enroll children of both races, and they appoint Negroes to important positions within the city government.

At the same time, the goals of the Negroes create considerable stresses and strains in other parts of the urban constituency. The diffusion of Negroes into new neighborhoods frequently arouses the fear of property owners that housing values will decline sharply or that lower income residents will alter the character of the neighborhood. Parents become concerned about the impact on educational instruction and workers about increasing job competition. All of these anxieties tend to spread gossip and rumor, provoke panic, and result in protest meetings and riots. So political leaders come to find that consideration of the Negro interests produces countervailing pressures, the so-called "backlash" effect. Urban renewal projects supported by business interests may be jeopardized, the tax base adversely affected, school problems multiplied. Hence the political system faces divided counsel as to what programs to adopt, how strictly to enforce building and health codes, and what weight to give the competing interests. With the migration expected to continue, these pressures will multiply in the years ahead.

THE DISPARITY IN THE DISTRIBUTION AND CONTROL OF INFLUENCE

In terms of the evolution in structure, political organization, and issues in big-city government during the past fifty years, two divergent trends are now clear. First, the importance of the city political system as a means for recruiting migrants into American life through the instrument of a tightly organized, boss-led machine has steadily declined. Second, the pressures upon the system to expand services, assume new roles, and make important decisions have steadily increased.

Revisions in the structures of city governments have been made to attempt adjustment to these new demands by improving the quality and enlarging the scope of administrative control exercised by officeholders—the city-manager form focusing on the service role and the strong-mayor emphasizing developmental decision-making. But the breakup of the early oligarchic patterns of influence distribution and the rise of separate power centers have substantially reduced the capacity of the political system itself to arrive at comprehensive and meaningful decisions. Voluntary agreements among principal actors have replaced settlements which were once more authoritatively determined.

Meanwhile, the types of decisions which the city system is called on to make are generated by forces often beyond its capacity to influence directly. Urban renewal is an organized effort to counteract the social and economic forces working to diffuse population and jobs and relies heavily on federal action. Urban transportation policy is basically shaped by technological changes, and the key decisions are again made at other levels of government. The Negro migration stems from important regional shifts in population, motivated by a minority drive for status and equity, and the city is a more or less passive recipient of these changes. Thus a system called upon to assume new roles and responsibilities finds itself internally disorganized, yet incapable of turning aside decisions the external world forces upon it. Except in structure, few large cities in the United States today possess the means to ensure comprehensive management of their internal conflicts or to guide the character of urban growth.

The Suburbs

When we leave the analysis of large central cities and turn to the municipalities that govern the rest of the nation's metropolitan areas, quite different local political systems appear. First, there is a greater variety of communities and governmental structures. Second, many more patterns in the distribution of influence are evident. Third, new functions and issues are emphasized.

Sunday supplements picture the typical suburb as an updated replica of the traditional American small town in a modern urban setting. In this ideal type, suburban residents are families with better than average incomes who own their own homes. They are friendly, civic-minded people who look upon their town as a place to escape the congestion, size, and impersonality of the city. Suburban government is "close to home" and represents the contemporary version of our grass-roots tradition.

This image of suburban living and politics is a sizable distortion of reality. It is true that most suburbs are small—under 25,000 in population and residential in character. Suburbanites do tend to own their own homes, often commute to work in another jurisdiction, and have a distinct attitude about local politics. But suburbs differ greatly among each other: in terms of size, the incomes, backgrounds, and occupations of their residents, their land uses, and their stages of development. Every large metropolitan area has its industrial suburb, its working-class suburb, its dormitory middle-class suburb where apartments and multifamily houses are numerous, or its suburbs that serve as retail trade centers and as recreational or honky-tonk areas. Each of these is likely to exhibit different political systems.[19]

---

[19] See Robert C. Wood, *Suburbia: Its People and Their Politics* (Boston, 1958).

Recognizing this suburban variety, social scientists have constructed several typologies designed to allow controlled observations of differences in behavior of suburbanites. Analyses of the economic functions of the suburbs (classifying them according to retail, wholesale, and manufacturing activities in various combinations) have been used as a basis for developing general theories of economic location and urban development. Occupational, housing, and ethnic typologies are employed to identify differences in social status and style among suburbs and to trace the interaction of class distinctions and choice of residences. When the primary objective is to understand public finance patterns in the urban area, typologies which identify community characteristics that are expenditure-generating have been developed to account for the widely different levels of taxes and services in the metropolitan area. All these analytical techniques permit us to classify suburbs into subspecies and modify the Sunday supplement picture.

From the point of view of political behavior, the most useful comparative indices are those that distinguish size, land use, social background, and rate of population growth of suburbs. Differences in these characteristics are closely associated with differences in governmental forms, the distribution of influence, political attitudes, and governmental roles and decisions.

GOVERNMENTAL STRUCTURES

Though local governmental forms are legally established on a statewide basis, over the years they often adapt to their particular environments. By home rule legislation, by special acts, by availing themselves of optional forms of organization offered by the state, communities in different stages of transition from rural to urban society rely on different sets of political institutions. In the suburbs, general-purpose municipalities—cities, towns, boroughs, and villages—share responsibilities in various combinations with counties and special districts. Whereas American large cities have most usually brought about a formal consolidation of programs within a single structure, suburban political systems use a variety of structures.

Suburbs in metropolitan areas of Northeastern, North Central, and Middle Atlantic states rely generally on small, autonomous general-purpose governments supplemented by the special districts. In New England, the prevalent forms are cities and towns, the latter not enjoying the legal status of cities but performing the same range of activities in smaller, less urbanized places. In New York, New Jersey, Pennsylvania, and Ohio, units are called villages, townships, and boroughs; but these units, like their town counterparts in New England, have preserved their independence. As new programs appropriate to urban conditions develop they are typically provided for by creating single-purpose special districts, such as fire protection, water supply and distribution, drainage, mosquito control, and sanitation. These small special districts, encompassing only a segment of a general-purpose government's jurisdiction, are to be distinguished from the giant public works districts that carry out programs across the territory of a number of local units. The "internal" districts usually carry out only routine tasks that can be financed by user-charges and special levies and are never applied to only part of the population. Because they are so convenient a way to finance new urban services, they are the most rapidly growing type of local government. Thus the local governments of the 212 metropolitan areas in the United States in 1960 break down into 310 counties, 4,142 municipalities, 2,575 townships, 5,411 special districts, and 6,004 school districts.[20]

Farther south and west, the county is likely to be the significant governmental structure in suburban territory. Many smaller-sized metropolitan areas are completely encompassed by a single county. Outside the incorporated central city, with the exception of a few other municipalities, the county provides whatever local public services are available. Even in large metropolitan areas, central-city and county functions may be consolidated as in Nashville and St. Louis or separated as in Baton Rouge, so that the county remains an important arm of suburban government. Around Washington, D.C., for example, although there are some sixty-seven separate local units of government, the important ones are the Maryland and Virginia counties surrounding the District of Columbia and the independent Virginia cities of Alexandria and Falls Church.

So far as the internal organization of suburban government is concerned, legal authority is usually distributed more widely than in the big city. Counties, suburban municipalities, and towns feature multiheaded structures in which no single office exists on which public attention can focus. There is a much higher proportion of city-manager governments in the suburbs than among large cities, and where there are mayor-council governments, it is more usual for the mayor's authority to be weak than strong.

Counties are usually directed by boards of supervisors or commissioners, sometimes representing smaller local units, and display more legislative than executive characteristics. Special districts are usually headed by multimember boards often appointed by county or local officials. The affairs of the famous New England town governments are directed by from three to five elected selectmen, and by an elected school committee supported by a number of special committees often appointed by the elected town moderator.

In both the number of units involved in political affairs and their organization of formal powers, then, suburbs are less centralized in their structures than are the large core cities, and usually political activists are less visible. These characteristics reflect the difference in the stage of urbanization of these governments and the fact that most suburban units concentrate on providing services and amenities rather than on operating as active agents of development or as arbiters of conflict.

THE DISTRIBUTION OF POLITICAL INFLUENCE

The fact that the jurisdictions of suburban governments in area and activities are more limited than urban ones, and their structures less unified, does not necessarily mean that their political systems are more divided. On the contrary, in many suburbs the political activists are much fewer in number and more alike in objectives than those in central cities. Thus, the burden of conflict-resolution upon the structures is much less.

Because suburbs are the most numerous local communities in the nation today and vary so greatly in their social characteristics, it is hard to gen-

---

[20] United States Department of Commerce, *op. cit.,* p. 71.

eralize about their patterns of influence distribution. Enough studies have been completed, however, to demonstrate the existence of several different patterns and to indicate types which range from single tightly organized power centers to ones as diverse as in large cities. Nevertheless, the number of suburbs falling in various classifications is still unknown, and all community factors associated with different patterns have by no means been identified.

In general terms, however, the student of suburban politics within any large metropolitan area can expect to find diverse patterns of influence distribution. At one extreme is the "vacuum" suburb, where residents are so similar in outlook and expectations that they agree about issues almost automatically. In these communities there will be few activists other than the office-holders themselves. In sharp contrast, large satellite industrial suburbs close to the metropolitan core often display interests as diverse as the central city. There are in addition a large number of two-group, duopolistic systems, with divisions initially established between old residents and newcomers, or stay-at-homes and commuters, or suburban bureaucracies and other citizens. These are likely to be further subdivided by ethnic and income factors, by attitudes toward spending and taxing, by families with children and those without, and by residential property owners and industrial and commercial ones.

Belmont, Massachusetts, for example, is a mature residential town of better than average income and relatively slow growth which exhibits a highly centralized power structure that has proved capable of assimilating an increasing number of descendants of Italian immigrants into a population originally largely Yankee Protestant, under a representative town meeting structure. Its next-door neighbor, Cambridge, a much larger suburb with a city-manager form of government, has such a highly decentralized pattern among ethnic, business, and university groups that no single interest can predominate and all but the most routine service decisions provoke controversies.

The political activists for whom an investigator of suburban politics looks initially are the "first families," representing the old-timers, and the so-called agitators, who represent the expectations of the new arrivals. For both groups he will analyze their social and economic backgrounds, paying particular attention to whether or not there are local divisions on ethnic and religious lines. Next he will identify the business groups in town, with special reference to their attitudes on taxes, and look to see if there are such countervailing civic organizations as Parent-Teacher Associations, welfare clubs, or a League of Women Voters. Finally, he will observe the political behavior of the suburban public employees and the women's groups made up of the wives of commuters.

A recent survey analyzed sixteen Boston suburbs according to extent of industrialization, population density, residential affluence, and proportion of hardship cases; the findings pointed to some major determinants of diffusion in political influence in these areas. The size of a suburb's population was closely associated with the number of activists who participated in major decisions on land use, taxes, and schools: the larger the suburb the more groups involved. A depressant factor which modified the impact of size was the homogeneity of the population—as it increased, the number of participants proportionately declined. An accelerating factor was the rate of population growth, which tended to increase the number of participants, especially among the smaller-sized suburbs. One finding, whatever the variations in these characteristics, was that the political systems were almost always self-contained; contacts and communications with, and information about, neighboring systems were either very limited or nonexistent.

Two other qualities besides the greater cohesiveness of the influentials' structure often serve to distinguish suburban from urban politics. One is the more amateur style of suburban politicians below the county level; the other, the correspondingly greater influence of professional administrators on general policy-making. There are, of course, full-time political organizations and leaders in suburbia: Westchester, Nassau, Hudson, and Bergen counties display this style in the New York metropolitan region and so do the counties around Washington and Pittsburgh. But at the municipality level outside the large, older suburbs the political activists are not likely to be career politicians. Mayors, councilmen, school board members, and selectmen are people who often have other occupations, and they appear as part-time participants, dabbling in local politics as an avocation or as a civic responsibility.

The Boston study indicated that the numerous boards, commissions, and study groups which link the influentials together in the suburbs are staffed mostly by volunteers, and similar findings are reported in Cleveland and St. Louis. Women activists in particular are distinguished from their big-city counterparts in being motivated by civic-service, programmatic ideals rather than by material rewards.

The volunteer quality of suburban politics does not mean that great numbers of citizens are involved or that all decisions are determined by an altruistic sense of the public interest. Sharp differences in participation rates and motives have been reported by Robert Gutman among Catholic, Jewish, and Protestant suburbs in New Jersey, with the Catholics having the greatest expectation and drive for wide community activities. Whatever the number of activists, suburban issues are more often resolved on the basis of idealistic and programmatic arguments than by personal bargains among participants. Hence, suburban politics is often a less serious game, because its consequences have fewer direct effects on the careers and individual lives of the participants, and it satisfies personality drives by providing recreation activity for many of them.

Contrasting with the amateur role of many suburban influentials is the significant role of the professional administrator. Two figures are likely to be of critical importance: the city manager and the school superintendent. In the suburbs these officers are less likely to be subject to close supervision and direction by their elected policy-making boards, who tend to delegate many responsibilities to the career executive. Thus, immediate decisions about the tax rate, the major spending programs, and land use are often in the hands of the professionals.

The city managers are usually schooled in engineering and business and are well paid and devoted to their professions. They bring a concern for efficiency and economy to the management of local affairs and tend to adopt a conservative posture with respect to taxes and new services. The school superintendent, with rigorous, specialized career training and certification from postgraduate schools of education, also is on a career ladder from small to large communities. His values are centered on the quest for better education, expressed in better buildings, more teachers with higher pay, an expanding curriculum, smaller classes. Quite frequently, the major suburban political conflicts arise out of the opposing objectives of these two professionals: the manager seeking to hold the tax rate down, the superintendent anxious to enlarge his budget. In these instances, the elected part-time officials often function as the disciples and supporters of the philosophy of the professional administrators they hired.

In summary, except for the large suburban units (counties or inner-ring municipalities) suburbs have a narrower distribution of political influence, with fewer independent power centers, and more communication and communality of interests than do the big cities. Though the formal structure of government is less executive-oriented and more divided, the informal political system seems more united. A wide net of volunteer activity, emphasizing the importance of citizen participation in community affairs and extolling the ideology of direct democracy, is directed either by a small number of influentials who manage affairs less spectacularly and more quietly than city politicians or by professional administrators. Suburban governments are likely to be "inner directed," neither informed nor especially concerned with the affairs of their neighbors.

PUBLIC ISSUES IN THE SUBURBS

We have already indicated that the formal structure and informal influence pattern of suburban politics are oriented toward the service and amenities roles of local government, and the stage of development of these communities makes this orientation a natural one. The principal public task in these areas is the accommodation of new families, industries, and commercial centers moving out from the central city. Except for the mature, inner-ring suburbs, the public problems are the reverse of those in the city: they arise from population growth rather than from decline.

Most suburbs face the challenge of providing new basic public facilities: schools, utilities, and streets—the "get-going" costs of a new enterprise. They do so from tax bases which are not as balanced (in terms of a mixture of types of property) as in the cities and in which the heaviest tax burden falls on residential holdings. To handle the expanded programs, they have the additional need to develop institutions and bureaucracies that were not required when the constituencies were rural.

It is this growth pressure that generates most of the issues of suburban politics, and it is the different community characteristics of the many suburbs which provoke such a variety of responses. Though the spread of metropolitan regions and the diffusion of different kinds of economic activity proceeds with considerable regularity, the political boundary lines of the suburbs dissect the growth process into many small pieces. One suburb receives a new factory to support its tax rates; the homes of the workers

Pointer in the Detroit *News*

"After We Added The Bedrooms, We Ran Out Of Roof."

Suburban tax bases are sometimes woefully inadequate.

are built in the next suburb, thereby increasing the pressure on the schools; a third receives a shopping center, and so on. Each of these units therefore faces a different economic situation and different growth problems.

Studies in Cleveland, St. Louis, New York, and other metropolitan areas have indicated that the growth pressure for public investment and spending (after variations in size of suburb have been taken into account) is predominately a function of the amount and kind of taxable property available, population density, and the social background of the inhabitants. That is, a suburb with a large industry to underwrite taxes will tend to maintain a high level of expenditures because the burden on residential taxpayers (who are voters) is low. High-density suburbs have high expenditures too, not from choice but from necessity—for a closely packed community requires more extensive services. If the residents have better than middle incomes and are college-educated, demands for high-quality services follow. Jewish communities, for example, usually spend more money on public schools than others, a function of their cultural emphasis on education and their preference for the use of public facilities.

In all these suburban situations, then, a continuing public issue is that of fiscal policy—the tax rate. On an internal basis, it is decided by the composition of the power structure: the relative influence of businessmen, property owners, and families with young children. This composition varies according to the intensity of the financial situations and the size of the particular groups. But the internal politics has limits in terms of the kinds of compromises which can be achieved, and so the suburbs come to focus on policies respecting new growth which can improve their immediate situation.

Today, three such issues concern them: (1) land-use planning; (2) schools; and (3) newcomers.

Land-use planning

The profession of planning emphasizes the interrelation of land and human activities across a broad area, a river basin, or an urban region. Suburban governments view the planning process from a different perspective. They are prone to use it and its companion programs of zoning, subdivision control, and building codes as ways for maintaining their independent operation and improving their social and economic status among their fellow jurisdictions. General land-use planning by a suburban government, when effectively applied, can allow the community to redirect the metropolitan area–wide economic and social trends. Planning can also secure for the community the choice new land uses which relieve pressures on the municipal budget. Thus, setting aside areas for industrial development, establishing minimum lot requirements, or excluding commercial developments are policy choices for suburban units which shape the character, finances, and style of the municipality. When supplemented by detailed zoning regulations and controls over subdivision development and building practices, they constitute regulatory techniques that powerfully influence densities, cost of housing, and the economic base of individual suburbs.

Generally, where these techniques are employed, they have been part of defensive strategies designed to preserve the semirural charm or the "good character" of the municipality. They operate to keep out "undesirable" land uses and to attract "desirable" ones, as the local political system chooses to define these terms. Thus, around New York City, Cleveland, Boston, and Denver there are suburban governments that have established five-acre minimum lot sizes (thus assuring that only expensive houses can be built); or have required that each house differ in design from five of its immediate neighbors (thus discouraging mass development); or have engaged in the public purchase of vacant land (thus controlling the rate of growth); or have required garages and detailed site location plans; or have set minimum costs for home construction—all these to the same effect.

Similarly, industry can be encouraged by setting aside large tracts of land for future development, building roads to assure easy access for expected workers, installing water and sanitation systems for the areas, and organizing development committees to seek out new industries and persuade them to locate in the municipality. Or mass developers may be required to pay special fees and taxes or donate land for schools, parks, and other facilities. All these regulatory policies go beyond the original intent of planning and zoning to ensure efficient land use and adequate health and safety standards. They are rather aimed toward securing for a particular suburb the best the region has to offer in terms of people and wealth.

Within individual suburban political systems, planning issues often provoke the most heated political conflicts. Groups concerned with the municipality's finances work to broaden the tax base by bringing in industrial and commercial establishments which pay more in property taxes than they require in local public services. Or they seek to permit only expensive residences, in which case a similar favorable balance between revenue and expenditures exists. But opposing the budget-watchers are real estate interests and construction companies anxious to build large-scale developments, residents who are opposed to local regulation on ideological grounds—even if tax rates zoom, and those who want to preserve the rural atmosphere of the community. There are also groups seeking a "balanced" community and prepared to admit young families and lower income groups for this purpose.

The controversies which arise from these conflicting interests have been dubbed "regime politics" by a research team of the University of Florida watching suburban behavior in that fast-growing state.[21] Because planning decisions often do determine the destiny of a suburb as an exclusive residential community, an industrial enclave, or a honky-tonk recreational or commercial town, they are likely to be especially contested. The opposing factions are in fact engaged in a struggle for control of the entire political and social system, and they compete with an aim to banish competitors from effective influence. Hence, the destiny politics of planning comes closer to revolutionary politics—the overthrow of an existing regime— than any other form of suburban decision-making.

The collective effect of these intense political battles within individual suburban communities is to create a competitive atmosphere across the large metropolitan areas and to strengthen the tendency for each suburb to go it alone. Suburbs which have preserved their residential quality dig in by trying to attract increasing numbers of well-to-do families leaving the metropolitan core. Suburbs with industrial bases work to get more, or try to use their ample financial resources to develop exclusive new neighborhoods. Large developers building in many parts of the metropolitan areas try to persuade local planning and zoning boards of the benefits of their proposals or seek out communities where no planning exists as places to speculate in land values.

The result is a game of musical chairs where each suburb tries to better its position against a backdrop of intergovernmental jostling, in which, however, common policy for land development on a metropolitan basis emerges. Thus, even though the suburbs are engaged in developmental decisions so far as their own jurisdiction is concerned, they do not influence the character of regional development significantly. Rather, the prime forces of diffusion continue to be the result of private economic decisions, and the suburb's choice is restricted to accepting or diverting the land pressures that population and economic growth set loose.

Schools

Of all the public facilities a community in process of transition to an urban stage is called upon to provide, the public school is the most significant one. School expenditures constitute the largest single item in most suburban budgets, ranging usually from 50 to 80 percent of total expenditures. Most suburbanites believe that the school program is the most important activity the government provides, and it affects the majority of voters in their capacity as parents and taxpayers directly. The search for better schools is a powerful motive for many people moving from the central city. And deci-

---

[21] Kammerer, *op. cit.*, Introduction.

sions about schools touch on some fundamental American beliefs about the school's role in the process of socialization.

Under these circumstances, it is not surprising that suburban school decisions evoke wide participation and a special set of activists who otherwise do not appear in suburban politics. The quantitative effect of schools on local taxes, their qualitative effect on the prospects for success of children from upwardly mobile families, and their role as cultivator and carrier of the American democratic tradition guarantee a special brand of politics. Moreover, since school government is almost everywhere in suburbia a separate government directed by independently elected officials often in geographically separate school districts, the processes for decision-making are distinct. There are separate school taxes, separate school bond issues, separate school elections, all based on the early American conviction that the schools were a "unique" governmental function to be kept out of general politics.

In the particularistic politics of the schools, the key political actor is the superintendent. As we have indicated, most school superintendents, even when elected, are career men. According to the doctrine of the superintendent's profession, he has the obligation to set standards for acceptable education and to determine the conditions—in terms of facilities, classroom size, personnel, and curriculum—which produce good education. Thereafter, he undertakes to explain these standards and to achieve them by assembling lay support. Typically, he does this by securing the consent of his school board or commission, building group support through teachers' associations and parents' organizations, and persuading more generally based civic associations to adopt his cause. Then he confronts his opposition, the officials and interests primarily concerned with the financial solvency of the local government.

Most suburbs record as their turning point from rural to suburban status the year in which schoolmen and their friends succeeded in overthrowing opposition to the establishment of a school system sufficiently endowed with new buildings, career teachers, and advanced salary schedules as to be classified, according to professional standards, as modern. Where such battles have been waged and lost, the character of the suburb is likely to move downward on the social and economic scale.[22]

Suburban school politics are concerned with more than the issue of finance, however. The separation of church and state provided by the national Constitution has in recent years raised special problems in school programs. Though a hundred years ago many states provided assistance to private and church-supported schools, successive decisions by the United States Supreme Court have made the relation between public and private schools more complex. Whether or not parochial schools can use public school buses or participate in special welfare, health, and guidance activities is a continuing question in many suburbs. The authority and duty of public school superintendents to supervise attendance and evaluate instruction in private schools is another troublesome matter. More informally, the existence

---

[22] See Warner Bloomberg, Jr., and Morris Sunshine, *Suburban Power Structures and Public Education* (Syracuse, 1963) for a systematic analysis of the factors accounting for school support.

of a large parochial school system is often interpreted as depressing efforts to develop the public schools. Many observers believe that the fact that Catholic families must pay both tuition and taxes tends to diminish their enthusiasm for public school improvements. At any rate, school politics becomes more complex as the ethnic and religious mix of a particular community increases.

Finally, the issue of what is taught in the schools frequently becomes a matter of controversy. Whether the curriculum is too progressive or too conservative, whether athletics and social studies are overemphasized or underemphasized, and whether kindergartens and special courses should be provided are all topics of public discussion. During the 1950s, the question of Americanism was raised in many suburbs; textbooks were examined, and teachers investigated to be sure that radical and unreliable doctrines (as defined by those groups concerned with the schools' role in political socialization) were not being taught.

Finances, religion, and patriotism, then, are all elements in suburban school politics. They require adept and careful handling by school administrators and their allies if their objective of improved education is to be achieved. The controversies they engender in the separate political system which governs the school almost guarantee that this type of politics will remain visible and volatile in suburbs across the nation.

Newcomers

Planning and school politics exemplify the role of suburban governments in developmental decisions which go beyond the routine and recurrent service and amenities issues. As we have seen, the degree of conflict over these decisions depends a great deal on the characteristics of size, heterogeneity, and growth rate of a given suburb. So long as these three factors are kept small in magnitude, the suburban political system with its amateur politicians and professional administrators is not likely to have to assume the role of arbiter between groups with extreme differences in values. Indeed, extremists in either planning or school politics tend to be in such small minorities that, though highly visible, their actual influence is slight.

But as we have also seen, the developmental decisions of suburbs are largely defensive in nature. If planning is instituted at an early stage of suburban development, the jurisdiction can select new activities from those decentralizing from the core city. If a judicious selection is made, a favorable balance between service demands and taxable resources is likely to be forthcoming. Then decisions about school quality can be reached. But the achievement of this orderly state of affairs turns on the magnitude of pressures generated from the private sector of the metropolitan economy and the policies of the central cities in retaining or attracting new growth. Because of their multiplicity and insularity, suburbs have little positive say in shaping the broad trends of urban development.

This defensive posture of most suburbs means that their political systems are constantly facing increasing growth forces. The metropolitan population grows, its density compared to cities of the past declines, jobs and households spread out farther and farther from the central city, land prices rise, housing markets expand, and the most restrictive of planning and zoning measures tend to crumble under pressures from the private market. This means that the key conditions for maintaining the informal casual style of suburban politics are constantly imperiled. With 40 million Americans destined to settle in the suburbs in the next generation, suburbs inevitably will change in size, heterogeneity, or growth rate.

The emerging issue in the suburbs, then, is one of conflict resolution, between newcomers and old residents. The particular form of conflict in the next decade or so will be the accommodation of Negro minorities. If existing trends continue, the Negro migration we described earlier would make one quarter of central-city populations nonwhite, but barely 4 percent of suburban residents would be Negro. But these trends are only straight-line projections of past history, and the Negro population is now pressing for open housing choices in all parts of the metropolitan area.

In the suburbs, the political position of the Negro is quite different from what it is in the larger cities. He does not have the numbers necessary to build strong voting blocs, and the population of each suburb is not likely to be heterogeneous enough to force public officials to construct coalitions among competing interests. Accordingly, the Negro has to rely more on the use of formal powers available to him and resort to judicial channels for the exercise of influence. This takes place by suits to require open occupancy in housing and to preclude so-called *de facto* segregation of school facilities. In the first instance, the Negro employs state antidiscrimination laws. In the second, where Negroes are likely to be already settled in one school area, he appeals to the federal courts to require that the suburban school system distribute Negro pupils more or less equally throughout elementary and junior high schools. By relying on formal channels and requiring major changes in local policy, these actions generate bitter political conflicts.

To date, the minority entry problem has occurred most frequently in older, mature suburbs where the quality of housing is declining and where the commuting trip to work is short. Typically it becomes critical after initial minority entry has occurred in housing and one neighborhood school becomes heavily Negro in enrollment. But as Negro incomes and occupational statuses rise, more and more suburbs become involved. Many old residents who disclaim any personal prejudices to the growth of a minority are disturbed because their image of their suburb as a grass-roots town of well-kept houses, good schools, sociability, hospitality, and conviviality seems threatened.

Viewed from the metropolitan perspective, the problem of accommodating the minority does not seem sizable. This minority accounts for only about 15 percent of total urban population in the next generation. But the present pattern is that of more concentration; as entry is secured in only a few suburbs, the proportion of Negroes climbs rapidly, exodus of old residents increases, and the final result is a community in which the minority unwittingly has become a majority. This is the so-called falling-domino pattern of population migration, with most of the Negro population concentrated in a few suburbs. Fair housing committees established in many Northern and Western suburbs work to counteract this pattern, but given the magnitude of the migration and the isolated positions of most suburbs, the expectation is that the arbiter role of suburban government will be expanded, and the stresses on its political system increased.

Rural Government

As the nation's population flows rapidly into metropolitan areas, the importance of rural government and that of "independent" cities serving as market centers for rural areas steadily declines in expenditures, manpower, activities, and decisions. The "emptying out" of the farmlands of the Middle West, South, and Northeast, the decline of population centers of less than 25,000 which are not a part of a metropolitan region, and the shifts in interstate transportation networks mean that the country communities for which the local government forms were originally designed are increasingly a minority. They are preoccupied (when their public decisions are consciously directed to new trends in American life at all) with the problem of making the process of community decline and dissolution reasonably orderly. Farmers and villagers in urban America are in disadvantageous economic positions, and as their societal bonds weaken, so does the performance of their governments.

Lane Lancaster, the most distinguished student of rural government in this generation, graphically describes rural government as being impoverished in financial resources, amateurish in administration, personalized in conduct, and lacking the disposition to change its structure to accommodate new conditions of rural life.[23] Lancaster sees the rural governments as holding on to the grass-roots ideology in terms of symbols and institutions, but actually depending on the state for financial largesse and decisions. Some centralization in consolidated school and drainage districts has occurred, but by and large long-established jurisdictions preside over dwindling resource bases and declining populations.

Whatever its future prospects and problems, however, the rural county or village political system is likely to be one of the most tightly organized in the nation. The qualities of limited size and homogeneity which produce centralized suburban systems are present without the disruptive pressures of growth. A small elite, expressing the inarticulate sentiments of a majority, is likely to rule (often without recourse to formal procedures and institutions) over a hopelessly outnumbered minority. A study of one upstate New York village discovered that governmental mechanisms were rarely employed in local politics, decisions were avoided whenever possible, or turned over to state or private bodies, and disagreement and conflict were studiously suppressed. In the classic ethos of intimacy and fraternity which a small town displays, the principal aim was to secure unanimity, not to deal rationally with the problems at hand. Active political participation and interest were therefore discouraged, and the small clique who possessed influence consciously refrained from using it.[24]

---

[23] Lane W. Lancaster, *Government in Rural America* (New York, 1937).

[24] Arthur J. Vidich and Joseph Bensman, *Small Town in Mass Society: Class, Power, and Religion in a Rural Community* (Princeton, 1958).

Rural and village politics do have importance in terms of who goes to the state legislature, who is employed by the county, how justice is administered. The "courthouse" gangs provide material for some of the best American political novels. But in terms of the relevance of these cohesive power centers to the major public decisions at the local level or their readiness or capacity to employ governmental power to resolve economic or social difficulties, rural local government is an anomaly on the local political scene: a strong system operating in low gear, indisposed to function whenever it can possibly do otherwise.

Summary

A review of the politics at the local level in America is a study of a mismatch between the efficiencies of the various political systems and the complexities and magnitude of the decisions they are required to make. Where the systems are well integrated, as in rural, some suburban, and district governments, the roles of government are often caretaker in form. Where the probability exists that government activities will have real geographical, social, or economic consequence, the system is diffused, fragmented, or limited in scope.

Nonetheless, it is important to recognize that in their traditional service and amenities roles the systems work. Schools are built, sewers dug, cement poured for roads, prisoners arrested, fires put out, law and order maintained. Moreover, the quality of local services is better than ever before; they are increasingly professional, they reach higher standards, they produce better products. Third, old battles against corruption and the exploitation of public office for personal gain have largely been won. Wrongdoing exists, the fix continues, but on a level more bureaucratic than political in most localities.

The issue which remains is the capacity of local government to assume the newer roles of developmental agent and arbiter in the metropolitan areas. Here the evidence is that on their own they seem to lack the capacity to make the decisions which would establish them as truly influential. But what if the systems are supported by other levels of government, and what if they alter their present pattern of behavior? These are the questions the next chapter examines.

29 / The Future of State and Local Governments: Interdependent Systems and Intergovernmental Politics

The last two chapters explored the "internal" workings of state and local political systems: how the various units manage conflict, make decisions, formulate and carry out policies. But at the same time the chapters made clear that a great deal of political action takes place *between* and *among* state and local governments and their units. So strong and recurrent have these relationships become in recent years that the *interdependence* of the separate systems and levels is an established, obvious fact of American political life.

Nevertheless, it is not easy to describe these informal systems tying together the different tiers of the American federal structure or involving several units at the same level. On first examination, the situation seems chaotic—"a marble cake" Morton Grodzins called our pattern of intergovernmental relations, with "unexpected whirls and imperceptible mergings of colors." And he went on to point out: "The multitude of governments does not mask any simplicity of activity. There is no neat division of functions among them. If one looks closely, it appears that virtually all governments are involved in virtually all functions. More precisely, there is hardly any activity that does not involve the federal, state, and some local governments in important responsibilities. Functions of the American governments are shared." [1]

To bring some order out of the apparent confusion, political scientists speak of three kinds of intergovernmental politics arising out of the interdependent federal structure the Constitution created. First is that web of relationships based on constitutional or statutory authority as well as on political practice that binds formal governments together. Chapter 4 treated this pattern in its discussion of American federalism. Principally, it consists of the involvement of each state in the election of national officials; amendments to the national Constitution; state obligations to the federal government with respect to national constitutional powers; state reciprocity regarding public acts; and grants-in-aid between levels of governments. More informally, the governments are joined in a general way through the mechanism of the party system, as Chapter 4 also made clear.

---

[1] Morton Grodzins, "Centralization and Decentralization in the American Federal System," *A Nation of States* (Chicago, 1963), p. 102.

Two other kinds of intergovernmental systems are in operation, less noticeable to the ordinary citizen but very important in the day-to-day activities of all American governments and our domestic politics. One is *vertical* (that is, involving all three levels of government) and *specialized* (that is, concerned principally with the bureaucracies of local, state, and national governments). The other is *horizontal,* involving the states and localities often as *general* governments in *regional* and *metropolitan* relations.

This chapter is an introduction to the politics of these last two systems, paralleling the analysis in Chapter 4 that probed the formal processes of American federalism. It first sketches the principal features of the vertical-specialist and horizontal-generalist patterns. It then identifies the forces of industrialization and urbanization that forged new communities in the United States and brought the systems into being. Finally, it examines efforts to formalize these systems by giving them a general legal base and general institutions—and the probable future direction and evolution of state and local governments. But always remember that at the present time, the systems remain examples of "invisible politics," real indeed to the professional politician and administrator, but rarely the subject of headlines or great public debates.

The Specialist System

By far the greatest number of interactions among levels of governments occurs in the communications, transfers of money, and collaborative activities of the respective bureaucracies. Great vertical axes of executive departments, agencies, bureaus, boards, and commissions engaged in common programs exist in transportation, welfare, housing, education, and resource development. Sometimes, as is the case in highways and public health, the axis is principally a federal-state one—though local officials, as we have seen, try energetically to use their influence. Sometimes, the axes are mainly state-local, as in education, though here the participation of Washington is growing. Sometimes, they are national-local, as is true in urban renewal. Whatever their focuses, these common programs, authorized by national and state statutes, fuse the separate levels together on a working base and are prime examples of intergovernmental interdependence.

In fact, so important are these shared functions that some observers believe they have transformed American federalism, and that a unitary bureaucracy now operates behind a legal façade of a geographical division of powers. It is argued that while we maintain a decentralized pattern of general politics in party organization and the activities of elected officials, our administrative structure is increasingly directed from Washington.[2]

Yet the intergovernmental politics of the specialists does not function this way. Like other American patterns, it consists of many separate power centers, exhibits continuing conflicts among its participants, and remains limited in its exercise of power. Two forces countervailing centralization are

---

[2] See Leonard White, *The States and the Nation* (Baton Rouge, 1953) and William Anderson, *The Nation and the States, Rivals or Partners?* (Minneapolis, 1955).

built into the systems, (1) the techniques of administrative collaboration that the American tradition and the separate legal structures of our government encourage bureaucracies to employ; and (2) the competition among specialists that originates in the separate programs they carry out and the separate professional skills they possess. These forces effectively continue to divide and constrain power.

ADMINISTRATIVE BARGAINING

Despite the existence of some forty common programs, involving grants-in-aid from one government to another and collaborative administrative action, it is a serious mistake to assume that an integrated administrative structure exists for any of these activities.[3] Even on a single level or in a single program, national, state, and local administrators do not often behave as a united band of political activists. There is no strong tradition in this country of professional career administrators trained to draft and execute general programs and equipped with powers to ensure their uniform application. Instead, our professional public servants have little prestige or status when compared with businessmen, doctors, or lawyers in private practice. They are rarely prepared to act in the independent and aggressive ways in which their European and English counterparts sometimes do. In the intergovernmental programs in particular, the national laws establish procedures that limit the authority and powers of federal administrators and place the responsibility for direct program management in the hands of state and local officials. Hence no orderly administrative hierarchy exists in which directives and policies flow from the top down.

Thus the key technique of administrators intent on implementing a particular program or solving a particular problem through intergovernmental channels is *persuasion*. The federal administrator, charged with the direction of a grant program in welfare or health or highways or renewal, receives initially an appropriation from the Congress, to be spent within a year. He believes that the funds are urgently required to meet the needs his program is designed to fulfill. At the same time, the actual expenditure of the funds depends on the plans and proposals offered by state and local authorities. If the program is an established one such as welfare, the allocation of money may be routine—although perhaps not in the amounts or for the purposes which the federal administrator prefers. If the program is a new one, as is the case currently with mass transportation and open-spaces grants, the administrator will probably have to encourage state and local officials to apply. In either event, he has few means for positively assuring that the actual operations of the program will meet the standards he considers ideal. If there are major deficiencies in state and local operations—either in the qualifications of personnel, the handling of money, or details of planning—he can withhold the money. But this defeats his basic purpose of meeting needs which he judges to be urgent.

---

[3] The United States Census reports that federal grants-in-aid to states and localities amounted to $7.1 billion in 1961 (United States Census Bureau, *Governmental Finances in 1961,* October 26, 1962). In addition, indirect contributions involved in federal programs with state and local impact were estimated by the Housing and Home Finance Agency to total some $13 billion in the same period.

"In Two Words, Yes And No"

From *The Herblock Book*, Beacon Press, 1952

Therefore, the politics of the specialist system is one of constant bargaining and negotiation involving the exchange of substantive benefits (money and technical skills) for compliance with procedural requirements (auditing, the filing of plans, personnel regulations) basically designed not to strengthen national control so much as to improve state and local performance. The federal agency has the power of the purse; state and local agencies have the influence which arises from an independent constitutional and ideological base, their contacts with Congressmen and party leaders, and the fact that the actual operations are in their hands.

A classic analysis of the politics of specialists was reported by Paul Ylvisaker in his study, *The Battle of Blue Earth County*.[4] This case dealt with the activation of the federal welfare assistance program in a rural county in Minnesota in the 1930s. Federal regulations prescribed that state welfare employees meet certain qualifications in education and experience. Blue Earth's political leaders, not sympathetic to the program from the beginning, rejected individuals who met the formal requirements and proposed a candidate who did not qualify. Thereafter, a long drawn-out controversy took place among local, state, and federal officials over the appointment, which was necessary before the county—or the state—could enter the program. (All counties in Minnesota had to participate before any one could receive funds.) In the end, Blue Earth triumphed. Ways were found, after a series of conferences, interpretations, and reinterpretations—fortuitously assisted by the promulgation of new regulations—for the county's candidate to be qualified, and months after the conflict began, Blue Earth entered the program.

The same pattern of negotiation has occurred frequently down through

---

[4] Paul Ylvisaker, *The Battle of Blue Earth County* (University, Ala., 1955), p. 6.

recent years. The city manager of Newburgh, New York, alarmed at the steady increase of welfare cases in that municipality, drafted a stringent set of requirements for individual welfare payments which conflicted with state and federal law. Ultimately, the courts ruled against Newburgh, but not until a major public airing of the problem had occurred and the Secretary of Health, Education and Welfare had ordered a thorough review and evaluation of national regulations. Similarly, the 1954 federal highway assistance program placed the Federal Bureau of Public Roads in conflict with state highway departments across the country in the application of regulations designed to prevent inflated payments in land-taking, favoritism in the award of contracts and the bonding and insurance of contractors, and noncompliance with contract specifications. Occasionally, the Bureau has felt compelled to stop payment of grants, but these decisions have provoked outcries from Congressmen and state officials that states' rights were being invaded and a program urgently demanded by American motorists jeopardized. In the urban renewal aid program, a similar conflict occurs between assuring quality projects, economically and honestly built, and authorizing a crash program large enough to arrest the spread of blight in a particular city.

Thus from the federal point of view, the process of administering a major grant is one of complex, tedious negotiations with companion specialists who work in different organizations and different political environments. Skills in diplomacy, not in executive management, often seem to be the major requirements for a successful federal official.

From the state or local perspective, the process often seems equally frustrating: well-conceived and urgently needed projects are delayed by the red tape of laborious federal review procedures, or made unworkable by requirements which do not fit local circumstances. In the give-and-take between specialists, money is ultimately spent, welfare payments made, hospitals and highways built. But the programs do not proceed under the direction of a single enterprise, either the dictates of Washington or of the state capital. By and large, they proceed by fits and starts, always subject to investigation and publicity by Congress, legislatures, or city halls, and in a manner commensurate with the talents, interest, and ability the individual governments can muster. Hence, program direction is more likely to be cautious and conservative than to be dynamic. Although the specialists form into distinct influence blocs within the federal system, power is divided within the blocs, and its locus is often found in the lower echelons.

PROFESSIONAL COMPETITION

Not only are individual intergovernmental administrative programs characterized by many separate power centers engaged in the process of haggling over money and procedures, but also each major program represents a separate political arena. Each professional specialist is naturally persuaded that his own activity should have top priority, and each develops separate channels of influence to the generalist system. Thus the politics of the interstate highway program involves one principal department in Washington, a parallel set in the states, a special subcommittee on appropriations in the Congress, and certain interest groups that support their activity. Health programs involve another and quite distinct group of institutions, referral procedures, and supporters; urban renewal, still a third.

The Housing and Home Finance Agency, for example, has its strongest working relations with municipalities, and mayors are its chief advocates. The Departments of Health, Education and Welfare and of Commerce still are most closely bound to the states, and their political power is at that level. Moreover, the professional training of each group of specialists tends to make communication difficult and to promote different approaches to public problems even when they are closely related. In the federal assistance programs which provide community facilities and services in metropolitan areas, for example, civil engineers plan and supervise highway construction; renewal operations are most probably under the direction of housing and real estate experts and planners; environmental health measures are designed by doctors. These different professional backgrounds mean that each group of specialists has different ideas about what is important in metropolitan or regional development, what techniques are best used in planning and carrying out programs, and what facilities ought to be built first.

Therefore, when the programs come into contact with one another, still another kind of dislocation in the bureaucratic power structure takes place. Specialists quarrel about the impact which one intergovernmental program has upon another. The highway engineer not unnaturally thinks of highways principally as a means to move goods and people from one place to another. His chief criterion in deciding new route locations is the cost compared to the benefits which users will receive, measured in terms of speed, time, and economic operation. The renewal expert or planner, on the other hand, is concerned with the land uses of the city. *He* regards a highway as one of the most important forces generating new land uses, by providing access to residential, commercial, or industrial areas and thereby creating new neighborhoods or accelerating the decline of old ones. Thus, his measures of costs and benefits are by means of less tangible, harder-to-calculate "social factors": how many houses will be destroyed by the new route, what losses in tax values will occur, what will be the consequence of an elevated highway cutting a community in two like the Berlin Wall, and what esthetic damage will be done to the skyline. He also will ask if mass transportation—buses, trains, or subways—might not move more people more rapidly.

In short, the highway engineer defines transportation needs in terms of what it takes to satisfy the preferences of the individual highway user—what the motorist's "desire lines" are. The city planner proceeds on the assumption that the best transportation system is one that produces a particular pattern of land uses and population densities and then moves the greatest number of people most rapidly in the shortest period of time. As a consequence of these different goals and calculations, the specialists frequently arrive at exactly opposite recommendations as to where highways and renewal projects should be located and what the total transportation network should be.

Another conflict arises between health and welfare specialists and renewal and planning experts. To many administrators working with low-income, poorly educated citizens, programs for the physical redevelopment of a city fail to take human problems of dislocation and adjustment into account. They see renewal projects as frequently destroying the fabric of long-established neighborhoods in which residents found great satisfactions even though their houses were in bad repair. They think that social planning—probing the causes of juvenile delinquency, providing adult education and vocational training, caring for the unemployables—is at least as important as physical planning. Thus they are concerned that both highway and renewal specialists may overlook or minimize the concerns of residents in areas where great new projects are pending. Once again, the intergovernmental subsystem of the specialist is subjected to tensions and strains caused by the need to give ample consideration to state and local interests and objectives.

Horizontal Relations: Regional and Metropolitan Political Systems

The behavior of the *vertical* political systems in intergovernmental relations indicates that state and local governments are not in the process of withering away. Their expenditures and employment rolls grow more rapidly than do those of the national government. Federal assistance comes to them under terms and conditions which allow considerable discretion in action; elected federal officials are most sensitive to local pressures; federal administrators have sizable compulsions to respect local prerogatives. All these conditions mean that intergovernmental relations among the three tiers operate in a manner designed to maintain the present set of dual systems. Moreover, there are signs that the *horizontal* relations among state governments and local governments have contributed new strength and resources to these levels in the past generation.

THE PATTERN OF INTERSTATE COLLABORATION

At the state level, both formally and informally, new links among the states have been forged in the twilight zone of public activities in which neither the states, limited in territory, nor Washington, restrained in legal authority, can operate effectively.

One such link is a set of well-established associations among state officials. The original impetus for voluntary cooperation was provided by the National Conference of Commissioners on Uniform State Laws established in 1892. Composed of from one to five commissioners appointed by the governors, the Conference now meets annually, trying to minimize differences in state laws covering similar subjects and recommending uniform model acts. Following the Conference, various other organizations of state officers were created: the Governors' Conference, the American Legislators' Association, the National Associations of Attorneys General and of State Budget Officers, for example. Since 1935, these organizations have been loosely grouped under a central agency called the Council of State Governments, the affairs of which are carried out by various commissions on interstate cooperation established by the states. The Council conducts research and assembles information for the officer associations. It also correlates their activity with the interests of such professional associations as the American Society of Planning Officials, the American Public Welfare Association, and the Civic Service Assembly.[5]

A more formal instrument for collaboration is the interstate compact. Virtually unused for more than a century, the compact device has been employed with increasing frequency since 1920 and has become especially popular since the end of the Second World War. Over 400 compacts have been concluded, covering matters which range from the settlement of boundary disputes to river development and management, conservation, interstate bridges, urban development for metropolitan areas that embrace two or more states, civil defense, and military assistance.

In the resource field, compact agencies have displayed considerable ability to use regulatory and developmental powers. The Ohio Valley Sanitation Compact polices stream pollution within eight states. The Interstate Commission of the Delaware River Basin has embarked on a broad program of research and development for four states;[6] the Colorado River Compact provides for water distribution among seven states. For the Missouri and Arkansas Red-White complex, similar developments are taking place.

Dramatic developments have also occurred in the fields of urban development and higher education. Under interstate compact, New York and New Jersey established the Port of New York Authority in 1921 which has developed a common system of vehicular tunnels, bridges, and terminals for the Hudson River, and has more recently taken over some mass transit facilities. Missouri and Illinois have provided a common development district for St. Louis and East St. Louis. A number of states have planned and constructed river crossings at state boundary lines with their neighbors. State regulatory commissions have sought to develop common policies with respect to commuter rail traffic. In education, the Southern Regional Educational Conference and the New England Board of Higher Education are examples of interstate undertakings which seek to avoid duplication of facilities for expensive professional education within their regions. The basic aim of these programs is to promote instruction, especially at the graduate level, in single-institution specialties for students of all participating states.

Much the same process of consolidation and pooling of resources seems to be taking place so far as institutional welfare programs are concerned. Small, poor states adjoining larger ones now have made arrangements for placing persons committed to their care in the facilities of their neighbors. The specialization in types of institutions for mental health, penal and corrective care, and child care has accelerated this process. Rhode Island and Massachusetts, for example, have negotiated for the transfer of women prisoners to Massachusetts reformatories, thus benefiting both states. Rhode Island profits by not having to make heavy capital investment to handle a small number of inmates. Massachusetts can operate its prisons more economically and provide additional specialized services.

---

[5] Council of State Governments, *The Book of the States* (Chicago, 1960).

[6] Roscoe C. Martin, *et al.*, *River Basin Administration in the Delaware* (Syracuse, 1960), Chapter 5.

Yet, as in the vertical-specialist system, the horizontal pattern of state collaboration remains one of the many power centers, each limited in influence. First, many compacts explicitly provide for a federal representative, usually designated by the President, who sometimes serves as chairman in order to offer a relatively impartial perspective with which to reconcile the different interests of the states. Frequently, too, a federal agency is designated as the principal research organization to do staff work for the compact agency.

Second, the capacity of states to work well together is limited to special areas. Experience has shown that forming compacts is most effective when a technical solution to the problem at hand is available and when an independent source of revenue exists (as is often the case in urban development projects). But the device is less useful when broad policies have to be determined. For one thing, the creation of a compact agency requires the unanimous consent of all states concerned, and protracted policy debates can cause the breakdown of arrangements. Also, the negotiation of compacts is a time-consuming business—the average time for some sixty compacts concluded in recent years was four years and nine months. Finally, the fact that the executive powers of most compact agencies are placed in a commission, without the direction of a single officer, weakens their administrative vigor and effectiveness in day-to-day operations. These characteristics indicate that while compacts are important instruments for interstate collaboration, their applications remain limited in scope.

INTERGOVERNMENTAL ARRANGEMENTS AT THE LOCAL LEVEL

Local governments, with the assistance and concurrence of the states, have also built patterns of horizontal collaboration. The most popular formal mechanism for achieving common action has been the large special district or authority, constructed along the same lines as the interstate compact agencies. In contrast to the suburban special districts (described in the preceding chapter) that are established *within* local jurisdictions to provide special utilities and public facilities, these districts embrace the territory of many local governments. They are usually established by state law for a specific purpose and often as public corporations with the power to raise income and spend money independently of the general-purpose local governments. Typically they are headed by a board of directors appointed by the governor of the state, and they are set up most often in large urban areas to deal with development problems. In the metropolitan areas of New York, Boston, St. Louis, Washington, Chicago, San Francisco, and Los Angeles—indeed across the country—the large district is the preferred means for carrying out metropolitan water, recreational, sewerage, transit, and park and port development programs.

The businesslike structure of the authorities and large districts encourages a pattern of influence distribution and a style of decision-making unlike any others currently on the local scene. For one thing, influence is centralized to an extent unknown since the decline of the city machine. The key authority officials are not elected, nor do they head an agency within any general state or local executive branch. Thus they are subject to only limited and sporadic supervision and control, as their governing boards are filled by long-term appointments made by state governors. Second, because they are engaged in moneymaking programs such as the construction and operation of turnpikes, tunnels, bridges, airports, and water systems, they are self-financing. They rarely require appropriations from general tax sources, and when they do, it is the states, not the local governments, which supply the funds. Third, they have broad legal authority to decide the particular activities in which they wish to engage, and they are rarely required to coordinate their decisions with those of other local governments.

Independence in management, finance, and programming endows the authorities and special districts with great political resources. They have the capacity to make decisions quickly—and thereby impress the public as effective agencies beset with none of the delays and compromises weaker political entities face. They can provide jobs, contracts, and benefits to state legislators and their constituencies—and they rarely need to ask for tax money in return. They can proceed informally without reference to the plans of other agencies and without the public sanction of individual decisions, through indirect channels of negotiation. Under these circumstances, it is not surprising that the new "strong men" in local government are the heads of these enterprises: Robert Moses and Austin Tobin in New York, or the late William Callahan in Massachusetts, for example.

Other devices besides the giant public works districts are being used to overcome the geographical limitations of local governments. The consolidated high school, for example, was originally inspired by the educational deficiencies which small, isolated, rural communities suffered, no one of which was able to provide on its own secondary schooling measuring up to modern standards. Now the same handicaps of size and limited tax resources have encouraged suburban school districts to make joint arrangements. Metropolitan library systems are groping for new forms of specialization and interchange; adult education programs try to build balanced curricula, and educational personnel exchanges for particular specialists— school psychologists, art instructors, and the like—are being made.

In public safety a similar pattern of collaboration and pooling of resources has emerged. Cities and towns in most metropolitan areas have made arrangements for mutual assistance in times of emergency. Fire departments respond to calls across local boundaries when major fires occur. Police have established metropolitan area–wide communications networks, use central crime laboratories, and have common procedures for pursuit and arrest and transfer of prisoners. Local jurisdictions have arrived at uniform methods for handling certain types of cases, principally traffic violations and juvenile cases, and common enforcement techniques often apply. In all these instances, the metropolitan policies have been worked out by voluntary negotiations and agreements among the local governments striving to counteract the effects of metropolitan area–wide public problems as they arise in areas in which a large number of separate jurisdictions exist.

METROPOLITAN "PARAPOLITICS"

Perhaps even more important evidence of local interdependence is found in the emergence of certain informal patterns of cooperation and consultation not established by law. Since the Second World War, embryonic political systems have emerged in many metropolitan areas that, to some observers, seem to have considerable potential for developing distinctive institutions and processes. At the present time, we often characterize these new associations and mechanisms as "parapolitical," inasmuch as they consist of both formal agencies and informal associations with participants drawn from both the public and the private sector.

The key components of these systems are the special-purpose authorities or large special districts beginning to assume new and broader responsibilities, and public and quasi-public bodies active in the field of urban development. The fifteen largest urban regions in the United States, for example, each have some kind of general-purpose planning agency. Every one has a special transportation agency and some kind of recreational or resource development agency. In every one, too, there is an association of private citizens concerned with metropolitan research planning and development. All these coexist with state and local agencies having responsibilities in these activities.

These new bodies are indicative of the new urban parapolitical system. Stimulating their appearance have been over a hundred large postwar research projects that have increased knowledge and improved communications among local officials and interest groups in metropolitan areas. Perhaps more important, established interest groups have come to recognize their stake in urban decisions. Business groups, such as the Committee for Economic Development and the Chamber of Commerce, labor unions, conservation associations, the League of Women Voters, and building contractors, have all come to take stands and articulate their special points of view. The beginning of a coalition of interests has been discernible as those active in health and welfare activities have pooled resources or merged programs on a united basis. Both public and private agencies have produced "images" of future urban development, goals toward which policy might be directed: the Year 2,000 plan for the Washington, D.C., area, the Regional Plan Association projections for New York. All these occurrences suggest that in many places the rudiments of a political system are in being: a communications network, an array of activists articulating their interests and engaging in negotiations, a set of goals which are distinct from the particular interests of any participant.

These evolutionary tendencies do not mean that a powerful political system is just around the corner, soon to be housed in a separate structure. For one thing, the interest groups are widely separated in objectives. Labor is suspicious of metropolitan collaboration as being designed primarily to protect downtown business investments. Some business interests are suspicious of new governments and new public policies in any form. Builders and contractors often favor metropolitan developmental policy, but chiefly in the hope that it will serve to substitute one set of zoning requirements and one building code for the many different and conflicting ones that complicate their business lives today. Many local officials fear that their own offices may lose prestige and power.

Moreover, a number of important interest groups are missing. Political parties, organized usually on a county basis and more concerned with control of offices than matters of policy, have usually kept aloof from efforts for metropolitan policy-making, however informally conducted. State highway departments have been concerned lest metropolitan plans interfere with the construction of their proposed new throughways. Legislators have viewed the civic leaders who appear in behalf of metropolitan programs as possible competitors. The public has yet to show serious and continuing concern.

Nonetheless, political agitation and action on the metropolitan level have sharply increased in the last decade. Partly, this has been the result of fortuitous circumstances: the decisions of national private philanthropic foundations and civic organizations to sponsor metropolitan research. Partly, it is explicable in terms of the political positions of big-city mayors and governors, the first needing relief from some of their problems, the second having to build a city-suburban coalition of voters to get elected. Partly, it has been due to the increased intellectual recognition that existing units of government and functional intergovernmental programs proceeding alone cannot succeed in shaping the forces in the private sector of the metropolitan economy. Whatever the relative importance of these factors, however, metropolitan politics is becoming a reality in most metropolitan areas across the country.[7]

The Underlying Pressures

What accounts for the rise of the informal, interdependent political systems among and between governments? Why have the vertical-specialist and horizontal-generalist patterns originated, persevered, and grown stronger when American folklore holds that our federal structure is, or at least ought to be, composed of two tiers of autonomous sovereign units, coexisting but rarely cooperating? The basic answer is that these new arrangements are the pragmatic political responses to the same vast social and economic changes that have affected state and local governments as well as Washington. These forces have created special pressures and problems for the lower political echelons. As the environment has become more complex, so have the political systems that direct public affairs.

In 1700, when the first versions of American state and local governments were firmly established as colony, New England town, and Virginia county, there were three settlements with populations over 4,000. Other Americans lived in hamlets, villages, plantations, farms, or forest cabins. By 1800, with the new national government just established, Boston, New York, and Philadelphia had grown to 12,000 people apiece and four other ports in New England and two south of the Potomac had reached the 5,000 mark in population. But the vast majority of the citizens were still farmers.[8] In no major program—transportation, education, welfare, public safety, or public works—did state and local governments function as professional mechanisms for shaping economic and social life. The first demands made on them by a rural and largely self-sufficient society were not great, and the low level

[7] For a provocative discussion of the "solution syndrome" in the governing of metropolitan areas, see Duane Lockard, *The Politics of State and Local Government* (New York, 1963).

[8] See Jean Gottmann, *Megalopolis: The Urbanized Northeastern Seaboard of the United States* (New York, 1961), p. 18.

and amateurish quality of public services was by and large what the populace expected.[9]

As the social and economic environment changed with increasing rapidity, however, the demands on government rose sharply. Political conflicts over the number and level of public services increased; the rule of the town fathers was first threatened, then overthrown. Increasingly, the effectiveness with which grass-roots government met demands, and settled disputes, and influenced community development was called into question by active groups within the electorate. Historically, then, two principal forces worked to reshape the state and local political systems. The first was urbanization, the process by which millions of Americans left the farm and village in the nineteenth century to take up residence in cities. The second is conventionally termed industrialization—the growing complexity and changing organizational pattern of the American economic system.

Urbanization increased the *scale* of organized community existence. Technological innovation in the form of improved farm machinery, fertilizers, seeds, and farm-to-market transportation led to vast increases in agricultural productivity and *pushed* population from the countryside. Simultaneously, technological innovation in the form of steam power plants, factory machinery, perfected techniques for manufacturing interchangeable parts which could be assembled in large quantities *pulled* displaced farmers into the urban labor force, along with hundreds of thousands of immigrants from Europe each year.[10] Contemporaneous inventions—the arc light, the electric elevator, macadam pavement, the cast-iron water main—at the same time made the congregation of a large number of people in small areas around the factories tolerable. This push and pull of technology stimulated the rapid growth of cities in the generations after the Civil War.

Of course, more than technology was involved. Although American philosophers celebrated the virtues of rural life throughout the nineteenth century, the city as the place of opportunity and adventure rivaled the Western frontier in providing the chance for men to seek their fortunes. By the end of the nineteenth century, Horatio Alger's novels symbolized the urban process by which poor country boys became city millionaires and their daughters found husbands from the ranks of European nobility.

So far as industrialization was concerned, when people gave up farming and small-town occupations, their economic dealings with one another became vastly more complex. As other chapters in this book have made clear, the American economy was transformed from a rural, mercantile one, in which the commercial towns and seaports on the Atlantic coastline operated as a trading "hinge" between Europe and the frontier, to an industrial one. In the burst of growth in the nineteenth century, the private economy shook off the doctrine of mercantilism, under which government had frequently regulated and directed economic growth, and functioned under a laissez-faire philosophy.

---

[9] See Carl Bridenbaugh, *Cities in the Wilderness: The First Century of Urban Life in America, 1625–1742* (New York, 1938).
[10] See Scott Greer, *Governing the Metropolis* (New York, 1962), Chapter 1.

In the late nineteenth and early twentieth centuries, this unfettered functioning of the private economy proved unsatisfactory to large segments of the public. A succession of depressions and panics, the rise of large business enterprises to monopolize entire industrial fields or to divide up their markets through trust agreement, made it clear that economic theories of pure and perfect competition were not working out in practice. Governments at every level were called on to intervene to maintain workable competition and to control sharp fluctuations in the business cycle, or to prevent arbitrary and highhanded decisions on the part of enterprises that were natural monopolies, such as railroads and public utilities.

These twin forces of urbanization and a maturing economic system triggered off important changes for both state and local governments just as they did in national political behavior. The rapid transformation of American society prompted state governments to attempt to ease the plight of the new urban worker and to protect the farmer who remained on the land. Primarily, this action took the form of new means of regulating private business action, though occasionally states undertook to own and manage businesses themselves; grain elevators in the Dakotas, for example; ice houses in the South; power plants in the far West. More often, however, as their constituencies became complex, states established a series of regulatory commissions and agencies designed to oversee the operation of railroads, insurance companies, and public utilities in order to ensure fair pricing and to prevent favoritism among shippers.

States also began to set standards for industrial workers: conditions under which women and children could be employed in factories, the maximum number of hours to be worked, minimum safety and fire protection requirements. Although these state laws were struck down frequently by the United States Supreme Court, which was then hostile to most public restrictions on private property rights, they provided the prototypes for many of the New Deal laws in the 1930s.

Furthermore, the states displayed growing concern for the farmer in the new economy. With the powerful assistance of federal grants-in-aid, agricultural research and educational facilities at the state level were expanded. Early attempts were made to stabilize prices and regularize processes of milk production and distribution. After 1900, when the automobile became a familiar sight on country roads, state after state established a highway department and turned its attention to providing farm-to-market roads.

As for the local governments, the principal force they felt was that of urbanization. Except as many localities came to own and operate their own power plants and to adopt zoning and planning regulations for the control of land use, local governments did not concern themselves directly with the regulation or management of the new economy. But, while the states, in company with the federal government, wrestled with the problem of how to eliminate the less satisfactory by-products of the new industrialization, cities felt the impact of larger and larger numbers of people living in compact spaces. As immigrants spilled into the cities from the farms and from abroad, the old ways of providing public services proved ineffective. The severe depressions that occurred in the last half of the nineteenth century demonstrated to many observers that temporary "outdoor" dole relief was not an adequate response to situations in which one quarter of the labor force was unemployed. With businesses requiring increasing skill and literacy among their employees, schools could not be the part-time, casually managed, and voluntary affairs they had been in most of the country throughout the first half of the nineteenth century. After city populations accounted for over one third of the total population in the United States in 1900, the scale of public investment required to underwrite city life rose sharply. Bridges, streets, water lines, and sewerage systems now became necessities. So did organized fire departments, more professional policemen,

CHART 29-1 / The Trend Toward Urbanization in the United States

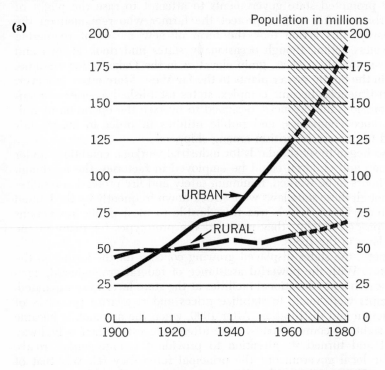

(a)

Population in millions

URBAN→

RURAL

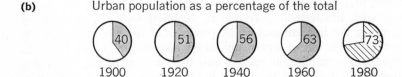

(b) Urban population as a percentage of the total

40 — 1900
51 — 1920
56 — 1940
63 — 1960
73 — 1980

SOURCES: (a) United States Bureau of the Census
(b) Philip M. Houser, "Population Perspectives" (projections)

city hospitals, and health departments empowered and equipped to control communicable diseases. Chart 29–1 shows the overwhelming growth of the urban population in this century. In response, local government produced a large "bundle of services" which was increasingly professional in nature.[11]

The Metropolitan Area and the Interstate Region

The steady trend toward urbanization and the increasing complexity of the private economy found geographical expression in two areas that the interdependent vertical and horizontal political systems now seek to manage. In effect, these areas made intergovernmental relations inevitable, for they expanded the scope of political conflicts and public problems far beyond the boundaries of established state and local jurisdictions. We speak today of *metropolitan areas* as the significant form of urban settlement, and we characterize the resource-mix from which economic development within a particular state goes forward as *regional* in character. That is, the urban population is no longer concentrated in single, compact, crowded munici-palities, and industries often draw their manpower, water, and raw ma-terials from beyond the boundaries of a single state. Two new types of com-munities, linking social and economic interests together, have thus arisen as the geographical expression of the industrial and urban trends. They com-plicate the functioning of our traditional state and local political systems as separate enterprises and encourage collaboration among governments and parapolitical innovations.

SPREAD CITIES

David W. Minar and Scott Greer have concisely summarized the resi-dential characteristics of the new metropolitan areas (whose geographic distribution is shown in Chart 29–2) that have resulted from the desires and incomes of the different kinds of people brought together to work in our large complex modern enterprises:

1. Toward the older centers of work and commerce are the oldest and densest neighborhoods. They are obsolete for the familistic popu-lations who want single-family housing. They are inhabited by (a) those with little choice—the very poor and the ethnic minorities, particularly Negroes and Puerto Ricans, and (b) those who choose an urban milieu—to be had only at the center. The latter take the better housing, or else "upgrade" neighborhoods, as has happened in the Georgetown district of Washington, D.C., and in the Near North district of Chicago.
2. In the outer neighborhoods of the older center city are still to be found many middle-rank, nonethnic populations. This housing is newer, more spacious, and frequently for single families. It is thus similar to the newer tract developments on the peripheries.
3. The edges are what is usually called "suburbia." Largely developed in tracts, these areas bring a range of prices from those appropriate to the craftsman and factory operative to those "fit" for the junior

---

[11] Solomon Fabricant, *The Trend of Government Activity in the United States Since 1900* (New York, 1952).

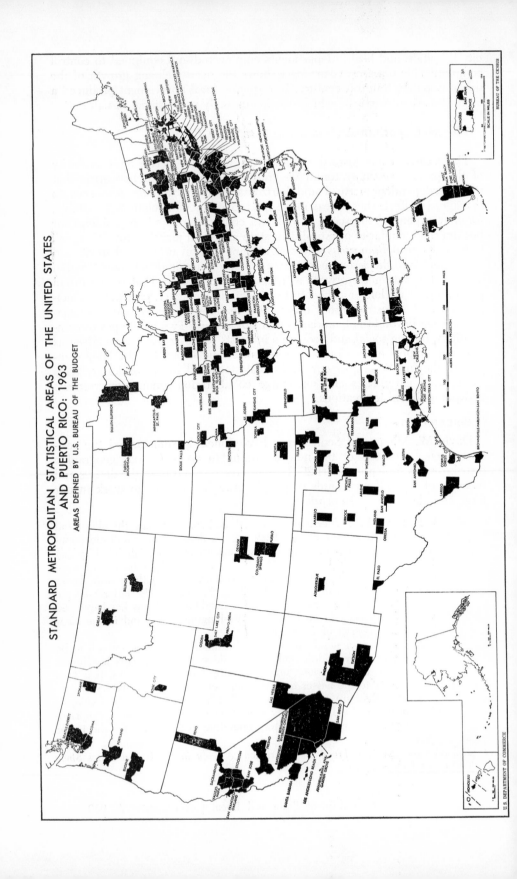

STANDARD METROPOLITAN STATISTICAL AREAS OF THE UNITED STATES
AND PUERTO RICO: 1963

AREAS DEFINED BY U.S. BUREAU OF THE BUDGET

U.S. DEPARTMENT OF COMMERCE

BUREAU OF THE CENSUS

CHART 29–2 / Standard Metropolitan Statistical Areas of the United States and
Puerto Rico: 1963

SOURCE: United States Department of Commerce, Bureau of the Census.

executive. "Park Forest"—the Chicago suburb studied by William
Holley Whyte—is the latter sort of development.

4. In the choicer locations by rivers and lakes and along the old
commuter-line railroads one finds the residential enclaves of the
wealthy and powerful. Protected by housing costs (and frequently
by informal agreements, building codes, and the actions of a
municipal government), these are the exclusive residential areas
sometimes called exurbia. The Main Line in Philadelphia, the
North Shore in Chicago, Westchester County in the New York
region are examples of such neighborhoods.[12]

In addition to special properties of residential location that distinguish
our new metropolitan areas from the first American settlements—seaports,
small towns, dispersed farms, and frontier outposts—and from the industrial
cities of the nineteenth century, there are other differences. Modern urban
complexes feature (1) a diffusion of industries and commercial establishments around the core city; (2) an increased reliance on the highway
as the principal communication and transportation link within the area;
(3) a considerable amount of cross-hauling and commuting between residence and work within the area; and (4) a sharp rise in the proportion of
service employment as compared to manufacturing.[13]

The result of the forces working for diffusion of social and economic
activities is the new "spread city," which contrasts sharply with the tight
cluster of buildings and people of the old city. Technology, especially in
the form of the automobile, is often singled out as a major factor in this
extension of the metropolis. As Webb S. Fiser writes,

> If the automobile becomes a nuisance and tends to distort many of the
> pleasures and purposes of life in our residential neighborhoods it
> threatens the very existence of our downtown areas. . . . Reliance
> upon the automobile results in exorbitant demands for highway and
> parking space. This makes it impossible to achieve that concentration
> of related activities traditionally associated with the center of cities.
> Victor Gruen has estimated that total dependence upon the auto-
> mobile in Manhattan would necessitate devoting the first nine stories
> of all structures to transportation space. Offices and stores would have
> to start at the tenth story.[14]

Looked at from the national perspective, the emergence of the metropolitan area as the predominant form of urban settlement distributes the

---

[12] David W. Minar and Scott Greer, "The Metropolis and Its Problems," *1963–64
American Government Annual* (New York, 1963), pp. 109–10.

[13] See Edgar M. Hoover and Raymond Vernon, *The Anatomy of a Metropolis* (Cambridge, Mass., 1959).

[14] Webb S. Fiser, *Mastery of the Metropolis* (Englewood Cliffs, 1962), p. 29.

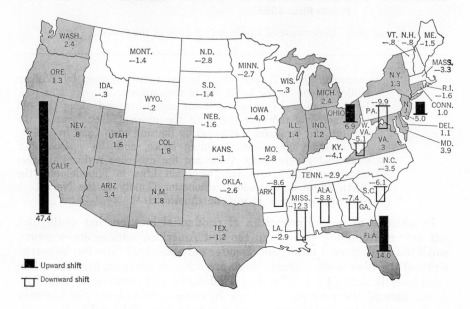

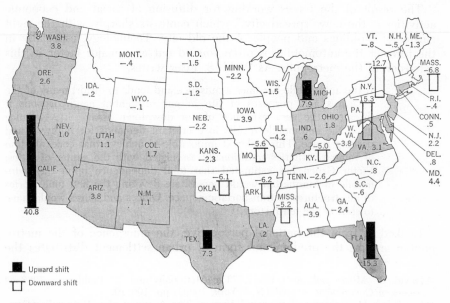

SOURCE: Harvey S. Perloff, with Vera W. Dodds, *How a Region Grows* (New York, 1963). Top: p. 66; bottom: p. 60.

present American population in a highly irregular and uneven way. In 1960, 113 million persons of the nationwide total of 179 million resided in standard metropolitan statistical areas. More important than this well-established trend toward urban living, however, are two patterns of concentration.

First, population is flowing to the largest urban areas. The five biggest metropolitan areas, those with over three million inhabitants, gained six million of the thirty million total population increase in the 1950–60 decade. Areas between one and three million increased from ten to nineteen, and collectively gained thirteen million. There are now twenty-nine regions with populations between half a million and a million, whereas ten years ago there were only twenty-one; they account for almost five million of the total population increase. But in the quarter-million to half-million category only four new areas have appeared in the United States (forty-eight in place of forty-four) and their total population increase in this decade of explosion has been a scant 700,000. In 1950 there were eighty-nine areas in the 25,000–100,000 category; in 1960 there were still eighty-nine areas of this size—with an overall population increase of about 400,000. And the number of standard metropolitan areas of under a hundred thousand has declined since the last census from forty-three to twenty-two, with 500,000 fewer people than they had before.

Second, especially since 1950, the "rims" of the continental United States, that is, the states along our coasts and boundaries, have grown at a much faster rate than the central area of the country. The eight Western states experienced a 24 percent increase in population between 1950 and 1960; the three Gulf coastal states, 41 percent; even the mature Atlantic seaboard, 17 percent. But the seventeen states of the "heartland" grew only 5 percent. Moreover, the emerging pattern is that of larger and larger metropolitan areas in these growing states, with little or no growth in the small and medium-sized towns. The maps reproduced here dramatically demonstrate the outward thrust of employment and population over the last twenty years.

As we examine this panorama of development, we find that a "typical" metropolitan area shows the following characteristics. First, the population of the old central city is declining while that of the surrounding suburbs is growing rapidly. Second, the boundaries of the metropolitan area have expanded to encompass 1,000 square miles or more and like fingers push into the rural countryside. Third, the density of the urban population is dropping from the high peaks reached in the cities at the turn of the century.

For the twenty-three largest metropolitan areas, with populations of over one million, these properties are intensified. In these areas, the central cities have experienced a decline in population averaging 17.3 percent over the last ten years, while the rate of suburban growth has risen sharply. Table 29–1 depicts this change for the twenty-two counties of the New York Metropolitan Region.

NEW REGIONS

If large metropolitan areas are now the places where most of our population resides and maintains its social relations, the interstate region is the basic unit for resource utilization and economic specialization. A hundred

TABLE 29-1 / Population of the New York Metropolitan Region by County, 1940, 1950, 1960

	1940		1950		1960			Change, 1950–60		
	Number (thousands)	Percent of region	Number (thousands)	Percent of region	Number (thousands)	Percent of region	Persons per square mile	Number (thousands)	Percent	Persons per square mile
Connecticut										
Fairfield	418	3.3	504	3.6	654	4.0	1,033	150	29.6	236
New Jersey	3,115	24.9	3,581	25.7	4,399	27.3	1,937	818	22.8	360
Bergen	410	3.2	539	3.9	780	4.8	3,320	241	44.7	1,026
Essex	837	6.7	906	6.5	924	5.7	7,249	18	1.9	138
Hudson	652	5.2	647	4.6	611	3.8	13,849	−36	−5.7	−832
Middlesex	217	1.7	265	1.9	434	2.7	1,405	169	63.8	547
Monmouth	161	1.3	225	1.6	334	2.1	701	109	48.4	229
Morris	126	1.0	164	1.2	262	1.6	548	98	59.2	204
Passaic	309	2.5	337	2.4	407	2.5	2,116	70	20.6	362
Somerset	74	0.6	99	0.7	144	0.9	472	45	45.3	147
Union	328	2.6	398	2.9	504	3.1	4,872	106	26.7	1,025
New York	8,984	71.8	9,865	70.7	11,086	68.7	2,746	1,221	12.4	300
Dutchess	121	1.0	137	1.0	176	1.1	216	39	28.7	48
Nassau	407	3.2	673	4.8	1,300	8.1	4,439	627	93.3	2,142
Orange	140	1.1	152	1.1	184	1.1	219	32	20.7	375
Putnam	17	0.1	20	0.1	32	0.2	135	12	56.2	49
Rockland	74	0.6	89	0.6	137	0.8	793	48	53.2	276
Suffolk	197	1.6	276	2.0	667	4.1	731	391	141.5	428
Westchester	574	4.6	626	4.5	809	5.0	1,799	183	29.3	407
N.Y. excl. N.Y.C.	1,529	12.2	1,973	14.1	3,304	20.5	889	1,331	67.4	358
Bronx	1,395	11.1	1,451	10.4	1,425	8.8	32,382	−26	−1.8	−601
Brooklyn	2,698	21.6	2,738	19.6	2,627	16.3	33,215	−111	−4.0	−1,401
Manhattan	1,890	15.1	1,960	14.0	1,698	10.5	75,816	−262	−13.4	−11,688
Queens	1,298	10.4	1,551	11.1	1,810	11.2	16,244	259	16.7	2,264
Richmond	174	1.4	192	1.4	222	1.4	3,681	30	15.9	505
New York City	7,455	59.6	7,892	56.6	7,782	48.2	24,311	−110	−1.4	−344
Region excl. N.Y.C.	5,063	40.4	6,059	43.4	8,357	51.8	1,262	2,298	37.9	347
Core	7,933	63.4	8,348	59.8	8,171	50.6	26,886	−177	−2.1	−583
Inner Ring	3,089	24.3	3,670	26.3	4,946	30.6	3,385	1,276	34.7	873
Outer Ring	1,546	12.3	1,933	13.9	3,022	18.7	584	1,089	56.4	211
REGION TOTAL	12,518	100.0	13,951	100.0	16,139	100.0	2,325	2,188	15.7	315

NOTE: Detail may not add to totals because of rounding.

SOURCE: New York Regional Plan Association, 1962.

years ago, a single city might owe its existence to proximity to a natural resource which supported its predominant industry—a mineral deposit, timber, or a crop that required processing. Thirty years ago one of the twelve great river basins of the country was thought of as providing that combination of agriculture, minerals, water power, and transportation facilities which provided economic self-sufficiency as well as certain cultural ties. Today, the sharp relative decline in long-haul transportation costs as compared to production and distribution costs has reduced city "specialization" (that is, dependence on the production of a particular product or on a single economic base) and expanded the area in which strong economic and business ties exist.

So planners have emphasized the "multipurpose" character of a drainage basin for a major river: providing water for cities in perhaps half a dozen states, irrigating farm lands in other states, generating power for industry, satisfying transportation and recreation needs, or providing game and fish for sportsmen. The Tennessee Valley, for example, has for more than a generation been the basis of coordinated planning and economic development programs carried out under the direction of the Tennessee Valley Authority. Although no comparable public agencies exist in any other major river basins in the United States, the techniques and concepts employed by the TVA have been adopted by other federal departments and state agencies charged with regional developmental responsibilities. Similarly, economists by "input-output" and "linear programming" techniques have come to identify complex networks of related goods and services that are needed to support industries producing finished products. Typically, these regions of suppliers, processors, and producers have no regard for state boundary lines.

Perhaps the most dramatic example of these new interstate regions is that stretching along the northeastern Atlantic seaboard from Portland, Maine, to Richmond, Virginia. Named "Megalopolis" by the geographer Jean Gottmann, this region consists of a continuous belt of densely populated urban counties 600 miles long and between 30 and 100 miles wide. Accounting for only 1.8 percent of the land area of the continental United States, Megalopolis' population totaled 37 million in 1960, 21 percent of the nation's population, and the density in its states is close to 700 per square mile, while that in California, their nearest rival, is 200.[15]

Megalopolis embraces six of the fifteen largest metropolitan areas with populations of over one million in the United States, and it is closely tied together by elaborate highway, rail, water, and air transportation. The region possesses great concentrations of industry, wealth, commerce, and educational enterprises. By virtue of specialized divisions of labor and land use, it has produced a new classification of population, rural *nonfarm*, and it has achieved a concentration of population *simultaneously* with a concentration of wealth and economic opportunity.

Thus, Megalopolis is the most advanced of the new regions that urbanization and the modern industrial economy have developed. Gottmann points out that it has achieved the heaviest concentration of decision-making activities in commerce, government, and education known in the Western world through a complex set of links joining the specialized occupations of its people. Thus, educators in Boston, financiers in New York, and government officials in Washington maintain daily contact with one another. Gottmann indicates the new region's visual form this way:

> As one follows the main highways or railroads between Boston and Washington, D.C., one hardly loses sight of built-up areas, tightly woven residential communities, or powerful concentrations of manufacturing plants. Flying this same route one discovers, on the other hand, that behind the ribbons of densely occupied land along the principal arteries of traffic, and in between the clusters of suburbs around the old urban centers, there still remain large areas covered with woods and brush alternating with some carefully cultivated

---

[15] Gottmann, *op. cit.*, p. 26.

patches of farmland. These green spaces, however, when inspected at closer range, appear stuffed with a loose but immense scattering of buildings, most of them residential but some of industrial character. That is, many of these sections that look rural actually function largely as suburbs in the orbit of some city's downtown. Even the farms, which occupy the larger tilled patches, are seldom worked by people whose only occupation and income are properly agricultural.[16]

A steady rhythm of movement characterizes the behavior of residents in Megalopolis. White-collar workers move every morning from the outlying portions of the region into its great cities and return at night. Seasonally, the city population flows to the seacoast resorts along the Atlantic Ocean— from Virginia Beach through Atlantic City and Long Island, to Maine—in the summer in search of relaxation, and it invades upper New York and New England for winter sports. Its behavior at work and play can be viewed as a single vast process using the land and resources of all the states from the mountain ranges of the Appalachians, the Poconos, and the Adirondacks to the sea in common ways. Even the spirit of its people, in Gottmann's view, is a common one: a sense of mission and calling to improve society, which the geographer classifies as a "Promethean endeavor."

The metropolitan area and the interstate region are intertwined, then, though it is useful to study the economic, social, and political functions of each separately.

> In this area, then, we must abandon the idea of the city as a tightly settled and organized unit in which people, activities, and riches are crowded into a very small area clearly separated from its nonurban surroundings. Every city in this region spreads out far and wide around its original nucleus; it grows amidst an irregularly colloidal mixture of rural and suburban landscapes; it melts on broad fronts with other mixtures, of somewhat similar though different texture, belonging to the suburban neighborhoods of other cities. Such coalescence can be observed, for example, along the main lines of traffic that link New York City and Philadelphia. Here there are many communities that might be classified as belonging to more than one orbit. It is hard to say whether they are suburbs, or "satellites," of Philadelphia or New York, Newark, New Brunswick, or Trenton. The latter three cities themselves have been reduced to the role of suburbs of New York City in many respects, although Trenton belongs also to the orbit of Philadelphia.[17]

To some observers, these new communities have disturbing implications. One of America's most distinguished urban philosophers, Lewis Mumford, believes they represent the rapid decline of American civilization.

> The city continues to grow inorganically, indeed cancerously, by a continuous breaking down of old tissues, and an overgrowth of formless new tissue. . . . Sometimes the expanding street system forms an orderly pattern, sometimes it produces only a crazy network that does not even serve traffic: but the difference between one type of order

---

[16] *Ibid.*, p. 5.
[17] *Ibid.*, pp. 5–6.

and another is merely a difference in the degree of sprawl, confusion, de-building.

As one moves away from the center, the urban growth becomes ever more aimless and discontinuous, more diffuse and unfocussed, except where some surviving town has left the original imprint of a more orderly life. . . . The loss of form, the loss of autonomy, the constant frustration and harassment of daily activities, to say nothing of gigantic breakdowns and stoppages—all these become normal attributes of the metropolitan regime. . . .

The form of the metropolis, then, is its formlessness, even as its aim is its own aimless expansion. . . .

The living memory of the city, which once bound together generations and centuries, disappears: its inhabitants live in a self-annihilating moment-to-moment continuum. The poorest Stone Age savage never lived in such a destitute and demoralized community.[18]

Others take a more hopeful view:

The picture of Megalopolis is not as dark as the outspoken pessimists and frequent protests would seem to paint it. Crowded within its limits is an extremely distinguished population. It is, *on the average*, the richest, best educated, best housed, and best serviced group of similar size (i.e., in the 25-to-40-million-people range) in the world. The area is still a focus of attraction for successful or adventurous people from all over America and beyond. It is true that many of its sections have seen pretty rural landscapes replaced by ugly industrial agglomerations or drab and monstrous residential developments; it is true that in many parts of Megalopolis the air is not clean any more, the noise is disturbing day and night, the water is not as pure as one would wish, and transportation at times becomes a nightmare. Many of these problems reflect the revolutionary change that has taken place as cities have burst out of their narrow bounds to scatter over the "open" countryside. In some ways this suburban sprawl may have alleviated a crowding that had threatened to become unbearable, for residential densities of population per square mile have decreased. But new problems have arisen because of the new densities of activities and of traffic in the central cities and because the formerly rural areas or small towns have been unprepared to cope with the new demands made upon their resources. New programs are needed to conserve the natural beauty of the landscape and to assure the health, prosperity, and freedom of the people. In spite of these problems, however, available statistics demonstrate that in Megalopolis the population is on the average healthier, the consumption of goods higher, and the opportunity for advancement greater than in any other region of comparable extent.[19]

Implications for Government

Whatever judgment one makes about the new communities, it is clear that they are the impetus for the new political patterns of intergovernmental

[18] Lewis Mumford, *The City in History: Its Origins, Its Transformations and Its Prospects* (New York, 1961), pp. 543–45.
[19] Gottmann, *op. cit.*, p. 15.

relations. Superimposing large and expanding economic and social systems upon smaller units of government created major stresses and strains on the old state and local political systems, and increased their interdependence. As the economic base of development became regional rather than state-wide, regulatory and promotional programs of individual states became increasingly ineffective. As the metropolitan area took the place of the city as the principal form of urbanization, it became more difficult to provide common services for the urban citizen and to find adequate and equitable tax resources. Hence, not only did the national government assume greater responsibilities in economic regulatory activity, but also the vertical pattern of grants-in-aid appeared to provide minimum levels of support for all states in welfare and transportation programs. As common needs in resource management—adequate water, sewerage, and recreational facilities —became obvious, the new mechanisms for horizontal collaboration in the form of interstate compacts, metropolitan districts, and authorities were perfected. As criminals moved across municipal borders and fires in one jurisdiction threatened homes in another, mutual aid agreements were concluded in public safety programs.

Three examples serve to demonstrate the new interdependence of state and local governments.

Consider first the question of how the water from a major river should be allocated. Residents of upstream communities may want to use it to dispose of sewage; those in downstream communities, to drink. Industries scattered across several states may require large amounts for processing purposes; fishermen may seek quiet streams for their sport. Since the upstream and industrial uses can result in pollution, making water unfit for household and recreational purposes, disagreements as to how the river should be developed and what importance ought to be attached to particular uses almost inevitably occur. In these circumstances the regular procedures of state governments are often not capable of resolving these issues except by an elaborate and time-consuming process of negotiation and bargaining. Hence, the growing importance of interstate compact agreements.

Take a second issue: economic development. When state governments within a regional economic complex undertake to make policy for improving transportation facilities or ensuring an adequate supply of trained manpower or supporting the indigent and unemployed by welfare programs, they find their present capabilities severely limited. The New York, New Haven and Hartford Railroad, for example, is a major facility for carrying commuters to New York City every day and for moving freight to New England industries and ports, and it is an important link between Northeastern cities and New England seashore resorts in handling the seasonal "surges" of Megalopolitan populations. When the railroad faced severe financial difficulties in the 1950s and sought public subsidies, however, the states of New York, Connecticut, Rhode Island, and Massachusetts were called upon to agree on a common policy of assistance. This proved such an extraordinarily difficult process of deliberation and negotiation that by the time a joint approach could be agreed upon the railroad had gone bankrupt. All the states could do, in company with the federal government, was to embark on a major study of transportation facilities for all of Megalopolis.

But if states move ahead on their own in stimulating economic development, they may find themselves in trouble. Different educational, welfare, and business development programs of the several states may offer special and "artificial" attractions or disabilities which influence population movements. Massachusetts educators believe that their program for the training of retarded children draws a large number of such persons from other states each year, and their families as well. Citizens in Midwestern farm states complain that they pay high costs for educating their young, only to see them disappear in the new cities of California. The more liberal welfare programs provided by Northern states are alleged to encourage the migration of indigent families from the South. The question arises how states can embark on quality programs without penalizing their own taxpayers. As a consequence, increased attention is paid to interstate planning arrangements and the pooling of educational and institutional facilities.

A third example of interdependence is found at the metropolitan level—at once more complex and more obvious than those at the state level. The 18,000-odd local governments in the 219 metropolitan areas face the question of what policies they wish to pursue in influencing the land use and economic development of their individual areas. Should major efforts be made to preserve and revitalize the old core cities? Should public agencies purchase land in the suburbs to preserve open spaces? Should more emphasis be given to mass transportation facilities throughout the area to slow down the diffusion of households and industries? These are the issues that have prompted the establishment of the quasi-public, quasi-private "halfway houses" of metropolitan councils, planning and development agencies that are the major components of the emerging metropolitan political system.

The Adequacy of Intergovernmental Arrangements

Have the state and local governments' collaborative responses to the new regional and metropolitan communities been sufficient? No hard and fast answer is possible of course, for the definition of "adequacy" is in the mind of the observer. Certainly, the new devices and mechanisms that now bind the levels and units of American government together have provided the basic facilities and services necessary for orderly community existence. They have also preserved autonomy in decision-making for state and local governments and, over recent years, have succeeded in vastly upgrading education, transportation, health, and welfare services. It is difficult to say that our political systems below the national level are in crisis.

Nevertheless, many experts believe that the intergovernmental patterns established so far fall far short of being satisfactory. They point out that in at least three ways, present arrangements create inequities, generate conflicts, and pose problems for the future.

VARIATIONS IN SERVICE LEVELS AND FINANCIAL RESOURCES

First, the persistence of a number of different governments within the confines of a single regional or metropolitan area results in great differences in the quantity and quality of services our state and local governments provide to their citizens. To many, it seems increasingly incongruous that within a single economic or social complex, the accident of location dictates the quality of public services and the tax burden of the residents. Why, for example, should the educational investment in children born and raised on the New Jersey side of the Hudson River be two thirds that of their neighbors in New York?

Thus, within a clearly defined river basin or economic region, or a metropolitan area, variations in government spending and taxation are very great, depending on the number of residents, the tax bases, and the political style of the region involved. In the New York metropolitan area, for example, one municipality spent $4.30 per capita for current operations in the 1950s while another was spending $351.20. One jurisdiction was levying $24.60 per capita in local real property taxes; another $376.89. The different fiscal policies of New Jersey and New York added further differentials in performance and effect. Because New Jersey relies heavily on property taxes, industries with large capital investment tend to seek new locations in New York, other things being equal. Because New York levies income and earnings taxes, businesses with high profit ratios often move in the opposite direction. The same situation exists in every large metropolitan area and between regions across the country.[20]

This pattern of sharp differences is the result, of course, of the blanket of relatively small state and local governments laid over highly interrelated regional and metropolitan areas. No longer is the contrast between rural and urban states or localities, but within urban and industrialized complexes. As differences in education, welfare, transportation, public safety, and utility programs become apparent, the pressure grows for a higher level of government to undertake financial and program responsibility in order to provide a measure of uniformity or to work to equalize resources and opportunities. Hence the push for federal legislation and grants-in-aid in many fields formerly the exclusive domains of state and local politics.

THE PRACTICE OF "DOMESTIC MERCANTILISM"

A second difficulty with the present systems of intergovernmental politics is that they fail to remove competitive struggles among states and localities that arise in the process of continued national economic growth and development. Each state tends to use economic planning programs as devices to secure faster growth than neighboring states have—to offer tax concessions, better public services, and the like. Advertisements in national magazines routinely call attention to the skilled, sober, and devoted labor force of Arkansas, the transportation facilities of New York, the tax advantages of New Jersey, or the climate of California. At the local level, municipalities have come to rely on land-use and tax policies to capture what they regard as the most advantageous new increments of urban growth—the higher-income residential development, the new light industry, or the shopping center.

These policies, state and local, are often dubbed "domestic mercantilism," the use of government power to gain economic advantages. The spectacle

---

[20] Robert C. Wood, *1400 Governments: The Political Economy of the New York Metropolitan Region* (Cambridge, 1961), p. 48.

of a suburb trying to get the "right" industry and planning to put the workers in the next-door town, or of a state which wants new business without public expenditures or the rise of trade unions is a common occurrence across the nation. A scramble for new tax values takes place as suburban jurisdictions use zoning and subdivision powers in a number of ways to build a better town. There is the case of an eastern suburb that bought all the vacant land within its borders to sell only to acceptable customers; frequently there is a rule that no "look alike" houses may be erected next to one another; and even more frequently there are minimum lot sizes and house prices that go beyond standards of health and safety.

From the point of view of the orderly development of the new communities, these strategies are not particularly useful nor is it at all certain that they are especially effective. Economic forces still seem to be the prime determinants of the pattern of industrial and residential location, and the policies of the states and localities caught up in much larger geographical complexes often seem to be "sound and fury" rather than influential directives which actually change the pattern of growth. Nevertheless, they constitute an important segment of the public business at the state and local levels and occupy a great deal of the time and attention of state and local officeholders and local pressure groups when they are not involved with nomination, election, and reelection concerns.

THE ABSENCE OF RESPONSIBLE DECISION-MAKING

A third defect of the present pattern, to many, is that comprehensive planning and decision-making about the future of our new communities is extraordinarily difficult to achieve. Each year our urban population increases by some two to three million—enough to create from ten to fifteen new "average" American cities, if we chose to adopt such a policy. Each year, our demands for water, recreational space, and energy sources grow apace, for we will build again one half of all existing structures—houses, factories, commercial districts, apartments—in the next generation. In effect, Americans are continually being asked what kinds of cities and regions they wish to inhabit.

Yet there are at present very few channels through which the citizen can express his choice. Without formal institutions of government with jurisdictions conterminous with the new areas, without comprehensive plans providing alternative directions for growth, without opportunity to react to new highway or mass transit proposals, the management of regional development is a hit-or-miss affair. Usually thousands of individual market decisions in the private sector of the economy, taken without calculation of public consequences, determine the form and shape of our new communities. So the Spread City and Megalopolis appear without any public consideration as to whether these are the preferred places for modern Americans to live.

This inability to look ahead, to plan, to guide a surging population expansion, and to assure that decisions of the special districts and interstate compact agencies are responsive to popular demands is often set down as the greatest liability of intergovernmental politics today. It implies that the governments can only keep spending and taxing—but cannot oversee democratically the major forces of change.

Proposals for Drastic Change

The service and resource inequities, the "beggar-thy-neighbor" economic policies of many states and localities, and the lack of comprehensive planning and development mechanisms have concerned students of state and local governments for at least two generations. In their view, however ingenious the grants-in-aid programs, the special district arrangements, and the informal techniques of collaboration may be, they are not sufficient responses to modern conditions. Indeed many students believe that resources are being wasted and economic growth impaired by the failure of states to acknowledge directly their responsibilities as resource managers. They argue that the landscape of metropolitan areas is being despoiled; that the central city is becoming abandoned; that needless expenditures are made on the wrong modes of transportation; that inefficient locations of industry and commerce are encouraged because of the inability of local governments to work more closely together. A larger, better-financed, more farsighted local government embracing the entire metropolitan area and interstate regional enterprises with vigorous executive organs and independent sources of revenue would, they think, make better politics and better policy below the national level.

Since the 1930s a whole battery of new institutions has been proposed, especially at the metropolitan level, to change state and local structures and strengthen their performance. Not many of these have succeeded, but at least three at the local level have been discussed and debated and are worth serious consideration.

ANNEXATION

The most obvious and straightforward of these proposals has been the annexation of newly urbanized territory by the core cities of metropolitan areas. In the nineteenth century and early twentieth, this practice of extending municipal boundary lines to keep pace with urban population growth was extensively used by almost every large American city. Now, it remains a fairly popular device in the Southwest and West.

Annexation cannot be considered a truly satisfactory response to the public problems raised by increased urbanization. Although effectively maintaining the coincidence of political, economic, and social boundary lines, the strategy often creates some financial, organizational, and land-use problems. If a core city annexes relatively undeveloped territory in anticipation of new development, it may have to undertake expensive investments in capital facilities long before any sizable revenues from the new area are forthcoming, and its administrative resources may be similarly strained. On the other hand, if a city waits until urbanization in outlying places has occurred, its opportunity to guide land-use policy is reduced or eliminated, and it risks almost certain opposition to annexation by residents of the fringe preferring their status as citizens of smaller communities and opposing the higher taxes which annexation often brings. Frequently these citizens move to establish separate municipalities rather than become absorbed by the metropolis. Even when annexation is successful the result is that the metropolis assumes responsibility over areas having few tax resources but requiring costly services, while the financially self-sufficient out-lying parts of the metropolitan area retain their separate identities. In older metropolitan areas, when suburban municipalities have long been in exist-ence, the annexation approach has proved almost completely impracticable.

REALLOCATIONS OF FUNCTIONS

A more typical approach to strengthening the capacities of local gov-ernment to deal with modern problems has been the piecemeal but more or less continuing process of reassigning local programs from one govern-mental level to another, or of consolidating major units. Primarily this in-volves assigning a new role to the American county. In the smaller metro-politan areas this approach has sometimes resulted in the consolidation of central-city and county functions, sometimes their separation. More often the readjustments have been made for specific programs.

City-county separation, first adopted in Baltimore more than a hundred years ago, has the disadvantage of seriously complicating the future expan-sion of central-city boundaries, for it often freezes the jurisdictions of the local governments involved. Only Virginia has devised a practical means for municipal expansion under the "separation" philosophy, by allowing the judiciary to adjust boundary lines to changing conditions. Consolidation plans of county and city, most recently demonstrated in Baton Rouge, Loui-siana, frequently achieve major structural simplifications but do not meet the problems of large multicounty metropolitan areas. A new version of consolidation, adopted by Nashville and Davidson County, Tennessee, in 1962, establishes one "expandable" urban service district designed to over-come the jurisdictional inflexibilities of the older plans, and this device may be applicable in other areas.[21]

At the present time, however, the most popular type of functional adjust-ment is the piecemeal merger of specific functions. In many metropolitan areas, public health, welfare, highway, and recreational programs have been established on a joint basis, most usually involving the central city and the county, and resulting in the emergence of the county as the principal metro-politan unit. Atlanta and Fulton County, Georgia, completed an extensive redistribution of functions along these lines in 1950, and Los Angeles County has assumed major responsibilities for traditional municipal services through the device of making separate service contracts with individual munici-palities. Known as the Lakewood plan after a municipality which initially turned over all its programs to Los Angeles County, this approach depends on voluntary agreements arrived at through a bargaining process between municipal and county officials. More than a thousand of these arrangements now apply to southern California metropolitan areas. They are widely heralded as a means by which politically autonomous units can overcome some of the administrative consequences of metropolitan fragmentation.[22]

---

[21] For an account of the Nashville plan, see David R. Grant and Lee S. Greene, "Surveys, Dust, Action," *National Civic Review* (October, 1961).

[22] Robert Warren, "The Organization of Metropolitan Areas: A Theoretical Inquiry," *American Political Science Review* (December, 1961), Vol. LV, No. 4, pp. 831–42.

METROPOLITAN FEDERATION

Progress in integrating local government by annexation and functional reallocations has seemed too slow and too limited to many. They advocate instead a metropolitan federal system as the most satisfactory way to solve the metropolitan problem on a comprehensive basis. Metropolitan federalism calls for the establishment of a government with jurisdiction over the entire metropolitan area (but with limited program responsibilities) and for the continuation of most existing local units to perform "purely local" functions. Usually, a federated plan provides for the participation of the smaller units in the policy-making process of the metropolitan government by some formula of representation on the latter's governing body.

New York City adopted its five-borough plan in 1897; this had the formal appearance of a federal system for the then urbanized area, but in practice the boroughs served principally as administrative units, and no further extension of the city has occurred since that time. Miami and Dade County, Florida, adopted a two-tiered form of government in 1957, but the experiment is limited to one county within a rapidly expanding area, and only cities with populations of more than 60,000 elect representatives to the county board of commissioners.

The most complete application of the federal principle in a metropolitan area was achieved in Toronto, Canada, in 1953, by prescription of the Ontario legislature. The municipality of metropolitan Toronto has jurisdiction over such areawide functions as water supply and distribution, sewerage, principal highways, public transportation, and planning; the area affected is the central city and twelve suburbs. A metropolitan council composed of the chief executives of the suburban governments and twelve elected public officials of Toronto directs the metropolitan municipality. The old units continue to carry out such functions as health, library, and welfare services, though the assumption of police responsibilities in 1957 by the metropolitan government has given rise to charges that the plan is "creeping annexation" and that ultimately full consolidation is intended. The Toronto plan has also been criticized because of its indirect and—on a population basis—unequal plan of representation and the fact that it was established without a popular referendum. Nonetheless, the metropolitan government's first ten years of operations establishes the plan as a vigorous and effective instrument.

The reasons for the defeat of these "radical" reform plans are many. The chief ones seem to be (1) the opposition of officeholders and bureaucracies of the existing governments; (2) the narrow base of the reform movements, which are often restricted to businessmen and academicians; (3) the unawareness of the public at large of the issues involved; (4) the desire of the public, when it is made aware of the reform proposals, to retain small governments "close to home and the grass roots." Indeed, those who have studied some of the major campaigns for metropolitan governments agree with Scott Greer's comment that the principal effect of the reform movements has been to produce "morality plays" that excite the actors but not the audiences.

The Future of Intergovernmental Politics

The poor reception accorded to bold new plans for structural reform suggests that continuous informal adjustment, not formal change, is the most likely path intergovernmental politics will follow in the future. Major revisions in legal and political systems—the vertical and horizontal patterns of politics—do take place without constitutional sanctions or much public visibility. But for those anxious to maintain pluralism and diverse centers of power in the United States, the future seems reassuring.

First, it seems likely that the initiative for domestic policy may be vested even more strongly in the lower echelons in the future. In the most recent grants-in-aid legislation for mass transportation and open spaces, the Congress has decreed that grants be made in conformity with comprehensive metropolitan plans. Administrative steps have also been taken at the federal level to assure that existing programs in highways, renewal, health and hospitals also are made parts of a general metropolitan plan. At the regional level, river basin planning increasingly proceeds through the combined deliberations of state, federal, and compact agency officials. Consequently, the outlook for these programs is that their basic framework will be shaped in terms of local or state plans, not by federal specifications, and the influence of the lower levels will be strengthened accordingly.

A second implication of the new political systems is that the formal structure of American federalism is an even less relevant guide to the allocation of decision-making responsibilities in our politics today than it was in the past. Public programs are now built around either a functional activity or problem as defined by specialists or a geographical area for which no general-purpose government exists. Elected officials, bureaucracies, and interest groups proceed by adopting mutually agreeable strategies and fashioning temporary coalitions. It is in this complex of multiple governments, agencies, and political activists that common policies are hammered out.

The continued involvement among levels and units of the American federal structure does not mean, however, that the principle of federalism does not work. If our polity looks like a marble cake, not a layer cake, in the way its institutions are arranged, the separate components are still distinguishable. The areal division of *powers* remains essentially intact. Each formally organized government has resources and legal authority of its own, each the capacity to decide how far and in what way it wishes to collaborate with its neighbors. So federalism has achieved the purpose of restraining arbitrary political action and preventing the concentration of political influence just as the separation of powers at the national level has worked to the same end. The fact that broad avenues of collaboration among the separate power centers have been created and that new arenas of politics have been established in the intergovernmental process of involvement does not vitiate the principle of divided powers any more than the Presidential assumption of initiative in matters of policy makes the Congress less "powerful." The different parts of the governmental machinery assume new functions, but the important point is that *persuasion,* not coercion, remains the basic technique by which government units influence one another.

The Challenge for State and Local Governments

The descriptions and analysis of these last four chapters have represented American state and local governments as vigorous enterprises that are increasingly involved with one another and the federal government in making important public decisions. Their number, their variety, the means which they possess to influence national politics and constrain the national government assure them of important and continuing roles in the general American political system. Although the federal government has expanded the size and number of its activities, the lower echelons have done so even more rapidly. Moreover, they have devised ways to collaborate with the federal government so as to continue to exercise influence in national affairs. Even in those areas which have always been the province of the national government—defense and foreign affairs—states and localities play their parts. The preparedness of our domestic defense arrangements, the effectiveness and equity of the selective service system, the image which foreign nations hold of the United States in the way we treat minority groups, or our administration of justice are all powerfully shaped by the decisions and policies of our lower levels of government.

What are the major problems of these levels today? One especially evident at the state level is ensuring that its institutions are popularly responsible. As the fulcrum of state political systems, legislatures in too many states have been ruled by powerful minorities. The decision of *Baker* v. *Carr* and subsequent decrees will make profound changes in the basis of representation, but if state governments are to match the federal one in responsiveness to public opinion, more than suitable apportionment procedures will be required. Public attention needs to be focused continually—and more strongly—on state politics; the party organizations in the states need to be more disciplined and more oriented to policy matters; the recruitment of state legislators needs to be broadened to bring in a wider variety of social, ethnic, and occupational backgrounds.

It is not only the states, as we have seen, that suffer from lack of public accountability. The affairs of many suburban and rural governments are directed by a few influentials, speaking probably for an apathetic and inarticulate majority but often cavalierly overriding minority interests. In large cities, portions of the public appear so alienated that key decisions are sometimes made by the collusion and connivance of a relatively small number of professional politicians. In the metropolitan arena, great public authorities and corporations often behave without consideration for public opinion or for the policies of general governments and elected officials. The need for visible politics, increased participation by representatives of diverse interests, open debate of important public issues, qualified candidates, and responsible parties is still great in these governments. Slogans concerned with the sanctity of states' rights and the purity of grass-roots democracy are not substitutes for majority-based political institutions, respect for minority rights, and orderly deliberations in full public view.

A second problem concerns the capacity of the institutions and the ability of the political systems to make decisions reasonably quickly, rationally, and with finality. Despite popular impressions we have seen that neither state nor local political systems are monolithic. On the contrary, they are composed of so many diverse and disparate interests and participants that they have chronic difficulty in achieving consensus or arriving at compromises. Today's legislative-oriented state governments and the fragmented local governments frequently fail to produce timely, comprehensive, and workable policies. It has been these poor performance records which have stimulated the proposals for strengthening the power of the governor, simplifying the state executive and administrative structure, increasing the power of the mayor, and speeding the development of the metropolitan institutions. All these proposals are designed to reduce the number of independent power centers in highly decentralized patterns of influence distribution and to compensate for the reaction against the town fathers and city bosses.

But improving the capacity of these governments to make meaningful decisions requires more than structural reform, especially since their major programs are formulated in the web of intergovernmental relations. Much more emphasis would have to be given to the recruitment of new political activists, not only for elected offices but for professional administrative posts. The report of the Municipal Manpower Commission for 1962, for example, revealed that most large cities are using manpower stock piles accumulated in Depression years to provide their administrative, technical, and professional personnel.[23] State personnel offices report much the same situation at the management levels where key decisions are so often made. Vacancies exist for engineers in highway departments, doctors in research laboratories, directors of state institutions. Only a few high-prestige positions—mental-hospital work attracting psychiatrists and psychologists, state police, city planning—have power comparable to the federal service in attracting college graduates. State and local governments have made few efforts to recruit or publicize their programs or to provide special career opportunities for young people entering their employ. Consequently, positions which are vital to the effective discharge of important public programs often go unfilled or are occupied by untrained personnel.

State and local governments need also to display greater imagination and creativity in devising new policies and new programs for collaborative action. As this chapter has stressed, the politics by which these governments will meet the demands made upon them is essentially the politics of intergovernmental relations. To institute and carry out new programs in this setting is in effect to work where no formal guidelines, institutions, or procedures clearly exist. Thus, governments which can only routinely discharge duties routinely assigned to them and which fail to explore new ideas and opportunities face the fate of disintegration and decline which all large organizations so oriented invite.

Yet neither more democratic nor more able state and local governments

---

[23] Municipal Manpower Commission, *Governmental Manpower for Tomorrow's Cities* (New York, 1963).

are likely to receive the full confidence and support of the public unless they have a clearer understanding of their mission or purpose in American life today. This clarification of objective is not easy, because of the competing glamour of national affairs and the persistence of old ideas about the proper role of these institutions. With our attention riveted to international maneuverings of the Soviet Union, the needs of newly developing nations, the latest accomplishments of the astronauts, we often find it difficult to consider the politics of everyday living. And old theories of state and local government encourage us in this, for they interpret the tasks of these governments to be essentially humdrum, concerned with the provision of routine services and facilities for material needs of the population. Digging sewers, arresting traffic violators, educating children, inspecting elevators, distributing vaccine, installing street lights, and interviewing welfare families do not seem, on first consideration, to be exciting, dramatic, and important activities.

Yet the work of state and local governments today is much more than the provision of an assortment of goods and services which the private marketplace has proven unwilling and unable to provide. In their new roles of resource managers and community developers, states and localities by their decisions or lack of decisions are prime shapers of the quality of American life and the face American civilization presents to the outside world. Whether or not our rivers are developed for recreation and conservation as well as for water-control purposes is an intergovernmental matter—one for state as well as federal decision. What shape our transportation system—and the consequent line of settlement in our new urban regions—will take is a state responsibility. Our present highway program has encouraged population diffusion and suburban sprawl as much as the federal mortgage insurance program has. What the future of old cities will be lies in the hands of mayors, city aldermen, city managers, renewal administrators, and planners at the local, as well as the state and national, level. How well, how rapidly, our children are educated is a matter which the initiative and energy of state and local school systems will decide. What cultural, civic, and recreational facilities will be open to the public depends on the attitudes of state and local budget makers.

All these choices fall now within the complex politics of intergovernmental relations, with the state and local levels given preference in initiating and executing programs. All are matters of quality: issues about how excellent our schools, civic centers, community services, state parks, mental institutions, hospitals, art galleries will be. Or they are matters of quality in another sense: the abilities of our courts to administer justice or of our police forces to achieve the professional pride that comes with honest and efficient execution of their duties.

These are the choices which set the style of a nation: the physical appearance of its cities, the morale and spirit of its people, the way they spend their time away from work. For America, no set of political activists will do more to set the tone and style of our civilization than the decision makers in the state capitol and city hall. If we are to achieve our future potential as a civilized nation, not just as a rich and powerful one, their competence, imagination, and integrity must be high.

THE CONSTITUTION
OF THE UNITED STATES OF AMERICA

We the people of the United States, in order to form a more perfect Union, establish justice, insure domestic tranquility, provide for the common defence, promote the general welfare, and secure the blessings of liberty to ourselves and our posterity, do ordain and establish this Constitution for the United States of America.

ARTICLE I

Section 1. All legislative powers herein granted shall be vested in a Congress of the United States, which shall consist of a Senate and House of Representatives.

Section 2. 1. The House of Representatives shall be composed of members chosen every second year by the people of all the several States, and the Electors in each State shall have the qualifications requisite for electors of the most numerous branch of the State Legislature.

2. No person shall be a representative who shall not have attained to the age of twenty-five years, and been seven years a citizen of the United States, and who shall not, when elected, be an inhabitant of that State in which he shall be chosen.

3. Representatives and direct taxes [1] shall be apportioned among the several States which may be included within this Union, according to their respective numbers, which shall be determined by adding to the whole number of free persons, including those bound to service for a term of years, and excluding Indians not taxed, three fifths of all other persons.[2] The actual enumeration shall be made within three years after the first meeting of the Congress of the United States, and within every subsequent term of ten years, in such manner as they shall by law direct. The number of representatives shall not exceed one for every thirty thousand, but each State shall have at least one representative; and until such enumeration shall be made, the State of New Hampshire shall be entitled to chuse three, Massachusetts eight, Rhode Island and Providence Plantations one, Connecticut five, New-York six, New Jersey four, Pennsylvania eight, Delaware one, Maryland six, Virginia ten, North Carolina five, South Carolina five, and Georgia three.

4. When vacancies happen in the representation from any State, the executive authority thereof shall issue writs of election to fill such vacancies.

5. The House of Representatives shall chuse their speaker and other officers; and shall have the sole power of impeachment.

Section 3. 1. The Senate of the United States shall be composed of two senators from each State, chosen by the legislature thereof,[3] for six years; and each senator shall have one vote.

2. Immediately after they shall be assembled in consequence of the first election, they shall be divided as equally as may be into three classes. The seats of the senators of the first class shall be vacated at the expiration of the second year, of the second class at the expiration of the fourth year, and of the third class at the expiration of the sixth year, so that one third may be chosen every second year; and if vacancies happen by resignation, or other-

---

[1] See the 16th Amendment.
[2] See the 14th Amendment.

[3] See the 17th Amendment.

wise, during the recess of the legislature of any State, the executive thereof may make temporary appointments until the next meeting of the legislature, which shall then fill such vacancies.[4]

3. No person shall be a senator who shall not have attained to the age of thirty years, and been nine years a citizen of the United States, and who shall not, when elected be an inhabitant of that State for which he shall be chosen.

4. The Vice President of the United States shall be President of the Senate, but shall have no vote, unless they be equally divided.

5. The Senate shall chuse their other officers and also a president pro tempore, in the absence of the Vice President, or when he shall exercise the office of President of the United States.

6. The Senate shall have the sole power to try all impeachments. When sitting for that purpose, they shall be on oath or affirmation. When the President of the United States is tried, the chief justice shall preside: and no person shall be convicted without the concurrence of two thirds of the members present.

7. Judgment in cases of impeachment shall not extend further than to removal from office, and disqualifications to hold and enjoy any office of honor, trust or profit under the United States: but the party convicted shall nevertheless be liable and subject to indictment, trial, judgment and punishment, according to law.

Section 4. 1. The times, places, and manner of holding elections for senators and representatives, shall be prescribed in each State by the legislature thereof; but the Congress may at any time by law make or alter such regulations, except as to the places of chusing senators.

2. The Congress shall assemble at least once in every year, and such meeting shall be on the first Monday in

[4] See the 17th Amendment.

December, unless they shall by law appoint a different day.

Section 5. 1. Each House shall be the judge of the elections, returns and qualifications of its own members, and a majority of each shall constitute a quorum to do business; but a smaller number may adjourn from day to day, and may be authorized to compel the attendance of absent members, in such manner, and under such penalties as each House may provide.

2. Each House may determine the rules of its proceedings, punish its members for disorderly behaviour, and, with the concurrence of two thirds, expel a member.

3. Each House shall keep a journal of its proceedings, and from time to time publish the same, excepting such parts as may in their judgment require secrecy; and the yeas and nays of the members of either House on any question shall, at the desire of one fifth of those present, be entered on the journal.

4. Neither House, during the session of Congress, shall, without the consent of the other, adjourn for more than three days, nor to any other place than that in which the two Houses shall be sitting.

Section 6. 1. The senators and representatives shall receive a compensation for their services, to be ascertained by law, and paid out of the Treasury of the United States. They shall in all cases, except treason, felony, and breach of the peace, be privileged from arrest during their attendance at the session of their respective Houses, and in going to and returning from the same; and for any speech or debate in either House, they shall not be questioned in any other place.

2. No senator or representative shall, during the time for which he was elected, be appointed to any civil office under the authority of the United States, which shall have been created, or the emoluments whereof shall have been encreased, during such time; and no person holding any office under the United States shall be a member of

either House during his continuance in office.

Section 7. 1. All bills for raising revenue shall originate in the House of Representatives; but the Senate may propose or concur with amendments as on other bills.

2. Every bill which shall have passed the House of Representatives and the Senate, shall, before it become a law, be presented to the President of the United States; if he approves he shall sign it, but if not he shall return it, with his objections to that House in which it shall have originated, who shall enter the objections at large on their journal, and proceed to reconsider it. If after such reconsideration two thirds of that House shall agree to pass the bill, it shall be sent, together with the objections, to the other House, by which it shall likewise be reconsidered, and if approved by two thirds of that House, it shall become a law. But in all such cases the votes of both Houses shall be determined by yeas and nays, and the names of the persons voting for and against the bill shall be entered on the journal of each House respectively. If any bill shall not be returned by the President within ten days (Sundays excepted) after it shall have been presented to him, the same shall be a law, in like manner as if he had signed it, unless the Congress by their adjournment prevent its return, in which case it shall not be a law.

3. Every order, resolution, or vote to which the concurrence of the Senate and the House of Representatives may be necessary (except on a question of adjournment) shall be presented to the President of the United States; and before the same shall take effect, shall be approved by him, or being disapproved by him, shall be repassed by two thirds of the Senate and House of Representatives, according to the rules and limitations prescribed in the case of a bill.

Section 8. The Congress shall have the power

1. To lay and collect taxes, duties, imposts, and excises, to pay the debts and provide for the common defence and general welfare of the United States; but all duties, imposts, and excises shall be uniform throughout the United States;

2. To borrow money on the credit of the United States;

3. To regulate commerce with foreign nations, and among the several States, and with the Indian tribes;

4. To establish an uniform rule of naturalization, and uniform laws on the subject of bankruptcies throughout the United States;

5. To coin money, regulate the value thereof, and of foreign coin, and fix the standard of weights and measures;

6. To provide for the punishment of counterfeiting the securities and current coin of the United States;

7. To establish post offices and post roads;

8. To promote the progress of science and useful arts, by securing for limited times to authors and inventors the exclusive right to their respective writings and discoveries;

9. To constitute tribunals inferior to the Supreme Court;

10. To define and punish piracies and felonies committed on the high seas, and offences against the law of nations;

11. To declare war, grant letters of marque and reprisal, and make rules concerning captures on land and water;

12. To raise and support armies, but no appropriation of money to that use shall be for a longer term than two years;

13. To provide and maintain a navy;

14. To make rules for the government and regulation of the land and naval forces;

15. To provide for calling forth the militia to execute the laws of the Union, suppress insurrections and repel invasions;

16. To provide for organizing, arming, and disciplining the militia, and for governing such part of them as may be employed in the service of the United States, reserving to the States respectively, the appointment of the officers, and the authority of training the militia

according to the discipline prescribed by Congress;

17. To exercise exclusive legislation in all cases whatsoever, over such district (not exceeding ten miles square) as may, by cession of particular States, and the acceptance of Congress, become the seat of the government of the United States, and to exercise like authority over all places purchased by the consent of the legislature of the State in which the same shall be, for the erection of forts, magazines, arsenals, dock-yards, and other needful buildings; and

18. To make all laws which shall be necessary and proper for carrying into execution the foregoing powers, and all other powers vested by this Constitution in the government of the United States, or in any department or officer thereof.

Section 9. 1. The migration or importation of such persons as any of the States now existing shall think proper to admit, shall not be prohibited by the Congress prior to the year one thousand eight hundred and eight, but a tax or duty may be imposed on such importation, not exceeding ten dollars for each person.

2. The privilege of the writ of habeas corpus shall not be suspended, unless when in cases of rebellion or invasion the public safety may require it.

3. No bill of attainder or ex post facto law shall be passed.

4. No capitation, or other direct, tax shall be laid, unless in proportion to the census or enumeration hereinbefore directed to be taken.[5]

5. No tax or duty shall be laid on articles exported from any State.

6. No preference shall be given by any regulation of commerce or revenue to the ports of one State over those of another: nor shall vessels bound to, or from, one State be obliged to enter, clear, or pay duties in another.

7. No money shall be drawn from the treasury, but in consequence of appropriations made by law; and a regu-

lar statement and account of the receipts and expenditures of all public money shall be published from time to time.

8. No title of nobility shall be granted by the United States: and no person holding any office of profit or trust under them, shall, without the consent of the Congress, accept of any present, emolument, office, or title, of any kind whatever, from any king, prince, or foreign State.

Section 10. 1. No State shall enter into any treaty, alliance, or confederation; grant letters of marque and reprisal; coin money; emit bills of credit; make any thing but gold and silver coin a tender in payment of debts; pass any bill of attainder, ex post facto law, or law impairing the obligation of contracts, or grant any title of nobility.

2. No State shall, without the consent of the Congress, lay any imposts or duties on imports or exports, except what may be absolutely necessary for executing its inspection laws: and the net produce of all duties and imposts laid by any State on imports or exports, shall be for the use of the treasury of the United States; and all such laws shall be subject to the revision and control of the Congress.

3. No State shall, without the consent of the Congress, lay any duty of tonnage, keep troops, or ships of war in time of peace, enter into any agreement or compact with another State, or with a foreign power, or engage in war, unless actually invaded, or in such imminent danger as will not admit of delay.

ARTICLE II

Section 1. 1. The executive power shall be vested in a President of the United States of America. He shall hold his office during the term of four years, and, together with the Vice President, chosen for the same term, be elected, as follows:

2. Each State shall appoint, in such manner as the legislature thereof may direct, a number of electors, equal to the whole number of senators and rep-

---

[5] See the 16th Amendment.

resentatives to which the State may be entitled in the Congress: but no senator or representative, or person holding an office of trust or profit under the United States, shall be appointed an elector.

The electors shall meet in their respective States, and vote by ballot for two persons, of whom one at least shall not be an inhabitant of the same State with themselves. And they shall make a list of all the persons voted for, and of the number of votes for each; which list they shall sign and certify, and transmit sealed to the seat of the government of the United States, directed to the president of the Senate. The president of the Senate shall, in the presence of the Senate and House of Representatives, open all the certificates, and the votes shall then be counted. The person having the greatest number of votes shall be the President, if such number be a majority of the whole number of electors appointed; and if there be more than one who have such majority, and have an equal number of votes, then the House of Representatives shall immediately chuse by ballot one of them for President; and if no person have a majority, then from the five highest on the list the said House shall in like manner chuse the President. But in chusing the President, the votes shall be taken by States, the representation from each State having one vote; a quorum for this purpose shall consist of a member or members from two thirds of the States, and a majority of all the States shall be necessary to a choice. In every case, after the choice of the President, the person having the greatest number of votes of the electors shall be the Vice President. But if there should remain two or more who have equal votes, the Senate shall chuse from them by ballot the Vice President.[6]

3. The Congress may determine the time of chusing the electors, and the day on which they shall give their votes; which day shall be the same throughout the United States.

[6] Superseded by the 12th Amendment.

4. No person except a natural born citizen, or a citizen of the United States, at the time of the adoption of this Constitution, shall be eligible to the office of President; neither shall any person be eligible to that office who shall not have attained to the age of thirty five years, and been fourteen years a resident within the United States.

5. In case of the removal of the President from office, or of his death, resignation, or inability to discharge the powers and duties of the said office, the same shall devolve on the Vice President, and the Congress may by law provide for the case of removal, death, resignation or inability, both of the President and Vice President, declaring what officer shall then act as President, and such officer shall act accordingly, until the disability be removed, or a President shall be elected.

6. The President shall, at stated times, receive for his services a compensation, which shall neither be increased nor diminished during the period for which he shall have been elected, and he shall not receive within that period any other emolument from the United States, or any of them.

7. Before he enter on the execution of his office, he shall take the following oath or affirmation:—"I do solemnly swear (or affirm) that I will faithfully execute the office of President of the United States, and will to the best of my ability, preserve, protect and defend the Constitution of the United States."

Section 2. 1. The President shall be commander in chief of the army and navy of the United States, and of the militia of the several States, when called into the actual service of the United States; he may require the opinion, in writing, of the principal officer in each of the executive departments, upon any subject relating to the duties of their respective offices, and he shall have power to grant reprieves and pardons for offenses against the United States, except in cases of impeachment.

2. He shall have power, by and with

the advice and consent of the Senate, to make treaties, provided two thirds of the senators present concur; and he shall nominate, and by and with the advice and consent of the Senate, shall appoint ambassadors, other public ministers and consuls, judges of the Supreme Court, and all other officers of the United States, whose appointments are not herein otherwise provided for, and which shall be established by law: but the Congress may by law vest the appointment of such inferior officers, as they think proper, in the President alone, in the courts of law, or in the heads of departments.

3. The President shall have power to fill up all vacancies that may happen during the recess of the Senate, by granting commissions which shall expire at the end of their next session.

Section 3. He shall from time to time give to the Congress information of the state of the Union, and recommend to their consideration such measures as he shall judge necessary and expedient; he may, on extraordinary occasions, convene both Houses, or either of them, and in case of disagreement between them with respect to the time of adjournment, he may adjourn them to such time as he shall think proper; he shall receive ambassadors and other public ministers; he shall take care that the laws be faithfully executed, and shall commission all the officers of the United States.

Section 4. The President, Vice President, and all civil officers of the United States, shall be removed from office on impeachment for, and conviction of, treason, bribery, or other high crimes and misdemeanors.

ARTICLE III

Section 1. The judicial power of the United States shall be vested in one Supreme Court, and in such inferior courts as the Congress may from time to time ordain and establish. The judges, both of the supreme and inferior courts, shall hold their offices during good behavior, and shall, at stated times, receive for their services, a compensation, which shall not be diminished during their continuance in office.

Section 2. 1. The judicial power shall extend to all cases, in law and equity, arising under this Constitution, the laws of the United States, and treaties made, or which shall be made, under their authority;—to all cases affecting ambassadors, other public ministers and consuls;—to all cases of admiralty and maritime jurisdiction;—to controversies to which the United States shall be a party;—to controversies between two or more States;—between a State and citizens of another State; [7]—between citizens of different States—between citizens of the same State claiming lands under grants of different States, and between a State, or the citizens thereof, and foreign States, citizens or subjects.

2. In all cases affecting ambassadors, other public ministers and consuls, and those in which a State shall be party, the Supreme Court shall have original jurisdiction. In all the other cases before mentioned, the Supreme Court shall have appellate jurisdiction, both as to law and fact, with such exceptions, and under such regulations as the Congress shall make.

3. The trial of all crimes, except in cases of impeachment, shall be by jury; and such trial shall be held in the State where the said crimes shall have been committed; but when not committed within any State, the trial shall be at such place or places as the Congress may by law have directed.

Section 3. 1. Treason against the United States shall consist only in levying war against them, or in adhering to their enemies, giving them aid and comfort. No person shall be convicted of treason unless on the testimony of two witnesses to the same overt act, or on confession in open court.

2. The Congress shall have power to declare the punishment of treason, but no attainder of treason shall work cor-

---

[7] See the 11th Amendment.

ruption of blood, or forfeiture except during the life of the person attainted.

ARTICLE IV

Section 1. Full faith and credit shall be given in each State to the public acts, records, and judicial proceedings of every other State. And the Congress may by general laws prescribe the manner in which such acts, records and proceedings shall be proved, and the effect thereof.[8]

Section 2. 1. The citizens of each State shall be entitled to all privileges and immunities of citizens in the several States.

2. A person charged in any State with treason, felony, or other crime, who shall flee from justice, and be found in another State, shall on demand of the executive authority of the State from which he fled, be delivered up to be removed to the State having jurisdiction of the crime.

3. No person held to service or labour in one State under the laws thereof, escaping into another, shall, in consequence of any law or regulation therein, be discharged from such service or labour, but shall be delivered up on claim of the party to whom such service or labour may be due.[9]

Section 3. 1. New States may be admitted by the Congress into this Union; but no new State shall be formed or erected within the jurisdiction of any other State; nor any State be formed by the junction of two or more States, or parts of States, without the consent of the legislatures of the States concerned as well as of the Congress.

2. The Congress shall have power to dispose of and make all needful rules and regulations respecting the territory or other property belonging to the United States; and nothing in this Constitution shall be so construed as to prejudice any claims of the United States, or of any particular State.

Section 4. The United States shall guarantee to every State in this Union a republican form of government, and shall protect each of them against invasion; and on application of the legislature, or of the executive (when the legislature cannot be convened) against domestic violence.

ARTICLE V

The Congress, whenever two thirds of both Houses shall deem it necessary, shall propose amendments to this Constitution, or, on the application of the legislatures of two thirds of the several States, shall call a convention for proposing amendments, which in either case, shall be valid to all intents and purposes, as part of this Constitution, when ratified by the legislatures of three fourths of the several States, or by conventions in three fourths thereof, as the one or the other mode of ratification may be proposed by the Congress; Provided that no amendment which may be made prior to the year one thousand eight hundred and eight shall in any manner affect the first and fourth clauses in the ninth section of the first article; and that no State, without its consent, shall be deprived of its equal suffrage in the Senate.

ARTICLE VI

1. All debts contracted and engagements entered into, before the adoption of this Constitution, shall be as valid against the United States under this Constitution, as under the Confederation.[10]

2. This constitution, and the laws of the United States which shall be made in pursuance thereof; and all treaties made, or which shall be made, under the authority of the United States, shall be the supreme law of the land; and the Judges in every State shall be bound thereby, any thing in the Constitution or laws of any State to the contrary notwithstanding.

---

[8] See the 14th Amendment, Section 1.
[9] See the 13th Amendment.

[10] See the 14th Amendment, Section 4.

3. The senators and representatives before mentioned, and the members of the several State legislatures, and all executive and judicial officers, both of the United States and of the several States, shall be bound by oath or affirmation to support this Constitution; but no religious test shall ever be required as a qualification to any office or public trust under the United States.

ARTICLE VII

The ratification of the conventions of nine States shall be sufficient for the establishment of this Constitution between the States so ratifying the same.

Done in Convention by the unanimous consent of the States present the seventeenth day of September in the year of our Lord one thousand seven hundred and eighty seven, and of the independence of the United States of America the twelfth. In witness whereof we have hereunto subscribed our names.

. . .

Articles in addition to, and amendment of the Constitution of the United States of America, proposed by Congress, and ratified by the legislatures of the several States, pursuant to the fifth article of the original Constitution.

AMENDMENTS

FIRST TEN AMENDMENTS PASSED BY CONGRESS SEPTEMBER 25, 1789. RATIFIED BY THREE-FOURTHS OF THE STATES DECEMBER 15, 1791.

AMENDMENT I

Congress shall make no law respecting an establishment of religion, or prohibiting the free exercise thereof; or abridging the freedom of speech, or of the press; or the right of the people peaceably to assemble, and to petition the government for a redress of grievances.

AMENDMENT II

A well regulated militia, being necessary to the security of a free State, the right of the people to keep and bear arms, shall not be infringed.

AMENDMENT III

No soldier shall, in time of peace be quartered in any house, without the consent of the owner, nor in time of war, but in a manner to be prescribed by law.

AMENDMENT IV

The right of the people to be secure in their persons, houses, papers, and effects, against unreasonable searches and seizures, shall not be violated, and no warrants shall issue, but upon probable cause, supported by oath or affirmation, and particularly describing the place to be searched, and the persons or things to be seized.

AMENDMENT V

No person shall be held to answer for a capital, or otherwise infamous crime, unless on a presentment or indictment of a grand jury, except in cases arising in the land or naval forces, or in the militia, when in actual service in time of war or public danger; nor shall any person be subject for the same offence to be twice put in jeopardy of life or limb; nor shall be compelled in any criminal case to be a witness against himself, nor be deprived of life, liberty, or property, without due process of law; nor shall private property be taken for public use, without just compensation.

AMENDMENT VI

In all criminal prosecutions, the accused shall enjoy the right to a speedy and public trial, by an impartial jury of the State and district wherein the crime shall have been committed, which district shall have been previously ascertained by law, and to be informed of the nature and cause of the accusation; to be confronted with the witnesses against him; to have compulsory process for obtaining witnesses in his favor, and to have the assistance of counsel for his defence.

AMENDMENT VII

In suits at common law, where the value in controversy shall exceed twenty dollars, the right of trial by jury shall be preserved, and no fact tried by a jury shall be otherwise re-examined in any court of the United States, than according to the rules of the common law.

AMENDMENT VIII

Excessive bail shall not be required, nor excessive fines imposed, nor cruel and unusual punishments inflicted.

AMENDMENT IX

The enumeration in the Constitution of certain rights shall not be construed to deny or disparage others retained by the people.

AMENDMENT X

The powers not delegated to the United States by the Constitution, nor prohibited by it to the States, are reserved to the States respectively, or to the people.

AMENDMENT XI

PASSED BY CONGRESS MARCH 5, 1794. RATIFIED JANUARY 8, 1798.

The judicial power of the United States shall not be construed to extend to any suit in law or equity, commenced or prosecuted against one of the United States by citizens of another State, or by citizens or subjects of any foreign State.

AMENDMENT XII

PASSED BY CONGRESS DECEMBER 9, 1803. RATIFIED SEPTEMBER 25, 1804.

The electors shall meet in their respective States, and vote by ballot for President and Vice President, one of whom, at least, shall not be an inhabitant of the same State with themselves; they shall name in their ballots the person voted for as President, and in distinct ballots, the person voted for as Vice President, and they shall make distinct lists of all persons voted for as President and of all persons voted for as Vice President, and of the number of votes for each, which lists they shall sign and certify, and transmit sealed to the seat of the government of the United States, directed to the President of the Senate;—The President of the Senate shall, in the presence of the Senate and House of Representatives, open all the certificates and the votes shall then be counted;—The person having the greatest number of votes for President, shall be the President, if such number be a majority of the whole number of electors appointed; and if no person have such majority, then from the persons having the highest numbers not exceeding three on the list of those voted for as President, the House of Representatives shall choose immediately, by ballot, the President. But in choosing the President, the votes shall be taken by States, the representation from each State having one vote; a quorum for this purpose shall consist of a member or members from two thirds of the States, and a majority of all the States shall be necessary to a choice. And if the House of Representatives shall not choose a President whenever the right of choice shall devolve upon them, before the fourth day of March next following, then the Vice President shall act as President, as in the case of the death or other constitutional disability of the President. The person having the greatest number of votes as Vice President shall be the Vice President, if such number be a majority of the whole number of electors appointed, and if no person have a majority, then from the two highest numbers on the list, the Senate shall choose the Vice President; a quorum for the purpose shall consist of two thirds of the whole number of Senators, and a majority of the whole number shall be necessary to a choice. But no person constitutionally ineligible to the office of President shall be eligible to that of Vice President of the United States.

AMENDMENT XIII

PASSED BY CONGRESS FEBRUARY 1, 1865. RATIFIED DECEMBER 18, 1865.
Section 1. Neither slavery nor involuntary servitude except as a punishment for crime whereof the party shall have been duly convicted, shall exist within the United States, or any place subject to their jurisdiction.

Section 2. Congress shall have power to enforce this article by appropriate legislation.

AMENDMENT XIV

PASSED BY CONGRESS JUNE 16, 1866. RATIFIED JULY 28, 1868.
Section 1. All persons born or naturalized in the United States, and subject to the jurisdiction thereof, are citizens of the United States and of the State wherein they reside. No State shall make or enforce any law which shall abridge the privileges or immunities of citizens of the United States; nor shall any State deprive any person of life, liberty, or property, without due process of law; nor deny to any person within its jurisdiction the equal protection of the laws.

Section 2. Representatives shall be apportioned among the several States according to their respective numbers, counting the whole number of persons in each State, excluding Indians not taxed. But when the right to vote at any election for the choice of electors for President and Vice President of the United States, representatives in Congress, the executive and judicial officers of a State, or the members of the legislature thereof, is denied to any of the male inhabitants of such State, being twenty-one years of age, and citizens of the United States, or in any way abridged, except for participating in rebellion, or other crime, the basis of representation therein shall be reduced in the proportion which the number of such male citizens shall bear to the whole number of male citizens twenty-one years of age in such State.

Section 3. No person shall be a senator or representative in Congress, or elector of President and Vice President, or hold any office, civil or military, under the United States, or under any State, who having previously taken an oath, as a member of Congress, or as an officer of the United States, or as a member of any State legislature, or as an executive or judicial officer of any State, to support the Constitution of the United States, shall have engaged in insurrection or rebellion against the same, or given aid or comfort to the enemies thereof. But Congress may by a vote of two thirds of each House, remove such disability.

Section 4. The validity of the public debt of the United States, authorized by law, including debts incurred for payment of pensions and bounties for services in suppressing insurrection or rebellion, shall not be questioned. But neither the United States nor any State shall assume or pay any debt or obligation incurred in aid of insurrection or rebellion against the United States, or any claim for the loss or emancipation of any slave; but all such debts, obligations, and claims shall be held illegal and void.

Section 5. The Congress shall have power to enforce, by appropriate legislation, the provisions of this article.

AMENDMENT XV

PASSED BY CONGRESS FEBRUARY 27, 1869. RATIFIED MARCH 30, 1870.
Section 1. The right of citizens of the United States to vote shall not be denied or abridged by the United States or by any State on account of race, color, or previous condition of servitude.

Section 2. The Congress shall have power to enforce this article by appropriate legislation.

AMENDMENT XVI

PASSED BY CONGRESS JULY 12, 1909. RATIFIED FEBRUARY 25, 1913.

The Congress shall have power to lay and collect taxes on incomes, from whatever source derived, without apportionment among the several States, and without regard to any census or enumeration.

AMENDMENT XVII

PASSED BY CONGRESS MAY 16, 1912. RATIFIED MAY 31, 1913.

The Senate of the United States shall be composed of two senators from each State, elected by the people thereof, for six years; and each senator shall have one vote. The electors in each State shall have the qualifications requisite for electors of the most numerous branch of the State legislature.

When vacancies happen in the representation of any State in the Senate, the executive authority of such State shall issue writs of election to fill such vacancies: *Provided,* That the legislature of any State may empower the executive thereof to make temporary appointments until the people fill the vacancies by election as the legislature may direct.

This amendment shall not be so construed as to affect the election or term of any senator chosen before it becomes valid as part of the Constitution.

AMENDMENT XVIII [11]

PASSED BY CONGRESS DECEMBER 17, 1917. RATIFIED JANUARY 29, 1919.

After one year from the ratification of this article, the manufacture, sale, or transportation of intoxicating liquors within, the importation thereof into, or the exportation thereof from the United States and all territory subject to the

[11] Repealed by the 21st Amendment.

jurisdiction thereof for beverage purposes is hereby prohibited.

The Congress and the several States shall have concurrent power to enforce this article by appropriate legislation.

This article shall be inoperative unless it shall have been ratified as an amendment to the Constitution by the legislatures of the several States, as provided in the Constitution, within seven years from the date of the submission hereof to the States by Congress.

AMENDMENT XIX

PASSED BY CONGRESS JUNE 5, 1919. RATIFIED AUGUST 26, 1920.

The right of citizens of the United States to vote shall not be denied or abridged by the United States or by any State on account of sex.

Congress shall have power to enforce this article by appropriate legislation.

AMENDMENT XX

PASSED BY CONGRESS MARCH 3, 1932. RATIFIED JANUARY 23, 1933.

Section 1. The terms of the President and Vice President shall end at noon on the 20th day of January, and the terms of Senators and Representatives at noon on the 3d day of January, of the years in which such terms would have ended if this article had not been ratified; and the terms of their successors shall then begin.

Section 2. The Congress shall assemble at least once in every year, and such meeting shall begin at noon on the 3d day of January, unless they shall by law appoint a different day.

Section 3. If, at the time fixed for the beginning of the term of the President, the President elect shall have died, the Vice President elect shall become President. If a President shall not have been chosen before the time fixed for the beginning of his term, or if the President elect shall have failed to qualify, then the Vice President elect shall act as President until a President shall have qualified; and the Congress may by law provide for the case wherein neither a President elect nor a Vice President elect shall have qualified, declaring who shall then act as President, or the manner in which one who is to act shall be selected, and such person shall act accordingly until a President or Vice President shall have qualified.

Section 4. The Congress may by law provide for the case of the death of any of the persons from whom the House of Representatives may choose a President whenever the right of choice shall have devolved upon them, and for the case of the death of any of the persons from whom the Senate may choose a Vice President whenever the right of choice shall have devolved upon them.

Section 5. Sections 1 and 2 shall take effect on the 15th day of October following the ratification of this article.

Section 6. This article shall be inoperative unless it shall have been ratified as an amendment to the Constitution by the legislatures of three-fourths of the several States within seven years from the date of its submission.

AMENDMENT XXI

PASSED BY CONGRESS FEBRUARY 20, 1933. RATIFIED DECEMBER 5, 1933.

Section 1. The Eighteenth Article of amendment to the Constitution of the United States is hereby repealed.

Section 2. The transportation or importation into any State, Territory, or possession of the United States for delivery or use therein of intoxicating liquors in violation of the laws thereof, is hereby prohibited.

Section 3. This article shall be inoperative unless it shall have been ratified as an amendment to the Constitution by conventions in the several States, as provided in the Constitution, within seven years from the date of the submission thereof to the States by Congress.

AMENDMENT XXII

PASSED BY CONGRESS MARCH 12, 1947. RATIFIED MARCH 1. 1951.

No person shall be elected to the office of the President more than twice, and no person who has held the office of President, or acted as President, for more than two years of a term to which some other person was elected President shall be elected to the office of the President more than once.

But this article shall not apply to any person holding the office of President when this article was proposed by the Congress, and shall not prevent any person who may be holding the office of President, or acting as President, during the term within which this article becomes operative from holding the office of President or acting as President during the remainder of such term.

This article shall be inoperative unless it shall have been ratified as an amendment to the Constitution by the legislatures of three-fourths of the several States within seven years from the date of its submission to the States by the Congress.

AMENDMENT XXIII

PASSED BY CONGRESS JUNE 16, 1960. RATIFIED MARCH 29, 1961.

Section 1. The District constituting the seat of Government of the United States shall appoint in such manner as the Congress may direct:

A number of electors of President and Vice President equal to the whole number of Senators and Representatives in Congress to which the District would be entitled if it were a State, but in no event more than the least populous state; they shall be in addition to those appointed by the states, but they shall be considered, for the purposes of the election of President and Vice President, to be electors appointed by a state; and they shall meet in the District and perform such duties as provided by the twelfth article of amendment.

Section 2. The Congress shall have power to enforce this article by appropriate legislation.

AMENDMENT XXIV

PASSED BY CONGRESS AUGUST 27, 1962. RATIFIED JANUARY 23, 1964.

Section 1. The right of citizens of the United States to vote in any primary or other election for President or Vice President, for electors for President or Vice President, or for Senator or Representative in Congress shall not be denied or abridged by the United States or any State by reason of failure to pay any poll tax or other tax.

Section 2. The Congress shall have the power to enforce this article by appropriate legislation.

Bibliography

The purpose of this bibliography is to present a sampling of the rich and varied literature in American government and politics. It is not an attempt to be exhaustive. The effort has not been made to mention all of the standard works on each of the topics treated in the text; highly specialized books and articles of interest primarily to professional political scientists have also been excluded. Some of the books listed are classic or pioneering works that merit consideration here because they redirected or reorganized men's thinking. Other books are chosen because the quality of their analyses and their literary excellence make them obvious introductions to an understanding of the areas with which they deal. Still others are included because they deal with current political problems in a stimulating, if impermanent, fashion.

Part I. Democracy and the American Way

POLITICAL SYSTEMS

G. E. G. Catlin, *The Science and Method of Politics* (New York: Knopf, 1927). An early effort to encourage systematic thinking about political behavior.

David Easton, *The Political System* (New York: Knopf, 1953). An attempt to construct an abstract model of the political process.

Robert MacIver, *The Web of Government* (New York: Macmillan, 1947). A sociologist's effort to isolate the factors which influence the operation of political systems.

Austin Ranney, *The Governing of Men: An Introduction to Political Science* (New York: Holt, 1958). The basic concepts of the discipline are set forth and explained.

Graham Wallas, *Human Nature in Politics*, 3rd ed. (London: Constable, 1920). A pioneering study of the insights afforded by Freudian psychology into political behavior.

GENERAL OVERVIEWS OF THE AMERICAN SYSTEM

James Bryce, *The American Commonwealth* (New York: Macmillan, 1888). A classic roadmap of late-nineteenth-century American government by a distinguished British scholar-statesman.

Harold J. Laski, *The American Democracy* (New York: Viking, 1948). An analysis of the American system from a Marxist viewpoint.

Max Lerner, *America as a Civilization* (New York: Simon and Schuster, 1957). An ambitious effort to reduce all the variety of the American experience to print.

Alexis de Tocqueville, *Democracy in America* (Henry Reeve, tr., H. S. Commager, ed., New York: Oxford Univ. Press, 1947).

SOCIAL BASIS

Margaret Mead, *And Keep Your Powder Dry* (New York: Morrow, 1942). An anthropologist's free-swinging effort to delineate American national character.

David Potter, *People of Plenty* (Chicago: Univ. of Chicago Press, 1954). A historian argues that American attitudes and expectations are, in large part, a function of material plenty.

David Riesman, *The Lonely Crowd* (New Haven, Conn.: Yale Univ. Press, 1950). A best-selling study of the changing characteristics of Americans.

W. W. Rostow, *The United States in the World Arena* (New York: Harper, 1960). A student of American foreign relations argues that a distinctive "style" exists which marks American reactions to international developments.

AMERICAN POLITICAL IDEAS

Daniel Boorstin, *The Genius of American Politics* (Chicago: Univ. of Chicago Press, 1953). Stresses the uniqueness of American democracy.

Ralph H. Gabriel, *The Course of American Democratic Thought*, 2nd ed. (New York: Ronald, 1956). A very useful survey of American intellectual development in the nineteenth and early twentieth centuries.

Louis Hartz, *The Liberal Tradition in America* (New York: Harcourt, Brace & World, 1955). Argues the centrality of Locke in American reflections on politics.

Richard Hofstadter, *The American Political Tradition* (New York: Knopf, 1951). A lucid exposition of the thought of eleven Americans from Jefferson to F. D. R.

Robert G. McCloskey, *American Conservatism in the Age of Enterprise* (Cambridge, Mass.: Harvard Univ. Press, 1951). Describes the fossilization of economic conservatism in the nineteenth century.

Charles H. McIlwain, *The Growth of Political Thought in the West* (New York: Macmillan, 1932). A useful history of ideas.

Charles E. Merriam, *American Political Ideas* (New York: Macmillan, 1920). This small volume is still the best primer to American political thought.

Vernon L. Parrington, *Main Currents in American Thought* (New York: Harcourt, Brace & World, 1927–30). The classic Jeffersonian rendering of American political ideas.

DEMOCRACY

Robert A. Dahl, *A Preface to Democratic Theory* (Chicago: Univ. of Chicago Press, 1956). Suggests that perhaps problems of democratic theory can be quantified and manipulated mathematically.

Anthony Downs, *An Economic Theory of Democracy* (New York: Harper, 1957). An attempted definition of democracy in terms of an economic "market" model.

Harold F. Gosnell, *Democracy, the Threshold of Freedom* (New York: Ronald, 1948). Postwar reconsideration of the democratic ethic and right of suffrage.

Walter Lippmann, *The Public Philosophy* (Boston: Little, Brown, 1955). An idealist critique of American democracy.

J. Roland Pennock, *Liberal Democracy: Its Merits and Prospects* (New York: Rinehart, 1950). A philosophic consideration of democracy—its strengths and limitations.

David Spitz, *Patterns of Anti-Democratic Thought* (New York: Macmillan, 1949). An attempt to clarify the idea of democracy by considering its opposites.

CONSTITUTIONALISM

Carl J. Friedrich, *Constitutional Government and Democracy* (Boston: Ginn, 1946). A comparative study of constitutional systems.

Charles H. McIlwain, *Constitutionalism, Ancient and Modern* (Ithaca, N.Y.: Cornell Univ. Press, 1947). A standard text.

Francis D. Wormuth, *The Origins of Modern Constitutionalism* (New York: Harper, 1949). A search for the genesis of constitutional ideas.

FRAMING THE CONSTITUTION

Charles A. Beard, *An Economic Interpretation of the Constitution of the United States* (New York: Macmillan, 1913). Argues that the most influential members of the Constitutional Convention acted on the basis of economically interested motives.

Robert E. Brown, *Charles Beard and the Constitution* (Princeton, N.J.: Princeton Univ. Press, 1956). Takes Beard to task for cavalier use of sources and over-hasty generalization.

Jonathan Elliot, *The Debates in the Several State Conventions on the Adoption of the Federal Constitution* (Philadelphia: Lippincott, 1836–59). Standard reference work.

Max Farrand, *The Framing of the Constitution* (New Haven, Conn.: Yale Univ. Press, 1926). The classic study.

———, ed., *The Records of the Federal Convention* (New Haven, Conn.: Yale Univ. Press, 1911, 1937). Primary source material.

Alexander Hamilton, James Madison, and John Jay, *The Federalist*, B. F. Wright, ed. (Cambridge, Mass.: Harvard Univ. Press, 1961). These essays, originally published in various New York newspapers, represented an effort by the authors to persuade the citizenry of that city and state that the new governmental instrument was worthy of support. Required reading for all who would approach the subject.

Forrest McDonald, *We the People: The Economic Origins of the Constitution* (Chicago: Univ. of Chicago Press, 1958). Refutes Charles Beard's conclusions.

FEDERALISM

William Anderson, *The Nation and the States, Rivals or Partners?* (Minneapolis, Minn.: Univ. of Minnesota Press, 1955). Sketch of a possible new cooperative federalism.

Arthur Maass, ed., *Area and Power* (Glencoe, Ill.: Free Press, 1959). Studies of the operational problems of divided power.

Arthur W. MacMahon, ed., *Federalism: Mature and Emergent* (New York: Doubleday, 1955). Essays considering American federalism from varying perspectives—law, administration, political parties, and others.

William H. Riker, *Federalism: Origin, Operation, and Significance* (Boston: Little, Brown, 1964). Recent theoretical and critical analysis of the causes and consequences of federal systems.

K. C. Wheare, *Federal Government* (London: Oxford Univ. Press, 1951). Standard comparative study of federalism.

Leonard D. White, *The States and the Nation* (Baton Rouge, La.: Louisiana State Univ. Press, 1953). Consideration of the problems and prospects of American federalism.

Part II. The Political Process

PARTY HISTORY AND DEVELOPMENT

Lee Benson, *The Concept of Jacksonian Democracy* (Princeton, N.J.: Princeton Univ. Press, 1961). An attempt to understand Jacksonian democracy through an analysis of its social phases.

Wilfred E. Binkley, *American Political Parties: Their Natural History*, 4th ed. (New York: Knopf, 1964). An excellent historical treatment of party development.

William N. Chambers, *Political Parties in a New Nation: The American Experience, 1776–1809* (New York: Oxford Univ. Press, 1963). A very useful study of the evolution of informal alignments into self-conscious parties.

Joseph Charles, *The Origins of the American Party System* (Williamsburg, Va.: Institute of Early American History and Culture, 1956). The ideas of early party leaders.

Marvin Meyers, *The Jacksonian Persuasion: Politics and Belief* (Stanford, Calif.: Stanford Univ. Press, 1957). An attempt to understand Jacksonian democracy through an analysis of its rhetoric.

Malcolm C. Moos, *The Republicans* (New York: Random House, 1956). A history.

M. Ostrogorski, *Democracy and the Organization of Political Parties* (New York: Macmillan, 1908). A classic study of parties in the American and British contexts.

FUNCTIONS OF PARTIES

Maurice Duverger, *Political Parties: Their Organization and Activity in the Modern State* (New York: Wiley, 1956). Seminal comparative study of the various types of political parties.

Bertram Gross, *The Legislative Struggle* (New York: McGraw-Hill, 1953). The congressional process rendered in terms of the continuing group struggle.

Pendleton Herring, *The Politics of Democracy* (New York: Norton, 1940). An early consideration of the importance of interest group activity.

V. O. Key, Jr., *Politics, Parties, and Pressure Groups,* 5th ed. (New York: Crowell, 1964). An excellent text by a distinguished scholar.

———, *Southern Politics in State and Nation* (New York: Knopf, 1949). A consideration of the causes and consequences of one-party rule in the South.

David Manwaring, *Render unto Caesar* (Chicago: Univ. of Chicago Press, 1962). A survey of how the Jehovah's Witnesses used legal processes to protect their members from state compulsion to salute the flag.

Peter Odegard, *Pressure Politics: The Story of the Anti-Saloon League* (New York: Columbia Univ. Press, 1928). Even today, a fascinating study of a powerful group in action.

Clement E. Vose, *Caucasian Only* (Berkeley and Los Angeles: Univ. of California Press, 1959). A study of how an interest group (the NAACP) utilizes the judicial process to further its objectives.

VOTING BEHAVIOR

America Votes (New York: Macmillan, 1956–). Very useful compilation of voting statistics; issued biennially.

Eugene Burdick and A. J. Brodbeck, eds., *American Voting Behavior* (Glencoe, Ill.: Free Press, 1956). A collection of essays on the components of voter choice.

James M. Burns, *The Deadlock of Democracy* (Englewood Cliffs, N.J.: Prentice-Hall 1962). Argues the disutility of present party alignments.

Angus Campbell, *et al., The American Voter* (New York: Wiley, 1960). The most recent and important major study of voting behavior.

V. O. Key, Jr., *Public Opinion and American Democracy* (New York: Knopf, 1961).

The role of public opinion in the American political process.

Paul Lazarsfeld, Bernard Berelson, and Hazel Gaudet, *The People's Choice* (New York: Columbia Univ. Press, 1948). The first major scientific study of voting behavior.

Samuel Lubell, *The Future of American Politics*, 2nd ed. (New York: Anchor, 1956). Lively treatment of the changing alignments within the electorate, keyed to an explanation of Truman's 1948 upset victory.

Austin Ranney and Willmoore Kendall, *Democracy and the American Party System* (New York: Harcourt, Brace & World, 1956). A standard text.

E. E. Schattshneider, *Party Government* (New York: Rinehart, 1942). Argues for a restructuring of American parties along the more disciplined lines of the British model.

PARTY ORGANIZATION

Hugh A. Bone, *Party Committees and National Politics* (Seattle, Wash.: Univ. of Washington Press, 1958). On the role of the formal party organs at the national level.

Alexander Heard, *The Costs of Democracy* (Chapel Hill, N.C.: Univ. of North Carolina Press, 1960). The standard work on party finance.

Frank Kent, *The Great Game of Politics* (Garden City, N.Y.: Doubleday, 1923). A journalist's classic exposition of the facts of life of urban politics.

V. O. Key, Jr., *American State Politics* (New York: Knopf, 1956). An important study of the weaknesses of state party organizations.

Duane Lockard, *New England State Politics* (Princeton, N.J.: Princeton Univ. Press, 1959). Six excellent case studies.

INTEREST GROUPS

Arthur F. Bentley, *The Process of Government*, new ed. (Bloomington, Ind.: Principia Press, 1949). The classic statement of the group theory of politics.

Bernard Berelson, Paul Lazarsfeld, and William McPhee, *Voting* (Chicago: Univ. of Chicago Press, 1954). Represents an intermediate stage in the development of theories of voting behavior.

Lawrence Fuchs, *Political Behavior of American Jews* (Glencoe, Ill.: Free Press, 1956). Case study of an ethnic voting pattern.

David B. Truman, *The Governmental Process* (New York: Knopf, 1951). A very important effort to apply modified group theory to the American political experience.

CHOOSING THE PRESIDENT

Paul T. David, Ralph M. Goldman, and Richard C. Bain, *The Politics of National Party Conventions* (Washington: Brookings Institution, 1960). This standard work considers conventions from historical and functional points of view.

——, Malcolm Moos, and Ralph M. Goldman, eds., *Presidential Nominating Politics* (Baltimore: Johns Hopkins Press, 1954). A compilation of case studies by a task force of political scientists.

Eugene H. Roseboom, *A History of Presidential Elections* (New York: Macmillan, 1957). Useful narrative.

Theodore H. White, *The Making of the President, 1960* (New York: Atheneum, 1961). Vivid journalistic account of 1960 Presidential battles.

Part III. The President, Congress, and the Executive Branch

THE PRESIDENT—TASKS AND RESOURCES

Edward S. Corwin, *The President: Office and Power*, 4th ed. (New York: New York Univ. Press, 1957). Standard catalog of tasks, powers, and precedents.

Louis W. Koenig, *The Chief Executive* (New York: Harcourt, Brace & World, 1964). Focuses on the obstacles in the path of an activist President.

——, *The Invisible Presidency* (New York: Holt, 1960). Study of Presidential alter egos.

Richard E. Neustadt, *Presidential Power* (New York: Wiley, 1960). Remarkable study of the dilemmas of the modern President who is compelled to rule rather than simply reign.

Clinton Rossiter, *The American Presidency* (New York: Harcourt, Brace & World, 1956). Discussion of the various Presidential roles in a historical context.

THE PRESIDENT IN ACTION

John M. Blum, *The Republican Roosevelt* (Cambridge, Mass.: Harvard Univ. Press, 1954). Lively study of the Presidential style of Theodore Roosevelt.

———, *Woodrow Wilson and the Politics of Morality* (Boston: Little, Brown, 1956). A consideration of the collisions between ideal and political reality in the Presidency of Woodrow Wilson.

James M. Burns, *Roosevelt: The Lion and the Fox* (New York: Harcourt, Brace & World, 1956). A sensitive exploration of the F. D. R. technique of governing.

Robert J. Donovan, *Eisenhower: The Inside Story* (New York: Harper, 1956). Glimpses of the inner workings of the White House during the early Eisenhower years.

Emmet John Hughes, *The Ordeal of Power: A Political Memoir of the Eisenhower Years* (New York: Atheneum, 1963). Caustic reflections of a former Eisenhower aide.

Rexford G. Tugwell, *The Democratic Roosevelt* (New York: Doubleday, 1957). F. D. R. in action as seen by a close associate.

THE PRESIDENT AND HIS INSTITUTIONAL ENVIRONMENT

Wilfred E. Binkley, *President and Congress* (New York: Knopf, 1947). A useful history of the various conceptions of what the Presidency should be.

Lawrence H. Chamberlain, *The President, Congress and Legislation* (New York: Columbia Univ. Press, 1946). Surveys the sources of initiative and effective sponsorship of legislation.

Richard F. Fenno, Jr., *The President's Cabinet* (Cambridge, Mass.: Harvard Univ. Press, 1954). The standard study of the Cabinet.

Joseph P. Harris, *The Advice and Consent of the Senate* (Berkeley: Univ. of California Press, 1953). An account of the confirmation and rejection of Presidential appointments.

Clinton Rossiter, *The Supreme Court and the Commander in Chief* (Ithaca, N.Y.: Cornell Univ. Press, 1951). Details of the development of the dimension of the Presidency.

Glendon A. Schubert, Jr., *The Presidency in the Courts* (Minneapolis, Minn.: Univ. of Minnesota Press, 1957). Examines the ways in which the Chief Executive has used and been used by the judiciary.

THE LEGISLATIVE PROCESS

Stephen K. Bailey, *Congress Makes a Law* (New York: Columbia Univ. Press, 1950). Case study of the passage of the Employment Act of 1946. Excellent picture of interest group behavior.

George B. Galloway, *The Legislative Process in Congress* (New York: Crowell, 1953). Standard text.

Ernest Griffith, *Congress: Its Contemporary Role*, 3rd ed. (New York: New York Univ. Press, 1961). Analysis by a sympathetic observer with long experience.

Malcolm E. Jewell, ed., *The Politics of Reapportionment* (New York: Atherton Press, 1962). Essays on the issues involved in reapportionment.

Neil MacNeil, *Forge of Democracy: The House of Representatives* (New York: McKay, 1963). Readable and sympathetic discussion by a skilled journalist.

Donald R. Matthews, *U.S. Senators and Their World* (Chapel Hill, N.C.: Univ. of North Carolina Press, 1960). Study of the Senate and its folkways.

Lindsay Rogers, *The American Senate* (New York: Knopf, 1926). Still a useful introduction to the subject.

David B. Truman, *The Congressional Party* (New York: Wiley, 1959). An effort to determine, through analysis of roll call votes, the structure and leadership roles of the parties in Congress.

———, ed., *The Congress and America's Future* (Englewood Cliffs, N.J.: Prentice-Hall, 1965). Essays on Congressional reorganization prepared for the American Assembly.

Julius Turner, *Party and Constituency: Pressures on Congress* (Baltimore: Johns Hopkins Press, 1952). The impact of constituency pressure upon legislative behavior.

John C. Wahlke and Heinz Eulau, eds., *Legislative Behavior: A Reader in Theory and Research* (Glencoe, Ill.: Free Press, 1959). Varied studies of the legislative process.

Woodrow Wilson, *Congressional Government: A Study in American Politics* (Boston: Houghton Mifflin, 1885). Classic study of the power in the Congressional committee leadership in the late nineteenth century.

CONGRESSIONAL INVESTIGATIONS

Alan Barth, *Government by Investigation* (New York: Viking, 1955). A journalist's denunciation of investigations.

Robert K. Carr, *The House Committee on Un-American Activities* (Ithaca, N.Y.: Cornell Univ. Press, 1952). Details the checkered career of this panel up to 1950.

Telford Taylor, *Grand Inquest* (New York: Simon and Schuster, 1955). A literate and informed warning concerning excesses of investigative zeal and misuse of Congressional power.

THE BUREAUCRACY

Paul H. Appleby, *Big Democracy* (New York: Knopf, 1945). Reflections on giant bureaucracies as a permanent feature of post–Second World War American life.

Marver H. Bernstein, *The Job of the Federal Executive* (Washington: Brookings Institution, 1958). Describes the world of top-level administrators, and discusses the problem of recruiting talent for these posts.

Peter M. Blau, *Bureaucracy in Modern Society* (New York: Random House, 1956). Brief, general discussion of the problem of bureaucracy.

J. Leiper Freeman, *The Political Process: Executive Bureau–Legislative Committee Relations* (New York: Random House, 1955). Provocative analysis of a complex problem.

Emmette S. Redford, *Ideal and Practice in Public Administration* (University, Ala.: Univ. of Alabama Press, 1958). Considers the values and the environment of the administrator.

Herbert A. Simon, *Administrative Behavior,* 2nd ed. (New York: Macmillan, 1957). Classic analysis of the process of bureaucracy.

Aaron Wildavsky, *The Politics of the Budgetary Process* (Boston: Little, Brown, 1964). The budget is treated as the focus of struggles over policy.

Peter Woll, *American Bureaucracy* (New York: Norton, 1963). Attempts to describe the impact of bureaucratic growth on the constitutional dispersion of power.

Part IV. Liberty, Justice, and Law

LAW, SOCIETY, AND POLITICS IN THE UNITED STATES

Henry J. Abraham, *Courts and Judges* (New York: Oxford Univ. Press, 1959). An introduction to the functions of operations of the judicial process.

Fred V. Cahill, *Judicial Legislation* (New York: Ronald, 1952). The significance of the growth of administrative law in America.

Benjamin N. Cardozo, *The Nature of the Judicial Process* (New Haven, Conn.: Yale Univ. Press, 1921). Urges the centrality of social utility in the job of judging.

Jerome Frank, *Courts on Trial* (Princeton, N.J.: Princeton Univ. Press, 1950). Emphasizes that the judge's choice is inevitably between competing social values.

————, *Law and the Modern Mind* (New York: Brentano's, 1930). A plea for "realism" in legal thinking and an end to the myth that the legal process is a mechanized and value-neutral exercise.

Oliver Wendell Holmes, *The Common Law* (Boston: Little, Brown, 1881). Classic study of the growth of law in response to the needs of society.

Willard Hurst, *The Growth of American Law* (Boston: Little, Brown, 1950). Useful history.

Jack W. Peltason, *Federal Courts in the Political Process* (New York: Random House, 1955). Attention is directed to the power exercised by the lower federal courts.

Victor G. Rosenblum, *Law as a Political Instrument* (New York: Doubleday, 1955). Analysis of courts as policy makers.

Glendon A. Schubert, Jr., ed., *Judicial Behavior: A Reader in Theory and Research* (Chicago: Rand McNally, 1964). A collection of papers and studies presenting behavioral approaches to the study of what courts and judges do.

Benjamin R. Twiss, *Lawyers and the Constitution: How Laissez-Faire Came to the Supreme Court* (Princeton, N.J.: Princeton Univ. Press, 1942). A fascinating study of the way in which the bar of the Supreme Court helped shape the opinions of the courts in the field of business regulation during the latter decades of the nineteenth century.

Alan F. Westin, *The Anatomy of a Constitutional Law Case* (New York: Macmillan, 1958). The nature of constitutional adjudication is explored.

JUDICIAL REVIEW

Charles A. Beard, *The Supreme Court and the Constitution* (New York: Macmillan, 1912). Contends that a majority of the founding fathers favored some sort of judicial negative over acts of Congress.

Alexander M. Bickel, *The Least Dangerous Branch* (Indianapolis: Bobbs-Merrill, 1962). Critical study of the work of the Court over the past decade.

Charles L. Black, Jr., *The People and the Court* (New York: Macmillan, 1960). Suggests that the "payoff" (functionality) of judicial review should be a more central concern than the intentions of the Framers.

James E. Clayton, *The Making of Justice* (New York: Dutton, 1964). A case study of the work of the Court during a single term (1962–63).

Edward S. Corwin, *Constitutional Revolution, Ltd.* (Claremont, Calif.: Claremont Colleges, 1941). A leading scholar's reaction to the new approaches taken by the Court after 1937.

———, *Court Over Constitution* (Princeton, N.J.: Princeton Univ. Press, 1938). Contradiction of Beard's argument.

Charles P. Curtis, Jr., *Lions Under the Throne* (Boston: Houghton Mifflin, 1947). Essay on the proper role of the Supreme Court.

Felix Frankfurter and James M. Landis, *The Business of the Supreme Court* (New York: Macmillan, 1927). A minor classic on the development of the Court's jurisdiction and its control over its docket.

Paul A. Freund, *On Understanding the Supreme Court* (Boston: Little, Brown, 1949). An excellent guide to the Court's ways of working, with special reference to Constitution consideration.

Charles G. Haines, *The American Doctrine of Judicial Supremacy*, 2nd rev. ed. (New York: Russell & Russell, 1959). Survey of the Court's "formative period," and the development of the doctrine of judicial review.

Charles Evans Hughes, *The Supreme Court of the United States* (New York: Columbia Univ. Press, 1928). An insight by a distinguished lawyer who had already sat upon the Court as an Associate Justice, and was to return as its Chief.

Robert G. McCloskey, *The American Supreme Court* (Chicago: Univ. of Chicago Press, 1960). Excellent short history of the Court.

C. Herman Pritchett, *The Roosevelt Court: A Study in Judicial Politics and Values, 1937–1947* (New York: Macmillan, 1948). An effort to discover the patterns of alignment among the justices with regard to various issues coming before the Court.

Charles Warren, *The Supreme Court in United States History* (Boston: Little, Brown, 1922). Dated, but still the standard history of the Court's development.

ON THE JUSTICES

A. Dunham and P. B. Kurland, eds., *Mr. Justice* (Chicago: Univ. of Chicago Press, 1956). Brief studies of nine justices dealing with both their work on the Court and their pre-Court experience.

Among the biographies and studies of particular Justices are:

Albert J. Beveridge, *The Life of John Marshall* (Boston: Houghton Mifflin, 1916–19).

Alexander M. Bickel, ed., *The Unpublished Opinions of Mr. Justice Brandeis* (Cambridge, Mass.: Belknap Press of Harvard Univ. Press, 1957).

Charles Fairman, *Mr. Justice Miller and the Supreme Court* (Cambridge, Mass.: Harvard Univ. Press, 1939).

John P. Frank, *Mr. Justice Black: The Man and His Opinions* (New York: Knopf, 1949).

Samuel Hendel, *Charles Evans Hughes and the Supreme Court* (New York: King's Crown Press of Columbia Univ. Press, 1951).

W. Melville Jones, ed., *Chief Justice John Marshall* (Ithaca, N.Y.: Cornell Univ. Press, 1956).

Willard L. King, *Melville Weston Fuller* (New York: Macmillan, 1950).

Samuel J. Konefsky, *Chief Justice Stone and the Supreme Court* (New York: Macmillan, 1945).

Max Lerner, ed., *The Mind and Faith of Justice Holmes* (Boston: Little, Brown, 1943).

Alpheus T. Mason, *Brandeis: A Free Man's Life* (New York: Viking, 1946).

———, *Harlan Fiske Stone: Pillar of the Law* (New York: Viking, 1956).

Joseph E. McLean, *William Rufus Day* (Baltimore: Johns Hopkins Press, 1946).

Donald G. Morgan, *Justice William Johnson, The First Dissenter* (Columbia, S.C.: Univ. of South Carolina Press, 1954).

Joel F. Paschal, *Mr. Justice Sutherland: A Man Against the State* (Princeton, N.J.: Princeton Univ. Press, 1951).

Henry F. Pringle, *The Life and Times of William Howard Taft* (New York: Farrar & Rinehart, 1939).

Merlo J. Pusey, *Charles Evans Hughes* (New York: Macmillan, 1951).

Carl B. Swisher, *Roger B. Taney* (New York: Macmillan, 1935).

——, *Stephen J. Field* (Washington: Brookings Institution, 1930).

CIVIL LIBERTIES

Ralph S. Brown, Jr., *Loyalty and Security* (New Haven, Conn.: Yale Univ. Press, 1958). The problem of ensuring that the interests of the government are protected while affording maximum "due process" to the individual employee.

Zechariah Chafee, Jr., *Free Speech in the United States* (Cambridge, Mass.: Harvard Univ. Press, 1941). A widely read history.

Robert E. Cushman, ed., *Safeguarding Civil Liberty Today* (Ithaca, N.Y.: Cornell Univ. Press, 1945). An effort to sketch the post–Second World War problems.

Osmond K. Fraenkel, *Our Civil Liberties* (New York: Viking, 1944). A survey.

Morton Grodzins, *The Loyal and the Disloyal* (Chicago: Univ. of Chicago Press, 1956). What sorts of people, sociologically and psychologically, commit disloyal acts.

John Stuart Mill, *On Liberty* (New York: Appleton-Century-Crofts, 1947). Originally published in 1851. Classic statement of the libertarian position on freedom of speech.

Leo Pfeffer, *Church, State, and Freedom* (Boston: Beacon, 1953). Written from a strict separationist viewpoint, this work details the areas of contention as they exist today.

Edward A. Shils, *The Torment of Secrecy* (Glencoe, Ill.: Free Press, 1956). The social-psychological costs of closed politics.

Samuel A. Stouffer, *Communism, Conformity, and Civil Liberties* (Boston: Heath, 1952). Seeks to determine, among other things, which groups within the community react to anticommunist excesses.

CIVIL RIGHTS

Harry S. Ashmore, *The Negro and the Schools* (Chapel Hill, N.C.: Univ. of North Carolina Press, 1954). Survey of segregated educational systems.

A. P. Blaustein and C. C. Ferguson, Jr., *Desegregation and the Law* (New Brunswick, N.J.: Rutgers Univ. Press, 1957). A useful introduction to the legal dimension of the civil rights revolution up to 1956.

Gunnar Myrdal, *An American Dilemma* (New York: Harper, 1944). Landmark study which became a potent weapon in the civil rights struggle.

Alan F. Westin, ed., *Freedom Now!* (New York: Basic Books, 1964). A collection of essays and articles treating various aspects of the civil rights struggle. Particular attention is paid to the debate over the means by which Negroes should seek to advance their cause.

Part V. Government in Action

GOVERNMENT AND THE ECONOMY

A. A. Berle, Jr., *Power Without Property* (New York: Harcourt, Brace & World, 1959). A widely read revisionist description of power distribution in the corporate world.

Marver H. Bernstein, *Regulating Business by Independent Commission* (Princeton, N.J.: Princeton Univ. Press, 1955). Reasoned analysis of the problems and prospects of these instruments.

Edward S. Corwin, *The Commerce Power versus States Rights* (Princeton, N.J.: Princeton Univ. Press, 1936). The constitutional aspects of federal regulation.

Robert A. Dahl and Charles E. Lindblom, *Politics, Economics, and Welfare* (New York: Harper, 1953). The American "style" in decision-making and value allocation.

Marshall E. Dimock, *The New American Political Economy* (New York: Harper, 1962). Survey of policy needs for a changed economy.

Merle Fainsod, Lincoln Gordon, and Joseph C. Palamountain, Jr., *Government and the*

American Economy (New York: Norton, 1959). An excellent text.

John K. Galbraith, *American Capitalism,* rev. ed. (Boston: Houghton Mifflin, 1956). An essay on the interaction of government, business, and labor.

Charles M. Hardin, *The Politics of Agriculture* (Glencoe, Ill.: Free Press, 1952). The Byzantine involvements of groups, parties, and governmental agencies with regard to the problem of soil conservation.

Industrial Relations Research Association, *Emergency Disputes and National Policy* (New York: Harper, 1955). Review of experience and of alternative policies in settlement of labor disputes.

James M. Landis, *The Administrative Process* (New Haven, Conn.: Yale Univ. Press, 1938). An enthusiastic account by a talented participant of the possibilities of administrative regulation of economic activity.

Earl Latham, *The Group Basis of Politics: A Study in Basing-Point Legislation* (Ithaca, N.Y.: Cornell Univ. Press, 1952). Impact of group pressures on Congress' consideration of legislation.

W. Arthur Lewis, *The Principles of Economic Planning* (London: Dennis Dobson and Allen and Unwin, 1949). A useful introduction.

Michael D. Reagan, *The Managed Economy* (New York: Oxford Univ. Press, 1963). Analysis of the challenge to democratic government in the development of corporate power.

Emmette S. Redford, *Administration of National Economic Control* (New York: Macmillan, 1952). Details the difficulties and possibilities of ministering to an unplanned economy.

———, *American Government and the Economy* (New York: Macmillan, 1965). A new, comprehensive text.

SCIENCE, TECHNOLOGY, AND NATURAL RESOURCES

James P. Baxter, *Scientists Against Time* (Boston: Little, Brown, 1946). Basic account of scientists' activities in the Second World War.

J. Stephan Dupre and Sanford A. Lakoff, *Science and the Nation: Policy and Politics* (Englewood Cliffs, N.J.: Prentice-Hall, 1962). An excellent overview of the emergence of science in government.

Philip O. Foss, *Politics and Grass: The Administration of Grazing on the Public Domain* (Seattle: Univ. of Washington Press, 1960). Recent analysis of land politics on the range.

Robert Gilpin, *American Scientists and Nuclear Weapons Policy* (Princeton, N.J.: Princeton Univ. Press, 1962). Excellent account of scientists' participation in high level policy-making.

——— and Christopher Wright, eds., *Scientists and National Policy-Making* (New York: Columbia Univ. Press, 1964). Collected analyses of political and policy roles of scientists and engineers.

Eli Ginzberg, ed., *Technology and Social Change* (New York: Columbia Univ. Press, 1964). Papers prepared by experts in a Columbia University Seminar.

Morton Grodzins and Eugene Rabinowitch, *The Atomic Age: Scientists in National and World Affairs* (New York: Basic Books, 1963). Scientists' views on major policy issues.

Herbert Kaufman, *The Forest Ranger: A Study in Administrative Behavior* (Baltimore, Johns Hopkins Press, 1960). Excellent analysis of public organization behavior under political pressure.

Arthur Maass, *Muddy Waters* (Cambridge, Mass.: Harvard Univ. Press, 1951). Study of interest group involvement in reclamation work.

Roscoe C. Martin, *River Basin Administration and the Delaware* (Syracuse, N.Y.: Syracuse Univ. Press, 1960). Study of interest group involvement and government in resource development.

Gifford Pinchot, *Breaking New Ground* (New York: Harcourt, Brace & World, 1947). Recollections of the patriarch of conservation.

President's Material Policy Commission, *Report* (Washington: United States Govt. Printing Office, 1952). The comprehensive, five-volume, mid-century study of United States natural resources.

Don K. Price, *Government and Science* (New York: New York Univ. Press, 1954). Authoritative survey of the growing involvement of the federal government in scientific research.

Philip Selznick, *TVA and the Grass Roots* (Berkeley: Univ. of California Press, 1949). A sociologist's assessment of the impact of TVA.

Charles P. Snow, *Science and Government* (Cambridge, Mass.: Harvard Univ. Press, 1961). Provocative treatise on political power and participation of national scientists.

Morgan Thomas and R. M. Northrup, *Atomic Energy and Congress* (Ann Arbor, Mich.: Univ. of Michigan Press, 1956). Treats the work of the Joint Committee on Atomic Energy.

Norman Wengert, *Natural Resources and the Political Struggle* (New York: Random House, 1955). Surveys the battles fought for conservation up to the early fifties.

GOVERNMENT AND WELFARE

Oscar E. Anderson, Jr., *The Health of a Nation: Harvey W. Wiley and the Fight for Pure Food* (Chicago: Univ. of Chicago Press, 1958). Study of the difficulties attendant upon performance in this most basic area.

E. M. Burns, *Social Security in Public Policy* (New York: McGraw-Hill, 1956). A general survey of performance and problems.

John J. Carson and John W. McConnell, *Economic Needs of Older People* (New York: Twentieth Century Fund, 1956). Useful survey, which is of particular reference to the Medicare debates of the early 1960s.

Michael Harrington, *The Other America* (New York: Macmillan, 1962). An attempt to dramatize the problem of poverty and create a climate conducive to greater governmental activity in this field.

Seymour Harris, *How Shall We Pay for Education?* (New York: Harper, 1948). A sketch and forecast of the problem which is now upon us.

Herman M. and Anne R. Somers, *Workmen's Compensation* (New York: Wiley, 1954). Penetrating analysis of experience with the nation's oldest social insurance legislation.

GOVERNMENT AND MONEY

Charles C. Abbott, *The Federal Debt* (New York: Twentieth Century Fund, 1953). A solid study of this little understood subject.

Jesse Burkhead, *Government Budgeting* (New York: Wiley, 1956). Thorough analysis of all aspects of budgeting.

Alvin H. Hansen, *Fiscal Policy and Business Cycles* (New York: Norton, 1941). The counter-cyclical checks which can be constructed by government taxing and spending.

Robert L. Heilbroner and Peter L. Bernstein, *A Primer on Government Spending* (New York: Vintage, 1963). A neatly written effort to part the clouds of myth and superstition that shadow much discussion of government borrowing and spending.

Harvey C. Mansfield, *The Comptroller General* (New Haven, Conn.: Yale Univ. Press, 1939). Standard analysis of financial control and accountability in the national government.

Frederick C. Mosher, *Program Budgeting* (Chicago: Public Administration Service, 1954). Analysis of theory and practice with particular reference to the United States Department of the Army.

Henry Simons, *Federal Tax Reform* (Chicago: Univ. of Chicago Press, 1950). A text.

Paul J. Strayer, *Fiscal Policy and Politics* (New York: Harper, 1958). An introduction and discussion of options.

Aaron Wildavsky, *The Politics of the Budgetary Process* (Boston: Little, Brown, 1964). Lively and imaginative discussion of the budget process.

FOREIGN POLICY AND DEFENSE

Gabriel A. Almond, *The American People and Foreign Policy* (New York: Harcourt, Brace & World, 1956). A valuable study of the domestic politics of foreign policy.

Paul Y. Hammond, *Organizing for Defense* (Princeton, N.J.: Princeton Univ. Press, 1961). An anatomy of the military establishment.

Roger Hilsman, *Strategic Intelligence and National Decisions* (Glencoe, Ill.: Free Press, 1956). Points up the importance of hard intelligence (and efficient intelligence gathering agencies) to the policy-making process.

Samuel P. Huntington, *The Common Defense* (New York: Columbia Univ. Press, 1961). Valuable survey of defense policy since the Second World War.

———, *The Soldier and the State* (Cambridge, Mass.: Harvard Univ. Press, 1957). Assessment of the character and strengths of the American officer corps, and an attempt to specify the proper relationship between civil authority and the military establishment.

George Kennan, *American Diplomacy 1900–1950* (Chicago: Univ. of Chicago Press, 1951). A minor classic by an exceptionally able scholar-diplomat.

Henry A. Kissinger, *Nuclear Weapons and Foreign Policy* (Garden City, N.Y.: Doubleday, 1957). An influential suggestion of alterations in our thinking about foreign policy necessitated by the new weapons technology.

C. O Lerche, Jr., *Foreign Policy of the American People,* 2nd ed. (Englewood Cliffs, N.J.: Prentice-Hall, 1961). A useful text.

Dexter Perkins, *Foreign Policy and the American Spirit* (Ithaca, N.Y.: Cornell Univ. Press, 1957). The ideological matrix of American foreign policy.

B. M. Sapin and R. C. Snyder, *The Role of the Military in American Foreign Policy* (Garden City, N.Y.: Doubleday, 1954). A brief but useful introduction to the changed (post–Second World War) role of the American military.

H. Bradford Westerfield, *The Instruments of America's Foreign Policy* (New York: Crowell, 1963). A survey of how the foreign policies of postwar America have evolved.

Part VI. The States and Communities

THE STATES

The books listed below are studies of general significance in the field and are intended to serve as introductory material. For each state and most major cities, specific bibliographies can be found, and the student should explore these for his own area.

American Assembly, *The Forty-eight States: Their Tasks as Policy-Makers and Administrators* (New York: Columbia Univ. Press, 1955). Excellent collection of papers covering state politics and government as of 1955.

Stephen K. Bailey, *et al., Schoolmen and Politics: A Study of State Aid to Education in the Northeast* (Syracuse, N.Y.: Syracuse Univ. Press, 1962). One of a twelve-volume series exploring the economics and politics of modern public educators.

Malcolm E. Jewell, *The State Legislature* (New York: Random House, 1962). A comprehensive treatment of modern American legislatures.

V. O. Key, Jr., *American State Politics: An Introduction* (New York: Knopf, 1956). Classic study of interaction of party and election procedures in our states.

Duane Lockard, *New England State Politics* (Princeton, N.J.: Princeton Univ. Press, 1959). An interesting comparative account of variations in state politics within an American region.

Davis McEntire, *Residence and Race* (Berkeley: Univ. of California Press, 1960). Authoritative final report to the Commission on Race and Housing on minority migration trends and problems.

Coleman B. Ransone, Jr., *The Office of Governor in the United States* (University, Ala.: Univ. of Alabama Press, 1956). Authoritative study of governors.

John C. Wahlke and others, *The Legislative System* (New York: Wiley, 1962). A comparative study of state legislators and their roles.

THE COMMUNITIES

Edward C. Banfield, *Political Influence* (Glencoe, Ill.: Free Press, 1961). An examination of the relative importance of various participants in selected cases of political struggle drawn from the Chicago experience.

——— and Morton Grodzins, *Government and Housing in Metropolitan Areas* (New York: McGraw-Hill, 1958). Useful study of local government capabilities in changing urban environment.

——— and James Q. Wilson, *City Politics* (Cambridge, Mass.: Harvard Univ. Press, 1963). Reappraisal of the functionality of the city political machine.

Robert H. Connery and Richard H. Leach, *The Federal Government and Metropolitan Areas* (Cambridge, Mass.: Harvard Univ. Press, 1960). Seeks to answer the question of how the federal government can best aid cities in meeting their responsibilities.

Robert A. Dahl, *Who Governs? Democracy and Power in an American City* (New Haven, Conn.: Yale Univ. Press, 1961). A study of how and by whom power is wielded in a test city, in this case, New Haven.

The Editors of Fortune, *Exploding Metropolis* (Garden City, N.Y.: Doubleday, 1958). A widely read collection of essays on urban areas.

Gladys Kammerer *et al., The Urban Political Community: Profiles in Town Politics* (Boston: Houghton Mifflin, 1963). One of the first comparative studies of local politics focused on city-manager governments.

William Riordon, *Plunkitt of Tammany Hall* (New York: Knopf, 1948). A lively picture of how the old-style city boss conducted business.

Wallace S. Sayre and Herbert Kaufman, *Governing New York City* (New York: Russell Sage Foundation, 1960). Informed and balanced overview.

Robert C. Wood, *Suburbia: Its People and Their Politics* (Boston: Houghton Mifflin, 1958). The escape from urbanism to a politics of nostalgia.

———— and Vladimir Almendinger, *1400 Governments* (Cambridge, Mass.: Harvard Univ. Press, 1960). The problem of fragmented authority in the metropolitan region.

INTERGOVERNMENTAL RELATIONS

Robert E. Agger, Daniel Goldrich, and Bert E. Swanson, *The Rulers and the Ruled* (New York: Wiley, 1964). Recent major comparative study of community power and decision-making.

Jean Gottman, *Megalopolis: The Urbanized Northeastern Seaboard* (New York: Twentieth Century Fund, 1961). A famous French geographer traces the evolution of America's first "linear city."

Scott Greer, *Governing the Metropolis* (New York: Wiley, 1962). Comprehensive treatment of the character and development of the modern urban community.

————, *Metropolitics: A Study of Political Culture* (New York: Wiley, 1963). Exploration of why metropolitan governmental reforms fail.

Edgar M. Hoover, Jr., and Raymond Vernon, *The Anatomy of a Metropolis* (Cambridge, Mass.: Harvard Univ. Press, 1960). The first of the nine-volume analysis by the New York Metropolitan Region Study of the economics and politics of our largest metropolitan area.

Floyd Hunter, *Community Power Structure* (Chapel Hill, N.C.: Univ. of North Carolina Press, 1953). Major analysis of city politics as elite-dominated, in contrast to the pluralistic interpretation of Dahl.

Lane W. Lancaster, *Government in Rural America*, 2nd ed. (New York: Van Nostrand, 1952). Classic treatment of this topic.

Roscoe C. Martin, *Metropolis in Transition* (Washington: Housing and Home Finance Agency, 1963). An analysis, based on selected case experience, of changes in response to new urban communities.

————, Frank J. Munger, and others, *Decisions in Syracuse* (Bloomington, Ind.: Indiana Univ. Press, 1961). Analysis of political patterns in a medium-sized American city.

Martin Meyerson and Edward C. Banfield, *Politics, Planning, and the Public Interest* (Glencoe, Ill.: Free Press, 1955). Detailed examination of political aspects of urban planning and redevelopment.

Lewis Mumford, *The City in History: Its Origins, Its Transformations, and Its Prospects* (New York: Harcourt, Brace & World, 1961). A major utopian analysis of the past and future of urban civilization.

Municipal Manpower Commission, *Governmental Manpower for Tomorrow's Cities* (New York: McGraw-Hill, 1963). Recent survey of municipal personnel needs and problems.

Charles Press, *Main Street Politics* (East Lansing, Mich.: Michigan State Univ. Press, 1962). An excellent guide to important articles and monographs on the nature of community politics.

Peter A. Rossi and Robert A. Dentler, *The Politics of Urban Renewal* (New York: Macmillan, 1962). Systematic account of decision-making for a renewal project.

Arthur J. Vidich and Joseph Bensman, *Small Town in Mass Society: Class, Power, and Religion in a Rural Community* (Princeton, N.J.: Princeton Univ. Press, 1958). Examination of the problems of rural life in modern circumstances.

James Q. Wilson, *Negro Politics: The Search for Leadership* (Glencoe, Ill.: Free Press, 1960). An excellent analysis of Negro politics in Chicago.

Index

Appeals, U.S. Court of, 413–94: judges of, 542–43
appellate courts, 489–90, 491
appointments: of judges, 530–32, 541, 545–46; Presidential, 295–97, 345, 531–32, 541; Senate approval of, 359–62
apportionment: of expenditures, 755; of Representatives, 381–84 (*see also* reapportionment)
Appropriations Committee: House, 406, 407, 408, 447, 751–54; Senate, 403, 408, 447, 751–54
armed forces (*see* Department of Defense; military services)
Arnow, Kathryn, 734*n.*
Aron, Raymond, 771
arraignment, and due process, 593–94
Articles of Confederation, 80–83, 605–06
Ashcraft v. *Tennessee*, 322 U.S. 143 (1942), 593*n.*
Asia, developments in, 775, 786
Associated Press v. *United States*, 326 U.S. 1 (1945), 568*n.*
associations, 51–54, 207–08: civil rights work of, 625–26 (*see also* groups; interest groups)
atomic energy, 678
Atomic Energy Commission, 339, 340, 651, 828–29: science research, 688, 692
atomic weapons (*see* nuclear weapons)
attitudes, political, 58–64
Attorney General, 432, 437, 547–50, 574
automatic incorporation, 476–78
automation, 31, 33
aviation, regulation of, 219–20, 652, 675–77

Bailey v. *Drexel Furniture Co.*, 259 U.S. 20 (1922), 719*n.*
Bailey v. *Patterson*, 369 U.S. 31 (1962), 623*n.*
Bailey v. *Richardson*, 341 U.S. 918 (1951), 580*n.*
Baker, Robert G., 364
Baker v. *Carr*, 369 U.S. 186 (1962), 382–84, 486*n.*, 487*n.*, 499*n.*, 714, 868, 956
balanced ticket, 53
ballot form, 201–03
Banfield, Edward C., 897*n.*, 901
Bank of the United States, 110, 116–17, 141, 146
banking, regulation of, 677 (*see also* Federal Reserve System)
Barber, James D., 875
Barden–La Follette Act of 1943, 718
Barenblatt v. *United States*, 360 U.S. 109 (1959), 582*n.*
Barkley, Alben, 331
Barron v. *Baltimore*, 7 Pet. 243 (1833), 475*n.*

Barsby v. *United States*, 334 U.S. 843 (1948), 580*n.*
Baruch, Bernard, 348
Bauer v. *Acheson*, 106 F. Supp. 445 (1952), 599*n.*
Baumgartner v. *United States*, 322 U.S. 665 (1944), 579*n.*
Baxter, J. P., III, 688*n.*
Baxter, Leone, 222*n.*
Beard, Charles A., 40, 75*n.*, 90, 501
Beard, Mary, 75*n.*
Beauharnais v. *Illinois*, 343 U.S. 250 (1952), 571
Beilan v. *Board of Education*, 357 U.S. 399 (1958), 582*n.*
Bell, David E., 327, 805
benign quota, 637
Bensman, Joseph, 922
Benson, Lee, 154*n.*
Berea College v. *Kentucky*, 211 U.S. 45 (1908), 612
Berelson, Bernard, 256*n.*, 714*n.*
Berlin, occupation of, 780, 823–24
Betts v. *Brady*, 316 U.S. 455 (1942), 595*n.*
Beveridge, Albert J., 82*n.*
Bill of Rights, 92, 97, 104, 475–77, 587
bills, procedures for, 393, 411–20
bills of attainder, 563
bills of rights, state, 77, 605
Bingham, Jonathan, 178
Binkley, Wilfred E., 152*n.*
Black, Hugo, 104–05, 468, 477, 508, 517, 537, 558, 564
Blackstone, Sir William, 68–69
Blaine, James G., 389
Bloomberg, Warner, Jr., 919*n.*
boards of education, 852–53
Bok, Curtis, 884
Bolling v. *Sharpe*, 347 U.S. 497 (1954), 619*n.*
Bone, Hugh A., 198*n.*
Boorstin, Daniel, 65*n.*, 76
boss, political, 173–77, 895–97, 899
Bosworth, Karl A., 874*n.*
Boudin v. *Dulles*, 136 F. Supp. 218 (1955), 599*n.*
Boykin, Joseph, 533*n.*, 534*n.*
Bradley, Joseph P., 538, 611
Brandeis, Louis D., 519, 536, 537, 579, 647, 668
Breard v. *Alexandria*, 341 U.S. 623 (1951), 582*n.*
Brennan, William J., Jr., 509, 517, 536
Bricker Amendment, 124, 817
Bridenbaugh, Carl, 840*n.*, 936*n.*
Brinegar v. *United States*, 338 U.S. 160 (1949), 592*n.*
British government, 66–69, **67**
Brown, Edmund A., 266

Brown, J. A. C., 230n.

Brown, Robert E., 79n., 90n.

Brown v. *Allen*, 344 U.S. 443 (1953), 596n.

Brown v. *Board of Education:* 347 U.S. 483 (1954), 221, 619; 349 U.S. 294 (1955), 620n.

Brown Shoe Co., Inc. v. *U.S.*, 370 U.S. 294 (1962), 499n.

Brownell, Herbert, 550

Bryan, William Jennings, 158–63, 276, 335, 523–24

Bryce, James, 863

Buchanan, James, 308

Buchanan, William, 875n.

budget, 742–56: defense, **811**; federal, 29, 30, 743, 748–56, 758; municipal, 743, 747; preparation of, 325–26, 745–54; state, 747; tax cuts and, 662, 744–45

Bull Moose Movement, 506

Bullitt, Stimson, 282n.

Bundy, McGeorge, 799–800, 824

Burdick, Eugene, 785n.

bureau, characteristics of, 433–35

Bureau of: Animal Industry, 433; Family Service, 727; Land Management, 698, 699, 700; Outdoor Recreation, 698; Public Assistance, 728; Reclamation, 436–37, 703–04; the Budget, 323, 325–28, 438–39, 743, 749–50, 752, 755, 816, 826

bureaucracies: federal, 423–52; interest groups and, 218–20, 434–35; intergovernmental, 925–30; operation of, 430–50; reorganization of, 437–39; state, 843, 877, 880–81, 885; urban, 898

Burke, Edmund, 375–76

Burkhead, Jesse, 743n., 748n., 848n.

Burns, Arthur F., 328

Burr, Aaron, 98, 143, 144–45

Burstyn v. *Wilson*, 343 U.S. 495 (1952), 569n.

Burton v. *Wilmington Parking Authority*, 365 U.S. 715 (1961), 623n.

Bush v. *Orleans Parish School Board*, 308 F. 2d 491 (5th Cir. 1962), 622n.

business (*see* capitalism; commerce)

Butler, Paul, 190

Byrd, Harry, 285, 411, 662, 745, 869

Byrnes, James F., 813

Cabinet, 334–48: activities of, March 8–15, 1889, 7–8; bureaus and, 435–37; departments of, 107, 431–33 (*see also* specific departments)

Cafeteria Workers v. *McElroy*, 376 U.S. 886 (1961), 445n.

Calendar Wednesday, 414

calendars, 383, 414–15

Calhoun, John C., 146, 155

California: government in, 953; politics in, 179; selection of judges in, 545–46

Campaign Committees, Congress, 391, 399

campaigns: expenses of, **183**, 191–96; Presidential, 264–65, 268–71, 278–83

Campbell, Alan, 833

Campbell, Angus, 167, 202n., 246n., 247n., 254n., 261n., 280n.

Cannon, Clarence, 355

Cannon, Joseph G., 390, 392

Cantwell v. *Connecticut*, 310 U.S. 296 (1940), 565n.

capitalism, 47, 54, 644: federalism and, 120; Supreme Court and, 121, 511–13, 518

Cardozo, Benjamin N., 538, 544, 563

Carlson v. *Landon*, 342 U.S. 524 (1952), 598n.

Carper, Edith T., 754n.

caucus, Congressional, 154–55

caucus chairmen, 391, 399

Celler, Emanuel, 353

censorship, 568–72

Central Intelligence Agency, 323, 798, 814–16

Chambers, William N., 142n., 161n.

Chandler, "Happy," 869, 882

Chaplinsky v. *New Hampshire*, 315 U.S. 568 (1942), 564n., 565n.

character, national, 43–44, 62–64

Charles River Bridge case, 648

charters, of colonies, 70

Chase, Samuel, 533

checks and balances, 67, 70, 352, 861

Chiari, Roberto, 821–22

child labor legislation, 718–19

Children's Bureau, 736

China, Communist, 792

Churchill, Winston, 776, 796

circuit court (*see* Court of Appeals)

cities (*see* metropolitan areas; urban government)

citizenship, 606: by naturalization, 574–75, 584

city-manager system, 839, 893–95, 898–99, 909, 914–15

Civil Aeronautics Act of 1938, 675

Civil Aeronautics Agency, 219

Civil Aeronautics Board, 219, 339, 652, 676–77

civil cases, 488–89, 493

civil law, 457

civil liberties, 10–11, 25–27, 56–57: due process and, 586–601; right of, 552–54, 562–86; Supreme Court decisions on, 475–78, 506, 514–15, 518

civil rights, 10–11, 25–27, 56–57, 92, 474, 602–40: demonstrations for, 627, 631–33, 639; as platform issue, 273; President's Committee on, 618; Supreme Court decisions on, 506, 514–15, 518–19, 611, 613 (see also Bill of Rights; civil liberties)

Civil Rights Act: of 1957, 623–24; of 1960, 624; of 1964, 417, 634–36

Civil Rights Cases, 109 U.S. 3 (1883), 611, 613

Civil Rights Commission, 623–24, 631, 634

civil rights organizations, 213, 221–22, 639

civil service, federal, 295: recruitment into, 439–48; tenure in, 447–48

Civil Service Commission, 341, 440–41

Civil War, 309–10: constitutional amendments after, 98, 475, 609; federalism and, 119; political parties and, 156–57; science research and, 687

Claims, Court of, 494

Clark, John D., 329

Clark, Mark, 585

Clark, Tom, 508, 539

Classification Act of 1949, 448

Clay, Henry, 146–48, 150–52, 521

Clay, Lucius, 823

Clayton Act, 664–66

"clear and present danger" test, 567, 579–80

Clement, Frank G., 273

Cleveland, Grover, 157–58, 283, 532

Clinton, George, 91, 143

closed shop, 671

cloture, 417

Coke, Sir Edward, 66, 68

Cold War, 659, 776–81, 786, 791–94, 796, 819, 823–25, 827

Cole v. *Young,* 351 U.S. 536 (1956), 445n., 581n.

Colegrove v. *Green,* 328 U.S. 549 (1946), 383n., 487n.

Colgate Palmolive Co. v. *FTC,* 310 F. 2d. 89 (1962), 461n.

collective bargaining (see labor-management relations)

colleges, state, 687–88, 699

Collins, LeRoy, 878

colonial period, 69–71

Commager, Henry S., 74n.

commerce: Constitutional provisions for, 503–04, 643; interstate, 104; regulation of, 342–45, 645–46 (see also economy)

commissions: municipal, 894; Presidential *ad hoc,* 347 (see also executive agencies; regulatory agencies)

Committee: Finance, 403; Joint Economic, 660–61; on Aeronautical and Space Sciences, 403; on Committees (House), 391; on Committees (Senate), 399; on Equal Employment Opportuni-

ties, 624–25; on Foreign Relations, 359, 403; Rules (House), 389, 392–95, 399, 406, 414; Un-American Activities, 366–67, 575, 581–82; Ways and Means (House), 406, 408

Committee of the Whole, 390, 418

committees, Congressional, 391–95, 399–408: appointment of, 390, 397, 400; ranking of, 405–08; standing, 403–05, 413

committees, state legislative, 874

Commodity Credit Corporation, 678

common law, 68–69, 456

Common Market, 789

Communism, expansion of, 774–82, 792 (see also subversive activities)

Communist Control Act of 1954, 574, 578

Communist party, 574–82

Communist Party v. *Subversive Activities Control Board,* 367 U.S. 1 (1961), 582n., 599n.

compacts, interstate, 128, 931–32, 948

compensation programs, 638

Compton, Karl T., 348

Comptroller General, 325, 755–56

Conant, James B., 348

concurrent resolution, 298, 326, 412, 438

conference chairmen: of House, 391; of Senate, 399

conference committees, 419–20

Congress: activities of, March 8–15, 1889, 6–7; activities of, March 8–15, 1964, 16–19; Cabinet and, 337; civil service recruitment and, 443–44; constitutional amendments and, 96, 100–01; constitutional provision for, 86, 114, 291–92; debates in, 394, 415–18; defense and foreign policies and, 816–18, 829; economic legislation of, 659–60, 663–66; executive agencies and, 339, 362–63, 434, 442, 452, 655–58, 701, 702–05, 751; investigative functions of, 363–68; legislative procedure in, 411–22; military functions of, 306; monetary activities of, 750–54; power structure of, 386–410; President and, 298–300, 349–50, 352–62, 385; staff for, 408–09; Supreme Court and, 482, 495, 496–97, 510, 517–19; welfare legislation of, 720–21

Congress of Racial Equality, 213, 632, 639

Congressional Court of Appeal, 517–18

Congressmen, 369–80

Connecticut, constitution of, 78

consent, popular: in Declaration of Independence, 75; in political system, 42

Consent Calendar, 393, 414–15

conservation, 686, 697–700

conservatives: Supreme Court and, 515–17; voting behavior of, 260

Constitution, United States, 41, 82–93:

equal protection clause, of Constitution, 504

equality: in American society, 45, 604; in Declaration of Independence, 74–75; rights of, 561–62, 602–40

equity, law of, 456–57

espionage, 814

ethnic background, voting behavior and, 254–57 (*see also* immigrants; Negroes)

Eulau, Heinz, 875*n*.

Europe, relations with, 767–68 (*see also* foreign affairs)

Everson v. *Board of Education*, 330 U.S. 1 (1947), 585*n*.

Ewing, Cortez A. M., 543*n*.

Ex parte McCardle, 7 Wall. 506 (1869), 496*n*.

Ex parte Quirin, 317 U.S. 1 (1942), 579*n*.

executive agencies, 339–42: procedures of, 651–54, 658; state, 885–87 (*see also* bureaucracies; Congress, executive agencies and; regulatory agencies)

executive agreements, 302–03

executive branch: activities of, March 8–15, 1964, 19–21; Presidency and, 294–97; state, 877, 880–81

Executive Office, 323–31, 346, 350, 692, 812–16

executive privilege, 365

expenditures: federal, 739–42, **740, 741,** 754–56, 833; local, **740, 742;** state, 739–42, **740, 741,** 833 (*see also* budget)

experts, administrative (*see* specialists)

Export-Import Bank, 678

expression, freedom of, 556, 563–86

Fabricant, Solomon, 939*n*.

factions, 138, 205: intraparty, 146, 872

Fainsod, Merle, 344*n*.

Fair Employment Board, 618

Fair Employment Practices Commission, 618–19, 634

fair hearing, 598

Fair Labor Standards Act of 1938, 719–20

fair procedure, 587 (*see also* due process)

family: influence of, in voting, 247, 258; law and, 461–62; mobility and, 48; public welfare and, 709–10, 714, 727–28

Farley, James A., 187

farms and farmers (*see* agriculture; rural population)

Farrand, Max, 83

fascists (*see* rightists)

Faubus, Orval, 621

Fay v. *New York*, 332 U.S. 261 (1947), 596*n*.

Federal Aviation Act of 1958, 675

Federal Aviation Agency, 31, 219–20, 438, 651, 675–76

Federal Bureau of Investigation, 427, 432, 437, 439, 442, 548, 549, 574

Federal Communications Commission, 339, 368, 654–55, 677

federal courts (*see* courts, federal; Supreme Court)

Federal Deposit Insurance Corporation, 127, 677

Federal Employers' Liability Act of 1908, 677

Federal Highway Act of 1956, 905

Federal Home Loan Bank, 732

Federal Housing Administration, 614, 619, 629, 677, 732

Federal Mediation and Conciliation Service, 672

Federal National Mortgage Association, 732

Federal Power Commission, 339, 343–44, 655–58

Federal Power Commission v. *Hope Natural Gas Co.*, 320 U.S. 591 (1944), 658*n*.

Federal Reserve Act, 121

Federal Reserve System, 127, 661, 677: Board of Governors of, 339, 343–45, 653, 661–62

Federal Savings and Loan Corporation, 732

Federal Security Agency, 438

Federal Service Entrance Examination, 443

Federal-State Action Committee, 129

federal-state-local interdependence, 127, 728, 925–30, 935, 947, 955–58

Federal Trade Commission, 339, 342, 460–61, 652–53, 735

Federal Trade Commission Act, 664–65, 735

federalism, 93, 863–64, 955: changes and constants in, 113–30, **126;** state systems and, 840–42

Federalist, The, 92, 643

Federalist party, 111, 137, 141–47, 152

Feiner v. *New York*, 340 U.S. 315 (1951), 566

Fenno, Richard F., Jr., 338, 751*n*., 752*n*.

Ferguson, LeRoy C., 875*n*.

Field, Stephen, 534, 537

Field v. *Clark*, 143 U.S. 649 (1892), 428*n*.

Fifteenth Amendment, 98, 112, 233, 475, 609, 611

Fifth Amendment, 367, 555, 556, 559, 647 (*see also* due process of law)

Fikes v. *Alabama*, 352 U.S. 191 (1957), 593*n*.

filibuster, 416–17

Finance Committee, 403

Finletter, Thomas, 899

First Amendment, 105, 514, 556, 563–64, 571, 582, 583

First Continental Congress, 80

Greene, Lee S., 953n.
Greene, Nathan, 670n.
Greene v. *McElroy*, 360 U.S. 474 (1959), 581n.
Greenewalt, Crawford, 518
Greer, Scott, 936n., 939–41, 954
Griggs v. *Allegheny County*, 369 U.S. 84 (1962), 558n.
Grimand v. *United States*, 220 U.S. 506 (1911), 428n.
Grodzins, Morton, 129n., 700n., 924
Grosjean v. *American Press Co.*, 297 U.S. 233 (1936), 568n.
gross national product, 29, 30, 738
groups, 51–54, 207–10: voting behavior of, 258–60, 278 (*see also* associations; interest groups)
Grovey v. *Townsend*, 295 U.S. 45 (1935), 613n.
Guinn v. *United States*, 238 U.S. 347 (1915), 613n.

Habeas corpus, 587
Habeas Corpus Act of 1867, 496
Hacker, Andrew, 873n.
Hall, Leonard, 196n.
Halleck, Charles, 408, 410
Hamilton, Alexander, 82, 111, 138, 643, 680, 827: Constitution and, 84, 86, 92; Federalists and, 140–41, 143–47; U.S. Bank and, 117, 141
Hammer v. *Dagenhart*, 247 U.S. 251 (1918), 718n.
Hampton and Co. v. *United States*, 276 U.S. 394 (1928), 428n.
Hancock, John, 91
Hanna, Mark, 159, 190, 310
Harbison, Winfred A., 71n.
Harding, Warren G., 162, 275, 284, 304, 327, 531
Harisiades v. *Shaughnessy*, 324 U.S. 580 (1952), 580n., 598n.
Harlan, John M., 206, 384, 509, 517, 536, 537, 539, 571
Harlan, John Marshall, 519, 537, 611–12
Harrington, James, 66
Harrington, Michael, 55n., 711, 737
Harris, Joseph P., 656n.
Harris, Louis, 257n.
Harris, Robert J., 604n.
Harrison, Benjamin, 5–6, 283
Harrison, William H., 152
Harrison v. *Day*, 106 S.E. 636 (Va. 1959), 620n.
Hartz, Louis, 44, 54, 76, 644
Hatch Acts, 191, 441–42, 443
Hawkins v. *Bleakley*, 243 U.S. 210 (1917), 726n.
Hay, John, 303, 771
Hayden, Carl, 334, 355

Hayes, Rutherford B., 157, 283, 611
Haynes, George H., 361n.
health (*see* public health)
Heard, Alexander, 194n.
Heller, Walter H., 328
Henkin, Louis, 783n.
Henry, Patrick, 91, 92, 101
Henry v. *United States*, 361 U.S. 98 (1959), 592n.
Herling, John, 667n.
Herndon v. *Lowry*, 301 U.S. 242 (1937), 579n.
Herring, E. Pendleton, 735n.
high court, state, 491
highway programs, 844–46, 880, 885–86, 905–07, 925, 928
Hirabayashi v. *United States*, 320 U.S. 81 (1943), 579n.
Hiss, Alger, 366, 445, 580
Hobbes, Thomas, 66
Hoffa, James R., 278
Hofstadter, Richard, 134n., 159n.
Hollingsworth v. *Virginia*, 3 Dallas 378 (1798), 298n.
Holmes, Oliver Wendell, Jr., 474, 500, 519, 537, 544, 567, 579, 586, 646
Holmes v. *Walton*, 883
Hooker, Richard, 605
Hoover, Edgar M., 941n.
Hoover, Herbert, 162, 164–65, 532, 536, 541
Hoover, J. Edgar, 437
Hoover Commissions, 129, 341, 705
Hoover Dam, 701
Hopkins, Harry, 347, 776, 799, 813
Hornig, Donald F., 331
Hospital Survey and Construction Act of 1946, 729
hospitals, public, 728–29, 730
House, E. M., 347, 799
House Calendar, 393
House of Representatives: foreign policy and, 303; legislative procedure in, 411–22; power structure of, 386–95, 400–11; relations with Senate, 354–56 (*see also* Congress)
housing: discrimination in, 614, 625, 629, 636–37; government activities in, 677, 678–79, 731–33; welfare and, 714
Housing Acts, 732–33
Housing and Home Finance Agency, 340, 929
Howe, Mark De Wolfe, 522n.
Hughes, Charles Evans, 504–05, 521, 536, 537
Hull, Cordell, 165, 769
Hull-Lothian Agreement, 303
Humphrey, Hubert, 267, 269–71, 276, 400, 752
Humphrey, West H., 533n.

"just compensation" clause, 555, 558
justice, law and, 471
justice of the peace, 490
justices, Supreme Court, 478, 507–10: appointment of, 531–32, 535, 544–45; characteristics of, 535–40; removal of, 532–35
"justiciable" questions, 486

Kammerer, Gladys, 894n., 918n.
Kaufman, Herbert, 218, 884n., 901
Kedroff v. *St. Nicholas Cathedral*, 344 U.S. 94 (1952), 584n.
Kefauver, Estes, 270, 274, 275, 366, 403, 666, 735, 900
Kelley, Stanley, Jr., 223, 731n.
Kelly, Alfred H., 71n.
Kelsey, Frances O., 735
Kelso, Robert, 709n.
Kennan, George, 57n., 777
Kennedy, Edward M., 182, 184
Kennedy, John F., 300, 304, 315, 327, 332–36, 349, 352, 394, 403, 655, 662, 682, 720, 731, 734: appointment of judges by, 509, 532, 543, 545; election of, 167, 192, 249–52, 256, 264–71, 274–76, 280–81, 283–84, 286; foreign policy of, 799, 813, 821, 823, 824–25
Kennedy, Robert, 264, 799, 815, 824
Kennedy Administration, 217–18, 295, 790–91
Kennedy v. *Martinez*, 372 U.S. 144 (1963), 598n.
Kent, Frank R., 172n., 176n.
Kent, James, 147
Kent v. *Dulles*, 357 U.S. 116 (1958), 581n., 599n.
Ker v. *California*, 374 U.S. 23 (1963), 592n.
Kerr bill, 656–57
Kerr-Mills Act, 730
Key, V. O., Jr., 157n., 160n., 163n., 171, 178n., 180n., 187, 221, 239n., 243n., 248n., 257n., 258n., 378n., 850, 864n.
Keynes, John M., 744
Keyserling, Leon H., 328–29
King, Martin Luther, Jr., 213, 632–33, 638
King, Rufus, 90
Kingsley Books, Inc. v. *Brown*, 354 U.S. 436 (1957), 568n.
Kirk, Russell, 860n.
"kitchen cabinet," 346
Know-Nothings, 608
Knowland, William F., 398
Knox, Frank, 336
Konigsberg v. *State Bar of California*, 366 U.S. 36 (1961), 582n.
Konvitz, Milton, 604n.
Korean War, 306, 580, 780–81, 786

Kovacs v. *Cooper*, 366 U.S. 77 (1949), 582n.
Ku Klux Klan, 162, 572, 614

La Follette, Robert M., 163, 189, 506, 542
labor: child, 718–19; hours of, 719–20; legislation for, 669–74; Supreme Court decisions on, 512–13, 515, 646–47 (*see also* employment)
Labor-Management Act of 1959, 600
labor-management relations, 669–74
labor racketeering, 673
Labor Reform Act of 1959, 671, 673–74
labor unions, 34: due process in, 600; freedom of association and, 572–73; as interest groups, 212–13; lawyers of, 527; Negroes in, 628; political contributions of, 193; reform of, 673–74; voting behavior and, 251
laissez-faire theory, 645–47, 663
Lakewood plan, 953
Lakoff, Sanford A., 690n., 695n.
Lancaster, Lane W., 922
land-grant colleges, 687–88, 699
land use: politics of, 697–701; in suburbs, 917–18; water development and, 702
Landis, James, 654
Landrum-Griffin Act, 600
Lane, Robert, 54n.
Langbridge's Case, 19 Edw. III 375, 471n.
Lasswell, Harold, 60n.
Latin America, 768–70, 789–91
law: changes in, in Revolution, 75–76; citizen's view of, 520, 528–29; classifications of, 456–57; in democracy, 63–64; English, 68; functions of, 458–70; politics and, 479–80; theories of, 471–79 (*see also* judicial system; legislative procedure)
law-enforcement: federal, 426–28, 854; local, 854–56; state, 854
law-enforcers, 546–51 (*see also* police)
Lawson v. *United States*, 339 U.S. 934 (1950), 580n.
law suits, for civil rights, 639 (*see also* specific suits)
lawyers: characteristics of, 525–28; government, 527, 547–51; role of, 521–24
Lazarsfeld, Paul F., 242n., 258n., 259n., 260n., 714n.
leaders: in Congress, 388–411; in state legislatures, 874–76
League of Nations, 302, 772
Lederer, William J., 785n.
leftists, measures against, 575–76
legislative procedure, 393, 411–22 (*see also* law)
Legislative Reorganization Act of 1946, 367, 408–09, 415, 753
legislative veto, 438, 439

Mason, George, 84, 85, 91, 605
Massachusetts: constitution of, 77–79; early government of, 605–06, 861; party organization in, 181–83, 184
Massachusetts Ballot, 201–02, **203**
Matthews, Donald M., 354*n*.
mayor, 957: role of, 893–95, 901, 904
medical care: for aged, 36, 729–31; government sponsored, 223; welfare and, 714–15, 727
medical research, 688, 690, 729
Megalopolis, 945–47
Meiklejohn, Alexander, 564
merger, and monopoly, 665–66
Merton, Robert K., 262*n*.
metropolitan area, 934, 939–43, **940, 944,** 945–56: federation in, 954 (*see also* special districts; urban government)
Meyer v. *Nebraska,* 262 U.S. 390 (1923), 715*n*.
Military Affairs Committee, House, 828–29
military services, 29, 30: scientific research and, 688, 692, 694–97; after Second World War, 776–77, 810, 826–29; in World Wars, 771–72, 774, 806–07
Miller, Ben R., 532*n*.
Miller, Samuel, 537
Miller, Warren E., 186*n*., 280*n*.
Miller, William, 276
Mills, Warner E., Jr., 649*n*.
Mills, Wilbur, 518
Minar, David W., 939–41
minerals (*see* mining)
minimum wage laws, 720–21
mining, regulation of, 698, 706, 707
minority groups, equality rights of, 617 (*see also* Negroes)
Mississippi, civil rights work in, 621, 631, 633
Missouri Basin development, 704–05
Mitchell, Billy, 772
mob action, 608
mobility: geographical, 36–38, 48–49; social, 48–49
monetary system, 121, 644
monopoly, 663–69: defense contracts and, 690
Monroe, James, 145–47
Monroe Doctrine, 768–69
Montesquieu, Charles, Baron de, 66–68
Morgan v. *Virginia,* 328 U.S. 373 (1946), 617*n*.
Morison, Samuel E., 74*n*.
Morrill Act of 1862, 119, 687, 699, 716
Morris, Gouverneur, 84, 85, 86, 88, 89
Morris, Robert, 83
Morse, Wayne, 416
Mosher, Frederick C., 748*n*.

Mountain Timber Co. v. *Washington,* 243 U.S. 219 (1917), 726*n*.
Mumford, Lewis, 946
Munger, Frank, 258*n*.
municipal court, 491
Municipal Manpower Commission, 890, 957
municipalities, 891, 892, 911–12: housing projects in, 732–33; public enterprise in, 678, 680 (*see also* urban government)
Munn v. *Illinois,* 94 U.S. 113, 134 (1877), 645*n*.
Murdock v. *Pennsylvania,* 319 U.S. 105 (1943), 584*n*.
Murphy, Frank, 478, 564
Murphy, Walter F., 525*n*.
Murray, Bill, 882
Murrow, Edward R., 804
Myers v. *U.S.,* 272 U.S. 52 (1926), 296*n*.
Myrdal, Gunnar, 604*n*.

NAACP, 615, 622–23, 639
NAACP v. *Alabama:* 357 U.S. 449 (1958), 572*n*., 583*n*., 622; 360 U.S. 240 (1959), 583*n*.
NAACP v. *Button,* 371 U.S. 415 (1963), 572
NAACP v. *State of Alabama,* 78 S. Ct. 1171, 207
Nardone v. *United States,* 302 U.S. 379 (1937), 591*n*.
National Academy of Sciences, 687
National Aeronautics and Space Administration, 340, 688, 696, 818
National Archives, 342
National Association for the Advancement of Colored People (*see* NAACP)
national chairman, of political party, 190
national committee, of political party, 189–91
National Conference of Commissioners on Uniform State Laws, 930
National Education Association, 848
National Institutes of Health, 31, 688, 690, 695
National Labor Relations Act of 1935, 121–22, 650, 671, 722
National Labor Relations Board, 122, 339, 650, 671, 674
National Labor Relations Board v. *Benne Katz,* 369 U.S. 736 (1962), 499*n*.
National Lawyers Guild, 526, 527
National Park Service, 698
National Recovery Administration, 720, 734
National Rivers and Harbors Congress, 702
National Science Foundation, 31, 688, 690, 692–93, 695, 697
national security (*see* defense policies)

National Security Act of 1947, 330, 807–08, 811, 813, 814
National Security Council, 323, 329–30, 799–800, 810, 812–14, 824
National Space Council, 697
national supremacy, 115, 117, 841 (see also federalism)
National Urban League, 639
Nationality Act of 1940, 574
Native-American party, 608
NATO, 318, **778–79**, 780, 791
Natural Gas Act of 1938, 656
natural gas industry, regulation of, 656–58
natural law, 471–72, 474, 477–78
natural resources, 684–87, 697–708, 931
naturalization, 574–75, 584
Navy (see Department of Defense; military services)
Near v. *Minnesota,* 283 U.S. 697 (1931), 568n.
Nebbia v. *New York,* 291 U.S. 502, 536 (1934), 647n.
Negroes: citizenship of, 607–09; in Congress, 379–80; equality rights of, 607–40; in interest groups, 213; migration of, 37, 908–09; political parties and, 168–69, 200, 909; in suburbs, 921–22; voting by, 112, 151, 237, 251–52, 254–55, 278, 608, 613–14, 623–24, 866, 908–09
Nelson, Gaylord, 267
Neustadt, Richard E., 263, 297, 321n., 325, 328, 337, 351n.
neutrality, 766–67, 772
Neutrality Acts, 772
New Deal, 522: legislation during, 449, 712–13, 722, 937; Supreme Court and, 482, 495, 506
New Jersey Plan, 85–86
New York: conservation program of, 699; constitution of, 78–79; elections in, 149–51, 545
Ng Fung Ho v. *White,* 259 U.S. 276 (1922), 598n.
Nineteenth Amendment, 98, 101, 112, 233, 616
Nixon, Richard, 167, 192, 249, 251, 267, 268, 273, 279–81, 285–86, 332, 366, 619, 790
Nixon v. *Herndon,* 273 U.S. 536 (1927), 613n.
nominating process, 186–89 (see also primary elections)
"nonjusticiable" questions, 486
nonvoters, 238–44
Norris, George W., 390, 542
Norris–La Guardia Act of 1932, 670
North: Congressmen from, 370; Democratic party in, 163; Negro rights in, 605, 607–10, 614, 619, 623–29, 639–40;

Republican party in, 156, 163; voting in, 257
North Atlantic Treaty Organization (see NATO)
Nourse, Edwin G., 328–29
nuclear weapons, 319, 781–84

Office of: Emergency Planning, 330–31, 816; Science and Technology, 331, 688, 692; Scientific Research and Development, 688; the Comptroller of the Currency, 435
oil industry, regulation of, 675, 706–07
old age, survivors, and disability insurance, 724–25
Olds, Leland, 656–57
Olmstead v. *United States,* 277 U.S. 438 (1928), 103, 591n.
Olney, Richard, 768–69, 771
On Lee v. *United States,* 343 U.S. 747 (1952), 591n.
open primaries, 267
Oppenheimer, Robert, 692–93
Oregon, primaries in, 267–68, 271
Organization of American States, 789, 822
organized crime, 900
Orlans, Harold, 691n.
Otis, James, 73
Owen, Wilfred, 905n.

Paine, Thomas, 73, 76, 474, 569
Palamountain, J. C., Jr., 344n.
Palko v. *Connecticut,* 302 U.S. 319 (1937), 476n.
Panama Canal Zone, 769, 821–22
Pan-American movement, 769
Parker, Alton, 161
Parker, Florence B., 722n.
Parker, John J., 536
Passman, Otto E., 407
passports, 575, 599
patents, 666
patriotism: characteristics of, 62; institutional, 354–56
Peace Corps, 818
Pendleton, Edmund, 91
Pendleton Act of 1883, 341, 440
Pennsylvania v. *Nelson,* 350 U.S. 497 (1958), 580n.
Perloff, Harvey S., 942n.
Permanent Investigating Committee, 575
Peters v. *Hobby,* 349 U.S. 331 (1955), 550, 581n.
petroleum production, 675, 706–08
Pfeffer, Leo, 527
Phillips Petroleum Co. v. *Wisconsin,* 347 U.S. 672 (1954), 657
Pierce, Franklin, 308
Pinkney, Thomas, 85, 143
Platform Committee, 272–73

platforms, political, 155–56, 272–73
Plessy v. *Ferguson,* 163 U.S. 537 (1896), 612, 618
pocket veto, 298
Point Four program, 780, 804
police, 547, 590–94: local, 854–56, 900, 902; state, 854, 881
Policy Committees: House, 392; Senate, 399–400
political attitudes, 58–64
political issues, voting and, 249–50, 260
political parties, 8–9, 22–25, 59, 63, 133–69; in Congress, 216, 371–73, 386–88, 396; Congressional committees of, 391–92, 399–400; development of, 110–11, 137–56; election procedures and, 200–04; finances of, 191–96; judges and, 531, 536, 539, 541, 546; national committee of, 189–91; national primary and, 277–78; in one-party states, 372, 870–72, 880; organization of, 170–89, **171**; President as leader of, 300–01; at state and local levels, 124, 837–39, 868–72, 876, 879–80, 897, 934; voting behavior and, 246–60; workers for, 196–200 (*see also* conventions; politicians)
politicians, 173–80, 196–200: occupations of, **197**; President's nomination and, 271–72; views of, 198–99 (*see also* machine, political)
politics: civil service and, 441–43; corruption in, 60; economic regulation and, 644–45, 654–58; factional, 138, 205; judges and, 529–46; law and, 457–58, 479–80; lawyers in, 522–23, 526; mobility and, 49; of public research, 691–97; in states, 139; in suburbs, 912–16, 920–21; urbanization and, 35 (*see also* machine, political; political parties)
poll tax, 98, 233–34
Pollock v. *Farmers' Loan & Trust Co.,* 157 U.S. 429 (1895), 758n.
polls (*see* surveys, voting)
poor (*see* poverty)
population, 29, 30: changes in, 34–38, **942,** 943, **944,** 949
positivism, in law, 472, 474, 477
Post Office, United States, 425, 432, 570, 678, 680
Potter, David M., 46, 50n., 711n.
Pound, Roscoe, 474, 526–28
poverty, 55: "war" on, 711, 737; welfare services and, 709–14, 727, 850
Powell, Adam Clayton, 179, 278
Powell, Thomas R., 510
Powell v. *Alabama,* 287 U.S. 45 (1932), 595n.
power: consent and, in political system, 42, 60, 75; delegation of, 114; prohibition of, 114–15; restraint of, 465–68 (*see also*

checks and balances; separation of powers)
power development, public, 679, 680 (*see also* utilities)
precinct politics, 172–80
preference polls, 267–68
Prendergast, Michael H., 300
Presidency: changes in, 5–6, 13–16, 308–20; succession to, 334
President: appointments by, 295–96, 510, 531–32, 535–37, 541, 548; budget activities of, 326–28, 749–50, 753; bureaucracies and, 322–31, 339–48, 437–39, 451–52; campaign of, 277–83; as Commander in Chief, 304–07, 806, 828; Congress and, 29, 349–50, 352–62, 385, 398; constitutional powers of, 294, 298, 299, 301, 304, 309; defense and foreign policies of, 124, 301–04, 799–818, 822, 826–29; diplomatic functions of, 301–04, 318–20; functions of, 292–320; in labor disputes, 670, 672–73; legislative powers of, 298–99, 412, 420–21; nomination of, 263–77; as party leader, 300–01; requirements for, 276; tenure of, 100
President's Committee on Civil Rights, 618
President's Science Advisory Committee, 688, 692–93
press, freedom of, 556, 563–64, 567–72
press conference, President's, 348–49
pressure groups (*see* interest groups)
Price, Don K., 651n., 801n.
Price, Hugh D., 217
price control, 312–13, 675
price-fixing (*see* monopoly)
primary elections: for Congress, 372; Presidential, 265–71, 277–78
Prince v. *Massachusetts,* 321 U.S. 158 (1944), 584n.
Pritchett, C. Herman, 525n.
privacy, right of, 563, 582–83
Private Calendar, 393, 415
private rights, 108–09, 603
procedural law, 457
production, national, 684–85, 738
production control, 675
Progressive party, 163, 166, 506
Progressives, in Republican party, 390
prohibited powers, in Constitution, 114–15
Prohibition, 97, 98–100
property: ownership of, 47; regulation of, 458–61, 643–45, 647; rights of, 552–62
property cases, 513–14
proportional representation, 898
Proxmire, William, 397
public accommodation, discrimination in, 611–13, 616, 619, 623, 625, 629–36
public enterprise, 678–81

public health, 31: regulation of, 674, 718–19, 728–31 (*see also* welfare)

Public Health Service, United States, 442, 728

public opinion: government influence on, 229–30; interest groups and, 221–26

Public Utilities Commission v. *Pollak*, 343 U.S. 451 (1952), 583*n*.

public works, 852, 856–58: special districts for, 932–33; under urban government, 902

punishment, 489, 596: in quasi-judicial procedure, 597–98

Quasi-judicial functions, of regulatory agencies, 339, 343, 429, 449–50: due process and, 596–99

Quesada, Elwood R., 219–20

Quock Walker case, 605–06

Racial discrimination, 611, 615–17 (*see also* Negroes, equality rights of)

radio, regulation of, 677

railroads, 846: regulation of, 648–49, 677

Railway Labor Act of 1926, 669–70, 672

Randolph, Edmund, 84–85, 88, 91

Ransom, Harry H., 806*n*., 812*n*., 827*n*.

ratification: of amendments, 96–97, 101–02; of Constitution, 90–92

Rayburn, Sam, 368, 389, 391, 392, 394, 623

real property cases, 493

reapportionment, 381–84, 867–68, 870, 889

recession, 661–63

Reciprocal Trade Agreements Acts, 303, 770

Reconstruction Finance Corporation, 678

Reconstruction forces, 609–11

Redford, E. S., 656*n*., 674*n*.

Reed, Daniel, 408, 541

registration, voting, 201

regulatory agencies, 339, 342–46, 518: federal courts and, 493; procedures of, 651–54, 658

Reich, Charles A., 697*n*.

Reid, Ogden, 188

Reinsch, Paul S., 863*n*.

religion: freedom of, 563, 583–86; of Presidential candidates, 163, 167; in public schools, 465–68, 479, 919–20; voting behavior and, 251–52, 256

removal from office: of judges, 532–35; by President, 296–97, 344–45; of President, 358

Rentler, Robert A., 903*n*.

representation: in Congress, 374–84; in state legislatures, 383–84, 865–70, 876

Representative: characteristics of, 373–74, 378–79; qualifications for, 369–73

Republican National Conventions, 265, 273–76

Republican party, 111, 136, 137, 156–69: campaigns of, 279–81; in Congress, 401–02; Congressional committees of, 391–92, 400; finances of, 192–96; origins of, 156; post–Civil War, 609–11; in states, 181–83, 184–86, 869–72; voting behavior and, 246–60

Republican party, Jeffersonian, 111, 137, 141–47, 152, 505

Republican party, National (*see* Whig party)

residence requirements, for voting, 235–36

resolution, 412

Reuther, Walter, 278

Revolution, 71–77, 840, 861

Reynolds v. *Sims*, 377 U.S. 533 (1964), 383*n*.

Reynolds v. *United States*, 98 U.S. 145 (1879), 584*n*.

Ribicoff, Abraham, 335, 880

Richards, Allan R., 861*n*., 862*n*., 863*n*.

Riesman, David, 45

"rif," 448

right to work, 561

rightists, 575–76

rights of man: in Constitution, 92; in Declaration of Independence, 74; English views of, 68–69; Locke's view of, 65–66, 73 (*see also* civil liberties; civil rights)

Rio Treaty, **778–79**, 789, 822

river-basin developments, 679–80, 702–05, 931, 945

Roberts, Owen J., 519, 536, 558, 647

Robinson, Frederick, 522

Robinson-Patman Act of 1936, 664

Rockefeller, Nelson, 270, 273, 878

Rogow, Arnold, 60*n*., 808*n*.

roll call vote, in Congress, 418–19

Roosevelt, Eleanor, 899

Roosevelt, Franklin D., 187, 297, 324, 327, 332–33, 347–48, 585, 618, 688, 704, 769: election of, 165–66, 230, 250, 256, 382; Great Depression and, 688, 713, 722; Second World War and, 124, 304–05, 336, 366, 773–74, 793, 812–13; Supreme Court and, 482, 495, 508, 532

Roosevelt, Theodore, 161, 268, 310–11, 313–14, 332, 346, 347, 348, 668, 697, 769

Root, Elihu, 526, 771

Roper poll, 246

Rosenblum, Victor G., 655*n*.

Rosenman, Samuel, 347

Rossi, Peter H., 903*n*.

Rossiter, Clinton, 71, 88*n*.

Rostow, W. W., 49–50, 62, 776

Roth v. *United States*, 354 U.S. 476 (1957), 570*n*.

social characteristics of voting behavior, **240**, 241–43, 250–60, **251–52**, 897

social class: of Congressmen, 378–79; voting behavior and, 254, 897 (*see also* social characteristics)

social groups (*see* associations; groups)

social security, 36, 311–12, 711, 714, 721–22, 724–25

Social Security Act of 1935, 713, 722–25, 730

social structure of community, 370–71

society, law and, 455, 464–65, 468

socioeconomic level (*see* social characteristics)

socioeconomic rights, 108–09

sociological theory of law, 473, 474, 478

Soil Conservation Service, 699

Solicitor General, 550

Somers, Anne R., 727*n.*

Somers, Herman M., 727*n.*

Sorauf, Frank J., 178*n.*

Sorensen, Theodore, 824

South: Congressmen from, 370; in Constitutional Convention, 86–87; Democratic party in, 156–57, 162, 165–66, 285, 613, 617; Negro rights in, 605–06, 609–16, 620–27, 630–33, 635; Republican party in, 167–68; voting behavior in, 257

South America (*see* Latin America)

Soviet Union, 576–77, 617, 773, 775–84, 786–87, 791–92, 800, 805, 823–25

space program, 696–97, 747

Speaker of the House, 350, 389–90

Special Assistant for: National Security Affairs, 799–800; Science and Technology, 692, 696

special districts, 835, 891, 911, 932, 934

special jurisdiction, court of, 491

specialists, administrative, 329, 347–48, 651–52, 654: interaction of, 925–30; state and local, 885–87, 957

speech, freedom of, 556, 563–67

Speiser v. *Randall*, 357 U.S. 513 (1958), 581*n.*

Standard Oil Co. of N.J. v. *United States*, 221 U.S. 1 (1911), 663

Stans, Maurice H., 327

Stassen, Harold, 271

state courts: organization of, 490–92; procedure in, 488–90, **494**; Supreme Court review of, 495–96

state governments, 11–12, 27–28, 833–36, **835**, 860–89: constitutional powers of, 114–19; due process in, 589–90; expenditures of, 739–42, **740**, **741**, 833, **844**, **845**, 849; federal government and, 119–30, **126**, 925–30, 935, 947, 955–58; laws of, 474, 476–78, 500, 644; licensing by, 674; local governments and, 924–30, 932, 935–37, 948–52, 955–58; loyalty-

security measures of, 573–75; natural resources regulation by, 686–87, 698, 699, 704, 705–07; public enterprise of, 678; after Revolution, 76–79; taxation by, 758, **760**, 762; welfare services of, 713, 718, 721, 725–27, 843, 849 (*see also* states)

State of the Union Message, 298

state political systems, 836–51, 859

states: education in, 716, 843, 847–49, 886; equality rights in, 605–08, 617, 619, 625; interaction among, 930–32, 943–52; political parties in, 171, 180–89

states' rights, 92, 97, 118

statutes, 107–09, 456 (*see also* law; legislative procedure)

statutory action cases, 493

Staub v. *City of Baxley*, 355 U.S. 313 (1958), 573*n.*

Stern, Philip M., 763*n.*

Stettinius, Edward, 801

Stevenson, Adlai, 167, 249, 250–52, 256, 266, 269, 270, 274, 275, 280, 335, 824

Stewart, Frank M., 898*n.*

Stewart, Potter, 468, 509, 517, 539

Stimson, Henry L., 336, 521, 524, 807, 814

Stokes, Donald E., 280*n.*

Stone, Harlan F., 360, 519, 532

Stone, I. F., 522

Straus, Oscar, 347*n.*

Strauss, Lewis L., 360–61

strict constructionist view of Constitution, 104–05

strikes, 310, 670 (*see also* labor-management relations)

Stromberg v. *California*, 283 U.S. 359 (1931), 579*n.*

strong-mayor-council plan, 893–95, 909

Student Non-Violent Coordinating Committee, 213, 639

Stueve v. *Cincinnati*, 168 N.E. 574 (1960), 559*n.*

Subcommittee on National Policy Machinery, 257, 266

substantive law, 457

suburbs, 35, 910–22, 951, 956: discrimination in, 628, 629; voting behavior and, 253–54, 256–57

subversive activities, 444–47, 574–76, 580: deportation for, 598

Subversive Activities Control Board, 574

suffrage, extension of, 111–12, 147, 233–34, 607–08 (*see also* voting; women's suffrage)

Sunday Closing Law Cases, 366 U.S. 420, 582, 599, 617 (1961), 585*n.*

Sunshine, Morris, 919*n.*

superior court, 491

Supreme Court, state, 491
Supreme Court, U.S., 474–79, 481–87: appeals to, 490, 495–98; changes in, 510–19; constant elements in, 502–10; constitutional change and, 102–07; constitutional provision for, 85–86; due process and, 589–90, 591–600; economic decisions of, 645–47, 657–58, 665; on equality rights, 611–13, 617, 619–23; federal-state powers and, 114, 116–19, 120, 121–25; judicial review by, 500–02; jurisdiction of, 494–99, **498**; on liberty and property, 553–54, 556, 563–86; on reapportionment, 868, 870 (*see also Baker* v. *Carr*); on taxation, 758; on welfare legislation, 718–20, 726 (*see also* justices, Supreme Court)
Survey Research Center, 167
surveys, voting, 244–46
Sutherland, George, 104, 537
Sweatt v. *Painter,* 339 U.S. 629 (1950), 618n.
Swisher, Carl B., 457n.

Taft, Robert, 270, 274, 276
Taft, William H., 161, 268, 292, 296n., 532
Taft-Hartley Act of 1947, 110, 574, 671–74
Talmadge, Herman, 188, 882
Taney, Roger, 104, 607
tariff, 644, 787–89: foreign relations and, 770; political parties and, 153, 157
taxation, 555, 712, 756–65: by state, 758, **760**, 762; in suburbs, 915–19; urban, 902 (*see also* income tax)
Taylor, John, 552
Taylor, Maxwell, 811, 815, 824
Taylor, W. R., 303n.
Taylor, Zachary, 301
Taylor Grazing Act of 1934, 698, 700
Taylor v. *Mississippi,* 319 U.S. 583 (1943), 579n.
technological change, 32–34 (*see also* science and technology)
television, 280, 677
Tennessee Valley Authority, 125, 339–40, 361, 679, 698, 703–05, 945
Tenth Amendment, 115–16
Terminiello v. *Chicago,* 337 U.S. 1 (1949), 565–66
territorial expansion, 769–70
Thirteenth Amendment, 98, 475, 609
Thomas v. *Collins,* 323 U.S. 516 (1945), 573
Thurmond, Strom, 166
ticket splitting (*see* ballot form)
Tilden, Samuel, 157, 283, 611
Times Film Corporation v. *Chicago,* 365 U.S. 43 (1961), 570n.

Tocqueville, Alexis de, 45, 46, 55, 56n., 59, 61n., 76, 152–53, 205, 315–16, 551, 602, 768, 841, 863
Torcaso v. *Watkins,* 367 U.S. 488 (1961), 585n.
Toronto plan, 154
tort law, 463, 493
Tower, John, 184
townships, 891, 911
Trade Agreements Acts, 788
Trade Expansion Act of 1962, 789
transportation, 30: interstate, 931, 944, 948; regulation of, 677, 682–83, 843–46; urban, 905–08 (*see also* air commerce; highways; railroads)
treason, 563
treaties, 123: collective defense, **778–79**; Presidential powers and, 301–02, 309; ratification of by Senate, 358–59, 816, 818
trial procedures, 488–90
Trop v. *Dulles,* 356 U.S. 86 (1958), 502, 596n.
Truman, David B., 53n., 195n.
Truman, Harry, 166, 223, 256, 284, 285, 304, 306, 308, 365–66, 444, 585, 618, 730–31: foreign policy and, 777–81, 813, 819, 828
Truman doctrine, 777
trusts, 663–69
Turner, Frederick J., 40
Turner, Julius, 188n.
Turner v. *Memphis,* 369 U.S. 350 (1962), 623n.
Tweed, William M., 173
Twelfth Amendment, 97–98, 144–45
Twentieth Amendment, 100
Twenty-first Amendment, 100
Twenty-fourth Amendment, 233
Twenty-second Amendment, 100, 332, 333
Twenty-third Amendment, 233, 283
two-party system, 133, 238

Un-American Activities Committee, 366–67, 575, 581–82
unemployment (*see* employment)
unemployment compensation, 722–24
Union Calendar, 393
unions (*see* labor unions)
United Nations, 318–20, 774, 785–87
United States Attorneys, 548–49
United States Bank, 110, 116–17, 141, 146
United States Information Agency, 341, 798, 804
United States Marshals, 548
United States v. *Aluminum Co. of America,* 148 F. 2d 416 (1945), 663
United States v. *Ballard,* 322 U.S. 78 (1944), 584n.